Persian Literature
Volume 1-2

Handbook of Oriental Studies

Handbuch der Orientalistik

SECTION ONE

The Near and Middle East

Edited by

Maribel Fierro (*Madrid*)
M. Şükrü Hanioğlu (*Princeton*)
Renata Holod (*University of Pennsylvania*)
Florian Schwarz (*Vienna*)

VOLUME 149/1-2

The titles published in this series are listed at *brill.com/ho1*

Persian Literature

A Bio-Bibliographical Survey

VOLUME 1-2

Biography, Additions, and Corrections

By

C.A. Storey

Prepared for Publication by

Joep Lameer

BRILL

LEIDEN | BOSTON

The Library of Congress Cataloging-in-Publication Data is available online at http://catalog.loc.gov
LC record available at https://lccn.loc.gov/2020055388

Typeface for the Latin, Greek, and Cyrillic scripts: "Brill". See and download: brill.com/brill-typeface.

ISSN 0169-9423
ISBN 978-90-04-43241-3 (hardback, set)
ISBN 978-90-04-44402-7 (hardback, vol. 1–1)
ISBN 978-90-04-44404-1 (hardback, vol. 1–2)
ISBN 978-90-04-44406-5 (hardback, vol. 2)
ISBN 978-90-04-44403-4 (hardback, vol. 3)
ISBN 978-90-04-44407-2 (hardback, vol. 4)
ISBN 978-90-04-44408-9 (hardback, vol. 5)

This book is printed on acid-free paper and produced in a sustainable manner

Contents

Foreword VII
Preface to the Original Edition X
List of Authorities and Abbreviations XI

2 **History, Biography, etc. (*continued from Volume 1–1*)**
13 Biography
13.1 *Poets* 615
13.2 *Saints, Mystics, etc.* 735
13.3 *Ambassadors* 860
13.4 *Calligraphists and Painters* 864
13.5 *Companions of the Prophet* 871
13.6 *Families, Tribes, Races* 872
13.6.1 Afghāns 872
13.6.2 Āfrīdīs 872
13.6.3 Barmecides 873
13.6.4 Bōhorahs 874
13.6.5 Khwēshgīs 874
13.6.6 Nā'iṭīs 875
13.6.7 Naubakhtīs 876
13.6.8 Appendix 877
13.7 *Kings* 877
13.8 *Munshīs* 878
13.9 *Officials (Ministers of State, Military Officers, etc.)* 879
13.10 *Orientalists* 893
13.11 *Philosophers, Physicians, etc.* 893
13.12 *Places (i.e. Inhabitants of Particular Towns, Provinces, or Countries)* 899
13.12.1 Ādharbāyjān 899
13.12.2 Aḥmadābād 900
13.12.3 Amrōhah 900
13.12.4 Aurangābād 901
13.12.5 Baihaq 901
13.12.6 Balkh 901
13.12.7 Barnāwah 901
13.12.8 Benares 902
13.12.9 Bhakkar (Bhak'har) 902
13.12.10 Bihār 902
13.12.11 Bījāpūr 902

13.12.12 Bilgrām 902
13.12.13 Bukhārā etc. 903
13.12.14 Calcutta 904
13.12.15 The Carnatic 905
13.12.16 Chittagong 905
13.12.17 Daulatābād 905
13.12.18 The Deccan 905
13.12.19 Delhi 905
13.12.20 Fārs 906
13.12.21 Gujrāt (Gujarat) 906
13.12.22 Ḥaidarābād 907
13.12.23 Harāt 907
13.12.24 India 907
13.12.25 Istānbūl 908
13.12.26 Jā'is 908
13.12.27 Jaunpūr 908
13.12.28 Kāshghar 909
13.12.29 Kashmīr 909
13.12.30 Khurāsān 910
13.12.31 Kōl 910
13.12.32 Lucknow 910
13.12.33 Murādābād 910
13.12.34 Rāprī 910
13.12.35 Samarqand 910
13.12.36 Shīrāz 910
13.12.37 Shūshtar 911
13.12.38 Sinandij 912
13.12.39 Sind 912
13.12.40 Tabrīz 912
13.12.41 Ṭihrān 912
13.12.42 Yazd 912
13.12.43 Ẓafarābād 913
13.13 *Shī'ites* 913
13.14 *Traditionists* 922
13.15 *Travellers, Pilgrims, Tourists* 923
13.16 *Women* 943
13.17 *General and Miscellaneous* 945
Some Miscellaneous Historical Works 963

Additions and Corrections 966

Foreword

The Royal Asiatic Society is delighted that Brill are to publish both a complete print edition and a searchable online version of C.A. Storey's *Persian Literature: A Bio-bibliographical Survey* that also includes all of Professor Storey's hitherto unpublished material. The *Bio-bibliography* was conceived as a work of reference similar to Carl Brockelmann's *Geschichte der arabischen Litteratur* (published between 1898 and 1902, with many subsequent editions and revisions, and also published online by Brill in 2009).

Charles Ambrose Storey (1888–1967) studied Classics and Oriental Languages at Cambridge. After graduation he taught at Sir Syed Ahmed Khan's College at Aligarh, in India. In 1919 he became Assistant Librarian and then, from 1927, the Librarian at the India Office. From 1933 he was Sir Thomas Adams's Professor of Arabic at Cambridge. After retirement in 1947 he continued his scholarly work until he died. In his will, he left all his academic materials, together with a generous legacy, to the Royal Asiatic Society in the hope that work on the Bibliography would be continued.

Storey had set out as an Arabist, with a distinguished list of publications dating from 1917. He became recognised as one of the great oriental scholars of his time. While at the India Office, Storey continued to research and publish in Arabic, but his increasing pre-occupation became the Persian bibliography, the first part of which was published in 1930. His approach was different to that of Brockelmann who had conceived his work as a general history of Arabic literature: Storey, by contrast, sought to provide a grand bibliographical guide that would list extant manuscripts, with details of their copies, locations, notations, and defects, together with printed books, biographical information about their authors, and data on editions and translations.

Although Storey was limited by the information available to him (for example, he did not have access to collections in Russia, Central Asia and Iran later included in Professor Yuri Bregel's greatly enlarged Russian translation of Storey's bibliography, published from 1974 onwards) the great strength of his work was, as Bregel has written, "the thoroughness with which it was prepared and printed, making it both an indispensable and generally reliable source of information"; and an early review, in 1935, by Vladimir Minorsky noted that 'the work has been so carefully done and such a mass of catalogues has been utilized that only longer use of the book may bring to evidence some occasional lacunae'.

Storey's approach was to classify Persian literature neither chronologically nor by name of author but according to genre and subject, with appropriate cross-referencing. During his lifetime he published, with Luzac, several fascicles covering Qur'anic literature, history, biography, mathematics, astronomy etc, designed to fit into an overall scheme of three volumes, together with cumulative indexes and corrections as publication proceeded. Between 1977 and 1990, the Society, drawing on the Storey Fund, continued publication (now with Brill) of Storey's accumulated manuscripts, largely without updating or correction. This still left in his papers material for further parts in the first three volumes and for the whole of a projected volume 4.

In the 1990s, François de Blois was commissioned to work on the Storey project, taking on the material relating to poetry. Publication of this part of the bibliography was begun in 1992 covering the pre-Mongol period, with subsequent parts brought together in a revised and corrected edition in 2004 as a fifth volume of the Storey design. De Blois's book, as appropriate for the state of knowledge quarter of a century after Storey's death, is, again in Bregel's words, "an essentially new work" drawing extensively on material not available to Storey and adopting new approaches to bibliographical research. It still left to be done a listing devoted to Persian poetry from the time of Saʿdī and Rūmī onwards.

And there the matter has rested until this online initiative by Brill. Included here is all the hitherto published material relating to the *Bio-bibliography*, together with all the remaining unpublished material from the Storey archive. Digital technology affords an opportunity to breathe new life into this enterprising work and besides the greater access to scholars across the world that online publication gives it offers the opportunity of future expansion and correction as further research is done. The original concept remains a powerful one: the provision of an excellent research tool to stimulate and facilitate study of a great body of world literature.

The Society is grateful to Dr Maurits van den Boogert at Brill who has worked with the Society to make this new edition possible, to Dr Joep Lameer, who has supervised the conversion process from Storey's handwritten pages to printed books on Brill's behalf, and to the production editor, Pieter te Velde, who also compiled the List of Authorities and Abbreviations.

An excellent account of Storey's scholarship and the bibliographical history of his *Bio-bibliography* written by the late Professor Bregel in 2005, is published in the *Encyclopaedia Iranica.*

As the Royal Asiatic Society approaches its 200th Anniversary in 2023, it is particularly gratifying that the intention of its founders—to promote 'the investigation and encouragement of the science, literature and the arts in relation to Asia'—is realised in so innovative a way; and that Professor Storey's lifetime of scholarship has been enabled by his generous benefaction to live on from generation to generation.

Gordon Johnson
The Royal Asiatic Society
December 2020

Preface to the Original Edition

Original Preface to Vol. 1–2, by C.A. Storey

The present instalment of my survey of Persian literature completes the first volume. In view of the inconveniently large size to which it has grown I have felt myself compelled, for purposes of binding, to regard the previous four fasciculi as Part 1 and the present instalment as Part 2.

Among those who since the date of my last acknowledgment have been so kind as to send me additions and corrections I remember particularly Professor A.J. Arberry, Mr. J.D. Pearson, Mr. G.M. Wickens and, above all, Professor V. Minorsky. To the Trustees of the "E. J. W. Gibb Memorial", who generously agreed to bear the cost of printing this second part of Volume I, I am greatly indebted.

C.A. Storey
April, 1953

Authorities and Abbreviations

This list does not include the recognised abbreviations for well-known periodicals nor the titles of Persian historical and biographical works (except in a few special cases).

A.H.S.	*Anno Hegirae Solaris*. I have prefixed these letters to dates in the Hijrī i shamsī era adopted some years ago in Persia.
A.S.B. Govt. Coll. 1903–07	*List of Arabic and Persian MSS. acquired on behalf of the Government of India by the Asiatic Society of Bengal during 1903–07*. Calcutta, 1908.
A.S.B. Govt. Coll. 1908–10	*List of ... MSS. acquired ... during 1908–10*. Calcutta, [1910 ?].
Aberystwyth	*The National Library of Wales. Catalogue of oriental manuscripts ... by H. Ethé*. Aberystwyth, 1916.
Adabīyāt Kutub-khānah-sī	The Adabīyāt Kutub-khānah-sī preserved in the University Library at Istanbul. (Historical MSS. cited from Tauer (*q.v. infra*).)
Afshār 1333	*Kitāb-shināsī i Īrān. Farwardīn-Isfand 1333. Gird-āwardah i Īraj i Afshār*. (in *Farhang i Īrān-zamīn* ii (Tihrān 1333/1954–5) pp. 397–400 (introductory) and 1–20 (separately paginated)).
Afshār 1334	*Kitāb-shināsī i Īrān 1334*. (French title on back wrapper: *Bibliographie de l'Irān. Février 1955–Mars 1956. Par Īraj Afshâr*). Tihrān 1335/1956. A defect from the bibliographical point of view is that the dates actually given on the title-pages or elsewhere in the books themselves, when different from 1334, are not specified.
Ahlwardt	*Verzeichniss der arabischen Handschriften der Königlichen Bibliothek zu Berlin von W.A.* Berlin, 1887–99.
Aḥmad thālith	The Library of Aḥmad III preserved in the Ṭōp Qapū Sarāy at Istanbul. (Historical MSS. cited from Tauer (*q.v. infra*).)
ʿAlīgaṛh Subḥ. MSS.	*Fihrist i nusakh i qalamī (ʿArabī, Fārisī wa-Urdū) Subḥān Allāh Ōriyenṭal Lāʾibrērī Muslim Yūnīwarsiṭī ʿAlī Gaṛh murattabah i Saiyid Kāmil Ḥusain* ... [A hand-list of the MSS. presented to the ʿAlīgaṛh Muslim University in 1927 by Saiyid Subḥān Allāh of Gōrakhpūr]. ʿAlīgaṛh, 1930.
ʿAlīgaṛh Subḥ. II	*Fihrist jild i duwwum maṭbūʿāt (ʿArabī, Fārisī wa-Urdū) Subḥān Allāh Ōriyenṭal Lāʾibrērī Muslim Yūnīwarsiṭī ʿAlī Gaṛh murattabah i Maulawī Muḥammad Abrār Ḥusain Ṣāḥib Fārūqī* ... ʿAlīgaṛh, 1932.

Amal al-āmil *A. al-ā. fī ʿulamāʾ Jabal ʿĀmil* [in Arabic], by M. b. al-Ḥasan al-Ḥurr al-ʿĀmilī. Ṭihrān, 1302.

Amīrī Efendī The Library of Amīrī (Emīrī) Efendī preserved in the Millat Kutub-khānah-sī at Istanbul. (Historical MSS. cited from Tauer (*q.v. infra*).)

ʿAmūjah Ḥusain Pāshā *Daftar i Kutub-khānah i ʿAmūjah Ḥusain Pāshā* [now preserved in the Millat Kutub-khānah-sī]. Istanbul, 1310. (Historical MSS. cited from Tauer (*q.v. infra*).)

Āqsarāy آقسرا یده والده جامعشریفی کتبخانه سی دفتری. درسعادت ۱۳۱۱

Arberry *Catalogue of the Library of the India Office. Vol. ii. Part vi. Persian books. By A.J. Arberry* ... London, 1937.

Asʿad *Daftar i Kutubkhānah i Asʿad Efendī*. Constantinople, n.d.

Āṣafīyah فهرست کتب عربی – فارسی واردو مخزونه کتب خانه آصفیه سرکار عالی . . . حیدراباد ۱۳۳۲ – ۱۳۳۳

Āṣafīyah III *Jild i siwwum i Fihrist i kutub i ʿArabī wa Fārisī wa Urdū makhzūnah i Kutub-khānah i Āṣafīyah i Sarkār i ʿālī* ... Ḥaidarābād, 1347/1928–9.

ʿĀshir *Daftar i Kutubkhānah i ʿĀshir Efendi*. Constantinople, 1306.

Ashraf ʿAlī Arab. Cat. *Catalogue of the Arabic books and manuscripts in the Library of the Asiatic Society of Bengal compiled by ... Mirza A. ʿA.* Calcutta, 1899–1904.

Ātash-kadah (circ. A.H. 1171–93/1760–79), by Luṭf-ʿAlī Bēg. References are given to the numbers assigned to the biographies in Ethé's description of the MS. Bodleian 384.

Āthār al-ṣanādīd [in Urdu], by S. Aḥmad Khān. Delhi, 1263/1847.

ʿĀṭif Efendī *Daftar i Kutub-khānah i ʿĀṭif Efendī*. Istanbul, 1310. (Historical MSS. cited from Tauer (*q.v. infra*).)

Aumer *Die persischen Handschriften der K. Hof- und Staatsbibliothek in Muenchen beschrieben von J.A.* Munich, 1866.

Āyā Ṣūfiyah *Daftar i Kutubkhānah i Āyā Ṣūfyah*. Constantinople, 1304.

B.S.O.S. *Bulletin of the School of Oriental Studies.*

Baghdād Köshkü The Baghdād Kiosk library preserved in the Ṭōp Qapū Sarāy at Istanbul. (Historical MSS. cited from Tauer (*q.v. infra*).)

Bānkīpūr *Catalogue of the Arabic and Persian manuscripts in the Oriental Public Library at Bankipore. Prepared* [so far as the Persian volumes are concerned] *by Maulavi Abdul Muqtadir*. Patna, 1908–

Bānkīpūr Arab. Hand-list فهرست دستی کتب قلمی لائبریری موقوفه خان بهادر . . . خدا بخش خان مرحوم . . . مسمی به مفتاح الکنوز الخفیه . . . مرتبه مولوی عبد الحمید . پٹنه ۱۹۱۸ – ۱۹۲۲

Bānkīpūr Pers. Hand-list فهرست نسخ خطی فارسی اورینٹل پبلک لائبریری بانکیپور مسمی به مراة العلوم . . . مرتبه مولوی عبد المقتدر . پٹنه ١٩٢٥–

Bānkīpūr Suppt. i, ii *Supplement to the Catalogue of the Persian manuscripts in the Oriental Public Library at Bankipore. Volume i* (*Volume* ii). *By Maulavi Abdul Muqtadir*. Patna (Calcutta printed) 1932, 1933.

Bashīr Āghā *Daftar i Kutubkhānah i Bashīr Āghā* [*Stambul*]. Constantinople, 1303.

Bāyazīd دفتر کتبخانهٔ ولی الدین سلطان بایزید جامعشریفی درو ننده واقعدر . درسعادت ١٣٠٤

Berlin *Verzeichniss der persischen Handschriften der Königlichen Bibliothek zu Berlin von W. Pertsch*. Berlin, 1888.

Blochet *Catalogue des manuscrits persans de la Bibliothèque Nationale*. Paris, 1905–12–

Bodleian *Catalogue of the Persian ... manuscripts in the Bodleian Library begun by ... Ed. Sachau ... completed ... by H. Ethé*. Oxford, 1889.

Bodleian iii *Catalogue of the Persian, Turkish, Hindustani and Pushtu manuscripts in the Bodleian Library. Part iii. Additional Persian manuscripts. By A.F.L. Beeston*. Oxford 1954.

Bodleian Nicoll and Pusey. See Nicoll-Pusey.

Bombay Fyzee *A descriptive list of the Arabic, Persian and Urdu manuscripts in the Bombay Branch, Royal Asiatic Society. By A.A. Fyzee*. [Reprinted from the *Journal of the B.B.R.A.S.*] [Bombay, n.d.]

Bombay Univ. *A descriptive catalogue of the Arabic, Persian and Urdu manuscripts in the Library of the University of Bombay. By Khān Bahādur Shaikh ʿAbdu'l-Ḳādir-e-Sarfarāz*. Bombay, 1935.

Brelvi and Dhabhar *Supplementary catalogue of Arabic, Hindustani, Persian and Turkish* MSS. *and descriptive catalogue of the Avesta, Pahlavi, Pazend and Persian* MSS. *in the Mulla Firoz Library* [at Bombay]. *Compiled by S.A. Brelvi ... and Ervad B.N. Dhabhar*. Bombay, 1917.

Breslau *Verzeichniss der arabischen, persischen, türkischen und hebräischen Handschriften der Stadtbibliothek zu Breslau von C. Brockelmann*. Breslau, 1903.

Brockelmann *Geschichte der arabischen Litteratur von C.B.* Weimar-Berlin, 1898–1902.

Browne Coll. *A descriptive catalogue of the Oriental* MSS. *belonging to the late E.G. Browne* [and at present deposited in the Cambridge University Library]. *By E.G. Browne. Completed & edited ... by R.A. Nicholson*. Cambridge, 1932.

Browne Hand-list — *A hand-list of the Muḥammadan manuscripts ... in the Library of the University of Cambridge by E.G.B.* Cambridge, 1900.

Browne Pers. Cat. — *A catalogue of the Persian manuscripts in the Library of the University of Cambridge by E.G.B.* Cambridge, 1896.

Browne Suppt. — *A supplementary hand-list of the Muḥammadan manuscripts ... in the Libraries of the University and Colleges of Cambridge by E.G.B.* Cambridge, 1922.

Bug͟hyat al-wuʿāt — *B. al-w. fī ṭabaqāt al-lug͟hawīyīn wa-'l-nuḥāt* [in Arabic], by al-Suyūṭī. Cairo, 1326.

Būhār — *Catalogue raisonné of the Bûhâr Library* [now in the Imperial Library, Calcutta]. *Vol. I. Catalogue of the Persian manuscripts ... Begun by Maulavî Qâsim Ḥasîr Raḍavî, revised and completed by Maulavi ʿAbd-ul-Muqtadir.* Calcutta, 1921.

Buk͟hārā Semenov — *Kalalog rukopisei istoricheskogo otdela Bukharskoi Tsentral'noi Biblioteki.* [By] *A.A. Semenov.* Tashkent, 1925.

But-k͟hānah (A.H. 1021/1612–13), by "Muḥammad" Ṣūfī, Ḥasan Bēg k͟hākī and ʿAbd al-Laṭīf ʿAbbāsī. References are given to the numbers assigned to the biographies in Ethé's description of the MS. Bodleian 366.

Caetani — *La fondazione Caetani per gli studi musulmani. Notizia della sua istituzione e Catalogo dei suoi MSS. orientali per cura di G. Gabrieli.* Rome, 1926.

Cairo — *Fihrist al-kutub al-Fārisīyah wa-'l-Jāwīyah al-maḥfūẓah bi-'l-Kutubk͟hānat al-k͟hidīwīyat al-Miṣrīyah ... jamaʿahu wa-rattabahu ʿAlī Efendī Ḥilmī al-Dāg͟histānī.* Cairo, 1306.

Calcutta Madrasah — *Catalogue of the Arabic and Persian manuscripts in the Library of the Calcutta Madrasah by Kamálu 'd-Dīn Aḥmad and ʿAbdu 'l-Muqtadir.* Calcutta, 1905.

Cambridge 2nd Suppt. — *A second supplementary hand-list of the Muḥammadan manuscripts in the university and colleges of Cambridge. By A.J. Arberry.* Cambridge 1952.

Cambridge Trinity. See Palmer Trinity.

Cataloghi — *Cataloghi dei codici orientali di alcune biblioteche d'Italia.* Florence, 1878–1904.

Chanykov — *Die Sammlung von morgenländischen Handschriften, welche die Kaiserliche Öffentliche Bibliothek zu St. Petersburg im Jahre* 1864 *von Hrn v. Chanykov enworben hat. Von B. Dorn.* St. Petersburg, 1865.

C͟helebī ʿAbd Allāh — *Daftar i Kutubk͟hānah i C͟helebī ʿA.A. Efendī.* Constantinople, 1311.

Christensen-Østrup — *Description de quelques manuscrits orientaux appartenant à la Bibliothèque de l'Université de Copenhague par A.C. et J.Ø.*

	(*Oversigt over det Kongelige Danske Videnskabernes Selskabs Forhandlinger*, 1915, no. 3–4, pp. 255–84.)
Const.	Constantinople.
Cureton-Rieu	*Catalogus codicum manuscriptorum orientalium qui in Museo Britannico asservantur Pars secunda, codices Arabicos amplectens.* [By W. Cureton and C. Rieu.] London, 1838–71.
D.M.G.	*Katalog der Bibliothek der Deutschen Morgenländischen Gesellschaft. Zweiter Band: Handschriften. Teil B: Persische und Hindustanische Handschriften bearbeitet von … Mahommed Musharraf-ul-Hukk.* Leipzig, 1911.
Dāmād Ibrāhīm	*Daftar i Kutub-khānah i Dāmād Ibrāhīm Pāshā* [now preserved in the Sulaimānīyah Kutub-khānah i ʿumūmī]. Istanbul, 1312. (Historical MSS. cited from Tauer (*q.v. infra*).)
Decourdemanche I	[A list by E. Blochet of MSS. presented to the Bibliothèque Nationale in 1905 by M.D.] (*Bibliographie Moderne*, Tome X, pp. 214–34.)
Decourdemanche II	*Une collection de manuscrits musulmans* (*donnée à la Bibliothèque Nationale par M.D.*). *Par E. Blochet.* (*Archives Marocaines*, XV, 2, pp. 193–282. Paris, 1909.)
Decourdemanche III	*Inventaire de la collection de manuscrits musulmans de M.D.* [presented to the Bibl. Nat. by Mlle. Wendling in 1916] *par E. Blochet.* (J.A. XIe série, Tome viii, pp. 305–423.)
Dhabhar	*Descriptive catalogue of some manuscripts bearing on Zoroastrianism and pertaining to the different collections in the Mulla Feroze Library. Prepared by Ervad Bomanji Nusserwanji Dhabhar.* Bombay, 1923.
Dorn	*Catalogue des manuscrits et xylographes orientaux de la Bibliothèque Impériale Publique de St. Pétersbourg.* [By B. Dorn.] St. Petersburg, 1852.
Dorn A. M.	*Das Asiatische Museum der Kaiserlichen Akademie der Wissenschaften zu St. Petersburg. Von … Dr. Bernh. D.* St. Petersburg, 1846.
Dresden	*Catalogus codicum manuscriptorum orientalium Bibliothecae Regiae Dresdensis. Scripsit … H.O. Fleischer.* Leipzig, 1831.
al-Durar al-kāminah	*al-D. al-k. fī aʿyān al-miʾat al-thāminah* (in Arabic), by Ibn Ḥajar al-ʿAsqalānī. Ḥaidarābād, 1348–50.
Edhem and Stchoukine	*Les manuscripts orientaux illustrés de la Bibliothèque de l'Université de Stamboul. Par Fehmi Edhem et Ivan Stchoukine* (*Mémoires de l'Institut Français d'Archéologie de Stamboul*, I). Paris, 1933.

Edinburgh	*A descriptive catalogue of the Arabic and Persian manuscripts in Edinburgh University Library. By Mohammed Ashraful Hukk …, H. Ethé …, and E. Robertson …* Edinburgh, 1925.
Edwards	*A catalogue of the Persian printed books in the British Museum compiled by Edward E.…* London, 1922.
Ellis	*Catalogue of Arabic books in the British Museum. By A.G.E.* London, 1894–1901.
Ellis-Edwards	*A descriptive list of the Arabic manuscripts acquired by the Trustees of the British Museum since* 1894 *compiled by A.G. Ellis and E. Edwards.* London, 1912.
Escurial	*Les Manuscrits Arabes de l'Escurial décrits par Hartwig Dérenbourg* (Publications de l'École des Langues Orientales Vivantes IIe série vol. x, xi fasc. 1) vol. i Paris, 1884. Vol. ii fasc. 1 Paris, 1903. *Décrits d'après les notes de H.D.… revues … par E. Lévi-Provençal* (Publ., École des Langues Or. Viv., Sér. 6 vol. iii) vol. iii Paris, 1928.
Ethé	*Catalogue of the Persian Manuscripts in the Library of the India Office by H. E.* Oxford, 1903–.
Eton	*Catalogue of the oriental manuscripts in the Library of Eton College compiled by D. S. Margoliouth.* Oxford, 1904.
Ewald	*Verzeichniss der orientalischen Handschriften der Universitäts-Bibliothek zu Tübingen.* Tübingen, 1839.
Fagnan	*Catalogue général des manuscrits des bibliothèques publiques de France. Départements. Tome xviii: Alger, Par E.F.* Paris, 1893.
Faiḍ Allāh Efendī	*Daftar i Kutub-khānah i Faiḍ Allāh Efendī wa-shaikh Murād etc.* [now preserved in the Millat Kutub-khānah-sī]. Istanbul, 1310. (Historical MSS. cited from Tauer (*q.v. infra*).)
Fātiḥ	*Daftar i Fātiḥ Kutubkhānah-sī.* Constantinople, n.d.
al-Fawā'id al-bahīyah	*al-F. al-b. fī tarājim al-Ḥanafīyah* [in Arabic], by M. 'Abd al-Ḥaiy Lakhnawī. Cairo, 1324.

Fawāt al-Wafayāt (in Arabic), by Ibn Shākir al-Kutubī. Būlāq, 1283.

Fleischer	*Catalogus librorum manuscriptorum qui in Bibliotheca Senatoria Civitatis Lipsiensis asservantur* (*Codices arabici persici turcici descripti ab H.O.F.*). Grimae, 1838.
Flügel	*Die arabischen, persischen und türkischen Handschriften der Kaiserlich-Königlichen Hofbibliothek zu Wien … beschrieben vom Professor Dr. G.F.* Vienna, 1865–7.
G.i.P.	*Grundriss der iranischen Philologie herausgegeben von W. Geiger und E. Kuhn.* Strassburg, 1896–1904.

Garcin de Tassy — *Histoire de la littérature hindouie et hindoustanie par M.G. de T.* 2nd ed. Paris, 1870–1.

Glasgow — *The Persian and Turkish manuscripts in the Hunterian Library of the University of Glasgow. By T.H. Weir.* (JRAS. 1906, pp. 595–609.)

Gotha — *Die persischen Handschriften der Herzoglichen Bibliothek zu Gotha. Verzeichnet von Dr. W. Pertsch.* Vienna, 1859.

Gotha Turkish — *Die türkischen Handschriften der Herzoglichen Bibliothek zu Gotha. Verzeichnet von Dr. W. Pertsch.* Vienna, 1864.

Gul i raʿnā (A.H. 1182/1768–9), by Lachhmī Narāyan "Shafīq" Aurangābādī. References are given to the pages of ʿAbd al-Muqtadir's description of the MS. Bānkīpūr viii 701.

Ḥ.Kh. — *Kashf al-ẓunūn ... Lexicon bibliographicum et encyclopaedicum a* ... Haji Khal[ī]fa ... *compositum ... edidit ...* (*G. Fluegel.* Leipzig, 1835–58.

Ḥabīb al-siyar — *Ḥ. al-s. fī akhbār afrād al-bashar.* By Khwāndamīr. Bombay, 1273/1857.

Ḥadā'iq al-Ḥanafīyah [in Urdu. Completed A.H. 1297], by Faqīr Muḥammad Lāhaurī. Lucknow, 1906.

Haft iqlīm, by Amīn Aḥmad Rāzī. The references are to the numbers given by Ethé to the biographies in his description of the I.O. MS. Ethé 724.

Ḥaidarābād Coll. — *Author-Catalogue of the Ḥaidarābād Collection of manuscripts and printed books* [presented by Nawwāb ʿAzīz Jang Bahādur of Ḥaidarābād to the Asiatic Society of Bengal]. Calcutta, 1913.

Ḥakīm-oghlu ʿAlī Pāshā — *Daftar i Ḥakīm-ūghlī ʿAlī Pāshā Kutub-khānah-sī* [now preserved in the Millat Kutub-khānah-sī]. Istanbul, 1311. (Historical MSS. cited from Tauer (*q.v. infra*).)

Ḥālat Efendī — *Daftar i Kutub-khānah i Ḥālat Efendī,* [now preserved in the Sulaimānīyah Kutub-khānah i ʿumūmī]. Istanbul, 1312. (Historical MSS. cited from Tauer (*q.v. infra*).)

Hamburg — *Katalog der orientalischen Handschriften der Stadtbibliothek zu Hamburg mit Ausschluss der hebräischen. Teil I. Die arabischen, persischen ... Handschriften beschrieben von C. Brockelmann.* Hamburg, 1908.

Ḥamīdīyah — حمیدیه کتبخانه سنده محفوظ کتب موجوده نک دفتریدر . دار الخلافة العلیة ١٣٠٠

Ḥasan Ḥusnī — The library of Ḥasan Ḥusnī Pāshā at Eyyūb. (Historical MSS. cited from Tauer (*q.v. infra*).)

Horn Pers. Hss. — *Persische Handschriften in Constantinopel. Von P. Horn.* (ZDMG. liv (1900), pp. 275–332 and 475–509.)

Houtum-Schindler	*The Persian manuscripts of the late Sir Albert Houtum-Schindler, K.C.I.E. By E.G. Browne.* (JRAS. 1917, pp. 657–94.)
Hudāʾī Efendī	The library of Hudāʾī Efendī preserved in the library of Salīm Aghā at Scutari. (Historical MSS. cited from Tauer (*q.v. infra*).)
I.Ḥ.	*Kashf al-ḥujub wal astār ʿan asmāʾ al-kutub wal asfār, or the Bibliography of Shīʿa literature, of Mawlānā Iʿjāz Ḥusain al-Kantūrī* [or rather al-Kintūrī]. *Edited by Mawlavi M. Hidayat Husain.* (Bibliotheca Indica.) Calcutta, 1912–14–
I.O.	India Office, London. These initials have been prefixed to the designations of certain manuscripts not described in Ethé's catalogue.
Ibn Quṭlūbughā	*Tāj al-tarājim, fī ṭabaqāt al-Ḥanafīyah* (in Arabic). *Die Krone der Lebensbeschreibungen … von Zein-ad-dîn Ḳâsim Ibn Ḳuṭlûbugâ … herausgegeben … von G. Flügel.* Leipzig, 1862.
Itḥāf al-nubalāʾ	*I. al-n. al-muttaqīn bi-iḥyāʾ maʾāthir al-fuqahāʾ al-muḥaddithīn*, by Ṣiddīq Ḥasan Khān. Cawnpore, 1288.
Ivanow	*Concise descriptive catalogue of the Persian manuscripts in the collection of the Asiatic Society of Bengal. By Wladimir I.* Calcutta, 1924.
Ivanow 1st Suppt.	*Concise descriptive catalogue of the Persian manuscripts in the collections of the Asiatic Society of Bengal. First supplement. By W. Ivanow.* Calcutta, 1927.
Ivanow 2nd Suppt.	*Concise descriptive catalogue of the Persian manuscripts in the collections of the Asiatic Society of Bengal. Second supplement. By W. Ivanow.* Calcutta, 1928.
Ivanow Curzon	*Concise descriptive catalogue of the Persian manuscripts in the Curzon Collection. Asiatic Society of Bengal. By W.I.* Calcutta, 1926.
Jackson-Yohannan	*A catalogue of the collection of Persian manuscripts … presented to the Metropolitan Museum of Art, New York, by A. S. Cochran. Prepared and edited by A. V. Williams Jackson … and A. Yohannan.* New York, 1914.
al-Jawāhir al-muḍīʾah	*al-J. al-m. fī ṭabaqāt al-Ḥanafīyah* [in Arabic], by ʿAbd al-Qādir b. Abī ʾl-Wafāʾ M. al-Qurashī. Ḥaidarābād, 1332.
de Jong	*Catalogus codicum orientalium Bibliothecae Academiae Regiae Scientiarum quem a clar. Weijersio inchoatum, post hujus mortem absolvit et edidit Dr. P. de J.* Leyden, 1862.
Kahl	*Persidskiya, arabskiya i tyurkskiya rukopisi Turkestanskoi publichnoi biblioteki.* [By] *E. Kalʹ.* Tashkent, 1889.

Kalimāt al-ṣādiqīn (A.H. 1023/1614), by M. Ṣādiq Hamadānī. References are given to the numbers assigned to the biographies in ʿAbd al-Muqtadir's description of the MS. Bānkīpūr viii 671.

Kamānkas̲h̲   *Daftar i Kutubk̲h̲ānah i Amīr k̲h̲wājah Kamānkas̲h̲.* Constantinople, n.d.

Karlsruhe   *Die Handschriften der ... Hof- und Landesbibliothek in Karlsruhe. II Orientalische Handschriften.* [The Arabic and Persian described by S. Landauer.] Karlsruhe, 1892.

K̲h̲āliṣ Efendī   The library of K̲h̲āliṣ Efendī preserved in the University Library at Istanbul. (Historical MSS. cited from Tauer *(q.v. infra)*.)

K̲h̲azīnat al-aṣfiyāʾ, by G̲h̲ulām Sarwar Lāhaurī. 3rd ed. Cawnpore, 1914.

K̲h̲izānah i ʿāmirah (A.H. 1176/1762–3), by G̲h̲ulām-ʿAlī "Āzād" Bilgrāmī. References are given to the numbers assigned to the biographies in Ethé's description of the MS. Bodleian 381.

K̲h̲ulāṣat al-afkār (A.H. 1206–7/1791–3), by Abū Ṭālib K̲h̲ān Iṣfahānī. References are given to the numbers assigned to the biographies in Ethé's description of the MS. Bodleian 391.

K̲h̲ulāṣat al-athar   *Kh. al-a. fī aʿyān al-qarn al-ḥādī ʿashar* [in Arabic], by al-Muḥibbī. Cairo, 1284.

K̲h̲ulāṣat al-kalām (A.H. 1198/1784), by ʿAlī Ibrāhīm K̲h̲ān. References are given to the numbers assigned to the biographies in Ethé's description of the MS. Bodleian 390 and in ʿAbd al-Muqtadir's description of the MS. Bānkīpūr viii 704–5.

K̲h̲usrau Pās̲h̲ā   *Daftar i Kutub-k̲h̲ānah i K̲h̲usrau Pās̲h̲ā.* Istanbul, n.d. (Historical MSS. cited from Tauer *(q.v. infra)*.)

Köprülü   *Köprülü-zāde Meḥmet Paşa Kütübḫānesinde maḥfūẓ kütüb i mevcūdenüñ defteridir.* [Istanbul] n.d. (Cf. Horn.)

Krafft   *Die arabischen, persischen und türkischen Handschriften der K.K. Orientalischen Akademie zu Wien, beschrieben von A.K.* Vienna, 1842.

Krause   *Stambuler Handschriften islamischer Mathematiker. Von Max Krause* (see PL. ii p. 1).

Lālah-lī   *Daftar i Kutubk̲h̲ānah i Lālah-lī.* Constantinople, 1311.

Lālā Ismāʿīl   The library of Lālā Ismāʿīl Efendī listed at the end of the *daftar* of the Ḥamīdīyah Library (for which see p. xvi of Section I). (Historical MSS. cited from Tauer *(q.v. infra)*.)

Leningrad Acad. i (Miklukho-Maklai)   *Akademiya Nauk SSSR. Institut Vostokovedeniya. N.D. Miklukho-Maklai. Opisanie tadzhikskikh i persidskikh rukopisei Instituta Vostokovedeniya* [Pt. 1 (see p. 3, l. 26)]. Moscow-Leningrad 1955.

Leningrad Asiatic Museum, Bukhārā Collection	*Arabskiye Rukopisi Bukharskoy kollektsii Aziatskogo Museya Instituta Vostokovedeniya* AN SSSR. By V. I. Belyaev. Leningrad, 1932.
Leyden	*Catalogus codicum orientalium Bibliothecae Academiae Lugduno-Batavae* [by Dozy, de Jong, de Goeje and Houtsma]. Leyden, 1851–77.
Lincei	Reale Accademia dei Lincei, Rome. The references are to the issues of the *Rendiconti* (Classe di scienze morali, storiche e filologiche) in which the manuscripts are catalogued.
Lindesiana	*Bibliotheca Lindesiana. Hand-list of Oriental manuscripts. Arabic, Persian, Turkish.* [Now in the John Rylands Library at Manchester.] Aberdeen, 1898.
Loth	*A catalogue of the Arabic manuscripts in the Library of the India Office. By O. L.* London, 1877.
Lu'lu'atā 'l-Baḥrain	*L. 'l-B. fī 'l-ijāzah li-qurratai al-ʿain* (in Arabic), by Yūsuf b. Aḥmad al-Baḥrānī [cf. Browne *Lit. Hist*, iv 356]. Bombay, n.d. For a Ṭihrān edition of 1269 see Harrassowitz's Bücher-Katalog 430, no. 641.
Lund	*Codices orientales Bibliothecae Regiae Universitatis Lundensis recensuit C. J. Tornberg.* Lund, 1850. *Supplementa.* Lund, 1853.
M. Idrīs	*Taṭyīb al-ikhwān bi-dhikr ʿulamāʾ al-zamān* [in Urdu], by M. Idrīs Nagarāmī. Lucknow, 1897.
Maʿārif	*Fihrist i kutub i khaṭṭī i Kitāb-khānah i ʿUmūmī i Maʿārif ... taʾlīf i ʿAbd al-ʿAzīz Jawāhir i Kalām* (English title on back cover of vol. i: *Catalogue of Persian and Arabic manuscripts of the Public Library of the Ministry of Education ... Arranged by Abdol-Aziz Javaher Kelam*), vol. i, Tihrān A.H.S. 1313/1934–5, vol. ii, A.H.S. 1314/1935–6 (Mihr Pr.).
Madras	*Alphabetical Index of manuscripts in the Government Oriental* MSS. *Library, Madras.* Madras, 1893.
Madrās iii	*A descriptive catalogue of the Islamic manuscripts in the Government Oriental Manuscripts Library, Madras. By T. Chandrasekharan ... Curator ... and the staff of the Library* [i.e., so far as this volume is concerned, "Janab Muhammad Yousuf Kokan" and "Syed Durwaish Khadari"]. *Volume iii. D. Nos. from 103 to 180 (Hindustani). D. Nos. from 219 to 289 (Arabic). D. Nos. 688 to 821 (Persian).* Madras 1954.
Maḥbūb al-albāb	*M. al-a. fī taʿrīf al-kutub wa-'l-kuttāb*, by Khudā Bakhsh. [A catalogue of Kh. B.'s private library now preserved in the Oriental Public Library founded by him at Bānkīpūr.] Ḥaidarābād, 1314.

Maḥmūd Efendī — The library of Maḥmūd Efendī preserved in the old *tekke* of Yaḥyā Efendī at Beshikṭāsh, Istānbūl (Historical MSS. cited from Tauer, q.v. p. xxxv).

Majālis al-mu'minīn, by Nūr Allāh Shūshtarī. Ṭihrān, 1299 [?].

Majālis al-'ushshāq. by Sulṭān Ḥusain b. Manṣūr. Cawnpore, 1287/1870.

Majlis — *Catalogue des manuscrits persans et arabes de la Bibliothèque du Madjless. Par Y. Etessami.* Ṭihrān, 1933.

Makhzan al-gharā'ib (A.H. 1218/1803–4), by Aḥmad 'Alī Sandīlī. References are given to the numbers assigned to the biographies in Ethé's description of the MS. Bodleian 395.

Manchester, Mingana — *Catalogue of the Arabic manuscripts in the John Rylands Library, Manchester, by A. Mingana* ... Manchester 1934.

Maqālāt al-ḥunafā': see *PL*. ii § 323 (6).

Marsigli — *Remarques sur les manuscrits orientaux de la collection Marsigli à Bologne ... par le Baron Victor Rosen.* (*Atti della R. Accademia dei Lincei.* Serie 3ª. Scienze morali. Vol. xii. Rome, 1885.)

Marteau — *Notices sur les manuscrits persans et arabes de la collection Marteau* [in the Bibliothèque Nationale] *par M. E. Blochet.* (*Notices et extraits*, Tome xli.) Paris, 1923.

Mashhad — *Fihrist i kutub i Kitāb-khānah i mubārakah i Āstān i quds i Riḍawī.* Mashhad, 1345/1926–.

Meherji Rana — *Descriptive catalogue of all manuscripts in the First Dastur Meherji Rana Library, Navsari. Prepared by Bamanji Nasarvanji Dhabhar.* Bombay, 1923.

Mehren — *Codices orientales Bibliothecae Regiae Hafniensis ... enumerati et descripti. Pars tertia. Codices persicos, turcicos, hindustanicos & c. continens.* [By A.F. Mehren.] Copenhagen, 1857.

Miklukho-Maklai. See Leningrad Acad. above.

Mir'āt al-khayāl (A.H. 1102/1690–1), by Shēr Khān Lōdī. References are given to the numbers assigned to the biographies in Ethé's description of the MS. Bodleian 374.

Mishkāt — *Fihrist i kitāb-khānah i ihdā'ī i Āqā-yi Saiyid Muḥammad Mishkāt bah kitāb-khānah i Dānish-gāh i Tihrān* (Publications of the University of Tihrān, 123, 168, 169, 181, 299 and —), vol. i (the Qur'ān, etc.), by 'Alī-Naqī Munzawī, A.H.S.1330–1/1952, vol. ii (Adab), by the same, A.H.S. 1333/1955, vol. iii, pt. 1 (Philosophy etc.), by M. Taqī Dānish-pazhūh, A.H.S. 1332/1953, pt. 2 (Medicine, Mathematics, etc.), by the same, A.H.S. 1332/1953, pt. 3 (Akhbār, Uṣūl, Fiqh), by the same, A.H.S. 1335/1956 (another volume, or part, is to follow: see pt. 3 p. [2111]).

Morley — *A descriptive catalogue of the historical manuscripts in the Arabic and Persian languages preserved in the Library of the Royal Asiatic Society ... By W. H. M.* London, 1854.

Muntahā 'l-maqāl — *M. al-m. fī aḥwāl al-rijāl* [in Arabic], by M. b. Ismāʿīl al-Karbalāʾī. Ṭihrān, 1302.

Muntakhab al-ashʿār (A.H. 1161/1748), by M. ʿAlī Khān Mashhadī. References are given to the numbers assigned to the biographies in Ethé's description of the MS. Bodleian 379.

Murād — *Daftar i Kutubkhānah i Dāmād-zādah Qāḍī-ʿaskar Muḥammad Murād.* Constantinople, 1311.

Muṣṭafā Efendī — The library of Muṣṭafā Efendī preserved in the Sulaimānīyah Kutub-khānah i ʿumūmī at Istanbul. (Historical MSS. cited from Tauer (*q.v. infra*).)

Nadhīr Aḥmad — *Notes on important Arabic and Persian MSS. found in various Libraries in India* [by Maulawī Ḥāfiẓ Nadhīr Aḥmad] (in the *Journal of the Asiatic Society of Bengal*, New Series, vol. xiii (1917), pp. lxxvii–cxxxix and vol. xiv (1918), pp. cxcix–ccclvi. The references are to the serial numbers in the Persian section of the latter.)

Nāfidh Pāshā — The library of Nāfidh Pāshā preserved in the Sulaimānīyah Kutub-khānah i ʿumūmī at Istanbul. (Historical MSS. cited from Tauer (*q.v. infra*).)

Nicoll-Pusey — *Bibliothecae Bodleianae codicum manuscriptorum Orientalium, ... catalogas ... Pars secunda ... confecit A. Nicoll ... Editionem absolvit et Catalogum Urianum aliquatenus emendavit E.B. Pusey.* Oxford, 1821–1835.

Nūr i ʿUthmānīyah — نور عثمانیه کتبخانه سنده محفوظ کتب موجوده نک دفتر یدر . استانبول ۱۳۰۳

Nuzhat al-khawāṭir — *N. al-kh. wa-bahjat al-masāmiʿ wa-l-nawāẓir* (in Arabic), a biographical dictionary of Indian celebrities in eight volumes (of which vol. i (1st-7th cent., published A.H. 1366/1947), vol. ii (8th cent., A.H. 1350/1931–2),[1] and vol. iii (9th cent., A.H. 1371/1951) have so far been printed at the press of the Dāʾirat al-Maʿārif al-ʿUthmānīyah, Ḥaidarābād, Deccan), by S. ʿAbd al-Ḥaiy b. Fakhr al-Dīn al-Ḥasanī (a former Director of the Nadwat al-ʿUlamāʾ, Lucknow, d. 15 Jumādā II 1341/2 Feb. 1923: see *N. al-kh.* vol. i pp. ḍād—ḥḥ (a biography by his son, S. ʿAbd

1 This second volume, printed some years in advance of the others, is meant when the *N. al-kh.* is cited in the present survey without mention of the volume-number.

	al-ʿAlī al-Ḥasanī), vol. ii pp. 181–92 (the same biography slightly altered); M. Idrīs [cf. p. xxi above] p. 40; Nad͟hīr Aḥmad p. lxxxi; Brockelmann Sptbd. ii p. 863).
Palmer Trinity	*A descriptive Catalogue of the Arabic, Persian and Turkish Manuscripts in the Library of Trinity College, Cambridge*. By E. H. Palmer. Cambridge and London, 1870.
Paris Arab. Accessions (1884–1924)	*Catalogue des manuscrits arabes des nouvelles acquisitions (1884–1924)*. By E. Blochet. Paris, 1925.
Peshawar	*Lubāb al-maʿārif al-ʿilmīyah fī maktabat Dār al-ʿulūm al-Islāmīyah*. By Maulawī ʿAbd al-Raḥīm. [The oriental section of the Library of the Islamiyah College, Peshawar.] Āgrah, 1918.
Philadelphia Lewis Coll.	*Oriental manuscripts of the John Frederick Lewis Collection in the Free Library of Philadelphia. A descriptive catalogue ... by Muhammed Ahmed Simsar*. Philadelphia, 1937.
PL.	*Persian literature*, i.e. the present survey, as has already been explained.
Princeton	*A catalogue of Turkish and Persian manuscripts belonging to Robert Garrett and deposited in the Princeton University Library*. By N. N. Martinovitch. Princeton, 1926.
Princeton, Arabic Catalogue	*Descriptive catalog of the Garrett Collection of Arabic Manuscripts in the Princeton University Library by Philip K. Hitti, Nabih Amin Faris, Buṭrus Abd-al-Malik*. Princeton, 1938.
Qarah Muṣṭafā	*Daftar i Qarah Muṣṭafā Pās͟hā wa Muṣallā Madrasah-sī*, etc. Constantinople, 1310.
Qarah-C͟helebī-Zādah	*Daftar i Kutub-k͟hānah i Qarah-C͟helebī-Zādah Ḥusām al-Dīn* [now preserved in the Sulaimānīyah Kutub-k͟hānah i ʿumūmī at Istanbul]. Istanbul, n.d. (Historical MSS. cited from Tauer (*q.v. infra*).)
Qilīj ʿAlī	*Qilīj ʿAlī Pās͟hā Kutubk͟hānah-sī daftarī*. Constantinople, 1311.
R.A.S.	*Catalogue of the Arabic, Persian, Hindustani, and Turkish MSS. in the Library of the Royal Asiatic Society*. (JRAS. 1892, pp. 501–69.)
Rāg͟hib Pās͟hā	The library of Rāg͟hib Pās͟hā at Istanbul. (Historical MSS. cited from Tauer (*q.v. infra*).)
Raḥmān ʿAlī	*Tad͟hkirah i ʿulamā i Hind*, by R. ʿA. Lucknow, 1894.
Raiḥānat al-adab	*R. al-a. fī tarājim al-maʿrūfīn bi-ʾl-kunyah au al-laqab* [on the title-pages is added *yā Kunā wa-alqāb*], a biographical dictionary (in Persian) of Islamic celebrities ancient and modern, mainly scholars and men of letters, not far short of 5,000

in number, by M. ʿAlī [b. M. Ṭāhir] Tabrīzī [Khiyābānī][2] *maʿrūf bah* Mudarris, who was born at Tabrīz (*R. al-a.* vi p. 13, l. 6 from foot) in 1296/1879 and died there (*vid. ibid.*) on 1 Shaʿbān 1373/5 April 1954 (*R. al-a.* vi p. 4^{10} [3] before completion of the printing of his work, which was seen through its final stages by his son, ʿAlī Aṣghar Mudarris,[4] and which consists of six volumes published at [Tihrān][5] and (vol. vi only) Tabrīz (Shafaq Pr.) from A.H. 1366/A.H.S. 1326/A.D. 1947 to [A.H.S. 1333, the preface to vol. vi being dated (on p. 34) 17 Isfand-māh 1333 (March 1955)] or more probably [A.H.S. 1334/1955] and containing (1) persons known by *alqāb* and *ansāb* (vols. i–iv), (2) persons known by *kunyahs* ((*a*) Abū, vol. v pp. 5–209, (*b*) Ibn, vol. v p. 209 to vol. vi p. 207, (*c*) Umm, vol. vi pp. 208–58, (*d*) Bint, vol. vi pp. 258–63, (*e*) Banī, vol. vi pp. 264–316, (*f*) Āl, vol. vi pp. 316–71) [the work being thus complete except for the list of corrigenda, *ghalaṭ-nāmah i judāgānah* (see vol. i p. 439^{12}), which the author hoped to append].

Rāmpūr — *Fihrist i kutub i Arabī maujūdah i Kutub-khānah i Riyāsat i Rāmpūr*. Rāmpūr, 1902.

Rashaḥāt, by ʿAlī b. Ḥusain Kāshifī. Cawnpore, 1911.

Rauḍāt al-jannāt — *R. al-j. fī aḥwāl al-ʿulamāʾ wa-'l-sādāt* [in Arabic], by M. Bāqir b. Zain al-ʿĀbidīn Khwānsārī. Persia, 1306.

Rawān Köshkü — The library of the Erivan Kiosk preserved in the Ṭōp Qapū Sarāy at Istanbul. (Historical MSS. cited from Tauer (*q.v. infra*).)

Rehatsek — *Catalogue raisonné of the Arabic, Hindostani, Persian and Turkish MSS. in the Mulla Firuz Library*. Bombay, 1873.

Riḍā Pāshā — The library of Riḍā Pāshā preserved in the University Library at Istanbul. (Historical MSS. cited from Tauer (*q.v. infra*).)

Rieu — *Catalogue of the Persian manuscripts in the British Museum. By C. R.* London, 1879–81–83.

---

2 Khiyābān is a *maḥallah* in Tabrīz (see Mujtahidī *Rijāl i Ādharbāyjān* … p. 73^{10}).

3 The author's autobiography is given in vol. iii, pp. 505–7 (under Mudarris, M. ʿAlī) and there is a biography by his son, ʿAlī Aṣghar Mudarris, in vol. vi, pp. 2–34. Both are accompanied by portraits.

4 About whom the author says a few words in vol. iii, p. 506^{30}–507^{2}.

5 The imprints are Chāp-khānah i Saʿdī [Tihrān?] (vol. i), Chāp-khānah i ʿIlmī (vol. ii, title-page), Chāp-khānah i Shirkat i Sihāmī i Ṭabʿ i Kitāb (vol. ii, cover, and vols. iii–v).

Riyāḍ al-shuʿarāʾ (A.H. 1162/1749), by ʿAlī-Qulī khān "Wālih" Dāghistānī. References are given to the numbers assigned to the biographies in Ivanow's description of the MS. Ivanow Curzon 57.

Rieu Suppt. — *Supplement to the Catalogue of the Persian manuscripts in the British Museum by C. R.* London, 1895.

Romaskewicz — *Indices alphabetici codicum manu scriptorum Persicorum Turcicorum Arabicorum qui in Bibliotheca Literarum Universitatis Petropolitanae adservantur. Supplementum confecit A. R.* Leningrad, 1925.

Rosen, Institut — *Les manuscrits persans de l'Institut des Langues Orientales (du Ministère des Affaires Étrangères) décrits par le Baron Victor R.* St. Petersburg, 1886.

Rosen, M.A. — *Notices sommaires des manuscrits arabes du Musée Asiatique par le Baron Victor R.* Première livraison. St. Petersburg, 1881.

Ross and Browne — *Catalogue of two collections of Persian and Arabic manuscripts preserved in the India Office Library by E. Denison R. and E. G. B.* London, 1902.

Safīnah i Khwushgū (A.H. 1137/1724–5), by Bindrāban Dās "Khwushgū". References are given to the numbers assigned by Ethé to the biographies in the MS. Bodleian 376 and to the pages of ʿAbd al-Muqtadir's description of the MS. Bānkīpūr viii 690.

Safīnat al-auliyāʾ, by Dārā-Shukūh. Cawnpore, 1884. References are given also to the numbers assigned by Ethé to the biographies in his description of the India Office MS. Ethé 647.

Salemann-Rosen — *Indices alphabetici codicum manuscriptorum persicorum turcicorum arabicorum qui in Bibliotheca Imperialis Literarum Universitatis Petropolitanae adservantur. Confecerunt C. S. et V. R.* St. Petersburg, 1888.

Salīm Aghā — *Daftar i Kutub-khānah i Ilḥāj Salīm Aghā*. Istanbul, 1310–11. (Historical MSS. cited from Tauer (*q.v. infra*).)

Salīmīyah — *Daftar i Kutubkhānah i Salīmīyah*. Constantinople, 1311.

Schefer — *Bibliothèque Nationale. Catalogue de la collection de manuscrits orientaux ... formée par M.C.S. et acquise par l'état publié par E. Blochet*. Paris, 1900.

Semenov *Ukazatel'* — *Ukazatel' persidskoi literatury po istorii Uzbekov v Srednei Azii.* [By] *A. A. Semenov*. Tashkent, 1926.

Semenov *Kurzer Abriss* — *Kurzer Abriss der neueren mittelasiatisch-persischen (tadschikischen) Literatur* (1500–1900). *Von A. A. Semenov* (in Otto Harrassowitz's *Litterae orientales*, Heft 46: April 1931, pp. 1–10).

Shahīd ʿAlī Pāshā — The library of Shahīd ʿAlī Pāshā at Istanbul. (Historical MSS. cited from Tauer (*q.v. infra*).)

al-Shaqāʾiq al-Nuʿmānīyah — *al-Sh. al-N. fī ʿulamāʾ al-daulat al-ʿUthmānīyah* [in Arabic], by A. b. Muṣṭafā Ṭāshkubrīzādah. Cairo, 1310.

Siyar al-auliyāʾ, by S.M. Mubārak ʿAlawī Kirmānī called Amīr Khwurd. Delhi, 1302.

de Slane — *Bibliothèque Nationale. Département des manuscrits. Catalogue des manuscrits arabes par M. le Baron de S.* Paris, 1883–95.

Smirnow — *Manuscrits turcs de l'Institut des Langues Orientales décrits par W. D. Smirnow*. St. Petersburg, 1897.

Sprenger — *A catalogue of the Arabic, Persian and Hindústány manuscripts, of the libraries of the King of Oudh, compiled ... by A. S. ... Vol. I containing Persian and Hindústány poetry*. Calcutta, 1854. [Most of these MSS. were destroyed or dispersed at the time of the Mutiny, but Sprenger's descriptions include manscripts in the Library of the Asiatic Society of Bengal and his own private Library (now in the Preussische Staatsbibliothek) as well as a number of printed or lithographed books.]

Stockholm — *Katalog över Kungl. Bibliotekets orientaliska handskrifter av W. Riedel*. Stockholm, 1923.

Subḥat al-marjān — *S. al-m. fī āthār Hindūstān* [in Arabic], by Ghulām ʿAlī "Āzād" Bilgrāmī. [Bombay], 1303.

Subkī — *Ṭabaqāt al-Shāfiʿīyat al-kubrā* [in Arabic], by ʿAbd al-Wahhāb b. ʿAlī al-Subkī. Cairo, 1324.

Ṣuḥuf i Ibrāhīm (A.H. 1205/1790), by ʿAlī Ibrāhīm Khān. References are given to the numbers assigned to the biographies in Pertsch's description of the MS. Berlin 663.

T.C.D. — *Catalogue of the manuscripts in the Library of Trinity College, Dublin ... by T. K. Abbott*. Dublin, 1900.

Tajallī i nūr — *T. i n. maʿrūf bah Tadhkirah i mashāhīr i Jaunpūr*, by S. Nūr al-Dīn "Zaidī" Ẓafarābādī. Pt. II. Jaunpur, 1900.

Tarkhān Khadījah Sulṭān — The library of Tarkhān khadījah Sulṭān listed at the end of the Yeñī Jāmiʿ *daftar* (for which see p. xxiii of Section I) and now preserved in the Sulaimānīyah Kutub-khānah i ʿumūmī. (Historical MSS. cited from Tauer (*q.v. infra*).)

Tashkent Acad. — *Akademiya Nauk Uzbekskoi SSR. Institut Vostokovedeniya. Sobranie vostochnykh rukopisei Akademii Nauk Uzbekskoi SSR ... pod redaktsiei i pri uchastii ... Professora A.A. Semenova*. Vols, i–iv. Tashkent 1952–57.

Tashkent Univ. ii	*A.A. Semenov. Opisanie tadzhikskikh, persidskikh, arabskikh i tyurkskikh rukopisei Fundamental'noi Biblioteki Sredneaziatskogo Gosudarstvennogo Universiteta im. V. I. Lenina. Vypusk* 2 (English title: *A.A. Semenov. A descriptive catalogue of the Persian, Tadjík, Arabic and Turkish manuscripts preserved in the Library of Middle Asiatic State University by name of V. I. Lenin*). Tashkent 1956.
Tauer	*Les manuscrits persans historiques des bibliothèques de Stamboul. Par Felix Tauer* (in *Archiv Orientální*, vol. iii (Prague, 1931), pp. 87–118, 303–26, 462–91, vol. iv (1932), pp. 92–107, 193–207).
Topkapı Sarayı	*Topkapı Sarayı Müzesi Kütüphanesi Farsça Yazmalar Kataloğu. Hazırlayan Fehmi Edhem Karatay*. Istanbul, 1961. [Only used for *Tales*.]
Turin	*I manoscritti arabi, persiani, siriaci, e turchi della Biblioteca Nazionale e della R. Accademia delle Scienze di Torino illustrati da C. A. Nallino*. (*Memorie della R. A. d. S. d. T.* Serie ii, tom. i. Turin, 1900.)
ʿUmūmī	*Kutubkhānah i ʿUmūmī daftarī*. Constantinople, n.d.
Upsala	*Codices Arabici, Persici et Turcici Bibliothecae Regiae Universitatis Upsaliensis. Disposuit et descripsit C.J. Tornberg*. Upsala, 1849.
Upsala Zetterstéen	*Die arabischen, persischen und türkischen Handschriften der Universitätsbibliothek zu Uppsala verzeichnet und beschrieben von K. V. Zetterstéen* (= *Le Monde oriental*, vol. xxii (1928). Upsala, 1930).
Uri	*Bibliothecae Bodleianae codicum manuscriptorum orientalium ... catalogus. Pars prima*. Oxford, 1787.
Vatican	*Aus italienischen Bibliotheken. I. Die persischen und türkischen Handschriften des Vatikans*. Von Paul Horn (ZDMG. li (1897), pp. 1–65).
Vatican, Levi della Vida	*Elenco dei manoscritti arabi islamici della Biblioteca Vaticana* ... [by] Giorgio Levi della Vida. Città del Vaticano 1935 (Studi e testi, 67).
Velyaminov-Zernov	*Vostochnyya rukopisi v bibliotekye pokoinago V.V. Vel'yaminova-Zernova. A. A. Semenova* (in *Izvyestiya Rossiiskoi Akademii Nauk*', 1919, pp. 855–72).
Vollers	*Katalog der islamischen ... Handschriften der Universitäts-Bibliothek zu Leipzig von K. V.* Leipzig, 1906.
Wahbī Efendī	The library of Wahbī Efendī preserved in the Sulaimānīyah Kutub-khānah i ʿumūmī at Istanbul. (Historical MSS. cited from Tauer (*q.v. supra*).)

Wilber	*Recent Persian contributions to the historical geography of Iran.* [By] *Donald N. Wilber* (see PL. ii D. Geography etc., beginning).
Yaḥyā Efendī	*Daftar i Kutubkhānah i Yaḥyā Efendī.* Constantinople, 1310.
Yeñī	يكى جامع كتبخانه سنده محفوظ كتب موجوده نك دفتر يدر. دار الخلافة العليه ١٣٠٠
Yildiz Köshkü	The library of the Yildiz Kiosk preserved in the University Library at Istanbul. (Historical MSS. cited from Tauer (*q.v. supra*).)
Zenker	*Bibliotheca Orientalis. Manuel de bibliographie orientale … Par J. Th. Z.* Leipzig, 1846–61.
Zuhdī Bey	The library of Zuhdī Bey preserved in the Sulaimānīyah Kutubkhānah i ʿumūmī at Istanbul. (Historical MSS. cited from Tauer (*q.v. supra*).)

The signs °, *, †, and ‡ appended to the dates of editions have the following meanings:

° described in one of the British Museum catalogues.

* preserved in the India Office.

† mentioned in one of the quarterly catalogues of Indian publications.

‡ in my own possession or at least seen by me.

13 Biography

13.1 *Poets*

A list of 51 sources of information concerning Persian poets (all *tadhkirahs* except one or two histories containing biographical sections) was prefixed by H. Ethé to his account of Persian poetical literature in the *Grundriss der iranischen Philologie*. An Urdu translation of this list was published in the *Oriental College Magazine*, vol. iii/2 (Lahore, Feb. 1927), pp. 21–37, by Dr. ʿAbd al-Sattār Ṣiddīqī. In a *takmilah* to Dr. ʿAbd al-Sattār's article (pp. 40–56) Prof. M. Shafiʿ enumerated 41 additional *tadhkirahs* (and other works) known to be extant as well as eleven which seem to be lost. In the next two issues of the OCM. (vol. iii/3 (May 1927) pp. 48–52 and vol. iii/4 (Aug. 1927) p. 31) he added four more and raised the total to 107. This total was successively increased to 135 and 142[1] by Ḥakīm S. Shams Allāh Qādirī (OCM. v/1 (Nov. 1928) pp. 1–7, v/4 (Aug. 1929) pp. 112–13) and to 143 by M. Shajāʿat-ʿAlī Khān, who described the *Maʾāthir al-Bāqirīyah* in OCM vi/2 (Feb. 1930) pp. 111–13. Subsequently Prof. M. Iqbāl described two more (nos. 144 and 145), both belonging to Prof. Maḥmūd Shērānī, namely the *Zubdat al-muʿāṣirīn* written in 1240/1824–5 by Mīr Ḥusain al-Ḥusainī, a resident of Shīrāz (OCM. x/1 (Nov. 1933) pp. 32–42 and x/2 (Feb. 1934) pp. 129–37, where extracts relating to Persian poetesses are published) and the *Laṭāʾif al-khayāl* written in 1076/1665 by a Persian who had visited India (OCM. xi/1 (Nov. 1934) pp. 58–73, where some extracts are given).

1088. Sadīd al-Dīn[2] M. b. M. b. Imām Sharaf al-Dīn Abī Ṭāhir Yaḥyā b. Ṭāhir b. ʿUthmān **al-ʿAufī** al-Bukhārī, who claimed descent from ʿAbd al-Raḥmān b. ʿAuf,[3] was probably born at Bukhārā and was certainly educated there. In 597/1200–1 he went to Samarqand, where his maternal uncle, the physician Majd al-Dīn M. b. ʿAdnān Surkhakatī (see no. 610 *supra*), was in the service of the Īlak Khān, Qilich Ṭamghāch Khān Ibrāhīm. The *Walī-ʿahd*, ʿUthman b. Ibrāhīm, appointed ʿAufī his secretary, but before long he had started on travels which took him to Khwārazm, Shahr i Nau, Nasā (in 600/1203–4), Khūjān = Khabūshān (in 603/1206–7), Isfarāyin, Nīshāpūr, Harāt, Isfizār (after 607) and other places.

1 One of these, however, the *Muʾnis al-aḥrār*, is an anthology without biographical information. A considerable proportion are histories containing biographical sections.

2 See Niẓām al-Dīn *Introduction* pp. 3–5. The authorities who give his *laqab* as Nūr al-Dīn are apparently in error.

3 A prominent *Ṣaḥābī*, for whom see *Ency. Isl.* and Caetani *Chronographia Islamica* pp. 341–2. He was one of *al-ʿAsharat al-Mubashsharah* and a member of the committee of six which elected ʿUthmān to the Caliphate. He died in 32/652–3.

 | DOI:10.1163/9789004444041_002

By 617/1220,[4] if not before, he was in Sind, ruled at that time by Nāṣir al-Dīn Qabājah, for whom, as mentioned below, two of his works were written. In a note discovered by A. H. M. Niẓām al-Dīn at the end of an India Office MS.[5] a contemporary who prefixes to ʿAufī's name, among other titles, those of *Qāḍī* and *Wāʿiẓ al-mulūk wa-'l-salāṭīn*, speaks of meeting him at Cambay, where he had been living for some time (*rūzī chand ān-jā sukūnat sākhtah būd*). It may be surmised that he was *Qāḍī* of that place, which was included in Nāṣir al-Dīn Qabājah's dominions. In 625/1228 he was in Bhakkar when Qabājah was besieged there by the troops of Īltutmish, the Sulṭān of Delhi. After Qabājah's capitulation and suicide ʿAufī became a subject of Īltutmish and the *Jawāmiʿ al-ḥikāyāt* is dedicated to that monarch's *Wazīr*, Qiwām al-Dīn al-Junaidī. He was still alive in 628/1230–1, the date of an event which is referred to in the *Jawāmiʿ al-ḥikāyāt* (see A. H. M. Niẓām al-Dīn *Introduction* p. 20).

In addition to the *Lubāb al-albāb* he wrote (1) *Tarjamah i kitāb al-Faraj baʿd al-shiddah*, a translation of al-Tanūkhī's work (for which see Brockelmann i 155, 519 (*ad* 155), *Supptbd.* i p. 253) written about 620/1223 for Malik Nāṣir al-Dīn Qabājah (see Niẓām al-Dīn *Introduction to the Jawámiʿu 'l-ḥikáyát* pp. 14–19, where it is shown that the I.O. MSS. Ethé 737 and 738 contain the second half of this translation), (2) *Jawāmiʿ al-ḥikāyāt wa-lawāmiʿ al-riwāyāt*, a collection of more than two thousand anecdotes planned at the request of Malik Nāṣir al-Dīn Qabājah, not yet finished at his death in 625, resuscitated at the suggestion of Sulṭān Īltutmish's *Wazīr* Niẓām al-Mulk Qiwām al-Dīn M. b. Abī Saʿīd al-Junaidī, to whom it was eventually dedicated not earlier than 628/1230–1 (see Niẓām al-Dīn *Introduction to the Jawámiʿu 'l-ḥikáyát*, G.M.S., N.S. viii, London 1929), (3) *Madāʾiḥ al-Sulṭān*, mentioned in the *Jawāmiʿ al-ḥikāyāt* but now apparently lost (see Niẓām al-Dīn *op. cit.* p. 14 n. 1).

Lubāb al-albāb,[6] notices of nearly 300 poets written probably in 618/1221–2 and dedicated to Malik Nāṣir al-Dīn Qabājah's *Wazīr*, ʿAin al-Mulk Fakhr al-Dīn al-Ḥusain b. Abī Bakr al-Ashʿarī: Sprenger no. 1 = **Berlin** 637 (defective. 15th cent.?), **Lindesiana** p. 124 no. 308 (16th or 17th cent.).

4 In a *khuṭbah* composed in this year and quoted in the *Lubāb al-albāb* (i pp. 115–16) ʿAufī referred to the conquests made on behalf of Nāṣir al-Dīn Qabājah by Malik Bahāʾ al-Dīn ʿAlī al-Jāmajī.

5 Ethé 737. See Niẓām al-Dīn *Introduction* pp. 16–17, where the Persian text is given.

6 A still earlier *tadhkirah*, the *Manāqib al-shuʿarāʾ* by Abū Ṭāhir al-Khātūnī, who flourished at the end of the 11th century, was known to Daulat-Shāh and is mentioned by Ḥājjī Khalīfah, who, however, seems to have known it only by name, since he does not give the opening words.

The *Bazm-ārāy* (Rieu Suppt. 106. Early 17th cent.), completed in 1000/1591–2 by S. ʿAlī b. Maḥmūd al-Ḥusainī and dedicated to the Kẖān i Kẖānān ʿAbd al-Raḥīm b. Bairam Kẖān (for whom see no. 698, Persian translations (3) *supra*) is largely plagiarized from the *Lubāb al-albāb* and may be regarded as virtually an additional manuscript (see M. Kẖān Qazwīnī's *muqaddimah* pp. h–w).

Edition: *Part II of the Lubábu 'l-albáb of Muḥammad ʿAwfí edited … by E. G. Browne*, **London and Leyden** 1903°* (Persian historical texts, vol. ii), *Part I of the Lubábu 'l-albáb … edited … by E. G. Browne and Mírzá Muḥammad ibn ʿAbdu 'l-Wahháb-i-Qazwíní*, **London and Leyden** 1906°* (Persian historical texts, vol. iv).

Corrections: *Taṣḥīḥ i Lubāb al-albāb*, by "Waḥīd" Dastgirdī (in *Armagẖān XI*, pp. 335–6, 652–4, 747–52, XII, pp. 843–4).

List of the poets (not quite complete): Sprenger, pp. 3–6.

Descriptions:

(1) *On the earliest Persian Biography of Poets, by Muhammad Aúfi, and on some other works of the class called Tazkirat ul Shuârá. By N. Bland* (in the *JRAS*. 1848, pp. 111–76),

(2) *An early Persian anthology* (in R. A. Nicholson's *Studies in Islamic poetry*, Cambridge 1921, pp. 1–42. With many verse translations).

[Autobiographical statements in the *Lubāb al-albāb* and the *Jawāmiʿ al-ḥikāyāt* (for these see the *muqaddimah* of M. Kẖān Qazwīnī and the preface of E. G. Browne to Part I of the *Lubāb al-albāb* and Niẓām al-Dīn's *Introduction to the Jawámiʿu 'l-ḥikáyát*); Rieu ii 749–50; Browne, *Lit. Hist*, ii pp. 477–9; *Ency. Isl.* under ʿAwfī (short and unsigned).]

1089. For the *Tārīkh i Guzīdah*, which was written in 730/1329–30 by **Ḥamd Allāh Mustaufī** Qazwīnī and of which the fifth and penultimate *bāb* (pp. 755–829 in the G.M.S. facsimile) is devoted to very brief notices of *imāms* and *mujtahids* (*Faṣl* 1 = pp. 755–9), ten *qurrāʾ* (*Faṣl* 2 = pp. 759–60), seven traditionists (*Faṣl* 3 = p. 760), *masẖāyikẖ* (*Faṣl* 4 = pp. 760–97), *ʿulamāʾ* (*Faṣl* 5 = pp. 797–812), and poets (*Faṣl* 6 = pp. 812–29), see no. 111 (2) *supra*. A translation of *Faṣl* 6 by E. G. Browne is mentioned there under Translations (5).

1090. For the *Firdaus al-tawārīkẖ*, which was written in 808/1405–6 by **Kẖusrau Abarqūhī** and which contains at the end a biographical dictionary of Arabic and Persian poets, see no. 114 *supra*.

1091. For the *Mujmal* of **Faṣīḥ** al-Dīn Aḥmad b. M. **Kẖwāfī**, a compendium of Islāmic history and biography to 845/1441–2, see no. 120 *supra*.

1092. The *Bahāristān*, a collection of anecdotes written in 892/1487 by the poet ʿAbd al-Raḥmān b. Aḥmad **"Jāmī"**, does not belong to this section, but it deserves a passing mention, since the seventh of its eight *rauḍahs* is devoted to short biographies of twenty-eight poets.

1093. **Daulat-Shāh** b. ʿAlāʾ al-Daulah Bakhtī-Shāh al-Ghāzī al-**Samarqandī**, as he calls himself (*T. al-sh.* pp. 11^{6}, 541^{1}), or Amīr[7] Daulat-Shāh, as he is called in the *Laṭāʾif-nāmah*, was the son of Amīr ʿAlāʾ al-Daulah Isfarāyinī (*Laṭāʾif-nāmah* p. 180^{7}), an intimate friend of Sulṭān Shāh-Rukh (*T. al-sh.* p. 337$^{19-20}$). He was present[8] at the battle of Chakman[9] Sarāy,[10] near Andkhūd, in which his sovereign, Abū 'l-Ghāzī Sulṭān Ḥusain defeated Sulṭān Maḥmūd Mīrzā, the third son of Sulṭān Abū Saʿīd,[11] but he did not rise to the dignities and influence of his ancestors, being apparently content to live a simple life as a landed proprietor (*az imārat u ʿaẓamat kih āyīn i ajdād i ū būd gudhasht*[12] *u sar rishtah i faqr u qanāʿat u dahqanat ba-dast āward, Laṭāʾif-nāmah* p. 180^{10}). Mīr ʿAlī-Shīr says in the *Majālis al nafāʾis*, which was begun in 896/1490–1, that news of his death had recently been received. According to the *Mirʾāt al-ṣafāʾ*, cited by Rieu, he died in 900/1494–5. He was about fifty years old when he began to write the *Tadhkirat al-shuʿarāʾ*.[13]

Tadhkirat al-shuʿarāʾ, notices of ancient and modern poets completed in 892/1487, dedicated to Mīr ʿAlī-Shīr (for whom see no. 1094 *infra*) and divided into a *muqaddimah* (on the art of poetry) seven *ṭabaqāt* ("each containing accounts of some twenty more or less contemporary poets and the princes under whose patronage they flourished") and a *khātimah* on seven poets contemporary with the author and the merits of Sulṭān Ḥusain: Ḥ. Kh. ii p. 262 no. 2819, Sprenger no. 3, **Cairo** p. 502 (AH 892, autograph[14]), p. 501 (AH 980/1572), p. 502 (n.d.), **British Museum** (AH 895/148–

7 This title was hereditary in families belonging to the aristocracy of high officialdom (see Barthold in *Mir-Ali-Shir* p. 113).

8 *dar ān muṣāff dar rikāb i ẓafar-maʾāb būdam* (*T. al-sh.* p. 533^{2}).

9 Vocalization not verified.

10 According to the *Ḥabīb al-siyar*, iii, pt. 3, p. 202^{19}, this battle took place at the end of 875/1471.

11 For whom see *Ency. Isl.* under Abū Saʿīd.

12 Cf. his own words *Az jāh u marātib i ābāʾ u ajdād bī bahrah māndah* (*T. al-sh.* p. 11^{19}).

13 *Chūn az rūy i muḥāsabat u murāqabat ba-rūz-nāmah i ḥayāt naẓar numūdam dīdam kih kārawān i ʿumr i girān-māyah dar tīh i gum-rāhī panjāh marḥalah qaṭʿ numūdah būd* (*T. al-sh.* p. 11^{10}. Cf. p. 12$^{5, 8}$).

14 The cataloguer may perhaps have been misled by the author's colophon, which is reproduced in some of the manuscripts (as in the G.M.S. edition).

90),[15] **Rieu** iii 977*b* (AH 973/1565), ii 809*b* (16th cent.), i 364*a*–365*b* (8 copies, one of the 16th cent. and three of the 17th), **Bodleian** 348 (AH 942/1536), 349 (AH 975/1567–8), 350 (AH 978/1571), 351–8, **Oxford** Ind. Inst. MS. Pers. A. ii. 21 (AH 994/1586), **Edinburgh** New Coll. p. 6 (AH 952/1545), **Ethé** 656 (AH 960/1553), 657–63, **I.O.** 3777 (18th cent.), **I.O. D.P.** 620, **Blochet** ii 1129 (AH 967/1560), 1130 (AH 974), 1131–41, iii 2452 (late 16th cent.), **Rosen** Inst. 31 (AH 971/1563–4), **Berlin** 638 (AH 974/1567), 639–42. **Dorn** 320 (AH 975/1567–8), **Flügel** ii 1199 (AH 979/1571), 1200 (AH 985/1577), **Browne** Pers. Cat. 113 (AH 979/1572), 112 (AH 984/1576–7), 114, Suppt. 292–5 (the last = King's 106), **Browne** Coll. J. 8 = Houtum-Schindler 36 (AH 908/1502–3 or 980/1572–3), **Būhār** 90 (AH 980/1572), **Krafft** p. 125 no. 312 (AH 982/1574), **Ivanow** 218 (AH 984/1576–7), Curzon 49, 50, **Kapurthala** (AH 999/1590–1. See *Oriental College Magazine* vol. iii/4 (Lahore, Aug. 1927) p. 11), **Tashkent** Univ. 69 (16th cent.), **Sipahsālār** ii pp. 475–7 (4 copies, one of 16th cent.), **Lindesiana** p. 132 no. 838 (not later than AD 1600), no. 54, no. 310, no. 309, **Rehatsek** p. 130 no. 15 (AH 1033/1623–4. LIST OF POETS), p. 95 no. 45, p. 103, no. 59 (apparently, though the title is given as *Maḥbūb al-qulūb*), **Bānkīpūr** viii 680 (AH 1051/1641), 681, **ʿAlīgaṛh** Subḥ. MSS. p. 61 no. 32, **Āṣafīyah** i p. 318 no. 36, iii p. 162 no. 119, **Aumer** 1 ("ziemlich alt"), **Bombay** Univ. p. 274 (old), **Bukhārā** Semenov 48, **Chanykov** 105, **Lahore** Panjab Univ. Lib. (2 copies. See *Oriental College Magazine* vol. iii, no 1 (Nov. 1926) p. 74), **Leningrad** Pub. Lib. (see *Mélanges asiatiques* iii (St. Petersburg 1859) p. 728), Mus. Asiat, (at least 3 copies. See *Mélanges asiatiques* vi (1873) p. 126, vii (1876) p. 402), **Madras** 440, **Majlis** 327, **Peshawar** 1451, **R.A.S.** P. 163, **Salemann-Rosen** p. 13 nos. 61*, 147*. A copy described as written by Sulṭān-ʿAlī Mashhadī (a celebrated calligraphist[16] contemporary with Daulat-Shāh) and adorned with six full-page miniatures occurred in Sotheby's sale catalogue for 22–23 May 1930.

Editions: (1) **Bombay** 1887°, (2) *The Tadhkiratu 'sh-Shuʿará ... of Dawlatsháh ... edited ... by E. G. Browne ...*, **London and Leyden** 1901°* (Persian historical texts, vol. i), (3) **Allāhabad** 1921* (*Ṭabaqahs* i–v only. Ed. S. M. Ḍāmin ʿAlī).

Extracts:

(1) [Life of "ANWARĪ"] *Vitae poetarum persicorum ex Dauletschahi Historia Poetarum ... excerptae ... persice edidit latine vertit ... J. A. Vullers. Fasc. II. Anvarii vitam tenens*, **Giessen** 1868°.

---

15 For information concerning this recently acquired MS. I am indebted to the kindness of Prof. A. J. Arberry.

16 Cf. *Laṭāʾif-nāmah* p. 170, *Tuḥfah i Sāmī* p. 69, *Ḥabīb al-siyar* iii pt 3, p. 344 antepenult., etc.

(2) [Life of "ANWARĪ"] *Ali Aukhadeddin Enveri. Materialy dlya ego biographii i kharakteristiki* [by V. A. Zhukovsky], **St. Petersburg** 1883°.

(3) [Life of "'AṬṬĀR"] *Pend-namèh, ou Le Livre des Conseils de Férid-eddin Attar, traduit et publié par M. le Bon Silvestre de Sacy,* **Paris** 1819°*, *Pand-nāmah i ... Farīd al-Dīn 'Aṭṭār* [reprinted from the Paris edition of 1819] **[Ṭihrān]** 1873°.

(4) [Life of "ḤĀFIẒ"] *Vitae poetarum persicorum ex Dauletschahi Historia Poetarum ... excerptae ... persice edidit latine vertit ... J. A. Vullers. Fasc I. Hâfizi Schirâzensis vitam tenens,* **Giessen** 1839°* (cf. no. 1 *supra*).

(5) [Life of "JĀMĪ"] *Tuhfat ul Ahrār, the Gift of the Noble: being one of the Seven Poems, or Haft Aurang, of Mullā Jāmī ... edited ... by F. Falconer* [with biographies of "Jāmī" from Daulat-Shāh's *tadhkirah*, the *Ātash-kadah* and the *Haft iqlīm*], **London** 1848°* (Society for the Publication of Oriental Texts).

(6) [Life of "NIẒĀMĪ"] *De expeditione Russorum Berdaam versus auctore inprimis Nisamio disseruit F. Erdmann* [with Daulat-Shāh's notice of "Niẓāmī"], **Kazan** 1826–32°.

(7) [Life of "NIẒĀMĪ"] *Behram-Gur und die russische Fuerstentochter. Muhammed Niszamiu-d-din, dem Gendscher, nachgebildet und durch ... Anmerkungen erlaeutert von F. von Erdmann* [with Daulat-Shāh's notice of "Niẓāmī"] *2te Auflage,* **Kazan** 1844°*.

(8) [Life of "SA'DĪ"] *The Persian and Arabick works of Sâdee* [edited by J. H. Harington and M. Rāshid. With Daulat-Shāh's notice of "Sa'dī" in Persian text and English translation], vol. i, **Calcutta** 1791°*.

Turkish translation (abridged): *Safīnat al-shu'arā',* written in 1233 by Fahīm Sulaimān Efendī (for whom see *Ency. Isl.* under Fehīm): **Flügel** ii 1258. Edition: **Istānbūl** 1259/1843 (cf. Babinger *Geschichtsschreiber der Osmanen* p. 351, n. 1).

English translation of *Ṭabaqahs* i–iii: *Translation with notes-critical and explanatory of Tadhkiratush-shu'ara ...* (*the portion prescribed for the B.A. Examination*) *of Dawlatshah-e-Samarqandi. By P. B. Vachha.* **Bombay** [1909*].

J. von Hammer-Purgstall's *Geschichte der schönen Redekünste Persiens, mit einer Blüthenlese aus zweyhundert persischen Dichtern* (Vienna 1818) is for the most part an abridged paraphrase of the *Tadhkirat al-shu'arā',* supplemented with selected notices from the *Tuḥfah i Sāmī* and a few from other sources.

Translations of extracts: (1) [Life of "ANWARĪ" (Latin)] see Extracts (1) above, (2) [Life of "ANWARĪ" (Russian)] see Extracts (2) above, (3) [Life of "'AṬṬĀR" (French)] see Extracts (3) above, (4) [Life of FIRDAUSĪ

(French)] *Tezkirat alschoara, Histoire des poëtes. Par Douletschah ... Par M. Silvestre de Sacy*, pp. 230–8 (in *Notices et extraits*, Tome iv (**Paris**, An 7 [= 1798°*])). (5) [Life of FIRDAUSĪ (German)] *Fragmente ueber die Religion des Zoroaster. Aus dem Persischen uebersetzt und mit einem ausfuhrlichen Commentar versehen nebst dem Leben des Ferdusi aus Dauletscha'h's Biographieen der Dichter. Von Dr. J. A. Vullers ...*, **Bonn** 1831°. (6) [Life of ḤĀFIẒ (French)] *Tezkirat alschoara. Histoire des poëtes. Par Douletschah ... Par M. Silvestre de Sacy*, pp. 238–45 (in *Notices et extraits*, Tome IV (**Paris**, An 7 [= 1798°*])). (7) [Life of "ḤĀFIẒ" (Latin)] see Extracts (4) above. (8) [Life of "SAʿDĪ" (English)] see Extracts (8) above. (9) [Account of the Sarbadār dynasty = Browne's ed. pp. 277–88[17] (French)] *Tezkirat alschoara. Histoire des poëtes. Par Douletschah ... Par M. Silvestre de Sacy*, pp. 251–62 (in *Notices et extraits*, tome iv (**Paris**, An 7 [= 1798°*])). (10) [Account of Sulṭān Ḥusain's conquests (abridged) = Browne's ed. pp. 522–39[18] (French)] *Tezkirat alschoara. Histoire des poëtes. Par Douletschah ... Par M. Silvestre de Sacy*, pp. 262–9 (in *Notices et extraits*, tome iv (**Paris**, An 7 [= 1798°*])).

Descriptions: (1) *Tezkirat alschoara.*[19] *Histoire des poëtes. Par Douletschah ben-Alaëddoulet algazi alsamarcandi ... Par M. Silvestre de Sacy* (in *Notices et extraits des manuscrits de la Bibliothèque nationale*, tome iv (**Paris**, An 7 [= 1798°*])), pp. 220–72 (with LIST OF POETS), (2) Sprenger 3.

Lists of the poets: (1) See under Descriptions (1) above, (2) Rehatsek pp. 130–1.

Sources: *The sources of Dawlatshāh ... By E. G. Browne* (in *JRAS*. 1899, pp. 37–45).

Metrical abridgment (about 250 verses): *Āsmān i sukhun*, a remodelling by Luṭf Allāh M. Muhandis b. Aḥmad, who lived in Aurangzēb's time, of a versification made in Akbar's time by "Fāʾidī" Kirmānī: Sprenger no. 15 (Top-khānah).

[Autobiographical statements (for which see Browne's English preface p. 15); *Majālis al-nafāʾis; Laṭāʾif-nāmah* p. 180; Rieu i p. 364; *Ency. Isl.* under Dawlat-Shāh (Huart); Browne *Lit. Hist*, iii pp. 436–7.]

17 In the notice of Ibn i Yamīn, the seventh biography in *Ṭabaqah* v.
18 In the final section of the Khātimah.
19 In the Arabic character, but transliterated in a footnote.

1094. Amīr, or Mīr,[20] Niẓām al-Dīn 'Alī-S͟hīr "Nawā'ī" and "Fānī"[21] b. Amīr G͟hiyāt͟h al-Dīn Kic͟hkīnah[22] was born at Harāt on 17 Ramaḍān 844[23]/9 Feb. 1441. He is said to have been a schoolfellow of Sulṭān Ḥusain b. Manṣūr, who, on becoming ruler of Harāt in 873/1469, appointed him Keeper of the Great Seal (*Muhr-dār*).[24] Before long, however, he resigned that appointment, being by nature averse from holding office. He continued nevertheless to occupy a position of great influence and intimacy at court, and in 876/1472 he was formally given the rank of *amīr* (*manṣab i 'ālī-marātib i imārat i dīwān i a'lā*).[25] On occasions when Sulṭān Ḥusain was absent from Harāt Mīr 'Alī-S͟hīr acted as Governor (*ḥākim*) of the town. In 892/1487 he reluctantly accepted the Governorship of Astarābād, but after little more than a year he returned to Harāt. On 12 Jumādā II AH 906/3 Jan. 1501 he died.

Barthold states (in the *Ency. Isl.* under Turks. III. Čag͟hatāi literature (English edition, Vol. IV p. 916)) that, although in European works Mīr 'Alī-S͟hīr is frequently described as a minister or vizier, he never in fact held any such official position.[26] "His influence on affairs of state and his activity as a patron of arts and sciences were the result of his friendship (not always unclouded) with his prince Sulṭān Ḥusain (1469–1506)."

20 'Alī-S͟hīr was an *amīr* (in Turkish *bēg*) by birth, this title being hereditary in families belonging to the aristocracy of high officialdom (Barthold in *Mir-Ali-Shir* p. 113. Cf. *Laṭā'if-nāmah* p. 218[12]: *Mīr masnad i imārat rā maurūt͟hī das͟ht*). In Turkish works he is called 'Alī-S͟hīr Bēg.
21 It is usually said that "Nawā'ī" was his *tak͟hallus* in Turkish poetry and "Fānī" in Persian (*Dar fārisī Fānī tak͟hallus kardah* (*Tārīk͟h i Ras͟hīdī*): *Dar s͟hi'r i turkī muṭlaqan tak͟hallus i īs͟hān Nawā'ī ast u dar dīwān i fārisī tak͟hallus-as͟h Fanā'ī* (sic. *Tuḥfah i Sāmī* p. 180[21])). This doubtless corresponds roughly to the facts, but it is shown by Berthels (*Mir-Ali-Shir* pp. 34–6: cf. *Der Islam* xix pp. 43–4, where, however, the sense is not quite correctly rendered) that "Fānī" is the *tak͟hallus* used in the *Lisān al-ṭair*, which is a Turkish work, and that according to Mīr 'Alī-S͟hīr's own statement at the end he used that *tak͟hallus* to emphasise the Ṣūfī character of the work.
22 *Ḥabīb al-siyar* iii, pt. 3, p. 179[6]. Kijīkīnah (Kījīkīnah, KJKNH) Bak͟hs͟hī according to the *Tārīk͟h i Rās͟hīdī*.
23 The authority for this date is K͟hwānd-Amīr's *Makārim al-ak͟hlāq* (see Rieu i p. 366).
24 *Ḥabīb al-siyar* iii pt. 3, p. 230[21] (*muḥāfaẓat i muhr i buzurg i humāyūn rā dar 'uhdah i ān-janāb kard*).
25 *Ḥabīb al-siyar* iii pt. 3, p. 231 [24seqq.]. The same rank was conferred immediately afterwards on Amīr S. Ḥasan [b.] Ardas͟hīr (*Ḥabīb al-siyar* iii pt. 3. p. 232[5]: *u ham-dar-ān rūz kih Amīr Niẓām al-Dīn 'Alī-S͟hīr bar masnad i imārat i dīwān nis͟hast Amīr Saiyid Ḥasan i Ardas͟hīr nīz ba-d-ān manṣab sarfarāz gas͟ht.*). Cf. Belin p. 15.
26 His contemporary K͟hwānd-Amīr mentions him several times incidentally in the *Dastūr al-wuzarā'*, but does not include him in the series of *wazīrs*.

Mīr ʿAlī-Shīr was the author of a Persian *dīwān*,[27] but his reputation as a Persian poet was not high.[28] In the history of Eastern-Turkish literature, on the other hand, he is an important figure. "Mīr ʿAlī Shīr," says Rieu, "has done more than any other to raise Turki to the rank of a literary language, and is universally considered as the most elegant, as he certainly is the most prolific, of Chaghatāi writers." His Turkī works (at least 29 in number[29]) include (1) four *dīwāns*,[30] (2) a *khamsah*,[31] (3) *Lisān al-ṭair* (AH 904/1498–9), modelled on ʿAṭṭār's *Manṭiq al-ṭair*, (4) *Khamsat al-mutaḥaiyirīn*, a memoir of his friend Jāmī,[32] (5) *Nasāʾim al-maḥabbah* (AH 901/1495–6), a translation of Jāmī's *Nafaḥāt al-uns*, (6) *Muḥākamat al-lughatain* (AH 905/1499–1500), on the superiority of Turkish to Persian,[33] (7) *Maḥbūb al-qulūb* (ASH 906/1500–1) on morals and manners.[34] According to the *Islâm Ansiklopedisi* the oldest and finest manuscripts of his *Kullīyāt* are (1) Istānbūl, Rawān Köshkü no. 808 (AH 901/1496), (2) Istānbūl, Fātiḥ no. 4059, (3) Paris, Suppl. turc. 316–17 (AH 933/1526) and (4) Leningrad Pub. Lib. [Dorn 558. Cf. ZDMG. ii pp. 248–56.]

---

27 *Dīwān i Fānī*. MSS.: Blochet iii 1765, 1766, Āyā Ṣōfyah 3882, Chorlulu ʿAlī Pāshā 295, Fātiḥ 3886–7 (*"Dīwān i Nawāʾī"*, but both described as Persian), Nūr i ʿUthmānīyah 3850, Yildiz 2781/30 (cf. Edhem and Stchoukine p. 43) etc.

28 Cf. the opinion expressed by Bābur (*Bābur-nāmah* tr. ʿAbd al-Raḥīm p. 109[1]: *baʿḍī abyāt i ū bad nīst wa-lī akthar sust u firūd and*),

29 For lists see Belin pp. 59–62, ZDMG. ii pp. 249–51 (Berezin), Rieu Turkish Cat. p. 265*b*, *Islâm Ansiklopedisi*, 5. cüz, pp. 353–6.

30 *Gharāʾib al-ṣighar* (Edition: Khīwah 1881 (*Isl. Ansikl.*). *Muntakhabāt* printed several times at Tashkent, Bukhārā, Tabrīz and Istānbūl acc. to *Isl. Ansikl.*), *Nawādir al-shabāb, Badāʾiʿ al-wasaṭ, Fawāʾid al-kibar*. For MSS. (some of them containing collections antedating the division into four *dīwāns* or selected from them) see Rieu Turkish Cat. pp. 294–7, Dorn 561–4, Jackson-Yohannan 21 (beg. *Zihī ẓuhūr*. No title, AH 905/1499–1500), 22 (*Nawādir al-shabāb*. AH 988/1580), Philadelphia Lewis 95 (beg. *Ai ṣafḥah*), Princeton 150–1, Tashkent 130, etc.

31 *Ḥairat al-abrār, Farhād wa Shīrīn, Majnūn wa Lailā, Sabʿah i saiyārah, Sadd i Iskandarī*. Editions: Khīwah 1880 and Tashkent 1904 (according to *Isl. Ansikl.*), Tashkent 1893 and 1901 (acc. to Tashkent Cat. no. 128). Cf. Rieu Turkish Cat. pp. 292–4, Dorn 560 (AH 898/1492–3), Tashkent 128 etc.

32 French translations of selected portions in Belin, *Notice*, pp. 101–58.

33 Editions: Paris 1841 (in Quatremère's *Chrestomathie turke-orientale* pp. 1–39), Istānbūl 1899, Khōqand 1918 (see *Isl. Ansikl.*).

34 Editions: Istānbūl 1889 (so *Isl. Ansikl.*, but perhaps 1289/1872–3 should be read, since an edition of that date is mentioned by Browne, *L.H.* iii p. 453), Bukhārā 1907 and Tashkent (so *Isl. Ansikl.*). Described at length by Belin in *Journal asiatique*, 6e série, tom. vii pp. 523–52, tom. viii pp. 126–54. For MSS., extracts and translations of extracts see Rieu Turkish Cat. pp. 275–6. The Persian translation made in 1204/1789–90 by "Aẓfarī" (see no. 808 *supra*) was described by S. M. ʿAbd Allāh from a MS. at Lahore (Panjāb Univ. Lib.) in OCM xi/4 (Aug. 1935) pp. 41–8.

Mīr ʿAlī-Shīr is famous also as a patron of writers and artists. Mīr Khwānd, Khwānd-Amīr, Ḥusain Kāshifī and Bihzād are among those who were indebted to his encouragement.

Majālis al-nafāʾis, short notices of contemporary Persian and Turkī poets, begun in 896/1490–1,[35] written in Eastern Turkish and divided into eight *majālis* ((1) deceased poets personally unknown to the author, (2) poets deceased before 896 whom the author had met, (3) living poets known to the author, (4) men of letters who occasionally wrote poetry, (5) noblemen of Khurāsān who occasionally wrote poetry (6) non-Khurāsānī poets, (7) kings and princes of Tīmūr's house, (8) Sulṭān Ḥusain): Ḥ. Kh. v p. 381 no. 11388 (cf. ii p. 263 no. 2822), **Flügel** ii 1209 (AH 903/1497–8 ?), **Blochet** iii 1765 (early 16th cent.), **Browne** Coll. J. 7 (AH 937/1530–1), **Rieu** Turkish Cat. p. 273*a* (AH 987/1579), p. 274*b* (AH 1232/1817), **Lindesiana** p. 244 no. 149 (AH 1031/1621–2), **Bukhārā** Semenov 28, 98, **Ethé** 664, **Leningrad** Asiat. Mus. (see Dorn p. 504), Institut (AH 1224/1809. See Smirnow p. 189 no. 96), Pub. Lib. nos. 558 (9) (in the *Kullīyāt i Nawāʾī*) and 553 (the latter only a fragment. See Smirnow p. 190[1], Dorn pp. 510, 503), Univ. no. 618 (see Salemann-Rosen p. 24), **Mashhad** iii p. 103, **Munich** Turkish Cat. p. 41 no. 148 (modern), **Velyaminov-Zernov** p. 861 no. 12, and probably also in the Istānbūl and Paris MSS. of the *Kullīyāt* mentioned above (no. 1094, ***Majālis al-nafāʾis***, MSS.).[36]

Editions: **Tashkent** 1326/1908 (together with the *tadhkirah* entitled *Bāgh i Iram* and Afḍal Makhdūm i Pīrmastī's *Afḍal al-tadhkār fī dhikr al-shuʿarīʾ wa-'l-ashʿār*, composed in 1322. See Semenov's Tashkent Cat., *vvedenie*, p. [3]), 1330/1912 (see Semenov's *Kurzer Abriss* p. 3, n. 1).

Extracts: (1) [The preface] Belin *Notice biographique et littéraire sur Mir Ali-Chir-Névâii* (tirage à part) pp. 65–8, (2) [parts of *Majlis* iii] Berezin *Chrestomathie turque* pp. 146–61, (3) [*Majlis* vii] Belin *op. cit.* pp. 73–82.

Translations of extracts: (1) [The preface (French)] Belin *op. cit.* pp. 68–72, (2) [*Majlis* vii (French)] Belin *op. cit. pp.* 83–100.

Description: Browne *Lit. Hist*, iii pp. 437–9.

---

35 On this date see Barthold's remarks in *Mīr-Ali-Shir*, p. 124, Hinz's trans. p. 35: Leider lässt sich die Schrift keiner bestimmten Zeit im Leben des Verfassers zuweisen, obschon sie ein Datum (896/1490–1491) enthält; denn dieses entspricht anderen Stellen der *Mağālis* nicht. So wird beispielsweise als Zeitgenosse des Verfassers von diesem als Beherrscher Samarqands der Sohn Sulṭān Maḥmūds genannt, Sulṭān ʿAlī Mīrzā; dieser herrschte in Samarqand zuerst kurze Zeit während des Jahres 1496, etwas länger sodann von 1498–1500 …

36 This list of Eastern-Turkish MSS. makes no claim to completeness.

Persian translations: (1) ***Laṭā'if-nāmah***, a translation made by Sulṭān-Muḥammad "Fakhrī" b. "Amīrī" Harawī (see no. 1099 *infra*), who added a ninth *majlis* (on living poets not mentioned in the original) and dedicated his work to the *Wazīr* Ḥabīb Allāh [Sāwajī] at the time of Sām Mīrzā's appointment to the [titular] Governorship of Khurāsān with Durmish Khān as his vice-gerent [i.e. in 927/1521 according to *Ḥabīb al-siyar* iii, *juz'* 4, p. 100]: **Lindesiana** p. 122 no. 55[37] (AH 939/1532–3), **Rieu** i 365*b* (AH 965/1558).

Editions:

(1) *Laṭā'if-nīmah i Fakhrī* [with preface, notes and indexes by S. M. 'Abd Allāh] (in the *Oriental College Magazine*, vol. vii no. 4 (**Lahore** Aug. 1931), vol. viii no. 1 (Nov. 1931), no. 2 (Feb. 1932), no. 3 (May 1932), no. 4 (Aug. 1932), vol. ix no. 1 (Nov. 1932) and no. 2 (Feb. 1933), (2) *The Majalis-un-Nafa'is* [*sic*] *"Galaxy of poets" of Mir 'Ali Shir Nava'i* [*sic*].

Two 16 th. century Persian translations edited with an introduction and annotations, etc., by Ali Asghar Hekmat, **Tihrān** AHS. 1323/1945 pp. 1–178.

(2) (***Tarjamah i Majālis al-nafā'is***), begun at Istānbūl in 927/1521, completed in 929/1522–3 and dedicated to Sulṭān Salīm by Ḥakīm [Shāh] M. b. Mubārak al-Qazwīnī (cf. *al-Shaqā'iq al-Nu'mānīyah* I pp. 371–2, Rescher's trans. p. 216), who compressed the matter of the original (with some additions) into seven *bihishts* and appended an eighth in two *rauḍahs* ((1) ancient and modern poets, mostly extracts from Jāmī's *Bahāristān*, (2) Salīm and the poets of his court): **As'ad** 3877, **Tihrān** Sa'īd Nafīsī's private library.

Edition: *The Majalis-un-Nafa'is* [sic] ... *Two 16th century Persian translations edited ... by Ali Asghar Hekmat*, **Tihrān** AHS. 1323/1945 pp. 179–409.

(3) ***Majālis al-nafā'is***, a translation made by Shāh 'Alī b. 'Abd al-'Alī in the time of Sulṭān Dīn Muḥammad [b. Jānī Bēg, who ruled over part of Khurāsān during the reigns of 'Abd Allāh Khān Uzbak (AH 991/1583–1006/1598) and 'Abd al-Mu'min Khān and after the latter's death in 1006/1598 was proclaimed Khān in Harāt, but was defeated soon afterwards by Shāh 'Abbās and died during his flight]: **Rieu** Suppt. 104 (breaks off in the middle of the account of Ulugh Bēg, the sixth in *Majlis* vii. 17th cent.).

37 Probably the *Laṭā'if-nāmah*, though this is not expressly stated in the catalogue. An inquiry addressed to the John Rylands Library failed to elicit the desired information, since the manuscript, owing to war-time precautions, was not available.

(4) *Majālis al-nafā'is*, a translation made by 'Abd al-Bāqī S͟harīf Riḍawī at the instance of G͟hulām G͟haut͟h K͟hān, Nawwāb of the Carnatic: **Madras** 445 (AH 1242/1827, probably autograph).

[Daulat-S͟hāh 494–509; Jāmī *Bahāristān* (the last notice in *Rauḍah* vii); *Makārim al-ak͟hāq*, a panegyric by K͟hwānd-Amīr (for whom see no. 125 *supra*) written in the rough before 'Alī S͟hīr's death but finished afterwards and dedicated to Sulṭān Ḥusain (MS.: Rieu i p. 367a); *Majīlis al-'us͟hs͟hāq* (the fourth biography from the end); *The Babur-nama in English* (see no. 698, 6th par. *supra*) i p. 271 (summarised in Browne's *Lit. Hist*, iii pp. 456–7); *Bābur-nāmah* tr. 'Abd al-Raḥīm pp. 108[18]–109[9]; *Laṭā'if-nāmah* pp. 218–23 (the first *qism* in *Majlis* ix); *Ḥabīb al-siyar* iii, *juz'* 3, pp. 217 etc.; *Tārīk͟h i Ras͟hīdī* (the passage, omitted in Ross's translation, is quoted in *Mélanges asiatiques* ix (St. Petersburg, 1888) pp. 358–60 and in *Oriental College Magazine*, vol. x no. 3 (Lahore, May 1934) pp. 155–7; *Tuḥfah i Sāmī*, Ṭihrān AHS 1314, pp. 179–81 (the first biography in *Ṣaḥīfah* vi. French translation by Silvestre de Sacy in *Notices et extraits*, tome iv (Paris, An 7 = 1798°*) pp. 290–3); *Mir'āt al-adwār* (Ethé 109, fol. 411b seq.); Taqī Kās͟hī *K͟hulāṣat al-as͟h'ār* (cf. Sprenger p. 20): Ḥasan Rūmlū *Aḥsan al-tawārīk͟h* xii pp. 55[9]–57[10], Seddon's trans, pp. 24–5; *Mir'āt al-k͟hayāl* (Bodl. 374) no. 57; *Safīnah i K͟hwus͟hgū* (Bodl. 376 no. 8); *Ātas͟h-kadah* no. 60 (Bombay 1277 p. 19[1]); *K͟hulāṣat al-afkār* no. 197; Elliot *Bibliographical index* pp. 114–16; M. Nikitski *Emir-Nizam-ed-Din-Ali-Shir, v gosudarstvennom i literaturnom ego znachenii*, St. Petersburg 1856 (diss. For a criticism see Barthold in *Mir-Ali-Shir*, Leningrad 1928, p. 101, Hinz's trans. p. 3); *Notice biographique et littéraire sur Mir Ali-Chir Névâii, suivie d'extraits tirés des œuvres du même auteur par M*. [F. A.] Belin (in the *Journal asiatique*, 5ᵉ série, tome xvii (1861) pp. 175–256, 281–357, published also as an offprint. For a criticism see Barthold, *op. cit.* pp. 101–2, Hinz's trans, pp. 3–4); Elliot and Dowson *History of India* iv pp. 527–8; Browne *Lit. Hist.* iii pp. 505–6 and elsewhere; *Mir-Ali-Shir: sbornik k pyatisotletiyu so dnya rozhdeniya*, Leningrad (Akademiya Nauk SSSR) 1928 (containing articles in Russian ((1) Contribution to the history of the literary language of Central Asia by A. Samoylovich pp. 1–23, (2) Nevāyi and 'Attār by E. Berthels, pp. 24–82, (3) A new C͟hag͟hatāy-Persian dictionary by A. Romaskevich, pp. 83–99, (4) Mīr 'Alī-S͟hīr and political life by W. Barthold pp. 100–64) as well as reviews of some books, mostly in Turkish, on Mīr 'Alī-S͟hīr. See a summary by H. Ritter in *Der Islam* xix (1930–1) pp. 42–9 and W. Barthold *Herat unter Husein Baiqara, dem Timuriden. Deutsche Bearbeitung* [of B.'s article in *Mir-Ali-Shir* pp. 100–64] *von W. Hinz* (D. M. G. Abhandlungen für die Kunde des Morgenlandes, xxii, 8 (Leipzig 1937)); *Oriental College Magazine* vol. x no. 2 (Lahore, Feb. 1934) pp. 3–34, vol. xi no. 2 (Feb. 1935) pp. 3–25 (articles in Urdu by S. M. 'Abd Allāh); *Ency. Isl.* in the section Č̣AG͟HATĀI LITERATURE

(Barthold), which forms part of the article TURKS (there is no separate article on Mir ʿAlī-S̲h̲īr); *Islâm Ansiklopedisi* under Ali Şîr (an article of 18 columns by A. Zeki Velidi Togan), where some further works are mentioned, including *Ali Şîr Beg, hayati ve eserleri* by A. Zeki Velidi Togan (a forthcoming publication of the University of Istanbul) and a Russian bibliography of ʿAlī-S̲h̲īr and his works by A. A. Semenov (Tashkent 1940); ʿAlī Aṣg̲h̲ar Ḥikmat's introduction to his edition of two Persian translations of the *Majālis al-nafāʾis* pp. z-KH; Portraits in the *Burlington Magazine*, Jan. 1931, plate IV B, and in Binyon, Wilkinson, and Gray's *Persian miniature painting*, London, 1933, pl. lxxvi.]

1095. For the (*Tārīkh̲ i Ṣadr i Jahān*), which was written, partly at least, in 907/1501–2 by Ṣadr i Jahān Faiḍ Allāh Banbānī and which concludes with a biographical chapter, see no. 127 *supra*.

1096. For the *Ḥabīb al-siyar* of **Khwānd-Amīr** which extends to 930/1524 and which contains biographies of celebrities at the end of reigns, see no. 125 (3) *supra*. In addition to this and other works he wrote

Makārim al-akh̲lāq, a pompous panegyric on Mīr ʿAlī-S̲h̲īr, who died in 906/1501 (see no. 1094 *supra*) before its completion: **Rieu** i 367*a* (AH 965/1558).

1097. At the end of his narrative of the year 911/1505–6 Bābur has inserted in the *Bābur-nāmah* (see no. 698 *supra*) short accounts of some poets, scholars, musicians and other celebrities contemporary with Sulṭān Ḥusain at Harāt. In the Bombay edition of ʿAbd al-Raḥīm's translation these will be found on pp. 112 antepenult.-116¹⁰. A corrected text of the passage was published by M. S̲h̲afīʿ in *OCM*. X/3 (May 1934) pp. 140–9.

1098. For the *Tārīkh̲ i Ras̲h̲īdī*, which was completed by Mīrzā Ḥaidar Dūg̲h̲lāt in 952/1546 and which contains biographies of poets and other celebrities, see no. 349 *supra*.

1099. Sulṭān-Muḥammad **"Fakh̲rī"** b. M. "Amīrī" al-Harawī was, according to "Ilāhī", a panegyrist of S̲h̲āh Ṭahmāsp (reigned 930/1524–984/1576). His *Laṭāʾif-nāmah* (for which see no. 1094, Persian translations (1) *supra*) was written at the time when S̲h̲āh Ismāʿīl's son, Sām Mīrzā (b. 923/1517) was appointed titular Governor of Khurāsān,[38] Durmis̲h̲ Kh̲ān, his tutor, being the real

---

38 I.e. in 927/1521, from which date he held the appointment, residing at Herāt, until his father's death in 930/1524.

Governor and Ḥabīb Allāh Sāwajī the *Wazīr*. It was to the latter that "Fakhrī" dedicated both the *Laṭā'if-nāmah* and the *Tuḥfat al-ḥabīb*, an anthology of ghazals.[39]

In the *Jawāhir al-ʿajā'ib*, according to Sprenger, "The author informs us that with the intention to perform the pilgrimage to Makkah, he came during the reign of Sháh Tahmásb Ḥosayny (reigned from 930 to 984) to Sind, the ruler of that country was then[40] Moḥammad 'ysá Tarkhán (died in 974), and it would appear that he wrote this book at his Court." M. ʿĪsā Tarkhān reigned from 961/1554 or 962/1555 to 974/1564 or 975/1565, but apparently "Fakhrī's" connexion with Sind began at an earlier date. In the *Tārīkh i Maʿṣūmī* (for which see no. 824 *supra*) "Maulānā Fakhrī Harawī"[41] is mentioned in a list of celebrities contemporary with Mīrzā Shāh Ḥasan [Arghūn], M. ʿĪsā Tarkhān's predecessor, who reigned from 930/1524 to 961/1554 and who is presumably identical with Abū 'l-Fatḥ Shāh Ḥasan Ghāzī,[42] the dedicatee of the *Rauḍat al-salāṭīn*.[43] To Shāh Ḥasan Arghūn he dedicated[44] also his *Ṣanā'iʿ al-ḥusn* [perhaps *Ṣanā'iʿ* al-Ḥasan, as ʿAbd al-Muqtadir transliterates], a work on poetical figures (MSS.: Bodleian 1371–2, Bānkīpūr ix 848 i).

(1) ***Rauḍat al-salāṭīn***, notices of royal poets in seven *bābs*, written at the request of Abū 'l-Fatḥ Shāh Ḥasan[45] Ghāzī: **Blochet** ii 1142 (early 17th cent.), 1143 (late 17th cent.), **Berlin** 644.

---

39 For which see Sprenger no. 6, Rieu Suppt. 375, Bānkīpūr xi 1101, Bānkīpūr Suppt. i 1993, Lindesiana p. 137 no. 864, Āṣafīyah i p. 716 no. 303, Peshawar 1892, and probably also Blochet iii 1978.

40 This word probably misrepresents the sense of the original.

41 *Maulānā Fakhrī Harawī mardī khwush-ṭabʿ u akābir būdah u shiʿr nīz mī-guftah. Baʿḍī taṣnīfāt dārad dar ṣanā'iʿ u badā'iʿ u ʿarūḍ u qāfiyah* (p. 206).

42 Blochet on the other hand says (tome iii p. 450) probably quite arbitrarily that the *Rauḍat al-salāṭīn* is dedicated "au sultan du Bengale, Aboul-Fath Shah Hoseïn Ghazi (†925 de l'hégire = 1519)." The Sulṭān of Bengal was called Ḥusain Shāh, not Shāh Ḥusain.

43 Curiously enough on the same page on which the *Tārīkh i Maʿṣūmī* speaks of Fakhrī Harawī it ascribes (according to the printed text) a work entitled *Rauḍat al-salāṭīn* to another author, who is described as follows: *Shāh Ḥusain* TKDRY [corrected in the index to NKDRY]: *dar silk i umarā-yi Mīrzā Shāh Ḥasan intiẓām dāsht. bah ḥiddat i ṭabʿ u jaudat i dhihn u makārim i akhlāq u maḥāsin i ādāb sar-āmad i fuḍalā-yi zamān i khwud būdah. u dar fann i shiʿr u tārīkh mahāratī kāmil dāsht. u Rauḍat al-salaṭīn az jumlah i muṣannafāt i ūst.*

44 According to ʿAbd al-Muqtadir the dedicatee's name is introduced into the following line of a *qiṭʿah* at the beginning of the work: *Rashk i Jam u Farīdūn naqd i Shujāʿ i Dhū 'l-Nūn* Chashm u chirāgh i Arghūn Shāh i Ḥasan-khaṣā'il.* Amīr Dhū 'l-Nūn was the father of Shāh-Bēg Arghūn, the founder of the Arghūn dynasty in Sind. Shujāʿ Bēg Arghūn, another son of Dhu 'l-Nūn, was the father of Shāh Ḥasan.

45 The Berlin MS. has Ḥusain according to Pertsch, and Blochet also writes Ḥusain.

(2) ***Jawāhir al-ʿajāʾib***, notices of 20 poetesses, written probably at the court of M. ʿĪsā Tarkhān:[46] Sprenger 5 (Tōp-khānah. 143 pp.), **Bodleian** 362 (apparently an abridgment (9 foll, only), AH 1185/1771), **Bānkīpūr** xi 1098 xxxii (abridgment (4 foll. only). 18th cent.), **Būhār** 482 (1) (abridgment (16 foll, only). 19th cent.)

Edition: **Lucknow** 1873°* (23 pp.).

List of the poetesses: Sprenger p. 11.

[*Tārīkh i Maʿṣūmī* p. 206; *Khazīnah i ganj i Ilāhī* (see Sprenger p. 83); *Makhzan al-gharāʾib*, no. 1901 (?); Sprenger p. 9; Rieu i p. 366.]

1100. Abū ʾl-Naṣr **Sām Mīrzā**, son of Shāh Ismāʿīl I, was born at Marāghah on 21 Shaʿbān 923/19 Sept. 1517 (*Ḥabīb al-siyar* iii, pt. 4, p. 83^{17}). Durmish Khān b. ʿAbdī Bēg [Shāmlū], a close friend of the Shāh, was appointed his tutor (*lalah, ibid.* p. 83^{22}). In 927/1521 the four-year-old prince was made titular Governor of Khurāsān with Durmish Khān as the real Governor (*Ḥ. al-s.* p. 100 ult.—101^{6}). Durmish Khān[47] reached Harāt in Dhū ʾl-Ḥijjah (*Ḥ. al-s.* p. 101^{12-13}), but it was not until the following year that Sām Mīrzā was actually sent to Khurāsān. He reached Harāt in Ramaḍān 928 (*Ḥ. al-s.* p. 104^{21}). In 939/1532–3 his brother Shāh Ṭahmāsp, who had acceded to the throne in 930/1524, appointed him for the second time Governor at Harāt[48] with Āghziwār[49] Khān as his guardian. They rebelled in 941/1534–5[50] and laid siege to Qandahār, at that time governed by Khwājah Kalān Bēg[51] on behalf of Mīrzā Kāmrān.[52] After a siege of eight months Āghziwār Khān was killed in battle outside Qandahār, and Sām Mīrzā sought and received his brother's forgiveness. In 951/1544 he and his brother Bahrām Mīrzā were sent by Shāh Ṭahmāsp to welcome Humāyūn,[53] the Mogul Emperor, who had gone to Persia as a refugee to seek the Shāh's help. Having

---

46 In the verse which Sprenger supposed to be a chronogram the word *tārīkh* is a corruption of *fārigh*.

47 After his death in 931 his brother Ḥusain Khān was appointed Governor of Harāt by Shāh Ṭahmāsp (*Aḥsan al-tawārīkh*. tr. Seddon, p. 94).

48 *Aḥsan al-tawārīkh* i p. 246 penult.

49 Vocalization unconfirmed.

50 *A. al-t.* i p. 260.

51 Formerly one of Bābur's chief amīrs. For an account of him see *Maʾāthir al-umarāʾ* iii pp. 179–81 (in the biography of his son Muṣāḥib Bēg).

52 Brother of the Mogul Emperor Humāyūn and Governor of Kābul, Qandahār and the Panjāb. For a summary of his career see Bānkīpūr Cat. ii pp. 217–22. Cf. *Ency. Isl.* under Kāmrān (H. Beveridge).

53 *A. al-t.* i p. 309^{8}. This seems to be the last mention of Sām in the *A. al-t.*

rebelled again in 969/1561–2,[54] he was punished by confinement in the fortress of Qahqahah,[55] and there he died in 974/1566–7,[56] when an earthquake destroyed the building in which he was seated.

Tuḥfah i Sāmī, notices of poets[57] who flourished from the later years of the 9th/15th century to the middle of the 10th/16th, composed, at least partly, in or about 957/1550,[58] and divided into seven *ṣaḥīfahs* ((1) Shāh Ismāʿīl and contemporary princes, p. 6 in the Ṭihrān edition, (2) Saiyids and *ʿulamāʾ*, p. 21, (3) *wazīrs* and other officials, p. 55, (4) persons of distinction who occasionally wrote poetry, p. 63, (5) poets best known by their pen-names (*shāʿirānī kih bi-takhalluṣ mashhūr-and*), p. 85, (6) poets of Turkish race, p. 179, (7) jesters and poets of the lower classes, p. 188): Ḥ. Kh. ii p. 263 no. 2823 (*Tadhkirat al-shuʿarāʾ fārisī li-Sām Mīrzā*), Sprenger p. 12 no. 7, **Bānkīpūr** viii 682 (AH 968/1561), 683 (AH 971/1564), **Rieu** i 368*a* (very defective, AH 969/1561–2), 367*b* (late 16th cent.), Suppt. 103 (AH 976/1569), **Flügel** ii 1201 (AH 972/1564–5), **Krafft** p. 126 no. 313 (AH 972/1565), **Lindesiana** p. 215 no. 317 (AH 977/1569–70), **Sipahsālār** ii

---

54 This is stated by Rieu and M. ʿAlī Tarbiyat apparently on the authority of the *Riyāḍ al-shuʿarāʾ* and the *Takmilat al-akhbār* (what is this work ?) respectively.

55 Iskandar Munshī in speaking of Qahqahah at a later date (p. 579[11]) mentions Sām Mīrzā, Ismāʿīl Mīrzā and Alqās Mīrzā as persons who had been confined there. He describes it as a fortress or castle (*qalʿah*) on a mountain peak in the region (*ulkā*) of Yāft [doubtless = "Yāft (Māft, or Bāft)," *Nuzhat al-qulūb* tr. le Strange p. 86] in the administrative division (*az aʿmāl*) of Qarājah-Dāgh [a mountainous tract rich in iron and other minerals stretching east of Marand in Northern Ādharbāyjān and including Ahar, the chief town. For a map of the region (on which, however, neither Yāft nor Qahqahah is marked) see S. M. ʿAlī Jamāl-Zādah's *Ganj i shāygān*, Berlin 1335, p. 102]. Cf. Seddon's note in *Aḥsan al-t.* ii (trans.) p. 293, and also Minorsky in BSOS. vii (1933–5) pp. 991–2, where it is stated that Yāft is "on the Qara-su". That Qahqahah was not in the immediate neighbourhood of Yāft is shown by the fact that Ismāʿīl ii, having left Qahqahah on Tuesday, 22 Safar 984, did not camp at Yāft until the following Thursday (*A. al-t.* trans. p. 205[11]).

56 According to M. ʿAlī Tarbiyat, who quotes (again apparently from the *Takmilat al-akhbar*: see n. 54 on this page) a chronogram (*Daulat i Ṭahmāsb shud bāqī*) by ʿAbdī Shīrāzī. Rieu on the other hand says (presumably on the authority of the *Riyāḍ al- shuʿarāʾ*) that "having rebelled in AH 969 against his brother Shāh Ṭahmāsp, he was thrown into prison, and afterwards put to death with other princes of the royal house, on the accession of Shāh Ismāʿīl II, A. 984." Iskandar Munshī mentions the names of some princes put to death by Ismāʿīl II, but Sām Mīrzā is not among them.

57 664 according to Sprenger, 663 in Berlin 643, but there are only 399 names in Silvestre de Sacy's list.

58 This date occurs in the notice of Humāyūn towards the end of *Ṣaḥīfah* i, where it is mentioned as the current year (*Notices et extraits* iv p. 281). In the Ṭihrān edition the passage (p. 17[4]) is corrupt (*tā aknūn kih sanah i khams wa-tisʿmiʾah i Hijrīst*). In the Bombay University MS. the date is given as 956 (*tā ḥāl kih 956 ast*).

p. 462 (probably *circ.* AH 983/1575), **Cairo** p. 501 (AH 997/1588–9), **Blochet** ii 1144 (AH 1001/1593), 1145 (late 16th cent.), 1146 (17th cent.), 1147 (early 18th cent.), **Bombay** Univ. p. 41 no. 25 (bears seal dated 1007/1598–9), **Aumer** 2, **Berlin** 643, 643*a*, **Browne** Suppt. 272, **Bukhārā** Semenov 41, **Ethé** 665 (about 579 biographies), 666 (only 474 biographies), **Leningrad** Asiat. Mus. (defective. See *Mélanges asiatiques* vii (St. Petersburg 1876) p. 402), **Leyden** iii p. 19 no. 933, **Madras** 305. Some other MSS. are mentioned in the Bombay University catalogue p. 42, including one dated 972 at Kābul (library unspecified). There are several at Istānbūl (e.g. Fātiḥ 4241–2, Ḥakīm-oghlū ʿAlī Pāshā 718).

Edition: **Ṭihrān** AHS. 1314/1936 (ed. Waḥīd Dastgirdī. Supplement to the periodical *Armaghān*, Year 16).

Edition of *Ṣaḥīfah* v: *The Tuhfa i Sami (Section V) of Sam Mirza Safawi edited ... by Mawlawi Iqbal Husain*, **Patna** (Allahabad printed) 1934* (Patna University).

Extracts: *Iqtibāsāt i Tuḥfah i Sāmī rājiʿ bah hunarwarān* [edited with notes by M. Shafīʿ in *Oriental College Magazine*, vol. x no. 2 (**Lahore**, Feb. 1934) pp. 73–128]. Abridgment: *Intikhāb i Tuḥfah i Sāmī*, by Ānand Rām "Mukhliṣ" (for whom see no. 780 *supra*): **I.O.** D.P. 718.

Descriptions:

(1) ... *Le présent sublime, ou Histoire des poëtes de Sam-mirza ... Par A. I. Silvestre de Sacy* (in *Notices et extraits des manuscrits de la Bibliothèque nationale*, Tome IV (**Paris**, An 7 = 1798°*) pp. 273–308. With LIST OF 399[59] POETS).

(2) *Ueber die morgenländischen Handschriften der königlichen Hof- und Central-Bibliothek in München. Bemerkungen von Othmar Frank*, **Munich** 1814°*, pp. 31–69 and Anhang pp. xv–xlix (LIST OF 518[60] POETS).

[*Ḥabīb al-siyar* iii pt. 4, pp. 83, 100, 104; Ḥasan Rūmlū *Aḥsan al-tawārīkh*, Seddon's trans., pp. 90[16], 118–19; *Khazīnah i ganj i Ilāhi* (Sprenger p. 77); *Safīnah i Khwushgū* (Bodl. 376 no. 58); *Muntakhab al-ashār* (Bodl. 379) no. 285; *Riyāḍ al-shuʿarā; Ātash-kadah*, Bodl. 384 no. 35, Bombay 1277 p. 14; *Makhzan al-gharāʾib* no. 1000; *Majmaʿ al-fuṣaḥāʾ* i 31 (where Sām is inadvertently described as a son of Shāh Ṭahmāsp); *Shamʿ i anjuman* p. 199; *Ency. Isl.* under Sām (Huart); M. ʿAlī Tarbiyat *Dānishmandān i Ādharbāyjān*, Ṭihrān AHS. 1314, pp. 173–4.]

59 The fifth *ṣaḥīfah* in the MS. described (Ancien fonds 247 = Blochet ii 1144) contains only 104 biographies, whereas there are 296 in the corresponding part of the Munich MS.

60 The Munich MS. is defective.

1101. Mīr ʿAlāʾ al-Daulah "Kāmī" b. Yaḥyā Saifī Ḥusainī[61] Qazwīnī was the second son of the author of the *Lubb al-tawārīkh* (see no. 129 *supra*), the younger brother and foster-son[62] of Mīr ʿAbd al-Laṭīf Qazwīnī, Akbar's teacher[63] and friend,[64] and the uncle of Naqīb Khān (for whom see no. 135 *supra*). When Shāh Ṭahmāsp sent orders from Ādharbāyjān in 960/1552–3 for the arrest of Mīr Yaḥyā and his family (cf. no. 129 *supra*) on the charge of excessive Sunnism, Mīr ʿAlāʾ al-Daulah, who was then in Ādharbāyjān (Badāʾūnī p. 98[10]), warned his father. The latter was arrested and died later in prison, but Mīr ʿAbd al-Laṭīf fled to the mountains of Gīlān. Invited to India by Humāyūn, Mīr ʿAbd al-Laṭīf arrived there shortly after Humāyūn's death and was received by Akbar in 963/1556, the first year of his reign (*Akbar-nāmah*, tr. Beveridge, ii, p. 35; Badāʾūnī i p. 30[15]). Naqīb Khān had accompanied him (*A.-n., ibid.*), but whether "Kāmī" reached India at this time or another is not recorded. A son of his, Mīr Yaḥyā Ḥusainī Saifī, is one of the poets included in the *Nafāʾis al-maʾāthir* (Sprenger p. 55).

Nafāʾis al-maʾāthir (a chronogram = 973/1565–6, the date of inception[65]), a *tadhkirah* dedicated to Akbar and containing (in the Munich MS.) a *maṭlaʿ* (subdivided into two *miṣraʿs*, (1) *dar kaifīyat i ṣudūr i shiʿr*, (2) *dar taʿrīf u taqsīm i shiʿr*), notices of about 350 poets, mainly of the 10th/16th century, arranged alphabetically in 28 *baits* (one for each letter), a fragment relating to the history of Gujrāt in the years 980–5,[66] and a *maqṭaʿ* dealing in three *maṭlabs* with the history of Bābur, Humāyūn and Akbar: Sprenger 10 (Mōtī Maḥall. LIST OF POETS), **Aumer** 3 (old), **Rieu** iii 1022*a* (only extracts, viz. the preface, table of contents, history of Bābur, Humāyūn and Akbar to Jumādā II 982/1574, and a few detached lives of

61 Ḥasanī according to the printed text of Badāʾūnī.

62 *Ham birādar i khurd i ʿAbd al-Laṭīf u ham tarbiyat-kardah i ū būd u ū-rā ḥaḍrat i āqā mī-guft* (Badāʾūnī iii 97[16]).

63 *Padshāh pīsh i īshān sabaqī chand az dīwān i Khwājah Ḥāfiẓ u ghair i ān khwāndah and* (Badāʾūnī iii 98[18]); *Dar sāl i duwwum ba-muʿallimī i ʿArsh-āshyānī iftikhār andūkht* (*Maʾāthir al-umarāʾ* iii 814[3]).

64 For ʿAbd al-Laṭīf see Badāʾūnī iii pp. 97–8; *Āʾīn i Akbarī* tr. Blochmann pp. 447–8; *Memoirs of Jahāngīr* tr. Rogers and Beveridge i pp. 28 n. 2, 264; *Maʾāthir al-umarāʾ* iii pp. 813–15; Raḥmān ʿAlī p. 132, etc.

65 Sprenger points out that considerably later dates occur in the MS. seen by him. The latest of those mentioned in his catalogue seems to be 996, the year of "Hādī's" death. He says further that "according to a Postscript" the work was completed in 979, and Aumer quotes, doubtless from the same "postscript", the chronogram *Tammat ʿalā yadaihi* (= 979).

66 Is this by any chance a portion of the history of Akbar misplaced ?

poets. Circ. AD 1850), **Ross-Browne** 247 (2) (circ. AD 1864. Cf. **Rehatsek** p. 169 no. 147, of which R.-B. 247 is probably a transcript).

Extracts (poets of Akbar's time in India only): *Muntakhab al-tawārīkh*, by ʿAbd al-Qādir Badāʾūnī (cf. no. 614 *supra*), iii pp. 170–390[67] (166 poets).

List of the poets: Sprenger pp. 47–55.

[*Muntakhab al-tawārīkh* iii pp. 97–8 (in the notice of Mīr ʿAbd al-Laṭīf); *Āʾīn Akbarī* tr. Blochmann p. 447 [37 and n.2]; *Mirʾāt i jahān-numā* (fol. 389 in a B.M. MS. cited by Rieu, iii p. 1022*b*); *Maʾāthir al-umarāʾ* iii p. 813 (in the life of Naqīb Khān).]

1102. S. Bahāʾ al-Dīn Ḥasan **"Nithārī" Bukhārī**,[68] or, as on the title-page[69] of Berlin 645, S. Ḥasan Khwājah[70] Naqīb al-Ashrāf[71] Bukhārī.

Mudhakkir i aḥbāb (a chronogram = 974/1566–7), notices of 275 poets who lived in Bukhārā or its dependencies after the time of Mīr ʿAlī-Shīr (for whom see no. 1094 *supra*), divided into a *maqālah* ((*a*) Chingīz-Khānī Sulṭāns, i.e. Shaibānī Khān etc., (*b*) Chaghatāy Sulṭāns, i.e. Bābur etc.), four *bābs* ((1) deceased poets not personally known to the author, (2) deceased poets known to the author, (3) living poets known to the author, (4) living poets unknown to the author) and a *khātimah* (the author's family): Ḥ. Kh. v p. 478, **British Museum** (AH 987/1579. See *British*

67 This section is headed *Dhikr i shuʿarā-yi ʿaṣr i Akbar-Shāhī kih dar Nafāʾis al-maʾāthir madhkūr-and kih maʾkhadh i īn ʿujālah ast u mashhūr bah Tadhkirah i Mīr ʿAlāʾ al-Daulah ast.* Similarly in his notice of "Kāmī" (p. 316) Badāʾūnī says that Mīr ʿAlāʾ al-Daulah's *tadhkirah* is *maʾkhadh i in ʿujālah.* Among the poets noticed by Badāʾūnī are an appreciable number who do not appear in Sprenger's account of the *Nafāʾis al-maʾāthir.* Badāʾuni may of course have used a later edition of the *N. al-m.* than that represented by the Lucknow MS. which Sprenger examined.

68 "Nitháry Bokháry, Bahâ aldyn Ḥasan" according to the *Nafāʾis al-maʾāthir.*

69 That the author does not mention his name in the preface seems probable from the fact that in the *British Museum Quarterly* the *Mudhakkir i aḥbāb* is described as anonymous. On the title-page (fol. 1a) of Berlin 645 his name is given in an ornate gold-lettered inscription quoted by Pertsch (*Tadhkirat al-shuʿarā afḍal al-mutaʾakhkhirīn Maulānā Saiyid Ḥasan Khwājah Naqīb al-Ashrāf Bukhārī sallama-hu ʾllāh taʿālā* ...). The dedicatee was Abū ʾl-Ghāzī Iskandar Bahādur Khān [the Shaibānid, 968/1561–991/1583: see *Ency. Isl.* under Iskandar Khān] according to Pertsch, Amir M. Badīʿ al-Ḥusainī according to the *BMQ*. Nawwāb Ṣadr Yār Jang and the *BMQ*. (but not Pertsch) describe the work as written in the time of ʿAbd Allāh Bahādur Khān, which suggests that he is mentioned in the preface.

70 This title is appended to the names of several of the author's relations in the *khātimah* (e.g. Bābā Khān Khwājah, ʿAbd al-Salīm Khwājah b. Pādshāh Khwājah, Walī Allāh Khwājah b. Mīram Khwājah).

71 For this office see *Ency. Isl.* s.v. Sharīf.

Museum Quarterly iv/4 (1930) p. 112), **Berlin** 645, **Ivanow** 219 (bad and defective. 17th cent.), **Leningrad** Institut Oriental de l'Académie (see an article by A. Boldyrev in *Musée de l'Ermitage, Travaux du Département oriental*, iii (1940) pp. 291–300).

Extracts relating to seven calligraphists: *OCM*. xi/2 (Feb. 1935) pp. 39–45 (ed. Nawwāb Ṣadr Yār Jang, from a MS. in his private library).

List of the poets: Berlin pp. 605–9.

[*Nafā'is al-ma'āthir* (Sprenger p. 54).]

1103. For the *Mīr'āt al-adwār*, a general history to 974/1566–7 by Muṣliḥ al-Dīn Lārī, which contains in the latter part biographies of writers and other celebrities inserted after the most important reigns, see no. 133 *supra*.

1104. For the *Aḥsan al-tawārīkh* of Ḥasan Rūmlū (AH 985/1577), which concludes the record of each year with obituary notices, mostly very short, see no. 381 *supra*.

1105. Taqī al-Dīn M. "Dhikrī" b. Sharaf al-Dīn 'Alī Ḥusainī Kāshānī, usually called **Taqī Kāshī**, was born circ. 943/1536–7[72] and was still alive in 1016/1607–8. He was a pupil of Muḥtasham Kāshī, who during the illness from which he died in 996/1588 sent for him and asked him to collect and arrange his poetical works. This he did and wrote a preface, which is prefixed to the British Museum MS. of Muḥtasham's *dīwān* (Rieu ii, p. 665).

Khulāṣat al-ash'ār wa-zubdat al-afkār, a remarkable *tadhkirah* containing "the fullest biographical details, the most copious and best chosen extracts (seldom less than a thousand verses[73] and in all 350,000 couplets), the soundest critical and most exact and complete bibliographical remarks on the Persian poets"[74] (Sprenger), divided into a *muqaddimah* (reasons for writing the work, four *faṣls* on *'ishq*, selections from 'Alī's *dīwān* with Persian paraphrase, and a *lāḥiqah* on poetry and the beginnings of

72 "He was born at Káshán about AH 946" according to Sprenger, who does not say how he obtained this information. If it is correct that when he wrote the *dhail* to the *khātimah* of the *Khulāṣat al-ash'ār* he had "now arrived at the fiftieth year of his age" (Bland p. 131) and if the date was then 993, as indicated by the chronogram quoted by Bland (who misinterpreted it) and Sprenger, he must have been born about 943.

73 Thus according to 'Abd al-Muqtadir the selections from Ḥāfiẓ amount to almost the whole *dīwān*.

74 "The only fault is that he dwells at too great a length on the love adventures of the subjects of his biography which are generally most disgusting."

Persian poetry), four *rukns* completed in 985/1577–8[75] ((1) (= *Mujallads* i and ii) 54 ancient poets, mainly *qaṣīdah*-writers from Subuktigīn's time to the 8th century, (2) (= *Mujallad* iii) 42 *ghazal*-writers and later *qaṣīdah*-writers of the 8th and early 9th centuries, (3) (= *Mujallad* iv) 49 modern poets of the 9th and a few of the 10th century, (4) (= *Mujallad* v) 101 poets from Sulṭān Ḥusain Mīrzā's time to that of the author), a *khātimah* added in 993/1585[76] (contemporary poets in 12 *aṣls* devoted to particular places,[77] (1) Kāshān, (2) Iṣfahān, (3) Qumm, etc.), and a short *dhail*,[78] the whole existing also in a revised and enlarged edition completed in 1016/1607–8, which ends with a [second] *khātimah* (poems, without biographies, of 60 poets, most of whom sent their *dīwāns* to the author after the completion of his work[79]) and an expanded *dhail* (the author's reflections on his work: see Bland pp. 131–2),[80] and of which there is an abridgment containing the biographies without the poetical quotations: Sprenger 8 (Mōtī Maḥall), 9 (Mōtī Maḥall. The abridged 2nd ed. LIST OF POETS[81]), **Blochet** iii 1242 (Notices of ʿAmʿaq, Sūzanī, Rashīd i Waṭwāṭ, Falakī, ʿImādī [from *Rukn* i]. "Ce volume est l'un des tomes du manuscrit original du grand tezkéré de Taki ed-Din ... el Kashani." Late 16th cent.), **Bānkīpūr** viii 684 (*Mujallad* iv = *Rukn* iii only.[82] Revised and annotated by the author. Late 16th or early 17th cent.), **Ethé** 667 (abridged 2nd ed. (without the poems), lacking *Rukn* IV), 668 (*Khātimah* only. 1st ed. (with

75 Rieu Suppt. 105, Berlin 647, Ethé 667 and Lindesiana 312 (Bland's MS.) contain at the beginning a eulogy on Shāh Ṭahmāsp, which must have been written before 984. Rieu Suppt. 105 contains also a later dedication to Shāh ʿAbbās, at the end of which the author says that the work was completed early in 996. In the Bland MS. *Rukn* ii opens with a dedication to Shāh ʿAbbās, but at the beginning of the work this MS. seems to contain no mention of Shāh ʿAbbās but (in its place ?) a dedication (dated 1006) to Ibrāhīm ʿĀdil-Shāh [II, of Bījāpūr, AH 987/1579–1035/1626]. In his *dhail* the author, writing in 1016, says that the work had occupied him during thirty years and that so much had been inserted in it, since its completion in its original form, that a sixth *mujallad* had become necessary.

76 After 14 years had been spent on the work (Sprenger p. 13).

77 The places of the poets' origins, their birthplaces.

78 Ethé 668, a MS. of 993, ends with a short *dhail*.

79 For the author's statements concerning this second *khātimah* see *JRAS*. ix (1848) p. 131.

80 It seems from Bland's description that the *dhail* in his MS. consists of the *dhail* of 993 (with its chronogram) supplemented by the author's final remarks and the chronogram for 1016.

81 For emendations of this list see Ethé 667.

82 On foll. 270–395 of this MS. there is a *tadhnīb* added after the completion of the work and containing quotations from about 250 poets concerning whom the author had been unable to obtain any biographical information.

the poems), AH 993/1585), **Dorn** 321 (*Rukn* iii only. AH 933/1526!! LIST OF 41 POETS), **Rieu** Suppt. 105 (introductory chapters and *Mujallad* i only, defective at end. 16th cent. LIST OF 22 POETS.), **Majlis** 334 (only *Khātimah, aṣls* 1–7. AH 1013/1604–5), **Lindesiana** p. 223 no. 312 (unabridged 2nd ed., lacking *Rukn* iv. AH 1038–9/1628–30. Bland's MS.), **Berlin** 647 (abridged 2nd ed. 19th cent.), 647a (only *Khātimah*, second *Khātimah* and *Dhail*. 19th cent. LIST OF POETS IN 2ND KHĀTIMAH), **Ivanow** 2nd Suppt. 932 (fragment of vol. iv = *Rukn* iii, viz. poets numbered 109–16 in Sprenger's list. Circ. AD 1873).

Description: *On the earliest Persian Biography of Poets, by Muhammad Aúfi, and on some other Works of the class called Tazkirat ul Shuârá. By N. Bland* (in *JRAS*. ix (1848), pp. 126–34).

[*Ṣuḥuf i Ibrāhīm* (Berlin Cat. p. 640); Bland in *JRAS*. ix (1848)pp. 131–2.]

1106. S. **ʿAlī b. Maḥmūd al-Ḥusainī** completed in 1000/1591–2 and dedicated to his patron, the *Khān i Khānān* ʿAbd al-Raḥīm[83] b. Bairam Khān, his

Bazm-ārāy, an anthology of ancient and modern poets with rhetorical and uninformative biographies largely plagiarized from the *Lubāb al-albāb* (see no. 1088 *supra*): **Rieu** Suppt. 106 (early 17th cent.).

1107. For the *Ṭabaqāt i Akbarī*, written in 1001–2/1592–4 by Niẓām al-Dīn Aḥmad Harawī, which contains brief notices of 81 poets of Akbar's time (Calcutta ed. vol. ii pp. 484–520) see no. 613 *supra*.

1108. The *Haft iqlīm*, completed in 1002/1594 by Amīn b. Aḥmad Rāzī, which contains geographically arranged notices of celebrities including many poets, will be described in the subsection of this work devoted to general biography.

1109. For the *Muntakhab al-tawārīkh* of ʿAbd al-Qādir Badāʾūnī, which was written in 1004/1595–6 and which contains notices of 166 poets of Akbar's time, see nos. 614 and 1101 (Extracts), *supra*.

1110. For the *Āʾīn i Akbarī*, which contains brief notices of poets of Akbar's time (Calcutta ed. pp. 235–62, Blochmann's trans. pp. 548–611) see no. 709 (2) *supra*.

83 For whom see no. 698, Persian translations (3), footnote *supra*.

1111. The *Majālis al-muʾminīn*, which was completed in 1010/1602 by Nūr Allāh Shūshtarī, and of which the 12th and last *majlis* deals with Persian poets, will be described in the subsection of this work devoted to general biography.

1112. Mullā **Muḥammad** "Muḥammad"[84] **Ṣūfī**[85] **Māzandarani,**[86] poet, mystic, traveller and in his time a celebrated personage,[87] was born at Āmul (*Mai-khānah* p. 345[5]), but early in life he migrated to Shīrāz and lived there for a prolonged period (*ibid.*). According to Taqī Kashī (Sprenger p. 33) he travelled much in Persia. In Akbar's reign (963/1556–1014/1605) he went to India[88] and settled at Aḥmadābād. It was there that he became the teacher and friend (*Maʾāthir al-umarāʾ* iii p. 450[17]) of Mīr S. Jalāl Bukhārī,[89] member of a saintly Gujrātī family, who was later (1052/1642) to become *Ṣadr* of Hindūstān. There too, until an estrangement supervened, he enjoyed the companionship of the poet "Naẓīrī" Nīshāpūrī (Bānkīpūr iii p. 61), and there he was visited repeatedly by Taqī Auḥadī (*ibid.*, doubtless on the authority of the *Khulāṣat al-ashʿār*). From time to time he travelled to other parts of India, and it was during a visit to Ajmēr that the author of the *Mai-khānah* had the felicity of meeting the devout, unworldly and evidently impressive *ṣūfī*, who informed him that he had lived for 15 years in Mecca (*Mai-khānah* p. 346[1]) and that there were few parts of the world he had not seen(!). It is said that he was summoned to

84 According to Sprenger and ʿAbd al-Muqtadir "Muḥammad" is the *takhalluṣ* used in the copies of the *dīwān* seen by them, though some of the *tadhkirahs* put him under "Ṣūfī". Bland says on the authority of the *Ṣuḥuf i Ibrāhīm*, but perhaps erroneously, that he used both pen-names.

85 *Chūn ṣūfī-ṭabīʿat u ṣāfī-ṭawīyat wāqiʿ shudah binā-bar-ān bi-Maulānā M. i Ṣūfī ishtihār yāftah* (*Mai-khānah*, p. 345).

86 ʿAbd al-Muqtadir says that the *tadhkirahs* mention several poets called Ṣūfī or M. Ṣūfī with various *nisbahs* (Māzandarānī, Shīrāzī, Kirmānī, Ardistānī, Hamadānī, Amulī, Iṣfahānī, Kashmīrī), but that some of these are merely repetitions of M. Ṣūfī Māzandarānī, since verses ascribed to them are to be found in the Bānkīpūr *dīwān*,

87 Taqī Kāshī describes him as "a mystical poet who enjoyed great celebrity during his life time" (Sprenger p. 33). In the *Maʾāthir al-umarāʾ* (iii p. 450) he is called *Mullā M. i Ṣūfī i Māzandarānī i mashhūr*.

88 With Abū Ḥaiyān i Ṭabīb and Mullā Ḥasan ʿAlī Yazdī according to the *Majmaʿ al-al-fuṣaḥāʾ*. Ṭāhir Naṣrābādī mentions in his account of Ḥusain [so in the printed text] ʿAlī Yazdī (*Tadhkirah* pp. 157–8) that he became a close friend of M. Ṣūfī (*Baʿd az ān ba-Hindūstān raftah bā Mullā M. i Ṣūfī marbūṭ shudah muddatī chūn shīr u shakar u āb u guhar ba-ham āmīzish dāshtand ba-ḥasb i taqdīrāt az yak-dīgar judā shudah and*). Cf. *Safīnah i Khwushgū* no. 626.

89 b. 1003/1595, d. 1057/1647.

Court by Jahāngīr and died on the way thither[90] at Sirhind[91] in 1032/1623[92] or 1035/1625–6.[93]

According to Taqī Kāshī "he was accused of being a freethinker by men learned in law" (Sprenger p. 33). He is one of the ten poets enumerated in the list of names at the end of the *Iqbāl-nāmah i Jahāngīrī* and in the *Haft iqlīm* his poetry is highly praised (*shiʿr dar ghāyat i jaudat u hamwārī dārad*). His *dīwān* is preserved at Bānkīpūr (iii no. 301), Hamburg (191 iv) and Munich (Aumer 18 (6)). A MS. in a private library was described by Sprenger (no. 382). His *sāqī-nāmah*, written in 1000/1591–2, is preserved at Bānkīpūr (two copies—iii p. 62 and xi p. 139), Berlin (18 ii 10 (a)), Hamburg (191 (4)) and Munich (Aumer 18 (3)). A Lucknow MS. was described by Sprenger (no. 187). His *But-khānah* was compiled in collaboration with Ḥasan Bēg Khākī, who was sent as *Bakhshī* to Gujrāt in 1007/1598–9 (see no. 138 *supra*).

But-khānah, a large selection from the *dīwāns* of 126 poets, mostly early, compiled in 1010/1601–2, but amplified in 1021/1612–13 by ʿAbd al-Laṭīf b. ʿAbd Allāh ʿAbbāsī Gujrātī,[94] who prefixed a preface and brief biographies

---

90 From Gujrāt (*Maʾāthir al-umarāʾ* iii p. 451), from Aḥmadābād (to Lahore, *Safīnah i Khwushgū*), from Kashmīr (*Ṣuḥuf i Ibrāhīm*). According to the *Muntakhab al-ashʿār* (no. 629) he died in Kashmīr.

91 So *Ṣuḥuf i Ibrāhīm*.

92 So Khwushgū.

93 So *Riyāḍ al-shuʿarāʾ* (according to Bānkīpūr i p. 61 antepenult.) and other works. According to the passage translated from the *Ṣuḥuf i Ibrāhīm* by Bland (JRAS. 1848 pp. 165–6) he was a resident of Aḥmadābād in Gujrāt in 1038 and afterwards, for some time, of Kashmīr, but the date is evidently corrupt, since the passage goes on to say that "by desire of the Emperor Jehangir [who died in 1037 !] he came from Kashmir, but arriving at Serhind, died there".

94 ʿAbd al-Laṭīf ʿAbbāsī after a period in the service of Lashkar Khān Mashhadī (*Dīwān* and afterwards *Ṣūbah-dār* of Kābul) became *Dīwān i Tan* with the title of ʿAqīdat Khān in Shāh-Jahān's fifth year. For some time he was Court Chronicler. He died in the twelfth year of the reign, 1048–9/1638–9. He was the author of (1) *Nuskhah i nāsikhah i Mathnawīyāt i saqīmah*, a revised and annotated edition of Jalāl al-Dīn Rūmī's *Mathnawī* completed in 1032/1622–3 (MSS.: Blochet iii 1340, Ethé 1088–90, 2993, Bodleian 663–5, Rieu ii 589*a*, 590*a*, Browne Pers. Cat. 227, etc.), (2) *Laṭāʾif al-maʿnawī min ḥaqāʾiq al-Mathnawī*, a commentary on the same work (Editions: Lucknow 1282/1866 (see Berlin p. 795[7]), Cawnpore 1876°. MSS.: Bombay Univ. p. 240, Ethé 1101, Rieu ii 590*a*, Bānkīpūr i 74, Ivanow 507, etc.), (3) *Mirʾāt al-Mathnawī*, another commentary on the same work (MS.: Ethé 1102), (4) *Laṭāʾif al-lughāt*, a glossary to the same work (Editions: Lucknow 1294/1877°*, Cawnpore 1905°*. MSS.: Bodleian 1748–51, Ethé 1091–7, Rieu ii 590*b*, 591*a*, 810*a*, iii 1000*a*, Bānkīpūr i 75, Eton 106, Glasgow, etc.), (5) *Laṭāʾif al-ḥadāʾiq min nafāʾis al-daqāʾiq*, a revised text of Sanāʾī's *Ḥadīqah* with a commentary begun in 1040/1630–1 and completed in 1042/1632–3 with help from Mīr ʿImād al-Dīn Maḥmūd "Ilāhī" (for whom see no. 1121 *infra*). (Edition: Lucknow 1887 (see Bānkīpūr i p. 29 [1 and 15]). MSS.: Edinburgh 273, Lahore Panjāb Univ., Bānkīpūr i 21, Būhār 283–4, ʿAlīgaṛh Subḥ. MSS. p. 49 no. 12), (6) *Sharḥ i Ḥadīqah*, the same

of the poets entitled *Khulāṣah i aḥwāl al-shuʿarāʾ*: **Bodleian** 366 (slightly defective. LIST OF POETS).

Edition of the selections from "Muṭahhar's" *dīwān:* OCM. xi/3 (May 1935) pp. 152–60, xi/4 (Aug. 1935) *ḍamīmah*, pp. 161–216 (ed. M. Shafīʿ).

[*Haft iqlīm* no. 1191 (a quotation from this in *Mai-khānah, ḥawāshī* p. 67); *Āʾīn i Akbarī* p. 254, Blochmann's trans. p. 590; Taqī Kāshī (Sprenger p. 33); Taqī Auḥadī; ʿAbd al-Nabī *Mai-khānah* pp. 345–60 and *ḥawāshī* pp. 67–9; *Safīnah i Khwushgū* no. 583; *Yad i baiḍāʾ; Muntakhab al-ashʿār* no. 629 (Bodl. col. 252. Passage quoted in *Mai-khānah, ḥawāshī* p. 67); *Riyāḍ al-shuʿarāʾ; Majmaʿ al-nafāʾis; Atash-kadah* no. 402 (under Iṣfahān. M. Zamān in the Bodl. Cat. is a corruption); *Maʾāthir al-umarāʾ* iii pp. 450–1; *Ṣuḥuf i Ibrāhīm* (summarised in *JRAS*. 1848 pp. 165–6); *Makhzan al-gharāʾib* no. 2434; *Nishtar i ʿishq; Majmaʿ al-fuṣahāʾ* ii p. 38; Bānkīpūr iii pp. 60–1.]

1113. **Taqī Auḥadī**,[95] or, as he calls himself, Taqī b. Muʿīn al-Dīn M.[96] b. Saʿd al-Dīn M. al-Ḥusainī al-Auḥadī[97] al-Daqqāqī[98] al-Balyānī[99] al-Iṣfahānī, was born at Iṣfahān in Muḥarram 973/1565. He was presented to Shāh ʿAbbās I (AH 985/1587–1038/1629) soon after his accession and enjoyed his favour for some years. In 1003/1594–5 he went on a pilgrimage to Najaf and other holy places, returning home in 1009/1600–1. In Rajab 1015/Nov. 1606 he left for India via Shīrāz, Kirmān and Qandahār. After staying for 18 months in Lahore and more than a year in Āgrah he went to Gujrāt (Gujarat) and lived there for three years, returning to Āgrah in 1020/1611–12. It was in that year, apparently while still in Gujrāt, that he compiled an anthology entitled *Firdaus i khayāl i Auḥadī*

---

revised text with an abridgment of the same commentary completed by the commentator himself in 1044/1634 (MSS.: Ethé 923–4, Ivanow 445, Ivanow Curzon 192).

[*ʿAmal i Ṣāliḥ* iii pp. 437–8; Rieu ii p. 589; Bānkīpūr i pp. 25–8.]

95 According to ʿAbd al-Muqtadir he "adopted the *takhalluṣ* Auḥadī", but this seems to be incorrect. Ivanow in describing a MS. of his *dīwān* calls it the *Dīwān i Taqī* and Sprenger, who had the same MS. before him, treats Taqī as the *takhalluṣ*. Similarly he is placed under the letter T in the *Makhzan al-gharāʾib* and elsewhere.

96 For his father, Sh. Muʿīn al-D. M. Auḥadī, see *Makhzan al-gharāʾib* no. 2297, where it is said that his *majlis* at Qazwīn was frequented by Shāh Ṭahmāsp, that from Qazwīn he went to Shīrāz and afterwards to India and that he died in the Deccan in 979.

97 Taqī was "descended by seven steps" (Bland p. 134) from Shaikh Auḥad al-Dīn ʿAbd Allāh Balyānī [b. Masʿūd b. M. b. ʿAlī b. Aḥmad b. ʿUmar b. Ismāʿīl b. Abī ʿAlī al-Daqqāq, d. 686/1287: see Sprenger p. 95, *Nafaḥāt al-uns* p. 291, *Safīnat al-auliyāʾ* p. 180 (no. 338)].

98 For Abū ʿAlī al-Daqqāq, who died in 405/1015 or 406/1016, see *Tadhkirat al-auliyāʾ* i pp. 187–201, *Nafaḥāt al-uns* pp. 328–31, *Safīnat al-auliyāʾ* p. 159 (no 283).

99 Balyān "bi-fatḥ i awwal bar wazn i GHLYĀN" is the name of a village in the *wilāyat* of Kāzarūn (*Burhān i qāṭiʿ*). Cf. *Shīrāz-nāmah* p. 140: *BLYĀN qaryaʾī az qurā i Kāzarūn ast.*

(a chronogram = 1020[100]), containing "all the specimens of poetry he had collected in the six years between Shiraz and Guzarat" (Bland p. 135). Later on at Āgrah one of the nobles of Jahāngīr's court "induced him to remodel the work, and to accompany the extracts with memoirs of the several authors quoted". Thus it became the *ʿArafāt al-ʿāshiqīn* completed at Āgrah in 1024. That he returned to Gujrāt is shown by the fact that his abridgment, the *Kaʿbah i ʿirfān* was written at Aḥmadabād[101] in 1036. The date of his death does not seem to be recorded, but the A.S.B. MS. of his *Tadhkirat al-ʿāshiqīn* (Ivanow 733) contains poems dated 1038 and 1039.[102]

His own list of his works, quoted from the *Kaʿbah i ʿirfān* in the *Guldastah* and thence in the Bānkīpūr catalogue, viii pp. 77–8, includes several *mathnawīs*[103] and several *dīwāns*.[104] Little of this large output seems to have survived. Of the *Tadhkirat al-ʿāshiqīn, a dīwān* of *ghazals*, the first half (*alif* to *dāl*) is preserved at Calcutta (Ivanow 733), and there is another *dīwān* (beginning *Īn charkh i gard-gard i kawākib-nigār chīst*) at Madras (no. 7). The *Surmah i Sulaimānī*, a dictionary of non-Arabic words utilised later (1062/1652) in the compilation of the *Burhān i qāṭiʿ*, is preserved at Leningrad (Salemann-Rosen p. 16 no. 174). The Lucknow (Tōp-khānah) MS. of the *Kullīyāt* (*sic*) described by Sprenger (p. 576) seems to have been only a comparatively small collection of his shorter poems.

(1) ***ʿArafāt* [?] *al-ʿārifīn*** [or ***al-ʿāshiqīn***] ***wa-ʿarasāt al-ʿāshiqīn*** [or ***al-ʿārifīn***],[105] begun at Āgrah in 1022/1613 and completed there in

100 "In later life," says Bland "he indulged his poetic inclination by compiling an anthology, which he named Firdúsi Khayáli Auhadi, of which the value of the letters contains also the date." Unfortunately Bland explains in a footnote that *Firdaus i khayāl* = 991, which is true but irrelevant, since at that date Taqī Auḥadī was eighteen years old.

101 This is stated in Taqī Auḥadī's own list of his works quoted from the *Kaʿbah i ʿirfān* by the author of the *Guldastah* and thence by ʿAbd al-Muqtadir in the Bānkīpūr catalogue viii p. 77 ult. (*Īn nuskhah kih Kaʿbah i ʿirfan-ast az ʿArafāt dar Aḥmadābād i Gujrāt sanah i* 1036 *muntakhab shud*.)

102 If these dates are correct, the poems in question must be later additions to the *Tadhkirat al-ʿāshiqīn*, which is already mentioned in Taqī's list of his own works in the *Kaʿbah i ʿirfān* written in 1036.

103 *Dar mathnawīyāt-ash ashʿār i shutur-gurbah ba-naẓar rasīd* (*Riyāḍ al-shuʿarā*ʾ, quoted in Bānkīpūr viii p. 78 ult.)

104 *Shiʿr i bisyār guftah ammā hamwār-ast* (Ṭāhir i Naṣrābādī p. 303).

105 In Taqī's own list of his works as quoted from the *Kaʿbah i ʿirfān* in the *Guldastah* the title of his *tadhkirah* is mentioned in two abbreviated forms, viz. *ʿ.rafāt and ʿ.rafāt al-ʿārifīn wa-ʿaraṣāt al-ʿashiqīn* (Bānkīpūr viii p. 77 penult, and p. 78[10]). Similarly the author of the *Guldastah* in his preface calls it *ʿ.rafāt al-ʿārifīn* (Bānkīpūr viii p. 117 antepenult.). In the Āṣafīyah catalogue it is called *gh.rafāt al-ārifīn*. The full title as given in the preface to the *tadhkirah* itself is, according to Bland, "Urfát u ghurfáti âáshikín wa ârsát u ârzáti

1024/1615, an alphabetically arranged dictionary of about 3000 poets divided into 28 *ʿarṣahs* (one for every letter of the alphabet) each subdivided into three *ʿarafahs* devoted respectively to ancient, mediaeval and modern poets:[106] **Bānkīpūr** viii 685–6 (apparently complete except for the omission of the 2nd and 3rd *ʿarafahs*, i.e. 138 poets, under *ḥāʾ*. AH 1050/1640–1), **I.O.** 3654 (= Lindesiana p. 223 no. 313. Circ. AD 1760), **Lindesiana** p. 223 no. 635 (verses only without biographies. Circ. AD 1780), **Āṣafīyah** iii p. 164 no. 209.

Description: *On the earliest Persian Biography of Poets ... By N. Bland* (in *JRAS*. 1848) pp. 134–6.

(2) ***Kāʿbah i ʿirfān***, an abridgment of the preceding made at Aḥmadābād[107] in 1036/1626: **Lindesiana** p. 223 no. 314 (AH 1036/1626).

(3) ***Intikhāb i Kaʿbah i ʿirfān***, an abridgment of the preceding made at Jahāngīr's request and divided into three *rukns* devoted respectively to ancient, mediaeval and modern poets: no MSS. recorded.

Selections from the *Intikhāb*: ***Guldastah*** compiled in 1155/1742 by ʿAbd al-Wahhāb ʿĀlamgīrī b. S. Manṣūr Khān, a grandson of S. Dilāwar Khān on his father's side and of Ghiyāth al-Dīn Khān b. Jumlat al-Mulk Islām Khān Riḍawī Mashhadī on his mother's side: **Bānkipūr** viii 692 (18th cent.).

[*ʿArafāt al-ʿāshiqīn*, preface (summarised in *JRAS*. ix (1848) pp. 134–5 and Bānkīpūr catalogue viii pp. 76–7); *Tadhkirah i Ṭāhir i Naṣrābādī* p. 303; *Safīnah*

âárifîn", which comes to the same thing as ʿAbd al-Muqtadir's "ʿUrafât wa Gurafât-i ʿÂshiqîn wa ʿAraṣât wa ʿAraḍât-i ʿÂrifîn". Neither the vocalisation nor the meaning can be regarded as obvious. That Bland did not understand the words is shown by his description of them as "one of those titles, in which, as in those of many Arabic books, the translatable sense is sacrificed to a sort of rhythm, if not rhyme." Since his time the *tadhkirah* has been generally known to European orientalists as the *ʿUrafāt al-ʿāshiqīn*, but no European seems to have ventured to translate these words. It seems probable that the first word should be read ʿArafāt (the name of the hill and adjoining plain 12 miles from Mecca, where the pilgrims assemble on the 9th day of the pilgrimage) and that the first element of the title means "The ʿArafāt of gnostics", the word ʿArafāt having been selected as suggesting a place of assembly. This interpretation receives perhaps a little support from the fact that the abridgment, *Kaʿbah i ʿirfān*, is named after another place of assembly for pilgrims. The word *ʿaraṣāt* may have been used in allusion to yet another place of assembly, the court of the last judgment. The transposition of *al-ʿashiqīn* and *al-ʿārifīn* may have been an afterthought of the author's.

106 "Wālih" (quoted in Bānkīpūr viii p. 78) says that this *tadhkirah* contains many idle tales (*muzakhrafāt i bisyār*). In the Bānkīpūr catalogue (iii p. 61) the *Majmaʿ al-nafāʾis* is credited with the strange statement that Taqī Auḥadī's *tadhkirah* [which contains some 3000 biographies] consists of selections from M. Ṣūfī's *But-khānah* [which, at least as represented by the Bodleian MS., deals with 126 poets].

107 See beginning of this entry, 1st par., last part.

i Khwushgū ii no. 364 (Bodleian col. 223); *Riyāḍ al-shuʿarāʾ; Majmaʿ al-nafāʾis* (I.O. D.P. 739 fol. 194*b*); *Khulāṣat al-afkār* no. 56; *Ātash-kadah* no. 685; *Ṣuḥuf i Ibrāhīm* (summarised in Bland's article pp. 135–6); *Makhzan al-gharāʾib* no. 424; *JRAS*. ix (1848) pp. 134–6; Sprenger p. 95 note.]

1114. For ʿAbd al-Bāqī Nihāwandī's *Maʾāthir i Raḥīmī*, which was completed in 1025/1616 and of which the *khātimah* (vol. iii, 1699 pp., in the Calcutta ed.) is devoted to contemporary celebrities, especially poets (pp. 66–1576), see no. 711 *supra*.

1115. ʿ**Abd al-Nabī** "Nabī" b. Khalaf **Fakhr al-Zamānī**[108] **Qazwīnī** was born at Qazwīn about 998/1590.[109] In his youth he had some poetical talent as well as a remarkable memory which enabled him to learn by heart without difficulty such tales as the *Qiṣṣah i Amīr Ḥamzah*. At the age of 19 he visited Mashhad and there met merchants and travellers who spoke to him of India and inspired him with a desire to see that country. Travelling via Qandahār and Lahore he reached Āgrah in 1018/1609–10. His relative Mīrzā Niẓāmī Qazwīnī, who was *Wāqiʿah-nawīs*, gave him employment, apparently as his *qiṣṣah-khwān*. In 1022/1613 at Ajmēr Mīrzā Amān Allāh b. Mahābat Khān[110] appointed him his librarian (*kitāb-dār*). Subsequently he was in Kashmīr for nearly two years

108 Fakhr al-Zamān, the maternal grandfather of ʿAbd al-Nabī, was *Qāḍī* of Qazwīn (*M.-kh.* p. 499[11]).

109 This is an inference from his statements that he was 19 years old when he went to Mashhad and that he reached Āgrah in 1018, apparently not many months later.

110 Amān Allāh "Amānī" Ḥusainī, who received the title of Khānah-zād Khān from Jahāngīr and that of Khān i Zamān from Shāh-Jahān. died in 1046/1637. In Jahāngīr's 17th year, AH 1031–2/1622–3, he was appointed to govern Kābul as deputy for his father, and he subsequently held other governorships. For his career, etc., see *Maʾāthir al-umarāʾ* i pp. 740–8, Beveridge's trans. pp. 212–19, *Memoirs of Jahāngīr* tr. Rogers and Beveridge i p. 252, ii pp. 44, 94, 99, 231, 239, 257, 275, *Tadhkirah i Ṭāhir i Naṣrābādī* pp. 59–60, etc. Among his works were (1) a *dīwān* (see Sprenger 97, Bodleian 1095), (2) *Ruqaʿāt i Amān Allāh i Ḥusainī*, a collection of 99 short letters on Ṣūfī matters addressed to numerous *shaikhs*, beg. *Hamd i wāfir*. MSS.: Āṣafīyah i pp. 114, 124, Bānkīpūr xi 1098 xviii, Berlin 62 (14), Brelvi-Dhabbar p. 59, Browne Suppt., 699 (King's 202), Būhār 270 ii, Ethé 1763 (7), 1893, 2934, Ethé ii 3046, Ross-Browne 191, Gotha Arabic Cat. p. 489, Ivanow 1st Suppt. 787 (3), 2nd Suppt. 951, Lahore (*OCM*. vii/3 (May 1931) p. 59). Editions: Calcutta, date ? (see Berlin p. 129), Lucknow 1269 (*v. ibid.*), 1871†, 1873°, Cawnpore 1271*, 1874†, 1881†, 1883†, 1885†, 1888†, 1899†. (3) *Inshā i Khānah-zād Khān*. a collection of political, social and other letters and prose compositions in four *faṣls*, beg. *Sar-nawisht i khāmah*. MSS.: Ethé 2077, Rieu ii 877*a*, Brelvi-Dhabbar p. 59. (4) *Umm al-ʿilāj* a treatise on purgatives written in 1036 and dedicated to Jahāngīr. MSS.: Rieu ii 794*a*, Ivanow 1554, Blochet ii 887 (6). Editions: Cawnpore 1873°*, 1880°. (5) *Chahār ʿunṣur i dānish*, an Arabic-Persian dictionary (MS. Rieu 509*a*), (6) *Ganj i bād-āward*, on agriculture (?). MS.: Āṣafīyah ii p. 968. Cf. Rieu ii 489*b*.

and then in Bihār for a time, when his patron Mīrzā Niẓāmī was successively *Dīwān* of those two provinces. In the former period he completed his *Dastūr al-fuṣaḥā'* a work now apparently lost, on the art of reciting the *Qiṣṣah i Ḥamzah*. In 1028/1619 at Patnah he came into contact with Nawwāb Sardār Khān[111] and experienced so much kindness at his hands that he dedicated to him the *Mai-khānah*, which was completed in that year. In 1041/1631–2 he wrote the preface to his collection of anecdotes, *Nawādir al-ḥikāyāt wa-gharā'ib al-riwāyāt*, which is preserved in MSS. at the British Museum (Rieu iii 1004*b*. Only the 1st of the 5 *Ṣaḥīfahs*) and in Manchester (Lindesiana p. 118 no. 194. What part or parts ?). In the *Mai-khānah* (p. 510) he tells us that in addition to his *sāqī-nāmah* he had written 1500 lines of poetry.

Mai-khānah, a collection of *sāqī-nāmahs* with biographies of their authors,[112] mostly contemporaries of the compiler, who began the work at Ajmēr in 1022/1613 or 1023/1614 and completed it at Patnah in 1028/1619:[113] **Rāmpūr** (AH 1039/1629–30. Cf. Nadhīr Aḥmad 96), **Lahore** Prof. M. Shafī''s private library, **Nūr i 'Uthmānīyah** 4328.

Edition: **Lahore** 1926* (ed. M. Shafī').

Description: *Tadhkirah i Mai-khānah aur us-kā mu'allif*, by M. Shafī' (in OCM. iii/1 (Nov. 1926) pp. 3–22, iii/2 (Feb. 1927) pp. 3–10). This differs little from the first 16 pages of the introduction to the Lahore edition.

Textual emendations: *Taṣḥīḥ i Mai-khānah*, by M. Shafī' (in OCM. iii/4 (Aug. 1927) pp. 79–90, iv/1 (Nov. 1927) pp. 55–62, iv/2 (Feb. 1928) pp. 43–55).

[*Mai-khānah* pp. 498–523 and the editor's Urdu introduction pp. *bā'-qāf*; OCM., *loc. cit.*; *Nawādir al-ḥikāyāt*, preface and fol. 35*a* (see Rieu iii 1004*b*); *Tarīkh i Muḥammad-Shāhī* (Berlin Cat. p. 479 no. 179).]

1116. A certain **"Qāṭi'ī"**[114] dedicated to Jahāngīr (reigned 1014/1605–1037/1628) his ***Majma' al-shu'arā' i Jahāngīr-Shāhī***, notices of 151 poets who wrote in praise of Jahāngīr, being the third *daftar* of a larger work: **Bodleian** 371 (autograph).

---

111 Khwājah Yādgār, brother of 'Abd Allāh Khān Fīrōz-Jang, received from Jahāngīr the title of Sardār Khān in 1022 (*Memoirs of Jahāngīr*, tr. Rogers and Beveridge, i p. 237) and the *jāgīr* of Monghyr in 1028 (*op. cit.* ii p. 89). For his career see *Ma'āthir al-umarā'* ii pp. 411–12.

112 In all 71 poets arranged in three *martabahs* ((1) 26 deceased authors of *sāqī-nāmahs* from Niẓāmī Ganjawī to Faghfūr Gīlānī (d. 1029), (2) 20 living authors of *sāqī-nāmahs*, (3) 25 living poets who had not yet written *sāqī-nāmahs*.

113 So according to the chronogram at the end, but later additions were made.

114 The *tadhkirah* of Mullā "Qāṭi'ī" is one of the sources of "Āzād's" *Khizānah i 'āmirah*. Sprenger says (p. 144) that he could find no account of the book or of its author.

1117. Shāh **Ḥusain b.** Malik **Ghiyāth al-Dīn Maḥmūd** has already been mentioned (no. 485 *supra*) as the author of a history of Sīstān, the *Iḥyā' al-mulūk*, completed in 1028/1619.

__Khair al-bayān__, begun in 1017/1608–9, completed in 1019/1610, revised and enlarged in 1035/1625–6, further enlarged in 1036/1626–7, and dedicated to Shāh 'Abbās, notices of ancient and modern poets in a *muqaddimah* (history of Muḥammad, the Twelve Imāms, and the Ṣafawī dynasty to 1033/1623–4), two *faṣls* ((1) ancient poets (2) modern poets), a *khātimah* (royal and noble poets), and a *khatm i khātimah* (scholars): **Rieu** Suppt. 108 (AH 1041/1631), 109 (defective. 18th cent.).

1118. **"Muṭribī" al-Aṣamm al-Samarqandī** was born in 966/1559 and was still alive in 1037/1628, when he went to Balkh.

__Tārīkh i Jahāngīrī__ (beg. *Ai nām i Tu iftitāḥ i har dīwānī ... Ba'd az tadhkirah i ḥamd i Ilāhī ta'ālā wa-ta'aẓẓam*), a *tadhkirah* begun in Rajab 1034/April–May 1625, dedicated to Jahāngīr [who died in 1037/1628] and divided into two *silsilahs* ((1) poets [of Transoxiana according to Ethé], who flourished at the courts of the Chaghatāy sulṭāns [Akbar and Jahāngīr], (2) poets of Transoxiana under the Uzbaks) and a *khātimah* (begun in Jumādā II AH 1036/Feb. 1627 and containing "a memoir of the author's own attachment to and personal attendance on the emperor Jahângîr ... together with an additional number of Transoxanian poets ..."): **Ethé** ii 3023 (AH 1075/1665).

1119. For Iskandar Munshī's *Tārīkh i 'ālam-ārāy i 'Abbāsī* (*Ṣaḥīfah* ii, *Maqṣad* 1 completed in 1025/1616 and *Maqṣad* 2 in 1038/1628–9) which concludes the record of Shāh Ṭahmāsp's reign with biographies of princes, high officials and other celebrities (pp. 95–136; poets on pp. 129–35) and which in the subsequent part contains obituary notices at the end of particular years, see no. 387 *supra*.

1120. **Ḥasan b. Luṭf Allāh Ṭihrānī Rāzī** was only a boy in 968/1560–1 when his father, Khwājah Luṭf Allāh, was appointed *Wazīr* of Khurāsān by Shāh Ṭahmāsp and went to Harāt. After his father's death in 981/1573–4 he succeeded him as *Wazīr*.

__Mai-khānah__, or *Kharābāt* (see Rieu Suppt. p. 76*b*[14]), notices of poets written for Ḥasan Bēg [Shāmlū, Bēglarbēgī of Khurāsān 1027/1618–1050/1640–1] and completed in 1040/1630–1: **Rieu** Suppt. 107 (very defective, AH 1227/1812).

List of the poets: Rieu Suppt. 107.

1121. Mīr **"Ilāhī" Hamadānī**, or, as he calls himself,[115] ʿImād al-Dīn Maḥmūd Ilāhī Ḥusainī, was the son of Ḥujjat al-Dīn[116] and was one of the Saiyids of Asadābād,[117] near Hamadān. In 1010/1601–2, he tells us,[118] he went to prosecute his studies at Shīrāz[119] and stayed there for 3½ years. After leaving Persia he spent some time at Kābul, where Ẓafar Khān "Aḥsan", a poet[120] and a patron of poets, was Governor[121] from 1033/1624, Jahāngīr's 19th regnal year, until 1037/1628,[122] the first year of Shāh-Jahān's reign. A poem addressed to him by Mīr "Ilāhī" in 1033 is mentioned by Rieu (ii 687*b*). It was at Kābul that he went to see the arrogant and irascible Ḥakīm Ḥādhiq[123] on the latter's return [in 1040/1630–1: see *Pādshāh-nāmah* i, pt. 1, p. 318 [12]] from his mission to Imām-Qulī Khān, of Bukhārā.

"After some years spent at Court, under Jahāngīr and Shāh-jahān," says Rieu,[124] "he accompanied Ẓafar Khan to Kashmīr, A/H. 1041–2,[125] and resided there till his death, the date of which, AH 1063,[126] is expressed in some verses engraved on his tomb, and quoted in the Vāḳiʿāt i Kashmīr, fol. 122a, by the chronogram *Būd sukhun-āfrīn*."

---

115 In his notice of "Ādharī", where also the title of his *tadhkirah* is mentioned (Sprenger p. 66).

116 Sprenger p. 435. Ḥujjat Allāh according to *Muntakhab al-ashʿār* no. 46.

117 See le Strange *L.E.C.* p. 196.

118 *Khazīnah* fol. 61*b*.

119 So Pertsch, correcting Sprenger, who said Iṣfahān.

120 For an autograph MS. of his *Kullīyāt* written in 1053 see Bānkīpūr ii no 329. For his *dīwāns* and other poems see Ethé 1601, Bānkīpūr iii 330, Ivanow 780, Sprenger 90, Madras 3, 3(*a*) and 3(*b*), Nadhīr Aḥmad 199 (Rāmpūr), Blochet iii 1900, *OCM*. VII/1 (Nov. 1930) p. 141. For his life see *Maʾāthir al-umarāʾ* ii pp. 756–62, Bānkīpūr Cat. iii pp. 117–18. In one of the prefaces contained in his *Kullīyāt* he mentions Mīr "Ilāhī" and four other poets with whom he associated at Kābul (Bānkīpūr Cat. iii p. 118[1]).

121 Technically Deputy Governor for his father, Khwājah Abū 'l-Ḥasan Turbatī, who was the absentee titular Governor.

122 When he was succeeded by Lashkar Khān Mashhadī (*Padshāh-nāmah* i, pt. 1, p. 120[10]).

123 For whom see *Maʾāthir i Raḥīmī* iii pp. 845–55, *Maʾāthir al-umarāʾ* i pp. 587–90, Bānkīpūr iii p. 109, Sprenger no. 238, Rieu Suppt. 325, etc.

124 Rieu's authority for all the statements, correct or incorrect, made in this sentence is doubtless the *Wāqiʿāt i Kashmīr*.

125 It was early in 1042 that Ẓafar Khān was sent to Kashmīr as deputy for his father, the absentee Governor. He was made Governor on his father's death in Ramaḍān 1042/1633 (*P.-n.* i pt. 1, p. 474[7]), was removed in 1048 (*P.-n.* ii p. 125 ult.) and was reappointed in 1051/1642 (*P.-n.* ii p. 283[2]).

126 Sprenger says (p. 436) that according to a chronogram by Ghanī he died in 1052, but that [Abū] Ṭālib places his death in 1060 and Sirāj in 1064. According to Rieu (iii p. 1091*b*) the date 1057 is given in the *Mirʾāt i jahān-numā*.

For a MS. of his *dīwān* transcribed in 1042/1632 see Rieu ii 687*b*, and for another, which contained (but seems no longer to contain) a chronogram for 1052/1642–3, see Sprenger 277 = Berlin 939.

Khazīnah i ganj i Ilāhī, alphabetically arranged notices of about 400 poets, chiefly of the 9th/15th and 10th/16th centuries: Sprenger 11 = **Berlin** 646 (unfinished autograph).

List of the poets (with some biographical details): Sprenger pp. 67–87. [Mubtalā *Muntakhab al-ashʿār* no. 46; *ʿAmal i Ṣāliḥ* iii pp. 415–16 (not very informative); Ṭāhir Naṣrābādī pp. 255–6; *Kalimāt al-shuʿarāʾ* (Sprenger p. 109); *Mirʾāt al-khayāl* no. 74 (p. 119 in the 1324 edition); *Hamīshah bahār* (Sprenger p. 117); *Wāqiʿāt i Kashmīr* p. 153; *Riyāḍ al-shuʿarāʾ*; *Dīwān i muntakhab* (Sprenger p. 150[3]); *Ātash-kadah* no. 598; *Khulāṣat al-afkār* no. 36; *Makhzan al-gharāʾib* no. 113; *Riyāḍ, al-afkār* (Bānkīpūr Suppt. i p. 50); *Haft āsmān* pp. 146–7; Rieu ii 687*b*, iii 1091*b*.]

1122. For the *Ṭabaqāt i Shāh-Jahānī* of M. Ṣādiq, in which 1046/1636–7 is spoken of as the current year and which contains 871 biographies of (1) Saiyids and saints, (2) scholars, physicians and men of letters (*ʿulamāʾ, ḥukamāʾ* and *fuḍalāʾ*), (3) poets, who lived under the House of Tīmūr, see the subsection of this work relating to General Biography.

1123. For the *Ṣubḥ i ṣādiq*, which was begun in 1041/1631–2 and finished in 1048/1638–9 by M. Ṣādiq Iṣfahānī and of which the 3rd *mujallad* is devoted to celebrated men of the first eleven centuries, see no. 142 *supra*.

1124. For the *Pādshāh-nāmah* of M. Amīn Qazwīnī, which contains a *khātimah* devoted to the *shaikhs*, scholars, physicians and poets of Shāh-Jahān's time, see no. 724 *supra*.

1125. For the *Muntakhab al-tawārīkh*, which was completed in 1056/1646–7 by M. Yūsuf Aṭakī Kanʿānī and of which the fifth *qism* is devoted to biographies of Imāms, saints, scholars and poets, see no. 144 *supra*.

1126. For the *Pādshāh-nāmah* of ʿAbd al-Ḥamīd Lāhaurī, which contains at the end of vol. i notices of 13 *mashāyikh* (pp. 328–39), 13 *fuḍalāʾ* (pp. 339–46), 8 physicians (pp. 346–51) and four poets (pp. 351–9), and at the end of vol. ii notices of 4 *mashāyikh* (pp. 753–4), six *ʿulamāʾ* (pp. 754–6), one physician (pp. 756–7), and two poets (pp. 757–9), see no. 734 *supra*.

1127. For the *ʿAmal i Ṣāliḥ* of M. Ṣāliḥ Kanbō Lāhaurī, which was completed in 1070/1659–60 and which contains at the end of vol. iii notices of 16 *Saiyids* and *shaikhs* (pp. 357–82), 13 scholars (pp. 382–93), 8 physicians (pp. 393–7), 18 poets (pp. 397–435), 14 prose-writers (pp. 435–43), and 7 calligraphists (pp. 443–6), see no. 738 (1) *supra*.

1128. The *tadhkirah* entitled *Laṭāʾif al-khayāl*[127] was written by a Persian, probably a native of Fārs, who was at Daulatābād in 1062/1652 and who also visited Aḥmadābād and Sūrat. In 1067/1656–7 he returned to Persia and met Ruknā "Masīḥ" Kāshī at Shīrāz and "Ṣāʾib", who showed him much kindness, at Iṣfahān. He went again to India at some date unspecified, and it was there that he wrote (part of ?) the *Laṭāʾif al-khayāl* in 1076/1665–6. Prof. M. Iqbāl in an article on the work (see below) demonstrated that the author was almost certainly **M. b. M. al-Dārābī**, who wrote the *Laṭīfah i ghaibī*,[128] a defence of Ḥāfiẓ against certain criticisms. From the *Laṭīfah i ghaibī* Rieu ascertained that M. b. M. al-Dārābī left his birthplace, Dārābjird, for Shīrāz, where he spent most of his life, and that in 1062/1652 he was at Aḥmadābād. From a passage absent from the B.M. MS. but occurring on p. 122 of the lithographed edition it appears that the *Laṭīfah i ghaibī* was written at Shīrāz in 1087/1676. Rieu adds that the author left also a Ṣūfī work, *Maqāmāt al-ʿārifīn*, and a treatise on the lawfulness of singing entitled *Shauq al-ʿārifīn wa-dhauq al-ʿāshiqīn*. Rieu says nothing about a *tadhkirah*, but Ṭāhir Naṣrābādī in a brief notice of him says that he had recently (*dar īn sāl*[129]) returned from India and was writing a *tadhkirah* of poets.[130]

Laṭāʾif al-khayāl, notices of 454 poets, mainly contemporary, arranged in 28 *ṭabaqahs* each devoted to a particular town, district or country ((1) Fārs and Shabānkārah, (2) tawābiʿ i Fārs, (3) Iṣfahān, and so on) and written (at least partly) in 1076/1665–6:[131] MS. (less than half of the work) in Prof. Maḥmūd Shērānī's private library at Lahore.

Description and extracts: *OCM*. xi/1 (Nov. 1934) pp. 58–73 (article by M. Iqbāl).

---

127 To be distinguished from the *Laṭāʾif al-khayāl* of Mīr M. Ṣāliḥ Nawwāb Riḍawī b. Mīrzā Muḥsin Nawwāb, which is an anthology without biographical information (see Bodleian 1143, Ethé 1739, Sipahsālār ii p. 479, *JRAS*. 1848 p. 168).

128 MSS.: Rieu Suppt. 417 (1), Ivanow 983. Edition: Ṭihrān 1304/1887° Cf. Browne *Lit. Hist.* iii pp. 300–1.

129 Unfortunately *dar īn sāl* does not always refer to the same year. Thus on p. 173 it is explained as 1077, but on p. 170 as 1083.

130 *Mullā Shāh Muḥammad—az wilāyat i Dārāb-ast ṭālib-ʿilm i munaqqaḥīst muddatī dar Hind būd dar īn sāl tashrīf āwardand tadhkirah i shuʿarā mī-nawīsad umīd kih muwaffaq bāshad* ...

131 According to Iqbāl this year is several times mentioned as the current year, but Ṭāhir Naṣrābādī, writing later than 1076 presumably, speaks of M. Dārābī's *tadhkirah* in terms which imply that it was not yet completed.

[Autobiographical statements in *Laṭā'if al-khayāl* (see OCM. xi/1 pp. 61–5) and *Laṭīfah i ghaibī* (see Rieu Suppt. 417 (1)); *Tadhkirah i Ṭāhir i Naṣrābādī* p. 186.]

1129. For the *Mir'āt al-'ālam*, which was written in 1078/1667 by Sh. M. Baqā Sahāranpūrī (nominally by Bakhtāwar Khān), and of which the *khātimah* contains alphabetically arranged notices of poets, see no. 151 (2) *supra*.

1130. **M. Ṭāhir Naṣrābādī** was born at Naṣrābād,[132] near Iṣfahān, probably in 1027/1618, since he tells us (*Tadhkirah* p. 458[12]) that in 1044/1634–5, when his father[133] died, he was seventeen years old. His great-grandfather, Khwājah Ṣadr al-Dīn 'Alī, was a wealthy landowner (*Tadhkirah* p. 457[6]) and the founder of three *madrasahs*,[134] but the family had become impoverished, and more than one of its members had gone to seek his fortune in India.[135] After a frivolous youth he went to live in a coffee-house frequented by scholars and poets and there he seems to have spent most of his life, since it was to it that he returned after his pilgrimage to Mashhad, Najaf, and Mecca some years before he wrote his *tadhkirah*. Enjoying the society and esteem of the learned, talented, and pious (such as Mīr 'Abd al-'Āl "Najāt"), winning by his compositions in prose and verse the approbation of men like Āqā Ḥusain Khwānsārī (for whom see no. 33, 2nd footnote *supra*, and *Tadhkirah* p. 152), and receiving from Shāh Sulaimān (1077/1666–1105/1694) on his visits to Naṣrābād marks of gracious favour, though not the material benefits he would have preferred, he lived no doubt happily enough, until the death of several friends, especially that

132 For information concerning Naṣrābād, a village now of five or six thousand inhabitants in the *dihistān* of Mārbīn half a parasang west of Iṣfahān, see the editor's introduction to the Ṭihrān edition of Ṭāhir's *tadhkirah*. Descendants of the author are still living in the village.

133 Ṭāhir does not mention his father's name. Rieu's statement that he was Mīrzā Ḥasan 'Alī is due apparently to hasty reading of a sentence (*Tadhkirah* p. 451, l. 5 *ab infra*), in which the author says that his father was a son of Mīrzā Ḥasan 'Alī's sister. It seems highly probable, however, that Ṭāhir's father was Mīrzā M. Taqī, since Mīrzā Ṣādiq, Ṭāhir's paternal uncle (see no. 142 *supra* and *Tadhkirah* pp. 64 and 452[18]), mentions in the *Subḥ i ṣādiq* (see Bānkīpūr vi p. 47, l. 12 *ab infra*) that his father, M. Ṣāliḥ, "died on the 18th Shawwâl, AH 1043 = AD 1638, leaving besides the author [i.e. M. Ṣādiq] three sons, viz. Muḥammad Taqî, who was then in Persia, Muḥammad Sa'îd and Muḥammad Ja'far, who were then living in Bengal."

134 One of these was at Naṣrābād, where the doorway is still standing (photograph in the Ṭihrān edition of the *Tadhkirah* p. *bā*).

135 E.g. Mīrzā Ṣāliḥ (*Tadhkirah* p. 452[17]) and Mīrzā Ismā'īl (p. 454[13]). In spite of Bland's statement (*JRAS*. 1848 p. 139[10]) there seems to be no evidence that Ṭāhir himself was ever in India.

of Ākhund Darwīsh Naṣīrā Qazwīnī in 1079[136] (*Tadhkirah* pp. 463[9] and 531[1]), robbed the coffee-house of its charm. He retired to a life of pious devotion in the mosque of Lunbān,[137] and had been there for seven years when he wrote his account of his own life. He had an only[138] son, Badīʿ al-Zamān (*Tadhkirah* p. 455), or Mīrzā Badīʿ Iṣfahānī, who became Malik al-shuʿarāʾ under Shāh Sulṭān-Ḥusain (according to "Ḥazīn": see Sprenger p. 138, *Kullīyāt i Ḥazīn* p. 993). His specimens of his own poetry, which in style resembles that of "Ṣāʾib" and "Kalīm" no longer admired in Persia (see the editor's introduction, p. *jīm*), include a *qaṣīdah* in praise of Shāh Sulaimān, lines from a *mathnawī* modelled on one by "Ahlī" Shīrāzī, and chronograms for the building of the Hasht Bihisht palace in 1080 (*Tadhkirah* p. 487). For his *Gulshan i khayālāt* (or *khayāl*), a short tract in ornate prose, see Rieu Suppt. 376, Bodleian 1636(6) and 1906: for his *Intikhāb i dīwān i Ṣāʾib* see Ethé 1623, Būhār 432 (1).

Tadhkirah i Ṭāhir i Naṣrābādī, short notices of more than 1,000[139] contemporary poets, begun in 1083/1672–3,[140] dedicated to Shāh Sulaimān and divided into a *muqaddimah* (kings and princes), five *ṣaffs* subdivided into *firqahs* ((1) (*a*) *amīrs* and *khāns* of Persia, p. 15, (*b*) *amīrs* of India, p. 53, (*c*) *wazīrs*, *mustaufīs*, and *kuttāb*, p. 69, (2) Saiyids and *nujabāʾ*, p. 95, (3) (*a*) scholars, p. 149, (*b*) calligraphists, p. 206, (*c*) *faqīrs*, p. 209, (4) professional poets of (*a*) ʿIrāq and Khurāsān, p. 212, (*b*) Transoxiana, p. 432, (*c*) India, p. 444, (5) the author and his relations, p. 451) and a *khātimah* (a collection of old and new chronograms, riddles, etc., p. 468): Sprenger p. 88, **Blochet** ii 1148 (ostensibly an autograph dated 1083/1672–3,

136 In 1089 according to the Bānkīpūr MS. If 1079 is correct and if Ṭāhir had subsequently spent seven years in the mosque at Lunbān, his account of his own life must have been written (or at any rate completed) later than 1083.

137 A village near Iṣfahān.

138 *munḥaṣir dar fard*. These words are the foundation for Bland's statement that Ṭāhir's son "was, at the time he wrote, still in Merv".

139 In the Berlin MS. 649 there are 838 notices according to a marginal numeration.

140 This date is mentioned in the preface (p. 5 ult.) and also, as the current year, at least once elsewhere (p. 170). Expressions like *dar-īn sāl* occur repeatedly in the work, but only very rarely (three times ?) are they further defined, and then (at any rate in the printed text) not always as the same year. Thus on pp. 170 and 173 *dar-īn sāl* is explained as meaning 1083 and 1077 respectively, while on p. 450 *al-ḥāl* is said to be 1081. "Current years" anterior to 1083 are probably corrupt, and so doubtless are some of the later dates that occur (always, it seems, in figures not words). The year 1089 found by Rieu on fol. 331 of a B.M. MS., apparently corresponds to 1081 in the printed edition (p. 450), Similarly the date of Darwīsh Naṣīrā's death is given as 1089 in the Bānkīpūr MS. (Cat. vol. viii p. 80[20]), but as 1079 in the printed text. According to Sprenger eight or nine biographies were added in 1092. This date does not seem to occur in the printed edition, where the latest dates appear to be 1085 (p. 326), 1086 (p. 342), 1112 (p. 20), and 1115 (p. 174).

although the date 1089[141] occurs in the biography of Mīr Luṭf Allāh), **Rieu** Suppt. 110 (AH 1097/1686. Lacunæ), i 368 b (18th cent.), **Bānkīpūr** viii 687 (AH 1105[142]/1694), **Lindesiana** p. 196 no. 315 (circ. AD 1700), **Berlin** 648 (AH 1114/1702), 649, **Edinburgh** 88 (AH 1118/1706. Lacunae), **Bodleian** 373 (AH 1132/1720), I.O. D.P. 587 (AH 1244/1829), **Ethé** 669, **Ivanow** 220 (AD 1870).

Edition: *Tadhkirah i Naṣrābādī*, **Ṭihrān** AHS. 1316–17/1937–8 (supplements to the periodical *Armaghān*).

Edition of *Ṣaff* iii, *firqah* 2 (calligraphists): *OCM*. xii/4 (Aug. 1935) pp. 154–9 (ed. M. Shafīʿ).

Description: *On the earliest Persian Biography of Poets ... By N. Bland* (in *JRAS*. ix (1848)) pp. 137–140.

List and epitome of the biographies in *Ṣaff* iii, *firqahs* 2–3, and *Ṣaff* iv: Sprenger pp. 88–108.

[*Tadhkirah i Naṣrābādī*, *Ṣaff* v, at end (pp. 457–68 in the printed edition. Summarised by Bland, Sprenger, Rieu, ʿAbd al-Muqtadir, etc.); *Safīnah i Khwushgū* (summarised in Bānkīpūr viii p. 85); *Ṣuḥuf i Ibrāhīm* (passage translated by Bland, pp. 139–40); Bland's article in *JRAS*. 1848 pp. 139–40 (see above); Rieu i 368b; Blochet ii 1148; Bānkīpūr viii 687; editor's introduction to the Ṭihrān edition.]

1131. For the *Jāmiʿ i Mufīdī*, a history of Yazd, which was completed in 1090/1679 and of which the 9th *faṣl* of the 2nd *maqālah* of the 3rd volume is devoted to the poets of Yazd, see no. 461 *supra*.

1132. Mīrzā M. Afḍal "**Sarkhwush**"[143] was, according to his pupil "Khwushgū", the second son of M. Zāhid[144] and was born in Kashmīr in 1050/1640–1 (Bānkīpūr viii pp. 92–3). M. Zāhid, says "Khwushgū", was in the service of ʿAbd Allāh Khān Zakhmī,[145] after whose death all Zāhid's five sons entered the Emperor's service. Naṣrābādī's statement that "Sarkhwush" was a Lāhaurī and was living in Lahore [in, or about, 1083] is described by "Khwushgū" as incorrect (Bkp. viii

141 1081 in the printed edition (p. 450).

142 The chronogram *Shud ākhir* = 1105, not 1150. Presumably therefore *panjāh* in the colophon is a *lapsus calami* for *panj*.

143 He "was generally called Chélá" according to Sprenger. This is a Hindī word meaning "servant, slave, disciple".

144 According to Shēr Khān (cited by Rieu) his grandfather was Mīr Laʿl Bēg, of Badakhshān. This fact is not mentioned in the 1324 edition of the *Mirʾāt al-khayāl*.

145 In the *Mirʾāt al-khayāl* (Bombay 1324 p. 290) "Sarkhwush" is described as "*az Mughūlān i ʿAbd-Allāh-Khānī*". For ʿAbd Allāh Khān see *Maʾāthir al-umarāʾ* iii p. 92[6].

p. 93¹⁻³). "Sark͟hwush" himself tells us (cf. Sprenger p. 108, Rieu i p. 369) that he was a hereditary servant of ʿĀlamgīr, that in his youth he had been anxious to acquire rank and wealth, but that when he wrote he was living in retirement at Delhi. According to "K͟hwushgū", his pupil, he died in Muḥarram 1126/1714[146] at the age of seventy-six.

"K͟hwushgū" says that his *Kullīyāt* consisted of about 45,000 verses (Bkp. viii p. 93⁶. Cf. *JRAS*. 1848 p. 169, where the number is given as nearly 40,000). They included six *mathnawīs*, (1) *Nūr ʿalā nūr*, modelled on Rūmī's *Mathnawī*, (2) *Ḥusn u ʿishq*, (3) *Sāqī-nāmah*, (4) *Qaḍā u qadar*, (5) *dar bayān i baʿḍī k͟huṣūṣīyāt i Hindūstān*, (6) *Jang-nāmah i M. Aʿẓam S͟hāh*, and, according to the *Gul i raʿnā* (cited Bkp. viii p. 82), two *dīwāns*, which (like his other poetical works ?) were lost through his son's carelessness. No MSS. of these works are recorded.

Kalimāt al-s͟huʿarāʾ (a chronogram = 1093/1682, but dates as late as 1108/1696–7 occur), very short notices of about 200 poets who flourished (nearly all in India) during the reigns of Jahāngīr, S͟hāh-Jahān, and Aurangzēb: Sprenger 13, **Ivanow** Curzon 51 (AH 1111/1700), 52 (defective at end. 18th cent.), 53 (19th cent.), 54 (defective at end. 19th cent.), **Ivanow** 221 (small portion only), 222 (portion only), **Rāmpūr** (AH 1129/1716. Pictures. See Nad͟hīr Aḥmad 88), **Madras** 441 (AH 1154/1741), 442–3, **Ethé** 670 (AH 1154/1742), 671 (n.d.), 672 (fragment), ii 3024 (AH 1270/1853–4), **I.O.** D.P. 709(e) (AH 1164/1750), **I.O.** 4046 (defective, AH 1237/1822), **Rieu** i 369a (AH 1156/1743), **Oxford** Ind. Inst. (AH 1157/1745) **Lindesiana** p. 216 no. 322 (circ. AD 1760), **Blochet** ii 1149 (18th cent.), 1150 (AH 1179/1765–6), **Berlin** 650 (1) (AH 1242/1826), 651 (AD 1784), **Āṣafīyah** i p. 318 no. 14 (AH 1222/1807–8), p. 322 no. 51 (circ. AD 1912), no. 54 (circ. 1912), no. 97 (circ. 1912), **Bānkīpūr** viii 688 (19th cent.), Suppt. ii 2175 (19th cent.), **Būhār** 91 (19th cent.), **Browne** Suppt. 296 (King's 92), **Peshawar** 1413.

List of the poets (with some biographical details): Sprenger pp. 109–115. [*Tad͟hkirah i Naṣrābādī* p. 450; *Kalimāt al-s͟huʿarāʾ* (see Sprenger p. 108, Rieu i p. 369); *Mirʾāt al-k͟hayāl* no. 106 (Bombay 1324 p. 290, but Rieu quotes from the work some information absent from this edition); *Hamīshah bahār* (Sprenger p. 123); *Safīnah i K͟hwushgū* (summarised in Bānkīpūr viii pp. 92–3); *Muntak͟hab al-as͟hʿār* no. 317; Sirāj *Dīwān i muntak͟hab* (Sprenger p. 150); *K͟hizānah i ʿāmirah* no. 60, pp. 263–4; *Gul i raʿnā* (cited Bānkīpūr viii p. 82); *Farḥat al-nāẓirīn* (*OCM*. IV/4 (Aug., 1928) p. 95); *Ṣuḥuf i Ibrāhīm* (passage translated by Bland, *JRAS*. 1848

---

146 So also *Tārīk͟h i Muḥammadī* (cited by Rieu iii 1086a), etc.: in 1125 according to Sirāj, in 1127/1715 according to the *Ṣuḥuf i Ibrāhīm*.

p. 169); *Khulāṣat al-afkār* no. 135; *Makhzan al-gharā'ib* no. 1034; *Nishtar i 'ishq*; Sprenger p. 108; Rieu i p. 369, iii p. 1086*a*; Bānkīpūr viii p. 82.]

1133. For the *Lubb al-lubāb*, which was composed in 1097/1685–6 by Ḥājjī Muḥammad-Qulī Qājār and of which the twenty-third *faṣl* contains short notices of 220 Persian poets, see no. 153 *supra*.

1134. For the *Mir'āt i jahān-numā*, an enlarged edition of the *Mir'āt al-'ālam* existing in two posthumous recensions completed in 1095/1684 and 1111/1699 respectively, which, like the original edition, contain towards the end alphabetically arranged notices of Persian poets, see no. 151 (3) *supra*.

1135. **Shēr Khān** b. 'Alī Amjad Khān **Lōdī**[147] spent at least part of his boyhood in Bengal, whither his father had gone in the service of Sulṭān M. Shāh-Shujā', Shāh-Jahān's second son.[148] He received some instruction there from Mullā Farrukh Ḥusain "Nāẓim",[149] who after completing his studies had left his home, Harāt,[150] and had settled in Jahāngīrnagar (D'hākah, i.e. Dacca in Eastern Bengal). He was, however, too young to profit fully from the Mullā's teaching, as his brothers had done, and he had read only some elementary Persian and Arabic text-books (*mukhtaṣarāt i fārisī u 'arabī*), when "Nāẓim" died on the day of 'Āshūrā' 1068/1657. His regular education then ceased, but he learned much from the conversation of his father and his father's erudite friends. In 1084/1673–4 his father died, in 1087/1676 his brother, 'Abd Allāh Khān, was killed (*sharbat i shahādat chashīd*) in the mountains of Kābul, and in 1090/1679 he sought employment under S. Shukr Allāh Khān [Khwāfī], who had been a

147 The author's name and the title of the work occur shortly before the notice of Rūdakī (p. 20^{10-11} in the 1324 edition). Lōdī is an Afghān clan-name (see *Ency. Isl.* under Afghānistān).

148 b. 1025/1616, Governor of Bengal 1048/1638, defeated by Aurangzēb at K'hajwah in 1069/1659, d. 1071/1660.

149 In spite of the *Ency. Isl.* (and the *Makhzan al-gharā'ib*, no. 2854) it is impossible to identify Farrukh Ḥusain "Nāẓim", who left Harāt evidently in early manhood, settled in Bengal and died there in 1068, with Mullā Nāẓim Harawī, who spent his whole life as court poet to the Bēglarbēgīs of Harāt (Rieu ii p. 692), never visited India (according to "Sarkhwush": see Sprenger p. 114), was upwards of 60 years old [in 1076], when the *Qiṣaṣ al-Khāqānī* was written (Rieu *loc. cit.*), died in 1081 (according to Sirāj: see Sprenger p. 151) and is best known as the author of a *Yūsuf u Zalīkhā*, begun in 1058 and completed in 1072, which is popular especially in Central Asia (Edition: Lucknow 1286/1870°*. MSS.: Ethé 1593–6, Ivanow 779, Bānkīpūr iii 336, Blochet iii 1901–4, iv 2195, Rieu ii 692*b*, Browne Suppt. 1381, Bodleian 1130, etc.).

150 *Aṣl-ash az Harāt ast ba'd az takmil i khwīsh az waṭan bar-āmadah ba-ḥasb i qismat ba-mulk i Bangālah uftād....*

friend of his father's in his Bengal days and who is described in the 1324 edition of the *Mir'āt al-khayāl* as *Faujdār* of the *chaklah* of Sirhind[151] and in Rosen's transcription of the same passage from a Leningrad MS. as *Faujdār* of the town of [Shāh-]Jahānābād[152]

Mir'āt al-khayāl, completed in 1102/1690–1, chronologically arranged notices of about 136[153] poets, viz. (1) 60[154] ancient poets from "Rūdakī" to "Āṣafī", p. 21, (2) 8 modern poets from Jalāl i "Asīr" to "Saḥābī", p. 75, (3) 28 poets of Shāh-Jahān's reign from "Qudsī" to "Fiṭrat", p. 85, (4) 11 living poets from 'Āqil Khān "Rāzī" to Aḥmad "'Ibrat", p. 238, (5) 9 living Indian poets whose fame had spread to Īrān and Tūrān from Nāṣir 'Alī Sirhindī to Sh. 'Abd al-Qādir (or to "Waḥshat", as in the Bombay edition, where there are some differences of arrangement) p. 291, (6) 15 poetesses from "Mihrī" to "Hamdamī", p. 334, the whole interspersed with short treatises on prosody, music, ethics, the interpretation of dreams and other subjects: Sprenger 14, **Bodleian** 374 (AH 1133/1721), 375 (AH 1213/1798–9), **Blochet** ii 1152 (early 18th cent.), 1151 (mid 18th cent.), **Bānkīpūr** Suppt. i 1785 (AH 1141/1728), **Ivanow** 223 (AH 1141/1729), 224 (late 18th cent.), **Ethé** 673 (AH 1147/1734), 674 (lacks the *tadhkirah* of poetesses at the end. N.d.), **Rieu** i 369*b* (18th cent.), 371*a* (AH 1183/1769), 371*a* (defective at end. 18th cent.), **Āṣafīyah** i p. 324 no. 25 (AH 1211/1796–7), no. 62 (n.d.), p. 170 no. 243, **Lindesiana** p. 222 no. 316 (circ. AD 1800), **Aumer 4** (AH 1220/1805), **Berlin** 650 (2) (little more than the 1st quarter of the work. AH 1242/1826), **Lahore** Panjab Univ. Lib. (defective at both ends. See *Oriental College Magazine*, vol. iii, no. 1 (Lahore, Nov. 1926), p. 74), **Rosen** Institut 32, **Bukhārā** Semenov 104, **Peshawar** 1471.

Editions: [**Calcutta**] 1246/1831*, **Barēli** 1264/1848* (cf. Sprenger 14), **Bombay** 1324/1906°.[155]

---

151 *kih ba-taqrīb i faujdārī dar chaklah i Sirhind kāmrawā'ī u kāmyābī dārad* (p. 120 ult.).

152 *kih ba-taqrīb i faujdārī dar shahr i Jahānābād u nawāḥī i ān kāmrānī u kāmyābī dārad* (Rosen Inst. p. 163³). Rieu cites the *Ma'āthir i 'Ālamgīrī*, p. 214, for the statement that Shukr Allāh Khān, a son-in-law of 'Āqil Khān Rāzī [for whom see no. 744 *supra*], was appointed *Faujdār* of Delhi in 1092. He wrote a commentary on Rūmī's *Mathnawī* (MSS.: Ivanow Curzon 211 and, probably, 'Alīgaṛh p. 49), and died in 1108 (Sprenger p. 151, from "Sirāj") or 1112 ("Khwushgū"). See also *Mir'āt al-khayāl* pp. 240–50, *Hamīshah bahār* (Sprenger p. 121), *Safīnah i Khwushgū* (Bānkīpūr viii p. 87), OCM. ix/i p. 66.

153 So in the Bodleian MS. Sprenger says that some of the numerous MSS. are abridgments. According to Bland the MS. described by him contained notices of seventy poets and fifteen poetesses.

154 So in the Bodleian MS.: Rosen says 61. The numbers for the succeeding classes are in accordance with Rieu's list.

155 Perhaps an abridgment. The date of printing (1324) will be found on p. 343.

Descriptions: (1) *On the earliest Persian Biography of Poets … By N. Bland* (in *JRAS*. 1848) pp. 140–2, (2) Rosen Institut pp. 161–8.

List of the poets (with some biographical details): Bodleian coll. 207–11.

Lists of the "modern" and contemporary poets: (1) Rieu i p. 370, (2) Rosen Institut pp. 161–8 (with epitomes of some biographies).

[*Mir'āt al-khayāl*, under Farrukh Ḥusain "Nāẓim" = Bombay 1324 pp. 120–1 (Persian text quoted by Rosen, Inst. pp. 162–3), and in *khātimah* = Bombay 1324 pp. 339–42 (summarised by Bland, pp. 141–2, and Sprenger p. 115); Rieu i 370 (where both passages are summarised).]

1136. Qāḍī **M. Badīʿ b. M. Sharīf Samarqandī** wrote in the reign of Subḥān-Qulī Khān, the Ashtarkhānī Sulṭān of Bukhārā (AH 1091/1680–1114/1702).

Tadhkirat al-shuʿarāʾ i Subḥān-Qulī-Khānī, notices of poets and scholars of Subḥān-Qulī Khān's time: **Bukhārā** Semenov 50 (cf. Semenov *Kurzer Abriss* p. 6).

1137. **Kishan Chand "Ikhlāṣ,"** son of Achal Dās and a pupil of ʿAbd al-Ghanī Bēg "Qabūl", was a K'hatrī (i.e. a Kshatriya) of Shāhjahānābād, who died in the reign of Aḥmad Shāh (1161/1748–1167/1754).

Hamīshah bahār, alphabetically arranged notices of about 200 poets who flourished (mainly in India) from the time of Jahāngīr (1014/1605–1037/1628) to the accession of Muḥammad Shāh (1131/1719) with a few of Akbar's time (963/1556–1014/1605), written in 1136/1723–4: Sprenger 16 (Tōpkhānah), **I.O.** 4401 (AH 1138/1726), **Ethé** 675 (AH 1139/1727), **Lindesiana** p. 156 no. 323 (circ. AD 1830), **Bānkīpūr** viii 689 (19th cent.), **Āṣafīyah** i p. 318 no. 13.

List and epitome of the biographies: Sprenger pp. 117–30.

[*Hamīshah bahār* (Sprenger p. 119); *Gul i raʿnā* (Bānkīpūr viii p. 129); *Ṣuḥuf i Ibrāhīm* (passage translated by Bland, *JRAS*. 1848 pp. 169–70); *Makhzan al-gharāʾib* no. 260; Sprenger p. 117; Beale *Oriental biographical dictionary*.]

1138. For the *Mir'āt i wāridāt*, of which the fourth *ṭabaqah* completed in 1142/1730 contains *inter alia* biographies of Indian poets and authors, see no. 779 (1) *supra*.

1139. **Bindrāban Dās "Khwushgū"** a Hindu "of the Bais tribe" (i.e. presumably of the Vaishya caste), was a native of Mat'hurā[156] (i.e. "Muttra", 30 miles N.N.W. of Āgrah). At the age of 14 he became a pupil of M. Afḍal "Sarkhwush",

156 So ʿAbd al-Muqtadir (Bkp. viii p. 83). According to the *Gul i raʿnā* as summarized in Bkp. viii p. 130 he was "a Hindû of the Bais tribe of Mathrâ", which perhaps does not necessarily

who suggested his *takhalluṣ* "Khwushgū"[157] and who died in 1126/1714 (see no. 1132 *supra*). Having spent the ten years 1137–47/1724–35 in compiling his *Safīnah*, he was prevented from making a fair copy and publishing the work by Nādir Shāh's invasion [1151/1739], in consequence of which he had to go with the army to Kōt Kāngrah (Sprenger p. 130). He remained seven or eight years[158] in the Panjāb, but in 1155/1742 he returned to Delhi and gave his *Safīnah* to "his master" Sirāj al-Dīn ʿAlī Khān "Ārzū", who wrote some notes and added a preface (*ibid.*). "Ārzū" himself says in his *Majmaʿ al-nafāʾis* (for which see no. 1149, 7th par. *infra*) that "Khwushgū" was his constant companion for 25 years (Bānkīpūr viii p. 84[1]). Among other distinguished friends of his were ʿAbd al-Qādir Bē-dil (for whom see Rieu ii 706*b*, Bānkīpūr iii pp. 194–5, viii p. 96, etc.), Saʿd Allāh "Gulshan" (for whom see Bānkīpūr viii p. 98) and ʿUmdat al-Mulk Amīr Khān "Anjām" (for whom cf. Sprenger pp. 153, 203). The last of these was, according to "Ārzū", the dedicatee of the *Safīnah* (Bkp. viii p. 84[2]). Towards the end of his life he renounced the world and lived piously at Allahabad. According to the *Gul i raʿnā* (quoted in Bānkīpūr viii p. 84) he died at ʿAẓīmābād (i.e. Patna) between 1161/1748 and 1170/1756–7.[159] For his uncle Sadānand "Bē-takalluf" see Bānkīpūr vii p. 94.

Safīnah i Khwushgū (a chronogram = 1137/1724–5, the date of inception), or *Safīnah i Khwushgūʾī* (a chronogram = 1147/1734–5, the date of completion), more or less chronologically arranged notices of poets in three *daftars* ((1) 362 ancient poets from "Rūdakī" to "Kāfī", (2) 811[160] "mediæval" poets from "Jāmī" to "Shugūnī" (d. some years after 1060), (3) modern and contemporary poets: Sprenger pp. 130–2 = **Berlin** 652–3 (*Daftars* I–II, defective), **Bānkīpūr** viii pp. 83–115 (*Daftar* III, apparently defective, AH 1182/1768–9), Suppt. i 1786 (*Daftar* II, defective, extending from "Jāmī" to "Surūrī" (no. 636 in Bodleian MS.). 19th cent.), **Majlis** 403 (*Daftar* II (?) AH 1268/1851–2), **Bodleian** 376 (*Daftar* II), **I.O.** 4023 (*Daftar* I), **Lahore** Panjāb Univ. (*Daftar* II, defective, 775 poets from Jāmī to Mīrzā Raḍī (no. 775 in Bodleian MS.). See *OCM.III*/1 (Nov. 1926) p. 75).

---

imply that he was born there. "Ḥairat" describes him (incorrectly ?) as "a Banya of Benares and a pupil of By-dil" (Sprenger p. 155).

157 This is stated by "Khwushgū" himself in his notice of "Sarkhwush" (see Rieu Suppt. p. 79 and Bānkīpūr viii p. 93).

158 Apparently an overestimate, if it was in 1155 that he returned to Delhi.

159 *dar ʿasharah i sābiʿ baʿd i miʾah wa-alf dar ʿAẓīmābād Paṭnah paikar i ʿunṣurī wā-gudhāsht.* ʿAbd al-Muqtadir understands this as meaning 1170 (Bkp. viii p. 84[2]).

160 So in the Bodleian MS. In the Berlin MS. there are 545, extending from Jāmī to Mīrzā Aḥmad Bēg (no. 554 in the Bodleian MS.).

List and epitome of the biographies: [*Daftar* II] Bodleian coll. 212–39 [*Daftar* III] Bānkīpūr viii pp. 84–115 (excellent epitome).

Alphabetical rearrangement ("991 notices")[161] made at S̲h̲ūshtar by "Durrī" S̲h̲ūshtarī and completed in 1241/1825: **Sipahsālār** ii p. 474 (770 poets. Some marginal notes in "Durrī's" hand), **Rieu** Suppt. Ill (AH 1252/1836).

[Autobiographical information in *Safīnah*, preface (?) (see Sprenger p. 130) and elsewhere (cf. Bānkīpūr viii pp. 87[14], 92[14], 93[3], 94[26], 95 ult., 98[18], 103[17], 108[9], 110[3], 112[18], 113[37], 114[17], 25 and many passages where "K̲h̲wus̲h̲gū" says that particular poets were friends of his, etc.); "Ḥairat" *Maqālāt al-s̲h̲uʿarāʾ* (Sprenger p. 155); *Gul i raʿnā* (passage summarised in Bānkīpūr viii pp. 130–1); *Majmaʿ al-nafāʾis; Mak̲h̲zan al-g̲h̲arāʾib* no. 736; Sprenger pp. 130–1.]

1140. For the *Burhān al-futūḥ*, which was composed in 1148/1735–6 by M. ʿAlī b. M. Ṣādiq Nīshāpūrī and of which the 16th *bāb* is devoted to poets, see no. 164 *supra*.

1141. **ʿAṭāʾ Allāh "Nudrat"**, entitled Dānis̲h̲war K̲h̲ān, is the author of a Persian dictionary, *ʿAin i ʿAṭā* (MS.: Ethé 2515), which he completed after twenty years' work in 1162/1749. The India Office MS. Ethé 1699 (*Kullīyāt i Nudrat*) is probably his *dīwān*.

    Tad̲h̲kirah i Nudrat, notices of ancient and modern poets in two *c̲h̲amans* ((1) the 3rd century, (2) the 4th century), seven *guls̲h̲ans* (the 5th to the 11th century) and one *ḥadīqah* or *k̲h̲ātimah* (contemporary poets of the 12th century), completed in Muḥammad S̲h̲āh's 19th regnal year, 1149–50/1737: **Ethé** 676 (breaks off in *Guls̲h̲an* III).

1142. For the *Tārīk̲h̲ i Hindī*, which was completed in 1154/1741–2 by Rustam ʿAlī S̲h̲āhābādī and of which the *k̲h̲ātimah* is devoted to contemporary or nearly contemporary *s̲h̲aik̲h̲s, ʿulamāʾ* and poets, see no. 630 *supra*.

1143. For the *Tārīk̲h̲ i Muḥammad-S̲h̲āhī*, or *Nādir-al-zamānī*, a history, mainly of India, to 1159/1746, by K̲h̲wus̲h̲-ḥāl C̲h̲and, which contains at the end of *Maqālah* ii short notices of 258 poets (list in Berlin cat. pp. 477–80), see no. 163 *supra*.

---

161 Although described (correctly, it seems) by Rieu as "taken from all three volumes of the original work", "Durrī's" recension is said in the Sipahsālāh catalogue to be a rearrangement of the second of the four [*sic* ?] *qisms*. The beginning (misplaced ?) of a third *qism* (= *daftar* apparently) is noted in Bānkīpūr viii p. 86[13].

1144. For the *Wāqiʿāt i Kashmīr*, which was completed in 1160/1747 by Khwājah M. Aʿẓam and which is devoted largely to the saints, poets, and scholars of Kashmīr, see no. 880 (1) *supra*.

1145. **Mardān ʿAlī Khān**[162] **"Mubtalā"** b. M. ʿAlī Khān Mashhadī composed in 1161/1748 his

Muntakhab al-ashʿār, a poetical anthology with short biographical notices: **Lahore** Prof. Maḥmūd Shērānī's private library (AH 1166/1753. See ʿAbd al-Nabī *Mai-khānah*, editor's preface p. BK), **Nadhīr Aḥmad** 94 (AH 1166/1753. ʿAbd al-Ḥusain, Lucknow. Perhaps the same MS. as the preceding), **Bodleian** 379.

List of the 755 poets (with some biographical details): Bodleian coll. 239–55.

[*Muntakhab al-ashʿār* no. 662.]

1146. **ʿAbd al-Ḥakīm "Ḥākim" Lāhaurī** b. Shādmān Khān Uzbak received a *manṣab* and the title of Ḥakīm Bēg Khān from Muḥammad Shāh at the beginning of his reign (1131/1719–1161/1748), but he subsequently left the royal service and became a wandering *faqīr*. "Āzād" Bilgrāmī made his acquaintance at Aurangābād. He was the author of a *dīwān* and of a *tadhkirah*, the title of which he changed at "Āzād's" suggestion from *Tuḥfat al-majālis* to *Mardum i dīdah* (see *Khizānah i ʿāmirah* p. 200[18]). When "Muṣḥafī" wrote his *ʿIqd i Thuraiyā* (in 1199/1784–5) he was still alive. According to the *Naghmah i ʿandalīb* he died in Kashmīr.

Muntakhab i Ḥākim (a chronogram = 1161/1748), or [?] *Nuskhah i pasandīdah dar dhikr i baʿḍī shuʿarā* [?], a small *tadhkirah* of poets including "Āfrīn", "Āzād", "Ummēd", and "Ārzū",[163] with a *takmilah* relating to Mīr ʿAbd al-Ḥaiy[164] and Sh. Nūr-Muḥammad: **Rehatsek** p. 133 no. 21 (AH 1175/1761–2 (?),[165] partly autograph), **Rieu** iii 1037*b* iv (extracts only (1 fol.), from a MS. in Munīr al-Mulk's library).

---

162 In the Bodleian catalogue the author's name is given (wrongly, it seems) as Muḥammad ʿAlîkhân bin Muḥammad.

163 The *Muntakhab i Ḥākim* is described by Rieu as compiled from the *Majmaʿ al-nafāʾis* of "Ārzū", with additional lives. If this is correct, "Ḥākim" must have used "Ārzū's" work before its completion in 1164.

164 Doubtless the editor of the *Maʾāthir al-umarāʾ*.

165 According to Rehatsek "this copy bears towards the end the date 1175". Presumably Rehatsek means that 1175 was the date of transcription, not that the year 1175 is mentioned in the text towards the end. It will be observed that apparently 1175 is the date assigned by "Azād" to the *Mardum i dīdah*.

It is not clear whether this work is identical with

> ***Mardum i dīdah***,[166] a small *tadhkirah* of poets whom the author had seen, composed, according to "Āzād" (*Khizānah i ʿāmirah* p. 200[18]), during a visit paid by "Ḥākim" to Aurangābād (evidently, to judge from the context, the second of the three visits mentioned by "Āzād", i.e. 15 Jumādā 'l-ūlā-19 Shawwāl 175/1761–2): no MSS. recorded.

[*Safīnah i Khwushgū* (Bānkīpūr viii p. 107); "Ḥairat" *Maqālāt al-shuʿarāʾ* (Sprenger p. 155); *Khizānah i ʿāmirah* pp. 200–4 (no. 37); *ʿIqd i Thuraiyā* (Rieu i 377*b*) fol. 42; *Makhzan al-gharāʾib* no. 642; *Naghmah i ʿandalīb* (Rieu iii 978*b*) fol. 70; Rieu iii 1086*b*.]

1147. Nawwāb Khān-i-Zamān Bahādur[167] Ẓafar-Jang[168] **ʿAlī-Qulī Khān "Wālih"** b. M. ʿAlī Khān Shamkhālī Lakzī Dāghistānī,[169] a descendant of the Shamkhāls, or rulers, of the Lesgians[170] of Dāghistān, was born at Iṣfahān in Ṣafar 1124/1712. His father, appointed in 1126/1714 Bēglarbēgī of Erivan, died in 1128/1716 or 1129/1717.[171] When still a schoolboy "Wālih" fell in love with his cousin, Khadījah Sulṭān, and was betrothed to her, but her forced marriage to Karīm-dād, the slave of Maḥmūd Khān,[172] and after his death to a succession of other persons saddened the rest of his life.[173] His father's uncle, Fatḥ-ʿAlī Khān, was

166 With the double meaning "pupil of the eye" and "men seen".

167 Kh.-i-Z. B., a title conferred by Aḥmad Shāh (*Khizānah i ʿāmirah* p. 448[14]).

168 Title conferred by Muḥammad Shāh (*Khizānah i ʿāmirah* p. 448[13]).

169 Usually known as ʿA.-Q. Kh. Dāghistānī, he is called ʿA.-Q. Kh. Lakzī in the *Ātash-kadah* (no. 15) and ʿA.-Q. Kh. Shamkhālī in the *Makhzan al-gharāʾib* (no. 3018). He appears to be the same person as "Nawāb ʿAlī Qulī Khān, commonly called Chhangā or Shash Angushtī (from having six fingers on each hand), a mansabdār of 5000 horse" (Beale), the father of Gannā Begam, Urdu poetess and wit, who became the wife of ʿImād al-Mulk Ghāzī al-Dīn Khān (see no. 797 penult. par. *supra* and Beale *Oriental Biographical Dictionary* under Ghazi-uddin Khan III) and who died in 1189/1775 (see Beale under "Gunna or Ganna Begam", Sprenger p. 227, Garcin de Tassy i pp. 488–90). P.S. This identification is confirmed by *Nujūm al-samāʾ* p. 47 penult.: *ʿAlī Qulī-Khān Wālih i Dāghistānī i Shash-angushtī dar Riyāḍ al-shuʿarā āwardah kih …*

170 For the Lesgians and their Shāmkhāls or Shamkhāls see *Ency. Isl.* under Dāghistān, *Ḥudūd al-ʿālam* tr. Minorsky p. 455, etc.

171 See Bānkīpūr viii p. 119[11–12].

172 Mīr Maḥmūd b. Mīr Wais, ruler of Qandahār, led an Afghān invasion of Persia in 1134/1721, defeated the Persians and sealed the fate of the Ṣafawī dynasty at the decisive battle of Gulnābād (some 3 leagues E. of Iṣfahān) in March 1722/Jum. II 1134, took Iṣfahān after a siege in October 1722 and forced Shāh Sulṭān-Ḥusain to abdicate (see Browne *Lit. Hist*, iv pp. 125–9, *Ency. Isl* under Ḥusain b. Sulaiman, etc.).

173 The romantic story of this 18th-century Majnūn and Lailā is the subject of a *mathnawī*, *Wālih u Sulṭān*, written in 1160/1747 at "Wālih's" request by Mīr Shams al-Dīn "Faqīr" Dihlawī (MSS.: Rieu Suppt. 343, Eton 144, Ivanow 866, Ivanow Curzon 297, Ethé 1711, I.O. D.P. 1262,

Prime Minister to S͟hāh Sulṭān-Ḥusain (reigned 1105/1694–1135/1722) and other relatives of his held high office, but in 1133/1720 they were all dismissed.[174] This calamity was followed by the Afg͟hān invasion (1721–2), the seven years of Afg͟hān rule and in 1144/1731 by the death of S͟hāh Ṭahmāsp II, to whom he had attached himself. "Wālih" left for India,[175] reached Delhi in 1147/1734–5,[176] and received in course of time from Muḥammad S͟hāh (reigned 1131/1719–1161/1748) a *manṣab* of 4000, the title of Ẓafar-Jang and the appointment of Second Mīr-Tūzuk. In Aḥmad S͟hāh's reign (1161/1748–1167/1754) he was promoted to a *manṣab* of 6000 and the title of K͟hān-i-Zamān Bahādur. In the reign of ʿĀlamgīr II (1167/1754–1173/1759) his *manṣab* was increased to 7000 and on 1 Rajab 1169/1 April 1756[177] he died at Delhi. For his *dīwān*, completed in 1157/1744–5, see Bodleian 1182, Ethé 1708, Edinburgh New Coll. p. 9, Āṣafīyah i p. 736 no. 345. A theological or Ṣūfī *mathnawī* composed in 1149/1736–7 and entitled *Najm al-hudā* (MSS.: Bānkīpūr Suppt. i 1921, Ivanow 855) is ascribed to "Wālih" Dāg͟histānī by Sprenger and Ivanow, but a verse quoted by ʿAbd al-Muqtadir shows that the author is a different "Wālih", namely S. M. Mūsawī, who was born in K͟hurāsān, migrated to Ḥaidarābād and then to Arcot and died in 1184/1770 (see Madras no. 61, *Gulzar i Aʿẓam* pp. 365–8, *Guldastah i Karnāṭak* (Ivanow 1st Suppt. 776 no. 68)). Another *mathnawī*, *Mīrzā-nāmah*, on the love adventures of Mīrzā S͟hīr-afgan (MS. Ivanow 856), is likewise ascribed to "Wālih" Dāg͟histānī by Sprenger and Ivanow, but probably this too is by S. M. Mūsawī.

Riyāḍ al-s͟huʿarāʾ, "alphabetically" arranged notices of "2500"[178] poets (very few of the author's contemporaries, especially of the contemporary poets of India, whom he held in small estimation) written mainly in 1160/1747 (a year often referred to, according to Ivanow) and completed in 1161/1748 (according to a chronogram quoted and explained

---

Bānkīpūr iii 413. English translation: *The story of Valeh and Hadijeh. Translated ... by Mirza Mahomed and C. Spring Rice*, London 1903°*).

174 For his dismissal see Malcolm *History of Persia* i p. 416 n. His successor, Muḥammad-Qulī K͟hān, was the maternal uncle of Luṭf-ʿAlī Bēg "Ād͟har".

175 According to "Āzād" (*K͟hizānah* p. 194[1]) "Wālih" and "Ḥazīn" travelled together from Kirmān to Bandar i ʿAbbāsī, but "Wālih", leaving by an earlier boat, reached Tattah ten days before "Ḥazīn". "Āzād" says (*K͟hizānah* p. 194[10]) that when Nādir S͟hāh was at Delhi "Ḥazīn" lay concealed in "Wālih's" house. "Ḥazīn" himself seems to make no mention of "Wālih", who according to "K͟hwus͟hgū" (Bkp. viii p. 110) was his disciple and pupil.

176 "Āzād," when returning in this year from Sīwistān, met "Wālih" at Lahore and accompanied him to Delhi (*K͟hizānah* p. 448[3]).

177 In support of this date Rieu (iii p. 1086*a*) cites the *Ṣūrat i ḥāl*, an autobiographic *mathnawī* by "Guls͟han" Jaunpūrī, who was employed by "Wālih" till his death (see Rieu ii 715*b*). The date 1170/1756–7 is given in the *K͟hizānah i ʿāmirah*.

178 "The notices," according to Rieu, "are stated to amount to 2500 in number."

by Bland, quoted without explanation by ʿAbd al-Muqtadir) or 1162/1749 (a year explicitly mentioned, according to Ivanow, as that in which the last portion was written):[179] Sprenger no. 18, **Berlin** 657 (an abstract containing only the biographies and one line by each poet. Autograph ?), 656 (2497 articles ? AH 1224/1809), **Ivanow** 230 (AH 1171/1757–8), **Ivanow** Curzon 57 (defective. A.D., 1794 ?), **Lindesiana**[180] p. 121 no. 311 (circ. AD 1770), no. 57 (AH 1210/1795–6), no. 58 (defective at end. Modern), **Būhār** 92 (AH 1191/1777–8), **Rieu** i 371*a* (AH 1203/1788) Suppt. 112 (AH 1216/1801), 113 (breaks off in *kāf*. 19th cent.), **Āṣafīyah** iii p. 164 no. 120 (AH 1258/1842), **Bānkīpūr** viii 693 (19th cent.), **Bodleian** 377 (n.d.), 378 (short fragment only), **I.O.** 3653, **Lahore** Panjab Univ. Lib. (extracts, 94 poets. See *Oriental College Magazine*, vol. iii, no. 1 (Lahore, Nov. 1926), p. 75).

Epitome (with some additions): ***Lubb i lubāb***, written by Qamar al-Dīn ʿAlī b. Sanā Allāh Ḥusainī Nāṣirī for Richard Johnson: **Ethé** 695 (AH 1194/1780, autograph).

Description: *On the oldest Persian Biography of Poets ... By N. Bland* (in *JRAS*. 1848) pp. 143–7.

List of the 2594 biographies in Ivanow 230 and Ivanow Curzon 57: **Ivanow** Curzon pp. 28–63.

[Autobiography in *Riyaḍ al-shuʿarāʾ, khātimah* (summarised by Rieu and ʿAbd al-Muqtadir); "Mubtalā" *Muntakhab al-ashʿār* no. 725; *Safīnah i Khwushgū* (summarised in Bānkīpūr viii p. 110); "Gulshan" Jaunpūrī *Ṣūrat i ḥāl* (Rieu ii p. 715*b*); "Ḥairat" *Maqālāt al-shuʿarāʾ* (Sprenger p. 160); *Khizānah i ʿāmirah* pp. 446–50 (Bodleian 381 no. 129); *Ātash-kadah* no. 841; *Ṣuḥuf i Ibrāhīm* (passage translated or summarised by Bland, pp. 145–6); *Khulāṣat al-afkār* no. 301 (cf. Bland p. 147); *Makhzan al-gharāʾib* no. 3018; *Riyāḍ al-ʿārifīn* pp. 263–4; *Majmaʿ al-fuṣaḥāʾ* ii p. 558; *Shamʿ i anjuman* p. 491.]

1148. Mīr **Ḥusain-Dōst** "Ḥusainī" b. S. Abī Ṭālib **Sanbhalī** left Sanbhal (i.e. "Sambhal", 22 miles S.W. of Murādābād) at the age of 19 for Delhi, where he spent his time in the company of poets. In 1173/1759–60, having left Delhi for Bareilly (Barēlī), he wrote a Persian grammar, *Tashrīḥ i nādir* (MSS.: Calcutta

179 The author, according to Rieu, claims as special excellences of his *tadhkirah* that he has confined his quotations to verses of undoubted merit and that he has inserted observations relating to prosody and poetical figures, historical information and critical judgments on poetical quality. "In India," says Sprenger, "this Tadzkirah is more esteemed than any other."

180 One of the three MSS. described in the Lindesiana catalogue is identical with the I.O. MS. mentioned below.

Madrasah p. 104, Rāmpūr (see Nadhīr Aḥmad 302)). In 1203/1789 he made a prose abstract of "Hātifī's" *Tīmūr-nāmah* (see no. 359 (2) *supra*).

Tadhkirah i Ḥusainī, completed in 1163/1749–50, short alphabetically arranged notices of about 200 ancient and modern poets (as well as some saints and princes) Sprenger no. 20 (Mōtī Maḥall), **Rieu** i 372*a* (18th cent.), 372*b* (18th cent.), **Bānkīpūr** viii 694 (different beginning. 19th cent.), **Berlin** 654 (breaks off in *sīn*), **Lahore** Panjāb Univ. (defective. See *OCM*. III/1 (Nov. 1926) p. 75).

Edition: **Lucknow** 1875°*.

Abridgment: **I.O.** 3847 (AH 1187/1773), **Ivanow** 2nd Suppt. 933 (AH 1250/1834).

1149. **Sirāj al-Dīn ʿAlī K͟hān "Ārzū"** Akbarābādī, entitled Istiʿdād K͟hān,[181] b. Sh. Ḥusām al-Dīn "Ḥusām"[182] was born at Gwalior[183] or Akbarābād in 1099/1687–8 or 1101/1689–90.[184] According to "Āzād"[185] he was descended on his father's side from Sh. Kamāl al-Dīn, the son of a sister of the great saint Naṣīr al-Dīn Maḥmūd called C͟hirāg͟h i Dihlī,[186] and on his mother's side from another celebrated saint M. G͟hauth Guwāliyārī[187] In 1132/1719–20 he went from Gwalior

---

181 See Bānkīpūr viii p. 112.
182 According to "K͟hwus͟hgū" (Bānkīpūr viii p. 87) "S͟hayk͟h Ḥusâm-ud-Dîn, father of the writer's master, Sirâj-ud-Dîn ʿAlî K͟hân Ârzû; was a Manṣabdâr under ʿĀlamgîr, and died AH 1115 (AD 1703)".
183 "Ḥairat" (Sprenger p. 153) says that he was born at Gwalior, studied first at Āgrah, proceeded thence to Delhi, and subsequently, with the sons of Nawwāb Isḥāq K͟hān, to Lucknow. In the *Ṣuḥuf i Ibrāhīm* also it is stated that he was born at Gwalior (see Berlin cat. p. 765⁵). Neither "Āzād", who had obtained a written autobiography from "Ārzū" (see the next note), nor "K͟hwus͟hgū" specifies the place of his birth. On the other hand both Rieu and ʿAbd al-Muqtadir say (on what authority?) that he was born at Akbarābād (i.e. Āgrah). If this is an inference from the *nisbah* Akbarābādī appended to his name (e.g. in the *K͟hizānah i ʿāmirah*), it is not of course necessarily correct. According to Sprenger (p. 133¹) "he was born in 1101 either at Agra or Gwályár, but brought up in the former city".
184 According to "K͟hwus͟hgū" (Bānkīpūr viii p. 112) the date 1099 has the authority of "Ārzū" himself and the support of a chronogram (*Nuzl i g͟haib*) composed by "Ārzū's" father. The date 1101/1689–90 is given by "Āzād", who had never met "Ārzū" but had written to him from the Deccan, when compiling his *Sarw i āzād*, and had obtained from him a written autobiography (*K͟hizānah i ʿāmirah* p. 119). Possibly therefore both dates are derived from "Ārzū" himself.
185 Doubtless on "Ārzū's" own authority (cf. the previous note).
186 d. 757/1356. See *Safīnat al-auliyā'* p. 100 (Ethé 647 no. 116); Beale *Oriental biographical dictionary* under Nasir-uddin Mahmud; *Ency. Isl.* under Čirāg͟h Dihlī; etc.
187 d. 970/1562–3, author of the Arabic Ṣūfī work *al-Jawāhir al-k͟hamsah* (see Brockelmann ii p. 418, *Supptbd.* ii p. 616, and, for the Persian translation, Ethé 1875–6, Bombay Univ. p. 227, etc.). Cf. *Ency. Isl.* under Muḥammad G͟hawth Gawāliyārī. For his tomb at Gwalior

to Delhi and found a patron in Anand Rām "Mukhliṣ" (d. 1164/1751: see no. 780 *supra*), who obtained for him a *manṣab* and a *jāgīr*. Influential support came to him also from Muḥammad Shāh's *Khān-sāmān*. Mu'taman al-Daulah Isḥāq Khān "Isḥāq" Shūstarī[188] and after his death in 1152/1739–40 from his eldest son Najm al-Daulah,[189] who paid "Ārzū" a monthly stipend of 150 rupees. In 1163/1750 Najm al-Daulah was killed, but his younger brother Sālār-Jang maintained the friendly relations of the family towards "Ārzū", and in 1168/1754–5, when Sālār-Jang went to Oudh, "Ārzū" accompanied him. Thus he reached the town of Awad'h (Ajōd'hyā, now part of Fyzabad), the home of his remote ancestor, the aforementioned Sh. Kamāl al-Dīn. Soon afterwards he was presented by Sālār-Jang to Shujā' al-Daulah, the Nawwāb-Wazīr of Oudh. He did not, however, enjoy for long the monthly stipend of 300 rupees granted to him by the Nawwāb-Wazīr, since he died at Lucknow on 23 Rabī' II 1169/26 Jan. 1756. He was buried at Delhi.

An incomplete list of "Ārzū's" works given in the preface to his *'Aṭīyah i kubrā* was reproduced by Blochmann in *JASB*. 37, pt. 1 (1868) pp. 70–1. They are (1) *Khiyābān*, a commentary on the *Gulistān* (MSS.: Sprenger 481, Bodleian 725, Berlin 49(2). Edition: Cawnpore 1293/1876–7°*), (2) *Shigūfah-zār*,[190] a commentary on the first part of the *Sikandar-nāmah* (MSS.: Sprenger 426, Rieu Suppt. 232, I.O. D.P. 1243A, 1243B, Lahore (Panjāb Univ.), 'Alīgaṛh p. 49, Āṣafīyah ii p. 1482, Berlin 736). This commentary "given in extenso, with a few additions, in the margins of the Iskandar Nāmah lithographed at Bombay A. H. 1277 [°*] ... forms the basis of the glosses in the Calcutta and Lucknow editions, as stated by Sprenger, Oude Catalogue, no. 426" (Rieu), (3) *Sharḥ i qaṣā'id i 'Urfī* (MSS.: I.O. D.P. 1286A, 1286C, 1286D, (4) *Sirāj i wahhāj, muḥākamah i shu'arā'*,[191] (5) *Sirāj i munīr, ajwibah i i'tirāḍāt i Mullā Munīr bar ash'ār i ba'ḍ i muta'akhkhirīn* [namely "Qudsī" (for whom see no. 727, *supra*) according to Bkp. iii p. 218], (6) *Risālah i adab i 'ishq, dar taḥqīq i adab i 'ishq*, (7) *Mi'yār al-afkār, dar qawā'id i ṣarfīyah u naḥwīyah i fārisī*, (8) *Mathnawī i Jūsh u khurūsh, ba-muqābalah i*

---

see V. A. Smith *Akbar* p. 435 (and the references given there), *Annual Report of the Director General of Archaeology in India* 1920–1 p. 14, 1921–2 pp. 37–8.

188 See *Ma'āthir al-umarā'* iii pp. 774–6, Bānkīpūr viii p. 103, Beale *Oriental biographical dictionary* under Is-haq Khan. His daughter became the wife of Shujā' al-Daulah, who succeeded Ṣafdar-Jang as Nawwāb-Wazīr of Oudh in 1754.

189 *See Ma'āthir al-umarā'* iii pp. 775–6.

190 This title apparently does not occur in the MSS. of the work, which is usually called *Sharḥ i abyāt i Iskandar-nāmah*.

191 This seems to be a conflation of two different works, since the list of "Ārzu's" works quoted in the Berlin catalogue, p. 765, from the *Ṣuḥuf i Ibrāhīm* describes the *Sirāj i wahhāj* as *dar ḥall i abyāt i Khwājah i Shīrāzī* and the *Dād i sukhun* (no. 19 below) as *dar muḥākamah i ash'ār i qaṣīdah i Qudsī u Shaidāb* [*sic*, apparently for *Shaidā-yi*] *Hindī*.

Sūz u gudāz i Mullā Nauʿī, (9) *Mathnawī i Sūz u sāz* [*sic*, apparently = *Shūr i ʿishq*, Sprenger p. 337] *dar barābar i Maḥmūd u Ayāz i Mullā Zulālī*, (10) *ʿĀlam i āb, dar jawāb i Sāqī-nāmah i Mullā Ẓuhūrī*, (11) *Mathnawī i ʿIbrat-fasānah, dar tatabbuʿ i Qaḍā u qadar i Mullā M.-Qulī Salīm*, (12) *Dīwān i ghazal, mushtamil bar panj hazār bait*,[192] (13) *Nathr i Payām i shauq dar jawāb i murāsalāt i aʿizzah*, (14) *Gulzār i khayāl, dar taʿrīf i faṣl i Hōlī i Hindūstān*, (15) *Ābrūy i sukhun, dar waṣf i ḥauḍ u fawākih u tāk*, (16) *qaṣāʾid u rubāʿīyāt u khuṭab*.

The *ʿAṭīyah i kubrā*, like most of "Ārzū's" works, seems to be undated, but the foregoing list is doubtless earlier than 1147/1734–5, since it does not include the *Sirāj al-lughah*, which was written in that year. To that list can be added (17) *ʿAṭīyah i kubrā*, on simile, metaphor and metonymy[193] (MSS.: Ivanow 394, Ivanow Curzon 177, Ivanow 2nd Suppt. 969 (4), Bānkīpūr ix 854 (2), Madras 482. Editions: [Calcutta] 1832* (followed by the *Mauhibati ʿuẓmā*), Cawnpore 1897°), (18) *Mauhibat i ʿuẓmā*, on rhetoric[194] (MSS.: Bānkīpūr ix 854 (1), Ivanow 2nd Suppt.969 (5), 970. Edition: [Calcutta] 1832* (preceded by the *ʿAṭīyah i kubrā*), (19) *Dād i sukhun, dar muḥākamah i ashʿār i qaṣīdah i Qudsī u Shaidā-yi* [*sic lege*] *Hindī*[195] (Berlin cat. p. 765). (MSS.: Ivanow 393, Lahore (Panjāb Univ. See OCM.V/4 (Aug. 1929) p. 17).) (20) *Zāʾid al-fawāʾid*, a dictionary of Persian verbs and the abstract nouns derived from them (MS.: Ivanow 2nd Suppt. 969 (11)), presumably related in some way to the*Zawāʾid al-fawāʾid*, a work on the same subject by ʿAbd al-Wāsiʿ Hānsawī (MS: Lahore, Panjāb Univ. See OCM. VIII/2 (Feb. 1932) p. 73). (21) *Sirāj al-lughah*, completed in 1147/1734–5, a dictionary of non-Arabic words used by the old poets (*mutaqaddimīn*) with many criticisms of the *Burhān i qāṭiʿ*, whose mistakes and to a much smaller extent

192 "Ārzū" wrote *dīwāns* in which he imitated those of "Sālim", "Athar" and "Fighānī", composing a counterpart to each poem in the same metre and rhyme (cf. Sprenger p. 337, Berlin Cat. p. 765). A MS. of the *dīwān* modelled on that of "Athar" is described by Sprenger, who says that "Arzú informs us in his Tadzkirah, *voce* Athar, that these poems formed first a separate Dywán as they do in this copy, but subsequently he incorporated them in his large Dywán". Ivanow Curzon 295 and 296 (both beginning *Chih parwarī*) seem to be copies of this same *dīwān*. Bānkīpūr iii 399 (*Dīwān i Ārzū: ghazals* beginning *Ai basmalah*, followed by *rubāʿīs* beginning *ʿĀlam bāghīst*) opens with the same poem as Sprenger 107, which is described as *Intikhāb az dīwān i Ārzū*.

193 On *bayān* only (*fa-qaṭ dar bayān*, Berlin cat. p. 765).

194 *dar fann i maʿānī wa-bayān* (Berlin cat. p. 765).

195 "A short treatise on various questions of style, versification, etc.... The author states that he undertook an analysis of a *qaṣīda* by Abū 'l-Barakāt Munīr (d. 1054/1644), and tried to be as impartial as possible. He refers also to Muḥammad Jān Qudsī (d. 1056/1646), and others." (Ivanow.) Presumably this work is concerned with "Shaidā's" *qaṣīdah*, "in which he enumerates at length the defects and the shortcomings of each and every couplet of a *ḳaṣīda* by his contemporary Ḳudsī ..." (*Ency. Isl.*, supplement, under Shaidā). For "Ārzū's" reply to "Munīr's" criticisms of "Qudsī" see no. 5 *supra* (*Sirāj i munīr*).

those of the *Farhang i Rashīdī* it was the author's primary purpose to correct[196] (MSS.: Ethé 2513, Lindesiana p. 216 no. 766, Ivanow 1434). For a description of this work and the *Chirāgh i hidāyat* see Blochmann in *JASB*.37, pt. 1 (1868) pp. 25–7. (22) *Chirāgh i hidāyat*, a dictionary of words used by modern poets (*muta'akhkhirīn*), forming the second *daftar* of the *Sirāj al-lughah* (MSS.: Rieu ii 501*b*, iii 997*a*, 1070*b*, Ivanow 1435–6, Ivanow Curzon 526, Bānkīpūr ix 807–9, Berlin 120 (1), Browne Pers. Cat. 147 I, Browne Suppt. 375 (King's 125), Ethé 2514, Lahore (Panjāb Univ. 2 copies). Editions (on the margin of Ghiyāth al-Dīn M. Rāmpūrī's *Ghiyāth al-lughāt*): Cawnpore 1868*, 1870*, 1874°, 1878°, 1307/1890*, Lucknow 1296/1879°, Bombay 1880–1°.)(23) [*Taṣḥīḥ i*[197]] *Gharā'ib al-lughāt*,[198] a corrected edition of 'Abd al-Wāsi' Hānsawī's *Gharā'ib al-lughāt*, which is a glossary of Urdū words with their equivalents in Persian, Arabic, and Turkish (MSS.: Rieu iii 1030*a*, Bānkīpūr ix 838, Ivanow 2nd Suppt. 969 (7), 'Alīgaṛh p. 56 nos. 16, 21, Lahore (Panjāb Univ. 2 copies).) (24) *Tanbīh al-ghāfilīn*, a criticism of the poems of "Ḥazīn"[199] (MSS.: I.O. D.P. 423 (*c*), Lahore (Panjāb Univ. See *OCM*.v/4 (Aug. 1929) p. 16)). Blochmann described this work briefly in *JASB*. 37, pt. 1 (1868) p. 27. A rejoinder, *Qual i faiṣal*, written in 1267/1850–1[200] by Maulawī Imām-Bakhsh "Ṣahbā'ī", was published at Cawnpore in 1862 (Blochmann *loc. cit.*) and in vol. iii of "Ṣahbā'ī's" *Kullīyāt*, Cawnpore and

196 "The Siráj is rather voluminous, as it contains the words of the Burhán with lengthy remarks attached to each" (Blochmann p. 27). "The critical remarks on the Burhán are so numerous, that the Burhán should never have been printed without the notes of the Siráj" (Blochmann p. 25).

197 So in the 'Alīgaṛh catalogue. The other cataloguers call "Ārzū's" revised edition by the same title as the original, *Gharā'ib al-lughāt*.

198 In the list of "Ārzū's" works quoted from the *Ṣuhuf i Ibrāhīm* in the Berlin catalogue, p. 765, there is mentioned *Nawādir al-alfāẓ dar bayān i lughāt i Hindīyah kih Fārisī u 'Arabī i ān shuhrat na-dārad*. According to Rieu "Ārzū's" revision of the *Gharā'ib al-lughāt* "is confined to those Hindī words the Arabic or Persian equivalents of which are not commonly known in India". Possibly, therefore, the *Nawādir al-alfāẓ* and the revised edition of the *Gharā'ib al-lughāt* are the same work.

199 "Being proud of his affluence and ability, Ḥazîn, remark some of his biographers, began to look down on the Amîrs and nobles, and commenced, says his friend Wâlih, as the poet's nature was, to write satires against the citizens, and did not even spare the king and his nobles. In spite of his friend Wâlih's advice, Ḥazîn continued his satirical writings, till, says Wâlih, the poet lost all esteem in the eyes of the public. Wâlih ... had at last, to his deep regret, to give up his friendship with Ḥazîn, and out off all communication with the poet.... Ḥazîn then began to criticise the eminent poets of the imperial court, and wrote satires against many of them, such as Sirâj-ud-Dîn 'Alî Khân Ârzû, ... Mîr Muḥammad Afḍal Sâbit, and others. In revenge Ârzû wrote the ... Tanbîh-ul-Ġâfilîn.... in which he collected a large number of frail verses from Ḥazîn's dîwân, and criticisingly pointed out mistakes therein" (Bānkīpūr cat. iii p. 225).

200 So Āṣafīyah ii p. 908.

Lucknow [1878–80°*]. According to Blochmann another rejoinder was written by a nephew of "Ārzū's", Mīr Muḥsin ʿĀlī, "and Ték Chand, Mirzá Qatíl and Wárastah take frequently occasion to justify Ḥazín." (25) *Iḥqāq al-ḥaqq*, another tract relating to "Ḥazīn". No MSS. seem to be recorded, but a rejoinder, *Iʿlāʾ al-ḥaqq*, was published in vol. i of "Ṣahbāʾī's" *Kullīyāt*, Cawnpore and Lucknow [1878–80°]. (26) *Mihr u Māh*, a *mathnawī* (MSS.: Lindesiana p. 216 no. 620, Lahore (Panjāb Univ. See *OCM*. VII/1 (Nov. 1930) p. 144)), (27) *Muthmir*, on the principles of the Persian language (*dar ʿilm i uṣūl i lughat*), a counterpart to al-Suyūṭī's *Muzhir*, (MS.: Ivanow Curzon 550).

Some others, of which no MSS. have yet been recorded, are mentioned by Sprenger and ʿAbd al-Muqtadir.

"Ārzū's" reputation as a scholar was, and still is, high in India, if not in Persia.[201] According to Blochmann (*Contributions to Persian lexicography* p. 25) "He is the best commentator whom India has produced. His commentaries to Nizámí's Sikandarnámah, the Qaçídahs of Kháqání and 'Urfí, and his *sharh* to the Gulistán, entitled Khiyábáni Gulistán, are of great value." Blochmann's opinion that the *Burhān i qāṭiʿ* should never have been printed without the notes of the *Sirāj al-lughah* has already been quoted. Another work commended by Blochmann is the *Tanbīh al-ghāfilīn* (*Contributions* p. 27[10]: "Of his other works which compilers ought to read, I may mention the *Tanbíh al ghāfilīn*.... As most remarks refer to Persian style and idiom, compilers [of dictionaries] and grammarians will do well to procure copies").

Several distinguished Urdū poets received instruction from "Ārzū" in the *ars poetica*, and thus he has a place in the history of Urdū poetry, though he himself rarely composed poetry in Urdū. His Persian poetry—if we may judge from the paucity of manuscripts—seems not to have retained such popularity as it may have enjoyed in his own day.

Majmaʿ al-nafāʾis, completed in 1164/1750–1, meagre alphabetically arranged notices[202] of 1419[203] or 1735[204] ancient and modern poets with extracts from their works: Sprenger 19, **Ethé** 680 (vol. ii only, beginning with *ḍād* (Ḍiyāʾ al-Dīn Fārisī) and ending with *yāʾ*. AH 1166/1753, transcribed from an autograph), **I.O.** D.P. 739 (omits preface, breaks off in

201 Cf. *Majmūʿah i naghz* i p. 24[11]: *Agar-chih zabān-dānān i Īrān az mamarr i ḥasad bā nafs al-amr az-ū ḥisābī na-mī-gīrand ammā ḥaqq ān-ast kih wujūd i īn chunīn kas dar khāk i pāk i Hindūstān ḥukm i iksīr i aʿẓam dārad.*

202 The biographies were added as an afterthought, the author's original intention having been to compile an anthology (*safīnah*), and he paid much less attention to the biographies than to the extracts.

203 So Sprenger.

204 So ʿAbd al-Muqtadir.

ṣād (Amīr Rūzbihan "Ṣabrī") and lacks the latter half of *thā'*, the whole of *jīm, ḥā', khā'* and *dāl* and the first part of *dhāl*), **Bānkīpūr** viii 695–6 (AH 1179/1765–6), **Bodleian** 380 (n.d.), **Ivanow** 231 (*alif* to *jīm* only. 19th cent.).

Abridgments: (1) ***Muntakhab i Majma' al-nafā'is***: Ethé 681 (AH 1243/ 1827), (2) **I.O.** 4015 (possibly identical with the preceding).

Selection of notices containing critical or other comments by "Ārzū" on the verses quoted: ***Jāmi' al-fawā'id***, compiled by K'harakpat Rāy Kāyat [i.e. Kāyat'h = Kāyast'ha] in 1195/1781 or 1196/1782, or both: **I.O.** 4081 (AH 1196/1782).

[Autobiography in *Majma' al-nafā'is; Hamīshah bahār* (Sprenger p. 118[6]); *Safīnah i Khwushgū* (passage summarised in Bānkīpūr viii p. 112); "Mubtalā" *Muntakhab al-ash'ār* no. 84; *Riyāḍ al-shu'arā'; Sarw i Āzād*; Sirāj *Dīwān i muntakhab* (Sprenger p. 150[2]); "Ḥairat" *Maqālāt al-shu'arā'* (Sprenger p. 153); *Khizānah i 'āmirah* pp. 116–21 (Bodleian 381 no. 11); *Dhikr i Mīr* pp. 63–4; *Khulāṣat al-kalām* no. 8 (passage summarised in Bānkīpūr viii p. 140); *Ṣuḥuf i Ibrāhīm* no. 393; *Khulāṣat al-afkār* no. 40; *Makhzan al-gharā'ib* no. 229; *Majmū'ah i naghz* i pp. 24–6; Sprenger pp. 132–3; Blochmann *Contributions to Persian lexicography* (in JASB. 37, Pt. 1 (1868)) pp. 25–8, 70–1; Garcin de Tassy i pp. 226–8; Beale *Oriental biographical dictionary* under Siraj-uddin 'Ali Khan; M. Ḥusain "Āzād" *Āb i ḥayāt* (in Urdu) pp. 123–5; Rieu ii 501–2; Raḥmān 'Alī p. 71; Bānkīpūr iii pp. 217–18, viii p. 112; Rām Bābū Saksēna *History of Urdu literature* pp. 47–8; S. Shams Allāh Qādirī *Qāmūs al-a'lām* (in Urdu), pt. 1 (Ḥaidarābād 1935), coll. 26–9, where several further references will be found.]

1150. Sh. Jamāl al-Dīn Abū 'l-Ma'ālī[205] M. 'Alī[206] **"Ḥazīn"** b. Abī Ṭālib Zāhidī[207] Lāhijī **Jīlānī** was born on 27 Rabī' II 1103/17 Jan. 1692 at Iṣfahān, to which his father had migrated from Lāhijān[208] Educated at his birthplace by his father and others[209] and subsequently at Shīrāz, he developed into a scholar, who both

205 So in the subscription to the *Ṣafīr i dil*, Bodleian 1185. There is no such subscription in the lithographed *Kullīyāt*.

206 *Muḥammad al-mad'ū* (or *al-mushtahir*) *bi-'Alī*, etc.

207 He was sixteenth (according to Balfour's text) in descent from a great saint, Sh. Zāhid Gīlānī, the spiritual director of Sh. Ṣafī al-Dīn Ardabīlī, the ancestor of the Ṣafawī kings (see Browne *Lit. Hist.* iv pp. 38–44).

208 At the age of ten (*Tadhkirat al-mu'āṣirīn* p. 951[15], Sprenger p. 136) "Ḥazīn" was taken by his father on a visit to Lāhijān and stayed there for nearly a year during which time he read the *Khulāṣat al-hiṣāb* with his uncle Sh. Ibrāhīm Zāhidī Jīlānī (d. 1119/1707–8).

209 The names of his teachers and the books which he studied under them are faithfully recorded in the autobiography. That M. Bāqir Majlisī (for whom see no. 247 *supra*) was not one of them (as alleged by "some of his biographers": see Bānkīpūr iii p. 223) seems

taught[210] and wrote on the subjects of his study. Even as a child he had composed poetry in spite of some early discouragement from his father (Autobiography pp. 19–20, 22, trans. pp. 18, 21). More remarkable than all this, however, is that in his desire for knowledge he associated at Iṣfahān with Christian priests like "the Caliph Avanus"[211] (Autobiog. p. 57, trans. pp. 62–3) and, secretly, with a Jew named Shuʿaib(*op. cit.* p. 58, trans. p. 63), read many Christian books and had a translation of the *Taurāt* written down for his use. Similarly at a later date[212] he obtained information concerning Zoroastrianism from a *dastūr* at Baiḍā (*op. cit.* p. 83, trans. p. 93).

Even before his father's death [in 1127/1715] "Ḥazīn" had visited many towns in Fārs[213] and some elsewhere, but until then and for a few years afterwards his main place of residence was Iṣfahān, and he was there when the Afghān invasion and the siege of 1134–5/1721–2 [cf. no. 1147, 6th footnote *supra*] brought misery to the inhabitants and compelled him to sell most of his possessions including two thousand volumes from his library, the rest of which was subsequently looted by the Afghāns. Before the end of the siege, however, "Ḥazīn" escaped in disguise, and the next eleven years were spent in wandering from place to place,[214] meeting scholars, composing poetry, writing philosophical and other treatises and occasionally teaching. More than once he came in contact with Shāh Ṭahmāsp (reigned 1135/1722–1144/1731): at Mashhad the king visited him (Autobiog. p. 161, trans. p. 174) and subsequently [early in 1142/1729]

clear from "Ḥazīn's" statement that he had seen him three or four times (Autobiography p. 32, trans. p. 32). He died when "Ḥazīn" was seven or eight years old.

210 Cf. Autobiography p. 59[9] (*u dar ḍimn i īn mashāghil kutub i mutadāwalah rā dars mī-guftam*), trans. p. 64, and other passages. His abandonment of the practice of teaching (apparently in 1143/1730–1) is recorded on p. 178, trans. p. 195. The last works taught by him were the *Uṣūl i Kāfī*, the *Man lā yaḥḍuruhu l-faqīh*, the *Ilāhīyāt i Shifāʾ* and the *Sharḥ i Tajrīd*.

211 Khalīfah Āwānūs, as he is called in Belfour's text, or AwānūsKhalīfah, as he calls himself at the beginning of his Persian work on Christian evidences completed in 1690 (MSS.: Rieu i p. 5, Browne Suppt. 1388), is judged by Rieu to have been a Roman Catholic, probably of French origin. Lady Sheil in her *Glimpses of life and manners in Persia* (London 1856, p. 349 [14]) speaks of being called on by "a Nestorian khaleefa, or bishop". According to Morier's *Adventures of Hajji Baba* (ch. 40) the Armenian patriarch of Echmiadzin was known in Persia as the Khalīfah.

212 Before his father's death in 1127/1715 (Autobiog. p. 100, trans. p. 110): it is not clear how long before.

213 In one journey alone "Ḥazīn" says that he saw most of Fārs (Autobiog. p. 91 penult. (*u dar ān safar kamtar nāḥiyah az mamlakat i Fārs māndah bāshad kih na-dīdah bāsham*), trans. p. 100).

214 An incomplete list of the towns visited in the course of these wanderings, which included pilgrimages to the holy places of al-Ḥijāz and al-ʿIrāq (nearly 3 years at Najaf), is given by Browne iv p. 279.

invited him to accompany the royal army on the march against Ashraf the Afghān (Autobiog. p. 175, trans. p. 192), later at Iṣfahān "Ḥazīn" gave the king advice and outlined measures calculated to preserve his dynasty (Autobiog. p. 190, trans. p. 206). These were years of revolution and disorder in Persia, and much space in "Ḥazīn's" autobiography is devoted to accounts of Afghān and Turkish invasions, local insurrections, the rise of Nādir Shāh and other historical events. Eventually the prevailing misery became so painful to him that he decided to leave the country.[215] Sailing from Bandar i ʿAbbāsī on 10 Ramaḍān 1146/14 Feb. 1734, "Ḥazīn" reached Tattah, in Sind, early in Shawwāl.[216] After a stay of more than two months[217] he continued his journey and halted successively at Khudā-ābād (7 months ill), Bhakkar[218] (nearly 1 month), a village near Multān (nearly 2 years), Lahore (3 months), Delhi (more than 12 months), Lahore again (where he heard that Nādir Shāh was besieging Qandahār[219] and where he remained through the period of the protracted siege and afterwards until Nādir Shāh entered the district of Kābul), Sulṭānpūr, Sirhind, and again Delhi, where he was during the period of Nādir Shāh's invasion[220] and where he had been living for more than three years at the time when he wrote his *Tadhkirat al-aḥwāl* late in 1154/1742 at the age of 53 [*sic*]. He had then spent eight unhappy years in India, constantly regretting his advent to a country which he found extremely uncongenial. His first return to Lahore was in fact intended to be only a stage on his way from India via Kābul and Qandahār to Khurāsān, where he hoped to settle, but this design was frustrated by Nādir Shāh's approach. After Nādir Shāh's departure "Ḥazīn" went back for the second time to Lahore, but here he incurred the enmity of the Governor, Zakarīyā Khān, and was in a position of some danger until "Wālih" (see no. 1147 *supra*)

215 According to the account given by ʿAbd al-Muqtadir (Bānkīpūr iii p. 224), presumably on the authority of "Ḥazīn's" acquaintance "Wālih" (for whom see no. 1147 *supra*), the immediate cause of "Ḥazīn's" departure was that he had incurred suspicion of complicity in the assassination of Walī-M. Khān Shāmlū, who had been sent to Lār as Governor by Nādir Shāh, and that he was consequently unsafe in Persia.

216 According to "Āzād" (*Khizānah i ʿāmirah* p. 194³) "Wālih" had reached Tattah ten days before.

217 The periods of residence up to the second arrival in Lahore make too large a total.

218 Here "Āzād", who was returning from Sīwistān to Delhi, met "Ḥazīn" and received from him an autograph copy of some verses as a memento (*Khizānah i ʿāmirah* p. 194⁴).

219 Nādir Shāh reached Qandahār before Naurūz 1149/March 1737 and the town capitulated on 2 Dhū 'l-Qaʿdah 1150/23 March 1738.

220 Nādir Shāāh won the battle of Karnāl on 15 Dhū 'l-Qaʿdah 1151/24 Feb. 1739, entered Delhi on 9 Dhū 'l-Ḥijjah/20 March and left the city on 7 Ṣafar 1152/16 May 1739. "Āzād" says that while Nādir was in Delhi "Ḥazīn" lay concealed in "Wālih's" house (*Khizānah i ʿāmirah* p. 194¹⁰).

arranged for his return to Delhi (*Khizānah i ʿāmirah* p. 19[410–13], Bānkīpūr iii p. 225[3–9]). ʿUmdat al-Mulk Amīr Khān "Anjām"[221] obtained for him a *suyūrghāl* from Muḥammad Shāh[222](*Khizānah i ʿāmirah* p. 194[14], Bānkīpūr iii p. 225), and his financial position was thus rendered secure, but his tactlessness and his disparagement of India and Indians aroused animosity against him at Delhi,[223] and it was not long before he moved first to Āgrah (*Khizānah i ʿāmirah* p. 194[18]) and then to Benares, which became his permanent place of residence. Apparently he continued for some time to cherish hopes of returning to Persia, since we are told by Ghulām-Ḥusain Khān that several times he went to Patnah and had made up his mind to leave India, when obstacles intervened (*Siyar al-mutaʾakhkhirīn*, Cawnpore, 1866, p. 615[17]: *chand bār ān ʿālī-miqdār tā ba-ʿAẓīmābād rasīdah ʿāzim i ba-dar raftan az khāk i siyāh i Hind būd: taqdīr musāʿadat nah numūd*). At Benares he was repeatedly visited by Ghulām-Ḥusain Khān (for whom see no. 802 *supra*) and more than once in 1177/1764 by the Emperor [Shāh-ʿĀlam], the *Wazīr* [Shujāʿ al-Daulah of Oudh] and Mīr Qāsim [the *Nāẓim* of Bengal], who were advised by him not to make war against the British (*Siyar al-mutaʾakhkhirīn*, ii 746[22–24]). When he finally became resigned to the prospect of spending the rest of his days in India, he built a tomb for himself at Benares, and in it he was buried when he died on the 10th, 11th, 13th, or 18th of Jumādā 11180/November 1766. According to ʿAbd al-Muqtadir the tomb and the two lines of poetry[224] inscribed thereon by his own hand can still be seen in the part of Benares known as Fāṭimān.

Ghulām-ḤusainKhān, who knew Ḥazīn well in his later years, was impressed by the depth of his learning and his omniscience (*Siyar al-mutaʾakhkhirīn* ii 615[6]: *makhfī na-mānad kih faqīr u kasānī-kih ba-hamah wujūh bihtar az-īn ḥaqīr būdah and itʿirāf dārand kih dar-īn juzw i zamān chūn ū kasī dīdah na-shudah bal-kih mutaraddidīn i ʿArab u ʿAjam nīz ba-jāmiʿīyāt i ān janāb dar jamīʿ i ʿulūm i ẓāhir u bāṭin aḥadī rā dar aṭrāf u aknāf i ʿālam nishān na-dādah and āyatī būd az āyāt i Ilāhī ...*). Raymond (Ḥājjī Muṣṭafā), the translator of the

221 For whom cf. no. 1139 1st par. *supra*.

222 According to Ghulām-Ḥusain Khān "Ḥazīn" more than once declined invitations from Muḥammad Shāh to undertake the office of *Wazīr* (*Siyar al-mutaʾakhkhirīn*. Cawnpore 1866, ii p. 615[11]: *Muḥammad Shāh ba-wasāṭat i ʿUmdat al-Mulk u dīgar muqarrabān i daulat-khwāh mukarrar paighām dādah masʾalat numūd kih mutaʿahhid i imḍā-yi umūr i wizārat gashtah raunaq-afzā-yi salṭanat i ū shawad ammā chūn sar firū āwardan ba-dunyā nang u ʿār i ān nuqāwah i akhyār būd rāḍī na-shud*).

223 One outcome of this animosity, "Ārzū's" *Tanbīh al-ghāfilīn*, has been mentioned above (no. 1149 (24)).

224 *Zabān-dān i maḥabbat būdah am dīgar na-mī-dānam * Hamīn dānam kih gūsh az Dūst paighāmī shunīd īn-jā. Ḥazīn az pāyi rah-paimā basī sar-gashtagī dīdam * Sar i shūrīdah bar bālīn i āsāyish rasīd īn-jā.*

Siyar al-muta'akhkhirīn, who visited him in 1764 and 1765, found him "a man of sense and also of knowledge". He was also a pious and devout man, but it is not clear whether his reputation as a saint was so great in his lifetime as it seems to have become after his death. According to the *Ārāyishi maḥfil* written in 1219–20/1804–5 (see no. 622, Free Urdu translation *supra*) he received revelations, performed miracles and was credited with some power over the sun. For the ill-nature which he seems to have shown in India a sufficient explanation can perhaps be found in the ill-health to which he so often refers in his autobiography.

In the course of the *Tadhkirat al-aḥwāl* (pp. 64, 97, 101, 163, trans. pp. 71, 106, 111, 176) "Ḥazīn" records the completion of four *dīwāns*, the third of which was collected at Shīrāz [evidently in, or soon after, 1127] and the fourth at Mashhad [evidently between 1139 and 1142]. The first three of these *dīwāns* do not seem to be extant, but the fourth may be more or less identical with an extant *dīwān* of 1155, which the author describes as his fourth, and which may be a re-issue or a later recension of that collected at Mashhad. The *dīwān* of 1155 (preserved in a B.M. MS., Rieu ii p. 715*a*, of about that date, as well as in other MSS.) opens with a prose preface (beginning *Iftitāḥ i nāmah*), which contains the statement that, having previously published three *dīwāns*, the author, then resident in India and over fifty years old, had collected in a fourth, AH1155, the remainder of his detached pieces, and that the four *dīwāns* together amounted to about 30,000 lines. This 1155 *dīwān* contains *qaṣīdahs, ghazals*, fragments of *ghazals* (*mutafarriqāt i ghazalīyāt*, mostly pieces of two or three lines), *rubāʿīs, muqaṭṭaʿāt* and parts of the four *mathnawīs*,[225] *Chaman u anjuman, Kharābāt*[226] (*mukhtaṣar*), *Maṭmaḥ al-anẓār* (prologue), and *Tadhkirat al-ʿāshiqīn*[227] (prologue and epilogue).

The 1155 *dīwān* seems to be the basis of the poetical portion of the Lucknow and Cawnpore *Kullīyāt*[228] (see 2nd next par.), in which, however, are included two other short *mathnawīs*, namely, the *Ṣafīr i dil*, composed in 1173, and the

225 In a prose preface prefixed to these four *mathnawīs* in a B.M. MS. (Rieu ii p. 716*b*) the author says "that the original drafts had been scattered in various countries, and that he had now written what he describes as a sample of each, in order to comply with the desire of a noble friend in India".

226 Cf. Autobiography pp. 164–73, trans. pp. 176–90, where it is stated that of the *Kharābāt*, a *mathnawī* modelled on Saʿdī's *Būstān*, 1200 verses had been written [apparently at Mashhad between 1139 and 1142], but that it had never been completed. Some extracts are quoted in the autobiography, and the same extracts with others occur in the Lucknow and Cawnpore editions of the *Kulliyāt*.

227 Cf. Autobiography pp. 97–99, trans. pp. 106–9, from which it appears that this *mathnawī* was begun at Iṣfahān [evidently before 1127] and that it consisted of about 4000 verses.

228 And indeed of all the later MSS. of his poems. It is noteworthy that among the *muqaṭṭaʿāt* in the lithographed *Kullīyāt* (p. 920) are the lines on his father's death, which are quoted

Farhangnāmah. A seventh *mathnawī*, the *Wadī'at al-badī'ah*, written on the model of "Sanā'ī's" *Ḥadīqah*, when the author was about 70 years old (and therefore circ. 1173), is preserved in several MSS.[229] Apparently "Ḥazīn" did not collect any fifth *dīwān*, but he seems to have made additions to the fourth, since a *dīwān* preserved in the British Museum and containing *qaṣīdahs* and *ghazals* (the latter defective at the end) is described by Rieu (ii p. 717*a*) as being "richer than the corresponding sections in the preceding copies".

Twenty prose works, several of them *ḥawāshī* on standard text-books, are mentioned by title in "Ḥazīn's" autobiography (pp. 59, 82, 84, 96–7, 150, 162, 201, 237; trans. pp. 64, 92, 93, 105, 163, 175, 219, 256). Of these the *Risālah i tajarrud i nafs* written at Kirmānshāh (Autobiog. p. 150, trans. p. 163) must be similar to, if not identical with, the *Risālah dar tajarrud i nafs* or *Risālah dar ḥaqīqat i nafs u tajarrud*, preserved in several MSS. (Ethé 1903, Bānkīpūr iii p. 231, Ivanow-Curzon 502 (2), Ivanow 2nd Suppt. 1043 (5)). The extant *Faras-nāmah* (Bānkīpūr iii pp. 232, 234, Lindesiana p. 152, Rieu ii p. 483) was written in India as a substitute for an unprocurable work on farriery composed by the author at Iṣfahān in his youth [about 1127: see Autobiog. p. 97, trans. p. 106], and is "a mere sample" of that earlier work. None of the other prose works mentioned in the autobiography seem to be recorded in library catalogues, but several prose works by him, mostly short tracts, are extant. These include (1) *al-Lam'ah [min ?] Mir'āt Allāh fī sharḥ Āyat Shahida 'llāh*, an Arabic commentary on Sūrah iii 16 composed at Ardabīl in 1139 (MSS.: Ethé 1904, Ivanow-Curzon 752 (4), I.O. Cat. of Arabic MSS. ii 1165 (2)), (2) *Shajarat al-Ṭūr fī sharḥ Āyat al-Nūr*, an Arabic commentary on Sūrah xxiv 35 composed in 1140 at Mashhad (MSS.: Ethé 1904, Ivanow-Curzon 752 (3), I.O. Cat. of Arabic MSS. ii 1165 (1)), (3) *Taḥqīq i ma'ād i rūḥānī* (Bānkīpūr iii p. 233, Ivanow-Curzon 752 (1), Ivanow 2nd Suppt. 1043 (3)), (4) *Risālah i auzān i shar'ī*, or *Risālah dar auzān i mithqāl u dirham u dīnār wa-ghairah* (Bānkīpūr iii p. 232, Rieu ii p. 483, Ivanow-Curzon 502 (7)), (5) *Mas'alah i ḥudūth u qidam* (Bānkīpūr iii p. 232, Ivanow-Curzon 502 (3), Ivanow 2nd Suppt. 1043 (4)), (6) *Jawāb i ruqa'āt i Shaikh Ḥasan i marḥūm* (Bānkīpūr iii p. 232), (7) *Sharḥ i Qaṣīdah i Lāmīyah*, a commentary on a *qasīdah* of his own in praise of 'Alī (Bānkīpūr iii pp. 232, 235), (8) *Risālah i ṣaidīyah*, or *Risālah dar khawāṣṣ i ḥayawān* ('Alīgaṛh Subḥ. MSS. p. 8, Bānkīpūr iii p. 232, Rieu ii p. 483), (9) a short note on the Persian invasions of India completed at Ḥusainābād in 1180 (see no. 784 (3) *supra*), (10) *Dastūr al-'uqalā'*, on

in the autobiography (pp. 16–17, trans. pp. 15–16) and which were written long before the collection of any fourth *dīwān*.

229 E.g. Bodleian 1185 (?), 1184 (5),Bānkīpūr iii407, Blochet iii 1940, Browne Suppt. 1139 (1), Ivanow 862 (1).

administrative ethics, etc., composed at Delhi in 1153/1740 (MSS.: I.O. D.P. 1207, Ivanow-Curzon 502 (1)), (11) *Mawāʾid al-asḥār*, on Shīʿite theology (Browne Suppt. 1280), (12) *Mudhākarāt fī ʾl-muḥāḍarāt* (I.O. D.P. 1207), (13) *Maṣābīḥ al-ẓalām fī ārāʾ al-kalām* (Āṣafīyah i p. 170, under Balāghat). A long, but confessedly incomplete, list of his own works evidently compiled late in "Ḥazīn's" life is quoted in the *Nujūm al-samāʾ* (pp. 287–93).

The *Kullīyāt i Ḥazīn* published by Nawal Kishōr at [Lucknow] in 1293/1876°* and at Cawnpore in 1893 (cf. Browne *Lit. Hist.* iv p. 281 n. 5) contains (1) *Tārīkh i aḥwāl bi-tadhkirah i ḥāl i Maulānā-yi Shaikh Muḥammad ʿAlī Ḥazīn kih khwud nawishtah ast*, pp. 2–144, (2) [Preface to the 1155 *dīwān*, beginning] *Iftitāḥ i nāmah*, etc., pp. 145–50, (3) *Qaṣāʾid*, pp. 150–255, (4) *Dīwān* [i.e. *ghazals*], pp. 257–689, (5) *Mutafarriqāt*, pp. 691–748, (6) *Rubāʿīyāt*, pp. 749–89, (7) *Mathnawīyāt* [viz. *Ṣafīr i dil*, pp. 791–822, *Chaman u anjuman*,[230] pp. 823–38, *Mukhtaṣarī az kitāb i mathnawī i musammā bi-Kharābāt*, pp. 839–61, *Dībāchah i Maṭmaḥ al-anẓār*, pp. 863–9, *Farhang-nāmah*, pp. 871–87, *Fātiḥah u khātimah i mathnawī i mausūm bi-Tadhkirat al-ʿāshiqīn*, pp. 889–902], (8) *Muqaṭṭaʿāt*, pp. 903–29, (9) *Tadhkirah* [*al-muʿāṣirīn*], pp. 931–1031.

(1) (***Tadhkirat al-aḥwāl***),[231] an autobiography containing a considerable amount of historical information written at the end of 1154/1742 in Delhi: Sprenger 22, **Bānkīpūr** vii 624 (AH 1162/1749), 625 (AH 1281/1865), **Ivanow** 225 (circ. AH 1180/1766–7), 226 (18th cent.), 227 (19th cent.), **Ivanow-Curzon** 55 (18th cent.), 56 (18th cent.), **Lindesiana** p. 151 no. 446 (circ. AD 1780–90), no. 447 (circ. AD 1800), no. 559 (AH 1218/1803–4), **Bodleian** 383 (AH 1197/1783), **Browne** Suppt. 300 (before AD 1788. King's 74), **Rieu** ii 823*a* (late 18th cent.), i 381*a* (AH 1216/1801), ii 843*b* (AH 1244/1829), **Rehatsek** p. 218 no. 11 (apparently, AH 1214/1799), **I.O.** D.P. 674*a* (AH 1223/1808), **Ethé** 677 (AH 1227/1812), **I.O.** 3952 (AH 1259/1843), 3967(c), **Ross and Browne** 240 (2) (AH 1280/1864), **Vollers** 987 (2).

Editions: **London** 1831°* (*The Life of Sheikh Mohammed Ali Ḥazin ... edited ... by F. C. Belfour.* Persian title: *Tārīkh i aḥwāl bi-tadhkirah i ḥāl i Maulānā-yi Shaikh Muḥammad ʿAlī Ḥazīn kih khwud nawishtah ast.* Oriental Translation Fund), **Benares** 1851* (title ?), [**Lucknow**] 1293/1876°* (*Kullīyāt i Ḥazīn* pp. 2–144), **Cawnpore** 1893 (*Kullīyāt i Ḥazīn* pp. 2–144. Cf. Browne *Lit. Hist.* iv p. 281 n. 5), **Delhi** 1319/1902°* (*Sawāniḥ i ʿumrī i ... ʿAlī Ḥazīn*).

Translations:

230 Doubtless only the "sample" referred to above (no. 1150, 4th par., 1st footnote).

231 The author having given his work no formal title, various quasi-titles are found on the title-pages of MSS. and editions, e.g. *Tārīkh i aḥwāl i Ḥazīn*, *Ḥālāt i Shaikh ʿAlī Ḥazīn*, etc.

(1) *The Life of Sheikh Mohammed Ali Hazin ... translated ... by F. C. Belfour*, **London** 1830°* (Oriental Translation Fund), **Bombay** [1901*. "Part 2" only ?], **Bombay** [1910*. 2 pts.],

(2) *The translation of the Tarikh-i-ahwal of Mowlana Muhammad Shaykh Ali Hazin. With an introduction and appendix. By M. C. Master.* **Bombay** 1911°*.

(2) (***Tadhkirat al-muʿāṣirīn***), notices of about 100 contemporary poets of Persia written in nine days towards the end of 1165/1752 and divided into two *firqahs* ((1) *ʿulamāʾ* who wrote poetry, (2) professional poets): Sprenger 21, **Bānkīpūr** iii 407 (AH 1178/1764), 408 (19th cent.), Suppt. ii 2350, **Rieu** ii 873*b* (before AH 1182/1768), i 372*b* (AH 1193/1779), ii 843*b* (AH 1244/1829), **Ivanow** 228 (18th cent.), 229 (19th cent.), **Ethé** 678 (AD 1806), 679 (probably AH 1227/1812), **I.O.** D.P. 493 (*p*) (early 19th cent.), **I.O.** 586 (*a*) (AH 1249/1833), **I.O.** 3967 (*a*) (early 19th cent.). ʿ**Alīgaṛh** Subḥ. MSS. p. 60 no. 11 (AH 1245/1829–30), **Berlin** 655 (breaks off in the notice of "Shaghaf" Qummī).

Editions: *Kullīyāt i Ḥazīn* [**Lucknow**] 1293/1876°*, pp. 931–1025, **Cawnpore** 1893 (cf. Browne *Lit. Hist.* iv p. 281 n. 5), pp. 931–1025.

List and epitome of the biographies: Sprenger pp. 135–41.

Description: *JRAS.* ix (1848) pp. 147–9 (by N. Bland).

[*Tadhkirat al-aḥwāl; Tadhkirat al-muʿāṣirīn* (contains no autobiography, but autobiographical statements occur here and there: see Sprenger pp. 135–41); *Safīnah i Khwushgū* (summarised in Bānkīpūr viii p. 110); "Mubtalā" *Muntakhab al-ashʿār* (Bodleian 379 no. 187); "Wālih" *Riyāḍ al-shuʿarāʾ* (the main source of ʿAbd al-Muqtadir's account of "Ḥazīn" in Bānkīpūr iii pp. 223–7); *Majmaʿ al-nafāʾis; Khizānah i ʿāmirah* pp. 193–200 (no. 36); *Tārīkh i Muḥammadī; Ātash-kadah* no. 783; *Siyar al-mutaʾakhkhirīn*, Lucknow 1866, vol. ii pp. 615 [2–26], 632 [17], 672 [4], 743 [23], 744 [3 22], 746 [22–3], 776 [18], trans. Calcutta 1926, vol. ii pp. 176–8, 433–4, 525 and footnote; *Khulāṣat al-kalām* no. 19; *ʿIqd i Thuraiyā; Khulāṣat al-afkār* no. 86; Short anonymous account of "Ḥazīn" (MS.: I.O. 4036); *Makhzan al-gharāʾib* no. 652; *Mirʾāt i āftāb-numā; Ārāyish i maḥfil* (see no. 622, Free Urdu translation *supra*. The passage relating to "Ḥazīn" is translated in Garcin de Tassy's *Mémoire sur les particularités de la religion musulmane dans l'Inde*, Paris 1869, pp. 104–6); *Nishtar i ʿishq; Naghmah i ʿandalīb; Majmaʿ al-fuṣaḥāʾ* ii p. 94 (3 lines !); *Haft āsmān* pp. 161–4; *Shamʿ i anjuman* p. 130; *Nujūm al-samāʾ* pp. 283–93 (on pp. 287–93 a long list by "Ḥazīn" of his own works); Rieu i p. 372, ii pp. 715–16; Bānkīpūr iii pp. 223–7 (an account of some length based mainly on the *Riyāḍ al-shuʿarāʾ*); Browne *Lit. Hist.* iv pp. 115–18, 277–81; *Ency. Isl.* under Ḥazīn (Hidayet Hosain); *Shaikh Muhammad ʿAli Hazin, his life, times and works. By Sarfaraz Khan Khatak*, Lahore 1944 (see *Luzac's Oriental list*, Jan.–March 1946, p. 6. Not utilised above); etc.]

1151. **Afḍal Bēg Khān Qāqshāl**[232] **Aurangābādī.**
Tuḥfat al-shuʿarāʾ, written in 1165/1751–2 and dealing with poets of the Deccan who flourished under Niẓām al-Mulk I: **Āṣafīyah** i p. 316 no. 10 (AH 1185/1771–2. Cf. Nadhīr Aḥmad 77), iii p. 162 no. 122, **Madrās** 439 (defective at end).

1152. Mīr **M. Taqī "Mīr"** b. Mīr M. ʿAlī[233] was born at Āgrah about 1137/1724–5.[234] His grandfather had been *Faujdār* of the environs of Āgrah (*Dhikr i Mīr* p. 4³: *bah faujdārī i gird i Akbarābād sar-afrāz gasht*): his father was a pious *darwīsh*. At the age of ten or eleven he lost his father, sought employment without success at Āgrah, went to Delhi, was presented to the Amīr al-Umarāʾ Ṣamṣām al-Daulah [Khān i Daurān],[235] a friend of his father's, and was granted by him a pension of one rupee a day (*op. cit.* p. 62). This pension (*rūzīnah*) came to an end when the Amīr al-Umarāʾ died [in 1151/1739] of a wound received in Nādir Shāh's invasion (p. 63⁶). "Mīr" went again to Delhi, lived for a time with his elder brother's maternal uncle[236] Sirāj al-Dīn ʿAlī Khān "Ārzū" (for whom see no. 1149 *supra*), and studied under some of his Delhi friends (p. 63¹³: *u kitābī chand az*

232 A Turkish clan-name. Two members of this clan were *amīrs* in Akbar's reign, Majnūn Khān Qāqshāl (see *Āʾīn i Akbarī* tr. Blochmann pp. 369–70, *Maʾāthir al-umarāʾ* iii 207–11) and Bābā Khān Qāqshāl (see *Āʾīn i Akbarī* tr. Blochmann p. 369 n. 3, *Maʾāthir al-umarāʾ* i pp. 391–3, Beveridge's trans. pp. 335–7).

233 *Dhikr i Mīr* p. 62¹¹ (*chūn marā dīd pursīd kih īn pisar az kīst guft az Mīr Muḥammad ʿAlī ast*). Elsewhere in the *Dhikr i Mīr* (e.g. pp. 5¹³, 16⁴, 25¹³) he calls his father ʿAlī Muttaqī (not *Mīr* ʿAlī Muttaqī) and on p. 5⁴ he describes this appellation as a *khiṭāb* (*Jawān i ṣāliḥī ʿāshiq-pīshah būd dil i garmī* (or *dil-garmī* ?) *dāsht ba-khiṭāb i ʿAlī Muttaqī imtiyāz yāft*). These passages seem to show that his real name was Mīr M. ʿAlī and that on account of his piety he was nicknamed or surnamed ʿAlī Muttaqī. Apparently those authorities who give his name as Mīr ʿAbd Allāh are wrong.

234 "Mīr" says in the *Dhikr i Mīr* (p. 152¹²) that he had reached the age of sixty (*aknūn kih pīrī rasīd yaʿnī ʿumr i ʿazīz ba-shaṣt-sālagī kashīd*). The date of the *dhikr i Mīr* appears to be 1197/1783 (according to a chronogram quoted in ʿAbd al-Ḥaqq's introduction but absent from the printed text of the work itself, presumably because it occurs in the *khātimah*, a collection of "facetiæ" omitted by ʿAbd al-Ḥaqq). It is true that on the page immediately preceding that on which "Mīr" gives his age as sixty he refers to the blinding of Shāh-ʿĀlam by Ghulām-Qādir, an event of 1202/1788, but this may well be a later insertion. In any case it cannot be supposed that his birth took place sixty years before 1202, i.e. in 1142, since in that case he would have been only nine years old in 1151/1738–9, whereas we know that he was at least ten when his father died (p. 54¹⁶: *al-Ḥamdu li-llāh kih dah-sālaʾī*, in his father's words), and that for some time after that event he had been in receipt of a pension from the Amīr al-Umarāʾ Ṣamṣām al-Daulah [Khān i Daurān], which terminated on the latter's death [in 1151/1739] from a wound received at the Battle of Karnāl.

235 Khwājah ʿĀsim, for whom see *Maʾāthir al-umarāʾ* i pp. 819–22.

236 *khālū-yi birādar i kalān* (p. 63¹⁶), that is to say, the mother of "Mīr's" half-brother was "Ārzū's" sister. Elsewhere (pp. 73⁸, 75¹) Mīr calls "Ārzū" *khālū* or *khālū-yi man*.

yārān i shahr khwāndam). He complains bitterly of the unfriendly treatment that he received from "Ārzū" (pp. 63^{18}–64^{7}). After leaving "Ārzū's" house he was for some time the protégé, or perhaps the employee, of Riʿāyat Khān (p. 67 ult.: *bā khwud rafīq-am kard tamattuʿī az-ū bastam u az qaid i tang-dastī rastam*); subsequently he was in the service of the Nawwāb Bahādur[237] (p. 71^{6}: *talāsh i rūzgār ba-khānah i Nawwāb Bahādur kardam u naukar shudam*), until his murder [in 1165/1752] deprived him of employment (p. 72^{7}). In the long period of his residence at Delhi he found either employers or patrons in a number of prominent Muslims and Hindus, but his autobiography contains several references to straitened circumstances. In 1197/1783[238] he migrated to Lucknow at the invitation of Āṣaf al-Daulah (p. 138 ult.), and there he lived in receipt of a stipend[239] from Āṣaf al-Daulah (d. 1212/1797) and his successor, Saʿādat-ʿAlī Khān (1798–1814), until his death in 1225/1810.

"Mīr" is regarded as one of the greatest Urdu poets. According to ʿAbd al-Ḥaqq (*Ency. Isl.* under Urdu) "his ghazals and mathnawīs are by far the best to be found in Urdū literature". His *Kullīyāt* were published at Calcutta in 1811 and at Lucknow in 1867 and 1874. Several of his works have been published separately. His Urdu writings do not concern us here, but the two following are in Persian.

(1) ***Nikāt al-shuʿarāʾ***, about 100 short notices of Rēkhtah (i.e. Urdu) poets written nearly one year after the death of "Mukhliṣ",[240] which occurred in 1164/1751 (see no. 780 1st par. *supra*): Sprenger no. 42, **Bodleian** 392 (AH 1211/1796), **Berlin** 668 (AD 1852), **Rāmpūr** (see *OCM*. VI/2 (Feb. 1930) p. 114).

Edition: **Aurangābād** (Badāyūn printed) [1920*] (Anjuman i Taraqqī i Urdu. With Urdu introduction by Ḥabīb al-Raḥmān Khān Shirwānī).

(2) ***Dhikr i Mīr***, an autobiography containing a good deal of historical information written (mainly ?) at the age of sixty:[241] Sprenger p. 627, **Etawah** K. B. Maulawī Bashīr al-Dīn Aḥmad's private library (AH 1222/1807), **Lahore** K. B. Maulawī M. Shafīʿ's private library.

237 Jāwīd Khān, a eunuch who became a great favourite of Aḥmad Shāh and was murdered by Ṣafdar-Jang (see Beale *Oriental biographical dictionary* under Jawid Khan).

238 This date, not mentioned by "Mīr", who seems to have had little interest in dates, is given in the Urdu *tadhkirahs Gulshan i Hind* and *Gulzār i Ibrāhīm* cited by ʿAbd al-Ḥaqq, *Dhikr i Mīr*, introduction p. *ṣād*).

239 *Majmūʿah i naghz* ii p. 229 penult.: *ba-ṣīghah i shāʿirī ba-mawājib i mablagh i dū ṣad rūpiyah mulāzim i sarkār i daulat-madār i Nawwāb i ghufrān-maʾāb Wazīr al-Mamālik Āṣaf al-Daulah Yaḥyā Khān Bahādur gashtah.*

240 *Qarīb i yak-sāl ast kih dar gudhasht* (p. 10 in the Berlin MS.).

241 See no. 1152 2nd footnote *supra*.

Edition: **Aurangābād** 1928* (Anjuman i Taraqqī i Urdū. With Urdu introduction by ʿAbd al-Ḥaqq).

[*Dhikr i Mīr* and the editor's Urdu introduction; *Makhzan al-gharāʾib* no. 2684; *Majmūʿah i naghz* ii pp. 229–54; *Gulshan i bī-khār*; various Urdu *tadhkirahs* and other works; Sprenger pp. 175, 627; Garcin de Tassy ii pp. 305–21; Blumhardt's Catalogue of Hindustani MSS. in the I.O. Library, p. 85 and elsewhere; Saksena *History of Urdu literature* pp. 70–80; *Ency. Isl.* under Mīr (Hidāyat Ḥusain) and under Urdū (ʿAbd al-Ḥaqq); T. Grahame Bailey *History of Urdu literature* pp. 47–50.]

1153. **Fatḥ-ʿAlī**, commonly called (*al-madʿū bi-*) ʿAlī, **Ḥusainī Gardēzī** or, as he is called in the *Majmūʿah i naghz*, S. (Mīr) Fatḥ-ʿAlī Khān Ḥusainī, was, according to that work (ii p. 20[14]), the elder brother of S. Ghālib ʿAlī Khān "ʿIyān", one of the Saiyids of Gardēz.[242] His father, therefore, was S. ʿIwaḍ Khān, who in the reign of Aḥmad Shāh was Deputy-Governor of the province of Lahore. S. Fatḥ-ʿAlī adopted the life of a *ṣūfī* and became an influential *shaikh*. In the *Majmūʿah i naghz*, which was completed in 1221/1806–7, his name is mentioned incidentally several times (vol. ii pp. 20, 184, 355, 369) and is followed by formulæ (*sallamahu Rabbuhu* and the like) showing that he was still alive at the time of writing (possibly long before 1221).

Tadhkirah i ʿAlī i Ḥusainī i Gardēzī, an alphabetically arranged *tadhkirah* of about 100 Urdu poets written at Delhi six years after the death of "Anjām" (and therefore in 1165/1751–2,[243] if the authorities cited by Sprenger, p. 203, are correct in saying that "Anjām" died in 1159): Sprenger no. 43, **Ethé** 698 (AH 1180/1766–7), 699 (AH 1216/1802), 700 (B.S. 1213/1805), **Ivanow** 233 (defective. Late 18th cent.), 1st Suppt. 767 (late 18th cent.), **Madras** 437 (*l*) (AH 1230/1815), **Bānkīpūr** Suppt. i 1787 (19th cent.), **Rieu** iii 1071*a* (19th cent.).

Edition: *Tadhkirah i Rēkhtah-gōyān*, **Aurangābād** date ? (Anjuman i Taraqqī i Urdu. With introduction by ʿAbd al-Ḥaqq. See a review in OCM. x/3 (May 1934) p. 134).

242 According to Khwājah ʿAbd al-Majīd's Urdu dictionary *Jāmiʿ al-lughāt*, s.v. Gardēzī, the Gardēzī Saiyids are a clan (*qabīlah*) of Saiyids settled at Muẓaffargaṛh (in the Panjāb). Gardēz, from which doubtless their ancestor, or ancestors, migrated, is in Afghānistān, some fifty miles from Ghaznī.

243 The date 1172 is mentioned in the *Oriental College Magazine* x/3, p. 134, and this, if based on Prof. ʿAbd al-Ḥaqq's researches, is doubtless more correct.

[*ʿIyār al-shuʿarāʾ* under Yūsuf (cf. Sprenger p. 178); *Majmūʿah i naghz* ii p. 20[14]; Garcin de Tassy i pp. 523–4; ʿAbd al-Ḥaqq's introduction to his edition (not utilised above).]

1154. Sh. M. Qiyām al-Dīn **"Qāʾim" Chāndpūrī** belonged to Chāndpūr (presumably the place of that name 19 miles S. of Bijnaur), but he went early in life to Delhi and obtained employment under the Emperor. According to Saksena he was *Dārōghah* of the Royal Armoury. When he wrote his *Makhzan i nikāt* (in 1168/1754–5), he had left Delhi owing to the decay of the empire. The date of his death is variously given (1202/1787–8, 1207/1792–3, 1208/1793–4, 1210/1795–6). He was himself an Urdu poet and the author of a *dīwān* (for which see Blumhardt's I.O. catalogue of Hindustani MSS., no. 143, and Sprenger p. 631). According to T. Grahame Bailey his poems were published in 1927.

Makhzan i nikāt (a chronogram = 1168/1754–5), a *tadhkirah* of Rēkhtah (i.e. Urdu) poets: Sprenger no. 44 (Mōtī Maḥall, autograph), **Ethé** 701.

Edition: **Aurangābād** 1929 (ed. ʿAbd al-Ḥaqq. See *BSOS*. v/4 (1930) p. 928).

[Autobiography at end of *Makhzan i nikāt* (summarised in Sprenger p. 179); Sprenger p. 179; Garcin de Tassy i pp. 360–71; Blumhardt *Catalogue of the Hindustani manuscripts in the Library of the India Office* pp. 74–5; Saksēna *A history of Urdu literature* p. 97; ʿAbd al-Ḥaqq's introduction to his edition of the *Makhzan i nikāt* (not utilised above): T. Grahame Bailey *A history of Urdu literature* p. 50.]

1155. Sirāj al-Dīn **"Sirāj"** Ḥusainī **Aurangābādī**, a Ṣūfī poet in Persian and Urdu, died in 1177/1763–4.

Majmūʿah i shuʿarāʾ or ***Dīwān i muntakhab***, an anthology completed in 1169/1755–6 from the works of about 680 poets without biographical details apart from dates of death: Sprenger no. 29 (F. Hall) = **Ethé** 691 (AH 1191/1777).

List of the poets: Sprenger pp. 149–51.

[*Majmūʿah i naghz* I p. 293; Sprenger pp. 148–9, 292; Garcin de Tassy III pp. 145–7; *Ṣubḥ i gulshan* p. 200; etc.]

1156. Nawwāb Ṣamṣām al-Daulah **Shah-nawāz Khān** Mīr ʿAbd al-Razzāq b. Ḥasan ʿAlī Ḥusainī Khwāfī **Aurangābādī** was born at Lahore on 28 Ramaḍān 1111/20 March 1700 and murdered at Aurangābād on 3 Ramaḍān 1171/11 May 1758. An account of his life will be given later in this fasciculus; when the time comes to deal with the *Maʾāthir al-umarāʾ*, his best-known work. At this point it will be sufficient to note that Ghulām-ʿAlī "Āzād" describes him as *shiʿr-fahm i bī-naẓīr*

(*Khizānah i ʿāmirah* p. 56[3]. Cf. *Maʾāthir al-umarāʾ* i p. 35[12]: *u dar shiʿr-fahmī dam i yaktāʾī mī-zad*).

Bahāristān i sukhun, a *tadhkirah* of ancient and modern poets left incomplete at the author's death in 1171/1758 and completed in 1194/1780 by his son, Mīr ʿAbd al-Ḥaiy (according to the *Sawāniḥ i Dakan* cited by Rieu iii p. 1025*a*): **Āṣafīyah** i p. 316 no. 17, iii p. 162 no. 121 (AH 1194/1780), no. 193 (AH 1204/1789–90) **Madras** p. 542 no. 528 (AH 1259/1843).

1157. S. **ʿAbd al-Wahhāb** "Iftikhār" Bukhārī **Daulatābādī**, a descendant of S. Jalāl Bukhārī called Makhdūm i Jahāniyān,[244] was born at Aḥmadnagar but settled at Daulatābād on his marriage to the daughter of S. Murtaḍā Khān, commandant of the fort.[245] His instructor in the art of poetry was Mīr Ghulām-ʿAlī "Āzād" Bilgrāmī (for whom see no. 1162 *infra*). M. Mīranjān, who did not know the precise date of his death, says that he died towards the end of the eighth decade of the twelfth century (*tā awākhir i ʿasharah i thāminah i miʾah i ithnā-ʿashar*).

Bī-naẓīr (a chronogram = 1172/1758–9), notices of 136 poets of the 12th/18th century.

Edition: *Tazkira-e-Benazir*, Allahabad 1940 (ed. S. Manẓūr ʿAlī. Allahabad Univ. Arabic-Persian Series, 1. See *JRAS*. 1941 p. 198).

[*Sarw i āzād; Khāzin al-shuʿarāʾ* fol. 38*a*]

1158. Mīr **ʿAlī Shēr "Qāniʿ" Tattawī**, born in 1140/1727–8, was still alive in 1202/1787–8 (see nos. 165, 828 *supra*).

Maqālāt al-shuʿarāʾ (a chronogram = 1174/1760–1, the date of completion), alphabetically arranged notices of the poets of Sind: **Rieu** ii 848*a* (AH 1246/1830), **I.O.** 4397 (AH 1271/1855).

1159. Sh. Qiyām al-Dīn **"Ḥairat"** b. Sh. Amān Allāh **Akbarābādī.**

Maqālāt al-shuʿarāʾ (a chronogram = 1174/1760–1), short notices of 150 poets who flourished from the time of Aurangzēb to that of ʿĀlamgīr II (d. 1173/1759): Sprenger no. 31 (Mōtī Maḥall), **Rāmpūr** (AH 1228/1813. See *OCM*. VI/2 (Feb. 1930) pp. '114–16).

List and epitome of the biographies: Sprenger pp. 153–60.

1160. **Naqsh ʿAlī** wrote in India.

Bagh i maʿānī (probably a chronogram = 1174/1760–1, but there are later additions), an extensive but concise dictionary of Persian poets: Sprenger

244 For whom see *Ency. Isl.* under Djalāl and the index to the present work.

245 For whom see *Maʾāthir al-umarāʾ* III pp. 644–5.

p. 152 (*Chamans* iii (Kings), iv (Wazīrs and Amīrs) and v (322 poets from time of Hārūn al-Rashīd to AH 800/1397–8). Mōtī Maḥall), **Bānkīpūr** viii 698 (*Chamans* vi and vii (?). Poets, mainly Indian or connected with India, from the 9th/15th century to the author's time, defective, ending with "Ẓarīf". Probably autograph), **Rieu** iii 1022*b* (extracts from *Chamans* iii and iv. Circ. AD 1850).

1161. **Durgā Dās.**

Safīnah i ʿishrat (a chronogram = 1175/1761–2), alphabetically arranged notices of ancient and modern poets: **Bānkīpūr** viii 699 (breaks off in *sīn*. 19th cent.).

1162. Ḥassān al-Hind[246] Mīr **Ghulām-ʿAlī "Āzād"** b. S. M. Nūḥ Ḥusainī Wāsiṭī[247] **Bilgrāmī** Ḥanafī Chishtī[248] was born at Bilgrām[249] on 25 Ṣafar 1116/29 June 1704. It was there that he received instruction in the *kutub i darsīyah* from Mīr Ṭufail Muḥammad Utraulawī Bilgrāmī (for whom see *Subḥat al-marjān* pp. 90–4, Raḥmān ʿAlī p. 98, etc.). In 1134/1721–2 he went to Delhi and remained there for two years studying Arabic lexicology (*lughat*), the Traditions and the life of the Prophet and belles lettres (*ḥadīth u siyar i Nabawī u funūn i adab*) with his maternal grandfather, Mīr ʿAbd al-Jalīl Bilgrāmī (for whom see no. 952 1st par. *supra*, footnote, and *Islamic culture* ii/1 (Jan. 1928) p. 133). Possibly it was in these same two years that his maternal uncle, Mīr M. b. ʿAbd al-Jalīl Bilgrāmī (for whom see no. 952 *supra*) taught him prosody and certain branches of *adab*. At the end of 1142/1730 he left Bilgrām for Sīwistān (i.e. Sehwan, in Sind) at the request of his uncle,[250] the aforesaid Mīr M. b. ʿAbd al-Jalīl Bilgrāmī, who was *Mīr Bakhshī* and *Waqāʾiʿ-nigār* at that town. Having appointed him, or caused him to be

246 Like Ḥassān b. Thābit (for whom see *Ency. Isl.*, etc.) "Āzād" composed Arabic *qaṣīdahs* in praise of the Prophet (quotations from some of these *qaṣāʾid i Nabawīyah* are made in the *Subḥat al-marjān*, e.g. twenty or so on pp. 218–20). The title dates back to "Āzād's" lifetime, since it occurs in the puff by his pupil, Qāḍī ʿAbd al-Qādir "Mihrbān" Aurangabadi, appended to the *Subḥat al-marjān* (p. 297 [19]).

247 For the Wāsiṭī Saiyids, who claim descent from a Saiyid said to have migrated from Wāsiṭ to India in the reign of Sulṭān Maḥmūd Ghaznawī (or at some other time), see *Āʾīn i Akbarī* tr. Blochmann i pp. 390–5, Blumhardt *Cat. of the Hindustani MSS. in the I.O. Library* pp. 21–22, etc.

248 *wa-'l-Ḥanafī madhhab*^{an} *wa-'l-Chishtī ṭarīqat*^{an} (*Subḥat al-marjān* p. 118 [16]).

249 15 miles South of Hardoi in Oudh. See *Ency. Isl. s.v.*

250 *Wa-fī sanati thalāth wa-arbaʿīn wa-miʾah wa-alf ṭalabanī 'l-khāl … ilā baldati Sīwistān* (*Subḥat al-marjān* p. 88[5]). In the *Khizānah i ʿāmirah* (p. 124[11]) Dhū 'l-Ḥijjah 1142 is given as the date of his leaving Bilgrām for Sīwistān.

appointed,[251] his *nā'ib*, Mīr Muḥammad went back to Bilgrām for four years. It was in 1147/1734 that "Āzād" on his return-journey from Sīwistān met "Ḥazīn" at Bhakkar, as has already been mentioned (no. 1150, 2nd par., 1st footnote *supra*). In Rajab 1150/Nov. 1737 he left Bilgrām on a pilgrimage to the Ḥijāz, sailed from Sūrat on 24 Dhū'l-Qa'dah, reached Jiddah on 18 Muḥarram 1151/8 May 1738, Mecca on 23 Muḥarram and al-Madīnah on 25 Ṣafar. Here he studied the *Ṣaḥīḥ* of al-Bukhārī under M. Ḥayāt Sindī Madanī (for whom see *Subḥat al-marjān* pp. 95–7, Raḥmān 'Alī pp. 186–7, Brockelmann Supptbd. ii p. 522). At the end of this year he performed the *ḥajj* and on 3 Jumādā I 1152/8 Aug. 1739 he sailed from Jiddah, reaching "Swally" on the 29th of that month and Sūrat on the 2nd of Jumādā II. After a stay of five months at Sūrat he settled at Aurangābād, where he spent the next seven years in seclusion at the *takyah* of Shāh Musāfir Ghujduwānī. Towards the end of 1159/1746 he became the friend and constant companion of Nawwāb Niẓām al-Daulah Nāṣir-Jang, Āṣaf-Jāh's second son,[252] who in 1161/1748 succeeded his father as *Ṣūbah-dār* of the Deccan (i.e. as Niẓām of Ḥaidarābād), and who was murdered in Muḥarram 1164/December 1750. According to Shams Allāh Qādirī "Āzād" received a stipend from Nāṣir-Jang, and this is not unlikely, but he resisted suggestions that he should seek office[253] and doubtless maintained this attitude to the end of his life. At any rate he describes himself in the *Khizānah i 'āmirah* (p. 125[12]) as living at Aurangābād in retirement at the age of sixty-one (*chand bār ba-tamāshā-yi aṭrāf i mulk i Dakan bar-khāstam aknūn dar dār al-amn i Aurangābād gūshah-gīr-am* ...). Shortly before this, in 1170/1757, when his great friend, the Prime Minister Ṣamṣām al-Daulah Shāh-nawāz Khān, was dismissed from office, "Āzād"—one of the few who remained faithful to the fallen minister—exerted himself on his behalf and took a prominent part in the negotiations which ended in his restoration to favour (*Ma'āthir al-umarā'* i pp. 28–9, Beveridge's trans. p. 22). In the following year, when Shāh-nawāz Khān's house was looted after his murder (3 Ramaḍān 1171/11 May 1758) and the unfinished manuscript of his great work, the *Ma'āthir al-umarā'*, disappeared, "Āzād" instituted a search, recovered eventually [most of] the dispersed fragments (see vol. i pp. 3, 11–12, trans.

251 *Wa-ja'alanī nā'ib[an] fī dhālika 'l-makān* (*Subḥat al-marjān* p. 88[6]): *u ān-janāb faqīr rā niyābat i har dū khidmat muqarrar kardah* (*Khizānah* p. 124[15]).

252 *wa-fī awākhiri sanati tis'ah* [*sic*] *wa-khamsīn wa-mi'ah wa-alf ḥaṣalat al-muwāfaqah bainī wa-bain al-Nawwāb Niẓām al-Daulah Nāṣir-Jang khalaf al-Nawwāb Niẓām al-Mulk Āṣaf-Jāh fa-aḥabbanī ḥubban 'ajaz al-qalam 'an bayānihi wa-rafa'anī makān[an] mā ḥāma aḥad[un] ḥauma arkānihi wa-kāna lā yada'unī fī 'l-ẓa'n wa-'l-iqāmah wa-lā yamallu min ṣuḥbatī ḥīn[an] min azminat al-istidāmah* (*Subḥat al-marjān* p. 122[5]).

253 *wa-lammā ... tawallā 'l-Nawwāb Niẓām al-Daulah Nāṣir-Jang ri'āsat al-Dakan ... bālagha 'l-aktharūna an akhtāra manṣib[an] min manāṣib al-imārah ... fa-nafaḍtu dhailī min al-habā' al-manthūr wa-mā miltu 'an jāddat al-istiqāmah ilā sharak al-ghurūr ...* (*Subḥat al-marjān* p. 122[16]).

pp. 3, 10), wrote a preface (*khuṭbah u tamhīd* = vol. i pp. 10–13) and a biography of Shāh-nawāz Khān (pp. 14–41) and inserted a few additional biographies.[254]

One of the last of the contemporary accounts of "Āzād" must be that published by William Chambers in the *Asiatick Miscellany*, vol. i, Calcutta 1785, pp. 496–7. It runs as follows:

> The author … [of the extracts mentioned in no. 1162 (17), Extracts *infra*] is at this day alive at Aurungabad, in the Decan, where, after a series of years spent in literary pursuits and extensive travels, he resides, in great repute, and with some splendour, at the age of eighty-five. The present Nizam has visited him twice in person at that city; and the Translator [i.e. W. Chambers] is in possession of the copy of a letter addressed to him, in the year 1775, by the celebrated Gâzy ud Dîn Khân, wherein he pays him the highest compliments. The work in question [i.e. the *Khizānah i ʿāmirah*] was published by him there in the sixty-first year of his age; and he is the author of several others in verse and prose: among which, he tells Gâzy ud Dîn Khân, in his answer to the above-mentioned letter, that his Arabick poems amounted to 4000 couplets, and his Persian to 8000; confessing, at the same time, that he was constantly adding something to each, though he had then passed the age of seventy. But his historical writings [e.g. the biographies of Āṣaf-Jāh and his sons, the account of the Marāṭ'hās, etc., in the *Khizānah i ʿāmirah*] are, to European readers, the most curious and valuable of his productions; and they have this particular recommendation, that he was the eye-witness of most of the facts which he relates, and has himself travelled over the countries which are the scene of his narrations:—circumstances that deserve to be more especially remarked, in regard to the ensuing Extracts, which have been the more readily selected, as they have a tendency to throw light on transactions, in which both the English and the French have been concerned, and, in their accounts of which, they have in some points differed from each other.

According to Wajīh al-Dīn Ashraf (*Baḥr i zakhkhār* (Rieu iii p. 976*b*) fol. 315) he died on 21 Dhū 'l-Qaʿdah 1200/15 September 1786[255] (see Rieu i

254 "Āzād's" edition, containing 260–290 biographies exists in several manuscripts. A much enlarged edition containing about 730 biographies, was completed in 1194/1780 by the author's son, Mīr ʿAbd al-Ḥaiy (Ṣamṣām al-Mulk) and was published at Calcutta in 1887–91 (Bibliotheca Indica. 3 vols.).

255 The date 1200 is given also in the *Khulāṣat al-afkār* and elsewhere. Rieu says that in the *Tārīkh i dil-afrūz* (cf. no. 1038 (1) *supra*) Ghulām-Ḥusain Khān "Jauhar", who saw "Āzād" at Aurangābād in 1198/1783–4, gives 1199/1784–5 as the date of his death.

p. 373b). He is buried at Rauḍah ("Rauza", "Roza", "Raoza") or K͟huldābād,[256] about seven miles from Daulatābād, and, according to T. W. Haig (*Historic landmarks of the Deccan*, Allahabad 1907, p. 58), "the fame of the poet's learning is such that parents take their children to his shrine in order that they may, by picking up with their lips a piece of sugar from the tomb, obtain both a taste for knowledge and the ability to acquire it.

Lists of "Āzād's" works are given in S. S͟hams Allāh Qādirī's Urdu *Qāmūs al-aʿlām* i coll. 33–5, the Bombay Univ. Cat. pp. 201–2 (based on the preceding), S. Wajāhat-Husain's article in the *JRASB*. 1936, Letters, pp. 123–30, and Brockelmann Supptbd. ii p. 600 (Arabic works only). The following list omits an Urdu work mentioned by S. Wajāhat-Ḥusain.

Arabic Works

(1) *Ḍauʾ al-darārī*, a commentary on al-Buk͟hārī's *Ṣaḥīḥ* to the end of the *kitāb al-zakāh* (*Subḥat al-marjān* p. 122 antepenult. No MSS. recorded?),

(2) *Subḥat al-marjān fī āt͟hār Hindustān*, written in 1177/1763–4 and divided into four *fuṣūl*, viz.:

(I, p. 4) on references to India in Qurʾānic commentaries and in the Traditions of the Prophet, originally an independent work completed at Arcot in S͟haʿbān 1163/1750 and entitled *S͟hammāmat al-ʿanbar fī-mā warada fī 'l-Hind min Saiyid al-Bas͟har*,[257]

(II, p. 24) biographies of Indian scholars, originally a part of the author's work *Tasliyat al-fuʾād*,[258] which also supplied material for *Faṣl* iii,

(III, p. 123) *fī muḥassināt al-kalām*, on certain rhetorical figures, viz., (*a*) 23 figures of Indian (i.e. Sanskrit) rhetoric, which the author exemplifies from Arabic poetry, especially his own (*maqālah* 1, p. 123), (*b*) 37 figures discovered or invented or first recognised as such by the author

---

256 For the vast cemetery of Rauḍah or K͟huldābād. which contains the tombs of Aurangzēb, Abū 'l-Ḥasan Quṭb-S͟hāh, Āṣaf-Jāh, some kings of Aḥmadnagar and several well-known saints, see Haig, *Historic Landmarks of the Deccan* pp. 56–8.

257 For MSS. of the S͟hammāmat al-ʿanbar see Āṣafīyah iii p. 258 nos. 853, 857, 859.

258 Cf. *Subḥat al-marjān* p. 122 antepenult. (*wa-Tasliyat al-fuʾād d͟hakartu fīhā baʿḍ qaṣāʾidī wa-fawāʾidī* [sic: read *fawāʾid?*] *uk͟har wa-qad naqaltu ʿanhā tarājim al-ʿulamāʾ wa-maṭālib uk͟hrā fī hād͟hā 'l-kitāb*), p. 123[10] (*al-maqālat al-ūlā fī 'l-muḥassināt allatī naqaltuhā ʿan al-Hindīyah ilā 'l-ʿArabīyah wa-'l-muḥassināt ḥilyah li-l-kalām muṭlaq*[an] *lākinna lahā jilwat*[an] *uk͟hrā fī 'l-kalām al-mauzūn fa-ʿalaiya an ad͟hkura hāhunā madḥ al-manẓūm min al-kalām wa-'l-ḥamāʾil al-manūṭah bi-ʿawātiq* [sic lege] *al-aqlām wa-qad ḥarrartu lahu faṣl*[an] *fī kitābī Tasliyat al-fuʾād fa-ajʿaluhu juzʾ*[an] [sic lege] *min hād͟hā 'l-sawād*).

himself (*maqālah* 2, p. 162: *fī 'l-muḥassināt allatī 'staḵhraja-hā 'l-mu'allif.* The first is *al-tafā'ul,* i.e. euphemism), (*c*) one figure invented by Amīr Ḵhusrau, namely *bū-qalamūn* (*maqālah* 3, p. 204), (*d*) two figures peculiar to the Arabs, viz. *ḥusn al-taḵhalluṣ* and *istiḵhdām al-muḍmar* (*maqālah* 4, p. 218), together with a *qaṣīdah badīʿīyah,* in which the foregoing figures are exemplified (*maqālah* 5, p. 220),

(IV, p. 234) *fī bayān al-maʿshūqāt wa-'l-ʿushshāq,* on the types of lovers depicted by the poets, in five *maqālahs,* (*a*) *fī bayān al-ghizlān,* introductory matter followed by an enumeration of the types of female lovers recognized by the Hindūs (*al-ṣāliḥah, al-muʿlinah, al-sūqīyah,* etc. p. 234), (*b*) types labelled by the author (*fī aqsām al-ghizlān allatī hiya min mustaḵhrajāt al-mu'allif,* p. 255. The first is *al-zā'irah fī 'l-ru'yā,* the second *al-nāfirah ʿan al-shaib,* and so on), (*c*) *al-qaṣīdat al-ghizlānīyah, a qaṣīdah* describing each of the foregoing types, p. 260, (*d*) *fī aqsām al-ʿushshāq,* on the types of male lovers, p. 263, (*e*) *al-qaṣīdat al-hayamānīyah,* a *qaṣīdah* on the types of male lovers, p. 295.

An edition of this curious work was published at [Bombay] in 1303/1886°*, and MSS. of it are preserved at Manchester (Cat. Arab. MSS. 292), the Calcutta Madrasah (p. 47 no. 88), and (extracts only) the British Museum (Rieu iii pp. 1022*b*, 1055*b*). A Persian translation of the third and fourth *faṣl* was made by the author himself and entitled *Ghizlān al-Hind* (a chronogram = 1178/1764–5). For MSS. see no. (12) below. A Persian translation of the first and second *faṣl* was made by S. Shams al-Dīn b. Shāh Wārith ʿAlī Ḥasanī Ḥusainī Banārasī at the request of the Rājah of Benares, Mahārāj Īsarī Parshād, in whose service the translator was in 1286/1869 (MS.: Bānkīpūr viii 653).

(3) *Dīwāns.* In the list of his own works given on pp. 122–3 of the *Subḥat al-marjān,* which was written in 1177/1763–4, "Āzād" mentions two Arabic *dīwāns* consisting of 3000 verses[259] (p. 122 penult.: *wa-l-dīwānān ... wa-jumlatu ashʿārī fī 'l-dīwānain thalāthatu ālāf wa-arsaltuhumā ila baʿḍ al-fuḍalā' bi-l-Madīnat al-Munawwarah*). Shams Allāh Qādirī in speaking of "Āzād's" Arabic *dīwān* [so—in the singular] says that it contains more than 3000 verses and that it was published in four volumes at Ḥaidarābād in 1300. The Āṣafīyah catalogue (i p. 696) records two MSS. and a printed (i.e. doubtless lithographed) edition, speaks of *har sih ḥiṣṣah,* but says nothing about place or date of publication. Sarkis (*Dictionnaire*

259 In the *Khizānah i ʿāmirah* written in 1176 only one Arabic *dīwān* is mentioned and this is said to consist of 3000 verses (p. 125[17]: *Dīwān i fārisī u ʿarabī i faqīr murattab ast. Dīwān i ʿarabī sih hazār bait bāshad*).

encyclopédique de bibliographie arabe, col. 1) records editions of (1) *al-dīwān al-awwal* completed in 1187[260] and lithographed at the Kanz al-ʿulūm Press, Ḥaidarābād, (2) *al-dīwān al-thānī* (pp. 59) printed (or lithographed) at the Lauḥ i maḥfūẓ Press, Ḥaidarābād,[261] and (3) *al-dīwān al-thālith* printed (or lithographed) at the Kanz al-ʿulūm Press without date. Seven *dīwāns* entitled *al-Sabʿat al-saiyārah* (beginning *Lamaḥat ilaiya bi-ʿainihā ʾl-kaḥlāʾu*) were begun in 1179 and completed in 1194 (Autograph MS.: Nawwāb Nūr al-Ḥasan's library, Lucknow. See Nadhīr Aḥmad in *JASB*. 1917 p. cxxxix, no. 152. According to S. Maqbūl Aḥmad Ṣamdanī, *Ḥayāt i Jalīl* ii p. 175 note 139, a selection from these seven *dīwāns* was published under the title *Mukhtār dīwān Āzād* at the Āsī Press, Lucknow, in 1328). A *dīwān i tāsiʿ* and a *dīwān i ʿāshir* are preserved at ʿAlīgaṛh (Subh. MSS. p. 126). For MSS. described simply as *Dīwān i Āzād* (*i Bilgrāmī*) see the ʿAlīgaṛh catalogue (Subḥ. MSS. p. 126), the Āṣafīyah catalogue (i p. 696) and the Rāmpūr Arabic catalogue (i p. 586).

(4) *Maẓhar al-barakāt*, a Ṣūfī *muzdawijah*, or *mathnawī*, in seven *daftars*, of which the first was completed in 1194/1780 and the second, third and fourth in 1195/1781, the rest being undated (MSS.: Āṣafīyah (autograph. See *Qāmūs al-aʿlām* col. 34), Manchester Arab. Cat. 481 (*a*), Princeton Arab. Cat. (1938) no. 136).

(5) *Shifāʾ al-ʿalīl fī iṣlāḥ*[262] *kalam Abī ʾl-Ṭaiyib al-Mutanabbī* (MS.: S. ʿAlī Ḥusain Bilgrāmī's library, Ḥaidarābād. See Nadhīr Aḥmad in *JASB*. 1917 p. cxxiii).

(6) *Kashkūl*[263] (MSS.: Āṣafīyah iii p. 642 nos. 242 (mainly autograph), 261).

Persian Works

(7) *Dīwān*, beginning *Bar-ār az madd i bi-smiʾllāhi tīgh i khwash-maqālī rā* (*Subḥat al-marjān* p. 123[8]. MSS.: Sprenger 146, Bānkīpūr iii 423, Ethé 1722, Ivanow-Curzon 304–6, Madras 75 (c) (*muntakhab*), and doubtless also Āṣafīyah iii p. 288 no. 830),

260 *Atamma taʾlīfahu sanata* 1187 according to Sarkis. If this *dīwān* is correctly described as *al-diwan al-awwal*, 1187 cannot be the date of collection. If 1187 is an error for 1287, that may be the date of printing (see the next note).

261 A copy of this second *diwān* is mentioned in the ʿAlīgaṛh catalogue (Subḥān Allāh Printed Books p. 25), and there 1287 is given as the date of printing.

262 Wajāhat-Ḥusain writes *iṣṭilāhāt* (as in the *Ḥadāʾiq al-Ḥanafīyah*), but the correctness of *iṣlāḥ* is shown by the words quoted by Nadhīr Aḥmad from the preface (*wa-lā yakhfā ʿalā ʾl-ṭabīb al-ṭārif bi-muʿālajat al-amrāḍ anna manṣib al-islāḥ aʿlā wa-arfaʿ min manṣib al-iʿtirāḍ fa-waqaʿa fī khāṭirī an uṣliḥa mā fī kalāmihi min al-fasād*).

263 Classed among the *Muḥāḍarāt i ʿArabī* in the Āṣafīyah catalogue. Shams Allāh Qādirī places it among "Āzād's" Persian works. It may of course contain extracts in both languages. Wajāhat-Ḥusain does not mention it.

(8) *Mathnawī ba-jawāb i Mathnawī i Mīr ʿAbd al-Jalīl i Bilgrāmī*[264] (MS.: Āṣafīyah iii p. 632),

(9) *Mathnawī i sarāpā-yi maʿshūq* (MS.: ʿAlīgaṛh Subḥ. MSS. p. 43 no. 90). It seems at least possible that this may be identical with the *Mirʾāt al-jamāl*, which is placed among the Persian MSS. in the catalogue of the Bibliotheca Lindesiana (p. 144 no. 592), though S. Wajāhat-Ḥusain, who gives references to *Itḥāf al-nubalāʾ* p. 331 and *Ḥadāʾiq al-Ḥanafīyah* p. 455, describes that work as "an Arabic poem containing 105 verses and describing the beauties of a beloved from head to foot". The language is not specified in the *Ḥadāʾiq al-Ḥanafīyah*: the *Itḥāf al-nubalāʾ* is not at the moment accessible.

(10) *Sanad al-saʿādāt fī ḥusn khātimat al-Sādāt* (*Subḥat al-marjān* p. 123[7]. MSS.: Āṣafīyah ii p. 1346 no. 372, iii p. 662 no. 101, Ethé 2670. According to Shams Allāh Qādirī an edition was published at Bombay in 1282/1865–6).

(11) *Ghizlān al-Hind* (a chronogram = 1178/1764–5), a translation of the third and fourth *faṣl* of the *Subḥat al-marjān* (no. 2 above) made at the request of the author's two friends, ʿAbd al-Qādir "Mihrbān" Aurangābādī (cf. no. 1162, 1st footnote *supra*) and Lachhmī Narāyan "Shafīq" Aurangābādī (cf. no. 641 *supra* and no. 1165 *infra*) (MSS.: Āṣafīyah i p. 168 no. 164, Berlin 1051, Ethé 2135, Nadhīr Aḥmad 310).

(12) *Shajarah i ṭaiyibah*, on the pedigrees and lives of the *shaikhs* of Bilgrām (*Qāmūs al-ʿalām* i col. 35. MSS.: Āṣafīyah i p. 322 no. 35, ii p. 1778 no. 114).

(13) *Rauḍat al-auliyāʾ*, written in 1161/1748, lives of ten saints buried at Rauḍah or Khuldābād, near Daulatābād, the first being al-Gharīb al-Hānsawī and the last "Āzād" himself (Edition: Aurangābād 1310/1892–3*. MSS.: Āṣafīyah i p. 320, iii p. 164, Ethé 655).

(14) *Maʾāthir al-kirām tārīkh i Bilgrām*, completed in 1166/1752–3 and divided into two *faṣls*, viz. (1) lives of about 80 *fuqarāʾ*, i.e. saints and mystics, connected, in some cases rather remotely, with Bilgrām and its neighbourhood, (2) lives of about 70 similar *fuḍalāʾ*, i.e. men of learning (Edition: Ḥaidarābād 1910 (with introduction by ʿAbd al-Ḥaqq. See *OCM*. III/2 (Feb. 1927) p. 33 footnote). MSS.: Āṣafīyah i p. 348 no. 105, Ethé 682 (sent by the author to Richard Johnson in 1785), Rieu iii 971*a*, Bānkīpūr viii 723, Berlin 603 (*Faṣl* 2 only. For a list of the biographies in this *faṣl* see Berlin pp. 567–8)).

264 Mīr ʿAbd al-Jalīl, "Āzād's" maternal grandfather, has already been mentioned (no. 1162, beginning *supra*). The *mathnawī* in question is doubtless that on the marriage of the Emperor Farrukh-siyar (Edition: Lucknow 1299/1882°*. MSS.: Nadhīr Aḥmad 210, Panjāb Univ. Lib., Āṣafīyah iii p. 632 (?). Cf. S. Maqbūl Aḥmad Ṣamdanī *Ḥayāt i Jalīl* ii pp. 62–72).

The second volume of this work is the *Sarw i āzād* (no. (16) below). The *Sharā'if i 'Uthmānī* of Ghulām-Ḥasan Ṣiddīqī Bilgrāmī (MSS.: Ivanow 277, I.O. 3913, Āṣafīyah iii p. 164) was written expressly for the purpose of correcting numerous alleged inaccuracies in the *Ma'āthir al-kirām*, and the *Sarw i āzād*. Another attack on the two volumes, more especially on "Āzād's" style and his poetry, is the *Taḥqīq al-sadād fī madhallat al-Āzād* written soon after 1167/1754 by M. Ṣiddīq "Sukhunwar" 'Uthmānī Bilgrāmī (MS.: Ivanow 397). A reply to the second attack is the *Ta'dīb al-zindīq fī takdhīb al-Ṣiddīq* of 'Abd al-Qādir Samarqandī Dihlawī (MS.: Ivanow 398).

(15) ***Yad i baiḍā'***,[265] alphabetically arranged lives of 532 ancient and modern poets, compiled originally at Sīwistān in 1145/1732–3 and thereupon published, later revised and enlarged at Allahabad in 1148/1735–6, and still further enlarged after the author's return from Mecca by additional matter sent to some friends for insertion: Sprenger no. 23, **Bānkīpūr** viii 691 (partly autograph), **I.O.** 3966 (b) (AH 1178/1764), **Āṣafīyah** iii p. 162 no. 186 (*Tadhkirah i Yad i baiḍā mausūm bah Tadhkirah i Ṣubḥ i khandān*. AH 1297/1880), no. 155 (*Tadhkirah i Ṣubḥ i khandān ya'nī Yad i baiḍā*).

(16) ***Sarw i āzād***, completed in 1166/1752–3 as the second volume of the work whose first volume is entitled *Ma'āthir al-kirām* (no. (14) above) and consisting likewise of two *faṣls*, viz. (1) notices of 143 poets who were born in India, or visited the country, after 1000/1591–2, including some learned men and poets of Bilgrām, (2) notices of 8 Rēkhtah (i.e. Urdū) poets: Sprenger no. 24, **Nadhīr Aḥmad** 86 (Ḥakīm 'Abd al-Ḥaiy, Lucknow. Autograph), **Āṣafīyah** i p. 320 no. 16 (AH 1194/1780), **Ivanow** 1st Suppt. 765 (AH 1223/1808), **Ivanow** Curzon 58 (19th cent.), **Lindesiana** p. 144 no. 330*g* (AH 1237/1821–2), **Ethé** 683 (n.d.), 684 (lacking *Faṣl* 2. AH 1265/1849), **Bānkīpūr** viii 697 (19th cent.), **Bombay** Univ. 122 (fragment only, 39 poets).

Edition: **Lahore** 1913* (published by the Āṣafīyah Book Depot, Ḥaidarābād. Cf. *OCM*. III/2 (Feb. 1927) p. 33 n. 2).

Lists of the poets: Ivanow-Curzon pp. 64–6 (132 Persian poets), Ivanow 1st Suppt. p. 7 (8 Urdu poets).

Criticisms: see under *Ma'āthir al-kirām* (no. (14) above).

(17) ***Khizānah i 'āmirah***, written in 1176/1762–3,[266] alphabetically arranged notices of about 135[267] ancient and modern poets, together with valuable

265 An alternative title, *Ṣubḥ i khandān*, is attributed to this work in the Āṣafīyah catalogue.

266 The death of Dargāh-Qulī Khān in 1180/1766 is recorded on p. 224 of the printed text.

267 In the Bodleian MS. the poets are 135, counting Āṣaf-Jāh, but not the other *amīrs*. Sprenger gives the number as 106.

biographies of Āṣaf-Jāh, his sons and some other contemporary nobles as well as historical accounts of the Marāṭ'hās and of Aḥmad S͟hāh Durrānī: Sprenger no. 25, **Lindesiana** p. 144 no. 319 (AH 1176/1762–3), no. 925 (AH 1196/1782), no. 320 (extracts. Circ. AD 1780), **Ethé** 685 (AH 1182/1768, transcribed from an autograph), 686(AH 1193/1779), 687–90 (four undated copies), 490 (historical extracts only), **I.O.** D.P. 644, **I.O.** 3991 (only the account of Āṣaf-Jāh, etc.), 4078, **Rieu** i 798*a* (first portion only, ending with the account of Aḥmad S͟hāh Durrānī, AH 1197/1783), 373*a* (fragment, breaking off in the notice of "Āzād". Late 18th cent.), 374*b* (extract, Āṣaf-Jāh to "Azād". Early 19th cent.), 374*b* (extract, Āṣaf-Jāh, his children, etc. AH 1232/1817), **Bodleian** 381 (AH 1199/1785), **Blochet** ii 1157 (18th cent.), 1158 (extracts. Late 18th cent.), **Āṣafīyah** i p. 318 no. 26 (AH 1221/1806–7), **Bānkīpūr** viii 700 (19th cent.), 658 (extract, Āṣaf-Jāh, etc. AH 1203/1789), Suppt. i 1788 (19th cent.), **'Alīgaṛh** Subḥ. MSS. p. 60 no. 20 (AH 1266/1849–50), **Ivanow** 232 (19th cent.), Curzon 59 (AH 1282/1865), **Browne** Pers. Cat. 115, **Browne** Coll. H. 23 (4) (only the account of Āṣaf-Jāh, etc.), **R.A.S.** P. 116 (possibly also P. 164 and P. 165).

Editions: **Cawnpore** 1871*, 1900°.

Extracts: (1) *A short history of the origin and progress of the Marratta State.*—[Persian text] *Extracted from the Khazanah e Aamerah* [Cawnpore editions pp. 39–47[13]], *and translated by William Chambers* (in *The Asiatick Miscellany*, vol. ii (**Calcutta** 1786*) pp. 86–122), (2) *Extracts from the Khazanah e Aamerah* [viz. *A short account of Naser Jung* (= Cawnpore editions pp. 54–56) and *A short account of Muzaffer Jung* (= Cawnpore editions pp. 59–60)].—*Translated by W. Chambers* [with the Persian text] (in *The Asiatick Miscellany*, vol. i (**Calcutta** 1785*) pp. 494–511).

Translations of extracts: (1) see Extracts (1) above, (2) see Extracts (2) above, (3) *History of Asof Jah, shewing by what means he acquired the Territory in the Dekhan, which is now in the Possession of his Son Nizaum-ul-Moolk; extracted from a Biographical Work, written in the Persian language* [= Cawnpore editions pp. 35^{8}–38^{2}], *and translated by Henry Vansittart* [without the Persian text] (in *The Asiatick Miscellany*, vol. i (**Calcutta** 1785*) pp. 327–31), (4) *The History of Ahmed Shah, King of the Abdallies, who are also called Duranees, from a Custom of wearing a Pearl in one of their Ears; extracted from the same Persian Book which furnished the History of Asof Jah* [= Cawnpore editions pp. 97–116 with omissions], *and translated by Henry Vansittart* [without the Persian text] (in *The Asiatick Miscellany*, vol. i (**Calcutta** 1785*) pp. 332–42).

List and epitome of the biographies: Bodleian coll. 255–60.

Descriptions: (1) *On the earliest Persian Biography of Poets ... By N. Bland* (in the *JRAS*. ix (1848)) pp. 152–3, (2) Sprenger pp. 143–5.

Sources: (1) Sprenger pp. 144–5, (2) Rieu i pp. 373–4, (3) Blochet ii pp. 328–9.

[Autobiographies in *Yad i baiḍā'* (AH 1148. Cf. Bānkīpūr viii pp. 115–16), *Rauḍat al-auliyā'* (AH 1161), *Ma'āthir al-kirām*, (AH 1166), *Sarw i āzād* (AH. 1166. Passage summarised in Bombay Univ. Cat. pp. 200–1), *Khizānah i 'āmirah* (AH 1176) no 13, pp. 123–45 (passage summarised by Bland, *JRAS*. ix (1848) pp. 150–2, Blochet, ii pp. 326–8, and much more briefly by Rieu, i p. 373, and 'Abd al-Muqtadir, Bānkīpūr iii pp. 252–3) and *Subḥat al-marjān* (AH. 1177) pp. 118–23; *Safīnah i Khwushgū* (passage summarised in Bānkīpūr viii p. 108[1-4]); *Riyāḍ al-shu'arā'*; *Gul i ra'nā* (a long biography by his pupil "Shafīq". Cf. Rieu iii p. 978*a*); *Asiatick Miscellany* i (Calcutta 1785) pp. 496–7 (passage quoted no. 1162, 3rd par. *supra* and in Bodleian Cat. col. 260); *Ṣuḥuf i Ibrāhīm* no. 199 (cf. Bland in *JRAS*. ix (1848) p. 152); *Khulāṣat al-afkār* no. 41 (summarised by Bland in *JRAS*. ix (1848) pp. 152–3); *Ārāyish i maḥfil* (for which see no. 622, Free Urdu translation *supra*. The passage is translated in Garcin de Tassy i p. 259); *Natā'ij al-afkār*; Bland in *JRAS*. ix (1848) pp. 150–3; Garcin de Tassy i pp. 259–60; *Ḥadā'iq al-Ḥanafīyah* (in Urdu) pp. 454–6; Raḥmān 'Alī pp. 154–5; Bānkīpūr iii pp. 252–3; *Ency. Isl.* under Ghulām 'Alī (unsigned); *Ḥayāt i Jalīl* (in Urdu), by S. Maqbūl Aḥmad Ṣamdanī, Allahabad 1929, vol. ii pp. 163–77; *Qāmūs al-a'lām* (in Urdu) by S. Shams Allāh Qādirī, pt. 1 (Ḥaidarābād 1935) coll. 32–5; Bombay Univ. Cat. pp. 200–3; *Āzād Bilgrāmī. By Sayyid Wajahat Husain* (in *JRASB*., 3rd series, Letters, vol. ii (1936) pp. 119–30); Brockelmann Supptbd. ii pp. 600–1.]

1163. As yet unidentified is—

A very large *tadhkirah* written probably between 1170/1757 and 1180/1766 and containing alphabetically arranged notices of 2200 poets, each letter forming a *ḥadīqah* subdivided into three *gulshans* ((1) ancient, (2) "mediaeval," (3) modern poets), the last of which comprises two *chamans* ((1) Īrān and Tūrān, (2) India): **Ethé** 692 (apparently a rough draft. No preface or colophon).

Here may be mentioned also—

Safīnat al-shu'arā', a large and apparently unfinished anthology of ancient and modern poets with useful biographies, written, at least partly, in 1170/1756–7 (mentioned on fol. 264*b* as the current year) by an unidentified author, who was an associate of Anand Rām "Mukhliṣ" (see no. 780 *supra*): **Ivanow** Curzon 326 (some 700 poets, about one-third of the work, very defective and much disarranged. Fol. 503. Late 18th cent. LIST OF POETS).

1164. For the *Tuḥfat al-kirām*, which was begun in 1180/1766–7 and completed in 1181/1767–8 by Mīr ʿAlī S͟hēr "Qāniʿ" Tattawī and which contains much biographical information concerning the celebrities of Sind and other places, see no. 828 (1) *supra*.

1165. **Lac͟hhmī Narāyan "Shafīq" Aurangābādī** has already been mentioned as the author of the *Ḥaqīqat-hā-yi Hindustān* (no. 641 (1) *supra*), the *Bisāṭ al-g͟hanāʾim* (p. 762), the *Tanmīq i s͟higarf* (p. 738), the *Maʾāthir i Āṣafī* (p. 750) and other works. For his life and other particulars see no. 641 *supra*.

(1) *C͟hamanistān i s͟huʿarāʾ*, notices of Rēk͟htah (i.e. Urdu) poets, written in 1761 and "taken largely from Mīr's *Nikāt us͟h S͟huʿarā*, 1752, and *Taẕkira e Fatḥ ʿAlī*, together with considerable additions of his own from earlier *taẕkiras*" (T. Grahame Bailey in *BSOS*. v/4 (1930) p. 927).

Edition: **Aurangābād** 1928 (ed. ʿAbd al-Ḥaqq. See *BSOS. loc. cit.*).

(2) *Gul i raʿnā*, begun in 1181/1767–8 and completed in 1182/1768–9, alphabetically arranged notices ("extremely rich in biographical detail") of Indian poets in two *faṣls*, (1) Muslims, (2) Hindus: **Bānkīpūr** viii 701 (1204 *Faṣlī*), **I.O.** 3692–3, **Rieu** iii 977*b* (extracts from *Faṣl* 1. 19th cent.), **Āṣafīyah** iii p. 162 no. 183 (ending with *fāʾ*), **Rehatsek** p. 161 nos. 121 (complete), 122 (defective, ending in *ẓāʾ*).

List and epitome of the biographies in *Faṣl* 2: **Bānkīpūr** viii pp. 129–34.

(3) *S͟hām i g͟harībān*, written in 1182/1768–9, a *tadhkirah* of poets of Persian birth who visited India (see Rieu iii 1085*b*): no MSS. yet recorded in any published catalogue ?

1166. It has already been mentioned (no. 167 *supra*) that **Yūsuf ʿAlī K͟hān** b. G͟hulām-ʿAlī K͟hān appended to his *Ḥadīqat al-ṣafāʾ* a k͟hātimah which is sometimes called the *Tadhkirah i Yūsuf ʿAlī K͟hān*.

(*Tadhkirah i Yūsuf ʿAlī K͟hān*), completed at Murshidābād in 1184/1770–1, short alphabetically arranged notices of about 300 ancient and modern poets with an appendix relating to 20 contemporary poets not included in "Ārzū's" *tadhkirah* (for which see no. 1149, *Majmaʿ al-nafāʾis*, *supra*): **Sprenger** no. 62, **Bodleian** 118 (autograph), **Berlin** 661 (AH 1213/1799), **Bānkīpūr** vi 480 (appendix only. 19th cent.), **Ivanow** 45.

List and epitome of the 20 biographies in the appendix: **Sprenger** pp. 193–4.

1167. For M. Aslam's *Farḥat al-nāẓirīn*, which was completed in 1184/1770–1 and of which the k͟hātimah contains notices of s͟haik͟hs, ʿulamāʾ and poets contemporary with Aurangzēb (published by M. S͟hafī' in *OCM*.), see no. 168 *supra*.

1168. Mīr **G͟hulām-Ḥasan** b. Mīr G͟hulām-Ḥusain b. Mīr 'Azīz Allāh Rātmanā'ī [?].
Tad͟hkirah i suk͟hun-āfrīnān i Hindī-zabān, meagre notices of a large number of Urdu poets written apparently in 1191/1777: **Ivanow** Curzon 62 (AD 1861).

1169. S. **G͟hulām-Ḥusain "S͟hōris͟h"**, familiarly called Mīr Bhainā, was a native of Patna. When he compiled his *tad͟hkirah* he had already written a Persian *dīwān* of about 4000 verses. According to Sprenger, who does not specify his authority, he died in 1195/1781.
Tad͟hkirah i S͟hōris͟h, short notices of 314 Urdu poets compiled probably in 1193/1779, "for the latest date that occurs in it is 1192, and men who died in 1194 are mentioned as being alive" (Sprenger): Sprenger no. 46 = **Bodleian** 387.
[Sprenger p. 182; Garcin de Tassy iii pp. 134–5.]

1170. Ḥājjī **Luṭf-'Alī Bēg "Ād͟har"** b. Āqā K͟hān Bēgdilī[268] S͟hāmlū Iṣfahānī was born at Iṣfahān on 20 Rabī' II 1134/7 Feb. 1722,[269] the year of Maḥmūd K͟hān's

---

[268] This Turcoman clan-name is explained by Luṭf-'Alī Bēg early in the historical introduction with which the second *Mijmarah* of the *Ātas͟h-kadah* opens. Bēgdil K͟hān, according to him, was the third of the four sons of Ildigiz K͟hān, who was the third of the six sons of Og͟hūz K͟hān. [For this eponymous ancestor of the Oghuz Turks see the articles Ghuzz, Toghuzghuz and Turks in the *Ency. Isl.*] In the time of Maḥmūd G͟haznawī, or in that of Chingīz K͟hān, the Bēgdilīs with other Turkish tribes migrated to Persia and, while some remained there, others went on and settled in Syria. In Tīmūr's reign Amīr Jahāngīr, when campaigning in Syria, recognized the Syrian Bēgdilīs as his countrymen and led them back to Persia with the intention of restoring them to Turkistān. On reaching Ardabīl, however, the Bēgdilī leaders had the honour of meeting Sulṭān 'Alī Siyāh-pūs͟h Ṣafawī [Sulṭān K͟hwājah 'Alī, as he is called in the *Silsilat al-nasab i Ṣafawīyah* p. 45 (=*JRAS*. 1921 p. 407)] and, having solicited his intercession, they obtained permission to leave the Tīmūrid camp (*urdū-yi Tīmūrī*) and stay at Ardabīl as *murīds* of that saintly personage. In the 250 years since S͟hāh Ismā'īls accession they had given faithful service to the Ṣafawī family and many of them had held high positions. The descendants of those Bēgdilīs who had returned from Syria were known as Bēgdilī S͟hāmlū, while the descendants of those who had never gone to Syria were called simply Bēgdilī [see *JRAS*. 1843 pp. 380–1, where a less corrupt text than that of the 1277 edition is summarised. Cf. the articles Ḳizil-bās͟h and S͟hāh-sewan in the *Ency. Isl.*].

[269] The incorrect date 1123/1711 given by Browne comes from the corrupt 1277 edition of the *Ātas͟h-kadah*. Its incorrectness is shown by the words which immediately follow: *u muqārin i īn ḥāl fitnah i Maḥmūd i G͟h.lijān* [sic, for *G͟hiljāy*] *i Afg͟hān rūy dādah*.

Afghān invasion,[270] on account of which his family fled from Iṣfahān to Qum, his home for the next fourteen years. At the beginning of Nādir Shāh's reign [AH 1147/1736–1160/1747] his father[271] was appointed Governor (*ḥākim*) of Lār and the coast of Fārs (*sawāḥil i Fārs*), and Luṭf-ʿAlī Bēg moved from Qum to Shīrāz. Two years later his father died near Bandar i ʿAbbāsī, and he went with his paternal uncle, Ḥājjī M. Bēg, on a pilgrimage to Mecca and al-Madīnah and then to the sanctuaries of al-ʿIrāq. Having spent a year in Fars, he set out on a pilgrimage to Mashhad and he was there when Nādir Shāh reached the town [in Shawwāl 1153/Dec. 1740] on his return from his campaigns in India and Turkistān. When Nādir Shāh left Mashhad for the Lesghian mountains [*Jibāl i Lakzīyah*, to punish the Lesghians[272] of Dāghistān for the murder of his brother, Ibrāhīm Khān], Luṭf-ʿAlī Bēg went with the army through Māzandarān to Ādharbāyjān. From there he returned to his birthplace, Iṣfahān. After Nādir Shāh's death he was in the service of ʿAlī Shāh,[273] Ibrāhīm Shāh,[274] Shāh Ismāʿīl[275] and Shāh Sulaimān[2764] (*baʿd az qatl i Nādir Shāh chandī dar silk i mulāzimān i rikāb i ʿAlī Shāh u Ibrāhīm Shāh u Shāh Sulaimān būdah*, to quote his own words). At the time when Ibrāhīm Mīrzā [afterwards Ibrāhīm Shāh] arrived in ʿIrāq, to the Governorship of which he had been appointed by his brother, ʿAlī Shāh, Luṭf-ʿAlī Bēg was *Dārūghah i Daftar i Dīwān i Aʿlā*. After these troubled years Luṭf-ʿAlī Bēg adopted the life of a ṣūfī and cultivated the society of scholars, mystics, poets and wits. Mīr S. ʿAlī "Mushtāq" instructed him in the art of poetry and became his intimate friend. According to the *Anjuman i Khāqān* and the *Majmaʿ al-al-fuṣaḥāʾ* he died in 1195/1781 (see Rieu Suppt.

---

270 Cf. no. 1147, 1st par., 6th footnote *supra*.

271 Several of Luṭf-ʿAlī Bēg's relations held prominent positions. His maternal uncle Muḥammad-Qulī Khān succeeded Fatḥ-ʿAlī Khān, "Wālih's" great-uncle (cf. no. 1147, 1st par., beginning *supra*), as Prime Minister to Shāh Sulṭān-Ḥusain. His paternal uncles, Walī-Muḥammad Khān and Muṣṭafā Khān Bēgdilī, and another maternal uncle, Riḍā-Qulī Khān Bēgdilī, were sent on missions to the Ottoman Sulṭān.

272 For the Lesghians, who have already been mentioned (no. 1147, beginning *supra*) in connexion with ʿAlī-Qulī Khān "Wālih" Dāghistānī, see the *Ency. Isl.* under Dāghistān.

273 ʿAlī Shāh = ʿĀdil Shāh = ʿAlī-Qulī Khān, who succeeded his uncle, Nādir Shāh, in 1160/1747 but was deposed in Shawwāl 1161/Sept. 1748 by his brother Ibrāhīm (see Malcolm *History of Persia* ii pp. 53–5, Watson *History of Persia* pp. 40–1, Sykes *History of Persia* ii pp. 272,275–6, Zambaur *Manuel de généalogie* p. 261).

274 ʿAlī Shāh's younger brother, deposed in Muḥarram 1163/Dec. 1749-Jan. 1750 (see Malcolm ii pp. 54–5, Watson p. 41, Sykes p. 276, Zambaur p. 261).

275 Shāh Ismāʿīl III [Ṣafawī], a boy of eight or nine, was proclaimed king at Isfahān in 1163 by ʿAlī Mardān Khān Bakhtyārī (see Malcolm ii p. 59, Watson p. 44, Zambaur p. 261).

276 Shah Sulaimān II [Ṣafawī] was proclaimed king at Mashhad in Muḥarram or Ṣafar 1163 (cf. no. 404 *supra*) and after reigning for 40 days was deposed and blinded (see Malcolm ii pp. 55–6, Watson p. 41, Zambaur p. 261).

p. 81a^{5-7}). It is true that in the *ʿIqd i Thuraiyā* "Muṣḥafī", writing in 1199/1785, said that Luṭf-ʿAlī Bēg "was then still alive in Iṣpahān, and was considered the greatest poet of the period" (Rieu[277] p. 375*a*), but "Muṣḥafī" lived in Delhi, and his information from Iṣfahān may not have been up to date.

MSS. of "Ādhar's" *dīwān* are preserved at Bānkīpūr (Cat. iii no. 400), Rāmpūr (*ghazals* only ? See Nadhīr Aḥmad 106) and Lahore (*ghazals* only. See *OCM*. VI/4 (Aug. 1930) p. 67). Extensive extracts from his *Yūsuf u Zalīkhā*, which is dated 1176/1762–3, are given in the *Ātash-kadah*.

His son, Ḥusain (or Ḥasan) ʿAlī Bēg "Sharar", is one of the poets noticed in the *Zīnat al-madāʾiḥ* (Rieu Suppt. 118) and the *Majmaʿ al-al-fuṣaḥāʾ* II p. 262.

Ātash-kadah,[278] notices of about 845 ancient and modern poets begun by the author at the age of forty[279] [and therefore about 1174/1760–1], continued or added to over a number of years (e.g. 1179, mentioned under Delhi as the current year, 1180,[280] described as the current year under "Anwarī", 1185, 1190, 1191 and 1193, dates given, with chronograms, for the deaths of "ʿUdhrī", "Ṭūfān", "Ṣahbā" and "Firībī"[281]), arranged for the most part geographically under towns or provinces and divided into two *mijmarahs* (*Mijmarah* I, ancient poets, subdivided into a *shuʿlah* (kings, princes and *amīrs* of all countries), three *akhgars* ((1) poets of Īrān, (2) poets of Tūrān, (3) poets of Hindūstān) and a *furūgh* (poetesses); *Mijmarah* II, about seventy contemporary poets alphabetically arranged, with a subdivision into two *partaus* ((1) contemporaries, preceded by a historical introduction mainly on the Afghān invasion and subsequent events, (2) autobiography): Sprenger no. 32, **Blochet** iv 2453 (Iṣfahān, AH 1180/1767, transcribed by Asad Allāh b. ʿAbd al-Raḥīm al-Shirwānī), ii 1153 (AH 1213/1799), 1154 (AH 1217/1802), 1155 (AH 1231/1816), 1156 (AH 1234/1819, collated with an autograph (?)), **Ethé** 693 (AH 1196/1782), 694 (AH 1215/1800, transcribed possibly by the author's son[282]), **Lindesiana** p. 182 no. 918 (AH 1202/1787–8), no. 56 (AH 1215/1800–1),

277 According to ʿAbd al-Muqtadir "Muṣḥafī, who composed his tadhkirah in AH 1199, speaks of Âḏur in the present tense, and says that the poet was then of about sixty years of age".

278 According to Blochet (ii p. 325) the *Ātash-kadah* "est un ouvrage très peu considéré en Perse.... Les lettrés persans prétendent que le choix des vers cités a été très mal fait...."

279 *Chūn shumār i sinīn i ʿumr az thalāthīn ba-arbaʿīn rasīd* (fol. $3b^9$ in the 1277 edition).

280 It will be noticed that a MS. dated 1180/1767 exists at Paris. According to Blochet the date is certain.

281 According to ʿAbd al-Muqtadir the Bānkīpūr MS. contains no mention of "Firībī" and no date later than 1187. The biography of "Firībī" is in the Bombay edition of 1277, as well as in Bodleian 384 and the MS. or MSS. described by Bland.

282 Ibn al marḥūm Luṭf-ʿAlī ʿAlī Muḥammad al-Shīrāzī maskin[an] al-Burūjirdī mauṭin[an], described by Ethé as the author's son, but, if these words are the sole evidence, it is not decisive.

Sipahsalar ii pp. 452–6 (four copies, one of 1207/1792–3), **Rieu** i 375*b* (defective. AH 1214/1800), Suppt. 114 (AH 1234/1818), i 375*a* (AH 1238/1823), **Oxford** Ind. Inst. MS. Whinfield 6 (AH 1219/1805), **Bodleian** MS. Pers. d. 80 (AH 1222/1807), Bodleian 384 (AH 1227/1812), 385 (AH 1228/1813), 386, **Berlin** 658 (AH 1223/1808), 659 (AH 1235/1820), 660, **Rehatsek** p. 68 no. 3 (AH 1224/1809–10), **Brelvi-Dhabhar** p. xiii (AH 1226/1811), **Majlis** 322 (AH 1225/1810), 321, **Bānkīpūr** viii 702 (AD 1823), **Browne** Suppt. 1 (AH 1273/1856–7), **As'ad** 2507–9, **Āṣafīyah** i p. 316 no. 4, **Leningrad** Pub. Lib. (2 copies. See *Mélanges asiatiques* iii (St. Petersburg 1859) p. 728), Institut (Rosen 33. AH 1230/1814–15), Mus. Asiat. (see *Mélanges asiatiques* vi (1873) p. 127), Univ. 1027*, 1183* (Romaskewicz p. 3), 1230 (AH 1241/1825–6. Romaskewicz p. 19), **Mas͟hhad** iii p. 157 (defective at end).

Editions: **Calcutta** 1249/1833*, **Bombay** 1277/1860° (a bad edition), 1299/1882°.

Extract (the S͟huʿlah only, i.e. the kings, princes and *amīrs*): The *Atesh Kedah, or Fire-temple, by Hajji Lutf Ali Beg, of Isfahan, now first edited ... by N. Bland*, **London** 1844°* (40 pp.).

Descriptions: (1) *Account of the Atesh Kedah, a biographical work on the Persian Poets, by Hajji Lutf Ali Beg, of Ispahan, by N. Bland* (in *JRAS*. vii (1843) pp. 345–92), (2) Browne *Lit. Hist*, iv pp. 282–4.

List and epitome of the biographies: Bodleian coll. 262–93.

Turkish translation: **Istānbūl** 1259/1843 (see *Ency. Isl.*).

Abridgment (the poems rearranged under four headings, (1) *qaṣāʾid*, (2) *muqaṭṭaʿāt*, (3) *g͟hazalīyāt*, (4) *rubāʿīyāt*, in the alphabetical order of the rhymes, with omission of the biographies): *Tad͟hkirah i Isḥāq*, by Isḥāq Bēg "'Ud͟hrī" Bēgdilī S͟hāmlū, a younger brother of Luṭf-ʿAlī Bēg, who died at an early age in 1185/1771–2:[283] **Sipahsālār** ii pp. 469–72.

[Autobiography in *Ātas͟h-kadah, Mijmarah* II, *Partau* 2 (passage translated by Bland, *JRAS*. 1843, pp. 381–3, and briefly summarised in Sprenger p. 161, Browne *Lit. Hist*, iv pp. 283–4 and Bodleian coll. 292–3), statements concerning his tribe, his ancestors and himself in the historical narrative (some 18 pp. in the 1277 edition) with which *Mijmarah* II begins (passage relating to the Bēgdilīs translated by Bland, *JRAS*. 1843, pp. 380–1); *Riyāḍ al-s͟huʿarāʾ* (passage summarised by Bland, *JRAS*. 1848 p. 161 n. 2); *Tad͟hkirah i Muṣḥafī* (for a translated extract see Bānkīpūr iii pp. 219–20); *Ṣuḥuf i Ibrāhīm* (passage summarised in *JRAS*. 1848 p. 161); *Mak͟hzan al-g͟harāʾib* no. 235; *Tad͟hkirah i Ak͟htar* (Berlin 664); *Tajribat al-aḥrār* (Rieu Suppt. 132); *Anjuman i K͟hāqān; Majmaʿ al-al-fuṣaḥāʾ* i

283 See *Ātas͟h-kadah, Mijmarah* ii, *Partau* i (Bodleian 384 no. 813; *JRAS*, 1843 p. 384); *Anjuman i K͟hāqān; Majmaʿ al al-fuṣaḥāʾ* ii p. 345.

pp. 73–5; *Sham' i anjuman* p. 65; Rieu i p. 375*a*; Bānkīpūr ii pp. 219–20, viii p. 135; Browne *Lit. Hist*, iv pp. 283–4; *Ency. Isl.* under Luṭf 'Alī Beg (Kramers).]

1171. Abu 'l-Ḥasan Amīr al-Dīn Aḥmad, known as (*al-mushtahir bi-*) **Amr Allāh Ilāhābādī**, travelled to 'Aẓīmābād (i.e. Patna) in Ṣafar 1192/1778 and there decided to write a *tadhkirah*. He composed it during his journey to Calcutta and finished it on 3 Jumādā II 1193/18 June 1779. On his return, as he tells us in his conclusion, he reached Lucknow in 1194/1780 and there he obtained much information about other poets but did not incorporate it in his work, since he felt obliged to confine himself to the poets of whom he had given a list in his introduction. The list referred to is dated 1197/1783. "Accordingly we have to suppose, that the preface and the work itself were composed AH 1193, but that the conclusion was added at the same time with the index of the poets, viz. AH 1197."

Tadhkirah i masarrat-afzā, alphabetically arranged notices of 247 Rēkhtah (i.e. Urdu) poets completed in 1193/1779:[284] **Bodleian** 388 (possibly autograph).

1172. Maulawī Gulshan 'Alī **"Gulshan" Jaunpūrī**, the younger brother of the grammarian and mathematician Raushan 'Alī "Naẓmī" Anṣārī Jaunpurī, was born at Jaunpūr, went as a young man to Delhi, where he witnessed Nādir Shāh's sack of the city (AH 1151/1739) and met the poets "Ḥazīn" and "Wālih", to the latter of whom he attached himself. After "Wālih's" death in 1169/1756 he returned home, but soon went in search of employment to Shamsābād (in the Farrukhābād District of the United Provinces), where Saiyid Basālat Jahān (d. 1176/1762–3) became his patron. He was already over sixty years of age when he wrote his autobiography. According to the *Tajallī i nūr* he died in 1200/1786 and was the author of a Persian *dīwān* and other works including treatises on *raml*, *jafr*, prosody and *mu'ammā*.

Ṣūrat i ḥāl, an autobiography in *mathnawī* verse: **Rieu** ii 715*a* (18th cent.). [*Makhzan al-gharā'ib* no. 2196; *Tajallī i nūr* II pp. 20–21.]

1173. For the *Ḥadīqat al-aqālīm*, which was written mainly in 1192/1778–1196/1782 by Murtaḍā Ḥusain Bilgrāmī and which contains biographies of poets and other celebrities, see no. 170 *supra*.

284 "The careful biographical information, along with the many and extensive extracts from Dîwâns, renders the work very valuable indeed. There occur many poets whom Garcin de Tassy (in his Histoire de la Littérature Hindouie et Hindoustanie) does not even mention, and the very useful list of Rêkhta poets given by A. Sprenger (in his Catalogue, p. 195 sq.) might be considerably enriched from this source with valuable biographical information."

1174. **Mōhan Laʿl "Anīs"** Kāyat'h[285] was the son of Rāy Tūlā (?) Rām, *Qānūngō* of the *parganah* of Gōpāmau in Oudh. In the art of poetry he was a pupil of Mirzā M. Fākhir "Makīn" Dihlawī[286] He had been resident at Lucknow for more than fifty years when he wrote the first edition of his *Anīs al-aḥibbāʾ* [in 1197/1783], and for more than ninety years when he completed the second edition [in 1235/1819–20]. The work was undertaken at the request of Mahārājah Tikēt Rāy,[287] who had been delighted with the *Tadhkirah* of "Ḥazīn" (for which see no. 1150 (2) *supra*) and had asked "Anīs" to write a counterpart to it on Indian poets. For his *dīwān* (MS. at Rāmpūr) see *OCM*. VI/4 (Aug. 1930) p. 75.

Anīs al-aḥibbāʾ, notices of "Makīn" and the poets of his school completed in 1197/1783 and divided into an *Iftitāḥ* (on "Makīn's" teacher, Mirzā ʿAẓīmā-yi "Iksīr" i Iṣfahānī),[2884] a *Fatḥ al-bāb* (on "Makīn"), a *Faṣl* (on 31 Muslim pupils of "Makīn"), a *Fāṣilah* (on six Hindū pupils), an *Ikhtitām* (on five Muslim pupils of "Makīn's" pupils) and a *Ḥusn i khātimah* (on six Hindū pupils of his pupils): Sprenger no. 33, **Rieu** i 376*a* (18th cent., apparently written or revised by the author), 377*a* (an enlarged recension begun in 1209/1794–5, completed in 1235/1819–20 and containing 50 notices in the *Faṣl*, 12 in the *Fāṣilah*, 11 in the *Ikhtitām* and 18 in the *Ḥusn i khātimah*. AH 1237/1822), **Berlin** 662 (AH 1218/1803–4), **Bānkīpūr** viii 703 (19th cent.).

List of the poets in the 1st edition: Sprenger pp. 162–3.

[Autobiography in *Anīs al-aḥibbāʾ* at end of *Fāṣilah*.]

1175. **Ghulām-Hamadānī "Muṣḥafī"** b. Walī-Muḥammad belonged to a family connected with Amrōhah (20 miles N. of Moradabad), but, if not born at Lucknow,[289] he lived there in early, or comparatively early, life. In, or about,

285 I.e. Kayast'h, the name of the Hindu caste of clerks and accountants.

286 Born at Delhi, migrated to Lucknow in 1173/1759–60, lived for some time at Faiḍābād and at Ilāhābād, where the Emperor Shāh-ʿĀlam became his pupil in the art of poetry, died at Lucknow in 1221/1806–7. See Rieu i 376*a*. Bānkīpūr iii pp. 258–9, Sprenger p. 481, *Ṣuḥuf i Ibrāhīm*, (penultimate biography under *Mīm*), *Khulāṣat al-afkār* no. 475, *Makhzan al-gharāʾib* no. 2699, *Tadhkirah i dil-gushā* (Berlin p. 672 no. 112).

287 *Dīwān* to Sarfarāz al-Daulah Mirzā Ḥasan Riḍā Khan, who was *Naʾib* of Āṣaf al-Daulah, the Nawwāb-Wazir of Oudh. Tikēt Rāy died in 1215/1800–1.

288 Went to Delhi [presumably from Persia] in Muḥammad Shāh's reign, and was afterwards invited by Nawwāb Mahābat-Jang (for whom see no. 960 *supra*) to Murshidābād, where he died in the time of Sirāj al-Daulah (AH 1169–70).

289 According to Rieu "he was born in Lucknow". Garcin de Tassy, citing the *Tadhkirah i Hindī* and paraphrasing doubtless the same words as Rieu, says "Mashafi habita d'abord Lakhnau". According to Saksena he was born at Akbarpūr. There is one place of that name near Fyzabad and another near Cawnpore. Shēftah (cited by Garcin ii p. 286) says that he was born at Delhi: Grahame Bailey that he "belonged to Amrohā, but went as a young man to Delhi, which he considered his native place".

1190/1776 he went to Delhi where he spent twelve years cultivating Rēkhtah (i.e. Urdu) poetry, which he found to be in vogue there, though his early predilection had been for Persian poetry. Eminent poets of the time used to forgather at his house. On returning to Lucknow he found a patron in Prince Sulaimān-Shukōh,[290] the second son of Shāh-ʿĀlam II and brother of Akbar-Shāh. He died in, or about, 1240/1824–5 at an advanced age. He was a facile writer of verse, and composed several *dīwāns*. In the *Tadhkirah i Hindī* he mentions three[291] in Persian and, apparently, four in Urdu. According to Sprenger, who cites the *Gulshan i bī-khār*, he subsequently wrote three more in Urdu. A volume of selections from four of his Urdu *dīwāns* was published at [Lucknow] in 1296/1879°. He enjoyed a considerable reputation in his time and he had many pupils.

(1) ***ʿIqd i Thuraiyā***, a *tadhkira* written at Delhi in 1199/1784–5 at the suggestion of Mīrzā "Qatīl" and devoted to 133 Persian poets who flourished, chiefly in India, from the time of Muḥammad Shāh (A.H. 1131–61/1719–48) to that of Shāh-ʿĀlam (A.H. 1173/1759–1221/1806): **Rieu** i 377*b* (late 18th cent.), **Bānkīpūr** viii 709 (A.H. 1244/1829).

Edition: **Aurangābād** date ? (ed. ʿAbd al-Ḥaqq. Anjuman i Taraqqī i Urdū. See a review in *OCM*. XI/4 (Aug. 1935) pp. 119–20.

(2) ***Tadhkirah i Hindī***, notices of about 350 Rēkhtah (i.e. Urdu) poets, from the time of Muḥammad Shāh to that of the author, written at the request of Mīr Mustaḥsan "Khāliq" and completed in 1209/1794–5: Sprenger no. 47 = **Ivanow** 1st Suppt. 769 (A.H. 1219/1804), **Rieu** i 378*a* (late 18th cent.), **Bānkīpūr** viii 710 (A.H. 1238/1822).

Edition: **Aurangābād** date ? (ed. ʿAbd al-Ḥaqq. Anjuman i Taraqqī i Urdū. See a review in *OCM*. XI/4 (Aug. 1935) pp. 131–4).

(3) ***Tadhkirah i Fārisī***, written in 1236/1820–1, notices of modern Urdu and Persian poets of India, with extracts, nearly all Urdū, from their works: **Bānkīpūr** viii 711 (A.H. 1237/1821–2).

(4) ***Riyāḍ al-fuṣaḥā'***, brief notices of about 325 contemporary Urdu poets.

Edition: **Aurangābād** date ? (ed. ʿAbd al-Ḥaqq. Pp. 378. Anjuman i Taraqqī i Urdū, no. 77. See a review in *OCM*. XI/4 (Aug. 1935) pp. 134–5.

[Autobiography in the *Tadhkirah i Hindī* (summarised by Rieu, i p. 377*b*, Sprenger, pp. 182–3, and Garcin de Tassy, ii pp. 284–5); *Tadhkirah i ʿIshqī*; *Majmūʿah i naghz* ii pp. 188–95; *Gulshan i bī-khār*; *Natā'ij al-afkār* p. 420;

290 See Garcin de Tassy iii pp. 171–3, Beale *Oriental biographical dictionary* p. 390.

291 Four according to Sprenger, who speaks of "a rough copy of a Persian Dywán in the style of Jalál Asyr, and one in the style of Nácir 'alyy", whereas ʿAbd al-Muqtadir regards these two as a single *dīwān* "in the style of Jalâl Asîr and Nâṣir ʿAlî".

Sprenger pp. 182–3, 625; Garcin de Tassy ii pp. 283–8 (under Mashafi); Rieu i p. 377*b*; M. Ḥusain "Āzād" *Āb i ḥayāt* (in Urdu), several editions; Beale *Oriental biographical dictionary* p. 246 (under Mas-hafi): Bānkīpūr viii pp. 149–50; Blumhardt *Catalogue of Hindustani manuscripts in the ... India Office* p. 125; *Ency. Isl.* under Maṣḥafī; Saksēna *History of Urdu literature* pp. 90–3; T. Grahame Bailey *History of Urdu literature* p. 53.]

1176. Nawwāb **'Alī Ibrāhīm Khān** "Khalīl" died in 1208/1793–4 (see no. 922 *supra*).

(1) ***Gulzār i Ibrāhīm***, notices of about 300 Rēkhtah (i.e. Urdū) poets completed in 119+8/1784: Sprenger 45, **Rieu** i 375*b* (18th cent.), iii 1069*a* (19th cent.), **Bānkīpūr** viii 707 (A.H. 1220/1806), **Ivanow** 1st Suppt. 768 (19th cent.), **Bodleian** 389.

Urdu translation made at the request of J.B. Gilchrist: **Browne** Suppt. 1084 (Corpus 159[1]).

(2) ***Khulāṣat al-kalām***, notices of 78 writers of *mathnawīs* completed in 1198/1784: **Lindesiana** p. 177 no. 318 (circ. A.D. 1790), **Bodleian** 390 (A.H. 1246/1831), **Bānkīpūr** viii 704–5 (lacks *dāl-ḍād*. 19th cent.), 706 (lacks the poetical extracts. 19th cent.).

Lists and epitomes of the biographies: (1) Bodleian coll. 295–302, (2) Bānkīpūr viii pp. 138–46 (lacking *dāl-ḍād*).

(3) ***Ṣuḥuf i Ibrāhīm***, notices of about 3278[292] ancient and modern poets completed at Benares in 1205/1790: **Berlin** 663, **Bānkīpūr** viii 708 (defective, ending with "'Urfī". 19th cent.).

Description: *On the earliest Persian Biography of Poets ... By N. Bland* (in *JRAS*. ix (1848)) pp. 158–61, 163–4.

List of the biographies: **Berlin** pp. 628–67.

1177. Maulawī M. **Qudrat Allāh "Shauq"** b. Sh. Qabūl Muḥammad has already been mentioned (no. 171 *supra*) as the author of the general history *Jām i jahān-numā* begun in 1191/1777 and completed in 1199/1785.

(1) ***Ṭabaqāt al-shu'arā'***: **Āṣafīyah** i p. 322 no. 40 (A.H. 1210/1795–6).

(2) ***Takmilat al-shu'arā' Jām i Jamshīd***, an alphabetically arranged *tadhkirah* of ancient and modern poets written after the *Jām i jahān-numā*: **Rāmpūr** (AH 1218/1803–4. See OCM. VII/1 (Nov. 1930) pp. 68–9 and Nadhīr Aḥmad 83).

292 Apparently the largest number of biographies in any *tadhkirah* yet described. The *Makhzan al-gharā'ib* (for which see no. 1181 *infra*) contains 3148.

1178. Mirzā **Abū Ṭālib Khān** Tabrīzī **Iṣfahānī**, the author of the *Lubb al-siyar u jahān-numā* (see no. 173 *supra*) and the *Tafḍīḥ al-ghāfilīn* (no. 934 *supra*), died at Lucknow in 1220/1805–6 or 1221/1806–7.

(1) ***Khulāṣat al-afkār***, notices of about 494 ancient and modern poets written in 1206–7/1791–3 on the basis of material collected during 25 years, divided into a *muqaddimah* (on Persian poetry and the rules to be observed in compiling *tadhkirahs*), 28 *ḥadīqahs* (one for each letter, under which the poets are arranged chronologically),[293] a *dhail* (160 supplementary notices) and a *khātimah* (on the author himself and 23 poets personally known to him) and followed in most manuscripts by five treatises, viz. (1) *Risālah dar ʿilm i akhlāq*, (2) *Muṣṭalaḥāt i musīqī*, (3) *dar ʿilm i ʿarūḍ u qāfiyah*, (4) *Mukhtaṣar dar funūn i khamsah i ṭibb*, (5) *Lubb al-siyar u jahān-numā* (see no. 173 *supra*):[294] Sprenger no. 34 (where parts of the preface are quoted), **Ethé** 696 (transcribed by G. Swinton[295] from an autograph and corrected by the author in 1804), 697 (lacks the first four of the appended treatises), **Bodleian** 391 (AH 1210/1796), **Rieu** i 378*b* (very imperfect. Early 19th cent.), iii 1003 *b* (poetical extracts only. Circ. AD 1850), Suppt. 116 (early 19th cent.), **Bānkīpūr** viii 712 (lacks the last three of the appended treatises. 19th cent.).

Description: *On the earliest Persian Biography of Poets ... By N. Bland* (in *JRAS*. ix (1848)) pp. 153–8, where the *muqaddimah* is summarised.

List and epitome of the biographies: Bodleian coll. 302–15.

(2) ***Masīr i Ṭālibī fī bilād i Afranjī***, a narrative completed in 1219/1804–5 from rough notes of a journey to Europe from 1 Ramaḍān 1213/6 Feb. 1799, when he left Calcutta, to 15 Rabīʿ I 1218/5 July 1803, when he reached Calcutta on his return: **Rieu** i 384*a* (AH 1221/1806),[296] 384*b* (vol. iii. Early 19th cent.), **Bodleian** 1855 (AH 1222/1807–8), **Blochet** i 647 (AH 1228/1813), **ʿAlīgaṛh Subḥ**. MSS. p. 57 no. 1, **Āṣafīyah** ii p. 836 no. 29, **Bānkīpūr** vii 627, **Browne** Pers. Cat. 116 (less than half the work), **Edinburgh** 90, **Ethé** 2727, **Madras** 449, **R.A.S.** P. 177.

Edition: *Masīrī* [*sic*] *Ṭālibī. Travels in Europe and Asia, by Mírza Abu Taleb Khán. Published and edited by his son Mírza Hasein* [*sic*] *Âli and Mír Kudrut Âli*. **Calcutta** 1812°* (pp. 865).

293 In his selections the compiler devotes special attention to *mathnawīs*, "from which he gives extracts of considerable extent" (Rieu i p. 379*b*).

294 The third *bāb* of the *Lubb al-siyar* contains biographies of celebrities including poets.

295 G. Swinton studied Persian under Abū Ṭālib Khān in London previously to his appointment to the Bengal Civil Service (see Ethé col. 357 ult.).

296 This MS., from which Major C. Stewart made his translation, is described by him in a note on a fly-leaf as "very superior to the printed edition".

English translation: *The Travels of Mirza Abu Taleb Khan, in Asia, Africa, and Europe, during the years* 1799, 1800, 1801, 1802, *and* 1803. *Written by himself, in the Persian language. Translated by C. Stewart.* **London** (Broxbourne printed) 1810° (2 vols.); *Second edition, with additions,* **London** (Broxbourne printed) 1814°* (3 vols.).

French translations (from the English): (1) *Voyages de Mirza Abu Taleb Khan ... Suivis d'une réfutation des idées qu'on a en Europe sur la liberté des femmes d'Asie; par le même auteur. Le tout traduit du persan en anglais, par C. Stewart ... et traduit de l'anglais en français par M. J. C. J.*[297] Paris 1811°. (2) *Voyages de Mirza Abou Taleb Khan ... trad. de l'anglais en français par Ch. Malo.***Paris** 1819 (see Zenker i no. 1025).

German translation (from the French of J. C. J.): *Reise des Mirza Abu Taleb Khan durch Asien, Afrika, und Europa, in den Jahren* 1799,1800, 1801,1802 *und* 1803. *Nebst einer Widerlegung der Begriffe, welche man in Europa von der Freyheit der asiatischen Weiber hat. Aus dem Französischen.* **Vienna** 1813°.

Urdu translation by Mīrzā ʿAlī Riḍā "Maḥzūn" Murādābādī: *Masīr i Ṭālibī,* **Murādābād** 1904* (Pt. 1 only ?).

Abridgment by David Macfarlane (beg. *Baʿd i ḥamd i mutakāthir*): **Berlin** 358.

Editions of the abridgment: *The Travels of Mirza Aboo Talib Khan. In the Persian language. Abridged by David Macfarlane* (*Masīr i Ṭālibī*). **Calcutta** 1827°* (pp. 157), 1836* (pp. 132).

1179. Sh. M. Wajīh [al-Dīn][298] **"ʿIshqī"** b. Ghulām-Ḥusain "Mujrim" ʿAẓīmābādī was for ten years *Taḥṣīldār* at Kharwar[299] and subsequently went to Dacca. In 1224/1809–10 he was still alive, but his sight was much impaired. For his *dīwān* see Sprenger 286.

Tadhkirah i ʿIshqī, short alphabetically arranged notices of 439 Rēkhtah (i.e. Urdū) poets, written probably in, or soon after, 1215/1800–1: Sprenger 48 = **Bodleian** 393 (n.d.).

[*Tadhkirah i ʿIshqī* no. 272, *Nishtar i ʿishq*; Garcin de Tassy ii p. 47; Sprenger pp. 183 and 441; *Nigāristān i sukhan* p. 65.]

---

297 I.e. Hendrik Jansen according to Edwards, col. 312.

298 The proper name of "Mujrim's" son is given as Miyān Raḥmat Allāh by Garcin (and, presumably on Garcin's authority, by Ethé in the Bodleian catalogue), but Miyān Raḥmat Allāh "ʿIshqī" (Sprenger p. 241, *Majmūʿah i naghz* II p. 396[2]) seems to be a different person.

299 Presumably K'harwar, described in the *Jāmiʿ al-lughāt* (an Urdu dictionary) as a village in the Midnāpur District [of Bengal].

1180. **Rafīʿ al-Dīn Qandahārī** died in 1241/1825–6.

Naubahār, notices of 57 ancient and modern poets written in 1216/1801–2: MS. in the possession of Ḥakīm S. S̲h̲ams Allāh Qādirī (see *OCM.* V/4 (Aug. 1929) p. 113).

1181. **S̲h̲. Aḥmad ʿAlī K̲h̲ān**[300] Hās̲h̲imī **Sandīlawī** (or Sandīlī)[301] b. S̲h̲. G̲h̲ulām-Muḥammad b. Maulawī M. Ḥājjī must have been born about 1163/1750, since according to his own statement in the preface he was in his fifty-fifth year when he compiled the *Mak̲h̲zan al-g̲h̲arāʾib*, a work in which 1217/1802–3 is mentioned[302] as the current year and which was completed in 1218/1803–4. Having been recommended to Nawwāb D̲h̲ū 'l-Faqār al-Daulah Mīrzā Najaf K̲h̲ān Bahādur G̲h̲ālib-Jang[303] by Nawwāb ʿIzzat al-Daulah Mīrzā Ḥasan Suhrāb-Jang,[304] he was enrolled through the former's influence in the *risālah* of S̲h̲āh-ʿĀlam (reigned 1173/1759–1221/1806). After Nawwāb Najaf K̲h̲ān's death [in 1196/1782], "which was followed by anarchy and a massacre of the inhabitants of Dihlī" (Bānkīpūr viii p. 154), Aḥmad ʿAlī began to cultivate the society of Persians from K̲h̲urāsān, ʿIrāq and Fārs and to collect Persian poems. Encouraged by his master, Mīrzā M. Ḥasan "Qatīl", he decided to compile a *tad̲h̲kirah*.

Mak̲h̲zan al-g̲h̲arāʾib, alphabetically arranged notices of 3148[305] ancient and modern poets completed in 1218/1803–4 at Delhi: Sprenger no. 27 (Faraḥ-bak̲h̲s̲h̲), **Bodleian** 395 (AH 1224/1809), **Bānkīpūr** viii 713–14 (AH 1224/1809), **Rieu** Suppt. 117 (1st half of 19th cent.), iii 1015*b* (34 notices only. AD 1850–1), **Lahore** Prof. Maḥmūd S̲h̲ērānī's private library (see ʿAbd al-Nabī *Mai-k̲h̲ānah,* editor's introduction, penultimate page), **Aʿẓamgaṛh** Dār al-Muṣannifīn (see *OCM.* III/2 (Feb. 1927) p. 36 n.).

List of the biographies (with epitomes of some): Bodleian coll. 317–96. [*Mak̲h̲zan al-g̲h̲arāʾib*, preface.]

---

300 So in the contemporary colophon quoted in Bānkīpūr viii p. 155.

301 Evidently a different person from S̲h̲. Aḥmad ʿAlī "K̲h̲ādim" Sandʾhīlawī [so], author of an anthology entitled *Anīs al-ʿus̲h̲s̲h̲āq,* if Sprenger is right in saying (p. 147) that the latter "flourished in India in 1165" [P.S. Cf. *Mai-k̲h̲ānah* ed. M. S̲h̲afīʿ p. 347 n. 3]. Sandīlah is a town 32 miles N.W. of Lucknow.

302 In the notice of G̲h̲ulām-Fak̲h̲r al-Dīn K̲h̲ān "Ḥairat" (see Bānkīpūr viii p. 154¹).

303 For Nawwāb Najaf K̲h̲ān see no. 637 footnote *supra,* Beale *Oriental biographical dictionary* under Najaf K̲h̲ān, etc.

304 Son of Mīrzā M. Muḥsin, the elder brother of Nawwāb Ṣafdar-Jang. The latter was *Nawwāb-Wazīr* of Awad̲h̲ ("Oudh") and died in 1167/1754.

305 Of the *tad̲h̲kirahs* hitherto described only the *Ṣuḥuf i Ibrāhīm* (for which see no. 1176 (3) *supra*) contains a larger number of biographies.

1182. For the *Mir'āt i āftāb-numā* of Nawwāb Shāh-nawāz Khān Dihlawī, which was written in 1218 and which contains biographies of Ṣūfīs, *'ulamā'*, poets and calligraphists, see no. 175 *supra.*

1183. **Bhagwān Dās "Hindī"**[306] (originally "Bismil") was the son of Dalpat Dās b. Harbans Rāy, a Kāyast'h[307] who held high offices at Lucknow. He was born in 1164/1750–1 and received his early education from Maulawī S. Yūsuf Sahāranpūrī. In the art of poetry his instructor was Mirzā M. Fākhir "Makīn" Dihlawī, who, as has already been mentioned (no. 1174 1st par. 2nd footnote *supra*), migrated to Lucknow in 1173/1759–60 and died there in 1221/1806–7. "In his youth, he held the post of Mîr Baḥr" (Bānkīpūr viii p. 156[28]), and subsequently, in the time of Āṣaf al-Daulah [1189–1212/1775–97], became *Dīwān* to Rājah Nid'hī [?] Sing'h Bahādur. After the Rājah's death he entered the service of Rājah Paṭar [?] Chand Bahādur and later that of Mahārājah Tikēt Rāy [who died in 1215/1800–1. See no. 1174 1st par. 3rd footnote *supra*]. He was the author of (1) *Silsilat al-maḥabbat, a mathnawī* modelled on "Jāmī's" *Silsilat al-dhahab,* (2) *Maẓhar al-anwār*, a *mathnawī* modelled on "Niẓāmī's" *Makhzan al-asrār*, (3) *Mihr i ḍiyā*, a *mathnawī* modelled on "Jāmī's" *Yūsuf u Zalīkhā*, (4) *Shauqīyah*, a *dīwān*, (5) *Dhauqīyah*, another *dīwān*, (6) *Tadhkirah i Ḥadīqah i Hindī*, on ancient and modern Indian poets to the year 1200/1786, (7) *Sawāniḥ al-nubuwwah*, an account of the Prophet and the Twelve Imams written at the request of S. Khairāt 'Alī, and

(8) ***Safīnah i Hindī***, alphabetically arranged notices of Persian poets who flourished in India from the accession of Shāh-'Ālam in 1173/1759 to 1219/1804–5, the date of completion: **Bānkīpūr** viii 715 (AH 1220/1805).

[Autobiography in *Safīnah i Hindī; Anīs al-aḥibbā'*.]

1184. For the *Zīnat al-tawārīkh*, a general history to 1221/1806–7 by M. Raḍī [not Riḍā apparently] Tabrīzī and 'Abd al-Karīm Ishtihārdī, which contains notices of poets and other celebrities at the end of *Pīrāyah* i, see no. 177 *supra.*

1185. S. Abū 'l-Qāsim, commonly called (*'urf*) Mīr **Qudrat Allāh** Qādirī (*Majmū'ah i naghz* ii p. 92 ult.), who used the *takhallus* **"Qāsim"**, studied medicine under Ḥakīm M. Sharīf Khān and poetics under Hidāyat Allāh Khān

306 In the *Anīs al-aḥibbā'* (AH 1197/1783) he is called Bhagwān Dās "Bismil". In the Bānkīpūr Catalogue Hindī is not expressly said to be a *takhallus*, but that is doubtless implied by the statement that "he at first adopted the *takhallus* Bismil". Moreover, his autobiography, to judge from its position (fol. 93*b* in a volume of 102 foll.), must be under "Hindī".

307 For this word see no. 1174 1st par. 1st footnote *supra.*

"Hidāyat" [of Delhi. See Sprenger p. 238], In his brief account of himself he says that he had written [doubtless in Urdū] a *dīwān* of about 7000 verses and two *mathnawīs*, the first of 3500 verses on the story of the *Miʿrāj* in the metre of Jalāl al-Dīn Rūmī's *Mathnawī*, and the second of about 5200 verses on the miracles of ʿAbd al-Qādir al-Jīlānī in the metre of the *Bustān*.

Majmūʿah i naghz[308] (a chronogram = 1221/1806–7, the date of completion), or (*Tadhkirah i Qāsim*), alphabetically arranged notices of about 800 Urdū poets: Sprenger no. 52, **Lahore** Panjāb Univ. Lib. (probably autograph. See OCM. III/1 (Nov. 1926) pp. 77–8 and the editor's introduction to the Lahore edition), **Bānkīpūr** Suppt. i 1789 (AD 1822), **Berlin** 669, **Ethé** 2849.

Edition: *Majmuʿa-i-Naghz, or Biographical notices of Urdu poets by Hakim Abu'l Qasim Mir Qudratullah Qasim. Edited by Hafiz Mahmud Shairani*, **Lahore** 1933 (Panjāb University Oriental Publications).

[Autobiography in *Majmūʿah i naghz* ii pp. 92–3 (summarised in Sprenger p. 186 and Bānkīpūr Suppt. i p. 65); Garcin de Tassy i pp. 353–6 (under Cacim); *Mīr Qudrat Allāh Khān "Qāsim" aur un kī tālīf Majmūʿah i naghz*, by Ḥāfiẓ Maḥmūd Shērānī (in OCM. IX/1 (Nov. 1932) pp. 28–51); the editor's Urdu introduction to the Lahore edition.]

1186. Nawwāb Aʿẓam al-Daulah Mīr **M. Khān "Sarwar"** b. Nawwāb Abu 'l-Qāsim Muẓaffar-Jang was the author of a large Urdu *dīwān*. He died in 1250/1834–5.

Tadhkirah i Sarwar, notices of about 1200 Urdu poets completed, according to a statement at the end (see Ethé 2850), on 9 Muḥarram 1222/19 March 1807, though other dates are indicated by various chronograms, including *ʿUmdah i muntakhabah* (1216), which Sprenger supposed to be the title: Sprenger no. 51, **Blochet** ii 1159 (AD 1829), **Ethé** 2850.

[*Gulshan i bī-khār*; Sprenger pp. 185, 285; Garcin de Tassy iii pp. 64–5.]

1187. Sh. **Ghulām-Muḥyī 'l-Dīn "ʿIshq"** (originally "Mubtalā") Qurashī Mēraṭ'hī was the son of Sh. Niʿmat Allāh "Niʿamī", whose bulky Persian *dīwān* he helped to arrange at the age of twelve. Having thus acquired a taste for poetry, he wrote a *dīwān* in which he used the *takhalluṣ* "Mubtalā". Subsequently he devoted much of his time to archery, without however neglecting his studies. "When Sháh 'álam came from Patna [or rather, from Ilāhābād ?] to Dilly [in 1185/1771] he gained the friendship of one of his courtiers, whose title was Nawáb Najaf

308 This is only the first of several chronograms given in the preface and is not stated to be the title, but it may now be accepted as such.

Khán, and his name Ibráhym Bég, and his takhalluç, Alam, he was induced by him to write another Dywán in which he used the takhalluç of 'ishq"[309] (Sprenger p. 187), and a Persian *mathnawī, Fusun i 'ishq*, telling the story of Shāh-Rukh and Māh-Rukh. He wrote also an *inshā'* entitled *Chahār daftar i sharq*,[310] as well as *Nuskhah i sarā'ir*, on chronograms, *Biḥār al-tashrīḥ*, composed in 1220/1805–6, and *Ash''āt* [*sic ?*] *al-'ishq*, on Ṣūfism, composed in the same year.

(1) ***Bāgh i gulhā-yi ḥusn*** (a chronogram = 1187/1773), or ***Majmū'ah i 'ishq***, or ***Chārchaman***, "a Persian Tadzkirah," which "fills about 1280 pages" (Sprenger): **'Alīgaṛh** Subh. MSS. p. 53 no. 8 (AH 1187, autograph).

(2) ***Ṭabaqāt i sukhun*** (a chronogram = 1222), biographies, which "have the advantage of being original" (Sprenger), divided into two *ṭabaqahs* ((1) Rēkhtah, i.e. Urdū, poets, 196 in number, (2) Persian poets of the same period): Sprenger no. 53 = **Berlin** 670 (lacking *Ṭabaqah* ii).

List of the poets in *Ṭabaqah* i: Berlin pp. 675–6.

[Autobiographical information in the *Ṭabaqāt i sukhun* under "'Ishq" and "Mubtalā" (summarised in Sprenger p. 187); *Majmū'ah i naghz*, ii p. 401.]

1188. **M. Ṣādiq "Humā"** Marwazī has already been mentioned (no. 427 *supra*) as the author of the *Tārīkh i jahānārā*.

Zīnat al-madā'iḥ, a collection of poems composed in praise of Fatḥ-'Alī Shāh from the first to the seventh year of his reign (AH 1218/1803–4) with a sequel (vol. ii) compiled in 1223/1808, together with notices of their authors: **Rieu** Suppt. 118, 119 (vol. ii), **Majlis** 397, 398 (AH 1223/1808–9).

Lists of the poets: Rieu Suppt. 118–19.

1189. Mirzā **M. 'Alī Kātib i Ṣafawī** was first employed by Shah-zādah Abū 'l-Naṣr Mirzā M. Sulaimān-Shukōh, Shāh-'Ālam's son,[311] to copy Persian and Urdū *dīwāns* and subsequently became *Muṣāḥib* and *Kātib*[312] to Sulṭān Abū 'l-Fatḥ Muḥammad "Ṭulū'ī" Ṣafawī [the last (nominal) king of the Ṣafawī dynasty, who was proclaimed at Ṭihrān in 1200/1785 by Āqā Muḥammad, fled to Sind in 1205/1790–1 and settled at Lucknow in 1210/1795–6 (cf. no. 402 *supra*)].

---

309 A [Persian] *Dīwān i 'Ishq* by Khalīfah Ghulām-Muḥyī 'l-Dīn 'Ishq is preserved at Ḥaidar-ābād (Āṣafīyah i p. 728 no. 483).

310 Or *shauq* ? This title is erroneously said by Sprenger to be a chronogram for 1199.

311 Cf. no. 1175 *supra*.

312 *Īn dharrah i khāksār ... dar sarkār i ... Sulṭān M. i Ṣafawī al-mutakhalliṣ Ṭulū'ī ... dar muṣāḥabat u shughl i sharīf i kitābat būd* (quoted by Nadhīr Aḥmad from the preface to the *Tadhkirah i Kātib*).

Tadhkirah i Kātib, alphabetically arranged notices of poets selected from the *Makhzan al-g͟harā'ib* (cf. no. 1181 *supra*) and completed in 1225/1810: **Rampūr** (see Nad͟hīr Aḥmad no. 81 and a more detailed description by M. Shajā'at 'Alī K͟hān in *OCM.* VI/2 (Feb. 1930) pp. 108–11).

1190. **Aḥmad Bēg "Ak͟htar"** Gurjī is one of the poets of Fatḥ-'Alī S͟hāh's time included in Bahman Mīrzā's *Tadhkirah i Muḥammad-S͟hāhī* (Rieu Suppt. 124 fol. 182*b*) and 'Alī Akbar S͟hīrāzī's *Tadhkirah i dil-gus͟hā* (Berlin p. 671 no. 45).

Tadhkirah i Ak͟htar, alphabetically arranged notices of contemporary poets written in 1227/1812–13: **Berlin** 664 (not later than 1264/1847).

List of the poets: Berlin pp. 665–7.

1191. Muns͟hī **D͟hū 'l-Faqār 'Alī K͟hān "Mast"** wrote in addition to the *Riyāḍ al-wifāq* several other works, of which the titles and subjects are mentioned by Sprenger.

Riyāḍ al-wifāq (a chronogram = 1229/1814), notices of 144 poets, mainly contemporaries of the author connected with Calcutta and Benares (at the latter of which places the work seems to have been compiled): Sprenger no. 36 = **Berlin** 665.

List and epitome of the biographies: Sprenger pp. 165–72.

1192. For the *Zubdat al-g͟harā'ib*, which was written in 1231/1816 by M. Riḍā "Najm" Ṭabāṭabā and of which the fifth volume contains biographies of philosophers, saints and poets, see no. 180 (1) *supra*.

1193. **Āqā Ḥusain-Qulī K͟hān "Ās͟hiqī"**[313] 'Aẓīmābādī b. Āqā 'Alī K͟hān S͟hāhjahānābādī was born at Patnah in 1194/1780. In the course of several visits to Akbarābād and S͟hāhjahānābād he met many learned men, from whom he collected numerous poems. In 1223/1808 he was shown a copy of "Wālih's" *tadhkirah* (for which see no. 1147 *supra*) by Mīr M. Ja'far "Masīḥ" Barēlawī, the *Taḥṣīl-dār* of Atraulī [in the 'Alīgaṛh District] and, finding the selections contained in it uninteresting,[314] he decided to write a *tadhkirah* himself[315] and

---

313   The statement that his *tak͟hallus* was "'Is͟hq" (Sprenger p. 644, Bānkīpūr VIII p. 157) seems to be erroneous.

314   Abū Ṭālib K͟hān Tabrīzī Iṣfahānī, on the other hand, regarded "Wālih's" *tadhkirah* as "abounding in beautiful poetry" and was greatly charmed with it (see *JRAS.* 1848 p. 155, where the preface to his *K͟hulāṣat al-afkār* is summarized).

315   According to Sprenger "he undertook it at the request of Mr. Elliot" and completed it in 1230. Perhaps Sprenger's copy was an early edition with a preface specially written for Mr. Elliot.

spent eight years in collecting material. According to Sprenger's summary of his biography in the *Gulshan i bī-khār* (under "ʿĀshiqī" if Sprenger is correct) "it is said that he now, 1252, resides at Lucnow, he is the author of the نشتر عشق in Persian, but as he does not know Arabic he fell into many errors" (Sprenger p. 205).

Nishtar i ʿishq, alphabetically arranged notices of 1470 ancient and modern poets with copious extracts, mainly *ghazals* and *rubāʿīs*, begun in 1224/1809–10 and completed in Rajab 1233/1818:[316] Sprenger no. 732, **Rāmpūr** (AH 1236/1820–1. See Nadhīr Aḥmad no. 97), **Bānkīpūr** viii 716–17 (late 19th cent.), **Lahore** Panjāb Univ. Lib. (slightly defective. See OCM. III/l (Nov. 1926) p. 76 and *Mai-khānah* ed. M. Shafīʿ p. *bā lām*).

[*Gulshan i bī-khār* (see Sprenger p. 205); Garcin de Tassy I p. 235 (under 'Aschiqui); *Nigāristān i sukhun* p. 59 (under "ʿĀshiqī"); *Ṣubḥ i gulshan* p. 271 (under "ʿĀshiqī").]

1194. **M. Fāḍil Khān**[317] **"Rāwī"** Bāyandurī **Garrūsī** was born in the district of Garrūs in Dhū 'l-Ḥijjah 1198/Oct.–Nov. 1784. After his father's death in 1214/1799–1800 he left his birthplace and pursued his studies in ʿIrāq and elsewhere, eventually reaching Ṭihrān, where he studied the art of poetry under the Malik al-Shuʿarāʾ, Fatḥ-ʿAlī Khān "Ṣabā" Kāshānī (for whom see no. 425 *supra*). Impressed by his abilities, which included a keen intelligence and a retentive memory, "Ṣabā" presented him to Fatḥ-ʿAlī Shāh, who appointed him Reciter of Panegyrics[318] at court. Subsequently he became Chief Herald[319] in constant attendance upon the Shāh. He committed "Ṣabā's" poems to memory and acted as his rhapsodist.[320] When the Shāh issued instructions that a collection of poems by the court poets should be compiled and two successive compilers, Aḥmad Bēg "Akhtar" (see no. 1190 *supra*) and M. Bāqir Bēg "Nashāṭī" Gurjī, had died before completing the task, Fāḍil Khān was ordered to undertake it and he accordingly compiled the *Anjuman i Khāqān*. After Fatḥ-ʿAlī Shāh's death [in 1250/1834] Fāḍil Khān retired and lived in receipt of a pension from Muḥammad Shāh Qājār. He died in 1252/1836–7.[321]

---

316 See the previous note.

317 So *Majmaʿ al-fuṣaḥāʾ*.

318 *Rāwī i madāyiḥ i Khāqānī shud* (*Majmaʿ al-fuṣaḥāʾ*).

319 *Bar jārchiyān i darbār buzurg u sālār shud dar safar u ḥaḍar az multazīmīn i rikāb i aʿlā būd* (*ibid.*): *manṣab i Jārchī-Bāshī yāft* (*Rauḍat al-ṣafā-yi Nāṣirī* vol. ix).

320 *Ashʿār i janāb i Malik* [*sc. al-Shuʿarāʾ*] *rā ḥāfiẓ u ḥāwī u nāqil u rāwī āmad* (*Majmaʿ al-fuṣaḥāʾ*).

321 So apparently *Majmaʿ al-fuṣaḥāʾ* and certainly *Rauḍat al-ṣafā-yi Nāṣirī* vol. ix.

Anjuman i Khāqān, notices of the poets of Fatḥ-ʿAlī Shāh's reign in four *anjumans* and a *khātimah*, undertaken at the Shāh's request in 1234/1818–19 and completed in five months: **Rieu** Suppt. 120 (AH 1234/1819), **Sipahsālār** ii p. 461 (AH 1236/1820–1), **Asʿad** 2075, **Lahore** Panjāb Univ. Lib. (See *OCM.* III/1 (Nov. 1926) p. 77), **Majlis** 324.

List of the poets: Rieu Suppt. p. 86.

[*Anjuman i Khāqān, khātimah; Tadhkirah i dil-gushā* (Berlin p. 672 no. 134); *Nigāristān i Dārā* fol. 92*b*; *Tadhkirah i Muḥammad-Shāhī* fol. 187*b*; *Majmaʿ al-fuṣaḥāʾ* ii p. 142; *Rauḍat al-ṣafā-yi Nāṣirī* vol. ix, 6th page from end.]

1195. **Maḥmūd Mīrzā** b. Fatḥ-ʿAlī Shāh **Qājār** has already been mentioned (no. 428 *supra*) as the author of the *Tārīkh i Ṣāḥib-qirānī*, completed in 1248/1832.[322] He died at Tabrīz in 1852 or 1853. His *Bayān al-Maḥmūd*, an anthology of initial lines of *ghazals* by contemporary poets (see Rieu Suppt. 377, Bānkīpūr Suppt. i 1997), was compiled in 1240/1824–5. For other works of his, mentioned in the preface to the *Safīnat al-Maḥmūd*, see Rieu Suppt. p. 87.

(1) ***Gulshan i Maḥmūd***, notices of forty-eight sons of Fatḥ-ʿAlī Shāh with specimens of their poetry, compiled by order of the Shāh in 1236/1820–1: **Rieu** Suppt. 121 (AH 1239/1823), **Asʿad** 2876.

List of the poets: Rieu Suppt. p. 87.

(2) ***Safīnat al-Maḥmūd***, notices of the poets of Fatḥ-ʿAlī Shāh's reign preceded in the B.M. MS. by two prefaces, the first of which gives *Majmaʿ i Maḥmūd* as the title and 1235/1819–20 as the date of compilation,[323] while the second says that in 1240/1824–5 the author was commanded by the Shāh to write an account of contemporary poets and that the title *Safīnat al-Maḥmūd* was given to it by the latter: **D.M.G.** 18 (lacks the earlier preface, AH 1256/1840), **Rieu** Suppt. 122 (mid 19th cent.), **Asʿad** 3874.

(3) ***Nuql i majlis***, notices of ancient and modern poetesses, composed in 1241/1825–6 at Nihāwand: MS. formerly in Vambéry's possession.

Extracts (biographies translated or summarised in German, verses in Persian and German): *Aus dem Geistesleben persischer Frauen. Von H. Vambéry* (in *ZDMG.* 45 (1891) pp. 403–28).

---

322 Another MS.: Leningrad Univ. 1142 (Romaskewicz p. 4).

323 According to Vambéry, however, the *Majmaʿ i Maḥmūd*, of which he possessed a MS. (see *ZDMG.* 45 (1891) pp. 403–5), is a collection of works by Maḥmūd Qājār, eleven in his MS., namely, (1) *Safīnat al-Maḥmūd*, (2) *Muntakhab al-Maḥmūd*, (3) *Gulshan i Maḥmūd*, (4) *Makhzan al-Maḥmūd*, (5) *Nuql i majlis*, (6) *Sunbulistān*, (7) *Parwardah i khayāl*, (8) *Maqṣūd i jahān*, (9) *Maḥmūd-nāmah*, (10) *Naṣāʾiḥ al-Maḥmūd* or *Durar al-Maḥmūd* (Rieu, Suppt. p. 87, gives these as two different works), (11) *Bayān al-Maḥmūd*.

1196. **'Alī Akbar "Bismil" Shīrāzī**, who has already been mentioned (no. 257 *supra*) as the author of the *Baḥr al-la'ālī*, died a few years before 1283/1866–7.

Tadhkirah i dil-gushā, on the poets of Fatḥ-'Alī Shāh's reign, begun in 1237/1821–2 by order of Ḥusain 'Alī Mīrzā and divided into a *gulzār* (subdivided in the Browne MS. into 3, in the Berlin MS. into 7, *gulbuns*, on Shīrāz, its history, buildings, gardens and celebrities, especially Sa'dī, Ḥāfiẓ and Waṣṣāf), two *būstāns* ((1) on Fatḥ-'Alī Shāh and 15 members of his family, (2) on 157 other poets arranged alphabetically under the *final* letter of the *takhalluṣ*, the first being "Bī-nawā", the second "Shaidā" and the last "Yārī"), and a *khātimah* (autobiography, ending (at least in the Browne MS.) with an account of the earthquake of 4 Shawwāl 1239/2 June 1824): **Browne** Coll. J. 18 = Houtum-Schindler 37 (apparently written by or for the author), **Berlin** 667 (AH 1252/1836).

List of the poets: Berlin pp. 669–73.

[See no. 257 *supra*, also *Riyāḍ al-'ārifīn* (Ṭihrān AHS 1316) pp. 422–4.]

1197. S. **'Abd al-Raḥīm "Munṣif"** al-Mūsawī b. Mīr M. Bāqir 'Alī-ābādī was born at Sārī in 1197/1783.

Badī' al-afkār, an anthology of ancient and modern poems with biographical notices, begun at Sārī in 1237/1821–2 for M. Kāẓim Mīrzā b. Muḥammad-Qulī Mīrzā b. Fatḥ-'Alī Shāh, completed in 1239/1824 and divided into six *qisms* ((1) *qaṣīdahs*, (2) *ghazals*, (3) *mathnawīs*, (4) *muqaṭṭa'āt*, (5) *rubā'īs*, (6) *tarjī'-bands*), in which the poets are arranged alphabetically except the royal princes, who come first: **Rieu** Suppt. 378.

[Autobiography at end of *Badī' al-afkār*.]

1198. Mīr **Ḥusain al-Ḥusainī**, having travelled from Shīrāz to 'Umān and thence to Sind, was admitted to the court of Mīr Karam 'Alī Khān and Mīr Murād 'Alī Khān Tālpur, the latter of whom has already been mentioned (no. 833 *supra*). On his return home (presumably to Shīrāz) Mīr Ḥusain compiled a *tadhkirah* as an *armaghān* for the two Sindī princes.

Zubdat al-mu'āṣirīn, a *tadhkirah* of contemporary poets compiled in 1240/1824–5: MS. in the possession of Prof. Maḥmūd Shērānī at Lahore.

Description with some extracts (verses by poetesses): *Fārisī kī ba'ḍ shā'ir 'auratēn aur un kā kalām* by M. Iqbāl (in OCM. X/1 (Nov. 1933) pp. 31–42).

1199. **'Abd al-Razzāq Bēg "Maftūn" b. Najaf-Qulī Khān Dunbulī** died in 1243/1827–8 (see no. 426 *supra*).

(1) *Tajribat al-aḥrār wa-tasliyat al-abrār*, personal memoirs with notices of his contemporaries written in 1228/1813: **Rieu** Suppt. 132, **Majlis** 534.

(2) *Nigāristān i Dārā*, notices of poets contemporary with Fatḥ-ʿAlī Shāh written in 1241/1825–6 and divided into five *nigār-khānahs* or *aiwāns* ((1) Fatḥ-ʿAlī Shāh, (2) 21 royal princes and noble amīrs, i.e. sons, grandsons and nephews of Fatḥ-ʿAlī Shāh, (3) 55 "favourites of the Shāh and of the princes, men of letters, Vazirs and other officials", beginning with "Ṣabā" and ending with "Humā", (4) about 120 other poets beginning with "Āzād" (M. ʿAlī Kashmīrī) and ending with "Yaghmā", (5) the author) and an appendix (on "ʿAndalīb"); **Rieu** Suppt. 123.

List of the poets in *Nigār-khānahs* i-iii: Rieu Suppt. pp. 88–9.

1200. Ḥakīm **ʿAlī-Riḍā** (in full, Ghulām-ʿAlī-Mūsā-Riḍā) **"Rāʾiq"**, usually known as **Bāqir Ḥusain Khān Nāʾiṭī**, was the son of Rukn al-Dīn Ḥusain Khān. He died in 1248/1832–3.

Guldastah i Karnāṭak (a chronogram = 1210/1795–6, the date of inception), alphabetically arranged notices of seventy poets who lived in the Carnatic towards the close of the eighteenth century and in the early years of the nineteenth, completed some time between 1244/1828–9 and 1248/1832–3, the date of the author's death: **Ivanow** 1st Suppt. 766 (early 20th cent.).

List of the poets: Ivanow 1st Suppt. pp. 8–10.

[Autobiography in *Guldastah i Karnāṭak; Natāʾij al-afkār* p. 189; *Ṣubḥ i waṭan* pp. 81–8; *Gulzār i Aʿẓam* p. 202; *Ishārāt i Bīnish* (Ivanow-Curzon p. 69 no. 49); M. Mahdī "Wāṣif" Madrāsī *Ḥadīqat al-marām* (in Arabic), Madras 1279/1862, pp. 23–4.]

1201. Rājah **Ratan Sing'h "Zakhmī"** who was born at Lucknow on 23 Muḥarram 1197/29 Dec. 1782 and died in 1851, has already been mentioned (no. 946 *supra*) as the author of the *Sulṭān al-tawārīkh*.

Anīs al-ʿāshiqīn, an alphabetically arranged *tadhkirah* of ancient and modern poets written at Lucknow in 1245/1829–30[324] and divided into a *muqaddimah* (in praise of Naṣīr al-Dīn Ḥaidar)[325] and 31 *ḥarfs*, in which are given brief biographies and selections, almost exclusively from the poets' *ghazals* and *rubāʿīs*: **Lahore** Panjāb Univ. Lib. (vol. i only, ending

324 It will be observed that the MS. described by Nadhīr Aḥmad is dated 1239. If this date is correct the MS. must represent an edition earlier than the *muqaddimah* in praise of Naṣīr al-Dīn Ḥaidar.

325 King of Awad'h ("Oudh") 1243/1827–1253/1837.

with "Ḍiyā'ī". See M. Shafīʿ in OCM. III/3 (May 1927) pp. 48–51), **Nadhīr Aḥmad** 73 (vol. ii only, beginning with "Ṭālib" Jājarmī and containing about 1176 notices. Gaurī Parshād, Lucknow, AH 1239/1820).[326]

[Autobiography in *Anīs al-ʿāshiqīn* under "Zakhmī" (summarised by M. Shafīʿ in OCM. III/3 (May 1927) pp. 49–50).]

1202. S. **M. ʿAlī** b. S. M. Ṭabāṭabā'ī **Zawārī** was born on 29 Ṣafar 1195/24 Feb. 1781 at Iṣfahān, to which his father had been forced by stress of circumstances to migrate from Zawārah,[327] the home of his family. At the age of nineteen S. M. ʿAlī went to Zawārah and pursued his studies there for two years, but misfortunes compelled him to leave the town and to wander for a period from place to place. In Fatḥ-ʿAlī Shāh's reign (1211/1797–1250/1834) he returned and obtained an appointment as clerk (*kātib*) in the Madrasah of Mīrzā ʿAbd al-ʿAẓīm at Ardistān. In the time of Saif al-Daulah Sulṭān-Muḥammad Mīrzā[328] an accusation having been laid against him and a summons issued, he fled from Ardistān, but some time afterwards successful intercession was made on his behalf, his offence was pardoned, and he was commanded to write a history of the Kākh i ʿAsharah [?].

Ma'āthir al-Bāqirīyah, notices of 52 panegyrists of S. M. Bāqir al-Mūsawī al-Ḥusainī, written in 1245/1829–30: **Rāmpūr** (AH 1247/1832. See a description by M. Shajāʿat ʿAlī Khān in OCM. VI/2 (Feb. 1930) pp. 111–13. Cf. Nadhīr Aḥmad no. 89).

[Autobiography in *khātimah* to *Ma'āthir al-Bāqirīyah* (summarised by Shajāʿat ʿAlī Khān).]

1203. **Khūb Chand "Dhakā'"** b. Bhawānī Chand Kāyat'h **Dihlawī**, a pupil of Mīr Naṣīr al-Dīn "Naṣīr",[329] lived at Sikandarābād and died in 1846. He was the author of a *dīwān* [in Urdu], of some Persian poetry, and of some compositions in ornate prose.

ʿIyār al-shuʿarā', an inaccurate and uncritical alphabetically arranged dictionary of nearly 1500 Rēkhtah (i.e. Urdū) poets, begun in 1208/1793–4 or 1213/1798–9[330] at the suggestion of "Naṣīr", but containing a date as late as 1247/1831–2: Sprenger no. 50 = (?) **Ethé** 702 (n.d.).

---

326 See two notes back.

327 For Zawārah, near Ardistān, see no. 22, 2nd footnote *supra*.

328 Who was appointed Governor of ʿIrāq in 1240/1824–5 (see no. 1204 *infra*).

329 d. at Ḥaidarābād in, or about, 1840 (see Sprenger p. 269, Garcin de Tassy ii pp. 418–20, Beale *Oriental biographical dictionary*, Saksēna *History of Urdu literature* pp. 146–7, T. Grahame Bailey *History of Urdu literature* p. 59, etc.).

330 "According to a rather ambiguous chronogram on fol. 2*b*, l. 8" (Ethé).

[Autobiography in *ʿIyār al-shuʿarāʾ*; Sprenger pp. 184–5; Garcin de Tassy iii pp. 350–1.]

1204. Saif al-Daulah **Sulṭān-Muḥammad** "Sulṭān" b. Fatḥ-ʿAlī Shāh **Qājār** was born on 26 Jumādā I 1228/27 May 1813.[331] In 1240/1824–5 he was appointed Governor of ʿIrāq and spent the next ten years at Iṣfahān, where learned and pious men frequented his court. After the death of Fatḥ-ʿAlī Shāh [in 1250/1834][332] he returned to Ṭihrān and in Muḥammad Shāh's campaigns against Gurgān and Harāt he had the rank of *mīrpanjah* (*Majmaʿ al-fuṣaḥāʾ* I p. 32⁴: *az Iṣfahān ba-Ṭihrān āmadah dar safar i Gurgān u Harāt dar kamāl i ʿizzat ba-manṣab i mīr-panjagī manṣūb u makhṣūṣ gardīd*). Some time later he visited Najaf and Karbalāʾ. In 1279/1862–3 he travelled via Gīlān and Shīrwān to Istānbūl, Alexandria, Cairo, Mecca, Damascus, Ḥimṣ, Aleppo, Diyārbakr, al-Mauṣil and Baghdād. After a year in Ṭihrān he made a pilgrimage to Mashhad. Apparently he was still alive when the *Majmaʿ al-fuṣaḥāʾ*, completed in 1288/1871, was written. Of his works Riḍā-Qulī Khān mentions (1) a dīwān of nearly twenty thousand verses, (2) *Mulūk al-kalām*, an anthology of passages in Arabic and Persian prose and verse on various subjects, (3) *Tuḥfat al-Ḥaramain wa-saif al-rasāʾil*, a *mathnawī*.

Tadhkirat al-salāṭīn (as it is called in the preface of the Sipahsālār MS.), or ***Bazm i Khāqān*** (as it is called in the preface of the Majlis MS.), written at Iṣfahān in 1245/1829–30, recast perhaps in 1250/1834–5,[333] and divided into a *muqaddimah* (consisting of the *Anīs al-ʿushshāq* of Sharaf al-Dīn "Rāmī" appropriated without acknowledgment) and three *bābs* ((1) kings and princes with verses by them, (2) a brief account of Fatḥ-ʿAlī Shāh and specimens of his poetry, (3) on the author's life and poems), or, as in the Majlis MS., into a *muqaddimah* (= the *Anīs al-ʿushshāq*) and five *anjumans* ((1) *dar baʿḍī az ashʿār u ḥālāt i salāṭīn u pādshāh-zādagān i pīshīn*, (2) *dar manāqib i pādshāh i ʿaṣr* [Fatḥ-ʿAlī Shah] *u ashʿārī az ū*, (3) *dar ashʿār u ḥālāt i shāh-zādagān*, (4) *dar ashʿār u aḥwāl i mīr-zādagān*, (5) *dar dhikr i ashʿār u ḥālāt i muʾallif*): **Sipahsālār** ii p. 477 (breaking off before the end of *Bāb* II), **Majlis** (containing in *Anjuman* v the author's biography only, not his poems. For some account of this MS., not described in the Majlis catalogue, see Sipahsālār ii p. 478, footnotes).

[*Majmaʿ al-fuṣaḥāʾ* i pp. 31–4 (summarised in Sipahsālār ii pp. 477–8).]

---

331 So *Nāsikh al-tawārīkh* (*Tārīkh i Qājārīyah* vol. i, at end. Quoted in Sipahsālār ii p. 477). The date 1227 is given in the *Majmaʿ al-fuṣaḥāʾ*.

332 Riḍā-Qulī Khān says 1249.

333 1245 is the date given in the preface of the Majlis MS. The Sipahsālār MS. seems to give the two dates 1250 and 1245 in a rather obscure way.

1205. **Bahman Mīrzā** b. Nā'ib al-Salṭanah 'Abbās Mīrzā[334] comes fourth in the list of 'Abbās Mīrzā's twenty-six surviving sons given in the *Rauḍat al-ṣafā-yi Nāṣirī* (vol. ix, fol. 166*a* (the 30th page from the end), l. 9). His eldest brother, Muḥammad Mīrzā, who acceded to the throne in 1250/1834 and died in 1264/1848, was born on 6 Dhū 'l-Qa'dah 1222/5 Jan. 1808. Probably therefore Bahman Mīrzā was born about 1225/1810. In the preface to the *Tadhkirah i Muḥammad-Shāhī* he "says that he was residing in Ardabīl, to the government of which he had been appointed by his father, when he was invited by his elder brother, Muḥammad Shāh, to join him, and, at his request, compiled the present work" (Rieu). The date of composition, 1247/1831–2, is indicated by a chronogram and at the end of the work 1249/1833–4 is given as the date of completion. He evidently returned to Ardabīl, since according to the *Rauḍat al-ṣafā-yi Nāṣirī* (x, fol. 2*a*, l. 11) he was there in Rajab 1250/Nov. 1834, when Muḥammad Shāh came to the throne. In that year he was appointed Governor of Burūjird (*op. cit.* x fol. 6*b*, l. 25, fol. 7*a*, l. 6 *ab infra*). In 1257/1841 (apparently) he was made Governor of Ādharbāyjān (*op. cit.* x fol. 26*a*, l. 6 *ab infra*), but in 1263/1847 he was superseded in favour of Nāṣir al-Dīn Mīrzā (*op. cit.* x fol. 42*a*, l. 18). He was then under suspicion of desiring to secure for himself the succession to the throne, and it was with some trepidation that he set out for Ṭihrān. Muḥammad Shāh gave him a friendly reception, but, when an inquiry into the finances of Ādharbāyjān revealed a large deficit, Bahman Mīrzā thought it prudent to take refuge in the Russian Embassy (*op. cit.* x fol. 42*b*, l. 21). Permission to live in Russian territory was granted to him, and there the remainder of his life was spent, though his recall was suggested early in Nāṣir al-Dīn Shāh's reign.[335] He seems to have gone to Georgia[336] and to have died there in 1883.[337]

---

334 For 'Abbās Mīrzā, Fatḥ-'Alī Shāh's eldest (surviving) son, see no. 434 *supra*.

335 Cf. R. G. Watson *History of Persia* p. 380: There were at this time absent from the kingdom, in banishment, two men who had been the most powerful, as well as perhaps the ablest, statesmen of Persia. One of the two was the Shah's uncle, Bahman Meerza, who had been implicated in the proceedings of the Asef-ed-Dowleh at Meshed. It was believed that the latter had offered to him the crown of Persia, and the discovery of this conspiracy had led to Prince Bahman being deprived of his government of Azerbaeejan, and to his being forced to retire to Georgia, where he remained under Russian protection. The other exiled Persian statesman was the Asef-ed-Dowleh, the uncle of the late Mahomed Shah. The Ameer-i-Nizam was urged to recall both of these illustrious exiles; but with regard to the case of Bahman Meerza, he observed that, should the prince be permitted to return to his country, his wealth, influence and popularity would quickly secure for him his former government of Azerbaeejan, which he would be likely to constitute an independent province.

336 See the preceding footnote.

337 "Mr. Churchill states in a letter that Bahman Mirza subsequently fled to the Caucasus and died there a few years ago " (Rieu Suppt. p. 90. From Rieu's preface it appears that the Churchill MSS. were acquired from 1884 to 1894). Cf. Browne Coll. p. 119, where it is

Tadhkirah i Muḥammad-Shāhī, notices of poets completed in 1249/1833–4 and divided into three *rishtahs* ((1) about 150 ancient and modern poets to the end of the 12th century of the Hijrah, (2) Fatḥ-ʿAlī Shāh and twelve Qājār princes, (3) 57 contemporary poets in alphabetical order): **Rieu** Suppt. 124 (AH 1257/1841).

List of the poets in *Rishtahs* 2 and 3: Rieu Suppt. pp. 90–1.

1206. Darwīsh Ḥusain **"Nawā"**[338] **Kāshānī** is described in the *Majmaʿ al-fuṣaḥāʾ* as a contemporary who after a period spent in travel (*muddatī siyāḥat kardah*) had settled in Tabrīz, where his *takyah* and its beautiful garden used to be visited by the children of the *Walī-ʿahd* and others. After his death [which must have occurred before 1288/1871] his *tadhkirah*, without preface or conclusion, had been seen by Riḍā-Qulī Khān, who mentions it in his *muqaddimah* (vol. i p. [8 8]) as well as in his notice of Darwīsh "Nawā". Riḍā-Qulī Khān did not regard him as a good judge of poetry (*quwwah i tashkhīṣ i shiʿr na-dāshtah*).

Tadhkirah i Darwīsh Nawā, short biographical notices of ancient and modern poets with extensive extracts from their works: **Rieu** Suppt. 115 (*Silsilah* i, *Ṭabaqah* 1 only, containing 50 ancient poets (specified by Rieu) in alphabetical order from Abū 'l-Faraj Rūnī to Niẓāmī Ganjawī.[339] Before AH 1253/1837, probably written by, or for, the author), **Browne** Coll v. 68 (contains not only the poets given in the preceding MS. but also in "*Ṭabaqa* i, *Silsila* 2" an enormous number of minor poets, some ancient, others "at least as modern as the Ṣafawí period", and in a third section (untitled and apparently incomplete, since it breaks off in the letter *Ṣād*) further poets, mostly quite modern).

[*Tadhkirah i Muḥammad-Shāhī* (Rieu Suppt. 124) fol. 221*a*; *Majmaʿ al-fuṣaḥāʾ* ii p. 527.]

---

said that a certain MS. "was originally transcribed in 1277/1860 for Prince Bahman Mírzá *Bahá'u'd-Dawla*, who according to a note in Schindler's writing attached to the volume, died in the Caucasus in AD 1883." [Bahman Mīrzā Bahāʾ al-Daulah, however, was not the same person as the Bahman Mīrzā who died in the Caucasus. The former was a son of Fatḥ-ʿAlī Shāh (47th in the list given in the *Rauḍat al-ṣafā-yi Nāṣirī* ix fol. 172*b*) and was Governor of Kāshān (*op. cit.* x fol. 22*a*, l. 21), Yazd (*op. cit.* x fol. 23*b*, l. 5), Simnān (*op. cit.* ix fol. 172*b* (17th page from end), l. 4) and doubtless of other places. He is presumably the Bahman Mīrzā who "died at Ṭihrán in Rabíʿ II, 1277 = Oct.-Nov. 1860" (Browne Coll. p. 90).]

338 "Bí-Nawá" according to the catalogue of the Browne Collection, but this is not supported by the *Tadhkirah i Muḥammad-Shāhī*, the *Majmaʿ al-fuṣaḥaʾ* or the "endorsement" on "Sipihr's" MS. seen by S. Churchill (cf. the next note).

339 The MS. described by Rieu was acquired through Sidney Churchill, who "states that a MS. belonging to Sipihr, of Teheran [for whom see no. 191 *supra*], and containing, besides the above Ṭabaḳah, two Silsilahs, treating of later and contemporary poets, is endorsed "Taẕkirah i Darvīsh Navā".

1207. Nawwāb ʿAẓīm al-Daulah Sarfarāz al-Mulk M. **Muṣṭafā Khān "Shēftah"**[340] Dihlawī Muẓaffar-Jang was a son of Nawwāb ʿAẓīm al-Daulah Sarfarāz al-Mulk Murtaḍā Khān, a Bangash Afghān, who in 1813 purchased the estate of Jahāngīrābād in the Bulandshahr District. He was born at Delhi in 1806[341] and educated by local scholars and *ṣūfīs*. In the art of poetry he received instruction from "Mūmin" and "Ghālib" (for the latter of whom see no. 694 *supra*). In Dhū 'l-Ḥijjah 1254/Feb. 1839 he started on a pilgrimage to Mecca and al-Madīnah and did not return to Delhi until Dhū 'l-Ḥijjah 1256/Feb. 1841. Of this journey he published (where ? when ?) an account entitled *Targhīb al-sālik ilā aḥsan al-masālik*, or *Rah-āward*, of which an Urdu translation, *Sirāj i munīr*, by S. Zain al-ʿĀbidīn, was published (where ?) in 1910. After the Mutiny of 1857 he was imprisoned for a time on a charge of seditious correspondence with the King of Delhi, but was subsequently pardoned. Thenceforward he lived mainly at Jahāngīrābād. He died in 1869 and was buried at Delhi.

He is the author of (1) the *safar-nāmah* mentioned above, (2) *Dīwān i Shēftah*, an Urdu *dīwān* published at Meerut, probably two or three years before 1857, and republished in the *Kullīyāt i Shēftah u Ḥasratī* (Badāyūn 1916), (3) *Dīwān i Ḥasratī*, a Persian *dīwān* published in the *Kulliyāt*, (4) a number of Persian *ruqaʿāt* published in the *Kullīyāt*, and

(5) ***Gulshan i bī-khār***, very short notices of about 600 Rēkhtah (i.e. Urdū) poets, "more correct than most other Tadzkirahs" (Sprenger), begun in 1248/1832–3 and completed in 1250/1834–5; **Rieu** iii 1069*a* (AH 1252/1837), **Bānkīpūr** viii 718 (AH 1255/1840).

Editions: **Delhi** 1253/1837–8 (see Sprenger p. 189 and *Kullīyāt i Shēftah u Ḥasratī*, introductory biography p. 43), 1843°*, **Lucknow** 1874°*.

For the *Gulistān i bī-khazān*, an Urdū *tadhkirah* written in 1265/1859 by Ḥakīm S. Ghulām-Quṭb al-Dīn "Bāṭin", of Āgrah, as an improved version of the *Gulshan i bī-khār*. which according to "Bāṭin" contains much satirical and unjust criticism, see Sprenger no. 57 and Blumhardt's *Catalogue of the Hindustani manuscripts in … the India Office* no. 61, as well as Blumhardt's catalogues of Hindustani printed books in the B.M. and I.O., where a lithographed edition (Lucknow 1875°*) is described. According to Sprenger it may be considered a translation of the *Gulshan i bī-khār* "into unintelligible Hindústány, with some idiotical remarks".

340 This *takhalluṣ* used by him in his Urdu poetry is better known than "Ḥasratī", which he used in his Persian poetry.

341 This is the date given by Niẓāmī Badāyūnī in the *Qāmūs al-mashāhīr*. If the catalogues are right in saying that he was 26 when he completed the *Gulshan i bī-khār* in 1250, he must have been bom in 1223 or 1224, i.e. in 1808 or 1809.

[Garcin de Tassy iii pp. 123–4; *Sham'i anjuman* 134–6; *Kullīyāt i Shēftah u Ḥasratī*, Badāyūn 1916 (published for his son, Nawwāb Ḥājjī M. Isḥāq K͟hān), introductory biography by Niẓāmī Badāyūnī; Niẓāmī Badāyūnī *Qāmūs al-mashāhīr* (in Urdū) ii p. 33; Rām Bābū Saksēna *A history of Urdu literature*, Allahabad 1927, pp. 150–1.]

1208. **Aḥmad**, known as (*al-shahīr bi-*) **Hulāgū** (or Halākū, which according to Blochet is the modern pronunciation), **"K͟harāb" Qājār** set out on a pilgrimage to Mecca and, being unaccompanied by friends who could speak his language, he sought to occupy his time by writing down such ancient and modern poetry as he could remember. Having visited Mecca and Medina, he went to Istānbūl (on an embassy, according to Blochet: *ba-jihat i muhimm i umūrāt i ẓāhirī i k͟hwud wārid i marz i Qusṭanṭīn u idrāk i sharaf-yābī i āstānah i A'lā Ḥaḍrat muyassar shud*, as "K͟harāb" himself says). The business of his embassy having kept him fully occupied during the year that he spent at Istānbūl, it was only after this delay that he could re-examine his manuscript. Finding the contemporary poetry most agreeable to his taste, he rejected the rest and confined his *Masṭabah i K͟harāb* to the poets of Fatḥ-'Alī S͟hāh's time. The Turkish poetry at the end of the work was collected by him during his visit to the Ottoman dominions.

Masṭabah i K͟harāb, brief notices of Fatḥ-'Alī S͟hāh's Persian, Indian and Turkish contemporaries who wrote Persian and Turkish poetry, compiled in 1253/1837–8: **Blochet** ii 1160 (AH 1271/1855).

[Autobiographical statements in the preface (summarised by Blochet, who quotes some of the original Persian).]

1209. H. H. Nawwāb Wālā-Jāh Amīr al-Hind A'ẓam al-Umarā' [afterwards 'Umdat al-Umarā'?][342] Muk͟htār al-Mulk Sirāj al-Daulah **M. G͟hauth K͟hān** [afterwards G͟hulām-M. G͟hauth K͟h?][343] "A'ẓam" Bahādur-Jang [afterwards S͟hahāmat-Jang?][344] was the last titular[345] Nawwāb of the Carnatic. He was born on 29 Dhū

---

342 'Umdat al-Umarā' in the *Madras almanac* for 1854.

343 In the *Ṣubh i waṭan* "he" calls himself M. G͟hauth K͟hān and says that his original name was M. G͟hauth (cf. *Madras almanac* for 1842). In the *Madras almanac* for 1854 and in the official announcement of his death he is called G͟hulām-M. G͟hauth K͟hān.

344 S͟hahāmat-Jang in the *Is͟hārat i Bīnis͟h* (Ivanow-Curzon p. 69 no. 10).

345 His grandfather 'Aẓīm al-Daulah in 1801 ceded his rights and authority in the Carnatic to the East India Company. Since the death of M. G͟hauth K͟hān the successive heads of this family have borne the title Prince of Arcot (*Amīr i Arkāt*). For the present Prince of Arcot see *Who's Who* under Arcot, Prince of. This house, to quote *The Times* of 3.12.1855, "was a century ago one of the most prominent in Southern India. His [i.e. M. G͟hauth K͟hān's] ancestor it was who was supported as Nawab by the English, in opposition to a

'l-Ḥijjah 1239/25 August 1824[346] and succeeded his father, Nawwāb Aʿẓam-Jāh, in 1825. During his minority his uncle, H. H. Prince ʿAẓīm-Jāh Bahādur Nāʾib i Mukhtār, acted as Regent. On 25 August 1842 he was installed as *Nawwāb Ṣūbah-dār* of the Carnatic at Chepauk Palace. After a life "spent in rioting and profligacy" (*The Times*) he died without issue on 7 October 1855 at the age of thirty-one years and was buried to the north of the Great Mosque at Triplicane. He "is said to have possessed considerable natural intelligence, but he never evinced any predilection for European society, and he had long forgotten the little knowledge of English he had once acquired. He was by nature of a lavish disposition, and the only value he seems to have set on money was to have it to give to his attendants" (*The [Madras] Athenaeum*). For his *dīwān*, the *Dīwān i Aʿẓam*, see Ivanow 1st Suppt. no. 814. A published edition of a work of his entitled *Bahāristān i Aʿẓam* (probably an anthology) is mentioned without date or place of publication under the heading *Dawāwīn* in the Āṣafīyah catalogue (i p. 714). M. Mahdī "Wāṣif" in his *Ḥadīqat al-marām* (p. 7) denies that he wrote any books and says that the poet "Rāqim"[347] wrote a work on prosody and a *tadhkirah* of poets which he ascribed to the Nawwāb.

(1) ***Ṣubḥ i waṭan***, notices of about 90 poets of the Carnatic with eleven *ghazals* by each, completed in 1257/1841 and intended to correct and supplement the *Guldastah i Karnāṭak* of "Rāʾiq" (see no. 1200 *supra*).

Edition: **Madras** 1258/1842* (cf. Sprenger p. 172). List of the poets common to the *Guldastah i Karnāṭak* and the *Ṣubḥ i waṭan*: Ivanow 1st Suppt. pp. 8–10.

(2) ***Gulzār i Aʿẓam*** (a chronogram = 1269/1852–3): **Āṣafīyah** i p. 322 no. 38 (AH 1302/1884–5).

Edition: [**Madrās** ?] 1272/1855–6 (see Ḥaidarābād Coll. p. 23 and Ivanow 1st Suppt. p. 40. The former gives Ḥaidarābād as the place of publication, the latter says "[Madras ?]").

[*Ṣubḥ i waṭan* pp. 3–8; *Madras almanac* 1842 pp. 282, 284: 1854 p. 109: and other dates; *Ishārāt i Bīnish* (Ivanow-Curzon p. 69 no. 10); *The Athenaeum*, [a

relative and rival, whose cause was espoused by the French. The struggle between the two European nations lasted long, but in the end, spite of the genius and devotion of men like Labourdonnais, Dupleix and Lally, the English triumphed and with them their ally the Nawab. But the power of his race was soon at an end. In 1801 Lord Wellesley, as Governor-General, entered into a treaty with the reigning Nawab by which that Prince ceded his rights and authority in the Carnatic to the British, one-fifth of the yearly revenues being guaranteed to him for the maintenance of himself and his retainers." For the Persian histories of the Carnatic see nos. 1082–87 *supra*.

346 1 Dhū 'l-Ḥijjah 1239 according to the *Ishārāt i Bīnish* (Ivanow-Curzon p. 69 no. 10).

347 Presumably M. Ḥusain "Rāqim" Qādirī, of whom there is a notice in the *Ishārāt i Bīnish* (Ivanow-Curzon p. 69 no. 50).

Madras newspaper] 9.10.1855 p. 482, 11.10.1855 p. 486; *The Times* [London newspaper] 3.12.1955 p. 8 col. 3; M. Mahdī "Wāṣif" Madrāsī *Ḥadīqat al-marām* (in Arabic), Madras 1279/1862, p. 7; Buckland *Dictionary of Indian biography* p. 73. Unfortunately some of the above works have not been available for the verification of certain details in the revision of this article.]

1210. **Wazīr ʿAlī "ʿIbratī" ʿAẓīmābādī** was born at ʿAẓīmābād (i.e. Paṭnah) and was a pupil of Rājah Piyārē Laʿl "Ulfatī" Dihlawī (d. 1254/1838).[348] After a period in the service of Nawwāb Raushan al-Mulk Mubārak al-Daulah M. Mahdī-Qulī Khān Bahādur Shaukat-Jang he was appointed *Munshī* to Nawwāb Mubāriz al-Mulk Ḍiyāʾ al-Daulah S. M. Ḥasan Khān Bahādur Tahawwur-Jang. Later he became the constant companion of Rājah Bhūp Sing'h.

He is the author of several works preserved at Calcutta, viz. *Iʿjāz al-maḥabbat*, written in 1247/1831–2, a prose version of "Faiḍī's" *Nal Daman* (Ivanow Curzon no. 259), *Miṣbāḥ al-akhlāq*, written in 1250/1834–5, a collection of 76 short bombastic letters (Ivanow Curzon no. 507), *Miʿrāj al-ushshāq*, written in 1251/1835–6, a prose version of "Hātifī's" *Lailā u Majnūn* (Ivanow Curzon no. 246) and *Sirāj al-maḥabbat*, written in 1252/1836, a prose version of "Minnat's" *mathnawī* on the story of Hīr and Rānjhā (Ivanow Curzon no. 314).

(1) ***Miʿrāj al-khayāl***, an alphabetically arranged dictionary of poets, chiefly Indians of the 18th and 19th centuries, completed in 1257/1841 (but later dates occur): **Ivanow** Curzon 60 (AH 1282/1865).

List of 23 contemporary poets: Ivanow-Curzon pp. 67–8.

(2) ***Riyāḍ al-afkār***, alphabetically arranged biographies of elegant prose-writers (many of them also poets), mostly of the 17th, 18th and 19th centuries and mostly Indians or Persians who settled in India, completed in 1268/1852 and divided into 28 *khiyābāns*: **Būhār** 93 (AH 1282/1866), **Bānkīpūr** Suppt. i no. 1784 (1272 *Faṣlī*).

List and epitome of the biographies: Bānkīpūr Suppt. i pp. 49–61.

[Autobiographies in *Miʿrāj al-khayāl* and *Riyāḍ al-afkār* (the latter summarised in Bānkīpūr Suppt. i p. 48).]

1211. M. **Qudrat Allāh Khān "Qudrat"** b. M. Kāmil Gōpāmawī "left his native place" (i.e. Gōpāmau[349] presumably) for the Carnatic in 1227/1812 and subsequently entered the service of the Nawwāb. In 1239/1823–4 the title of Khān was conferred upon him and he was appointed custodian of the late Nawwāb's tomb. He was the author of two *dīwāns*.

---

348 For accounts of his life see *Miʿrāj al-khayāl* and *Riyāḍ al-afkār* (the latter summarised in Bānkīpūr Suppt. i p. 50).

349 14 miles East of Hardoi in Oudh.

Natā'ij al-afkār, about 525 short notices of ancient and modern poets completed in 1258/1842 and dedicated to Nawwāb M. G͟hauth K͟hān (for whom see no. 1209 *supra*): Sprenger no. 730, **Rieu** iii 1024*b* (extracts only. Circ. AD 1850), **I.O.** 4027 (AD 1895).

Edition: **Madras** 1843 (see Sprenger p. 644).

[*Natā'ij al-afkār*, preface (summarised by Rieu); *Guldastah i Karnāṭak* (Ivanow 1st Suppt. p. 9 no. 51); *Ṣubḥ i waṭan* pp. 148–53; *Is͟hārāt i Bīnis͟h* (Ivanow-Curzon p. 69 no. 48); M. Mahdī "Waṣif" Madrāsī *Ḥadīqat al-marām* (in Arabic), Madras 1279/1862, pp. 47–8; *S͟ham' i anjuman* p. 392.]

1212. **M. Riḍā "Najm"** b. Abī 'l-Qāsim Ṭabāṭabā has already been mentioned as the author of the general histories *Zubdat al-g͟harā'ib* (begun in 1231/1816. See no. 180 (1) *supra*) and *Majma' al-mulūk* (begun about 1260/1844. See no. 180 (2)), and of the Indian histories *Ak͟hbārāt i Hind* (completed in 1264/1848. See no. 656 *supra*), and *Mafātīḥ al-ri'āsat* (extending to 1251/1835–6. See no. 691 *supra*).

Nag͟hmah i 'andalīb (a chronogram == 1261/1845), or *Chahār bāg͟h* (?),[350] a *tad͟hkirah* of 226 foll, dedicated to Wājid 'Alī S͟hāh, King of Oudh, and divided into two *rauḍahs*, of which the first is subdivided into five *bahārs* ((1) on Persian grammar, fol. 7*b*, (2) forms of Persian poetry, fol. 11*a*, (3) poetical figures, fol. 13*a*, (4) metre and rhyme, fol. 15*b*, (5) short alphabetically arranged notices of ancient and modern poets, not usually very informative biographically except in the case of Indian poets, especially the more recent, foll. 19*a*–200*b*), and the second into two *ḥadīqahs* ((1) on Greek music, fol. 201*a*, (2) on Indian music, fol. 203*b*), **Rieu** iii p. 978*b* (circ. AD 1850. Received by H. M. Elliot from the author), 1014*b* (extracts only), 1018*b* (extracts only).

1213. Mīrzā **Amīr Bēg "Amīr"** Banārasī was in the service of the rulers of Oudh from the time of Sa'ādat-'Alī K͟hān [1212–29/1797–1814] to that of M. Amjad 'Alī S͟hāh [1258–63/1842–7].

Ḥadā'iq al-shu'arā', begun in 1211/1796–7 at the request of Ẓafar al-Daulah Fatḥ-'Alī K͟hān Kaptān, completed on 7 S͟ha'bān 1262/31 July, 1846, and containing alphabetically arranged and biographically not very informative notices of 2609 poets (the first "Ābrū", the last M. Yūnus K͟hān "Yūnus" Abharī) in 31 *ḥadīqahs* (foll. 8–166*b*), followed by 30 *s͟hajarahs* on the correct forms of the titles of kings and poets (foll. 166*b*–183), 31 *dauḥahs* on the correct forms of geographical names (foll. 183–217), two *thamarahs* on the names, dates of accession and length of reign of kings in Pre-Islamic Persia and the Muḥammadan world (foll. 217–29),

---

350 This second title, written on the fly-leaf of Elliot's MS., does not appear in the text.

seven *nakhlahs* on the seven dialects of Persian (Harawī, Sagzī, etc., foll. 229*b*–230), and 30 *natījahs* forming a large anthology of poetical quotations arrayed alphabetically according to the rhymes (foll. 230–853): **Ivanow** Curzon 702 (probably autograph), **Būhār** Arabic cat. pp. 529–30 (*ḥadīqahs* and *shajarahs* only).

1214. **M. ʿAlī "Bahār"** b. Āqā Abū Ṭālib mudhahhib **Iṣfahānī** was, like his father, an illuminator by trade. According to *al-Maʾāthir wa-'l-āthār* he lived for a time in Ṭihrān, but returned to Iṣfahān and died there. He is the author of the facetious tales entitled *Yakhchālīyah* (Editions: [Persia] 1290/1873°, 1298/1881°).

Madāʾiḥ al-Muʿtamadīyah, poems in praise of Muʿtamad al-Daulah Minūchihr Khān,[351] a memoir of whom by "the late" Āqā ʿAlī Rashtī is prefixed to the work, with rhetorical and mostly uninformative notices of their authors: **Rieu** Suppt. 127 (AH 1259/1843, apparently the copy presented to Minūchihr Khān. "whose portrait is found inside the original painted cover"), 128 (AH 1263/1847, an enlarged edition, in which the opening memoir is brought down from 1259/1843 to Minūchihr Khān's death on 5 Rabīʿ i 1263/21 Feb., 1847, and notices of 19 additional poets are given).

List of the poets (87 + 19): Rieu Suppt. pp. 93–5. [*al-Maʾāthir wa-'l-āthār* p. 213.]

1215. S. **ʿAlī Kabīr**, commonly called (*al-madʿū* or *ʿurf*) **M. Mīranjān**, "Saiyid," originally "Ajmalī", b. S. ʿAlī Jaʿfar Ḥusainī **Muḥammadī** Ḥanafī Naqshbandī **Ilāhābādī** has already been mentioned (no. 299, Persian translation *supra*) as the author of a translation of ʿAbd al-ʿAzīz Dihlawī's *Sirr al-shahādatain*, completed at Ghāzīpūr in 1251/1835 and entitled *Iẓhār al-saʿādah fī tarjamat Asrār al-shahādah*. He was born on 28 Muḥarram 1212/1797, both his father and his mother being descendants of a well-known scholar and mystic, Shāh Khūb Allāh (properly M. Yaḥyā) Ilāhābādī[352] In addition to a number of theological and other works in prose[353] he wrote a *dīwān* and several *mathnawīs*.[354]

351 Minūchihr Khān Gurjī Tiflīsī, a Georgian eunuch taken captive in Fatḥ-ʿAlī Shāh's Georgian Campaign of 1219/1804, became Īch-Āqā-sī in charge of the royal Ḥaram and was given the title of Muʿtamad al-Daulah after the death of the previous holder of the title, ʿAbd al-Wahhāb "Nashāṭ", on 5 Dhū 'l-Ḥijjah 1244/8 June 1829 (cf. *Rauḍat al-ṣafā-yi Nāṣiri* ix fol. 146*b*, l. 20). Early in 1258/1842 he was appointed Governor of Iṣfahān, Luristān and ʿArabistān (*op. cit.* x fol. 24*a* antepenult). Cf. Browne, *A year amongst the Persians* pp. 60, 201.

352 d. 1144/1731. See *Khāzin al-shuʿarā* fol. 173*a* (under "Yaḥyā"), Raḥmān ʿAlī pp. 58–9.

353 Titles in *Kh. al-sh.* fol. 185*b*.

354 Titles in *Kh. al-sh.* fol. 186*a*.

Khāzin al-shuʿarā' (a chronogram = 1260/1844, the date of inception), or *Wāqiʿāt al-nādirāt* (= 1265/1848–9, the date of completion), notices of 190 modern[355] poets, nearly all Indians and most of them disciples, pupils, friends, or relatives of Shāh Khūb Allāh, his uncle M. Afḍal "Muḥaqqar" Ilāhābādī, or of someone connected with them: **I.O.** 3899 (AD 1908).

[*Khāzin al-shuʿarā', khātimah* (foll. 180–96).]

1216. Mīrzā **ʿAbd Allāh "Raunaq"** b. M. Āqā Kurdistānī was born at Sinandij,[356] to which an ancestor of his had migrated from Hamadān. He was appointed *Munshī Bāshī*, or Chief Secretary, by Amān Allāh Khān II, who was made Governor (*Wālī*) of Kurdistān by M. Shāh Qājār in 1262/1846, was deposed after a year's tenure, and was reinstated by Nāṣir al-Dīn Shāh in 1265/1848–9.

Ḥadīqah i Amān-Allāhī, notices of the poets of Sinandij, completed in 1265/1848–9, and dedicated to Amān Allāh Khān II, the Governor: **Rieu** Suppt. 129 (AH 1266/1850).

[Autobiography in the *khātimah* to the *Ḥadīqah i Amān-Allāhī* (summarised by Rieu); *Majmaʿ al-fuṣaḥā'* ii pp. 150–1.]

1217. S. **Murtaḍā "Bīnish"** b. Ṣādiq ʿAlī Riḍawī Ḥusainī Madrāsī, whose family came from Gulbargah, was born in 1226/1811 at Madrās.

Ishārāt i Bīnish, (a chronogram = 1265/1848–9, the date of completion), notices of 69 (66 ?) contemporary poets of the Carnatic, dedicated to Nawwāb M. Ghauth Khān Shahāmat-Jang (for whom see no. 1209 *supra*): **Ivanow** Curzon 61 (many additions and emendations, possibly by the author).

Edition: *Tadhkirah i Bīnish*, [**Madras**] 1268/1851–2*.

List of the poets: Ivanow-Curzon pp. 68–70.

[Autobiography in *Ishārāt i Bīnish; Ṣubḥ i waṭan* pp. 38–42; *Ṣubḥ i gulshan* p. 75.]

1218. Qāḍī **Nūr al-Dīn "Fā'iq"**[357] b. Qāḍī S. Aḥmad Ḥusain Riḍawī.

Makhzan i shuʿarā', (a chronogram = 1268/1851–2), a *tadhkirah* of the Rēkhtah (i.e. Urdu), poets of Gujrāt: **Bombay** Univ. (see *JBBRAS*, n.s. iv (1928), p. 142).

Edition: **Aurangābād** (Delhi printed) date ? (Anjuman i Taraqqī i Urdū. With introduction by ʿAbd al-Ḥaqq. See review in *Oriental College Magazine* x/3 (May 1934), p. 135).

355 Nāṣir ʿAlī Sirhindī (d. 1108/1697) seems to be among the earliest.

356 The capital of Persian Kurdistān: see *Ency. Isl.* under Senna.

357 Qāḍī Nūr al-Dīn Ḥusain Khān Riḍawī Fā'iq according to the *Oriental College Magazine.*

1219. ʿAbd al-ʿAlīm **Naṣr Allāh Khān**"Qamar" Aḥmadī Khwēshgī[358] Khūrjawī, who died in 1299/1881, has already been mentioned (no. 1043) as the author of a *Tārīkh i Dakan*.

Gulshan i hamīshah-bahār, brief and almost dateless notices of 414 Indian, mostly Urdū, poets, written by the author at the age of thirty[359] after reading "Shēftah's" *Gulshan i bī-khār* (cf. no. 1207 (5) *supra*) at Bijnaur and finding it unsatisfactory: Fatḥ al-akhbār Press, **Kōl** [i.e. ʿAlīgaṛh], AH 1270/1854* (p. 173 in Arberry).

[Autobiography in *G. i h.-b.* pp. 92–4; see also no. 1043 *supra*.)

1220. Mīrzā **Ṭāhir "Shiʿrī" Iṣfahānī**, surnamed (*mulaqqab bah*) Dībājah-nigār, one of the Iṣfahānī shaikhs descended, like "Ḥazīn" (see no. 1150 *supra*), from Sh. Zāhid Jīlānī, was born at Iṣfahān in 1224/1809. Educated at his birthplace and at Ṭihrān, he entered the service of Nawwāb Iʿtiḍād al-Salṭanah (for whom see no. 316 *supra*). His death must have occurred between 1272/1856, the date of the *Ganj i shāygān*, and 1288/1871, the date of the completion of the *Majmaʿ al-fuṣaḥāʾ*, in which, apparently through a misprint, he is said to have died in 1270. The same date is given in *al-Maʾāthir wa-'l-āthār*.

Ganj i shāygān, notices of 41 or 42 panegyrists of the Ṣadr i Aʿẓam, Mīrzā Āqā Khān, written in 1272/1856[360] and divided into a *durj i nukhustīn* (*dar dhikr i āthār u aṭwār i shāh-zādagān*), a *durj i duwum* (*dar sharḥ i ḥasab u nasab i Ṣadr i Aʿẓam u marātib i faḍl u adab i shuʿarā-yi buzurgwār*) and a *silk* (*dar tarjamah i aḥwāl u shammaʾī az aqwāl i muʾallif i kitāb*): **Majlis** 428.

Edition: [**Ṭihrān**] 1272/1856°.

Description with a list of the poets: *Mélanges asiatiques* iv (St. Petersburg 1863), pp. 57–60.

[*Ganj i shāygān, silk; Majmaʿ al-fuṣaḥāʾ* ii, pp. 246–7; *al-Maʾāthir wa-'l-āthār* p. 204.]

1221. For the *Rauḍat al-ṣafā-yi Nāṣirī*, which was completed in 1274/1857 by Riḍā-Qulī Khān and which contains biographies of celebrities including poets (e.g. vol. ix, foll. 173*a*–179*a*), see no. 1225 (16) *infra*.

358 For this Afghān clan-name see *An Afghan colony at Qasur*, by M. Shafīʿ (in *Islamic culture* iii/3 (July 1929) pp. 452–73).

359 Naṣr Allāh Khān does not mention the date of his birth.

360 The chronogram quoted in the Majlis catalogue (*Āgandah shud ba-durj i guhar Ganj i shāygān*) really indicates 1273, but is apparently intended to indicate 1272.

1222. For the *Khwurshīd i jahān-numā*, which was begun in 1270/1853–4 and completed in 1280/1863–4 by S. Ilāhī Bakhsh Angrēzābādī and of which the ninth *burj* contains biographies of saints, poets, etc., see no. 190 *supra*.

1223. S. **ʿAbd al-Laṭīf "Alṭaf"** Ḥusainī is the author of an Urdu verse translation of Jāmī's *Iʿtiqād-nāmah* published with the Persian text at Madrās in 1272/1855–6*.

Shamʿ i maḥfil i sukhan, notices of Persian and Indian poets: **Madrās** 1279/1862*.

1224. **Maulawī Āghā Aḥmad ʿAlī** "Aḥmad" b. Āghā Shajāʿat-ʿAlī was born at D'hākā (Dacca) in Eastern Bengal on 10 Shawwāl 1255/17 Dec. 1839. In 1862 he founded at Calcutta the Madrasah i Aḥmadīyah, over which he presided until his death. In 1864 he was appointed a Persian teacher in the Calcutta Madrasah, and on 6 Rabīʿ ii AH 1290/6 June 1873 he died of fever at Dacca. He was the author of (1) *Muʾaiyid i Burhān*, a defence of the *Burhān i qāṭiʿ* against the criticisms of "Ghālib"[361] (475 pp. Maẓhar al-ʿajāʾib Press, Calcutta 1865),[362] (2) *Shamshīr i tīz-tar*, a reply to "Ghālib's" rejoinder, the *Shamshīr i tīz* (106 pp. Calcutta 1868),[2] (3) *Risālah i tarānah* (*A treatise on the Rubáʿí entitled Risálah i Taránah by Ághá Ahmad 'Alí ... with an introduction and explanatory notes by H. Blochmann*, Calcutta 1867°*, pp. 11, 17), (4) *Risālah i ishtiqāq*, an elementary Persian grammar (1872). He was editor, or co-editor, of the Bibliotheca Indica editions of the *Akbar-nāmah* (see no. 709 (1), Editions *supra*), the *Iqbāl-nāmah i Jahāngīrī* (see no. 717, Editions *supra*), the *Maʾāthir i ʿĀlamgīrī* (see no. 717, Editions *supra*), the *Muntakhab al-tawārīkh* (see no. 614, Editions *supra*), the *Sikandar-nāmah i baḥrī*, and the *Wīs u Rāmīn*.

Haft āsmān, an account of Persian *mathnawīs* and their writers, begun in 1869 and intended to consist of an *auj* (on the nature of *mathnawī* verse, the earliest writers of *mathnawīs* and "Niẓāmī", the "imām" of *mathnawī-gūyān*), seven *āsmāns* (each devoted to *mathnawīs* in one of the seven metres used in that kind of verse) and an *ufuq*, but never continued beyond the *auj* and the first *āsmān* (on *mathnawīs* in the *sarīʿ* metre).

Edition: *The Haft ásmán or History of the Masnawí of the Persians. By the late Maulawí Ághá Ahmad 'Alí ... with a biographical notice of the author, by H. Blochmann.* **Calcutta** 1873°* (Bibliotheca Indica).

[Blochmann's biographical notice.]

---

361 For whom see no. 694 *supra*.

362 Neither the British Museum nor the India Office seems to have the *Muʾaiyid i Burhān* or the *Shamshīr i tīz-tar*.

1225. Amīr al-Shuʿarāʾ **Riḍā-Qulī Khān "Hidāyat"** b. M. Hādī Ṭabaristānī[363] as born at Ṭihrān on 15 Muḥarram 1215/8 June 1800. His father, who died in 1218/1803–4 at Shīrāz, had been Treasurer[364] to Āqā Muḥammad Shāh Qājār (reigned 1193/1779–1211/1797) and after serving Fatḥ-ʿAlī Shāh for a short time in the same capacity had been appointed Treasurer of the province of Fārs[365] under the Governor, Ḥusain ʿAlī Mīrzā. Having lost his father in early childhood, Riḍā-Qulī lived for some years with relatives of his mother at Bārfurūsh,[366] and later, having returned to Fārs, he was cared for by another relative, M. Mahdī Khān "Shiḥnah" Māzandarānī,[367] who held high office in the province. On the completion of his education he entered the service of the Governor, Ḥusain ʿAlī Mīrzā,[368] and held various appointments in attendance upon him and his sons.[369] In 1245/1829–30, when Fatḥ-ʿAlī Shāh visited Shīrāz (3 Rajab/29 Dec. to 11 Shaʿbān/5 Feb.), Riḍā-Qulī was presented and was given the titles of Khān and Amīr al-Shuʿarā.[370] After Muḥammad Shāh's accession [in 1250/1834] and the defeat and arrest of Ḥusain ʿAlī Mīrzā the province of Fārs came under

363 The autobiographies in the *Majmaʿ al-fuṣaḥāʾ* and the *Rauḍat al-ṣafā-yi Nāṣirī* are headed Hidāyat i Ṭabaristānī and Hidāyat i Māzandarānī respectively.

364 *Dar ḥaḍrat i … M. Shāh Qājār … ba-manṣab i khazīnah-dārī maḥsūd i aqrān būdah* (*Riyāḍ al-ʿārifīn* p. 627[11]): *Āqā M. Shāh wai rā rīsh-safīd i ʿamalah i khalwat u ṣandūq-dār i jinsī i khwud kardah* (*Majmaʿ al-al-fuṣaḥāʾ* ii p. 581[21]).

365 *Pas az intiqāl i ān daulat ba-ḥaḍrat i … Fatḥ-ʿAlī Shāh … dar ān darbār … ba-manṣab i madhkūr* [i.e. *manṣab i khazīnah-dārī*] *muftakhir u ḥasb al-amr maʾmūr ba-khidmatgudhārī i Farmān-farmā-yi mamlakat i Fārs shudah ba-Shīrāz āmadah* (*Riyāḍ al-ʿārifīn* p. 627[12]); *Baʿd az sālī dū ba-Taḥwīl-dārī u Ṣāḥib-jamʿī i kull i mutawajjihāt i dīwānī i Fārs maʾmūr u ba-khidmat i … Ḥusain ʿAlī Mīrzā-yi Farmān-farmā-yi Fārs mashghūl būd* (*Majmaʿ al-fuṣahāʾ* ii p. 581[23]).

366 *Majmaʿ al-al-fuṣaḥāʾ* ii p. 581[25]. It appears from *Rauḍat al-ṣafā-yi Nāṣirī* ix fol. 95, l. 12, that he was there in 1224/1809 at the age of nine.

367 For accounts of him see *Anjuman i Khāqān. Nigāristān i Dārā, Tadhkirah i Muḥammad-Shāhī, Rauḍat al-ṣafā-yi Nāṣirī* ix fol. 177*b* penult. (7th page from end), *Majmaʿ al-fuṣaḥāʾ* ix pp. 252–3. He died in 1247/1831–2.

368 Son of Fatḥ-ʿAlī Shāh and for thirty years Governor of Fārs, he became a pretender to the throne on his father's death but was defeated and he died on his way to the fortress prison of Ardabīl.

369 *Chūn zamān i khurd-sālī dar-gudhasht ba-mulāzamat i Shāh-zādah i Farmān-farmā u farzandānash ba-sar mī-raft u muʿazzaz u mukarram mī-zīst u manāṣib i munāsib dāsht* (*Majmaʿ al-fuṣaḥāʾ* ii p. 581); *rūzgārī chand nīz ba-ḥukm i wirāthat mulāzamat numūd ʿāqibat ba-khwud sitīzān u az khidmat gurīzān dar kunj i ʿuzlat pā ba-dāman kashīd hamginān-rā kārash shigift āmadah* etc. (*Riyāḍ al-ʿārifīn* p. 628[2]). In speaking of Riḍā Qulī Mīrzā, Ḥusain ʿAlī Mīrzā's eldest son, Riḍā-Qulī Khān says *Bandah i muʾallif sāl-hā dar khidmatash ḥarīf i ḥujrah u garmābah u gulistān būdah am* (*Rauḍat al-ṣafā-yi Nāṣirī* x fol. 5*a*, l. 19).

370 *Rauḍat al-ṣafā-yi Nāṣirī* ix fol. 148*b*, l. 10 *ab infra*, *Majmaʿ al-fuṣaḥāʾ* ii p. 581 penult.

the authority of Fīrūz Mīrzā[371] and Muʿtamad al-Daulah Minūchihr Khān (for whom see no. 1214 2nd par. footnote *supra*). Riḍā-Qulī Khān was appointed Companion[372] to the former and held this position for a year or two, but when Fīrūz Mīrzā was transferred to the Governorship of Kirmān, he remained in Shīrāz at the court of the new Governor, Farīdūn Mīrzā.[373] In 1254/1838 he was sent to Ṭihrān by Farīdūn Mīrzā with presents for Muḥammad Shāh,[374] who had just returned from his unsuccessful expedition against Harāt.[375] Muḥammad Shāh instructed him to remain at court and in 1257/1841 appointed him guardian to his son ʿAbbās Mīrzā.[376] He became the constant companion of the king, with whom he used to discuss history and poetry.[377] At the end of 1263/1847 he was appointed Governor of the district of Fīrūzkūh and in accordance with a recognized custom sent his eldest son, ʿAlī-Qulī, to administer the district as his deputy.[378] After the accession of Nāṣir al-Dīn Shāh in 1264/1848

---

371 The Shāh's brother, twelfth in the list of the sons of ʿAbbās Mīrzā b. Fatḥ-ʿAlī Shāh given in the *Rauḍat al-ṣafā-yi Nāṣirī* ix fol. 166*a*.

372 *Faqīr-rā ba-munādamat i Nawwāb Fīrūz Mīrzā manṣūb dāshtand* (*Majmaʿ al-fuṣaḥāʾ* ii p. 582^{4}); *chūn man i bandah.... dar ān zamān ba-ṣawāb-dīd i Muʿtamad al-Daulah ba-munādamat u muṣāḥabat i amīr-zādah i madhkūr muftakhir u maʾmūr būdam u jamʿī az mutaʿalliqīn u ʿiyāl dar mauṭin i māʾlūf yaʿnī Shīrāz dāshtam li-hādhā Nawwāb i ashraf Farmān-farmā-yi jadīd i Fārs Farīdūn Mīrzā marā az ḥarakat manʿ u ba-sukūn amr farmūd u ba-khilʿat u inʿām u raḥmat u ikrām dar ḥaḍrat i khwud muʿazzaz u mashʿūf hami-dāsht chunān-kih dar tahniyat i wurūdash midḥatī kih ziyādah az hashtād bait būd mauzūn u maʿrūḍ dāshtam ba-ʿadad i abyāt ashrafī i tūmānī jāʾizah jāʾiz shumurd u adā farmūd* (*Rauḍat al-ṣafā-yi Nāṣirī* x fol. 10*b*, l. 1).

373 Another of Muḥammad Shāh's brothers, fifth in the list referred to in footnote 375.

374 *u dar īn aiyām Nawwāb ... Farīdūn Mīrzā ... bandah i muʾallif u ʿAlī-Qulī Khān Sartīb i Afshār rā bā baʿḍī tuḥaf u hadāyā rawānah i Dār al-khilāfah numūd u pas az sharaf-yābī i ḥuḍūr i ḥaḍrat i sulṭānī u maʿrūfiyat dar khidmat i janāb i Ḥājjī* [Mīrza Aqāsī] *i Airawānī ba-tawaqquf i rikāb māʾmūr shudīm* (*Rauḍat al-ṣafā-yi Nāṣirī* x fol. 22*a*, l. 22). Riḍā-Qulī Khān reached Ṭihrān on 15 Ramaḍān and stayed at the house of Ḥājjī Mīrzā Āqāsī, the Prime Minister (*Majmaʿ al-fuṣaḥāʾ* ii p. 582^{7}).

375 For this expedition see R. G. Watson, *History of Persia* pp. 297–319.

376 *Ham dar īn sāl Shāh-zādah ʿAbbās Mīrzā pas az faut i birādar i akbar i khwud dar shab i iḥyā-yi Ramaḍān muṭawallid gardīd u samī i birādar i raftah shud u ḥaḍrat i Shāhanshāhī bandah i muʾallif rā ba-tarbiyat u khidmat i ū maʾmūr farmūd* (*Rauḍat al-ṣafā-yi Nāṣirī* x fol. 25*a*, l. 19).

377 *Majmaʿ al-fuṣaḥāʾ* ii 582^{9-11}. Cf. *op. cit. i* fol. 5*a*, l. 13: *ba-khidmat i tarbiyat i yakī az shāh-zādagānam māʾmūr u ba-manṣab i tarkhānī i ḥuḍūr i bāhir al-nūr dar safar u ḥaḍar u khalwat u jalwat masrūr dāsht*. For the word *tarkhānī* cf. *op. cit.* ii p. 515^{1}: *dar zamān i jawānī dar khidmat i ... Fatḥ-ʿAlī Shāh simat i munādamat dāshtah dar khalawāt ba-kitāb-khwānī u dar jalawāt ba-tarkhānī makhṣūṣ būdah kamāl i maḥramīyat dar ān-ḥaḍrat yāftah*.

378 *Rauḍat al-ṣafā-yi Nāṣirī* x fol. 41 *b* penult.: *u ḥukūmat i wilāyat i Fīrūzkūh nīz ba-īn-ghulām mufawwaḍ gardīd u ʿAlī-Qulī pisar i akbar i khwud rā bah niyābat rawānah kardam.*

he retired from official life for a time,[379] but on 5 Jumādā II 1267/7 April 1851 he left for Khīvah on the embassy which he has described in his *Sifārat-nāmah i Khwārazm*. On his return after an absence of eight months[380] he was appointed Principal of the newly founded Dār al-Funūn College, or École polytechnique, at Ṭihrān.[381] About the same time he was instructed to bring the *Rauḍat al-ṣafā'* up to date.[382] For nearly fifteen years he remained at the College and then he was appointed *Lālah-bāshī*, or Tutor, to the Crown Prince, Muẓaffar al-Dīn Mīrzā, who had just been nominated Governor of Ādharbāyjān and with whom he spent some years at Tabrīz. He died at Ṭihrān on 10 Rabī' II 1288/30 June 1871. Gobineau says of him: "J'ai vu dans un diner Ryza-Kouly-Khan, ancien gouverneur du frère du roi, ambassadeur à Bokhara, historiographe, grammairien, et poëte excellent en persan littéraire et en dialecte. C'est un des hommes les plus spirituels et les plus aimables que j'aie rencontrés dans aucune partie du monde."[383]

Riḍā-Qulī Khān's works[384] include (1) *ghazalīyāt* and *qaṣā'id*. In the *Riyāḍ al-'ārifīn*, completed in 1260/1844,[385] his *Dīwān i ghazalīyāt* is described as consisting of 8,000 verses and his *qaṣā'id* as amounting to more than 10,000 verses. In the *Majma' al-fuṣaḥā'*, completed in 1288/1871,[386] his *qaṣā'id* and *ghazalīyāt* together are said to comprise more than 30,000 verses. A MS. *dīwān* transcribed in 1283/1866 and consisting mainly of *ghazals* is preserved

---

379 *Majma' al-fuṣaḥā'* ii p. 582 [14]: *ba-rikāb-būsī sharaf-yāb gashtah ba-khidmat i muqarrarah ma'mūr āmadam ba-sababī chand az ān khidmat isti'fā numūdam u ba-kunj i 'uzlat uftādam.*

380 *az safar i dūr i Khwārazm kih hasht-māh imtidād yāftah būd* (*Rauḍat al-ṣafā-yi Nāṣirī* x fol. 106, l. 8).

381 *pas ba-riyāsat u nāẓimīyat i Madrasah i Dār al-Funūn ... muftakhir gashtam u dar-īn ḍimn ḥasb al-amr ba-itmām i tārīkh i Rauḍat al-ṣafā ḥukmī raft ...* (*Majma' al-fuṣaḥā'* ii p. 582 [17]). The Dār al-Funūn was opened on 5 Rabī' II 1268/28 January 1852 (*al-Ma'āthir wa-'l-āthār* p. 111).

382 See work no. (16) *infra*.

383 *Trois ans en Asie*, Paris 1859, tome ii pp. 454–5 (chapitre v: les caractères).

384 Of the twenty works enumerated below all but the *Jāmi' al-asrār* (no. 14), the *Nizhād-nāmah* (no. 17) and the *Farhang* (no. 18) are mentioned in the *Majma' al-fuṣaḥā'* (ii p. 582). The *Jāmi' al-asrār* is mentioned without information concerning its subject in the author's list of his own works in the *Riyāḍ al-'ārifīn* (pp. 628–9). That list, although it immediately follows a statement that 1260 was the current year and that the author's age was then forty-five, contains (at least in the printed edition of AHS 1316) several works written after 1260, since it includes all the twenty enumerated below except the *Sifārat-nāmah* (no. 15), the *Nizhād-nāmah* (no. 17) and the *Farhang* (no. 18).

385 That it contains later additions (at least in its printed form) is clear from the preceding note.

386 For the date see work no. (20) *infra*.

in the British Museum (Rieu Suppt. 365). (2)–(8) seven *mathnawīs*,[387] namely (2) *Anwār al-wilāyah* in the metre of the *Makhzan al-asrār*, (3) *Gulistān i Iram* or *Baktāsh-nāmah*, on the love-story of Baktāsh and Rābiʿah (Edition: [Ṭihran[388]] 1270/1854°), (4) *Baḥr al-ḥaqāʾiq* in the metre of "Sanāʾī's" *Ḥadīqah*, (5) *Anīs al-ʿāshiqīn*, "a religious and mystic poem, with anecdotes of saints and Sufis" (M.S.: Rieu Suppt. 364 ii, dated 1253/1837), (6) *Khurram bihisht* (metre *mutaqārib*) completed in 1277/1860–1 (MS.: Majlis 433), (7) *Hidāyat-nāmah* (metre *ramal*), "a poem containing moral and religious precepts illustrated by apologues and anecdotes in the style of the Masnavi of Jalāl ud-Dīn Rūmi and in the same metre" (MS.: Rieu Suppt. 364 i, dated 1253/1837), (8) *Manhaj al-hidāyah*, (9) *Madārij al-balāghah*, "(lith. 1331) … a glossary of rhetorical and poetical terms with many examples taken from different poets" (*Ency. Isl.*), (10) *Maẓāhir al-anwār* (see no. 303 *supra*), (11) *Miftāḥ al-kunūz*, a commentary on the *dīwān* of Khāqānī (MS.: Rieu Suppt. 221 ii, dated 1259/1843), (12) *Laṭāʾif al-maʿārif*,[389] (13) *Fihris al-tawārīkh* a concise chronology presented to Nāṣir al-Dīn Shāh just before the author's departure on his embassy to Khīwah (*Rauḍat al-ṣafā-yi Nāṣirī* x, fol. 70*a*, l. 5 *ab infra*), which "appears to have been lost save that portion which was lithographed at Tabríz in AH 1280, but which has never been distributed" (S. Churchill in *JRAS*. 1887 p. 318), (14) *Jāmiʿ al-asrār* (see footnote 383 *supra*), (15) *Sifārat-nāmah i Khwārazm* (see no. 440 (1) *supra*), (16) *Rauḍat al-ṣafā-yi Nāṣirī*, an edition of the seven volumes of the *Rauḍat al-ṣafāʾ* (see no. 123 *supra*), followed by a continuation in three[390] volumes extending to 1274[391]/1857 (Edition: Ṭihrān 1270–4/1853–7°), (17) *Nizhād-nāmah i pādshāhān i Īrānī-nizhād* (see no. 317 (2) *supra*), (18) *Farhang i anjuman-ārāy i Nāṣirī*, a dictionary of which the introductory remarks were written in 1286/1869–70 and which is devoted mainly to words used by the poets (Edition: Ṭihrān 1288/1871°*. For a description see *JRAS*. 1886 pp. 200–3),

(19) ***Riyāḍ al-ʿārifīn***, notices of saints who were also poets with selections from their poems, completed in 1260/1844, dedicated to Muḥammad Shāh and divided into a *ḥadīqah* (on Ṣūfism, the life of the Ṣūfīs and their conventional terms), two *rauḍahs* ((1) *dar dhikr i ʿurafā u mashāyikh ba-tartīb i tahajjī*, notices of about 170 saints and mystics who composed poetry, (2) *dar dhikr i fuḍalā u muḥaqqiqīn i ḥukamā*, alphabetically arranged

387 The first six have the title *Sittah i ḍarūrīyah*.

388 Tabrīz according to *Ency. Isl.* (Massé).

389 Probably the work referred to in S. Churchill's statement that "The Latáif ul-'Árifin is a Súfi tract in prose mixed with verse" (*JRAS*. 1887 p. 318).

390 The *R. al-ṣ. i N.* is in ten volumes, each with its own title-page. In the B.M. description "2 vols." should properly be "10 vols. in 2".

391 Not 1270, as stated in the *Ency. Isl.*

notices of about 100 poets and philosophers (the first Avicenna, the last Yaḥyā Lāhijī), who at times wrote mystical poetry), a *firdaus* (*dar sharḥ i ḥāl i muta'akhkhirīn u mu'āṣirīn*, alphabetically arranged notices of about 70 modern and contemporary Ṣūfī poets) and a *khuld* (autobiography): **Rieu** Suppt. 126 (19th cent.).

Editions: **Ṭihrān** 1305/1888°, AHS. 1316/1937‡.

(20) ***Majma' al-fuṣaḥā'***, notices of 862 ancient[392] and modern poets completed in 1288/1871[393] and divided into four chapters[394] ((1) 115 kings and princes who wrote poetry, the first being Nāṣir al-Dīn Shāh, the last Yūsuf 'Ādil-Shāh (vol. i, fol. 10*b*–p. 63), (2) 323 ancient poets from AH 173/789–90 to 800/1397–8,[395] the first Abū Ḥafṣ Sughdī, the last Yūsuf Ghaznawī (vol. i pp. 64–657), (3) 66 "mediaeval" poets (*shu'arā-yi mutawassiṭīn*), the first "Āhī" Turshīzī, the last Yaḥyā Gīlānī (vol. ii pp. 2–57), (4) 358 modern and contemporary poets, the first "Adīb" Marāgha'ī, the last two "Yaghmā" and "Hidāyat" (vol. ii pp. 58–678): **Rieu** Suppt. 125 (an early recension dedicated to Muḥammad Shāh. The MS. breaks off in the notice of Niẓāmī,

---

392 Riḍā-Qulī Khān criticises his predecessors for including in their so-called *tadhkirahs* only inferior specimens of ancient poetry.

393 1288 is given as the date of completion on p. 678 [1] of vol. ii. In the preface (vol. i, fol. 6*a*, l. 7) and in the heading to *Bāb* ii (vol. i p. 64) 1284 and 1285 respectively are mentioned as the current year, but earlier years are elsewhere described as current, e.g. 1274 (vol. ii p. 548[15]) and 1275 (vol. ii p. 81 [13]). The work, based in part on material collected over a period of thirty years (see vol. i, fol. 4*b* ult.), would doubtless have remained unfinished, if the author had not been instructed first by Muḥammad Shāh (vol. i, fol. 5*a*, l. 14) and later by Nāṣir al-Dīn Shāh (fol. 6*a*, l. 4) to finish it.

394 The word *bāb* is applied to these divisions at the end of the preface (vol. i, fol. 6*a*, l. 14), at the beginning of the biography of Nāṣir al-Dīn Shāh (fol. 10*b*, ll. 1 and 5) and in the heading to *Bāb* ii (vol. i p. 64. *Bābs* iii and iv are without headings). On the other hand the word *rukn* is used, but doubtless only by way of comparison, a few lines before the divisions are called *abwāb* (vol. i, fol. 6*a*, l. 10: *u ān-rā murattab u mubawwab sākhtam u bunyān i ān-rā mānand i 'ālam i jusmānī bar chār rukn nihādam*). On p. 657 of vol. i the words *qismat* and *ṭabaqah* are used.

395 These dates are given in the heading to the table of contents on fol. 7*b* in vol. i, but there is some confusion in the arrangement of the poets, since, although *Bāb* ii includes some poets of the eighth century (e.g. Ṣafī al-Dīn Ardabīlī, d. 735, vol. i p. 313, and 'Alī Hamadānī, d. 786, p. 340), there are far more in *Bāb* iii (e.g. Ibn i Yamīn, d. 763, vol. ii p. 2, Ḥāfiẓ, d. 791, p. 11, Khwājū. d. 734, p. 15, Salmān i Sāwajī, d. 769, p. 19). The *mutawassiṭīn* in *Bāb* iii seem to be poets who died between 701 and 1151 (AH 1150 being given on p. 56 (cf. *Ṭarā'iq al-ḥaqā'iq* iii p. 42 [33]) as the date of the death of "Hāshimī" Dihlawī b. M. Mu'min "'Arshī", who is erroneously described as the author of the *Maẓhar al-āthār* (cf. Rieu ii 802, Ethé 1765), a *mathnawī* really written in 940). Here again, however, there is some overlapping, since *Bāb* iv contains Fatḥ Allāh "Janāb" Iṣfahānī, who died in 1146 (vol. ii p. 92).

vol. i p. 639 in the Ṭihrān edition. Circ. AH 1250/1835, said to be partly autograph).

Edition: **Ṭihrān** 1295/1878°* (2 vols.).

Descriptions: 1) *Relation de l'ambassade au Kharezm* (see no. 440 (1), Edition *supra*), introduction, pp. xx–xxi; (2) *JRAS*. 1886 pp. 203–4 (by S. Churchill. With list of *tadhkirahs* mentioned in the preface).

In addition Riḍā-Qulī Khān was editor of (1) the *Dīwān i Minūchihrī* (*Ṭihrān, date? See JRAS*. 1886 p. 200. The Ṭihrān edition of 1297/1880° was based on his edition), (2) the *Qābūs-nāmah* and the *Tuzuk i Tīmūrī* (Ṭihrān 1285/1868°), (3) the *Nafthat al-maṣdūr* (Ṭihrān AHS 1307–8/1928–30[396]).

[Autobiographies in *Riyāḍ al-ʿārifīn*, last chapter (Ṭihrān 1316 pp. 627–52), *Rauḍat al-ṣafā-yi Nāṣirī* ix foll. 178*b* (5th page from end), *Majmaʿ al-fuṣaḥā'* ii pp. 581–677; biography by Mānakjī (cf. no. 317 (2), footnote *supra*) prefixed to the *Farhang i anjuman-ārāy i Nāṣirī* (Ṭihrān 1288/1871°*); *Relation de l'amhassade au Kharezm de Riza Qouly Khan traduite et annotée par C. Schefer* (see no. 440 (1), Edition *supra*), introduction, pp. xv–xxiv; *A modern contributor to Persian literature, Rizá Ḳulí Khan and his works. By Sidney Churchill* (in *JRAS*. 1886 pp. 196–206. Cf. *JRAS*. 1887 pp. 163 and 318); *al-Ma'āthir wa-'l-āthār*, p. 189; Berthels *Ocherk istorii persidskoi literatury*, Leningrad 1928 pp. 110–13; *Ency. Isl.* under Riḍā Ḳulī Khān (Massé).

Portraits: *Farhang i anjuman-ārāy i Nāṣirī*, plate; *Nafthat al-maṣdūr*, frontispiece; *Riyāḍ al-ʿārifīn* AHS. 1316, frontispiece; Browne *Lit. Hist.* iv p. 344.]

1226. Nawwāb M. **Siddīq Ḥasan Khān**"Nawwāb" died in 1890 (see no. 48 *supra*).

Shamʿ i anjuman, notices of 989 ancient and modern poets, completed in 1292/1875.

Edition: [**Bhōpāl**,] 1292–3/1876°*.

[See no. 48 *supra* as well as *Shamʿ i anjuman* pp. 474–86 and Brockelmann *Supptbd.* ii pp. 859–61.]

1227. [Nawwāb] Raḍī al-Daulah Niẓām al-Mulk[397] S. Abū 'l-Khair **Nūr al-Ḥasan Khān** "Ṭaiyib",[398] originally "Nūr", b. M. Ṣiddīq Ḥasan Khān, elder son of the author of the *Shamʿ i anjuman* (see § 1226 *supra*) by his first wife, a daughter

396 1307 *Shamsī* on title-page, 1308 on cover, but 1341 [*Qamarī* = 1922–3] in the lithographer's colophon.

397 These two titles, conferred doubtless by the State of Bhōpāl, are mentioned in *Ma'āthir i Ṣiddīqī* (cf. no. 48, end *supra*) iv p. 216.

398 *Ma'āthir i Ṣiddīqī* p. 216.

of the Prime Minister of Bhōpāl, M. Jamāl al-Dīn K͟hān Dihlawī, was born at Bhōpāl on 21 Rajab 1278/22 January 1862. Among his teachers was Maulawī Ilāhī Bak͟hsh Faiḍābādī, Head Teacher of the Madrasah i Sulaimānī at Bhōpāl. His publications include (1) *'Arf al-jādī min jinān hudā 'l-hādī* (Edition: Bhōpāl 1296/1879. See Āṣafīyah iii p. 444, from which it would seem to be a Persian work on Ḥanafī Law, though Sarkis (*Dictionnaire encyclopédique*, col. 1873) treats it as an Arabic work), (2) *al-Nahj al-maqbūl min s͟harā'i' al-Rasūl* (Edition: place ? 1296/1879. See Āṣafīyah iii p. 446, where it is placed among the Persian works on Ḥanafī Law), (3) *al-Jawā'iz wa-'l-ṣilāt min jam' al-asāmī wa-'l-ṣifāt* (an Arabic work "on Muḥammadan names, titles, and epithets." Edition: Delhi[399] 1297/1880°), (4) *al-Raḥmat al-muhdāh ilā man yurīd ziyādat al-ilm 'alā aḥadīth al-Mis͟hkāh*, in Arabic (Edition: place ? 1301/1883–4. See Sarkis, col. 1873, and Āṣafīyah i p. 628, from the latter of which it appears that Nūr al-Ḥasan was the editor rather than the author of this *Takmilah i Mis͟hkāt*), (5) *Sulṭan al-ad͟hkār min aḥādīth Saiyid al-abrār*, an abridgment of the *'Amal al-yaum wa-'l-lailah* of Ibn al-Sunnī[400] (Edition: Ḥaidarābād 1318/1900–1. See Sarkis, col. 1873).

In the Āṣafīyah catalogue, vol. i, published in 1332/1914, he is described as *maujūd* (i.e. still alive), but on p. 49 of the *Ma'āthir i Ṣiddīqī*, vol. ii, published in 1342/1924, his name is followed by the word *marḥūm*.

(1) **Nigāristān i suk͟han**, a supplement to the *S͟ham' i anjuman*, devoted primarily to poets of Bengal and elsewhere whose verses sent for inclusion in that work arrived too late but containing also many other ancient and modern poets, 651 in all. Edition: [**Bhōpāl**], 1293/1876*°.

(2) **Tad͟hkirah i Ṭūr i Kalīm.** Edition: place ? 1299/1881–2 (see Āṣafīyah i p. 318).

[*S͟ham' i anjuman* pp. 486–7; *Nigāristān i suk͟han* pp. 130–3; Ellis ii col. 446; Edwards col. 599; Sarkis *Dictionnaire encyclopédique de bibliographie arabe*, col. 1873; *Ma'āthir i Ṣiddīqī* (cf. no. 48, end *supra*), iv p. 216; Brockelmann *Supptbd.* ii p. 861. Very full information would doubtless be obtainable from the fifth volume of the *Ma'āthir i Ṣiddīqī*, if ever published, since that volume was to deal with Ṣiddīq Ḥasan K͟hān's descendants. Only vols. i–iv have been accessible to me.]

1228. Nawwāb Ṣafi al-Daulah Ḥusāin al-Mulk[401] S. Abū Naṣr M. 'Alī Ḥasan K͟hān "Ṭāhir", originally "'Ās͟hiqī", b. M. Ṣiddīq Ḥasan K͟hān was the younger

---

399 So Ellis. Sarkis says Bhōpāl.
400 See Brockelmann i p. 165.
401 For these titles see *Ma'āthir i Ṣiddīqī* vi p. 216 and the description of the author's work *Ta'līm u tarbiyat* on the back covers of the *Ma'āthir i Ṣiddīqī*.

son of the author of the *Sham' i anjuman* (see no. 1226 *supra*) by his first wife, a daughter of the Prime Minister of Bhōpāl, M. Jamāl al-Dīn Khān Dihlawī. He was at one time Honorary Director of the Department of Education in the State of Bhōpāl. Among his works were *al-Bunyān al-marṣūṣ min bayān ījāz al-fiqh al-manṣūṣ*, a Persian work on Ḥanafī Law (Edition: place ? 1299/1881–2. See Āṣafīyah iii p. 444), *Khirman i gul*, a Persian *dīwān, Nālah i dil*, an Urdu *dīwān, Ma'āthir i Ṣiddīqī*, a detailed Urdu biography of his father (Edition: Lucknow 1342/1924–1343/1925), and several other Urdu works (e.g. *Fiṭrat al-Islām, Sīrat al-Islām, al-Madanīyah fī 'l-Islām, Intiẓām i khānah-dārī*), of which descriptions (without dates and places of publication) are given on the back covers of the *Ma'āthir i Ṣiddīqī*.

(1) ***Ṣubḥ i gulshan***, a supplement to the *Sham' i anjuman* (see no. 1226 *supra*) and the *Nigāristān i sukhan* (see no. 1227 (1) *supra*), begun in 1294/1877 and completed in 1295/1878.
   Edition: Bhōpāl 1295/1878° (cf. *OCM* iii/2 (Feb. 1927) P. 51).)

(2) ***Bazm i sukhan***, biographies of Urdu poets, written in 1297/1880.
   Edition: place ? date ? (see Āṣafīyah iii p. 162 no. 133 and Peshawar 1482 (1)).

[*Ma'āthir i Ṣiddīqī* iv p. 216. Very full information would doubtless be obtainable from the fifth volume of the *M.i.Ṣ.*, if ever published, since that volume was to deal with Ṣiddīq Ḥasan Khān's descendants. Only vols. i–iv have been accessible to me.]

1229. M. **Muẓaffar Ḥusain "Ṣabā"** Gōpāmawī[402]
   Rūz i raushan, written in 1297/1880 as a supplement to the *Sham' i anjuman* (see no. 1226 *supra*), the *Nigāristān i sukhan* (see no. 1227 (1) *supra*), and the *Ṣubḥ i gulshan* (see no. 1228 (1) *supra*).
   Edition: **Bhōpāl** 1297/1880° (cf. *OCM*. iii/2 (Feb. 1927) p. 51).)

1230. Qārī **Raḥmat Allāh "Wāḍiḥ"** b. 'Ashūr Muḥammad Bukhārī[403] was a contemporary of the Manghit Amīr Muẓaffar al-Dīn (reigned 1277/1860–1303/1885).
   Tuḥfat al-aḥbāb fī tadhkirat al-aṣḥāb, usually called *Tadhkirah i Qārī Raḥmat Allāh*, notices of Central Asian poets of the nineteenth century: **Bukhārā** Semenov 38.

402 Gōpāmau is 14 miles East of Hardoi in Oudh.

403 Ibn-i-Aschur-Muhammad-Rahmatullah-i-Bukhari according to Semenov's *Kurzer Abriss* p. 9. This might conceivably represent M. Rahmat Allāh b. 'Ashūr Bukhārī. According to Semenov's Bukhārā catalogue the name appears as Ibn-e 'Ashur-Rehmetolla-ol-Bokhari in the lithographed edition.

Edition: *Tuḥfat al-aḥbāb ... maʿ Tārīkh i kathīrah u Majmūʿah i Salīmī*, **Tashkent** 1332/1913–14 (with additions by Mīrzā Salīm Bēk. Cf. no. 506, Edition *supra* and Semenov *Kurzer Abriss* pp. 9–10).

1231. **Abū 'l-Qāsim Muḥtasham** was the son of M. ʿAbbās "Rifʿat" Shirwānī (for whom see nos. 308, 600 *supra*) and the grandson of Aḥmad b. Muḥammad al-Yamanī al-Shirwānī (for whom see no. 308 footnote *supra*, Brockelmann *Sptbd* ii pp. 850–1, *Dānishmandān i Ādharbāyjān* p. 31 and Sarkis *Dictionnaire encyclopédique de bibliographie arabe* coll. 1120–1).

Akhtar i tābān, or *Tadhkirat al-nisāʾ*, brief notices of 82 poetesses.

Edition: **Bhōpāl** 1299/1881–2 (see M. Shafīʿs description in OCM. iii/3 (May 1927) p. 52).

1232. Mīrzā **Muḥammad b. M. Rafīʿ**, entitled Malik al-kuttāb, **Shīrāzī** has already been mentioned as the author of the *Zīnat al-zamān* or *Tāj al-tawārīkh* (no. 662 *supra*, where some biographical information will be found), the *Iksīr al-tawārīkh* (no. 263, Persian translations (3) *supra*), the *Tārīkh i Ingilistān* and the *Tārīkh i qadīm i Yūnān* (no. 609 *supra*) and the *Mirʾāt al-zamān* (no. 611 (2) *supra*).

Tadhkirat al-khawātīn, alphabetically arranged notices of Arabian, Persian, Indian, and Turkish poetesses.

Edition: [**Bombay**] 1306/1889°.

1233. Kunwar[404] **Durgā-Parshād** "Mihr" **Sandīlī** has already been mentioned as the author of the *Gulistān i Hind* (no. 661 *supra*, where some biographical information will be found) and the *Būstān i Awadʾh* (no. 951 *supra*).

Ḥadīqah i ʿishrat, notices of poetesses[405] written in 1893.

Edition: **Sandīlah** 1894°*.

1234. **"Afḍal" Makhdūm i Pīrmastī** is described by Semenov (Bukhārā Catalogue p. 5) as a contemporary Bokharan poet and prose-writer.

Afḍal al-tadhkār fī dhikr al-shuʿarāʾ wa-'l-ashʿār, notices of Central Asian poets of the nineteenth century written in 1322/1904: **Bukhārā** Semenov 4.

Edition: Tashkent 1326/1908 (see Semenov *Kurzer Abriss* p. 10).

[Mīrzā Salīm Bēk's additions to the *Tuḥfat al-aḥbāb* (see no. 1230, Edition *supra*), Tashkent 1332/1913–14, pp. 2, 6, 310–11.]

404 A Hindi word meaning "prince (son of a Rājah)".

405 So Edwards. Arberry says "famous women".

1235. **Dīnshāh** Jījībhā'ī **Īrānī**, a Bombay solicitor (B.A. 1902, from St. Xavier's College, Judge Spencer Prizeman 1904, Muncherji Nowroji Banaji Scholar 1904, LL.B. 1905 from the Government Law School), was President of the Iranian Zoroastnan Anjuman in 1928. Among his publications are (1) *The Resurrection of the ancient sovereigns of Iran in the ruins of Madayen. A Persian operetta by Syed Mirzadeh Eshqi* [i.e. "'Ishqī's" *Rastākhīz*]. *Translated* [and edited] *by Dinshaw J. Irani*, Bombay 1924*. (2) *The divine songs of Zarathustra*, London 1927. (3) *Paik i Mazdayasnān* [essays on Zoroastrianism, originally written in English or Gujarati, translated into Persian by Pūr-Dāwud. Pts. 1–8], Bombay 1927–9*. (4) *Pouran-dokht-nâmeh* [*Pūrān-dukh-nāmah*]. *The poems of Poure-Davoud.* [Edited] *with their English translation by D. J. Irani*, Bombay 1928*. (5)*Akhlāq i Īran i bāstān*, Bombay [1930*], Ṭihrān 1932. (6) *Falsafah i Īrān i bāstān*, Bombay 1933, as well as English translations of a number of Persian texts prescribed for Bombay University examinations

Poets of the Pahlavi regime [selections from the works of contemporary poets with English translations and short biographies (in Persian with English epitomes)], **Bombay** 1933 (vol. i, 98 poets).

[Bombay University Calendar; list of publications facing title-page of *Poets of the Pahlavi regime*; portrait in group with R. Tagore and members of the Literary Society, Ṭihrān, reproduced as frontispiece to the same work.]

1236. **Sa'īd Nafīsī**, the son of Dr. Mīrzā 'Alī Akbar Khān Nafīsī Nāẓim al-aṭibbā, was born at Ṭihrān in AHS 1274/1895. After completing his education in Europe[406] he returned to Persia in AHS 1297/1918–19 and received an appointment in the Ministry of Public Works. In AHS 1306/1927–8 (so Īrānī) or 1308/1929–30 (so Ishaque) he entered the service of the Ministry of Education and was nominated to lectureships in Literature and History in the Faculties of Law and Literature [presumably at the University of Ṭihrān]. His works, of which seventeen are mentioned in a list accompanying his edition of the *Rubā'īyāt* of Bābā Afḍal Kāshānī (Ṭihrān AHS 1311/1933, with bio-bibliographical introduction), include novels, a French-Persian dictionary, a life of Sh. Zāhid Gīlānī (Rasht AHS 1307/1928–9. Cf. no. 1150, 1st par., 3rd footnote, *supra*), and editions of classical Persian texts (e.g. 'Umar Khaiyam's *Rubā'iyāt*, Ṭihrān. AHS 1306/1927–8, 2nd ed. AHS 1309/1930–1, the *Qābūs-nāmah*, Ṭihrān AHS 1312/1933, Sanā'ī's *Sair al-'ibād ilā 'l-ma'ād*, Ṭihrān AHS 1316/1937, Khwand-Amīr's *Dastūr al-wuzarā'*, Ṭihrān AHS 1317/1938, Ḥusain Kāshifī's *Lubb i lubāb i Ma'nawī*, Ṭihrān (see *Luzac's Oriental List* 1940, p. 108), "'Aṭṭār's" *Dīwān i qaṣā'id u ghazalīyāt*, Ṭihrān AHS 1319/1940–1, and the *Tārīkh i Baihaqī*, vol. i, Ṭihrān AHS 1319/1940).

406 Neither Īrānī nor Yāsimī specifies the part or parts of Europe to which he went.

(1) ***Aḥwāl u muntakhab i ash'ār i Khwājū-yi Kirmānī***: Ṭihrān AHS 1307/1928.
(2) ***Aḥwāl u ash'ār i ... Rūdakī i Samarqandī***: vol. i. **Ṭihrān** AHS 1309–10/1930–2; vol. ii. **Ṭihrān** AHS. 1310/1931–2.
(3) ***Majd al-Dīn i Hamgar i Shīrāzī***: **Ṭihrān** AHS. 1314/1935–6.
(4) ***Aḥwāl u ash'ār i fārisī i Sh. Bahā'ī***: **Ṭihrān** 1316/1937–8. [Īrānī *Poets of the Pahlavi regime* pp. 344 i-344 xviii (portrait); Rashīd Yāsimī *Adabīyāt i mu'āṣir* pp. 57–9 (portrait), 110, 114, 116.]

1237. Ghulam-Riḍā Khān **Rashīd Yāsimī** is the son of M. Walī Khān, Mīr Panj, Īl i Gūrān, Qal'ah i Zanjī, and was born in 1314/1896–7 at Kirmānshāh. In 1333/1914–15 he went to Ṭihrān and after completing his education served for a time in the Ministry of Education and subsequently in the Ministry of Finance. At the time when Ishaque and Īrānī wrote [circ. 1932] he held an appointment at the Imperial court. On the title-page of his *Adabīyāt i mu'āṣir* [1937–8] he is described as a Professor in the University of Ṭihrān. A list of his published works printed on the cover of his translation of E. G. Browne's *Literary History of Persia*, vol. iv, comprises twenty titles and includes seven translations. The *Dīwān i Mas'ūd i Sa'd i Salmān* published at Ṭihrān in AHS. 1318/1939 was edited by him.
(1) ***Aḥwāl i Ibn i Yamīn***: **Ṭihrān** AHS 1303/1924.
(2) ***Tatabbu'u intiqād i aḥwāl u āthār i Salmān i Sāwajī***: **Ṭihrān**[circ. 1928 ?].
(3) ***Adabīyāt i mu'āṣir***, mainly notices of contemporary poets[407] followed by brief sketches of other branches of literature: **Ṭihrān** AHS 1316/1937–8 (printed as an appendix to the *Tārīkh i adabīyāt i Īrān*, i.e. Rashīd Yāsimī's translation of the fourth volume of E. G. Browne's *Literary History of Persia*).
[Ishaque *Sukhanvarān-i-Īrān* i pp. 92–105 (portrait); Īrānī *Poets of the Pahlavi regime* pp. 284–307 (portrait).]

1238. Dr. **Qāsim Ghanī**, a medical graduate of the American University at Bairūt, is a physician practising in Ṭihrān. In 1924–5, five or six years after graduating at Bairūt, he spent eighteen months in Paris, and he was there for a second visit in 1928. Two of Anatole France's novels, *Thaïs* and *La révolte des anges*, have

407 As sources of biographical information concerning contemporary poets Rashīd Yāsimī mentions (in addition to the works of Ishaque and Īrānī) the *Bihtarīn ash'ār* of "Pizhmān" Bakhtyārī [Ṭihrān 1313/1934*], the *Muntakhabāt i āthār* of M. Diyā' Hashtrūdī [AH 1342/1023–4], the *Gulhā-yi adab* of Sa'ādat Nūrī [Iṣfahān AHS 1342/1923–4], and the *Asrār i khilqat* of Muṭī'ī [cf. Ishaque *Modern Persian poetry* p. 195, from which it appears that this work is the *A. i kh.* of Sarhang Aḥmad Akhgar, ed. Ḥusain Muṭī'ī Ṭihrān AHS 1314/1935–6].

been translated by him into Persian. He and M. b. ʿAbd al-Wahhāb Qazwīnī were joint editors of the *Dīwān i Ḥāfiẓ* published at Ṭihrān in AHS 1320/1941.

Baḥth dar āthār u afkār u aḥwāl i Ḥāfiẓ. Vol. i: *Tārīkh i ʿaṣr i Ḥāfiẓ*, **Ṭihrān** AHS. 1321/AH 1361/1942 (with preface by Prof. M. Qazwīnī); vol. ii pt. 1: *Tārīkh i taṣawwuf dar Islām*, Ṭihrān AHS 1322/AH 1362/1943.

[M. Qazwīnī's preface.]

1239. **Badīʿ al-Zamān Furūzān-far** b. Āqā Sh. ʿAlī Bushrūya'ī Khurāsānī was born at, or near, Bushrūyah in AHS. 1318/1900–1. Educated first at local schools and later at Mashhad under the well-known poet "Adīb" Nīshāpūrī (d. 1344/1926), he went to Ṭihrān early in AHS. 1303/1924 and studied philosophy and other subjects. In 1308/1929 he was appointed Lecturer in Persian Literature (as well as Arabic Literature and Logic, according to Īrānī) at the Teachers' Training College (*Dār al-Muʿallimīn*, now called *Dānish-sarāy i ʿĀlī*). When the Madrasah i Sipahsālār was reconstituted as the Faculty of Theology and Philosophy (AHS. 1313/1934–5), he was made Assistant Director(?) (*muʿāwin i ān dānish-kadah gardīd*). In 1316/1937–8 he became Director of the newly-founded Institute for the Training of Preachers. On the title-page of his life of Rūmī [1315/1937] he is described as a Professor in the University of Ṭihrān (*ustād i Dānish-gāh i Ṭihrān*), a title doubtless held concurrently with more than one of the aforementioned appointments.

(1) ***Sukhan u sukhanwarān***, a poetical anthology with a biographical and critical introduction to the selections from each poet: vol. i (44 poets of Khurāsān and Transoxiana from the third to the sixth century), **Ṭihrān** AHS. 1308–9/1930; vol. ii, pt. 1 (11 poets of ʿIrāq and Ādharbāyjān in the fifth and sixth centuries), **Ṭihrān** [AHS 1312/1933]; *in progress ?* (Vols. i and ii, pt. 1, reviewed by R. A. Nicholson in *JRAS*. 1936 pp. 122–3).

(2) ***Risālah dar taḥqīq i aḥwāl u zindagānī i Maulānā Jalāl al-Dīn i Rūmī***: **Ṭihrān** 1315/1937‡ (vol. i).

[Autobiographical statements in the *muqaddimah* to no. (2); Ishaque *Sukhanvarān-i-Īrān* i pp. 32–7 (portrait); Īrānī *Poets of the Pahlavi regime* pp. 178E–194 (portrait); Yāsimī *Adabīyāt i muʿāṣir* pp. 27–9 (portrait)].

1240. **M. Isḥāq** (M. Ishaque), M.A., B.Sc., Ph.D., Lecturer in Arabic and Persian in the Post-Graduate Department of the University of Calcutta and formerly Assistant Lecturer in the Department of Arabic and Islamic Studies at the University of Dacca, was born at Calcutta in 1900 and educated at Calcutta University. He visited Persia in 1930 and 1934 and in the eight months that he spent in the country he made the acquaintance of many prominent writers and collected the literary and biographical material which formed the basis for his *Sukhanwarān i Īrān dar 'aṣr i ḥāḍir*. Subsequently he obtained the degree of Ph.D. at the University of London for a thesis substantially identical with his work *Modern Persian Poetry* (Calcutta 1943).

Sukhanvarān-i-Īrān dar 'aṣr-i-ḥāẓir. *Poets and poetry of Modern Persia, vol. i* [notices of 33 poets] *with thirty-two portraits and two Musical Notes ... Calcutta* (Delhi printed), 1933‡, *vol. ii* [notices of 51 poets] *with fifty-one portraits and one Musical Note ...* **Calcutta** (Delhi printed), 1937‡ [vol. iii, devoted to prose-writers, is to follow].

[*Armaghān* xi/7 (Sept.–Oct. 1930), pp. 559–60 (with portrait).]

1241. **Ḥabīb Yaghmā'ī** b. Mīrzā Asad Allāh is a grandson of the poet "Yaghmā" and was born in 1320/1902–3 at the village of Khūr in the district (*bulūk*) of Jandaq and Biyābānak. Educated at the Teachers' Training College (*Dār al-Mu'allimīn*) in Ṭihrān, he was for two years Director of Education and Charitable Bequests at Simnān (*ba-riyāsat i ma'ārif u auqāf i Simnān manṣūb gasht*) before being appointed Lecturer in Persian Literature at the Dār al-Funūn in Ṭihrān and a member of the staff of the Press Department (*u ba'dan ba-mu'allimī i adabīyāt i Fārisī dar Dār al-Funūn u 'uḍwīyat i Idārah i Kull i Inṭibā'āt bar qarār gardīd*). His poems have been published mainly in newspapers and periodicals. An edition of Asadī's *Karshāsp-nāmah* was published by him at Ṭihrān in AHS 1317/1938. Several unpublished works of his are mentioned by Ishaque.

Sharḥ i hāl i Yaghmā, an account of the poet "Yaghmā",[408] who died on 16 Rabī' II 1276/13 Nov. 1859, preceded by a description of the district of Jandaq and Biyābānak: **Ṭihrān** [circ. 1927 ?‡],

[Ishaque *Suhhanvarān-i-Īrān* i pp. 64–9 (portrait); Yāsimī *Adabīyāt i mu'āṣir* pp. 96–7 (portrait).]

1242. For 'Abd al-Ḥusain "Āyatī's" *Tārīkh i Yazd*, which was completed in AHS. 1317/1938–9, and of which pp. 268–351 are devoted to the poets of Yazd, see the Additions and Corrections to this work.

1243. Appendix

(1) ***Bazm i wiṣāl***, a metrical account by "Ṣabūrī" of his journey from Persia to India and his doings there: **Lucknow** 1873°*.

(2) ***Ḥisār i Nāy: sharḥ i hāl i Mas'ūd i Sa'd i Salmān***, completed in AHS. 1317/1938 by Suhailī Khwānsārī: Islāmīyah Press [**Ṭihrān** ? 1938 ? ‡].

(3) ***Life and Times of Hafiz of Shiraz***, by M. Ḥamīd Allāh: [**Allahabad** 1892*].

408 Cf. Browne, *List. Hist.* iv pp. 337–44.

(4) *Madhāq i sukhan*, "a biographical dictionary of famous Persian poets,"[2] by S͟hāh Ḥaidar Ḥasan b. S͟hāh M. Ḥasan Ilāhābādī: [**India**] 1300/1883*.

(5) *S͟harḥ i aḥwāl i Nāṣir i K͟husrau*, drawn up for Charles Schefer by the Persian Minister of Public Instruction and Jaʿfar-Qulī K͟hān b. Riḍā-Qulī K͟hān: **Blochet** i 637.

(6) *Tad͟hkirah i muk͟htaṣar dar ḥāl i Rēk͟htah-gōyān i Hind*, by M. Ṣadr al-Dīn: **Browne** Suppt. 304 (Corpus 159[409]).

(7) *Tad͟hkirah i mutaʾak͟hk͟hirīn i shuʿaraʾ i Fārs*, short notice of modern poets, mainly of Fārs, with copious extracts from their works: **Browne** Coll. J. 19 (apparently only about half of the work).

(8) *Tad͟hkirah i shuʿārāʾ*, by Maulawī ʿAbd al-G͟hanī "G͟hanī" Farruk͟hābādī. Edition: place ? 1916 (Āṣafīyah iii p. 162 no. 198).

(9) *Tad͟hkirah i shuʿarāʾ i Qāʾināt*, notices of thirty poets of Qāʾināt or Bīrjand, by Ḍiyāʾ al-Dīn Qāʾinātī (contemporary): **Nad͟hīr Aḥmad** 80 (W. Ivanow's collection, AH 1330/1912, transcribed from an autograph).

(10) *Tad͟hkirah u tabṣirah*, notices of popular Persian poets, by Mahdī Ḥusain Nāṣirī: **Allahabad** [1915*].

(11) *Tad͟hkirat al-nisāʾ*, on the poetesses of India, without author's name: **Nad͟hīr Aḥmad** 82 (Ḥājjī Ḥabib Allāh's library, Nellore. AH 1182/1768).

(12) *Tad͟hkirat al-shuʿarāʾ*, by Bahāʾ al-Dīn Ḥasan K͟hān "ʿUrūj", probably the author of the *Payām i ulfat* (Ivanow 402, 1st Suppt. 793): **Āṣafīyah** i p. 318 nos. 12, 99.

(13) *Tad͟hkirat al-shuʿarāʾ*, by Ṣiddīq K͟hān b. Amīr Muẓaffar: **Buk͟hārā** Semenov 49.

(14) *Yag͟hmā-yi Biyābānak*, a life of "Yag͟hmā" (cf. no. 1241 *supra*) by ʿAlī Muqaddam: Ṭihrān AHS. 1313/1934*.

13.2 Saints, Mystics, etc.

[The series of works enumerated in the preceding subsection includes not only the *tad͟hkirahs* primarily concerned with poets but also a number of histories containing biographies of poets in appendices or special sections or otherwise. Most of these histories treat similarly of saints and other celebrities, but except in special cases they are not mentioned below. For information concerning them the preceding subsection should be consulted. Works concerned primarily with the utterances of saints are not included in the following subsection, unless they contain an appreciable amount of biography.]

---

409 So Arberry. According to the Quarterly Catalogue it contains lives of the poets of Allahabad.

1244. The *Kashf al-maḥjūb* written probably about 450/1058 by ʿAlī b. ʿUthmān al-Jullābī al-Hujwīrī is a general work on Ṣūfism and does not belong to this subsection,[410] but of the 420 pages to which it extends in Nicholson's translation pp. 70–175 are biographical and deserve mention, here.

1245. Shaikh al-Islām Abū Ismāʿīl ʿ**Abd Allāh** b. M. b. ʿ**Alī al-Anṣārī** al-Harawī al-Ḥanbalī, who in his poems calls himself "Anṣārī", "Pīr i Harī", or "Pīr i Harāt", and who in Ṣūfī works is often called simply Shaikh al-Islām, was born at Quhunduz[411] on 2 Shaʿbān 396/4 May 1006. He was a disciple of Abū 'l-Ḥasan al-Kharaqānī (for whom see no. 1247 1st footnote, *infra*) and is one of the most famous Ṣūfīs. He was a learned man, especially in Arabic linguistics, the Traditions, history, genealogy, and Qurʾānic exegesis, but his uncompromising Ḥanbalism and his polemics against non-Ḥanbalīs made him the victim of more than one heresy-hunt.[412] He died in Dhū 'l-Ḥijjah[413] 481/Feb.–March 1089 and is buried near Harāt[414]

ʿAbd Allāh Anṣārī's extant works, and more especially the MSS. of them preserved at Istānbūl, are the subject of H. Ritter's *Philologika* viii/1 (in *Der Islam* 22/2 (1934) pp. 89–100). The Arabic works are enumerated by Brockelmann. They include the *Manāzil al-sāʾirīn*, the *Dhamm al-kalām*, and *al-Arbaʿīn fī 'l-ṣifāt*, an anthropomorphic tract (MS.: Baghdād Köshkü 510. See *Der Islam* 17/3–4 (1928) p. 255 (*Philologika* ii), where the work is briefly described by Ritter). The surviving Persian works are mostly brief Ṣūfī tracts in rhymed prose.[415] According to Ḥ. Kh. (iii p. 293) Anṣārī was the author of three Persian

410 It may nevertheless be permissible to record two articles dealing with Hujwīrī's work, namely (1) *Persian Sufiism, being a translation* [by Sidney Jerrold] *of* [the literary portions of] *Professor Zhukovsky's introduction to his edition of the Kashf al-Maḥjūb* (in BSOS, v/3 (1929) pp. 475–88), and (2) *The Kashfu-l-Maḥjūb of Abū-l-Ḥasan ʿAlī al-Jullābī. By L. S. Dugin* (in JRASB., Letters, viii/2 (1942) pp. 315–79).

411 *Man ba-Quhunduz zādah am* (*Nafaḥāt* p. 377[1]): *maulūdash ... dar Quhunduz min maḥallāt i Ṭūs* (*Riyāḍ al-ʿārifīn* p. 50[21]): *dar Quhunduz i Ṭūs mutawallid shudah* (*Majmaʿ al-fuṣaḥāʾ* p. 65). It seems probable that the Quhunduz referred to was at Harāt rather than Ṭūs.

412 *Wa-kāna saif[an] maslūl[an] ʿalā 'l-mukhālifīn wa-jidhʿ[an] fī aʿyun al-mutakallimīn wa-'mtuḥina ghaira marrah* (*Ṭabaqāt al-Ḥanābilah* p. 401).

413 So *Ṭabaqāt al-ḥuffāẓ*. The *Safīnat al-auliyāʾ* says 9 Rabīʿ II.

414 For a description of his shrine see Yate, *Northern Afghanistan* pp. 33–7, and for some views see Niedermayer and Diez *Afganistan*, Leipzig 1924, p. 61.

415 The best known is the *Munājāt*, of which there are several editions. The *Naṣīḥat-nāmah i wazīr* or *Naṣīḥah i Niẓām al-Mulk* was published by Berthels in the *Izvestiya Akademii Nauk*, series vi, vol. 20 (Leningrad 1926) pp. 1139–50.

dīwāns. No copies of these are recorded, but twenty *ghazals* occurring in the Persian tract or collection of tracts which passes in Central Asia under the incorrect title of *Manāzil al-sāʾirīn* (see Berthels in *Islamica* iii/1 (1927) p. 10) and which Zhukovski called the *Pseudo-Manāzil al-sāʾirīn*[416] were published by him in an article entitled *Pesni Kheratskago Startsa*, which he contributed to the *Vostochnyya Zametki* (St. Petersburg 1895), pp. 79–113, and of which an English translation, *The songs of the Elder of Herat*, was published by L. Bogdanov in the *JRASB.*, Letters, vol. v, 1939, pp. 205–55. A small collection of *rubāʿīyāt* ascribed to Anṣārī has been published several times in the East.

Anṣārī finds a place in the *ṭabaqāt al-mufassirīn*,[417] and a *tafsīr* by him *"ba-zabān i darwīshān"* is mentioned in the *Majālis al-ʿushshāq* (p. 56. Cf. *Islamica* iii/1 (1927) p. 15). Of this Ṣūfī *tafsīr* no copies seem to have survived. A MS. at Mashhad containing a Persian commentary on *Sūrahs* xxi 6–xxv is indeed described in the catalogue (vol. i, fṣl. 3, MSS., p. 11 no. 30) as the *Tafsīr i Khwājah ʿAbd Allāh i Anṣārī*, but this Mashhad *tafsīr*, which deals separately with translation, explanation and *taʾwīl* in three *naubats*, is apparently the same as that of which *Sūrahs* vi–ix are preserved in the Sipahsālār Library (Catalogue, vol. i p. 148) and which, though it often quotes Anṣārī in the third

416 Three MSS. of this work were known to Zhukovski, one in the Leningrad Public Library (III.2.8., called *Manāzil al-sāʾirīn* in the copyist's colophon) and two in his own possession (one of which has the title *Manāzil al-sāʾirīn* written in a later hand on the first leaf). This tract, or collection of tracts, begins with the words *Ḥamd i bī-ḥadd Ilāhī rā u durūd i bī-ʿadad (thanā-yi bī-ʿadd) pādshāhī rā kih bardāsht az dīdah i dilhā ramad* (*Vostoch. Zam.* p. 82), which, as Ritter has pointed out, are the opening words of the tract or collection of tracts usually called *Kanz al-sālikīn* (Āṣafīyah i p. 466 no. 303, Bānkīpūr Suppt. i 1995 xxii, Bombay Univ. p. 139 no. 65, Browne Coll. D.7, Būhār 165, Cairo p. 422, Dresden 172 (1), Ethé 1919 (5), Ivanow 1158–9, Lahore (see *OCM*. VIII/3 (May 1932) p. 133), Leipzig Fleischer 110 (5), Rieu ii 738*a*, Shahīd ʿAlī Pāshā 1383 (see *Der Islam* 22/2 pp. 97–8, where other Istānbūl MSS. are mentioned)). Some of these MSS. (e.g. the Asiatic Museum MS. Nov. 3, of which the sections are enumerated by Berthels (*Islamica* III/I (1927) p. 11), and Ivanow 1158) contain far more matter than others and appear to be extensively interpolated.

417 A precise statement concerning his activities in this field occurs in the biographical note written in 746/1345–6 by M. b. M. sibṭ al- … al-Mālikī on the first leaf of the B.M. MS. of the *Dhamm al-kalām* and quoted in Cureton-Rieu p. 711. It runs as follows: … *ʿālim bi-'l-ḥadīth ṣaḥīḥihi wa-saqīmihi wa-bi-āthār al-salaf wa-lughāt al-ʿArab wa-'khtilāfihā wa-bi-tafsīr al-Kitāb al-ʿAzīz wa-maʿānīhi wa-aqwāl al-mufassirīn iftataḥa 'l-Qurʾān al-ʿAzīz fa-fassarahu ilā qaulihi Yuḥibbūnahum ka-ḥubbi 'llāhi* [II 160] *fa-'ftataḥa majālis fī 'l-ḥaḍrah … fī hādhihi 'l-āyah muddah ṭawīlah min ʿumrihi wa-kadhā fī qaulihi ʿazza wa-jalla Inna 'lladhīna sabaqat lahum minnā 'l-ḥusnā* [XXI 101] *fa-fassara fīhā thalāth-miʾah wa-sittīn majlisan, Wa-qad jamaʿa ʿAbd al-Qādir al-Ruhāwī kitāban sammāhu 'l-Mādiḥ wa-'l-mamdūḥ … muʿẓam al-kitāb fī tarjamatihi fa-man ṭālaʿa dhālika ʿarafa manzilatahu wa-jalālatahu fī 'l-ummah….*

naubat, cannot be the work of Anṣārī himself (see the cataloguer's remarks on p. 149). [P.S. See the Additions and Corrections.]

Ṭabaqāt al-Ṣūfīyah,[418] notices of 120 saints based on the Arabic *Ṭabaqāt al-Ṣūfīyīn* of M. b. al-Ḥusain al-Sulamī (d. 412/1021, see Brockelmann i 200, *Sptbd.* ipp. 361–2), apparently taken down from ʿAbd Allāh Anṣārī's oral discourses and arranged after his death by an anonymous disciple: **Nāfidh Pāshā** 426 (AH 771/1370. See *Der Islam* 22/2 (1934) p. 93), **Nūr i ʿUthmānīyah** 2500 (AH 839/1436. See *Der Islam* 22/2 p. 93), **Ivanow** 234 (collated AH 1015/1606–7).

Extracts: (1) L. Massignon *La passion d'al-Hallaj*, Paris 1922, i pp. 368–9 (with French translation). (2) L. Massignon *Essai sur les origines du lexique technique de la mystique musulmane* 1922, pp. 99–100.

List of the saints: Ivanow pp. 80–82.

Description of the work and discussion of the language: *Tabaqat of Ansari in the Old Language of Herat. By W. Ivanow* (in *JRAS*. 1923 pp. 1–34 and 337–82).

[*Ṭabaqāt al-Ḥanābilah taʾlīf al-Qāḍī Abī 'l-Ḥusain M. b. Abī Yaʿlā M.... ikhtiṣār Shams al-Dīn Abī ʿAbd Allāh M. b. ʿAbd al-Qādir ... al-Nābulusī* (cf. Brockelmann *Sptbd.* i pp. 308, 557), Damascus 1350/1931, pp. 400–1; *Kharīdat al-qaṣr* (see Leyden cat., 2nd ed., ii/1 p. 217); al-Dhahabī *Taʾrīkh al-Islām*, apparently under AH 481 (B.M. Or. 50 (Cureton-Rieu p. 739) fol. 176. See Cureton-Rieu p. 710*b* n., where this biography is described as *notitia uberrima*); Idem *Tadhkirat al-ḥuffāẓ* iii pp. 354–60; *Tārīkh i Guzīdah* pp. 785–6; biographical note written in 746/1345–6 by M. b. M. sibṭ al- ... al-Mālikī on the first leaf of the B.M. MS. of the *Dhamm al-kalām* and quoted in Cureton-Rieu p. 711 (cf. footnote 416, *supra*, where a part of it is quoted); al-Yāfiʿī *Mirʾāt al-janān* under AH 481 (vol. iii p. 133); al-Subkī *Ṭabaqāt al-Shāfiʿīyat al-kubrā* iii p. 117; al-Ṣafadī *al-Wāfī bi-'l-Wafayāt* (cf. Gabrieli *Indice* p. 105); *Mujmal i Faṣīḥī* under AH 481; al-Suyūṭī *Ṭabaqāt al-mufassirīn* p. 15, *Ṭabaqāt al-ḥuffāẓ* iii p. 24; *Nafaḥāt al-uns* pp. 576–80; *Majālis al-ʿushshāq* no. 8; *Haft iqlīm* no. 619; *Safīnat al-auliyāʾ* pp. 165–6 (no. 300); *Shadharāt al-dhahab* iii pp. 365–6; *Riyāḍ al-shuʿarāʾ*; *Ātash-kadah* no. 287; *Khulāṣat al-afkār* no. 2; *Makhzan al-gharāʾib* no. 4; *Rauḍāt al-jannāt* p. 450; *Khazīnat al-aṣfiyāʾ* ii pp. 235–6; *Riyāḍ al-ʿārifīn* pp. 50–1; *Majmaʿ al-fuṣaḥāʾ* i p. 65; Rieu i p. 35; V. A. Zhukovsky *Pesni Kheratskago Startsa* (in *Vostochnyya Zametki*, St. Petersburg 1895, pp. 79–113) and L. Bogdanov's English translation, *The songs of the Elder of Herat* (in *JRASB.*, Letters, vol. v, 1939, pp. 205–55); *Ṭarāʾiq al-ḥaqāʾiq* ii pp. 162–3; *GIP*. ii p. 282; Ethé col. 974; Browne

418 This work is one of the main sources of Jāmī's *Nafaḥāt al-uns* (see W. Ivanow *The sources of Jami's Nafahat* (in *JASB*. 1922, pp. 385–91)).

Lit. Hist. ii pp. 269–70; *Ency. Isl.* under Anṣārī (unsigned) and Herewī (M. Ben Cheneb); Ivanow pp. 78–9; Berthels *Grundlinien der Entwicklungsgeschichte des ṣūfischen Lehrgedichts in Persien* (in *Islamica* iii/1 (Leipzig 1927), pp. 1–31) pp. 7–15; Brockelmann i p. 433, *Sptbd.* i pp. 773–5.]

1246. For *al-Qand fī maʿrifat ʿulamāʾ Samarqand*, an Arabic work on the holy places, graves of holy men, etc., at Samarqand by ʿUmar b. M. al-Nasafī (d. 537/1142), which seems not to have survived in its original form but only in the Persian translation of an Arabic abridgment, see no. 496 *supra*.

1247. Of unknown date but certainly earlier than 698/1299, the date of the. British Museum MS., is an account of Abū 'l-Haṣan al-Kharaqānī,[419] the teacher of Abū Saʿīd b. Abī 'l-Khair (see no. 1248, 2nd par., footnote, *infra*), abridged from a work entitled *Nūr al-ʿulūm*.

Nūr al-ʿulūm *min kalām al-Shaikh Abī 'l-Ḥasan al-Kharaqānī*: no MSS. recorded.

Abridgment: *al-muntakhab min kitāb Nūr al-ʿulūm min kalām al-Shaikh Abī 'l-Ḥasan al-Kharaqānī*,[420] an account of the utterances and mode of life of Abū 'l-Ḥasan al-Kharaqānī in ten *bābs*: **Rieu** i p. 342*a* (lacks much of *Bābs* iii and vi. AH 698/1299).

Edition with Russian translation by E. Berthels: *Nūr al-ʿulūm. Zhizneopisanie sheykha Abū-l-Ḥasana Kharakānī* (in *Iran* iii (**Leningrad** 1929) pp. 155–224).

1248. In the preface to the *Asrār al-tauḥīd* (see § 1249 *infra*) M. b. al-Munawwar says that a cousin (*pisar i ʿamm*) of his [who must, like himself, have been a great-great-grandson of Abū Saʿīd b. Abī 'l-Khair] had written a work in five chapters entitled *Ḥālāt u sukhanān i shaikh i mā*. M. b. al-Munawwar does not mention his name, but Zhukovsky, who identified an untitled British Museum

419 d. 425/1033, aged 73. See *Kashf al-maḥjūb* tr. Nicholson p. 163; Samʿānī *Ansāb* fol. 194b^{9}; *Tadhkirat al-auliyāʾ* ii pp. 201–55; *Nafaḥāt al-uns* pp. 336–8; *Majālis al-ʿushshāq* no. 6; *Haft iqlīm* no. 837; *Safīnat al-auliyāʾ* p. 74 (no. 67); *Majmaʿ al-gharāʾib* no. 5; *Riyāḍ al-ʿārifīn* pp. 47–8; *Khazīnat al-aṣfiyāʾ* i pp. 522–7; Nicholson *Mystics of Islam* pp. 133–8, *Studies in Islamic mysticism* pp. 42–4. Kharaqān, four leagues from Bisṭām on the road to Astarābād, is spelt *bi-fatḥ al-khāʾ wa-'l-rāʾ wa-'l-qāf al-maftūḥāt* according to Samʿānī (*Ansāb* fol. 194b^{7}), and he had visited the place (according to a quotation, not from the *Ansāb* apparently, in Yāqūt's *Muʿjam al-buldān* s.v.). In the *Qāmūs*, on the other hand, it is said to be pronounced "like Saḥbān" (*wa-taḥrīkuhu laḥn*), and al-Suyūṭī (*Lubb al-lubāb* p. 91) spells it *bi-'l-ḍamm wa-'l-qāf* (cf. le Strange L.E.C. p. 366).

420 These are the words of a heading in the MS., whereas in the subscription the tract is called *Nūr al-ʿulūm*.

manuscript as the *Ḥālāt u sukhanān*, came to the conclusion that his name was Muḥammad and that he was probably the son of Abū Rauḥ Luṭf Allāh b. Abī Saʿīd [b. Abī Ṭāhir b. Abī Saʿīd b. Abī 'l-Khair]. Most of this work (nearly five-sixths apparently) is incorporated in the *Asrār al-tauḥīd*.

***Ḥālāt u sukhanān i Shaikh Abū Saʿīd Faḍl Allāh b. Abī 'l-Khair al-Maihanī*,**[421] written probably about 540/1145–6: **Rieu** i 342*b* ii (AH 699/1299).

Edition: *Zhizn' i ryechi startsa Abu-Sa'ida Meykheneyskago* (*Ḥālāt u sukhunān etc.*). **St. Petersburg** 1899°* (ed. V. A. Zhukovsky. Publications of the Faculty of Oriental Languages in the University of St. Petersburg, no. 2).

Many passages of this work are translated in R. A. Nicholson's essay *Abú Saʿíd ibn Abi 'l-Khayr* (*Studies in Islamic mysticism*, Cambridge 1921, pp. 1–76).

Descriptions: (1) Browne *Lit. Hist.* ii 263; (2) Nicholson *op. cit.* p. 1.

1249. **M. b. al-Munawwar** b. Abī Saʿīd b. Abī Ṭāhir b. Abī Saʿīd b. Abī 'l-Khair Maihanī was, like the author of the *Ḥālāt u sukhanān*, a great-great-grandson of Abū Saʿīd.

***Asrār al-tauḥīd fī maqāmāt al-Shaikh Abī Saʿīd*,** an account of the saint much larger than the *Ḥālāt u sukhanān*, most of which it incorporates, written probably in 574/1178–9,[422] or at any rate not earlier than 552/1157, the date of Sanjar's death, and not later than 599/1202, since Ghiyāth al-Dīn M. b. Sām, King of Ghōr, to whom it is dedicated, died in that year: **Mehren** 16 (lacks foll. 1–13. AH 711/1311), **Leningrad** Pub. Lib. (defective. 8th/14th cent.), **Cairo** p. 412.

Editions: **St. Petersburg** 1899°* (*Tainy edineniya s Bogom v podvigakh startsa Abu-Sa'ida. Tolkovanie na chetverostishie Abu-Sa'ida* [Persian text edited by V. A. Zhukovsky and followed (pp. 487–93) by the *Risālah i Ḥaurāʾīyah*, an explanation of one of Abū Saʿīd's quatrains by ʿUbaid Allāh

421 b. 357/967 at Maihanah (between Abīward and Sarakhs, not the place of this name south of Turbat i Ḥaidarī), d. there 440/1049. See Nicholson's *Studies in Islamic Mysticism* pp. 1–76 and his article in the *Ency. Isl.*; Browne *Lit. Hist.* ii pp. 261–9; *Kashf al-maḥjūb* tr. Nicholson, pp. 164–6; *Tadhkirat al-auliyā'* ii pp. 322–37; Subkī iv p. 10; *Nafaḥāt al-uns* pp. 339–47; *Haft iqlīm* no. 525; *Safīnat al-auliyā'* pp. 162–3 (no. 294); *Makhzan al-gharā'ib* no. 1; *Khazīnat al-aṣfiyā'* ii pp. 228–9; etc.

422 Bahmanyār draws attention to statements of the author implying that his work was written 100 + 34 years (*sī u chahār sāl* according to the Copenhagen MS.) or 100 + 30 or 40 years (*sī sāl u chihil sāl* [*sic*] according to the Leningrad MS., Ṭihrān ed. p. 287[2]) after Abū Saʿīd's death [in 440], i.e. in 574, if the former reading is correct, in 570 or 580, if the latter reading be accepted.

b. Maḥmūd S͟hās͟hī. Publications of the Faculty of Oriental Languages in the University of St. Petersburg, no. 1]); Ṭihrān AHS 1313/1934–5 (ed. Aḥmad Bahmanyār. Based on Zhukovsky's edition and containing the *Risālah i Ḥaurā'īyah* as well as a Persian translation of Zhukovsky's preface but modernised in spelling and shorn of textual notes).

Many passages of this work are translated in R. A. Nicholson's essay *Abú Sa'íd ibn Abi 'l-Khayr* (*Studies in Islamic mysticism*, Cambridge 1921, pp. 1–76).

Descriptions: (1) Browne *Lit. Hist.* ii pp. 262–3, (2) Nicholson *Studies in Islamic mysticism* pp. 1–3.

1250. The celebrated mystic and poet **Farīd al-Dīn M. b. Ibrāhīm al-'Aṭṭār** was born at Kadkan or S͟hādyāk͟h, villages near Nīs͟hāpūr. He spent thirteen years of his youth at Mas͟hhad and after many wanderings settled finally in Nīs͟hāpūr. Like his father he was a druggist by profession. According to Daulat-S͟hāh he died in 627/1230, possibly the correct date, but various other dates are given.

Tad͟hkirat al-auliyā', notices (practically confined to sayings and anecdotes) of about 70 saints mainly of the first three Islāmic centuries, to which is added in some MSS. an appendix (called sometimes vol. ii) containing 20–25 notices of later saints: H. K͟h ii p. 258 no. 2797, **Blochet** iv 2306 (slightly defective at both ends. Early 13th cent.), i 403 (late 13th or early 14th cent.), 404 (late 13th or early 14th cent.), 405 (AH 888/1483), 406 (16th cent.), 407 (AH 1049/1639), 153 (1) (defective. 18th cent.), **Berlin** 580 (AH 687/1288 or 689/1290), 578 (old), 579 (AH 999/1591), 581 (with appendix (20 saints)), 582 (with appendix, AH 1099/1688), 583 (defective), 584 (fragments), **Bānkīpūr** viii 659 (AH 724/1324. LIST OF THE 77 NOTICES), 660 (AH 830/1426–7), 661 (AH 939/1532–3), **Upsala** Zetterstéen 408 (defective, AH 791/1388–9), **Peshawar** 1053B (14th cent.), **Rieu** i 344*a* (14th cent.), 344*b* (17th cent.), **Ivanow** 235 (defective, late 15th or early 16th cent.), 236 (AH 1094/1683(?)) 237 (AH 1171/1757–8), 238 (late 18th cent.), Curzon 63 (slightly defective. 17th–18th cent.), 1st Suppt. 770 (part only. 19th cent.), 771 (part only. AH 1112/1700), **I.O. D.P.** 584A (AH 920/1514–15 ?), 584B (slightly defective. 17th cent.), **Ethé** 1051 (with appendix, AH 1091/1680), 1052 ("very old"), 1053 (n.d.), 1054 (fragment), **Leyden** iii p. 17 no. 930 (AH 941/1534–5), no. 929 (old), **Āṣafīyah** i p. 316 nos. 3 (AH 978/1570–1), 11 (AH 1082/1671–2), 15, 31, 34, **Rehatsek** p. 190 no. 29 (?) (author not stated, AH 984/1576–7), no. 28 (?) (author not stated. Defective at both ends), **Būhār** (with appendix. 16th cent.), **Leningrad** Mus. Asiat. (AH 1003/1594–5. See *Mélanges asiatiques* vii (St. Petersburg 1876) pp. 505–11), Pub. Lib. (Chanykov 104), Univ. nos. 579*, 580* (Salemann-Rosen p. 13), **Bodleian**

622 i–ii (with appendix (23 saints). Seals dated 1020/1611–12), 623 i (*ah* 1026–7/1617–18), 624 i–ii (with appendix, *ah* 1078/1668), 625 ix–x (with appendix, n.d.), **ʿAlīgaṛh** Subḥ. MSS. p. 61 no. 22 ("old"), **Browne** Suppt. 291 (King's 75), **Browne** Coll. J. 4 (9) (only 40 notices, AH 1269/1852–3), J. 3 (7) (selections, AH 1297/1880), V.7 (14 (1) ("of no great antiquity"), **Cairo** p. 501 (four copies, one dated 1267/1850–1, the rest undated).

Editions: Fakhr al-maṭābiʿ [**Delhi** ? circ. 1852 ?*], Mujtabāʾī Press, **Delhi** (date ? see Ḥaidarābād Coll. p. 27), **Lahore** 1306/1889*, 1308/1891*, **Lucknow** 1891°, **London and Leyden** 1905–7°* (ed. R. A. Nicholson. 2 vols. Persian Historical Texts, iii, v).

Translated extracts:

(1) [Life of Ḥallāj], F. A. D. Tholuck *Blüthensammlung aus der morgenländischen Mystik*, **Berlin** 1825, pp. 310–27.

(2) [Shaqīq Balkhī, Ḥātim Aṣamm, Aḥmad Khiḍrūyah Abū Ḥafṣ Ḥaddād] *Vier turkestanische Heilige. Ein Beitrag zum Verständnis der islamischen Mystik. Von P. Klappstein*, **Berlin** 1919 (Türkische Bibliothek, 20. A Kiel dissertation).

(3) J. Hallauer *Die Vita des Ibrahim b. Edhem in der Tedhkiret el-Ewlija des Ferid ed-din Attar, eine islamische Heiligenlegende*, **Leipzig** 1925 (Türkische Bibliothek, 24. A Zürich dissertation. Cf. H. H. Schaeder's review in *Islamica* iii/2 (1927) pp. 282–94).

Lists of the saints: (1) Leyden iii pp. 17–19, (2) *Mélanges asiatiques* vii (St. Petersburg 1876), pp. 505–11, (3) Ethé coll. 622–5 (includes appendix), (4) Bānkīpūr viii pp. 17–18.

Abridgments:

(1) by ʿAbd al-Wāḥid Bilgrāmī, i.e. probably Sh. ʿAbd al-Wāḥid "Shāhidī" Bilgrāmī, who died in 1017/1608–9 (see *Āʾīn i Akbarī* tr. Blochmann p. 547, Badāʾūnī *Muntakhab al-tawārīkh* iii pp. 65–6, Raḥmān ʿAlī p. 136), **Berlin** 585.

(2) **Mehren** 15 (45 saints. 41st regnal year [of Aurangzēb ?]).

Swedish translation: *Ur Tazkiratú 'l-Awliyá skrifven af Shaikh Farídu 'd-Dín 'Attár öfversatt af Baron Erik Hermelin efter Professor Reynold A. Nicholson's text.* **Stockholm** 1931–2* (2 vols.).

Persian metrical version: *Walī-nāmah*, composed by Ḥāfiẓ ʿAllāf for Ibrāhīm Sulṭān, Shāh-Rukh's son, and completed at Mecca in 821/1418: **Rosen** Institut 79 (AH 887/1482).

Turkish translations:[423]

(1) [Eastern Turkish] **Paris** Bib. Nat. 100 (Uighur script), **Fātiḥ** 2848 (Arabic script. See *Islâm Ansiklopedisi* ii p. 10*a*). Edition: *Tezkereh-i evliâ.*

423 This list makes no claim to completeness. No attempt has been made to search the catalogues of Turkish MSS.

Manuscrit ouïgour de la Bibliothèque Nationale reproduit par l'héliogravure typographique, **Paris** 1890. French translation: *Tezkereh-i evliâ. Le Mémorial des saints traduit sur le manuscrit ouïgour de la Bibliothèque Nationale par A. Pavet de Courteille*, **Paris** 1889.

(2) [Eastern Turkish] by Khwājah Shāh b. S. Aḥmad b. S. Asad Allāh ... al-Khuwārazmī: **Leningrad** Mus. Asiat. (AH 1234/1828–9). See *Mélanges asiatiques* vii (1876) pp. 511–12).

(3) [Eastern Turkish. Unidentified] **Bukhārā** Semenov 44, **Schefer** 989 (14 saints only ? 19th cent.), **Upsala** Zetterstéen 636.

(4) [Old Anatolian Turkish] a translation dedicated to Āydīn-oghlū Meḥmed Bey (AH 707–34. See *Islâm Ansiklopedisi* ii p. 10, which is the authority for the date just given), **Bāyazid** 1643.

(5) [Ottoman Turkish] by Sinān al-Dīn Yūsuf b. Khiḍr, called Khwājah Pāshā (d. 891/1486. See *Ency. Isl.* under Sinān Pasha I), Ḥ. Kh ii p. 258 no. 2798, **Nūr i 'Uthmānīyah** 2299 (presumably the autograph referred to in *Ency. Isl.*).

(6) [Ottoman Turkish] by 'Alī Riḍā Qarāḥiṣārī (see *Islâm Ansiklopedisi* ii p. 10*b*[3]).

(7) [Miscellaneous, including unidentified or inadequately described MSS.] **Browne** Handlist 232 (first 20 notices only. AH 931/1524), **Dresden** 18 (a translation or adaptation by M. b. Ghāzī), 99, 141 (different from 99. AH 1018/1608–10), 174 (AH 1039/1629–30 and 1093/1682), **Leyden** iii p. 19 no. 931 (AH 952/1545), **Upsala** 306 (*Maqālat al-auliyā'*, written by order of Sulṭān Abū 'l-Fatḥ Malik Isfandiyār [if Tornberg's Effendijar is to be so read] Bahādur Khān), and the Istānbūl MSS. mentioned in *Islâm Ansiklopedisi* ii p. 10*b*.

Urdu translation by Mīrzā Jān: *Anwār al-adhkiyā'*, **Cawnpore** 1914*.

[*Lubāb al-albāb* ii pp. 337–9; Daulatshāh pp. 187–92; *Majālis al-mu'minīn, majlis* 6 (pp. 296–300); *Rauḍāt al-jannāt* iv pp. 196–7; Rieu i 344*a*; *Grundriss der iranischen Philologie* ii 284–5; M. Qazwīnī's *muqaddimah i intiqādī dar sharḥ i aḥwāl i Sh. 'Aṭṭār* prefixed to vol. ii of R. A. Nicholson's edition of the *Tadhkirat al-auliyā'*; Browne *Lit. Hist.* ii 506–15; *Ency. Isl.* under 'Aṭṭār (less than one column, unsigned); Bombay Univ. Cat. pp. 60–4; *Philologika. Von Hellmut Ritter X. Farīdaddīn 'Aṭṭār* (in *Der Islam* 25/2 (1938) pp. 134–73); *Islâm Ansiklopedisi* under Attâr (12 columns by H. Ritter); etc., etc.]

1251. Nūr al-Dīn 'Alī b. Yūsuf **al-Shaṭṭanūfī**[424] al-Lakhmī al-Shāfi'ī was born at Cairo in Shawwāl 647/Jan.–Feb. 1250 and died there on 19 Dhū

424 Shaṭṭanūf (*bi-'l-fatḥ wa-tashdīd al-ṭā'* according to Suyūṭī's *Lubb al-Lubāb*) or Shaṭanūf (*ka-ḥalazūn* according to the *Qāmūs*) is in Egypt, *min a'māl al-Manūfīyah* according to the

'l-Ḥijjah 713/6 April 1314 (see *al-Durar al-kāminah* iii p. 141, *Bug͟hyat al-wuʿāt* pp. 358–9, Brockelmann ii 118, *Sptbd* ii p. 147).

Bahjat al-asrār wa-maʿdin al-anwār, an Arabic biography of ʿAbd al-Qādir al-Jīlānī:[425] Ḥ. K͟h. ii p. 71 (inaccurate), **Ahlwardt** ix nos. 10,072–6, **Cureton-Rieu** p. 737, etc.. etc. (see Brockelmann).

Editions: **Cairo** 1301/1883–4 (Sarkis col. 1127), 1304/1887 (Ellis i col. 262, Sarkis *loc. cit.*), **Tunis** 1302–4/1884–7 (Sarkis *ibid*).

Persian translations:

(1) *Kas͟hf al-āt͟hār* (a chronogram = 1133/1720–1), written in the reign of Muḥammad S͟hāh (1131–61/1719–48) by M. Ḥabīb Allāh Akbarābādī (*maulid*ⁿ) Dihlawī (*tawaṭṭun*ⁿ), the author of the *D͟hikr i jamīʿ i auliyāʾ i Dihlī* (see no. 1349 *infra*): **I.O.** **D.P.** 711 (A H 1140/1727, transcribed from an autograph), **Āṣafīyah** i p. 462 no. 431 (A H 1270/1853), iii p. 200 no. 1338.

(2) *Zubdat al-āt͟hār muntak͟hab i Bahjat* **al-asrār**, an abridged translation by ʿAbd al-Ḥaqq Dihlawī (for whom see no. 243 *supra*): **I.O.** **D.P.** 759*a* (defective. Early 19th cent.).

Edition: **Delhi** [1890°. With Urdu translation].

Another translation, *Maqāmāt i G͟haut͟h al-t͟haqalain*, was made by Badr al-Dīn b. Ibrāhīm Sihrindī (see no. 1323 *infra*), but no copies seem to be recorded.

1252. **Ibrāhīm** b. S͟haik͟h al-Islām Ṣadr al-Dīn **Rūzbihān** b. Fak͟hr al-Dīn Aḥmad b. Rūzbihān wrote the life of his great-grandfather[426] in response to a request made ninety-four years after his death, i.e. in or about 700/1300–1.

Tāj al-ʿarūs. The spelling S͟haṭṭanaufī comes from Veth's edition of the *Lubb al-Lubāb*, but this seems to be a mistranscription.

425 For this celebrated saint (b. 470/1078 or 471/1079 in Gīlān, d. 561/1166 at Bag͟hdād) see al-D͟hahabī *Taʾrīk͟h al-Islām* (published in Margoliouth's article *Contributions to the biography of ʿAbd al-Ḳādir of Jīlān, JRAS*. 1907 pp. 267–310); al-Yāfiʿī *Mirʾāt al-janān* iii pp. 347–66; *Fawāt al-Wafayāt* ii pp. 2–3; *Nafaḥāt al-uns* pp. 586–90; *Ak͟hbār al-ak͟hyār* pp. 9–22; *Haft iqlīm* no. 1195, *Safīnat al-auliyāʾ* pp. 43–58 (no. 36); M. al-Dīlāʾī *Natījat al-taḥqīq* (partially translated by T. H. Weir in *JRAS*. 1903 pp. 155–66); *K͟hazīnat al-aṣfiyāʾ* i pp. 94–5; *Ency. Isl.* under ʿAbd al-Ḳādir (Margoliouth); Brockelmann i pp. 435–6, *Sptbd* i pp. 777–9, where numerous biographies are mentioned.

426 Rūzbihān b. Abī Naṣr al-Baqlī, of whose works the best known is an Arabic Ṣūfī commentary on the Qurʾān entitled *ʿArāʾis al-bayān fī ḥaqāʾiq al-Qurʾān*, died at S͟hīrāz in 606/1209. See *S͟hīrāz-nāmah* p. 116; *S͟hadd al-izār* (Rieu Arab. Suppt. p. 462); *Nafaḥāt al-uns* pp. 288–90; *Majālis al-ʿus͟hs͟hāq* no. 17; *Haft iqlīm* no. 173; *But-k͟hānah* (Bodleian 366) no. 119; *Safīnat al-auliyāʾ* p. 176 (no. 324); *Majmaʿ al-g͟harāʾib* no. 812; *Riyāḍ al-ʿārifīn* p. 128; *K͟hazīnat al-aṣfiyāʾ* ii pp. 253–4; *Majmaʿ al-fuṣaḥāʾ* i pp. 235–6; *Ṭarāʾiq al-ḥaqāʾiq* ii pp. 286–7; Massignon *La passion d'al Ḥallāj* pp. 374–7, 45* (at end of book), *Recueil de textes inédits concernant l'histoire de la mystique* pp. 113–14; Brockelmann i p. 414, *Sptbd*. i pp. 734–5; etc.

(***Sīrat-nāmah i Shaikh Rūzbihān***),[427] or (***Aḥwāl i Rūzbihān***), a life of Rūzbihān b. Abī Naṣr al-Baqlī divided into seven *bābs* ((1) on his birth and early life, (2) on the great *shaikhs* who were his contemporaries, (3) anecdotes concerning him and his miracles (*dar ḥikāyāt u karāmāt i shaikh*), (4) his observations relating to Qurʾānic exegesis, the Traditions, etc., (5) various observations of his to his associates (*dar fawāʾid i mutafarriqah bar aṣḥāb*), (6) on his children and grandchildren and some merits (*shaṭrī az faḍāʾil*) of the author's father Shaikh al-Islām Ṣadr al-Millah wa-'l-Dīn Rūzbihān al-Thānī al-Shaikh al-Thānī, (7) on his death): MS. (two fragments of 36 and 9 leaves (early 13th cent.) containing portions of *Bābs* 1, 3, 4, and 7) acquired at Shīrāz by W. Ivanow.

Description: (1) [1st fragment] *A biography of Ruzbihan al-Baqli. By W. Ivanow* (in *JASB*. xxiv/4 (1928) pp. 353–61, (2) [2nd fragment] *More on biography of Ruzbihan al-Baqli* [with the Persian text of the surviving portion of *Bāb* i]. *By W. Ivanow* (in *JBBRAS*. vii (1931) pp. 1–7).

1253. **Farīdūn** b. Aḥmad **Sipah-sālār**, a high military officer under the Saljūqids, says that he was Jalāl al-Dīn Rūmī's disciple for forty years.

(***Risālah i Sipah-sālār***) or (***Manāqib i Jalāl al-Dīn i Rūmī***), an account of Jalāl al-Dīn Rūmī and his successors, dependent largely upon the *Walad-nāmah* of Sulṭān Walad and including a supplement by the Sipah-sālār's son which brings it down to the period when Chelebī ʿĀbid (d. 739/1338) was head of the order: **Heidelberg** P. 233 (AH 1006/1597. See *Zeitschrift für Semitistik* Bd. 6 (1928) p. 223), **Breslau** Richter 89 (?) (*Manāqib al-Ḥusain al-Khaṭībī al-Balkhī*, called at the end of the MS. *Risālah i Sipah-sālār*, but described by Richter as a biography of Bahāʾ al-Dīn Walad. AH 1292/1875).

Editions: place ? 1302/1884–5 (see Āṣafīyah i p. 428 no. 984), **Cawnpore** 1319/1901 (Maḥmūd al-Maṭābiʿ. See the bibliography to Nicholson's article on Tibrīzī in the *Ency. Isl.*); **Tihrān** (*Aḥwāl i Maulawī*. Date ? See *Luzac's Oriental list* 1947 p. 41).

Turkish translation: *Manāqib i ḥaḍrat i Khudāwandgār*, tr. Midḥat Bahārī Ḥusāmī, **Salonica** (so Kramers in *Ency. Isl.* under Sulṭān Walad) or **Constantinople** (so Nicholson in *Ency. Isl.* under Tibrīzī) 1331/1913.

[Nicholson in *Ency. Isl.* under Tibrīzī.]

427 The place in the preface where the title should come has been left blank, but the author uses the expression *sīrat-nāmah* at least twice in referring to his work.

1254. ʿAfīf al-Dīn ʿAbd Allāh b. Asʿad **al-Yāfiʿī**, already mentioned (no. 89 *supra*) as the author, or epitomator, of *al-Durr al-naẓīm fī faḍāʾil al-Qurʾān al-ʿaẓīm*, was born in the Yemen, settled at Mecca in 718/1318, and died there in 768/1367.

I. ***Rauḍ al-rayāḥīn fī ḥikāyāt al-ṣāliḥīn***, five hundred anecdotes of saints, Ḥ. Kh. iii p. 488 (for MSS. and editions see Brockelmann ii 177, *Sptbd* ii p. 228).

Persian translations:

(1) ***Tuḥfat al-murshidīn min ḥikāyāt al-ṣāliḥīn***, by Jalāl [al-Dīn] M. b. ʿAbbādī [or ʿUbādī or ʿIbādī] Kāzarūnī[428] [with a *dhail* on the life of the translator's *murshsid* Sh. Bū Isḥāq Kāzarūnī[429]]: **Lahore** Panjāb Univ. (AH 818/1415. See *OCM*. viii/3 p. 140), **Āyā Ṣōfyah** 1702.

(2) ***Tarjamah i Rauḍat*** [*sic*] ***al-rayāḥīn***, written in the reign of Sulṭān M. Quṭb-Shāh (AH 1020–35/1612–26) by Faḍl Allāh "Jahānī" b. Asad Allāh al-Ḥusainī al-Aʿrābī al-Simnānī: **Ethé** 642 (AH 1026/1617).

II. ***Khulāṣat al-mafākhir*** *fī 'khtiṣār manāqib al-shaikh ʿAbd al-Qādir wa-jamāʿah mimman ʿaẓẓamahu min al-shuyūkh al-akābir*,[430] about 200 anecdotes, mainly of ʿAbd al-Qādir Jīlānī,[431] written as a supplement (*ʿalā sabīl al-takmilah*) to the *Rauḍ al-rayāḥīn*: **Ahlwardt** 8804, **Loth** 708 ii, **Būhār** 275, etc.

Persian translations:

(1) (***Tarjamah i Khulāṣat al-mafākhir***) or (***Tarjamat al-Takmilah***), written by an anonymous disciple[432] of S. Jalāl al-Dīn Bukhārī,[433] at whose suggestion the work was undertaken: **Bodleian** 332 (before AH 910/1504), 333 (M. Shāh's reign (AD 1719–48)), **Bānkīpūr** viii 670 (AH 991/1584), **Āṣafīyah** i p. 410 no. 720 (*Takmilah i Imām ʿAbd Allāh i Yāfiʿī* by Mīrān Muḥyī 'l-Dīn. ASH 999/1590–1), **I.O.** D.P. 640 (AH 1012/1604), D.P. 596 (AH 1031/1621), **Ethé** 643 (AH 1089/1678), **Cairo** p. 502 (AH 1020/1611),

428 Jalāl al-Dīn M. b. al-ʿ.bādī al-Kāzarūnī according to the Āyā Ṣōfyah catalogue.

429 Presumably different from the work published at Istānbūl in 1945 as Vol. 14 of the Bibliotheca Islamica (Maḥmūd b. ʿUṯmān, *Die Vita des Scheich Abū Isḥāq al-Kāzarūnī*. Hrsg. von F. Meier). For Abū Isḥāq Ibrāhīm b. Shahryār Kāzarūnī, who died in 426/1035, see *Kashf al-maḥjūb*, tr. Nicholson, pp. 172, 173; *Tadhkirat al-auliyā'* ii pp. 291–304; Ibn Baṭṭūṭah (ii p. 89); *Haft iqlīm* p. 206 (no. 162); *Safīnat al-auliyā'* p. 161 (no. 292); *Khazīnat al-aṣfiyā'* ii pp. 225–7; *Der Islam* xix/1–2 (1930) pp. 18–26; etc.

430 This, according to al-Yāfiʿī's preface, is the *laqab* of the work, its *ism* being *Aṭrāf ʿajāʾib al-āyāt wa-'l-barāhīn wa-ardāf gharāʾib ḥikāyāt Rauḍ al-rayāḥīn* (see the passage quoted in Bānkīpūr viii p. 32; … *wa-sammaituhu kitāb Aṭrāf … wa-laqqabtuhu bi-Khulāṣat al-mafākhir …*).

431 See footnote 424, *supra*.

432 In the copyist's colophon of I.O. D.P. 640 the work is ascribed to Mīrān Saiyid Muḥyī 'l-Dīn and in the Āṣafīyah catalogue Mīrān Muḥyī 'l-Dīn is given as the name of the author.

433 See no. 1260 *infra*.

Edinburgh 242 (old), **Ivanow** 242 (AH 1177/1763–4), Curzon 75 (late 18th or early 19th cent.), 1st Suppt. 857 (slightly defective at both ends. Early 19th cent.), **Būhār** 185 (lacunæ. 19th cent.), **Berlin** 19 (1) (begins with 101st anecdote).

(2) ***Tarjamah i Takmilah***, a verse translation in 105 *ḥikāyats* made by "'Abdī", who completed it in 1051/1641–2 in Shāh-Jahān's reign: Sprenger 63 = **Ivanow** 742 (18th cent.).

[Subkī vi p. 103; *al-Durar al-kāminah* ii pp. 247–9; *Nafaḥāt al-uns* pp. 681–2; *Safīnat al-auliyā'* p. 68 (no. 62); *Khazīnat al-aṣfiyā'* i 114; *Rauḍāt al-jannāt* p. 457; *Ency. Isl.* under Yāfi'ī (Krenkow); Brockelmann ii pp. 176–7, *Sptbd.* ii pp. 227–8, where further references will be found.]

1255. For the *Shīrāz-nāmah*, which was completed in 744/1343–4 by Aḥmad b. Abī 'l-Khair Shīrāzī and which contains notices of holy persons connected with Shīrāz, see no. 459 *supra*.

1256. Shams al-Dīn Aḥmad **Aflākī** was a disciple of Jalāl al-Dīn Rūmī's grandson, Jalāl al-Dīn al-'Ārif, at whose request he wrote the *Manāqib al-'ārifīn*.

Manāqib al-'ārifīn, lives of Jalāl al-Dīn Rūmī, his father, successors and associates, begun in 718/1318–19,[434] completed in 754/1353–4[435] and divided into ten *faṣls* ((1) Bahā' al-Dīn Walad, his father, d. 628/1231, (2) Burhān al-Dīn Tirmidhī, his spiritual guide, (3) Jalāl al-Dīn himself, b. 604/1207, d. 672/1273, (4) Shams al-Dīn M. b. 'Alī Tabrīzī, his friend and guide, (5) Ṣalāḥ al-Dīn Farīdūn Qūnawī known as Zarkūb, a friend and *khalīfah*, d. 657/1258, (6) Ḥusām al-Dīn Ḥasan b. Akhī Turk, a *khalīfah*, d. 683/1284, (7) Bahā' al-Dīn Sulṭān Walad, Jalāl al-Dīn's son d. 712/1312,[436] (8) Jalāl al-Dīn Farīdūn, known as Chelebī Amīr 'Ārif al-Balkhī, Sulṭān Walad's son, b. 670/1272, d. 719/1320, (9) Chelebī Shams al-Dīn Amīr 'Ābid, another of Sulṭān Walad's sons, d. 739/1338 and succeeded by his brother Ḥusām al-Dīn Amīr Wājid, who died in 742/1342, (10) descendants of the foregoing *shaikhs*): Ḥ. Kh. vi p. 154, **Blochet** i 409 (AH 964/1556), 410 (*Faṣls* i-iii only. 16th cent.), 411–14 (all 17th cent.), 415 (18th cent.), **Rieu** i 345 *b* (slightly defective, AH 997/1589), 344*b* (17th cent.), **Ethé** 630 (AH 1027/1618), **I.O.** D.P. 734 (AH 1034/1624), 1120 (defective. 19th cent.),

434 Or 710/1310–11, according to some MSS. (e.g. Ethé 630).

435 This date is given in a note which occurs at the end in some of the MSS., e.g. Ethé 630 (*Ta'rīkh taṣnīf al-muṣannif ... Maulānā Sh. al-D. A.* [*al-*]*Aflākī al-'Ārifī raḥimahu 'llāh sanat arba' wa-khamsīn wa-sab'-mi'ah*). In the B.M. MS. Add. 25,025 the word *taṣnif* is absent from the note.

436 As Rieu mentions, notices of the foregoing seven shaikhs are given in the same order in the *Nafaḥāt al-uns*, pp. 528–44.

Flügel ii 1206 (1041/1632); **Ivanow** 240 (slightly defective, AH 1177/1763–4), **Āṣafīyah** i p. 324 no. 23, **Berlin** 587 (defective), **Chanykov** 103, **Salemann-Rosen** p. 19 no. 589, **Upsala** Zetterstéen 409, as well as several of the Istānbūl catalogues (see Horn p. 292).

Edition: *Sawāniḥ i ʿumrī i ḥaḍrat i Maulānā Rūmī musammā bah Manāqib al-ʿārifīn*, **Āgrah** 1897°.

French translation: *Les saints des derviches tourneurs, récits traduits … et annotés par Cl. Huart*, **Paris** 1918*, 1922* (Bibliothèque de l'École des Hautes Études, sciences religieuses, vols. 32 and 36).

Abridged Turkish translation of *Faṣls* i–viii: *Hasht bihisht* (beginning *Ḥamd i nā-maḥdūd awwal Munshiʾ i kāʾināt*), by an unknown translator: **Flügel** ii 1207 (AH 1015/1606).

English translation of extracts: *The Mesnevī … of … Jelālu-'d-Dīn … er-Rūmī. Book the first … translated … by J. W. Redhouse*, **London** 1881°* (Trübner's Oriental Series), pp. 1–135.

Abridgment (with excision of all passages savouring of unorthodoxy): ***Khulāṣat al-Manāqib***, by Aḥmad b. M., apparently a disciple of Jalāl al-Dīn Bukhārī (d. 785/1383. See no. 1260 *infra*), **Ivanow** 241 (18th cent.).

Revised version: ***Thawāqib al-manāqib i auliyāʾ Allāh*** (a chronogram = 947/1540–1), by ʿAbd al-Wahhāb b. Jalāl al-Dīn M. al-Hamadānī,[437] who "revised and corrected the original work, curtailed it in some places by omitting superfluous stories and traditions, increased it in others by adding much needed explanations.… paid particular attention to dates, genealogy, etc." and divided the new edition into a *muqaddimah*, nine *dhikrs* or biographies (the tenth of the original being omitted) and a *khātimah* (containing the *tārīkh* and a *munājāt*): Ḥ. Kh. p. 154, **Ross-Browne** 218 (16th cent.), **Ethé** 631 (17th cent.).

Turkish translation of the revised version: *Tarjamah i Manāqib i thawāqib* [?], written in 998/1590[438] by Darwīsh Maḥmūd al-Maulawī and dedicated to the Sulṭān Murād [iii]: **Browne** Suppt. 1251 (Trinity R. 13, 1, Palmer p. 7), probably also **Flügel** ii 1208 (defective, beginning in the third biography).

437 So Ross-Browne and Ethé. Ḥ. Kh. calls him al-Sh. ʿA. al-W. al-Ṣābūnī al-Hamadānī.

438 Ḥ. Kh. is the authority for this date. The dedication to Murād is mentioned by Palmer, not by Ḥ. Kh.

1257. **Tawakkulī** b. Ismāʿīl b. Ḥājjī **al-Ardabīlī** known as (*al-mushtahir bi-*) **Ibn i Bazzāz**[439] mentions his uncle (*ʿamm i muʾallif*) Pīrah Aḥmad al-Ardabīlī[440] as one of the disciples of the celebrated saint Ṣafī al-Dīn Isḥāq al-Mūsawī,[441] the ancestor of the Ṣafawīs, and says that he himself and Shams al-Dīn Ardabīlī called on the saint to condole with him on the death of his eldest son, Khwājah Muḥyī ʾl-Dīn[442] In 726/1325 he was with the same Shams al-Dīn at Marāghah.[443]

Ṣafwat al-ṣafāʾ, or *al-Mawāhib al-sanīyah fī ʾl-manāqib al-Ṣafawīyah*[444] (beginning *al-Ḥ. l. ʾlladhī tajallā li-auliyāʾihi*),[445] an account of the life, sayings and miracles of the aforementioned Sh. Ṣafī al-Dīn Isḥāq (d. 12 Muḥarram 735/12 Sept. 1334), written in the time of his son and successor Ṣadr al-Dīn Mūsā,[446] completed in, or not very long before, 759/1358[447] and divided into a *muqaddimah*, twelve *bābs* and a *khātimah*:[448] Ḥ. Kh. iv p. 105, **Ethé** 1842 (AH 759/1358, said to be an autograph), **Leyden** v p. 231 no. 2639 (AH 890/1485), **Āyā Ṣōfyah** 3099 = Tauer 434

---

439 Tawakkulī ... Bazzāz: so in the Bombay edition p. 6[1] (four lines above the table of contents with which the author's preface ends). This passage has perhaps been removed by Abū ʾl-Fatḥ from his revised edition, since Rieu does not refer to it but says that "the author's name appears incidentally in the text, fol. 553*a*, as Tavakkulī, "توكلى". A person of this name, Tawakkulī ʿAtīqān [= b. ʿAtīq] Ardabīlī, figures in an anecdote on p. 261 of the Bombay edition (*Bāb* vii, *faṣl* 5, *ḥikāyat* [24]). Browne says (*Lit. Hist.* iv p. 34) that in a note in A. G. Ellis's MS. the name is written Tūklī.

440 Bombay edition p. 354[13]. The author's brother, Pīrah Yaʿqūb, who according to Rieu is mentioned among the saint's disciples, does not seem to be among those enumerated in *Bāb* xii of the Bombay edition.

441 For whom see *Ḥabīb al-siyar* iii, 4 pp., 5–9. *Majālis al-muʾminīn* p. 273 (*majlis* 6); *Haft iqlīm* no. 1359; *Silsilat al-nasab i Ṣafawīyah* pp. 10–38 (cf. *JRAS*. 1921 pp. 397–404); Browne *Lit. Hist.* iv pp. 38–44; *Dānishmandān i Ādharbāyjān* pp. 231–4.

442 Bombay edition p. 293[17] (*Bāb* viii, *faṣl* 16).

443 Bombay edition p. 262[2] (*Bāb* vii, *faṣl* 5).

444 See the Bombay edition p. 6[2–3], where, however, the text is corrupt.

445 These are the opening words of Ethé 1842 and all the Istānbūl MSS. described by Tauer. On the other hand the Bānkīpūr MS. begins *Sitāyish u niyāyish mar Khāliqī rā* and the Bombay edition *al-Ḥ. l. ʾl-Walī al-Ḥamīd wa-ʾl-ṣalāt wa-ʾl-salām ... ammā baʿd īn miskīn i kam-biḍāʿat*. The first words of the Leyden and Leningrad MSS. are not given in the catalogues.

446 According to the *Silsilat al-nasab i Ṣafawīyah* (p. 39 = *JRAS*. 1921 p. 404) he was born in 704/1305 and died in 794/1392. According to Rieu (iii p. 1085*b*) the date of his death is given as 779/1377–8 in the *Qiṣaṣ al-Khāqānī*, fol. 5*a*.

447 It will be noted that Ethé 1842, described as an autograph, is dated 759. According to Rieu the author "states that, in the very year in which he wrote, Malik Ashraf (who reigned AH 745–758) had dismissed his Vazīr ʿAbd ul-ʿAlī".

448 The subjects of the chapters are given by Browne (*Lit. Hist.* iv pp. 38–9).

(AH 896/1491), 2123 = Tauer 435 (AH 914/1509), **Ḥakīmoghlū ʿAlī Pāshā** 775 = Tauer 436 (AH 947/1540), **Bānkīpūr** viii 662 (AH 1035/1625–6), **Adabīyāt Kutubkhānah-si** 4675 = Tauer 437 (AH 1049/1639), **Chanykov** 90 (cf. *Mélanges asiatiques* i (St. Petersburg 1852) p. 543), **Dorn** 300 (from Ardabīl). A MS. written at Ardabīl in 1030/1621, which belonged to the late A. G. Ellis (= Ellis Coll. M. 163), is mentioned by Browne (*Lit. Hist.* iv p. 35). Ellis Coll. M. 164 is dated 964/1557.

Edition: **Bombay** 1329/1911°*[449] (ed. Aḥmad b. Karīm Tabrīzī).

Extracts (containing references to the Shīrwān-Shāhs): *Mélanges asiatiques* i (St. Petersburg 1852) pp. 543–8 (with French translation by Chanykov, pp. 549–52).

Description: Browne *Lit. Hist.* iv pp. 34–5, 38–9.

Revised edition (beginning *Sharīftarīn dhikrī*) prepared at the command of Shāh Ṭahmāsp (reigned 930/1524–984/1576) by Abū 'l-Fatḥ al-Ḥusainī (cf. no. 21 *supra*), whose additions, according to Rieu, "appear to be confined to the preface and to the Khātimah, in which an account of the descendants of Ṣafī ud-Din is brought down to Shāh Ṭahmāsp": **Rieu** i 345*b* (16th cent.), **Browne** Suppt. 837 (King's 87), **Mashhad** iii fṣl. 14, MSS., no. 68.

Turkish translation written in 949/1542–3, in Shāh Ṭahmāsp's reign by M. Kātib "Nashāṭī" Shīrāzī (*M. al-Kātib yuʿraf bi-Nashāṭī*): **Rieu** Turkish Cat. p. 281 (16th cent.), **Chanykov** 91.[450]

1258. To Shāh Shujāʿ [i.e., according to Ethé, the Muẓaffarid, who reigned from 760/1359–786/1384] was dedicated—

A life of ʿAbd al-Qādir al-Jīlānī[451] (beginning *Sazāwār i ḥamd u thanā Pādshāhīst*): **Ethé** 1800 (AH 1052/1642).

---

449 This edition contains also (1) an account of Ardabīl, pp. 25–7 marg., (2) an account of Ādharbāyjān, pp. 28–65 marg., (3) *al-Ṭibb al-jadīd al-kīmiyāʾī*, an Arabic medical work, being Part IV of Ṣāliḥ b. Naṣr Allāh al-Ḥalābi's *Ghāyat al-itqān* (see Brockelmann ii p. 365, *Sptbd.* ii p. 666), pp. 66–158 marg., (4) an Arabic translation of the *Basilica chymica* of Crollius, pp. 158–239 marg., (5) extracts from the Arabic *tafsīr* entitled *ʿArāʾis al-bayān* (see Brockelmann i p. 414, *Sptbd.* i p. 735) by Rūzbihān al-Baqlī (cf. no. 1252 *supra*), pp. 241–358 marg., 359–383, (6) the *Gulshan i rāz* of Maḥmūd Shabistarī, pp. 384–98, (7) an extract from "ʿAṭṭār's" *Manṭiq al-ṭair*, pp. 384–98 marg.

450 No attempt has been made to trace other MSS. of this translation.

451 For whom see footnote 424 *supra*.

1259. **S. M. b. Mubārak** b. M. ʿAlawī **Kirmānī**, called Amīr, or Mīr, i Khwurd,[452] was the grandson of S. M. b. Maḥmūd Kirmānī,[453] a merchant who in the course of his journeyings between Kirmān and Lahore used to meet Sh. Farīd al-Dīn Ganj i Shakar[454] at Ajōd'han and became his disciple. After Farīd al-Dīn's death [in 664/1265] he became the friend of Sh. Niẓām al-Dīn Auliyā.[455] He died in

---

452 Cf. *Rashaḥāt* p. 47², where two persons called Amīr [i] Buzurg and Amīr [i] Khwurd are mentioned.

453 For biographies (based probably on the *Siyar al-auliyā'*) see *Akhbār al-akhyār* p. 96; *Kalimāt al-ṣādiqīn* no. 38; *Khazīnat al-aṣfiyā'* i p. 320.

454 Farīd al-Dīn Masʿūd called Ganj i Shakar or Shakar-ganj, the *khalīfah* of Quṭb al-Dīn Bakhtyār, died on 5 Muḥarram 664/17 Oct. 1265 aged 95 and was buried at Ajōd'han or Pattan (now called Pāk Pattan on his account), about half-way between Lahore and Multān in the Montgomery District of the Panjāb. Some Ṣūfī tracts by him are extant and there are two collections of his utterances, (1) *Rāḥat al-qulūb*, collected by Niẓām al-Dīn Auliyā (Edition: place ? date ? (Āṣafīyah iii p. 198). MSS.: ʿAlīgaṛh Subḥ. MSS. p. 18 no. 5, p. 19 no. 23, Āṣafīyah i p. 420, Bānkīpūr xvi 1357, xvii 1641, Būhār 170, Ivanow 1181, Lindesiana p. 204). (2) *Asrār al-auliyā'*, collected by Badr al-Dīn Isḥāq (Editions: Lucknow 1876°*, place ? 1301/1883–4 (Āṣafīyah i p. 398), Cawnpore 1890†. MSS.: ʿAlīgaṛh Subḥ. MSS. p. 13, Āṣafīyah i p. 396, nos. 354, 650, Browne Suppt. 47 (King's 35), Rieu iii 973*b* (extracts)). See *Siyar al-ʿārifīn* no. 5; *Akhbār al-akhyār* pp. 52–4; Firishtah ii pp. 383–91; *Gulzār i abrār* nos. 14 and 21; *Jawāhir i Farīdī; Safīnat al-auliyā'* pp. 96–7 (no. 113); *Mir'āt al-asrār, ṭabaqah* 19; *Sawāṭiʿ al-anwār* (Ethé col. 329 no. 17); *Ātash- kadah* no. 755; *Ṣuḥuf i Ibrāhīm; A brief account of Masúd, known by the name of Faríd Shakarganj or Shakarbár. By Munshí Mahan* [*sic*] *Lal* (*in JASB. V* (1836) pp. 635–8); *JASB. VI* (1837) pp. 190–3 (an account of Pākpattan in an article (pp. 169–217) entitled *Journal of Captain C. M. Wade's voyage from Lodiana to Mithankot by the river Satlaj on his mission to Lahór and Baháwulpur in 1832–33. By Lieut. F. Mackeson*); *Khazīnat al-aṣfiyā'* i pp. 287–305; Garcin de Tassy, *Mémoire sur ... la religion musulmane dans l'Inde*, 2nd ed., Paris 1869, pp. 94–5; Beale *Oriental biographical dictionary* under Farid; *The shrine of Bābā Farīd Shakarganj at Pakpattan. By Miles Irving* (in *Journal of the Punjab Historical Society*, i (1911–12) pp. 70–6); *Iʿlān i siyādat i Farīdī* (in Urdu), by Rashīd Aḥmad, Amrōhah 1915; Bānkīpūr xvii pp. 112–14; *Babā Farīd Ganj i Shakar, Sh. Ibrāhīm, aur Farīd i Thānī*, an Urdu article by Mōhan Sing'h "Dīwānah" in *OCM*. xiv/2 (Feb. 1938) pp. 75–81, xiv/3 (May 1938) pp. 25–37, xiv/4 (Aug. 1938) pp. 88–90, xv/1 (Nov. 1938) pp. 67–84, xv/2 (Feb. 1939) pp. 44–71 (and later issues ?); *Nasab-nāmah i ḥaḍrat i Bābā Farīd al-Dīn Ganj i Shakar*, an Urdu article by Baldēv Sing'h in *OCM*. xvii/2 (Feb. 1941) pp. 118–27.

455 N. al-D. M. b. A. Badā'ūnī, the most celebrated of the saints of Delhi, was born in 636/1238–9 at Badā'ūn, to which his grandfather is said to have migrated from Bukhārā. After spending four years at Delhi he went to Ajōd'han and in 655/1257 became a disciple of Farīd al-Dīn Ganj i Shakar. Returning to Delhi he settled in the neighbouring village of Ghiyāthpūr (now called Niẓām al-Dīn Auliyā kī bastī, i.e. N. al-D. A.'s village) and died there in 725/1325. Among his disciples were Chirāgh i Dihlī and the poets Khusrau (see no. 665 *supra*) and Ḥasan Dihlawī. Discourses of his are extant in four collections, (1) *Afḍal al-fawā'id*, collected (in part ?) by Khusrau before the *Rāḥat al-muḥibbīn*, in which it is mentioned as an earlier work (see Bānkīpūr xvii p. 115. According to Waḥīd Mirzā the first of its four parts was presented to the saint in 719 [i.e. long after the time

711/1311–12 and was buried at Delhi. His grandson M. b. Mubārak, received his initiation into Ṣūfism in childhood from Sh. Niẓām al-Dīn. Subsequently he became the disciple of Naṣīr al-Dīn Maḥmūd Chirāgh i Dihlī[456] It is stated in the *Khazīnat al-aṣfiyā'* on the authority of the *Shajarah i Chishtīyah* that he died in 770/1368–9.

at which the discourses of the *Rāḥat al-muḥibbīn* were collected] and permission was then obtained to continue the work, but the second part [unlike the third and fourth? According to Waḥīd Mirzā the work "is divided into four parts".] remained incomplete). Edition: Delhi 1887°. Description: Waḥīd Mirzā *Life and works of Amir Khusrau* pp. 225–7. (2) *Rāḥat al-muḥibbīn*, "discourses relating to the accounts of prophets and saints" and apparently to other matters taken down by Khusrau from 20 Rajab 689 to 9 Muharram 691 (MSS.: Bānkīpūr xvii 1642, Rieu 973*b* (extracts)). (3) *Fawā'id al-fu'ād*, taken down by Ḥasan Dihlawī in 707–19 and 719–22 and containing according to Ivanow "much biographical material concerning early Chishtī saints" (Edition: Lucknow 1885°. MSS.: 'Alīgaṛh Subḥ. MSS. p. 18, Ivanow 239, Rieu iii 972, 973*b* (extracts), 1040*b* (extracts)). (4) *Durar i Niẓāmīyah*, taken down by 'Alī b. Maḥmūd Jāndār ... (presumably = 'Alī-Shāh b. Maḥmūd Jāndār, *Gulzār i abrār* no. 85. MS.: Būhār 183). His collection of the utterances of his master Ganj i Shakar, the *Rāḥat al-qulūb*, is mentioned in the preceding note. See *Nafaḥāt al-uns* pp. 584–6; *Siyar al-'ārifīn* no. 7; *Akhbār al-akhyār* pp. 54–60; *Haft iqlīm* no. 385; Firishtah, [Lucknow] 1281, ii pp. 391–8; *Gulzār i abrār* no. 78; *Kalimāt al-ṣādiqīn* no. 25; *Safīnat al-auliyā'* pp. 97–8 (no. 114); *Mir'āt al-asrār, ṭabaqah* 20; *Maṭlūb al-ṭālibīn* (Ethé 653); *Sawāṭi' al-anwār* (Ethé col. 331 no. 21); "Mubtalā" *Muntakhab al-ash'ār* no. 665; *Tadhkirah i Ḥusainī* p. 330; *Makhzan al-gharā'ib* no. 2716; *Khazīnat al-aṣfiyā'* i pp. 328–9; Garcin de Tassy *Mémoire sur les particularités de la religion musulmane dans l'Inde*, 2nd ed., 1869, pp. 97–9; *Ḥadā'iq al-Ḥanafīyah* pp. 277–8; *Nuzhat al-khawāṭir* pp. 122–8; Beale *Oriental biographical dictionary* under Nizam-uddin Aulia; Raḥmān 'Alī p. 240; Bānkīpūr xvi p. 19; *Ency. Isl.* under Niẓām al-Dīn (Hidayet Hosain); Waḥīd Mirzā *Life and works of Amir Khusrau* pp. 112–19.

456 Naṣīr al-Dīn Maḥmūd b. Yaḥyā Awad'hī called Chirāgh i Dihlī was born at Awad'h, i.e. Ajōd'hya. At the age of forty he became a disciple of Niẓām al-Dīn Auliyā and in 724/1324 was nominated by him as his successor (*khalīfah*). He died at Delhi in 757/1356. Among his disciples were Gēsu-darāz (see p. 950 n. 1) and M. b. Ja'far Makkī (see no. 228 *supra*). A collection of his utterances, *Khair al-majālis*, begun in 755/1354 and completed in 756/1355 or 760/1359 by his disciple Ḥamīd Shā'ir Qalandar (*Akhbār al-akhyār* p. 86[15]), or Ḥamīd Qalandar (*op. cit.* p. 86[18], *Khazīnat al-aṣfiyā' i* p. 365), or Ḥamīd al-Dīn b. Tāj al-Dīn al-Qalandar al-Dihlawī (*Nuzhat al-khawāṭir* p. 37), is described in the last-mentioned work (p. 38[1]) as well-known (*mutadāwal fī aidī 'l-nās*), but no copies seem yet to be recorded in any published catalogue. See *Siyar al-'ārifīn* no. 12; *Akhbār al-akhyār* pp. 80–6; *Haft iqlīm* no. 402; Firishtah ii pp. 398–400; *Gulzār i abrār* no. 131; *Kalimāt al-ṣādiqīn* no. 33; *Safīnat al-auliyā'* pp. 100–1 (no. 116); *Mu'nis al-arwāḥ*; *Mir'āt al-asrār, ṭabaqah* 20; *Sawāṭi' al-anwār* (Ethé col. 331 no. 22); *Khazīnat al-aṣfiyā'* i pp. 353–7; Beale *Oriental biographical dictionary* under Nasir-uddin Mahmud; Raḥmān 'Alī p. 238; *Nuzhat al-khawāṭir* pp. 158–60; *Ency. Isl.* under Čirāgh Dihlī (Hidayet Hosain); *Shaikh Nasīruddīn Mahmūd Chirāgh-i-Dehlī as a great historical personality*, by M. Ḥabīb (in *Islamic Culture* xx/2 (April 1946)).

Siyar al-auliyāʾ fī maḥabbat al-Ḥaqq jalla wa-ʿalā, lives of Chishtī[457] saints, written in the reign of Fīrōz-Shāh Tughluq (752–90/1351–88), when the author was fifty years old, and divided into ten *bābs* ((1) *shaikhs* of the order from the Prophet to Niẓām al-Dīn,[458] (2) *khalīfahs* of Muʿīn al-Dīn Sijzī,[459]

457 Chisht, a village near Harāt (marked as Khwajah Chisht on some maps), was the burial-place of Abu Aḥmad Abdāl Chishtī, the real founder of the Chishtī order, who died in 355/966 (see *Nafaḥāt* pp. 366–7, *Haft iqlīm* no. 622; *Safīnat al-auliyāʾ* p. 89 (no. 102); *Sawāṭiʿ al-anwār* (Ethé col. 328 no. 9); *Khazīnat al-aṣfiyāʾ* i pp. 241–3).

458 See footnote 453 *supra*.

459 Muʿīn al-Dīn M. b. Ghiyāth al-Dīn Ḥasan Sijzī Chishtī, the founder of the Indian branch of the Chishtī order and one of India's most famous saints, is said to have been born in Sijistān but to have grown up in Khurāsān. Having resided for long or short periods at various places in Persia and the neighbouring countries (twenty years, according to Dārā-Shukōh, at Hārūn ("*az nawāḥi i Nīshāpūr*") with his *pīr*, Khwājah ʿUthmān Hārūnī), he eventually settled at Ajmēr and died there in 633/1236 at an advanced age. A collection of 28 discourses by him was made by Quṭb al-Dīn Ūshī and entitled *Dalīl al-ʿārifīn* (Editions: Cawnpore 1889°, Lucknow 1890°. MSS.: Āṣafīyah i p. 418 nos. 417 and 964, iii p. 196 no. 1505, Bānkīpūr xvii 1639, Rieu iii 973*b* (extracts), Ivanow-Curzon 460, ʿAlīgaṛh Subḥ. MSS. p. 18 no. 9, p. 19 no. 17). He himself made a collection of ʿUthmān Hārūnī's utterances under the title *Anīs al-arwāḥ* (Edition: Lucknow 1890°. MSS.: Āṣafīyah i p. 402 nos. 599, 801, p. 404 no. 963, iip. 848, Bānkīpūr xvii 1638, Būhār 169, I.O. D.P. 1153(*a*), Ivanow-Curzon 460 (1)). A *dīwān* of Ṣūfī poems by a poet who uses the *takhalluṣ* "Muʿīn" is ascribed to him (Editions: [Lucknow] 1285/1868°*, Lucknow 1316/1898°, 1327/1909*, Cawnpore 1288/1871*. 1875*, 1910‡, Lahore 1886*, [1904*], [1934*]. MS.: Bānkīpūr i 53). See *Siyar al-ʿārifīn* no. 1; *Akhbār al-akhyār* pp. 22–5; Firishtah II pp. 375–8; *Gulzār i abrār* no. 5; *Safīnat al-auliyāʾ* pp. 93–4 (no. 110); *Muʾnis al-arwāḥ* (no. 1322 (1) *infra*); *Mirʾāt al-asrār, ṭabaqah* 17; ʿAbd al-Ḥamīd *Pādshāh-nāmah* i, 1, p. 81; *Sawāṭiʿ al-anwār* (Ethé col. 329 no. 15); "Mubtalā" *Muntakhab al-ashʿār* no. 609; *Ātash-kadah* no. 756; *Ṣuḥuf i Ibrāhīm*; *Makhzan al-gharāʾib* no. 2280; *Riyāḍ al-ʿārifīn* pp. 220–1; *Miftāḥ al-tawārīkh* p. 57; *Waqāʾiʿ i Shāh Muʿīn al-Dīn Chishtī* (no. 1411 (124) *infra*); *Khazīnat al-aṣfiyāʾ* i pp. 256–67; Garcin de Tassy *Mémoire sur ... la religion musulmane dans l'Inde*, Paris 1869, pp. 59–63; *Majmaʿ al-fuṣaḥāʾ* i p. 542; *Ḥadāʾiq al-Ḥanafīyah* p. 250; Beale *Oriental biographical dictionary* under Muʿin-uddin Chishti; *Muʿīn al-auliyāʾ* (no. 1406 *infra*); *Tārīkh i Khwājah i Ajmēr maʿruf bah Aḥsan al-siyar* (in Urdu), by M. Akbar Jahān, Āgrah [1905*]; Bānkīpūr i p. 77; *Ency. Isl.* under Čishtī (unsigned); *Sawāniḥ i Khwājah i gharīb-nawāz rāh-numā i Ajmēr i sharīf* (in Urdu), by ʿĀshiq Ḥusain "Sīmāb" Akbarābādī, Āgrah 1921*; *Maḥfil i Khwājah ʿurf Tārīkh i Sarwar i Ajmērī* (in Urdu), by Ghulām-Aḥmad Khān "Sarwar" Ajmērī, Āgrah [1924*]; *Tārīkh al-salaf* (in Urdu), by "Maʿnī" Ajmērī, Āgrah 1344/1925–6; etc.

Quṭb al-Dīn Bakhtyār,[460] and Farīd al-Dīn,[461] (3) descendants of Farīd al-Dīn, relatives of Niẓām al-Dīn and Saiyids of the author's family, (4) *khalīfahs* of Niẓām al-Dīn, (5) some friends[462] who had the honour of being *murīds* and intimates of Niẓām al-Dīn (*baʿḍī yārān i aʿlā kih bi-sharaf i irādat u qurbat i Sulṭān al-mashāyikh ... makhṣūṣ u musharraf būdah and ...*), (6) duties of *khalīfahs* and *murīds*, (7) forms of prayer used by Farīd al-Dīn and Niẓām al-Dīn, (8) mystic love and visions of God, (9) *samāʿ* (music, trances and dancing), (10) sayings and letters of Niẓām al-Dīn): **Ivanow** 243 (defective, AH 1040/1630–1), **I.O.** D.P. 668 (AH 1093/1682), **Berlin** 586 (lacks end of *Bāb* v and most of *Bāb* vi), **Rieu** iii 976*a* (extracts only. Circ. AD 1850), **Āṣafīyah** i p. 444 no. 939 (*Bāb* ix only. AH 1277/1860–1).

Edition: **Delhi** 1302/1885°*.

Urdu translation: *Urdū tarjamah i kitāb i S. al-a.*, **Lahore** [1923*].

[Autobiographical statements in the *Siyar al-auliyā'; Akhbār al-akhyār* p. 97; *Maṭlūb al-ṭālibīn, maṭlab* 16 (Ethé col. 325 no. 45); *Dhikr i jamīʿ i auliyā' i Dihlī; Khazīnat al-aṣfiyā'* i p. 366; *Nuzhat al-khawāṭir* p. 142; Raḥmān ʿAlī p. 82]

1260. S. **Jalāl al-Dīn** Ḥusain b. Aḥmad Ḥusainī **Bukhārī**, surnamed **Makhdūm i Jahāniyān**, one of the great saints of India and a grandson of that S. Jalāl Bukhārī, called S. Jalāl i Surkh, who migrated from Bukhārā to India and died at Uchh,[463] was born at Uchh in 707/1308. He became a disciple of Sh. Rukn al-Dīn Abū 'l-Fatḥ (see no. 1280, 3rd par. (8) footnote *infra*), associated with

460 Q. al-D. B. Ūshī, known as (*al-maʿrūf bah*) Kākī (in allusion to the cakes of bread (*kāk*) which used to appear miraculously for his sustenance), was born at Ūsh or Ōsh (both spellings are used by Barthold) in Farghānah. He became a disciple of Muʿīn al-Dīn Chishtī and it is said that in the course of his travels he met Shihāb al-Dīn Suhrawardī at Baghdād. He died at Delhi in 633/1235, the same (Hijrī) year as his *pīr* Muʿīn al-Dīn. A collection of his discourses was made under the title *Fawā'id al-sālikīn* by Farīd al-Dīn Ganj i Shakar (MSS.: Bānkīpūr xvii 1640, Ivanow Curzon 413). A *dīwān*, in which "Quṭb", or "Quṭb i Dīn", is the *takhalluṣ* used, is ascribed to him (Editions: Lucknow 1879°, 1882‡, Cawnpore 1904*. MSS.: Sprenger453, Rieu Suppt. 238), and also a *mathnawī, Mathnawī i mai-rang* (Edition: Cawnpore 1890°). See *Siyar al-ʿārifīn* no. 4; *Akhbār al-akhyār* pp. 25–6; *Haft iqlīm* no. 1520; Firishtah ii pp. 378–83; *Gulzār i abrār* no. 13; *Kalimāt al-ṣādiqīn* no. 1; *Safīnat al-auliyā'* pp. 94–6 (no. 112); *Mir'āt al-asrār, ṭabaqah* 18; *Rauḍah i aqṭāb; Sawāṭiʿ al-anwār* (Ethé col. 329 no. 16); *Riyāḍ al-shuʿarā'; Makhzan al-gharā'ib* no. 2047; *Riyāḍ al-ʿārifīn* p. 206; *Khazīnat al-aṣfiyā'* i pp. 267–76; Garcin de Tassy *Mémoire sur les particularités de la religion musulmane dans l'Inde*, 2nd ed., Paris, 1869, pp. 89–92; *Shamʿ i anjuman* p. 387; Beale *Oriental biographical dictionary* under Qutb-uddin Bakhtiar; Bānkīpūr xvii pp. 110–11.

461 See footnote 452 *supra*.

462 *Yārān i aʿlā* seems to be a term applied to friends of Niẓām al-Dīn, not, as Rieu supposed, the friends of the author.

463 See *Akhbār al-akhyār* p. 61; Firishtah, Bombay 1831–2, ii pp. 774–5, [Lucknow] 1281 ii pp. 412–13; *Khazīnat al-aṣfiyā'* ii pp. 35–8; etc. Uchh is now in the State of Bahāwalpūr.

al-Yāfiʿī (see no. 1254 *supra*) at Mecca, and received the Chishtī investiture from Sh. Naṣīr al-Dīn Chirāgh i Dihlī (see p. 942 n. 1). In consequence of his travels, which took him to Egypt, Syria, the two ʿIrāqs, Khurāsān. Balkh and Bukhārā, he is called Jahān-gasht. He died on 10 Dhū 'l-Ḥijjah 785/3 Feb. 1384 and is buried at Uchh. Two or three Ṣūfī works by him are recorded in the catalogues (e.g. ʿAlīgaṛh Subḥ. MSS. p. 18 nos. 14, 15, Princeton 99). Collections of his utterances and teachings are the *Khizānah i Jalālī* (by Abū 'l-Faḍl b. Ḍiyāʾ ʿAbbāsī, if Ivanow 1st Suppt. 856 is indeed a part of that work), the *Khulāṣat al-alfāẓ Jāmiʿ al-ʿulūm*, by ʿAlī b. Saʿd b. Ashraf (Ivanow 1209), the *Sirāj al-hidāyah* (I.O. D.P. 1038), and a work of unknown title written by a descendant of the *shaikh* and divided into *majlises*, of which Ivanow 1210 is a fragment. A work based on his teachings is the *Khizānat al-fawāʾid al-Jalālīyah* composed in 752/1351 by Aḥmad Bahā b. Yaʿqūb (Ethé 2561, I.O. D.P. 998).

(***Safar-nāmah i Makhdūm i Jahāniyān***), an account of travels (but perhaps not genuine, since the work seems not to be mentioned by the biographers and the MSS. are (all ?) late): **I.O.** D.P. 1107 (AH 1130/1718), 1123 (18th cent.), **Āṣafīyah** i p. 442 nos. 775 (AH 1159/1746), 429, ii p. 836 no. 16 (AH 1188/1774), **Lindesiana** p. 159 no. 624 (AH 1240/1824–5), **Madrās** i *448*.

Urdu translations: (1) *Safar-nāmah i ḥaḍrat i Makhdūm i Jahāniyān Jahān-gasht*, by M. ʿAbbās, **Lucknow** 1908* (described as 4th edition), (2) *S.-n. i M. i J.*, **Lahore** 1909 (possibly the same translation).

[Shams i Sirāj *Tārīkh i Fīrōz-Shāhī* pp. 514–16; "Yūsufī" *Maḥbūbīyah* (see no. 1273 *infra*); *Siyar al-ʿārifīn* no. 13; *Akhbār al-akhyār* pp. 141–3; Firishtah, Bombay 1831–2, vol. ii pp. 779–84, [Lucknow] 1281/1864–5 pp. 415–17; *Gulzār i abrār* no. 128: *Dabistān i madhāhib*, tr. Shea and Troyer, New York 1937, p. 280; *Safīnat al-auliyāʾ* p. 116 (no. 157); *Mirʾāt al-asrār, ṭabaqah* xxi; *Sawāṭiʿ al-anwār* (Ethé col. 332[29]); ʿAbd al-Rashīd *Tārīkh i Qādirīyah* fol. 47*b*; *Khazīnat al-aṣfiyāʾ* ii pp. 57–63; Beale *Oriental biographical dictionary* under Shaikh Jalal; *Nuzhat al-khawāṭir* (in Arabic) pp. 28–35; *Ency. Isl.* under Djalāl (unsigned)].

1261. **Ḥājjī Rūmī** was a *khalīfah* of Maulānā Taqī al-Dīn M. Naqawī [Taqawī ?].

Taḥrīr al-muʿtaqid fī ḥālāt al-murshid, a life of Taqī al-Din M. Naqawī[464] and his father ʿAlī Murtaḍā, surnamed Māh i Shaʿbān i Biyābānī and Shaʿbān al-Millah:[465] **Rieu** iii 1042*a* (circ. AD 1850).

464 A Bhakkarī Saiyid and Suhrawardī *shaikh*, who was born at Jhūnsī [Jhūsī, near Allahabad] in 720/1320–1 and died on 7 Dhū 'l-Ḥijjah 785/31 Jan. 1384. Cf. *Nuzhat al-khawāṭir* p. 93, where the authority is the *Manbaʿ al-ansāb* (by Taqī al-Dīn's great-grandson Muʿīn al-Ḥaqq. See no. 1264 *infra*), but where there is a discrepancy, since T. al-D. is called (not M. but) ʿAlī b. ʿAlī b. M. al-Ḥusainī al-Bhakkarī al-Shaikh T. al-D. al-Jhūnsawī.

465 Cf. *Nuzhat al-khawāṭir* p. 92, where it is said on the authority of the *Manbaʿ al-ansāb* that ʿAlī b. M. b. M. b. M. b. Shujāʿ b. Ibrāhīm al-Ḥusainī al-Bhakkarī thumma 'l-Jhūnsawī al-mashhūr bi-Shaʿbān al-Millah was born at Bhakkar on 24 Shaʿbān 630 [in 660/1261–2

1262. S. Nūr Allāh Shūshtarī in his *Majālis al-mu'minīn* (p. 311[23]) cites the *Khulāṣat al-manāqib* as the work of **Nūr al-Dīn Ja'far Badakhshī**,[466] a disciple of S. 'Alī Hamadānī (*Maulānā N. al-D. J. B. kih az afāḍil i talāmidhah i ūst dar kitāb i Kh. al-m. dhikr numūdah kih ...*). The ascription of the work to "'Alā'ī" (OCM. iii/1, p. 70: *muṣannif kā nām "'Alā'ī" lik'hā hai*) may be an inference from a poetical quotation, since "'Alā'ī" (in addition to "'Alī") was used by S. 'Alī Hamadānī as a *takhalluṣ* (see Rieu ii p. 825*a* iii). Ethé's reason for ascribing the work to S. 'Alī himself is not clear.

Khulāṣat al-manāqib, an account of the life and more especially the sayings of Amīr S. 'Alī b. Shihāb al-Dīn Hamadānī,[467] begun in 787/1385–6 in

---

according to the *Taḥrīr al-mu'taqid*. See Rieu iii p. 1042*a*], that he travelled at the age of thirty to Multān, whence he moved successively to Bihār, Shaikhpūrah, and finally to the neighbourhood of Allahabad, where large numbers were converted by him to Islām, and that he died on 3 or 13 Dhū l-Ḥijjah 760/26 Oct. or 5 Nov. 1359 [at Jhūnsī according to the *Taḥrīr al-mu'taqid*].

466 One of the authorities cited in the commentary on the *Aurād i Fatḥīyah* described in Rieu Suppt. 20.

467 S. 'A, H., the "Second 'Alī" (*'Alī al-Thānī*) travelled extensively before settling in Kashmīr, where his influence contributed greatly to the spread of Islām in the country. His arrival is said (e.g. by Firishtah, ii p. 339 penult., and by Abū 'l-Faḍl, *Ā'īn* p. 583[11]) to have occurred in the reign of Sulṭān Quṭb al-Dīn (AH 780/1378–796/1393–4 according to W. Haig's tentative determination in *JRAS*. 1918 p. 468), but different authorities give different dates, e.g. 741 (!) (see Ethé 1850), 773 or 780 (*Nuzhat al-khawāṭir* p. 88[3]), 781 (Rieu p. 447, perhaps from the *Wāqi'āt i Kashmīr*). His migration from Khurāsān (cf. *Nuzhat al-khawāṭir* p. 88[2]) or, more probably, from Transoxiana (cf. *Majālis al-mu'minīn* p. 313[20]) was prompted by a desire to escape the wrath of Tīmūr. The statement that he was expelled by Tīmūr from Hamadān cannot be correct, since Tīmūr did not reach Hamadān until after S. 'Alī's death, which occurred on 6 Dhū 'l-Ḥijjah 786/19 January 1385 at the age of seventy-three. He was buried by his own desire in Khuttalān (which may perhaps be the place from which he migrated to Kashmīr). He "may be regarded as a sort of patron saint of the Musulmán section of the population" [of Kashmīr] and "the mosque of Sháh-i-Hamadán is perhaps the most reverenced in the town" [of Srīnagar. *Tārīkh i Rashīdī* tr. Ross, p. 432 n. 2]. His works, of which forty-three are enumerated in the *Nuzhat al-khawāṭir* are mostly short Ṣūfī tracts, and some are in Arabic. Collections of ten or more are preserved in the MSS. Rieu ii 835*b*, Blochet i no. 156, iv no. 2249, and Cairo p. 529. The best known are the *Aurād i fatḥīyāh*, an Arabic litany repeatedly lithographed in India, and the *Dhakhīrat al-mulūk*, a fairly large treatise on political ethics (Edition: [Lahore] 1323/1905–6°*. MSS.: Leyden iv p. 220 nos. 1958–60, Berlin 6 (5), 295–7, Blochet ii 760–6, Rosen Inst. 110, Mashhad 9, MSS., no. 22, Bānkīpūr ix 943, Flügel iii 1853, Rieu ii 447*b*, 448*a*, 835*b*, Būhār 213–14, Āṣafīyah ii p. 1220, Bodleian 1451–3, Browne Suppt. 640 (King's 189), Browne Coll. N. 6, Ethé 2176–9, Lindesiana p. 121, Ivanow Curzon 490, Ivanow 1380, 'Alīgaṛh Subḥ. MSS. p. 11, Dresden 5, Panjāb Univ. (OCM. ix/2 (Feb. 1933) p. 44), Leningrad Univ. 1174 (Romaskewicz p. 9), Madras 425–6, Princeton 67, Upsala 456). For poems by him see Bānkīpūr i 150 (a "*dīwān*" of 14 foll.), Blochet iv 2249 (some *ghazals*), Rieu ii 825*a* (some *ghazals*), Āṣafīyah i p. 464 (*Gulshan i asrār*), p. 716 (*Chihil asrār*, an edition (place ?) of 1303. Cf. Edwards col.

Khuttalān:[468] **Berlin** 6 (8), **Bodleian** 1264, **Lahore** Panjāb Univ. Lib. (see *OCM*. iii/1 (Nov. 1926) p. 70).

1263. **Ṣalāḥ b. Mubārak al-Bukhārī** became a disciple of Khwājah ʿAlāʾ al-Dīn ʿAṭṭār[469] in 785/1393 and was by him introduced to Bahāʾ al-Dīn Naqshband, after whose death in 791/1389 he began to write his *Anīs al-ṭālibīn*.

Anīs al-ṭālibīn wa-ʿuddat al-sālikīn, or *Maqāmāt i Khwājah Naqshband*, an account of Bahāʾ al-Dīn Naqshband,[470] his teachings and miracles: Ḥ. Kh. i p. 487, **Bānkīpūr** xvi 1377 (an abridgment (foll. 55) beginning *Ammā baʿd chunānkih dar ẓuhūr aḥwāl u āthār i auliyā rā*. AH 856/1452, ostensibly transcribed by ʿAbd al-Raḥmān Jāmī), 1376 (AH 994/1586), **Ivanow** 244 (beg. as Bānkīpūr xvi 1377. AH 952/1545–6), **Ivanow** Curzon 64 (AH 993/1585), **Ethé** 1851 (AH 1008/1599–1600), **I.O.** D.P. (Bilg. 428) (AH 1041/1631–2), D.P. 1185 (an abridgment), **Blochet** i 113 (11) (AH 1009/1600),[471] **Āṣafīyah** iii p. 362 no. 236, **Berlin** 4 (23), **Cairo** p. 423 (apparently), **Istānbūl** (several copies, e.g. Fātiḥ 2560. See Horn p. 290, Brockelmann *Sptbd.* ii p. 282), **Lahore** Panjab Univ. Lib. (defective at end. See *OCM*. iii/1 (Nov. 1926) p. 70), **Romaskewicz** p. 3 no. 966*a*, **Upsala** Zetterstéen 472 (13) (defective).

112, where a *takhmīs* by Mastān Shāh (Edition: Lahore 1313/1897° in M. Sh.'s *Ātash-kadah i waḥdat*) is mentioned). See "Ādharī" *Jawāhir al-asrār* (Rieu i p. 43) fol. 121; *Nafaḥāt al-uns* p. 515; Daulat-Shāh p. 325⁹; *Majālis al-ʿushshāq* no. 36; *Ḥabīb al-siyar* iii, 3, p. 87 (based on the *Nafaḥāt*); *Tārīkh i Rashīdī*, tr. Ross, p. 432; *Haft iqlīm* no. 1019; *Majālis al-muʾminīn* pp. 311–13; Firishtah, [Lucknow] 1281, vol. ii p. 339 penult.; *Safīnat al-auliyāʾ*, pp. 107–8 (no. 135); *Wāqiʿāt i Kashmīr* pp. 36–7; *Makhzan al-gharāʾib* no. 1582; *Riyāḍ al-ʿārifīn* pp. 178–9; *Khazīnat al-aṣfiyāʾ* ii pp. 293–9; *Majmaʿ al-fuṣaḥāʾ i* p. 340; Rieu II p. 447; Beale *Oriental biographical dictionary* under Sayyad ʿAli; Raḥmān ʿAlī p. 148; T. W. Arnold *The preaching of Islam*, 2nd ed., p. 292; ʿAbd al-Ḥaiy Lak'hnawī *Nuzhat ai-khawāṭir* (in Arabic) pp. 87–90; Ethé no. 1850; Bānkīpūr Cat. i pp. 229–31; Brockelmann ii p. 221, *Sptbd* ii p. 311; etc.

468 Khuttal or Khuttalān (pronounced also Khutlān or Khatlān) was the name of a district between the Panj and the Wakhsh (tributaries of the Oxus) west of Badakhshān. See le Strange *L.E.C.*. p. 438, Barthold *Turkestan* p. 69, *Ency. Isl.* under Khuttal (Barthold).

469 d. 802/1400, a disciple of Bahāʾ al-Dīn Naqshband. See *Rauḍat al-sālikīn* no. 5, *Rashaḥāt* pp. 79–90, *Haft iqlīm* no. 1490, *Safīnat al-auliyāʾ* p. 80 (no. 85), *Khazīnat al-aṣfiyāʾ* i pp. 551–4.

470 See no. 13 1st footnote, *supra; Rauḍat al-sālikīn* no. 4; *al-Shaqāʾiq al-Nuʿmānīyah*, tr. Rescher, pp. 165–6; *Haft iqlīm* no. 1489; *Safīnat al-auliyāʾ* pp. 78–9 (no. 82); *Ency. Isl.* under Nakshband (Margoliouth); Brockelmann *Sptbd.* ii p. 282 (where some further references will be found).

471 Blochet gives the author's name as Mullā Ḥusām al-Dīn Khwājah Yūsuf. Ḥāfiẓī Bukhārī and describes the ascription to Ṣalāḥ b. Mubārak as incorrect.

1264. S. **Muʿīn al-Ḥaqq** b. Shihāb al-Ḥaqq b. M. Abū Jaʿfar b. Shāh Taqī al-Dīn[472] b. Shaʿbān al-Millah,[473] a Bhak'harī Saiyid by descent, was a native of Jhūnsī [Jhusi, near Allahabad], where his great-grandfather, Shāh Taqī al-Dīn died in 785/1384.[474] His father, Shihāb al-Ḥaqq, was born in 760/1359 and died in 800/1397, leaving him an orphan at an early age. Desiring to ascertain his pedigree, he went via Multān, where he stayed with Sh. Kabīr, to Bhak'har and was affectionately received by his relatives. He obtained from them a copy of an old *nasab-nāmah* alleged to have been brought to Bhak'har by their ancestor, S. M. Makkī, who according to him was born in 540/1145–6 and died in 644/1246–7. On this *nasab-nāmah* he based the *Manbaʿ al-ansāb*, which cannot have been completed earlier than 830/1426–7, the latest date mentioned in his genealogical account of his family.

Manbaʿ al-ansāb, an account of the Saiyids of Bhak'har and of various matters relating mainly to Ṣūfism in eleven[475] *faṣls* ((1) genealogy of Muḥammad, (2) genealogy of the Prophets, (3) history of Muḥammad, the twelve Imāms and the fourteen Maʿṣūms, (4) genealogical account of the Saiyids in Arabia and elsewhere, (5) account of the four *Pīrs*, of the fourteen *khānawādahs* and of some minor orders, (6) rules, observances and prayers of the Ṣūfīs, (7) doctrines of the philosophers and the Ṣūfīs concerning the soul, (8) differences of opinion on some *ḥadīths* relating to Ṣūfism, (9) the meaning of the words *Āmantu bi-'llāh*, (10) eulogies on the early Caliphs and the twelve Imāms, (11) the origin and destiny of man and the various classes of *faqīrs*), being Muʿīn al-Ḥaqq's work retouched and greatly enlarged by his lineal descendant in the sixth degree, S. ʿAlī Ghaḍanfar, commonly called Jār Allāh,[4762] who lived probably about the close of the 10th/16th century, and who "professes to have added genealogical accounts of Sayyids of various countries, extracted from some standard historical works; further, a sketch of the Ṣūfī orders, borrowed from the Aḥvāl ul-Aṣfiyā and the Laṭāif i Ashrafī and finally the last six chapters of the work" (Rieu): **Rieu** i 348*a* (AH 1175/1761), iii 1042*a* (extracts

---

472 See footnote 462 *supra*.

473 See footnote 463 *supra*.

474 This is the date given in the *Taḥrīr al-muʿtaqid* (see no. 1261 *supra* and Rieu iii p. 1042*a*). For two apparently corrupt dates given in the Bānkīpūr MS. of the *Manbaʿ al-ansāb* see the Bānkīpūr catalogue, Suppt. ii p. 59 n.

475 So Rieu. A twelfth *faṣl* (on the genealogy of the Imāms and of Shāh Taqī al-Dīn) is mentioned in the preface of the Bānkīpūr copy but is absent from that MS.

476 This editor, not mentioned by ʿAbd al-Muqtadir, is doubtless responsible for the references to Jāmī and his *Nafaḥāt*, which led ʿAbd al-Muqtadir to suppose that the author wrote the work at a very advanced age.

only. Circ. AD 1850), **Bānkīpūr** Suppt. ii 2069 (lacunae. AD 1876), **Āṣafīyah** iii p. 718.

1265. **M. ʿAlī Sāmānī.**

Siyar i Muḥammadī, a biography of the Chishtī saint S. M. b. Yūsuf Ḥusainī known as Gēsū-darāz and Bandah-nawāz,[477] written in 831/1427–8: **Āṣafīyah** iii p. 198 no. 1374 (AH 1312/1894–5).

1266. **Abū ʾl-Makārim b. ʿAlāʾ al-Mulk Jāmī**[478]

Khulāṣat al-maqāmāt, a biography of Sh. Aḥmad i Jām,[479] written at least partly in 840/1436–7, which is mentioned as the current year in *Bāb*

---

477 S. M. b. Yūsuf Ḥusainī, born at Delhi in 721/1321, became a disciple of the Chishtī *shaikh* Naṣīr al-Dīn Maḥmūd Chirāgh i Dihlī (d. 757/1356: no. 1259, 1st par., 5th footnote *supra*), migrated after the latter's death to Gujrāt, remained there many years with Khwājah Rukn al-Dīn Kān i Shakar, and in 815/1412–13 settled at Gulbargah, where he died on 16 Dhū ʾl-Qaʿdah 825/1 Nov. 1422, "at the age of 105 lunar years, leaving numerous descendants in the enjoyment of great wealth and honours" (Rieu i p. 347*b*). He wrote several Ṣūfī works, including *Asmār al-asrār* (Edition: Ḥaidarābād 1350/1931–2. MSS*.: Ivanow 1220, 1219 (3), Princeton 120 (?), Ethé 1861, Bombay Univ. p. 158, Āṣafīyah iii pp. 194, 198), *Khātimah* (MSS.: Ethé 1920 (12), 1856–8, 1869 vi, Ivanow 1222, Āṣafīyah i p. 416), *Ḥadāʾiq al-uns* (MSS.: Ethé 1869 v, Ivanow 1228, Āṣafīyah i p. 418), *ʿIshq-nāmah* (Ḥ. Kh. iv p. 212. MSS.: Ethé 1869 iii, Ivanow 1229, Āṣafīyah i p. 430. Turkish translation by Firishtah-Zādah: Flügel iii 1968 I. Edition of the Turkish translation: Istānbūl 1288/1871), *Wujūd al-ʿāshiqīn* (MSS.: Bānkīpūr xvi 1374, Ivanow 1223–7, Ethé 1858–60, Āṣafīyah i p. 496), *Istiqāmat al-sharīʿah bi-ṭarīq al-ḥaqīqah* (MSS.: Ivanow 1219 (2), Bodleian 1267 (1), Ethé 1861–2). A collection of discourses by him, *Jawāmiʿ al-kalim* or *Malfūẓāt i Bandah-nawāz*, was made by his disciple M. b. M. Akbar Ḥusainī (MSS.: Āṣafīyah iii p. 196, i pp. 412, 486 (?), ii p. 1722 (?), Ivanow 1231, Rieu i 347). See *Tārīkh ḥabībī* (no. 1269 (2) *infra*), *Khawāriqāt* (no. 1293 *infra*), *Akhbār al-akhyār* pp. 131–6; Firishtah, Bombay 1831–2, vol. i p. 607, vol. ii p. 748, [Lucknow] 1281/1864–5, vol. i pp. 319–20, vol. ii p. 399, Briggs's trans. vol. ii pp. 388, 398; *Gulzār i abrār* no. 158 (Ivanow p. 100[16]); *Riyāḍ al-auliyāʾ*; *Sawāṭiʿ al-anwār* (Ethé col. 331 no. 22 (*a*)); *Khazīnat al-aṣfiyāʾ* i pp. 381–2; Rieu i pp. 347–8; Beale *Oriental biographical dictionary* under Muhammad Gesu Daraz; Raḥmān ʿAlī p. 82; *Ḥālāt i dil-gudāz maʿrūf bah Sawāniḥ i Bandah-nawāz* (in Urdū), by Ḥakīm M. ʿUmar Dihlawī, Delhi 1320/1902–3; two views of his shrine at Gulbargah in *Pictorial Hyderabad ... by K. Krishnaswamy Mudiraj*, vol. i, Ḥaidarābād 1929, [plates] pp. 98, 99.

478 The author's name, absent from the three MSS. mentioned here, is given in the *Ṭarāʾiq al-ḥaqāʾiq* (see Ivanow p. 88) and in Khanikoff's *Mémoire sur la partie méridionale de l'Asie centrale*, Paris, 1861, p. 116 (see Ivanow 1st Suppt., p. 158).

479 Shaikh al-Islām Abū Naṣr A. b. Abī ʾl-Ḥasan Nāmaqī Jāmī, called Zhandah Pīl, is said to have been born in 441/1049–50 and to have died in 536/1142. His tomb at Jām, or Turbat i Shaikh Jām, about half-way between Harāt and Mashhad [cf. *Ency. Isl.* under Turbat-i Shaikh-i Djām] is described in C. E. Yate's *Khurasan and Sistan*, pp. 36–7. The works ascribed to him are some Ṣūfī tracts (e.g. *Miftāḥ al-najāt* begun in 522/1128, Flügel iii 1679, and *Uns al-tāʾibīn*, Ivanow 1169) and a *dīwān* (Editions: Cawnpore 1879°, 1881°, 1885†,

3 (*JRAS*. 1917 p. 355[12]), and divided into ten *bābs* and a *faṣl*: **Ivanow** 245 (foll. 106. Lacunæ. Late 17th cent.), **I.O.** D.P. 641 (17th cent.), **Leningrad** Asiat. Mus V 21 (a fragment corresponding to foll. 4–46 of Ivanow 245 and breaking off early in *Bāb* 8. 16th cent. ?).

Edition based on the Leningrad fragment: *A biography of Shaykh Ahmad-i-Jam. By W. Ivanow* (in *JRAS*. 1917, pp. 291–365).

1269. **ʿAbd al-ʿAzīz b. S͟hēr Malik**[480] b. M. **Wāʿiẓī** wrote the two works mentioned below in the time of ʿAlāʾ al-Dīn Aḥmad S͟hāh II, the Bahmanid ruler of the Deccan, who reigned from 838/1435 to 862/1457 and whose father, S͟hihāb al-Dīn Aḥmad S͟hāh I (825/1422–838/1435), was not only a disciple and patron of the famous saint of Gulbargah, S. M. b. Yūsuf Ḥusainī surnamed Gēsū-darāz,[481] but also an admirer of the still more famous saint, S͟hāh Niʿmat Allāh Walī, of Māhān, to whom he sent two missions.[482]

1898†. MSS.: Bānkīpūr i 23, Ethé 2863, 910, Brelvi-Dhabhar p. xxiv, Rieu ii 551*b*, Ivanow 436, Ivanow-Curzon 191, Bombay Univ. p. 224, Āṣafīyah i p. 716, Panjāb Univ. (*OCM*. iii/2 p. 75), Sprenger 88). See *Nafaḥāt* pp. 405–17; *Haft iqlīm* no. 667; *Majālis al-muʾminīn* pp. 271–2; *Safīnat al-auliyāʾ* pp. 168–9 (no. 308); *Makhzan al-gharāʾib* no. 3; *Riyāḍ al-ʿārifīn* pp. 51–3; *K͟hazīnat al-aṣfiyāʾ* ii pp. 243–4; *Majmaʿ al-fuṣaḥāʾ* I pp. 67–8; Bānkīpūr i pp. 30–1; *Ency. Isl.* under Aḥmed Jāmī (A. S. Beveridge); *JRAS*. 1917 pp. 300–6 (*q.v.* together with Ivanow 245 for further references).

480 An *amīr* named S͟hēr Malik was put to death by S͟hihāb al-Dīn Aḥmad S͟hāh, who was his maternal uncle (see *Burhān i maʾāt͟hir* p. 73[21], W. Haig *The religion of Aḥmad S͟hāh Bahmanī* (in *JRAS*. 1924) p. 78).

481 See W. Haig *op. cit*, pp. 74–5.: "He had always shown an inclination for the society of holy men. In AD 1399, in the reign of his brother and predecessor, Fīrūz, the saint Sayyid Muhammad Gīsū Darāz, whose shrine is still the best known in the Dakan, came from Dihlī and settled at Gulbarga. He was at first received with much honour, but the accomplished and cultured Fīrūz soon wearied of the rude and unlettered saint, and treated him with neglect. Aḥmad, simpler and more devout than his brother, built a hospice for Gīsū Darāz, and was unremitting in his devotion to him. The misfortunes of Fīrūz in the latter part of his reign were attributed by many to his neglect of the saint, and Aḥmad certainly enjoyed the active sympathy of Gīsū Darāz in his intrigues to supplant his brother.... Aḥmad S͟hāh, on his accession to the throne, distinguished Sayyid Muhammad Gīsū Darāz with an even greater measure of his favour, with the result that the cult of the saint became the fashion among all classes. The predecessors of Aḥmad on the throne of the Dakan had been disciples of the family of Muhammad Sirāj-al-dīn Junaidī, but Aḥmad forsook the representative of this family and became the professed disciple of Gīsū Darāz, on whom he bestowed large endowments which were long enjoyed by his descendants."

482 The purpose of the first mission was to seek the saint's acceptance of the Sulṭān as a disciple: the second mission conveyed a request that the saint would send a son to India to act as the Sulṭān's spiritual guide (see Firis͟htah i p. 433, W. Haig *op. cit.* pp. 76–7, and Rieu ii p. 832*b* xv, where a document entitled *Nasab i k͟hirqah i Aḥmad S͟hāh* is recorded). Three of the saint's grandsons went to the Deccan, and at least two of them seem to have settled

(1) ***Manāqib i ḥaḍrat i shāh Niʿmat Allāh Walī,***[483] dedicated to ʿAlāʾ al-Dīn Aḥmad Shāh: **Rieu** ii 833*a* (17th cent.).

(2) ***Tārīkh ḥabībī wa-tadhkirat murshidī,*** a biography of Gēsū-darāz,[484] completed in 849/1445–6: **Ivanow** 246 (AH 1159/1746).

1270. **Mīm,**[485] who was a khalīfah of Shāh M. Ṣalāḥ Dūndē,[486] himself a *khalīfah* of Shāh ʿUthmān Akbar, wrote—

Ḥālāt i Shāh ʿ Uthmān Akbar, an account of Shāh ʿUthmān Akbar (b. at Jhūnsī in 737/1336–7, d. 821/1418–19), a son of Maulānā Taqī al-Dīn M. Naqawī (for whom see no. 1261, 1st footnote *supra*): **Rieu** iii 1042*b* (extract only. *Circ.* AD 1850).

1271. **M. b. Abī ʾl-Qāsim** was a disciple of Sh. Aḥmad i K'haṭṭū (کهتّو), who is called also Sh. Aḥmad i Maghribī.[487]

---

there permanently (Haig, *op. cit.* pp. 77–8; H. K. Sherwani *Maḥmūd Gāwān*, Allahabad 1942, p. 26, and elsewhere).

483 For this saint and poet, who was a disciple of al-Yāfiʿī (see no. 1254 *supra*) and who died at Māhān (near Kirmān) in 834/1431, see Daulat-Shāh pp. 333–40; *Ḥabīb al-siyar* iii, 3, p. 143; Taqī Kāshī no. 102 (Sprenger p. 19); *Majālis al-muʾminīn* pp. 275–6 (in *Majlis* 6); *Khazīnah i ganj i Ilāhī* (Sprenger p. 86); *Jāmiʿ i Mufīdī; Mirʾāt al-khayāl* p. 60 (no. 43); Mubtalā *Muntakhab al-ashʿār* no. 664; *Ātash-kadah* no. 250; *Khulāṣat al-afkār* no. 277; *Makhzan al-gharāʾib* no. 2710; *Riyāḍ al-ʿārifīn* pp. 241–8; *Majmaʿ al-fuṣaḥāʾ* ii pp. 42–8; Rieu ii pp. 634–5; Bānkīpūr ii pp. 10–11; Browne *Lit. Hist.* iii pp. 463–73; *Ency. Isl.* under Niʿmat Allāh Walī (Berthels); "Āyatī" *Tārīkh i Yazd* pp. 229–32; etc. Editions of his *dīwān* have been published at [Ṭihrān] in 1276/1860° and AHS 1316/1938 (for MSS. see Sprenger 419, Rieu Suppt. 279, Rieu ii 634*b*, Bānkīpūr ii 168–9, Berlin 856–8, Ivanow Curzon 234, Browne Suppt. 625, R.A.S. P. 299, etc.). For prose works by him see Ivanow 1239–40, Rieu ii 831–833*a*, 635*b*, 828*b*, 829*a*, Āṣafīyah i p. 472, etc.

484 For whom see footnote 475 *supra*.

485 For this name cf. Bānkīpūr viii p. 107, where an eighteenth-century "Shāh Mīm, with the *takhalluṣ* Mīm" is mentioned.

486 For this name no. 815 1st footnote.

487 A saint much revered in Gujrāt, who was born at Delhi, became the disciple and eventually the *khalīfah* of Bābā Isḥāq Maghribī (d. 776/1375. See *Khazīnat al-aṣfiyāʾ* ii pp. 289–90, *Nuzhat al-khawāṭir* p. 13) at K'haṭṭū, a village near Nāgaur (for which see no. 9 2nd footnote *supra*), settled in Gujrāt, where he died on 10 Shawwāl 849/9 Jan. 1446 and was buried at Sark'hēj, 6 miles S.W. of Aḥmadābād (cf. Murray's *Handbook to India, Burma, and Ceylon*, 4th ed., p. 117: "To the rt. is the Tomb of the Saint Shaik Ahmad Khattu Ganj Bakhsh, called also Maghrabi. Ganj Bakhsh lived at Anhalwada, and was the spiritual guide of Sultan Ahmad I., and a renowned Mohammedan saint; he retired to Sarkhej, and died there in 1445 [*sic*] at the age of 111. This magnificent tomb and mosque were erected to his memory. The tomb is the largest of its kind in Guzerat, and has a great central dome and many smaller ones …"). See *Akhbār al-akhyār* pp. 156–61; *Āʾīn i Akbarī* tr. Blochmann p. 507; *Gulzār i abrār* no. 164; *Tūzuk i Jahāngīrī* ed. S. Aḥmad p. 212[11], Rogers and Beveridge's trans. i p. 428; *Mirʾāt al-asrār, ṭabaqah* 22; *Riyāḍ al-auliyāʾ; Mirʾāt i Aḥmadī, khātimah* pp. 33–4,

Malfūẓāt i Aḥmad i Maghribī, an account of the life and sayings of Sh. Aḥmad i K'haṭṭū in sixteen *faṣls* (166 foll.): **Ivanow** 247 (18th cent.).

1272. Aḥmad b. M., called **Muʿīn al-fuqarāʾ**, flourished probably in the 9th/15th century.

(***Kitāb i Mullā-zādah***), or (***Risālah i Mullā-zādah***), a list with some biographical details of celebrities, especially saints, buried at Bukhārā:[488] **Leningrad** Mus. Asiat. (at least two copies, one of AD 1600 and another of 1289/1872. See *Mélanges asiatiques* vii (St. Petersburg 1876) p. 173), **Leningrad** Univ. 947*b* (Salemann-Rosen p. 49), 948*b* (*ibid.*), probably also 593*c* (*Tadhkirah i shuyūkh i Bukhārā*, by A. b. M. called M. al-f. See Salemann-Rosen p. 13), **Tashkent Univ.** Semenov 64 (AH 1230/1814–15), **R.A.S.** P. 159 (2) ("An Account of the Holy and Learned Men of Bukhārā from AH 54 to 814". Author not stated, AH 1246/1830–1), **Majlis** 225 (AH 1301/1883–4), **Bukhārā** Semenov 92.

Edition: **Bukhārā** 1904 (with the *Tārīkh i Bukhārā of Narshakhī* (cf. no. 495, Editions (2) *supra*). See the Tashkent Univ. catalogue no. 64).

Extracts: W. Barthold *Turkestan v epokhu Mongolskago nashestviya* i p. 166–72.

Description: Barthold *Turkestan*, London 1928, p. 58.

1273. **"Yūsufī,"** the author of the *Maḥbūbīyah*, is probably to be identified with Najm al-Dīn Yūsuf ibn Rukn al-Dīn M. Niʿam Allāh Gardēzī, the author of the *Aurād i Yūsufī* (for which see Ivanow 1st Suppt. 859). He was a disciple of S. Ḥāmid Kabīr and S. Rukn al-Dīn Abū 'l-Fatḥ, who were respectively the grandson and the great-grandson of the celebrated saint S. Jalāl al-Dīn Bukhārī called Makhdūm i Jahāniyān (d. 10 Dhū 'l-Ḥijjah 785/3 Feb. 1384 at Uchh: see no. 1260 *supra*). Probably, therefore, he flourished in the latter half of the 9th/15th century. S. Rukn al-Dīn Abū 'l-Fatḥ was (no doubt considerably) his junior and received instruction from him in the *Qurʾān* and some other Arabic books (cf. *Maḥbūbīyah*, I.O. D.P. 1107 foll. 2*a*, 97*b*), but this did not prevent Yūsufī from becoming his pupil in the *ʿulūm i bāṭin*.

Maḥbūbīyah, anecdotes of S. Jalāl al-Dīn Bukhārī, called Makhdūm i Jahāniyān, of his son, S. Maḥmūd Nāṣir al-Dīn, his grandson, S. Ḥāmid

English trans. pp. 32–3; *Khazīnat al-aṣfiyāʾ* ii pp. 314–20; Beale's *Oriental biographical dictionary* under Ahmad Khattu; etc.

488 Cf. *Manāqib i mazārāt i Bukhārā-yi-sharīf* (Leningrad Univ. no. 390. Salemann-Rosen p. 17) and *Risālah i mazārāt i Bukhārā sharīf* (Peshawar 999A).

Kabīr, and his great-grandson, S. Rukn al-Dīn Abū 'l-Fatḥ: **I.O.** D.P. 1107*a* (AH 1130/1718), D.P. 658 (AH 1268/1851).

1274. The well known poet, scholar and mystic Nūr al-Dīn 'Abd al-Raḥmān b. Aḥmad **Jāmī** was born at Kharjird in the district of Jām[489] on 23 Sha'bān 817/7 Nov. 1414 and died at Harāt on 18 Muḥarram 898/9 Nov. 1492.

Nafaḥāt al-uns min ḥaḍarāt al-quds, more or less chronologically arranged notices of about 567 saints from Abū Hāshim al-Ṣūfī (2nd/8th cent.) to Qāsim al-Anwār (d. 837/1433–4), as well as of 13 Ṣūfī poets from "Sanā'ī" to "Ḥāfiẓ" and 34 female saints, begun in 881/1476–7 at the request of Mīr 'Alī Shīr (for whom see no. 1094 *supra*), completed in 883/1478–9 and constituting an enlarged, extended and linguistically modernized recension of 'Abd Allāh Anṣārī's *Ṭabaqāt*, which, as already mentioned (no. 1245 *supra*), is itself an enlarged Persian version of the *Ṭabaqāt al-Ṣūfiyah* of M. b. al-Ḥusain al-Sulamī: Ḥ. Kh. vi p. 367 no. 13922, **'Āshir** p. 109 no. 177 (autograph according to Brockelmann *Sptbd.* ii p. 286), **Blochet** iv 2307 (AH 883/1478–9, transcribed from an autograph), iii 1676 (AH 895/1490, transcribed from an autograph), i 416 (AH 907/1501), 417 (AH 934/1527), iv 2300 (2) (AH 968/1561), i 418–20, **Dorn** 422 (2) (AH 883/1478 (?)), **Leyden** iii p. 19 no. 932 (AH 896/1491), **Browne** Coll. J. 6 (10) = Houtum-Schindler 35 (AH 902/1497), **Browne** Pers. Cat. 276 (16th–17th cent.), Suppt. 1321 (AH 1100/1688–9), 1322 (fairly old. King's 118), **Rieu** i 349*b* (AH 916/1510. Said to have been collated with an autograph), 349*a* (AH 961/1554), 350*a* (Āgrah, AH 1012/1603. Calligraphic with 17 fine pictures), 350*b* (16th cent.), 350*b* (16th cent.), 350*b* (17th cent.), **Flügel** iii 1944 (AH 919/1513), **Dresden** no. 408 (AH 930/1524), **Bānkīpūr** Suppt. i 1780 (AH 932/1525–6), **Bānkīpūr** ii 181 (5) 204, 205, 206 (AH 1074/1663–4) 181 (5), **Madras** 446 (AH 939/1532–3), **Bodleian** 894 (3) (AH 941/1534), 895 (3) (AH 963/1556), 957 (old), 958 (n.d.), **Peshawar** 889 (AH 942/1535–6) **Būhār** 84 (AH 954/1547), **Upsala** 301 (AH 958/1551), **Princeton** 103 (AH 962/1554–5), Berlin 592 (AH 971/1563), 593 (AH 1021/1612), 594, 595, 596, 38 (2) (AH 1096/1684–5), **Bombay** Fyzee 4 (AH 972/1565), **Ethé** 1357 (8) (612 biographies, AH 980/1572), 1366 (549 biographies, AH 987/1579), 1362 (AH 990/1582), 1361 (611 biographies, AH 1023/1614), 1359 (620 biographies, n.d.), 1360 (612 biographies,

489 *Wilādat i īshān Kharjird i Jām būdah ast* (*Rashaḥāt* p. 133[8]): *Aṣl u maulid i bandagī i Maulānā wilāyat i Jām ast u masqaṭ i ra's i mubārakash qaryah i Kharjird u mansha'ash dār al-salṭanah i Harāt* (Daulat-Shāh p. 483[23]). For the town of Jām see footnote 477 *supra*. Kharjird, some seventy-five miles from the town of Jām, is about twenty-five miles south of Khwāf.

n.d.), 1363–4, 1365 (597 biographies. AH 1065/1654–5), 1367, **I.O.** D.P. 774 (AH 1032/1622), 774B, **Cairo** p. 428 (AH 983/1575), p. 534 (AH 985/1577–8), pp. 427–8 (3 undated copies), **Turin** 94 (AH 995/1587), **Rehatsek** p. 104 no. 61 (AH 1002/1593–4), **Āṣafīyah** i p. 350 nos. 98 (AH 1007/1598–9), 32, 52, 53, 74, 113, **Leningrad** Asiat. Mus. (AH 1008/1599. See *Mélanges asiatiques* vii (1876) p. 401), Univ. 591–2 (Salemann-Rosen p. 20), 1184 (Romaskewicz p. 15), **Ivanow** Curzon 65 (with Lārī's glosses, AH 1014/1605–6), 66, **Ivanow** 612 (2) (old), 248 (AH 1133/1720–1), 249 (AH 1144/1731–2), 250, **Lindesiana** p. 165 no. 527 (*circ.* AD 1700), **ʿAlīgaṛh** Subḥ. MSS. p. 16 no. 88, **Bukhārā** Semenov 112, **Chanykov** 102, **Eton** 39, 40 (selections), **Lahore** Panjāb Univ. (3 copies. See *OCM*, iii/i (Nov. 1926) pp. 71–2), **Majlis** 564, **Tashkent Univ.** 75, etc.

Editions: **Calcutta** 1858–9°* (*The Nafahtáal-ons* [*sic*] *min hadharát al-qods, or the lives of the Soofis…. Edited by Mawlawis Gholám 'Iisa* [,] *'Abd al Hamíd and Kabír al-Dín Ahmad, with a biographical sketch of the author, by W. Nassau Lees….* Lees' Persian Series); [**Bombay**] Ḥaidarī Press, 1289/1872* (followed by the *Silsilat al-dhahab*); **Cawnpore** 1885† (followed by the *Silsilat al-dhahab*), 1893† (followed by the *Silsilat al-dhahab*); **Lahore** 1897† (with Lārī's *Takmilah*); **Tashkent** 1915 (with Lārī's commentary. See Harrassowitz's *Bücher-Katalog* 405 (1926) no. 856 and Bukhārā Semenov pp. 14, 26).

Eastern-Turkish translation (abridged): *Nasāʾim al-maḥabbah min shamāʾim al-futuwwah*, begun in 901/1495–6 by Mīr ʿAlī-Shīr "Nawāʾī" (see no. 1094 *supra*), who omitted many notices (e.g. all the female saints), added some new ones (e.g. 33 Indian saints from Shakar-ganj onwards) and concluded the work with an account of "Jāmī" himself: **Rieu** Turkish Cat. p. 274*b*.

Ottoman Turkish translation: *Futūḥ al-mujāhidīn li-tarwīḥ qulūb al-mushāhidīn*,[490] completed in 927/1521 by "Lāmiʿī":[491] Ḥ. Kh. vi p. 367 ult., **Schefer** MSS. turcs 1052 (AH 986/1579), **Fleischer** p. 522 no. 279, **Vatican** (see *ZDMG*. 51 (1897) p. 40 no. 25).

Edition of the Ottoman Turkish translation: **Istānbūl** 1270/1854 (see Harrassowitz's *Bücher-Katalog* 405 (1926) no. 1096, Zenker ii p. 39).

Arabic translation by Tāj al-Dīn b. Zakarīyāʾ b. Sulṭān al-ʿAbshamī al-Umawī al-ʿUthmānī al-Hindī al-Ḥanafī al-Naqshbandī:[492] **de Slane** 1370 (AH 1104/1693), **Cairo** Arab. Cat. ii p. 75, **Rāmpūr** Arab. Cat. i p. 370.

490 So Fleischer. Ḥ. Kh. writes *F. al-mushāhidīn li. t q. al-mujāhidīn.*

491 Maḥmūd b. ʿUthmān Bursawī, for whom see *Ency. Isl.* under Lāmiʿī.

492 d. 1050/1640. See footnote 517 *infra*.

Urdu translation: *Tarjamah i Nafaḥāt al-uns*, by S. Aḥmad ʿAlī Chishtī Niẓāmī. Edition: place ? date ? (Āṣafīyah iii p. 184 no. 249).

Commentaries:

(1) *Ḥāshiyah i Nafaḥāt al-uns*, "very meagre and almost of no importance" (Ivanow), written[493] at the request of Jāmī's son, Ḍiyāʾ al-Dīn Yūsuf, by ʿAbd al-Ghafūr Lārī,[494] who had heard the author explain difficult passages in the *Nafaḥāt* and who appended a *khātimah*,[495] or *takmilah*,[496] on Jāmī's life and utterances, often absent from MSS. of the *Ḥāshiyah* and often transcribed as an independent work: Ḥ. Kh. vi p. 367^{9}, **I.O.** D.P. 1152(*c*) (*Khātimah* only. AH 947/1540–1), **Ethé** 1362 marg. (selections only ? AH 1042/1632–3), 1923 (37) (*Khātimah* only. N.d.), **Blochet** i 421 (without *Khātimah*. AH 963/1555), **Cairo** p. 428 (*Khātimah* only ? AH 983/1575), **Ivanow** Curzon 65 (with *Khātimah*. AH 1014/1605–6), **Ivanow** 249 marg. (without *Khātimah*. AH 1144/1731–2), Curzon 67 (defective. Without *Khātimah*), 68 (without *Khātimah*), **Berlin** 593 marg. (without *Khātimah*. AH 1021/1612), 594 marg. (without *Khātimah*. Defective), 595 marg. (without *Khātimah*. Portion only), 596 (with *Khātimah*), 597 (without *Khātimah*. Defective), **Āṣafīyah** i p. 346 no. 112 (AH 1156/1743–4), p. 414 no. 201, **Rieu** i 350*b* (with *Khātimah*. 18th cent.), 351*b* (*Khātimah* only. AH 1133/1721), **ʿAlīgaṛh** Subḥ. MSS. p. 13 no. 27, **Bodleian** 960 (without *Khātimah*), 958 (*Khātimah*), **Būhār** 85, **Bukhārā** Semenov 52–3 (both without *Khātimah*), **Tashkent Univ.** 75 (*Khātimah* only), etc.

(2) *Ḥāshiyah i Nafaḥāt al-uns*, meagre notes by Khwājah M. Dihdār "Fānī" Shīrāzī:[497] **I.O.** D.P 682 (AH 1108/1696), 990 (18th cent.), **Bodleian** 961 (fragment only).

---

493 In 896/1490–1 according to Ethé (Bodleian 960), but hardly any of the other cataloguers mention this date. The *Khātimah*, written immediately after the completion of the *Ḥāshiyah* proper, contains the date of Jāmī's death.

494 Raḍī al-Dīn ʿA. al-Gh. L., both a pupil (*shāgird*) and a disciple (*murīd*) of Jāmī's, wrote also Arabic annotations on *al-Fawāʾid al-Ḍiyāʾīyah*, Jāmī's incomplete Arabic commentary on Ibn al-Ḥājib's *Kāfiyah* (for which see Brockelmann i p. 304, *Sptbd. i* p. 533, Loth 928–9, Ellis coll. 30–1, Fulton-Ellis col. 34 etc.). He died on 5 Shaʿbān 912/21 Dec. 1506. See *Rashaḥāt* pp. 163–73; *The Bābur-nāmah in English* i p. 284; *Bābur-nāmah* tr. ʿAbd al-Raḥīm p. 113 (text edited by M. Shafīʿ in OCM. x/3 (May 1934) pp. 141–2); *Tārīkh i Rashīdī* (the passage, omitted by Ross, is quoted by M. Shafīʿ in OCM. x/3 (May 1934) p. 153); *Safīnat al-auliyāʾ* p. 84 (no. 91); *Khazīnat al-aṣfiyāʾ* i p. 598.

495 So styled by the author himself in the preface to the *Ḥāshiyah* (cf. Berlin p. 560^{22-3}).

496 The title most frequently given to the work by copyists.

497 M. b. Maḥmūd *al-mulaqqab bi-*Dihdār, as he calls himself in the preface to the *Ḥāshiyah*, belonged to a family of Arab descent which had migrated from Ḥuwaizah, in Khūzistān, to Shīrāz. According to the *Miʿyār i sālikān i ṭarīqat* (as quoted in Rieu, iii p. 1094*b*) he "stayed many years at the court of Burhān Niẓām Shāh [ruler of Aḥmadnagar

(3) *Mukāshafāt i ʿAlī Akbar Wahbī* (a chronogram = 1198/1784, the date of completion), explanations of the Ṣūfī terms by ʿAlī Akbar b. Mīrzā Asad Allāh b. Sirāj al-Ḥaqq Amr Allāh al-Maudūdī: **Bānkīpūr** ii 208 (2 vols., ending with the notice of M. b. al-Faḍl al-Balkhī, the 119th in the Calcutta edition (pp. 130–1). 18th cent.).

Description: *Notices et extraits* xii pp. 287–436 (by Silvestre de Sacy, whose description relates to the MS. Blochet i 419).

Sources: *The sources of Jami's Nafahat*, by W. Ivanow (in. *JASB*. N.S. 18 (1922) pp. 385–402); *More on the sources of Jami's Nafahat*, by W. Ivanow (in *JASB*. N.S. 19 (1923) pp. 299–303).

Abridgments:

(1) *Khulāṣat al-Nafaḥāt*, an abridgment containing utterances and often explanations of them but scarcely any dates or other biographical information, written not later than 923/1517, the date of the Bānkīpūr MS., by Jalāl, i.e. probably, as ʿAbd al-Muqtadir suggests, Sh. Jalāl Harawī:[498] **Bānkīpūr** ii 207 (AH 923/1517), **I.O.** D.P. 642 (AH 968/1560–1).

914–61/1508–53], who made him Nāẓir of his kingdom. After the death of that prince's successor (AH 972) he retired to Sūrat, where he died AH 1016. If this is correct, he must have gone to India before Akbar's reign (963–1014/1556–1605), not in it, as Rieu says (ii p. 816*a*). He does not seem to be mentioned in the *Burhān i maʾāthir*, but some connexion with Aḥmadnagar is indicated by the title of a Ṣūfī tract of his, *Risālah i Niẓām-Shāh*, or *Risālah ba-jihat i Niẓām-Shāh* (Bodleian 1298 (2)). It was doubtless after his retirement (if that is the right word) to Sūrat, that he "became intimate" (Rieu ii p. 816*a*) with the Khān i khānān ʿAbd al-Raḥīm (cf. no. 698, Persian translations (3), footnote *supra*), to whom are dedicated at least three of his works, the *ʿAsharah i kāmilah* (Bānkīpūr xvii 1517, etc.), the *Alif al-insānīyah* (Bkp. xvii 1525, etc.) and the *Sharḥ Khuṭbat al-bayān* (Bkp. xvii 1527, Ethé 1922 (27)). He is not, however, one of the adherents of the Khān i khānān to whose biographies the *khātimah* of the *Maʾāthir i Raḥīmī* (cf. no. 711 *supra*) is devoted. Although according to the *Miʿyār i sālikān i ṭarīqat* he died at Sūrat, Taqī Auḥadī (cited in Bānkīpūr xvii p. 34[12–13]) says that he died at his birthplace, Shīrāz. Seventeen of his works, mostly short Ṣūfī tracts, are described in the Bānkīpūr catalogue, xvii 1516–32. For smaller collections see Rieu ii 816 *a* (eleven), Leningrad Univ. 997 (ten. Romaskewicz pp. 3, 6, 9, 11, 12, 15), Flügel iii 1964 (seven), Bodleian 1298 (7)—(13) (seven) and Āṣafīyah p. 202 no. 1447 (five). Bodleian 1281 is a *Ḥāshiyah i Faṣl al-khiṭāb*. *Ḥāshiyahs* on the *Rashaḥāt* and the *Gulshan i rāz* are mentioned by Sprenger and Rieu, but no copies seem to be recorded. Of his poetical works a *Maulūd-nāmah*, on the birth of Muḥammad, is preserved at Princeton (no. 86). A *mathnawī* entitled *Haft dilbar* dedicated to Akbar and a *dīwān* containing *qaṣāʾid* and *tarjīʿ-bands* were described by Sprenger from MSS. in the Mōtī Maḥall and the Tōp-khānah.

498 Sh. J. Harawī, the son of a high official, Khwājah M. b. ʿAbd al-Malik (*kih dar silk i aʿāẓim i ahl i qalam intiẓām dāsht*), early devoted himself to Ṣūfism and became the disciple of Shams al-Dīn M. Rūjī (d. 904/1499. See *Rashaḥāt* pp. 187–98, *Safīnat al-auliyāʾ* pp. 189–90 (no. 361); *Khazīnat al-aṣfiyāʾ* i pp. 590–2). At the time when Khwānd-Amīr wrote his biography (i.e. probably in 929/1523) he was in the habit of preaching a weekly sermon in

(2) *Khulāṣat al-Nafaḥāt*, an abridgment made in 927/1521 by Maḥmūd b. Ḥasan b. Maḥmūd al-Ḥasanī al-Āmulī and containing 232 biographies, some of which relate to saints of Fārs and ʿIrāq not mentioned by Jāmī: **Bodleian** 959 (n.d.).

[Some biographical sources are mentioned in no. 18 *supra*: a fuller list will be given in the section POETRY. Meanwhile the following may be added—ʿAbd al-Ghafūr Lārī's *Khātimah* to his *Ḥāshiyah* (see no. 1274, Commentaries (1) *supra*); Mīr ʿAlī-Shīr *Majālis al-nafāʾis* (cf. no. 1094 *supra*), first notice in *Majlis* iii (but this contains no biographical information), *Khamsat al-mutaḥaiyirīn* (cf. no. 1094, 2nd par., Turkī works (4) *supra*. Translated extracts in Belin's *Notice biographique* pp. 101–58), *Nasāʾim al-maḥabbah* (see no. 1094, 2nd par., Turkī works (5) *supra*), at end; *Laṭāʾif-nāmah* pp. 96–7 (no biographical information); *Tārīkh i Rashīdī* (passages quoted in *Mélanges asiatiques* ix pp. 327, 355–8, and one of them in OCM. x/3 p. 153); *Tuḥfah i Sāmī* pp. 85–90; *Haft iqlīm* no. 264; *Khazīnat al-aṣfiyāʾ* i pp. 586–90; *Jāmī ... taʾlīf i ʿAlī Aṣghar Ḥikmat*, Tihrān, AHS 1320/1942.]

1275. **ʿAlī b. Maḥmūd al-Abīwardī al-Kūrānī**[499] ***Rauḍat al-sālikīn***, a detailed life of the Naqshbandī shaikh ʿAlāʾ al-Dīn M. b. M. b. Muʾmin al-Ābizhī [or al-Ābīzī][500] al-Qūhistānī, who was a disciple of Saʿd al-Dīn al-Kāshgharī and who died in 892/1487,[501] preceded by short notices of ten other shaikhs (from ʿAbd al-Khāliq Ghujduwānī to ʿUbaid Allāh Aḥrār), who occur in the Naqshbandī pedigree: **Būhār** 186 (AH 948/1541), **Ethé** 632 (defective at end).

List of the biographies: Ethé coll. 260–1.

1276. Abū ʾl-Ghāzī Sulṭān **Ḥusain** b. Sulṭān Manṣūr b. Bāyqarā b. ʿUmar Shaikh b. Tīmūr, virtually the last of the Tīmūrid kings of Khurāsān, was born at Harāt[502] in Muḥarram 842/June-July 1438. After Sulṭān Abū Saʿīd's death (25 Rajab 873/8 Feb. 1469) he seized Harāt and ascended the throne there in Ramaḍān 873/March 1469. Having reigned for thirty-eight years he died on 11 Dhū ʾl-Ḥijjah 911/5 May 1506. His patronage and that of his celebrated friend Mīr ʿAlī-Shīr "Nawāʾī" (see no. 1094 *supra*) made his court a brilliant centre of

---

the *masjid i jāmiʿ* at Harāt. According to the *Ṣuḥuf i Ibrāhīm* (cited by ʿAbd al-Muqtadir) he was a grandson of Jāmī's. See *Ḥabīb al-siyar* iii, 3, p. 348; *Ṣuḥuf i Ibrāhīm*; *Makhzan al-gharāʾib* no. 500.

499 Kūrān was a village near Isfarāyin (Samʿānī 489*b*, *Lubb al-Lubāb* 226).

500 Ābizh or Ābīz was a village in Qūhistān (*Rashaḥāt* p. 176^6, where it is spelt Apīz).

501 For notices of him see *Rashaḥāt* pp. 176–86, *Gulzār i abrār* no. 237; *Khazīnat al-aṣfiyāʾ* i pp. 578–80.

502 *Ḥabīb al-siyar* iii, 3, p. 203^{18}.

letters and art. "Jāmī," "Hātifī," "Hilālī," Ḥusain Kāshifī, ʿAbd Allāh Marwārīd, Mīr Khwānd, Khwānd-Amīr, Daulat-Shāh, Bihzād and Sulṭān ʿAlī Mashhadī were among the famous men who found encouragement there. Sulṭān Ḥusain himself wrote poetry. A MS. of his Turkī *dīwān* is preserved in the Bibliothèque nationale at Paris. The *Majālis al-ʿushshāq*, which is ostensibly[503] the work of Sulṭān Ḥusain, is said by Khwānd-Amīr (*Ḥabīb al-siyar* iii, 3 p. 330[7]) and Bābur (*Bābur-nāmah* tr. ʿAbd al-Raḥīm p. 112[8]. Cf. Browne *Lit. Hist.* iii p. 457) to be the work of Mīr[504] **Kamāl al-Dīn Ḥusain** b. Maulānā Shihāb al-Dīn Ṭabasī **Kāzargāhī**[505] Kamāl al-Dīn Ḥusain, who, according to Khwānd-Amīr, was well acquainted with the usual subjects of study and occasionally wrote poetry, laid claim to special knowledge of *jafr* and *taṣawwuf*. Leaving Ṭabas, he went to Ādharbāyjān and lived for a time under the patronage of Sulṭān Yaʿqūb [Āq-quyūnlū, AH 884–96/1479–90]. He then migrated to Harāt, was appointed Warden of the shrine of Khwājah ʿAbd Allāh Anṣārī,[506] and wrote a commentary on the *Manāzil al-sāʾirīn.*[507] In 904/1498–9 Sulṭān Ḥusain appointed him to the office of Ṣadr.[508] The date of his death is not mentioned in the *Ḥabīb*

503 Except in so far as verses by Kamāl al-Din Ḥusain occurring in the book are headed "by the author" (cf. Bābur's statement quoted by Browne, *Lit. Hist.* iii p. 458).

504 His mother, a sister of Amīr [i.e. Mīr] Rafīʿ al-Dīn Ḥusain (*Laṭāʾif-nāmah* p. 161[3]), belonged to a distinguished family of Nīshāpūrī Saiyids (*dar silk i banāt i sādāt i ʿiẓām i Nīshāpūr intiẓām dāsht, Ḥabīb al-siyar* iii, 3, p. 330[2]).

505 Or Gāzargāhī ? His claim to this *nisbah*, which is applied to him in the *Bābur-nāmah*, but not in the *Laṭāʾif-nāmah* or the *Ḥabīb al-siyar*, is presumably based on his connexion with the shrine of ʿAbd Allāh Anṣārī at Kāzargāh or Gāzargāh, some two miles to the north-east of Harāt. A description of the shrine is given in C. E. Yate's *Northern Afghanistan* pp. 33–7, where the name of the place is spelt Gazargah. Doubtless this represents the modern, if not the ancient, pronunciation, though Kāzargāh would be expected, since the place is said to have received its name (properly Kārzār-gāh, battlefield) from a battle fought there in 206/821–2. See Barthold *Herāt unter Ḥusein Baiqara*, tr. Hinz, p. 78 n. 1; *Istorico-geagrafichesky obzor Irana* p. 40.

506 *Ḥabīb al-siyar* iii, 3 p. 330[4]: *Khāqān i manṣūr amr i shaikhī i tauliyat i mauqūfāt i mazār i muqarrab i ḥaḍrat i Bārī Khwājah ʿAbd Allāh i Anṣārī rā ba-ān-janāb mufawwaḍ gardānīd.* The Warden who was at the shrine when Yate visited it in 1885 is called by him "the Mutawali [read Mutawallī], or superintendent of the endowment of the shrine". For ʿAbd Allāh Anṣārī see no. 1245 *supra*.

507 For the *Manāzil al-sāʾirīn*, an Arabic work on Ṣūfism by ʿAbd Allāh Anṣārī, see Brockelmann i p. 433, *Sptbd.* i p. 774. No MS. of Kamāl al-Dīn's commentary seems to be recorded.

508 *Ḥabīb al-siyar* iii, 3, p. 330[5]: *manṣab i ṣadārat u pursīdan i muhimm i dād-khwāhān rā nīz ba-rāy i ṣawāb-numāyash tafwīḍ farmūd.* For the functions of a *ṣadr* see *Tadhkirat al-mulūk*, tr. Minorsky, p. 111. The number of these officials was increased by Sulṭān Ḥusain (*Ḥabīb al-siyar* iii, 3, p. 327, l. 5 *ab infra: chūn dar zamān i khujastah-nishān i Khāqān i ʿalī-makān mauqūfāt i bilād i Khurāsān ba-martabaʾī rasīdah būd kih yak kas az ʿuhdah i ḍabṭ i ān bīrūn na-mī tuwānist āmad paiwastah ān pādshāh i ʿālī-jāh dū sih kas az aʿāẓim i sādāt u fuḍalā rā ba-taʿahhud i manṣab i ṣadārat sarfarāz mī sākht binā bar-ān dar awān*

al-siyar, but he seems to have been dead at the time of writing (930/1524 probably), since the past tense is used in speaking of him.

Majālis al-ʿushshāq, romantic and panegyrical accounts in ornate prose and verse of about seventy-six great mystics (beginning with Jaʿfar al-Ṣādiq), famous lovers (e.g. Majnūn), and kings, of whom the last is Sulṭān Ḥusain himself, begun in 908/1502–3 and completed in the following year:[509] Ḥ. Kh. v p. 380, **Leningrad** Univ. 1024 (AH 909/1503–4. See Romaskewicz p. 13), 1076 (AH 972/1564–5. See Romaskewicz p. 13), 915 (see Salemann-Rosen p. 18), **Bodleian** 1271 (AH 959/1552. PICTURES), 1272 (AH 1029/1619–20), 1273, **Ethé** 1870 (AH 973/1565), 1871 (defective and disordered. PICTURES), **Ḥakīm-oghlū ʿAlī Pāshā** 667 (AH 982/1574. See Duda *Ferhād und Schīrīn* p. 206), **Nūr i ʿUthmānīyah** 4211 (AH 987/1579. See Duda *Ferhād und Schīrīn* p. 205), **Blochet** i 423 (late 16th cent. PICTURES described in *Revue des Bibliothèques*, 1898, p. 392), 424 (16th cent.), 425 (late 16th cent. PICTURES described in *Revue des Bibliothèques* 1898, p. 391), 426 (late 16th cent. PICTURES described in *Revue des Bibliothèques* 1900 p. 195), 427 (AH 988/1580. PICTURES described in *Revue des Bibliothèques* 1899, p. 60), **Bānkīpūr** viii 663 (16th cent. PICTURES), **Lālā Ismāʿīl** 578 (AH 1050/1640–1. See Duda *Ferhād und Schīrīn* p. 206), **Rieu** i 351*b* (AH 1215/1800), 353*a* (first 26 *majālis* only. Early 18th cent.), **Amīrī Efendī** Pers. 93 (see Duda *Ferhād und Schīrīn* p. 206), **Āṣafīyah** i p. 472 no. 861 (AH 1146/1733–4), **Āyā Ṣūfiyah** 4238 (see Duda *Ferhād und Schīrīn* p. 206), **Berlin** 598 (PICTURES), 599 (defective at beginning), **Browne** Suppt. 1140 (n.d.), Coll. D. 21(3), **Flügel** iii 1949, **Leyden** v p. 232 no. 2642, **Majlis** 671 (defective), **Rāmpūr** (Nadhīr Aḥmad 90. PICTURES).

Editions: **Lucknow** 1870*; 1293/1876*; **Cawnpore** 1312/1897°.

Lists of the biographies: (1) G. Ouseley *Biographical notices* pp. 247–50, (2) Flügel iii pp. 427–8, (3) Rieu i pp. 352–3, (4) Ethé coll. 1036–9.

[For Sulṭān Ḥusain see Daulat-Shāh pp. 521–40 (abridged French translation by Silvestre de Sacy in *Notices et extraits* iv (An 7 [= 1798]) pp. 262–6); *Majālis al-nafāʾis, majlis* 8; *Bābur-nāmah* in the year 911 (pp. 103 penult-105[16] in the Bombay edition of ʿAbd al-Raḥīm's translation); *Laṭāʾif-nāmah* pp. 215–16 (*majlis* 8); *Rauḍat al-ṣafāʾ; Ḥabīb al-siyar* iii, 3, pp. 201 foll. (H. Ferté's *Vie de Sultan Hossein Baïkara traduit de Khondémir* (Paris 1898) contains the early

i salṭanat i ān-ḥaḍrat jamʿī kathīr az arbāb i ʿamāʾim ba-saranjām i mahāmm i ān manṣab mashghūlī numūdand.)

509 The work is severely criticized, by Bābur, who calls it "a miserable production, mostly lies, and insipid and impertinent lies to boot, some of which raise a suspicion of heresy. Thus he [i.e. Kamāl al-Dīn Ḥusain] attributes carnal loves to many prophets and saints, inventing for each of them a paramour" (see Browne *Lit. Hist.* iii pp. 457–8).

part of this narrative and, according to Bouvat,[510] goes as far as p. 254 of Vol. iii [evidently in the Ṭihrān edition[511]], in which according to the same authority the life of Sulṭān Ḥusain occupies pp. 239–83); *Tuḥfah i Sāmī* pp. 11–12; *Maṭlaʿ al-saʿdain*; *Ency. Isl.* under Ḥusain Mīrzā (H. Beveridge); Browne *Lit. Hist.* iii pp. 390–1; W. Barthold *Herat unter Ḥusein Baiqara, dem Timuriden. Deutsche Bearbeitung von W. Hinz*, Leipzig (D.M.G.) 1938 (a translation of Barthold's article *Mir-Ali-Shir i politicheskaya zhizn'* in *Mir-Ali-Shir. Sbornik k pyatisotletiyu so dnya rozhdeniya*, Leningrad 1928, pp. 100–64); etc.

For Kamāl al-Dīn Ḥusain see *Ḥabīb al-siyar* iii, 3, p. 330; *Bābur-nāmah* towards the end of the account of the year 911 (p. 112[6] in the Bombay edition of ʿAbd al-Raḥīm's translation); *The Bābur-nāma in English* i p. 280; *Laṭāʾif-nāmah* p. 161; *Haft iqlīm* pp. 192–3 (no. 154); Browne *Lit. Hist.* pp. 440, 457–8.]

1277. Fakhr al-Dīn **ʿAlī b. al-Ḥusain** al-Wāʿiẓ **al-Kāshifī** known as (*al-mushtahir bi-*) al-Ṣafī[512] was the son of Ḥusain b. ʿAlī al-Wāʿiẓ al-Kāshifī (for whom see nos. 20, 268 *supra*). In order to visit Khwājah ʿUbaid Allāh he went twice from Harāt (*L.-n.* p. 166[9]) to Samarqand: towards the end of Dhū 'l-Qaʿdah 889/ Dec. 1484 and again early in Rabīʿ ii 893/March 1488, as he himself tells us (*Rashaḥāt* p. 2[5]), he was admitted to the presence of the saint and after every conversation made a written record of what he had heard. After his father's death [in 910/1504–5] he succeeded him as preacher in the *masjid i jāmiʿ* at Harāt (*H. al-s.* iii, 3, p. 341). In 939/1532–3 after one year's confinement at Harāt he went to Gharjistān and there completed his collection of anecdotes, the *Laṭāʾif al-ṭawāʾif*[513] for the amusement of the Sulṭān, Shāh Muḥammad, who had received him kindly. Rieu says that he died in 939/1532–3, probably on

510 *L'empire mongol* (2me *phase*), Paris 1927, p. 163.

511 In the Bombay edition the account of Sulṭān Ḥusain begins on p. 201 of vol. iii, pt. 3, and ends with his burial on p. 327 (after which come notices of his children and the celebrities of his reign), but a good deal of the intervening space is devoted to Bābur.

512 Fakhr …Ṣafī: so in the preface to the *Rashaḥāt*. The *tadhkirahs* give some curious variations—Maulānā Ṣafī al-Dīn (*Laṭāʾif-nāmah*), Fakhrī called Mullā-Zādah ("his name is Fakhr aldyn b. Ḥosayn Wāʾitz Káshify, sometimes he used the takhalluç of Çafyy". *Nafāʾis al-maʾāthir*, Sprenger p. 52), Ṣafī al-Dīn Muḥammad (!) (*Khazīnah i ganj i Ilāhī*, first notice, Sprenger p. 80, but Fakhr al-Dīn ʿAlī Ṣafī in the second notice, Sprenger p. 83), Maulānā Fakhrī Kāshifī (*Makhzan al-gharāʾib* no. 1902). The *Tuḥfah i Sāmī*, which calls him correctly Fakhr al-Dīn ʿAlī, says nothing about his *takhalluṣ*. In the verses quoted at the end of the *Rashaḥāt* (p. 363[12], p. 363 ult., p. 364[1]) he calls himself Ṣafī.

513 MSS.: Berlin 1013–15, Oxford Ind. Inst. MS. Pers. A. iv. 12, Bodleian 454–6, Lindesiana p. 154 no. 617, Lahore, Rieu ii 757b, 758*a*, Blochet iv 2091, Ivanow 297, Ivanow 1st Spt. 775, Būhār 443–4, Ethé 778–9, Bānkīpūr viii 732–4, Rehatsek p. 230, Browne6t Coll. x. 5, Bombay Univ. p. 229, Edinburgh New Coll. p. 10, Eton 86–7, Leyden v p. 295, Majlis 622 (2).

the authority of the *Tuḥfah i Sāmī*, though the printed text gives the incorrect date 909.

Of his works only the *Maḥmūd u Ayāz* is mentioned by name in the *Ḥabīb al-siyar* and the *Tuḥfah i Sāmī*. This *mathnawī*, which according to the former was written in the same metre as the *Lailā u Majnūn* [of Niẓāmī] and was well known (*dar miyān i mardum mashhūr ast*), seems now, if extant at all, to be extremely rare. Possibly the Berlin MS. 692 (2), which begins with the words *Ai nām i tu ganj-nāmah i rāz* and which contains the hemistich *Sulṭān i jahān Ḥusain i ghāzīst*, may be a copy of it,[514] since the Sulṭān Ḥusain referred to is more likely to be Sulṭān Ḥusain of Harāt than Shāh Sulṭān-Ḥusain the Ṣafawī, who is suggested in the Berlin catalogue. Neither the *Maḥmūd u Ayāz* nor the *Rashaḥāt* is mentioned in the *Rauḍāt al-jannāt*, which speaks only of the *Laṭā'if al-ṭawā'if*, the *Ḥirz al-amān min fitan al-zamān*,[515] a work entitled *Anīs al-'ārifīn* (*fī 'l-mawā'iẓ wa-l-naṣā'iḥ wa-tafsīr al-āyāt wa-'l-akhbār wa-'l-qiṣaṣ wa-'l-ḥikāyāt al-gharībah*)[516] and an abridgment of his father's *Asrār i Qāsimī*[517]

Rashaḥāt i 'ain al-ḥayāt, or simply *Rashaḥāt* (a chronogram = 909/1503–4, the date of completion), a memoir of Nāṣir al-Dīn 'Ubaid Allāh b. Maḥmūd Shāshī called Khwājah Aḥrār,[518][3] with notices of some other Naqshbandī *shaikhs*, divided into a *maqālah* (chronologically arranged

514 Bodleian 1084 may be a fragment of this poem.

515 On the talismanic virtues of letters of the alphabet, Qur'ānic verses, etc. MSS.: Lindesiana p. 120 no. 676, Ivanow Curzon 656, Āṣafīyah i p. 56, Ḥakīm-oghlū 453.

516 A work of this title in 32 *bābs* appears on p. 429 of the Cairo Persian catalogue (Section: *'Ilm al-mawā'iẓ*), where the author is said to be Ḥusain b. al-Raṣadī al-mushtahir bi-'l-Wā'iẓ.

517 The *A. i Q.*, a work of doubtful authorship, ostensibly by Ḥusain Wā'iẓ (d. 910) but dedicated to Qāsim al-anwār (d. 837), on the five occult sciences *Kīmiyā, Līmiyā, Hīmiyā, Sīmiyā* and *Rīmiyā*, has been lithographed at Lūd'hiyānah in 1289/1872* and at Bombay in 1302/1885° and (a different recension, *Kashf al-asrār i Qāsimī*) in 1312/1894°*. MSS.: Mehren 132 (AH 907/1501–2, said to have been transcribed from an autograph in the author's lifetime), Browne Coll. Q. 3, Bānkīpūr Suppt. ii 2055, Peshawar 1954, Āṣafīyah ii p. 1690 nos. 5, 203, 193, p. 1692 no. 198. No copy of the abridgment seems to be recorded.

518 Head of the Naqshbandī order in his time and dedicatee of Jāmī's *Tuḥfat al-aḥrār*, born in 806/1404, doubtless at or near Shāsh, i.e. Tāshkand (both his father and his maternal grandfather were Shāshīs, and when he was one year old they were living at Bāghistān (*Rashaḥāt* p. 220[18]), which is near Tāshkand, *az kūh-pāyah-hā-yi Tāshkand, op. cit.* p. 208[11]), settled in Samarqand, where he acquired great wealth by farming and trade and where he died on 29 Rabī' i 895/20 (21?) Feb. 1490. See *Nafaḥāt al-uns* pp. 465–74; *al-Ḍau' al-lāmi'* (in Arabic) v p. 120 (three lines only); *Rauḍat al-sālikīn* no. 10; *Majālis al-'ushshāq* no. 54; *Ḥabīb al-siyar* iii, 3, pp. 200–1; *al-Shaqā'iq al-Nu'mānīyah* (in Arabic), tr. Rescher, pp. 167–71; *Haft iqlīm* no. 1533; *Gulzār i abrār* no. 187; *Safīnat al-auliyā'* pp. 80–1 (no. 87); *Khazīnat al-aṣfiyā'* i pp. 582–6; JRAS. 1916 pp. 59–75 (the article cited below under Description). Several small Ṣūfī works by him are extant, e.g. (1) *Wālidīyah* (MSS.: Browne Suppt. 684 (Trinity), Ethé 1923 (13), Tashkent Univ. 19 (1) (?), 20 (1)); (2) *Fiqarāt* (Edition: Ḥaidarābād,

notices of Naqshbandīs, p. 4 ult.), three *maqṣads* ((1) on Aḥrār, his parentage, early life, wanderings, etc., p. 207, (2) his sayings, p. 242, (3) his miracles, with notices of the disciples by whom they were related, p. 287), and a *khātimah* (on his death, p. 360): Ḥ. Kh. iii p. 461 no. 6453, **Lahore** Panjāb Univ. Lib. (2 copies dated 978/1570–1 and 1006/1597–8. See OCM. iii/1 (Nov. 1926), p. 72), **Ethé** 633 (AH 984/1577), 634 (collated in 1041/1632), 635 (n.d.), **I.O.** D.P. 653 (AH 985/1577), **Ivanow** 252 (AH 995/1587), 253 (AH 1005/1596–7), 254 (AH 1141/1728–9), 255 (defective. 19th cent.), **Ivanow** Curzon 69 (AH 1013/1605), 703 (early 19th cent.), **Āṣafīyah** i p. 320 no. 1 (AH 1000/1591–2), no. 5 (AH 1017/1608–9), p. 346 no. 61 (AH 1085/1674–5), p. 438 no. 128, **Velyaminov-Zernov** p. 865 no. 9 (AH 1023/1614), **Bānkīpūr** viii 664 (AH 1036/1627), Suppt. i 1781 (defective. 17th cent.), **Rieu** i 353*a* (AH 1074/1664), **Berlin** 600 (AH 1080/1669), **Princeton** 460 (AH 1092/1681), **Blochet** i 422 (17th cent.), **Edinburgh** 243 (17th cent.), **Tashkent Univ.** Semenov 72 (17th cent.), 71 (AH 1250/1834), **Peshawar** 978 (AH 1111/1699–1700), **Būhār** 86 (AH 1286/1869), **ʿAlīgaṛh** Subḥ. MSS. p. 60 no. 7, **Bodleian** 360 (n.d.), **Bukhārā** Semenov 73, **Chanykov** 101, **Dorn** 310, **Gotha** p. 121 no. 32*a* (contains the *Maqālah* only), **Salemann-Rosen** p. 16 no. 293.

Editions: **Lucknow** 1890°; **Cawnpore** 1911–12* (described as a seventh edition); **Tashkent** 1329/1911 (see *Ency. Isl.* under Ṣafī and Barthold's *Ulug Beg*, tr. Hinz, p. 234).

Description: *The Rashahat-i-ʿainal-hayat* (*Tricklings from the fountain of life*). *By H. Beveridge* (in JRAS. 1916, pp. 59–75).

List of the biographies in the *maqālah*: Gotha pp. 122–26.

Persian commentary: *Tauḍīḥ al-Rashaḥāt*, by M. Ḥusain b. M. Hādī al-ʿAqīlī al-ʿAlawī al-Shīrāzī, who based it on the explanations of his spiritual guide Ḥabīb Allāh: **Bānkīpūr** viii 665 (AH 1186/1772).

Arabic translation: *Taʿrīb* (or *Tarjamat*) *Rashaḥāt ʿain al-ḥayāt* written in 1029/1620 by Tāj al-Dīn b. Zakarīyāʾ b. Sulṭān al-ʿAbshamī al-Umawī al-ʿUthmānī al-Hindī al-Ḥanafī al-Naqshbandī:[519] **Cairo** Arab. Cat. ii p. 75, 2nd ed. i p. 202, **Paris** de Slane 2044.

---

date ? (Āṣafīyah iii p. 200). MSS.: Āṣafīyah i p. 458, Gotha 21, Lindesiana p. 119, Tashkent Univ. 19 (3), Ethé 1919 (3), Būhār 190 (1)).

519 An Indian who settled in Mecca and died there in 1050/1640. See *Khulāṣat al-athar* i p. 464–70, Raḥmān ʿAlī p. 35, Bānkīpūr Arab. Cat. xiii pp. 154–5, Brockelmann ii p. 419, *Sptbd* ii p. 618. For his translation of the *Nafaḥāt al-uns* see no. 174, Arabic translation *supra*.

Edition of an Arabic translation:[520] **Mecca** 1307/1889–90 (with a continuation (*dhail*), *Nafā'is al-sāniḥāt fī tadhyīl al-bāqiyāt al-ṣāliḥāt*,[521] by M. Murād b. 'Abd Allāh al-Qāzānī al-Manzilawī (*tawallud^{an}*) al-Makkī (*tawaṭṭun^{an}*), who was alive at the time of publication. See Sarkis *Dictionnaire encyclopédique de bibliographie arabe* col. 1481, Brockelmann *Sptbd.* ii p. 287, and the catalogue of the Bombay bookseller Ghulām-Rasūl Sūratī for 1914–15 p. 177).

Turkish translations: (1) completed in 993/1585 by M. Ma'rūf b. M. Sharīf al-'Abbāsī, Qāḍī of Smyrna: Ḥ. Kh. iii p. 463, **Rieu** Turkish cat. p. 74 (less than the first half of the *Maqālah*). Editions of M. Ma'rūf's translation: **Istānbūl** 1236/1820–1; **Būlāq** 1256/1840–1. (2) by 'Ārif Chelebī: **Bānkīpūr** (AH 1046/1636–7, autograph. See Bānkīpūr Pers. Cat. viii p. 26), **Berlin** Turkish Cat. p. 31 (small portion only).

It is not clear from the description whether **Velyaminov-Zernov** 5 (p. 859) is one of the above translations or another.

[*Laṭā'if-nāmah* p. 166; *Ḥabīb al-siyar* iii, 3, p. 341; *Tuḥfah i Sāmī* p. 68 (in *Ṣaḥīfah* iv); *Nafā'is al-ma'āthir* under "Fakhrī" (Sprenger p. 52); *Khazīnah i ganj i Ilāhī* (Sprenger pp. 80 and 83); *Makhzan al-gharā'ib* no. 1902; *Rauḍāt al-jannāt* p. 257[21] (quotes from the *Riyāḍ al-'ulamā'*); Bānkīpūr viii p. 24; *Ency. Isl.* under Ṣafī (V. F. Büchner); Brockelmann *Sptbd.* ii p. 286.]

1278. M. b. Burhān al-Dīn Samarqandī called Maulānā **M. Qāḍī**[522] became a disciple of the great Naqshbandī saint, Khwājah 'Ubaid Allāh Aḥrār,[523] in 885/1480 (*Rashaḥāt* p. 344[13]) and waited upon him for nearly twelve years. After 'Ubaid Allāh's death he went to Tāshkand (*Tārīkh i Rashīdī* tr. Ross p. 213) and remained there until the destruction of the town [by Shaibānī Khān Uzbak in 908/1503]. Having migrated to Bukhārā, he was well received by Maḥmūd Sulṭān, Shaibānī's brother, who became his disciple for one winter (*ibid.*). In 916/1510 after the crushing defeat of the Uzbaks at Marw by Shāh Ismā'īl's forces he left Bukhārā for Andujān and Akhsī (*op. cit.* pp. 214 and 277, in the latter of which places he is said to have left Samarqand [*sic*] and gone to Andujān). While resident in Farghānah he was often visited by Ḥaidar Mīrzā Dūghlāt (*op. cit.* p. 278. Ḥaidar Mīrzā, born in 905/1499–1500, was then a mere boy), and he gained many followers and devotees (*op. cit.* p. 342). He was between sixty and seventy

520 Perhaps not Tāj al-Dīn's translation, since both Sarkis and Ghulām-Rasūl Sūratī describe M. Murād as the translator.

521 Cf. Cairo Arab. Cat. 2nd ed. v p. 394.

522 An explanation of this appellation is given in *Tārīkh i Rashīdī*, tr. Ross, p. 212 (correctly translated ?).

523 d. 895/1490 or 896/1491 at Samarqand. See footnote 516 *supra*.

years of age when he died in 921/1516[524] at Tāshkand, where he had gone from Akhsī on a visit to Suyunjuk Khān (*ibid.*).

(1) ***Silsilat al-ʿārifīn***, an account of Khwājah ʿUbaid Allāh: Ḥ. Kh. iii p. 607 no. 7211, ʿ**Alīgaṛh** Subḥ. MSS. p. 15 no. 71.

(2) ***Tadhkirat al-auliyāʾ*** (beg. *Bi-gū, ai murgh i zīrak, ḥamd i Maulāʾī kih hast ū-rā * Sipās* etc.), perhaps identical with the preceding work: **Chanykov** 100 (AH 1189/1775).

[*Bayān i aḥwāl i Maulānā* M.Q. (see no. 1285 *infra*); *Rashaḥāt* pp. 344–7; *Tārīkh i Rashīdī*, tr. Ross, pp. 212–14, 277–9, 341–2, and elsewhere (see the index under Hazrat Mauláná Muhammad Kázi (but the Maulānā M. who escaped with Ḥaidar to Badakhshān was a different person), and under Muhammad Kazi); *Gulzār i abrār* no. 195; *Ṭabaqāt i Shāh-Jahānī*; *Sanawāt al-atqiyāʾ* fol. 271*b*; *Khazīnat al-aṣfiyāʾ* i pp. 597–8; Rieu ii 859*b*.]

1279. Quṭb al-ʿālam[525] **ʿAbd al-Quddūs** b. Ismāʿīl b. Ṣafī al-Dīn Ḥanafī[526] **Gangōhī**[527] was the disciple, brother-in-law and *khalīfah* of Sh. M. b. ʿĀrif b. Aḥmad ʿAbd al-Ḥaqq [Rudaulawī], "but got besides an investiture from almost all the Khânwâdas or Ṣûfic branches" (Ethé col. 336). He spent thirty-five years in Rudaulī,[528] migrated thence in 896/1491, early in the reign of Sulṭān Sikandar Lōdī [894–923/1489–1517], at the suggestion of his disciple ʿUmar Khān Kāsī, one of the Sulṭān's *amīrs*, to Shāhābād, "near Delhi,"[529] where he remained another thirty-five years. In 932/1525–6, when Bābur defeated and killed Sulṭān Ibrāhīm b. Sikandar Lōdī and sacked Shāhābād, ʿAbd al-Quddūs moved to Gangōh, where after fourteen years he died in 944/1537 or 945/1537 at the age of eighty-four.

Ṣūfī works by him are (1) *Nūr al-hudā* (MS.: Ethé 1924 (14)), (2) *Qurrat al-aʿyun* (MS.: Ethé 1924 (16)), (3) *Rushd-nāmah* or *Risālah i Rushdīyah* (Edition: Jhajjar 1312/1897°.[530] MSS.: ʿAlīgaṛh Subḥ. MSS. p. 16 no. 75, Princeton 113). A collection of his letters on Ṣūfī subjects (*Maktūbāt i ʿAbd al-Quddūs* or *Maktūbāt i Quddūsīyah*) was made by his disciple Bud'han Jaunpūrī (Edition: Delhi 1287/1870°*. MSS.: Bodleian 1275, Ethé 1873), and there exists a collection of Ṣūfī

524 The chronogram *Naqd i Khwājah ʿUbaid Allah* comes to 921, not 922.
525 According to the *Sawāṭiʿ al-anwār*.
526 He is said to have been a descendant of Abū Ḥanīfah (*Safīnat al-auliyāʾ* p. 101).
527 Gangōh is 23 miles S.W. of Sahāranpūr in the United Provinces.
528 38 miles from Bārā Bankī in Oudh.
529 Shāhābād, formerly in the *sarkār* of Sirhind (*Ṣūbah* of Delhi), is now in the Anbālah ("Ambala") District of the Panjāb. It is about 110 miles N. of Delhi.
530 One of these dates (given in the B.M. catalogue) is presumably incorrect, since they do not correspond.

dicta, *Laṭā'if i Quddūsī*, compiled by S͟h. Rukn al-Dīn (Edition: Delhi 1311/1894. MS.: I.O. D.P. 1099).

Anwār al-ʿuyūn fī asrār al-maknūn, anecdotes of Aḥmad ʿAbd al-Ḥaqq Rudaulawī:[531] **Aṣafīyah** i p. 486 no. 575 (? *Malfūẓ i S͟h. A. ʿA. al-Ḥ.*).

Editions: ʿ**Alīgaṛh** 1905*; **Lucknow** [1909*. With an Urdū translation by K͟halīl al-Raḥmān C͟haud'hurī].

[*Ak͟hbār al-ak͟hyār* pp. 221–4; *Zubdat al-maqāmāt* pp. 96–101; *Safīnat al-auliyā'* p. 101 (no. 118); *Mir'āt al-asrār, ṭabaqah* 23; *Sawāṭiʿ al-anwār* no. 30 (Ethé col. 336); *K͟hazīnat al-aṣfīyā'* i pp. 416–18.]

1280. Ḥāmid b. Faḍl Allāh known as (*al-maʿrūf bi-*) Darwīs͟h Jamālī (*Siyar al-ʿārifīn*, Ethé 637, fol. 2*b*²), i.e. S͟haik͟h, or Mullā, "**Jamālī**" Kanbō[532] **Dihlawī**, used at first the *tak͟halluṣ* "Jalālī",[533] but changed it to "Jamālī" at the suggestion of his *pīr*, Samāʾ al-Dīn,[534] who died in 901/1496. He himself tells us that after visiting the two holy cities, the Mag͟hrib, the Yemen, Palestine, Rūm, Syria, the two ʿIrāqs, Ād͟harbāyjān, Gīlān, Māzandarān and K͟hurāsān[535] he returned to Delhi and to the presence of his revered master, Samāʾ al-Dīn. The names of some Ṣūfīs met in the course of these wanderings are mentioned in the *Siyar al-ʿārifīn*[536] and these might provide clues to the chronology. "Jamālī's" visit to Harāt, for example, and his meetings with Jāmī cannot have taken place later than 898/1492, the year in which Jāmī died. It seems probable that at the time of his travels he was still quite young. According to ʿAbd al-Ḥaqq[537] his career began in the reign of Sulṭān Sikandar Lōdī [894–923/1488–1517]. He was one of

---

531 A C͟his͟htī saint, who died in 836/1433 or 837/1434. See *Ak͟hbār al-ak͟hyār* pp. 187–90; *Mir'āt al-asrār, ṭabaqah* 23 (summarized in Bānkīpūr viii p. 62); *Riyāḍ al-auliyā'* (cited by Rieu, iii p. 1086a); *Sawāṭiʿ al-anwār* no. 27 (Ethé col. 336); *K͟hazīnat al-aṣfīyā'* i pp. 384–7.

532 Cf. *Ṭabaqāt i Akbarī* i p. 340², *Muntak͟hab al-tawārīk͟h* i p. 325⁵. Kanbōh, spelt also Kanbōh, Kambō and Kambōh, is the name of a mainly agricultural caste in the Panjāb and western United Provinces. According to "Āzād" (*K͟hizānah* p. 177 ult.) the *qāḍīs* and *muftīs* of Delhi were usually members of this caste (*k͟hidamāt i s͟harʿīyah i Dār al-k͟hilāfah i Dihlī mit͟hl i qaḍā u iftā ak͟htar bah qaum i Kanbō taʿalluq dās͟ht u dārad*).

533 As "Jamālī" himself gives his name as Ḥāmid b. Faḍl Allāh, it is difficult to understand the statement that his original name was Jalāl K͟hān or Jalāl (*Ak͟hbār al-ak͟hyār* p. 227 ult.: *Nām i aṣl i ū Jalāl K͟hān ast*).

534 See *Siyar al-ʿārifīn* no. 14 (Ethé col. 264); *Ak͟hbār al-ak͟hyār* pp. 211–12; *Kalimāt al-ṣādiqīn* no. 77; *K͟hazīnat al-aṣfīyā'* ii pp. 74–6 (S͟h. S. al-D. Suhrawardī); *Ḥadā'iq al-Ḥanafīyah* p. 355; Raḥmān ʿAlī p. 80. Badā'ūnī calls him S͟h. S. al-D. Kanbō-yi Dihlawī (*M. al-t.* i p. 326¹).

535 According to a passage quoted in *OCM.* ix/3 p. 38 he visited Ceylon.

536 It is not clear what authority Sprenger had for his statement that "Jamālī" wrote an account of his travels (*safar-nāmah*).

537 *A. al-a.* p. 227⁷: *Ibtidā-yi ū az zamān i Sulṭān Sikandar b. Buhlūl ast*.

the Sulṭān's intimate friends.[538] An elegy (*marthiyah*) on this Sulṭān is one of the poems from which quotations are given by Nawwāb Ṣadr-Yār-Jang (OCM. x/1 p. 156). Odes were written by him also in praise of Bābur [932–7/1526–30] and Humāyūn [937–63/1530–56]. He accompanied the latter on his expedition to Gujrāt and died there on 10 Dhū 'l-Qa'dah 942/1 May 1536.[539] "His tomb, a very elegant little building of white marble, is a short distance S.E. of the Koṭob minár, eleven miles from Dilly" (Sprenger p. 446). He left two sons, of whom the elder, Sh. 'Abd al-Raḥmān[540] Gadā'ī Kanbō,[541] became *Ṣadr* in Akbar's reign.

Badā'ūnī, who describes "Jamālī" as a famous poet[542] (*shā'ir i mashhūr, M. al-t.* iii p. 76[8]), says that in addition to the *Siyar al-'ārifīn* he wrote other works in prose and verse (*u ghair i ān naẓm u nathr i dīgar dārad, M. al-t.* i p. 326[1]), including a *dīwān* of 8,000 or 9,000 verses. Of his *dīwān* only two manuscripts are at present known to exist, one, probably complete or nearly so, at Rāmpūr (described briefly by Nadhīr Aḥmad (no. 179) and much more fully by Imtiyāz 'Alī "'Arshī" (OCM xi/1 pp. 76–8)), and another, defective at both ends and containing only *qaṣā'id,*[543] *tarkīb-bands* and *marāthī,* in the private library of Nawwāb Ḥabīb al-Raḥmān Khān Shirwānī (see OCM. x/1 pp. 147–59). The latter library possesses also a Ṣūfī *mathnawī, Mir'āt al-ma'ānī* (OCM. x/1 pp. 145–7), which according to Imtiyāz 'Alī is not rare [though no copies seem to be recorded in published catalogues]. Another *mathnawī, Mihr u māh* (OCM. xi/1 p. 75), seems not to be extant.

Siyar al-'ārifīn,[544] completed in Humāyūn's reign [i.e. not earlier than 937/1530, nor later than 942/1536, the year of the author's death] and devoted to the lives of fourteen[545] Chishtī[546] saints, namely (1) Mu'īn al-Dīn Ḥasan Sijzī Chishtī,[547] (2) Badr al-Dīn Maḥmūd Mūyīnah-dūz

538 *az muṣāḥibān u ham-zabānān i ū būd* (*Ṭabaqāt i Akbarī* i p. 340[2]); *ibtidā az nudamā-yi Sulṭān Sikandar Lōdī būdah* (*Ma'āthir al-umarā'* ii p. 539[5]).

539 *A. al-a.* p. 228[14–16].

540 OCM. xi/1 p. 74 on the authority of the *Ā'īnah i Muḥammadī* of M. Ḥārithī Badakhshī.

541 See Badā'ūnī iii pp. 76–7; *Ma'āthir al-umarā'* ii pp. 539–41, Beveridge's trans. pp. 568–70; etc.

542 He is to be distinguished from "Jamālī" (Pīr Jamāl) Ardistānī, who died in 879/1474–5 (see no. 232 *supra*).

543 According to 'Abd al-Ḥaqq Dihlawī his *qaṣā'id* are better than his *ghazals* and *mathnawīs*.

544 According to Badā'ūnī (*Muntakhab al-tawārīkh* i p. 325 penult.) this work *khālī az suqmī u tanāquḍī nīst*.

545 Thirteen according to Rieu, who omits no. 2.

546 See no. 1259 3rd par. 1st footnote *supra*.

547 See no. 1259 3rd par. 3rd footnote *supra*.

Khujandī,[548] (3) Bahā' al-Dīn Zakarīyā' [Multānī],[549] (4) Quṭb al-Dīn Bakhtyār Ūshī,[550] (5) Farīd al-Dīn Mas'ūd [Ganj i Shakar],[551] (6) Ṣadr al-Dīn 'Ārif,[552] (7) Niẓām al-Dīn M. [Auliyā'] Badā'ūnī,[553] (8) Rukn al-Dīn Abu 'l-Fatḥ,[554] (9) Sh. Ḥamīd al-Dīn [Siwālī] Nāgaurī,[555] (10) Najīb [al-Dīn] Mutawakkil,[556] (11) Jalāl al-Dīn Abū 'l-Qāsim Tabrīzī,[557] (12) Naṣīr al-Dīn

548 Presumably identical with Khwājah Maḥmūd Mūyīnah-dūz, who is described as a disciple of Qāḍi Ḥamīd al-Dīn Nāgaurī (d. 643/1246 (?). See no. 9 *supra*) and an associate (*muṣāḥib*) of Khwājah Quṭb al-Dīn [Bakhtyār Ūshī, d. 633/1235]. See *Akhbār al-akhyār* p. 50; *Kalimāt al-ṣādiqīn* no. 16; *Khazīnat al-aṣfiyā'* pp. 284–5.

549 One of the great saints of India, born in 566/1170–1 (*Safīnat al-auliyā'* p. 115[10]) or 578/1182–3 (Firishtah ii p. 404[20]), disciple and *khalīfah* of Shihāb al-Dīn 'Umar Suhrawardī (d. 632/1234), with whom he associated at Baghdād on his way back from a *ḥajj*, and *pīr* of the poet "'Irāqī", died in 666/1267 at Multān. See *Nafaḥāt al-uns* pp. 583–4; *Akhbār al-akhyār* pp. 26–8; Firishtah ii pp. 404–9; *Safīnat al-auliyā'* pp. 114–15 (no. 152); *Mir'āt al-asrār, ṭabaqah* 18; *Makhzan al-gharā'ib* no. 280; *Khazīnat al-aṣfiyā'* ii pp. 19–26; Garcin de Tassy *Mémoire sur les particularités de la religion musulmane dans l'Inde* 2nd ed., Paris 1869, pp. 92–3; Beale *Oriental biographical dictionary* under Baha-uddin Zikaria [*sic*]; Raḥmān 'Alī p. 32; *Ency. Isl.* under Bahā' al-Dīn Zakarīyā' (Arnold).

550 See no. 1259 3rd par. 4th footnote *supra*.

551 See no. 1259 2nd footnote *supra*.

552 Son, disciple and successor of Bahā' al-Dīn Zakarīyā' Multānī (no. 3 above), died in 684/1286 and was buried at Multān near his father. See *Akhbār al-akhyār* pp. 61–3; Firishtah ii pp. 409–11; *Safīnat al-auliyā'* p. 116 (no. 155); *Khazīnat al-aṣfiyā'* ii pp. 28–31.

553 See no. 1259 3rd footnote *supra*.

554 Son and successor of Ṣadr al-Dīn 'Ārif (no. 6 above), died in 735/1335 and was buried at Multān near his father. See *Akhbār al-akhyār.* pp. 63–6; Firishtah ii pp. 411–12; *Safīnat al-auliyā'* p. 116 (no. 156); *Maṭlūb al-ṭālibīn, majlis* 10; *Khazīnat al-aṣfiyā'* ii pp. 47–51.

555 See no. 9 4th par. *supra*.

556 Brother and successor of Ganj i Shakar (no. 5 above), died at Delhi in 669/1271 (*Sawāṭi' al-anwār*) or 671/1272–3 (*Khazīnah*). See *Akhbār al-akhyār* pp. 60–1; *Kalimāt al-ṣādiqīn* no. 26; *Mir'āt al-asrār, ṭabaqah* 19; *Sawāṭi' al-anwār* (Ethé, col. 331 no. 18); *Khazīnat al-aṣfiyā'* i pp. 305–7.

557 Originally a disciple of Badr al-Dīn Abū Sa'īd al-Tabrīzī (who according to the *Safīnat al-auliyā'*, p. 93[15], was visited at Tabrīz by Mu'īn al-Dīn Chishtī), he went after Abū Sa'īd's death to Baghdād and for seven years consorted with Shihāb al-Dīn 'Umar Suhrawardī (d. 632/1234), accompanied Auḥad al-Dīn Kirmānī (d. 697/1297–8) on a journey to Mecca, travelled much in company with Bahā' al-Dīn Zakarīyā' Multānī (d. 666/1267), went to Delhi in the reign of Īltutmish (607–33/1210–36), associated with Quṭb al-Dīn Ūshī (d. 633/1235), migrated from Delhi to Badāyūṅ and from there to Bengal, where he died after making many converts to Islām. According to the *Khazīnat al-aṣfiyā'* he died in 642/1244–5, but this date must be incorrect, and some of the other particulars given above are scarcely credible if, as seems probable, he is the same person as the aged Sh. Jalāl al-Dīn Tabrīzī, whom Ibn Baṭṭūṭah visited [probably about 740/1339–40] in the mountains of Kāmarū (i.e. Kāmrūp, or Western Assam), and who died not long afterwards at the alleged age of 150 years (Ibn Baṭṭūṭah iv p. 217[1]). He himself told Ibn Baṭṭūṭah that he was in Baghdad when the Caliph al-Musta'ṣim was put to death (in 656/1258). See

Maḥmūd Awad'hī,[558] (13) S. Jalāl al-Dīn Makhdūm i Jahāniyān Bukhārī,[559] (14) Samā' al-Dīn: **Lindesiana** p. 162 no 115 (AH 964/1556–7), **Rieu** i 354*a* (omits no. 2. AH 1019/1610), 355*a* (AH 1131/1719), **Ethé** 637 (AH 1043/1634), 638 (lacks no. 2. N.d.), 639 (a shorter redaction, AH 1123/1711), **Berlin** 590 (lacks no. 14. AH 1085/1674), 591, **Ivanow** Curzon 71 (18th cent.), **Bānkīpūr** Suppt I 1782 (late 18th cent.).

Edition: **Delhi** 1311/1893°.

Description: *OCM.* ix/3 (May 1933) pp. 44–7 (by Yā-Sīn Khān Niyāzī).

[*Tārīkh i Shēr-Shāhī* (an Urdū translation of the passage is given in *OCM.* ix/3 p. 35); *Akhbār al-akhyār* pp. 227–9; *Ṭabaqāt i Akbarī* i p. 340; *Haft iqlīm* no. 393; Badā'ūnī *Muntakhab al-tawārīkh* i pp. 325–6; *Kalimāt al-ṣādiqīn* no. 91; *Ṭabaqāt i Shāh-Jahānī*; *Khazīnah i ganj i Ilāhī*; *Mir'āt al-'ālam*; *Riyāḍ al-auliyā'*; *Safīnah i Khwushgū* no. 43; *Muntakhab al-ash'ār* no. 137; *Riyāḍ al-shu'arā'*; *Khizānah i 'āmirah* pp. 177–9 (no. 27); *Ātash-kadah* no. 751; *Ṣuḥuf i Ibrāhīm*; *Khulāṣat al-afkār* no. 67; *Makhzan al-gharā'ib* no. 493; *Nishtar i 'ishq*; *Natā'ij al-afkār*; S. Aḥmad Khān *Āthār al-ṣanādīd* (in Urdu), Delhi 1270/1853, p. 47; *Khazīnat al-aṣfiyā'* ii p. 84; *Sham' i anjuman* p. 106; Carr Stephen *The archæology … of Delhi* pp. 171–3; Rieu i p. 354*a*; Raḥmān 'Alī p. 43; Bānkīpūr Suppt. i pp. 43–4; *Sikandar Lōdī aur us-kē ba'd fārisī muṣannifīn*, by Yā-Sīn Khān "Niyāzī" (in *OCM.* ix/3 (May 1933) pp. 37–48); *Taṣānīf i Shaikh "Jamālī" Dihlawī* (in Urdu) by Nawwāb Ḥabīb al-Raḥmān Khān Shirwānī (in *OCM.* x/1 (Nov. 1933) pp. 145–59); *Istidrākāt* (in Urdu) by Imtiyāz 'Alī "'Arshī" (in *OCM.* xi/1 (Nov. 1934) pp. 74–8).]

1281. M. b. Yaḥyā b. Yūsuf al-Raba'ī **al-Tādifī**, or al-Tādhifī, al-Ḥalabī al-Ḥanbalī was born in 899/1493–4 and died at Aleppo in Sha'bān 963/1556.

Qalā'id al-jawāhir fī manāqib al-Shaikh 'Abd al-Qādir, an Arabic account of 'Abd al-Qādir al-Jīlānī[560] and some of his disciples and contemporaries: Ḥ. Kh. iv, p. 565, no. 6557, **Bānkīpūr** xii 752, etc. (see Brockelmann *Sptbd.* i p. 777, ii p. 463).

Edition: **Cairo** 1303/1886° (see Ellis ii, col. 274).

Persian translation of selected parts written in 1012/1603–4 by Ḥusain b. Sh. Ṣābir Sindī: ***Qalā'id al-jawāhir***, **I.O.** D.P. 704 (defective at the end and elsewhere. 18th cent.).

[M. Rāghib al-Ṭabbākh *I'lām al-nubalā' bi-ta'rīkh Ḥalab al-shahbā'* pp. 25–6; Sarkis *Dictionnaire encyclopédique de bibliographie arabe*, col. 287; Brockelmann *Sptbd.* ii p. 463.]

Akhbār al-akhyār pp. 44–6; *Khazīnat al-aṣfiyā'* ipp. 278–83; *Nuzhat al-khawāṭir* pp. 20–2; *Dānishmandān i Ādharbāyjan* p. 97 (based on the *Khazīnat al-aṣfiyā'*).

558 i.e. Chirāgh i Dihlī, for whom see no. 1259 last footnote of 1st par. *supra*.

559 See no. 1260 *supra*.

560 See no. 1251 2nd par. footnote *supra*.

1282. Abū 'l-Muḥsin **M. Bāqir b. M.ʿAlī** wrote in 947/1540–1—***A history of the Naqshbandī order*** in a *muqaddimah*, four *maqṣads* ((1) *shaikhs* prior to Bahāʾ al-Dīn, (2) Bahāʾ al-Dīn, (3) *shaikhs* from the time of Bahāʾ al-Dīn to that of Aḥrār, (4) Aḥrār) and a *khātimah*: **Ethé** 636 (16th cent.).

1283. An unknown disciple of Makhdūm i Aʿẓam Aḥmad b. Saiyid Jalāl al-Dīn Khwājagī Kāsānī[561] completed in 949/1542—

Maqāmāt i ḥaḍrat i Makhdūm i Aʿẓam: **Tashkent Univ.** Semenov 74 (1).

1284. **Maḥmūd** b. Sh. ʿAlī b. ʿImād al-Dīn **Ghujduwānī.**

Miftāḥ al-ṭālibīn, a large biography of Sh. Kamāl al-Dīn Khwārazmī,[562] at one time head of the Kubrawī order, written in 950/1543–4: **Samarqand** V. L. Vyatkin's private library (see Semenov *Kurzer Abriss* p. 4).

Extracts: *Zapiski Vostochn. Otd. Imp. Russ. Arkheol. Obshchestva* xv pp. 205–12 (ed. W. Barthold).

1285. An unknown author, who had received his information from disciples of Maulānā M. Qāḍī, wrote—

Bayān i aḥwāl i ḥaḍrat i Maulānā M. Qāḍī, an account of M. b. Burhān al-Dīn Samarqandī called Maulānā M. Qāḍī (for whom see no. 1278 *supra*): **Rieu** ii 859*b* (19th cent.).

1286. **Shams al-Dīn al-Qādirī** or, more fully, Shams al-Dīn Abū 'l-Fatḥ Muḥammad b. Sh. Isḥāq Walī Allāh al-Qādirī b. Quṭb al-Anām Shaikh al-Islām Shams al-Dīn Muḥammad al-Qādirī al-Multānī, was fifty years old when he wrote his *Makhāzin al-Qādirīyah* in the second half of the 10th/16th century,[563] apparently at Bīdar[564] in the Deccan. He had previously written in Arabic an account of his grandfather's miracles.

Makhāzin al-Qādirīyah, a defence of ʿAbd al-Qādir al-Jīlānī against the attacks of ignorant persons: **Rieu** ii 874 (AH 1130/1717), **Ivanow** 1326 (2) (lacking the first three of the eleven *makhzans*. AH 1142/1729–30),

561 For this saint, who was born at Kāsān in Farghānah, became the spiritual director of ʿUbaid Allāh Khān Shaibānī and who, according to Semenov, died probably in 1512 (misprint for 1542 ?) see Semenov *Kurzer Abriss* p. 3 and no. 1300 *infra*.

562 Cf. no. 219 2nd par. *supra* and no. 1287 *infra* as well as *Laṭāʾif-nāmah* p. 17 and *Majālis al-muʾminīn* pp. 321–9.

563 This follows from his statements that he was "at present" (*ḥālā*) fifty years old (I.O. D.P. 730, fol. 218, l. 4) and that his father died in Shawwāl 945/1539 at the age of fifty-two (fol. 220*a*, l. 9).

564 He states that his father was buried *dar-īn shahr i Bīdar*. His grandfather, Shaikh Muḥammad al-Qādirī al-Multānī, who died in 935/1529 (fol. 218*b*, ll. 12–13), was also buried at Bīdar.

Āṣafīyah i p. 474 no. 919 (AH 1199/1785), **I.O.** D.P. 730 (defective at end. 18th cent.).

1287. In 972/1564–5[565] was written—

Risālah dar aḥwāl i ḥaḍrat i Kamāl al-Dīn i Khwārazmī:[566] **Āṣafīyah** iii p. 164 no. 168.

1288. Maulānā Kamāl al-Dīn Maḥmūd Andujānī, [=Maḥmūd Ghujduwānī ?], who was a friend and confidant of "the great and highly renowned" Sh. Quṭb al-Dīn [Kamāl al-Dīn ?] Ḥusain [Khwārazmī ?], wrote in 949/1542–3 a work entitled *Miftāḥ al-ṭālibīn* [cf. no. 1284 *supra*]. An abridgment of that work was made by a pupil of Sh. Quṭb al-Dīn Ḥusain and enlarged by the addition of "many new and valuable details". In 973/1565–6 the same pupil, whose name has not been ascertained,[567] abridged his own abridgment under the title *Jāddat al-ʿāshiqīn*.

Jāddat al-ʿāshiqīn, on the mystical doctrine, especially on the life and miracles of Sh. Quṭb al-Dīn [Kamāl al-Dīn ?] Ḥusain: **Ethé** 1877 (AH 989/1581), **ʿAlīgaṛh** Subḥ. MSS. p. 18 no. 1.

1289. **Ḥusain** Ḥāfiẓ **Qazwīnī** (or **Tabrīzī**)[568] settled in Damascus and there met Sh. Bahāʾ al-Dīn al-ʿĀmilī.

Rauḍāt al-jinān wa-jannāt al-janān,[569] completed in 975/1567–8: **Mashhad** 14, MSS., no. 35 (*"jild i thānī"*, i.e. *Rauḍah* vii to the end of the work).

1290. **Nūr al-Dīn M. b. Ḥusain** b. ʿAbd Allāh b. Pīr Ḥusain b. Shams al-Dīn **al-Qazwīnī.**

Silsilah-nāmah i Khwājagān i Naqshband, a spiritual pedigree of Naqshbandī shaikhs with biographical information about some of them,

565 The Āṣafīyah catalogue adds *Dar Samarqand nawishtah shud*, but it is not clear whether this refers to the composition of the work or to the transcription of this particular MS.

566 Cf. no. 1284 *supra*.

567 In the catalogue of the Subḥān-Allāh MSS. at ʿAlīgaṛh the *Jāddat al-ʿāshiqīn*, described as the *malfūẓāt* of Sh. Khwārazmī, is said to be the work of Sh. Sharaf al-Dīn Ḥusain commonly called (*ʿurf*) M. Maʿṣūm.

568 *Qazwīnī yā Tabrīzī ba-tardīdī kih dar khātimah i Mustadrakāt al-wasāʾil dar tarjamah i Shaikh Bahāʾī madhkūr ast* (Mashhad catalogue).

569 The precise subject of this work is not stated in the Mashhad catalogue, where it appears in the section *Tārīkh u afsānah*. That it is concerned with saints may be inferred from the chronogrammatic verse

*Chu pursīdam zi tārīkhash khirad guft * Ziyārāt i qubūr i auliyā shud.*

composed in 978/1570–1: **Blochet** i 428 (AH 993/1585, copied from an autograph), **Lālah-lī** 1381, **Ḥamīdīyah** p. 110 no. 155.

1291. Bābā **Dāwud Khākī** Kashmīrī Suhrawardī, a devoted disciple of Sh. Ḥamzah Kashmīrī,[570] used often to visit the members of his order at Multān. He was hostile to the Chak dynasty, accompanied the army sent by Akbar to invade Kashmīr and died in 994/1586, soon after their arrival in the country. Of his works M. Aʿẓam mentions (1) *Wird al-murīdīn*, (2) *Dastūr al-sālikīn*, a commentary on the preceding, (3) *Qaṣīdah i Jalālīyah*, and (4) *Risālah i ghuslīyah*.

Wird al-murīdīn, a short metrical life of Sh. Ḥamzah Kashmīrī: **Lahore** 1894° (in a pamphlet of 31 pp. with the title *Ḍarūrī i kalān, Ḍarūrī i khwurd, Wird al-murīdīn*, containing five short works, of which the first and the third are by Dāwud Khākī).

[*Wāqiʿāt i Kashmir* pp. 108–10; *Khazīnat al-aṣfiyā*ʾ ii pp. 88–9.]

1292. Khwājah **Isḥāq. Qārī**,[571] another disciple of Sh. Ḥamzah Kashmīrī, lived in seclusion at Shīwah [spelling ?] for twenty-two years and died at al-Madīnah after performing a pilgrimage.

Ḥilyat al-ʿārifīn, a biography of Sh. Ḥamzah Kashmīrī written in 980/1572–3: **Rieu** iii 972*b* (acephalous. AH 1139/1726).

[*Wāqiʿāt i Kashmīr* pp. 121–2.]

1293. **Mann Allāh** b. ʿAlī Allāh M. Ḥusainī.[572]

Khawāriqāt (so Ethé), or *Tabṣirat al-khawāriqāt* (*al-khawāriq*) *i Gēsū-darāz i Ḥusainī*, on the life and miracles of Gēsū-darāz,[573] his descendants and spiritual successors, composed in 981/1573–4:[574] **Ethé** 1869 vii, **Āṣafīyah** i p. 406 nos. 337, 817 (AH 1311/1893–4:), iii p. 194 no. 1378 (AH 1311/1893–4).

1294. **Ḥusain b.** Mīr **Ḥusain** Ḥusainī **Sarakhsī**.

Saʿdīyah, biographies of the Jūybārī Khwājahs Muḥammad Islām, a contemporary of the Shaibānids ʿUbaid Allāh Khān (AH 940–6) and ʿAbd Allāh Khān (AH 946–7/1539–40), and Khwājah Saʿd, written in 984/1586:

570 Sh. Ḥamzah, one of the great saints of Kashmir, died on 24 Ṣafar 984/23 May 1576. See *Wāqiʿat i Kashmīr* pp. 104–6; *Khazīnat al-aṣfiyā*ʾ ii pp. 86–7.

571 *Az ʿilm i qirāʾat ḥifẓ i wāfir dāsht.*

572 The Āṣafīyah Catalogue is the authority for the author's name, which is not mentioned by Ethé.

573 d. 825/1422. See no. 1265 footnote *supra*.

574 So Ethé and Āṣafīyah iii p. 194, but AH 891 according to Āṣafīyah i p. 406.

Tashkent A. A. Semenov's private library (AH 984/1586, autograph. See Semenov *Kurzer Abriss* p. 4), **Bukhārā** private libraries (see Semenov *Ukazatel'* p. 26, where the work is called *Manāqib i Sh. Khwājah M. Islām*, and where a reference is given to Zimin *Materialy k istorii Turkestana v XVI v.* (*Izv. T. Otd. Russ. Geogr. Obshchestva*, Tashkent 1918) p. 30).

1295. S. **Murshid**, a Yasawī dervish, says in the preface to his *Ḥujjat al-abrār* that in accordance with Ṣūfī tradition he had left his monastery and travelled to Transoxiana, Syria, Egypt, al-Madīnah, Persia and Asia Minor. His *Tasallā'* [*sic*] *al-qulūb*, a diffuse commentary on the first three verses of Jalāl al-Dīn Rūmī's *Mathnawī* (Blochet iii 1377 (1)), is dedicated to the memory of Prince Mubāriz al-Dīn Shirwān Girāy, a son of the Khān of the Crimea, Abū 'l-Muẓaffar M. Girāy Khān b. Daulat Girāy Khān, who reigned from 985/1577 to 992/1584.

Ḥujjat al-abrār, a *mathnawī* completed in 996/1588, dedicated to Sulṭān Murād b. Salīm [982–1003/1574–95] and dealing with the orders of dervishes at Istānbūl and their chiefs, especially Aḥmad Yasawī:[575] **Blochet** iii 1377 foll. 103*b*–173 (17th cent.).

1296. The *Riyāḍ al-auliyā'*,[576] as it is called in an inscription of doubtful authority on a fly-leaf, is there said to be the work of Mu'īn al-Dīn Minbarī (?). The author, whatever his name may have been, was a disciple of Muḥammad Balkhī (M. al-Zāhid al-Jāmī al-Balkhī b. Abī Bakr b. M. b. Abī Sa'īd b. Khalīl Allāh al-Jāmī). The latter, whose biography is the last in the biographical part of the work, was born in 899/1493–4, lived in Balkh and Badakhshān, and died on 10 Rabī' i 979/2 Aug. 1571. Probably therefore the *Riyāḍ al-auliyā'* was written towards the end of the 10th/16th cent.

Riyāḍ al-auliyā' (?), biographies of the ancient prophets (foll. 1*b*–45, beginning *al-Ḥ. l. ... ammā ba'd 'ulamā-yi ḥadīth u khabar*, possibly not a part of the main work), Muḥammad (fol. 45*b*, beginning *Ḥamd i bī-ghāyat u shukr i bī-nihāyat mar ān pādshāhī rā*), the first Caliphs, early and later Ṣūfīs (the latest being a number connected with Khurāsān) followed by discussions of various Ṣūfī topics: **Ivanow** Curzon 704 (late 17th cent.).

575 For Aḥmad Yasawī, who died in 562/1166–7 and is buried at his birthplace, Yasī, the town now called Turkistān, or Ḥaḍrat i Turkistān, see *Rashaḥāt* pp. 8–9; *Safīnat al-auliyā'* p. 76 (no. 75); *Khazīnat al-aṣfiyā'* i pp. 531–2; *Legenda pro Khakim Atà* [an Eastern-Turkish biography of Ḥakīm Atā (for whom see *Ency. Isl.* under Ḥakīm Atā) with extracts from several Persian works relating to his teacher Aḥmad Yasawī and his spiritual successors]. *Soobshchil K. G. Zaleman* [i.e. C. Salemann], *Ottisk iz Izvestiy Imperatorskoy Akademii Nauk*, T. ix, no. 2 (St. Petersburg 1898) pp. 105–50; *Ency. Isl.* under Aḥmed Yesewī (Melioransky); *Der Islam*, xiii (1923) p. 106 (Babinger), xiv (1925) p. 112 (Barthold).

576 This is the title of a work completed in 1090/1679–80 by M. Baqā (see no. 1337 *infra*).

List of the 15 principal biographies of later s͟haik͟hs: Ivanow Curzon pp. 467–8.

1297. **Abū 'l-Maʿālī M. "Muslimī"** (*Tuḥfat al-Qādirīyah,* foll. $2b^9$, $3a^2$) or S͟hāh S. K͟hair al-Dīn Abū 'l-Maʿālī Qādirī Kirmānī Lāhaurī b. S. Raḥmat Allāh b. S. Fatḥ Allāh (*K͟hazīnat al-aṣfiyāʾ* i p. 149^{12}) was born in 960/1553 and became a disciple of S͟h. Dāwud C͟hūnī-wāl,[577] presumably at or near C͟hūnī.[578] Subsequently he settled in Lahore, where he died on 16 Rabīʿ i 1024/15 April 1615 and was buried outside the Mōtī Darwāzah in a tomb which the *K͟hazīnat al-aṣfiyāʾ* describes as visited by hundreds of people on the anniversary of his death. In addition to the *Tuḥfat al-Qādirīyah* a work entitled *Ḥilyah i Saiyid i ʿālam* and a *dīwān* (in the possession of his descendants) are mentioned in the *K͟hazīnat al-aṣfiyāʾ*.

Tuḥfat al-Qādirīyah, a life of ʿAbd al-Qādir Jīlānī[579] in 21 *bābs*: **Lahore** Panjāb Univ. (AH 1101/1689–90. See OCM. viii/4 (Aug. 1932) p. 41), **Ethé** 1803 (AH 1137/1725), **Ivanow** 266 (18th cent.), **Ivanow** Curzon 77 (18th cent.), **Āṣafīyah** i p. 408 no. 495, ii p. 848 nos. 31, 32, **Tashkent Univ.** 18 (4).

Edition: **Siyālkōt** 1317/1899° (in a collectaneous volume entitled *Ism i aʿẓam* containing several Ṣūfī works, three of them by Abū 'l-Maʿālī).

Urdu translations (1) *Sīrat al-G͟haut͟h,* by M. Bāqir, **Lahore** 1905*, (2) *Urdū tarjamah i kitāb T. al-Q.*, by M. ʿAbd al-Karīm, **Lahore** 1906†, (3) **Lahore** [1919*].

Abridgment by the author himself: *Muk͟htaṣar i Tuḥfah i Qādirīyah,* in two *qisms* ((1) on ʿAbd al-Qādir, (2) on his associates): **Ivanow** Curzon 267 (AH 1101/1689–90).

[*Safīnat al-auliyāʾ* pp. 195–6; *K͟hazīnat al-aṣfiyāʾ* i pp. 149–51.]

1298. **ʿAbd al-Ḥaqq** b. Saif al-Dīn al-Turk[580] **al-Dihlawī** al-Buk͟hārī, who died in 1052/1642–3, has already been mentioned as the author of the *Madārij al-nubuwwah* (no. 243 *supra*), the *S͟harḥ Sufar al-saʿādah* (no. 224, Persian commentary *supra*), the *D͟hikr al-mulūk* or *Tārīk͟h i Ḥaqqī* (no. 615 *supra*), the *Aḥwāl i Aʾimmah i It͟hnāʿas͟har* (no. 273 *supra*) and the *Jad͟hb al-qulūb ilā diyār al-maḥbūb* (no. 607 *supra*).

---

577 For whom see Badāʾūnī *Muntak͟hab al-tawārīk͟h* iii pp. 28–39; *Safīnat al-auliyāʾ* p. 193 (no. 369), *K͟hazīnat al-aṣfiyāʾ* i pp. 128–31. His tomb is at S͟hērgaṛh (*kih dīhī az muḍāfat i qaṣabah i C͟hūnī ast, K͟hazīnah* i p. 130^{14}). According to the *K͟h. al-a.* Abū 'l-Maʿālī was not only his *murīd* and *k͟halīfah* but also his *birādar-zādah i ḥaqīqī.*

578 *Qaṣabah i C͟hūnī kih ba-fāṣilah i c͟hihal kurūh az Lāhaur ba-janūb wāqiʿ ast* (*K͟hazīnah* i p. 129^{19}).

579 For whom see no. 1251 2nd par. footnote *supra.*

580 Not al-Turkī. The incorrect form should be corrected in no. 243 *supra.*

(1) ***Akhbār al-akhyār fī asrār al-abrār***, lives of 255 Indian saints preceded by a notice of ʿAbd al-Qādir Jīlānī (for whom no. 1251, 2nd par., footnote *supra*) and followed by a *khātimah* or *takmilah* on the author's ancestors and his own life, compiled before 996/1588 but revised and completed in 999/1590–1: **Bodleian**363 (AH 1095/1684), **I.O.** D.P. 572 (AH 1107/1695–6, said to have been transcribed from a MS. corrected by the author), **Ethé**640 (n.d.), **Browne**Suppt. 21 (AH 1109/1697–8. King's 18), 22 (AH 1243/1827–8. Corpus 126), **Bānkīpūr** viii 666 (AH 1133/1720), 667 (AH 1278/1861–2), **Blochet** i 431 (18th cent.), **Rieu** i 355*a* (AH 1218/1803), **Ivanow**258 (19th cent.), **Āṣafīyah** i p. 346 nos. 33 and 99, **Berlin**588 (defective), 52 (11)-(12) (extracts), **Bukhārā** Semenov 1, **Lahore**Panjāb Univ. Lib. (see *OCM.* iii/1 (Nov. 1926) p. 72).

Editions: Aḥmadī Press [**Delhi** presumably[581]] 1270/1853–4 (see Bānkīpūr viii p. 28), Muḥammadī Press, **Delhi**1282/1865–6 (see ʿAlīgaṛh Subḥān Allāh ii p. 57 no. 19), **Delhi** 1309/1891–2 (see Āṣafīyah iii p. 182 no. 215 and Waḥīd Mirzā *Life and works of Amir Khusrau* p. 241 (5)), Mujtabāʾī Press, **Delhi** 1332/1914‡.[582]

(2) ***Zād al-muttaqīn fī sulūk ṭarīq al-yaqīn***, written in 1003/1594–5 and devoted to the lives of two Indian saints resident at Mecca in the 10th/16th century, namely ʿAlī b. Ḥusām al-Dīn al-Muttaqī[583] and ʿAbd al-Wahhāb

581 One of the publications of the Aḥmadī Press at Delhi was the 1285 edition of the *Sirr al-shahādatain* mentioned on no. 299 *supra*.

582 The last is the edition cited in this work. It contains also the *rasāʾil* or *makātīb* entitled *Irsāl al-makātīb wa-ʾl-rasāʾil ilā arbāb al-kamāl wa-ʾl-faḍāʾil* (cf. *Taʾlīf qalb al-alīf*, ed. Shams Allāh, pp. 39–43).

583 ʿA. b. H. al-D. Muttaqī Qādirī Shādhilī Madyanī Chishtī, born at Burhānpūr in 885/1480 or 888/1483 (*al-N. al-s.* p. 317[3]), went after his father's death (*A. al-a.* p. 259[2]) to Multān, where he became a pupil of Sh. Ḥusām al-Dīn Muttaqī Multānī (for whom see *A. al-a.* p. 213), lived for a time at Aḥmadābād in the reign of Bahādur Shāh (932–43/1526–36), departed thence when Bahādur Shāh was defeated by Humāyūn [in 941/1535], migrated [immediately ?] to Mecca [in 953/1546 according to *S. al-m.*, but this date seems to be incorrect], associated with Abū ʾl-Ḥasan al-Bakrī [who died in 952/1545 according to *Shadharāt al-dhahab* viii p. 293, if the same person is meant] and Ibn Ḥajar [al-Haitamī (d. 974/1567), not al-ʿAsqalānī (d. 852/1449)], died on 2 Jumādā i 975/4 Nov. 1567 at the age of 87 or 90 and was buried at al-Maʿlāh (*al-N. al-s.* p. 315[15]), the cemetery outside Mecca. Of his numerous works the best known at the present day is the collection of traditions entitled *Kanz al-ʿummāl*, which was printed at Ḥaidarābād in 1312–15/1894–7. See *Akhbār al-akhyār* pp. 257–69; *al-Nūr al-sāfir* (in Arabic) pp. 315–19; *Ẓafar al-wālih* (in Arabic) i pp. 315–17; *Safīnat al-auliyāʾ* p. 191 (no. 365); *Maʾāthir al-kirām; Mirʾāt i Aḥmadī, khātimah* pp. 85–7, English trans. pp. 73–5; *Subḥat al-marjān* p. 43; *Khazīnat al-aṣfiyāʾ* i pp. 429–31; *Ḥadāʾiq al-Ḥanafīyah* p. 382; Rieu i p. 356; Raḥmān ʿAlī p. 146; Bānkīpūr Arabic Cat. v p. 142; *Ency. Isl.* under al-Muttaqī al-Hindī (Hidāyat Ḥusain); Brockelmann ii p. 384, *Sptbd.* ii pp. 518–19. Biographies entitled *Itḥāf al-naqī* and *al-Qaul al-naqī* were written

b. Walī Allāh al-Muttaqī[584] as well as to short notices of some contemporary Meccan *shaikhs* and *faqīrs*:[585] **Rieu** i 356*a* (AH 1260/1844), **Peshawar** 1462 (1).

(3) ***Zubdat al-āthār muntakhab i Bahjat al-asrār***,[586] an abridgment of al-Shaṭṭanūfī's life of ʿAbd al-Qādir al-Jīlānī (for which see no. 1251 *supra*): I.O. D.P. 759*a* (defective. Early 19th cent.).

Edition: *Zubdat al-āthār … aur kitāb i Urdū Kuḥl al-abṣār tarjamah i Zubdat al-asrār* [*sic*[587]], **Delhi** [1890°. With an Urdū translation],

1299. **M. Ṣāliḥ b. Amīr ʿAbd Allāh** b. Amīr ʿAbd al-Raḥmān wrote in the time of ʿAbd al-Muʾmin Khān b. ʿAbd Allāh Khān Ūzbak (AH 1006/1598).

Tārīkh i mazārāt i Balkh: **Kābul** National Library (see *Journal asiatique*, Jan.-March 1924, p. 150).

Presumably this is different from the

Tārīkh i madfūnīn i Balkh, (u ḥālāt i Samarqand): **Āṣafīyah** i p. 346 no. 168 (author's name not stated in the catalogue).

1300. A disciple of Khwājah Iṣḥāq wrote—

Ḍiyāʾ al-qulūb, a biography of Khwājah Isḥāq (d. 1007/1598), the son of Makhdūm i Aʿẓam (d. 949/1542): see no. 1283, footnote *supra*): MS. in private possession (see Semenov *Ukazatel'* p. 20, where a reference is given

(see Bānkīpūr Cat. v. p. 143) by his pupils ʿAbd al-Wahhāb al-Muttaqī (for whom see the next note) and al-Fākihī (for whom see Brockelmann ii p. 388, *Sptbd* ii p. 529), but no copies seem to be recorded in published catalogues.

584 ʿA. al-W. M., born at Mandū [usually spelt Māndū], went to Mecca before the age of twenty [*A. al-a.* p. 269[13]], attached himself in 963/1556 [*A. al-a.* p. 270[8]], apparently the year of his arrival, to ʿAlī al-Muttaqī, a friend of his father's, transcribed and collated many copies of his works, was recognized as his successor, taught Fiqh, Ḥadīth and other subjects for many years in the Ḥaram i Sharīf and died in 1001/1592–3. ʿAbd al-Ḥaqq Dihlawī was his pupil for upwards of two years from 996/1588 and derived from him most of the information concerning ʿAlī al-Muttaqī which is contained in the *Zād al-muttaqīn*. See *Akhbār al-akhyār* pp. 269–78; *Mirʾāt i Aḥmadī, khātimah* p. 88, English trans, p. 75; *Khazīnat al-aṣfiyāʾ* i pp. 138–40: *Ḥadāʾiq al-Ḥanafīyah* p. 392; Raḥmān ʿAlī p. 139.

585 For a list of these 26 persons see S. Shams Allāh Qādirī, *A treatise of Shaikh Abd-ul-Haq Dehlawi …* (*Tadhkirah i muṣannifīn i Dihlī*) pp. 12–13.

586 Mentioned in ʿAbd al-Ḥaqq's own list of his works *Taʾlīf qalb al-alīf* (Shams Allāh Qādirī's edition p. 31) and also, according to Shams Allāh Qādirī, in the *Akhbār al-akhyār*.

587 Described by Edwards as "Zubdat ul-āṣār. ʿAbd ul-Ḥakk's own Persian abridgment of his Arabic work Zubdat ul-asrār, anecdotes and sayings of ʿAbd ul-Kādir Gīlānī. With the omitted passages of the Z. ul-asrār, translated into Persian by Amānat Khān, and a Hindustani translation of the original Arabic by the latter". In ʿAbd al-Ḥaqq's list of his own works there is no suggestion that the *Zubdat al-āthār* was abridged from a work entitled *Zubdat al-asrār*.

to Validov *Vostochnye rukopisi v Ferganskoi oblasti* (in *Zapiski Vostochn. Otd. Imp. Russ. Arkheol. Obshchestva*, xxii) p. 304).

1301. A different work on the same subject was written by **"the son of Mullā Mīr Muḥammad ʿIwaḍ"**

Manāqib i Maulānā Isḥāq: MS. in private possession (see Semenov *Ukazatel'* p. 27, where references are given to Validov *op. cit.* p. 312, Zimin *Materialy k istorii Turkestana v* xvi *v.* (*Izv. T. Otd. Russ. Geogr. Obshchestva*, Tashkent 1918) pp. 29–30, and Barthold *Otchet o komandirovke v Turkestan* (*Zapiski Vostochn. Otd. Imp. Russ. Arkheol. Obshchestva* xv) pp. 61–3).

1302 **ʿUbaid Allāh Naqshband Samarqandī**, a disciple of Sh. Luṭf Allāh Chūstī, wrote probably at the beginning of the seventeenth century.

Sirāj al-sālikīn wa-laṭāʾif al-ʿārifīn, a biography of Sh. Luṭf Allāh Chūstī, who died in 979/1571–2, with information concerning other Naqshbandīs: MS. in private possession (see Semenov *Ukazatel'* p. 19, where a reference is given to Barthold *Otchet o komandirovke v Turkestan* (*Zapiski Vostoch. Otd. Imp. Russ. Arkheol. Obshchestva*, xv) pp. 61–3. Cf. Semenov *Kurzer Abriss* p. 5, where the title (apparently of this same work) is given as *Manāqib i Maulānā-yi Luṭf Allāh i Chūstī* and a MS. in Semenov's possession transcribed in 1173/1759–60 from one dated 1022/1613–14 is mentioned, and Semenov *Ukazatel'* p. 27, where references are given to Zimin *Materialy k istorii Turkestana* (*Izv. T. Otd. Russ. Geogr. Obshchestva*, Tashkent 1918) pp. 29–30 and Validov *Vostochnye rukopisi v Ferganskoi oblasti* (*Zapiski Vostochn. Otd. Imp. Russ. Arkheol. Obshchestva*, xxii) p. 312).

1303. M. Amīn[588] **"Ḥashrī" Tabrīzī** Anṣārī lived for a time at ʿAbbāsābād, near Iṣfahān, on friendly terms with[589] Nawwāb Mīrzā Ḥabīb Allāh, the *Ṣadr*, and in receipt of a stipend from the Office of Pious Foundations (*mablaghī az sarkār i mauqūfāt waẓīfah dāsht*, Naṣrābādī p. 280⁸). Subsequently he went to Tabrīz and died there. His poetical works (of which no copies seem to be recorded) included a *mathnawī* on the campaigns of Shāh ʿAbbās I (reigned 985–1038/1587–1629) written by royal command and another entitled *Rauḍah i abrār*, which was composed in 1011/1602–3 in the same metre as the *Makhzan*

588 So *Dānishmandān i Ādharbāyjān* p. 118⁹. Naṣrābādī and "Āzād" call him simply Ḥashrī Tabrīzī without mentioning his name.

589 *az muṣāhibān i Nawwāb būd* (Naṣrābādī p. 280¹⁰).

al-asrār and which, like the *Rauḍah i aṭhār*, dealt with the saints, mystics and poets buried at Tabrīz. In the preface to the *Rauḍah i aṭhār* he mentions an earlier work of his on persons buried at Shīrāz.

Rauḍah i aṭhār, a prose work composed in 1011/1602–3 and devoted to a bare enumeration[590] of the saints, etc., buried in Tabrīz and its neighbourhood: **Flügel** ii 836 (AH 1021/1612–13), **Chanykov** 111–12.

Edition: **Tabrīz** 1303/1885–6 (see *D. i Ā. p.* 118[18]). [*Tadhkirah i Naṣrābādī* p. 280; *Khizānah i ʿāmirah* p. 193; *Danishmandān i Ādharbāyjān* pp. 117–18.]

1304. "**Ḥusainī**" an Afghān of Peshawar and a disciple of the local Qādirī *pīr* Qāsim b. Qadam, was born in 977/1569–70.

Tuḥfah i Qāsimī, a *mathnawī* on the miracles of Mīr Dād and other Afghān saints, begun in 1009/1600–1 and completed in 1012/1603–4: **Ivanow** Curzon 261 (18th–19th cent.).

1305. ʿ**Abd al-Ṣamad b. Afḍal M.** b. Yūsuf Anṣārī, the son of a sister of Abū 'l-Faḍl (for whom see no. 709 *supra*), completed in 1015/1606–7 the collection of his uncle's official letters entitled *Mukātabāt i ʿAllāmī*, which has been mentioned in no. 709, 3rd par., beginning *supra*.

Akhbār al-aṣfiyā', short notices of about 250 saints, mostly the same as in the *Akhbār al-akhyār* (see no. 1298 (1) *supra*), completed in 1014/1605–6, in the reign of Jahāngīr: **Peshawar** 1057 (AH 1089/1678–9), **Ethé** 641 (AH 1098–9/1687–8), **Bānkīpūr** viii 668 (lacunae. 18th cent.), 669 (transcribed from the preceding).

1306. ʿ**Abd al-Qādir ibn Hāshim** ibn M. al-Ḥusainī.

Ḥadīqat al-auliyā', biographies of saints who lived in Sind, completed in 1016/1607–8: **I.O.** 4399 (19th cent.).

1307. Khwājah **Kamāl**.

Tuḥfat al-suʿadā' (beg. *al-Ḥ. li-walīyihi wa-'l-ṣ. ʿalā Nabīyihi ... ʿārifān ḥājjī 'l-Ḥaramain bandagī i Shaikh Qiwām al-Dīn i ʿAbbāsī i Lak'hnawī*), short lives of the Chishtī saints, Sh. Saʿd (d. 988/1580),[591] Qiwām al-Dīn

590 eine schlichte Aufzählung (Flügel).

591 This date is given by Nadhir Aḥmad doubtless on the authority of the *Tuḥfat al-suʿadā'*. Neither the *Akhbār al-akhyār* nor the *Khazīnat al-aṣfiyā'* contains a biography of Sh. Saʿd.

(d. 840/1436–7),[592] and S̲h̲āh Mīnā (d. 870/1465–6),[593] composed in 1016/1607–8 at the request of the author's son, S̲h̲āh Ḥamīd Abū 'l-Faiḍ: Rāmpūr (AH 1175/1761. See Nad̲h̲īr Aḥmad 75).

1308. Sh. ʿAlīm (or ʿĀlīm ?) ʿAzīzān was born in 972/1564 and died in 1041/1632. *Lamaḥāt min nafaḥāt al-quds*, biographies of s̲h̲aik̲h̲s belonging to a branch of the Naqs̲h̲bandī order. Edition: **Tas̲h̲kent** 1327/1909 (see Semenov *Kurzer Abriss* p. 5).

1309. For the *Tārīk̲h̲ i K̲h̲ān-i-Jahānī u Mak̲h̲zan i Afg̲h̲ānī* which was completed in 1021/1613 by Niʿmat Allāh b. Ḥabīb Allāh Harawī and of which the k̲h̲ātimah contains notices of 68 Afg̲h̲ān saints, see no. 544 (1) *supra*. The third *daftar* of the shorter recension, *Mak̲h̲zan i Afg̲h̲ānī* (no. 544 (2) *supra*), is likewise devoted to Afg̲h̲ān saints.

1310. **M. G̲h̲aut̲h̲ī** b. Ḥasan b. Mūsā S̲h̲aṭṭārī,[594] as he calls himself, or M. b. al-Ḥasan al-Manduwī, as he is called in the *Nuzhat al-k̲h̲awāṭir* (p. 61[10]),[595] or Mullā G̲h̲aut̲h̲i Māndū-wālē,[596] as he is called in (the heading of ?) the extract contained in Ivanow-Curzon 74, was the son of Ḥasan b. Mūsā Aḥmadābādī, whose biography is the last in the *Gulzār i abrār* (or at any rate in Ivanow 259). He had contemplated writing the *Gulzār i abrār* as early as 998/1590, but circumstances compelled the postponement of the work until after 1010/1602. "In fact, the greater part of his book was written between 1020/1611 (cf. f. 29v) and 1022/1613 (cf. ff. 172v, 182v, 184v, etc.). Only once he mentions 1008/1599 as current (f. 65)" (Ivanow).

---

592 Cf. *Ak̲h̲bār al-ak̲h̲yār* p. 155; *Sawāṭiʿ al-anwār* (Ethé col. 332[45]); *K̲h̲azīnat al-aṣfiyāʾ* i pp. 388–9. Q. al-D. was a disciple of Chirāg̲h̲ i Dihlī (for whom see no. 1252 5th footnote *supra*) and of Mak̲h̲dūm i Jahāniyān (see no. 1260 *supra*).

593 S̲h̲āh Mīnā, the saint of Lucknow, was a disciple of Sh. Qiwām al-Dīn and of Sh. Sārang. See *Ak̲h̲bār al-ak̲h̲yār* p. 156; *Malfūẓāt i S̲h̲āh Mīnā* (*Tuḥfat-i-Saʿdīyah* ? no. 1411 (123) *infra*); *K̲h̲azīnat al-aṣfiyāʾ* i pp. 398–9; *Lucknow District Gazetteer* p. 214.

594 Possibly identical with Maulānā G̲h̲aut̲h̲ī, who is mentioned under Aḥmadābād in the *Haft iqlīm*, (p. 88, no. 31) as a person known to everyone and of whose poetry four verses are quoted. "G̲h̲authî, a poet of Gujarât," whose "name was Ḥasan", occurs in the *Mak̲h̲zan al-g̲h̲arāʾib* (no. 1816), but, if his name is correctly given as Ḥasan, he cannot be identical with the author of the *Gulzār i abrār*. Cf. *Riyāḍ al-s̲h̲uʿarāʾ* 688 (Ivanow-Curzon p. 37), where there is another notice of Ḥasan G̲h̲aut̲h̲ī. There seems to be no mention of M. G̲h̲aut̲h̲ī or of Ḥasan G̲h̲aut̲h̲ī in the k̲h̲ātimah to the *Mirʾāt i Aḥmadī*.

595 Merely in a citation of the *Gulzār i abrār*.

596 Māndūwālī (*sic* ?) according to Ivanow.

Gulzār i abrār, bombastic, but valuable,[597] notices of 575 Indian saints, many of them Gujrātīs, dedicated to Jahāngīr and divided into five *chamans* ((1)–(3) seventh, eighth and ninth century respectively, (4) tenth and early eleventh century, (5) S̲h̲aṭṭārīs): **Lindesiana** p. 143 no. 185 (AH 1078/1667–8), **Buk̲h̲ārā** Semenov 94 (AH 1078/1667–8), **Ivanow** 259 (AH 1155/1742–3), **Ivanow** Curzon 74 foll. 67*b*–70 (Muʿīn al-Dīn Chishtī only), **Āṣafīyah** iii p. 162 no. 177, **Rieu** iii 1041*b* (extracts only. *Circ*.AD 1850).

List of the saints: Ivanow pp. 97–180

1311. **M. Ṣādiq Kas̲h̲mīrī Hamadānī** is best known as the author of the *Ṭabaqāt i S̲h̲āh-Jahānī*, which he wrote, partly at any rate, in 1046/1636–7. Another work of his, the *Silsilat al-ṣādiqīn*, is referred to in the *Kalimāt al-ṣādiqīn*.

Kalimāt al-ṣādiqīn, biographies of 125 saints buried at Delhi, completed in 1023/1614: **Bānkīpūr** viii 671 (18th cent.).

List and epitome of the biographies: Bānkīpūr viii pp. 35–45.

1312. **Naṣīb i Kas̲h̲mīr**,[598] as he calls himself, or Abū 'l-Fuqarāʾ Bābā Naṣīb, as M. Aʿẓam calls him, or Bābā Naṣīb al-Dīn Suhrawardī Kas̲h̲mīrī, as he is called in the *K̲h̲azīnat al-aṣfiyāʾ*, was a disciple of Bābā Dāwud K̲h̲ākī, who has already been mentioned in this work (no. 1291). One of the great saints of Kas̲h̲mīr, he was renowned for his austerity and for his kindness to the poor and wretched.[599] He died on 13 Muḥarram 1047/7 May 1637.

(*Rīs̲h̲ī-nāmah*),[600] lives of Kas̲h̲mīrī saints, especially of Bābā Nūr al-Dīn Walī Rīs̲h̲ī,[601] the subject of the first and by far the longest biography (foll.

---

[597] "because of its exactitude in dates, richness in details, and its abundant information about a great many persons otherwise unknown, but especially for its large number of references to the history of Gujrāt and India in general" (Ivanow).

[598] Rhyming with *faqīr i ḥaqīr*.

[599] *Masākīn dar k̲h̲idmatas̲h̲ rujūʿ i tamām dās̲h̲tand dar waqt i k̲h̲wud maljaʾ u maʾāb i g̲h̲urabā u bī-chāragān būd* (*Wāqiʿāt i Kas̲h̲mīr* p. 142¹¹).

[600] Cf. *Wāqiʿāt i Kas̲h̲mīr* p. 63¹⁴: *Rīs̲h̲ī kasī rā gūyand kih az zumrah i zāhidān u ʿābidān dar riyāḍat sak̲h̲t u ṣulb-tar bās̲h̲ad u k̲h̲wud rā az aulād u izdiwāj fārig̲h̲ dārad dast az jamīʿ i ārzūhā u hawā u hawas bar-dārad chih jāy i mulk u māl*; *K̲h̲azīnat al-aṣfiyāʾ* ii p. 334¹⁵: *Darwīs̲h̲ān i Rīs̲h̲ī firqah dar Kas̲h̲mīr az k̲h̲ānadān i Kubrawīyah būdand darwīs̲h̲* [sic, but read *u Rīs̲h̲ī*] *ba-zabān i Kas̲h̲mīrī mard i ʿābid u zāhid rā gūyand kih faiḍ i Uwaisī dās̲h̲tah bās̲h̲ad*. It is the Sanskrit word *rishi*, meaning "saint" or "anchorite". See *Some Account of the Rishis or Hermits of Kashmir*, by Lieut.-Col. D. J. F. Newall (in *JASB*. xxxix, pt. 1 (1870) pp. 265–70).

[601] Who died in 842/1438–9. See *Waqiʿāt i Kas̲h̲mīr* pp. 63–4; *K̲h̲azīnat al-aṣfiyāʾ* ii pp. 312–13; Lawrence, *The Valley of Kashmir* pp. 287–8.

169b–332 in Ivanow 260), Bābā Bām al-Dīn,[602] Bābā Zain al-Dīn,[603] Bābā Laṭīf al-Dīn,[604] Bābā Naṣr al-Dīn,[605] Bābā Rajab al-Dīn,[606] Bābā S͟hukr al-Dīn,[607] Bābā Laṭīf al-Dīn's disciples, Bābā Naurōz Rīs͟hī[608] [Malik Saif al-Dīn, Mirzā Ḥaidar Kās͟hg͟harī],[609] S͟h. Ḥamzah[610] and several of his disciples, with a long preliminary discourse on the merits of the first four Caliphs, etc.: **Ivanow** 260 (defective at the beginning and elsewhere. Foll. 519. Early 17th cent.), **Edinburgh** 245 (foll. 428), **I.O. D.P. 731** (18th cent.). [*Wāqi'āt i Kas͟hmīr* p. 142; *K͟hazīnat al-aṣfiyā'* ii p. 95: Rieu iii 1085a.]

1313. **Bahā' al-Dīn "Bahā"**, whose *Rīs͟hī-nāmah* seems to be based on that of Naṣīb, is placed here for convenience in the absence of information concerning his date (which will probably be revealed approximately as soon as a cataloguer particularizes the latest Qādirīs mentioned in his poem).

Rīs͟hī-nāmah, a metrical account of the saints of Kashmir in three *daftars* ((1) S͟h. Nūr al-Dīn, his followers and contemporaries, (2) S͟h. Ḥamzah and some other *Rīs͟hīs*, (3) 'Abd al-Qādir Gīlānī and the *s͟haikhs* of his *silsilah* in Kashmir): **Bānkīpūr Suppt.** i 1894 (AH 1284–5/1867–9), **I.O.** 3684, **London** S.O.A.S.

1314. **'Alī Aṣg͟har b. S͟h. Maudūd b. S͟h. M. C͟his͟htī Hindālawī (?)**[611] Fathpūrī wrote his *Jawāhir i Farīdī* primarily to elucidate the complex genealogical relations of the descendants of S͟h. Farīd al-Dīn Ganj i S͟hakar,[612] who were so numerous that he had been surnamed Ādam i T͟hānī and many impostors had been able to claim privileges to which they were not entitled.

Jawāhir i Farīdī, an elaborate work on the lives of some C͟his͟htī saints, especially Farīd al-Dīn Ganj i S͟hakar and his descendants, completed in 1033/1623 under Jahāngīr (but evidently supplemented later)[613] and divided into five *bābs* ((1) the Prophet, his wives and children, the

---

602 *Wāqi'āt i Kas͟hmīr* p. 64.
603 *W. i K.* p. 64.
604 *W. i K.* p. 65.
605 *W. i K.* p. 65.
606 *W. i K.* p. 70.
607 *W. i K.* p. 70.
608 *W. i K.* p. 73.
609 See no. 349 *supra*; *JRAS*. 1918, p. 461, etc.
610 See no. 1291, footnote *supra*.
611 Ivanow writes Handālawī, 'Abd al-Muqtadir Bîdâlawî.
612 See no. 1259 3rd footnote *supra*.
613 According to Ivanow the years 1036 and 1038 are referred to as current and at the end of the work an event of 1057 is mentioned.

early Caliphs and some *Tābiʿīn*, (2) Muʿīn al-Dīn Chishtī,[614] Quṭb al-Dīn Bakhtyār Ūshī,[615] Farīd al-Dīn Ganj i Shakar, Najīb al-Dīn Mutawakkil,[616] their wives, children and disciples, (3) Zain al-ʿĀbidīn Chishtī Hindālawī, a descendant of Ganj i Shakar in the fourth generation and a contemporary of Sikandar Lōdī (894–923/1488–1517), who settled at Hindālī (?), near Fatḥpūr, (4) a list of *aʿrās*, i.e. days of the month on which the anniversaries of the death of different saints are celebrated, together with some information concerning the affiliations of the author's father, (5) on the descendants of Sh. Saʿd Ḥājjī (so Ivanow), or Saʿīd Ḥājjī (so Būhār), a relation of Ganj i Shakar, and those of Sh. ʿAbd Allāh Ghaffārī, known as Shaikh al-Islām, etc.): **Ivanow** Curzon 72 (late 19th cent.), **Būhār** 87 (AH 1314/1896).

Edition: **Lahore** 1301/1884* (author's name given as Aṣghar ʿAlī).

1315. **S. M. Qāsim "Riḍwān"** was the younger son of the Yasawī saint Jamāl al-Dīn Khwājah Dīwānah S. Atāʾī of Khwārazm and Khīwaq (i.e. Khīwah). The latter, a son of S. Pādshāh Khwājah Pardah-pūsh and a descendant of Sulṭān Khwājah Aḥmad Yasawī called Atā,[617] was born shortly before Shāh Ismāʿīl's invasion, i.e. in 916/1510,[618] and died in 1016/1607–8.

Maqāmāt i Saiyid Atāʾī, an account of the life, miracles and teachings of the aforementioned saint, completed on 1 Muḥarram 1036/22 September 1626 on the basis of a work by Ākhund Maulānā Darwīsh Tāshkandī and the *Maqāmāt al-ʿārifīn* of Qāḍī Jān M. b. Qāḍī Khān BJĀRĪ (read Bukhārī ?) and divided into a *muqaddimah*, four *maqāms* and a *khātimah:* **Ethé** 644 (slightly defective at end).

1316. **M. Hāshim** b. M. Qāsim al-Nuʿmānī (?) **al-Badakhshānī**,[619] who mentions his name not in the preface[620] to the *Zubdat al-maqāmāt* but in the second

614 See no. 1259 3rd par. 3rd footnote *supra*.

615 See no. 1259 3rd par. 4th footnote *supra*.

616 See no. 1280 3rd par. (10), with footnote, *supra*.

617 See no. 1295 2nd par., footnote *supra*.

618 Ethé quotes the passages *Chūn ḥaḍrat i īshān chahār māyah* [*sic*, apparently for *chahārmāhah*] *shudand fitnah i Shāh Ismāʿīl wāqiʿ gardīd* (fol. 14b ult.) and *Ḥaḍrat i īshān dar hangām i shīr-khwāragī būdand kih fatarāt i gharībah numūd u bi-sabab i hujūm i Qizil-bāsh u fitnah i Shāh Ismāʿīl kār i akthar i ān-ḥudūd ba-qatl anjāmīd* (fol. 31a, l. 1).

619 M. al-Hāshim [*sic*] b. M. al-Qāsim al-Nuʿmānī al-Badakhshānī in I.O.D.P. 1034 fol. 105b (no other MS. is at present accessible to me). The Cawnpore edition has al-NBGHĀNĪ instead of al-Nuʿmānī, but otherwise agrees with the MS. Al-Nuʿmānī, if correct, refers doubtless to his *pīr*, Mīr M. Nuʿmān.

620 Not at any rate in the preface as given in the Cawnpore edition and the Bānkīpūr MS.

faṣl of the second *maqṣad* (p. 130[14] in the Cawnpore edition), and whom a later author[621] calls **Hāshim Kishmī**,[622] tells us that, although his ancestors were Kubrawīs, he had even in his youth been attracted towards the Naqshbandī order. Having gone to India, he made the acquaintance of Mīr M. Nuʿmān[623] at Burhānpūr and in 1031/1621–2 visited Aḥmad Sirhindī. For nearly two years he was in constant attendance upon the latter. He is evidently identical with the poet "Hāshim", i.e. Khwājah Hāshim b. M. Qāsim, who, as Sprenger ascertained from his *dīwān*, was at Burhānpūr in 1030/1621 and was apparently still alive in 1056/1646. For this *dīwān*, which contains at least two poems in praise of Aḥmad Fārūqī, see Ivanow 747 = Sprenger 250, Ethé 2898, Rehatsek p. 144 no. 67, Madras 64 (?), Āṣafīyah i p. 437 (?).

(1) ***Zubdat al-maqāmāt***, or ***Barakāt al-Aḥmadīyat al-bāqiyah***, an account of the life, miracles and teachings of Sh. Aḥmad Fārūqī Sirhindī,[624] his

621 M. Iḥsān, author of the *Rauḍat al-Qaiyūmīyah*, who in his list of authorities mentions Hāshim Kishmī's *Zubdat al-maqāmāt wa-barakāt al-Aḥmadīyah* (see Ivanow-Curzon p. 87[5]). In S. ʿAlī Bilgrāmī's description of the I.O. MS. D.P. 994(b) (Bilg. 480) the author's name is given as Khwājah Muḥammad Hāshim, probably on the authority of a colophon or a note on the title-page.

622 Evidently from Kishm in Badakhshān, like M. Ṣiddīq Kishmī, who is said to have come from Kishm in Badakhshān (*Zubdat al-maqāmāt* p. 372[10]: *wai az Kishm i Badakhshān-ast*). Kishm, once the chief town of Badakhshān, still exists (see *Ency. Isl.* under Badakhshān) and is marked even on fairly small maps.

623 One of Aḥmad Sirhindī's *khalīfahs*. He was born at Samarqand *circ.* 977/1569–70 (*Zubdat al-maqāmāt* p. 328[5]), though his father, Shams al-Dīn Yaḥyā known as Mīr Buzurg, belonged to Kishm (*op. cit.* p. 327[1])

624 Badr al-Dīn Aḥmad b. ʿAbd al-Aḥad Fārūqī Kābulī Sirhindī Naqshbandī, called Imām i Rabbānī, Maḥbūb i Subḥānī and Mujaddid i Alf i Thānī (i.e. the Renovator of the Second Millennium, in allusion to the tradition *Inna 'llāha yabʿathu li-hādhihi 'l-ummati ʿalā ra'si kulli mi'ati sanatin man yujaddidu lahā dīnahā*, Abū Dāwud, *malāḥim*, 1), was born in, or about, 971/1563–4 at Sirhind (or Sihrind, as it is also spelt) of a family Kābulī in origin but resident in India for many generations. In 1028/1619 he was imprisoned at Gwalior by Jahāngīr, who took exception to the apparent arrogance of some sentences in his *Maktūbāt*, but in the following year he was pardoned and dismissed with a *khilʿat* and a present of 1,000 rupees. In 1032/1623 he received from Jahāngīr a present of 2,000 rupees, and on 29 Ṣafar 1034/11 December 1624 he died at Sirhind. Among his works were (1) *Maktūbāt*, a large collection of letters in three *daftars* (Editions: Delhi 1288/1871*, 1290/1873*, Lucknow 1294/1877°*, Amritsar 1339/1921* (incomplete ?), etc. MSS.: Bānkīpūr xvi 1392–3, Ethé 1891, Ivanow 1268, etc.), (2) *Mabda' u maʿād* (Editions: Cawnpore 1309/1891°, Amritsar 1330/1912*. MSS.: Peshawar 1067(6), Nadhīr Aḥmad 37, Panjāb Univ. (OCM. viii/4 p. 41). Urdu trans.: Lahore [1923*]), (3) *Maʿārif i ladunīyah* (Edition: [Lahore] 1351/1933*. MSS.: Peshawar 1916(5) (?), Panjāb Univ. (OCM. viii/4 p. 41). Urdu trans.: Lahore [1923*]),(4) *Sharḥ i rubāʿīyāt i Sh. M. Bāqī* (MSS.: Peshawar 1067(8), Panjāb Univ. (OCM.

preceptor, Khwājah M. Bāqī,[625] and their children, *khalīfahs* and friends, written at the request of Aḥmad Sirhindī's children and completed in 1037/1627–8: **Bānkīpūr** viii 672 (18th cent. FULL ANALYSIS), **I.O.** D.P. 994*b*, 1034 (much damaged. AH 1150/1737–8).

Editions: **Lucknow** 1885† **Cawnpore** 1890°.

Urdu translation: *Urdū tarjamah i kitāb i Zubdat al-maqāmāt....*, **Lahore** [1909*].

Evidently this author is the M. Hāshim b. Qāsim who wrote-

(2) ***Nasamāt al-quds min Ḥadā'iq al-uns***, a continuation of the *Rashaḥāt i 'ain al-ḥayāt* (see no. 1277 3rd par. *supra*) written in 1031/1622 for Aḥmad Fārūqī Sirhindī and containing biographies of Naqshbandīs from the beginning of the tenth/sixteenth century to the first quarter of the eleventh/seventeenth: **Leningrad** Univ. no. 305 (*Nasamāt fī manāqib al-mashāyikh al-Naqshbandīyah*, by M. H. b. Q. Salemann-Rosen p. 19. Cf. Semenov *Ukazatel'* p. 19, where a reference is given to Validov *Vostochnye rukopisi v Ferganskoi oblasti* (in *Zapiski Vostochn. Otd. Imp. Russ. Arkheol. Obshchestva*, xxii) pp. 306–8).

---

viii/4 p. 41)). See *Gulzār i abrār* no. 537; *Kalimāt al-ṣādiqīn* no. 123; *Tūzuk i Jahāngīrī* pp. 272 penult., 308[7], 370[28], Rogers and Beveridge's trans. ii pp. 91–3, 161, 276; *Safīnat al-auliyā'* pp. 197–8 (no. 376); *Ḥaḍarāt al-quds, daftar* 2; *Manāqib al-haḍarāt* (no. 1320 *infra*); *Rauḍat al-qaiyūmīyah* (no. 1359 *infra*); *Subḥat al-marjān* pp. 47–52; *Khazīnat al-aṣfiyā'* i pp. 607–19; Beale *Oriental biographical dictionary* under Ahmad Sarhindi; Raḥmān 'Alī pp. 10–12; *Maqāmāt i Imām i Rabbānī Mujaddid i Alf i Thānī* (in Urdu), by M. Ḥasan, Lahore [1923*]; *Sīrat i Mujaddid* (in Urdu), by Wilāyat 'Alī Shāh, Lahore, 1928; Ivanow-Curzon p. 85; etc. Accounts of his teachings are *Anwār i Aḥmadīyah* and *Hadīyah i Mujaddidīyah*, by Maulawī Wakīl Aḥmad "'Ājiz" Sikandarpūrī published in one volume at Delhi in 1309–11/1892–4°*, *Kanz al-hidāyat* by M. Bāqir b. Sharaf al-Dīn Lāhaurī (Amritsar 1335/1917*), *Imam-i-Rabbani Mujaddid i Alf i Thani Shaikh Ahmad Sirhindi's Conception of Tawhid*, by B. A. Fārūqī, Lahore, date ? (*Luzac's Oriental List* 1940 p. 148).

625 M. al-Bāqī, or M. Bāqī or M. Bāqī bi'llāh, b. Qāḍī 'Abd al-Salām Uwaisī Naqshbandī was born at Kābul about 971/1563–4 or 972/1564–5 (*Z. al-m.* p. 5 penult.) and died at the age of forty or so in 1012/1603 at Delhi. His influence contributed much to the spread of the Naqshbandī order in India. It has been mentioned in the preceding note that his *rubā'īyāt* are extant with a commentary by his disciple, Aḥmad Sirhindī. A collection of his letters has also been preserved (cf. Rieu iii 1058*b*, Ivanow 1328(5), I.O. D.P. 1058(*b*). Urdu trans.: *Maktūbāt i sharīf i ḥaḍrat i Khwājah Bāqī bi 'llāh Dihlawī*, Lahore 1923*). According to the *Kalimāt al-ṣādiqīn* he wrote a commentary on some *sūrahs* of the *Qur'ān* and a *mathnawī*. The I.O. MS. D.P. 1095 is a copy of his *Kullīyāt*. See *Gulzār i abrār* no. 520; *Kalimāt al-ṣādiqīn* no. 120; *Safīnat al-auliyā'* p. 85 (no. 93); *Ḥaḍarāt al-quds*, at end of *ḥaḍrat* 1; *Riyāḍ al-auliyā'*; *Khazīnat al-aṣfiyā'* i pp. 605–7; Beale *Oriental biographical dictionary* under Muḥammad Bāqī: *Ḥayāt i bāqiyah* (in Urdu), Delhi [1905°].

1317. On 22 Sha'bān 1042/22 February 1633 **Pīr Muḥammad Shaṭṭārī** b. 'Āqil Muḥammad Farkhārī and some friends of his were at the tomb of Saiyid al-Shuhadā' Shāh Ismā'īl Ghāzī 'Arabī and heard the story of the martyr from some of the guardians of the shrines at Kāntā-Duwār and Jalā-Maqām[626] Impressed by the wonderful tale, his friends urged him to put it into writing and in response to their request he wrote the *Risālat al-shuhadā'* in Shāh-Jahān's reign (1037–69/1628–59).

Risālat al-shuhadā', a short (18 pp.) account of Shāh Ismā'īl, a Saiyid said to have gone from Mecca to Bengal in the reign of Bārbak Shāh (864–79/1459–74), for whom he defeated the rebel Rājah of Madāran and conquered Kāmrūp but by whose order he was beheaded on 14 Sha'bān 878/ 4 January 1474:[627] MS. found by G. H. Damant "in the possession of the Faqír in charge of Ismá'íl Ghází's tomb at Káṇṭá Dúár, Rangpúr".

Edition: *Notes on Sháh Ismá'íl Ghází, with* [the Persian text and] *a sketch of the contents of a Persian MS., entitled "Risálat ush-Shuhadá", found at Káṇṭá Dúár, Rangpúr. By G. H. Damant* (in JASB. xliii (1874), pt. 1, pp. 215–39).

1318. **M. b. Jalāl Shāhī Riḍawī** is the author of a Ṣūfī tract entitled *Istiqāmat al-sharī'ah 'alā manhaj al-ḥaqīqah* (Ethé 2916 (1)).

al-As'ilah wa-'l-ajwibah, answers to seventeen questions received in 1042/1632–3 from S. M. Bhuwah concerning important dates in the lives of eminent *shaikhs*: Ethé 2916 (2).

1319. Mīr **'Alī Akbar** Ḥusainī **Ardistānī** dedicated his *Majma' al-auliyā'* to Shāh-Jahān, who reigned from 1037/1628 to 1068/1658.

Majma' al-auliyā', more fully *Maḥfil al-aṣfiyā' wa-majma' al-auliyā'*, or chronogrammatically *Majma' i faiḍ* (= 1043/1633–4, the date of

626 "There are four Dargáhs, or shrines, in Rangpúr, erected to the memory of Sháh Ismá'íl Ghází. They are all situate a few miles to the north-east of G'hoṛág'háṭ, in thánah Pírganj. The principal one is at Káṇṭá Dúár, a place marked in the survey maps at Chatra Hát, and as Katta Doar on Sheet 119 of the Indian Atlas. It is said to have been erected over his body. About three miles west is another at a place called Jalá Maqám.... These two dargáhs are under the care of the same faqīr, who has a large jágír and claims to be a descendant of one of the servants of Ismá'íl, who came with him from Arabia. The head of the saint is said to be buried at Káṇṭá Dúár, and his body at Madáran, in Jahánábád, west of Húglí" (JASB. 1874 p. 215).

627 "The account given in the MS. corresponds most strangely in many particulars with the legend which Mr. Blochmann heard at Húglí (see Asiatic Society's Proceedings, April, 1870, page 117)."

completion), lives of about 1,400 or 1,500 saints in a *muqaddimah* (on Ṣūfī technical terms), twelve *babs* ((1) the first four Caliphs, the Twelve Imāms, the *Ṣaḥābah*, the *Tābiʿīn*, etc., 304 biographies, (2) Ḥasan Baṣrī and 142 of his order, (3) Ibrāhīm b. Adham and 62 of his order, (4) Maʿrūf Karkhī and 73 of his order, (5) Bāyazīd Bisṭāmī and 53 of his order, (6) Junaid Baghdādī and 89 of his order, (7) 162 Naqshbandīs and Turkish *shaikhs*, (8) 65 Qādirīs, (9) 64 Suhrawardīs, Kubrawīs and Chishtīs, (10) 277 Indian saints of Delhi, Gujrāt, etc., (11) 36 saints who were poets, (12) 38 female saints) and a *khātimah* (on the merits of the Prophet's family and the first four Caliphs with some account of al-Khiḍr and Ilyās): **Ethé** 645 (AH 1043/1633, autograph), 646 (apparently a later redaction. *Muqaddimah* and *Bābs* 1–6 only), **Ivanow** 261 (*Bābs* 1–4 only. 18th cent.), **Bukhārā** Semenov 99.

1320. The *Manāqib al-ḥaḍarāt* is one of the authorities cited by M. Iḥsān in his *Rauḍat al-qaiyūmīyah*, where it is described as the work of M. Amīn, a *khalīfah* of Ādam Banūrī (see Ivanow-Curzon p. 87). This information is confirmed and amplified in the *Khazīnat al-aṣfiyāʾ* (I p. 632[9]), where the author is called Ḥājjī **M. Amīn Badakhshī.**

Manāqib al-ḥaḍarāt, or more fully *Manāqib i Ādamīyah u ḥaḍarāt i Aḥmadīyah*, lives of Naqshbandī saints, especially Aḥmad Fārūqī Sirhindī (for whom see no. 1316 (1) 1st footnote *supra*), his sons, M. Saʿīd ʿUmarī[628] and M. Maʿṣūm,[629] his disciple Sh. Ādam Banūrī,[630] and their disciples and contemporaries, in a *muqaddimah*, three *maṭlabs*, eleven *bābs* and a *khātimah:* **Ethé** 652 (defective and disarranged.[631] AH 1139–40/1726–8).

628 His second son, b. Shaʿbān 1005/1597, d. 1070/1659–60. See *Zubdat al-maqāmāt* pp. 308–15, *Khazīnat al-aṣfiyāʾ* I pp. 638–9, Raḥmān ʿAlī 190.

629 His third son, b. 1007/1599 or 1009/1600–1, d. 1070/1659, or 1079/1668–9 or 1080/1669–70. See *Zubdat al-maqāmāt* pp. 315–26, *Khazīnat al-aṣfiyāʾ* I pp. 639–42; Raḥmān ʿAlī p. 212.

630 d. at al-Madīnah in 1053/1643. A collection of his sayings and letters entitled *Natāʾij al-Ḥaramain* is preserved at Peshawar (990B). See *Khazīnat al-aṣfiyāʾ* I pp. 630–5. Banūr, some twenty miles from Sirhind, is now in the State of Patiala.

631 The three *basmalahs* found by Ethé in the MS. (on foll. 1*b*, 40*b* and 189*b*) may be the beginnings of the *Manāqib al-ḥaḍarāt* and of two other works quoted therein. The *Natāʾij al-Ḥaramain* referred to on the margin of the first beginning is, as mentioned in the preceding note, a collection of Ādam Banūrī's sayings and letters. Ethé's suggested identification of M. Murād b. Ḥabīb Allāh b. Saʿdī (mentioned, perhaps as author, on the margin of the third beginning) with the Kashmīrī saint, M. Murād Naqshbandī (d. 1134/1722), is not possible, since the latter's father was M. Ṭāhir (see *Khazīnat al-aṣfiyāʾ* I p. 658).

1321. Sulṭān M. **Dārā-Shukōh**[632] "Qādirī", the eldest son of the Mogul Emperor Shāh-Jahān (1037–68/1628–58) and Mumtāz-Maḥall, was born at Ajmēr in Ṣafar 1024/March 1615. In Shaʿbān 1042/Feb. 1633 he married Nādirah Bēgam, the daughter of his uncle, Sulṭān Parwēz. From 1043/1633, when he received his first *manṣab* (12,000/6,000) and the *sarkār* of Ḥiṣār as his fief, he was rapidly promoted and eventually reached unprecedented rank (60,000/40,000) in the State Service. He was appointed to several governorships (Allahabad in 1055/1645, the Panjāb in 1057/1647, Gujrāt (Gujarat) in 1059/1649, Multān, and Kābul in 1062/1652), but these provinces were administered for him by deputies, and Lahore was the only provincial capital to which he ever paid a visit of any length. In 1063/1653 he was in command at the unsuccessful siege of Qandahār, which forms the subject of Rashīd Khān's *Laṭāʾif al-akhbār* (see no. 733 *supra*). Although he had been recognized by Shāh-Jahān as heir to the throne, his claim was disputed in 1067/1657, when Shāh-Jahān fell ill, by his younger brothers, Shāh-Shujāʿ, Aurangzēb and Murād-Bakhsh. He was twice defeated in battle by Aurangzēb, first at Samūgaṛh, near Āgrah, in Ramaḍān 1068/June 1658 and then at Ajmēr in Jumādā II 1069/March 1659. On 26 Dhū 'l-Ḥijjah 1069/14 September 1659 he was executed at Delhi by order of Aurangzēb, who had obtained from the *ʿulamāʾ a fatwā* declaring him to be a *kāfir*.

Dārā-Shukōh and his sister Jahān-ārā were, according to the latter (see OCM. xiii/4 p. 16[16–17]), the first of Tīmūr's line to set their feet upon the path of *Khudā-ṭalabī* and *Ḥaqq-jūʾī*. Dārā-Shukōh himself says (*Sakīnat al-auliyāʾ*, Urdu trans. p. 5[3]) that *darwīshes* had always fascinated him and that much of his time had been spent in seeking them out. Then on the 10th,[633] or the 29th,[634] of Dhū 'l-Ḥijjah 1049, at the age of twenty-five, he had been admitted to the society of a saint (*ēk dōst i Khudā*[635] *kī ṣuḥbat mēn phunchā*) and had been treated by him with great kindness.[636] That which others used to obtain after a month he had

632 The words Dārā and Shukōh in this name form a compound idea ("Majestic as Dārā," the ancient Persian king), and the second element is not, strictly speaking, separable from the first, but Manucci, Bernier and other Europeans speak of "Prince Dara". Contemporary Indians may possibly have done the same in conversation.

633 So Bānkīpūr viii p. 49.

634 So Urdu trans. p. 5[11].

635 So in the Urdu translation, but apparently not in the Persian original, since Rieu speaks of an "eminent master" and ʿAbd al-Muqtadir of the "great master".

636 The unnamed saint was of course Mullā Shāh. Rieu interprets Dārā-Shukōh's statements in this place as meaning that "he had received the initiation to the Ḳādirī order in AH 1049", but this is not expressly stated in the text (at any rate not in the Urdu translation). His admission to the Qādirī order seems to have occurred before this month with Mullā Shāh, since in the *Safīnat al-auliyāʾ* completed in Ramadān 1049 he already describes himself as M. Dārā-Shukōh Ḥanafī Qādirī. According to his sister (*Ṣāḥibīyah*, Urdu trans. in OCM.

obtained on the first night, and in a month that for which others needed a year. He had reached immediately and without austerities an aim usually attained only through years of severe discipline (*sālhā-sāl kē mujāhadoṅ aur riyāḍatōṅ sē*). Of Dārā-S͟hukōh's works the best known by far is the *Safīnat al-auliyāʾ* completed in 1049/1640, which may be described as a standard work of reference. Somewhat similar in content, but of narrower scope and much less known is the *Sakīnat al-auliyāʾ* completed in 1052/1642–3. The *Risālah i Ḥaqq-numā*, written in 1055/1645, is a small Ṣūfī tract.[637] The *Ḥasanāt al-ʿārifīn*, composed in 1062/1652 is an annotated collection of ecstatic or paradoxical utterances (*s͟haṭaḥāt* or *s͟haṭḥīyāt*[638]) ascribed to various mystics.[639] A work entitled *Rumūz i taṣawwuf*, which is described by Arberry as a catechism of Ṣūfī doctrine, was published with an Urdu translation at Lahore in [1923*]. Whether this is a genuine work of Dārā-S͟hukōh's and whether it contains a date are matters for investigation. The works of Dārā-S͟hukōh's last years are a remarkable series resulting from an interest in Hindu mystīcīsm and a desire to reconcile Hinduism and Islām. Apparently the earliest literary outcome of this interest was not actually a work of his but a record of some seventy questions posed by him to the Hindu ascetic Bābā Lāl[640] and the answers given by the

xiii/4 p. 14[17]) he was a *murīd* of Miyāṅ Mīr (*Mērē bhāʾī ḥaḍrat Miyāṅ-jīw sē nisbat i irādat rak'htē haiṅ*). In the *Safīnat al-auliyāʾ* he says only that he had visited Miyāṅ Mīr twice (p. 72[12]: *īn faqīr dū bār ba-mulāzamat i īs͟hān rasīdah*) and that one of these occasions was when at the age of twenty he was taken to the saint by S͟hāh-Jahān and through his intercession was cured of an illness which had baffled the physicians.

637 Editions: Lucknow 1881°, 1883†, 1888†. English translation: *The Compass of Truth; or, Risala-i-Haqnuma. By Muhammad Dara Shikoh ... Rendered into English by Rai Bahadur Śriśa Chandra Vasu*, Allahabad 1912°*. MSS.: Āṣafīyah i p. 416, Bānkīpūr xvi 1398, Ivanow Curzon 444 ii, 462 xix, Lahore Panjāb Univ. (*OCM*. VIII/4 p. 40). Description: Qanungo i pp. 141–3

638 Cf. Dozy and *Ency. Isl.* under S͟haṭḥ.

639 Edition: Delhi 1309/1892°. MSS.: ʿAlīgaṛh Subḥ MSS. p. 18, Āṣafīyah i p. 414 nos. 553, 685, 875, Berlin 1022, Būhār 179, Ivanow 1270, Ivanow Curzon 441 i, Lahore Panjāb Univ. (*OCM*. VIII/4 p. 42), Princeton 111, 130 (4). Urdu translation: Lahore [1921*]. Description: Qanungo i pp. 154–8.

640 Bābā Lāl (spelt also Laʿl), or Lāl Dās, or Lāl Dayāl, as he is variously called in different MSS., is said by Huart and Massignon (p. 287) on the authority of the Urdu translation of the *S͟haṭaḥāt*, i.e. the *Ḥasanāt al-ʿārifīn*, (p. 44) to have been a Kabīr-pant'hī. Qanungo (I p. 336) doubts whether he was "a Kabirpanthi out and out". For information concerning him see H. H. Wilson's article, *Sketch of the religious sects of the Hindus*, in *Asiatic Researches* xvii (Calcutta 1832) pp. 294–8, Garcin de Tassy (mainly dependent on Wilson) i pp. 273–4, Qanungo i pp. 332–3, Garcin de Tassy *Mémoire sur les particularités de la religion musulmane dans l'Inde*, 2nd ed., Paris 1869, pp. 100–1 and Sujān Rāy *K͟hulāṣat al-tawārīk͟h* pp. 68–9 (under D'hyānpūr).

The text of these questions and answers translated from the "Hinduwī" by C͟handarbhān "Barahman" (cf. no. 730 2nd par., end *supra*) and headed in the MSS. by

latter.[641] In 1065/1654–5 he completed the *Majmaʿ al-baḥrain,*[642] in the preface[643] to which he says that in his intercourse with Hindu *faqīrs* he had ascertained that their divergence from the Ṣūfīs was merely verbal and that he had written the work with the object of reconciling the two systems. In 1067/1657 was completed at Delhi after six months' labour the *Sirr i akbar* or *Sirr al-asrār*, a translation of 50[644] or 52[645] Upanishads undertaken by Dārā-Shukōh with the help of some pandits of Benares.[646] These works were congenial to him

---

various titles or quasi-titles, such as *Suʾāl n jawāb i Dārā-Shukōh u Bābā Lāl, Jawāb u suʾāl i Bābā Laʿl-Dās u Dārā-Shukoh, Nādir al-nikāt*, etc., has been published with a French translation by Cl. Huart and L. Massignon under the title *Les entretiens de Lahore* [*entre le prince impérial Dârâ Shikûh et l'ascète hindou Baba Laʿl Das*] in the *Journal asiatique*, tome CCIX (July–Dec. 1926) pp. 285–334. An edition (undated ?) is mentioned in the Āṣafīyah catalogue, i p. 444. For MSS., which show some differences of recension and some of which are only abstracts, see ʿAlīgaṛh Subḥ. MSS. p. 14, Āṣafīyah i p. 444, Bānkīpūr xvi 1454, Bānkīpūr Suppt. ii 2267, Berlin 1081(2), Bodleian 1241(14), 1821, Brelvi-Dhabhar p. 73 no. 3, Browne Suppt. 776 (King's 14[1]), Rieu ii 841*b*, iii 1034*a*. According to Garcin de Tassy, i p. 274, there is an Urdu translation entitled *Risālah i aswilah u ajwibah i Dārā-Shukōh u Bābā Lāl*. An English translation of some extracts is given by Qanungo (i pp. 337–47).

641 An indication of date is provided by the opening words quoted by Massignon (*op. cit.* p. 333) from a MS. acquired by W. Ivanow in 1926. According to Massignon they run as follows: *Suʾālāt i Dārā-Shukōh i shāh-zādah jawāb i Gōsāʾīṅ* [*sic lege*] *Bābā Lāl sākin i* KYTL [read *Kait'hal* ?] *MḤRĀN* [read *Muḥarrirān*?] *Ray Chandarbhān i Barahman munshī i shāh-zādah sih sih* [dittographed ?] *rūz dū* [read *dar* ?] *majlis shudah u sābiq Rāy Jādau Dās dar bayāḍ i khāṣṣ nawishtah būdand dar* NYWLĀ [read certainly *dar-īn-wilā*] *baʿd i fatḥ i Qandahār bāz ittifāq uftād.*

642 Edition with English translation: *Majmaʿ-ul-baḥrain; or, The mingling of the two oceans ... Edited ... with English translation, notes and variants by M. Mahfuz-ul-Haq*, Calcutta 1929* (Bibliotheca Indica). MSS.: Āṣafīyah i p. 472, Aumer 351 (1), Bānkīpūr xvi 1452, Bodleian 1241 (13), 1820–1, Brelvi-Dhabhar p. x no. 9, Eton 36, Ivanow Curzon 681, Rieu ii 828*a*, 841*b*. Description: Qanungo pp. 143–6. Arabic translation: *Tarjamah i Majmaʿ al-baḥrain* written before 1185/1771 by M. Ṣāliḥ b. al-Shaikh Aḥmad al-Miṣrī: Būhār Arab. Cat. 133.

643 This preface occurs in one of the two B.M. MSS.

644 So Rieu.

645 So Qanungo i p. 147, Ivanow-Curzon 678.

646 MSS.: Āṣafīyah ii p. 1540 nos. 1, 2, 52, Bānkīpūr xvi 1453, Bānkīpūr Suppt. ii 2083, Berlin 1077(2), Blochet I 216–17, Bodleian 1329–31, Būhār 107, Ethé 1976–82, Ivanow 1708, 1714(4), Ivanow-Curzon 678–9, Ivanow 2nd Suppt. 1093, Lindesiana p. 131 no. 340, Princeton 145, Rieu i 54–55*a*, ii 841*b*. Edition: *Sirr i akbar*, Benares 1909* (Pt. 1 (15 Upanishads) only. Ed. Brij Mōhan Lāl). Latin translation: *Oupnek'hat* (*id est, Secretum Tegendum*): *opus ipsa in India rarissimum, ... ad verbum, e persico idiomate, samskreticis vocabulis intermixto, in latinum conversum ...: studio et opera Anquetil Duperron*, Strasbourg 1801–2°*. German translation: *Das Oupnek'hat ... Aus der sanskrit-persischen Uebersetzung des Fürsten Mohammed Daraschekoh in das Lateinische von Anquetil Duperron, in das Deutsche übertragen von F. Mischel*, Dresden 1882°. Descriptions: (1) *The unpublished translation of the Upanishads by Prince Dara Shukoh*, by Mahesh Das (in *Dr. Modi Memorial Volume*, Bombay 1930, pp. 622–38), (2) Qanungo i pp. 147–54.

because "although he had perused the Pentateuch, the Gospels, the Psalms, and other sacred books, he had nowhere found the doctrine of Tauḥīd, or Pantheism, explicitly taught, but in the Beds (Vedas) and more especially in the Upnikhats (Upanishads), which contain their essence".[647] Another work, the *Ṭarīqat al-ḥaqīqah*, described by Edwards as a tract in prose and verse on the Vēdānta philosophy, was published at Gūjrānwālah in [1895°*]. An Urdu translation by Aḥmad ʿAlī Batālawī appeared at Lahore in [1923*]. A translation of the *Yōgavāsishṭ'ha* (*Tarjamah i Jōg Bās͟his͟ht*) made in 1066/1655–6 (by a certain Ḥabīb Allāh according to Ethé 2927) under the auspices of Dārā-S͟hukōh is preserved in several MSS.[648] There is also a translation of the *Bhagavad-gītā*, called in some MSS. by the title *Āb i zindagī*,[649] which is ascribed on very doubtful authority[650] to Dārā-S͟hukōh. According to Qanungo (i p. 139) the *Gulzār i ḥāl*, Walī Rām's translation of the *Prabōd'ha-c͟handrōdaya* (see no. 620 1st par. *supra*), was written "for the use of Dara Shukoh". No authority is cited for this statement. In any case the *Gulzār i ḥāl* was not completed until 1073/1662–3, i.e. more than three years after Dārā-S͟hukōh's death.

Dārā-S͟hukōh wrote poetry in which he used the *tak͟hallus̤* "Qādirī". His *dīwān* is mentioned by "Sark͟hwus͟h", who describes it as short, and also by Kis͟han C͟hand "Ik͟hlāṣ". G͟hulām-Sarwar Lāhaurī had seen a copy of it (*K͟hazīnat al-aṣfiyā'* i p. 174[15]), but it is now extremely rare.[651] Finally it may be noted that Dārā-S͟hukōh was a calligraphist. Two pages from an autograph MS. of his *Safīnat al-auliyā'* are reproduced in *OCM*. x/3, where they face p. 114, and other specimens of his writing are in existence.[652]

(1) ***Safīnat al-auliyā'***, completed on 27 Ramaḍān 1049/21 Jan. 1640 and devoted to short notices[653] of holy men, namely the Prophet (p. 17), the

647 Rieu i p. 54, from Dārā-S͟hukōh's preface.

648 Bānkīpūr Suppt, ii 2080, Berlin 1077(1), Browne Pers. Cat. 35(2), Ethé 1972–4, 2927, Ross-Browne 194, Ivanow 1700, Ivanow-Curzon 680. Cf. Qanungo i pp. 159–60.

649 Ethé 1949, Ivanow 1707, Rieu i 59*a*.

650 To quote Ethé's words "In the British Mus. copy it is wrongly ascribed to Abû-alfaḍl; the real translator was, as a note on fol. 1*a* in the present copy proves [!], prince Dârâ Shukûh".

651 The only copy traceable at present belongs to the private library of K͟hān Bahādur Maulawī Ẓafar Ḥasan, Superintendent, Archæological Survey, Northern Circle, Āgrah, who has published a description of it under the title *Manuscript copy of the Dīwān of Dārā Shikūh* in the *JRASB*., Letters, Vol. V, 1939, pp. 155–73. The statement of Massignon (*Textes inédits* i p. 256) that "Le dîwân de Dârâ Shikouh est à Londres (MS. Or. 9492)" is incorrect. The B.M. MS. Or. 9492 is the *dīwān* of "Dārā", a poet of Fatḥ-ʿAlī S͟hāh's time. Dārā-S͟hukōh's *tak͟hallus̤* was not "Dārā", but "Qādirī".

652 On p. 172 of the article referred to in the preceding note Ẓafar Ḥasan speaks of "the specimens of his writing, still available". Cf. no. 1321 (1), MSS., **Lahore** *infra*.

653 Particularly valuable on account of "a comparative strictness in the chronological order and the full dates they give" (Ethé).

first three Caliphs (p. 19), the Twelve Imāms (p. 22), Salmān Fārisī (p. 30), Uwais Qaranī (p. 30), Ḥasan Baṣrī (p. 31), Qāsim b. M. b. Abī Bakr (p. 31), the four Imāms (Abū Ḥanīfah, etc., p. 32), Abū Yūsuf (p. 34), M. S̲h̲aibānī (p. 34), *shaik̲h̲s* of the QĀDIRĪ (previously Junaidī) order[654] (pp. 35–73, nos. 27–65[655]) from Maʻrūf Kark̲h̲ī (d. 200/815) to Miyān Mīr (d. 1045/1635), K̲h̲wājahs, i.e. NAQSHBANDĪS (previously Ṭaifūrīs) (pp. 73–85, nos. 66–94) from Abū Yazīd Bisṭāmī (d. 261/875) to Ṣāliḥ K̲h̲wājah Dahbīdī (d. 1048/1638 at Balk̲h̲), CHISHTĪS (pp. 86–102, nos. 95–119) from K̲h̲wājah ʻAbd al-Wāḥid [b.] Zaid (d. 177/793) to S̲h̲. Jalāl T'hānēsarī (d. 989/1582. Cf. no. 25 *supra*), KUBRAWĪS (pp. 102–9, nos. 120–39) from Abū Bakr Nassāj to Sulṭān Walad (d. 712/1312), SUHRAWARDĪS (pp. 110–19, nos. 140–59) from Mims̲h̲ād Dīnawarī (d. 299/911–12) to S̲h̲āh-ʻĀlam (d. 880/1475 at Aḥmadābād[656]), miscellaneous *shaik̲h̲s* (*mashāyikh i mutafarriqah*, pp. 119–99, nos. 160–377) from Mālik [b.] Dīnār (d. 137/754–5) to S̲h̲. Bilāwal Lāhaurī (d. 1046/1637), and holy women (pp. 199–216, nos. 378–411), i.e. the wives and daughters of the Prophet and some female saints from Zā'idah, ʻUmar's slave-girl, to Bībī Jamāl K̲h̲ātūn, Miyān Mīr's sister, who was still alive in 1049 at the time of writing:[657] **Lahore** private library of Dīwān Anand Kumār, Reader in Biology in the Panjāb University (an autograph described by M. S̲h̲afīʻ in *OCM*. x/3 (May 1934) pp. 109–15), **Bānkīpūr** viii 673 (revised and corrected by the author), 674 (AH 1108/1697), **Lindesiana** p. 131 no. 164 (AH 1063/1652–3), no. 193 (AD 1701), **Rieu** i 356*b* (17th cent.), iii 976*b* (extracts only. *Circ.* AD 1850), **Blochet** i 432 (17th cent.), **Ethé** 647 (17th cent.), 648 (AH 1120/1709), 649 (AH 1179/1765), **Ross and Browne** 124 (AH 1151/1738–9), **I.O.** D.P. 666 (AH 1151/1739), **Āṣafīyah** i p. 320 no. 24 (4th yr. of Farruk̲h̲-siyar /1127–8/1715–16), no. 101 (AH 1113/1701–2), iii p. 164 no. 118, **Ivanow** 262 (AH 1137/1724–5 ?), **Rehatsek** p. 203 no. 54 (AH 1143/1730–1), **Lahore** Panjab Univ. Lib. (2 copies dated AH 1153/1740 and Samwat 1896), **Berlin** 17 (1), 576 (3).

List and epitome of the biographies: Ethé coll. 274–315.

---

[654] At the end of the notice of S̲h̲āh Madār (no. 358, p. 188 = *OCM*. x/3 p. 115) the author says that of the people of India [i.e. presumably of those who belonged to Ṣūfī orders] half, mostly from the upper classes (*ashrāf*), were followers (*murīd*) of ʻAbd al-Qādir, a quarter, mostly from the lower classes (*ajlāf*), followed S̲h̲āh Madār (see no. 1329 (6), 2nd footnote *infra*), an eighth followed Muʻīn al-Dīn Chishtī (see no. 1259, 2nd par., 3rd footnote *supra*) and an eighth Bahā' al-Dīn Zakarīyā' (see no. 1280, 3rd par., (3) footnote *supra*).

[655] These are the numbers assigned to the notices in Ethé's description of the I.O. MS. Ethé 647. In the Nawal Kis̲h̲ōr editions the notices are not numbered.

[656] Cf. *Mir'āt i Aḥmadī, k̲h̲ātimah* pp. 37–8, English trans. pp. 35–6.

[657] She died in 1057 (see no. 1321 (2), 4th footnote *infra*).

Editions: **Āgrah** 1269/1853*, **Lucknow** 1872°, **Cawnpore** 1884†‡, 1318/1900°.

(2) ***Sakīnat al-auliyā'***, an account of the great saint of Lahore, Miyāṅ, or Mīyāṅ[658] Mīr[659] and some of his disciples, especially Mullā Shāh,[660] completed in 1052/1642–3:[661] **Bānkīpūr** viii 675 (18th cent.), **Ivanow** Curzon 73 (18th cent.), **Rieu** i 357 (AH 1276/1859). Urdū translation:[662] *Urdū tarjamah i kitāb i Sakīnat al-auliyā'*, **Lahore** [*circ.* 1920 ?‡].

[Autobiographical statements (relating mainly to meetings with Ṣūfīs and visits to graves) in the *Safīnat al-auliyā'* (collected by M. Shafī' in OCM. x/3 pp. 110–15) and the *Sakīnat al-auliyā'*; other autobiographical statements in the preface

---

658 This Hindī word, meaning "lord" or "master", is a title of respect and not a part of the saint's name.

659 Miyāṅ Mīr, or Shāh Mīr, whose real name was Mīr Muḥammad (*Sakīnat al-auliyā'*, Urdu trans., p. 19, *'Amal i Ṣāliḥ* iii p. 363 ult.), or Muḥammad Mīr (*Khazīnat al-aṣfiyā'* i p. 154[4]: *Shaikh M. Mīr al-mashhūr bi-Miyān-Mīr Bālā Pīr Qādirī Lāhaurī*), was a Fārūqī (not a Saiyid apparently) and was born at Sīwistān (i.e. Sehwan, in Sind) in 938/1531–2 (*Sakīnah*, Urdu trans., p. 19 ult.), or 957/1550 (*Safīnah* p. 70[10]), or 975/1567–8 (*Sakīnah*, Urdu trans., p. 75 ult.). He settled in Lahore (at the age of twenty-five according to *Khazīnah*. i p. 154[14]) and had been living there for more than sixty years when he died on the 7th (*Safīnah* p. 72[19]), or the 17th (*Sakīnah*, Urdu trans., p. 74 ult.) of Rabī' I 1045/21st or 31st August, 1635 (so both *Safīnah* and *Sakīnah*) or in 1044/1634–5 (*Pādshāh-nāmah* i, 2, p. 331[1], *'Amal i Ṣāliḥ* iii p. 366[10]). His tomb to the east of Lahore at the place now called Miyāṅ Mīr is close to the military cantonment. The *jī* or *jīw* sometimes appended to the word Miyāṅ is a Hindī affix indicative of respect. See *Tūzuk i Jahāngīrī* p. 286 antepenult., Rogers and Beveridge's trans. ii p. 119; *Safīnat al-auliyā'* pp. 70–3 (no. 65); *Pādshāh-nāmah* i, 2, pp. 329–31; *'Amal i Ṣāliḥ* iii pp. 363–6; *Khazīnat al-aṣfiyā'* i pp. 154–60; Rieu i p. 358*a*; Beale *Oriental biographical dictionary* under Shāh Mīr (the *Ḍiyā' al-'uyūn*, however, is by Shāh Mīrzā (for whom see no. 93 *supra*), not Shāh Mīr); *Ency. Isl.* under Mīrāndjī (*sic* ?) (Hidayet Hosain).

660 See no. 1332 3rd par. footnote *infra*.

661 This date occurs at the end of the preface (Urdu trans. p. 6[10]). At the beginning of the account of Bībī Jamāl Khātūn, the saint's sister, (Urdu trans. p. 101[4]) 1050 is mentioned as the current year. Two or three dates are later insertions. Thus the notice of Sh. 'Abd al-Wāḥid, which speaks of him in the present tense, ends with a statement that he died in 1056 (Urdu trans. p. 170[12]). Similarly Bībī Jamāl Khātūn, who is described as "now, in 1050, alive and well" (Urdu trans. p. 101[4]), is said to have died on Tuesday, 27 Rabī' I 1057 "after the writing of this book" (Urdu trans. p. 102 penult.). A reference to the *Safīnat al-auliyā'* occurs in the chapter headed *Bayān i faḍīlat i silsilah i Qādirīyah* (Urdu trans. p. 12[6]). Curiously enough the *Safīnat al-auliyā'* contains a reference (inserted either subsequently or in anticipation of a future event) to the *Sakīnat al-auliyā'*. It comes near the end of the notice of Miyāṅ Mīr and in the autograph described by M. Shafī' it runs as follows: *Chūn ba'd az-īn risāla'ī dar bayān i aḥwāl u auḍā' i ān-ḥaḍrat u pīr u murīdān i īshān nawishtah shud dar-īn kitāb ba-hamīn qadr iktifā numūd* (OCM x/3 p. 111[11]). In the Nawal Kishōr text (p. 72[17]) *pīsh az-īn* takes the place of *ba'd az-īn*, and *risāla'ī* is expanded into *risāla'ī musammā ba-Sakīnat al-auliyā*.

662 I have failed to trace an edition of the Persian text.

to the *Sirr i akbar*; Manucci *Storia do Mogor*, tr. W. Irvine, i pp. 221–7, etc.; the travels of Bernier, Tavernier, etc.; contemporary and later histories of India; *Kalimāt al-shuʿarā'* (Sprenger p. 113); *Hamīshah bahār* (Sprenger p. 128); *Ṣuḥuf i Ibrāhīm*; *Makhzan al-gharā'ib* no. 2083; *Tadhkirah i khwush-nawīsān* p. 54; *Riyāḍ al-ʿārifīn* pp. 208–9; *Khazīnat ai-aṣfiyā'* i pp. 174–5; Elliot and Dowson *History of India* vii pp. 220–32, 236–41, 242–6 (extracts from the *Muntakhab al-lubāb*); *Facsimiles of several Autographs of Jahángír, Sháhjahán, and Prince Dárá Shikoh, together with Notes on the Literary Character and the Capture and Death of Dárá Shikoh. -By H. Blochmann* (in JASB. xxxix, pt. 1 (1870) pp. 271–9); Beale *Oriental biographical dictionary* under Dárá Shikoh; *Ency. Isl.* under Dārā Shikōh (H. Beveridge); *Dārā Shikoh as an author*, by Pandit Sheo Narain (in *Journal of the Panjab Historical Society*, ii (1913–14) pp. 21–38); *Court painters of the Grand Moguls*, by L. Binyon and T. W. Arnold, London 1921, pp. 25–29 and plates xx–xxii; *Un essai de bloc islamo-hindou au XVIIe siècle: l'humanisme mystique du prince Dârâ*, by L. Massignon and A. M. Kassim (in *Revue du monde musulman* lxiii (1926) pp. 1–14); *L'Inde mystique au moyen âge*, by Yūsuf Ḥusain, Paris 1929, last chapter; *Dara Shukoh. Vol I. Biography.* [By] *Kalika-Ranjan Qanungo*, Calcutta [1935]. For portraits of Dārā-Shukōh see *Indische historische Porträts* by H. Goetz (in *Asia Major* ii (1925)) p. 238; *Court painters of the Grand Moguls* by Binyon and Arnold, plates xx-xxii; Rieu ii 780*b*, 781*b*, 785*b*; Ethé 1980 (?); etc.]

1322. **Jahān-ārā** Bēgam, sometimes called simply Begam Ṣāḥib[663] or Bēgam Ṣāḥibah[664] by contemporary historians, was the second child of Shāh-Jahān and Mumtāz-Maḥall. She was born on 21 Ṣafar 1023/23 March 1614, almost exactly a year before her eldest brother, Dārā-Shukōh (for whom see no. 1321 *supra*). Devoted to her father, whom she attended in his captivity, and also to Dārā-Shukōh, she shared the latter's interest in Ṣūfism, and was initiated into the Qādirī order by his *pīr*, Mullā Shāh,[665] early in 1050/1650, when she and her father were on a visit to Kashmīr (OCM. xiii/4 (Aug. 1937) pp. 14–15). "Shāh's" opinion of her ("She has attained to so extraordinary a development of mystical knowledge that she is worthy of being my representative") and her description of one of her own mystical experiences are quoted (from the *Nuskhah i aḥwāl i Shāhī*) by Macdonald in *The religious attitude and life in Islam*, p. 205,[666]

663 e.g. *Pādshāh-nāmah* i, 1, p. 178^4,^7, *ʿAmal i Ṣāliḥ* i p. 80^13.

664 Cf. *Ma'āthir al-umarā'* i p. 10^4.

665 See no. 28 *supra*, no. 1332 3rd par., footnote *infra*, and Additions and Corrections.

666 As Qanungo points out, Macdonald (or rather von Kremer, since the former is only quoting the latter) calls her Fāṭimah through a misunderstanding of the complimentary title Fāṭimat al-Zamānī.

and thence by Qanungo in *Dara Shukoh*, i pp. 351–2. In spite of her Qādirī connections she had a fondness for the Chishtī order:[667] in the preface to the *Muʾnis al-arwāḥ* she calls herself a votary (*murīdah*) of Muʿīn al-Dīn Chishtī and on her tomb she is described as a disciple of the saints of Chisht. She died unmarried in Ramaḍān 1092/1681 and was buried at Delhi in a tomb built by herself,[668] and still standing, to the south of the tomb of Niẓām al-Dīn Auliyā (for whom see no. 1259 4th footnote *supra*). "The events of Jahánárá's life, such as they are, have suffered on the one hand from sentiment which adorns her 'with every virtue that a woman possesses'; and on the other by the court-tattle of Bernier which I need not repeat here."[669]

(1) ***Muʾnis al-arwāḥ***, a biography of Muʿīn al-Dīn Chishtī.[670] with notices of some of his disciples, completed in 1049/1640: **Brit. Mus.** (a MS. presented by W. Irvine, who believed it to be an autograph),[671] **Rieu** i 357*b* (17th cent.), 357*a* (18th cent.), **Āṣafīyah** i p. 492 no. 770 (AH 1198/1783–4), no. 237 (AH 1320/1902–3), **Ivanow** Curzon 74 (18th cent.), **Bodleian** 372, **Eton** 38, **Lahore** Panjāb Univ. (see *OCM*. III/1 (Nov. 1926) p. 73).

Urdu translation:[672] **Lahore** [1908*].

(2) ***Ṣāḥibīyah***, an account of Mullā Shāh (see no. 1332 3rd par., footnote *infra*) written (completed ?) on 27 Ramaḍān 1051/30 December 1641: **Aḥmadābād** Āpā-Rāō Bhōlā-Nāt'h Library (19 foll.).

Description and Urdu summary: *Jahān-ārā Bēgam kī ēk ghair-maʿrūf taṣnīf: Ṣāḥibīyah*, by M. Ibrāhīm (in *OCM*. xiii/4 (Aug. 1937) pp. 3–19).

[Autobiographical statements (relating almost entirely to the years 1049–50 and especially to her connexions with Mullā Shāh) at the end of the *Ṣāḥibīyah; Pādshāh-nāmah* i, 1, p. 94 and elsewhere; *ʿAmal i Ṣāliḥ* i p. 80 and elsewhere; *Maʾāthir i ʿĀlamgīrī* p. 213; N. Manucci *Storia do Mogor*, tr. W. Irvine, vol. i, London 1907, p. 217 (see also index); Carr Stephen *The archaeology and monumental remains of Delhi*, Ludhiana and Calcutta [1876] pp. 108–9; Rieu i

667 Doubtless because Muʿīn al-Dīn Chishtī was (to quote Qanungo *Dara Shukoh* p. 104) " the patron saint of the house of Akbar".

668 For this tomb see S. Aḥmad Khān *Āthār al-ṣanādīd* (in Urdu), Delhi 1853, *Bāb* 3, p. 73; *The Indian antiquary* ii p. 120; Carr Stephen *The archæology ... of Delhi* p. 108; etc.

669 Carr Stephen *loc. cit.* For Peter Mundy's accusation against her see *The Indian antiquary* xliv pp. 24, 211.

670 For whom see no. 1259 2nd par. 3rd footnote *supra*.

671 See Manucci *Storia do Mogor*, tr. W. Irvine, iv p. 423. According to M. Ibrāhīm (*OCM*. xiii/4 (Aug., 1937) p. 3 footnote) there is an autograph MS. of this work in the Lucknow [Public ?] Library.

672 I have failed to trace an edition of the Persian text, although according to Ivanow the work "has been repeatedly lithographed in India, in the original Persian and in Hindustani translations".

357; Beale *Oriental biographical dictionary*, 2nd ed., under Jahan Ara Begam; *Jahān-ārā* (in Urdu), by Maḥbūb al-Raḥmān "Kalīm", 'Alīgaṛh 1907* and 2nd ed. [1918*]; *Persian letters from Jahān Arā, daughter of Shāh Jahān, ... to Raja Budh Parkash of Sirmur*, by H. A. Rose (in *JASB*. 1911 pp. 449–78); *Ency. Isl.* under Djahānārā Bēgam (H. Beveridge); *Jahānārā*, by G. Yazdani (in *Journal of the Panjab Historical Society* ii/2 (Calcutta 1914) pp. 152–69, where many references are given); K. R. Qanungo *Dara Shukoh*, vol. i, biography, Calcutta [1935], p. 10 and elsewhere; the afore-mentioned article by M. Ibrāhīm].

1323. Shaikh **Badr al-Dīn** b. Ibrāhīm **Sirhindī** became a disciple of the great saint Aḥmad Sirhindī (for whom see no. 1316 (1), 1st footnote *supra*) in 1018/1609–10, remained in close association with him for seventeen years, and was present when he was washed after death. Among works of his own that he mentions are (1) *Wiṣāl i Aḥmadī*, on some miracles which occurred just before and after the saint's death, (2) *Karāmāt al-auliyā'*, in support of the belief that saints can perform miracles after death, (3) *Majma' al-auliyā'*,[673] biographies of 1,500 saints completed in 1044/1634–5, (4) a Persian translation of the *Futūḥ al-ghaib* of 'Abd al-Qādir al-Jīlānī, (5) *Maqāmāt i Ghauth al-thaqalain*, a Persian translation of the *Bahjat al-asrār*, a life of 'Abd al-Qādir by 'Alī b. Yūsuf al-Shaṭṭanūfī (see no. 1251 *supra*), (6) a Persian translation of another life of 'Abd al-Qādir entitled *Rauḍat al-nawāẓir*, i.e. presumably the *Rauḍat al-nāẓir*, which Ḥ. Kh. ascribes to al-Fīrūzābādī (see Ahlwardt 10080–1, Brockelmann ii, p. 119, l. 2), (7) an unfinished Persian translation of the *'Arā'is al-bayān fī ḥaqā'iq al-Qur'ān*, a Ṣūfī *tafsīr* by Rūzbihān al-Baqlī (for which see Brockelmann i 414, *Sptbd.* i 735; *Catalogue of the Arabic MSS. in the Library of the India Office*, vol. ii, no. 1106). The last three were undertaken at the request of Sulṭān M. Dārā-Shukōh.

(1) ***Sanawāt al-atqiyā'***, very brief biographies of distinguished persons, with special reference to the dates of their death, from the time of Adam to 1044/1634–5: **I.O.** D.P. 672 (AH 1085/1674).

(2) ***Ḥaḍarāt al-quds***, biographies of Naqshbandī saints in two *daftars*, of which the first in one *ḥaḍrat* begins with Abū Bakr al-Ṣiddīq and ends with M. Bāqī (for whom see no. 1316 (1) footnote *supra*) and the second deals in *Ḥaḍarāt* ii-xii with Aḥmad Sirhindī, his life, sayings, miracles, children and disciples, completed not earlier than 1053/1643, since Ādam Banūrī's death, which occurred in that year (cf. no. 1320 2nd par. 3rd footnote *supra*), is mentioned: **I.O.** D.P. 630 (*Daftar* ii only. 17th cent.), **Tashkent Univ.** 70 (*Daftar* ii. AH 1248/1832), 70-*a* (*Daftar* ii apparently. AH 1257/1841).
Urdu translation: by Khwājah Aḥmad Ḥusain Khān, **Lahore** 1923*].

673 For a work of this title containing about the same number of biographies and completed in 1043/1633–4 by Mīr 'Alī Akbar Ḥusainī Ardistānī see no. 1319 *supra*.

1324. Probably soon after 1054/1644–5, the latest date mentioned in the work, an anonymous disciple wrote-

Fātiḥ al-qulūb, an account (32 foll.) of the life and miracles of the saint, calligrapher and poet Mīr ʿAbd Allāh "Waṣfī" b. Mīr Muẓaffar Ḥusainī Tirmidhī, who received from Akbar or Jahāngīr the title of *Mushkīn-qalam* and who died in 1025/1616 or 1035/1626:[674] **Ethé** 650.

1325. **Ilāh-diyah,**[675] or Allāh-diyah, b. Sh. ʿAbd al-Raḥīm b. Sh. Bīnā Ḥakīm **Chishtī** ʿUthmānī, a descendant of Sh. Jalāl al-Dīn Pānīpatī,[676] was a disciple of Shāh Aʿlā Pānīpatī[677] and lived at Kairānah,[678] near Pānīpat. His grandfather, Sh. Bīnā, or Bhīnā,[679] was a noted surgeon of Akbar's time, and his paternal uncle, Muqarrab Khān,[680] Jahāngīr's surgeon and friend (cf. no. 246 *supra*), was Governor of Gujrāt, Bihār and Āgrah in Jahāngīr's reign and on his retirement in Shāh-Jahān's reign was given the *parganah* of Kairānah, his birthplace, as a *jāgīr*. Ilāh-diyah and his two brothers, Sh. Qāsim and Sh. Fuḍail, took part in Shāh-Jahān's march towards Kābul.

Siyar al-aqṭāb, begun in 1036/1626–7 completed in 1056/1646–7 and devoted to the lives of twenty-seven persons from ʿAlī b. Abī Ṭālib to Shāh Aʿlā Pānīpatī, who form the author's spiritual pedigree and each of whom, according to the Chishtīs, became Quṭb al-aqṭāb: **Rieu** i 358*b* (17th cent.), **I.O.** D.P. 669 (AH 1019/1610 [!], perhaps a mistake for 1119/1707), **ʿAlīgaṛh** Subḥ. MSS. p. 60 no. 15 (AD 1867).

Editions: **Lucknow** 1877°*, 1881†, 1889†.

List of the saints: Rieu i p. 359.

---

674 See Badāʾūnī iii pp. 383–4 (cf. Sprenger p. 65); *Āʾīn i Akbarī* p. 115[5] (merely the name Mīr ʿAbd Allāh in a list of calligraphists), Blochmann's trans. p. 103[7]; *Ṣuḥuf i Ibrāhīm; Makhzan al-gharāʾib* no. 2951; Rieu i p. 154; Beale *Oriental biographical dictionary* under ʿAbdullah Tirmizi. For his son M. Ṣāliḥ "Kashfī" see no. 274 *supra*.

675 *diyah* (or *diyā*, as it is usually written) is a Hindī word meaning "given".

676 d. 765/1363. See *Siyar al-aqṭāb; Mirʾāt al-asrār, ṭabaqah* 22; *Sawāṭiʿ al-anwār* no. 26; *Khazīnat al-aṣfiyāʾ* i pp. 361–5.

677 d. 1033/1624. See *Siyar al-aqṭāb* (last biography: summarized by Rieu, i p. 359*a*); *Khazīnat al-aṣfiyāʾ* i pp. 459–61.

678 Kairānah, now in the Muẓaffarnagar District of the United Provinces, is about twenty miles east of Pānīpat, which is in the Karnāl District of the Panjāb. Muqarrab Khān "built many edifices" in Kairānah, "and laid out a beautiful garden with an immense tank" (*Āʾīn i Akbarī*, tr. Blochmann p. 544[1]). He also "constructed a mausoleum near the tomb of the renowned Saint Sharafuddín of Pánípat" (*op. cit.* p. 543 penult.).

679 See Badāʾūnī *Muntakhab al-tawārīkh* iii p. 169; *Āʾīn i Akbarī* p. 234[11] (merely his name in the list of physicians), Blochmann's trans. p. 543.

680 Ḥakīm Sh. Ḥasan, d. at Kairānah in 1056/1646, aged ninety. See *Memoirs of Jahāngīr*, tr. Rogers and Beveridge, p. 27 and elsewhere (see index); *Maʾāthir al-umarāʾ* iii pp. 379–81; *Āʾīn i Akbarī* tr. Blochmann pp. 543–4; Rieu iii p. 1086*a*, l. 3.

1326. Abū 'l-'Abbās **M. Ṭālib.**

Maṭlab al-ṭālibīn, a history of the Jūybārī *shaikhs* written about 1056/1646: **Tashkent** A. A. Semenov's private library (AH 1235/1819–20. See Semenov *Kurzer Abriss* p. 6).

1327. In 1060/1650 was written—

Ḥikāyat[681] ***al-ṣāliḥīn***, anecdotes of famous saints, stated to be a translation from the Arabic: **Browne** Suppt. 407 (AH 1217/1802–3. Corpus 228[6]), **Blochet** iv 2134 (AH 1228/1813).

1328. Mīr **Muḥammad Fāḍil**, called (*al-mad'ū bi-*) Maẓhar al-Ḥaqq, b. S. Aḥmad b. S. Ḥasan al-Ḥusainī al-Tirmidhī **al-Akbarābādī** died in Rabī' ii AH 1106/ Nov.-Dec. 1694 (according to the chronograms given by his nephew at the end of the *Mukhbir al-wāṣilīn*). One of the opening sections of the *Mukhbir al-wāṣilīn* is in praise of Shāh-Jahān, who was on the throne when he began the work.

Mukhbir al-wāṣilīn (a chronogram = 1060/1650, the date of inception), a series of chronogrammatic poems containing the dates of the death of the Prophet, the first four Caliphs, the Twelve Imāms, numerous saints and a few other persons from the first century of Islām to AH 1105/1693–4 (often with the place of burial but usually little else except laudatory phrases): **Āṣafīyah** i p. 252 no. 756 (AH 1140/1727–8), no. 405, **Ivanow** 759 (AH 1151/1738–9), **Ivanow** Curzon 268 (19th cent.), **'Alīgaṛh** Subḥ. MSS. p. 16 no. 83, **Rieu** iii 1035*b* (extracts only. *Circ.* AD 1850).

Editions: **Calcutta** 1249/1833–4*, **Lucknow** (Muṣṭafā'ī Press) 1265/1849 (see Sprenger p. 489).

1329. '**Abd al-Raḥmān** b. 'Abd al-Rasūl b. Qāsim b. Shāh Bud'h 'Abbāsī 'Alawī **Chishtī** was a descendant of the saint Aḥmad 'Abd al-Ḥaqq Rudaulawī,[682] and succeeded in 1032/1622, on his brother's death, to the headship of a local branch of the Chishtī order at Rudaulī.[683] According to the *Mir'āt al-'ālam*, the author of which was a personal acquaintance, he lived at D'hanītī,[684] a village in the *sarkār* of Lucknow, and died there in 1094/1683 (see Rieu iii p. 973*a*). Among his works were (1) *Mir'āt al-makhlūqāt*, a translation and Islamising explanation, written in 1041/1631–2, of a Sanskrit verse treatise on Hindu cosmogony

681 In the singular, not *Ḥikāyāt*.
682 See no. 1279 3rd par. footnote *supra*.
683 Thirty-eight miles from Bārā Bankī in Oudh.
684 Not confirmed.

in the form of a dialogue between Mahādēv and Pārbatī handed down by the Munī Bās̲his̲ht (Vāsishṭ'ha) (MSS.: Rieu iii 1034*a*, Āṣafīyah ii p. 1386, Bodleian 1823), (2) *Mir'āt al-ḥaqā'iq*, an abridged translation and Islamising explanation of the *Bhagavad-gītā* (MSS.: Rieu iii 1034*b*, Bombay Univ. p. 134, Āṣafīyah ii p. 1356), (3) *Nafas i Raḥmānī* (Edition: place ? 1307/1889–90. See Āṣafīyah i p. 494), (4) *Aurād i C̲his̲htīyah* (MS.: Āṣafīyah iii p. 24),

(5) ***Mir'āt al-asrār***, biographies of numerous saints from the early days of Islām to Ḥusām al-Dīn Mānikpūrī (d. 853/1449), begun in 1045/1635–6, completed in 1065/1654 and divided into a preface (on Ṣūfism, the degrees of spiritual knowledge, the origin and contents of the work), a *muqaddimah* (on the *k̲hirqah i k̲hilāfat*, the four Pīrs, Ḥasan, Ḥusain, Kumail, Ḥasan Baṣrī, the fourteen *k̲hānawādahs*, and twelve of the forty derivative orders or *silsilahs*) and twenty-three *ṭabaqāt* devoted to successive generations of *s̲haik̲hs*: **Ivanow** 264 (AH 1088/1677–8), **Lindesiana** p. 118 no. 196 (*circ.* AD 1750), **Rieu** i 359*b* (AH 1189/1775), iii 973*b* (extracts only. *Circ.* AD 1850), **Bānkīpūr** viii 676 (AH 1220/1806), Suppt. ii 2074 (*Muqaddimah* only. 19th cent.), **Būhār** 89 (probably transcribed from Bānkīpūr viii 676. B.S. 1301/1894), **Āṣafīyah** iii p. 166 no. 167 (AH 1309/1891–2).

List and epitome of the biographies: Bānkīpūr viii pp. 55–63.

(6) ***Mir'āt i Madārī***, a life of the saint of Makanpūr,[685] Badīʿ al-Dīn surnamed Quṭb al-Madār and commonly called S̲hāh Madār,[686] written in 1064/1654 at Makanpūr and based mainly on the *Īmān i Maḥmūdī*, a biography by the saint's *k̲halīfah*, Qāḍī Maḥmūd Kintūrī,[687] and the *Laṭā'if i As̲hrafī* (see Rieu iii 1042*a*, Ivanow 1214, etc.), whose author was a friend

685 A village 8 miles N.W. of Bilhaur and 40 miles from Cawnpore.

686 S̲h. Madār, "one of the most popular saints of India and the subject of the most fabulous legends" (Rieu), is said in the *Mir'āt i Madārī* to have been a Jew born at Aleppo in 715/1315, who visited Mecca, embraced Islām at al-Madīnah, migrated to India, and settled at Makanpūr, where he died in 840/1436 after spending thirty-five years of his life in Syria, forty at Mecca, al-Madīnah and al-Najaf and fifty in India. He was treated with great respect by Ibrāhīm S̲hāh S̲harqī, who built his tomb. According to a pedigree quoted in the *K̲hazīnat al-aṣfiyā'* he was descended on his father's side from Abū Hurairah and on his mother's from ʿAbd al-Raḥmān b. ʿAuf (!). See *Ak̲hbār al-ak̲hyār* p. 164; *Gulzār i abrār* no. 60; *Kalimāt al-ṣādiqīn* no. 21; *Safīnat al-auliyā'* pp. 187–8 (no. 358); *Dabistān i mad̲hāhib*, trans., New York 1937, p. 279; *K̲hazīnat al-aṣfiyā'* ii pp. 310–12; *Ā'īn i Akbarī*, tr. Jarrett, iii p. 370; Garcin de Tassy *Mémoire sur … la religion musulmane dans l'Inde* (2nd ed. Paris 1869) pp. 52–9; S. M. Amīr Ḥasan *Tadhkirat al-muttaqīn* (see no. 1410 *infra*); *Siyar al-Madār* (in Urdu), by Ẓahīr Aḥmad "Ẓahīrī", Pt. i Lucknow 1900, Pt. ii Badāyūn 1920; *Cawnpore District Gazetteer* (Allahabad 1909) pp. 309–10; Jaʿfar S̲harīf *Islam in India or the Qānūn-i-Islām*, tr. G. A. Herklots, revised W. Crooke, Oxford 1921, pp. 195–6; Bānkīpūr Cat. viii pp. 64–66 (where the *Mir'āt i Madāri* is summarized).

687 Kintoor (officially so spelt) is a village near Bārā Bankī.

of Shāh Madār's: **Ivanow** 263 (AH 1146/1733–4), **Rieu** i 361*a* (18th cent.), iii 973*a* (19th cent.), **Bānkīpūr** viii 677 (18th cent.), **I.O.** D.P. 657(c), **Būhār** 88 (transcribed from the Bānkīpūr MS. in 1304/1886).

Urdū translation: *Thawāqib al-anwār li-maṭāliʿ Quṭb al-Madār*, by M. ʿAbd al-Rashīd Ẓuhūr al-Islām, **Farrukhābād** 1328/1910*.

(7) ***Mirʾāt i Masʿūdī***, a life of the legendary hero and martyr Sulṭān al-Shuhadāʾ Sālār Masʿūd Ghāzī,[688] said to be based on a contemporary history by Mullā M. Ghaznawī, a servant of Sulṭān Maḥmūd: **Ivanow** Curzon 103 (AH 1233/1818), **Rieu** iii 1029*a* (*circ.*AD 1850), **ʿAlīgaṛh** Subḥ. MSS. p. 59 no. 6.

Abridged English translation by B. W. Chapman: **B.M.** MS. Add. 30776.

Extracts from Chapman's translation: Elliot and Dowson *History of India* ii pp. 513–49.

Abridged Urdu translation: *Khulāṣah i tawārīkh i Masʿūdī*, by Akbar ʿAlī b. M.-Bakhsh, [**Lucknow** ?] 1288/1871°.

Abridgment by the author himself: *Qiṣṣah i Sālār Masʿūd i Ghāzī*: **Rieu** iii 1042*b* (*circ.* AD 1850).

[Autobiographical statements in *Mirʾāt al-asrār* (summarized by Rieu and ʿAbd al-Muqtadir) and *Mirʾāt i Madārī; Sawāṭiʿ al-anwār* no. 29 (Ethé col. 336[22]).]

1330. **ʿAlāʾ al-Din M. Chishtī Barnāwī.**[689]

Chishtīyah i bihishtīyah, or ***Firdausīyah i qudsīyah***,[690] a large work on the saints of the Chishtī order completed perhaps in 1066/1655–6, the date of Prof. Maḥmūd Shērānī's MS. (such dates as 1069/1658–9, 1071/1660–1 and 1076/1665–6, which occur in Ivanow-Curzon 78, being presumably later insertions), and divided into a *muqaddimah*, twenty-eight *dhikrs* (of which the first twenty-one are short notices of the early saints, etc., from

688 An alleged nephew of Sulṭān Maḥmūd Ghaznawī, born at Ajmēr in 405/1014 and killed in battle against the Hindu idolaters in 424/1033 at Bahrāʾich, where his tomb is a celebrated place of pilgrimage. See *Safīnat al-auliyāʾ* p. 160 (no. 290); *Mirʾāt al-asrār, ṭabaqah XII; Khazīnat al-aṣfiyāʾ* ii pp. 217–24; Garcin de Tassy *Mémoire sur ... la religion musulmane dans l'Inde* (2nd Ed., Paris 1869) pp. 72–9; *Ghazā-nāmah i Masʿūd* (in Urdū), by ʿInāyat-Ḥusain Bilgrāmī, Cawnpore 1293/1876°*; Rieu iii 1015; Beale *Oriental biographical dictionary* under Masaʿud Ghazi; Ivanow 322; *Ency. Isl.* under Ghāzī Miyān (Hidayat Ḥusain), where some further references will be found.

689 At the beginning of Professor Maḥmūd Sherānī's article mentioned below the name of this author is followed by the dates 1007 and 1088, presumably as those of his birth and death, but the authority for them is not specified.

690 *Īn risālah īst musammā bi'sm i Firdausīyah* [*i qudsīyah ?*] *yaʿnī* [*!*] *nām i īn nuskhah Chishtīyah i bihishtīyah* etc. (Ivanow-Curzon 78, fol. 2). In the Āṣafīyah catalogue it is called *Chishtīyah i bihishtīyah musammā bah Firdausīyah i qudsīyah.*

the Prophet to Naṣīr al-Dīn Chirāgh i Dihlī (cf. no. 1259 1st par. last footnote *supra*), while the twenty-second to the twenty-eighth are much longer notices of the local saints of Barnāwah and Rāprī,[691] namely Badr al-Dīn b. Sharaf al-Dīn Anṣārī (d. 788/1386), Naṣīr al-Dīn i Buzurg (d. 855/1452), ʿAlāʾ al-Dīn i Buzurg (d. 875/1471), Pīr Būd'han (d. 29 Shaʿbān in an unspecified year), Badr al-Dīn i Thānī (d. 949/1543), Farīd al-Dīn b. Bāyazīd b. Pīr Būd'han (d. 987/1579), Bahāʾ al-Dīn b. ʿAlāʾ al-Dīn,[692] grandson of the preceding (d. 1038/1628), whose biography occupies more than half the work), a *khātimah* (additional information concerning descendants of the foregoing *shaikhs*), and a *waṣl al-khātimah*, (eulogies of the Chishtī order): **Lahore** Prof. Maḥmūd Shērānī's private library (AH 1066/1655–6, possibly autograph), **Ivanow** Curzon 78 (AH 1209/1795), **Āṣafīyah** i p. 412 no. 562 (AH 1258/1842).

1331. **Niẓām al-Dīn Aḥmad b. M. Ṣāliḥ** Ṣiddīqī Ḥusainī lived in the time of Shāh-Jahān and composed in 1060/1650 a work on poetical figures entitled *Majmaʿ al-ṣanāʾiʿ*.[693]

Karāmāt al-auliyāʾ, on the miracles of saints in all periods of the history of Islam, completed in 1068/1658: **Ivanow** 265 (18th cent.), **Rieu** iii 974*a* (*circ.* 1850).

1332. **Tawakkul Bēg Kūlālī**[694] was a son of the *Qūsh-bēgī* to Iʿtiqād Khān, Governor of Kashmīr. At the age of sixteen[695] he became a disciple of the Qādirī saint, Mullā Shāh Badakhshī,[696] who was then resident in Kashmīr, and he kept in touch with him, visiting him at intervals, until 1071/1660–1, when he

691 Rāprī is a village, once a large town, in the Shikohābād *taḥṣīl* of the Mainpūrī District of the United Provinces. Barnāwah is not mentioned either in the Mainpūrī District Gazetteer or in the Imperial Gazetteer of India.

692 For Sh. Bahāʾ al-Dīn Barnāwī, who was not only a saint but also a musician, see an Urdu article by Professor Maḥmūd Shērānī based mainly on the *Chishtīyah i bihishtiyah* and entitled *Makhdūm Shaikh Bahāʾ al-Dīn Barnāwī* in the *OCM*. iii/4 (Aug. 1927) pp. 41–58, iv/1 (Nov. 1927) pp. 9–26, and v/4 (Aug. 1929) pp. 72–99. This article includes a summary of the information contained in the *Chishtīyah i bihishtīyah* concerning the earlier *shaikhs* of Barnāwah.

693 Lindesiana p. 205 no. 754, Ross and Browne 68, Ethé 2937–3, Bānkīpūr ix 850–2, xi 1098 liii, Būhār 263–4, Ivanow 1st Suppt. 788, Ivanow Curzon 176, Rieu ii 814*b*, 821*b*, iii 999*b*, Browne Suppt. 1144–5 (Corpus 23[1] and 28), Leyden v p. 160, etc.

694 Meaning of this *nisbah* not ascertained. A Mīr Yūsuf Kūlālī is mentioned in ʿAbd al-Ḥamīd's *Pādshāh-nāmah* i, 2, p. 320[2].

695 As Tawakkul Bēg says that he had availed himself of Mullā Shāh's teaching for forty years, this discipleship must have begun in, or about, 1031/1622.

696 See second next footnote below.

saw his master for the last time. For a period anterior to 1053/1643–4 he was in the service of Shāh-Shujāʿ, Governor of Bengal. In 1054/1644 he went with a letter of introduction from Mullā Shāh to Dārā-Shukōh (see no. 1321 *supra*), who gave him the rank of *dū-ṣadī* and subsequently on several occasions sent him with messages to Mullā Shāh. After Aurangzēb's accession in 1069/1659 he obtained a post in the government service at Kāngrah.

It seems likely that he is identical with Tawakkul Bēg b. Tūlak Beg,[697] who in Shāh-Jahān's 26th regnal year, A.H. 1063/1653, was sent by Dārā-Shukōh, at that time *Ṣūbah-dār* of Kābul, to Ghaznīn as *Amīn* and *Waqāʾiʿ-nawīs* and who at the request of Shamshēr Khān Tarīn, the *T'hānah-dār* of Ghaznīn, wrote the *Shamshēr-Khanī*, an abridgment of Firdausī's *Shāh-nāmah* (see Rieu ii 539–40, Ethé 883–90, etc.).

Nuskhah i aḥwāl i Shāhī (a chronogram = 1077/1666–7), an account of Mullā Shāh[698] and his teachings: **Rieu** Suppt. 130 (early 19th cent.), **Āṣafīyah** iii p. 56 no. 349.

French summary: *Mollâ-Shâh et le spiritualisme oriental, par M. A. de Kremer* (in *Journal Asiatique*, viᵉ série, tome xiii (1869), pp. 105–59).

[Autobiographical statements in the *Nuskhah i aḥwāl i Shāhī* (see Rieu and *Journal asiatique, loc. cit.*)]

1333. ʿ**Abd Allāh**[699] Khwēshgī[700] Qaṣūrī,[701] i.e. Ghulām-Muʿīn al-Dīn ʿAbd Allāh known as al-Khalīfah al-Khwēshgī al-Chishtī (Ross-Browne 56), or

697 Rieu mentions that in one of the B.M. MSS. of the *Shamshēr-Khānī* he is called Tawakkul Muḥammad son of Tūlak Muḥammad al-Ḥusainī.

698 Mullā, or Maulānā, Shāh, whose name was Shāh Muḥammad (Shāh being part of his name, not a title), though Miyān Mīr used to call him Muḥammad Shāh (*Sakīnat al-auliyā*', Urdu trans. p. 117², Bānkīpūr viii p. 50²), was born in Badakhshān AH 992/1584, settled in India in 1023/1614–15 and died at Lahore in 1072/1661. See no. 28 *supra;* Jahān-ārā *Ṣāḥibīyah* (cf. no. 1322 (2) *supra*); *Sakīnat al-auliyā*' foll. 86–118 (pp. 116–58 in the Urdu translation); *ʿAmal i Ṣāliḥ* iii pp. 370–2; *Tadhkirah i Naṣrābādī* p. 63; *Wāqiʿāt i Kashmīr* pp. 161–2; *Riyāḍ al-shūʿarā*' (cf. Bland in *JRAS.* 1848 p. 147); *Farḥat al-nāẓirīn* (passage quoted in *OCM.* iv/3 (May 1928) pp. 95–6); *Riyāḍ al-ʿārifīn* pp. 161–2; Beale *Miftāḥ al-tawārīkh* (Āgrah 1849) pp. 401–2; S. M. Latif *Lahore: its history*, etc., pp. 59, 175–6, 178; *Ency. Isl.* Suppt. under Shāh Muḥammad; K.-R. Qanungo *Dara Shukoh. Vol. i. Biography* (Calcutta [1935]) pp. 348–58; *Jahān-ārā Bēgam kī ēk ghair-maʿrūf taṣnīf: Ṣāḥibīyah*, by M. Ibrāhīm (in *OCM.* xiii/4 (August 1937) pp. 3–19).

699 It will be seen that his proper name was ʿAbd Allāh but that he was known as ʿUbaid Allāh (or *vice versa*, since there is some disagreement in the MSS.). Similarly his father was properly called ʿAbd al-Ḥaqq but was known as ʿAbd al-Qādir.

700 The name of an Afghān clan (cf. no. 840 1st footnote *supra*).

701 Qaṣūr is 34 miles S.E. of Lahore. "The Afghâns of Qasûr belong mostly to the Khweshgî clan, whose eponym appears to have flourished in the eleventh century [AD]" (M. Shafīʿ

"'Abdallâh, known as 'Ubaid-allâh, with the epithet Khalîfah Ḥayy [read K͟halîfah-jī]⁷⁰² bin 'Abd-alḥakk (known as 'Abd-alḳâdir al-khwîshî [sic ?] alćishtî)" (Ethé 1271), or "'Abdu'l-lah K͟halīfa-jī b. 'Abdi'l-Ḥaqq, known as 'Abdu'l-Qādir K͟hwīshagī" (Ivanow 273), or "'Abdu'l-lah K͟hwīshagī Chishtī, surnamed K͟halīfah, of Qaṣūr" (Ivanow 1294), or 'Ubaid Allāh known as (al-ma'rūf bah) 'Abd Allāh al-K͟hwēs͟hgī al-C͟his͟htī, who used the takhalluṣ "'Ubaidī" (OCM. iii/4 p. 21), was born at Qaṣūr (Ross-Browne 56) and it was there that in S͟hāh-Jahān's reign after finishing his studies (taḥṣīl i 'ulūm sē farāghat pā-kar, OCM. iii/4 p. 23¹) he completed the first volume of his first commentary on Ḥāfiẓ, the Baḥr al-firāsah, which he had begun while still a student. The second and final volume was completed long afterwards at Bījāpūr (OCM. iii/4 p. 23³). From the preface to his second commentary, the K͟hulāṣat al-baḥr, also a production of his early life, it appears that "he was for a time attached to the Shaikh Maulânâ 'Abd-alrashîd (known as Muḥammad Rashîd) Yuwânjî and afterwards in the service of⁷⁰³ Shaikh Pîr Muḥammad of Lak͟hnau" (Ethé 1271). In 1077/1666–7 he was at Aurangābād, where he had gone in the service of Dilēr K͟hān,⁷⁰⁴ and it was there that he wrote the Ak͟hbār al-auliyā' (Islamic culture iii/3 p. 453). In 1133/1720–1, Muḥammad S͟hāh's second regnal year, he was again at Qaṣūr, evidently towards the end of a long life, and there he wrote his Asrār i Mathnawī at the instigation of two K͟hwēs͟hgī chiefs, Ḥasan [Ḥusain ?] K͟hān and Sa'īd K͟hān (Ross-Browne 56). In the preface to his Asrār i Mathnawī u anwār i ma'nawī, a commentary on the first daftar of Rūmī's Mathnawī completed in 1133/1720–1 (MSS.: Ross-Browne 56 (AH 1133/1721, perhaps autograph), Sprenger 373 (Mōtī Maḥall)) he gives a list of his earlier works, which is quoted verbatim by Sprenger. These are firstly three commentaries on the dīwān of Ḥāfiẓ, (1) Baḥr al-firāsah [in the preface of which S͟hāh-Jahān (AH 1037–68/1628–58) is praised. MSS.: Kapūrt'halah 123 (see OCM. iii/4 p. 21), Peshawar 1028], (2) K͟hulāṣat al-baḥr fī 'ltiqāṭ al-durar, a larger commentary

---

    in the article mentioned below). See also an article entitled S͟hahr i Qaṣūr kē muta'alliq iqtibāsāt by M. S͟hafi' in OCM. xiii/2 (Feb. 1937) pp. 92–8.

702 The jī appended to the word k͟halīfah is the same Hindi affix indicative of respect that occurs, for example, in Miyān-jī (cf. no. 1321 (2), 2nd footnote).

703 Or rather, visited. Sh. Pīr Muḥammad Lak'hnawī died at Lucknow in 1080/1669–70 or 1082/1671–2. See K͟hazīnat al-aṣfiyā' i pp. 482–3 (where there is a quotation from the Ma'ārij al-wilāyat telling how 'Abd Allāh K͟hwēs͟hgī on his way to Bengal [ba-safar i Bangālah, possibly with Dilēr K͟hān, who took part in the campaign of Mu'aẓẓam K͟hān Mīr Jumlah against S͟hāh-S͟hujā' at the beginning of Aurangzēb's reign] visited him at Lucknow, showed him the Baḥr al-firāsah and was invested by him with the C͟his͟htī k͟hirqah); Tajallī i nūr i pp. 81–2.

704 i.e. Jalāl K͟hān Dāwud-za'ī, for whom see Ma'athir al-umarā' ii pp. 42–56, Beveridge's translation pp. 495–505.

(MSS.: Āṣafīyah (transcribed by Dārā-Shukōh, "who was a disciple of Sayyid Ādam Rasūl[705] of Māwarā' al-Nahr as would appear from the colophon." See Nadhīr Aḥmad 129), Ethé 1271), (3) *Jāmiʿ al-baḥrain* (no MSS. recorded), then (4)*Rāḥat al-ashbāḥ*, a commentary on the *Nuzhat al-arwāḥ* [of Ḥusain b. ʿĀlim al-Ḥusainī] (no MSS. recorded), (5) *Makhzan al-ḥaqā'iq*, a commentary on the *Kanz al-daqā'iq*, (6) *Sharḥ i ḤRF* [*sic* ?] *ʿāliyāt*, and (7) *Maʿārij al-wilāyat "kih dar bayān i mashāyikh i Hindūstān-ast."* In this list he mentions neither the *Akhbār al-auliyā'* nor the two Ṣūfī works *Taḥqīq al-muḥaqqiqīn fī tadqīq al-mudaqqiqīn* (Ivanow 1294 (1)) and *Fawā'id al-ʿāshiqīn* (Ivanow 1294 (2)).

(1) ***Akhbār al-auliyā' min lisān al-aṣfiyā'***, an account of Khwēshgī and other saints written in 1077/1666–7 at Aurangābād and divided into six *bābs* ((1) *dar bayān i aḥwāl i Khwēshgiyān*, (2) *dar bayān i mashāyikh i sā'ir i Afghānān*, (3) *dar bayān i aḥwāl i nisā' i ʿārifāt*, (4) *dar nasab i Afghānān u sabab i āmadan az Bait al-Maqdis ba-Kūhistān*, (5) *dar aḥwāl i mashāyikh i Qaṣūr u nawāḥī i ān*, (6) *dar aḥwāl i īn aḥqar i ʿibād Allāh* (*ʿAbd Allāh Khwēshgī Chishtī*): **Ivanow** 273 (A.H. 1294/1877, transcribed at Qaṣūr for H. Blochmann).

This work is one of the sources of M. Shafīʿ's article *An Afghan colony at Qasur I*. in *Islamic culture* iii/3 (July 1929) pp. 452–73.

(2) ***Maʿārij al-wilāyat*** (*dar bayān i mashāyikh i Hindūstān*), mentioned by the author in the above-mentioned list of his own works and often quoted in the *Khazīnat al-aṣfiyā'* but not yet recorded in any published catalogue.

[Autobiography (without exact dates according to Ivanow p. 620) in *Bāb* 6 of the *Akhbār al-auliyā'* (a biography based on this chapter was to be included in Part II of M. Shafīʿ's article mentioned above, but no such second part seems to be traceable in *Islamic culture* from 1929 to 1937).

1334. Ḥāfiẓ **M. Saʿīd** b. Ḥāfiẓ [*sic* ?] began the *Rāḥat al-arwāḥ* in Rajab 1084/October 1673 and completed it in 1085/1674–5.

Rāḥat al-arwāḥ, a biography of Sh. ʿAzīz Allāh, who was born at Lahore on 3 Jumādā II 1047/23 Oct. 1637 and died on 20 Shawwāl 1084/28 Jan. 1674: **Ethé** 651 (AH 1108/1696).

705 Not identified. It is not clear why Dārā-Shukōh (presumably the well-known son of Shāh-Jahān and disciple of Mullā Shāh) should describe himself as a disciple of this person, who seems not to be mentioned in the *Safīnat al-auliyā'* or the *Sakīnat al-auliyā'*.

1335. S. **Zindah ʿAlī** al-Muftī wrote towards the end of the eleventh/seventeenth century.

__Thamarāt al-mashāyikh__, on Central Asian *shaikhs* of various orders: **Bukhārā** Central Library (AH 1277/1860–1. See Semenov *Kurzer Abriss* p. 7).

1336. For Sh. **Ḥusain b.** Sh. **Abdāl Zāhidī's** *Silsilat al-nasab i Ṣafawīyah*, which was dedicated to Shāh Sulaimān (reigned 1077–1105/1667–94) and which deals mainly with Ṣafī al-Dīn Isḥāq (cf. no. 1257 1st par. *supra*) and mystics descended from him, see no. 396 *supra*.

1337. For **M. Baqā** "Baqā" Sahāranpūrī (b. 1037/1627–8, d. 1094/1683) and **Bakhtāwar Khān** (d. 1096/1685) see no. 151 *supra*. Another of the works written by the former but by a "courteous fiction" ascribed to the latter is the *Riyāḍ al-auliyāʾ*.

__Riyāḍ al-auliyāʾ__ (a chronogram = 1090/1679–80, the date of completion), lives of saints, etc., in four *chamans* ((1) the first four Caliphs, (2) the Imāms, (3) saints, (4) Indian saints): **Rieu** iii 975*a* (AD 1851), **Āṣafīyah** i p. 320 no. 115, **Browne** Suppt. 728 (Corpus 126).

1338. In the only recorded copy of the *Adhkār al-aḥrār* all of the preface except the last 6½ lines is missing and the name of the author does not appear. He was, however, a disciple of Mīr Abū 'l-ʿUlā Naqshbandī Akbarābādī, and he completed his biography in Safar 1093/1682.

__Adhkār al-aḥrār__, an account of the saint Amīr Abū 'l-ʿUlā ibn Amīr Abī-Wafāʾ ibn Amīr ʿAbd al-Salām, or as he is called in the *Khazīnat al-aṣfiyāʾ* (i p. 636) Mīr Abū 'l-ʿUlā Naqshbandī Akbarābādī, who was born in 990/1582 at Nārēlah near Delhi and who died on 9 Ṣafar 1061/1651 and was buried at Akbarābād (i.e. Āgrah): **I.O.** D.P. 576*a* (defective at beginning. 11th year of M. Shāh = AH 1142/1730).

1339. **M. Ṣādiq Shihābī Saʿdī Qādirī** wrote the *Manāqib i Ghauthīyah* at the request of his *murshid*, S. ʿAbd al-Qādir b. S. ʿAbd al-Jalīl al-Ḥasanī al-Ḥusainī Gharīb Allāh, who was a descendant and *khalīfah* of ʿAbd al-Qādir al-Jīlānī at Aḥmadābād. The work cannot have been written earlier than the 17th century, since the *Takmīl al-īmān* of ʿAbd al-Ḥaqq Dihlawī, who died in 1052/1642 (cf. no. 243 *supra*), is mentioned in the preface, nor later than 1160/1747, the date of Ivanow-Curzon 76.

Manāqib i Ghauthīyah, an account of ʿAbd al-Qādir al-Jīlānī, called al-Ghauth al-aʿẓam (for whom see no. 1251 2nd par. footnote *supra*), divided into a *muqaddimah* and fifty or more[706] *manqabahs* and dealing with *manāqib* not contained in such well-known works as the *Bahjat al-asrār* (see no. 1251 *supra*) and the *Takmilah* of al-Yāfiʿī (see no. 1254 II *supra*): **Ivanow** Curzon 76 (AH 1160/1747), **Ivanow** 268–70 (all 18th cent.), **Āṣafīyah** i p. 490 nos. 813 (AH 1179/1765–6), 428 (AH 1260/1844–5), ii p. 1556 no. 52, p. 1558 no. 43, **I.O.** D.P. 751B (*a*) (AH 1211/1797), 751A (AH 1248/1832), **Ethé** 1799, **Bānkīpūr** xvii 1589 (AH 1253/1837–8), **Būhār** 181 (19th cent.), **Lahore** Panjāb Univ. (see *OCM*. iii/1 p. 69), **Peshawar** 1014.

Edition: **Bombay** 1886†.

Urdu translation: *M. i Gh.*, **Lucknow** 1907* (2nd ed.).

1340. In 1109/1697–8 an anonymous author wrote-

Khawāriq al-sālikīn (a chronogram), some anecdotes of early Ṣūfīs of Kashmīr, etc.: **Ivanow** Curzon 79 (4) (foll. 106–15. Mid 19th cent.).

1341. **M. Būlāq** b. Sh. Abū M. Khālidī **Dihlawī** b. Sh. ʿAlī Akbar was a descendant of the great saint Niẓām al-Dīn Auliyā (for whom see no. 1259 1st par. 4th footnote *supra*).

Maṭlūb al-ṭālibīn, a detailed biography of Niẓām al-Dīn Auliyā with short accounts of his relations, disciples and spiritual descendants and of the other Chishtī *pīrs* and the different branches of the Chishtī order, divided into seventeen *maṭlabs* and completed in 1111/1699–1700: **Ethé** 653 (AH 1137/1724–5).

Urdu translation: *Shawāhid i Niẓāmī* (a chronogram = 1317/1899–1900), by M. Ḍāmin ʿAlī, **Delhi** 1900°.

List of the saints: Ethé coll. 318–26.

Probably identical with the above-mentioned M. Būlāq is M. Bulāq[707] (spelt without *wāw*), who wrote the *Rauḍah i aqṭāb*).

Rauḍah i aqṭāb (a chronogram = 1124/1712), biographies of Quṭb al-Dīn Bakhtyār Ushī Kākī (for whom see no. 1259 2nd par. 4th footnote *supra*) and some saints buried near him: **Rieu** iii 974*a* (extracts only. *Circ.* AD 1850).

706 Fifty followed by a *khātimah* and a *tadhyīl* (the last on ʿAbd al-Qādir's pedigree and the more celebrated of his 49 children) in Ethé 1799, sixty-seven in I.O. D.P. 751B(*a*), ninety-one (the number of years in ʿAbd al-Qādir's life) in I.O. D.P. 751A.

707 Edwards prefixes the title Sayyid to M. Bulāq's name, doubtless on the authority of a title-page, but the text of the work itself (to judge from Rieu and Blumhardt) seems to give no warrant for this. Rieu writes Muḥammad Yalāq, but this is presumably a corruption.

Editions: **Delhi** 1304/1887°, **Lahore** 1890†.
Urdu translation: *Rauḍah i aqṭāb*, **Delhi** 1892*.

1342. Sh. **Manṣūr b. Sh̲āh Chānd Muḥammad** b. S̲h̲āh M. Mīr b. S̲h̲āh Ḥāmid b. S̲h̲āh ʿAbd al-Qawī b. S̲h̲āh Chānd M. b. S̲h̲āh Ḥamīd al-Dīn known as S̲h̲aikh Chāʾildah was forty years old in 1119/1707–8, when he wrote the *Tuḥfat al-qāriʾ*.

Tuḥfat al-qāriʾ, biographies of saints in three parts ((1) Ḥaḍrat i ʿAbbās, (2) S̲h̲āh ʿAlī Sarmast and how he settled in Gujrāt, (3) S̲h̲āh Chāʾildah (d. 7 Ṣafar 911/1515) and Qāḍī Maḥmūd Maḥbūb Allāh (d. 941/1534–5) and his sons) and two appendices ((1) S̲h̲aikh al-Islām S̲h̲āh Lār Muḥammad, (2) S̲h̲āh Jamāl Muḥammad (d. 985/1577–8)): **Bombay** Fyzee 16 (AH 1261/1845).

1343. S. **Aḥmad b.** S. **Ḥusain Akbarābādī**.
Maqāmāt i ḥaḍrat i Sh̲āh Naqshbandi, written in 1119/1707–8: **Brelvi and Dhabhar** p. xliii no. 7 (defective at beginning).

1344. At the beginning of his notice of Sh̲. Saʿdī Lāhaurī the author of the *Khazīnat al-aṣfiyāʾ* mentions a certain Sh̲. **M. ʿUmar Pash̲āwarī** who was a disciple and friend of Sh̲. Saʿdī and who wrote under the title *Jawāhir al-asrār* a biography of his master extending from his birth to the date of his death. Probably this Sh̲. M. ʿUmar Pash̲āwarī is identical with M. ʿUmar b. Ibrāhīm al-Nīshāpūrī [sic ?], who wrote the *Ẓawāhir al-sarāʾir*. Doubtless the work was written in the first half of the eighteenth century.

Ẓawāhir al-sarāsir [sic, for *al-sarāʾir* presumably], on the lives and teachings of Saʿdī Lāhaurī,[708] ʿAbd al-Raḥmān Sulamī Nīshāpūrī, and S. Ādam Banūrī:[709] **Nadh̲īr Aḥmad** 40 (S̲h̲āh M. Muḥaddith's library, Rāmpūr).

1345. For Kāmwar Kh̲ān's *Haft gulshan i Muḥammad-S̲h̲āhī*, a history of India which extends to 1132/1719–20 and of which the seventh *gulshan* is devoted to Indian saints, see no. 625 *supra*.

---

708 Sh̲. Saʿdī BLKH̲ĀRĪ Mujaddidī Lāhaurī, a *khalīfah* of Sh̲. Ādam Banūrī, died in 1108/1696. See *Khazīnat al-aṣfiyāʾ* i pp. 647–53. BLKH̲ĀRĪ is not a misprint for Bukhārī. since a chronogram for the date of his death requires the presence of the *lām*.

709 Cf. no. 1320 2nd par. 3rd footnote *supra*.

1346. Sh. **Abū 'l-Faiyāḍ** Qamar al-Ḥaqq[710] **Ghulām-Rashīd**, born on 8 Rabīʿ al-Awwal 1096/12 Feb. 1685, was the son [?[711]], disciple and successor (*sajjādah-nishīn*) of Sh. Badr al-Ḥaqq M. Arshad b. M. Rashīd ʿUthmānī Jaunpūrī. In 1147/1734–5 his discourses were attended by Ghulām-Sharaf al-Dīn b. Imām al-Dīn, who has given an account of his life and teachings in the *Ganj i Faiyāḍī* (see no. 1354 *infra*). He died at Jaunpūr on 5 Ṣafar 1167/2 Dec. 1753. Among his works were an Arabic commentary on [his father's [?] Arabic grammar] the *Hidāyat al-naḥw*[712] and a Persian commentary on the *Qaṣīdah i Ghauthīyah*.[713]

Ganj i Arshadī, an account of the life and sayings of the above-mentioned Badr al-Ḥaqq M. Arshad b. M. Rashīd ʿUthmānī Jaunpūrī,[714] compiled in 1134–5/1721–3 from rough notes written by Sh. Shukr Allāh: ʿ**Alīgaṛh** Subḥ. MSS. p. 19 no. 19, **Rieu** iii 1013*b* (preface, table of contents and extracts only. *Circ.* A.D. 1850).

[*Tajallī i nūr* i p. 74 (from the *Baḥr i zakhkhār*).]

1347. Mullā **Niẓām al-Dīn M. Sihālawī**[715] was the third son of Mullā Quṭb al-Dīn Sihālawī, a celebrated teacher who was murdered in 1103/1692 (cf. no. 1401 2nd par. 2nd footnote *infra*). Having studied under Ghulām-Naqshband Lak'hnawī (cf. Brockelmann *Sptbd.* ii p. 611, Raḥmān ʿAlī p. 158) and others, he, like his father, became famous in India as a teacher. He died in Jumādā I 1161/May 1748, and the scholarly tradition of the family was carried on by his

---

710 So Rieu iii 1013*a*.

711 *Pisar u murīd u sajjādah-nishīn i Shāh Arshad ast* (*Tajallī i nūr* p. 74[8]). Browne in his description of the *Ganj i Faiyāḍī* describes him as the son of Shaikh Muḥibb Allāh. If this is a real discrepancy and Muḥibb Allāh is not merely a description of M. Arshad, the information derived from the *Ganj i Faiyāḍī* is likely to be correct.

712 See no. 1346 last footnote.

713 A well-known Arabic *qaṣīdah* ascribed to ʿAbd al-Qādir al-Jīlānī (see Brockelmann *Sptbd.* i p. 779 no. 44).

714 M. Arshad, according to the *Tajallī i nūr* (i p. 73), was the son of Dīwān M. Rashīd [evidently the same person as ʿAbd al-Rashīd Jaunpūrī, who died in 1083/1672 and whose works include the *Rashīdīyah*, well known in India: see Raḥmān ʿAlī p. 119; *Tajallī i nūr* i p. 71; Būhār Arab. cat. p. 513; Brockelmann *Sptbd.* ii p. 621; etc.]. Born in 1041/1631–2, he became one of the best scholars of Jaunpūr as well as an influential Ṣūfī affiliated to the Chishtī, Suhrawardī and Qalandarī orders. The [anonymous] Arabic syntax entitled *Hidāyat al-naḥw* [for which see Ellis col. 637, Brockelmann i p. 305, *Sptbd.* i 535] was one of his works according to the *Tajallī i nūr*, which does not mention the titles of any other works by him. He died on 24 Jumādā II 1113/26 Nov. 1701 and was buried at Jaunpūr, near his father.

715 *Sihālī* (*ba-kasr i sīn i muhmalah u hā-yi hawwaz u alif u lām i maksūr u yā-yi taḥtānī i maʿrūf*) *qaṣabah īst az tawābiʿ i Lak'hnaʾū* (Raḥmān ʿAlī p. 168).

son, Mullā ʿAbd al-ʿAlī M. Baḥr al-ʿulūm Lak'hnawī (for whom see Raḥmān ʿAlī p. 122, *Ency. Isl.* under Baḥr al-ʿulūm, Brockelmann *Sptbd.* ii p. 624). His works, nearly all commentaries or *ḥawāshī* on standard text-books, include (1) annotations on Ṣadrā's commentary on al-Abharī's *Hidāyat al-ḥikmah* (see Brockelmann *Sptbd.* i p. 840 antepenult.), (2) a commentary on Muḥibb Allāh al-Bihārī's *Musallam al-thubūt* (see Brockelmann *Sptbd.* ii p. 623, 1. 5 *ab infra*), (3) *Ṣubḥ i ṣādiq*, a commentary on Ḥāfiẓ al-Dīn al-Nasafī's *Manār al-anwār* (see Brockelmann *Sptbd.* ii p. 264, l. 4 *ab infra*), (4) annotations on the *Shams i bāzighah* of Maḥmūd Jaunpūrī (see Brockelmann *Sptbd.* ii p. 621), (5) annotations on Jalāl al-Dīn Dawānī's commentary (*ʿAqāʾid i Jalālī*) on the *ʿAqāʾid* of ʿAḍud al-Dīn al-Ījī (see Brockelmann *Sptbd.* ii p. 292[12]).

Manāqib al-Razzāqīyah, a life of the author's *pīr*, the Qādirī saint, S. ʿAbd al-Razzāq Bānsawī, who died on 6 Shawwāl 1136/1724 at Bānsī in the Bastī District of the United Provinces:[716] **Bānkīpūr** xvii 1592, **I.O.** D.P. 729.

Edition: **Lucknow** 1896° (pp. 20).

[*Malfūẓ i Razzāqī* pp. 148–59; *Maʾāthir al-kirām* p. 220; *Subḥat al-marjān* pp. 94–5; *Ḥadāʾiq al-Ḥanafīyah* p. 445; Raḥmān ʿAlī p. 241; Alṭāf al-Raḥmān *Aḥwāl i ʿulamāʾ i Farangī Maḥall* (in Urdu), Lucknow [1907*] p. 77; Bānkīpūr xvii p. 78.]

1348. **Bahāʾ al-Ḥaqq al-Qādirī** cannot have lived earlier than the 17th century, since he several times quotes ʿAbd al-Ḥaqq Dihlawī, who died in 1052/1642. If the Rāmpūr MS. is correctly described by Nadhīr Aḥmad as an autograph, he was living in 1138/1725–6.

Anīs al-Qādirīyah, an account of ʿAbd al-Qādir al-Jīlānī with brief notices of some earlier saints: **Rāmpūr** (A.H. 1138/1725–6, autograph. See Nadhīr Aḥmad 31), **I.O.** D.P. 577 (18th cent.).

1349. **M. Ḥabīb Allāh** b. Shaikh Jahān **Akbarābādī** Dihlawī was born at Akbarābād [i.e. Agrah] in 1082/1671–2. At the age of twelve he left his *maktab* and entered the *madrasah* of Malik al-ʿUlamāʾ Sh. ʿAṭāʾ Allāh,[717] with whom he read the Arabic *ʿulūm* until the age of twenty.[718] He then married and spent five years in straitened circumstances as a teacher at Delhi. Having entered the service of Zēb al-Nisāʾ, Aurangzēb's daughter [who died in 1114/1702],[719] he was for

716 An Urdu work on this saint is *Karāmāt i Razzāqīyah* by Nawwāb M. Khān Shāhjahānpūrī, Hardoi [1907*].

717 A biography of this scholar, who seems not to be mentioned by Raḥmān ʿAlī, is given in the *Dhikr i jamīʿ i auliyāʾ i Dihlī* (foll. 101*a*–103*b* in D.P. 594, foll. 85*a*–87*a* in D.P. 634).

718 Reading *bist-sālagī* instead of the impossible *sī-sālagī*.

719 For Z. al-N. see Jadunāt'h Sarkār's *Studies in Mughal India* pp. 79–90.

a time engaged in translating the *Fatāwī i ʿĀlamgīrī.*[720] Later in association with Muḥammad-Yār Khān, the Governor of Delhi, he compiled a lexicographical work or works.[721] At the same time he wrote annotations (*ḥāshiyah*) on the *Qāmūs*.[722] Having composed a work entitled *Muzīl al-aghlāṭ* he submitted it to the Khān i Khānān,[723] and was taken into the service of Bahādur Shāh (1119–24/1707–12) with a *manṣab* of 150. An advantageous intimacy with the Wazīr al-Mulk [i.e. the Khān i Khānān] ensued.[724] After receiving the appointments of Lecturer to the Emperor and Librarian to the Khān i Khānān,[725] he accompanied the Imperial army to Ḥaidarābād [in the campaign of 1120/1708–9 against Kām-bakhsh, Bahādur Shāh's brother]. When they reached the Narbadā on the return journey, he wrote a *risālah i ḥurūf i sabʿah* [so D.P. 594, but for *sabʿah* D.P. 634 has *ṣīghah* (?)] and submitted it to the Emperor, who rewarded him with a *khilʿat*, a present of 1,000 rupees, promotion to a *manṣab* of 400, and a *jāgīr*. In the reign of the *Shahīd i marḥūm* [i.e. Farrukh-siyar, 1124–31/1713–19] he became Keeper of the Treasury at Delhi and also Superintendent of the Holy Shrines[726] At this time, he says, he undertook and completed his translation of the *Bahjat al-asrār* (for which see no. 1251 *supra*, where it has been recorded that in the work itself the date of completion is given as 1133). At the beginning of Muḥammad Shāh's reign (1131–61/1719–48) he was appointed *wakīl i sharʿī* to the king and received the title of Khān.[727] At the time of writing the *Dhikr i jamīʿ i auliyāʾ i Dihlī* he was hoping to resign his *manṣab* and go on a *ḥajj*. In 1147/1735 he completed and dedicated to Muḥammad Shāh a Persian

720 *Chandī dar sarkār i Z. al-N.... tarjamah i Fatāwī i ʿĀlamgīrī numūd.* There seem to be no extant MSS. of this translation undertaken at the instance of Zēb al-Nisāʾ and perhaps never completed. A translation of the *kitāb al-ḥudūd* and the *kitāb al-jināyāt* made at a much later date by Qāḍī 'l-quḍāt M. Najm al-Dīn Khān Kākōrawī, who died in 1229/1814 (see Raḥmān ʿAli pp. 233–5, Sprenger p. 166), was printed at Calcutta in 1813°*. For the Arabic original, compiled by Sh. Niẓām Burhānpūrī (cf. Raḥmān ʿAlī p. 242) and others (five of whom are mentioned in Bānkīpūr xix p. 63), see Brockelmann ii p. 417, *Sptbd.* ii p. 604.

721 *u muddatī dar ṣuḥbat i M. Y. Kh. Nāẓim i Dār al-khilāfah tālīf i kitāb* [D.P. 634 has *kutub*] *i lughat mī-kard.*

722 No MSS. of this *ḥāshiyah* seem to be recorded. His Persian translation of the *Qāmūs* is mentioned below.

723 i.e. Munʿim Khān, who died in 1123/1711. See *Maʾāthir al-umarāʾ* iii pp. 667–77, Irvine *Later Mughals* i pp. 19, 36, 38, 125, etc.

724 *u bā Wazīr al-Mulk muṣāḥabat u muʿāsharat numūdah fawāʾid i bisyār girift.*

725 *u ba-khidmat i tadrīs i ḥuḍūr sar-buland gardīd u dāroghagī i kitāb-khānah wa-ghairah khidamāt az sarkār i nawwāb i ʿālī-janāb yāft.* I do not feel sure that I have translated this correctly.

726 *ba-khidmat i Amānat i Khizānah i ʿāmirah i Dār al-khilāfat u Amānat i Mazārāt i mutabarrakah sar-buland gardīdah.*

727 *u dar shurūʿ i ʿahd i mubārak ba-khidmat i wakālat i sharʿī i ḥaḍrat i Khidīw i Gaihān ba-iḍāfah i ṣadī u khiṭāb i khānī ʿizz i imtiyāz yāft.*

translation of the *Qāmūs* to which he gave the title *Qābūs* (MSS.: Āṣafīyah iii p. 618 nos. 373–4, Bodleian 1674, Būhār 253–4, Calcutta Madrasah 157–60, Rieu ii 511*a*, 511*b*). According to the *Tārīkh i Muḥammadī* (cited by Rieu. iii 1089*a*) he died at Delhi in 1160/1747.

Dhikr i jamīʿ i auliyāʾ i Dihlī (a chronogram = 1140/1727–8), lives of the saints of Delhi arranged according to the dates of their *aʿrās*: **I.O.** D.P. 594 (18th cent.), 634 (AH 1242/1827), **Rieu** iii 975*b* (*circ.* A.D. 1850) and probably also **Āṣafīyah** i p. 316 ult. (*Tadhkirah i j. i a. i D.* Author not stated, A.H. 1180/1766–7).

[Autobiography in the *khātimah* to the *Dh. i j. i a. i D.*]

1350. **M. Akram** b. Sh. M. ʿAlī b. Sh. Ilāh-bakhsh al-Ḥanafī al-**Barāsawī**,[728] a disciple of Sh. Saund'hā Safīdūnī,[729] by whom he was invested with the *khirqah i khilāfat* in 1111/1699–1700, began his *Sawāṭiʿ al-anwār* at Delhi in 1135/1722–3 and completed it in Muḥarram 1142/July-August 1729.

***Sawāṭiʿ al-anwār*, or *Iqtibās al-anwār*,**[730] a large work on the saints of the Chishtī order in four chapters called *iqtibās* ((1) Muḥammad, the first four Caliphs and the Imāms, (2) from Ḥasan Baṣrī to ʿUthmān Hārūnī, (3) from Muʿīn al-Dīn Chishtī to M. b. ʿĀrif b. Aḥmad ʿAbd al-Ḥaqq Rudaulawī,[731] (4) from ʿAbd al-Quddūs Gangōhī (cf. no. 1279 *supra*) to the author's father), these chapters being subdivided into sections called *nūr* and, in the case of the third *iqtibās*, into subsections called *sāṭiʿ*, *lāmiʿ*, and *shuʿāʿ*: **Ethé** 654, **I.O.** D.P. 667.

Edition: *Iqtibās al-anwār*, **Lahore** 1895°* (pp. 349).

List and epitome of the biographies: Ethé coll. 327–39.

1351. M. ʿ**Abd al-Rashīd** b. Nadhr-Muḥammad Qādirī **Kairā-nawī** was a disciple of Ḥājjī Shāh Fatḥ-Muḥammad Qādirī Kairānawī, called Miyān-jīw.[732] The latter, who was both the maternal uncle and the father-in-law of Nadhr-Muḥammad, ʿAbd al-Rashīd's father, was born at Anbālah (i.e. Ambala in the Panjāb), received the *khirqah i khilāfat* from Sh. Muḥyī 'l-Dīn (so Rieu), or

728 Barās is a village situated a few miles west of Karnāl in the Panjāb.

729 For Sh. Saund'hā see Ethé col. 338 no. 36, *Khazīnat al-aṣfiyāʾ* i p. 487. Safīdūn is now in the State of Jīnd.

730 This is given as an alternative title in the author's preface according to the I.O. MSS., but as the sole title in the lithographed edition, which (1) omits from the author's preface his statement concerning the date of composition, (2) inserts after the preface a *muqaddimah* on Ṣūfism, the 14 main orders, etc. (3) differs elsewhere from the text of the I.O. MSS.

731 For A. ʿAbd al-Ḥaqq Rudaulawī see no. 1279, 3rd par., footnote *supra*.

732 This is an Indian title of respect (cf. no. 1321 (2), 1st and 2nd footnote, *supra*).

Sh. Yaḥyā (so ʿAbd al-Muqtadir), Madanī at al-Madīnah, settled at Kairānah[733] and died there on 29 Rabīʿ al-Awwal 1130/2 March 1718.

(1) ***Taḥāʾif i Rashīdīyah***, biographies (each headed *Tuḥfah*) of thirty-seven persons from the Prophet to Shāh Fatḥ-Muḥammad, who form the author's spiritual pedigree in the Qādirī order, begun in 1137/1724–5 and completed in 1143/1730–1: **Rieu** i 361*b* (AH 1146/1733).

List of the biographies: Rieu i p. 362*a*.

(2) ***Tarīkh i Qādirīyah***, a shorter work on the lives of the same persons, written in 1150/1737: **Rāmpūr** (AH 1193/1779. See Nadhīr Aḥmad 74), **Bānkīpūr** viii 678 (18th cent.).

List of the biographies: Bānkīpūr viii p. 67.

1352. Quṭb al-Dīn Aḥmad, known as (*al-maʿrūf bi-*) **Walī Allāh**, b. ʿAbd al-Raḥīm b. Wajīh al-Dīn i Shahīd b. Muʿaẓẓam b. Manṣūr al-ʿUmarī al-Naqshbandī al-Muḥaddith **al-Dihlawī**, who was born in 1114/1703 and died in 1176/1762–3, has already been mentioned as the author of the *Fatḥ al-Raḥmān* (no. 35 (1) *supra*), *al-Fauz al-kabīr* (no. 35 (2) *supra*), the *Surūr al-maḥzūn* (no. 222 *supra*, Persian translation of the abridgment) and the *Qurrat al-ʿainain* (no. 285 *supra*). Twenty of his works are mentioned by Brockelmann, and Hidāyat Ḥusain's list, which includes only "the most important" and omits "many pamphlets on religious subjects", enumerates seventeen. His life, spent in teaching and writing, was uneventful, but he exercised great influence in India as a theologian.

(1) ***Anfās al-ʿārifīn***, on the lives, sayings and miracles of the author's kinsmen, teachers, etc., in three *qisms*, namely (1) *Bawāriq al-wilāyah*, on the author's father, ʿAbd al-Raḥīm Dihlawī (d. 1131/1719. See Raḥmān ʿAlī p. 119), (2) *Shawāriq al-maʿrifah*, on the author's paternal uncle, Abū 'l-Riḍā Muḥammad,(3) in five separately-titled and detachable *faṣls*, of which the first is *Imdād fī maʾāthir al-ajdād*, the second *al-Nubdhat al-ibrīzah* [*al-ibrīzīyah* ?] *fī 'l-laṭīfat al-gharīzah* [*al-gharīzīyah* ?] (*dar nashr i aḥwāl i Shaikh ʿAbd al-Azīz Dihlawī u aslāf u akhlāf i īshān*), the third *al-ʿAṭīyat al-Ṣamadīyah fī* [*'l-?*] *anfās al-Muḥammadīyah* (*dar dhikr i manāqib … i ḥaḍrat i Shaikh Muḥammad al-PHLTĪ*), the fourth *Insān al-ʿain fī mashāyikh al-Ḥaramain*, and the fifth *al-Juzʾ al-laṭīf fī tarjamat al-ʿabd al-ḍaʿīf*, a brief autobiography extending to 14 Rajab 1145/31

733 Kairānah is a town on the Jumna 31 miles S.W. of Muẓaffarnagar.

Dec. 1732, the date of the author's return home from his pilgrimage to Mecca:[734] **I.O.** 3985 (only the *Imdād. Circ.* AD 1895).

Edition: *Anfās al-ʿārifīn*, **Delhi** 1315/1897* (pp. 196).

Edition and English translation of *Qism* iii, *faṣl* 5: *The Persian autobiography of Shāh Walīullah bin ʿAbd al-Raḥīm al-Dihlavī: its English translation and a list of his works. By Mawlavi M. Hidayat Husain* (in *JASB*. N.S. viii (1912) pp. 161–75).

Edition of *Qism III, fasl* 5: *Saṭaʿāt maʿah ... Juzʾ al-laṭīf* [Delhi 1890°].

(2) ***al-Intibāh fī salāsil auliyāʾ Allāh***, an enumeration of the spiritual pedigrees of the author with incidental expositions of Ṣūfī practices and other matters, divided (in the I.O. MS.) under the headings *Muqaddimah* fol. 1*b*, *Silsilah i Ṣūfīyah i ʿulamāʾ* fol. 7*b*, *Silsilah i bishārah* fol. 8*b*, *Silsilah i Khwājah* [*sic*] *i Qādirīyah* fol. 10*b*, *Ṭarīqah i Naqshbandīyah* fol. 21*a*, *Ṭarīqah i Chishtīyah* fol. 42*a*, *Ṭarīqah i Kubrawīyah* fol. 55*a*, *Ṭarīqah i Madyanīyah* fol. 58*a*, *Ṭarīqah i Shādhilīyah* fol. 61*a*, *Ṭarīqah i Shaṭṭārīyah* fol. 62*a*: **Āṣafīyah** i p. 402 no. 584 (AH 1174/1760–1), **I.O.** D.P. 776 (late 18th cent.).

Edition: **Delhi** 1311/1893–4 (see *JASB*. 1912 p. 168).

[To the biographical sources mentioned on p. 22 may be added *Khazīnat al-aṣfiyāʾ* ii p. 373; *Ḥayāt i Walī* (in Urdu. 360 pp.), by M. Raḥīm-Bakhsh, Delhi 1319/1901–2*; Bānkīpūr xiv pp. 134–5; Brockelmann *Sptbd.* ii pp. 614–5. For an anonymous work defending Walī Allāh against the charge that he had insufficient respect for the Imāms, see Bānkīpūr xvii 1619.]

734 This autobiography of five pages tells of his birth (4 Shawwāl 1114), his going to *maktab* (in his 5th year), his beginning to pray and fast, his circumcision, his finishing the *Qurʾān* and beginning to read Persian books (7th year), his reading the *Sharḥ i Mullā* [Jāmī on Ibn al-Ḥājib's *Kāfiyah*] (10th year), marriage (14th year), his introduction to the practices of the Ṣūfīs, especially the Naqshbandīs, as his father's disciple and his completion of the traditional course of studies (15th year), his father's death after giving him licence to accept *baiʿat* and give *irshād* (17th year), some twelve years of teaching, of progress in Ṣūfism, study of the books of the four *madhāhib* and acceptance of the *rawish i fuqahā-yi muḥaddithīn*, his departure for the pilgrimage (end of 1143), his visits to Mecca and Medina, his intercourse with the traditionist Sh. Abū Ṭāhir [M. b. Ibrāhīm al-Kurdī al-Madanī, d. 1145: see *JASB*. 1912 p. 166], by whom he was admitted to several Ṣufī orders (*khirqah i jāmiʿah i Sh. A. Ṭ. kih ḥāwī i jamīʿi khiraq i Ṣūfīyah tuwān guft pūshīd*), his performance of the *ḥajj* at the end of this year, his departure for India (beginning of 1145) and his arrival home on 14 Rajab. Many of the books read by him in the course of his studies are specified.

1353. For the *Burhān al-futūḥ*, which was composed in 1148/1736–7 by M. ʿAlī b. M. Ṣādiq Ḥusainī Nīshāpūrī Najafī Burhān-pūrī, and of which the fifteenth *bāb* is devoted to notices of *ṣūfīs*, see no. 164 *supra*.

1354. **Ghulām-Sharaf al-Dīn**[735] b. Sh. Imām al-Dīn b. Sh. Karīm al-Dīn was the son of a daughter of Hidāyat Allāh Qādirī Rashīdī Arshadī Faiyāḍī Manērī. He was a disciple of Sh. Abū 'l-Faiyāḍ Ghulām-Rashīd (see no. 1346 *supra*), whose discourses he attended and noted down from 11 Muḥarram to 12 Ramaḍān 1147/13 June 1734 to 5 February 1735.

Ganj i Faiyāḍī, a biography of the above-mentioned Sh. Abū 'l-Faiyāḍ Ghulām-Rashīd with a collection of his letters and sayings: **Browne** Pers. Cat. 111 (AH 1150/1738), **Ivanow** Curzon 80 (18th cent.).

1355. **M. b. Yār-Muḥammad**[736] b. Rājī Kamman **Kōlawī** tells us that he was born on 2 Dhū 'l-Ḥijjah 1098/9 October 1697.

Ashjār al-jamāl or alternatively *Akhbār al-jamāl*, short notices of prophets and saints including some Ṣūfīs of Kōl (i.e. ʿAlīgaṛh), completed in 1151/1738: **Ivanow** Curzon 81 (defective. Late 18th cent.) = Nadhīr Aḥmad 57.

1356. M. **Qiyām al-Dīn**, commonly called (*ʿurf*) Qaḍī Khān, b. Abū 'l-Ḥasan Chishtī Fārūqī.

Ḥaqā'iq al-auliyā', written in 1154/1741–2: **Āṣafīyah** iii p. 100 no. 1293 (Precise subject not stated, AH 1154/1741–2).

1357. **M. Najīb Qādirī Nāgaurī** Ajmērī wrote his *Makhzan al-aʿrās* in 1155/1742 and 1156/1743 (and possibly subsequent years) on the basis of a work by Sharaf al-Dīn b. Qāḍī Shaikh M. Nahrawālī[737]

735 Similar personal names consisting of the word Ghulām followed by the name of a saint are Ghulām-Jīlānī (cf. no. 915 *supra*), Ghulām-Hamadānī (no. 1175 *supra*), Ghulām-Muḥyī 'l-Dīn (nos. 547, 852 *supra*), and Ghulām-Naqshband (cf. Brockelmann *Sptbd.* ii p. 611). The Sharaf al-Dīn referred to is evidently Sharaf al-Dīn Yaḥyā Manērī (for whom see no. 1404 (2) footnote).

736 Nadhīr Aḥmad gives the author's name as "Yār Md. B. Rājī Kamman", and this indeed appears to be the form in which the name first occurs in the MS., since Ivanow in quoting the opening words [*al-Ḥ. l.... ammā baʿd fa-qāla ...* (*M. b.*) *Yār M. b. Rājī ...*] brackets *M.b.* as though supplied from another place.

737 Nahrawālah = Pattan in Gujrāt.

Makhzan al-aʿrās, dates of the deaths of saints arrayed under the months: **Ivanow** 1631 (slightly defective at end. Late 18th cent.), 1632 (late 18th or early 19th cent.), **Ivanow** 1st Spt. 869 (early 19th cent.).

Edition (presumably of this work): *Kitāb i aʿrās*, by M. Najīb Qādirī Nāgaurī, [**Āgrah**] 1300/1883°.

1358. Miyāṅ **Aḥmad b. Maḥmūd Uwaisī** Chanābī.

Laṭāʾif i nafīsīyah[738] ***dar faḍāʾil i Uwaisīyah***, anecdotes of Uwais al-Qaranī,[739] written in 1156/1743: **Lahore** Panjāb Univ. Lib. (see OCM. viii/4 p. 42).

Edition: **Delhi** 1314/1896°.

Urdu translation: *Nasīm i Yaman fī ḥālāt i Uwais i Qaran*, by S. M. Ishfāq[740] Ḥusain Shāh Razzāqī, **Lahore** 1328/1910*.

1359. Abū 'l-Faiḍ Kamāl al-Dīn **M. Iḥsān** b. Ḥasan Aḥmad (d. 1149/1736) b. M. Hādī b. M. ʿAbd Allāh b. Aḥmad Mujaddid i Alf i Thānī was a great-great-grandson of the celebrated Naqshbandī saint Aḥmad Sirhindī and was apparently a *khalīfah* of the saint in Oudh or Bengal.

Rauḍat al-qaiyūmīyah, begun before 1152/1739 but then interrupted until about 1154/1741 and containing in the concluding lines a reference to the reigning sovereign Muḥammad Shāh (d. 1161/1748), though some later dates (e.g. 1164/1751) occur in the narrative, a detailed account of the lives (narrated laudably year by year) and miracles, etc., of the great saint Aḥmad Fārūqī Sirhindī, called here the first *qaiyūm* (*qaiyūm i awwal i īn ummat*), who died in 1034/1624 (see no. 1316 (1), 1st footnote *supra*), and his first three successors (the second, third and fourth *qaiyūm*), namely, his (third) son, M. Maʿṣūm called ʿUrwat al-wuthqā (b. 1007/1599, d. 1079/1668),[741] M. Naqshband Ḥujjat Allāh (b. 1034/1625, d. 1114/1702), the son of the preceding, and M. Zubair (b. 1093/1682, d. 1152/1740), with an

738 So called because "*maḍāmīn u maʿānī laṭīfah i nafīsah par mabnī hai*" (Urdu trans., p. 9, l. 5 from below).

739 For Uwais al-Qaranī, who is said to have been killed at the Battle of Ṣiffīn (AH 37/657) or to have died at some other date (AH 18, 22, 32, etc.), see *Kashf al-maḥjūb*. tr. Nicholson, pp. 83–4; *Tadhkirat al-auliyāʾ* i pp. 15–24; *Haft iqlīm* pp. 19–22 (no. 1); *Majālis al-muʾminīn* pp. 120–1 (3rd biography *in Majlis* 4); *Safīnat al-auliyāʾ* p. 30(no. 18); *Khazīnat al-aṣfiyāʾ* ii pp. 118–21; Caetani *Chronographia Islamica* i pp. 214 (AH 18) and 423 (AH 37), where other references will be found.

740 Or Ashfāq in accordance with the usual, though corrupt, Indian pronunciation in such names as this.

741 Cf. no. 1320 2nd par. 2nd footnote *supra* and *Qaiyūm i thānī*, a short (48 pp.) Urdu biography by M. ʿAẓīm Fīrōzpūrī, Lahore [1905*].

enormous number (probably more than two thousand) of short notices of their descendants and disciples, interspersed with incidental references to historical events, e.g. Nādir Shāh's invasion, which the author, an eye-witness, describes at some length: **Ivanow** Curzon 82 (AH 1218/1804).

1360. **M. Amān b. M. Yūsuf** b. M. Raḥīm seems to have followed the army of Niẓām al-Mulk Āṣaf-Jāh to Arcot [in 1156/1743]. He had visited the shrines of saints at Aurangābād, Gwalior and elsewhere.

Safīnat al-ʿārifīn, notices of numerous holy men, mostly Indian, from the first four Caliphs to the end of the eleventh century of the Hijrah, the latest date being 1103/1692, the year of the death of S. Ḥasan Rasūl-numā:[742] **Rieu** i 362*b* (18th cent.).

1361. For the *Wāqiʿāt i Kashmīr*, begun by M. Aʿẓam in 1148/1735–6, completed in 1160/1747, and devoted largely to the lives of Kashmīrī saints, see no. 880 (1) *supra*.

1362. Mir **Ghulām-ʿAlī "Āzād" Bilgrāmī**, who was born at Bilgrām in 1116/1704 and died, doubtless at Aurangābād, in 1200/1786, has already been mentioned (no. 1162 *supra*) as the author of the *Khizānah i ʿāmirah* and other works.

(1) ***Raudat al-auliyā'***, lives of ten saints buried at Rauḍah ("Rauza", "Roza", "Raoza"), or Khuldābād (cf. no. 1162, 4th par., 2nd footnote *supra*), namely Burhān al-Dīn M, called al-Gharīb al-Hānsawī[743] (p. 4), Muntajab al-Dīn Zarzarī Zar-bakhsh (p. 14), Ḥasan Dihlawī (p. 16), Rājū Qattāl (p. 18), Gēsū-darāz (p. 19), Farīd al-Dīn Adīb (p. 25), Khwājah Ḥusain b. Maḥmūd Shīrāzī (p. 26), Zain al-Dīn Dāwud b. Khwājah Ḥusain Shīrāzī (p. 26), Shāh Jalāl Ganj i Rawān (p. 41), Shāh Khāksār (p. 42), followed by brief notices of three rulers buried there (Aurangzēb, Niẓām al-Mulk Burhān Shāh, Niẓām al-Mulk Āṣaf-Jāh) and an autobiography of the author, who wrote the work in 1161/1748: **Āṣafīyah** iii p. 164 no. 148 (AH 1167/1753–4), i p. 320 no. 22 (AH 1232/1816–17), **Ethē** 655.

742 For whom see *Dhikr i jamīʿ i auliyā' i Dihlī* (I.O. D.P. 594 foll. 90*b*–92*a*); Khāfī Khān ii pp. 552–3; *Chahār gulshan* (I.O. 3944 fol. 23a ult.); *Āthār al-ṣanādīd* (in Urdu), *bāb* iii p. 74; *Khazīnat al-aṣfiyā'* i p. 180 margin. A collection of his sayings taken down by a disciple named Khalīl is preserved in an I.O. MS. (D.P. 590).

743 B. al-D. Gh., who is the person commemorated in the name of Burhānpūr, was a disciple of Niẓām al-Dīn Auliyā (cf. no. 1259, 4th footnote) and died in 738/1337 (or thereabouts). See *Akhbār al-akhyār* pp. 93–4; *Haft iqlīm*, no. 390; Firishtah ii pp. 400–1; *Safīnat al-auliyā'* p. 101 (no. 117); *Khazīnat al-aṣfiyā'* i pp. 346–8; *Nuzhat al-khawāṭir* pp. 143–4; Beale *Oriental biographical dictionary* under Burhan-uddin Gharib; etc.

Edition: **Aurangābād** 1310/1892–3*.

Urdu translation by Saif Allāh Qādirī: *Tarjamah i R. al-a.*, **Ḥaidarābād** (see Ḥaidarābād Coll. p. 52, where neither the date of publication nor the name of the original author is mentioned).

(2) ***Ma'āthir al-kirām tārīkh i Bilgrām***, completed in 1166/1752–3 and divided into two *faṣls*, namely (1) lives of about eighty *fuqarā'*, i.e. saints and mystics, firstly those of Bilgrām and its neighbourhood and secondly those incidentally mentioned in the preceding biographies, (2) lives of about seventy *fuḍalā'*, i.e. learned men, firstly those of India and secondly those of Oudh and Bilgrām: **Āṣafīyah** i p. 348 no. 105 (AH 1180/1766–7), **Ethé** 682 (sent by the author to Richard Johnson in 1785), **I.O.** 3923 (*circ.* AD 1880 ?), **Bānkīpūr** viii 723 (early 19th cent.), **Rieu** iii 971*a* (AH 1266/1850), **Berlin** 603 (*Faṣl* 2 only).

Edition: **Ḥaidarābād** 1910 (with introduction by 'Abd al-Ḥaqq. See *OCM*. iii/2 (Feb. 1927) p. 33 footnote).

List of the biographies in *Faṣl* 2: Berlin pp. 567–8.

The *Sarw i āzād*, which is the second volume of this work, though for all practical purposes it may be regarded as independent, has already been dealt with (no. 1162 (16) *supra*).

1363. Ḥanīf al-Dīn **'Abd al-Qādir** b. Qāḍī S. M. Sharīf b. Qāḍī S. M. Ḥanīf **Kintūrī**[744] Nīshāpurī died in 1204/1789–90 (according to the Āṣafīyah catalogue).

Kuḥl al-jawāhir fī manāqib 'Abd al-Qādir, written in 1167/1753–4: **Āṣafīyah** i p. 460 no. 633.

1364. For the *Chahār gulshan* of Rāy Chaturman, which was completed in 1173/1759–60 and of which the fourth *gulshan* is devoted to Muslim and Hindu saints, see no. 631 *supra*.

1365. For the *Mir'āt i Aḥmadī*, which was completed by 'Alī Muḥammad Khān in 1175/1761, and of which the *khātimah* contains *inter alia* accounts of the saints and Saiyids buried in, or near, Aḥmadābād, see no. 984 *supra*.

1366. **M. Ṣādiq Kāshgharī.**

Tadhkirah i Khwājagān, or ***Tadhkirah i 'Azīzān***, a Turkī work on the lives of certain saints of Kāshghar, written in 1182/1768–9: **Leningrad** Institut (see *Manuscrits turcs de l'Institut des Langues Orientales décrits par W.*

744 Presumably in reference to Kintūr, a village 21 miles N.E. of Bārah Bankī in Oudh.

D. Smirnow (St. Petersburg 1897) pp. 156–60. Cf. Semenov *Ukazatel* p. 15, where no MSS. are mentioned).

English epitome: *The history of the Khojas of Eastern-Turkistān summarized from the Tazkira-i-Khwājagān of Muḥammad Ṣādiq Kāshgharī, by the late Robert Barkley Shaw ... Edited with introduction and notes by N. Elias.* **Calcutta** 1897 (*Journal of the Asiatic Society of Bengal,* vol. lxvi, part 1, extra no.).

Persian version (?):[745] MSS. ?

1367. **M. ʿĀbid.**

Ḥālāt i Saiyid Sālār Masʿūd Ghāzī, an account, written in 1188/1774–5, [presumably of the Saiyid who is said to have founded Ghāzīpūr (cf. no. 1411 (64) footnote *infra*) rather than of the legendary hero who has already been mentioned (no. 1329 (7) *supra*) as the subject of the *Mirʾāt i Masʿūdī*]: **Āṣafīyah** iii p. 362 no. 251 (AD 1831).

1368. S. **Ghulām-Ḥusain Khān** b. Hidāyat-ʿAlī Khān b. S. ʿAlīm Allāh b. S. Faiḍ Allāh[746] **Ṭabāṭabāʾī** Ḥasanī, who was born at Delhi in 1140/1727–8, has already been mentioned (pp. 625–40) as the author of the *Siyar al-mutaʾakhkhirīn,* which he began in 1194/1780 and completed in 1195/1781.

Bishārat al-imāmah, a *mathnawī,* written before the *Siyar al-mutaʾakhkhirīn,*[747] on the lives of the author's ancestors, especially the miracles of his great-grandfather, S. Faiḍ Allāh Ṭabāṭabāʾī, and his grandfather S. ʿAlīm Allāh Ṭabāṭabā, the latter of whom died at ʿAẓīmābād (*i.e.* Patna) in Shaʿbān 1156/1743:[748] **Bānkīpūr** Suppt. i 1991 (AH 1277/1860).

1369. "From various incidental allusions in his book it is possible to conclude that" a certain **Sabzawārī** (*khāk-sār i Sabzawārī,* as he calls himself) "wrote shortly after 1188/1774" (Ivanow). S. Qamar al-Dīn Aurangābādī (d. 1193/1779 or 1195/1781: cf. no. 36 *supra*), the subject of the 26th *sāniḥah,* and Mīr Ghulām-ʿAlī "Āzād" (d. 1200/1786: cf. no. 1162, 4th par. *supra*), the subject of the 27th, were still alive at the time of writing.

(*Sawāniḥ*), a work in 31 *sāniḥahs* on the saints buried or still living in or near Aurangābād (the first being Burhān al-Dīn Gharīb, who died in

745 That the work exists in a Persian form is implied by its inclusion in Semenov's *Ukazatel',* but the inclusion may be inadvertent.

746 Cf. *Siyar al-mutaʾakhkhirīn* i p. 3^{13}, ii p. 374^{11} (Lucknow editions).

747 The *B. al-i.* is mentioned in the *S. al-m.* ii pp. 523^{16}, 613^{13} (Lucknow editions).

748 *S. al-m.* ii p. 613^{11-12} (Raymond's trans. (1926) ii p. 171).

738/1337, the last Miyāṅ Ghulām-Ḥusain, still living), with descriptions of their graves and of the city: **Ivanow** 285 (late 18th cent.), possibly also **Rehatsek** p. 197 no. 43 ("*Resáláh Sowáneh* ... This little MS. contains the legends of the saints who lived during the time of Aurung-zyb, who amounted to about a dozen or so; it contains also a description of the city of Aurangábád, which he restored and looked upon with peculiar favour, and of the mausoleum of one of his Begums; it was composed during his lifetime,[749] but bears no date").

List of the biographies, etc.: Ivanow pp. 122–3.

1370. **M. Aʿẓam T'hattawī.**

Tuḥfat al-ṭāhirīn, an account of the saints buried at Tattah and on Maklī hill (no. 1373 (2) footnote *infra*), written in 1194/1780: **Rieu** iii 1061*b* (extracts only).

1371. It was at the request of Ṭīpū Sulṭān (ruler of Mysore 1197–1213/1782–99: cf. no. 1070) that a certain **M. Sharīf** compiled the *Ṣaḥīfat al-aʿrās*.

Ṣaḥīfat al-aʿrās, or *Tarīkh i wafāt i buzurgān*, an almanac giving the names of the holy personages who died on each day of the Muḥammadan year: **Ethé** 2733, **Ivanow** 1634.

1372. Mīr Shihāb al-Dīn[750] "Niẓām", entitled **ʿImād al-Mulk[751] Ghāzī al-Dīn Khān Fīrōz-Jang** [III], was a son of the Amīr al-umarāʾ Ghāzī al-Din Khān Fīrōz-Jang [II, i.e. Mīr M. Panāh, d. 1165/1752[752]] and a grandson of Niẓām al-Mulk Āṣaf-Jāh[753] His mother was a daughter of Iʿtimād al-Daulah Qamar al-Dīn Khān,[754] who became *Wazīr* to Muḥammad Shāh in 1136/1724 and died in 1161/1748. In the reign of Aḥmad Shāh (1161–7/1748–54) he was *Mīr Bakhshī* (Quartermaster General[755]) and subsequently *Wazīr*. He directed the military

749 If this work was really written in Aurangzēb's lifetime, Ivanow 285 is presumably an expanded recension of it.

750 This name was borne also by his great-grandfather, who like him had the title Ghāzī al-Dīn Khān Firōz-Jang (but not ʿImād al-Mulk) and who died in 1122/1710. See *Maʾāthir al-umarāʾ* ii pp. 872–9, Beveridge's trans. pp. 587–92; Beale *Oriental biographical dictionary* under Ghazi-uddin Khan i.

751 By the title ʿImād al-Mulk he is distinguished from his father and his great-grandfather, both of whom bore the title Ghāzī al-Dīn Khān Fīrōz-Jang.

752 See *Maʾāthir al-umarāʾ* i pp. 361–2; *Khizānah i ʿāmirah* pp. 49–50.

753 Mīr Qamar al-Dīn. See *Maʾāthir al-umarāʾ* iii pp. 837–48; *Khizānah i ʿāmirah* pp. 35–49.

754 Mīr M. Fāḍil. See *Maʾāthir al-umarāʾ* i pp. 358–61.

755 See BSOS.ix/1 p. 225.

operations against Ṣafdar-Jang[756] and, with Marāṭʰā help, against Sūraj Mal, the Jāṭ. In 1167/1754 he deposed Aḥmad S̲h̲āh and placed ʿĀlamgīr II upon the throne. In 1169/1755 Mīr Muʿīn al-Mulk, Governor of the Panjāb,[757] who had perforce submitted to Aḥmad S̲h̲āh Abdālī, died, and his widow and her favourite Ādīnah Bēg K̲h̲ān[758] seized the reins of government. ʿImād al-Mulk, desiring to restore the province to the empire, captured Lahore, where he left Ādīnah Bēg K̲h̲ān in charge, removed Mug̲h̲ulānī Bēgam to Delhi and married her daughter. Aḥmad S̲h̲āh Abdālī at once marched on Lahore (AH 1170/1756), expelled Ādīnah Bēg K̲h̲ān, and went on to Delhi, which he entered victoriously with ʿĀlamgīr II and ʿImād al-Mulk in his train. ʿImād al-Mulk then took part on behalf of Aḥmad S̲h̲āh Abdālī in the operations of Jahān K̲h̲ān against Sūraj Mal and in unsuccessful hostilities against S̲h̲ujāʿ al-Daulah of Oudh. Aḥmad S̲h̲āh Abdālī, displeased with ʿImād al-Mulk, appointed Najīb al-Daulah *Amīr al-Umarāʾ* and left for Lahore. ʿImād al-Mulk marched from Farruk̲h̲ābād against Najīb al-Daulah and with Marāṭʰā help besieged him and ʿĀlamgīr II in Delhi. In 1174/1760 the growing power of the Sikʰs and Marāṭʰās brought Aḥmad S̲h̲āh Abdālī for the fourth time to India, and the Marāṭʰās were defeated at Pānīpat. ʿImād al-Mulk, knowing that ʿĀlamgīr II desired an Abdālī victory, had murdered him [8 Rabīʿ II 1173/29 Nov. 1759] on Aḥmad S̲h̲āh's approach.

The days of ʿImād al-Mulk's power were now over. For a time he stayed with Sūraj Mal [who died in 1177/1763], then with Aḥmad K̲h̲ān Bangas̲h̲ [d. 1185/1771] at Farruk̲h̲ābād, and he fought on the side of S̲h̲ujāʿ al-Daulah of Oudh against the British. In 1187/1773 he went to the Deccan and received some land in Mālwah from the Marāṭʰās. Then after living for a time at Sūrat he went on a pilgrimage to Mecca. In 1195/1781 according to the *Gulzār i Ibrāhīm*, (cited in Sprenger p. 273) he was in Sind. Subsequently he was at the court of Tīmūr S̲h̲āh Abdālī (who reigned 1187–1207/1773–93), and in 1211/1797, when Zamān S̲h̲āh (1207–16/1793–1801) invaded the Panjāb, ʿImād al-Mulk is said to have been in his service. He died at Kālpī on 10 Rabīʿ II 1215/1 September 1800.[759]

ʿImād al-Mulk, who originally used the *tak̲h̲alluṣ* "Āṣaf" but abandoned it later for "Niẓām", wrote poetry in Persian, Urdu, Arabic and Turkī. His Persian *dīwān*, of which there are MSS. in the British Museum (Rieu ii 719*b*) and at Leningrad (Romaskewicz p. 9), was published in 1301/1883–4 (see Āṣafīyah iii

---

756   See *Maʾāt̲h̲ir al-umarāʾ* i pp. 365–8.
757   He was a son of Iʿtimād al-Daulah Qamar al-Dīn K̲h̲ān and therefore a maternal uncle of ʿImād al-Mulk.
758   Cf. no. 843 *supra*.
759   See *JASB*. xlviii/1 (1879) p. 130.

p. 296, where the place of publication (presumably Ḥaidarābād) is not mentioned). A poem in praise of ʿAlī (*Manqabat i Niẓām dar madḥ i ʿAlī*) and a *qaṣīdah* are preserved in MS. (autograph ?) at ʿAlīgaṛh (Subḥ. MSS. p. 37 nos. 7, 8). His *mathnawīs* included one on the miracles of Maulānā Fakhr al-Dīn (*Fakhrīyat al-Niẓām*), but no MSS. seem to be recorded.

Manāqib i Fakhrīyah, a biography of Maulānā M. Fakhr al-Dīn called Muḥibb al-Nabī Dihlawī,[760] written in 1201/1786–7: **I.O.** D.P. 728 (AH 1227/1812), **Lindesiana** p. 158 no. 741 (AH 1240/1824–5), **Āṣafīyah** i p. 490 no. 342 (AH 1312/1894–5).

Edition: **Delhi** 1315/1897*.

[*Khizānah i ʿāmirah* pp. 50–4; *Maʾāthir al-umarāʾ* ii pp. 847–56; *Gulzār i Ibrāhīm*; Muṣḥafī *Tadhkirah i Hindī*; *Makhzan al-gharāʾib* no. 2922; *Majmūʿah i naghz* ii pp. 277–80; *Tadhkirah i Sarwar*; *Tadhkirah i khwush-nawīsān* p. 76; *ʿIyār al-shuʿarāʾ*; *Gulshan i bī-khār; Tārīkh ʿImād al-Mulk* (see no. 797 *supra*); *Naghmah i ʿandalīb*; Sprenger p. 273; Garcin de Tassy ii pp. 476–7; W. Irvine *The Bangash Nawábs of Farrukhábád* (in JASB. xlviii/I (1879)) pp. 128–30; Rieu ii 719–20, iii 1092*b*; Beale *Oriental biographical dictionary* under Ghazi-uddin Khan III.]

1373. Mīr **ʿAlī Shēr "Qāniʿ" Tattawī**, who was born in 1140/1727–8 and was still alive in 1202/1787–8, has already been mentioned (no. 828 *supra*) as the author of the *Tuḥfat al-kirām* and other works.

(1) ***Miʿyar i sālikān i ṭarīqat*** (a chronogram = 1202/1787–8), lives of saints from the time of Muḥammad to the close of the twelfth century of the Hijrah in twelve *miʿyārs* each devoted to a century: **Rieu** ii 847*b* (AH 1246/1830), **I.O.** 4396 (*circ.* AD 1852 probably).

(2) ***Maklī-nāmah***, accounts of the saints buried on Maklī hill[761] (beside Tattah): **Rieu** iii 1061*b* (extracts only).

---

760 Fakhr al-Dīn Fakhr i Jahān Shahjahānābādī Chishtī, as he is called in the *Khazīnat al-aṣfiyāʾ*, was the son and *khalīfah* of Sh. Niẓām al-Dīn Aurangābādī (cf. no. 1380 3rd before last footnote *infra*). Born at Aurangābād in 1126/1714, he migrated to Delhi at the age of twenty-five and died there in Jumādā II 1199/April-May 1785. See *Dhikr al-aṣfiyāʾ; Miftāḥ al-tawārīkh* p. 360; *Khazīnat al-aṣfiyāʾ* i pp. 498–505; Beale *Oriental biographical dictionary* under Fakhr-uddin (Maulana) (Beale's statement that he was styled Saiyid al-shuʿarāʾ seems to be based on the fact that the chronogram on his tomb is followed by the words *min kalām S. al-sh. Fakhr al-Dīn Maqbūl i Ilāhī sanah i* 1199, but presumably the author of the chronogram was his disciple S. Fakhr al-Dīn "Mast", who is mentioned in the *Khazīnat al-aṣfiyāʾ* i p. 500³).

761 Cf. no. 1370 *supra*.

1374. Autobiographical statements in the text of the *Baḥr i zakhkhār* show that the author, **Wajīh al-Dīn Ashraf**, lived at Lucknow and that he was writing the work in 1203/1788–9.

Baḥr i zakhkhār (beginning: *Ḥamd i bī-ḥadd Qadīmī rā*), a "vast compilation" (595 foll, in the very imperfect B.M. MS.) devoted to the lives of saints and mystics, mostly Indian and many contemporary with the author, divided into eight *lujjahs*, which are subdivided into *nahrs* and again into *maujs* (viz.[762] (1) Muḥammad's children and wives, the Caliphs and the Companions, (2) 'Alī, Fāṭimah, the Imāms, the *Tābi'īn*, traditionists, jurists and Qur'ān-readers, (3) (*a*) Ḥasan Baṣrī[763] and his disciples, (*b*) Chirāgh i Dihlī (cf. no. 1259 1st par. last footnote *supra*) and his disciples, (*c*) Sirāj al-Dīn 'Uthmān[764] and his order, (*d*) 'Alī Ṣabīr,[765] etc., (4) (*a*) Ma'rūf Karkhī,[766] etc., (*b*) 'Abd al-Qādir Gīlānī (cf. no. 1251 2nd par. footnote *supra*), and the Qādirīs, (*c*) Abū Najīb Suhrawardī,[767] etc., (*d*) Najm al-Dīn Kubrā,[768]

---

762 The analysis which follows is based on the table of contents prefixed to the work in the B.M. MS. (foll. 1–70).

763 Celebrated traditionist and ascetic, d. 110/728 at al-Baṣrah. See Ibn Qutaibah *Ma'ārif* p. 225; *Kashf al-maḥjūb*, tr. Nicholson p. 86; *Tadhkirat al-auliyā'* i pp. 24–40; Ibn Khallikān no. 155; *Haft iqlīm* p. 144 (no. 88); *Safīnat al-auliyā'* p. 31 (no. 19); *Khazīnat al-aṣfiyā'* i pp. 222–5; *Rauḍāt al-jannāt* pp. 208–11; *Ency. Isl.* under al-Ḥasan (unsigned); Caetani *Chronographia Islamica* p. 1396 (where many further references will be found); Massignon *Essai sur les origines du lexique technique de la mystique musulmane* pp. 152–79; *Der Islam*. XIV (1925) pp. 1–75.

764 One of Niẓām al-Dīn Auliyā's disciples, d. 758/1357. See *Maṭlūb al-ṭālibīn* (Ethé col. 324[22]); *Sawāṭi' al-anwār* (Ethé col. 333[6]); *Khazīnat al-aṣfiyā'* i pp. 357–8; *Nuzhat al-khawāṭir* (in Arabic) p. 77; etc.

765 'Alā' al-Dīn 'Alī b. Aḥmad Ṣābir Kalyarī, founder of the Ṣābirī branch of the Chishtī order and a disciple of Ganj i Shakar (for whom see no. 1259 3rd footnote *supra*), died in 690/1291 and is buried at Pīrān Kalyar, near Roorkee, in the Sahāranpūr District of the United Provinces. See *Akhbār al-akhyār* p. 69; *Sawāṭi' al-anwār* (Ethé col. 334 no. 24); *Khazīnat al-aṣfiyā'* i pp. 315–19; *Sawāniḥ i 'umrī i ḥaḍrat i Ṣābir ... mukammal tārīkh i Pīrān Kalyar i sharīf* (in Urdu), by Sulṭān Maḥmūd b. Mushtāq Aḥmad Murādābādī, Murādābād [1911 ?]; *Tadhkirah i Ṣābirīyah ma'rūf bah Siyāḥat i Kalyar* (in Urdu), by Walī Aḥmad Khān. Badāyūṅ [1922]; etc.

766 For M. al-K., a celebrated Ṣūfī who died in 200/815–16 and is buried at Baghdād, see *Kashf al-maḥjūb* tr. Nicholson pp. 113–15; *Tadhkirat al-auliyā'* i pp. 269–74; Ibn Khallikān no. 371; *Nafaḥāt* pp. 42–3; *Haft iqlīm* p. 105 (no. 38); *Majālis al-mu'minīn* p. 266; *Safīnat al-auliyā'* p. 35 (no. 27); *Khazīnat al-aṣfiyā'* i pp. 76–8; *Rauḍāt al-jannāt* iv pp. 216–17; *Ency. Isl.* under Ma'rūf (Nicholson); etc.

767 'Abd al-Qāhir b. 'Abd Allāh, d. 563/1168 at Baghdād. See Ibn Khallikān (Cairo 1310) i p. 299; Subkī iv p. 256; *Nafaḥāt* p. 478; *Safīnat al-auliyā'* p. 103 (no. 122); *Khazīnat al-aṣfiyā'* ii p. 11; Brockelmann i p. 436, *Sptbd.* i p. 780; etc.

768 Founder of the Kubrawī order, d. 618/1226 at Khwārazm. See *Tārīkh i Guzīdah* p. 789; Subkī v p. 11; *Nafaḥāt* p. 480; *Majālis al-'ushshāq* no. 19; *Haft iqlīm* no. 1401; *Majālis al-mu'minīn*

(5) (*a*) saints of the Maghrib, (*b*) Qalandarīs, (*c*) martyrs, (*d*) Bāyazīd Bisṭāmī;[769] Bahā' al-Dīn Naqshband (cf. no. 1263 2nd par. 1st footnote *supra*); Shaṭṭārīs; Shāh Madār (cf. no. 1329 (6) *supra*), (*e*) Wais [i.e. Uwais] Qaranī (cf. no. 1358 *supra*), (6). saints of unknown affiliation, (7) ecstatics (*majdhūbān*), (8) female saints): **Rieu** iii 976*b* (*Lujjahs* 1–3 and first two sections of *Lujjah* 4, defective at end. *Circ.* AD 1850).

Edition of the portion relating to the Ṣābirīs: *Shuʿbah* [= Mauj ?] *i siwum az nahr i duwum*[770] *i lujjah i siwum i kitāb i Baḥr i zakhkhār*, **Allahabad** 1313/1895* (51 pp.).

1375. **M. Naʿīm Allāh Bahrā'ichī** Ḥanafī Naqshbandī, born in 1153/1740–1, doubtless at Bahra'ich (65 miles north-east of Lucknow), was the son of Ghulām-Quṭb al-Dīn, commonly called (*ʿurf*) Malik Kālī (or Kālē ?). b. Malik Ghulām-Muḥammad. In 1171/1757–8 he went to Lucknow and pursued Arabic studies there. Subsequently he studied at Shāhjahānpūr, Bareilly, Delhi, Murādābād and elsewhere. In 1186/1772–3 he was initiated into the Naqshbandī order by M. Jamīl, one of Mīrzā Jān-i-Jānān "Maẓhar's" *khalīfahs*, who had come from Delhi to Lucknow. Not long afterwards he visited "Maẓhar" at Delhi and spent four months there. In 1189/1775–6 he returned to Delhi and remained in constant association with "Maẓhar" for four years, receiving from him the *khirqah* and his *ijāzat* as a member of the Naqshbandī, Qādirī, Chishtī and Suhrawardī orders. Thenceforward he lived mainly in Lucknow. When he wrote his autobiography in 1208/1793–4, he had visited Delhi four times, the *bilād i Afāghinah* (i.e. probably Rohilkhand) several times and Pānīpat twice. He died at Bahrā'ich in 1218/1803–4.

(1) ***Bishārāt i Maẓharīyah dar faḍā'il i ḥadarāt i ṭarīqah i Mujaddidīyah***[771] (beginning: *al-Ḥ. l. 'lladhī aẓhara fī Mir'āt al-ḥudūth anwār al-qidam*), a

---

p. 286 (*Majlis* 6); *Safīnat al-auliyā'* p. 103 (no. 124); *Riyāḍ al-ʿārifīn* p. 239; *Khazīnat al-aṣfiyā'* ii p. 258; *Rauḍāt al-jannāt* p. 81; Browne *Lit. Hist*, ii pp. 491–4; *Ency. Isl.* under Nadjm al-Dīn (Berthels); Brockelmann i p. 440, *Sptbd. i* p. 786; *Doklady Akademii Nauk*, Leningrad 1924, series B, April-June, p. 36 (an article by Berthels on Kubrā's quatrains with biography and bibliography).

769 Abū Yazīd Ṭaifūr b. ʿĪsā al-Bisṭāmī, d. 261/875 or 264/878 at Bisṭām. See *Kashf al-maḥjūb* tr. Nicholson pp. 106–8; *Tadhkirat al-auliyā'* i pp. 134–79; IbnKhallikān under Ṭaifūr; *Nafaḥāt* p. 62; *Majālis al-ʿushshāq* no. 4; *Haft iqlīm* no. 836; *Majālis al-mu'minīn* p. 263; *Safīnat al-auliya'* p. 73 (no. 66); *Riyāḍ al-ʿārifīn* p. 46; *Khazīnat al-aṣfiyā'* i pp. 519–22; *Rauḍāt al-jannāt* pp. 338–41; *Ency. Isl.* under Bāyazīd (unsigned); Massignon *Essai sur les origines du lexique technique de la mystique musulmane* pp. 243–56; etc.

770 This division seems to diverge from that of the B.M. MS.

771 i.e. the branch of the Naqshbandī order founded by Aḥmad Sirhindī called Mujaddid i Alf i Thānī (for whom see no. 1316 (1) 1st footnote *supra*).

life of the saint and poet Mirzā "Maẓhar",[772] founder of the Shamsīyah Maẓharīyah branch of the Naqshbandī order, with accounts of twelve other Naqshbandī *shaikhs* (the first Aḥmad Sirhindī, the last M. ʿĀbid Sunāmī[773]) and some forty-five of "Maẓhar's" *khulafāʾ* (the first Thanāʾ Allāh Pānīpatī (cf. *Khazīnat al-aṣfiyāʾ* i p. 689, Raḥman ʿAlī p. 38, etc.) the last Nūr-Muḥammad Qandahārī), written in 1204/1789–90 at the suggestion of Mīr M. Māh Bahrāʾichī and divided into a *muqaddimah*, two *maqṣads* (subdivided into five and six *bābs* respectively), and a *khātimah*: **Rieu** i 363*a* (AH 1207/1792), **I.O.** 4431 (late 18th cent.).

772 Mīrzā Shams al-Dīn Ḥabīb Allāh (cf. Rieu i 363*b*, where the information concerning his "real name" comes evidently from the *Bishārāt i Maẓharīyah*), or Mīrzā Jān-i-Jānān "Maẓhar" (*Jān-i-Jānān mutakhalliṣ bi-"Maẓhar" pisar i Mīrzā Jān "Jānī" takhalluṣ*, as he calls himself in the autobiographical preface to his *dīwān*) is said to have owed the name or nickname Jān-i-Jān (upon which Jān-i-Jānān is apparently a later improvement: cf. Sprenger p. 488) to a punning suggestion by Aurangzēb that Jān-i-Jān would be a suitable name for the new-born son of Mīrzā Jān, who was a *manṣabdār* in the Imperial service. He was born at Kālābāgh, Mālwah, in 1111/1699–1700 or 1113/1701–2 or thereabouts ("Maẓhar's" own statements on this subject seem to have varied: see OCM. xviii/1 pp. 37–8), but most of his life was spent at Delhi, where he was murdered by a Shīʿite fanatic in Muḥarram 1195/January 1781 (other dates, 1192, 1194, seem to have less good authority). Although "Maẓhar" wrote little in Urdu, his influence on the development of Urdu poetry is regarded as important. In Persian he is represented by (1) a *dīwān* of some 1,000 verses (Editions: Calcutta 1267/1851*, Cawnpore 1271/1855°*, Madras 1272/1855–6, Lahore [1922*]. MSS.: Āṣafīyah i p. 732, iii p. 294, Browne Suppt. 609–10, Edinburgh 321, Lindesiana p. 186, Blochet iii 1945, Bānkīpūr Suppt. i 1966, Ivanow 875–6, Ivanow-Curzon 745(4), Edinburgh New Coll. p. 9, etc.), (2) *Kharīṭah i jawāhir*, an anthology of single lines and a few *rubāʿīs* selected [by "Maẓhar", not by M. ʿAbd al-Raḥmān as stated in the B.M. and I.O. catalogues] from the works of many ancient and modern poets (Editions (appended to the *dīwān*): Cawnpore 1271/1855°*, Lahore [1922*]. MS.: I.O. D.P. 1328), (3) *Maktūbāt*, Ṣūfī letters compiled by M. Naʿīm Allāh Bahrāʾichī (MSS.: ʿAlīgaṛh Subḥ. MSS. p. 53 no. 13, p. 18 no. 12 (it is not clear from the catalogue whether the second MS. contains the same collection as the first)). See "Maẓhar's" brief autobiographical preface to his *dīwān* (quoted in Sprenger p. 488); *Maqāmāt i Maẓharī* (see no. 1376 *infra*); *Safīnah i Khwushgū* (see Bānkīpūr viii p. 111); *Nikāt al-shuʿarāʾ; Sarw i āzād;* "Ḥairat" *Maqālāt al-shuʿarāʾ* (Sprenger p. 159); *Gul i raʿnā; Gulzār i Ibrāhīm; ʿIqd i Thuraiyā; Ṣuḥuf i Ibrāhīm; Khulāṣat al-afkār* no. 448; *Makhzan al-gharāʾib* no. 2693; *Majmūʿah i naghz* ii pp. 198–200; *Ṭabaqāt i sukhun*; *Nishtar i ʿishq; Natāʾij al-afkār; Khāzin al-shuʿarāʾ* fol. 152*a* ult.; Sprenger p. 256 (information from several Urdu *tadhkirahs*): *Khazīnat al-aṣfiyāʾ* i pp. 784–7; Garcin de Tassy ii pp. 297–300; Rieu i 363, iii 1086*a*; *Ḥadāʾiq al-Ḥanafīyah* p. 453; Beale *Oriental biographical dictionary* under Jan Janan; Raḥmān ʿAlī p. 226; Saksēna *History of Urdu literature* pp. 49–51; *Ency. Isl.* under Maẓhar (Hidayet Hosain); T. Grahame Bailey *History of Urdu literature* p. 46; Bānkīpūr Suppt. i pp. 214–15; OCM. xviii/1 (Nov. 1941) pp. 27–43 (part of an Urdu article entitled *Tanqīd bar Ab i ḥayāt i Maulānā, M. Ḥusain "Azād"* by M. Maḥmūd Shērānī); etc.

773 Sunām is now in the State of Patiala.

(2) ***Maʿmūlāt i Maẓharīyah***, "an account of the Maẓharī sect of Ṣūfīs with special reference to the doctrines of its founder Maẓhar Jān-jānān" (Arberry). Editions: **Cawnpore** 1284/1867*, **Lahore** 1893† (in both of these editions the *M. i M.* is followed by *Maḥbūb i ʿārifīn*, "a short tract on the duties of the mystic" (Arberry), by ʿAlī Rāstīnī).

(3) (***Aḥwāl i Naʿīm Allāh Bahrāʾichī***), a brief autobiography (beginning: *Baʿd i ḥamd u ṣalāt az faqīr Naʿīm Allāh ʿufiya ʿanhu birādar i girāmī-qadr Bakhsh Allāh wa-ghairah birādarān zāda qadruhum daryāband kih* ...) written in 1208/1793–4 at the age of fifty-six: **I.O.** 4431 foll. 142*b*–145*b* (late 18th cent.).

[Autobiography mentioned above; statements, in the *Bishārāt i Maẓharīyah* (summarized by Rieu); Raḥmān ʿAlī p. 243.]

1376. Shāh ʿAbd Allāh, commonly called (*al-mashhūr bi-*) **Ghulām-ʿAlī**,. b. S. ʿAbd al-Laṭīf Mujaddidī ʿAlawī **Dihlawī** was born in 1158/1745 at Baṭālah in the Gūrdāspūr District of the Panjāb. At the age of thirteen he went to Delhi and associated with well-known Ṣūfīs like Fakhr al-Dīn Fakhr i Jahān (cf. no. 1372, 4th par., footnote *supra*) and Khwājah Mīr "Dard". In 1180/1766–7 at the age of twenty-two he became a disciple of Mīrzā "Maẓhar" (cf. no. 1375 (1), 2nd footnote *supra*) and in due course received from him the *khirqah i khilāfat* of the four main orders. After "Maẓhar's" death Ghulām-ʿAlī succeeded him as superior of his community (*jā-nishīn u ṣāḥib-sajjādah i īshān shud*). He died on 22 Ṣafar 1240/1824. Collections of his letters (*Makātīb i sharīfah*. Edition: Madras 1334/1916*) and of his utterances (*Durr al-maʿārif.*[774] Edition: Delhi [1927*]) were made by his disciple Shāh Raʾūf Aḥmad Muṣṭafā-ābādī (for whom see *Khazīnat al-aṣfiyāʾ* i p. 703, *Ḥadāʾiq al-Ḥanafīyah* p. 472, Raḥmān ʿAlī p. 66). The former is presumably the work *dar bāb i maktūbāt u maqāmāt i ān-janāb* referred to in the *Khazīnah* i p. 703 antepenult.

Maqāmāt i Maẓharī, or *Laṭāʾif i khamsah*, "memoirs, with some letters, of Shams ul-Dīn Habīb Ullāh Maẓharī" [*sic*, but read Maẓhar]: ʿ**Alīgaṛh** Subḥ. MSS. p. 18 no. 10 (?) (*Risālah dar ḥālāt i ... Mirzā Jān i Jānān wa-ghairah*, by Shāh Ghulām-ʿAlī).

Edition: **Delhi** 1309/1892°, probably also [**Delhi**] Aḥmadī Press, 1269/1853* (a biography of "Maẓhar" epitomized from Maulawī Naʿīm Allāh's work (see no. 1375 (1) *supra*) by Ghulām-ʿAlī Mujaddidī ʿAlawī, without title-page but beginning with the words *Īn risālah i sharīfah dar bayān i ḥālāt u maqāmāt i ḥaḍrat i Shams al-Dīn Ḥabīb Allāh* ...).

774 So Arberry, but *Dār al-maʿārif* according to the *Khazīnah*, the *Ḥadāʾiq* and Raḥmān ʿAlī.

Probably this author is the same as 'Abd Allāh *ma'rūf bah* G͟hulām-'Alī who wrote

Karāmāt u irs͟hādāt i Mujaddid i Alf i T͟hānī:[775] Āṣafīyah i p. 460 no. 288. [*K͟hazīnat al-aṣfīyā'* i pp. 693–700; Raḥmān 'Alī p. 155.]

1377. **Mullā M. Ṣādiq Yārkandī.**
Majma' al-muḥaqqiqīn, a history of the K͟hwājahs of Kās͟hghar to 1208/1793–4: no MSS. recorded?

Eastern-Turkish translation by Mullā M. Sātqīn: MS. in private possession (see Semenov *Ukazatel'* p. 24, where a reference is given to Validov *Vostochnye rukopisi v Ferganskoi oblasti* (*Zapiski Vostochn. Otd. Imp. Russ. Arkheol. Obshchestva* xxii) p. 304).

1378. **Turāb 'Alī** b. M. Kāẓim Qalandarī 'Alawī **Kākōrawī**,[776] a descendant of Niẓām al-Dīn Qārī known as S͟h. Bhīkan Kākōrawī,[777] was born in 1181/1767–8 and died on 5 Jumādā I 1275/11 December 1858. Among his works were a *dīwān* (described by Raḥmān 'Alī as *mas͟hhūr*), *Maṭālib i ras͟hīdī* (on ethics and Ṣūfism. Editions: Lucknow 1280/1863°, 1875°*, 1896†) and *S͟harā'iṭ al-wasā'iṭ* ("on the duties and observances of Ṣūfī instructors and their disciples". Edition: Lucknow 1293/1876*). Of the *Maktūbāt i S͟hāh Mujtabā Lāharpūrī*,[778] compiled by him in 1224/1809, there is a MS. at Ḥaidarābād (Āṣafīyah i p. 484). To the south-east of the town of Kākōrī are the *dargāhs* of S͟hāh M. Kāẓim[779] and S͟hāh Abū Turāb, "in whose memory annual festivals are celebrated and a great fair is held, attended by large numbers of people from Lucknow and the neighbouring villages" (*Lucknow: a gazetteer*, by H. R. Nevill, Allahabad 1904, p. 191).

(1) **Kas͟hf al-mutawārī fī ḥāl i Niẓām al-Dīn i Qārī**, a biography of the aforementioned S͟h. Bhīkan. Edition: **Lucknow** 1318/1901°.

---

775   Cf. no. 1316 (1) 1st footnote *supra*.
776   Kākōrī is about eight miles due west of Lucknow.
777   Qārī Amīr Niẓām al-Dīn b. Amīr Saif al-Dīn, called S͟h. Bhīkan, or Bhikārī, or Bhīk, was born in 890/1485 and died in 981/1573–4. According to Raḥmān 'Alī he wrote works entitled *Manhaj* (*dar uṣūl i ḥadīt͟h*), *Ma'ārif* (*dar taṣawwuf*) and *Tarjamah i risālah i Mulhamāt i Qādirī*, the last being described as a translation of a work by S. 'Abd al-Razzāq, one of 'Abd al-Qādir al-Jīlānī's sons. See *Ṭabaqāt i Akbarī* ii p. 478 (only his name in a list); Badā'ūnī *Muntak͟hab al-tawārīk͟h* iii p. 24; Raḥmān 'Alī p. 33.
778   S͟hāh Mujtabā is the eighth of the *s͟haik͟hs* whose biographies are given in the *Uṣūl al-maqṣūd*.
779   S͟hāh M. Kāẓim, Turāb 'Alī's father, died in 1221/1806.

(2) *Uṣūl al-maqṣūd,* accounts of twelve Qalandarī shaikhs, the spiritual ancestors of the author,[780] written in 1225–6/1810–11 and divided into twelve chapters called *aṣl*: **Ivanow** Curzon 83 (AH 1275/1858), **Bānkīpūr** viii 679 (latter half of 19th cent.).

Edition: place ? 1312/1894–5 (see Āṣafīyah i p. 316).

Lists of the biographies: (1) Ivanow-Curzon p. 88, (2) Bānkīpūr viii p. 69. [*al-Rauḍ al-azhar* p. 190 onwards; *Mawāhib al-qalandar* p. 25[8]; Raḥmān ʿAlī p. 36.]

1379. A certain **"Girāmī"** appears to be the author of the *Riyāḍ al-wāṣilīn.*

Riyāḍ al-wāṣilīn (a chronogram = 1229/1814), or *Tadhkirah i wāṣilān,* a metrical account of famous saints composed by order of M. Raḥīm Khān, of Khīwah (who reigned 1221–41/1806–25): **Leningrad** Mus. Asiat. (see *Mélanges asiatiques* vii (St. Petersburg 1876) p. 402).

1380. **Gul Muḥammad** Maʿrūfī Karkhī[781] Chishtī **Aḥmadpūrī** is described in a marginal note on p. 1 of the Delhi edition of his *Dhikr al-aṣfiyāʾ* as the eldest son of Ḥakīm Allāh-Yār Maʿrūfī Karkhī and as a resident of Aḥmadpūr Sharqīyah in the State of Bahāwalpūr. He is mentioned in the Bahāwalpūr State Gazetteer (p. 179) as a disciple and *khalīfah* of Khwājah M. ʿĀqil, a saint buried at Kōṭ Miṭ'han[782] in the Ḍērah Ghāzī Khān District. According to the list of *aʿrās* printed at the end of the *Dhikr al-aṣfiyāʾ* (p. 226) he died on 9 Muḥarram 1243/3 August 1827.

---

780 In giving this account of his spiritual ancestors the author professes to follow the custom observed in the Chishtī affiliation. The twelve shaikhs are ʿAbd al-ʿAzīz Makkī, Khiḍr Rūmī, Najm al-Dīn Ghauth al-dahr, Quṭb al-Dīn Bīnā-dil Jaunpūrī (d. 925), M. Quṭb [Jaunpūrī], ʿAbd al-Salām [Jaunpūrī] (d. 976), ʿAbd al-Quddūs Jaunpūrī (d. 1052), Mujtabā Lāharpūrī (d. 1084), Fatḥ Jaunpūrī (d. 1118), Ilāh-diyah Aḥmad Lāharpūrī (d. 1147), Bāsiṭ ʿAlī Ilāhābādī (d. 1196) and M. Kāẓim (d. 1221), the author's father, of whom a very long and detailed account is given. "The work sheds no light on the origin and the history of the Qalandars and the flourishing period of their movement in India, where it acquired great importance. The author's more or less authentic information begins only with the x/xvi c., when Qalandarīs had finally degenerated, lost their importance, and when their different branches had become amalgamated with other Sufic orders which still flourished at that time, especially the Qādirīs and Chishtīs" (Ivanow). The *muqaddimah* to the *Tārīkh i maẓhar i buzurgān* (Bodleian 1997) contains a brief account of the Qalandarī order.

781 For Maʿrūf al-Karkhī see no. 1374 2nd par. (4) a *supra.*

782 "The shrine of Muhammad Aqil Sáhib at Koṭ Miṭhan was in the old town of Koṭ Miṭhan, but when in S. 1919 both town and shrine were washed away by the Indus, the coffin containing the body of Muhammad Aqil Sáhib was disinterred and brought to the present shrine" (H. A. Rose *Glossary of the tribes and castes of the Punjab and North-West Frontier Province* i p. 599).

Dhikr al-aṣfiyāʾ fī takmilat Siyar al-auliyāʾ dar manqabat i Shams al-Hudā,[783] a continuation of the *Siyar al-auliyāʾ* of S. M. Kirmānī (see no. 1259 *supra*) divided into a *muqaddimah* (on the *ḥilyah* of the Prophet and the dates of the death of the Chishtī saints down to Chirāgh i Dihlī),[784] two *bābs* (on the lives of Kamāl al-Dīn ʿAllāmah,[785] Sirāj al-Dīn b. Kamāl al-Dīn,[786] ʿAlam al-Dīn M.,[787] Sh. Rājan,[788] Sh. JMN (Jumman ?),[789] Sh. Ḥasan M.,[790] Sh. M. b. Ḥasan M.,[791] Muḥyī ʾl-Dīn Yaḥyā Madanī,[792] Kalīm Allāh Jahānābādī,[793] Niẓām al-Dīn Aurangābādī,[794] Fakhr al-Dīn b. Niẓām al-Dīn Aurangābādī,[795] Nūr-M. Mahārawī,[796] M. ʿĀqil,[797] and their disciples) and a *khātimah* (on the *aʿrās*). Edition: Delhi 1312/1894°*.
[*Dhikr al-aṣfiyāʾ* p. 208 foll.]

---

783 So in the author's preface. On the title-page, however, we read "*Kitāb i maḥāmid-intisāb ... al-mausūm bah Dhikr al-aṣfiyā maʿrūf Takmilah Siyar al-auliyā dar manqabat i Shams al-Hudā*, the words *Takmilah Siyar al-auliyā* being put in the boldest type.

784 See no. 1259 1st par. last footnote *supra*.

785 One of Chirāgh i Dihlī's disciples, d. 756/1355. See *Khazīnat al-aṣfiyāʾ* i p. 353; Raḥmān ʿAlī p. 173.

786 Son of the preceding, mentioned incidentally *Khazīnah* i p. 436² in the pedigree of Sh. Ḥasan M., whose great-great-grandfather he was.

787 A disciple of Chirāgh i Dihlī, mentioned incidentally *Khazīnah* i p. 536⁴.

788 A disciple of the preceding, mentioned incidentally *Khazīnah* i p. 536⁴ as Sh. Maḥmūd al-maʿrūf (i.e. known as) Sh. Rājan.

789 A disciple of the preceding mentioned incidentally *Khazīnah* i p. 436³ as Sh. Jamāl al-Dīn al-mashhūr (i.e. known as) Sh. JMN. Cf. *Mirʾāt i Aḥmadī, khātimah*, p. 75⁶, Eng. trans. p. 65¹³, where there is another incidental mention. In the English trans. the surname is spelt Jumman. In the *Tadhkirat al-kirām* (Bānkīpūr Suppt. i 1783 fol. 146) there is a notice of a certain Shāh Jamāl Muḥammad alias Jumman.

790 *Khalīfah* of the preceding, d. 980/1572–3 or 982/1575. See *Mirʾāt i Aḥmadī, khātimah*. pp. 75–6, Eng. trans. pp. 65–6; *Khazīnah* i p. 436.

791 Son of the preceding, d. 1040/1630. See *Mirʾāt i Aḥmadī, khātimah*, pp. 76–9, Eng. trans. pp. 66–8.

792 Grandson of the preceding, d. 1101/1689. See *Mirʾāt i Aḥmadī, khātimah* pp. 79–83, Eng. trans. pp. 68–70.

793 Disciple of the preceding, d. 1140/1727. See *Khazīnah* i pp. 494–5; *Ḥadāʾiq al-Ḥanafīyah* pp. 438–9; Raḥmān ʿAlī p. 172.

794 Disciple of the preceding, d. 1142/1730. See *Khazīnah* i pp. 495–7.

795 Son and *khalīfah* of the preceding, d. 1199/1785. See no. 1372 antepenult. par., footnote *supra*.

796 Disciple of the preceding, d. 1205/1791. See no. 1396 2nd par. footnote.

797 Disciple of the preceding, d. 1229/1814 and is buried at Kōṭ Miṭʾhan. See *Khazīnah* i p. 507 antepenult.; H. A. Rose *Glossary of the, tribes and castes of the Punjab* i p. 599. Cf. no. 1380 2nd footnote.

1381. Qāḍī M. **Irtaḍā ʿAlī K͟hān** "K͟hwushnūd" **Gōpāmawī**[798] was born in 1198/1783–4. He was a pupil of Maulawī Ḥaidar ʿAlī Sandīlī[799] and Maulawī M. Ibrāhīm Bilgrāmī. In 1225/1810–11 he went to Madrās, where his father, Muṣṭafā ʿAlī K͟hān, was *Qāḍī*, and after his father's death he himself became *Qāḍī* of Madrās. He died in 1251/1835–6. Of his works Raḥmān ʿAlī mentions (1) commentaries or *ḥawāshī* on Ṣadrā,[800] Mīr Zāhid Mullā Jalāl[801] and other text-books, (2) *Nafāʾis i Irtaḍāʾīyah*, (3) *Nuqūd al-ḥisāb*, (4) *risālah i Farāʾiḍ*,[802] (5) *Sharḥ i qaṣīdah i Burdah*. For a MS. of his *Fatāwā* see Āṣafīyah ii p. 1062 no. 97.

(1) *Fawāʾid i Saʿdīyah*, " lives of famous saints and Ṣūfīs." Edition: **Lucknow** 1885°.

(2) *Tuḥfah i Aʿẓamīyah*,[803] catalogued under the heading *Tadhkirah i Fārisī*, but whether it is a *tadhkirah* of poets or saints is not stated: **Āṣafīyah** i p. 316 no. 96 (AH 1235/1819–20).

[*Ishārāt i Bīnish*; *Ṣubḥ i waṭan* pp. 65–8; *Ḥadīqat al-marām* p. 4; *Shamʿ i anjuman* p. 145; Raḥmān ʿAlī p. 21; Brockelmann *Sptbd.* ii p. 854.]

1382. **Imām al-Dīn K͟hān** b. G͟hulām-Ḥusain K͟hān b. G͟hulām-Gīlānī K͟hān was a dependent of M. Amīr K͟hān [Nawwāb of Tōnk 1817–34: cf. no. 898 *supra*].

Majmaʿ al-karāmat (sing.), a life of Shāh Dargāhī Naqshbandī,[804] of Rāmpūr: **Nadhīr Aḥmad** 91 (AH 1236/1820–1. Ḥāfiẓ Aḥmad ʿAlī K͟hān's library, Rāmpūr).

1383. **Niẓām al-Dīn Balk͟hī Mazārī b. Mīr M.ʿAzīz Anṣārī Mutawallī**[805] was born on 1 Ramaḍān 1195/21 August 1781. At Balk͟h in 1213/1798–9 he met for the first time Shāh Faḍl i Aḥmad Maʿṣūmī, a Naqshbandī *shaikh*, one of whose

---

798 Gōpāmau is a small town 14 miles north-west of Hardoi in Oudh.
799 d. at Sandīlah (cf. no. 1181 2nd footnote *supra*) in 1225/1810. See Raḥmān ʿAlī pp. 54–5. One of his pupils was the Shīʿite *Mujtahid*, S. Dildār ʿAlī Lakʾhnawī (for whom see Raḥmān ʿAlī pp. 60–1, Brockelmann *Sptbd.* ii p. 852).
800 i.e. the commentary of Ṣadr al-Dīn M. b. Ibrāhīm al-Shīrāzī on the first *fann* of the second part (physics) of Athīr al-Dīn al-Abharī's *Hidāyat al-ḥikmah* (for which see Brockelmann i p. 464, *Sptbd.* i pp. 839–41).
801 i.e. the annotations of Mīr M. Zāhid al-Harawī on the commentary of Jalāl al-Dīn al-Dawānī on the first part (logic) of al-Taftāzānī's *Tahdhīb al-manṭiq wa-'l-kalām* (for which see Brockelmann ii p. 215, *Sptbd.* ii pp. 302–4).
802 *Furaiz-i-Irtazeeah: a treatise on the Mohammedan law of inheritance. By Moulavie Mohummud Irtaza Alee Khan Bahadur*, Madras, 1825*.
803 Dedicated presumably to Nawwāb M. G͟hauth K͟hān "Aʿẓam", for whom see no. 1209 *supra*.
804 Who died in 1226/1811. See *K͟hazīnat al-aṣfiyāʾ* i pp. 690–2.
805 i.e. Warden of the alleged shrine of ʿAlī at Balk͟h.

khulafā' he subsequently became. Among his writings were a *dīwān* and a biographical work entitled *Aḥsan al-tawārīkh fī dhikr al-ʿulamā' wa-'l-fuqarā' wa-'l-mashāyikh*. No copies of these works seem to be recorded. His *Tuḥfat al-murshid* was completed at Balkh in Shawwāl 1240/May-June 1825.

Tuḥfat al-murshid, on the life, sayings and devotional practices of Shāh Faḍl i Aḥmad Maʿṣūmī, known as Ḥaḍrat-jīw[806] Ṣāḥib, who was born in 1151/1738–9 and died at Peshawar in 1231/1815–16 or 1232/1816–17. Edition: **Lahore**[1912*].

[Autobiography in *Tuḥfat al-murshid*, pp. 175–84.]

1384. M. **Abū 'l-Ḥayāt Qādirī P'hulwārī**[807] Bihārī wrote the *Tadhkirat al-kirām* in 1249/1833–4.

Tadhkirat al-kirām, biographies of forty-five Bihārī *shaikhs*, mostly of the 18th and early 19th century, the first being M. Wārith Rasūl-numā (b. 1084/1673, d. 1166/1753), the thirty-fifth M. ʿAlī Akbar (d. 1247/1832) and the last Burhān al-Dīn (d. 1107/1696): **Ivanow** 1st Suppt. 772 (19th cent.), **Bānkīpūr** Suppt. i 1783 (19th cent.).

Edition: **Lucknow**[1880°].

Lists of the biographies: (1) Ivanow 1st Suppt. pp. 12–13, (2) Bānkīpūr Suppt. i pp. 46–7.

1385. Āqā **Taqī**, of Khōy, the author of the *Ādāb al-musāfirīn*, is doubtless identical with Taqī b. M., who in the *Dānishmandān i Ādharbāyjān* (p. 87) is described as one of the well known *ʿurafā'* of Khōy and is there stated to have written at Shīrāz in 1257/1841 a metrical commentary entitled *Nuqṭah i asrār* in about two thousand verses on the first verse of Rūmī's *Mathnawī*.

Ādāb al-musāfirīn, notices of Ṣūfī saints: **Browne** Suppt. 7 (A.H. 1256/1840–1).

1386. For the *Riyāḍ al-ʿārifīn*, completed by Riḍā-Qulī Khān "Hidāyat" in 1260/1844 and devoted to notices of saints who were also poets, see no. 1225 (19) *supra*.

1387. The author of the *Makhzan i Aḥmadī* was "Sayyid Muḥammad ʿAlî" according to the Bānkīpūr Catalogue, "**Muhammad ʿAlī**, called[808] ʿAlī" according to

806 For the affix *jīw* see no. 1321 (2) 2nd footnote *supra*.
807 Phulwārī is a village in the Patna Division of Bihār.
808 In the terminology of the British Museum "called" is used to represent *mutakhalliṣ*, but also *madʿū, maʿrūf, mashhūr, mulaqqab, mukhāṭab* and the like.

the Catalogue of Persian printed books in the British Museum. "A faithful disciple of Aḥmad Shâh," he "spent most of his time in the company of his *Pîr*".[809]

Makhzan i Aḥmadī, completed in 1261/1845 and dedicated to Wazīr al-Daulah,[810] a life of S. Aḥmad Shāh[811] from his birth at Rāy

---

809 On pp. 203–4 of his *Tadhkirah i ʿulamāʾ i Hind* Raḥmān ʿAlī gives a biography of Maulawī [not Saiyid, be it noted] Muḥammad ʿAlī Ṣadrpūrī b. Shaikh Ramaḍān ʿAlī, a resident (*mutawaṭṭin*) of Ṣadrpūr in the parganah of Malīḥābād near Lucknow. He was a Ṣūfī and a poet using the *takhalluṣ* "Muḥammad" [not "ʿAlī"]. Born early in the second decade of the thirteenth century of the Hijrah, he studied Ḥadīth and Tafsīr under Mirzā Ḥasan ʿAlī Muḥaddith Lak'hnawī and entered the Naqshbandī Mujaddidī order of Ṣūfīs as a *murīd* of Maulawī Shāh Bishārat-ʿAlī Bahrāʾichī. He strove earnestly to promote fidelity to the *Sunnah* and to extirpate *bidʿah*, and was himself a man of deep piety. In 1258/1842 he went to Ṭōnk and entered the service of Wazīr al-Daulah Nawwāb Wazīr M. Khān [to whom the *Makhzan i Aḥmadī* is dedicated]. He died in Rajab 1289/1872 in the time of Nawwāb M. ʿAlī Khān. Among the works of his which Raḥmān ʿAlī mentions is [not *Makhzan i Aḥmadī* but] *Waqāʾiʿ i Aḥmadīyah* (*dar ḥālāt i Saiyid Aḥmad i Mujāhid i Rāy Barēlī*). In spite of the discrepancies noted above it seems difficult to believe that M. ʿAlī Ṣadrpūrī is not identical with the author of the *Makhzan i Aḥmadī* [which, we may note, "is intermixed with numerous poems and verses"].

810 Wazīr al-Daulah Wazīr M. Khān succeeded his father Amīr Khān (for whom see no. 898 *supra*) as Nawwāb of Ṭōnk in 1834 and died in 1864.

811 S. Aḥmad Mujāhid Rāy-Barēlawī, as Raḥmān ʿAlī calls him, or S. Aḥmad Barēlawī, as he is more commonly called, was the son of M. ʿIrfān and belonged to the family of the Saiyids of the Rāy Barēlī *takyah* (*az khānadān i Sādāt i takyah i Rāy Barēlī*, Raḥmān ʿAlī p. 81). In 1222/1807 he became a disciple of Shāh ʿAbd al-ʿAzīz Dihlawī (for whom see no. 41 *supra*) and assimilated the latter's puritanical views and hostility towards all "idolatrous" or superstitious innovations. On leaving Delhi he started a revivalist movement, in the course of which he "performed miracles and attracted a large number of followers", becoming "a terror to the Shîʿahs of Lucknow and Naṣîrâbâd". In 1821 he visited Calcutta and gained numerous adherents. In 1822 he made a pilgrimage to Mecca with his two chief disciples M. Ismāʿīl Dihlawī (cf. *Ency. Isl.* under Ismāʿīl al-Shahīd) and ʿAbd al-Ḥaiy Dihlawī, who were respectively the nephew and the son-in-law of his old teacher, Shāh ʿAbd al-ʿAzīz, and of whom the former expounded S. Aḥmad's doctrines in the Persian work *Ṣirāṭ al-mustaqīm* (Calcutta 1238/1823°). On 7 Jumādā II 1241/17 Jan. 1826 he set out from Rāy Barēlī with a view to conducting *jihād* against the Sik'hs, whom he accused of oppressing the Muslims in the Panjāb, of prohibiting the *adhān* and the killing of cows. After inciting the people of Kābul and Qandahār, he with ten or twelve thousand adherents from India and Afghānistān attacked the Peshawar district. For some years he engaged Ranjīt Sing'h's forces with varying success until he was killed in battle at Bālākōṭ on 24 Dhū 'l-Qaʿdah 1246/6 May 1831. His works include short tracts entitled *Tanbīh al-ghāfilīn* (Delhi 1285/1868*) and *Mulhimāt* [*sic*] *i Aḥmadīyah fī 'l-ṭarīq al-Muḥammadīyah* (Āgrah 1299/1882°). See *JASB*. i (1832) pp. 479–98 (cf. Beale *Oriental biographical dictionary*, London 1894, pp. 354–5); *The Indian Musalmans*, by W. W. Hunter, London 1871, pp. 12–18, 52–3, etc.; *Tawārīkh i ʿajībah* or *Sawāniḥ i Aḥmadī* (in Urdu), by M. Jaʿfar, Delhi 1891*, Sād'haurah [1914*]; Raḥmān ʿAlī pp. 81–2; *Ḥayāt i ṭaiyibah* (in Urdu), by Mīrzā Ḥairat Dihlawī, Delhi 1895*; Buckland Dictionary of Indian biography

Barēlī[812] in Ṣafar[813] 1201/Nov.-Dec. 1786 to his return thither from Mecca in 1239/1823: **Bānkīpūr** xvi 1415 (AH 1263/1847).

Edition: **Āgrah** 1299/1882°.

1388. Miyāṅ **Khair Muḥammad** Munshī, by whom the MS. referred to below is signed at the end, may be the author of the biography.

(Aḥwāl i Shāh Gul[814] Imām Chū[815] walad i Saiyid Aḥmad ʿAlī Shāh Chū) (beg. *Shāh-ṣāḥib S. A. ʿA. Shāh Chū walad i Shāh Fatḥ Nūr Shāh*), a notice of Shāh Gul Imām, a Saiyid and *faqīr* of great sanctity, who settled at Ūchh (now in the state of Bahāwalpūr) and in Samwat 1810 (AD 1754) erected various buildings there, together with an account of his family extending to the death of his successor, S. Gul M. Shāh, in 1209/1794–5: **Rieu** iii 977*a* (foll. 9. AH 1267/1850).

1389. ʿAbd al-ʿAlīm **Naṣr Allāh Khān** Aḥmadī Khwēshgī Khūrjawī, who died in 1299/1881, has already been mentioned as the author of the *Tārīkh i Dakan* (no. 1043 *supra*) and the *Gulshan i hamīshah-bahār* (no. 1219).

Bayāḍ i dil-gushā (probably intended to be a chronogram for 1268/1851–2 (though actually amounting to 1168), like four alternative titles (e.g. *Maʿlūmāt i Khwājagān*), which do in fact come to 1268), a detailed biography of the author's *pīr*, Shāh ʿAbd al-ʿAlīm (b. Ākhūnd Jān Muḥammad, *B. i d.-g.* p. 21^{8}) Lōhārawī[816] (d. 13 Muḥarram 1266/29 Nov. 1849: see *B. i d.-g.* p. 219 antepenult.) with shorter accounts of the latter's *pīr*, Shāh Iḥsān-ʿAlī Pāk-Pattanī, and of Ṣūfīs associated with them.

Edition: **Kōl** [i.e. ʿAlīgaṛh. Probably A.H. 1268/1851–2 or 1269/1852–3].[817]

---

p. 8; *Ency. Isl.* under Aḥmad b. Muḥammed ʿIrfān (Blumhardt); Niẓāmī Badāyūnī *Qāmūs al-mashāhīr* (in Urdu) i pp. 314–15.

812 Rāy (Rai, or Rae) Barēlī, the chief town of a district in Oudh 48 miles S.E. of Lucknow, is to be distinguished from Barēlī (officially Bareilly) in Rohilkhand.

813 So *Makhzan i Aḥmadī*, but the *Ency. Isl.* gives the date 1 Muḥ. 1201/24 Oct. 1786.

814 Rieu writes Kul, but Gul seems more probable.

815 Perhaps a misreading of Jīw (for which see no. 1321 (2) 2nd footnote).

816 According to *B. i d.-g.* p. 22^{6} Lōhārī, known as Lōhārī-Jalālābād, is in the District of Muẓaffarnagar "*az mutaʿalliqāt i Sahāranpūr*".

817 The date 1270 given by Arberry has perhaps been taken inadvertently from a short pamphlet printed at the same press which comes next to the *Bayāḍ i dil-gushā* in the collectaneous India Office volume.

1390. **Faḍl Allāh b. Shaikh al-Mulūk** enjoyed the patronage of Mīr Ṭahmāsp b. Daulat-Shāh b. Fatḥ-ʿAlī Shāh, Governor of Fārs. Shortly after reaching Shīrāz from ʿIrāq in 1272/1855–6 he wrote his *Ḍiyāʾ al-ʿārifīn.*

Ḍiyāʾ al-ʿārifīn, on the lives and sayings of 96 *ʿurafāʾ* who flourished in the first four centuries of Islām: **Rieu** Suppt. 102.

1391. Muftī M. **Ghulām-Sarwar** b. Muftī Ghulām-Muḥammad b. Muftī Raḥīm Allāh Quraishī Asadī al-Hāshimī **al-Lāhaurī** wrote the Urdu works *Guldastah i karāmāt*, on the life of ʿAbd al-Qādir Jīlānī (Delhi 1867*, Lucknow 1875*, Lahore 1878*), *Akhlāq i Sarwarī* (Lahore 1288/1871°*, Lucknow 1878°), *Makhzan i ḥikmat*, moral tales and sayings (Lahore 1871°* [Lucknow] 1878°), *Dīwān i Sarwarī*, verses in praise of ʿAbd al-Qādir Jīlānī (Lahore 1872°*, 1873*, 1292/1876°), *Naʿt i Sarwarī*, verses in praise of Muḥammad (Lahore 1290/1873°*, 1877*, Lucknow 1878°, 1880°), *Gulshan i Sarwarī*, ethics in verse (Lahore 1874*, Lucknow 1295/1878°), *Ḥadīqat al-auliyāʾ* (Lahore 1875*, Cawnpore 1877*, 1889*), *Bahāristān i tārīkh* or *Gulzār i shāhī*, a history of India followed by a sketch of English history (Lucknow 1877°*), *Tārīkh i Makhzan i Panjāb*, a gazetteer of the Panjāb (Lucknow 1877°*), *Zubdat al-lughāt* or *Lughāt i Sarwarī*, a dictionary of Arabic, Persian and other foreign words explained in Urdu (Lucknow 1294/1877°*), and *Dīwān i ḥamd i Īzadī* (Lucknow 1881°).

(1) ***Khazīnat al-aṣfiyāʾ*** (a chronogram = 1280), biographical notices of saints begun in 1280/1863–4, completed in 1281/1864–5 (but with some later additions) and divided into seven *makhzans* ((1) the Prophet, the first four Caliphs and the Imāms, not only the Twelve but also Abū Ḥanīfah, Mālik, Abū Yūsuf, Shaibānī, Shāfiʿī and Aḥmad b. Ḥanbal, vol. i p. 4,[818] (2) Qādirīs, vol. i p. 76, (3) Chishtīs, vol. i p. 222, (4) Naqshbandīs, vol. i p. 516, (5) Suhrawardīs, vol. ii p. 2, (6) miscellaneous orders, vol. ii p. 118, (7) in four *ḥiṣṣahs* (*a*) the Prophet's wives, vol. ii p. 397, (*b*) his daughters, vol. ii p. 404, (*c*) saintly women, vol. ii p. 406, (*d*) deranged saints (*majānīn u majādhīb*), vol. ii p. 428).

Editions: **Lahore** 1284/1867–8 (pp. 1072, 18. See *JASB*. xxxix, pt. 1 (1870), p. 274 n.); **Lucknow** (Thamar i Hind Pr.) 1873*; **Cawnpore** (N.K.) 1312/1894*; 1902°; 1914‡.

(2) ***Ganjīnah i Sarwarī***, or, chronogrammatically, ***Ganj i tārīkh*** (= 1284), chronograms for the birth and death of famous Muslims.

Editions: **Lahore** 1285/1868*, **Lucknow** (N.K.) 1877°*, 1307/1889*.

818 The references are to the Cawnpore edition of 1914.

1392. **M. Ḥusain** b. M. Masʿūd Chishtī Ṣābirī[819] Quddūsī[820] **Murādābādī**, a disciple of S. Amānat ʿAlī Ḥusainī Chishtī,[821] completed his *Anwār al-ʿārifīn* in 1286/1870.

Anwār al-ʿārifīn, lives of numerous ancient and modern saints, especially of the Chishtī, Qādirī and Naqshbandī orders, including a number buried at Murādābād. Editions: **Barēlī** ("Bareilly") 1290/1873*, **Lucknow** 1876°*.

1393. **Ghulām-Muḥammad Khān Jhajjarī** became a disciple of Khwājah M. Sulaimān Chishtī Taunsawī[822] in 1255/1839.

Manāqib i Sulaimānī, a life of Khwājah M. Sulaimān Chishtī Taunsawī, written in 1255/1839–40, with a continuation (*takmilah*) to the time of the saint's death, written in 1287/1870–1.

Editions: **Delhi** [1871*], **Jhajjar** 1897†.

1394. Ḥāfiẓ **Aḥmad Yār**, a resident of Pākpattan, wrote a biography of Khwājah M. Sulaimān Taunsawī (cf. no. 1393 1st par. *supra*) entitled *Manāqib i Sulaimānīyah*[823] An abridgement of this, containing some additional information but devoted mainly to the saint's utterances (*malfūẓāt*), was made by **Yār-Muḥammad b. Tāj-Muḥammad**, who was himself one of the saint's associates.

Intikhāb i Manāqib i Sulaimānīyah. Edition: **Lahore** 1325/1907°*.

1395. **Aḥmad ʿAlī Khairābādī** was a disciple of Shāh Sulaimān Taunsawī (for whom see no. 1393 1st par. *supra*).

---

819 For ʿAlī Ṣābir see no. 1374 2nd par. (3) (*d*) *supra*.

820 For ʿAbd al-Quddūs Gangōhī see no. 1279 *supra*.

821 Perhaps Maulawī A. A. Chishtī, who lived at Amrōhah and died in 1280/1864. See *Khazīnat al-aṣfiyāʾ* i p. 515.

822 M. S., born at Gargōjī, in the hill-country west of Taunsah in the Ḍērah Ghāzī Khān District of the Panjāb, was educated at the *madrasah* of Qāḍī M. ʿĀqil (cf. no. 1380 2nd par. last footnote) at Miṭ'hankōṭ and afterwards became a disciple of Nūr-Muḥammad Mahārawī (for whom see no. 1396 2nd par. footnote). He settled at Taunsah and died there on 7 Ṣafar 1267/12 December 1850. His grave is marked by a mausoleum erected by M. Bahāwal Khān III, Nawwāb of Bahāwalpūr 1825–52, who was one of his disciples. See *Manāqib al-maḥbūbain; Khazīnat al-aṣfiyāʾ* i p. 514; *Anwār al-ʿārifīn; Qaṣr i ʿārifān*; Dera Ghazi Khan Gazetteer (1898) p. 54; Bahawalpur State Gazetteer (1904) p. 74; *Khātam i Sulaimānī* (in Urdu), by Ilāh-Bakhsh Khān Balōch, Lahore 1325/1907*; *Note on the shrine of Taunsa*, by D. C. Phillott (in *JASB*. 1908 pp. 21–9); Griffin and Massey *Chiefs and families of note in the Panjab*, revised ed., Lahore 1909–11, vol. ii p. 388; H. A. Rose *Glossary of the tribes and castes of the Panjab and North-West Frontier Province* i (Lahore 1919) pp. 602–3.

823 In his *Intikhāb* Yār-Muḥammad regularly calls this work *Manāqib i sharīfah*. The publisher calls it *Manāqib i Sulaimānīyah*.

Qaṣr i ʿārifān, notices of Chishtī, Qādirī, Suhrawardī and Naqshbandī saints to the time of Shāh Sulaimān Taunsawī: **Lahore** Panjab Univ. Lib. (AH 1291/1874, copied from an autograph. See *OCM*. iii/1 p. 73).

1396. **Najm al-Dīn Nāgaurī** is mentioned among the *khulafāʾ* of Khwājah M. Sulaimān Taunsawī (for whom see no. 1393 1st par. *supra*) on p. 84 of *Ghulām-Muḥammad Khān's Manāqib i Sulaimānī*, where he is called Najm al-Dīn Jhunjhunuwī and described as a descendant of Sulṭān al-tārikīn Ḥamīd al-Dīn Nāgaurī (for whom see no. 9, 4th par. *supra*) resident at Jhunjhunū[824]

Manāqib al-maḥbūbain, lives of Nūr-Muḥammad Mahārawī,[825] his *khalīfah*, Shāh Sulaimān Taunsawī, and other Chishtī saints, followed by a short life of the author. Editions: [**Rāmpūr**, 1890?°], **Lahore** 1312/1895°.

1397. Shāh **Ḍiyāʾ Allāh** Fakhrī Qādirī Ḥanafī died in 1292/1875–6 and was buried at Lahore.

Maktūb i Ḍiyāʾī (a chronogram = 1289/1872–3), or, as on the title-page but not in the preface, *Nasab-nāmah i kalān*, pedigrees of the Prophet and of fourteen Ṣūfī "families" with short biographical notes, followed by an account of the seventy-two Islāmic sects derived from the *Ghunyat al-ṭālibīn* of ʿAbd al-Qādir al-Jīlānī (cf. Brockelmann i p. 435). Editions: **Lahore** 1289/1872°, 1293/1876*, 1296/1879*, 1309/1891°.

1398. Maulawī Abū Muḥammad **Ḥasan "Shiʿrī" Qādirī** b. Ṣadr al-Dīn M., or Khwājah Ḥasan Kaul [or Kōl ?] "Shiʿrī", as he is called in the *Taḥāʾif al-abrār*, was a Kashmīrī but spent most of his life as a trader in the Panjāb and Hindūstān. He died in 1298/1881 and was buried at Amritsar. He is the author of (1) a *dīwān* entitled *Dīwān i Shiʿrī* or *Mīrʾāt al-khayāl* (Edition: Amritsar 1304/1887°), (2) a cosmography entitled *Zubdat al-akhbār* (Edition: Amritsar 1282/1865°) and (3) a metrical *Chār darwīsh*.

824 Jhunjhunū is "about 90 miles north-by-north-west of Jaipur city" (*Imperial Gazetteer of India, Provincial series, Rājputāna*, Calcutta 1908, p. 262). Nāgaur is in the State of Jōd'hpūr (cf. no. 9, 2nd par., footnote *supra*).

825 This saint, surnamed Qiblah i ʿālam, has through his disciples "exercised a profound influence over the whole of the south-western Punjab" (Rose). Born in 1142/1730, he went to Delhi and obtained the *khirqah i khilāfat* from Fakhr al-Dīn Muḥibb al-Nabī (for whom see no. 1372 4th par. *supra*). He died in 1205/1791 and was buried at Chishtiyān, near Mahārān, in the State of Bahāwalpūr. See *Khazīnat al-aṣfiyāʾ* i pp. 506–8; *Bahawalpur State Gazetteer* (1904) pp. 176–8; H. A. Rose *Glossary of the tribes and castes of the Punjab and North-West Frontier Province* i (Lahore 1919) p. 533.

Gulzār i Khalīl, a life of the Kashmīrī saint Khwājah M. Khalīl b. ʿAbd al-Ghafūr Qādirī (b. 1175/1761, d. 1242/1827) followed by an account of the author's ancestors, completed in 1290/1873. Edition: **Lahore** 1291/1874*.

[*Gulzār i Khalīl* pp. 35–6; *Taḥāʾif al-abrār* p. 351.]

1399. Maulawī Shāh **Taqī ʿAlī Qalandar Kākōrawī** was the younger son of Shāh Turāb ʿAlī Qalandar Kākōrawī (for whom see no. 1378 *supra*). He was born in 1213/1798–9 and after a life devoted to teaching at Kākōrī died on 17 Rajab 1290/10 September 1873.

al-Rauḍ al-azhar fī maʾāthir al-Qalandar, or *Laṭāʾif al-adhkār fī manāqib ʿumdat al-akhyār*, a detailed biography of the author's father, Shāh Turāb ʿAlī, with some account of his spiritual ancestors, the Qalandarī order and other matters, divided into a *muqaddimah* (in three *faṣls*, of which the third is *dar taʿrīf i ahl i sulūk az firaq i Ṣūfīyah i Malāmatīyah u ḥikāyāt u kalimāt u iṣṭilāḥātashān*) and ten *laṭīfahs* ((1) on the Prophet, his parents, ʿAlī b. Abī Ṭālib etc., (2) on the meaning of the word *qalandar*, etc., biography of ʿAbd al-ʿAzīz Makkī, (3) biographies of ten *shaikhs* from Khiḍr Rūmī to Bāsiṭ ʿAlī Ilāhābādī [the same ten as in the *Uṣūl al-maqṣūd*, no. 1378 (2) *supra*], (4) biographies of Masʿūd ʿAlī Ilāhābādī and the author's grandfather M. Kāẓim (cf. no. 1378, 1st par., end), (5) on Shāh Turāb ʿAlī and his ʿAlawī pedigree, M. b. al-Ḥanafīyah, the meaning of the expression Āl i Nabī, etc., (6) *dar dhikr i mabādī i ḥāl i ān-ḥaḍrat*, (7) *dar bayān i maslak i ḥaḍrat i īshān dar uṣūl wa-ghair i ān*, (8) *dar dhikr i maslak i ḥaḍrat i walī-niʿmat dar taʿabbud u tanassuk* etc., (9) *dar dhikr i samāʿ i ghinā*, and (10) [supplied after the author's death by ʿAlī Anwar Qalandar] *dar bayān i ʿishq u maḥabbat*). Edition: **Rāmpūr and Lucknow** 1331–6/1913–18[-19*] (with an introduction, *Mawāhib al-qalandar li-man yuṭāliʿ al-Rauḍ al-azhar*, on the life of Taqī ʿAlī etc., completed in 1333/1915 by Shāh Ḥabīb Ḥaidar Qalandar, and a continuation, *Ḥauḍ al-Kauthar fī takmilat Rauḍ* [*sic*] *al-azhar*, completed in 1291/1874 by ʿAlī Anwar Qalandar).

[*Mawāhib al-qalandar* p. 11 ult.-22; *al-Rauḍ al-azhar* pp. 707 ff.; Raḥmān ʿAlī p. 37.]

1400. ʿ**Alī Anwar** Qalandar b. ʿAlī Akbar b. Ḥaidar ʿAlī, who was born in 1269/1853, completed in 1291/1874 the *Ḥauḍ al-Kauthar fī takmilat Rauḍ* [*sic*] *al-azhar*, which has been mentioned above (no. 1399 2nd par., end).

(1) ***Intiṣāḥ ʿan dhikr ahl al-ṣalāḥ***, biographies of famous Ṣūfīs with some account of the Ṣūfī orders: [**Lahore**] Majmaʿ al-ʿulūm Pr. [1877*] (pp. 120);

Lucknow 1327/1910* (with a continuation (p. 164 onwards) entitled *al-Īḍāḥ fī tatimmat al-Intiṣāḥ* by M. Ḥabīb Ḥaidar. Pp. 214).

(2) ***Taḥrīr al-Anwar fī tafsīr al-Qalandar***, an account of the Qalandars: [**Lucknow**] ʿAlawī Pr. 1290/1873°* (pp. 32).

[*Mawāhib al-qalandar* (cf. no. 1399, last par. *supra*) pp. 20 ult., 22.]

1401. Maulawī **Walī Allāh** b. Mullā Ḥabīb Allāh b. Mullā Muḥibb Allāh Anṣārī **Lak'hnawī** Farangī-Maḥallī, one of the well-known family of *ʿulamāʾ* who have taught for several generations at Farangī Maḥall,[826] Lucknow, died on 10 Ṣafar 1270/12 November 1853. Among his works were *ʿUmdat al-wasāʾil*, on the *manāqib* of the saint S. ʿAbd al-Razzāq Bānsawī (cf. no. 1347 2nd par. *supra*), a commentary on the *Qurʾān* entitled *Maʿdin al-jawāhir*, as well as commentaries and *ḥawāshī* on several standard text-books.

al-Aghṣān al-arbaʿah li-l-shajarat al-ṭaiyibah, a life of the saintly Mullā Aḥmad Anwār al-Ḥaqq Farangī-Maḥallī[827] and other descendants of the celebrated teacher Quṭb al-Dīn Sihālawī,[828] the ancestor of the *ʿulamāʾ* of Farangī Maḥall, Lucknow, in a *muqaddimah* (on the genealogy of Quṭb al-Dīn) and four *aṣls* devoted to the lives and descendants of Quṭb al-Dīn's four sons,[829] with additions by the author's son, M. Inʿām Allāh, Deputy Collector, bringing the information down to 1296/1879.

Edition: **Lucknow** 1298/1881*.

[Raḥmān ʿAlī p. 252; Alṭāf al-Raḥmān *Aḥwāl i ʿulamāʾ i Farangī Maḥall* (in Urdu), Lucknow [1907*], p. 80.]

1402. Ḥājjī Mullā **M. Bāqir** b. M. Ismāʿīl b. ʿAbd al-ʿAẓīm b. M. Bāqir Māzandarānī Kujūrī (*aṣlan*) **Ṭihrānī** (*maulidan wa-maskinan*).

826 Cf. Raḥmān ʿAlī p. 168: *Farangī Maḥall aknūn maḥallah īst az maḥallāt i shahr i Lak'hnaʾū dār al-imārah i ṣūbah i Awad'h sābiq qiṭʿah i zamīn būd kih dar-ān tājirī az Farangistān sukūnat dāsht az-īn wajh ān qiṭʿah i zamīn ba-Farangī Maḥall shuhrat girift baʿd i murūr i aiyām ba-wajh i na-māndan i aʿqāb i tājir i Farangī zamīn i madhkūrah dar nuzūl i shāhī dar-āmad baʿd i qatl i Mullā-yi shahīd* [i.e. Quṭb al-Dīn Sihālawī] *aulādashān jihat i qiyām i khwud jā-yi madhkūr muʿāf yāftand u dar-ān-jā hanūz aulād i sharīfash qiyām-padhīr and u ān mauqiʿ bah Farangī Maḥall shuhrat dārad.*

827 A. A. al-Ḥ. F.-M. b. Aḥmad ʿAbd al-Ḥaqq b. M. Saʿīd b. Quṭb al-Dīn Sihālawī died in 1236/1821. See Raḥmān ʿAlī p. 13.

828 Q. al-D. Sihālawī was murdered in 1103/1692. See *Maʾāthir al-kirām* i no. 24; *Subḥat al-marjān* p. 76; Raḥmān ʿAlī p. 167; etc. Sihālī is a village near Lucknow (cf. no. 1347 1st footnote *supra*).

829 For the third of these four sons, Mullā Niẓām al-Dīn M. Sihālawī, see no. 1347 *supra*.

Jannat al-naʿīm wa-'l-ʿaish al-salīm fī aḥwāl Maulānā ʿAbd al-ʿAẓīm (so in the Arabic preface p. 3 ult., but *J. al-n. fī a. ʿA. al-ʿA. ʿalaihi 'l-salām wa-'l-takrīm*, in the Persian preface p. 10^{2}), an account, written in 1296/1879 (see p. 6^{15}), of the Imām-zādah ʿAbd al-ʿAẓīm b. ʿAbd Allāh al-Ḥasanī (b. ʿAlī b. Ḥasan b. Zaid b. Ḥasan b. ʿAlī b. Abī Ṭālib. Cf. *J. al-n.* p. 479 antepenult.; *Rauḍāt al-jannāt* p. 356; *Muntahā 'l-maqāl* p. 179; etc.), who is said to have died at Raiy about AH 250/864 and whose shrine is at the place called after him Shāh ʿAbd al-ʿAẓīm, five or six miles south of Ṭihrān (cf. Browne *A year amongst the Persians* pp. 82, 158–61, etc.), together with notices of his ancestors and of some holy, learned or pious persons buried near Ṭihrān.

Edition: [**Ṭihrān**] 1296–8/1879–81* (pp. 548. Portrait of the author at end).

1403. **Ghulām-Naqī** b. M. Fatḥ-ʿAlī **Bilgrāmī** Chishtī Ṣābirī[830] was born on 17 Ramaḍān 1231/11 August 1816.

Manbahāt* [*Munabbihāt* ?] *fī ʿilm al-amwāt, biographies of well-known Indian saints, chiefly Chishtīs, and of a few poets, princes and noblemen, completed at the Jāmiʿ Masjid Madrasah, Ḥaidarābād, in 1298/1881: **Ivanow** Curzon 84 (autograph ?).

1404. **Amīn Aḥmad** "Thabāt" Firdausī.

(1) ***Gul i bihishtī***, a metrical account of some Chishtī saints: [**Lucknow**] 1881° (242 pp.).

(2) ***Gul i firdaus***, a metrical biography of Sharaf al-Dīn Aḥmad b. Yaḥyā Munyarī,[831] with interwoven notices of other Chishtī saints: **Lucknow** 1884° (266 pp.).

---

830 Cf. no. 1374 2nd par. (3) (*d*) footnote.

831 Sh. al-D. A. b. Y. Munyarī or Manērī, born at Manēr, a village in the Patna Division of the Province of Bihār, went to Delhi either before or shortly after the death of Niẓām al-Dīn Auliyā (for whom see no. 1259 4th footnote *supra*) and became a disciple of Najīb al-Dīn Firdausī. After his return to Bihār he spent many years of seclusion and austerity in the Rajagriha hills. Later he settled outside the town of Bihār (now a place of pilgrimage called on his account Bihār Sharīf) and died there on 7 Shawwāl 772/1371 or 781/1380 or 782/1381. See *Akhbār al-akhyār* pp. 117–22; *Gulzār i abrār* no. 99; *Mir'āt al-asrār, ṭabaqah* 20, last biography; *Makhzan al-gharā'ib* no. 1143; *Khazīnat al-aṣfiyā'* ii pp. 290–2; Ḍamīr al-Dīn *Sīrat al-Sharaf* (cited in *Nuzhat al-khawāṭir* p. 10^{2} and Bānkīpūr xvi p. 25); Rieu ii 402; Beale *Oriental biographical dictionary* under Sharafuddin Ahmad Ahia [*sic*] Maniri and also under Shah Sharaf-uddin; Raḥmān ʿAlī p. 84; *Nuzhat al-khawāṭir* (in Arabic) pp. 8–10; Bānkīpūr xvi p. 25. Among his works were (1) *Maktūbāt*, well known Ṣūfī letters, of which there are three or four collections (MSS.: Āṣafīyah i p. 486 nos.

(3) ***Rauḍat al-naʿīm***, metrical biographies of ʿAbd al-Qādir Jīlānī and other saints: Sharaf al-akhbār Pr. [**Lucknow** ?] 1301/1883–4*.

1405. M. **Ḍiyāʾ al-Raḥmān** Shāhqulīpūrī was a disciple of S. Shāh ʿAlī ʿAbd al-Qādir Shams al-Qādirī called Murshid ʿAlī Qādirī Baghdādī (*aṣl*[an]) Mēdnīpūrī (*maulid*[an]), who was himself (see p. 13, l. 7 from foot) a disciple of S. Ṭufail ʿAlī Qādirī Razzāqī Dhākirī (d. 1251/1836: see p. 187[3]), the nephew (*birādar-zādah*, p. 152[8]), son-in-law and successor of S. Shāh Dhākir ʿAlī.

Mudhākarah i Quṭb al-ʿālamīn, or *Madārij i sanīyah i Dhākirīyah*, or *Adhkār i baiyinah i Qādirīyah* (all chronograms = 1309/1891–2), a life of S. Shāh Abū ʾl-Ḥasan M. Dhākir ʿAlī Qādirī Razzāqī Baghdādī, called Ghauth i Thānī, a son of S. Shāh Abū M. ʿAbd Allāh al-Qādirī al-Baghdādī and a descendant of ʿAbd al-Qādir al-Jīlānī, who was born at Baghdād in 1111/1699–1700 (see p. 193), migrated to India in 1180/1766–7, settled at Mangalkōṭ, north of Bardwān in Bengal, and died there in 1192/1778, based on the *Risālah i Dhākirīyah* (a chronogram = 1232/1817) of an unnamed disciple of the *shaikh*: **Cawnpore** (Aḥmadī Press) 1310/1893‡.

1406. Qāḍī S. **Imām al-Dīn Ḥasan Khān**, Deputy Collector at Ajmēr, may be presumed to have written his *Muʿīn al-auliyāʾ* shortly before publication.

68, 69, 461, 683, 810, Bānkīpūr xvi 1361–5, xvii 1585, 1615, Brelvi-Dhabhar p. 72, Ethé 1843–7, Ivanow 1205–7, Ivanow-Curzon 756, Ivanow 1st Suppt. 855, Kapurthala (OCM. iii/4 (Aug. 1927) p. 10), Lahore (OCM. viii/3 (May 1932) p. 138), Leyden v p. 42 no. 2304, Peshawar 940*b*, Princeton 98. Editions: *Maktūbāt i ṣadī* [*sic* ?], [Arrah] 1287/1870* (vol. i only, pp. 165), *Maktūbāt*, Lucknow 1885° (pp. 400). Translation: *Letters from a Sûfî teacher, Shaikh Sharfuddîn Manerî or Makhdûm-ul-Mulk. Translated ... by Baijnath Singh*, Benares [1909*] (pp. 130)), (2) *Ajwibah* (MSS.: Bānkīpūr xvii 1569, Bombay Univ. p. 231 no. 151 Ivanow-Curzon 462 IV. Edition (?): *Maktūbāt i jawābī*, Lucknow 1884°), (3) *Fawāʾid i Ruknī*, extracts from the *Maktūbāt* (MS.: Bānkīpūr xvii 1612). Edition: place ? 1328/1910 (Āṣafīyah iii p. 200)), (4) *Irshād al-sālikīn* (MSS.: Bānkīpūr xvii 1583, Ethé 1849, Ivanow-Curzon 462 iii), (5) *Maʿdin al-maʿānī*, a collection of *malfūẓāt* (MSS.: Āṣafīyah i p. 488 no. 70, Bānkīpūr xvi 1360, Ivanow-Curzon 425, Lahore (OCM. viii/3 (May 1932) p. 138), Vollers 902 (?)). (6) *Mukhkh al-maʿānī*, a collection of *malfūẓāt*. Edition: Āgrah 1321/1904*. The name of his birthplace, officially spelt Maner (i.e. Manēr presumably), is spelt Munair in the Bānkīpūr catalogue (xvi p. 25) and Manīr (*bi-fatḥ al-mīm wa-kasr al-nūn*) in the *Nuzhat al-khawāṭir* (p. 9[1]), but the spelling Munyar (or Manyar ?) is attested, though perhaps only as a poetic licence, by several verses in the *Sharaf-nāmah i Aḥmad i Munyarī*, a dictionary dedicated to his memory in 877/1472 or 878/1473 by a dweller at his shrine, Ibrāhīm Qiwām Fārūqī Bīhārī (e.g. *Mughīth i jahān sarwar i Munyar ast * kih khāk i dar i rauḍah ash ʿanbar ast* (quoted Ethé ii 3052), *Samī-yi Nabī Aḥmad i Munyarī * kih dārad ba-d-ū dīn i ḥaqq bartarī* (Sipahsālār Cat. ii p. 190), *Sarāpā kih mamlū zi durr i darīʾ st * Sharaf-nāmah i Aḥmad i Munyarī ʾst*).

Muʿīn al-auliyāʾ, a life of Muʿīn al-Dīn Chishtī Ajmērī,[832] his successors and his spiritual descendants: **Ajmēr** [1894°. Pp. 308].[833]

1407. Ṣāḥib-zādah **M. Ḥasan** b. ʿAbd al-Raḥmān **Mujaddidī Naqshbandī**, a descendant of Aḥmad Sirhindī (for whom see no. 1316 (1) 1st footnote *supra*), was resident at Amritsar in 1910.

Anīs al-murīdīn, a life of the author's father, Pīr ʿAbd al-Raḥmān b. ʿAbd al-Qaiyūm (b. 1244/1828–9, d. 1315/1897), written in 1316/1898–9. Edition: **Amritsar** 1328/1910*.

1408. **Maʿṣūm ʿAlī** b. Raḥmat-ʿAlī **Niʿmat-Allāhī al-Shīrāzī** (see *Ṭarāʾiq al-ḥaqāʾiq*, author's preface, 1. 2), or Āqā-yi Ḥājjī Mīrzā Maʿṣūm[834] *Nāʾib al-Ṣadr*, as "Furūghī" calls him in his prefixed *taqrīẓ* (so also on the title-page of Vol 1), or al-Ḥājj Maʿṣūm ʿAlī Shāh al-Niʿmat-Allāhī al-Shīrāzī, as he is called on the other title-pages, was the son of Ḥājjī Zain al-ʿĀbidīn known as (*maʿrūf bi-*) Ḥājjī Mīrzā Kūchak Nāʾib al-Ṣadr and surnamed (*mulaqqab bi-*) Raḥmat-ʿAlī Shāh (see "Furūghī's" *taqrīẓ* p. 5[8]). He was born at Shīrāz on 14 Rabīʿ al-Awwal 1270/15 Dec. 1853. In the course of extensive travels he visited various parts of Persia, ʿIrāq, India, Turkistān and Turkey, meeting numerous men of learning and piety. His visit to Mecca and al-Madīnah he described in a *safar-nāmah* entitled *Tuḥfat al-Ḥaramain*.

Ṭarāʾiq al-ḥaqāʾiq, biographical notices of saints and mystics completed at Ṭihrān in Ṣafar 1318/1900 and divided into a *muqaddimah* (on Ṣūfism, etc.), six *waṣls* (1) companions of ʿAlī b. Abī Ṭālib, vol. ii pp. 2–27, (2) the *silsilah* of Ḥasan i Baṣrī, vol. ii pp. 27–39, (3) the *silsilah* of Kumail b. Ziyād, vol. ii pp. 39–51, (4) the *silsilah* of Ibrāhīm b. Adham, vol. ii pp. 51–68, (5) the *silsilah* of Bāyazīd i Bisṭāmī, vol. ii pp. 68–114, (6) the *silsilah* of Maʿrūf i Karkhī and its fourteen branches including the Niʿmat-Allāhī *shaikhs*, whose biographies are the primary concern of the work, vol. ii pp. 114–311, vol. iii pp. 2–220) and a *khātimah* (an account of the author and some of his contemporaries, vol. iii pp. 220–354).

Edition: **Ṭihrān** 1316–19/1898–1901‡ (cf. Mashhad iii p. 137).

[Autobiography in *khātimah* to *Ṭarāʾiq al-ḥaqāʾiq*: *taqrīẓ* by M. Ḥusain "Furūghī" Iṣfahānī prefixed to vol. i: portrait following the *taqrīẓ*.]

---

832 For whom see no. 1259 2nd par. 3rd footnote *supra*.

833 The Āṣafīyah Library has two copies of this work dated 1312 [i.e. 1894–5] which the catalogue [iii p. 166 nos. 131, 173] describes, probably by inadvertence, as manuscripts.

834 His father calls him Muḥammad Maʿṣūm in a note recording the date of his birth which is quoted in the *Ṭarāʾiq al-ḥaqāʾiq* iii p. 220 antepenult.

1409. Ḥājjī Abū Muḥammad **Muḥyī 'l-Dīn "Miskīn"** b. Mullā M. Shāh Aḥmadī Kubrawī Ḥanafī Naqshbandī was born in 1282/1865–6. He was a pupil of Ḥajjī M. Yaḥyā, whom he accompanied in 1307/1889–90 on a pilgrimage to Mecca. In 1309/1891–2 he wrote a work entitled *ʿAin al-jārī sharḥ Arbaʿīn al-Qārī*. When he wrote the preface to his *Taḥāʾif al-abrār* he was resident in the district of Amīrākadal.

Taḥāʾif al-abrār [so in the author's preface, but on the title-page *Tārīkh i kabīr i Kashmīr al-mausūm bah T. al. a. fī dhikr al-auliyāʾ al-akhyār*], a mainly biographical work on Kashmīr begun in 1310/1892–3, completed in 1321/1903–4 and divided into ten *taḥāʾif* ((1) Saiyids, (2) *rīshīs*, i.e. anchorites [cf. no. 1312 *supra*], (3) *mashāyikh u ṣāliḥān*, (4) scholars, (5) *majdhūbān*, (6) poets, (7) sacred relics, (8) sulṭāns, (9) geography, (10) on the permissibility of certain foods and drugs).

Edition: **Amritsar** 1321–2/1905°* (only the first seven *taḥāʾif*, being the first of the two volumes).

[*Taḥāʾif al-abrār* pp. 363–4.]

1410. Maulawī S. M. **Amīr Ḥasan Madārī Fanṣūrī**[835] b. Saiyid Shāh Ākhūn is described on the title-page of the *Tadhkirat al-muttaqīn* as a (still-living) *raʾīs* of Makanpūr[836]

Tadhkirat al-muttaqīn (the title-page adds *fī aḥwāl khulafāʾ Saiyid Badīʿ al-Dīn*), biographies of Shāh Madār (for whom see no. 1329 (6) 2nd footnote *supra*), his *khulafāʾ* and prominent members of his order down to the author's time. Edition: **Cawnpore** 1315/1898* (vol. i) and 1322–3/1905* (vol. ii).

1411. Appendix

(1) ***Adhkār al-adhkiyāʾ fī bayān manāqib mashāyikh al-ṭuruq*** (beg.: *Aʿlāʾ i ajnās i ḥamd u sipās*): **Cairo** p. 498 (AH 1126/1714).

(2) (***Aḥwāl Ibn al-Khafīf***), an Arabic biography of Abū ʿAbd Allāh M. b. al-Khafīf al-Shīrāzī,[837] by his pupil Abū 'l-Ḥasan ʿAlī b. M. al-Dailamī (cf.

835 This *nisbah* indicates descent from Saiyid Abū Turāb Fanṣūr (d. 899/1494), Shāh Madār's immediate successor, whose biography is given on pp. 22–31 of the first volume of the *Tadhkirat al-muttaqīn*. The word Fanṣūr is not explained. For its use as a geographical name see *Ḥudūd al-ʿālam*, tr. Minorsky, p. 87.

836 A village 8 miles N.W. of Bilhaur and 40 miles from Cawnpore, owing its celebrity to the shrine of Shāh Madār.

837 For this saint, who died in 371/981–2, see *Kashf al-maḥjūb* tr. Nicholson p. 158; ʿAbd Allāh Anṣārī *Ṭabaqāt al-Ṣūfīyah* (Ivanow 234, no. 110); ʿAṭṭār *Tadhkirat al-auliyāʾ* ii pp. 124–31;

Brockelmann *Sptbd.* i p. 359 and R. Walzer in *JRAS* 1939 pp. 407–22): no MSS. recorded.

Persian translation in thirteen *bābs* prepared by Rukn al-Dīn Yaḥyā b. Burhān al-Dīn b. Junaid at the request of an unnamed Atābak described as *Atābak i sāʿīd i marḥūm i shahīd*: **Berlin** 605 (breaks off in *Bāb* x. 62 foll. Old), **Köprülü** 1589 foll. 379*a*–406*b*.

Extracts: Massignon *Recueil de textes inédits* p. 81.

(3) ***Aḥwāl u aqwāl i ḥaḍrat i Saiyidnā ʿAbd al-Qādir i Jīlānī:*** **Āṣafīyah** i p. 396 no. 876 (AH 1232/1816–17).

(4) ***Anecdotes of saints in the first three Islāmic centuries*** (beginning: *al-Ḥ. l. R. al-ʿā.... Thanā u sitāyish mar Khuday rā kih āfrīdgār i jahānast u āfrīdgār i hamah i jānwarān ast*) divided according to subject into twenty *bābs* (I. *Andar khwurdan i ḥalāl*, etc.) and written apparently in the fifth/eleventh century: **Rieu** Suppt. 393 (defective at end. 13th cent.).

(5) ***(Ansāb i mashāyikh i Kashmīr)***, genealogical tables and chains of spiritual succession relating to prophets and other holy persons, especially Kashmīrī saints, with occasional dates (of which 1101/1690 and 1128/1716 seem to be the latest): **Ivanow** Curzon 79 (3).

(6) ***Anwār al-Raḥmān li-tanwīr al-janān***, the life and teachings of Shāh ʿAbd al-Raḥmān, by M. Nūr Allāh. Edition: **Lucknow** 1321/1903°*.

(7) ***Aʿrās i buzurgān*** (beginning, without preface, *Shahr i Rabīʿ al-Awwal* 1. *Wafāt yāft Saiyid al-Mursalīn*) the Persian version of an Arabic obituary calendar relating to holy persons from the first Islāmic century onwards, especially to members of the Bā-ʿAlawī family (about whom particulars are given mainly on the authority of *ʿIqd al-jawāhir wa-'l-durar* (Brockelmann ii p. 383, *Sptbd.* ii p. 516), *al-Nūr al-sāfir* (Brockelmann ii p. 419, *Sptbd.* ii p. 617) and similar works), composed evidently in India[838] and doubtless soon after 1160/1747 (the date of the latest death recorded, that of S. M. b. Ḥāmid b. ʿAbd Allāh b. ʿAlī Bā-ʿAlawī, of Malabar, p. 34, 27th Rajab) apparently by a son of S. Shaikh b. ʿAlawī b. ʿAbd Allāh Bā-ʿAbbūd Bā-ʿAlawī (who on p. 28 is called *al-Saiyid al-jalīl al-ʿallāmah al-wālid*[839]), probably S. ʿAlawī b. Shaikh Bā-ʿAbbūd Bā-ʿAlawī, who is mentioned on p. 74 ult. as the author of the preceding biography and whose name

Haft iqlīm no. 171; *Safīnat al-auliyāʾ* p. 110 (no. 144); Massignon *La passion d'al-Hallaj* pp. 363–4; Brockelmann *Sptbd.* i pp. 358–9 (where further references will be found).

838 For Indian saints the compiler's chief authority is the *Mirʾāt al-asrār* (cf. no. 1329 (5) *supra*).

839 The last word is queried in the printed text.

occurs also on pp. 7[9] and 34[7] (as the subject of statements in the third person, however).

Edition: *The Á'aras-i-bozorgán, being an obituary of pious and learned Moslims from the beginning of Islám to the middle of the twelfth century of the Hijrah. Edited [from a MS., containing also, it seems, the Arabic original, in the Library of the College of Fort William]*[840] *by W. Nassau Lees, and Mawlawi Kabir al-Dín Ahmad. Published by W. N. Lees.* [**Calcutta**] 1855°* (pp. 91).

(8) ***Asrār al-mashāyikh***, by Bahā' al-Dīn b. Maḥmūd b. Makhdūm Qāḍī Ḥamīd al-Dīn Nāgaurī[841] *al-ma'rūf bah* Rājah: **Āṣafīyah** iii p. 362 no. 192 (AH 1077/1666–7).

(9) ***Badā'i' al-āthār***, an account of the visit of 'Abd al-Bahā' to the United States in 1912, by Maḥmūd Zarqānī: **Bombay** 1332/1914°* (Vol I only ?).

(10) ***Bhagat-māl:*** see ***Bhakta-māla.***

(11) ***Bhagat-nāmah:*** see ***Bhakta-māla.***

(12) ***Bhakta-māla***, translations of Nābhājī's Hindī biographies of Vaishnava saints, (1) *Srī Bhagat-māl*, with introduction, marginal notes, and glossary, **Meerut** 1269/1853* (pp. 12, 6, 468,50), (2) *Gangā-sāgar 'urf Bhagat-nāmah*, a metrical translation by Nat'han Lāl from Tulasī-Rāma's Urdu version, **Delhi** 1897° (18 pts.).

(13) ***Dār al-asrār fī khawāriq Badī' al-Dīn Shāh Madār:***[842] **Peshawar** 1957 (9).

(14) ***Dhikr i Khwājah 'Abd al-Khāliq i Ghujduwānī:***[843] **Leyden** v p. 232 no. 2641 (22 foll. AH 900/1494–5).

The same saint, who died in 575/1179–80, is the subject of **Rieu** ii 862*a* i (beginning *Az ān shaikh i rabbānī*. 18th cent.) and **Ethé** 1923 (1) (*Dhikr i Khwājah i Khwājahā Khwājah i jahān 'Abd al-Khāliq i Ghujduwānī*, beginning *Ān shaikh i 'alā 'l-iṭlāq*).

(15) ***Dhikr i maqāmāt i Imām i A'ẓam*** (i.e. presumably Abū Ḥanīfah): **Āṣafīyah** ii p. 1556 no. 44.

(16) ***Ḍiyā' al-qulūb***, "a treatise on Ṣūfī orders," by Imdād Allāh Fārūqī: **Delhi** [1877 ?°*]; place ? 1914 (Āṣafīyah III p. 200); and in the *Kullīyāt i Imdādīyah*, **Cawnpore** 1315/1898°, pp. 127–81.

840 The MS. should presumably be now either in the library of the Royal Asiatic Society of Bengal or in that of the India Office, but it seems not to be traceable in the catalogues of those libraries.

841 For Qāḍī Ḥ. al-D.N. see no. 9 *supra*.

842 Cf. no. 1329 (6) 2nd footnote *supra*.

843 See *Nafaḥāt al-uns* p. 431; *Rashaḥāt* p. 18; *Haft iqlīm no.* 1486; *Safīnat al-auliyā'* p. 76 (no. 76); *Khazīnat al-aṣfiyā'* i p. 532; *Ency. Isl.* under Ghudjduwānī (unsigned).

(17) ***Durr al-dārain fī manāqib Ghauth al-Thaqalain,***[844] by S. Ghulām-ʿAlī Qādirī Mūsawī: **Āṣafīyah** iii p. 662 (author's name given as ʿAlī al-Mūsawī).
Edition: place ? 1308/1890–1 (Āṣaf. ii p. 1556 nos. 16–17).

(18) ***Gangā-sāgar:*** see ***Bhakta-māla.***

(19) ***Genealogies of Shīʿite and Ṣūfī families:*** **Lindesiana** p. 142 no. 789 (circ. AD 1750).

(20) ***Ḥālāt i ḥaḍrat i Shāh Balāwal i Lāhaurī***[845] (in Persian ?): no MSS. recorded. Urdu translation: *Urdū tar-jamah i kitāb i Ḥ. i ḥ. Sh. B. L.*, **Lahore** [1923*].

(21) ***Ḥālāt i Saiyid Muḥammad i Jaunpūrī,*** a life of S. M. b. S. Bud'h Uwaisī Jaunpūrī, who claimed to be the Mahdī, founded a sect in Gujrāt[846] and died in 910/1504–5:[847] **Āṣafīyah** ii p. 848 no. 34 (AH 1267/1850–1).

(22) *Mathnawī i* ***Ḥālāt i shahādat i Muḥammad Ghauth Qādirī:*** **Āṣafīyah** i p. 468 no. 679 (AH 1240/1824–5).

(23) ***Ḥālāt u karāmāt i ḥaḍrat i Shāh Ṣafī u Shāh Miyān u Shāh Ilhām-Allāh u Shāh Qudrat-Allāh,*** by Shāh Faiḍ Allāh: **Āṣafīyah** iii p. 196 no. 1454.

(24) *Risālah i* ***ḥasab u nasab i ḥaḍrat i Ḥāfiẓ M. ʿAlī-Shāh Khairābādī,***[848] an autobiography: **Āṣafīyah** iii p. 362 no. 208 (AH 1310/1892–3).

(25) *Risālah i* ***ḥasab u nasab i Makhdūm Abū 'l-Fatḥ b. S. Niẓām al-Dīn Shanūzānī (?) al-MLKI al-Khurāsānī,*** apparently an autobiography: **Āṣafīyah** iii p. 362 no. 208 (AH 1310/1892–3).

(26) ***Ḥikāyāt al-ṣāliḥīn,*** anecdotes in twenty *bābs* each containing ten *ḥikāyāt*, by ʿUthmān b. ʿUmar called Kahf: Ḥ. Kh. iii p. 81 (beginning not quoted).
Arabic translation: **Lahore** 1298/1881° (pp. 108).

(27) ***Ḥikāyāt i auliyā i ṣāliḥīn:*** **Āṣafīyah** i p. 416 no. 639.

---

844 The Ghauth al-Thaqalain is of course ʿAbd al-Qādir al-Jīlānī (for whom see no. 1251 2nd par. footnote).

845 S. Shāh B. b. S. ʿUthmān b. S. ʿĪsā Qādirī Lāhaurī, was born at Shaikhūpūrah, became a disciple of S. Shams al-Dīn Qādirī Lāhaurī and died on 28 Shaʿbān 1046/25 Jan. 1637. See *Safīnat al-auliyā'* p. 198 (no. 377); ʿAbd al-Ḥamīd *Pādshāh-nāmah* i, 2 p. 334; *ʿAmal i Ṣāliḥ* iii p. 366; *Khazīnat al-aṣfiyā'* i pp. 161–3.

846 See *Ency. Isl.* under Mahdawīs; Raḥmān ʿAlī pp. 188–9; etc.

847 See *Ẓafar al-wālih* (in Arabic) i pp. 34–6; *Ma'āthir al-umarā'* i pp. 124–5, Beveridge's translation pp. 116–7; Raḥmān ʿAlī pp. 197–201; *Sawāniḥ i Mahdī i mauʿūd* (in Urdu), by S. Walī Sikandarābādī, Āgrah 1321/1903*; *Intikhāb i tawārīkh al-Aghyār* (no. (28) below); etc. For a work entitled *Ithbāt i madhhab i Saiyid Muḥammad Ṣāḥib i Jaunpūrī*, by Shihāb al-Dīn Mahdawī (d. circ. 1275/1858–9), see Āṣafīyah ii p. 1354 no. 50.

848 Presumably the same person as the subject of the *Manāqib i Ḥāfiẓīyah* mentioned below (no. 48).

(28) ***Intikhāb i tawārīkh al-Aghyār***, notices of S. M. Jaunpūrī (see no. (21) above) and his followers (called *Ghair-mahdī* by their enemies: see *Ency. Religion and Ethics* vi p. 189). Edition: place ? date ? (Peshawar no. 1549).

(29) ***'Iqd al-la'ālī'***, on the life and merits of Shāh Abū 'l-Ma'ālī,[849] by Maulawī Mushtāq Aḥmad Ṣābirī:[850] **Sād'haurah** 1331/1913*.

(30) ***Kanz al-ansāb***, the genealogy of eminent saints and other famous men, by 'Abd al-Razzāq 'Aṭā Ḥusain: **Bombay** 1883° (pp. 344).

(31) ***Karāmāt al-auliyā':*** **Āṣafīyah** i p. 460 nos. 706 (AH 1236/1820–1), 894.

(32) ***Karāmāt i Qādir Walī***, in verse, by M. Najīb b. Aḥmad 'Alī. Edition: place ? 1267/1851 (Āṣafīyah ii p. 850).

(33) ***Khulāṣat al-'ārifīn:*** **Āṣafīyah** i p. 416 (2 copies).

(34) ***Lam'at al-shams***, a metrical account of Shams al-Dīn [Tabrīzī ?] and of Ni'mat Allāh Walī (presumably N. A. W. Kirmānī. Cf. no. 1269 (1), footnote *supra*), by ?: **Āṣafīyah** ii p. 850 no. 50.

(35) ***Maḥāmid i Ḥammādīyah***, a life of S. Shāh Ghulām-Muḥammad Qādirī *al-mukhāṭab min 'ind Rasūl Allāh bah* Ḥammād i Thānī, by Maulawī S. M. Burhān al-Dīn Khān. Edition: place ? 1308/1890–1 (Āṣafīyah iii p. 202 no. 1494).

(36) ***Majmū'ah i fawā'id i 'Uthmānī***, life, letters, and sayings of M. 'Uthmān Damānī, by M. Akbar 'Alī Shāh Dihlawī: **Delhi** 1316/1899°.

(37) ***Makhzan i 'irfānī***, "the life, sayings and writings of the Peshawari saint S. Amīr called Ḥaḍrat-jī," by Sulṭān M. Ajnālawī: **Amritsar** [1920*].

(38) ***Malfūẓ i asrār al-makhdūmīn***, sayings of Shāh Karak Karawī and anecdotes concerning him, compiled by Karīm-Yār, Ra'īs of Yuhan: **Fatḥpūr** 1893°.

(39) ***Malfūẓ i Razzāqī***, the life and sayings of 'Abd al-Razzāq Bānsawī (cf. no. 1347 2nd par. *supra*), by M. Khān Razzāqī, edited by S. Ghulām-Jīlānī: **Lucknow** 1896°, [1905*].

(40) ***Malfūẓāt i Ḥājjī Wārith 'Alī Shāh***, life and sayings of W. 'A. Sh., by Khudā-Bakhsh "Shā'iq":[851] Anwār i Muḥammadī Press [**Lucknow**] 1293/1876*.

(41) ***Malfūẓāt i Shāh Mīnā:*** see *Tuḥfat al-Sa'dīyah* below.

(42) ***Malfūẓāt i Sharīfī***, life and sayings of Sharīf al-Dīn M. Chishtī: **Ambala** 1917* (with preface by Mushtāq Aḥmad Chishtī).

---

849 Presumably Abū 'l-Ma'ālī b. S. M. Ashraf Chishtī Ṣābirī, of Anbahtah ("Ambahta") near Sahāranpūr, who was a disciple of M. Ṣādiq Gangōhī and a *khalīfah* of his son, M. Dāwud b. M. Ṣādiq Gangōhī Chishti, and who died in 1116/1704–5. See *Sawāṭi' al-anwār* (Ethé col. 338 no. 35(d)), *Khazīnat al-aṣfiyā'* i pp. 485–6.

850 Author of the Ṣūfī tract *Ḍābiṭah dar taḥṣīl i rābiṭah*, Ludiana 1893*.

851 "Shā'iq" is the author of a *Mathnawi* in six *daftars* published at Lucknow in 1294/1877°*.

(43) ***Manāqib al-aṣfiyā'***, lives of famous saints, by Shāh Shu'aib Firdausī: **Calcutta** 1895° (152 pp.).

(44) ***Manāqib i Amīr Kulāl:***[852] **Peshawar** 1003.

(45) **(*Manāqib i auliyā i kirām*)**, short lives of saints (Luqmān i Ḥakīm, Ja'far i Ṣādiq, Uwais i Qaranī, etc.): **Berlin** 589 (69 foll.).

(46) ***Manāqib i Ghauthīyah,***[853] **Peshawar** 1094 (1).

(47) ***Manāqib i ḥaḍrat i Shaikh Jīw Khunuk*** [?], by 'Abd al-Ḥalīm: **Āṣafīyah** i p. 490 (AH 1177/1763–4).

(48) ***Manāqib i Ḥāfiẓīyah***, a life of M. 'Alī Khairābādī,[854] by Ghulām M. Hādī 'Alī Khān Chishtī Kashmīrī: **Cawnpore** 1305/1888° (256 pp.).

(49) ***Manāqib i mazārāt i Bukhārā-yi sharīf:*** **Leningrad** Univ. 390 (Salemann-Rosen p. 17), possibly also **Peshawar** 999A (*Risālah i mazārāt i Bukhārā sharīf*).

(50) ***Manāqib i Qādirīyah:*** **Peshawar** 995.

(51) ***Maqāmāt i Amīr Kulāl:***[855] Ḥ. Kh. vi p. 54, **Lahore** Panjāb Univ. Lib. (defective at end and disarranged. See *Oriental College Magazine*, vol. iii, no. 1 (Lahore, Nov. 1936) p. 70).

(52) ***Ma'qūlāt*** [*sic*] ***i auliyā' Allāh***, sayings and biographies of saints (beginning *Wa-'an Abī 'l-Dardā'*): **Ethé** 1895 (1).

(53) ***Mazārāt i Bukhārā:*** see ***Manāqib i mazārāt i Bukhārā*** (no. 49 above).

(54) ***Mishkāt al-nubuwwah***, an account of the saints of Ḥaidarābād, etc., by S. 'Alī: **Āṣafīyah** iii p. 166 no. 194.

(55) ***Mukhbir al-auliyā'***, an account of Chishtī and other saints, most of them buried at Aḥmadābād, by Rashīd al-Dīn Maudūd Lālā [?] b. Sh. Aḥmad Chishtī al-Fārūqī b. Sh. Ḥusām al-Dīn M. Farrukh al-Ṣūfī al-Chishtī, who was a native of Aḥmadābād and whose spiritual guide was S. M. Aḥsan al-Sijzī, the head of the Chishtī order: **Bombay** Fyzee 14 (19th cent.).

(56) ***Munājāt i Khākī***, a metrical Naqshbandī pedigree, by Ḥakīm Qamar al-Dīn Siyālkōtī: **Lahore** [1911*].

---

852 Presumably S. Amīr Kulāl, who died in 772/1370. See *Maqāmāt i Amīr Kulāl* (no. (51) below; perhaps another copy of the same work); *Nafaḥāt al-uns; Rashaḥāt* pp. 42–3; *Haft iqlīm* no. 1488; *Safīnat al-auliyā'* p. 77 (no. 81); *Khazīnat al-aṣfiyā'* i pp. 546–8.

853 Whether this is the work of M. Ṣādiq Shihābī (see no. 1339 *supra*) does not appear from the catalogue.

854 Probably identical with the subject of the (*Risālah i*) *ḥasab a nasab i ... Ḥāfiẓ M. 'Alī-Shāh Khairābādī* mentioned above (no. (24)).

855 For S. Amīr Kulāl see no. (44) above. According to *Rashaḥāt* p. 45, the author of the *Maqāmāt i Amīr Kulāl* was a grandson of Amīr Ḥamzah, Amīr Kulāl's second son (*dar Maqāmāt i Amīr Kulāl kih nabīrah i Amīr Ḥamzah ta'līf kardah*). This passage is probably the source of Ḥ. Kh.'s information. According to the OCM. the author's name does not occur in the preface. The cataloguer inferred from a passage on fol. 15 that Amīr Ḥamzah himself was the author.

(57) ***Nāfiʿ al-sālikīn***, a life of M. Sikandar "Wāṣil" Khāliṣ-pūrī, by Sh. Dāwud Pūtrīk: **Bombay** 1310/1893° (appended to M. Sikandar's *Tuḥfat al-ʿulamāʾ*, for which see Ellis).

(58) ***Nasab-nāmah i ḥaḍrat i S. Shāh Ismāʿīl i Bukhārī:*** **Āṣafīyah** i p. 494 no. 123.

(59) ***Nasab-nāmah i nāmī i shaikh-zādagān***, "genealogies of certain noted saints": **Lucknow** 1876*.

(60) ***Nasab-nāmah i Shāh Wajīh al-Dīn***,[856] by S. Yaḥyā b. S. Ḥusain: **Bombay** Fyzee 15 (incomplete).

(61) ***Nasāʾim i Ghauthīyah***, a life of ʿAbd al-Qādir al-Jīlānī (cf. no. 1251 2nd par. footnote *supra*) in eleven *nasīms*: **Ivanow** 271 (18th cent.), **Ethé** 1801 (n.d.). Abridgment: *Nasāʾim al-Qādirīyah*, likewise in eleven *nasīms*:: **Ethé** 1802 (AH 1154/1741), probably also **Āṣafīyah** ii p. 882 no. 79.

(62) ***Nasāʾim al-Qādirīyah:*** see under *Nasāʾim i Ghauthīyah* above.

(63) ***Nawādir al-safar***, notices of 22 Chishtī saints with descriptions of their shrines, by Farīd al-Dīn: **Ivanow** 272 (defective at end ?. 18th cent.).

(64) ***Qiṣṣah (Ḥālāt) i Sālār Masʿūd i Ghāzī***,[857] "a fiction of the wildest character" (Rieu), being one form of the legend of Sālār Masʿūd (cf. no. 1329 (7) *supra*): **Ivanow** 322 (early 19th cent.), **Rieu** iii 1015*a* (AD 1850).

(65) ***Rauḍat al-abrār***, lives of Kashmīrī saints, by Abū 'l-Ḥasan M., known as Muḥammad al-Dīn Qādirī Lāhaurī: **Jēlam** [i.e. Jihlam, Jehlam, or "Jhelum"] 1302/1885° (80 pp.).

(66) ***Rauḍat al-auliyāʾ***, *tadhkirah i auliyāʾ i Bījāpūr*, by M. Ibrāhīm: **Āṣafīyah** iii p. 164 no. 169 (AH 1310/1892–3).

(67) ***Rauḍat al-auliyāʾ fī aḥwāl al-aṣfiyāʾ***, a life of Muḥammad and brief notices of Naqshbandī saints, by M. Ḥusain b. M. Riḍā. Edition: **Amritsar** 1333/1915*.

(68) ***Risālah i amīrīyah***, a life of Bahāʾ Allāh, by M. Muṣṭafā al-Baghdādī: see no. (73) below.

---

856 Presumably Wajīh al-Dīn ʿAlawī Gujrātī, a well-known scholar and mystic, who died in 998/1590 and whose grave at Aḥmadābād is marked by a beautiful tomb. See Badāʾūnī iii pp. 43–4; *Maʾāthir i Raḥīmī* iii pp. 17–18; *Safīnat al-auliyāʾ* p. 193 (no. 371); *Maʾāthir al-kirām*; *Mirʾāt i Aḥmadī, khātimah* pp. 68–70, Eng. trans. pp. 60–61; *Subḥat al-marjān* p. 45; *Majmūʿah i ḥālāt i ḥaḍrat i Shāh W. al-D. ʿA. G.* ("in Urdu, Persian, and Arabic"), by M. Yūsuf b. Aḥmad Khatkhatī, Shihābī Press, Bombay (see Ḥaidarābād Coll. p. 36); Raḥmān ʿAlī pp. 249–50; Brockelmann *Sptbd.* i p. 534 and elsewhere.

857 In the B.M. MS. the title is given as *Ḥālāt i Saiyid Sālār Masʿūd i Ghāzī*. The attribution of the title Saiyid to Sālār Masʿūd is perhaps due to a confusion with Saiyid Masʿūd Ghāzī, the founder of Ghāzīpūr, who is said to have died in 767/1365–6. See *A short history of Syed Masud Gházi and his descendants*, by S. Ali Azhar, in the *Journal of the United Provinces Historical Society*, iii pp. 49–53.

(69) ***Risālah i Bahāʾīyah fī maqāmāt i ḥaḍrat i Khwājah Bahāʾ al-Dīn***, by Abū ʾl-Qāsim b. M. b. Masʿūd: **ʿAlīgaṛh** Subḥ. MSS. p. 12 no. 11 (AH 1062/1652).

(70) ***Risālah i buzurgān i Samarqand:*** **Bukhārā** Semenov 71.

(71) ***Risālah dar ḥālāt i Shāh Pīr Muḥammad***, by Maulawī ʿAẓamat Allāh: **ʿAlīgaṛh** Subḥ. MSS. p. 62 no. 41.

(72) ***Risālah i Quṭbīyah i ʿishqīyah***, a panegyric in honour of the anonymous author's spiritual guide, Mihr ʿAlī Shāh, followed by a metrical *silsilah* of Chishtī saints; **Lahore** [1916*].

(73) ***al-Risālat al-tisʿ-ʿasharīyah***, a life of Bahāʾ Allāh, by Aḥmad Suhrāb, preceded by biographies of Sh. Aḥmad al-Aḥsāʾī and S. Kāẓim al-Rashtī and followed (p. 103) by the *Risālah i amīrīyah* of M. Muṣṭafā al-Baghdādī on the life of Bahāʾ Allāh: **Cairo** 1338/1919* (128 pp.).

(74) ***Riyāḍ al-nūr maʿrūf bah Gulzār i surūr***, chronograms on the births and deaths of Muslim celebrities, especially Ṣūfīs, by M. Imām al-Dīn: **Lahore** 1333/1915*.

(75) ***Sālik i ṭarīqat***, a list of famous *shaikhs* of various orders: **Lucknow** 1300/1883° (the first work in a *Majmūʿah i rasāʾil* (50 pp.) containing also (2) *Rauḍat al-ʿibrat*, (3) *Ḥadīqat al-masāʾil*, and (4) *Ṣirāṭ al-jannah*).

(76) ***Sawāniḥ i mukhtaṣar i Shāh Wājid ʿAlī Qalandar***, by Maulawī M. Ikrām ʿAlī Qalandar: **Calcutta** 1919* (with an Urdu translation entitled *Lawāʾiḥ i naẓar*).

(77) ***Sawāniḥ i Shāh Niʿmat Allāh Walī*** (beg. *Bar ḍamīr i khwurshīd-iqtibās*), by Ṣunʿ Allāh Niʿmat-Allāhī, abridged, according to Nadhīr Aḥmad, from the *Jāmiʿ i Mufīdī* (see no. 461 *supra*) and therefore later than 1090/1679: **Nadhīr Aḥmad** 87 (W. Ivanow's collection, AH 1281/1864), perhaps also **Āṣafīyah** i p. 442 no. 815 ("*Silsilat al-ʿārifīn*," author not named. Defective). Edition (?): *Sawāniḥ al-aiyām fī mushāhadāt al-aʿwām mausūm ba-Silsilat al-ʿārifīn*: **Bombay** 1307/1890°.

(78) ***Sayings and miracles of Khwājah ʿAlāʾ al-Dīn ʿAṭṭār:***[858] **Rieu** ii 862*b* (18th cent.).

(79) ***Shaikh Aḥmad Bībī-Khānī***, a metrical biography by Ghulām-Muḥyī ʾl-Dīn "Sanjī": **Lahore** 1924* (18 pp.).

(80) ***Shajarah i ʿāliyah i Naqshbandīyah***, a metrical Naqshbandī pedigree, by Ḥabīb Allāh Naqshbandī: **Ludhiana** 1888°.

858 ʿAlāʾ al-Dīn M. Bukhārī, one of the chief disciples of Bahāʾ al-Dīn Naqshband, died in 802/1400. See *Nafaḥāt al-uns* p. 448; *Rashaḥāt* pp. 79–90; *Haft iqlīm* no. 1490; *Safīnat al-auliyāʾ* p. 80 (no. 85); *Khazīnat al-aṣfiyāʾ* i pp. 551–3.

(81) ***Shajarah i ʿāliyah i ṭarīqah i Qādirīyah i Mujaddidīyah***, a metrical pedigree down to M. Shēr, the author's *pīr*, by M. Yūsuf ʿAlī Qādirī: **Agrah** 1322/1904*.

(82) ***Shajarah i ansāb i pīrān i ṭarīqah i Naqshbandī i Mujaddidī khānadān i Maulānā*** [Raḥīm-Bakhsh called] ***M. Masʿūd Shāh***, in prose and verse: Ḥasanī Press [**Delhi** 1869*].

(83) ***Shajarah i Chishtī u Qādirī u Qalandarī u Ṣābirī***, prose and verse pedigrees of the author, Ghulām-Bhīk,[859] in several orders, with a panegyric on Maulawī Qādir-Bakhsh Sahāranpūrī: **Murādābād** [1912*].

(84) ***Shajarah i khānadān i Naqshbandīyah***, followed by *Shajarah i khānadān i Qādirīyah*, metrical pedigrees by Abū ʾl-Ḥasan Ṣiddīqī Nānautawī: **Agrah** 1873*.

(85) ***Shajarah i khānadān i Qādirīyah:*** see no. (84) above.

(86) ***Shajarah i mubārakah i Chishtīyah i Ṣābirīyah i Quddūsīyah i Muḥibbīyah i Muḥammadīyah***, followed (p. 20) by *Shajarah i sharīfah i manẓūmah i Qādirīyah*, a metrical pedigree by Shāh Ḥabīb Allāh Thānī Muḥibb-Allāhī: **Allahabad** [1926*].

(87) ***Shajarah i mutabarrakah i manẓūmah:*** see no. (90) below.

(88) ***Shajarah i Naqshbandīyah***, a metrical pedigree of S. Imām ʿAlī: Fārūqī Press [**Delhi** 1874*].

(89) ***Shajarah i Qādirī***, prose and verse pedigrees of Shāh Mardān, by Ghulām-Nabī: **Lahore** 1330/1912*.

(90) ***Shajarah i Qādirīyah***, "a genealogy of the Qādirī order," followed (p. 5) by *Shajarah i mutabarrakah i manẓūmah*, "a metrical genealogy of certain saints of the same order, and (p. 10) by a similar work in Panjabi verse by Raḥīm-bakhsh": **Lahore** [1879*].

(91) ***Shajarah i sharīfah i manẓūmah i Qādirīyah***, by Shāh Ḥabīb Allāh Thānī Muḥibb-Allāhī: see no. (86) above.

(92) ***Shajarah i ṭaiyibah*** (on title-page: … *Shajarah i ʿāliyah i Naqshbandīyah*), "a genealogy of certain branches of the Naqshbandī order," by Ḥusain Allāh Ghaznawī. Followed (p. 5) by *Munājāt*, prayers of Shāh ʿAbd Allāh Abū ʾl-Khair (p. 6), an account of his death (p. 7), *Naʿt i nūrānī*, metrical devotions by Shāh Ḥusainī: **Ludhiana** [1923*].

(93) ***Shajarah i ṭaiyibah i khānadān i Chishtīyah***, "genealogies of various branches of the Chishtī order: Niẓāmīyah, Ṣafawīyah, Khādimīyah. and Khalīlīyah": **Lucknow** 1920*.

(94) ***Shajarah i ṭaiyibah i Qādirīyah***, pedigree of Shāh ʿAlī M. Lāhaurī: **Lahore** [1904*].

859 For proper names of this type see no. 1354 footnote. For Sh. Bhīk see no. 1378 2nd footnote.

(95) ***Shajarah i ṭaiyibah i silsilah i ʿāliyah i Naqsh- bandīyah:*** **Lahore** [1889°].

(96) ***Shajarah i ṭaiyibah i silsilah i ʿalīyah i Suhrawardīyah i ḥaḍarāt i Rafīqīyah***, "succession list of the Shaikhs of the Rafīkī order of Ṣūfīs, in verse, with a genealogical table of the posterity of Abū M. Shihāb ul-Dīn Kilīj down to the author," ʿAbd al-Salām Rafīqī Nūrpūrī: **Lahore** [1899°].

(97) ***Shajarahā-yi salāsil i Qādirīyah u Chishtīyah wa-ghairah***, metrical pedigrees, by M. Asad Allāh Khān and M. Ḥāfiẓ Allāh: **Jhajjar** [1897°].

(98) ***Shajarat al-ʿārifīn***, a brief metrical account of the family of Shāh M. Rafīʿ al-Zamān Ilāhābādī, by M. ʿAlī "Ulfat": **Allahabad** 1297/1880° (followed by selections from the *dīwān* of Shāh M. Ḥasan "Ashraf" Ilāhābādī[860]).

(99) ***Shams al-ansāb***, on the genealogy of ʿAbd al-Qādir Jīlānī, by M. Maʿṣūm Sharīf Iṣfahānī: **Āṣafīyah** ii p. 1778 no. 110.

(100) ***Sharḥ i ḥāl i auliyā:*** **Lindesiana** p. 116 no. 790 (circ. AD 1650).

(101) ***Silsilah i ʿāliyah***, "an account of the Shaikhs of Kanbuh," by ʿInāyat Ḥusain b. Fatḥ Allāh, with supplements by Faiḍ Aḥmad b. Dildār Aḥmad: **Meerut** 1306/1889° (196 pp.).

(102) ***Silsilah i ʿalīyah***, a genealogy of Khwājah ʿUbaid Allāh Aḥrār (see no. 1277 3rd par. footnote n. 3 *supra*) and his family, by ʿAbd al-Ḥaiy b. Abū 'l-Fatḥ al-Ḥusainī, a descendant of Khwājah Aḥrār: **Tashkent** Univ. 74 (5).

(103) ***Silsilah i ʿāliyah i Chishtīyah i Fakhrīyah i Niẓāmīyah i Sulaimānīyah***, the spiritual pedigree of the author, M. Sulaimān: **Lahore** 1870*.

(104) ***Silsilah i ʿalīyah i Chishtīyah i Niẓāmīyah i Fakhrīyah i Sulaimānīyah i Laṭīfīyah***, the spiritual pedigree of the author, Shāh ʿAbd al-Laṭīf, successor of M. Sulaimān: **Tippera** 1917*.

(105) ***Silsilah i Qādirīyah***, the spiritual pedigree of the author, ʿAbd al-Ḥaqq Shāh: **Fīrōzpūr** [1918]*.

(106) ***Silsilah i ṭarīqah i Naqshbandīyah***, by Ḍiyāʾ al-Dīn Khālid al-Mujaddidī al-Baghdādi: **Cairo** p. 415 (AH 1276/1860).

(107) ***Silsilat al-laʾāliʾ***, spiritual genealogies of the Naqshbandī, Qādirī, Chishtī and Suhrawardī orders, by Muʿīn al-Din "Thabāt": **Lucknow** [1883°].

(108) ***Sketch of the life of ʿAbd al-Qādir al-Jīlānī*** (cf. no. 1251, 2nd par., footnote *supra*) written by Muḥsin at the request of Sh. M. b. Sh. M. Ashraf Lāhaurī: **Tashkent** Univ. 18 (3).

---

860 A biography of "Ashraf" without dates is given in the *Khāzin al-shuʿarāʾ* (fol. 46*b*). He was apparently alive at the time of writing (1260–5/1844–9).

(109) *Spiritual pedigrees of Ṣūfic shaikhs of Kashmīr:* **Ivanow** Curzon 79.

(110) *Sulṭānī*, a metrical biography of Sulṭān al-ʿārifīn Ḥamzah Makhdūmī[861] and his descendants, by Mullā Bahāʾ al-Dīn MTW Kashmīrī: **Lahore** [1933*].

(111) *Ṭabaqāt i mashāyikh i Naqshbandīyah i Bukhārā:* **Leningrad** Univ. no. 854 (Salemann-Rosen p. 17).

(112) *Tadhakkur al-mashāyikh*, biographies of a few *shaikhs*, beginning with the affiliation of Nūr al-Dīn ʿAbd al-Raḥmān b. M. al-Isfarāyinī (d. 639), by an anonymous Kubrawī *darwīsh*: **Blochet** i 159 (10) (AH 877/1472).

(113) *Tadhkirah i ḥaḍrat i khwājah Muʿīn al-Dīn Chishtī:*[862] **Āṣafīyah** ii p. 848.

(114) *Tadhkirah i Khwājagān i Naqshbandīyah:* **Peshawar** 1015.

(115) *Tadhkirah i Ṣūfīyah*, by Rashkī b. Dīwān Mannū Lāl Falsafī: **Āṣafīyah** i p. 318 no. 100 (defective at end).

(116) *Tadhkirat al-auliyāʾ*, lives of Aḥmad Zain al-Dīn Aḥsāʾī,[863] Kāẓim b. Qāsim Rashtī,[864] and M. Karīm Khān Kirmānī,[865] by Niʿmat Allāh Riḍawī: **Bombay** 1313/1896° (pp. 143).

(117) (*fī Tārīkh i ajdād u farzandān u aṣḥāb i ḥaḍrat i Maulānā Jalāl al-Millah wa-'l-Dīn Muḥammad i Rūmī*): **Leyden** v p. 232 no. 2640 (22 foll. A.H. 900/1494–5).

(118) *Tarjamat Ibn al-Khafīf:* see *Aḥwāl Ibn al-Khafīf.*

(119) *Thamarāt al-quds*, biographies of saints and pious women, mostly of the Chishtī order, by Laʿl Bēg: **Rāmpūr** (defective. See Nadhīr Aḥmad 84).

(120) *Tuḥfaḥ i Akmalīyah*, on the life and sayings of Akmal al-Dīn Badakhshī and his successors, by Abū M. Ḥasan b. Ḥāfiẓ Walī Allāh Kubrawī Kashmīrī: **Lahore** 1350/1932* (appended to the same author's mystical *mīmīyah* entitled *Mukhbir al-asrār*).

(121) *Tuḥfah i nāznīn*, a biography in prose and verse of M. Saif al-Dīn Qādirī, by S. Bahāʾ al-Dīn M. Naqshbandī Kashmīrī: **Lahore** [1920*].

(122) *Tuḥfat al-auliyāʾ*, a biography of S. ʿAbd al-Wahhāb Ṣābirī called Akhūn Panjū, by Maulawī Mīr Aḥmad Shāh Riḍwānī Pashāwarī: **Lahore** 1321/1903*.

---

861 I.e. presumably either Sh. Ḥamzah Kashmīrī (for whom see no. 1291 footnote *supra*) or someone descended from him.

862 For whom see no. 1259 2nd par. 3rd footnote *supra*.

863 Founder of the Shaikhī sect, d. 1242/1827. See Browne *Lit. Hist.* iv pp. 410–11, 421–2; Brockelmann *Sptbd.* ii pp. 844–5, and the authorities there cited.

864 One of Aḥsāʾī's pupils. See Browne *op. cit.* iv p. 421; Brockelmann *Sptbd.* ii p. 845.

865 One of Kāẓim Rashtī's pupils, d. 1288/1871. See Browne *op. cit.* iv. p. 421; Brockelmann *Sptbd.* ii p. 846.

(123) ***Tuḥfat al-Saʿdīyah***[866] or (***Malfūẓāt i Shāh Mīnā***), on the life and teachings of Shāh Mīnā,[867] by Muḥyī 'l-Dīn b. Ḥusain Riḍawī Ḥusainī: **Ivanow** Curzon 70 (defective and damaged. Early 19th cent.), **Rāmpūr** (see Nadhīr Aḥmad 76).

Edition: *Malfūẓāt i ... Mīnā*, **Hardoi** (1900°).

(124) ***Waqāʾiʿ i Shāh Muʿīn al-Dīn i Chishtī***,[868] by Bābū Lāl. Editions: **Lucknow** 1879°, 1881†, 1883† (cf. Āṣafīyah ii p. 850).

(125) ***Ẓafar al-Islām***, a life of Muʿīn al-Dīn Chishtī (cf. no. 1259 2nd par. 3rd footnote *supra*), by S. Ẓafar ʿAlī "Ẓafar": **Delhi** [1904*].

13.3 *Ambassadors*

1412. For the embassies sent by Sulṭān Shāh-Rukh to China and India see no. 363, Extracts (4), (5), (6) *supra*.

1413. For the (*Tārīkh i Īlchī i Niẓām-Shāh*), by Khwurshāh b. Qubād al-Ḥusainī, which contains an account of the author's mission to Shāh Ṭahmāsp, see no. 131 *supra*.

1414. S. **Ghulām-ʿAlī Khān** was sent to Istānbūl in 1200/1786 by Ṭīpū Sulṭān of Mysore, (for whom see no. 1070 *supra*) in the vain hope of enlisting Ottoman support against the British. The instructions issued to him are preserved in a MS. at Calcutta (Ivanow 1677).

Waqāʾiʿ i manāzil i Rūm, a diary of the journey to Istānbūl in 1200–1, completed on 19 Rabīʿ al-Awwal 1201/9 January 1787: **Ivanow** 1678 (foll. 123).

1415. **Quṭb al-Mulk** and **ʿAlī Riḍā** were sent as envoys to Ḥaidarābād by Ṭīpū Sultān, of Mysore, (for whom see no. 1070 *supra*). The instructions issued to them are preserved in a MS. at Calcutta (Ivanow 1679), which is dated 1217 Maulūdī[869] [circ. 1205/1790–1].

(***Rūz-nāmah i wukalāʾ i Ḥaidarābād***), a report on the above-mentioned mission, dealing chiefly with the expenses incurred on the journey: **Ivanow** 1680.

866 This is the title given (incorrectly ?) by Nadhīr Aḥmad.
867 For whom see no. 1307 3rd footnote *supra*.
868 Cf. no. 1259 2nd par. 3rd footnote *supra*.
869 For Ṭīpū's Maulūdī era see no. 1070 (3) 3rd par. 2nd footnote *supra*.

1416. In return for the mission of Captain (afterwards Sir) John Malcolm to Persia (in 1799–1801) Fatḥ-ʿAlī S͟hāh dispatched Ḥājjī K͟halīl K͟hān Qazwīnī Malik al-Tujjār as his envoy to the Government of India. In 1802 K͟halīl K͟hān was killed at Bombay in a quarrel between his servants and the Hindu soldiers provided as his bodyguard. To succeed him the S͟hāh appointed his relative[870] M. Nabī K͟hān Qazwīnī, who returned to Persia in January, 1807. An account of the mission of these two envoys was written by an unnamed grandson of the second. [*Rauḍat al-ṣafā-yi Nāṣirī* ix foll. 81*b*–82*a* (AH 1219); Watson *History of Persia* pp. 129–30; Sykes *History of Persia* ii p. 302].

Tārīk͟h i sifārat i Ḥājjī K͟halīl K͟hān u M. Nabī K͟hān ba-Hindūstān 1802–1805: **Bombay** 1886°.

1417. Ḥājjī Mīrzā **Abū 'l-Ḥasan** K͟hān b. Mīrzā M. ʿAlī **S͟hīrāzī**, nephew and son-in-law[871] of the late Prime Minister Ḥājjī Ibrāhīm K͟hān S͟hīrāzī, left Ṭihrān on 22 Rabīʿ I 1224/7 May, 1809, accompanied by James Morier, on a mission to London of which the main purpose was to ascertain how the subsidy promised to Persia under the preliminary treaty of March, 1809, was to be paid (*Rauḍat al-ṣafā-yi Nāṣirī* ix fol. 95*b*, Watson *History of Persia* p. 163, Sykes *History of Persia* ii p. 308, etc.). On 18 July, 1810, he set sail on his return journey with Sir Gore Ouseley and Morier (*Rauḍat al-ṣafā'* ix fol. 99*a* penult., etc.). In 1815 he was sent as envoy to St. Petersburg (*R. al-ṣ.* ix fol 111*a* penult.) and in 1818 as envoy extraordinary to Great Britain (*R. al-ṣ.* ix fol. 116*a*). Subsequently he became Minister for Foreign Affairs, and he continued to hold this office until 1250/1834, the last year of Fatḥ-ʿAlī S͟hāh's reign (*R. al-ṣ.* ix fol. 171*a*).[872]

Ḥairat-nāmah i sufarā, a diary of the author's mission to England in 1224–5/1809–10, apparently left unfinished since both the recorded MSS. end before the departure from England: **Bānkīpūr** vii 630 (ends with 10 Ṣafar 1225/17 March, 1810. Written in 1228/1813 for Sir G. Ouseley), **Rieu** i 386*b* (spaces for the dates left blank. Early 19th cent.).

[*Rauḍat al-ṣafā-yi Nāṣirī*, passages specified above and others (e.g. ix fol. 147*b*, x fol. 42*a*); J. Morier *A journey through Persia, Armenia, and Asia Minor to Constantinople, in ... 1808 and 1809*, London 1812, pp. 220–3, *A second journey through Persia ... to Constantinople*, 1810–16, London 1818, appendix; W. Ouseley *Travels in various countries of the East*, i, London 1819, p. 2 *et passim*; W. Price

870 A nephew (*hams͟hīrah-zādah*) according to Riḍā-Qulī K͟hān, a brother-in-law according to Sykes.

871 *hams͟hīrah-zādah u dāmād* (*Rauḍat al-ṣafā-yi Nāṣirī* ix fol. 95*b* penult.).

872 Mīrzā Masʿūd Ād͟harbāyjānī was appointed Foreign Minister by Muḥammad S͟hāh shortly after his accession (*R. al-ṣ.* x fol. 6*b*, l. 24).

Journal of the British embassy to Persia, London 1825; J. B. Fraser *A winter's journey (tâtar) from Constantinople to Tehran*, ii, London 1838, p. 3; *A memoir of ... Sir Gore Ouseley ... by the Rev. James Reynolds* (prefixed to G. Ouseley's *Biographical notices of Persian poets*, London 1846); Portrait by Sir W. Beechey at the India Office. A caricature of Abū 'l-Ḥasan K͟hān was drawn by J. Morier in his romance *The adventures of Hajji Baba, of Ispahan, in England*, London 1828, reprinted 1835, 1942.]

1418. Ḥusain K͟hān Muqaddam[873] Ajūdān-bās͟hī was descended from Āqā K͟hān Muqaddam, an *amīr* of S͟hāh Ṣafī's time (*Rauḍat al-ṣafā-yi Nāṣirī* x fol. 29*b*, l. 4). After a period in the service of the Nā'ib al-Salṭanah ['Abbās Mīrzā, d. 1249/1833: cf. no. 434 *supra* and corrections] he became an officer in the army and rose to the rank of Adjutant General. In 1254/1838 Muḥammad S͟hāh sent him on a special mission to Great Britain, France, and Austria in the hope of obtaining the recall of the British Minister at Ṭihrān, Sir John McNeill (*op. cit.* x fol. 29*b*, l. 20, Watson *History of Persia* pp. 324, 328–31, Sykes *History of Persia* ii p. 336). Having visited Istānbūl and Vienna he reached Paris on 1 Ṣafar 1255/16 April, 1839, and London shortly afterwards (*R. al-ṣ.* x fol. 30*a*, l. 20). Here he interviewed Lord Palmerston and was given a memorandum containing nine demands of the British Government. In 1258/1842 he was appointed Governor of Yazd (*op. cit.* x fol. 30*a*, l. 25), and held this office for two years (*op. cit.* x fol. 30*b*, l. 1). Presumably it was about this time that the title of Niẓām al-Daulah was conferred upon him. In the early days of the Bābī movement he was Governor of Fārs and in that capacity he interviewed and imprisoned the Bāb at S͟hīrāz (*op. cit.* x fol. 35–36*a*, Watson pp. 349–51, Sykes p. 341, and the Bābī histories). In the disturbances which followed the death of Muḥammad S͟hāh (in 1264/1848) Ḥusain K͟hān was besieged in the fort of Karīm K͟hān's citadel until rescued by his supersessor, Bahrām Mīrzā (*op. cit.* x fol. 46*b*, l. 19 foll.).

According to Riḍā-Qulī K͟hān (*op. cit.* fol. 22*a* ult.) an account of Ḥusain K͟hān's mission to Europe was written by Mīrzā **'Abd al-Fattāḥ Garmrūdī**,[874] who accompanied the envoy as his deputy (*nā'ib*. Cf. fol. 30*a*, l. 11, where he is called Mīrzā Fattāḥ). It is not clear whether Chanykov's MS. contains this account or another.

873 A Turkish tribal name.

874 Cf. *Dānishmandān i Ād͟harbāyjān* p. 258, where it is stated that 'A. al-F. Garmrūdī Tabrīzī wrote (1) *Chahār faṣl*, an account of the Ajūdān-bās͟hī's mission, (2) *S͟hab-nāmah*, on the licentiousness of European life, and that numerous copies of both works are in existence.

Travels of Ḥusain Kẖān, Ajūdān-bāsẖī, in Germany [Austria ?], France, and England in 1254/1838 beginning: *Kẖudāwandī-rā bandah īm*): **Chanykov** 116.

1419. Ḥājjī Mīrzā **Muḥammad Kẖān b. Fatḥ-ʿAlī Bēg Lawāsānī** was sent on a mission to Russia at the beginning of Nāṣir al-Dīn S̱ẖāh's reign [1264–1313/1848–96]. He was editor of the *dīwān* of "Nas̱ẖāṭī" Kẖān Hazārjarībī published at [Ṭihrān[875]] in [1845 ?ᵒ].

Mirʾāt al-arḍ, an account of the above-mentioned mission to Russia written in 1264/1848: **Majlis** 702.

1420. For Riḍā-Qulī Kẖān "Hidayat's" *Sifārat-nāmah i Kẖwārazm*, an account of his embassy to Khiva in 1267/1851, see no. 440 (1) *supra*.

1421. Mīrzā **Ḥusain b. ʿAbd Allāh Sarābī Tabrīzī**.

Makẖzan al-asfār, an account of Farrukẖ Kẖān Kās̱ẖānī's[876] mission to Europe in the course of which he negotiated the Anglo Persian treaty of March 1857[877] at Paris and subsequently visited London: **Browne** Coll.

---

875   Cf. Browne *Press and poetry of modern Persia* p. 8: The well-known Mashhadí Asad Áqá "*Básma-chí*" ("the Printer") of Tabríz ... also relates that Mírzá Ṣáliḥ of Shíráz, the *Wazír* of Ṭihrán, sent at great expense one Mirzá Asaduʾlláh, of the province of Fárs, to St. Petersburg to learn the art of printing, and that on his return thence he founded at Tabríz, with the assistance of the late Áqá Riḍá, father of the above-mentioned Mashhadi Asad Áqá, a lithographic press, the first book lithographed at which was the Holy Qurʾán in the hand-writing of Mírzá Ḥusayn the famous calligraphist. Five years later, at the Sháh's command, this press and its appurtenances were transferred to Ṭihrán, where the first book printed was the *Díwán* of Nisháṭí Khán the poet.

876   Amīn al-Mulk F. Kẖ. K. Kẖāzin i Sulṭānī was in the service of four S̱ẖāhs of Persia (*Rauḍat al-ṣafā-yi Nāṣirī*; x fol. 107*b*, l. 26). In M. Ḥasan Kẖān's list of the successive Heads of Government Departments in Nāṣir al-Dīn S̱ẖāh's reign (*al-Maʾāthir wa-ʾl-āthār* pp. 15–29) he appears under the headings *Riyāsat i ʿamalah i kẖalwat i kẖāṣṣah i humāyūnī* (p. 20*a*), *Idārah i ṣandūq-kẖānah i mubārakah* (ibid.), *Idārah i muhr i mubārak u kẖizānat i kẖātam i humāyūn* (p. 20*b*), *Idārah i ṣarf i jaib i mubārak* (ibid.), *Mukẖāṭabīn i salām i ʿāmm* (p. 22*b*), and *Pīshkhidmat-bāshiyān i ḥuḍūr i mubārak* (p. 23*a*). His appointment to the *Ṣāḥib-jamʿī i kẖāṣṣ* took place in 1270/1854 (*Rauḍat al-ṣafā* x fol. 92*b*,l. 7 from foot). He must have been an elderly man at the time of his mission to Europe (for which see *Rauḍat al-ṣafā* x fol. 107*b*, l. 21–109*a*, l. 5, fol. 122*a*, l. 18–123*a*, l. 2, fol. 128*a*, l. 1–129*b*, l. 17, fol. 130*a*, ll. 13–27, Watson *History of Persia* pp. 430, 456, 459, 461). A *Siyāḥat-nāmah* of Farrukẖ Kẖān is mentioned in Browne's *Press and poetry of modern Persia* p. 20*n*, as having been circulated in manuscript.

877   The date 11 Ḏẖū ʾl-Qaʿdah 1273/3 July 1857 given in the catalogue of the Browne collection as that of Farrukẖ Kẖān's departure from Ṭihrān is, of course, incorrect.

K. 7 = Houtum-Schindler 38 (AH 1276/1860), **Mashhad** iii, *Faṣl* 14, MSS., p. 28 (*Makhzan al-waqāʾiʿ*).

1422. Mushīr al-Daulah Mīrzā **Jaʿfar Khān** Ḥusainī, the son of Mīrzā Taqī Ḥusainī Wazīr i Tabrīzī, was, like Mīrzā M. Ṣāliḥ Shīrāzī (see no. 1607 *infra*), one of the young Persians sent to England in 1230/1815 for the completion of their education. He spent four years in Europe, mainly in London (*Rauḍat al-ṣafāʾ* x fol. 27*b*, l.1), and later, having specialized in Mathematics and Geometry, he wrote a book on arithmetic printed at Ṭihrān in 1263/1847 and known as the *Khulāṣat al-ḥisāb i Mushīr al-Daulah*. In 1252/1836–7 he was *Muhandis-bāshī i ʿAsākir i Manṣūrah* when he was sent as Persian Ambassador to Istānbūl and in the course of his residence there he negotiated the commercial treaty of 1257/1841 with Belgium and the treaty of 1258/1842 with Spain. In 1260/1844 he was on his way to the Erzerum conference (see Watson *History of Persia* p. 365) when he fell ill at Tabrīz and was replaced as Persian Commissioner by Mīrzā Taqī Khān Farāhānī. In 1264/1848 he went to Baghdād and Muḥammarah to discuss the delimitation of the frontier between Persia and Turkey with representatives of Turkey, Russia, and Great Britain. The results of his investigations into the question of the frontier were recorded in a booklet, of which, according to M. ʿAlī "Tarbiyat", many copies are in existence. In 1275/1858–9 he was appointed President of the Dār al-Shūrā and in 1277/1860–1 he was sent as Envoy Extraordinary on a mission to England. He died at Mashhad after a period as *Mutawallī* of the Shrine of the Imām Riḍā (cf. *al-Maʾāthir wa-'l-āthār* p. 15).

(***Siyāḥat-nāmah i Jaʿfar Khān Mushīr al-Daulah***), an account of the above-mentioned journey to England in 1277/1860–1: **Ṭihrān** 1277/1861 (in the *Rūz-nāmah i Daulat i ʿalīyah i Irān* no. 513, 29 Rajab 1277/10 Feb., 1861. See *Dānishmandān i Ādharbāyjān* p. 345 penult.[878])

[*Rauḍat al-ṣafā-yi Nāṣirī* x fol. 27*a*, l. 4 from foot, fol. 56*a*, l. 24, 81*b*, l. 25; *Dānishmandān i Ādharbāyjān* pp. 344–7 (portrait).]

13.4 *Calligraphists and Painters*

In the parts of this work devoted to the biography of poets and saints, attention has been drawn to a number of historical works containing biographical sections. Some of these contain notices of calligraphists (in addition to such poets

878 *Sharḥ u tafṣīl i īn siyāḥat u māmūrīyat dar shumārah i 513 i Rūz-nāmah i D. i ʿa. i Ī … nawishtah shudah ast.* M. ʿAlī "Tarbiyat" does not say that the account was written by Jaʿfar Khān himself.

as were also calligraphists), but no attempt is made here to give a complete list of such works.

In an article entitled *Khaṭṭ u khaṭṭāṭān*, which he contributed to the OCM. x/4 (Aug. 1934), pp. 3–72, Prof. M. Shafīʿ published extracts relating to calligraphists from (1) the *Khaṭṭ u sawād* of Majnūn b. Maḥmūd Rafīqī, (2) an unidentified general history, possibly the *Khulāṣat al-tawārīkh* of Aḥmad Ibrāhīmī (cf. no. 1431 *infra*), (3) the *Mirʾāt al-ʿālam* of Bakhtāwar Khān, (4) the *Khulāṣat al-makātīb* of Sujān Rāy and (5) the *Mirʾāt al-iṣṭilāḥ* of Ānand Rām "Mukhliṣ". An index to the names of the calligraphists noticed in these extracts is given on p. 70 of M. Shafīʿ's article. Further information concerning the first three of these sets of extracts will be found below.

1423. The second chapter of Majnūn b. Maḥmūd al-Rafīqī's *Khaṭṭ u sawād* (written after 909/1503–4: see Bodleian 1369 (1); Rieu ii 531*b*; Ivanow 1623 (1), 1624; Ethé 1763 (4), 2931) is devoted to very brief notices of calligraphists and has been published by M. Shafīʿ in OCM. x/4 (Aug. 1934), pp. 17–18. The whole work has been published by Yā-Sīn Khān "Niyāzī" in OCM. xi/2 (Feb. 1935), pp. 46–74.

1424. For the *Laṭāʾif-nāmah*, which was written in 927/1521 by Sulṭān-Muḥammad "Fakhrī" b. "Amīrī" Harawī and of which the fifth *qism* of the ninth *majlis* is devoted to *arbāb i hunar*, including calligraphists and painters, see no. 1094, Persian translations (1) *supra*.

1425. For the *Bāburnāmah*, which contains brief notices of Sulṭān-ʿAlī Mashhadī, the calligraphist, and Bihzād, the painter, (published in ʿAbd al-Raḥīm's Persian translation by M. Shafīʿ in OCM. x/3 pp. 147–8), see no. 698 *supra*.

1426. For M. Ḥaidar Dūghlāt's *Tārīkh i Rashīdī*, of which the second *daftar*, completed in 948/1541, contains biographies of scholars, poets, calligraphists, painters, etc., see no. 349 *supra*. The Persian text of the whole of this biographical section has been published by C. Salemann in *Mélanges asiatiques* ix (St. Petersburg 1888) pp. 323–80 and by M. Shafīʿ in OCM. x/3 (Lahore, May 1934) pp. 150–70. An English translation of the notices of painters and gilders was published by T. W. Arnold under the title *Mīrzā Muḥammad Ḥaydar Dughlāt on the Harāt school of painters* in the BSOS. v/4 (1930) pp. 671–4.

1427. **Dūst-Muḥammad** al-Kātib, as he calls himself (*Ḥālāt i hunarwarān* p. 8[8]), was according to his own statement (*op. cit.* p. 307) one of the *kuttāb i kitāb-khānah i sharīfah i aʿlā ʿillīyūn*. Probably he is identical with Dūst-Muḥammad Harātī, who is mentioned by Aḥmad Ibrāhīmī (cf. no. 1431 *infra*) and others[879] as a calligraphist of Shāh Ṭahmāsp's time and who according to the former (see BSOS. x/1 p. 205 n. 2) was the king's favourite and was retained in his service when all the other calligraphists were dismissed.

(***Ḥālāt i hunarwarān***[880]), a sketch of the history of Muslim calligraphy and painting written as an introduction (*dībāchah*, p. 31[1]) to an album of ancient and modern paintings and specimens of calligraphy arranged and embellished by the author in 953/1546 at the command and for the library of Abū 'l-Fatḥ Bahrām Mīrzā:[881] **Istānbūl** Tōp Qapū Sarāy.

Edition: *A treatise on calligraphists and miniaturists, Ḥālāt i hunarwarān, by Dōst Muhammad, the Librarian of Behram Mirza (d.* 1550), *edited by M. Abdullah Chaghtai*, **Lahore** 1936‡.

1428. For the *Tuḥfah i Sāmī*, which was composed, at least partly, in or about 957/1550, and which contains notices of a number of calligraphists, painters, musicians, etc., see no. 1100 *supra*. The notices of these calligraphists, painters, etc., extracted from the various parts of the *Tuḥfah i Sāmī* were published by M. Shafīʿ in an article entitled *Iqtibāsāt i Tuḥfah i Sāmī rājiʿ bah hunarwarān* in the OCM. x/2 (Feb. 1934) pp. 73–128 (the last two pages being an alphabetical index).

1429. For the *Mudhakkir i aḥbāb*, written in 974/1566–7 by "Nithārī" Bukhārī, from which extracts relating to seven poets who were also calligraphists have been published by Nawwāb Ṣadr Yār Jang in OCM. xi/2 (Feb. 1935) pp. 39–45, see no. 1102 *supra*.

1430. Extracts relating to calligraphists from an unidentified general history[882] written apparently in the second half of the tenth/sixteenth century were published by M. Shafīʿ in OCM. x/4 (Aug. 1934) pp. 23–30.

---

879 Cf. *Paidāyish i khaṭṭ u khaṭṭāṭān* p. 157. In a list of *nastaʿlīq*-writers who died in Shāh Ṭahmāsp's reign Iskandar Munshī gives the name, but no further particulars, of Maulānā Dūst (so, not Dūst-Muḥammad) Harātī (*ʿĀlam-ārāy i ʿAbbāsī* p. 124).

880 This title, which by chronogrammatic licence indicates 952 (instead of 953), is the invention of the editor, M. Abdullah Chaghtai.

881 One of Shāh Ṭahmāsp's younger brothers. He died on 19 Ramaḍān 956/11 Oct. 1549 at the age of 33 and was buried at Mashhad (Ḥasan Rūmlū p. 342, Seddon's trans. p. 155).

882 Possibly the *Khulāṣat al-tawārīkh* of Aḥmad Ibrāhīmī (for which see no. 1431 infra). According to the owner, Prof. Maḥmūd Shērānī, of Lahore, the title *Khulāṣat al-tawārīkh* was written on the back of the MS., from which both the beginning and the end are missing.

1431. Qāḍī **Aḥmad Ibrāhīmī** Ḥusainī [Qummī] b. Mīr Munshī Sharaf al-Dīn Ḥusain was the great-grandson of Ḥāfiẓ Qanbar Sharafī, an Abyssinian slave who was a calligraphist and poet in the service of Qāḍī Sharaf al-Dīn, Governor of Qum (*BSOS*. x/1 (1939) p. 200). His father, who "was successively *munshī* to Sām Mīrzā[883] in Harāt, scribe to the secretariat under the vakīl Aḥmad Beg Nūr Kamāl, and vazīr at the court of the famous Ibrāhīm Mīrzā, when that prince was governor in Mashhad" (*BSOS*. x/1 p. 201), received from Shāh Ṭahmāsp (AH 930–84/1524–76) the title of *Mīr Munshī* and died in 990/1582 at the age of seventy-six (*ibid.*). Qāḍī Aḥmad, when still a boy (*dar aiyām i ṣibā*, *BSOS*. p. 204 penult.), went in 964/1556–7 to Mashhad and remained there for eight years, during which time he received instruction in penmanship from Shāh Maḥmūd Zarrīn-Qalam Nīshāpūrī (d. 972/1564–5). Shāh Ismāʿīl II (AH 984–5/1576–8) instructed him to write a history extending from the accession of Shāh Ismāʿīl I (AH 907–30/1502–24) to the current reign (*ZDMG*. 89 p. 319), and this task he fulfilled by composing the fifth volume of the *Khulāṣat al-tawārīkh*,[884] which he completed down to 999/1590–1[885] and dedicated to Shāh ʿAbbās (AH 985–1038/1587–1629). Other works of his, mentioned in the *Khulāṣat al-tawārīkh* but not yet recorded in any published catalogue, were *Majmaʿ al-shuʿarāʾ wa-manāqib al-fuḍalāʾ*, a *tadhkirah* of poets (*ZDMG*. 89 p. 317. Cf. *BSOS*. x p. 200), and *Jamʿ al-khiyār*, a *tadhkirah* in at least six volumes on the scholars and poets of Ādharbāyjān, Arabian ʿIrāq and ʿArabistān (*ZDMG*., *loc. cit.*).

(***Tadhkirah i khwush-nawīsān u naqqāshān***[886]), written [*circ.* 1006/1597–8] about twenty years after the execution of Shāh Ṭahmāsp's daughter, Parī-Khān Khānum [3 Dhū 'l-Ḥijjah 985/11 Feb. 1578. See *ʿĀlam-ārāy i ʿAbbāsī* p. 162] and divided into three *faṣls* ((1) *thulth*-writers, (2) *taʿlīq*-writers, (3) *nastaʿlīq*-writers) and a *khātimah* (on a few of the most recent painters, illuminators, and other craftsmen): **London** (?) private library of Mrs. C. C. Edwards (84 foll., lacking introduction and a leaf or leaves at end), **Ḥaidarābād** private library of Āqā S. M. ʿAlī (lacks a page or more of the introduction), **Moscow** Museum of Oriental Civilisations.

883 Cf. no. 1100 *supra*.

884 A MS. of this fifth volume was acquired in 1895 by the Preussische Staatsbibliothek and has been described by W. Hinz in an article entitled *Eine neuentdeckte Quelle zur Geschichte Irans im 16. Jahrhundert* (*ZDMG*. 89/3–4 (1935) pp. 315–28). See also second previous footnote.

885 The Berlin MS., which is defective at the end, breaks off in the year 1592. Persian histories often extend beyond the limits indicated in their prefaces.

886 Correct title unknown.

Edition: announced as in preparation by Miss Zahrā Dāʿīzādah for the M.A. degree at Ḥaidarābād (cf. BSOS. x/1 (1939) p. 211).

Russian translation: *Kazi Ahmed. Traktat o kalligrafakh i khudozhnikakh ... Vvedenie, perevod i kommentarii Professora B. N. Zakhodera.* **Moscow** 1947.

Descriptions:

(1) *Calligraphers and artists: a Persian work of the late 16th century. By C. C. Edwards* (with the text and translation of two extracts (Shāh Maḥmūd and Āqā Riḍā) and an index to the calligraphers and artists. In BSOS. x/1 (1939) pp. 199–211),

(2) *Tadhkirah i khwush-nawīsān u naqqāshān*, by Zahrā Dāʿī-zādah (in *Armaghān* xix (1318)/5–6 pp. 344–5).

1432. For the *Maʾāthir i Raḥīmī*, which was completed in 1025/1616 by ʿAbd al-Bāqī Nihāwandī, and of which the third volume is devoted to notices of contemporary celebrities including towards the end some calligraphists and painters, see no. 711 *supra*.

1433. For the *ʿAmal i Ṣāliḥ* of M. Ṣāliḥ Kanbō Lāhaurī, which was completed in 1070/1659–60 and which contains at the end of vol. ii notices of seven calligraphists (pp. 443–6), see no. 738 (1) *supra*.

1434. For the *Mirʾāt al-ʿālam*, which was composed in 1078/1667 ostensibly by Bakhtāwar Khān but really by M. Baqā Sahāranpūrī and of which the first *numūd* of the *afzāyish* is devoted to notices of calligraphists (published by M. Shafīʿ in OCM. x/4 (Aug. 1934) pp. 33–65), see no. 151 (2) *supra*.

1435. For the *Tadhkirah i Ṭāhir i Naṣrābādī*, which was begun in 1083/1672–3 and of which the second *firqah* of the third *ṣaff* is devoted to calligraphists, see no. 1130 *supra*. The Persian text of this second *firqah* was published by M. Shafīʿ on the basis of a British Museum MS. (Rieu i p. 368) in the OCM. xi/4 (Aug. 1935) pp. 154–9.

1436. Notices of some Sindī calligraphists from the third volume (p. 241 in the 1304 edition) of ʿAlī-Shēr "Qāniʿ" Tattawī's *Tuḥfat al-kirām* (for which see no. 828 (1) *supra*) have been published on the basis of an autograph MS. by M. Shafīʿ under the title *Khaṭṭāṭān i Sind* in OCM. xi/2 (Feb. 1935) pp. 131–4.

1437. Khalīfah Sh. **Ghulām-Muḥammad "Rāqim"** Haft-qalamī Akbar-Shāhī Dihlawī, a calligraphist of note in his time, is mentioned by "Qāsim" in his *Majmūʿah i naghz*, a *tadhkirah* composed in 1221/1806, as a young man who "twelve or thirteen years ago before going to Lucknow" had read with him the *Sharḥ i Shamsīyah* [i.e. Quṭb al-Dīn al-Rāzī's commentary on al-Kātibī's manual of logic entitled *al-Risālat al-Shamsīyah*] and the *Ḥāshiyah i Mīr* [i.e. the annotations of al-Saiyid al-Sharīf al-Jurjānī (see no. 53 *supra*) on the *Sharḥ al-Shamsīyah*], had submitted Urdu verses to him and who, having returned to Delhi, was at that time studying medicine under Mirzā Muḥammad "ʿIshq". He must have been born some years before 1194/1780, since he was a pupil of the calligraphist M. Ḥafīẓ Khān, who died in that year and, if the date AH 1261/1845 is not a later addition to the work mentioned as no. iii below, he must have lived to an advanced age.

I. (***Tadhkirah i khwush-nawīsān***) (beg. *ai qiṭʿah i luṭf zīr-mashq i karamat*), chronologically arranged notices of celebrated calligraphists preceded by instructions in prose and verse concerning the choice of a pen, the making of ink, etc.: **Rieu** ii 532a (defective, AD 1863), **Ivanow** Curzon 86 (defective. Mid 19th cent.).

Edition: *The Tadhkira-i-khushnavīsān of Mawlānā Ghulām Muḥammad Dihlavī edited with prefaces, notes, and indices by M. Hidayet Husain*, **Calcutta** 1910°* (*Bibliotheca Indica*).

II. ***Musawwadah i Tadhkirah i khaṭṭ u khwush-nawīsān az ibtidāy*** [*sic*] ***tā zamān i ākhir i sanah i*** 1239 (beg. *Ḥamdī kih qalam az taḥrīr i ān qāṣir ast*), a work of which the contents are "to some extent identical" with those of the preceding **Rieu** ii 532*b* (incomplete and out of order. 19th cent.), **Rāmpūr** (see *Oriental College Magazine*, vol. vi, no. 2 (Lahore, Feb. 1930), pp. 113–14, where the work is called *Tadhkirat al-kātibīn*). Probably **Bānkīpūr** xi 1077, in which the preface, defective at the beginning, mentions a division into a *muqaddimah*, three[887] *bābs* and a *khātimah* and gives 1239/1823 as the date of completion, is another copy of this work or of this recension.

III. (***Risālah i mutaḍammin i ḥālāt i khwush-nawīsān i khuṭūṭ***[888]), notices of Indian calligraphists from the time of Akbar to that of Bahādur Shāh II divided into four *faṣls* ((1) nastaʿlīq writers, (2) shikastah and shafīʿāʾī writers, (3) naskhī and ṭughrā writers, (4) seal-engravers), the latest date mentioned being AH 1261/1845: **Rieu** iii 1033*a* (circ. AD 1850).

[*Majmūʿah i naghz* I 264; *Gulshan i bē-khār* 125; Sprenger p. 280 ult.; Garcin de Tassy ii p. 567.]

887 Only two *bābs* ((1) seventy calligraphists, mainly *nastaʿlīq*-writers, (2) thirty-six *shikastah*-writers) are mentioned in M. Shajāʿat-ʿAlī Khān's description of the Rāmpūr MS.

888 These are the opening words of the B.M. MS.

1438. Mīrzā **Sanglākh Khurāsānī**, surnamed (*mulaqqab*) Dānā-yi Irān and Āftāb i Khurāsān, calligraphist, poet, and Ṣūfī, one of the celebrities of his time in Persia, excelled especially in the writing of *nastaʿlīq*. In the course of his travels, which are described at some length in the *Imtiḥān al-fuḍalāʾ*, he visited not only many parts of Persia but also Turkistān, ʿArabistān, Kurdistān, Turkey, and Egypt. At Istānbūl he made a prolonged stay. He died at Tabrīz in 1294/1877 at the age of one hundred and ten "approximately". A poem of his in praise of Smyrna was published with a Turkish paraphrase (*Tarjamah i qaṣīdah i Sanglākh dar madḥ i Izmīr*) at Būlāq in 1261/1845°.

Imtiḥān al-fuḍalāʾ, or *Tadhkirat al-khaṭṭaṭīn*, bombastic notices of calligraphists in four unnumbered parts ((1) ancient and modern calligraphists, (2) an account of Sanglākh's travels, dated 1288/1871, (3) Sanglākh's pupils, (4) Ottoman calligraphists), described on the title-page as the work of Sanglākh but written actually, as is not concealed, by his pupil, Munshī "Ghaibī": [**Tabrīz**] 1291/1874° (foll. 465, unpaginated. Described as Vol I). [*Imtiḥān al-fuḍalāʾ* (portrait facing 2nd title-page); *al-Maʾāthir wa-ʾl-āthār* p. 216.]

1439. Ḥājjī Mīrzā ʿ**Abd al-Muḥammad Khān** Iṣfahānī **Īrānī** is, or was, editor of the illustrated weekly newspaper *Chihrah-numā* published from 1322/1904–5 onwards first for a short time at Alexandria and subsequently at Cairo[889] In the preface to his *Paidāyish i khaṭṭ u khaṭṭāṭān*, of which he wrote the *khātimah* in Ramaḍān 1346/1928, he mentions works of his entitled *Amān al-tawārīkh* and *Fuʾād al-tawārīkh.*

Paidāyish i khaṭṭ u khaṭṭāṭān, a sketch of the history of writing from its beginning to the early ʿAbbāsid period followed by (1) notices of Ibn Muqlah (p. 90), Ḥasan b. Muqlah (p. 107), Ibn Bawwāb (p. 109), and al-Bukhārī (p. 115), (2) more or less alphabetically arranged notices of 104 calligraphists, none of them, except Abū ʾl-Faḍl Sāwajī (d. 1312/1894–5. p. 153, under Mīrzā), later than the first half of the 18th century, the first being Ibrāhīm Mīrzā Ṣafawī (p. 117) and the last Yaḥyā-yi Ṣūfī (7th/13th cent.), (3) *Sargudhasht i ijmālī i barkhī az khaṭṭāṭān i gum-nām* (p. 249), (4) *Sargudhasht i khwush-nawīsān i muta-ʾakhkhirīn u maʿāṣirīn*, containing after a brief historical introduction notices of ʿAbd al-Wahhāb "Nashāṭ;" (d. 1244/1829, p. 252), ʿAlī Khān Amīn al-Daulah (p. 254), M. Ḥusain Mushkīn-qalam (d. 1330/1912. p. 256), Qāsim Āqā Tabrīzī (d. 1292/ 1875. p. 258), M. ʿAlī b. Ḥusain ʿAlī Bahāʾ (b. 1270/1853–4. p. 260) and Najīb Bēk Hawāwīnī: **Cairo** 1345–6/1927–8‡.

889 Cf. Browne *Press and poetry of modern Persia* pp. 72–3.

1440. Appendix

(1) ***Tārīkh i Kalām al-mulūk***[890] (*fī bayān ẓuhūr wa-ījād al-khaṭṭ wa-aḥwāl al-khaṭṭāṭīn*. Beginning of the first Cairo MS.: *Bi-dān-kih aṣl i khaṭṭ nuqṭah ast*), by Mīrzā Yūsuf al-Lāhijī: **Cairo** p. 500 (part only. Foll. 49), *ibid.* (the same part ? Foll. 36. AH 1275/1858).

13.5 *Companions of the Prophet*

See also Traditionists, nos. 1583–88 *infra*, and Biography: General, no. 1644 *seqq. Infra.*

1441. **ʿUbaid Allāh b. ʿAbd Allāh al-Ḥusainī** known as (*al-mashhūr bi-*) ***Murshid b. Aṣīl*** was presumably the son of S. Aṣīl al-Dīn ʿAbd Allāh al-Ḥusainī (for whom see no. 229 *supra*). He tells us that he had long cherished the idea of waiting on the *Ṣaḥābīs* cited as authorities in the six collections, but that his intention could not be carried out until in Shaʿbān 884/1479 it won the approval of the Amīr Niẓām al-Daulah wa-'l-Dīn ʿAlī-Shīr (for whom see no. 1094 *supra*).

(1) ***Tuḥfat al-faqīr al-ḥaqīr ilā ḥaḍrat al-Amīr al-Kabīr*** (beg. *al-Ḥ. l. 'l. jaʿala rijāla*), short notices[891] of the Prophet's contemporaries who are cited as authorities for traditions in the six canonical collections, in four *bābs* ((1) the *ʿAsharah i Mubashsharah*, (2) persons best known by their *asmāʾ*, (3) persons best known by their *kunyahs*, (4) the Prophet's wives and daughters: **I.O.** D.A. 157 fol. 31–58 (17th cent.), **Rāmpūr** (see Nadhīr Aḥmad 78).

(2) ***Tuḥfah i Murshidī*** (beg. *al-Ḥ. l. 'l-Muwaffiqi 'l-Muʿīn*), the same biographical notices arranged alphabetically: **Rāmpūr** (see Nadhīr Aḥmad 79).

1442. Other works:

(1) ***Aṣḥāb i kirām***, popular biographies of the Prophet's Companions, translated (from what language ?) by S. Riḍā ʿAlī-Zādah: **Lahore** 1344–5/1926–7* (2 vols).

(2) ***Manāqib al-Aṣḥāb wa-'l-Tābiʿīn***, by ʿAbd Allāh al-Naisābūrī. Anonymous Persian translation (beginning: *Ḥ. u sipās u sitāyish lāʾiq*): **Cairo** p. 504 (AH 1274/1760–1).

---

890 Two works with this title have already been mentioned (nos. 430–31 *supra*). Whether the title has good authority in this case is not clear.

891 The information given relates to the name, or names, of each *Ṣaḥābī* and, if necessary, the spelling of them, the collections in which his traditions occur, the total number of traditions related by him, the number occurring in each collection, and the date of his death.

13.6 *Families, Tribes, Races*

13.6.1 Afghāns

For some works containing genealogical information concerning the Afghāns and the Afghān tribes see nos. 544–77 *supra*. For the Bangash Nawwābs of Farrukhābād see nos. 906–08. For the Rohillas see nos. 609–18. For the Āfrīdīs and Khwēshgīs see nos. 1444 and 1449–50 *infra*.

1443. **Shēr Muḥammad Khān Gan̤dah-pūr**,[892] who came of a well-known family resident at Kulāchī in the Ḍērah Ismāʿīl Khān District of the Panjāb, visited many parts of Afghānistān in quest of the *nasab-nāmahs* and other genealogical, historical, and sociological information on which he based his *Khwurshīd i jahān*. He died in 1302/1885. Among his works were a *Safar-nāmah i Īrān u Turkistān* and a *risālah i kaifīyat i jamʿ i Qurʾān*.

> ***Khwurshīd i jahān***, a detailed work on the genealogies of the Afghān tribes and clans with information concerning their history and customs: **Lahore** 1894° (pp. 320. Cf. Peshawar 1546).

[Peshawar catalogue p. 291]

13.6.2 Āfrīdīs

1444. **Qāsim ʿAlī Khān Āfrīdī** b. Burhān (d. 1194/1780) b. Nēk-nām Khān (d. 1145/1732) was born on 20 Rajab 1183/19 Nov. 1769 and was the great-grandson of an Afghān who had settled in India and whose descendants were scattered in different parts of the country, ignorant of their family connexions and almost all ignorant of Pashtō. His home, for at any rate a large part of his life, was at Farrukhābād, but his career (as a soldier ?) took him to various parts of India and he saw service under Jaswant Rāō Hōlkar, Nawwāb Amīr Khān, Mīr Jaʿfar "Masīḥ" and others. In 1222/1807 he was appointed Superintendent of the Criminal Court Prison at Farrukhābād and in 1223/1808 Superintendent of the Civil Court Prison. According to a note in the Bānkīpūr MS. of his works he died on 15 Jumādā i 1241/26 Dec. 1825. In addition to the *Tuzuk i Āfrīdī* described below several other works of his are preserved in the Peshawar MS. 1910A (*Kullīyāt i Āfrīdī*) and in the similar MS. Bānkīpūr Suppt. ii 2245–50. These are (1) *Shafāʿat i Āfrīdī*, forty-one Persian poems, *qaṣīdahs* and *ghazals*, in praise of the Prophet, the Imāms and eminent *shaikhs*, Bānkīpūr Spt. ii 2246 (foll. 60b–71a. Probably identical with the *Qaṣāʾid i Āfrīdī*, Peshawar 1910A (4), described as in Persian and Pashtō), (2) *Dīwān i Hindī*, *ghazals* in alphabetical order intermixed with some Persian *ghazals* and completed (according to

892 This is an Afghān tribal name (see *Ency. Isl.* under Afghānistān).

the concluding verse) in Rajab 1216/Nov.-Dec. 1801, Bānkīpūr Spt. ii 2247 (foll. 72b–178a. Doubtless more or less identical with Peshawar 1910A(3) (*Dīwān i Āfrīdī ba-zabān i Urdū*)), (3) *Āfrīdī-nāmah*, a vocabulary of Persian words (the first of which is *Āfrīdī*) with Pashtō, Kashmīrī, English, and Hindi translations, Bānkīpūr Spt. ii 2248 (foll. 179b–207a. Evidently identical with *Farhang i Āfrīdī*, Peshawar 1910A (5)), (4) *Dīwān i Pashtō*, Bānkīpūr Spt. ii 2249 = Peshawar 1910A (2). (5) *Khwāb-nāmah, mustazāds* in Pashtō, Bānkīpūr Spt. ii 2250 = Peshawar 1910 (4) (b). In addition to "Āfrīdī" or "Afrīdī" "Qāsim ʿAlī" occurs in these poems as a *takhalluṣ*.

Tuzuk i Āfrīdī (so Peshawar), or ***Risālah i Āfrīdī*** (so Bānkīpūr), a family history and autobiography in twenty-one *bābs* completed in 1222/1807 with a twenty-second *bāb* (on the death of the author's brother, Aʿẓam ʿAlī Khān) added in 1225/1810 and a twenty-third added in 1239/1823 (concerning relatives about whom he had subsequently collected information): **Peshawar** 1910A (acephalous. Transcribed for the author in 1230/1815. Number of *bābs* not stated in the catalogue), **Bānkīpūr** Suppt. ii 2245 (probably autograph. Many additions and marginal notes).

13.6.3 Barmecides

1445. The anonymous history of the Barmecides published by ʿAbd al-ʿAẓīm Khān Garakānī is assigned by him on linguistic, stylistic and other grounds to the fourth/tenth or fifth/eleventh century.

(***Akhbār i Barāmikah***), beginning: *al-Ḥ. l. R. al-ʿā. wa-'l-ṣ. ʿalā khairi khalqihi M. wa-ālihi 'l-ṭāhirīn. Riwāyat kard Abū 'l-Qāsim b. Ghassān girdāwarandah i akhbār i Āl i Barmak guft Barmak mardī būd az farzandān i wuzarā-yi mulūk i Akāsirah*: MS. in the possession of the editor mentioned below.

Edition: *Akhbār i Barāmikah* [so on title-page], or *Tārīkh i B.* [so on wrapper], **Ṭihrān** AHS 1312/1935* (edited with a long introduction by Mīrzā ʿAbd al-ʿAẓīm Khān Garakānī[893]).

893 ʿA. al-ʿA. Kh. "Qarīb" b. Mīrzā ʿAlī Akbar, born at Garakān in 1296/1879, went to Ṭihrān in 1311/1893–4 and studied French among other subjects. In 1317/1899–1900 he was appointed teacher in the Madrasah i ʿIlmīyah and since then he has taught the Persian language and literature in several of the schools and colleges of Ṭihrān. When Ishaque wrote his *Sukhunvarān* [circ. 1932] he was on the staff of the Madrasah i ʿAlī i Niẓām (Military College). His works include (1) *Qawāʿid i Fārisī*, a Persian grammar in three volumes, (2) *Dastūr i zabān i Fārisī*, in four volumes, (3) *Farāʾid al-adab*, an anthology with biographies of the authors, (4) an edition of *Kalīlah wa-Dimnah*, (5) an edition of the *Gulistān*. See Ishaque *Sukhanvarān* i pp. 219–24 (portrait), *Modern Persian poetry* pp. 9, 20, etc.

1446. **Ḍiyā' al-Dīn Baranī** has already been mentioned (no. 666 *supra*) as the author of a *Tārīkh i Fīrōz-Shāhī* completed in 758/1357.

Akhbār i Barmakiyān (beginning *Ḥ. u thanā mar Khudā'ī rā kih ba-faḍl i khwīsh*), anecdotes of the Barmecides translated from the Arabic of Abū 'l-Qāsim M. al-Ṭā'ifī or Abū M. 'Abd Allāh b. M. Lābarī (the latter apparently a writer of the third/ninth century: see Rieu), or both,[894] and dedicated to Fīrōz-Shāh:[895] **Ethé** 569 (AH 1097/1686), **I.O.** D.P. 363 (a) (small fragment only), **Rieu** i 333*b* (17th cent.), **Bodleian** 308 (seal dated 1124/1716), **Ivanow** Curzon 85 (AH 1285/1868).

Edition: place ? 1280/1863–4 (Āṣafīyah i p. 222 no. 880), **Bombay** [1889°].

1447. '**Abd al-Jalīl** b. Niẓām al-Dīn Yaḥyā **Yazdī**.

Tawārīkh i Āl i Barmak, a history of the Barmecides begun in 762/1360, dedicated to Shāh Shujā', the Muẓaffarid, and based on material collected by the author's father: **Blochet** i 633 (late 15th cent.), 634 (AH 926/1520).

Extracts: C. Schefer, *Chrestomathie persane*, **Paris** 1883–5°*, ii pp. 1–54 (notes, etc., pp. 1–64 at other end).

13.6.4 Bōhorahs

1448. **M. 'Abbās** "Rif'at" **Shīrwānī** has already been mentioned as the author of the *Tārīkh i Āl i amjād* (no. 308), the *Sulṭān-nāmah* (no. 600) and the *Bāgh i chahār-chaman* (no. 1005).

Qalā'id al-jawāhir fī aḥwāl al-Bawāhir,[896] composed in 1287/1870–1. Edition: place ? 1301/1883–4 (Āṣafīyah i p. 248).

13.6.5 Khwēshgīs

1449. Some sources of information concerning the Khwēshgī clan have already been mentioned in connection with Pīr Ibrāhīm Khān Khwēshgī (no. 840) and

894 Both of these persons are described in different places as *mu'allif i aṣl, mu'allif i awwal i īn kitāb, mu'allif i 'Arabī*, etc.

895 The date "A.H 755 = A.D 1356" [*sic !*] given in the Bodleian catalogue as that of the completion of the work seems to be a lapsus calami for 757 [=1356], which, however, is mentioned in Rieu' description [incorrectly for 758] as that of the *Tārīkh* [*i Fīrōz-Shāhī*], not of the *Akhbār i Barmakiyān*.

896 For the Bohoras, or Bohrahs, a caste in Western India, mostly Ismā'īlī Shī'ites in the Bombay Presidency, see *Ency. Isl.* under Bohorās (T. W. Arnold).

ʿAbd Allāh K͟hwēs͟hgī (no. 1333). The former's *Sairistān*, which includes a short account of the K͟hwēs͟hgīs, is mentioned on no. 840 3rd par.

1450. For ʿAbd al-ʿAlīm Naṣr Allāh K͟hān K͟hwēs͟hgī see no. 1043.

13.6.6 Nāʾiṭīs

1451. **G͟hulām-ʿAbd al-Qādir**[897] **"Nāẓir"**, surnamed Qādir ʿAẓīm K͟hān, b. G͟hulām-Muḥyī 'l-Dīn "Muʿjiz" **Naʾiṭī** S͟hāfiʿī was born in 1200/1786 and died in 1243/1827–8.

Gulistān i nasab, a genealogical work (124 foll.) on the Nāʾiṭī (or Nāʾiṭī) tribe or clan[898] completed in 1224/1809 and divided into three *bābs* ((1) *dar bayān i faḍīlat i qaum i Banū Nāʾiṭ*, (2) *dar bayān i nasab i rāqim i suṭūr*, (3) *dar bayān i faḍīlat i aslāf i buzurgān i k͟hwud*) and a *k͟hātimah* (*dar bayān i tafṣīl i nasab u mustaqīm s͟hudan i silsilah i aqārib i īn k͟hānadān*): **Ivanow** 1st Suppt. 774 (1) (circ. AH 1251–8/1835–42).

[*Ṣubḥ i waṭan* p. 168; *Is͟hārāt i Bīnis͟h; Gulzār i Aʿẓam* pp. 360–1.]

1452. The manuscript containing the *Gulistān i nasab* just described contains also five short works on the Nāʾiṭī tribe, three of them in Persian, one in Arabic, and one in Urdu.[899] Those in Persian are:—

(1) ***Aḥwāl al-qaum*** by M. Akram K͟hān: *Ivanow* 1st Suppt. 774 (2).

(2) ***Kas͟hf al-nasab***, by an anonymous author who refers to the *Gulistān i nasab* and M. Akram's work: **Ivanow** 1st Suppt. 774 (4).

(3) ***al-Nāʾit*** (so spelt here, with tāʾ not ṭāʾ, as also in M. Akram's work), by M. Saʿīd known as (*s͟hahīr*) Ustād: **Ivanow** 1st Suppt. 774 (3) (AH 1251/1835).

Another Persian work relating to this tribe is

Qābūs li-muʿtariḍ ṣāḥib al-Qāmūs, "a refutation" by M. ʿAbd al-Razzāq b. ʿAlī Aḥmad K͟hān "of the claim put forward by G͟hulām Dastgīr, in a work

897 For names of this type see no. 1354 footnote *supra*.

898 The Nāʾiṭīs, Navāyat, Navayet, Nawāʾit, who claim Arab descent, are a largely sea-faring tribe living on the coast of the Bombay Presidency and elsewhere in southern India: cf. Yule and Burnell *Hobson Jobson*, under Navait, Naitea, Nevoyat, etc. Among the best known members of the tribe are ʿAlī b. Aḥmad al-Mahāʾimī, author of the *Tabṣīr al-Raḥmān*, an Arabic commentary on the Qurʾān written in 831/1427–8 (see the *Catalogue of Arabic MSS. in the … India Office* ii no. 1142, Brockelmann *Sptbd.* ii p. 310) and Nawwāb ʿAzīz-Jang (see no. 1045 *supra*). See also no. 1084 1st par. footnote.

899 It has been mentioned in no. 1045 1st par. that an Urdu *Tārīk͟h al-Nawāʾiṭ* was written by Nawwāb ʿAzīz-Jang, the former owner of Ivanow 1st Suppt. 774.

entitled *Qawānīn i Dastgīrī*, that the tribe of Nawāyat is descended from the Quraish": **Madras** 1331/1913*.

13.6.7 Naubakhtīs

1453. ʿ**Abbās** Khān **Iqbāl** Āshtiyānī, who in 1342/1924[900] and AHS 1312/1933–4[901] was described as a *Muʿallim* in the *Dār al-Muʿallimīn* (Teachers' Training College) and in 1938[902] as a Professor in the University of Ṭihrān, visited Europe for the first time in 1925[903] and was here again thirteen years later, since his introduction to the *Ṭabaqāt al-shuʿarāʾ al-muḥdathīn* was written at Paris in September, 1938. Among his works are *Tārīkh i mufaṣṣal i Īrān* (vol. i, Ṭihrān, AHS 1312/1933–4. See no. 321 (*a*) (9) *supra*), *Tārīkh i ʿumūmī wa Īrān* (*Luzac's Oriental List* 1940 p. 107), and *Tārikh i tamaddun i jadīd* (*Luzac's Oriental List* 1942 p. 9), as well as biographies of ʿAbd Allāh b. al-Muqaffaʿ, (see no. 1667 (31) *infra*) and Qābūs b. Washmgīr (no. 1457 *infra*). Persian and Arabic[904] works edited by him include (1) Rashīd al-Dīn *Waṭwāṭ's Ḥadāʾiq al-siḥr*, Ṭihrān, AHS 1308/1929*, (2) the *Bayān al-adyān* of Abū 'l-Maʿālī M. Ḥusainī, Ṭihrān, AHS 1312/1933*, (3) the *dīwān* of Hātif Iṣfahānī, Ṭihrān, AHS 1312/1934‡, (4) the *Tabṣirat al-ʿawāmm fī maʿrifat maqālāt al-anām*, Ṭihrān, AHS 1313/1934*, (5) the *Tajārib al-salaf* (cf. no. 110 *supra*), Ṭihrān, AHS 1313/1934*, (6) Ibn Shahrāshūb's *Maʿālim al-ʿulamāʾ* (A.), Ṭihrān AH 1353/1934‡, (7) al-Thaʿālibī's *Tatimmat al-Yatīmah* (A.), Ṭihrān AH 1353/1934‡, (8) the *Ṭabaqāt al-shuʿarāʾ al-muḥdathīn* of Ibn al-Muʿtazz (A.), London 1939 (Gibb Memorial Series).

Khānadān i Naubakhtī[905] (*Les Naubakht, leur biographie, leurs œuvres politiques, littéraires et intellectuels; histoire sommaire des principales sectes musulmanes jusqu'au Ve siècle de l'Hégire; secte Imamienne et ses premiers théologiens; liste alphabétique des différentés sectes chiites; abrégé de leurs doctrines et références bibliographiques les concernant: avec table généálogique*): **Ṭihrān** AHS 1311/1933* (see *Luzac's Oriental List* 1933 p. 13 and a review by R. Levy in *JRAS*. 1935 pp. 739–40).

[Portrait in *Qābūs i Washmgīr*, frontispiece.]

900 *Qābūs i Washmgīr*, title-page.
901 *Tārīkh i mufaṣṣal i Irān*, title-page.
902 *Ṭabaqāt al-shuʿarāʾ al-muḥdathīn* introduction, at end.
903 *Op. cit.* introduction p. xxviii.
904 Marked (A) in the list which follows.
905 For the Āl i Naubakht see Massignon *La passion d'al Hallâj* pp. 142–59; *Die Sekten der Schîʿa von al-Ḥasan ibn Mūsā an-Naubaḫtī herausgegeben von H. Ritter*, Istanbul 1931, introduction. For Abū Sahl Ismāʿīl b. ʿAlī Ibn Naubakht, the denouncer of al-Ḥallāj, see also *Rauḍāt al-jannāt* p. 31; *Tanqīḥ al-maqāl* i p. 139; Brockelmann *Sptbd.* i p. 319; etc.

13.6.8 Appendix

1454.
(1) ***Nasab-nāmah i Sādāt i Bārhah:***[906] **Āṣafīyah** ii p. 1778 no. 119 (AH 1314/ 1896–7).
(2) ***Tārīkh i Imām-zādahā i Shaft u Fūman u Kahdam wa-ghairuhā***: **Leningrad** Mus. Asiat. (see *Mélanges asiatiques* iv (1863) p. 499).

13.7 *Kings*

1455. **M. b. ʿAlī** b. M. b. al-Ḥasan al-Kātib **al-Samarqandī** (so Leyden iii p. 14), or Bahāʾ al-Dīn[907] M. b. ʿAlī b. M. b. Ḥusain[908] al-Ẓahīr[909] al-Kātib al-Samarqandī (cf. Rieu ii p. 748*b*, *al-Muẓaffrīyah* p. 255) is said by ʿAufī,[910] who calls him Ẓahīr al-Dīn ... M. b. ʿA. al-Samarqandī al-Kātib, to have been for a time (*muddatī*) Minister (*ṣāḥib-dīwān i inshaʾ*) to Qilich Ṭamghāch Khān. His *Aʿrāḍ al-siyāsah* is dedicated to "Abū ʾl-Muẓaffar Qilich Ṭamghāch Khāqān b. Jalāl al-Dīn", i.e. according to Barthold (*Turkestan* p. 18) Qilich Ṭamghāch Khān Masʿūd b. ʿAlī (cf. *op. cit.* pp. 334, 336).[911] His *Sindbād-nāmah*,[912] of which there are MSS. at the British Museum (Rieu ii 748) and the Royal Asiatic Society (see S. Oldenburg's article *O persidskoi prozaicheskoi versii "Knigi Sindbāda"* in *al-Muẓaffarīyah: Sbornik statei uchenikov ... bar. V. R. Rozena*, St. Petersburg 1897, pp. 255–8) begins with a long eulogy of the same monarch, who is there called Rukn al-Dīn ... Quṭlugh Bilgā [Bēg ?[913]] Abū ʾl-Muẓaffar Qilich Tamghāch Khān b. Qilich Qarā-Khān and is described as having vanquished his foes in Tūrān in the year fifty-six (i.e. 556/1161. See Rieu ii p. 748*a*). A third work, *Samʿ al-Ẓahīr*

---

906 For the Bārhah Saiyids see Blochmann's translation of the *Āʾīn i Akbarī* pp. 390–5; W. Irvine *Later Mughals* i pp. 201–2; Blumhardt *Catalogue of Hindustani manuscripts in the ... India Office* p. 22; etc.

907 *Sindbād-nāmah*, B.M. MS. Or. 255 fol. 11*b* (quoted by Rieu): *mī-gūyad muqarrir i īn kalimāt ... al-ṣadr al-ajall al-auḥad malik al-udabāʾ wa-ʾl-kuttāb Bahāʾ al-Dīn saʿd al-Islām ṣāḥib al-naẓm wa-ʾl-nathr muʿjiz al-bayānain mafkhar al-lisānain ... M. b. ʿA. b. M. b. ʿUmar al-Ẓahīrī al-Kātib al-Samarqandī.*

908 So in the R.A.S. MS. It will be noticed that the B.M. MS. has ʿUmar, probably a corruption.

909 So in the R.A.S. MS., while the B.M. MS. has al-Ẓahīrī.

910 *Lubāb al-albāb* i p. 91.

911 He "ascended the throne, judging from his coins, in 558/1163. In 560/1165 he restored the city walls of Bukhārā on a foundation of baked bricks ..." (Barthold *Turkestan* p. 336). For the word Ṭamghāch see M. Qazwīnī's remarks in his edition of the *Chahār maqālah*, notes, pp. 92–4, English translation p. 102.

912 This work is in prose, not in "prosaic Persian verses", as stated by Barthold (*Turkestan*, London 1928, p. 18). P.S. It is now accessible in the edition published at Istānbūl in 1948 by Ahmed Ateş.

913 Cf. Barthold *Turkestan* p. 336 n. 1.

fī jamʿ al-Ẓahīr, is mentioned by ʿAufī (cf. *Haft iqlīm* and Ḥ. Kh., both probably dependent on ʿAufī).

Aʿrāḍ al-siyāsah fī aghhrāḍ al-riʾāsah, biographies of 74 persons, nearly all kings,[914] from Jamshīd to Sanjar, "largely anecdotal in character, and of little interest on the whole, with the exception of the narrative of contemporary events during the reign of Qilich-Ṭamghāch-Khān inserted at the end of the book" (Barthold *Turkestan* p. 28): Ḥ. Kh. i p. 368 (*Aghrāḍ al-siyāsah*), **Leyden** iii p. 14 no. 927 (AH 948/1541–2), **Āṣafīyah** ii p. 1218 no. 107, **Āyā Ṣōfyah** 2844.

Extracts (contemporary events): Barthold *Turkestan v epokhu mongolskago nashestviya*, **St. Petersburg** 1900°* i, Teksty, pp. 71–2.

[*Lubāb al-albāb* i pp. 91–2; *Haft iqlīm* no. 1422; Rieu iip. 748.]

1456. For the *Futūḥāt i Fīrōz-Shāhī* see no. 667 *supra*.

For the *Bābur-nāmah*, or Memoirs of Bābur, see no. 698 *supra*.

For the "autobiography" of Shāh Ṭahmāsp see no. 380 *supra*.

For the *Jahāngīr-nāmah* or *Tūzuk i Jahāngīrī* see no. 715 *supra*.

For Mīrzā Jawān-bakht's account of his escape from Delhi see no. 799 *supra*.

For the autobiography of Ṭīpū Sulṭān see no. 1070 (1) *supra*.

For the autobiography of Shāh Shujāʿ al-Mulk see no. 562 *supra*.

For Nāṣir al-Dīn Shāh Qājār's diaries of his journeys to Europe and elsewhere see no. 439 *supra*.

For the autobiography of ʿAbd al-Raḥmān Khān, Amīr of Afghānistān, see no. 575 *supra*.

For Muẓaffar al-Dīn Shāh Qājār's diary of his visit to Europe in 1900 see no. 448 *supra*.

1457. ʿ**Abbās** Khān **Iqbāl** Āshtiyānī (see no. 1453 *supra*).

Qābūs i Washmgīr i Ziyārī: *zindagānī i ʿilmī u adabī i ū*: **Berlin** 1342/1924‡ (Intishārāt i Īrānshahr, i).

13.8 *Munshīs*

1458. For the *Riyāḍ al-afkār* completed in 1268/1852 by Wazīr ʿAlī "ʿIbratī" ʿAẓīmābādī see no. 1210 (2) *supra*.

See also the subsection BIOGRAPHY: (*j*) OFFICIALS.

914 Among the others are Ptolemy (al-Ḥakīm), Plato, Aristotle, and Abū Muslim.

13.9 *Officials (Ministers of State, Military Officers, etc.)*

1459. It has been convincingly demonstrated by M. Qazwīnī[915] that Muḥammad i munshī, the author of the *Nafthat al-maṣdūr*, is the same person as **M. b. Aḥmad** b. ʿAlī b. M. al-munshī **al-Nasawī**,[916] who in 639/1241–2 wrote the Arabic *Sīrat al-Sulṭān Jalāl al-Dīn Mankubirnī* (for which see Brockelmann i p. 319, *Sptbd.* i p. 552). Born at Kharandiz [?[917]], a fort near Nasā for many generations in the possession of his family, he was for some time in the service of the local rulers, the Āl i Ḥamzah (to use the name suggested by Qazwīnī for the dynasty), and about the year 621/1224 was sent by one of them, Nuṣrat al-Dīn Ḥamzah b. M. b. M. b. ʿUmar b. Ḥamzah, on a mission to Sulṭān Ghiyāth al-Dīn, the brother of the Khwārazm-Shāh Sulṭān Jalāl al-Dīn Mankubirnī.[918] Before he could carry out his mission Sulṭān Ghiyāth al-Dīn was defeated at Ray by his brother, and M. Nasawī, proceeding to the latter's camp near Hamadān, was taken into his service. In 622/1225, at Marāghah he was appointed to the office of secretary (*kātib al-insha*ʾ), and thenceforward he was in constant attendance on the Sulṭān in his campaigns. After the conquest of Akhlāṭ in 627/1230 he was sent on a mission to the Malāḥidah of Alamūt. In the following year the Sulṭān was severely defeated near Āmid by the Mongols, but escaped from the battlefield only to be killed by Kurds near Maiyāfāriqīn. Nasawī escaped in a different direction and with two or three others reached Āmid, where he was imprisoned for three months by the Ortuqid Malik Masʿūd. Thence he went successively to Mārdīn, Irbil, Urūmiyah, Khōy, Pergerī (Muḥarram 629/ Oct. 1231) and finally after great hardships, to Maiyāfāriqīn. There he settled

915 In a pamphlet of forty pages printed with a preface of three pages by ʿAbbās Iqbāl at the Maṭbaʿah i Majlis, Ṭihrān, in 1308/1929* under the title *Maqālaʾī tārīkhī u intiqādī az ḥaḍrat i ʿallāmah i ustād Āqā-yi Mīrzā M. Khān Qazwīnī dar bāb i nuskhah i Nafthat al-maṣdūr taʾlīf i Nūr al-Dīn Muḥammad i munshī.*

916 Qazwīnī's main evidence is provided by a series of parallel passages, which could not conceivably have been written by two different persons (*Maqālah* pp. 9–15).

917 This place, spelt Khrndr or the like (with incomplete punctuation) in the very old Paris MS. of the *Sīrat Jalāl al-Dīn* (and perhaps identical with the Kharāndīz described by Yāqūt as being, he thought, in Khurāsān), is mentioned several times in the *Sīrah* (pp. 30, 53, 57–8, 60–1), and more than once as the author's birthplace and home (e.g. p. 30: *qalʿat Kharandiz masqaṭ raʾsī wa-mansha*ʾ *asāsī*). In the *Nafthat al-maṣdūr*, on the other hand, a place spelt ZYDR is mentioned twice (pp. 34^2 and 63^7), in the latter case as the author's birthplace (*turbat i aṣlī*). M. Qazwīnī's suggestion that Zaidar may be merely a corruption of Kharandiz will probably commend itself to most students. In any case it was doubtless on the strength of the second passage that "Hidāyat" appended the *nisbah Zaidarī* to the author's name. See Qazwīnī's *Maqālah* pp. 17–21.

918 For whom see *Ency. Isl.* under Djalāl al-Dīn Mangubartī (an unsigned article of which the authorship is acknowledged by Brockelmann, *GAL. Sptbd.* i p. 552).

under the protection of Malik Muẓaffar S̲h̲ihāb al-Dīn G̲h̲āzī, the Aiyūbid, and it was there that he wrote the *Naft͟hat al-maṣdūr* four years later.

(***Naft͟hat al-maṣdūr***[919]) (beg. *Dar īn-muddat kih talāṭum i amwāj i fitnah*), an account of the author's adventures in four months of 628/1231 between his separation from Sulṭān Jalāl al-Dīn at Āmid and his arrival at Maiyāfāriqīn: Ṭihrān two modern MSS. in private ownership (see Mujtabā Mīnuwī's footnote on p. 2 of M. Qazwīnī's *Maqālah*).

Edition: *Kitāb i Naft͟hat al-maṣdūr* ...[920] *ta'līf i K̲h̲wājah Nūr al-Dīn*[921] *Muḥammad Zaidarī*[922] *K̲h̲urāsānī* ... *bā muqaddimah i marḥūm Riḍā-Qulī K̲h̲ān Hidāyat i Ṭabarī Lalah-bās̲h̲ī*. Ṭihrān AHS 1307–8[923]/1928–9‡ (*S̲h̲irkat i Ṭabʿ i kitāb*. Pp. 105, of which 2–26³ are devoted to the introduction, written in 1281/1864–5, by "Hidāyat").

1460. Of unknown authorship is:—

Nasā'im al-as̲h̲ār, biographies of *wazīrs* completed in Ṣafar 725/1325 and used extensively by the author of the *Āt͟hār al-wuzarā'*: **Āyā Sōfyah 3487** (see Viqār Ahmad Hamdānī's remarks on this work in *JRAS*. 1938 p. 563).

1461. **Saif al-Dīn Ḥājjī b. Niẓām al-Faḍlī** (or al-ʿUqailī ?) was in the service of K̲h̲wājah Qiwām al-Dīn Niẓām al-Mulk K̲h̲wāfī, who became Governor of Qum and Rai in 873/1468–9, was appointed Wazīr by Sulṭān Ḥusain in 875/1470–1 and was deposed in 892/1487.

At͟hār al-wuzarā', notices of celebrated *wazīrs*, composed in 883/1478–9, dedicated to Niẓām al-Mulk K̲h̲wāfī and divided into two *maqālahs* ((1) in twelve *bābs* devoted to the *wazīrs* of particular dynasties, namely

---

[919] This expression, meaning "complaint of one's misfortunes", "*dard i dil*," occurs twice in the text (p. 31⁷: *az naft͟hat al-maṣdūrī kih mahjūrī ba-d-ān rāḥatī tuwānad yāft*, and p. 58¹⁰: *Bi-yā tā ba-sar i naft͟hat al-maṣdūr i k̲h̲wīs̲h̲ bāz s̲h̲awīm kih īn muṣībat nah az ān qabīl ast kih ba-bukā u ʿawīl dar muddat i ṭawīl ḥaqq i ān tuwān gud̲h̲ārd*) and forms a convenient and appropriate title, though there is no reason to suppose that the author intended it to serve as such (see M. Qazwīnī's *Maqālah* p. 21).

[920] The words omitted (*fī futūr zamān al-ṣudūr wa-zamān ṣudūr al-futūr*) are apparently an arbitrary addition based on the title of Anūs̲h̲irwān b. K̲h̲ālid's memoirs (see no. 335 *supra* and M. Qazwīnī's *Maqālah* pp. 23–5).

[921] The author himself does not mention his *laqab*, but Juwainī in the *Jahān-gus̲h̲ā* (ii p. 153) speaks of Nūr al-Dīn mun s̲h̲ī as the Sulṭān Jalāl al-Dīn's *mun s̲h̲ī* and the *mudabbir* of his kingdom. It was doubtless this passage or a similar passage in some later historian that "Hidāyat" had in mind when he called our author Nūr al-Dīn. See Qazwīnī's *Maqālah* pp. 16–17.

[922] See five notes back, ad K̲h̲arandiz.

[923] 1307 on the title-page, 1308 on the cover, and [AH] 1341 [*sic* ? = 1922–3] in the lithographer's colophon.

(*a*) Pre-Islāmic kings of Persia, (*b*) the first four Caliphs, (*c*) Umaiyads, (*d*) ʿAbbāsids, (*e*) Sāmānids, (*f*) G͟haznawids, (*g*) Buwaihids, (*h*) Saljūqids, (*j*) K͟hwārazm-S͟hāhs, (*k*) Chingiz K͟hān and his descendants, (*l*) Muẓaffarids and G͟hōrids. (*m*) Tīmūrids to Abū Saʿīd, (2) on K͟hwājah Qiwām al-Dīn, apparently imperfect in all the MSS.): **Bānkīpūr** viii 654 (AH 1044/1634), **Rieu** Suppt. 101 (17th cent.), iii 969*b* (AH 1239/1824), **Āṣafīyah** iii p. 92 no. 1059 (defective at both ends), **Bodleian** 347 (n.d.), **Browne** Pers. Cat. 109, **Ethé** 621, **Majlis** 619 (4).

1462. G͟hiyāt͟h al-Dīn surnamed (*mulaqqab*) **K͟hwānd-Amīr**, who died probably in 942/1535–6, has already been mentioned as the author of the *Maʾāt͟hir al-mulūk* (no. 125 (1) *supra*), the *K͟hulāṣat al-ak͟hbār* (no. 125 (2)), the *Ḥabīb al-siyar* (no. 125 (3)), the *Humāyūn nāmah* (no. 700), and the *Makārim al-ak͟hlāq*, a panegyric on Mīr ʿAlī S͟hīr (no. 1096).

Dastūr al-wuzarāʾ (a chronogram = 915/1509–10[924]), lives of eminent *wazīrs* arranged—apart from the first two, Āṣaf and Buzurjmihr—under dynasties from the Umaiyads to the Tīmūrids, the last being ministers of Sulṭān Ḥusain:[925] Ḥ. K͟h. iii p. 228, **Bodleian** 87 (AH 965/1558), **Chanykov** 66 (AH 974/1566), **Berlin** 604 (AH 1013/1604), **Rieu** i 335*a* (AH 1036/1627), **Ivanow** 212 (AH 1222/1807–8), **Browne** Coll. J. 11 (12) (AH 1268/1852), **Buk͟hārā** Semenov 70, **Flügel** ii 1204, **Leningrad** Mus. Asiat. (see *Mélanges asiatiques* iv (St. Petersburg 1863) p. 54).

Edition: **Ṭihrān** AHS 1317/1938‡ (ed. Saʿīd Nafīsī).

---

924 Not 906 as stated in the third note on p. 8 of the printed edition. This chronogram, as the author tells us in his preface (p. 8), indicates the date of completion. The work must have been begun several years earlier, since Abū ʾl-Fatḥ Sulṭān Ḥusain Bahādur K͟hān (d. 911/1506) is spoken of in the preface as a living sovereign (p. 5). It is dedicated to one of his *wazīrs*, whose name, not mentioned in the British Museum MS., is given in the printed edition (p. 6) as Kamāl al-Millah wa-l-Dunyā wa-ʾl-Dīn K͟hwājah Maḥmūd [*sic* ?]. According to Saʿīd Nafīsī, whose edition is based on two MSS. belonging respectively to ʿAbbās Iqbāl (undated) and ʿAbd al-Rahīm K͟halk͟hālī (AH 1010), the work exists in two forms (*dū riwāyat*), of which the first, composed in 906 [a date based apparently on his miscalculation of the chronogram], is represented by ʿAbbās Iqbāl's MS., while the second, containing twelve additional biographies at the end and completed after 914 (the latest date mentioned) and before 916 (the date of the death of S͟haibānī K͟hān, who is three times mentioned towards the end as a living ruler), is represented by ʿAbd al-Raḥīm K͟halk͟hālī's MS. It is at any rate a fact that the final biographies are not the same in all MSS.

925 Darwīs͟h Aḥmad (d. 912/1507) is the last *wazīr* in the printed edition, which contains—on the basis of ʿAbd al-Raḥīm K͟halk͟hālī's MS.—biographies of some contemporary *wazīrs* apparently absent from most of the MSS. According to the catalogues, Bodleian 87 and Rieu i 335*a* end with Majd al-Dīn M. (printed ed., pp. 400–18), Flügel ii 1204 and Ivanow 212 with Afḍal al-Dīn M. Kirmānī (printed ed., pp. 433–41).

Extracts: [Faḍl Isfarāyinī, Aḥmad Maimandī and Ḥasanak, Ghaznawid wazīrs] Elliot *Bibliographical index* ..., Calcutta 1849, *muntak͟habāt* pp. 25–7.

Translation of the same extracts: Elliot *Bibliographical index* pp. 117–20; Elliot and Dowson *History of India* iv pp. 148–53.

List of the biographies: *Wiener Jahrbücher*, Bd. 74 Anz.-Bl. pp. 1–4 (Hammer).

1463. For the memoirs of Asad Bēg Qazwīnī, which extend from 1011/1602 to 1014/1605 see no. 712 *supra*.

1464. For the *Ma'āthir i Raḥīmī*, completed in 1025/1616 by 'Abd al-Bāqī Nihāwandī, see no. 712 *supra*.

1465. Sh. Farīd b. Sh. Ma'rūf **Bhakkarī**.[926]

D͟hak͟hīrat al-k͟hawānīn, lives of Indian nobles from the time of Akbar to 1060/1650, dedicated to Nawwāb S͟hāyistah K͟hān[927] and divided into three chapters ((1) Akbar's, (2) Jahāngīr's, and (3) S͟hāh-Jahān's contemporaries): Ḥaidarābād Prof. 'Abd al-Ḥaqq's private library (foll. 230, one leaf missing at end. Bears a librarian's note of 1069/1659 or 1169/1756. See M. Abdulla Chughtai's description in *Islamic culture* ix/3 (July, 1935) pp. 411–22, where information is given concerning a number of nobles associated with the arts, especially building).

Almost the whole of this work seems to have been incorporated with little alteration in the *Ma'āthir al-umarā'*. In S͟hāh-nawāz K͟hān's preface (vol. i p. 8³, Beveridge's trans. p. 7) it is referred to in the words *Agar-chih dar-īn waqt kitābī mausūm ba-D͟hak͟hīrat al-k͟hawānīn taṣnīf i S͟haikh Ma'rūf Bhakkarī mutaḍammin i aḥwāl i umarā ba-naẓar rasīd u akthar i maṭālib i ān ḍamīmah i īn nuskhah gardīd līkin chūn bināyi ān bar ak͟hbār i samā'ī i muk͟hālif i taḥqīq i ahl i īn fann būd u ma'k͟hadh i īn*

---

926 M. Abdulla Chughtai's summary of the preface to the *D͟hak͟hīrat al-k͟hawānīn* (*Islamic culture* ix/3 (July, 1935) p. 412) begins with the sentence "After offering praise to the Almighty God and asking blessings on the Prophet, Sheykh Farīd son of Sheykh Ma'rûf *Ṣadr Sarkar Bhakkar* (District Officer of Bhakkar) says that volumes have been devoted by historians to accounts of the former and the present Sultans". It appears from the *Ma'āthir al-umarā'*, iii p. 73, that a S͟h. Ma'rūf, presumably S͟h. Farīd's father, was Ṣadr of Bhakkar shortly after 1007/1598–9. Consequently the words quoted above do not necessarily mean that S͟h. Farīd was himself Ṣadr of Bhakkar, though he may of course have held the same post as his father.

927 Mīrzā Abū Ṭālib S͟hāyistah K͟hān Amīr al-Umarā' died in 1105/1694. See *Ma'āthir al-umarā'* ii pp. 690–706; Beale *Oriental biographical dictionary* under Shaista Khan.

nuskhah kutub i muʿtabarah i t͟hiqāt ast rujḥānī badīhī u mazīyatī ẓāhir bar-ān mutaḥaqqaq u t͟hābit gas͟ht. It will be noticed that here, apparently by inadvertence, the author of the *D͟hak͟hīrat al-k͟hawānīn* is called S͟h. Maʿrūf Bhakkarī[928] The same thing occurs in the apparently spurious preamble of Ivanow 215, in which S͟h. Maʿrūf Bhakkarī is made to speak as though the work contained in the MS. were the *D͟hak͟hīrat al-k͟hawānīn*, whereas it appears to be a defective copy of the *Maʾāt͟hir al-umarāʾ*.[929]

1466. Ṣadr al-Dīn M. "Fāʾiz" b. Zabardast K͟hān is the author of poetical works in Persian and Urdu, including a Persian *mat͟hnawī* dated 1134/1721–2, which are preserved with some Persian *ruqaʿāt* in the Bodleian MS. 1177 (*Kullīyāt i Fāʾiz*). The Urdu *mat͟hnawī* describing a bang-seller has been translated into French by Garcin de Tassy (i pp. 436–8). He wrote a short astronomical (or astrological ?) work entitled *Najm al-Ṣadr* (MS.: Panjāb Univ. Lib. (dated 1135/1723 and probably autograph). See *OCM*. x/3 p. 106) and doubtless also the treatise on gardening entitled *Zīnat al-basātīn* (MS.: Panjāb Univ. Lib. See *OCM*. x/1 (Nov. 1933) p. 99, where the date of transcription, given as "probably 1032", should perhaps be read 1132).

Irs͟hād al-wuzarāʾ, short notices of celebrated viziers written (according to Elliot *History of India* iv p. 148) in Muḥammad S͟hāh's reign (1131–61/1719–48) and divided into twelve *maqālahs* devoted for the most part to particular dynasties, the last being concerned with the viziers of the Indian Tīmūrids: **Rieu** i 338*b* (foll. 65, breaking off in the notice of D͟hū 'l-Faqār K͟hān b. Asad K͟hān, vizier to Jahāndār S͟hāh. 18th cent.), iii 1014*b* (extracts only. Circ. AD 1850), 1046*a* (extract only).

1467. Early in 1160/1747 **Mīran** [?[930]] **Lāl** wrote:

Tad͟hkirah i aḥwāl i Saiyid M. K͟hān (beginning *Az ān-jā kih pīs͟h-gāh i Dāwar i ḥaqīqī*), an account of the career of a contemporary official: **Ivanow** Curzon 159 (7) (foll. 301*b*–317. AH 1207/1792–3).

The same official's career, especially the events of 1160–1/1747–8, is the subject of another short tract with the same title but of unstated authorship (beginning *Īn sipihr i luʿbat-bāz rā rasmī ast qadīm*): **Ivanow** Curzon 159 (3) (foll. 249–256*b*. AH 1207/1792–3).

---

928   He is called S͟h. Farīd Bhakkarī in *Maʾāt͟hir al-umarāʾ* ii p. 788 and also in ʿAbd al-Ḥaiy's preface.
929   The biographies are alphabetically arranged, without any grouping in three chapters, and include a life of Amīr K͟hān Sind'hī, a noble of Aurangzēb's time.
930   As the second consonant is unpointed, the name could be read Mitran, Manran, etc.

1468. M. ʿAbbās K͟hān "ʿAbbās" Afg͟hānī b. M. Ziyārat Allāh died in 1188/1774 according to Nad͟hīr Aḥmad, who gives a reference to *Ak͟hbār al-ṣanādīd*.[931] part i, pp. 373–5.

Ḥālāt i ʿAbbās K͟hān, an autobiography: Rāmpūr Ḥāfiẓ Aḥmad ʿAlī K͟hān's library (see Nad͟hīr Aḥmad 66).

Extracts: *Ak͟hbār al-ṣanādīd, loc. cit.*

1469. Rāy **Kēwal Rām**, son of Rag'hunāt'h Dās, describes himself as an Aggarwālah by caste and a resident of Kāsnah in the *ṣūbah* (province) of Delhi.

*Tadhkirat al-umarā*ʾ, concise notices of Indian nobles (k͟hāns from *nuh-hazārī* to *dū-ṣadī*, untitled *amīr*s from *s͟hash-hazārī* to *hazārī*, Hindū *zamīndār*s, and Deccan *amīr*s from *haft-hazārī* to *pānṣadī*) who served under Akbar and his successors to the death of Aurangzēb [AH 1119/1707], completed in 1140/1727–8 (so Bodleian 258), or 1184/1770–1[932] (so Rieu i 339 and Sprenger, MSS. of the late Sir H. Elliot (*JASB*. xxiii (1854) p. 239), or 1194/1780 (so Ethé 629, Ivanow 216, and Elliot *History of India* viii p. 192), and divided into two *bāb*s ((1) Muslims, in two *faṣl*s, (a) those who bore the title *k͟hān*, with a *d͟hail* devoted to those who bore such other titles as Amīr al-umarāʾ, Amīn al-Daulah, and Iʿtimād al-Daulah, (b) those without official titles, such as Ibrāhīm Mīrzā, S͟h. Ibrāhīm, S͟h. Abū ʾl-Faḍl, Ḥakīm Abū ʾl-Fatḥ, (2) Hindūs, in two *faṣl*s, (a) those who bore the titles Rānā, Mahārājah, Rājah, Rāō, Rāwat, Rāwal, Rāy-Rāyān, or Rāy, (b) Rājpūts and others without these titles): **Rieu** i 339*a* (AH 1195/1781), ii 876*b* (18th cent.), iii 971*b* (circ. A.D 1850), **Ivanow** 216 (probably defective in middle. Late 18th cent.), **Bodleian** 258, **Ethé** 629.

1470. For the *Ṭahmās-nāmah*, the memoirs of Ṭahmās K͟hān, written in 1193/1779, see no. 800 *supra*.

1471. **S͟hāh-nawāz K͟hān Aurangābādī**, i.e. Mīr ʿAbd al-Razzāq b. Mīr Ḥasan ʿAlī Ḥusainī K͟hwāfī **Aurangābādī**, entitled Nawwāb **Ṣamṣām al-Daulah S͟hāh-nawāz K͟hān** Ṣamṣām-Jang, the descendant of a Saiyid who had

---

931 Presumably an Urdu work, but not traceable in the Urdu catalogues of the British Museum, India Office, Āṣafīyah Library, or the Subḥān Allāh collection at ʿAlīgaṛh. From the number of pages in part i it would appear to be a much larger work than Sir Saiyid Ahmad's *Āthār al-ṣanādīd* (cf. no. 654, 5th par. *supra*), the first part of which in the Lucknow edition of 1876 has only 98 pages.

932 Ethé's argument that the date 1184 is impossible in view of the fact that a former owner's seal on fol. 1*a* of Bodleian 258 bears the date 1181 is of course invalid, since seals were often used long after the dates inscribed on them.

migrated from Khwāf to India in Akbar's reign, was born on 28 Ramaḍān 1111/20 March 1700 at Lahore,[933] where his father had died fifteen days before at the age of nineteen.[934] His grandfather, M. Kāẓim Khān,[935] who died in 1135/1722–3, had been appointed *Dīwān* of Lahore and subsequently of Multān by Aurangzēb, but many of his relations were resident in Aurangabad,[936] and there Mīr ʿAbd al-Razzāq settled in the year in which the Amīr al-Umarāʾ Ḥusain ʿAlī Khān went to the Deccan [i.e. in 1127/1715].

In his twenties[937] he entered the service of Nawwāb Niẓām al-Mulk Āṣaf-Jāh (the first of the "Niẓāms" of Ḥaidarābād) and in 1145/1732–3 he was appointed *Dīwān* of Barār ("Berar"). In 1155/1742[938] he was dismissed for taking part in the rebellion of Nāṣir-Jang, Āṣaf-Jāh's second son, who had been vice-gerent during his father's absence in the north,[939] and he had five years of leisure, which he devoted to the compilation of his great work, the *Maʾāthir al-umarāʾ*. In 1160/1747 Āṣaf-Jāh reappointed him *Dīwān* of Barār. In 1161/1748 Nāṣir-Jang succeeded his father and made Shāh-nawāz Khān *Dīwān* of the Deccan, i.e. Prime Minister.

Nāṣir-Jang's succession, however, was contested by a nephew, Muẓaffar-Jang, who sought French help to further his designs. On Nāṣir-Jang's assassination in December 1750, Dupleix, the Governor of Pondicherry, installed Muẓaffar-Jang

933 So according to "Āzād", *Maʾathir al-umarāʾ* i p. 18[1]. Shāh-nawāz Khān himself (*M. al-u.* iii p. 721[16]) does not say expressly that he was born at Lahore, though he says that his father died there and that he was born fifteen days afterwards. Rieu (on what authority ?) says that he was bom at Multān.

934 So according to Shāh-nawāz Khān (*M. al-u.* iii p. 72114). "Āzād" says twenty (*M. al-u.* i p. 16[18]).

935 For his life see *M. al-u.* iii pp. 715–21.

936 Shāh-nawāz Khān's great-grandfather, Mīrak Muʿīn al-Dīn Aḥmad entitled Amānat Khān (for whose life see *M. al-u.* i pp. 258–68, Beveridge's trans. pp. 221–30), was appointed *Dīwān* of the Deccan in Aurangzēb's 22nd year (1089/1678) and died in 1095/1684. The same office was held by his son, Mīr ʿAbd al-Qādir Diyānat Khān, his grandson, ʿAlī Naqī Diyānat Khān, and his great-grandsons, Mīrak M. Taqī Wizārat Khān and Mīr M. Ḥusain Khān Yamīn al-Daulah Manṣūr-Jang.

937 *M. al-u.* i p. 6[5]: *dar ʿasharah i thālithah i sinīn i nadāmat-qarīn ... zamānah ba-kashākash i mulāzim-pīshagī afkand.*

938 *M. al-u.* i p. 6[14].

939 Muḥammad Shāh summoned Āṣaf-Jāh to help him against the Marāṭ'hās, who in 1737 suddenly appeared on the outskirts of Delhi. Āṣaf-Jāh was out-generalled by them near Bhōpāl in 1738 and, without any actual fighting, obtained peace by ceding the province of Mālwah. These events were followed by Nādir Shāh's invasion. Āṣaf-Jāh was one of the commanders at the Battle of Karnāl in 1739 and took a prominent part in the subsequent negotiations with Nādir Shāh. See *De Voulton's Noticia. Translated ... by L. Lockhart* (in BSOS. iv/2 (1926) pp. 223–15); L. Lockhart *Nadir Shah* pp. 124, 132–3, 136, 139–42. 148, and the various authorities cited by Lockhart.

as *Ṣūbah-dār* of the Deccan and provided him with a bodyguard of French troops and sepoys under the command of M. Bussy[940] Muẓaffar-Jang, however, was murdered in February, 1751, and his uncle, Ṣalābat-Jang, was proclaimed *Ṣūbah-dār* by Bussy, who now made French influence predominant at Aurangābād, Ṣalābat-Jang's capital. In 1165/1752 Ṣalābat-Jang appointed S̲h̲āh-nawāz K̲h̲ān *Ṣūbah-dār* of Ḥaidarābād, but he was soon dismissed at Bussy's instance. In 1167/1753, again at Bussy's instance, he was appointed Prime Minister[941] with the rank of a *haft-hazārī* and the title of Ṣamṣām al-Daulah.

S̲h̲āh-nawāz K̲h̲ān now made an effort to terminate the French predominance in the Niẓām's dominions, and at his advice Ṣalābat-Jang dismissed Bussy. Bussy, however, marched on Ḥaidarābād, took up a strong position in which he withstood a siege for nearly two months and was then reinstated by Ṣalābat-Jang. In 1170/1757 S̲h̲āh-nawāz K̲h̲ān's downfall was precipitated by his failure to satisfy the demands of the army, whose pay was much in arrear. Rising against him, they obtained his dismissal and he fled to Daulatābād with his family and nearly five hundred followers. His property was confiscated and troops were sent to besiege him. His friend G̲h̲ulām-ʿAlī "Āzād", one of the few who remained faithful to the fallen minister, exerted himself on his behalf and eventually secured his return to favour. Shortly afterwards, however, Ḥaidar-Jang, Bussy's right-hand man, seized an opportunity of putting him under arrest and five weeks later, on 3 Ramaḍān 1171/11 May 1758, he was murdered by one of Bussy's Hindu soldiers. With other members of his family he lies buried to the south of Aurangābād.

His *tad̲h̲kirah*, the *Bahāristān i suk̲h̲un*, has already been mentioned (no. 1156 *supra*). His *muns̲h̲aʾāt* are highly praised by G̲h̲ulām-ʿAlī "Āzād", who expresses regret that they had never been collected (*Maʾāt̲h̲ir al-umarāʾ* i p. 36⁸). A small collection of them (87 foll.) is preserved in an acephalous MS. at Bombay (Bombay Univ. p. 110 no. 39).

Maʾāt̲h̲ir al-umarāʾ, biographies of Indian nobles from the reign of Akbar to the author's time (*pānṣadīs* and upwards in Akbar's reign, *sih-hazārīs* and upwards thereafter to the middle of Aurangzeb's reign, thenceforward *panj-hazārīs* or *haft-hazārīs*) arranged in groups alphabetically according to the initial letter of the title and within these groups chronologically according to the dates of death, begun in 1155/1742

940 Charles Joseph Patissier, Marquis de Bussy-Castelnau (1718–85), for whom see Buckland's *Dictionary of Indian biography*, p. 64.

941 *Nawwāb Ṣamṣām al-Daulah rā ba-ʿaṭā-yi k̲h̲ilʿat i wakālat i muṭlaq i k̲h̲wud ... bar-nawāk̲h̲t. U ū muddat i c̲h̲ahār sāl ba-manṣab i wakālat i muṭlaq pardāk̲h̲t* (*M. al-u.* i p. 21^{14-17}).

(author's preface p. 6[14], Beveridge's trans. p. 6[18]), worked at for five years ("Āzād's" preface p. 11[4], Beveridge's trans.p. 10[1]), neglected then for some twelve years ("Azad's" preface p. 11[8], Beveridge's trans. p. 10[6]) and still unfinished at the author's death, after which the MS. was lost until eventually recovered a year or more later[942] in fragments and incomplete by the author's friend Ghulām-ʿAlī "Āzād" Bilgrāmī (cf. no. 1162 *supra*), who prepared an edition extant in several MSS., but soon superseded by the greatly enlarged edition of Mīr ʿAbd al-Ḥaiy, the author's son.[943]

I. Ghulām-ʿAlī "Āzād's" edition, containing a preface by the editor (beg. *Ḥamd i Shāhanshāhī*), his life of the author (beg. *Nawwāb Ṣamṣām al-Daulah ... Nām i aṣlī i ū, Mīr ʿAbd al-Razzāq ast*), the author's preface (beg. *al-Ḥ. l. wa-salām ʿalā ʿibādihi*), and a series of biographies (two hundred and thirty-four in Bodleian 166, two hundred and sixty in Morley 101–2, two hundred and eighty-seven in Bānkīpūr 655) beginning with Adham Khān Kōkah, ending with Yāqūt Khān Ḥabashī, and including three (S. ʿAbd Allāh Khān Quṭb al-Mulk, Nawwāb Āṣaf-Jāh, and Nawwāb Niẓām al-Daulah Nāṣir-Jang) added by the editor from his *Sarw i Āzād* (for which see no. 1162 (16) *supra*): **Lindesiana** p. 219 no. 824 (circ. AD 1770. Not described in the catalogue as "Āzād's" edition, but if the conjectural date is correct it can be nothing else), **Madrās** i 444 (AH 1192/1778), **Ethé** 622 (AH 1199/1785), 623 (AH 1203/1789), 624–5, **R.A.S.** P. 104–5 = Morley 101–2 (AH 1204/1789), P. 106–7 (AH 1261/1845), **Ivanow** 213 (AH 1221/1806–7), 215 (some differences, for which see Ivanow's description. The beginning partly spurious), **Lahore** Panjab Univ. Lib. (AH 1244/1828. See *Oriental College Magazine*, vol. iii, no. 1 (Lahore, Nov. 1926), p. 68), **Bānkīpūr** viii 654 (287 biographies. 19th cent.), **Bodleian** 166 (234 biographies), 167 ("quite modern").

---

942 *Baʿd i yak sāl i kāmil az shahādat i muṣannif* ("Āzād's" preface p. 11 ult.). ʿAbd al-Ḥaiy says *Baʿd az chand sāl qadrī ajzā ba-dast āmad* (p. 3[12]).

943 Ṣamṣām al-Mulk (previously for a time Ṣamṣām al-Daulah) Mīr ʿAbd al-Ḥaiy "Ṣārim" Aurangābādī was born in 1142/1727–30. In 1162/1749 Nāṣir-Jang (cf. no. 1471 2nd par. end) appointed him to a *manṣab*, conferred upon him the title of Khān and made him *Dīwān* of Barār ("Berar"). In the time of Ṣalābat-Jang (cf. no. 1471 3rd par.) he became Governor (*Nāẓim*) of Aurangābād and Commandant of the fort of Daulatābād. His father's downfall (in 1170/1757) involved him too, but Niẓām-ʿAlī (cf. no. 1032 1st par.) restored him to favour and appointed him *Dīwān* of the Deccan. He was with Niẓām-ʿAlī's army before the fort of Kaulās, when he fell ill and died on 15 Jumādā 'l-Ūlā 1196/28 April 1782. It has already been mentioned (no. 1156 2nd par.) that he completed his father's *tadhkirah*, the *Bahāristān i sukhun*. See *Maʾathir al-umarāʾ* iii pp. 973–9 (a brief autobiography); *Khizānah i ʿāmirah* pp. 296–7; *Sawāniḥ i Dakan*; Rieu i pp. 340*b*, 342*a*.

II. ʿAbd al-Ḥaiy's edition, begun in 1182/1768–9 some time after the recovery of further fragments of the author's MS., completed in 1194/1780 and containing ʿAbd al-Ḥaiy's preface (beg. *Sitāyish i bī-karān*), the author's preface, "Āzād's" preface, "Āzād's" life of the author, a list of the biographies (in which the many added by ʿAbd al-Ḥaiy are marked with a Q as an abbreviation for *Ilḥāq*), the series of biographies, seven hundred and thirty[944] in number according to a statement prefixed by ʿAbd al-Ḥaiy to his list, the first being Ismāʿīl Bēg DWLDĪ, the last Yalangtōsh Khān, and finally a *khātimah* devoted to a brief autobiography of the editor and specimens of his poetry: **Ethé** 627 (apparently autograph first brouillon, lacking seventy-two leaves between foll. 4 and 5 and containing about three hundred and seventy-one biographies), 626 (containing, without preface or *khātimah*, a series of biographies beginning with Ismāʿīl Bēg DWLDĪ and ending with Yalangtōsh Khān, perhaps ʿAbd al-Ḥaiy's biographies separately copied. Received by Richard Johnson from Mīr M. Ḥusain at Ḥaidarābād in 1788), **I.O.** 3903–5 (transcribed probably in 1886), **Rieu** i 339*b* (AH 1196/1782) 341*b* (two copies, both dated 1196/1782), 342*a* (two 18th-cent. copies), **Blochet** i 639–40 (late 18th cent.), 641 (late 18th cent.), **Ivanow** 214 (18th cent.), **R.A.S.** P. 108 = Morley 103 (AH 1242/1826), **Bānkīpūr** viii 656–7 (19th cent.), **Āṣafīyah** i p. 252 no. 520 (from *dāl* to *mīm*).

Edition (of ʿAbd al-Ḥaiy's recension): *The Maásir-ul-umará by Nawāb Samsámud-Dowla Shah Nawáz Khan ... Edited ... by Maulaví 'Abd-ur-Rahím (and Maulaví Mirzá Ashraf 'Alí)*. **Calcutta** 1888 [1887]-91°* (3 vols. Bibliotheca Indica).

English translation (rearranged): *The Maaṣiru-l-umarā* [fasc. 7 The *Maāthir-ul-umarā*], being biographies of the Muḥammadan and Hindu officers of the Timurid sovereigns of India from 1500 to about 1780 AD *by Nawāb* [fasc. 7 *Nawwāb*] *Ṣamṣāmu-d-Daula Shah Nawāz Khān and his son 'Abdul Ḥaqq* [*sic*, but correctly on fasc. 7 *'Abdul-Ḥayy*]... *Translated by H. Beveridge* ... [fasc. 7 adds *and revised, annotated and completed by Baini Prashad, D. Sc., F.R.A.S.B.*]. **Calcutta** 1911- °*, *in progress* [fasc. 1–6, 600 pp., published in 1911–14°*, and fasc. 7, pp. 601–840, published in 1941°*, form "Vol I" and contain the biographies of those persons whose names

944 On this approximately correct number see Beveridge's remarks in his translation p. 32 n. 1. As he says, however, "the number of the biographies contained in the three volumes [sc. of the printed edition] is considerably more than 726, for most of the notices end with accounts of the sons and grandsons of the subject of the biography."

or titles,[945] when transliterated, begin with the letters A-L, the first being ʿAbd al-ʿAzīz K͟hān Bahādur (Persian text, vol. ii p. 836), and the last Luṭf Allāh K͟han Ṣādiq (Persian text., vol. iii p. 177). Bibliotheca Indica.]

[*Maʾāt͟hir al-umarāʾ* iii pp. 721–8 (an autobiography appended to the biography of his grandfather, M. Kāẓim K͟hān), i pp. 14–40 (a biography prefixed to the work by the editor, G͟hulām-ʿAlī "Āzād". English translations of this biography have appeared in the *Quarterly Oriental Magazine* (Calcutta 1825) p. 269 onwards and in Beveridge's translation of the *M. al-u.* pp. 12–32); *K͟hizānah i ʿāmirah* pp. 62–3 (in the account of Ṣalābat-Jang); contemporary European writers such as Orme and Dupleix; *Mirʾāt al-ṣafāʾ* (B.M. Add. 6540) foll. 103–4, etc.; Persian histories of Ḥaidarābād; M. Wilks *Historical sketches of the south of India*, i (London 1810) pp. 382, 387, 389; J. Grant Duff *History of the Mahrattas* (1826), revised edition, Oxford 1921, vol. i pp. 434, 460, 463, 476, 486–7, 494–9, 500; H. G. Briggs *The Nizam* (London 1861) i pp. 124–33; Elliot and Dowson *History of India* viii pp. 187–91; Rieu i p. 340; Buckland *Dictionary of Indian biography* p. 385; Bānkīpūr catalogue viii pp. 11–12; *Ency. Isl.* under Ṣamṣām al-Dawla (H. H. Schaeder); *Pictorial Hyderabad compiled ... by K. Krishnaswamy Mudiraj*, Hyderabad 1929, vol. i pp. 183–4; etc.]

1472. Nawwāb **ʿAlī Ibrāhīm K͟hān** died in 1208/1793–4 (see no. 922 *supra*).
Declaration concerning his governorship [*sic ?*] *of Benares*: **Rieu** Suppt. 405A (see no. 922 (1) *supra*).

1473. For the *Ḥairat-nāmah i sufarāʾ* of Mīrzā Abū ʾl-Ḥasan S͟hīrāzī, Persian envoy in London, and afterwards Minister for Foreign Affairs, see no. 1417 *supra*.

1474. **M. Riḍā "Najm" Ṭabāṭabā** (see no. 180 *supra*).
Notice of S͟hāh-nawāz K͟hān [***Dihlawī***],[946] ***S͟hāh-ʿĀlam's Wazīr***: **Rieu** iii 1018b viii (AD 1849).

945 Some persons entered in the original under their titles are entered by Beveridge under their names and *vice versa*. Thus Ḥaidar-Qulī K͟hān Muʿizz al-Daulah will be found under M in the original but under H in the translation. The original not infrequently departs from the best usage in entering persons under such prefixed titles as S͟haik͟h, Ḥakīm, Mīr, and Qāḍī. Beveridge's arrangement is occasionally affected by eccentricities of transliteration, e.g. Ekatāz K͟hān (the only entry under E !).

946 For S͟hāh-nawāz K͟hān Dihlawī see no. 175 *supra*. He is, of course, to be distinguished from S͟hāh-nawāz K͟hān Aurangābādī (for whom see no. 1471 *supra*).

1475. Rājāyān-rājah Rājah **Chandū La'l** "Shādān" Mahārājah Bahādur has already been incidentally mentioned in this work (no. 333, Persian translations (2) footnote, no. 1038 1st par.). A member of a family claiming descent from Rājah Tōdar Mal, Akbar's Finance Minister, he was born in 1766 and, like his paternal uncle before him, became *Kaṛōṛgīr* of the town of Ḥaidarābād in the time of Mīr Niẓām-'Alī Khān (AH 1175–1218/1761–1803). In 1221/1806 Mīr-'Ālam (for whom see no. 1034) obtained the Niẓām's sanction for his appointment as *Peshkār* (*Mīr-'Ālam Rājah Chandū, La'l rā bah pēshkārī i khwēsh az pēshgāh i Ḥuḍūr i pur-nūr sarfarāz u sarbuland u mumtāz gardānīdah, Gulzār i Āsafīyah* p. 101[13]). After the death of Mīr-'Ālam in 1223/1808 Munīr al-Mulk was appointed *Dīwān*, but the administration of the state was in the hands of Chandū La'l, its virtual ruler (*Gulzār i Āṣafīyah* p. 105 penult.[947]). In 1235/1820 the title of Mahārājah Bahādur was conferred upon him (*G. i Ā.* p. 109[10]), in the time of Mīr Farkhundah 'Alī Khān (1829–57) he received the additional title of Rājāyān-rājah (*G.i Ā.* p. 234[10]), and on 15 April 1845 he died.

He was the author of *dīwāns* in Persian and Urdu and was a generous patron of letters. Some information about his lavish benefactions will be found in the *Gulzār i Āṣafīyah*, pp. 234[12]–36.

One of his descendants was Mahārājah Sir Kishun Pershad [i.e. Kishan Parshād], G.C.I.E., "Hereditary Peshkar and President of the Executive Council of the State [of Ḥaidarābād]," who was born in 1864 and died on 13 May 1940 (see *Who was Who* 1929–40 under Kishun Pershad).

'Ishrat-kadah i āfāq, in three *fuṣūl*[948] ((1) *dar aḥwāl i khānadān i Āṣafīyah* ... [*bā* ?] *nabdhī az aḥwāl i ābā wa-ajdād i kirām i khwud*, (2) *dar dhikr i ghazalīyāt u rubā'īyāt u afrādī kih bī mashīyat u fikr sar-zad i khāmah ... gardīdah*, (3) *dar dhikr i ḥikāyāt i 'ajībah u nikāt i gharībah*): **I.O.** 4386.

Edition: place ? [presumably **Ḥaidarābād**] 1325/1907 (see Āṣafīyah iii p. 6 no. 264).

[*Gulzār i Āsafīyah* pp. 233–6, 101, 109, and elsewhere; Briggs *The Nizam* i pp. 149–54; Garcin de Tassy iii pp. 90–2; Buckland *Dictionary of Indian biography* p. 79; Niẓāmī Badāyūnī *Qāmūs al-mashāhīr* (in Urdu) i p. 191; Saksena *History of Urdu*

947 Cf. *op. cit.* 234[2]: *Dar dīwānī i Munīr al-Mulk Bahādur az pēshgāh i khudāwand i ni'mat ḥaḍrat i Maghfirat-manzil* [i.e. Sikandar-Jāh, 1803–29] ... *ba-darajah i buland i arjmand i mukhtārī i umūr i riyāsat u wakālat i Angrēz Bahādur ... ma'mūr gashtah.*

948 The subjects of the three *fuṣūl* are given here in the author's own words as quoted in the 1938 catalogue of the Ibrāhīmī Bookshop (Maktabah i Ibrāhīmīyah), Ḥaidarābād, Deccan, p. 46. According to Saksena "He also wrote a book entitled *Ishrat Qada* [*sic*] *Afaq* in which he narrates the incidents of his life, the history of his family, and his own services in the Nizam's dominions."

literature p. 201; K. Krishnaswamy Mudiraj *Pictorial Hyderabad* i p. 196 (portrait, p. 195); see also no. 333, Persian translations (2) footnote *supra.*]

1476. **Ḥasan Chelebī "Shaidā"** was evidently a dependent of Dāwud Pāshā, Governor of Baghdād.[949]

Durrat al-tāj wa-ghurrat al-ibtihāj, described as the fourth volume of the *Khamsah i Dāwud-Shāhī* and devoted mainly to a metrical chronicle of Dāwud Pāsha's movements and the daily occurrences at his residency from Rajab 1236/April 1821 to Ramaḍān 1237/May-June 1822 (foll. 56–212), but also to six prose tracts (foll. 5–55) and the author's *dīwān* (foll. 213–77): **Rieu** Suppt. 356 (AH 1237/1822).

1477. An as yet unidentified author born at Iṣfahān on 16 Jumādā 1197/19 May 1783, who traces his descent to Ḥājjī Qiwām al-Dīn Shīrāzī, of Shāh Shujā''s time [AH 760–86/1359–84], and mentions brothers named Mīrzā 'Alī Akbar, Mīrzā 'Alī Riḍā, and Fatḥ Allāh Khān, and a great-uncle named 'Abd al-Raḥīm Khān, began in Dhū 'l-Ḥijjah 1239/Aug. 1824 at the request of some friends to note down the events of his life and thus produced an autobiography, from which it appears that he held various positions in the reign of Fatḥ-'Alī Shāh.

Autobiography (beginning: *Bas bi-gardīd u bi-gardad rūzgār dil ba-dunyā dar na-bandad hūshyār*), divided into four *bābs* ((1) *dar kaifīyat i nasab*, (2) *az zamān i wilādat ilā awān i maghḍūb shudan az sulṭān i jahāniyān ...*, (3) *dar inḥirāf i mizāj i mubārak i sulṭānī ...*, (4) *tafṣīl i aḥwāl ba'd az siyāsat u yāsā ...*) and followed by (1) Mīrzā Kūchak ["Wiṣāl"] Shīrāzī's poetical description of an earthquake at Shīrāz some years before the composition of the autobiography, fol. 53*a*, (2) a concise account of the ancient Persian kings (*guftār dar dhikr i mukhtaṣarī az waqā'i' i auḍā' u aḥwāl i mulūk i pasandīdah-shiyam i 'Ajam ...*, foll. 61*a*–139): **Ethé** 706 (transcribed AH 1253/1837 by Abū 'l-Qāsim b. 'Abd-al-Riḍā Qazwīnī).

1478. Mīrzā **M. Ja'far** b. Mīrzā M. Khān, better known as M. Jān, was the grandson of Nawwāb Mīrzā Mahdī 'Alī Khān Bahādur Ḥashmat-Jang Khurāsānī, whose father, Mīrzā M. Ṣādiq Khān, was *Ḥakim-bāshī* to the Persian court after the murder of Nādir Shāh.

Majmū'ah i Ja'farī, a biography of the above-mentioned Nawwāb Mīrzā Mahdī 'Alī Khān (b. 1168/1755, sent to Turkey as envoy by Shāh-Rukh Mīrzā, invited to India by Nawwāb Dhū 'l-Faqār al-Daulah Najaf 'Alī Khān[950]

949 See *Ency. Isl.* under Dā'ūd Pasha.

950 More commonly called Najaf Khān.

[d. 1196/1782, cf. no. 637, footnote, no. 798 (2)], reached Sūrat in 1193/1779, Shāhjahānābād in 1195/1781, and ʿAẓīmābād in 1198/1783–4, entered the E.I. Co.'s service, was given an appointment in the Customs and Revenue Department at G͟hāzīpūr, became a friend of Jonathan Duncan, Collector of Benares, who later, when Governor of Bombay, invited him thither and sent him on a mission to Fatḥ-ʿAlī S͟hāh, was granted a pension by the Marquis Wellesley and died on 17 Rabīʿ II 1219/5 July 1804): **Bombay Univ.** p. 148.

1479. **S͟hafīʿ al-Dīn Ḥasan** b. Niʿmat Allāh al-Mūsawī **al-S͟hūs͟htarī** completed in Ṣafar 1259/March 1843:—

Muʿtamadīyah, a life of Muʿtamad al-Daulah Minūchihr K͟hān (cf. no. 1214 2nd par. footnote): **Berlin** 31 (8) (AH 1259/1843), 31 (1) (a few additions (*mulḥaqāt*) only).

1480. ʿAbd al-ʿAlīm M. **Naṣr Allāh K͟hān** K͟hwēs͟hgī **K͟hūrjawī**, who died in 1299/1881, has already been mentioned (no. 1043) as the author of a *Tārīk͟h i Dakan*.

Jāmiʿ i Fatḥ-K͟hānī (a chronogram = 1263/1847), a biography of the author's maternal uncle, Fatḥ K͟hān b. Ṣadr K͟hān, who was born in 1193/1779 and died in 1262/8 Nov. 1846 after serving as *Taḥṣīldār* at Niẓāmābād (Aʿẓamgaṛh District) and elsewhere, with much autobiographical information: **Delhi** 1848*.

Urdu translation by Pandit Dayā Nātʾh "Ārām" Dihlawī: *Jāmiʿ i Fatḥ-K͟hānī*. **Delhi** 1849*.

1481. S. **Ḥaidar Ḥusain K͟hān** b. M. Ḥusain K͟hān **S͟hāhjahānābādī** wrote in 1264/1848:—

Tārīk͟h i aḥwāl i Islām K͟hān Mas͟hhadī:[951] **Āṣafīyah** iii p. 94 no. 1135.

1482. Mubāriz al-Daulah **Pīr Ibrāhīm K͟hān** K͟hwēs͟hgī Qaṣūrī has already been mentioned (no. 840 *supra*) as the author of a history of Bahāwalpūr.

Sairistān, a brief account of the author's visit to England in 1851–2 together with a short history of his tribe.

Edition: [**Multān** according to M. S͟hafīʿ, **Bahāwalpūr** according to Edwards] 1854°.[952]

---

951 For a biography of this *amīr* of S͟hāh-Jahān's time see *Maʾāthir al-umarāʾ* i pp. 162–7. Cf. no. 725 1st par. *supra*.

952 In the B.M. catalogue this work is mistakenly entered under "Mubāriz ul-Daulah, *Nawab of Bahawalpur*"

Description (by M. Shafīʿ): *Islamic culture* iii no. 3 (July 1929) pp. 454, 472.

1483. Sh. **Aḥmad ʿAlī "Rasā" Lak'hnawī** was a *taḥṣīldār* in British India until 1857.
Dhikr i yārān i zamān, an autobiography with accounts of the author's contemporaries: **Āṣafīyah** ii p. 848 no. 39 (AH 1276/1859–60, autograph).

1484. Appendix.

(1) ***Ḥālāt i Āṣaf-Khānān***, short accounts of four persons entitled Āṣaf Khān, viz., (1) Khwājah ʿAbd al-Majīd Harawī, who became Ā. Kh. in Akbar's fifth year, (2) Khwājah Ghiyāth al-Dīn ʿAlī Qazwīnī, who became Ā. Kh. in Akbar's eighteenth year, (3) Jaʿfar Bēg, who became Ā. Kh. in Akbar's twentieth year, and (4) Abū 'l-Ḥasan b. Iʿtimād al-Daulah: **Edinburgh** 413 (AH 1161/1748).

(2) (***Tārīkh i Mīrzā Masʿūd***), a history of ʿAbbās Mīrzā Nāʾib al-Salṭanah: see no. 434 *supra*.

13.10 *Orientalists*

1484A. **Abū 'l-Qāsim Saḥāb.**
Farhang i khāwar-shināsān dar sharḥ i hāl u khidamāt i dānishmandān i Irān-shinās u mustashriqīn, notices of some 570 orientalists (based in some cases on information supplied by themselves) with about sixty portraits: **Tihrān** AHS 1317/1938 (375 pp.)

13.11 *Philosophers, Physicians, etc.*

[See also BIOGRAPHY: GENERAL.]

1485. Abū Sulaimān M. b. Ṭāhir b. Bahrām al-Manṭiqī al-Sijzī (or al-Sijistānī), a philosopher of the 4th/10th century (see M. Qazwīnī *Abû Sulaïmân Manṭiqî Sidjistânî*, Publications de la Société des Etudes Iraniennes [Paris] no. 5, 1933; Brockelmann *Sptbd.* i pp. 377–8; etc.) wrote in Arabic a work entitled *Ṣiwān al-ḥikmah* (the Repository of philosophy) on the Greek (and some Islāmic ?) philosophers and their ideas. Of this work no complete copy is known to exist, but extracts from it are preserved in at least four MSS. (Bashīr Āghā 494 foll. 1–95, Murād 1408 (incorrectly 1431 in the *daftar*) foll. 1–88, Köprülü 902 foll. 1–123, Leyden ii p. 292 no. 888 foll. 1–73, and probably also Uri (Bodleian) p. 121 no. 484[953]).

---

953 Cf. M. Plessner's observations on all these MSS. in Islamica iv/4 (1931) pp. 534–8.

A supplement to this work was written between 553/1158[954] and 565/1169–70[955] by Ẓahīr al-Dīn Abū 'l-Ḥasan **ʿAlī b. Zaid al-Baihaqī**, who has already been mentioned (no. 466 *supra*) as the author of a *Tārīkh i Baihaq*.

Tatimmat Ṣiwān al-ḥikmah,[956] an Arabic work on the lives and sayings of 111 philosophers, physicians, mathematicians, etc., many of them contemporary or nearly contemporary with the author, the first being Ḥunain b. Isḥāq and the last Ismāʿīl al-Jurjānī, author of the *Dhakhīrah i Khwārazmshāhī*: **Murad** 1408 (*b*) (AH 639/1241–2), **Bashīr Āghā** 494 (*b*) (AH 689/1290), **Leyden** ii p. 292 no. 888 (*b*) (AH 692/1293), **Köprülü** 902 (14th cent.), **Mashhad** iii, *fṣl* 14, MSS., no. 24, **Ahlwardt** ix no. 10052 (18th cent.), and probably **Uri** p. 121 no. 484.

Edition of the Arabic text: *Tatimma Ṣiwān al-ḥikma of ʿAlī b. Zaid al-Baihaḳī, edited by Mohammad Shafīʿ. Fasciculus I*[957]*- Arabic text.* **Lahore** 1351/1935‡. (For a review by M. Krause see *Der Islam* 24/1 (1937) pp. 90–2).

Extract: *The earliest account of ʿUmar Khayyām*[958] By E. D. R[oss] and H. A. R. G[ibb] (in *BSOS*. v/3 (1929) pp. 467–70, with English translation, pp. 470–3).

Translations of the same extract: (1) [German] *Zu ʿOmer-i-Chajjâm. Von G. Jacob und E. Wiedemann* (in *Der Islam* iii/1 (1912) pp. 42–7). (2) [English] see above under Extract.

Description and discussion: *Abû Sulaïmân Manṭiqî Sidjistânî*, savant du IVe siècle de l'Hégire. Par M. Muḥammad Khan Qazvînî (Publications de la Société des études iraniennes [Paris], no. 5, 1933), pp. 1–7, etc.

Persian translation: ***Durrat al-akhbār wa-lumʿat al-anwār***, written probably about 730/1330[959] and dedicated to Sulṭān Abū Saʿīd's *Wazīr*, Khwājah Ghiyāth al-Dīn M. b. Khwājah Rashīd al-Dīn Faḍl Allāh (d. 736/1336) by an as yet unidentified-author who appended biographies of Shihāb al-Dīn [Yaḥyā b. Ḥabash] Qatīl al-Suhrawardī, Fakhr al-Dīn

954 The date of the death of Abū Bakr b. ʿUrwah mentioned on p. 141[7].

955 The date of Baihaqī's death.

956 This title, though not mentioned in the work itself, is that by which the author designates the work in his *Mashārib al-tajārib* (quoted in Yāqūt *Irshād al-arīb* v p. 212[9]).

957 Fasc. II is the Persian translation mentioned below. Fasc. III containing the "introduction, etc." may perhaps not yet have appeared.

958 Shahrazūrī's account is an abridged reproduction of Baihaqī's with the addition of three Arabic poems and two rubāʿīs.

959 The period of Ghiyāth al-Dīn's vizierate is referred to near the end (1935 ed. p. 133[9]) as *īn muddat i dū sih sāl*, which may not be meant quite literally. The precise date of Ghiyāth al-Dīn's appointment does not seem to be recorded, but it followed the killing of Dimashq Khwājah on 5 Shawwāl 727/24 Aug. 1327 (*Guzīdah*, trans. p. 150).

al-Rāzī, Naṣīr al-Dīn M. al-Ṭūsī and Rashīd al-Dīn Faḍl Allāh: **Lahore** Panjāb Univ. Lib.

Editions: (1) *Tārīkh al-ḥukamā' al-musammā bah D. al-a. w. l. al-a.* (ed. M. Shafīʿ. In OCM. v/2 (**Lahore** Feb. 1929) *ḍamīmah*, pp. 1–56, v/3 (May 1929) *ḍamīmah*, pp. 57–80, vi/1 (Nov. 1929) *ḍamīmah*, pp. 81–152). (2) *Tatimma Ṣiwān al-ḥikma of ʿAlī b. Zaid al-Baihaḳī, edited by Moḥammad Shafīʿ... Fasciculus II—Persian version,* **Lahore** 1350/1935‡ (Panjab University Oriental Publications Series, no. 20. Title on Persian title-page as in OCM.). (3) **Ṭihrān** (see *Luzac's Oriental List* 1940, no. 1, p. 15, where the date is not mentioned).

1486. ʿAlī b. Yūsuf **al-Qifṭī** was born in 568/1072 at Qifṭ in Upper Egypt and died at Aleppo in 646/1248 [Brockelmann i p. 325, *Sptbd.* i p. 559; *Ency. Isl.* under Ibn al-Ḳifṭī (Mittwoch) and al-Ḳifṭī (Brockelmann)]

Ikhbār al-ʿulamā' bi-akhbār al-ḥukamā': no MSS. recorded (?).[960]

Arabic abridgment: *al-Muntakhabāt wa-'l-multaqaṭāt min kitāb Ta'rīkh al-ḥukamā'*, written in 647/1249–50 by M. b. ʿAlī b. M. al-Khaṭībī al-Zauzanī: **Ahlwardt** ix 10053–4, **Cureton-Rieu** p. 684, **Flügel** ii 1161–2, **Leyden** 2nd ed. ii (1) p. 130, etc. (see Brockelmann).

Edition of the Arabic abridgment: *Ibn al-Qifṭī's Ta'rīḫ al-Ḥukamā'. Auf Grund der Vorarbeiten Aug. Müller's herausgegeben von Prof. Dr. J. Lippert.* **Leipzig** 1903°*.

Persian translation of the abridgment: ***Tarjamah i Ta'rīkh al-ḥukamā'***, written in the time of Shāh Sulaimān Ṣafawī (AH 1077–1105/1666–94) by an anonymous translator and dedicated to Mīrzā M. Ibrāhīm, *Mustaufī i Mamālik i Īrān*: **Majlis** 536 (AH 1099/1688), 535, **Mashhad** iii, *fṣl.* 14, MSS., no. 10 (AH 1296/1879), **Vatican** Pers. 133 (Rossi p. 137).

1487. Shams al-Dīn M. b. Maḥmūd **al-Shahrazūrī** al-Ishrāqī, who completed his *Rasā'il al-Shajarat al-Ilāhīyah fī ʿulūm al-ḥaqā'iq al-Rabbānīyah* (cf. Brockelmann i p. 469, *Sptbd.* i p. 851) in 680/1282 (as appears from Weisweiler's description of the Tübingen MS.[961]), wrote also *al-Rumūz wa-'l-amthāl al-lāhūtīyah fī 'l-anwār al-mujarradat al-malakūtīyah* (*fī maʿrifat al-nafs wa-'l-rūḥ*. See Escurial

960 As MSS. of the "Grundwerk" Brockelmann gives "Halet 619 (622*h*), Mešh, xiv, 5". The first words of Mashhad iii, *faṣl* 14 p. 5 no. 14 [*Ta'rīkh al-ḥukamā'*, beginning *al-Ḥ. l. al-Qadīm al-Azal* (*sic*)] suggest that it is a copy of Shahrazūrī's *Nuzhat al-arwāḥ*.

961 "Am Schluss findet sich die Angabe, dass der Verfasser das Werk am 23. Dū'l-Ḥiǵǵa 680/1282 vollendet habe."

(Derenbourg) i 696, Vatican (Levi della Vida) 299,[962] etc.) as well as commentaries on two works of Shihāb al-Dīn Yaḥyā b. Ḥabash al-Suhrawardī al-Maqtūl (d. 587/1191), namely, *Sharḥ Ḥikmat al-ishrāq* (MSS. Yeñī 767, Sarāy, Aḥmad III 3230, Lālah-lī 2525. See Ritter in *Der Islam* 24/3–4 (1937) p. 278) and *al-Tanqīḥāt fī sharḥ al-Talwīḥāt* (MSS.: Köprülü 880, ʿĀṭif 1588, Nūr i ʿUthmānīyah 2693–4. See Ritter *loc. cit.* p. 273).

Nuzhat al-arwāḥ wa-rauḍat al-afrāḥ,[963] an Arabic work on the lives and especially the sayings of about 34 Pre-Islāmic "philosophers" from Adam to Galen and about 77 Post-Islāmic from Ḥunain b. Isḥāq to Yaḥyā b. Ḥabash al-Suhrawardī, based mainly, it seems,[964] on the *Mukhtār al-ḥikam* of Mubashshir b. Fātik (Brockelmann i p. 459, *Sptbd.* i p. 829) and the *Tatimmat Ṣiwān al-ḥikmah* (see no. 1485 *supra*), of which latter a large part has been incorporated: Ḥ. Kh. vi p. 321, **Ahlwardt** 10056 (AH 782/1380), 10055 (circ. AH 1100/1688), **I.O.** 4613 (15th cent. See *JRAS*. 1939 p. 383), **Cureton-Rieu** p. 601 (AH 995/1587), p. 688 (AH 996/1658), **Leyden** iii p. 343 (undated, but modern), **Mashhad** iii, *fṣl* 14, MSS., p. 77 (5) no. 14 (cf. no. 1486 footnote, *supra*), etc. (see Brockelmann i p. 469, *Sptbd.* i p. 851).

Persian translation: ***Tarjamah i Taʾrīkh al-ḥukamāʾ***, begun in 1011/1602–3 by Maqṣūd ʿAlī Tabrīzī[965] at the request of Sulṭān Salīm Shāh [who succeeded to the throne in 1014/1605 as the Emperor Jahāngīr]: **Ethé**

962 "La sottoscrizione a f.77ᵛ in data 611 è certamente falsa." This date, which is quoted in the Leyden catalogue (iii p. 345) and was inadvertently taken by Sachau for the date of the Leyden MS. of the *Nuzhat al-arwāḥ*, was one of the bases for his conclusion that that work was written after 586 [the date of Yaḥyā Suhrawardī's death: Alhwardt read the same date as 587] and before 611.

963 This title, not mentioned in the work itself, is inscribed on some of the MSS. and is that by which the work was known to the Persian translator and to Ḥājjī Khalīfah. A variant, which transposes the two halves (*R. al-af. wa-n. al-ar.*), seems to be based on the sole authority of the Leyden MS.

964 For al-Shahrazūrī's unacknowledged debt to the *Mukhtār al-ḥikam* see Leyden iii p. 344. The extent to which he has reproduced the *Tatimmat Ṣiwān al-ḥikmah* can be judged from M. Shafīʿ's textual notes to his edition of that work.

965 M. ʿA. T., of whom a biography containing no mention of the *Tarjamah i Taʾrīkh al-ḥukamāʾ* is given on pp. 59–60 of the first *qism* (*aḥwāl i ʿulamā u fuḍalā*) of the *khātimah* to the *Maʾāthir i Raḥīmī* (completed in 1025/1616: cf. no. 711 *supra*), is described there as an incomparable Ṣūfī, a scholar and a man of austere piety. In spite of his unworldly character he was prevailed upon by ʿAbd al-Raḥīm Khān (Governor of Gujarat: cf. no. 698, Persian translations (3) *supra*) to accept the life of a courtier and official and served him for many years (*muddat-hā dar silsilah i ʿAlīyah i īn sipahsālār mulāzim u jāgīrdār būd*). He became *Ṣadr* of the province of Gujarāt, but eventually through the intrigues of an enemy was dismissed and imprisoned in the fortress of Gwalior.

614 (pt. 1 dated Āgrah AH 1019/1610, pt. 2, in a different hand, undated), 615 (AH 1039/1630, collated with an autograph at Āgrah), 616 (AH 1041/1631–2), 617, **Ivanow** 274 (AH 1033 (?)/1623–4), **Rieu** Suppt. 100 (AH 1088/1677), **Lahore** Panjāb Univ. Lib. (AH 1120/1708. See *OCM*. iii/1 p. 68), **Lindesiana** p. 191 no. 435 (?)[966] (circ. AD 1770), **Browne** Suppt. 232 (King's 97), **Būhār** 94 (defective. 19th cent.), **Āṣafīyah** i p. 224 no. 247, **Tashkent Univ.** 68 (1).

Abridgment: *Intikhāb i Tārīkh, al-ḥukamā'* (beg.: *Sipās u sitāyish Ḥakīmī rā, kih awwal i bī-awwal-ast*), written in 1054/1644 (*intikhāb* is a chronogram) for presentation to 'Abd Allāh Quṭb-Shāh by an unknown author,[967] a resident of Muḥammadābād,[968] who wrote also the ethico-theological *Risālah i kalām* (Bānkīpūr Spt. ii 2298, Calcutta Madrasah 180 (2), Būhār 210) and the ethico-political *Akhlāq i bādshāhī* (a chronogram = 1055. Bānkīpūr Spt. ii 2299, Calcutta Madrasah 180 (3), Bodleian 1469, Browne Suppt. 30 (King's 7), Ivanow 1391, I.O. 4625 (2)): **Bānkīpūr** viii 651 (LIST OF BIOGRAPHIES. 18th cent.), Suppt. i 1778, Suppt. ii 2297 (18th cent.), **Calcutta** Madrasah 180 (1) (late 17th cent.), probably also **Ivanow** 275 (AH 1100 (?)/1688–9), **Ethé** 618 (not later than AD 1788), **Berlin** 71 (1) ("rec^{d} Juny [Jany ?] 1797 from Moonshy Sudder ul Deen"), **Rieu** ii p. 834 no. xix (foll. 166–70: evidently only a fragment or a drastic abridgment. Late 17th cent.).

1488. Ḥā[jjī ?] Ḥmd [= Aḥmad or Muḥammad ?] b. 'Alī b. al-Ḥājj Jamāl al-Dīn Ḥusain **al-Anṣārī**, a son of Zain al-Dīn 'Alī al-'Aṭṭār, the author of the *Ikhtiyārāt i Badī'ī*, a well-known work on materia medica, was born at Shīrāz in 760/1359. He had spent forty years in attendance upon his father, who died in 806/1403–4, and he had written works entitled *Miftāḥ al-kunūz*, on medicaments, *Dastūr al-muta'ākilīn*,[969] on sweetmeats, *Tuḥfat al-mulūk*, on intoxicating drinks, *Dastūr al-zirā'ah*, on agriculture, *Dastūr al-su'adā'*, on the sayings of sages, and some shorter treatises. [Autobiographical statements in the notice of his father at the end of the MS. described below.]

966 "Translated from the Arabic by 'Azīzī."

967 Ethé 618 is described as an abridgment or extract from Maqṣūd 'Alī's translation "made by Munshî Mîr Sayyid Ṣadr-aldîn bin Mîr Muḥammad Ṣādiḳ bin Mîr Muḥammad Amîn" On the ... first page Mr. Richard Johnson states that he has received this little book from Munshî Ṣadr aldîn (that is, from the compiler himself), being an extract from his common-place book, AD 1778." A note at the end of Berlin 71(1) describes the work as *jam' kardah i Saiyid Ṣadr al-Dīn az kutub i mu'tabar*. It may be doubted whether S. Ṣadr al-Dīn's contribution to the work extended beyond copying it into his commonplace book. All the manuscripts begin with the words given above.

968 I.e. doubtless Bīdar, now in the state of Ḥaidarābād.

969 *al-muta'akkilīn* according to Rieu, but this seems improbable.

Unidentified work, of which the first *qism* is divided into two *ḥarfs* ((1) on the value of learning. Notices of Pre-Islāmic philosophers, (2) meagre accounts of the lives and sayings of Muslim philosophers, beginning with Muḥammad and ʿAlī and ending (according to the preface)[970] with ʿAlāʾ al-Dīn Manṣūr, a physician whose brother ʿIzz al-Dīn Masʿūd is stated to have died in 813/1410–11 and one of his nephews in 817/1414–15, the latest date mentioned): **Rieu** ii 873*a* (a fragment containing *Qism* I and possibly a part of *Qism* II. Beg. *Qism i awwal dar faḍīlat i ʿilm u ḥikmat u tawārīkh i ḥukamā*,… 18th cent.).

1489. Mullā **Aḥmad** b. Naṣr Allāh **Tattawī**, who was murdered at Lahore in 996/1588, has already been mentioned no. 135 *supra*) as the chief author of the *Tārīkh i alfī*.

Khulāṣat al-ḥayāt, on the lives[971] and sayings of philosophers, written at the request of [Ḥakīm] Abū "lFatḥ b. ʿAbd al-Razzāq [Gīlānī, one of Akbar's physicians[972]] and divided, according to the preface, into a *fātiḥah* (5 introductory discourses), two *maqṣads* (on Pre-Islāmic and Islāmic philosophers respectively), and a *khātimah* (*dar bayān i madhāhib i millatain*), but probably left unfinished, since no MS. hitherto described extends beyond Socrates in *Maqṣad* i: **Upsala** Zettersté en 390 ("Theil I". AH 1037/1628), **Bānkīpūr** Suppt. i 1779 (AH 1078/1668), **I.O.** D.P. 639 (*Fātiḥah* and *Maqṣad* i. 17th cent.), **Āṣafīyah** i p. 318 no. 33, **Ivanow** Curzon 497 (*Fātiḥah* and *Maqṣad* i, defective and much damaged. Early 19th cent.), **Majlis** 541 (ends with Socrates), **Rieu** iii 1034*b* (description and some extracts only. AD 1851).

1490. ʿ**Abd al-Sattār b. Qāsim Lāhaurī** has already been mentioned (no. 205) as collaborator with Jerome Xavier (d. 1617) in the translation of the latter's biographies of Christ and the Twelve Apostles into Persian and (no. 356 (1), Abridgments (3)) as epitomator of Sharaf al-Dīn ʿAlī Yazdī's *Ẓafar-nāmah*.

Thamarat al-falāsifah (presumably identical with the "*Aḥwāl i Farangistān*", Rieu iii p. 1077*a*), an account of Greece and Rome and of the lives (doubtless more especially the sayings) of the Greek and

970 The last notice is in fact that of the author's father.

971 The contents of *Maqṣad* i give this work little claim to be regarded as biographical but, as in the earlier works of this kind, the biographical element would doubtless have been greater in the portion dealing with Islāmic times.

972 See *Āʾīn i Akbarī tr.* Blochmann pp. 424–5; *Maʾathir al-umarāʾ* i pp. 558–62, Beveridge's trans. pp. 107–10; Beale *Oriental biographical dictionary* under Abul-Fath Gilani.

Roman philosophers (cf. Sir E. Maclagan *The Jesuits and the Great Mogul*, London 1932, p. 218): **Mashhad** iii p. 78 ("*Tadhkirat al-ḥukamā*". Not later than AH 1145/1732–3), **Lindesiana** p. 177 no. 445 (AH 1185/1771), **Browne** Suppt. 770 ("*Samar al-falāsifah*", AH 1197/1783, King's 222), **B.M.** Or. 5893 (see Maclagan *op. cit.* p. 218), **Āṣafīyah** i p. 346 nos. 118 (AH 1236/1820–1), 169, **Patiala** Victoria Library (see Maclagan *op. cit.* p. 218).

1491. Hakīm al-Mamālik Mīrzā **ʿAlī-Naqī b. Ismāʿīl**, physician to Nāṣir al-Dīn Shāh Qājār, had a knowledge of French and had studied medicine and other subjects abroad (doubtless in France). He was also a poet.

Rūz-nāmah i Ḥakīm al-Mamālik: **Ṭihrān** 1286/1869–70 (see *Āṣafīyah* iii p. 350. Apparently identical with the *Ruz-nāmah* describing Nāṣir al-Dīn Shāh's visit to Khurāsān in 1867. See no. 439 *supra* and Additions and Corrections *infra*).

[*al-Maʾāthir wa-ʾl-āthār* p. 194.]

1492. APPENDIX.

(1) ***Aḥwāl i ḥukamāʾ***, "biographical notices and sayings of ancient philosophers," the first Idrīs, the last two Ibn Sabʿīn and Abū Naṣr M. b. M. al-Turk: **Bānkīpūr** Suppt. i 1986 foll. 83*a*–98*b*.

(2) ***Tadhkirat al-ḥukamāʾ***: **Rehatsek** p. 77 no. 16 (AH 1211/1796–7. "The book is not scarce, and may be had in the bazar." Probably therefore it is one of the works mentioned above.)

13.12 *Places (i.e. Inhabitants of Particular Towns, Provinces, or Countries*[973]*)*

13.12.1 Ādharbāyjān

1493. **M. ʿAlī Khān "Tarbiyat"** Tabrīzī, recently (AHS 1314/1935–6),[974] a Deputy in the Majlis, was presumably the proprietor of the Tarbiyat Library, which "lasted from AH 1316 to 1326 (= AD 1898–1908)", serving as a centre "of distribution and interchange for most of the Persian, Arabic, and Turkish papers published in Persia" and maintaining "epistolary and other relations with the chief educational centres".[975] Under the management of that Library appeared

973 References have been given to a number of works already described which may be regarded as dealing with the biography of particular localities. Such references could be multiplied, especially by the inclusion of works dealing with single saints.

974 See the first title-page of the *Dānishmandān i Ādharbāyjān* and Ḥasan Isfandiyārī's *taqrīẓ*.

975 *The press and poetry of modern Persia* p. 1.

in 1320–1/1903–4 the fortnightly scientific magazine *Ganjīnah i funūn*,[976] which published "Tarbiyat's" work *Hunar-āmūz*.[977] The date of the closure of the Library (1908) is doubtless the year in which "Tarbiyat" went into exile at Istānbūl,[978] from which place he sent to E. G. Browne, apparently in 1912, the manuscript of his work *Waraqī az daftar i tārīkh i maṭbūʿāt i Īrānī u Fārisī*, which the latter translated, enlarged, and published under the title *The press and poetry of modern Persia* (Cambridge 1914). ʿAbd al-ʿAzīz "Jawāhir al-Kalām" mentions him as the founder of two libraries, the Public Library (*Kitāb-khānah i ʿUmūmī*) at Tabrīz (about 7,000 volumes) and his own private library of about 5,000 volumes. A work of his entitled *Zād u būm*, a geography of Persia, is mentioned in *The press and poetry of modern Persia*, p. 163 no. 123.

Dānishmandān i Ādharbāyjān, a biographical dictionary of celebrities, mainly poets and scholars: **Ṭihrān** AHS 1314/1935–6. (For a review by Minorsky see *BSOS*. ix/1 (1937) pp. 251–3).

[Browne *The press and poetry of modern Persia*, pp. ix, 1–2, 130, 163, etc.; ʿAbd al-ʿAzīz "Jawāhir al-Kalām" *Kitāb-khānahā-yi Īrān* [Ṭihrān], AHS 1311/1932–3, pp. 91–2; Ḥasan Isfandiyārī's *taqrīẓ* prefixed to the *Dānishmandān i Ādharbāyjān*].

13.12.2 Aḥmadābād

1494. For the *Mirʾāt i Aḥmadī*, which was completed by ʿAlī Muḥammad Khān in 1175/1761, and of which the *khātimah* contains *inter alia* accounts of the saints and Saiyids buried in, or near, Aḥmadābād, see no. 984 *supra*.

1495. For the *Mukhbir al-auliyāʾ* of Rashīd al-Dīn Maudūd Lālā, which is concerned mainly with saints buried at Aḥmadābād, see no. 1411 (55) *supra*.

13.12.3 Amrōhah

1496. It was in 1296/1879 that Saiyid **M. Āl i Ḥasan** b. S. Nadhīr Aḥmad b. S. Imām al-Dīn Aḥmad Maudūdī Amrōhawī completed his:—

976 *Op. cit.* p. 130.
977 *Ibid.*
978 *Op. cit.* pp. x, 2 n. 1, 6.

Nukhbat al-tawārīkh, on the saints and other celebrated men of Amrōhah,[979] in a *muqaddimah* ((*a*) genealogical information concerning the patriarchs, etc., the Prophet and his family, (*b*) a sketch of the history of Amrōhah), four *bābs* ((1) the Saiyids, (2) the Shaikhs, (3) the Mughuls and Afghans, (4) the Kambōhs and Kalāls) and a *khātimah* (further saints, etc., *manṣabdārs*, the author's teachers and friends).

Edition: **Amrōhah** 1880°*.

13.12.4 Aurangābād

1497. For the (*Sawāniḥ*) of Sabzawārī, written shortly after 1188/1774 and dealing with the saints of Aurangābād, see no. 1369 *supra*.

13.12.5 Baihaq

1498. For the *Tārīkh i Baihaq*, which was completed in 563/1168 by ʿAlī b. Zaid al-Baihaqī and which is mainly biographical, see no. 466 (2) *supra*.

13.12.6 Balkh

1499. For the *Faḍā'il i Balkh*, an Arabic work which was completed in 610/1213 and translated into Persian at some date later than 676/1278 and of which the third section contains biographies of seventy famous *shaikhs* of Balkh and its neighbourhood, see Additions and Corrections ad no. 471 (471*a* (2)) *infra*.

1500. For the *Tārīkh i mazārāt i Balkh*, of M. Ṣāliḥ b. Amīr ʿAbd Allāh (AH 1006/1598), see no. 1299 *supra*, where another work (?) of the same kind is mentioned.

13.12.7 Barnāwah

1501. For the *Chishtīyah i bihishtīyah* of ʿAlā' al-Dīn M. Barnāwī, which was written about 1066/1655–6 and deals more especially with the Chishtīs of Barnāwah and Rāprī, see no. 1330 *supra*.

979 Amrōhah is an old town 19 miles W.N.W. of Murādābād. Several of the celebrities mentioned by Āl i Ḥasan are mentioned also in the official *Gazetteer of Moradabad* (Allahabad, 1911).

13.12.8 Benares

1502. For the *Riyāḍ al-wifāq* (a chronogram = 1229/1814) of Dhu 'l-Faqār 'Alī Khān "Mast", which is concerned mainly with contemporaries of the author connected with Calcutta and Benares, see no. 1191 *supra*.

13.12.9 Bhakkar (Bhak'har)

1503. For the *Manbaʿ al-ansāb*, an account of the Saiyids of Bhak'har written by S. Muʿīn al-Ḥaqq some time after 830/1426–7 and enlarged probably about the close of the 10/16th century by S. 'Alī Ghaḍanfar, see no. 1264 *supra*. The *Taḥrīr al-muʿtaqid* (no. 1261) and the *Ḥālāt i Shāh 'Uthmān Akbar* (no. 1270) are concerned with the same family.

13.12.10 Bihār

1504. For the *Tadhkirat al-kirām* of M. Abū 'l-Ḥayāt P'hulwārī, which was written in 1249/1833–4 and deals with Bihārī *shaikhs*, see no. 1384 *supra*.

1505. S. M. **Jawād Ḥusain.**

Tārīkh i Ḥasan, a short history of Islām in India, followed by notices of the Saiyids of Bihār: **Cawnpore** 1329/1912*.

13.12.11 Bījāpūr

1506. For the *Rauḍat al-auliyā'*, a *tadhkirah* of the saints of Bījāpūr, by M. Ibrāhīm, see no. 1411 (66) *supra*.

13.12.12 Bilgrām

1507. In 1110/1698–9 (according to the Āṣafiyah catalogue) S. **Junaid** b. S. Darwēsh M. Ḥātim **Bilgrāmī** composed his

Junaidīyah or *Nasab-nāmah i sādāt i Bilgrām u Bārhah*, on the genealogy of the Saiyids of Bilgrām[980] and Bārhah[981] **Rieu** iii 1021*b* (extracts only ? Circ. AD 1850), **Āṣafīyah** ii p. 1778 no. 115 (AH 1309/1891–2).

---

980 The genealogies of the Saiyids of Bilgrām form the subject of an Urdu work, *Rauḍat al-kirām shajarah i Sādāt i Bilgrām* (236 pp.), by S. Waṣī al-Ḥasan (Gōrak'hpūr 1920).

981 Cf. no. 1454 (1) footnote *supra*.

1508. For the *Maʾāthir al-kirām tārīkh i Bilgrām* completed in 1166/1752–3 by Ghulām-ʿAlī "Āzād" Bilgrāmī, see no. 1411 (66) *supra*. For the same author's *Sarw i āzād*, which includes some biographies of Bilgrāmīs, see no. 1162 (16) *supra*.

1509. **Ghulām-Ḥasan "Thamīn"** Ṣiddīqī Farshūrī[982] **Bilgrāmī** has already been mentioned no. 791 *supra*) as the author of an account of Aḥmad Shāh Abdālī's third invasion of India written in 1197/1783 at the request of Jonathan Scott.

Sharāʾif i ʿUthmānī, biographies of eminent Bilgrāmīs belonging to the ʿUthmānī clan, composed in 1179/1765–6 and written primarily to correct alleged mis-statements in "Āzād's" *Maʾāthir al-kirām* [which was completed in 1166/1752–3: see no. 1362 (2) *supra*]: **Ivanow** 277 (many blank spaces, AD 1875), **I.O.** 3913, **Āṣafīyah** iii p. 164 no. 202.

1510. For the *Tabṣirat al-nāẓirīn*, composed in 1182/1768 by Mīr S. Muḥammad b. ʿAbd al-Jalīl Bilgrāmī and dealing mainly with events in the lives of Bilgrāmī Saiyids, see no. 952 *supra*.

1511. Other works:—

(1) ***Musajjalāt fī taʾrīkh al-quḍāt***, on the Qāḍīs of Bilgrām, by Qāḍī Aḥmad Allāh Bilgrāmī, commonly known as (*ʿurf*) M. ʿUthmān b. Qāḍī M. Iḥsān, who, according to Raḥmān ʿAlī (p. 15), was Qāḍī of Bilgrām until 1196/1782: **I.O.** 3913*b*.

(2) ***Naẓm al-laʾālī fī nasab āl ʿAlāʾ al-Dīn al-ʿālī***, or, chronogrammatically, *Subḥat al-durr wa-ʾl-yawāqīt*, on the genealogy of the Saiyids of Bilgrām, by S. M. b. S. Ghulām-Nabī b. al-Saiyid al-shahīd al-musammā bi-ʾl-Arshad: **Aṣafīyah** iii p. 720.

13.12.13 Bukhārā etc.

1512. For the *Kitāb i Mullā-zādah*, which was written probably in the 9th/15th century by Aḥmad b. Maḥmūd called (*madʿū*) Muʿīn al-fuqarāʾ and which contains notices of shaikhs and others buried at Bukhārā, see no. 1272 *supra*.

1513. For the *Manāqib i mazārāt i Bukhārā-yi sharīf* see no. 1411 (49) *supra*.

For the *Ṭabaqāt i mashāyikh i Naqshbandīyah i Bukhārā* see no. 1411 (111) *supra*.

982 In the bibliography to the unsigned article on Bilgrām in the *Ency. Isl.* this word is [correctly ?] spelt Firshawrī. FRSHWR (vocalization ?) is an old form of the name Peshawar (cf. ʿIṣāmī *Futūḥ al-salāṭīn* p. 401, l. 7863 (also li. 7866, 7870), *Ṭabaqāt i Akbarī* i p. 37[3]), but this may have nothing to do with Ghulām-Ḥasan's *nisbah*.

1514. For the *Mudhakkir i aḥbāb* (a chronogram = 974/1566–7) of "Nithārī", which contains notices of 275 poets who lived in Bukhārā or its dependencies after the time of Mīr ʿAlī-Shīr, see no. 1102 *supra*.

1515. **ʿAbd al-Karīm b. Maḥmūd Qāḍī** b. Nūr al-Dīn M. Qāḍī, known as Qāḍī **Ikhtiyār**. began in 1009/1600–1:—

ʿAwālim al-asrār fī gharāʾib al-asfār (beginning: *Majmūʿah i ʿAwālim al-a. fī gh. al-a. az ṣādirāt i ʿawālim i āfāqī … u bayān i aḥwāl i akābir i maḥrūsah i Bukhārā*), an interesting account of travels in Transoxiana and Khurāsān, to Kābul, etc., together with biographies of distinguished men, *shaikhs*, poets, and others, who lived at Bukhārā in the author's time: **Ethé** 2723.

1516. For the *Tārīkh i Jahāngīrī*, which was begun in 1034/1625 by "Muṭribī" al-Aṣamm al-Samarqandī and which deals with poets of Transoxiana, see no. 1118 *supra*.

1517. For the *Tārīkh i Mīr Saiyid Sharīf Rāqim*, a collection of chronograms relating to kings, divines, men of letters, etc., who flourished in Central Asia from the birth of Tīmūr in 736/1336 to 1054/1644–5, see no. 506 *supra*.

1518. For the *Maṭlab al-ṭālibīn* of Abū 'l-ʿAbbās M. Ṭālib, which was written about 1056/1646 and deals with Jūybārī *shaikhs*, see no. 1326 *supra*.

1519. For the *Thamarāt al-mashāyikh* of S. Zindah ʿAlī, which was written towards the end of the eleventh/seventeenth century and deals with Central Asian *shaikhs* of various orders, see no. 1335 *supra*.

1520. For the *Tuḥfat al-aḥbāb* of Raḥmat Allāh "Wāḍiḥ", which deals with Central Asian poets of the nineteenth century, see no. 1230 *supra*.

1521. For the *Afḍal al-tadhkār*, notices of Central Asian poets of the nineteenth century written in 1322/1904 by "Afḍal" Makhdūm i Pīrmastī, see no. 1234 *supra*.

13.12.14 Calcutta

1522. For the *Riyāḍ al-wifāq* (a chronogram = 1229/1814) of Dhū 'l-Faqār ʿAlī Khān "Mast", which is concerned mainly with contemporaries of the author connected with Calcutta and Benares, see no. 1191 *supra*.

13.12.15 The Carnatic

1523. For the *Guldastah i Karnāṭak* (a chronogram = 1210/1795–6) of "Rā'iq", see no. 1200 *supra.*

1524. For the *Ṣubḥ i waṭan*, completed in 1257/1841, ostensibly by Nawwāb M. Ghauth Khān, see no. 1209 (1) *supra.*

1525. For the *Ishārāt i Bīnish* (a chronogram = 1265/1848–9), see no. 1217.

13.12.16 Chittagong

1526. **'Abd al-'Alī Islāmābādī** b. Minnat 'Alī was born in 1262/1846, presumably at Chittagong. Educated at the Calcutta Madrasah, he was appointed Professor of Persian in that institution and subsequently became Professor of Arabic in the Hoogly Madrasah.

Ṣaḥīfat al-a'māl wa-Mir'āt al-aḥwāl, a history of Islāmābād (i.e. Chittagong) and its famous men: **Āgrah** [1889°] (pp. 276).

[Raḥmān 'Alī p. 124; M. Idrīs p. 47.]

13.12.17 Daulatābād

1527. For the *Rauḍat al-auliyā'*, which was written in 1161/1748 by Mīr Ghulām-'Alī "Āzād" Bilgrāmī and which is concerned with ten saints buried in the cemetery called Rauḍah or Khuldābād near Daulatābād, see no. 1362 (1) *supra.*

13.12.18 The Deccan

1528. For the *Tuḥfat al-shu'arā'*, written in 1165/1751–2 by Afḍal Bēg Khān Qāqshāl Aurangābādī and dealing with poets of the Deccan who flourished under Niẓām al-Mulk I, see no. 1151 *supra.*

13.12.19 Delhi

1529. For the *Kalimāt al-ṣādiqīn*, completed in 1023/1614 by M. Ṣādiq Kashmīrī Hamadānī and dealing with saints buried at Delhi, see no. 1311 *supra.*

1530. For the *Rauḍah i aqṭāb* (a chronogram = 1124/1712) of M. Bulāq, which is concerned with Quṭb al-Dīn Bakhtyār Kākī and some saints buried near him, see no. 1341 *supra.*

1531. For the *Dhikr i jamīʿ i auliyāʾ i Dihlī* (a chronogram = 1140/1727–8) of M. Ḥabīb Allāh Akbarābādī, see no. 1349 *supra*.

1532. Nawwāb **Dargāh-Qulī Khān Sālār-Jang** Muʾtaman al-Daulah [afterwards Muʾtaman al-Mulk] b. Khānadān-Qulī Khān b. Naurōz-Qulī Khān was the great-great-grandson of Khānadān-Qulī Khān Dhū ʾl-Qadr Turkmān Būrbūr, who settled in India in the reign of Shāh-Jahān. Born in 1122/1710 at Sangamnēr,[983] at which place his father was for a time *Waqāʾiʿ-nigār* (*Khizānah* p. 222 antepenult.), he entered the service of Nawwāb Niẓām al-Mulk Āṣaf-Jāh and at the age of twenty became one of the Nawwāb's suite. He accompanied Āṣaf-Jāh to Delhi [in 1150/1737] and while there wrote the *Risālah i Sālar-Jang*. In the reign of Nawwāb Ṣalābat-Jang [1164–75/1750–62] he was given the rank of *Shash-hazārī*. the title of Muʾtaman al-Daulah, and the Governorship (*Ṣūbah-dārī*) of Aurangābād. Nawwāb Niẓām-ʿAlī [1175–1217/1762–1802] promoted him to the rank of *Haft-hazārī* and conferred upon him the *Māhīmarātib* and the title of Muʾtaman al-Mulk. In 1179/1765 he was dismissed from the Governorship of Aurangābād, and on 18 Jumādā I 1180/22 October 1766 he died.

(***Risālah i Sālār-Jang***), or (***Ābādī i Dihlī***), (beg. *Waqtī kih Nawwāb Dargāh-Qulī Khān ... ba-rafāqat i Nawwāb Niẓām al-Mulk*), an account of Delhi, its buildings, pleasure-grounds, festivals, etc., and its contemporary *shaikhs*, poets, singers, and dancers: **Rieu** ii 858*b* (apparently either AH 1192/1778 or 1200/1786), **Rehatsek** p. 218 no. 11 (AH 1214/1799), **Ross and Browne** 240 (transcribed from the preceding MS. in 1280/1864).

[*Khizānah i ʿāmirah* pp. 221–4; *Ḥadīqat al-ʿālam* ii p. 283 (summarized in Rieu ii p. 858*b*).]

13.12.20 Fārs

1533. For "Furṣat's" *Āthār i ʿAjam*, which contains numerous notices of celebrities connected with Fārs and other parts of south-western Persia, see no. 465 *supra*.

13.12.21 Gujrāt (Gujarat)

1534. For the *Gulzār i abrār* completed in, or about, 1022/1613 by M. Ghauthī and containing biographies of saints, many of whom were Gujrātīs, see no. 1310 *supra*.

---

983 *Presumably SNGMYR* (*Khizānah* p. 223[1]) should be so emended. Sangamnēr is 49 miles N.W. of Aḥmadnagar.

1535. For the *Makhzan i shuʿarā*ʾ (a chronogram = 1268/1851–2), which is a *tadhkirah* of the Urdu poets of Gujrāt by Nūr al-Dīn “Fāʾiq”, see no. 1218 *supra*.
See also PLACES (2) AHMADĀBĀD above.

13.12.22 Ḥaidarābād

1536. For the *Mishkāt al-nubuwwah*, an account of the saints of Ḥaidarābād, by S. ʿAlī, see no. 1411 (54) *supra*.
See also PLACES (18) THE DECCAN.

13.12.23 Harāt

1537. For the *Maqṣad al-iqbāl al-sulṭānīyah* of ʿAbd Allāh b. ʿAbd al-Raḥmān al-Ḥusainī see no. 469 *supra*. Presumably this is the same work as *Mazārāt i Harāt* by ʿA. A. b. ʿA. al-R. Ḥusainī, Harāt AHS 1310/1931–2 [Lescot].

13.12.24 India

1538. The Arabic work *Subḥat al-marjān fī āthār Hindustān* written in 1177/1763–4 by Mīr Ghulām-ʿAlī “Āzād” Bilgrāmī has already been described (no. 1162, Arabic works (2) *supra*). It can relevantly be mentioned here, since the second *faṣl*, containing biographies of Indian scholars, has been translated into Persian (*see* no. 1162, Arabic works (2), last par. *supra*).

1539. M. ʿAbd al-Shakūr commonly called **Raḥmān ʿAlī** b. Ḥakīm Shēr ʿAlī[984] was born in 1244/1829 at Aḥmadābād Nārah. After his father's death he was brought up by an elder brother at Fatḥpūr. In 1267/1851 he went to the Central Indian State of Rēwān (otherwise Rewa), where the eldest son of the Hindu Rājah, disliking his name ʿAbd al-Shakūr, changed it to Raḥmān ʿAlī. Having held various offices, including those of Civil Judge and Magistrate of the First Class, he became in 1284/1867–8 a member of the Council of the State. In 1887 he received from the Government of India the title of Khān Bahādur. He wrote a number of works, most of them in Urdu.

Tadhkirah i ʿulamāʾ i Hind, or *Tuḥfat al-fuḍalāʾ fī tarājim al-kumalāʾ*, biographies of ancient and modern Indian scholars:

Edition: **Lucknow** 1894°*.

[Raḥmān ʿAlī pp. 258–61; M. Idrīs p. 26.]

984 For a notice of Ḥakīm Shēr ʿAlī see Raḥmān ʿAlī p. 89.

13.12.25 Istānbūl

1540. For the *Ḥujjat al-abrār*, a *mathnawī* completed in 996/1588 by S. Murshid and dealing with the orders of dervishes at Istānbūl and their heads, see no. 1295 *supra*.

13.12.26 Jā'is

1541. For ʿĀbid Ḥusain's *Tārīkh i Jā'is* see no. 953 *supra*.

13.12.27 Jaunpūr

1542. **Khair al-Dīn M. Ilāhābādi**, who died about 1827 (see no. 687 *supra*), has already been mentioned as the author of works entitled *ʿIbrat-nāmah* (see no. 805 *supra*), *Jaunpūr-nāmah* (see no. 919 *supra*), *Guwāliyār-nāmah* (see no. 997 *supra*) and *Tuḥfah i tāzah* (no. 923).

Tadhkirat al-ʿulamā', completed on 25th September, 1801 (15 Jumādā I AH 1216), and containing biographies of 28 scholars connected with Jaunpūr together with that of the author, which forms the *Khātimah*: **Ivanow** 203 (19th cent.), **I.O.** 4028 (transcribed in 1903 from the preceding MS.).

Edition with English translation: *Tazkirat-ul-ʿUlama, or, A memoir of the learned men (of Jaunpur) by Mawlana Khairud-Din Muhammad of Jaunpur, edited ... with English translation, notes, etc., by Muhammad Sana Ullah*, **Calcutta** 1934‡.

1543. Munshī **M. Mahdī** b. Khalīl Aḥmad was the head of an old family, which had held the zamīndārī of Mariahu (Maṛiyāhū, Maḍiyāhū, or Manḍiyāhū) near Jaunpūr and the hereditary office of *Qāḍī* since the time of Akbar. He was *Taḥṣīldār* at Mariahu during the Mutiny and protected the treasury and records. He was still living in 1888.

Tadhkirah i Mahdī or (*mulaqqab bah*) *Baḥr al-marām*,[985] a metrical autobiography: **Allahabad** 1888°*.

[*Jaunpūr District Gazetteer* 1908, p. 104.]

1544. S. **Nūr al-Dīn** "Zaidī" **Ẓafarābādī** Jaunpūrī indicates by a chronogram that 1881 was the year in which he composed the first part of his *Tajallī i nūr*.

---

985 This is what the author himself calls the work in the last line.

Tajallī i nūr or (*ma'ruf bah*) *Tadhkirah i mashāhīr i Jaunpūr*, biographies of the famous men of Jaunpūr in three *shigarf-nāmahs* ((1) saints and mystics, (2) scholars and poets, (3) amīrs).

Edition: Pt I, **Jaunpūr** 1889*, Pt. II, **Jaunpūr** 1900°*. It seems possible that Part III (amīrs) was never written.

See also PLACES (43) ẒAFARĀBĀD.

13.12.28 Kāshghar

1545. For the *Tadhkirah i Khwājagān*, a Turkī work written in 1182/1768–9 by M. Ṣādiq Kāshgharī, see no. 1366 *supra*.

1546. For the *Majma' al-muḥaqqiqīn*, a history of the Khwājahs of Kāshghar to 1208/1793–4 by M. Ṣādiq Yārkandī, see no. 1377 *supra*.

13.12.29 Kashmīr

1547. For the *Rīshī-nāmah* of Bāhā Naṣīb Kashmīrī, who died in 1047/1637, see no. 1312 *supra*.

1548. For the *Rīshī-nāmah* of "Bahā" see no. 1313 *supra*.

1549. For the *Khawāriq al-sālikīn* (a chronogram = 1109/1697–8), anecdotes of early Ṣūfīs of Kashmīr, etc., by an anonymous author, see no. 1340 *supra*.

1550. For the *Wāqi'āt i Kashmīr* (a chronogram = 1148/1735–6) of M. A'ẓam, which is devoted mainly to biographies of the saints, poets, and scholars of Kashmīr, see no. 880 (1) *supra*.

1551. For the *Taḥā'if al-abrār*, which was completed in 1321/1903–4 by Muḥyī 'l-Dīn "Miskīn" and which deals mainly with saints and other celebrities of Kashmir, see no. 1409 *supra*.

1552. For the *Rauḍat al-abrār* of Muḥammad al-Dīn Lāhaurī see no. 1411 (65) *supra*.

For spiritual pedigrees of certain *shaikhs of Kashmīr* see no. 1411 (5) and no. 1411 (109) *supra*.

13.12.30 Khurāsān

1553. For the *Maṭlaʿ al-shams of M. Ḥasan Khān Marāghī,* which includes notices of Khurāsānī celebrities, see no. 471 *supra.*

13.12.31 Kōl

1554. For the *Ashjār al-jamāl* of M. b. Yār-Muḥammad Kōlawī, which includes notices of some Ṣūfīs of Kōl, see no. 1355 *supra.*

13.12.32 Lucknow

1555. For *al-Aghṣān al-arbaʿah,* Walī Allāh Lak'hnawī's life of Aḥmad Anwār al-Ḥaqq Farangī-Maḥallī and other descendants of Quṭb al-Dīn Sihālawī, the ancestor of the ʿulamāʾ of Farangī Maḥall, see no. 1401 *supra.*

13.12.33 Murādābād

1556. For the *Anwār al-ʿārifīn* of M. Ḥusain Murādābādī, which includes notices of some Ṣūfīs buried at Murādābād, see no. 1392 *supra.*

13.12.34 Rāprī

1557. For the *Chishtīyah i bihishtīyah* of ʿAlāʾ al-Dīn M. Barnāwī, which was written about 1066/1655–6 and deals more especially with the Chishtīs of Barnāwah and Rāprī, see no. 1330 *supra.*

13.12.35 Samarqand

1558. For *al-Qand fī maʿrifat ʿulamāʾ Samarqand,* see no. 496 *supra.*
For a *Risālah i buzurgān i Samarqand* see no. 1411 (70) *supra.*

13.12.36 Shīrāz

1559. Muʿīn al-Dīn Abū 'l-Qāsim **Junaid** b. Najm al-Dīn Abī 'l-Fatḥ Maḥmūd al-ʿUmarī **al-Shīrāzī** was the son of a devout Ṣūfī and preacher who died in 740/1339–40 and the great-grandson of Ṣadr al-Dīn al-Muẓaffar b. M. al-ʿUmarī al-ʿAdawī, author of the *Marmūzāt al-ʿishrīn* (Ḥ. Kh. v p. 500) and many other works, who died in 688/1289. He was himself a *khaṭīb* and must have lived to a very advanced age.

Shadd al-izār fī ḥaṭṭ al-auzār ʿan zuwwār al-mazār, usually called *Hazār mazār*, an Arabic work on the celebrated men buried at Shīrāz written probably in 791/1389, the latest date mentioned: Ḥ. Kh. iv p. 16, **Rieu** Arabic Suppt. 677 (19th cent.), **Majlis** 559.

Persian translation: ***Multamas al-aḥibbā khāliṣ min al-riyāʾ*** made by the author's son ʿĪsā b. Junaid al-ʿAdawī: **Rieu** i 346*b* (18th cent.).

13.12.37 Shūshtar

1560. For the *Tadhkirah i Shūshtarīyah* of S. ʿAbd Allāh b. Nūr al-Dīn Shūshtarī, which includes notices of celebrated men connected with Shūshtar, see no. 486 *supra*.

1561. **ʿAbd al-Laṭīf** b. Abī Ṭālib b. Nūr al-Dīn b. Niʿmat Allāh al-Ḥusainī al-Mūsawī **al-Shūshtarī**, a Nūrī Saiyid and the nephew of ʿAbd Allāh b. Nūr al-Dīn Shushtarī (for whom see no. 486 *supra*), was born in 1172/1758–9. After visiting Shīrāz, Kirmānshāhān, and Baghdād he left Baṣrah in 1202/1787–8 for Bengal. In 1211/1796–7 he went to Lucknow and in 1214/1799–1800 to Ḥaidarābād, where in 1215–16/1800–2 he wrote his *Tuḥfat al-ʿālam*, dedicated to Mīr-ʿĀlam (for whom see no. 1034 *supra*). In 1216/1801–2 he went to Bombay, where he met Abū Ṭālib Khān Landanī (for whom see no. 173 *supra*), and in 1219/1804–5 he returned to Ḥaidarābād, where he died in 1220/1806 (see Rieu Suppt. 84 ii).

Tuḥfat al-ʿālam, a narrative of the author's life and travels preceded by an account of Shūshtar, of some neighbouring places and of the Nūrī Saiyids and followed, in some MSS., by an appendix, *Dhail al-Tuḥfah*, written in 1219/1804–5 at the request of Āqā Aḥmad b. M. ʿAlī Bihbahānī (for whom see no. 1575 *infra*): **Būhār** 95 (autograph (?), AH 1214/1799 (?)), **Edinburgh** 85 (AH 1222/1807) **Bodleian** 323 (AH 1229/1814), **Bānkīpūr** Suppt. i 1777 (AH 1229/1814), **Ivanow** Curzon 98 (defective at both ends. Contains part of the *Dhail*. Early 19th cent.), **Rieu** i 383*a* (contains the *Dhail*. Early 19th cent.), Suppt. 84 ii (contains the *Dhail*. AH 1258/1842), **Leningrad** Univ. 1101 (AH 1255/1839. See Romaskewicz p. 4), **I.O.** 4624 (AH 1258/1842. See Arberry in *JRAS*. 1939 p. 389), **Ross and Browne** 238 (circ. AD 1864), **Blochet** i 646 (contains the *Dhail*. 19th cent.), **Āṣafīyah** i p. 232 no. 634, **Berlin** 98 (contains the *Dhail*), **Majlis** 685 (?), **Rehatsek** p. 69 no. 5.

Editions: **Bombay** 1263/1847 (cf. Rieu i 383*b*, Zenker i p. 61, and Mashhad iii p. 118. In the last work Ḥaidarābād is given as the place of printing); **Ḥaidarābād** n.d.°; place ? 1297/1880 (Āṣaf. i p. 232 no. 870).

Analyses of the work: (1) Rehatsek pp. 70–1. (2) Rieu i pp. 383–4.

List of 21 poets and theologians whose biographies are given in the work: Ivanow-Curzon p. 101.

13.12.38 Sinandij

1562. For the *Ḥadīqah i Amān-Allāhī*, notices of the poets of Sinandij completed in 1265/1848–9 by ʿAbd Allāh "Raunaq", see no. 1216 *supra*.

13.12.39 Sind

1563. For the *Ḥadīqat al-auliyāʾ* completed in 1016/1607–8 by ʿAbd al-Qādir b. Hāshim, see no. 1306 *supra*.

1564. For the *Maqālat al-shuʿarāʾ* (a chronogram = 1174/1760–1) of ʿAlī Sher "Qāniʿ" Tattawī see no. 1158 *supra*.

1565. For the same author's *Tuḥfat al-kirām* (a chronogram = 1180/1766–7), the third volume of which is concerned to a large extent with celebrities of Sind, see no. 828 (1) *supra*.

1566. For the same author's *Maklī-nāmah* see no. 1373 (2) *supra*.

1567. For the *Tuḥfat al-ṭāhirīn*, written in 1194/1780 by M. Aʿẓam T'hattawī, see no. 1370 *supra*.

13.12.40 Tabrīz

1568. For the *Rauḍah i aṭhār* of "Ḥashrī" Tabrīzī see no. 1303 *supra*.

13.12.41 Ṭihrān

1569. For the *Jannat al-naʿīm* of M. Bāqir Ṭihrānī, see no. 1402 *supra*.

13.12.42 Yazd

1570. For the *Jāmiʿ i Mufīdī*, which in its third *mujallad* contains numerous notices of famous men of Yazd, see no. 461 *supra*. M. Mufīd Mustaufī wrote also -

An autobiographical memoir "very rich in words and poor in facts" extending over the years 1077–85/1666–75 (beg.: *Ḥ. u s. i bī-qiyās Mālik al-mulkī rā kih rifʿat*): **Bodleian** 423 (91 foll.).

1571. For the *Tārīkh i Yazd* of ʿAbd al-Ḥusain "Āyatī", which was completed in 1317/1938–9 and which contains biographies of many Yazdī celebrities, especially poets, see Additions & Corrections ad 457 (457*d*) *infra*.

1572. S. **Muḥammad ʿAlī b. S. Jaʿfar Yazdī** after twenty years of unprofitable study in his birthplace Yazd and twenty years of wandering in Persia, Turkey, Arabia, Turkistan, and the Deccan settled in 1226/1811 at Sūrat. He had spent nearly twenty years in service under British patrons (Wm. Forbes. Judge at Sūrat, J. Romer, J. Sutherland[986]) when in 1244/1827 he completed his *Mīzān al-akhlāq* and dedicated it to Sir John Malcolm, the Governor of Bombay.

Mīzān al-akhlāq, a record of the author's life and a eulogy of British rule in India: **Rieu** i 388 (AH 1244/1827).

13.12.43 Ẓafarābād

1573. S. ʿ**Abd al-Aḥad** b. S. Barakat ʿAli **Ẓafarābādī** was living in 1914 and himself corrected the proofs of his *Maẓhar al-aḥadīyah*.

Maẓhar al-aḥadīyah fī bayān al-ansāb [*sic*] ***al-sādāt al-Zaidīyah***, on the genealogy of the Zaidī Saiyids of Ẓafarābād (4¾ miles S.E. of Jaunpūr) from Ādam to the author's time.

Edition: **Jaunpūr** 1914°*.

13.13 *Shīʿites*

1574. Qāḍī S. **Nūr Allāh "Nūrī"**[987] b. S. Sharīf b. S. Nūr Allāh Ḥusainī Marʿashī **Shūshtarī** was born at Shūshtar[988] in 956/1549 (?).[989] In early manhood (*fī mabādiʾ al-shabāb*[990]) he went to Mashhad and he subsequently settled in India.

986 For the last-named see Buckland's *Dictionary of Indian biography*.

987 *Dar fann i shāʿirī kamāl i qudrat u mahārat dāsht takhalluṣ i wai Nūrī būd dar jawāb i qaṣīdah i S. Ḥasan i Ghaznawī qaṣīdaʾī guftah kih īn chand bait az ānjāst*: *Shukr i Khudā kih nūr i ilāhīst rahbaram*, etc. (*Riyāḍ al-shuʿaraʾ*; as quoted in *Nujūm al-samāʾ* p. 12). The author of the *Nujūm al-samāʾ* goes on to say *Rāqim al-ḥurūf rā bisyārī az ashʿār i ābdār i ān sulālat al-akhyār ba-naẓar rasīdah*. Cf. Badāʾūnī iii p. 137^{16}: *ṭabʿ i naẓmī dārad u ashʿār i dil-nishīn mī-gūyad*. No *dīwān* or other collection of his poems seems to be recorded in the catalogues, but the list of his works in the *Nujūm al-samāʾ* includes a *dīwān i qaṣāʾid* (p. 16 antepenult.) and a *dīwān i ashʿār* (p. 17^{7}).

988 *Majālis al-muʾminīn* p. 31, l. 10 from foot (*dar ān-diyār i faiḍ-āthār maulid i īn khāksār ast*), *Iḥqāq al-ḥaqq, khātimah*, quoted in *Nujūm al-samāʾ* p. 10 (*idh baʿda mā rakibtu ghārib al-ightirāb fī mabādiʾ al-shabāb li-taḥsīl al-ḥikam wa-takmīl al-fuyūḍ wa-ʾl-niʿam min waṭanī Shūshtar al-maḥrūsah ilā ʾl-Mashhad al-muqaddasat al-Riḍawīyat al maʾnūsah ramānī zamānī ilā ʾl-Hind al-manḥūsah qāmat tilka ʾl-shauhāʾ al-maʾyūsah ʿalā ʾzdiyād ghammī*, etc.).

989 *Nujūm al-samāʾ* p. 13^{2}, *Shahīd i thālith* p. 4. It is not clear whether this date has good authority.

990 See the passage from the *Iḥqāq al-ḥaqq* quoted in the second previous footnote. Mirzā M. Hādī says, on the authority of a note in an old MS. of the *Masāʾib al-Nawāṣib*, that he went to Mashhad in 979/1571–2. In that year he must have reached the age of twenty-three, if 956 is the correct date for his birth.

He was there apparently in 992/1584, if not earlier, since his work *al-Jalālīyah*[991] completed in that year (I.Ḥ. 775) is stated by I'jāz Ḥusain to have been written in the time of Jalāl al-Dīn M. Akbar Bahādur, Sulṭān of Delhi, a statement based doubtless on the author's own words. In Rajab 993/July 1585[992] he began at Lahore his best known work, the *Majālis al-mu'minīn*. In 995/1587 he wrote and dedicated to the Khān i Khānān 'Abd al-Raḥīm Khān[993] *al-'Asharat al-kāmilat al-Khān-i-Khānānīyah* (I Ḥ 2116).

It must have been in 994/1586 or 995/1587[994] that Akbar, to whom he had been presented by Ḥakīm Abū 'l-Fatḥ Gīlānī,[995] appointed him, though a Shī'ite, *Qāḍī* of Lahore in place of the aged Sh. Mu'īn, who after falling down through infirmity in the imperial *darbār* had been retired and who died in 995/1587.[996] 'Abd al-Qādir Badā'ūnī speaks in high praise of his integrity as a judge, his strict control of corrupt *muftīs* and *muḥtasibs*, and his personal piety and learning. His last years seem to have been spent in Āgrah, since it was there that he completed his *Iḥqāq al-ḥaqq* in 1014/1605 and there that he was flogged to death by order of Jahāngīr on 18 Jumādā ii 1019/7 Sept. 1610. Authorities disagree concerning the precise reason for his execution. According to the *Amal al-āmil* (p. 73[6]) he was put to death *bi-sabab ta'līf Iḥqāq al-ḥaqq*, and this may well be correct. Not only does that work indicate a fanatical hatred of Sunnism, but as Horovitz has shown, it contains at least one passage which Jahāngīr might have considered personally offensive. The statement in the *Riyāḍ al-shu'arā'* that the cause of his undoing was the evidence of his Shī'ism provided by the *Majālis al-mu'minīn* is highly improbable. As Horovitz observes, his Shī'ism was no secret[997] and would in itself have been no sufficient ground for execution.[998] Another account says that he incurred Jahāngīr's wrath by a disparaging remark about the latter's patron saint Sh. Salīm Chishtī.[999] In any

991 Presumably so called in allusion to Akbar's *laqab*.

992 Cf. Rieu i. p. 338*a*, where it is recorded that "at the end [of Add. 23,541, Rieu i p. 337*a*] is a marginal note, apparently transcribed from the author's autograph, stating that the work had been commenced in Lahore, in Rajab, A H. 993, and completed on the 23rd of Zulka'dah, AH 1010.

993 For whom see no. 698, Persian translations (3) and no. 711 2nd par. *supra*.

994 Akbar reached Lahore on 27 May, 1586 (see *Akbar-nāmah* tr. Beveridge iii p. 748) and he was there until 1589 (*ibid.* pp. 817–18).

995 For whom see no. 1489 2nd par. *supra*. He was a brother of Ḥakīm Humām, who has been mentioned in no. 135 1st par. *supra*.

996 Badā'ūnī iii p. 96.

997 Cf. Badā'ūnī iii p. 137: *agarchih Shī'ī-madhhab ast.*

998 There were, of course, many Shī'ites among the prominent men of Jahāngīr's time in India.

999 Cf. *JASB*. 1875 p. 116.

case Nūr Allāh is regarded by the Shīʿites as a martyr and those in India call him *al-Shahīd al-thālith*.[1000]

Of his numerous works the lists given in the *Nujūm al-samāʾ* and in M. Hādī's *Shahīd i thālith* contain 89 and 109 titles respectively. They include a number of *ḥawāshī* on well-known text-books, but few of them seem to have become popular. Concerning those mentioned by Brockelmann (*Sptbd.* ii pp. 607–8) it may be noted that the *Maṣāʾib al-nawāṣib* (IH 2954) is preserved also at the India Office (Arab. MSS. Cat. ii no. 2158) and a Persian translation of it by M. Ashraf at Mashhad (I *fṣl.* i no. 260), the *Iḥqāq al-ḥaqq* (IH 111) also at the India Office (Arab. MSS. Cat. ii no. 2149), the British Museum (Ellis-Edwards p. 8), Bānkīpūr (x 623), and the R.A.S.B. (Ashraf ʿAlī, Arab. Cat. p. 23. 3 copies), and a Persian translation of it at Bānkīpūr (xiv 1332), and the *Ḥāshiyah ʿalā tafsīr al-Baiḍāwī* also at Calcutta (A.S.B. Govt. Coll. 1903–7 p. 16). The *Sirāj al-qulūb wa-ʿilāj al-dhunūb* mentioned by Brockelmann as a work of Nūr Allāh's is by Zain al-Dīn al-Maʿbarī (cf. Sarkis *Dictionnaire encyclopédique de bibliographie arabe* col. 1762). Nūr Allāh's annotations on the fifth *maqṣad* (*al-Imāmah*) of al-Qūshjī's commentary (*al-Sharḥ al-jadīd*, Brockelmann i p. 509[17], *Sptbd.* i p. 926[12]) on Naṣīr al-Dīn al-Ṭūsī's *Tajrīd al-ʿaqāʾid*) are preserved at the India Office (Loth 471 xv). Badāʾūnī describes Nūr Allāh as *ṣāḥib i taṣānīf i lāʾiqah*, but he specifies only a *tauqīʿ* "beyond all praise" (*kih az ḥaiyiz i taʿrīf u tauṣīf bīrūn-ast*) on the undotted[1001] *tafsīr* of "Faiḍī".

Majālis al-muʾminīn, begun in Rajab 993/1585 at Lahore and completed on 23 Dhū 'l-Qaʿdah 1010/1602,[1002] biographies of eminent Shīʿites (including a number who according to the author passed as Sunnites though they were really Shīʿites practising *taqīyah*) divided into a

1000 That the third place among the martyrs was still regarded as vacant by some at least of the Shīʿites of Persia in the 19th century is shown by the fact that the title *Shahīd i thālith* was given to Ḥājjī Mullā M. Taqī Burghānī, who was assassinated by a Bābī in 1848 (sec *Qiṣaṣ al-ʿulamāʾ* p. 19 seq.; *Nujūm al-samāʾ* pp. 407–11; *Aḥsan al-wadīʿah* pp. 30–5; *Tārīkh i jadīd* pp. 274–80; Browne *Lit. Hist*, iv p. 421; Brockelmann *Sptbd.* ii p. 829; etc.). For the *Shahīd i awwal* see *Majālis al-muʾminīn* p. 249; *Luʾluʾatā 'l-Baḥrain* pp. 142–8; Brockelmann i 108, *Sptbd.* ii p. 131 and for the *Shahīd i thānī* no. 1582 (3) *infra*. In the *Nujūm al-samāʾ* p. 330, the title *Shahīd i rābiʿ* is given to Mīrzā M. Mahdī b. Hidāyat Allāh Mūsawī Iṣfahānī Mashhadī.

1001 *Tauqīʿī bar tafsīr i muhmal i Sh. Faiḍī nawishtah.* Several orientalists have misunderstood the word *muhmal* and spoken of the "worthless" *tafsīr* of "Faiḍī". The peculiarity of "Faiḍī's" *tafsīr*, the *Sawāṭiʿ al-ilhām* (Brockelmann ii p. 417, *Sptbd.* ii p. 610), is that it consists entirely of words containing no dotted (*manqūṭ*) letters. His *Mawārid al-kilam wa-silk durar al-ḥikam* is another specimen of this kind of composition.

1002 The authority for these dates is a marginal note "apparently transcribed from the author's autograph" at the end of the B.M. MS. Add. 23, 541. Mirzā M. Hādī gives 990/1582 as the date of composition, and so does E. G. Browne (on what authority ?).

fātiḥah (on the term Shīʿah) and twelve *majālis* ((1) places with Shīʿite associations, p. 11, (2) some Shīʿite tribes and families, p. 52, (3) Shīʿite contemporaries of the Prophet, p. 66, (4) Shīʿites of the next generation (Tabiʿūn), p. 118, (5) Shīʿite scholars of the succeeding generations, p. 141, (6) Ṣūfīs, p. 255, (7) philosophers, p. 329, (8) Shīʿite kings and 16 Shīʿite dynasties, p. 354, (9) governors, generals, etc., p. 420, (10) *wazīrs* and calligraphists,[1003] p. 433, (11) Arab poets, p. 458, (12) Persian poets, p. 496): IH 2738, **I.O.** D.P. 745 (AH 1016/1608), 732 (breaks off in *Majlis* v. AH 1051/1641–2 (earlier part only)), **Ethé** 704 (n.d.), 2829 ii (fragments), **I.O.** 3834, 3869, **Lindesiana** p. 207 no. 363 (circ. AD 1600), **Bānkīpūr** vii 720 (AH 1045/1635), 721 (18th cent.), **Berlin** 601 (AH 1051/1641), 602 (defective), **Leningrad** Univ. 1039 (AH 1052/1642–3. See Romaskewiez p. 13), **Mashhad** iii p. 100 (AH 1054/1644–5), **Majlis** 556 (AH 1058/1648), **Rieu** i 337a (17th cent.), 338*a* (17th cent.), 338*a* (17th cent.), 338*b* (17th cent.), **Ivanow** 276 (1st 5 *majālis*. 17th cent.), 1st Suppt. 773 (last 6 *majālis*. AH 1077/1667), *Bodleian* 367 (n.d.), 368 (AH 1102/1690) 369 (n.d.), 370 (n.d.), **Blochet** i 429 (AH 1104/1692), 430 (defective at end. 17–18th cent.), **Edinburgh** 244 (AH 1157/1744, copied from a MS. of 1028/1618), **Asʿad** 1280, **ʿUmumīyah** 5148.

Editions: **Ṭihrān** 1268/1852° (unpaginated), 1299/1881–2‡.

[Biography of his grandfather, S. Nūr Allāh b. M.-Shāh Shūshtarī, in *Majālis al-muʾminīn* pp. 223–5; brief autobiographical passage in *Iḥqāq al-ḥaqq, khātimah* (quoted in Goldziher's *Beiträge zur Literaturgeschichte* (see below) pp. 486–8, *Nujūm al-samāʾ* pp. 10–11, *Shahīd i thālith* (see below) pp. 26–30); *Āʾīn i Akbarī* p. 234 (only his name in a list), Blochmann's trans. p. 545 (where a few facts are added from unspecified sources); *Ṭabaqāt i Akbarī* ii p. 468 (only *Imrūz* [i.e. in 1002 presumably] *ba-qaḍā-yi Lāhaur mashghūlast u ba-diyānat u amānat u faḍāʾil u kamālāt ittiṣāf dārad*); Badāʾūnī *Muntakhhab al-tawārīkh* iii 137–8; *Mirʾāt al-ʿālam* (among the *ʿulamāʾ* at the end of *Ārāyish* vii)*; Amal al-āmil* p. 73; *Riyāḍ al-shuʿarāʾ* (the passage, or parts of it, quoted in *Nujūm al-samāʾ* pp. 12–13, 14–16, and thence, so far as the account of the martyrdom is concerned, in *Der Islam* iii pp. 66–7); *Tadhkirah i Shūshtar* p. 36; *Khulāṣat al-afkār* no. 290; *Makhzan al-gharāʾib* no. 2821; *Rauḍāt al-jannāt* iv pp. 222–3; *Nujūm al-samāʾ* pp. 9–17; I. Goldziher *Beiträge zur Literaturgeschichte der Sîʿâ und der sunnitischen Polemik* (Sitzungsberichte der K. Akademie der Wissenschaften [zu Wien], phil.-hist. Classe, 78. Bd., Vienna 1874) pp. 486–513 (on the *Iḥqāq al-ḥaqq* mainly. A review of the *Beiträge* was published in *ZDMG*.

1003 The calligraphists are Ibn al-Bawwāb (p. 456), Mīr ʿAlī Tabrīzī, Sulṭān-ʿAlī Mashhadī and Mīr ʿAlī Mashhadī.

29 (1876) pp. 673–81 by O. Loth, who added some details); Rieu i 337; Raḥmān ʿAlī p. 245; *Taqijja, von J. Horovitz* (in *Der Islam* iii (1912) pp. 63–7, where the text of ʿAlī-Qulī Khān "Wālih's" account of the martyrdom is quoted from the *Nujūm al-samāʾ*); *Shahīd i thālith*, an Urdu biography by Mirzā M. Hādī "ʿAziz" Lak'hnawī, Lucknow 1916* (photograph of the tomb as frontispiece); *Saḥīfah i nūr*, an Urdu biography by S. Ṣaghīr Ḥasan "Shams" Zaidī Wāsiṭī, Delhi 1919*; Būhār Arabic Cat. pp. 124–7; Bānkīpūr viii pp. 161–2; *Ency. Isl.* under Nūr Allāh (Hidayet Hosain); Brockelmann *Sptbd.* ii pp. 607–8.]

1575. **Aḥmad b. M. ʿAlī** b. M. Bāqir al-Iṣfahānī commonly called (*al-mashhūr bi-*) **al-Bihbahānī**,[1004] a member of the Majlisī family which produced several famous Shīʿite theologians,[1005] was born at Kirmānshāhān in 1191/1777. His father, a bitter enemy of the Ṣūfīs, whom he denounced in his *Risālah i Khairātīyah* (Rieu i p. 33*b*), was "the chief priest of Kermanshah", whom Sir John Malcolm met in 1800 (*History of Persia*, London 1829, ii pp. 271, 297–8) and who died in 1216/1801–2 (see *Mirʾāt al-aḥwāl i jahān-numā, Maṭlab* 4; *Rauḍāt al-jannāt* iv pp. 121–2; *Qiṣaṣ al-ʿulamāʾ* p. 157, in the notice of his father). Aḥmad b. M. ʿAlī had visited the Mesopotamian sanctuaries and various towns in Persia before leaving Mashhad in 1219/1804–5 on the journey which took him via Bandar i ʿAbbās, Ṣuḥār, and Masqaṭ to Bombay in Ṣafar 1220/1805. From Bombay he went to Ḥaidarābād (Deccan) and, among other places, Calcutta (1221/1806), Murshidābād, ʿAẓīmābād (Patna), Faiḍābād (Fyzabad) (1222/1807), Lucknow, Faiḍābād again (1223/1808), ʿAẓīmābād again, Murshidābād again, Jahāngīrnagar (i.e. Dacca) and again ʿAẓīmābād, where he wrote his autobiography in 1224–5/1809–10. A list of his own works, nineteen in number, is given in the *Mirʾāt al-aḥwāl i jahān-numā* (*Maṭlab v, maqṣad* 2, near the end) and is quoted in the Bānkīpūr Catalogue (vii pp. 184–5). Of the *Tuḥfat al-muḥibbīn* (no. 9, composed at Faiḍābād) and the *Tanbīh al-ghāfilīn* (no. 15, composed at Lucknow in 1222/1807 = I.Ḥ. 709, on the *akhbārīs* and *ʿulamāʾ* suspected of Ṣūfism) there are MSS. at Bānkīpūr (xiv nos. 1321 and 1322). The *Risālah i wilādat u wafāt i Chahdārdah Maʿṣūm* (= no. 12 (?), I.Ḥ. 1542) is preserved at Calcutta (Ivanow 2nd Suppt. 1063 (2)). A later work, the *Sabīl al-najāt* completed at ʿAẓīmābād in 1225/1810 or 1226/1811 and dedicated to M. ʿAlī Khān Qājār, is preserved at Calcutta in two copies (Ivanow 1128 and Ivanow-Curzon 392).

1004 The first syllable of this *nisbah* is vocalized with a *kasrah* on the margin of *Rauḍāt al-jannāt* p. 123.

1005 For the most famous of these, M. Bāqir b. M. Taqī al-Majlisī, see no. 247 *supra*; Brockelmann *Sptbd.* ii pp. 572–4.

Mirʾāt al-aḥwāl i jahān-numā, an account of the author's ancestors and relations, of his own life and travels, and of the persons whom he met, completed (so far as the first *mujallad*, the only one extant,[1006] is concerned) in 1225/1810 at ʿAẓīmābād [i.e. Patna], dedicated to M. ʿAlī Khān Qājār [Fatḥ-ʿAlī Shāh's eldest son, d. 1237/1821[1007]] and divided into five *maṭlabs* ((1) M. Taqī b. Maqṣūd ʿAlī Majlisī[1008] and his descendants, (2) M. Bāqir b. M. Taqī Majlisī,[1009] (3) M. Ṣāliḥ b. Aḥmad Māzandarānī,[1010] pupil and son-in-law of M. Taqī, (4) M. Bāqir b. M. Akmal Iṣfahānī Bihbahānī,[1011] grandson of M. Ṣāliḥ and grandfather of the author, (5) the author's memoirs in three *maqṣads*, (*a*) from his birth to his landing at Bombay, (*b*) his life in India, (*c*) account of Europe and the English) and a *Khātimah* (advice to kings and rulers and a sketch of Persian history from the decline of the Ṣafawīs to the author's time): **Rieu** i 385*a* (AH 1225/1810), Suppt. 131 (AH 1281/1864, containing on the margins of foll. 69–79 some additional notices written in Nāṣir al-Dīn Shāh's reign by M. Ṣādiq b. S. M. Mahdī b. Amīr S. ʿAlī), **Bānkīpūr** vii 628 (lacking the sketch of recent Persian history at end of *Khātimah*. 19th cent.) 629 (AH 1225/1810–11), **Būhār** 96 (AH 1225/1810–11), **I.O.** D.P. 748 (not later than AH 1226/1811), **I.O.** 3941 (defective at both ends and damaged. 19th cent.), **Ivanow** 278 (AH 1227/1812), 2nd Suppt. 935 (lacks *Maqṣad* 3 of *Maṭlab* v and *Khātimah*. Mid-19th cent.), **Āṣafīyah** i p. 252 no. 195, **Nadhīr Aḥmad** 71 (S. Zain al-ʿĀbidīn, Murshidābād).

[Rieu i pp. 385–6; *Nujūm al-samāʾ* pp. 382–6 (based on the *Mirʾāt al-ahwāl*); Bānkīpūr vii pp. 180–5.]

1576. In 1231/1816 an anonymous author dedicated to Ghāzī al-Dīn Ḥaidar, King of Oudh,

Āʾīnah i ḥaqq-numā, notices of contemporary Shīʿite scholars, especially S. Dildār ʿAlī,[1012] his teachers and pupils and some persons who vis-

1006 It will be observed that in this volume the narrative is carried down to the time of composition.

1007 26 Ṣafar 1237. See *Rauḍat al-ṣafā-yi Nāṣirī* ix fol. 124*b*, l. 21.

1008 Cf. *Luʾluʾatā ʾl-Baḥrain* pp. 49–50; *Rauḍāt al-jannāt* pp. 129–31; *Qiṣaṣ al-ʿulamāʾ* pp. 181–3; Browne *Lit. Hist*, iv p. 409.

1009 See no. 247 *supra*; Brockelmann *Sptbd.* ii pp. 572–4.

1010 Cf. *Rauḍāt al-jannāt* p. 331, *Qiṣaṣ al-ʿulamāʾ* pp. 179–80; *Nujūm al-samāʾ* p. 106; Brockelmann Sptbd. ii p. 578.

1011 Cf. *Rauḍāt al-jannāt* pp. 123–4, *Qiṣaṣ al-ʿulamāʾ* pp. 157–61; Brockelmann *Sptbd.* ii p. 504.

1012 For whom see Raḥmān ʿAli p. 60; Brockelmann *Sptbd.* II p. 852.

ited Lucknow in his time: **I.O.** D.P. 259 (*b*), **Āṣafīyah** ii p. 1330, iii p. 182, **Bānkīpūr** Suppt. ii 2062 (19th cent).

1577. **M. ʿAlī b. Ḥājjī M. Ḥasan** known as Hindī went from Persia to India in 1193/1779 and returned home after an absence of thirty-seven years, fifteen of which were spent in the service of Nawwāb Āṣaf al-Daulah (Nawwāb-Wazīr of Oudh 1189–1212/1775–97) and those from 1227/1812 onwards (evidently, therefore, only two or three) in that of the Governor General[1013]

Majmaʿ al-nuqūl, stories of persons who honoured the memory of al-Ḥusain by means of *taʿziyahs*, pilgrimages to Karbalāʾ, and lamentation (*taʿziyah-dārān u zawwārān u giryah-kunandagān i Saiyid al-Shuhadāʾ*): **Berlin** 1020.

1578. Mīrzā M. **Ḥaidar-Shukōh** b. Mīrzā M. Kām-bakhsh Bahādur b. Mīrzā M. Sulaimān-Shukōh b. Muḥammad Shāh, apparently a great-grandson of the Mogul Emperor Muḥammad Shāh (1131–61/1719–48), flourished in the third quarter of the 13th/19th century.

Majmūʿah i Ḥaidar-Shukōh (beginning: *Fātiḥah i kull i kalām ... ammā baʿd īn Shīʿī i maurūthī M. Ḥaidar-Shukōh b. Mīrzā M. Kām-bakhsh*, etc.), memoirs, correspondence (some of the letters being dated 1270/1853–4), and a declaration of allegiance to Shīʿism, which, according to the author, was the faith of the earlier Indian Tīmūrids: **Ivanow** 2nd Suppt. 930 (21 foll., defective at end. Late 19th cent.).

1579. **M. b. Sulaimān** b. M. Rafīʿ b. ʿAbd al-Muṭṭalib b. ʿAlī **al-Tunakābunī**[1014] was born in 1234/1818–19 or 1235/1819–20.[1015] His father, a scholar and physician, was for some years in attendance on Muḥammad-Qulī Mīrzā, Governor of Māzandarān. It is stated in the Mashhad catalogue (iii p. 142) on the authority of Ḥājj S. M. (Mujtahid i) Tunakābunī that M. b. Sulaimān died in 1308/1890–1. His works, of which he gives a list in the *Qiṣaṣ al-ʿulamāʾ*, amounted to more than two hundred. Of these *al-Fawāʾid fī uṣūl al-dīn, a manẓūmah*, was published at Ṭihrān in 1283/1866–7 (*Aḥsan al-wadīʿah* i p. 122[10]), the *Mawāʿiẓ al-muttaqīn* at [Ṭihrān] in 1297/1880°, and the *Sabīl al-najāt* in the same volume as the *Qiṣaṣ*

1013 *Hākim i Gawarnar M H R Ā Nāʾib i Kanpūnī Angrēz Bahādur*, which Pertsch interprets as meaning Lord Moira who, however, as Pertsch points out, did not reach India until 1228/1813.

1014 For Tunakābun, the most westerly district of Māzandarān (capital Khurramābād), see Rabino *Mázandarán and Astarábád* pp. 21–4, 105–7, etc.

1015 *Qiṣaṣ al-ʿulamāʾ* 1309 ed., p. 61[11]: *u maulid i īn faqīr dar sanah i hazār u duwīst u sī u chahār yā sī u panj būdah.*

al-ʿulamāʾ at [Ṭihrān] in 1304/1886° and 1309/1891‡. In his list of his works are mentioned an alphabetically arranged *Tadhkirat al-ʿulamāʾ* (*Qiṣaṣ al-ʿulamāʾ* p. 69[19]. Cf. p. 7[14]), a work entitled *Karāmāt al-ʿulamāʾ* (*op. cit.* p. 69[20]) and an autobiography entitled *Mudhakkir al-ikhwān* (*op. cit.* p. 723).

Qiṣaṣ al-ʿulamāʾ, notices of 153 ancient and modern Shīʿite scholars completed 17 Rajab 1290/10 Sept. 1873, arranged *ba-tartīb i ijāzāt u tartīb i azminah u aʿṣār* and beginning with the author's teacher S. Ibrāhīm Qazwīnī: **Āṣafīyah** i p. 348 nos. 114–5 (AH 1301/1883–4).

Editions: [**Persia** ?] 1296/1879°; [**Ṭihrān**] 1304/1886° (followed by (1) M. b. Sulaimān Tunakābunī's *Sabīl al-najāt*, (2) S. Murtaḍā's *Tabṣirat al-ʿawāmm*); [**Ṭihrān**] 1308–9/1891‡ (followed by the same two works on p. 350 and p. 358 respectively); **Bombay** or Lucknow (?) 1306/1888–9 (cf. *Aḥsan al-wadīʿah* i p. 122[6], Browne *Lit. Hist*, iv p. 354); **Tabrīz** 1320/1902–3 (cf. *Aḥsan al-wadīʿah* i p. 122[6]).

Description: *A traveller's narrative written to illustrate the episode of the Bàb edited ... and translated ... by E. G. Browne*, ii (Cambridge 1891) pp. 197–8.

Urdu translation by Mīr Nādir ʿAlī "Raʿd": *Qiṣaṣ al-ʿulamāʾ*, **Ḥaidarābād** 1340–1/1921–3*.

[*Qiṣaṣ al-ʿulamāʾ*, 1308–9 ed., pp. 58–74; *al-Maʾāthir wa-ʾl-āthār* p. 157; *Aḥsan al-wadīʿah* i pp. 121–3.]

1580. Maulawī Mīrzā **Muḥammad ʿAlī** (so on the title-page and in the three prefixed *taqārīẓ*) al-Kashmīrī *aṣl*[an] *thumma* 'l-Lak'hnawī (so in the third *taqrīẓ*, p. iv, l. 3) or, as he calls himself in the preface, Muḥammad b. Ṣādiq b. Mahdī, was a pupil of S. M. ʿAbbās Shūshtarī[1016] and an old friend of S. Ḥāmid Ḥusain.[1017]

Nujūm al-samāʾ fī tarājim al-ʿulamāʾ, lives of Shīʿite scholars of the eleventh (p. 4), twelfth (p. 157), and thirteenth (p. 313) Islāmic centuries, begun in 1286/1869–70[1018] at the request of S. Ḥāmid Ḥusain[1019] and divided,

1016 *wa-huwa mimman qaraʾa ʿalaiya baʿda ʾl-kutubi ʾl-adabīyah wa-shaṭr*[an] *min kitābī Rawāʾiḥ al-Qurʾān fī faḍāʾil umanāʾ al-Raḥmān* (first *taqrīẓ*, p. i, l. 5 from foot). M. ʿA. Sh. is the author of a *mathnawī* entitled *Mann u salwā* (I.H. p. 564. Editions: [Delhi ?] 1263/1847°, Amrōhah 1894°) and other works.

1017 S. H. H. Mūsawī Nīshāpūrī Lak'hnawī wrote the large Shīʿite work *ʿAbaqāt al-anwār fī imāmat al-Aʾimmat al-aṭhār*, of which the British Museum has a number of parts published from 1293/1876 to 1314/1896 (Edwards col. 243). Cf. *al-Maʾāthir wa-ʾl-āthār* p. 168.

1018 A prefixed *taqrīẓ* by S. Ḥāmid Ḥusain is dated 1290/1873, but the printed text contains quotations from the *Qiṣaṣ al-ʿulamāʾ* (e.g. pp. 410[10], 412[9], 415[6]), which were doubtless inserted some years later than 1290.

1019 *wa-qad ṣannafa biʾltimāsī kitāb*[an] *rāʾiʿ*[an] as Ḥāmid Ḥusain says in his *taqrīẓ*, p. ii antepenult.

according to the preface, into three *najms*, one for each century, and a *khātimah*, of which the subject is not stated: **Lucknow** 1303/1886° ("Vol I (*jild i awwal*)," apparently the only one published, consisting of 424 pages and ending with Muftī S. Muḥammad-Qulī Khān b. S. M. Ḥusain b. S. Ḥāmid Ḥusain, who died at Lucknow in 1260/1844).[1020]

1581. ʿ**Abd al-ʿAzīz "Jawāhir al-Kalām"** is the author of *Kitāb-khānahā-yi Īrān* (Firdausī Press [Tihrān] AHS 1311/1932–3), at the end of which is printed a list of other works by the same author. These are (1) *Athār al-Shīʿat al-Imāmīyah* (see below), (2) a Persian translation of Ibn Khaldūn's *Muqaddimah* (described as having been sent to the Persian Ministry of Education in the hope that it would be published), (3) a commentary [doubtless in Arabic] on the *Kifāyat al-uṣūl* of Mullā M. Kāẓim Khurāsānī[1021] (in three volumes, of which half of the first volume is described as having been lithographed at Tihrān), (4) *Nahj al-faṣāḥah*, a collection of the Prophet's short speeches, sayings etc., modelled on the *Nahj al-balāghah* (unfinished), (5) philosophical and other essays published in periodicals at Cairo, Bairūt and Istānbūl. According to a statement on the back cover of the *Kitāb-khānahā-yi Irān* the author had collected much material for two further works, namely (6) *Tārīkh i Tihrān* and (7) *Kitāb i makhṭūṭāt i Īrān*, on the Arabic and Persian MSS. in the libraries of Persia.

Āthār al-Shīʿat al-Imāmīyah *rājiʿ ba-ʿaqāʾid u afkār u adwār i siyāsī u adabī u tārīkh i bilād u mamālik u āthār i adabī u māddī u sharḥ i ḥāl i mardumān i nāmī i ʿilmī u siyāsī i Shīʿah az ibtidā-yi tashkīl i īn firqah tā ʿaṣr i ḥāḍir* ... in twenty volumes, of which only two are described at the end of the *Kitāb-khānahā-yi Īrān* as having been printed, namely vol. iii (in Arabic [Tihrān 1342/1924‡ (according to the title-page, but 1348 [1929–30] according to the cover)] and also in a Persian translation, *shāmil i ḥālāt i salāṭīn u farmānrawāyān i Shīʿah az ibtidā-yi Islām, tā kunūn*) and vol. iv (*shāmil i ḥālāt i kāffah i wuzarāʾ u umarāʾ i īn firqah*), the latter (biographies of wazīrs arranged chronologically under the dynasties and then (*Bāb* 2, p. 125) biographies of amīrs similarly arranged) having been printed in a Persian translation at the Maṭbaʿah i Majlis [**Tihrān**] in AHS 1307/1928–9‡. From the colophon of vol. iv it appears that the subject of vol. v is the history of modern Persia from Qājār times to the present.

1020 There is nothing to show whether or not this is the end of the third *najm*.
1021 Cf. Brockelmann *Sptbd.* ii p. 799; Browne *Lit. Hist*, iv p. 371.

1582. Other works:—

(1) ***Kākh i dil-āwīz yā Tārīkh i Sharīf i Raḍī***,[1022] by S. ʿAlī Akbar Burquʿī Qummī (in, and offprinted from, *Armaghān* xix/5–6 (Murdād 1317/1938) pp. 357–71, xix/7 (Mihr 1317) pp. 451–8, xix/8 (Ābān 1317) pp. 505–12, xix/9–10 (Ispand 1317) pp. 593–608 (cf. *Luzac's Oriental List* 1940 p. 107)).

(2) ***Risālah dar faḍīlat i ʿilm u ʿulamāʾ***, a short treatise written not earlier than 1052/1642 (Shāh Ṣafī being referred to as dead) by M. Muqīm al-Ḥusainī al-Astarābādī[1023] on the spiritual advantages of theological learning, with eulogies of some famous Shīʿite divines and especially an encomiastic biography of M. Bāqir Dāmād (d. 1040/1630–1 or 1041/1631–2. See Brockelmann *Sptbd.* ii p. 579 and the authorities there cited): **Ivanow** Curzon 705 (late 18th cent.).

(3) ***Risālah dar sabab i shahādat i Shahīd i Thānī***, on the death of Zain al-Dīn al-ʿĀmilī[1024] at Istānbūl: **Ivanow** 1st Spt. 827(6) (AH 1252/1837).

13.14 *Traditionists*

1583. For the *Tuḥfat al-faqīr al-ḥaqīr* and the *Tuḥfah i Murshidī of ʿUbaid Allāh b. ʿAbd Allāh al-Ḥusainī* known as Murshid b. Aṣīl, the former of which was written in 884/1479, see no. 1441 (1) *supra*.

1584. Muḥammad, entitled **Khawāṣṣ Khān**, Ḥanafī Qādirī Qurashī Madanī[1025] Bījāpūrī was a contemporary of the Mogul Emperor Farrukh-siyar.

Muhimmat al-muḥaddithīn (a chronogram = 1128/1716), a short biographical dictionary of Ḥanafī traditionists: **Āṣafīyah** i p. 348 (= Nadhīr Aḥmad 95).

1585. **Walī Allāh** b. ʿAbd al-Raḥīm **Dihlawī** was born in 1114/1703 and died in 1176/1762–3 (see nos. 35, 224 (Edition of the Arabic translation), 285, 1352 *supra*).

Āthār al-muḥaddithīn: **Āṣafīyah** i p. 346 no. 81 (AH 1174/1760–1).

1022 For whom see *Ency. Isl.* under al-Sharīf al-Raḍī (Krenkow), Brockelmann I p. 82, *Sptbd* I pp. 131–2.

1023 Presumably identical with M. Muqīm b. Jamāl al-Dīn Ḥusain al-Husainī al-Astarābādī, who wrote for "Quṭb-Shāh" a *Risālah fī ʾl-maʿād* (IḤ 1523).

1024 Cf. *Luʾluʾatā ʾl-Baḥrain* pp. 25–31; etc.

1025 So Nadhīr Aḥmad. The Āṣafīyah catalogue calls him Imtinān [*sic* ?] Khawaṣṣ Khān Ḥanafī Qādirī Bījāpūrī.

1586. ʿ**Abd al-ʿAzīz** b. Walī Allāh **Dihlawī**, who was born in 1159[1026]/1746 and died in 1239/1824, has already been mentioned as the author of the *Fatḥ al-ʿAzīz* (no. 40 (5)) and the Arabic work *Sirr al-shahādatain* (p. 223).

Bustān al-muḥaddithīn, a bibliography of works on the Traditions with biographies of their authors: **Bānkīpūr** viii 652 (mid 19th cent.).

Editions: **Delhi** [12]93/1876°* **Lahore** [1884*], [1893°].

1587. Nawwāb M. **Ṣiddīq. Ḥasan Khān**, who was born at Bareilly in 1248/1832 and died at Bhōpāl in 1890, has already been mentioned as the author of the *Ifādat al-shuyūkh bi-miqdār al-nāsikh wa-'l-mansūkh* (no. 48 (1)), the *Iksīr fī uṣūl al-tafsīr* (no. 48 (2)) and the *Shamʿ i anjuman* (no. 1226).

Itḥāf al-nubalāʾ al-muttaqīn bi-iḥyāʾ maʾāthir al-fuqahāʾ al-muḥaddithīn, a bibliography of works on the Traditions followed by biographies of traditionists: **Cawnpore** 1289/1872* (446 pp.).

1588. Other works:

(1) ***Kitāb al-dīn al-mubīn fī sharḥ uṣūl al-ḥadīth wa-bayān aḥwāl al-mashāhīr min al-muḥaddithīn***, one (evidently the first)[1027] of the twenty-four volumes of the *Rauḍāt i Shāhī* (a work *mutaḍammin i aḥwāl i buzurgān u dar aḥādīth u tafsīr wa-ghairah* according to Raḥmān ʿAlī) composed in 1077/1666–7 by S. M. Jaʿfar Badr i ʿĀlam Aḥmadābādī Gujrātī b. S. Jalāl al-Dīn M. Maqṣūd i ʿĀlam, who was born in 1023/1614 and died, in 1085/1675 (see Raḥmān ʿAlī p. 214): **Nadhīr Aḥmad** 85 (M. ʿAlī Ḥusain's library, Ḥaidarābād.AH 1077/1667, apparently autograph).

(2) ***Silsilat al-ʿasjad fī dhikr mashāyikh al-sanad.*** Edition: place ? date ? (Āṣafīyah i p. 346).

13.15 *Travellers, Pilgrims, Tourists*

See also nos. 1412–22 *supra*

1589. Ḥakīm Abū Muʿīn **Nāṣir** "Ḥujjat" **ibn Khusrau** Qubādiyānī Marwazī, born in Dhū 'l-Qaʿdah 394/Aug.-Sept. 1004 apparently at Qubādiyān, was by profession an official in the revenue department. In Rabīʿ ii 437/Oct.-Nov. 1045, when Chaghrī Bēg Dāwud b. Mīkāʾīl b. Saljūq was *Amīr* of Khurāsān, Nāṣir went on revenue business from Marw to Panj-dīh, near Marw al-Rud, and from there

1026 Ghulām-Ḥalīm. the pseudonym adopted by him in the *Tuḥfah i Ithnā-ʿAsharīyah*, is a chronogram indicating this year.

1027 According to the colophon (quoted by Nadhīr Aḥmad) it is followed "*fī 'l-sifr al-thānī*" by "*al-kitāb al-thānī wa-huwa 'l-musammā bi-kitāb al-muʿjizāt wa-'l-āyāt al-baiyināt.*"

to Jūzjānān. Here he dreamt a dream which caused him to abandon the practice of drinking and undertake a pilgrimage to Mecca. Returning to Marw he resigned his official appointment and set out on the journey which he has described in his *Safar-nāmah*. In Egypt, then flourishing under Fāṭimid rule, he came in contact with Ismāʿīlī theologians, and presumably it was there that he became a convert to the Ismāʿīlī creed. At this time or later he was appointed *ḥujjat* or leader of propaganda for Khurāsān. Some time after his return, however, his religious views or his propagandist activities met with disapproval from the authorities and he was forced to leave Balkh. He seems to have gone for a time to Māzandarān, but eventually he settled at Yumgān (or Yamkān ?) in the mountains of Badakhshān, and there he died and was buried probably in, or about, 481/1088.

Among his works were (1) a *dīwān* (Editions: Tabrīz 1280/1864°, Tihrān AHS 1304–7/1925–8 (*Dīwān i ashʿār i Ḥakīm ... Nāṣir b. Khusrau ... ba-inḍimām i Rūshanāʾī-nāmah ... u Saʿādat-nāmah ...* with introduction, notes and indexes by Mujtabā Mīnuwī). Selections: (*a*) *Auswahl aus Nâṣir Chusrau's Kaṣîden* [with translation]. *Von ... H. Ethé* (in ZDMG. 36 (1882) pp. 478–508): (*b*) *Kürzere Lieder und poetische Fragmente aus Nâçir Khusraus Dîvân. Von H. Ethé* (in *Nachrichten der Gesellschaft der Wissenschaften*, Göttingen 1882, pp. 124–52). (2) *Rūshanāʾī-nāmah*, a philosophical poem (Editions: (1) *Nâṣir Chusrau's Rûśanâinâma ... oder Buch der Erleuchtung in Text und Uebersetzung, nebst Noten und kritisch-biographischem Appendix. Von H. Ethé* (in ZDMG. 33 (1879) pp. 645–65, 34 (1880) pp. 617–42): (2) Berlin 1341/1923* (*Safar-nāmah i Ḥakīm N. i Kh. ba-inḍimām i Rūshanāʾī-nāmah u Saʿādat-nāmah*. A reprint of Ethé's text): (3) Tihrān AHS 1304–7/1925–8 (see above under *dīwān*): (3) *Saʿādat-nāmah*, a didactic poem (Editions: (1) *Le Livre de la Félicité ..., par Nâçir ed-Dîn ben Khosroû* [with a French translation] *par E. Fagnan* (in ZDMG. 34 (1880) pp. 643–74: (2) Berlin 1341/1923* (see above under *Rushanāʾī-nāmah*): (3) Tihrān AHS 1304–7/1925–8 (see above under *dīwān*). Emendations: ZDMG. 36 (1882) pp. 96–114: (4) *Zād al-musāfirīn*, a prose handbook of Ismāʿīlī theology and metaphysics (Edition: Berlin 1341/1923* (ed. M. Badhl al-Raḥmān)): (5) *Wajh i dīn* (Edition: Berlin 1343/1925* (with preface by T. Īrānī)).

(*Safar-nāmah i Ḥakīm Nāṣir i Khusrau*) an account of a journey which started from Jūzjānān on 6 Jumādā II 437/19 Dec. 1045 and during which the author visited among other places Shāburqān, Marw, Nīshāpūr, Qūmis (i.e. Bisṭām), Dāmghān, Simnān, Qazwīn, Tabrīz (where he met "Qaṭrān"), Vān, Akhlāṭ, Bitlīs, Arzan (Erzerum), Maiyāfāriqīn, Āmid, Aleppo, Maʿarrat al-Nuʿmān (where he met Abū 'l-ʿAlāʾ), Ḥamāh, Tripoli, Bairūt, Sidon, Tyre, Acre, Ḥaifā, Jerusalem, Mecca (to which he made four pilgrimages), Damascus, Jerusalem again, Egypt (where he stayed two or three years) and finally the Ḥijāz, the Yemen, Laḥsā, Qaṭīf, Baṣrah, Arrajān, Iṣfahān, Nā'īn, Ṭabas, Tūn, Sarakhs and Marw (26 Jumādā II 444/23 Oct. 1052): **Rieu** i 379 (AH 1102/1691), iii 979*a* (abstract only. Circ. AD 1850), **Blochet** i 644 (AD 1874), 645 (AH 1296/1878), **Ivanow** 279 (AH 1292/1875).

Editions: **Paris** (Vienne printed) 1881°* (*Sefer Nameh, relation du voyage de Nassiri Khosrau ..., publié, traduit et annoté par C. Schefer.* Publications de l'École Spéciale des Langues Orientales Vivantes, Série ii, vol. 1), **Delhi** 1882°* (*Safar-nāmah i Ḥakīm Nāṣir i Khusrau.* With a biographical preface by M. Alṭāf Ḥusain "Ḥalī"), **Bombay** 1309/1892°, **Ṭihran** 1312/1894–5 (*Siyāḥat-nāmah.* See Mashhad, fṣl. 14, ptd. bks., no. 130), [**Ṭihrān** ?] 1314/1896–7 (with the *dīwān*: see Ghanī-zādah's *muqaddimah* to the 1341 edition, p. *dāl*, and Taqī-zādah's *muqaddimah* p. NB n.), **Berlin** 1341/1923*.

French translation: see Editions above.

Russian translation: *Safar-name. Kniga puteshestviya* [translation and introduction by E. E. Berthels] **Leningrad**[1028] (or Moscow ?[1029]) 1933.

Translations of extracts: (1) *An account of Jerusalem translated ... from the Persian text of Násir ibn Khusru's* [*sic*] *Safar-námah. By ... Major A. R. Fuller* (in *JRAS*. 1873 p. 142 *et seqq.*). (2) *Diary of a journey through Syria and Palestine by Nâsir-i-Khusrau, in* 1047 AD *Translated ... and annotated by G. le Strange.* **London**, 1888° (Palestine Pilgrims' Text Society).

[Autobiographical statements in his works especially the *Safar-nāmah* and the *dīwan* (most fully discussed in S. Ḥasan Taqī-zādah's *muqaddimah* to the 1304–7 edition of the *dīwān* and very briefly summarised in C. N. Seddon's review, *JRAS*. 1930 pp. 671–4. A spurious autobiography (of which an abridgment is printed in the Tabrīz edition of the *dīwān*) is the source of incorrect and legendary information given in the *Khulāṣat al-ash'ār*, the *Haft iqlīm*, the *Ātash-kadah* and elsewhere (cf. Browne *Lit. Hist*, ii pp. 218–20)); Zakarīyā' al-Qazwīnī *Āthār al-bilād* (in Arabic) pp. 328–9 (s.v. Yumgān. Cf. Browne *Lit. Hist*, ii p. 218); *Tārīkh i Guzīdah* p. 826; *Bahāristān, Rauḍah* 6, 8th. notice; Daulat-Shāh pp. 61–4; *Khulāṣat al-ash'ār; Haft iqlīm* no. 863; *But-khānah* no. 3; *Mir'āt al-khayāl* pp. 27–8 (no. 7); *Ātash-kadah* pp. 187-[194] (no. 425 (under Iṣfahān). Based on the spurious autobiography. Summarized by Bland in *JRAS*. vii (1843) pp. 360–1); *Majma' al-gharā'ib* no. 2711; Sprenger pp. 428–9; *Majma' al-fuṣaḥā'* i pp. 607–33; *Rauḍāt al-jannāt* iv p. 223; Bieu i pp. 379–81; H. Ethé *Nasir Khusrau's Leben, Denken und Dichten* (in *Travaux ... du Congrés international des orientalistes à Leyde*, vol. ii, Leyden 1884); *Náṣir-i-Khusraw, poet, traveller and propagandist. By E. G. Browne* (in *JRAS*. 1905 pp. 313–52); Browne *Lit.*

1028 So *Ency. Isl.* under Nāṣir-i-Khusraw.

1029 So Harrassowitz's *Litterae orientales* 58 (April 1934) p. 22

Hist, ii pp. 218–46; M. G͟hanī-zādah's *muqaddimah* to the 1241 edition of the *Safar-nāmah; Ency. Isl.* under Nāṣir-i K͟husraw (Berthels); S. Ḥasan Taqī-zādah's *muqaddimah* to the 1304–7 edition of the *dīwān* (very briefly summarised in C. N. Seddon's review, *JRAS.* 1930 pp. 671–4)].

1590. S͟h. Abū 'l-Faiḍ "**Faiḍī**" b. Mubārak was born at Āgrah in 954/1547 and died there in 1004/1595 (see no. 706 *supra*).

A short account of the pilgrimage of Rafīʿ al-Dīn S͟hāh Abū Turāb (cf. no. 982 *supra*) *to Mecca in 986/1578 and his return in 987/1579 with the Qadam i Rasūl* (beginning: *Qadam i qalam dar taiy i masālik i maḥāmid i Ilāhī kūtāh ast*): **Bānkīpūr** Suppt. i 1995 vii (foll. 68b–70a. 18th cent.).

1591. For the *ʿAwālim al-asrār fī g͟harāʾib al-asfār*, begun in 1009/1600–1 by Qāḍī Ik͟htiyār, see no. 1515 *supra*.

For the *Baḥr al-asrār*, which concludes with an account of Maḥmūd b. Amīr Walī's extensive travels from 1034/1624–5 onwards, see no. 505 *supra*.

1592. **Ṣafī b. Walī Qazwīnī** has already been mentioned as the author of the *Zēb i tafāsīr* (no. 30 *supra*) and the *Tuḥfat al-ak͟hyār* (no. 148 *supra*).

Anīs al-ḥujjāj, an account of a journey to Mecca and Medina in 1087–8/1676–7 after the completion of the *Zēb i tafāsīr*: **Rieu** iii 980a (defective and disarranged. Circ. AD 1850).

1593. **M. Mufīd** Mustaufī b. Najm al-Dīn Maḥmūd Bāfqī Yazdī has already been mentioned as the author of the *Jāmiʿ i Mufīdī*, begun at Baṣrah in 1082/1671 and completed at Multān in 1090/1679 (see no. 461 *supra*), and of the *Muk͟htaṣar i Mufīd*, begun in the Deccan in 1087/1676–7 and completed at Lahore in 1091/1680–1 (see no. 312 (2) *supra*). The fifth *maqālah* of the third *mujallad* of the former work is devoted to an account of the author's life and travels.

A memoir (beg. *Ḥamd u sipās i bī-qiyās Mālik al-mulkī rā kih rifʿat i sarā-pardah i ʿaẓamatas͟h*), "very rich in words and poor in facts", extending over the years 1077–85 but dealing mainly with the author's journey to India (Iṣfahān, Bag͟hdād, Baṣrah, Sūrat, S͟hāhjahānābād, Ḥaidarābād, Sārangpūr, Burhānpūr, Aurangābād, Golconda) in 1081–5: **Bodleian** 423.

1594. For Anand Rām "Muk͟hliṣ's" account of his journey from Delhi to Muktēsar in 1156/1743 (?), see no. 780 (10) *supra* and the additions and corrections relating to that page.

For the *Bayān i wāqiʿ* of K͟hwājah ʿAbd al-Karīm b. ʿĀqibat-Maḥmūd Kas͟hmīrī, who entered Nādir S͟hāh's service at Delhi in 1151/1739, reached Qazwīn with him in 1154/1741, travelled thence to ʿIrāq, Syria and Arabia, returned to Delhi in 1156/1743 and wrote an account of these travels and of contemporary history to 1198/1784, see no. 411 *supra*.

1595. **Iʿtiṣām al-Dīn** b. S͟h. Tāj al-Dīn, of Tājpūr (described by him as in the Nadiyah District [of Bengal]), began his official career as a *muns͟hī* under Jaʿfar ʿAlī K͟hān ["Mīr Jaʿfar", Nawwāb-Nāẓim of Bengal 1170–4/1757–60 and again 1763–5. Cf. no. 802 3rd, 5th par. *supra*]. On the accession of Mīr Qāsim [in 1174/1760. Cf. no. 802 5th par. *supra*] he entered the service of Major Yorke and took part in the campaign against the Rājah of Bīrbhūm. He later fought on the British side against Mīr Qāsim [in 1177/1763. Cf. no. 802 5th, 6th par. *supra*]. Then after a short period in the service of General Carnac [1765–6] he entered that of S͟hāh-ʿĀlam. In 1180/1767, when Captain Archibald Swinton came to England with a letter from S͟hāh-ʿĀlam to George III, Iʿtiṣām al-Dīn accompanied him.[1030] He embarked at Hijilī[1031] on 9 S͟haʿbān 1180/10 January 1767[1032] and returned to Bengal in 1183/1769 after an absence of two years and nine months.[1033] In 1189/1775 he was sent to Poonah to help in the negotiations of the East India Company with the Marāṭ'hās.

S͟higarf-nāmah i wilāyat, or ***Wilāyat-nāmah***, an account written in 1199/1785 of the author's voyage to England in 1180/1767 and of his experiences there, but not of his return journey, which brought him back to Bengal in 1183/1769: **Rieu** iii 981*b* (AD 1810), i 383*a* (AH 1227/1812), **I.O.** D.P.

1030 Cf. *Bengal: past and present*, vol. 45 (1933) p. 135, where the following extract from Captain Swinton's diary is quoted from p. 105 of the *Swinton family records* (Edinburgh 1908, privately printed): In the end of the year 1765 the Emperor Shah Alam requested the English Army to conduct him to Delhy, and assist in placing him on the throne of his Fathers, but as Lord Clive could not promise him that, he resolved with Lord Clive's approbation to send a letter to the King of Great Britain to solicit his assistance. As I was about to return to Europe and was well known to the King of Hindostan, the Vizier Monyr ul Dowla requested me to be the bearer of it. This I mentioned to Lord Clive who readily consented: accordingly in December, 1765, the letter was delivered to Lord Clive, and the same time put into my hand by his Lordship.... He also requested me to carry a Munshy to Europe with me in case it should be thought proper to send an answer in the Persian language. Having obtained Lord Clive's consent, I engaged the Munshy to go to Europe. Monyr ul Dowlah [so] however insisted on paying Rs. 2,000 towards his charges.

1031 Cf. W. Foster's *Early travels in India 1583–1619* p. 25 n. 1: "Hijili, on the west side of the Hūgli river, at the mouth of the Rāsulpur river. It was for a long time a place of importance, as cargoes were landed there for transport up the Hūgli, but was gradually washed away."

1032 This date does not seem to tally with the statement in Captain Swinton's diary (if correctly reproduced) that S͟hāh-ʿĀlam's letter was delivered to him in December 1765.

1033 This would imply that he returned in, or about, the beginning of Jumādā I 1183/September 1769.

685 (Samwat 1869/1812), 595 (AH 1231/1816), **I.O.** 4021, **Āṣafīyah** iii p. 350 no. 94 (AH 1230/1815), ii p. 836 no. 25, **Bodleian** 1854, **Ivanow** Curzon 96 (19th cent.).

Urdu translation: **R.A.S.** H.2.

Abridged Urdu and English translations: *Shigurf namah i Velaët, or Excellent intelligence concerning Europe; being the travels of Mirza Itesa modeen, in Great Britain and France. Translated from the original Persian manuscript into Hindoostanee, with an English version and notes, by J. E. Alexander*[1034] [and Munshī Shamshēr Khān: cf. Garcin de Tassy iii pp. 109–10], **London** 1827°*.

[Autobiographical statements, summarized in Rieu i 383, Bodleian, and Buckland's *Dictionary of Indian biography*].

1596. Mīr **M. Ḥusain** b. ʿAbd al-Ḥasanī [read perhaps ʿAbd al-Ḥusain] **al-Iṣfahānī**. (***Risālah i aḥwāl i mulk i Farang u Hindūstān***), an account of a journey in 1188/1774 via Calcutta to Lisbon and London and of a year's residence in the latter place, followed by a sketch of European astronomy: **Rehatsek** p. 19 no. 33, p. 99 no. 51.

1597. [Mīr] **Jamāl al-Dīn Ḥusain b.** Mīr [?[1035]] **Aḥmad al-Ḥusainī al-Mūsawī** b. Mīr Ibrāhīm b. Mīr Amīn al-Dīn b. Mīr Jamāl al-Dīn Ḥusain b. Mīr Fakhr al-Dīn Ḥasan[1036] b. Mīrzà ʿImād al-Dīn Ḥusain surnamed (*al-mulaqqab*) Injū b. Mīr Sharaf al-Dīn Rāhūlī[1037] was evidently the great-great-grandson of the author of the *Farhang i Jahāngīrī*[1038] (not, as Pertsch seems to have supposed, the author of the *Farhang i Jahāngīrī* himself).

1034 Sir James E. Alexander 1803–85: see the *Dictionary of national biography* and Buckland *Dictionary of Indian biography*.

1035 Queried by Pertsch for some reason unspecified.

1036 Ḥusain according to Pertsch.

1037 *Sic ?* Read perhaps Rāhūyī.

1038 Mīr J. al-D. Ḥu. b. Fakhr al-Dīn Ḥa. Injū, a member of a Shīrāzī Saiyid family, went to the Deccan and eventually became *Wakīl*, or Prime Minister, to Murtaḍā Niẓām-Shāh (reigned 972–96/1565–88). Entering Akbar's service in the 30th regnal year (993–4), he held high positions both in his reign and in that of Jahāngīr and died at Āgrah in 1035/1625–6 (according to the *Tārīkh i Muḥammadī*, cited by Rieu iii p. 1088b). See *Burhān i maʾāthir* pp. 397[7], 452[22], 453[1], 454[5], 456[3], 456 antepenult., 567[4]; *Āʾīn i Akbarī* p. 226*b* no. 164 (only his name in a list of *Nuh-ṣadīs*), Blochmann's trans. p. 450; *Memoirs of Jahāngīr*, tr. Rogers and Beveridge, i 46 and elsewhere; *The Embassy of Sir T. Roe to India ... edited by Sir W. Foster*, new ed., Oxford, 1926, pp. 209–12; *Maʾāthir al-umarāʾ* iii pp. 358–60 (quoted and translated in Blochmann's *Contributions to Persian lexicography* (JASB. 37 (1868)) pp. 66–8, translated in *Āʾīn i Akbarī*, tr. Blochmann, pp. 450–1); Rieu ii pp. 496–7.

Brief memoirs (beg. *al-Ḥ. I. 'l. ta'abbada lahu*), divided into a *muqaddimah*, a *faṣl* and a *khātimah* and dealing mainly with persons met by the author on his travels, especially on a journey to Mecca and Medina: **Berlin** 13 (7) (only 9 or 10 leaves. Defective at end).

1598. **Ghulām-Muḥammad Khān**, who may possibly be identical with the author of the *Nawādir al-qiṣaṣ* (no. 1603), undertook his travels of 1196–1201/1782–7 at the request of Warren Hastings, the Governor-General of India.

Account of a journey in and beyond northern India, especially of the part from Shāhjahānābād [i.e. Delhi] to Kābul and Qandahār with reports on contemporary historical events: **Ethé** 2725 (defective at end).

1599. S. Shāh **'Azīz Allāh Bukhārī**, "Moonshy to Sir John Murray, Bart.",[1039] was in the 68th year of his age in Ramaḍān 1209/March 1795, when he wrote at Calcutta for his employer "Seven alphabets with the combinations of all the letters in each" (Rieu ii 533). Berlin 997 and 1084 are MSS. transcribed by him for Sir J. Murray in 1210/1796.

Reminiscences of a journey from Farrukhābād in 1201/1786–7 (beg. *Huwa 'l-Muta'ālī. Rūzī dar siyāḥat i īn bī-biḍā'at dar aiyām i bī-kārī kih kamāl i bī-qarārī-st dar sanah i 1201*), written in 1203/1789 at the request of Sir J. Murray:[1040] **Berlin** 15 (1) (4 foll.).

It appears from the opening words of the reminiscences just mentioned that 'Azīz Allāh Bukhārī was unemployed in 1201/1786–7 and it may be conjectured that his employment by John Murray began not earlier than that year. If so, it must have been someone else who accompanied Murray and at his request kept a diary of his journey from Calcutta to Rāmpūr and back in the period 25 June 1783 to 1 January 1784.

Diary of a journey made in the company of John Murray from Calcutta along the Ganges via Mīrzāpūr, Allahabad, Cawnpore, Farrukhābād and Āgrah to Rāmpūr and back by another route (Barēlī etc.), beginning *Dar*

1039 John Macgregor Murray, who was Military Secretary to the Commander-in-Chief in the Rohilla War (1774) and subsequently First Secretary and Member of the Military Board, became a Lieutenant-Colonel in 1787, was created a Baronet in 1795, retired in 1798 and died in 1822 (see *East India Military Calendar* London 1823, vol. ii p. 461; Rieu i 409*b*). Two volumes containing respectively Persian letters received by him in the years 1788–96 and Persian letters sent by him in the same period to various Indians of rank are described in Rieu i p. 410. Two volumes described in Rieu i pp. 409*b* and 410*a* contain miscellaneous papers collected by him on the history and administration, land-tenure and revenue of Bengal and Bihar, etc.

1040 In his description of this MS. (Berlin p. 52) Pertsch does not say that Sir John Murray was present on this journey, but he says so, perhaps erroneously, later in the catalogue (p. 380).

bayān i ān-kih ba-mūjab i farmūdah i khudāwand i niʿmat and containing not only dates of arrival and departure etc. but also information about topography, local customs, industry, trade, revenue, history and other matters: **Berlin** 361 (apparently the original draft. 139 foll.), 362 (AH 1204/1790, fair copy by S. Shāh ʿAbd al-Laṭīf. 203 foll).

1600. Maulawī **Rafīʿ al-Dīn** b. Farīd al-Dīn Khān **Murādā-bādī**, a pupil of Walī Allāh Dihlawī (see nos. 35, 222 4th par., 285, 1352 *supra*) and an associate of ʿAbd al-ʿAzīz Dihlawī (see nos. 40, 299), died at Murādābād on 15 Dhū ʾl-Ḥijjah 1218/27 March 1804. Several works of his (*Tārīkh i Afāghinah, Tadhkirat al-mashāyikh, Suluww al-kaʾīb bi-dhihr al-ḥabīb, Qiṣar al-āmāl bi-dhikr al-ḥāl wa-ʾl-maʾāl, Kanz al-ḥisāb, Sharḥ i Arbaʿīn i Nawawī, Tarjamah i ʿAin al-ʿilm, Ḥālāt al-Ḥaramain* and others) are mentioned without specification of the language by Ṣiddīq Ḥasan, Ghulām-Sarwar and Raḥmān ʿAlī.

(*Ḥālāt al-Ḥaramain*),[1041] an account of a journey from Murādābād to Mecca and Medina in 1201–3/1786–8: **Bānkīpūr** vii 626 (19th cent.).

[*Itḥāf al-nubalāʾ* p. 251; *Ḥadāʾiq al-Ḥanafīyah* p. 463; Raḥmān ʿAlī p. 66.]

1601. **M. Baqā** is described by Major Yule[1042] in a manuscript note as "my friend Muhummud Buqqa".

Short account of the author's journey from Cawnpore to Benares and back through Jaunpūr and Partābgaṛh to Lucknow from 23 April to 8 October 1798 with descriptive and historical notes on the places visited: **Rieu** ii 841*b* (late 18th cent.).

1602. **ʿAlī b. Mīrzā Khairāt-ʿAlī.**

Manāzil i ḥajj, a short account of a pilgrimage from Persia to the Shīʿite shrines in Mesopotamia and thence to Mecca and Medina, written in 1214/1799 and dedicated to Muḥammad Mīrzā b. Ḥusain, grandson of Shāh Ṭahmāsp II: **Ivanow** 287 (early 19th cent.).

1603. **Ghulām-Muḥammad Khān** left his birthplace, Sirhind, at the age of twelve and [in course of time ?] wandered eastwards in pursuit of learning and a livelihood. He seems to have been for a time in the service of Shujāʿ al-Daulah (*Nawwāb-Wazīr* of Oudh 1167–88/1754–75), and he was wounded at the battle of Baksar ("Buxar", AH 1178/1764). In 1214/1799, when Colonel John

1041 No title is mentioned in the preface.

1042 William Yule, father of Sir Henry Yule.

Collins[1043] was sent from Farrukhābād to Jaipūr in pursuit of Wazīr-ʿAlī, the fugitive *Nawwāb-Wazīr* of Oudh,[1044] Ghulām-Muḥammad Khān was veterinary surgeon to his detachment. The surrender of Wazīr-ʿAlī by the Mahārājah of Jaipūr seems to have made an unfavourable impression on him, since in writing the *Nawādir al-qiṣaṣ* at the request of his fourteen-year-old son Faḍl i Ḥusain "his main object was to disparage the court of Jaipūr".

Nawādir al-qiṣaṣ, narratives and notes relating to Lahore, Qaṣūr, Kashmīr, Tibet, Multān, Siyālkōṭ, Bilāspūr (Sirhind) etc., Delhi, Jaipūr, Qāsim ʿAlī Khān [Mīr Qāsim: cf. no. 802 5th par. *supra*], the Rōhēlahs of Kaṭ'hēr and Najīb Khān [cf. nos. 909–18 *supra*], the Jāts, Farrukhābād [cf. nos. 906–08], the Marāt'hās and the battle of Pānīpat [cf. nos. 555, 792], Shujāʿ al-Daulah's wars with the Rōhēlahs, etc.: **Rieu** iii 981*b* (circ. AD 1854, said to have been transcribed from an autograph).

1604. For the *Masīr i Ṭālibī fī bilād i Afranjī*, Abū Ṭālib Khān's narrative of his journey to Europe in 1213–18/1799–1803, see no. 1178 (2) *supra*.

1605. Ra'īs al-Umarā' Ḥāfiẓ M. **ʿAbd al-Ḥusain** Karbalā'ī Hindī **Karnātakī** is doubtless identical with the Nawwāb Ra'īs al-Umarā' who in the period 1 Shaʿbān 1234/26 May 1819 to 17 Rabīʿ I 1236/23 Dec. 1820 made a pilgrimage from Karbalā' via Ṭihrān to Mashhad, of which an account (*Tadhkirat al-Riḍā?*) was written by S. Muḥibb Ḥusain Khān b. Jaʿfar al-Mūsawī (Berlin 360). He completed on 21 Shawwāl 1233/24 Aug. 1818:

Tadhkirat al-ṭarīq fī maṣā'ib ḥujjāj Bait al-ʿAtīq, an account of a pilgrimage from Karbalā' to Mecca and al-Madīnah in the period 26 Shawwāl 1230/1 Oct. 1815 to 17 Jumādā I 1232/4 April 1817: **Berlin** 359.

1606. Ḥājjī **M. Ḥusain Khān** b. Bāyram ʿAlī Khān succeeded to the princedom of Merv in 1202/1787–8, his father having died while repelling an invasion of Shāh Murād, the Sulṭān of Bukhārā. For some years the son continued hostilities but, having made peace, he accepted an invitation to Bukhārā and was treacherously detained there with his chief supporters while Shāh Murād took possession of Merv and deported to Bukhārā nearly one thousand families.[1045] After seven years' detention M. Ḥusain Khān escaped to Shahr i Sabz and

1043 For whom see Buckland *Dictionary of Indian biography* p. 89.

1044 He was wanted for the murder of George Frederick Cherry (for whom see Buckland *op. cit.* p. 80).

1045 "An almost mortal blow was dealt it at the end of the 18th century when the Amīr of Bukhārā Shāh Murād destroyed the dam on the Murghāb and drove away almost all the inhabitants of Merw." (*Ency. Isl.*, Suppt., under Merw al-Shahidjān (Jakoubovsky)).

went from there to Khujand, Khōqand, Yārkand, Khutan, Chitrāl, Wakhān, Kāfiristān, Jalālābād, Kābul, Ghaznī, Qandahār, Isfizār, Ṭabas and eventually to Ṭihrān. It was there that he met Sir Gore Ouseley and he had been living there for eighteen years as the guest of Fatḥ-ʿAlī Shāh when at the age of fifty-odd years he wrote his brief account of his wanderings.

Translation: *Narrative of the travels of Haji Muhammed Hussein Khan, Prince of Marv, written in 1818;*[1046] *translated from the original,*[1047] *which the Prince wrote at the request of Sir Gore Ouseley* (in *Biographical notices of Persian poets ... by the late ... Sir Gore Ouseley, Bart.*, **London** 1846, pp. 332–51).

1607. **M. Ṣāliḥ** b. Ḥājjī Bāqir Khān **Shīrāzī**, known as (*al-shahīr bi-*) Kāzarānī [*sic*], who accompanied Sir Gore Ouseley's embassy from Iṣfahān to Ṭihrān in 1812 and had been attached to the service of Colonel D'Arcy,[1048] was one of five Persians sent by the Prince Qāʾim-maqām [ʿAbbās Mīrzā b. Fatḥ-ʿAlī Shāh] to England in 1815 under the guardianship of Colonel D'Arcy for the purpose of gaining proficiency in European subjects (English, French, Latin and Natural Science in his case). He is identified by Rieu, doubtless correctly, with "Mirza Salih, one of the public secretaries of H.M. the Shah of Persia, who has been employed on a diplomatic mission in this country" and who, according to an unsigned article (*Persian newspaper and translation*) in the *JRAS*. v (1839) pp. 355–71, was editor of a Ṭihrān newspaper "undertaken a few years since".[1049] Presumably also he is the same person as "Mírzá Ṣáliḥ of Shíráz, the *Wazír* of Ṭihrán", who, according to Browne's *Press and poetry of modern Persia* p. 8, sent at great expense one Mírzá Asadu'lláh, of the province of Fárs, to St. Petersburg to learn the art of printing, and ... on his return thence ... founded at Tabríz, with the assistance of the late Áqá Riẓá ... a lithographic press, the first book lithographed at which was the Holy Qur'án in the handwriting of Mírzá Ḥusain the famous calligraphist." A collection of Persian dialogues (*Suʾāl u jawāb*) composed by him for Sir Gore Ouseley, probably in

1046 Sir Gore Ouseley left Persia in 1814. M. Husain Khān's account of his wanderings was sent to him by letter.

1047 The original does not seem to be among the Ouseley MSS. described by Ethé in the Bodleian catalogue.

1048 Attached to Sir G. Ouseley's mission in 1810, he subsequently entered the Persian service.

1049 The specimen described in the *JRAS*., "lithographed on two large folios, printed on one side only" and "surmounted by the Persian emblem of the Lion and Sun", began with the headings *Akhbār u waqāʾiʿ i shahr i Muḥarram al-Ḥarām 1253* * *Dar Dār al-Khilāfah i Ṭihrān inṭibāʿ yāftah* * *Akhbār i mamālik i sharqīyah*. The second part of the paper, devoted to European news, is headed *Akhbār i mamālik i gharbīyah*. This newspaper seems not to be mentioned in Browne's *Press and poetry of modern Persia*.

1812, is preserved in MS. at Oxford (Bodleian 1857) and is doubtless the same as the *Persian dialogues ... with an English translation by W. Price* published at Worcester in 1822° and reissued in W. Price's *Grammar of the three principal Oriental languages, Hindoostanee, Persian, and Arabic ... to which is added a set of Persian dialogues ... by Mirza Mohammed Saulih, of Shiraz ... with an English* [and French] *translation* (London, Worcester printed, 1823°*).

(1) ***Account of a journey from Iṣfahān to Ṭihrān*** [with Sir Gore Ouseley's embassy ?], "containing topographical and historical information about these two towns and the places lying between," and "dated at the end, AH 1227, the 11th of Jumâdâ I = AD 1812, 23rd of May": **Bodleian** 1856 (40 foll.).

(2) **(*Siyāḥat-nāmah i M. Ṣāliḥ i Shīrāzī*)**, in four *faṣls* ((1) circumstances leading to the author's departure, (2) his journey from Tabrīz (10 Jumādā II 1230/19 April 1815) through Erivan, Tiflis, Moscow, St. Petersburg and thence by sea, (3) his arrival in England (29 Shawwāl 1230/4 October 1815) and his stay there, (4) his return journey by sea to Istānbūl and thence by land towards Persia from 2 Shawwāl 1234/4 July 1819 to Ṣafar 1235/Nov.- Dec. 1819, at which point the MS. breaks off with an account of his stay at Erzerum: **Rieu** i 387*b* (presented by the author to George Willock).

1608. In 1237/1822 S. **M. b. Aḥmad al-Ḥasanī** completed

Risālah i S. M. b. A. al-Ḥ., a brief account of the author's journey to Kurdistān with Claudius James Rich:[1050] **Leningrad** Mus. Asiat. (see *Mélanges asiatiques* ii (St. Petersburg 1852–6) p. 54).

1609. **Zain al-ʿĀbidīn** b. Iskandar **Shīrwānī** Niʿmatallāhī, born at Shamākhī on 15 Shaʿbān 1194/1780, was taken as a child of five to Karbalā', where he received his education. Finding his teachers biased and narrow-minded, he started at the age of seventeen on a long series of travels in search of knowledge and enlightenment, associating with scholars, mystics and others. Among the places visited by him were ʿIrāq, various parts of Persia, Kābul, where he became the disciple of a celebrated *murshid* named Ḥasan ʿAlī Shāh, Peshawar, which he left after the death of Ḥasan ʿAlī Shāh in 1216/1801, Delhi, Bengal, the Deccan and other places in India, Ṭukhāristān, Turkistān, Southern Arabia, Abyssinia, the Ḥijāz, Egypt, Syria, Asia Minor, Greece, Constantinople and Morocco. Having returned to Persia, he went to Ṭihrān and was at first well received but later, having been traduced by enemies to Fatḥ-ʿAlī Shāh, he went successively

1050 For C. J. Rich (1787–1821) see the *Dictionary of national biography*, Rieu iii p. xi, etc.

to Hamadān, Shīrāz and Kirmān. Returning to Shīrāz in 1236/1820, he married and decided to settle there, but, having been declared an infidel by the *mujtahids*, he fled to Yazd. Thence he went to Iṣfahān. Shortly afterwards he returned to Shīrāz and taking his wife to Qūmishah settled there in 1237/1821. He died in 1253/1837. This remarkable man was both intelligent and broad-minded. His works contain varied and interesting information.

(1) ***Riyāḍ al-siyāḥah***, a geographical work interspersed with much biographical and historical information, of which the first volume (on Persia) was completed at Qūmishah in 1237/1821–2 and the second (on extra-Persian countries which the author had visited or about which he had received information) in 1242/1827: **Chanykov** 115 (autograph. See *Mélanges asiatiques* i (St. Petersburg 1849–52) p. 556), **Leningrad** Mus. Asiat. (AH 1258/1842. See *Mélanges asiatiques* ii, p. 57), **Rieu** Suppt. 139 (vol. ii only. Before AH 1246/1830), **Cairo** p. 531 ("*Risālah manqūlah min kitāb Riyāḍ al-siyāḥah awwaluhā Dar chigūnagī (sic lege) i taqsīm i zamīn ba-ḥukm i ḥukamā i ḥikmat.* AH 1240/1824–5).

Edition: **Iṣfahān** 1329/1911 (see Harrassowitz's *Bücher-Katalog* 430 (1931) no. 897).

Extract: Dorn (B.) *Muhammedanische Quetten zur Geschichte der südlichen Küstenländer des Kaspischen Meeres*, iv (St. Petersburg 1858°*) pp. 455–67.

(2) ***Bustān al-siyāḥah***, an alphabetically arranged geographical dictionary interspersed with much biographical and historical information completed at Shīrāz in 1247/1832: **Rieu** Suppt. 140 (lacks the four chapters which in the 1310/1892–3 edition precede the *Sair* (see Browne *Lit. Hist.* iv p. 451). Apparently A.H 1248/1832), **D.M.G.** 17 (only 19 of the 28 *gulshans*. Circ. AH 1250/1834–5), **Leningrad** Pub. Lib. (see *Mélanges asiatiques* iii (St. Petersburg 1859), p. 732).

Editions: **Ṭihrān** 1310/1892–3 (see Browne *Lit. Hist.* iv p. 450 n. 3); 1315/1898°; **Shīrāz** 1342/1923–4 (see Harrassowitz's *Bücher-Katalog* 430 (1931) no. 896).

Description: Browne *Lit. Hist.* iv, pp. 450–2.

(3) ***Ḥadā'iq al-siyāḥah***, an earlier and shorter recension of the *Bustān al-siyāḥah* completed at Shīrāz in 1242/1827: **Rieu** Suppt. 141 (AH 1273/1857), **Blochet** i 673 (AH 1274/1857–8).

The "*Risālah fī bayān aḥwāl al-jānī [I]bn Iskandar Zain al-'Ābidīn al-Shirwānī*" (**Cairo** p. 531. AH 1240/1824–5) may be a part of the *Riyāḍ al-siyāḥah* or a short independent autobiography.[1051]

1051 The opening words are given as *al-Ḥamdu lillāhi Rabbi 'l-'ālamīn.*

[*Ḥadāʾiq al-siyāḥah*, preface; *Bustān al-siyāḥah*, preface and under Shamākhī; *Mélanges asiatiques*, tome iii (1857–9), pp. 50–9 (Lettre de M. Khanvkov à M. Dorn) = *Bulletin histor-phil. de l'Acad. des Sciences*, tome xiv, N. 16; *Rauḍat al-ṣafā-yi Nāṣirī* ix foll. 166*b*, l. 19, 171*b*, p. 4, x foll. 5*b*, l. 14, 7*a*, l. 19, and elsewhere; Rieu Suppt. pp. 99–102; Browne *Lit. Hist.* iv pp. 450–2; *Dānishmandān i Ādharbāyjān* pp. 169–71.]

1610. ʿ**Alī Mirzā** "Maftūn" b. Mirzā Abū Ṭālib **Dihlawī** (*mutawaṭṭan*[an]) ʿ**Azīmābādī** (*maskin*[an]).

Zubdat al-akhbār fī sawāniḥ al-asfār, an account of pilgrimages to Mecca and Mashhad in 1241–3/1825–7 dedicated to Amīn al-Daulah Nāṣir-Jang [*Wazīr* to the King of Oudh, dismissed in 1263/1847. Cf. Rieu iii, p. 963*a*] and divided into three *muḥīṭs* subdivided into *anhār* ((1) ʿAẓīmābād by boat to Bārh, Bhāgalpūr, Rājmaḥall, Hūglī, Calcutta, thence to Ceylon, Mokhā, Jiddah, Medina and Mecca, (2) Jiddah to Muscat, Shīrāz, Kāzarūn, Iṣfahān, Kāshān, Naṣrābād, Qumm, Ṭihrān, Simnān, Dāmghān, Nīshāpūr, Mashhad, (3) return journey to Ṭihrān etc.): **Bānkīpūr** vii 631 (*Muḥīṭ* i. Written in 1246/1831 by the author's brother, Mirzā Amīr ʿAlī), 632 (*Muḥīṭ* ii. AH 1249/1833, autograph).

1611. M. **Qādir Khān "Munshī"** Bīdarī has already been mentioned as the author of the *Tārīkh i Āṣaf-Jāhī* (no. 1041), the *Tawārīkh i farkhundah* (*ibid.*), and the *Tārīkh i Qādirī* (no. 1026 (2)).

Sair i Hind u gulagsht i Dakan, composed in 1247/1831–2: **Āṣafīyah** i p. 242 nos. 754 (AH 1254/1838), 286.

1612. Nawwāb M. **Muṣṭafā Khān** "Shēftah" and "Ḥasratī" who was born at Delhi in, or about, 1806 and who died in 1869, has already been mentioned (no. 1207 *supra*) as the author of the *Gulshan i bī-khār*.

Targhīb al-sālik ilā aḥsan al-masālik, or *Rah-āward*, an account of a pilgrimage to Mecca and Medina in 1254–6/1839–41.

Edition: place ? 1283/1866–7 (Āṣafīyah ii p. 836, Peshawar 1941).

Urdu translation by S. Zain al-ʿĀbidīn: *Sirāj i munīr*, place ? 1910.

1613. **Yūsuf Khān Gilīm-pōsh.**

Tārīkh i Yūsufī, an account of a journey from Ḥaidarābād to Europe, especially England, in 1828, composed in 1259/1843 and dedicated to Queen Victoria: **Ivanow** 289 (late 19th cent.).

1614. The anonymous Frenchwoman who speaks in the first person in the *Rūz-nāmah i safar i Shīrāz* seems to have been a teacher in the service of the Shāh,[1052] though Boré, the former owner of the MS., has written thereon a note saying that she went to Persia to trade in jewellery.

Rūz-nāmah i safar i Shīrāz, account of a journey in 1251/1835–6 from Ṭihrān to Shīrāz and from Shīrāz to Iṣfahān, "évidemment rédigé par un mirza persan sur les notes ou d'après les souvenirs de la voyageuse": **Blochet** i 649 (1st half of 19th cent.).

1615. Nawwāb Riḍā-Qulī Mīrzā[1053] Nā'ib al-Iyālah [Deputy Governor of Fārs], Nawwāb **Najaf-Qulī Mīrzā** "Wālī", Governor of Kūhgīlūyah and Bihbahān as well as "a well known Persian and Arabic scholar, an excellent poet, and consulted as an oracle on many subjects, being exceedingly fond of literature", and Ḥusām al-Daulah Taimūr Mīrzā,[1054] "a celebrated warrior, horseman, and hunter," who "governed Bushir for many years and had seen many English who visited the Persian Gulf", are respectively the first, the third, and the fifth of the seventeen sons of the Farmān-farmā Ḥusain-ʿAlī Mīrzā b. Fatḥ-ʿAlī Shāh enumerated in the *Rauḍat al-ṣafā-yi Nāṣirī* (x fol. 5*a*, ll. 17, 21, 23). When their father the Governor of Fārs was defeated in his attempt to supplant his brother Muḥammad Shāh and to seize the throne after the death of Fatḥ-ʿAlī Shāh [19 Jumādā II 1250/23 October 1834], they managed to escape from Shīrāz (*op. cit.* x fol. 4*b*, l. 7 from foot) and after visiting England in the summer of 1836 settled in Baghdād. An account of these events was written by Najaf-Qulī Mīrzā and a copy of it was obtained from him, or from one of his brothers, at Baghdād by Asʿad Yaʿqūb Khaiyāṭ,[1055] a Syrian Christian who had been for more than five years Principal Interpreter to the British Consul General at Damascus and had accompanied the princes as their interpreter. Another account of the visit was written by their British *mihmāndār*, James Baillie Fraser,[1056] under the title *Narrative of the residence of the Persian princes in London in 1835* [*sic*[1057]] *and*

1052 *Chūn īn kamīnah i namak-khwārah i daulat-khwāh i Shāhanshāh i gītī-panāh madām i muʿallim kih zan i Farangsīs-am* (quoted by Blochet from fol. 1*b*).

1053 Cf. no. 1225 6th footnote.

1054 Spelt "Taymoor Meerza" by Asʿad Y. Khaiyāṭ, and "Timour Meerza" by J. B. Fraser. "Teymur" and "Taymur" are given in the *Farhang i Nafīsī* as the ways of pronouncing the name of the founder of the Tīmūrid dynasty (Tamerlane). Taimūr Mīrzā, best known as the author of the *Bāz-nāmah i Nāṣirī*, died in 1291/1874 (according to Phillott's introduction to his translation of the *Bāz-nāmah*).

1055 *Cf.* Fraser's *Narrative* i p. 58.

1056 For whom see the *Dictionary of national biography* and Buckland's *Dictionary of Indian biography*.

1057 The princes did not reach England until 1836.

1836, with an account of their journey from Persia and subsequent adventures (2 vols., London 1838).

English translation: *Journal of a residence in England, and of a journey from and to Syria, of their Royal Highnesses Reeza Koolee Meerza, Najaf Koolee Meerza, and Taymoor Meerza, of Persia, to which are prefixed some particulars respecting modern Persia, and the death of the late Shah. Originally written in Persian, by H.R.H. Najaf Koolee Meerza, son of Prince Firmân Firmân* [*sic*], *grandson of H.M. Fathali Shah, the late Emperor of Persia; and translated, with explanatory notes, by Assaad Y. Kayat. In two volumes. Printed for private circulation only*. **London** 1839°*.

[A portrait of the three princes forms the frontispiece to Fraser's *Narrative*.]

1616. Ḥājj Mīrzā **ʿAlī Khān** Marāghī, entitled Ḥājib al-Daulah and later **Iʿtimād al-Salṭanah**, was the father of M. Ḥasan Khān Marāghī Iʿtimād al-Salṭanah (for whom see no. 192 *supra*). From the latter's list of successive Heads of Government Departments in Nāṣir al-Dīn Shāh's reign (*al-Maʾāthir wa-ʾl-āthār* pp. 15–29) it appears that he became Minister of Justice in 1278/1861–2 (*op. cit.* p. 16*b*) and Minister of *Waẓāʾif* in the nineteenth year of the reign (i.e. in 1282/1865–6. *Op. cit.* p. 17*b*). Other offices held by him are mentioned without dates in the aforesaid list under the headings *Idārah i Farrāsh- khanah u Ḥijābat i Daulat* (p. 19*a*), *Idārah i Bannāʾī i Dīwān i* Aʿlā (p. 21*b*),[1058] *Idārah i Bāghāt i Mubārakah i Daulatī* (p. 22*a*) and *Idārah i Khāliṣajāt i Dīwānī* (p. 23*b*). He was at different times Governor of ʿArabistān and Khūzistān (*op. cit.* p. 31*b*), Luristān (*op. cit.* p. 32*a*) and Gīlān (*ibid*). According to the Mashhad catalogue he died in 1285/1868–9.

(*Safar-nāmah i Ḥājj Mīrzā ʿAlī Khān i Marāghī*),[1059] an account of a journey to Mecca written in 1263/1847: **Mashhad** iii p. 90 (AH 1306/1888–9).

1617. Mubāriz al-Daulah **Pīr Ibrāhīm Khān** Khwēshgī Qaṣūrī, who was born at Qaṣūr in 1794 and died in 1856, has already been mentioned (no. 840 *supra*) as the author of a history of Bahāwalpūr.

(1) ***Autobiography*** (in Persian ?): see no. 840, last par. *supra*.

(2) ***Sairistān***, an account of a visit to England in 1851–2 together with a brief history of his tribe: **Multān**[1060] 1854° (pp. 237).

1058 Cf. *Rauḍat al-ṣafā-yi Nāṣirī* x fol. 141*a* (fifth page from end) ult

1059 Called *Safar-nāmah* simply in the Mashhad catalogue, but it is not clear whether this is a formal title or a description.

1060 So M. Shafīʿ in *Islamic culture* iii/3 pp. 454, 472 (cf. no. 840 3rd par. 1st footnote *supra*).

1618. **Khudā-dād Khān** b. Rāḍō Khān Tarīn has already been mentioned (no. 834 *supra*) as the author of the *Lubb i tārīkh i Sind'h*, completed in 1318/1900.

Waqā'i' al-sair i Jaisalmēr, an account of a tour to Jaisalmēr in 1859: **Karāchī** 1875*.

1619. Maulawī Abū Rajā **M. Zamān Khān** Shāhjahānpūrī, *Mudarris* in a *madrasah* at Ḥaidarābād and one of the instructors who educated Mīr Maḥbūb 'Alī Khān (Niẓām of Ḥaidarābād, b. 1866, succeeded his father 1869, d. 1911), wrote an Urdu work *Hadīyah i Mahdawīyah* (Editions: Cawnpore 1867*, 1877*) in refutation of the teachings expounded in four tracts by S. 'Īsā, commonly called (*'urf*) 'Ālim Miyān, Mahdawī Ḥaidarābādī, the leader of the Mahdawī sect (cf. no. 1411 (21)). On 6 Dhū 'l-Ḥijjah 1292/3 Jan. 1876 he was murdered in a mosque at Ḥaidarābād by an alleged Mahdawī. According to Niẓāmī Badāyūnī an annual *'urs* is celebrated at his tomb in the court of his *madrasah*.

Dāstān i jahān, an account of a journey to Egypt, Syria, and Mesopotamia in 1283/1866 (pp. 3–92 = *Kitāb* i), followed by a geography of the world (pp. 92–309 = *Kitāb* ii), a history of Jerusalem (pp. 309–360 = *Kitāb* iii) and a history of the Ottoman Sulṭāns (pp. 360–92 = *Kitāb* iv): **Badāyūn** [1906°, 1911*].

[Raḥmān 'Alī pp. 188–90; Niẓāmī Badāyūnī *Qāmūs al-mashāhīr* (in Urdu) ii pp. 191–2 (evidently based mainly on Raḥmān 'Alī or on some common source).]

1620. For Nāṣir al-Dīn Shāh's diaries of his journeys in Europe and Asia see no. 439.

1621. Ḥājjī **Ḥabīb Punnōchhī**.

Manāzil al-safar i ḥajj, a metrical account of a pilgrimage in 1287–8/1870–1: **Lahore** 1875* (24 pp.).

1622. Nawwāb M. **Kalb-'Alī Khān** succeeded his father, Yūsuf 'Alī Khān, as Nawwāb of Rāmpūr in 1865. He was a member of Lord Lytton's Council and was created G.C.S.I. He died in 1887 and was succeeded by his son Mushtāq 'Alī Khān. His works include (1) *Shigūfah i khusrawī*, addresses, prefaces and other compositions, Rāmpūr 1287–9/1870–3°*, and (2) *Tarānah i gham*.

Qindīl i Ḥaram, an account in rhymed prose of a pilgrimage in 1872: **Rāmpūr** 1290/1873°*.

[*Nigāristān i sukhun* pp. 128–30; *Būstān i Awad'h* p. 188; *Who's who in India*, 1911; Rām Bābū Saksēna *A history of Urdu literature* pp. 177–9; portrait in the Urdu translation of R. B. Saksēna's work.]

1623. For the diary of M. Ḥasan Khān Marāghī Iʿtimād al-Salṭanah, describing his journey with Nāṣir al-Dīn Shāh from Tiflīs to Ṭihrān in 1290–1/1873–4, see no. 444 (4) *supra*. The journey on which he accompanied Nāṣir al-Dīn Shāh to Mashhad in 1300/1882 is described in the *Maṭlaʿ al-shams* (for which see no. 471 *supra*).

1624. **Farhād Mīrzā** b. ʿAbbās Mīrzā b. Fatḥ-ʿAlī Shāh, who died in 1888, has already been mentioned in connexion with the works *Qamqām i zakhkhar* (no. 259 *supra*) and *Jām i Jam* (no. 193 *a* (3)).

Hidāyat al-sabīl wa-kifāyat al-dalīl, diary of a pilgrimage to Mecca in 1292–3/1875–6: **Shīrāz** 1294/1877* (362 pp.), **Ṭihrān** 1294/1877° (385 pp.).

1625. **Sulṭān-Murād Mīrzā** Ḥusām al-Salṭanah is the eleventh of the twenty-six sons of ʿAbbās Mīrzā b. Fatḥ-ʿAlī Shāh enumerated by Riḍā-Qulī Khān (*Rauḍat al-ṣafāʾ* ix, fol. 166*a*, 1. 11). He held at different times the governorships of several towns[1061] and provinces,[1062] but he is more especially associated with Khurāsān, of which province he was Governor at least five times (*al-Maʾāthir wa-ʾl-āthār* pp. 29*b*, 30*a*). It was he who dealt with the rebellion of the Sālār (M. Ḥasan Khān b. Allāh-Yār Khān Qājār Dawālū) and besieged him in Mashhad after the death of Muḥammad Shāh (Watson *History of Persia* pp. 368, 380, 383–4). He was for a time Minister of War (*al-Maʾāthir wa-ʾl-āthar* p. 16).

Dalīl al-anām fī sabīl ziyārat Bait Allāh al-ḥarām, the journal of a pilgrimage to Mecca in 1297/1880: **Majlis** 693 (AH 1323/1905).

[*Rauḍat al-ṣafā-yi Nāṣirī* ix foll. 155*a*, l. 17, 166*a*, l. 11, x foll. 18*b*, l. 2, 58*b* antepenult., 71*b*, l. 19, 91*b*, l. 7, 113*b*, l. 16, 118*b*, l. 17, 120*a*, l. 15, and elsewhere.]

1626. Ḥājjī **Pīr-zādah Nāʾīnī.**

Safar-nāmah i Ḥājjī Pīr-zādah i Nāʾīnī, an account of a journey to Paris, Istānbūl and Cairo in 1303/1885–6: **Majlis** 695 (AH 1321/1903).

1627. Nawwāb Mīr **Lāʾiq ʿAlī Khān** ʿImād al-Salṭanah Sir **Sālār-Jang** [II], K.C.I.E., elder son of the great Prime Minister of Ḥaidarābād, Nawwāb Mīr Turāb ʿAlī Khān Sir Sālār-Jang [I], G.C.S.I., was born at Ḥaidarābād in 1862[1063] or 1863,[1064]

1061 e.g. Iṣfahān (*al-Maʾāthir wa-ʾl-āthār* p. 21a penult.), Yazd (*ibid.* p. 33*a*), Kirmānshāh (*ibid.*, p. 35*a*).

1062 e.g. Fārs (*al-M. wa-ʾl-ā.* p. 21*a*), Kurdistān (*ibid.* p. 32*a*).

1063 So Buckland.

1064 1280/1863 according to Niẓāmī Badāyūnī.

and was educated with Mīr Maḥbūb ʿAlī K͟hān (b. 1866, succeeded his father as Niẓām in 1869, d. 1911). After his father's death in 1883 he was appointed Secretary to the Council of Regency and in 1884 he became Prime Minister. Having resigned in April 1887 owing to differences with the Niẓām, he visited England and was created K.C.I.E. He died in July 1889. His son, Mīr Yūsuf ʿAlī K͟hān (Sālār-Jang III), was Prime Minister in 1912–14.

The travels in Europe of Nawab Mir Laik Ali Khan Imadul Saltana Sir Salar Jang Bahadur (*Waqāʾiʿ i musāfarat* etc.[1065]): **Bombay** 1305/1888°.

[Buckland *Dictionary of Indian biography* p. 371; Niẓāmī Badāyūnī *Qāmūs al-mashāhīr* (in Urdu) i p. 278.]

1628. **S. M. Riḍā b.** Muftī S. **Dildār Ḥusain** Hāshimī was Mīr Munshī to Amīr al-Daulah Saʿīd al-Mulk Rājah M. Amīr Ḥasan K͟hān Mumtāz-Jang,[1066] Rājah of Maḥmūdābād (near Sītāpūr in Oudh), whom he accompanied on the journey described in his *Dalāʾil al-ẓafar*.

Dalāʾil al-ẓafar fī tadhkirat al-safar, an account of a journey in 1306/1889 to the Shīʿite sanctuaries of Mesopotamia.

Edition: **Lucknow** [1893°*].

1629. **Maḥmūd Ṭarzī** b. G͟hulām-Muḥammad K͟hān Ṭarzī, a descendant of Sardār Raḥm-dil K͟hān, brother of Amīr Dōst-Muḥammad K͟hān (who reigned 1242–80/1826–63), was born at G͟haznī in 1285/1870. In the reign of ʿAbd al-Raḥmān K͟hān (1296–1319/1879–1901. Cf. no. 575 *supra*) his father, having been accused of high treason and banished from Afg͟hānistān, settled with all his family at Damascus, and here Maḥmūd married a Syrian wife. After the father's death the family was pardoned by Ḥabīb Allāh K͟hān (1319–37/1901–19) and Maḥmūd returned to Kābul, where in 1329/1911 he founded the fortnightly newspaper, *Sirāj al-ak͟hbār*, "the ancestor of all the present periodical publications in Afghanistān" (Bogdanov). In 1919 after the accession of his son-in-law, Amān Allāh K͟hān (1919–29), he was appointed Minister of Foreign Affairs. In 1922 he became Afg͟hān Minister to France and Belgium, but in 1924 he was reappointed Minister of Foreign Affairs. In 1927 he went to France on leave for the sake of his health.

He played a prominent part in the literary renaissance which occurred in the reign of Ḥabīb Allāh K͟hān. Among his works are (1) *Rauḍah i ḥikam*, "moral, literary and political essays" (Arberry), Kābul 1331/1913*, (2) *Az har dahan suk͟hanī*

[1065] In the Āṣafīyah catalogue (ii p. 836) the work is called *Safar-nāmah i Sālār Jang i marḥūm*, but this cannot be the actual title.

[1066] b. 1849, succeeded his father 1858: see Sir R. Lethbridge *The Golden Book of India* pp. 331–2.

u az har chaman samanī, a commonplace book in prose and verse, Kābul 1331/1913*, (3) *Adab dar fann* or *Maḥmūd-nāmah*, a small collection of odes (45 pp.), Kābul 1331/1913* (I.O. V.T. 3754*a*), (4) *Tārīkh i muḥārabah i Rūs u Zhāpān* (see no. 609 [Russo-Japanese War] *supra*), as well as the following translations of the Turkish versions of novels by Jules Verne, (5) *Siyāḥat dar jaww i hawā* (=*Robur le Conquérant*=*A clipper of the clouds*), Kābul 1332/1913*, (6) *Jazīrah i pinhān* (= *L'île mystérieuse*), Kābul 1332/1914* (vol. i), (7) 20,000 *farsakh siyāḥat dar zīr i baḥr* (= *Vingt mille lieues sous les mers*), Kābul 1332/1914*. According to Bogdanov he "found time to translate (from the Arabic and Turkish versions) several novels by Victor Hugo and most of the novels by Jules Verne". Few of these seem to have reached Europe.

Siyāḥat-nāmah i sih qiṭʿah i rūy i zamīn dar 29 rūz, an account of a journey in Asia, Europe and Africa in 1308/1890–1: **Kābul** 1333/1915* (674 pp.).

[L. Bogdanov *Notes on the Afghan periodical press* (in *Islamic culture* iii/1 (Jan. 1929) pp. 126–52) p. 127 n. 2.]

1630. Colonel **Shāh Bēg Khān** b. Raḥmān Bēg b. Yūsuf Bēg Shughnānī was born in 1288/1871, his father being *Aq-saqāl* of some villages in Shughnān. In 1301/1884 he was taken to Kābul and became a protégé of the Amīr ʿAbd al-Raḥmān, who arranged for the continuance of his education and subsequently gave him employment at court. After his return from his first pilgrimage he was appointed by the Amīr Ḥabīb Allāh to membership of the Common Council (p. 117[7]: *dar jumlah i mimbarān i Shūrā-yi ʿĀmm*) and six months later to the Privy Council (*sharaf i bār-yābī i Shūrā-yi Khāṣṣ nīz ʿaṭā farmūdand*). Later he became Afghān Minister in Bombay.

Safar i aiyām i saʿīdah bā nikāt i mufīdah (so at top of p. 1 and in the preface, but on the cover *Safar-nāmah i Ḥijāz ... mushtamil-bar ḥālāt i S. i a. i s....*), accounts of pilgrimages from Kābul to Mecca in 1320–1/1903 and 1322–3/1904–5 (pp. 19–34), together with extracts (*nikāt i mufīdah*) from the *Anwār i Suhailī* and elsewhere (pp. 35–116) and a biography of the author (pp. 8–19), the whole accompanied by an Urdu translation by the editor, M. Fāḍil Khān b. M. Ḥusain, *Mīr Munshī* to the Afghān Legation: **Lahore** [1915*].

[Biography referred to above. Portrait frontispiece. Portrait of the translator at end.]

1631. Other works:—

(1) ***Adventures of Columbus***, *Discoverer of America. Translated by Mirza Mahommad Munshi.* (*Aḥwāl i Kristōfar Kulambas*): **Calcutta** 1910*.

(2) ***Aḥwāl i Kristōfar Kulambas***: see ***Adventures, etc.***, above.

(3) ***Armaghān i Hindūstān***, by S. Luṭf-ʿAlī Shāh Maudūdī Chishtī. Edition: place? 1311/1893–4 (Āṣafīyah ii p. 836).

(4) ***Fawāʾid al-nāẓirīn***, an account of al-Ṭāʾif and Mecca translated from J. L. Burckhardt's *Travels in Arabia* (London 1829, vol. i p. 101–vol. ii p. 87) by M. Najm al-Dīn: **Rieu** iii 993*b* (AH. 1254/1838 ?).

Edition: *Fowaid oon Nazireen, or Travels of the late Mr. John Lewis Burckhardt on the Hedjaz, as far as Mecca. Abridged and translated into Persian by Robert Neave, Esq., and arranged for the press by Nuzmood Deen Mahomud*, **Calcutta** 1832°*.

(5) ***Guldastah i Ḥakīm mausūm bah Safar i Ḥijāz***, an account of a pilgrimage by ʿAbd Allāh Khān "Ḥakīm" Kāndilī: **Lahore** 1322/1904*.

(6) ***Guldastah i Ingilistān***, a short account in prose and verse of a visit to London, by S. ʿAbd Allāh b. M.: **Calcutta** 1271/1854°*.

(7) ***ʿIbrat al-nāẓirīn safar-nāmah i ʿIrāq***: **Āṣafīyah** ii p. 836.

(8) ***Nuh sāl dar Amrīkah***, by ʿAbd Allāh Dashtī: **Ṭihrān**, date ? (see *Luzac's Oriental List* 1934 p. 107).

(9) ***Rūz-nāmah i Mīrzā M. Shafīʿ Gushtāsb Māzandarānī*** (Travels ? cf. no. 14 below): **Leningrad** Univ. 866*b* (Salemann-Rosen p. 16).

(10) ***Rūz-nāmah i safar i Mīrzā Naṣīr Allāh Sulṭān***: **Leningrad** Univ. 407 (Salemann-Rosen p. 16).

(11) ***Rūz-nāmah i safar i Piṭirburgh***, by Mīrzā Masʿūd: **Leningrad** Univ. 680 (Salemann-Rosen p. 16).

(12) ***Safar i Ḥijāz***. See ***Guldastah i Ḥakīm***.

(13) ***Safar-nāmah i janāb i Qāḍī Taqī Muttaqī***, the travels of Q.T.M., of Ambala, by S. Amīn Allāh b. M. Munīr: **Ambala** [Anbālah], [1909*].

(14) ***Safar-nāmah i Mīrzā M. Shafīʿ Gushtāsb Māzandarānī*** (cf. no. 9 above): **Leningrad** Univ. 866*a* (Salemann-Rosen p. 16).

(15) ***Safar-nāmah i Mūsyū Farānsīsī***: **Āṣafīyah** ii p. 836.

(16) ***Safar-nāmah i Qum***, by Mīrzā Ghulām-Ḥusain Afḍal al-Mulk: **Majlis** 697 (AH. 1324/1906).

(17) ***Safar-nāmah (Mimwār) i Sar Antwān Sharlī u Sar Rubart Sharlī***, a translation made by Ḥājj ʿAlī-Qulī Khān Sardār i Asʿad: **Ṭihrān** 1330/1912 (see Mashhad iii p. 136).

(18) ***Safar-nāmah i Wāmbirī***, a translation made in 1302/1884–5 by Āwānus[1067] Masīḥī b. Ustād Ibrāhīm Zargar-bāshī (cf. no. (22) below) from the French version of A. Vámbéry's *Travels in Central Asia, being the account of a journey from Teheran ... performed in* 1863 (London 1864): **Majlis** 698 (ends in *Faṣl* xv).

1067 For this name cf. no. 1150 1st par. penult. footnote *supra*.

(19) ***Sarbāz i Pārsī***, an account of travels in Persia by Khalīl Wazīr: **Bombay** AHS 1311/1933* (96 pp.).
(20) ***Sawāniḥ i safar al-Ḥijāz***: **Leningrad** Univ. 1141*i* (Romaskewicz p. 10).
(21) ***Siyāḥat i Turāb***, by Turāb ʿAlī: **Lindesiana** p. 228 no. 349 (circ. AD. 1820).
(22) **(*Siyāḥat-nāmah*)**, a translation made in 1890 by Āwānus Khān (cf. no. (18) above) from a French version of H. M. Stanley's *In darkest Africa* (London 1890): **Majlis** 699 (AH. 1308/1890–1).
(23) ***Siyāḥat-nāmah***, account of an expedition sent in Nāṣir al-Dīn Shāh's reign to extend the telegraph to Iṣfahān, Yazd, Kirmān and the ports of the Persian Gulf: **Majlis** 700.
(24) ***Ṭalīʿah i shams***, a translation by Ibrāhīm Khān Ṣaḥḥāf-bāshī of an account of Christopher Columbus: **Mashhad** 1327/1909 (see Mashhad 14, ptd. bks., no. 139).
(25) ***Tuḥfat al-bāṣirīn***, a diary of a pilgrimage by M. ʿAlī b. M. Qāsim: **Karāchī** 1858°.
(26) ***Tūshah i rāh***, a *mathnawī* describing a journey from Kashmīr to India and meetings with persons of distinction by M. Anwar Shāh "Anwar":[1068] **Lahore** 1874* (18 pp. Cf. Arberry p. 306).

13.16 *Women*

1632. For the memoirs of Gulbadan Bēgam see no. 703 *supra*.

1633. For the *Jawāhir al-ʿajāʾib* of "Fakhrī" b. "Amīrī" Harawī see 1099 (2) *supra*.

1634. **Gaston Bruit** composed his account of Bībī Juliyānā[1069] at the request of Colonel Jean-Baptiste Joseph Gentil,[1070] who had come to India in 1165/1752, twenty-two years before the date of composition, and had married Bībī Juliyānā's great grand-niece.

1068 Another work by the same author is *Manẓūm i Anwar*, poems in praise of Kalb-ʿAlī Khān. Nawwāb of Rāmpūr (for whom see no. 1622 *supra*), Amritsar 1293/1876°* (220 pp.).

1069 For whom see Gentil's *Mémoires sur l'Indoustan* pp. 367–80; J. A. Ismael Garcias *Uma doña portuguesa na corte do Grão Mogol*, Nova Goa 1907; E. Maclagan *The Jesuits and the Great Mogul*, London 1932, pp. 181–9; etc.

1070 For whom see Buckland *Dictionary of Indian biography* p. 161. He was at this time in the service of Shujāʿ al-Daulah, the *Nawwāb-Wazīr* of Oudh and "was most generous in helping less fortunate fellow countrymen, and enrolled a body of them to serve under the Nawab.". He was born at Bagnols in 1726 and died there in 1799. His collection of Persian MSS. is now in the Bibliothèque Nationale.

Aḥwāl i Bībī Juliyānā, an account of a Portuguese woman who was taken captive in childhood, apparently at Hūglī, by S͟hāh-Jahān's forces and who, having in course of time entered the service of Prince M. Muʻaẓẓam (S͟hāh-ʻĀlam Bahādur S͟hāh), rose to an influential position in his household and died (according to the *Tārīk͟h i Muḥammadī* cited by Rieu) at Delhi in Rabīʻ I 1147/August 1734: **Rieu** ii 822*a* (late 18th cent.), **Browne Suppt.** 16 (King's 20).

French translation: *Histoire de Donna Juliana (Ahwál-i Bíbí Julyáná). Traduite d'un manuscrit persan de la bibliothèque du King's College, Cambridge ... Par Edward Henry Palmer* (in, and offprinted from, *Nouvelles annales des voyages*, tome ii, May 1865, pp. 161–84).

1635. For a biography of Bēgam Samrū see no. 900 *supra*.

1636. For the verses by poetesses contained in the *Zubdat al-muʻāṣirīn* of Mīr Ḥusain al-Ḥusainī see no. 1198 *supra*.

1637. For the *Nuql i majlis*, notices of poetesses composed in 1241/1825–6 by Maḥmūd Mīrzā Qājār, see no. 1195 (3) *supra*.

1638. For S͟hāh-Jahān Bēgam's history of Bhōpāl, the *Tāj al-iqbāl*, see no. 990 *supra*.

1639. For the *Ak͟htar i tābān* or *Tadhkirat al-nisā*ʾ of Abū ʼl-Qāsim Muḥtasham and the *Tad͟hkirat al-k͟hawātīn* of M. b. M. Rafīʻ S͟hīrāzī see nos. 1231–32 *supra*.

1640. For the *Ḥadīqah i ʻishrat* of Durgā-Pars͟hād "Mihr" Sandīlī see no. 1233 *supra*.

1641. M. Ḥasan K͟hān Marāg͟hī, entitled Ṣanīʻ **al-Daulah** and afterwards **Iʻtimād al-Salṭanah**, died at Ṭihrān in 1896 (see no. 192 *supra*).

Khairāt ḥisān,[1071] lives of eminent Muslim women, in 3 vols. Edition: [Ṭihrān,] 1304/1887°–1307/1889°.

1642. For an anonymous *Tad͟hkirat al-nisā*ʾ on Indian poetesses see no. 1243 (11) *supra*.

1071 Cf. *Qurʾān* lv 70.

1643. Other works:—

(1) ***Aḥwāl i Bānū … Mumtāz-Maḥall:***[1072] **Lindesiana** p. 111 no. 351 (AD. 1844).
(2) ***Khulāṣah i aḥwāl i Bānū Bēgam*:** **Lahore** Panjāb Univ. Lib. (see *OCM*. ii/4 (Lahore, August 1926) p 53).

13.17 *General and Miscellaneous*

1644. M. b. Manṣūr b. Saʿīd … b. Abī Bakr al-Ṣiddīq al-Taimī al-Qurashī, surnamed (*al-mulaqqab*) **Mubārak-Shāh** known as (*maʿrūf bi-*) **Fakhr i Mudabbir**, as he calls himself ("*Tārīkh*", ed. Ross, p. 62[3], *Ādāb al-ḥarb*, preface[1073]), was descended on his mother's side from the *amīr* Bilgā-tagīn, the father-in-law of Sulṭān Maḥmūd Ghaznawī (Rieu ii p. 488*a*). Fifteen years after the defeat of Khusrau Shāh by ʿAlāʾ al-Dīn Ghōrī [i.e. in or about 565/1169–70, since according to Ibn al-Athīr, *Kāmil* xi p. 108, Khusrau Shāh was defeated in 550/1155] he was in Multān and was then a mere youth (*kūdakī*, Rieu *ibid.*). "Several other references to Multān make it probable that it was his native place" (Rieu, *ibid.*). After the defeat of Khusrau Malik by Muʿizz al-Dīn M. b. Sām [in 582/1186] Mubārak-Shāh went to Lahore and caused a search to be made for title-deeds and other family papers long inaccessible to him. His family pedigree having been found and taken to Lahore, he conceived the idea of working out genealogical tables of the Prophet and the ʿAsharah i Mubashsharah, one of whom was his ancestor Abū Bakr. This led to further study and eventually after more than thirteen years of research he completed a volume of genealogical tables, which earned the warm commendation of his erudite father, the pupil of many great scholars of Ghaznah ("*Tārīkh*", p. 70[5]) and the master of more than twenty branches of learning (*ibid.* p. 68[10]). In the autumn of 602/1206, when Muʿizz al-Dīn M. b. Sām was in Lahore, he was told about these tables and asked to see them, but before they could be shown to him he left Lahore and was murdered on his way to Ghaznah. When his successor, Quṭb al-Dīn Aibak, entered Lahore, he too was told about Mubārak-Shāh's tables. The author was presented and the tables, or some of them, were read to the Sulṭān, who expressed his approval and gave orders that they should be transcribed and bound for the royal library. A later work by this author, the *Ādāb al-ḥarb wa-'l-shajāʿah* (so Rieu ii p. 487 and Ivanow 1608), or *Ādāb al-mulūk wa-kifāyat*

1072 For other accounts of Mumtāz-Maḥall see the works relating to Āgrah and the Tāj Maḥall in the geographical and topographical section of this work.

1073 In the latter place the name, as quoted by Rieu, is Sharīf M. [b.] Manṣūr [b.] Saʿīd … Quraishī *mulaqqab* bi-Mubārak-Shāh maʿrūf bi-Fakhr i Mudabbir.

al-mamlūk (so in Ethé 2767), seems to be undated, but it is dedicated to Sulṭān Īltutmish, who reigned at Delhi from 607/1210 to 633/1236.[1074] In both of these works he speaks of himself as an infirm old man (*pīr i ḍaʿīf, "Tārīkh"* p. 62³).

(***Shajarah i ansāb i Mubārak-Shāhī***),[1075] 137 genealogies relating to the Prophet, the ʿAsharah i Mubashsharah, the Muhājirūn, the Anṣār, the Prophets mentioned in the *Qurʾān*, the Ghassānids, the Tabābiʿah, Pre-Islāmic and Islāmic poets, the Pre-Islāmic Persian kings, the Umaiyads and ʿAbbasids, Arab tribes, the Umarāʾ of Umaiyad and ʿAbbāsid times, the Ṭāhirids, Ṣaffārids, Sāmānids, Subuktagīnids, Ghōrids and others, preceded by an introduction containing some historical information about the last Ghōrids and their first successors in India as well as a number of pages in description and praise of the Turks: **Ellis Coll. M.** 253 (16th cent.).

Edition of the introductory matter and of the account of Adam and Eve and their immediate descendants (i.e. foll. 1–48*a* and 50*b*–55*b* out of 125): *Taʿríkh-i* [*sic*] *Fakhru'd-Dín Mubáraksháh, being the historical introduction to the Book of Genealogies of Fakhru'd-Dín Mubárakshàh Marvar-rúḍí* [*sic*[1076]] *completed in* A.D. *1206. Edited from a unique manuscript by E. Denison Ross*, **London** 1927* (R.A.S., Forlong Fund).

Description with an abridged translation of most of the introductory portion: *The genealogies of Fakhr-ud-Dín Mubárak Sháh.* [Signed E. Denison Ross. In *ʿAjab-nāmah: a volume of oriental studies presented to E. G. Browne*, Cambridge, 1922, pp. 392–413].

Elucidation of Mubārak-Shāh's statements concerning the Turks: *On Mubarakshah Ghuri* [*sic*]. *By Ahmet-Zeki Validi* (in BSOS. vi/4 (1932) pp. 847–58. Pp. 856²⁷–858 are devoted to a description of the *Raḥīq al-taḥqīq* of Fakhr al-Dīn M.-Sh. Ghōrī, who, as indicated below, seems to be a different person).

In spite of some curious resemblances it seems impossible to identify Fakhr al-Dīn Mubārak-Shāh Qurashī (M. b. Manṣūr) with Fakhr al-Dīn Mubārak-Shāh Marwarrūdhī. The latter, according to Ibn al-Athīr

1074 The title Nāṣir Amīr al-Muʾminīn appended to the name of Īltutmish in the preface (see Rieu ii p. 488*a*, Ethé col. 1493) would imply, if really a part of the author's text, that the work was completed late in the reign. Some fifty pages of extracts relating to the Ghaznawids have been published with English translation and prefatory remarks by Miss Iqbāl M. Shafīʿ in *Islamic culture* for April 1938.

1075 No formal title is given to the work by the author, but he refers to it as *īn shajarah* (e.g. pp. 68⁸, 69⁸, 73²), *ānshajarah i ansāb* (p. 71 penult.), *īn shajarah u* [*sic ?*] *ansāb* (p. 62⁸).

1076 As indicated below, F. al-D. M.-Sh. Marwarrūdhī seems to be a different person from the author of this work.

(*al-Kāmil*, ed. Tornberg, xii p. 160 ult.), was Fakhr al-Dīn Mubārak-Shāh b. al-Ḥasan [so in Tornberg's text, not b. Abī 'l-Ḥasan, as Ross states] al-Marwarrūdhī. a good Arabic and Persian poet, the owner of a guest-house containing books for the learned and chess-boards for the ignorant [evidently therefore a rich man], who stood high in the regard of Ghiyāth al-Dīn the Great, Lord of Ghaznah and Harāt, and who died in Shawwāl 602/May-June 1206[1077] [i.e. several years before Mubārak-Shāh Qurashī can have died]. According to the *Ṭabaqāt i Nāṣirī* (p. 28⁸, where he is called Malik al-kalām Maulānā Fakhr al-Dīn Mubārak-Shāh Marwarrūdhī) he wrote *in verse* a genealogy of the Ghōrids (*nisbat-nāmah i īn salāṭīn i nāmdār rā dar silk i naẓm kashīdah*). Minhāj i Sirāj had himself in 602/1205–6 [i.e. at, or about, the age of thirteen: see no. 104 *supra*] seen a copy of this metrical genealogy in the *ḥaram* of Māh i Mulk, Ghiyāth al-Dīn M. b. Sām's daughter, who told him [*Ṭabaqāt* p. 69⁷⁻¹³] that the work was originally dedicated to Sulṭān 'Alā' al-Dīn Ḥusain Jahānsūz [who died in 551/1156[1078]] but was put aside by the author in an unfinished state until eventually completed with a new dedication to Ghiyāth al-Dīn M. b. Sām [d. 599/1202]. In the *Haft iqlīm* (no. 516, Ethé col. 415. Text quoted by Ross in *Ta'ríkh-i Fakhru'd-Dín*, introd., pp. iii–v) there is a notice of a certain Fakhr al-Dīn Mubārak-Shāh, who, though placed under Marw i Shāhjān, is evidently the same person as Fakhr al-Dīn Mubārak-Shāh Marwarrūdhī. He is described as *Ṣadr i Saḥbān-bayān i daryā-banānī*,[1079] an intimate friend of Sulṭān Ghiyāth al-Dīn Ghōrī and a dispenser of lavish hospitality.[1080] Amīn Rāzī quotes two verses from a *qaṣīdah* of his in praise of Malik Saif al-Dīn Ghōrī [who died in 558/1162[1081]]. Finally Mubārak-Shāh Marwarrūdhī is probably identical with the poet Mubārak-Shāh Ghūrī, who according to the *Ḥabīb al-siyar* (Bombay ed. ii p. 155, translated by Ross in *'Ajab-nāmah* p. 394) wrote verses in praise of Ghiyāth al-Dīn [Ghōrī] as well as the astronomical work *al-Madkhal al-manẓūm fī baḥr al-nujūm*,[1082] and who, as Ahmet-Zeki

1077 Ibn al-Athīr's words are: *wa-fīhā fī Shawwāl tuwuffiya Fakhr al-Dīn Mubārak Shāh b. al-Ḥasan al-Marwarrūdhī wa-kāna ḥasan al-shi'r bi-'l-Fārisīyah wa-'l-'Arabīyah wa-lahu manzilah 'aẓīmah 'inda Ghiyāth al-Dīn al-kabīr ṣāḥib Ghaznah wa-Harāh wa-ghairihimā wa-kāna lahu dār ḍiyāfah fīhā kutub wa-shiṭranj fa-'l-'ulamā' yuṭāli'ūn al-kutub wa-'l-juhhāl yal'abūn bi-'l-shiṭranj.*

1078 Mubārak-Shāh Qurashī, if a *kūdak* in 565 (see no. 1644, beginning), cannot have been much more than a child in 551.

1079 I have conjecturally emended the text printed by Ross.

1080 *Finā' i suddah i ū maḥaṭṭ i raḥl i afāḍil u marji' u ma'āb i amāthil mī būd.*

1081 In 565, as we have noted above, Mubārak-Shāh Qurashī was a *kūdak*.

1082 Cf. Ḥ. Kh. v p. 472, where the author's name is corrupted into Mubārak 'Udhī.

Validi has shown (BSOS. vi/4 pp. 856–8), completed in Muharram 584/March 1188 the metrical work on ethics *Raḥīq al-taḥqīq* (*min kalām Fakhr al-Dīn Mubārak-Shāh Ghōrī*. MS.: Āyā Ṣōfyah 4792).

1645. Shams al-Dīn A. b. M. b. Ibrāhīm b. Abī Bakr **Ibn Khallikān** al-Barmakī al-Irbilī al-Shāfiʿī was born at Arbela in 608/1211 and died at Cairo, as a professor in the Madrasat al-Amīnīyah, in 681/1282. His Arabic biographical dictionary, the *Wafayāt al-aʿyān wa-anbāʾ abnāʾ al-zamān*, was begun at Cairo in 654/1256 and completed in 672/1274. The Arabic text has been published at Göttingen (ed. F. Wüstenfeld) in 1835–50, at Paris (only as far as no. 678, ed. MacGuckin de Slane) in 1838–42, at Būlāq in 1275/1859° and 1299/1882°, at Cairo in 1299/1882° and 1310/1892‡ and at [Ṭihrān ?] in 1284/1867°. An English translation by MacGuckin de Slane was published in the Oriental Translation Fund Series, Paris and London, 1842–71°. [See Brockelmann i pp. 326–8, *Sptbd.* i p. 561; *Ency. Isl.* under Ibn Khallikān; etc.]

The following Persian translations are extant:—

(1) ***Manẓar al-insān fī tarjamat Wafayāt al-aʿyān***, an abridged translation begun in 893/1487 and completed in 895/1489 by Yūsuf b. Aḥmad b. M. b. ʿUthmān b. ʿAlī b. Aḥmad al-Shujāʿ al-Sijzī or al-Sanjarī for Maḥmūd Shāh Bēgaṛah of Gujrāt (reigned 863–917/1458–1511): **Rieu** ii 809*a* (latter half of the work. 16th cent.), i 334*a* (AH 1012/1603), 335*a* (16th cent.), **Bānkīpūr** viii 719 (AH 1018/1609).

(2) (***Tarjamah i Wafayāt al-aʿyān***) an incomplete (?)[1083] translation made for Sulṭān Salīm I (AH 918–26/1512–20) by [ʿAbd al-] Kabīr b. Uwais b. M. al-Laṭīfī (i.e. Ẓahīr al-Dīn al-Ardabīlī al-Ḥanafī known as (*al-shahīr bi-*) Qāḍī-zādah),[1084] who completed the first part (nos. 1–204) at Istānbūl on 5 Dhū 'l-Qaʿdah 926/17 Oct. 1520 and the second part (nos. 205–453) in 928/1521–2; Ḥ. Kh. vi p. 455, **Browne** Suppt. 1359 (Pt I, autograph, AH 926/1520, Pt. II, transcribed from an autograph, AH 1019/1610–11. King's 110), **Majlis** 538 (Pt I, AH 926/1520), **Bodleian** 361 (Pts I–II, AH 1197/1783).

1083 According to the translator's statement (see Ḥ. Kh. vi p. 455[5], Bodleian col. 193) he had translated half of the work when Salīm died. It will be observed that the two parts extant in manuscript contain 453 of the 865 biographies. At that point presumably the work was discontinued.

1084 Kabīr b. Uwais was deported from Tabrīz to Istānbūl by Salīm after the battle of Chāldirān [in 920/1514] and was granted a stipend of eighty dirhams a day. His account of Salīm's campaigns of 922–3/1516–17, which included the conquest of Egypt, has already been mentioned (no. 588 *supra*). In 930/1524 he was put to death at Cairo with Aḥmad Pāshā "al-Khāʾin". See *al-Shaqāʾiq al-Nuʿmānīyah*, Cairo 1310, i p. 506, Rescher's trans. p. 289; *Shadharāt al-dhahab* viii p. 173; *Dānishmandān i Ādharbāyjān* pp. 249–50; *Majālis al-nafāʾis* tr. Qazwīnī pp. 396–7.

1646. For the *Bahjat al-tawārīkh*, which was completed in 861/1456–7 by Shukr Allāh b. Shihāb al-Dīn Aḥmad al-Rūmī and which is largely biographical (the 13 *bābs* being devoted respectively to (1) cosmography, geography and ethnology, (2) the Pre-Islāmic prophets, (3) Muḥammad's genealogy, (4) his birth, life, etc., (5) his wives, children, and other relations, (6) his ten principal associates, (7) his other companions, (8) the Twelve Imāms, (9) the famous *shaikhs*, (10) the ancient philosophers, (11) the Pre-Islāmic Persian kings, (12) the Umaiyad and ʿAbbāsid Caliphs, (13) the Ottoman Sulṭān), see no. 122 *supra*.

1647. For the *Tārīkh i Ṣadr i jahān*, which was written at least partly in 907/1501–2 by Faiḍ Allāh b. Zain al-ʿĀbidīn Banbānī and which contains biographies of poets, Companions of the Prophet, scholars, etc., see no. 127 *supra*.

1648. ***Abū Bakr b. Hidāyat Allāh Ḥusainī*** wrote his *Riyāḍ al-khulūd* in 989/1581.
Riyād al-khulūd, on the lives and sayings of amirs, scholars, and divines: **Majlis** 549 (AH 1316/1898–9).

1649. **Amīn** [ibn] Aḥmad **Rāzī**[1085] was born at Rai,[1086] of which town his father, Khwājah Mīrzā Ahmad,[1087] a favourite of Shāh Ṭahmāsp, was for some years *Kalāntar*. Khwājah M. Sharīf "Hajrī" Rāzi,[1088] *Wazīr* successively of Khurāsān, Yazd and Iṣfahān, was his paternal uncle, and Iʿtimād al-Daulah (Ghiyāth Bēg b. M. Sharīf), Nūr-Jahān's father and Jahāngir's *Wazīr*, was his first cousin. That Amīn Rāzī was resident in India when he wrote the *Haft iqlīm*, is shown by incidental references to Akbar and his court, such, for example, as the statement that "Ṭarīqī" Sāwajī (*Haft iqlīm* no. 1011: cf. Badāʾūnī iii p. 263) was for about fifteen years *mulāzim i īn dargāh*.

Haft iqlīm, biographical notices of about 1560 poets, saints, scholars, and other celebrities completed in 1002/1593–4[1089] and arranged geo-

---

1085 At the beginning of the preface to the *Haft iqlīm* he calls himself Amīn i Aḥmad i Rāzī. The *iḍāfat* has commonly been ignored by Orientalists and the name read as Amīn Aḥmad, but we know on Amīn's own authority that his father's name was Aḥmad and the presence of the *iḍāfat* is made clear in the chronogrammatic *rubāʿī* at the end of the preface. It runs as follows:— *Īn nuskhah kih hast hamchu firdaus nikū Tā mū na-shawī darū nah bi-shkāfī mū. Gar az tu kasī suʾāl i tārīkh kunad, Taṣnīf i Amīn i Aḥmad i Rāzī gū.*

1086 *Shahr i Rai kih maulid u manshaʾi īn faqīr ast* (Bombay Univ. p. 72).

1087 *Haft iqlīm* no. 1117.

1088 "Hajrī" (this vocalisation seems more probable than "Hijrī" hitherto favoured by Orientalists) died in 984/1576–7. See *Haft iqlīm* no. 1114; *Makhzan al-gharāʾib* no. 3051; etc. For his *dīwān* see Bānkīpūr ii 244 and Ethé 1440.

1089 The chronogram indicating this date is quoted in note 1 on p. 1169. As Ethé pointed out (I.O. Cat. col. 498), the mention of Muḥammad III (acc. 1003/1595) in the list of Ottoman

graphically under their towns or countries, of which in many cases geographical accounts are given: Ḥ. Kh. vi p. 501 no. 14411, **Sipahsālār** ii p. 485 no. 1123 (AH 1025/1616), nos. 1124–5, **Bodleian** 416 (AH 1039/1630), 417 (AH 1075/1665), 418 (AH 1199/1785), 419 (3rd and 5th *iqlīms* only. N.d.), 420 (4th *iqlīm* only. N.d.), MS. Pers. c. 24 (AH 1052/1642), **Oxford** Ind. Inst. MS. Whinfield 20 (defective. N.d.), **Cairo** p. 509 (AH 1052/1643), **Rieu** i 335*b* (17th cent.), 336*b* (AH 1059/1649), 337*a* (17th cent.), 337a (the first two-thirds of the work. 17th cent.), iii 970*a* (AH 1261/1845), Suppt. 138 (17th cent.), **Leningrad** Univ. 1134 (AH 1066/1655–6. See Romaskewicz p. 15), 1154 (*vid. ibid.*), **Blochet** 642 (AH 1068/1657–8), 643 (AH 1094/1683), **Ethé** 724, 725 (AH 1089/1678), 726 (defective, beginning in 3rd *iqlīm*. AH 1093/1682), **I.O.** 4541 (AH 1006/1597–8 or 1106/1694–5 ? date indistinct), **Bānkīpūr** vii 636 (17th cent.), **Āṣafīyah** iii p. 162 no. 190 (17th cent.), i p. 232 no. 465, **Ivanow** 282 (AH 1166/1752–3), 283 (AD 1871), Curzon 706 (19th cent.), **Lindesiana** p. 113 no. 712 (extracts only. Circ. AD 1750), **Majlis** 456 (AH 1273/1856–7), **Būhār** 100 (19th cent.), **Bombay** Univ. 36 (portion only, corresponding to nos. 985–1558 in Ethé's description), **Browne** Pers. Cat. 110, **Browne** Coll. K. 5 (13) = Houtum-Schindler 39, K. 4 (= I.O. 4541 above), **Eton** 56 (imperfect), **Kapurthala** 49 (see *Oriental College Magazine* vol. iii/4 (Lahore, Aug. 1927) p. 19), **Lahore** Panjab Univ. Lib. (2 copies. See *Oriental College Magazine*, vol. iii, no. 1 (Lahore, Nov. 1926), p. 68).

Edition: *Haft Iqlîm, or the geographical and biographical encyclopaedia of Amîn Aḥmad Râzî. Edited by E. Denison Ross and ... ʿAbdul Muqtadir (Fasc 2. Edited by A. H. Harley and ʿAbdul Muqtadir. Fasc 3. Edited by A. H. H., ʿA. M. and M. Mahfuz-ul Haq)*, **Calcutta** 1918°* (Fasc. 1), 1927°* (Fasc. 2), 1939 (Fasc. 3). These three fasciculi, which form "vol. i", extend to "Partawī" of Shīrāz (no. 260 in Ethé's enumeration).

Abridgment: *Intikhāb i Haft iqlīm* by Faiḍ Allāh "Himmat" Anṣārī Jaunpūrī, dedicated to Wajīh al-Dīn ʿAlī Khān Bahādur: **Ethé** 727.

Extracts: **(1)** [on Māzandarān, Gīlān, etc.] B. Dorn *Muhammedanische Quellen zur Geschichte der südlichen Küstenländer des Kaspischen Meeres*, **St. Petersburg** 1850–8°*, Theil iv pp. 88–100, **(2)** [on Turkistān] *Description ... de Boukhara par Mohammed Nerchakhy, suivie de textes relatifs à la Transoxiane. Texte persan publié par C. Schefer*, Paris 1892°*, pp. 243–91, **(3)** [on Africa] *Documents persans sur l'Afrique publiés et*

Sultans shows that some parts of the *Haft iqlīm* are later than 1002, but Browne's statement (*Lit. Hist.* iv p. 448) that it was "composed in 1028/1619" is doubtless a mistake.

traduits par C. Huart (*in Recueil de mémoires orientaux. Textes et traductions publiés ... à l'occasion du XIV*^{e} *Congrès International des Orientalistes réuni à Alger avril 1905. Publications de l'École des Langues Orientales Vivantes*, V^{e} série, vol. 5, **Paris** 1905°*, pp. 104–14 (text), 114–30 (trans.)).

For one or two other extracts see Edwards.

Translations of extracts: **(1)** [on Kāshghar (French)] *Notice de l'ouvrage persan qui a pour titre Matla-assaadeïn ... Par M. Quatremère* (in *Notices et extraits des manuscrits de la Bibliothèque du Roi ... tome xiv* (**Paris** 1843°*)), pp. 474–89. **(2)** [on Africa] see Extracts (**3**) above.

Lists and epitomes of the biographies: ((1) Ethé coll. 381–499, (2) [nos. 985–1558 only, i.e. from "Qudsī" Tafrishī to Amīr Aḥmad Ḥājjī of Kāshghar] Bombay Univ. pp. 68–107.

1650. M. Ṣādiq, the author of the *Ṭabaqāt i Shāhjahānī*, who mentions a brother of his, Mullā M. Yūsuf Kashmīrī Hamadānī (d. 1033/1623–4) among the poets of Jahāngīr's reign, may be regarded as certainly identical with **M. Ṣādiq Hamadānī**, the author of the *Kalimāt al-ṣādiqīn* (see no. 1311 *supra*), who in the *Tārīkh i Muḥammadī* is called Maulānā Ṣādiq Kashmīrī (see Rieu iii p. 1096*b*). From the *Ṭabaqāt i Shāhjahānī* Rieu ascertained that the author was born about 1000/1591–2, that he spent his life in Delhi, studied under Sh. Fā'iḍ (d. 1022/1613), and was a favourite disciple of Sh. ʿAbd al-Ḥaqq Dihlawī (for whom see nos. 243, 1298 *supra*). The author of the *Kalimāt al-ṣādiqīn*, who often refers to Sh. ʿAbd al-Ḥaqq Dihlawī as *ḥaḍrat i makhdūmī*, mentions a maternal grandfather, Ḥājjī M. Hamadānī, who went to Multān and finally settled in Delhi, where he died in 1006/1597 (Bānkīpūr viii pp. 34–5). He speaks of an earlier work of his entitled *Silsilat al-ṣādiqīn* and expresses a hope of being able to write a *Ma'āthir i Jahāngīrī* (*ibid.* p. 35).

Ṭabaqāt i Shāhjahānī, lives of 871 celebrities who lived under Tīmūr and his successors, divided into ten *ṭabaqāt* ((1)) Tīmūr, 770–807/1369–1405, (2) Mīrān-Shāh and Shāh-Rukh, 807–50/1405–47, (3) Mīrzā Sulṭān-Muḥammad and Ulugh Bēg, 850–3/1447–9, (4) Abū Saʿīd, 854–73/1450–69, (5) ʿUmar Shaikh, 873–99/1469–94, (6) Bābur, 900–37/1495–1530, (7) Humāyūn, 938–63/1531–56, (8) Akbar, 963–1014/1556–1605, (9) Jahāngīr, 1014–37/1605–27, (10) Shāh-Jahān, from 1037/1627 to the date of composition, which is not specified in the preface, though 1046/1636–7 is mentioned early in *Ṭabaqah* 10 as the current year), each *ṭabaqah* being subdivided into three *bābs* ((1) Saiyids and saints, (2) scholars, physicians and men of letters (*ʿulamā', ḥukamā', fuḍalā'*), (3) poets): **Āṣafīyah** i p. 246 no. 721 (before AH 1156/1743), **Ethé** 705 (n.d.), **Rieu** iii 1009*b* (19th cent.).

1651. For the *Ṣubḥ i ṣādiq*, which was completed in 1048/1638–9 by Mirzā M. Ṣadiq b. M. Ṣāliḥ Iṣfahānī and of which the third *mujallad* is devoted to celebrated men of the first eleven centuries, see no. 142 2nd par. *supra*. The same author's *Shāhid i ṣādiq* (for which see no. 142 1st par. *supra*) contains some biographical matter (e.g. *Bāb* iii, *faṣl* 79, which is devoted to "notices of remarkable events and of the death of celebrated men in chronological order from the Hijrah to AH 1042" (Rieu ii p. 776), and the *khātimah*. which is "an alphabetical list of proper names of places and men, with fixation of their spelling, and short notices" (*ibid.*)).

1652. For the *Mir'āt al-ʿālam*, which was composed in 1078/1667 ostensibly by Bakhtāwar Khān but really by M. Baqā Sahāranpūrī and which contains biographies of celebrities, see no. 151 (2) *supra*.

1653. Mīrzā Nūr al-Dīn M. "**ʿAlī**" b. Ḥakīm Fatḥ al-Dīn Shīrāzī, entitled **Niʿmat Khān** and **Dānishmand Khān**, who died at Delhi in 1122/1710, has already been mentioned as the author of the *Waqāʾiʿ i Ḥaidarābād* (no. 751 (1) *supra*) and other works.

> ***Rāḥat al-qulūb*** (beg. *Āfrīn Sukhan-āfrīnī rā kih dar ṣalā-yi thanāyash*), satirical notices of some contemporaries, whose names are indicated by means of riddles: **Rieu** ii 796*a* (18th cent.), **Edinburgh** 375 (1) (18th cent.).

1654. For the *Farḥat al-nāẓirīn*, which was completed in 1184/1770–1 by M. Aslam Parasrūrī and of which the *khātimah* is devoted to geography, the lives of scholars, saints and poets, and the family of Shujāʿ al-Daulah, see no. 168 *supra*.

1655. For the *Ḥadīqat al-aqālīm*, which was written mainly in 1192–6/1778–82 by Murtaḍā Ḥusain Bilgrāmī and which, like the *Haft iqlīm*, consists largely of geographically arranged biographies, see no. 170 *supra*.

1656. For the *Lubb al-siyar u jahān-numā*, which was compiled in 1208/1793–4 by Mīrzā Abū Ṭālib Khān Iṣfahānī and of which the third bāb contains biographies of philosophers, Companions of the Prophet, scholars, poets, etc., see no. 173 *supra*.

1657. For the *Zubdat al-gharāʾib*, which was composed in 1231/1816 by M. Riḍā "Najm" Ṭabāṭabā and of which the fifth volume contains lives of philosophers, saints, poets, etc., see no. 180 (1) *supra*.

1658. For the *Yādgār i Bahādurī*, which was completed in 1249/1833–4 by Bahādur Sing'h b. Hazārī-Mal, and of which the third *sāniḥah* contains *inter alia* biographies of philosophers, saints (Muslim and Hindu), scholars, poets and others, see no. 182 *supra*.

1659. Maulawī S. **Ashraf al-Dīn Aḥmad** b. Nawwāb Wazīr al-Sulṭān S. M. Amīr ʿAlī Khān Bahādur, who was born in 1855 and received the title of Khān Bahādur in 1893, has already been mentioned (no. 975 *supra*) as the author of the *Ṭabaqāt i Muḥsinī-yah* (Calcutta 1889*). In addition to the *Nau ratan* referred to there he wrote some essays on education published under the title *Chār dīwār* at Calcutta in 1894*.

Dur-dānah i khayāl, an autobiography: **Lucknow** (N.K.) 1889*.

1660. According to M. ʿAlī "Tarbiyat"[1090] as translated by E. G. Browne in *The Press and poetry of modern Persia*, pp. 165–6, the *Nāmah i dānishwarān i Nāṣirī* was "compiled by a committee of scholars consisting of Mírzá Abu'l-Faẓl of Sáwa, Mīrzā Hasan of Ṭálaqán,[1091] ʿAbdu'l-Wahháb of Qazwín,[1092] known as "Mullá Áqá", and Muḥammad, called al-Mahdí[1093] This work, which was not completed, is a detailed Dictionary of Biography of the notable and eminent persons, men of letters, divines, philosophers, mystics, etc., who were most celebrated in Islám, and contains accounts of their biographies, adventures, characteristics and writings. Its publication was begun in AH 1296 (= a.d. 1879) under the supervision of ʿAlí-qulí Mírzá *Iʿtiẓádu's-Salṭana*.[1094] On his death in AH 1298 (= AD 1881), after the publication of two volumes,[1095] the editorial committee

1090 For whom see no. 1493 *supra*.

1091 In the British Museum catalogue the *Nāmah i dānishwarān* [vol. i only] is entered under Ḥusain [*sic*], Ṭaliqānī, to whom also the *Lisān al-ʿAjam*, a Persian grammar of 172 pp. published at Bombay in 1317/1899°, is there ascribed. According to the Bombay Quarterly Catalogue (1900, 4th quarter) the author of the *Lisān al-ʿAjam* was Mīrzā Ḥasan b. M. Taqī Ṭālaqānī. The other collaborators in the *Nāmah i dānishwarān* are not mentioned by Edwards, but the Āṣafiyah catalogue (i p. 348) gives the four names-Mīrzā Abū 'l-Faḍl Sāwī, Mīrzā Ḥasan Ṭālaqā'ī [*sic*], Mullā ʿAbd al-Wahhāb Qazwīnī and Mullā M. Mahdī.

1092 He died in Muḥarram 1306/Sept. 1888. See *al-Maʾathir wa-'l-āthar* p. 161; *Bīst maqālah i Qazwīnī*, pt. 1, p. 5.

1093 Shams al-ʿUlamāʾ Sh M. Mahdī Qazwīnī ʿAbd-al-Rabb-ābādī, who died at Ṭihrān on 24 Dhū 'l-Ḥijjah 1331/24 November 1913. See *Bīst maqālah i Qazwīnī*, pt. 1, p. 8, and the periodical *Yādgār* v/3, p. 60.

1094 Cf. no. 316 *supra*.

1095 The second volume did not appear until 1312 (see below).

made over the supervision to Muḥammad Ḥasan Khán *I'timádu's-Salṭana*,[1096] so that the last five volumes (iii–vii) were published as appendices to the Year Books (*Sál-náma*) of AH 1318, 1319, 1321, 1322, and 1323 (= a.d. 1900–5)."

Nāmah i dānishwarān i Nāṣirī, a large unfinished dictionary of learned men, vol. i (beginning with Ibn Bābawaih[1097] and ending with Abū Isḥāq Ibrāhīm b. Aḥmad b. M. Ṭabarī[1098]) [**Ṭihrān**] 1296/1879°, vol. ii (beginning with Abū 'l-Baqā' 'Abd Allāh b. al-Ḥusain al-'Ukbarī[1099] and ending with Ibn Abī 'l-'Azāqir, i.e. M. b. 'Alī al-Shalmaghānī[1100]) **Ṭihrān** 1312/1894 (cf. Browne *Lit. Hist.* iv p. 447 and Āṣafīyah i p. 348 no. 57), vols. iii–vii appended to the *Sāl-nāmahs* specified above.

1661. **M. Ḥasan Khān** Marāghī, entitled **Ṣanī' al-Daulah** and afterwards **I'timād al-Salṭanah**, who died at Ṭihrān in 1896, has already been mentioned several times (nos. 192, 306, 328, 444, 471, 480, 609 [America, 2nd work]). His work *al-Ma'āthir wa-'l-āthār* is mentioned as no. 444 (2), but, since it contains a considerable amount of biography, it deserves further attention and more precise description here.

al-Ma'āthir wa-'l-āthar, memorabilia of the first forty years of Nāṣir al-Dīn Shāh's reign, written in 1306/1888–9 and divided into sixteen chapters ((1) on the Shāh's personal appearance, mental and spiritual gifts, etc., p. 4, (2) his children and grandchildren, p. 11, (3) the mothers of his children, p. 13, (4) list of high officials, p. 15, (5) list of provincial governors, p. 29, (6) list of wars, rebellions, riots, punitive expeditions, etc., p. 37, (7) buildings erected, repaired or decorated, parks and gardens laid out, etc., p. 53, (8) social reforms, innovations, discoveries, etc., p. 91, (9) the Shāh's journeys in Persia and elsewhere, p. 132, (10), biographies of scholars, divines, writers, physicians, etc., p. 135, (11) list of persons honoured with the *Nishān i Timthāl i Humāyūn*, p. 227, (12) list of titles conferred, p. 230, (13) the national revenue of 1268/1851–2 compared with that of 1303/1885–6, p. 242, (14) contemporary rulers in all parts of the world, p. 245, (15) diplomatic representatives of foreign countries in Ṭihrān, p. 253, (16) a year-by-year record of remarkable events outside Persia, p. 257), to all of which is appended a separately paginated list of

1096 Cf. no. 192 *supra*.

1097 Cf. no. 262 *supra*.

1098 A Mālikī who died at Baghdad in 393/1003.

1099 Cf. Brockelmann i 282, *Sptbd.* i p. 495. He died in 616/1219.

1100 Burnt at Baghdād as a heretic in 322/934. Cf. *Tusy's List of Shy'ah books* p. 305; *Shadharāt al-dhahab* ii p. 293; Brockelmann *Sptbd* I p. 189 n. 1.

officials in the ministries at Ṭihrān and in the offices of the provincial governments, etc.: **Tihrān** 1306–7/18890*. (Pp. 294, 62. The date 1306 is given on the title-page, but 8 Muḥarram 1307 in the colophon on p. 294.)

1662. Ḥājj S͟h. ʿAbbās b. M. Riḍā **Qummī** is described as *marḥūm* on the title-page of the Tihrān edition of the *Hadīyat al-aḥbāb*.

Hadīyat al-aḥbāb fī d͟hikr al-maʿrūfīn bi-l-kunā wa-ʾl-alqāb wa-ʾl-ansāb, short alphabetically arranged notices of ancient and modern S͟hīʿite and Sunnite scholars, poets, etc., composed in 1349/1930–1 (according to the Sipahsālār catalogue i p. *Yā-Alif*) and divided into three *bābs* ((1) names beginning with Abū, (2) names beginning with Ibn, (3) *nisbahs*, surnames, descriptions, etc.): **Najaf** 1349/1930–1 (Sipahsālār cat., *loc. cit.*); **Tihrān** AHS 1329/1950‡ (281 pp.).

1663. Ḥājī Mīrzā **Yaḥyā** "Yaḥyā" b. S. Ḥādī **Daulatābādī**, well known as a writer, an educationist and a prominent figure in the Persian revolution, was born at Daulatābād in 1281/1864–5. In the second volume of M. Ishaque's *Sukhanvarān-i-Īrān dar ʿaṣr-i-ḥāẓir*, published in 1937, it was stated that for some years he had been resident in Belgium and was acting as guardian to the Persian students in that country. In the same author's *Modern Persian poetry*, published in 1943, the date of his death is given as 1318 (!), possibly a misprint for 1361/1942, since his son in his preface to the *Ḥayāt i Yaḥyā* speaks of the eighty years of his life. Among his published works is *Urdībihisht* (vol. i only, Tihrān AHS 1304/1925*, a collection of his poems).

Ḥayāt i Yaḥyā, an autobiography in four volumes: **Tihrān** AHS 1328/1950-, *in progress* (the date is that of the editor's preface to vol. ii, the only volume so far published. Title on cover: *Tārīk͟h i muʿāṣir yā Ḥayāt i Yaḥyā*).

[Browne *The press and poetry of modern Persia* pp. 54, 102, 157, *Lit. Hist*, iv pp. 225, 307; D. J. Irani *Poets of the Pahlavi regime* pp. 668B–690 (portrait); M. Ishaque *Sukhanvarān-i-Īrān* ii pp. 416–22 (portrait), *Modern Persian poetry* pp. 9, 17, 87, 165, etc.; Ḥabīb Allāh Muk͟htārī *Tārīk͟h i bīdārī i Īrān* p. 28 (portrait).]

1664. Mīrzā **Muḥammad** b. ʿAbd al-Wahhāb b. ʿAbd al-ʿAlī **Qazwīnī**, whose father has already been mentioned (no. 1660) as one of the compilers of the *Nāmah i dānis͟hwarān*, was born at Ṭihrān on 15 Rabīʿ al-Awwal 1294/30 March 1877, and it was at Ṭihrān that he received an education in the usual subjects of the traditional Islamic curriculum. Of all these subjects the Arabic *adabīyāt*, and especially Arabic grammar, appealed to him most strongly (*Bīst maqālah i Qazwīnī*, pt. 1, p. 6: *Az miyān i īn hamah ʿulūm i mutadāwalah na-mī-dānam* *ba-chih sabab az hamān ibtidā-yi amr shauqī shadīd ba-adabīyāt i ʿArab girībān-gīr i man shud tā akthar i aiyām i ṣibā u shabāb dar shuʿab i mukhtalifah i īn fann ba-khuṣūṣ naḥw ṣarf gardīd u ʿumr i girān-māyah dar ishtighāl ba-ism u fiʿl u ḥarf gudhasht u aknūn kih taʾammul i aiyām i gudhashtah mī-kunam u bar ʿumr i talaf-kardah taʾassuf mī-khwuram bāz yakī az bihtarīn i tafrīḥāt i man muṭālaʿah i Sharḥ i Raḍī u Mughnī ʾl-labīb ast kih barā-yi man aḥlā min waṣl al-ḥabīb ast! Al-ʿādah ka-ʾl-ṭabīʿat al-thāniyah*). Apart from his teachers in various *madrasahs* he came into close contact with several persons of culture and distinction, such as Sh. Hādī Najmābādī. S. Aḥmad "Adīb" Pīshāwarī, Shams al-ʿulamāʾ Sh. M. Mahdī Qazwīnī ʿAbd-al-Rabb-ābādī (cf. no. 1160 1st footnote, *supra*) and M. Ḥusain Khān "Furūghī" Iṣfahānī (cf. no. 319 *supra*). One of the sons of the last-named, M. ʿAlī Khān Dhakāʾ al-Mulk (cf. no. 320 *supra*), became his pupil in Arabic, his instructor in French and soon his intimate friend. For some years too he gave instruction in Arabic grammar to the two sons of Sh. Faḍl Allāh Nūrī (who was crucified at Ṭihrān on 13 Rajab 1327/31 July 1909). In 1322/1904 at the suggestion of his brother, Mīrzā Aḥmad Khān, who was then in London, he came to see the manuscripts of the British Museum, and he remained in London for nearly two years. In 1324/1906, having accepted the invitation of the Trustees of the E. J. W. Gibb Memorial to prepare an edition of the *Tārīkh i Jahān-gushāy i Juwainī* (for which see no. 340 (1) *supra*), he moved to Paris, where several good manuscripts of that work are preserved. At the end of 1333/1915, when it became impossible for him to continue his work in Paris (*ba-ʿilalī kih īn-jā mauqiʿ i dhikr i ān nīst dīgar barāy i man dar Pārīs ba-hīch wajh idāmah i kārhāʾī kih ba-dast dāshtam mumkin na-būd*), he welcomed the proposal of his old friend, Ḥusain-Qulī Khān Nawwāb, the newly appointed Persian Minister to Germany, that they should travel together through Switzerland to Berlin. There he and the other members of the Persian colony, among whom were S. Ḥasan Taqī-zādah (cf. no. 321 (*a*) (1) *supra*), S. M. ʿAlī Khān Jamāl-zādah, Mīrzā Maḥmūd Khān Ghanī-zādah, Mīrzā Ḥusain Kāẓim-zādah, M. ʿAlī Khān Tarbiyat (cf. no. 1493 *supra*) and Mīrzā Ibrāhīm Pūr-Dāwud (cf. Browne *Press and poetry of modern Persia* pp. xviii, 289), suffered hardships which some of them mitigated by engaging in propagandist activities (cf. Browne *Lit. Hist*, iv p. 483). When the war came to its end, Qazwīnī was eager to resume his work on the *Tārīkh i Jahān-gushāy i Juwainī*, but travel from one European country to another was difficult in those days and it was not until 16 Jumādā II 1338/8 January 1920 that he again reached Paris. His return had been facilitated by his old friend M. ʿAlī Khān "Furūghī" (cf. no. 320 *supra*), one of the Persian delegates to the Peace Conference, who soon afterwards was instrumental in obtaining for him a modest stipend from the Persian Government. He was by this time recognized as by far the most learned and critical of living Persians in historical and linguistic matters.[1101] In 1939 he returned to Persia and accepted an invitation to teach in the University of Ṭihrān. He died on 6 Khurdād 1328/28 Rajab 1368/27 May 1949. In addition to several well-known volumes of the Gibb Memorial Series edited by him with copious learned notes his works include articles contributed to Persian periodicals. Twenty of these have been collected and published under the title *Bīst maqālah i Qazwīnī*[1102] (pt. i, Bombay [1928*], pt. ii, Ṭihrān AHS 1313/1934*).

(1) ***Maqāla'ī tārīkhī u intiqādī ... dar bāb i nuskhah i Nafthat al-maṣdūr ...***[1103] see no. 1459 1st footnote.

(2) ***Sharḥ i ḥāl i Abū Sulaimān i Manṭiqī i Sijistānī***[1104] (French title: *Abû Sulaimân Manṭiqî Sidjistânî ...*), Chalon-sur-Saone 1352/1933 (46 pp. Publications de la Société des Études Iraniennes et de l'Art Persan, 5).

(3) ***Wafayāt i muʿaṣirīn***, alphabetically arranged biographies of the author's contemporaries, begun in the periodical *Yādgār* iii/3, continued in the succeeding issues of that volume, then interrupted for reasons explained in iv/3 pp. 73–4, resumed in v/1–2 (Sept.-Oct. 1948) pp. 89–110 (letters Z and S), v/3 pp. 51–72 (Sh[1105]), v/4–5 pp. 63–91 (Ṣ-Ẓ), v/6–7 pp. 122–8 (part of ʿAin), v/8–9 pp. 66–72 (ʿAin continued), interrupted at that point by the author's death[1106] and concluded in v/10 pp. 44–54 by a life of Qazwinī himself [unsigned, but presumably by the editor, ʿAbbās Iqbāl].

[Autobiography in *Bīst maqālah i Qazwīnī*, pt. i (Bombay [1928]) pp. 5–23; *Yādgār* v/8–9 pp. 1–8 (portrait frontispiece), v/10 pp. 44–5; *The Times* 4.6.49; BSOAS. xiii/2 (1950) pp. 547–50 (an obituary by Mojtabā Mīnovī); Īraj Afshār *Nathr i Fārsī i muʿāṣir* pp. 57–66 (portrait).]

1101 "Mais le premier qui commença à étudier l'histoire de la Perse d'une manière critique fut Moḥammad b. ʿAbdu 'l-Wahhāb Ḳazwīnī, auteur qui s'acquit une haute autorité scientifique, même parmi les savants de l'Occident. La recherche et l'analyse critique des documents historiques persans (*isnād*) furent le domaine principal de son activité scientifique ... Son hypercriticisme et sa pédanterie ne lui permirent, jusqu'á présent, de composer aucun grand ouvrage digne de lui." (F. Machalski, *Quelques remarques sur l'état actuel de l'historiographie persane*, in *Rocznik Orientalistyczny* xv (1939–49) p. 100.)

1102 This is actually the title of Pt I only, Pt. II being called *B. m. az maqālāt i tārīkhī u intiqādī u adabī bi-qalam i ... Muḥammad Khān Qazwīnī.*

1103 This *maqālah* is not included in the *Bīst maqālah i Qazwīnī.*

1104 Cf. no. 1485 *supra* and *Bīst maqālah i Qazwīnī* ii pp. 102–23 (in an article on the *Tatimmat Siwān al-ḥikmah*).

1105 Including Shams al 'Ulamā' M. Ḥusain Qarīb Garakānī.

1106 It is highly desirable that these biographies should be published as an independent work, with or without any further biographies for which Qazwīnī may have left materials, especially as the first three volumes of *Yādgār* seem to be now unprocurable.

1665. **ʿAbd Allāh Mustaufī** was born according to Machalski (*Rocz. Or.* xv p. 106³) in "1294 h. (1875)", i.e. presumably either in 1292/1875 or in 1294/1877.

Sharḥ i zindagānī i man yā Tārīkh i ijtimāʿī u idārī i daurah i Qājārīyah, a history of Qājār times incorporating autobiographical memoirs and a highly interesting picture of Persian domestic and social life: **Ṭihrān** AHS 1324/1945–6 onwards (cf. Additions and corrections ad no. 451 (4) end, (11) *infra*).

Description of vols. i–ii: F. Machalski *Quelques remarques sur l'état actuel de l'historiographie persane* (in *Rocznik Orientalistyczny* xv (1939–49)) pp. 105–7.

1666. **Īraj Afshar.**

Nathr i Fārsī i muʿāṣir: *muntakhabātī az bihtarīn i āthār i muwarrikhīn u muḥaqqiqīn i nāmī i Īran az ṣadr i mashrūṭīyat tā muʿāṣir* [with short biographies[1107] and portraits], **Ṭihrān** AHS 1330/1951 (to be followed by a similar volume on novelists, etc., and dramatists by Saʿīd Nafīsī).

1667. Other biographical works:—

(1) ***Abraham Lincoln; sa vie et son oeuvre***, by Khān Bahādur Mīrzā Muḥammad (for whom see under *Dūstdārān i bashar* below): **Berlin** AH 1343/1924 (Publications Iranschähr, no. 8. See the R.A.S.'s *Catalogue of printed books*, p. 278).

(2) ***Adhkār al-kirām al-bararah fī manāqib Imām Dār al-Hijrah***, a biography of Mālik b. Anas, by Maulawī S. M. Jalāl al-Dīn: **Madras** 1310/1893* (116 pp.).

(3) ***Aḥwāl i Amīr ʿAṭā' Allāh Faʿfarī Zainabī***, an account of A. ʿA. A., who migrated from Delhi to Bengal [sc. Bihār], became *Wazīr* to Shēr Shāh at Sahasrām ("Sasseram" in Bihār) and eventually settled at P'hulwārā, near Patna, by Shāh Nūr al-Ḥaqq: **Bankipur** Suppt. ii 2272 (AH 1298/1881).

(4) ***Aḥwāl i aulād u jāydād i Saiyid Aḥmad Sāndawī***, "compiled by ʿAlī Naqī Khān, under instructions from the Governor-General of India, to clear up certain complications which had arisen in regard to the disposal of the estate in Oudh in the possession of the descendants of Sayyid Aḥmad Sāndwī": **Edinburgh** 89 (159 foll., with a large map of Fatḥ-ganj. AH 1230/1814).

1107 Unfortunately too late in their arrival to be used adequately in the present survey.

(5) *Aḥwāl i Sar Jamshēd-jī Jījī-bhā'ī*, a metrical biography of Sir Jamsetjee Jejeebhoy [probably the first Baronet of that name (1783–1859),[1108] but the B.M. catalogue does nor make this clear], by Farāmarz Naurōz-jī Kuṭār: **Bombay** A.Y. 1264/1895° (63 pp.).

(6) *Armag͟hān i aḥbāb* (*Tadhkirah i mashāhīr mausūm bah A. i* a.), brief biographies of poets, kings, and other celebrities, mainly Persian, by S͟hams al-'ulamā' Maulawī M. Ḥusain [b. M. Sirāj al-Dīn], Professor, Mission College, Lahore,[1109] whose preface is dated 1 November 1890 and who compiled in 1906 a work entitled *al-'Ajā'ib* (see index): **Lahore** 1890° (68 pp.); 1917* (116 pp.); **Sād'haurah** 1893° (64 pp.).

(7) *al-Aslāf*, a biographical dictionary of famous men, ancient Greeks and Muslims, prophets, etc., by M. S͟hajā'at 'Alī K͟hān: **Badāyūn** 1916* (114 pp.).

(8) *Chahār Ā'īn i Maḥbūbī*, by Maulawī Abu 'l-Faiḍ Najm al-Dīn b. Aḥmad 'Alī 'Abbāsī Chirīyākōtī [who died in 1306/1888–9: see Raḥmān 'Alī pp. 235–6]: **Āṣafīyah** iii p. 162 no. 145 (under *Tadhkirah i fārisī*, but without further indication of the subject, which may not be biographical, AH 1334/1915–16).

(9) *Dūstdārān i bashar*, biographies of famous philanthropists, male (vol. i) and female (vol. ii,[1110] of which the preface is dated Masqaṭ, 28 Ṣafar 1330 [1912]), by [Mīrzā] Muḥammad [b. Aḥmad,[1111] Muns͟hī], M.R.A.S.,[1112]

[1108] See Buckland's *Dictionary of Indian biography* p. 223; D.N.B. under Jeejeebhoy; *Ency. Brit.*, 11th ed., *ibid.*

[1109] In spite of the British Museum catalogue this person (still alive when the 1917 edition was published) is clearly different from S͟hams al-'ulamā' M. Ḥusain "Azād" b. M. Bāqir (b. Delhi 1827, 1828 or 1830, d. Lahore 22.1.1910), who was Professor of Arabic in the Government College, Lahore (1870 ?–1889), wrote some Persian and Urdu readers for the Panjab Education Department, and whose name is illustrious in the history of Urdu literature. For his life and works (which include Urdu works on Persian literature) see Prāg Nārāyan Bhārgava *Ṣaḥīfah i zarrīn* (in Urdu), Lucknow 1902, Panjab section, p. 8; *Civil and military Gazette* [a newspaper], Lahore, 23.1.1910, p. 10b; Rām Bābu Saksēna *History of Urdu literature* pp. 219–22, 274–9, *Tārīkh i adab i Urdū* [Urdu translation of the preceding work], Lucknow [1929], *ḥiṣṣah i nathr*, pp. 46–52 (portrait facing p. 50); *Maulana M. Husain Azād* [a short Urdu biography, 48 pp.] by Ṭālib Ilāhabādī, Allahabad 1931; T. Grahame Bailey *History of Urdu literature* pp. 87, 96; *S͟hams al-'Ulama' Maulānā M. Ḥusain "Azād"*, by Āg͟hā M. Bāqir [his grandson] (in OCM. xv/2 (Feb. 1939), *ḍamīmah*, pp. 41–118 (portrait facing p. 41)); etc.

[1110] Vol. iii is described as in the press in a list of Kāvayānī publications at the end of the Berlin ed. of vol. ii.

[1111] So in the *Ṭulū' i tamaddun*.

[1112] K͟hān Bahādur Āg͟hā Mīrzā Muḥammad, C.I.E., The Sheikh's Market, Ashar, Basrah, Iraq, appears in the lists of Members published in the *JRAS.* from 1924 to 1932. On the title-page of the *Dūstdārān i bashar*, vol. ii, are mentioned the titles of nineteen works by him, including *Aḥwāl i Kristōfar Kulambas* (cf. no. 1631 (2) *supra*), *Ṭulū' i tamaddun* (cf. no. 193 (a) (16)

Order of the Lion and the Sun (2nd Class), Nishān i ʿIlmī (3rd Class): **Bombay** [printed, but published at Najaf] 1914† (138 pp. Vol. i only ?); **Berlin** (Kāvayānī Pr.) 1343/1925* (the date of vol. ii, which alone is in the I.O. Library).

(10) ***Faḍl i Ṣafdarī***, on the merits of ʿAlī b. Abī Ṭālib, by M. Najm al-Dīn Qādirī: **Ārah** ["Arrah"], Nūr al-Anwār Pr., 1294/1877* (pp. 8, 76).

(11) ***al-Farʿ al-nāmī min al-aṣl al-sāmī***, on *ansāb* (according to *Maʾāthir i Ṣiddīqī* iv, appended *fihrist i kutub*, p. 14), by Ṣiddīq Ḥasan Khān (for whom see pp. 27–8, 913, 1137): **Bhōpāl** (so *M. i Ṣ.*, without date) 1301/1883–4 (so Āṣafīyah ii p. 1556, without place, but Sarkīs and Brockelmann say India 1291: there may, therefore, be two editions).

(12) ***Jaur [u] jafā*** (?), love-story of the author, M. Riḍā, son of the late Amīr M. Zamān Khān Durrānī Fufalzai, and a dancing-girl named Murād-Bakhsh at Ḍērah Ghāzī Khān [once seat of the Durrānī Governors], written in 1221/1806: **Rieu** i 384*b* (cf. iii 1087*a*. 36 PICTURES).

(13) ***Jawāhir i arbaʿah***. Edition: place ? date ? (Āṣafīyah. i p. 346, under *Tarājim i Fārisī*, but without further indication of the subject).

(14) ***Kār-nāmah i suturgān i shurafā i Pārsiyān i mamlakat i Hindūstan***, biographies of eminent Parsees, by Āmūzandah Shērmand Īrānī: [**Poona** 1917*] (48 pp.).

(15) ***Kitāb i Ṣubḥī***, an autobiographical apologia, composed (so far as pt. i is concerned) AHS 1312/1933[1113] by Faiḍ Allāh. Muhtadī *maʿrūf ba-*Ṣubḥī, who after some years as a Bahāʾī missionary became private secretary to ʿAbd al-Bahāʾ (d. 28.11.1921[1114]) at Ḥaifā and who has much to say about the history of Bahāʾism and its leading personalities: **Ṭihrān** AHS 1312/1933–4‡ (*Daurah* i. 216 pp.).

(16) ***Maṭlaʿ al-anwār***, by M. Shafīʿ Khān al-Wazīr [b. ?] ʿAbd al-Bāqī al-Sharīf al-Baghdādī: **Āṣafīyah** ii p. 1556 (*Manāqib*) no. 9.

(17) ***Maẓhar al-ḥaqq*** (*Taḥqīq al-ansāb al-mashhūr bi'sm i tārīkhī Maẓhar al-ḥaqq* [= 1284/1867–8]), on the races and genealogies of Indian Muslims (Shaikhs, Saiyids, Mughals, Pat'hāns, etc.), by ʿAbd al-Razzāq Kalyānawī: N.K. [**Lucknow**] 1292/1875°*.

---

supra), *Inshāʾ i aʿlā, Inshaʾ i jadīd, Zabān i Ingilīsī, Aḥwal i Gārfild, Tārīkh i Almān* and *Ḍarb al-amthāl i fārsī*. His portrait forms the frontispieces to S. Ahmad Kasrawī's *Nāmhā-yi shahrhā u dīhhā-yi Irān, daftar* i (Ṭihrān AHS 1308/1929–30) and *daftar* ii (Ṭihrān AHS 1309/1930–1). Kasrawī made his acquaintance in the course of his visit to ʿIrāq and Khūzistān (cf. no. 489 *supra*).

1113 Five years (p. 4^4) after the circulation, in 1307/1928 (p. 2, l. 5 from foot), of an attack on his orthodoxy and character.

1114 For an obituary notice by E. G. Browne see *JRAS*. 1922 pp. 145–6.

(18) ***Miftāḥ al-jannah***, by Mullā M. al-shahīr bah Zanjānī. Edition: 1290/1873 (Āṣafīyah ii p. 1556 (*Manāqib*) no. 10).
(19) ***Mir'āt al-kaunain***, by Ghulām-Nabī Firdausī. Edition: place ? 1312/1894–5 (Āsafīyah i p. 324).
(20) ***Mi'yār al-faḍā'il li-khilāfat al-akhyār wa-'l-radhā'il*** "a Persian version of a work (originally written in Arabic) on the exploits of famous Muslim champions" (Arberry), by Maulawi Nasīm Ḥasan: **Amrōhah** 1334/1917* (308 pp.).
(21) ***Nasab-nāmah***, by Faḍl Allāh Shihāb al-Dīn b. al-Qāḍī Ḥasan: **Cairo** p. 529.
(22) ***Niẓām al-ansāb***, written in 1307/1889–90 (vol. i) and 1310/1892–3 (vol. ii) by S. M. Mansur 'Alī "Khirad" Naqawī al-Bukhārī b. S. Zain al-'Ābidīn Shikārpūrī: **Āṣafīyah** iii p. 720 (AH 1307 and 1310).
(23) ***Qur'ān*** [sic, possibly for ***Qirān***] ***al-su'adā***, by M. Ḥusainī Madanī Aurangābādī: **Āṣafīyah** i p. 322 no. 18 (under the heading *Tadhkirah*).
(24) ***Risālah fī bayān nasl al-mulūk wa'l-ashrāf min Ādam:*** **Leningrad** Univ. 384 (Salemann-Rosen p. 17).
(25) ***Risālah i dhikr i mughanniyān i Hindūstān***, composed in Aḥhmad Shāh's fifth regnal year (AH 1165–6) by 'Ināyat Khān "Rāsikh" (fl. 1163/1750: see Ethé 411): **Bānkīpūr** xvii 1734 (15 foll. 19th cent.).
(26) ***Riyaḍ i laṭīf***, *Reyaz-i-Latif, or Biographical sketches of the Persian authors for the use of ... candidates of the Universities, Calcutta, Bombay, Madras, Panjab and Allahabad*, by Abū 'l-Munīf M. Laṭīf: **Calcutta** 1904°* (64 pp.).
(27) ***Safīnah i Raḥmānī***, by Ḥafiẓ 'Abd al-Raḥmān "Ḥairat". Edition: place ? 1884 (Āṣaflyah i p. 320).
(28) ***Saḥā'if i sharā'if***, composed in 1231/1816 by M. 'Askarī Ḥusainī Bilgrāmī: **Āṣafīyah** i p. 322 no. 19 (autograph).
(29) ***Shajarah i ṭaiyibah***, by Ghulām-'Alī "Āzād" Bilgrāmī: see no. 1162 Persian works (12) *supra*.
(30) ***Shams al-manāqib***, by M. 'Alī Khān "Surūsh" Iṣfahānī (d. 1285/1868–9: see *Majma' al-fuṣaḥā'* ii pp. 184–95): [**Ṭihrān**] 1301/1884 (122 foll. See Karatay p. 121).
(31) ***Sharḥ i ḥāl i 'Abd Allāh b. al-Muqaffa'***, by 'Abbās Iqbāl (cf. no. 1453 *supra*): **Berlin** 1926* (Intisharāt i Īranshahr, 15).
(32) ***Sharḥ i ḥāl i Kulunil Muhammad Taqī Khān*** (*Colonel Mohamed Taghi Khan* (*Biography of*) *by some of his friends and admirers* [Riḍā-zādah "Shafaq"[1115] and others]): **Berlin** 1927* (Intishārāt i Īrānshahr, 20).

1115 Dr. Sādiq Khān R.-z. "Shafaq", Professor of Modern Philosophy in the University of Ṭihrān, was born at Tabrīz in 1310/1892–3 and was in 1328/1910 owner and editor of the Tabrīz weekly newspaper *Shafaq* (Browne *The press and poetry of modern Persia* p. 111).

(33) ***Sharḥ i ḥāl u āthār i Saiyid Jamāl al-Dīn i Asadābādī***[1116] (French title: *Seyed Djemal-ud-Din Afghani. Par son neveu M. Lutfullah Khan* [Asadābādī] *avec quelques appendices par des savants différents*): **Berlin** 1926* (tom. i. 128 pp. Intishārāt i Īranshahr, 13); **Tabrīz** AHS 1326/1947–8 (an augmented edition. See Yādgār iv/1–2 p. 127).

(34) ***Sharh i ḥāl u iqdāmāt i Shaikh Muḥammad i Khiyābānī***[1117] (*Cheikh Mohammad Khiabani. Sa biographie et son activité politique et sociale. Par ses amis et ses admirateurs* [Riḍā-zādah "Shafaq"[1118] and others]. **Berlin** 1926* (Intishārāt i Īranshahr, 14).

(35) ***Tadhkirah i Allāhī***, a biography of Muẓaffar ʿAlī Shāh Allāhī, of Āgrah, by M. Abū 'l-Ḥasan Farīdābādī: **Lucknow** 1887° (122 pp.).

(36) ***Tadhkirat al-akhyār***, brief notices of Prophets, Imāms, kings and philosophers, by ʿAlī Akbar Sharīf Gīlānī: **Lahore** Panjāb Univ. (AH 1224/1809. See *OCM*. viii/4 (Aug. 1932) p. 45).

(37) ***Taḥqīq al-ansāb:*** see ***Maẓhar al-ḥaqq*** above.

(38) ***Tarānah i gham***, a panegyric in rhymed prose on Maulānā M. ʿAbd al-Rashīd, by M. Kalb-ʿAlī Khān, Nawwāb of Rāmpūr (cf. no. 1622): [**Rāmpūr**] 1289/1872°*.

(39) ***Tārīkh i jāwīd***, short biographical notices and portraits of Persian officers killed on active service: **Ṭihrān** (Ministry of War) AHS 1325/1946–7 (vol. i, covering the years 1320–5), 1326 (vol. ii, covering the years 1300–26), 1327 (vol. iii, additional biographies for the years 1300–27).

(40) ***Ṭarīq al-bukāʾ***, stories of saints and martyrs, by Mullā M. Ḥusain "Giryān" Shahrābī: **Bombay** 1343/1925*.

Subsequently he studied at Robert College, Istānbūl, and at the University of Berlin. His works include a *Tārīkhi adabīyāt i Irān barāy i dabīristānhā* [Ṭihrān AHS 1321/1942] and a *Farhang i Shāh-namah* (Luzac's OL. 1942 p. 10). See Rashīd Yāsamī *Adabīyāt i muʿāṣir* p. 59 (portrait); D. J. Irani *Poets of the Pahlavi regime* pp. 345–348B (portrait); Ishaque *Sukhanvarān-i-Irān* ii pp. 241–6 (portrait), *Modern Persian poetry* pp. 10 n. 3, 11, 26; Mahdī Mujtahidī *Rijāl i Adharbāyjān* pp. 97–99; *Tarīkh i jarāʾid u majallāt i Irān* iii p. 74; Īraj Afshār *Nathr i Fārsi i muʿāṣir* pp. 138–44 (portrait).

1116 Born 1254/1838–9, died at Istānbūl 9 March 1897. See Zaidān *Mashāhīr al-sharq* ii pp. 54–66, *Taʾrīkh ādāb al-lughat al-ʿarabīyah* iv pp. 312–13; Browne *The Persian revolution* pp. 2–30, etc. (portrait frontispiece); *Encyl. Isl.* under Djamāl al-Dīn (Goldziher); *Armaghān* xii (AHS 1310/1931–2) pp. 586–601 (an article by Ṣifāt Allāh Jamālī); Brockelmann *Sptbd.* iii pp. 311–15; etc. A biography of 96 pp. published at Tihrān is mentioned in *Luzac's OL*. 1951 p. 32, where the title is given as "Seyed Jamal Afgani" and the author's name is not mentioned.

1117 Cf. Ḥabīb Allāh Mukhtārī *Tārīkh i bīdārī i Īrān* p. 54 (portrait); M. Ṣadr Hāshimī *Tarikh i jaraʾid u majallāt i Irān* ii p. 106 (portrait).

1118 Cf. (32) *supra*.

(41) *Yādgār i Hindī*, "Poems in Persian entitled Yadgar-i-Hindee, containing a brief account of the great prophets, kings, rulers, and philosophers of the world by Rai Kunhya Lall" i.e. Kanhaiyā Lāl "Hindī" (for whom see no. 861 *supra*): **Lahore** 1290/1873°*.

(42) *Zindagāni i Mānī*, by Malik al-Shu'ara' ["Bahār" presumably. Cf. Additions & Corrections ad 452 (452*e* (5))[17]: **Ṭihrān** (see *Luzac's O.L.* 1938 p. 186).

(43) *Zubdat al-'ulūm*, by 'Iwaḍ Ḥiṣārī,[1119] a collection of legends and traditions of Muḥammad, his Companions, celebrated scholars, saints, etc., with an account of the miracles of 'Abd al-Qādir al-Jīlānī and a description of Heaven and Hell: **Bodleian** 334 (n.d.).

Some Miscellaneous Historical Works

1668.

(1) ***al-'Ajā'ib***, accounts of marvellous events in the reigns of Akbar and Jahāngīr extracted from the *Iqbāl-nāmah i Jahāngīrī* (cf. no. 717 *supra*), by Shams al-'ulamā' Maulawī M. Ḥusain [b. M. Sirāj al-Dīn[1120]], Professor, Mission College, Lahore, whose preface is dated 16 Muharram 1324/12 March 1906 and who is described as *marḥūm* on the title-page of the 1924 edition [but who was still alive in 1917, when an edition of his *Armaghān i aḥbāb* was published (see no. 1667 (6) *supra*): **Lahore** [1906*] (38 pp.); 1924* (36 pp.). English translation: *The curiosities of Indian history. Being an English translation of Al-'Ajaib ... by K.M. Maitra*: **Lahore** 1922* (55 pp.).

(2) ***Chār chaman***, by 'Abd al-Wadūd: **Āṣafīyah** iii p. 100.

(3) ***Ḍiyā' i qamar***, composed in 1305/1887–8 by Ākhund Shēr Ḥasan Khān: **Āṣafīyah** i p. 246 no. 627.

(4) ***Ḥaqq al-Sulṭān***, on the merits of the Ottoman dynasty, by M. Nuṣrat 'Alī: **Delhi** (Nusrat al-Maṭābi') 1295/1878* 184 pp.).

(5) ***Ḥilyat al-'adhrā'*** stories of the Prophets for children, by M. 'Abd al-Ḥalīm "Sharar":[1121] **Lucknow** 1921* (100 pp.).

1119 Who was a protégé of a certain Khwājah Bāqī Jān Ghiyāth al-Millah wa-'l-Dunyā wa-'l-Dīn [ibn ?] 'Imād al-Dīn.

1120 A *marthiyah* on the compiler's father by Maulawī 'Azīz al Dīn, calligraphist to the Nawwāb of Bahāwalpūr, is appended to *al-'Ajā'ib* (p. 36 in the 1924 edition).

1121 A well-known Urdu novelist, historian and journalist (1860—December 1926). See R. B. Saksena *History of Urdu literature* pp. 334–41; T. Grahame Bailey *History of Urdu literature* p. 91.

(6) *Jahān-nāmah*, a metrical sketch of general and Indian history composed in the reign of Aurangzēb not earlier than 1099/1688 by "Fanā'ī", a disciple of Sh. Luqmān b. Sh. 'Uthman Khalīl Sulaimānī: **Rieu** ii 701*b* (*Jild* i only, on the Creation, the Prophets, etc., from Adam to Luqmān and the early kings of Persia. Late 17th cent.).

(7) *Jang-nāmah i Mashriqī*, by Bhawānī Parshād "Mashriqī" Kāyast'h, a resident of Qinnauj: **Āṣafiyah** iii p. 100 no. 1134 (A.H. 1208/1793–4).

(8) *Kitāb-khānah i Iskandarīyah*, a translation by S. M. Taqī Fakhr Dā'ī Gīlānī of an Urdu pamphlet by M. Shiblī Nu'mānī[1122] in rebuttal of the allegation that the library at Alexandria was destroyed by 'Umar: **Ṭihran** AHS 1315/1936–7 (67 pp. See Harrassowitz's *Litterae orientales*, Oct. 1938 p. 14).

(9) *Laṭa'if al-tawārīkh*, a sketch, mainly catechetical, of Oriental history (Chaldaea, Media, Persia, Macedonia, Carthage, Egypt, Arabia, etc.), mostly ancient and mediaeval, but in the case of Egypt brought down to 1914, by Āqā Mīrzā Hājjī Āqā[1123] b. Ḥājjī Abū 'l-Ḥasan Kāzarūnī, Principal of the Madrasah i Khaz'alīyah at Muḥammarah: **Bombay** 1332–3/1915* (*Daurah* i. 272 pp.).

(10) *Ma'ārif i shattā*, composed in 1306/1888–9 by S. M. Manṣūr 'Alī "Khirad" Naqawī Bukharī Shikārpūrī: **Aṣafīyah** iii p. 110 (AH 1306/1888–9).

(11) *Mukhtaṣar i tārīkh i Rūsiyah*, translated [from a Turkish original ?] by S. Riḍā 'Alī-zādah: **Lahore** 1345/1927* (Mufīd i 'āmm Pr. 122 pp.).

(12) *Muntakhab al-tawārīkh*, by Abū 'l-Barakāt b. M. Naṣr Allāh: **Lindesiana** p. 107 no. 401 (AH 1111/1699).

(13) *Nuskhah i Dhakā*, composed in 1265/1849 by Ghulām-Aḥmad Maḥmud "Dhakā", a resident of Ṭēkmāl: **Aṣafīyah** iii p. 102.

(14) *Shams al-madhāhib*, composed in 1251/1835–6 by Munshī M. Qādir Khān (cf. no. 1026): **Āsaflyah** i p. 246 no. 851 (AH 1251/1835–6. Under *Tārīkh*. but without further indication of the subject).

1122 b. 1857, d. 18 Nov. 1914, the author of several well-known biographical, historical and other works in Urdu (e.g. *al-Ma'mūn, Sīrat al-Nu'mān* [i.e. Abū Ḥanīfah], *al-Fārūq, al-Ghazālī, Sīrat al-Nabī, Shi'r al-'Ajam, al-Kalām*) as well as of some Persian poetry. Of the five parts of his *Shi'r al-'Ajam* at least three have been translated into Persian by M. Taqī Fakhr-Da'ī Gīlanī ((1) *Luzac's OL.* 1938 p. 10, (2) *LOL.* 1948 p. 68, (5) *LOL.* 1939 p. 179). See *Ency. Isl.* under Shiblī (A. Siddīqī); R. B. Saksena **History of Urdu literature** pp. 287–94; T. Grahame Bailey *History of Urdu literature* pp. 88–9; R. P. Bhajiwalla *Mauláná Shibli and Umar Khayyám*, Surat 1932, pp. 19–50 (portrait); Brockelmann *Sptbd.* ii p. 862; translator's preface to Persian trans. of *Shi'r al-'Ajam*, vol. i; etc.

1123 A.M.Ḥ.A., so on the title-page: M. Ḥ. Ā. Kāzarūnī on the cover, but in the Quarterly Catalogue (Bombay 1917 (1)) he is called Aghá Mirzá Háji Ráza [*sic*] Kazráni [sic].

(15) ***Sharaf-nāmah***, by M. Auliyā Nā'iṭī entitled (*al-mukhāṭab bah*) Ḥāfiẓ-Yār-Jang: **Āṣafīyah** i p. 246 no. 530.
(16) ***Tanbīh al-sālikīn***, by Ḥasan 'Alī b. S. 'Alī known as (al-shahīr bi-) Mīrzā Buzurg Ṭabīb Shīrāzī: **Āṣafīyah** i p. 234 no. 692.
(17) ***Tārīkh i adabīyāt i Īrān***, by Jalāl al-Dīn "Sanā" Humā'ī Iṣfahānī:[1124] **Tabrīz** 1348/1929–30* (vols. i–ii only (from the beginnings to the Mongol conquest). Pp. 332; 408).
(18) ***Tarīkh i badāyi'*** (a chronogram=1298), or ***Tarjamah i Ḥaqā'iq al-kalām fī ta'rikh al-Islām***, a translation by Iskandar Efendī, *ṣāhib-imtiyāz i "Akhbār i Dār al-Khilāfah"*, of the Turkish work of 'Abd al-Laṭīf Ṣubḥī Pāshā (d. 1303/1886: see Babinger *Geschichtsschreiber der Osmanen* p. 369): **Istānbūl** 1298/1880‡ (vol. i only (from Muhammad to 'Alī). 301 pp. Maḥmud Bey's Pr. Cf. Karatay p. 166).
(19) ***Tārīkh i Iskandarī***, by Ṭāhir b. Ḥasan b. 'Alī Mūsā al-Ṭūsī: **Āṣafīyah** ip. 222 no. 429 (defective at end).
(20) ***Tārīkh i milal i mashriq***, a revised and enlarged edition of the work of Seignobos, by M. 'Alī Khān Dhakā' al-Mulk ["Furūghī": cf. no. 320]: **Ṭihrān** 1327/1909 (Mashhad cat. p. 121).
(21) ***Tārīkh i Qipchāqī***:[1125] **Leningrad** Univ. no. 964c (AH 1238/1822–3. Romaskewicz p. 4).
(22) ***Tārīkh i 'umūmī***, Pt. i (the ancient world) by M. 'Alī Khān. **Lahore**, Mufīd i 'āmm Pr., AHS 1306/1928* (440 pp.), Pt. ii (the middle ages) by Abū 'l-Ḥasan Arjmand Sāwajī and M. Ḥusain Khān, **Lahore** AHS 1305/1927* (571 pp.).
(23) ***Tārīkh i 'umūmī i qurūn i wusṭā***, by 'Abd al-Ḥusain Shaibānī: **Ṭihrān** [1932*-], *in progress* [?].
(24) ***Tārīkh i Yahūd***, by Paiwīz Rāhbar: **Ṭihrān** 1946 (see Probsthain's *Orientalia nova*, 2 (1946–8) p. 28).
(25) ***Tuḥfah i A'ẓamīyah***,[1126] by Badr al-Daulah, Muftī of Madrās (cf. nos. 297 and 652 *supra*): **Āṣafīyah** ii p. 876 ("*Siyar i Fārsī*") nos. 111 (a.h. 1236/1820–1), 24 (A.H. 1259/1843).

1124 Born 1317/1899–1900 at Iṣfahān. See D. J. Irani *Poets of the Pahlavi regime* pp. 336–9 (portrait); Ishaque *Sukhanvarān-i-Īrān* ii pp. 214–19 (portrait), *Modern Persian poetry* pp. 12, 30; Burqa'ī *Sukhanwarān i nāmī i mu'āṣir* pp. 124–6 (portrait); Īraj Afshar Nathr i Fārsi i mu'āṣir pp. 205–11 (portrait).
1125 Possibly = *Tārīkh i Qipchāq-Khānī* (for which see no. 161).
1126 For a work of this title described as by Irtaḍā 'Alī Khān see no. 1381 (2).

Additions and Corrections

P. xxviii, ad M. Idrīs: *Read Nagrāmī.* For Nagrām, a village near Lucknow, see Raḥmān ʿAlī p. 124[16], where the name is spelled out.

No. 1, penult. par., MSS. [*Tarjamah i Tafsīr i Ṭabarī*]. Also **Ṭihrān** National Museum (vols. i–iv and vi (last), AH 606–8/1209–11. From the shrine of Sh. Ṣafī at Ardabīl. See A. Romaskewicz's article *Persidski "tafsir" Tabarī* in *Zapiski Kollegii Vostokovedov v* (1930) pp. 801–6), **Mashhad** i, *fṣl.* 3, MSS., no. 19 (S. xxiii 58–xxxiv 19), **Āṣafīyah** iii p. 230 no. 572.

No. 1, 2nd par., footnote. al-Mufaqqih is apparently a corruption of al-Mutafaqqih.

No. 2, end. Among the MSS. of old commentaries as yet unidentified are **Fātiḥ** 301 (S. xlix–lxiv. AH 630. Language archaic. Translation of xliv 1 begins *Ai girawandagān pīshī ma- kunīt bar Muḥammad.* Magnificent MS.) [Ritter, *OLZ.* 1928 col. 1123], **Browne** Coll. A. 2 (probably composed in 5th/11th cent. S. xxxviii 20–xcv. 13th cent.) and **Blochet** iv 2211 (S. vii–x. An isolated volume of a large commentary (in 14 or 15 vols. ?). Early 13th cent.). A fragment of 46 leaves (S. ii 61–146) from an old *tafsīr* has been described with some extracts and an exposition of its linguistic features in an Urdu article (*Qurʾān Pak kī ēk qadīm tafsīr*) contributed by Prof. Maḥmūd Shērānī (probably the owner of the fragment) to *OCM.* viii/3 (May 1932) pp. 1–96.

No. 3, 2nd par., MSS. [*Tafsīr al-Sūrābādī*]. Also **Brit. Mus.** (S. xix–xxv. AH 535/1140–1. See *British Museum Quarterly* vi/2 (1931) p. 55). For a MS. dated 684/1285 of the first quarter of this commentary in the private library of the late M. ʿAlī Khān "Tarbiyat" (cf. no. 1493 *supra*) at Tabrīz see ʿAbd al-ʿAzīz Jawāhir al-Kalām's *Kitāb-khānahā-yi Īrān*, [Ṭihrān] AHS 1311, p. 91, and Mahdī Bayānī's article *Sargudhasht i hasht qarn i yak nuskhah i khaṭṭī i Qurʾān* in the periodical *Payām i nau* i/7 (Ṭihran [1945]) p. 45.

No. 4, 2nd par., MSS. [*Tāj al-tarājim*]. Also **Fātiḥ** 302 foll. 1–127 and 280–528 (S. xviii–cxiv. AH 506/1112–13. See Ritter in *OLZ.*1928/12 col. 1123), **Sipahsālār** i pp. 78–80 no. 138 (S. xix–cxiv. 15th cent.).

No. 5, 1st par. [Abū Naṣr etc.]. According to the editor's Arabic preface in the MS. Fātiḥ 303 the author's name is A. N. Aḥmad b. al-Ḥasan b. Aḥmad al-Daranī (?) and he is there said to have died in 549 [1154–5]. According to the copyist's

 | DOI:10.1163/9789004444041_003

colophon his surname [*Beiname*] is Zāhid, not Zāhidī. [Ritter, OLZ. 1928/12 col. 1123]. Among the forms in which the name occurs are Saif al-Dīn A. N. b. A. b. Ḥusain b. Sulaimān DRWĀJKĪ (Mashhad cat.), A. N. b. A. b. al-Ḥusain b. A. b. S. Darwājakī or Wardājakī (Ivanow Curzon 332) and A. N. A. b. al-Ḥasan b. A. Sulaimānī al-RĀRWḤKĪ (Bānkīpīr xiv p. 2). The words *Qāla 'l-Shaikh al-Imām al-Zāhid* recur fairly often in the text (Ivanow Curzon 333).

No. 5, 2nd par. [*Tafsīr i Zāhidī*]. The work is so called in some of the colophons (e.g. Ivanow Curzon 332, 333, Bānkīpūr xiv 1112–13). According to the already cited Arabic editorial preface in Fātīḥ 303 the title is *Laṭā'if al-tafsīr* [Ritter, OLZ. 1928/12 col. 1123], Other MSS.: **Mashhad** i, *fṣl.* 3, MSS., no. 26 ("*Tafsīr i Saif al-Dīn*"; Apparently complete. AH 829/1425–6), **Fātiḥ** 303 (S. i–xviii. AH 877/1472–3. See Ritter, OLZ. 1928/12 col. 1123).

No. 5, 2nd par., MSS. **Bānkīpūr** Pers. Hand-list 1121–2 = **Bānkīpūr** xiv 1112–13.

No. 5, end. *Insert:*

5*a*. **Rashīd al-Dīn** Abū 'l-Faḍl **Aḥmad b. M.** b. Aḥmad b. Mihrpazd **al-Maibudī** al-Yazdī.

Kashf al-asrār wa-'uddat al-abrār (beg. *Khair kalimāt al-shukr*), a large commentary begun in 520/1126, based in part on the concise *tafsīr*[1] of 'Abd Allāh al-Anṣārī (for whom see no. 1245 *supra*) and having the comments on each verse arranged in three *naubats* ((1) a literal Persian translation, (2) explanation of the sense, variant readings, occasion of the revelation, legal application, traditions and anecdotes, (3) Ṣūfī explanation): Ḥ. Kh. v p. 202 no. 10674 (incorrect), **As'ad** 146 (S. xxvi–cxiv, described as vols. 7 and 8. AH 726), 145 (S. i–xvii. AH 889), **Nūr i 'Uthmānīyah** 474 (S. vi–x. Early 8th/14th cent.), 444 (S. iv 147–ix 119, described as vol. 3. 8th/14th cent. ?), **Yeñī** p. 80 no. 43 (complete. Written for the *Wazīr* Faṣīḥ al-Dīn Aḥmad Pāshā and bearing the seal of Bāyazīd II) [Ritter, OLZ. 1928/12 col. 1123], **Mashhad** i, *fṣl.* 3, MSS., nos. 176 (S. i–ii 193), 30 (S. xxi 6–xxv), **Sipahsālār** i p. 148 no. 209 (S. vi–ix, 13th cent.).

No. 6, 2nd par., MSS. **Bānkīpūr** Pers. Hand-list 1137–9 = **Bānkīpūr** xiv 1114–16 (first two leaves missing).

1 Cf. the words quoted in the Mashhad catalogue from the preface: *Chūn nuskhah i tafsīr Abī Ismā'īl 'Abd Allah b. M. b.* [*sic*] *Anṣārī rā dīdam kih dar kamāl i ījāz ast khwāstam Fārisī kunam....* For Anṣārī's *tafsīr* no. 1245, 3rd par. *supra*.

No. 6, 2nd par., MSS. [*Rauḍ al-jinān*]. Also **Mashhad** i, *fṣl.* 3, MSS., nos. 129–36 (of which 134 (S. xxxiii–xlviii) and 136 (S. lxxiv–cix) are dated 556/1161 and 557/1162 respectively), **Majlis** ii 811 (vols. i–x (out of 20 vols.). AH 1058/1648), **Sipahsālār** i pp. 129–34 no. 194 (S. xii–xvii), **ʿAlīgaṛh Subḥ**. MSS. p. 6 no. 11 (“*juzw i thānī*”). Edition: **Ṭihrān** (Maṭbaʿah i Majlis) AH 1323/1905–6 (vol. i, i.e. S. i–iv 61 and vol. ii, i.e. S. iv 62–ix), AHS 1313–15/ 1934–6 (vols. iii–v, i.e. S. x–cxiv). According to the Sipahsālār catalogue Muẓaffar al-Dīn Shāh gave orders in 1319/ 1901–2 for the printing of this work and at the time of his death (Dhū ’l-Qaʿdah 1324/ Jan. 1907) “vols. i–ii”; and 173 pages of “vol. iii”;, i.e. more than ten of the author’s twenty *mujallads*, had been printed. In Riḍā Shāh’s reign the printing was resumed and completed (cf. Mashhad iv, p. 491, Majlis ii p. 27[16]).

No. 7, 2nd par., MSS. [*Tafsīr i Baṣāʾir i Yamīnī*]. “The Tafsīr described by me in the first catalogue as No. 956 is apparently *not* identical with Rosen 45. But it *is* identical, as Professor Houtsma has written, with Leyden iv, 45 (No. 1710) …” [W. Ivanow, in a letter.]

No. 7, 2nd par., MSS. [*Tafsīr i Baṣāʾir i Yamīnī.*] **Bāyazīd** 68 should be deleted, since that MS. (217 foll. 8th/14th cent. ?) contains the *Baṣāʾir al-naẓāʾir*, an introduction to the *Qurʾān* and a Qurʾānic glossary, by Abū ’l-Faḍāʾil M. b. al-Ḥusain al-Muʿīnī [Ritter, *OLZ*. 1928, col. 1123]. Other MSS.: **Mashhad** i, *fṣl.* 3, MSS., nos. 12–13 (1st half only. AH 610/1213) and probably **Leyden** iv p. 45 no. 1710 (S. xviii–xxxiv 32. N.d. See previous correction).

No. 9, 2nd par. [Qāḍī Ḥamīd al-Dīn Nāgaurī.] His tomb is near that of Bakhtyār Kākī. For the inscription, which gives 695/1296 as the date of his death, see Beale *Miftāḥ al-tawārīkh* (1867) p. 73.

No. 9, 3rd par. [Qāḍī Ḥ. al-D. Nāgaurī.] Also *Āʾīn i Akbarī* tr. Jarrett p. 367; *Gulzār i abrār* no. 20; *Kalimāt al-ṣādiqīn* no. 5; *Riyāḍ al-ʿārifīn* (AHS 1316) p. 104.

No. 9, penult. par. [Sh. Ḥamīd al-Dīn Nāgaurī.] Also *Āʾīn i Akbarī* tr. Jarrett p. 367; *Gulzār i abrār* no. 50; *Makhzan al-gharāʾib* no. 566.

No. 11, 2nd par., MSS. [*al-Asʾilah wa-’l-ajwibah.*] Āyā Ṣōfyah 1033*a* and 69*b* are dated 826 and 885 respectively. Ā. Ṣ. 71 belonged to the library of Bāyazīd II (886–918). The words “(probably also 66)”; should be deleted: Ā. Ṣ. 66 contains the Ḥurūfī commentary described in the addendum to no. 12, end. [Ritter, *OLZ*. 1928 col. 1123.]

No. 11, 2nd par., MSS. [*al-As'ilah wa-'l-ajwibah*]. Also **Nāfidh Pāshā** 108 (modern). [Ritter.] *Delete* (also 98 ?). Fātiḥ 98 is the Ḥurūfī commentary described in the addendum to no. 12, end.

No. 12. This record should be deleted. For the *Kashf al-asrār wa-ʿuddat al-abrār* (erroneously ascribed by Ḥ. Kh. to al-Taftāzānī) see the addendum to no. 5.

No. 12, end. *Insert:*

12*a*. (***Tafsīr i Ḥurūfī***) (beg. *Ibtidā* (5 times) *khilqat az īn-jā nah az aurāq*), a curious Ḥurūfī commentary stated to have been composed in 796/1394: **Āyā Ṣōfyah** 66 (bears seal of Bāyazīd II (886–918)), **Fātiḥ** 98 (same seal), probably also **Kamānkash** 230 (acephalous. AH 914). [Ritter, *OLZ.* 1928 col. 1123.]

No. 13, 2nd par. [*Tafsīr i M. Pārsā.*] This work was composed at Bukhārā in 820, as appears from the author's colophon in Asʿad 84 (AH 1059). [Ritter, *OLZ.* 1928 col. 1124.]

No. 13, 2nd par., end. Delete the note of interrogation. [Ritter, *ibid.*]

No. 13, penult. par., ult. *Delete* probably. [Ritter, *ibid.*]

No. 13, last par. [M. Pārsā.] Also *Khazīnah i ganj i Ilāhī* (Sprenger p. 84); *Haft iqlīm* no. 1492; Rieu ii p. 863; Ethé no. 1855; Brockelmann *Sptbd.* ii pp. 282–3.

No. 14 (2), end. [Niʿmat Allāh Walī.] Also *Khazīnah i ganj i Ilāhī* (Sprenger p. 86); *Ātash-kadah* no. 250; *Khazīnat al-aṣfiyā'* i pp. 114–15; Bānkīpūr ii pp. 10–11. Photograph of his tomb (erected in 840 by Aḥmad Shah Bahmanī) in Sykes *History of Persia* ii, facing p. 156.

No. 15, 1st par. Charkh is a small place on the road from Kābul to Ghaznī and is nearer to the former than to the latter.

No. 15, 2nd par., MSS. [*Tafsīr i Yaʿqūb i Charkhī.*] Fātiḥ 299 and Asʿad 88 are dated 924 and 933. [Ritter, *OLZ.* 1928 col. 1124.]

No. 15, 2nd par., MSS. Yeñī p. 79 no 22 should be deleted, since it contains a small (20 foll.) anonymous commentary on the *Fātiḥah* (beg. *Fātiḥah i futūḥāt i Ilāhī*) with an appendix on the *khawāṣṣ* of the *sūrah*. [Ritter, *ibid.*] Other

MSS.: **Lahore** Panjāb Univ. (2 copies, one dated 1089–91/1678–80. See *OCM*. xi/2 p. 77), **Ivanow** 2nd Suppt. 988 (late 18th cent.), **Bānkīpūr** xiv 1156 (18th cent.), **Nāfidh Pāshā** 59 (AH 1234/1818–19. See Ritter, *OLZ*. 1928 col. 1124), **Blochet** iv 2212 (AH 1239–42/1823–7), **Vatican** Pers. 158 (AH 1270/1853. Rossi p. 151), **ʿAlīgaṛh** Subḥ. MSS. p. 6.

No. 15, 3rd par. Also **Bombay** 1308/1890–1 (Mashhad i, *fṣl*. 3, ptd. bks., no. 8).

No. 16, 2nd par., MSS. [*Baḥr i mawwāj*.] **Bānkīpūr** Pers. Hand-list 1105–8, 1109 and 1110–11 = **Bānkīpūr** xiv 1117–20 (complete, AH 1265/1849), 1121 (S. xxxviii–cxiv. AH 1101/1689–90) and 1122–3 (S. i–xviii. 17th cent.).

No. 16, 2nd par., penult. [*Baḥr i mawwāj*.] *Read* **Nūr i ʿUthmānīyah** 234 (S. i–xii. AH 984), 235 (S. xiii–cxiv. AH 984). [Ritter, *OLZ*. 1928 col. 1124.]

No. 16, 2nd par., MSS. [*Baḥr i mawwāj*.] Also **ʿAlīgaṛh** Subḥ. MSS. p. 5 nos. 1–2 (S. xxxvi–cxiv. AH 1087/1676–7), p. 6 no. 26 (defective).

No. 16, last par. *Akhbār al-akhyār* (Delhi 1332) pp. 180–1.

No. 16, last par. [Shihāb al-Dīn Daulatābādī] Also *Khazīnat al-aṣfiyāʾ* i pp. 390–2.

No. 17, 2nd par. [*al-Muḥammadīyah* or *Tafsīr i Muṣannifak*.] Correct title: *k. al-Shifāʾ fī tafsīr kalām Allāh al-munazzal min al-samāʾ*. It was begun in 862 (not 863) and completed in 866. [Ritter, *OLZ*. 1928 col. 1124.]

No. 17, 3rd par. [*Tafsīr i Muṣannifak*.] *Read* **Fātiḥ**; 636 (S. i. Author's brouillon presented in 863), **Bāyazīd** 260 (S. i, 307 foll., of which 1–234*a* are autograph), 261 (S. lxxvii–cxiv. AH 1123), **Āyā Ṣōfyah** 285 (S. lxxvii–cxiv. After AH 1000). [Ritter, *OLZ*. 1928 col. 1124.]

No. 17, last par. [Muṣannifak.] Also *Ency. Isl.* under al-Bisṭāmī (Huart).

No. 18. This record should be deleted, since Salīmīyah 49 contains a part (S. i and lxxviii–cxiv. AH 974) of Kāshifī's *Mawāhib i ʿalīyah* (for which see no. 20 (2)). [Ritter, *OLZ*. 1928 col. 1124.]

No. 19 (1), MSS. **Bānkīpūr** Pers. Hand-list 1128 = **Bānkīpūr** xiv 1139.

No. 19 (2), MSS. **Bānkīpūr** Pers. Hand-list 1123–6 = **Bānkīpūr** xiv 1140–3 (1140 and 1141 of 17th cent., 1142 dated 1104, 1143 19th cent.).

No. 19 (2), MSS. [*Tafsīr i Sūrah i Yūsuf.*] Also **Mashhad** iv p. 438 nos. 335 (AH 986/1579), 336, **Bānkīpūr** Suppt. ii 2056 (AH 1098/1687), **Majlis** ii 789 (early 19th cent.), **Lahore** Panjāb Univ. (AH 1273/1856–7. See *OCM*. xi/2 p. 77).

No. 19, 4th par. [*Tafsīr i Sūrah i Yūsuf.*] Also **Lucknow** 1309/1891–2 (under the title of *Tafsīr i nuqrah-kār.*[2] See Mashhad iv p. 481).

No. 19, last par. [Muʿīn al-Dīn Farāhī] Also *Majālis al-nafāʾis* (tr. Fakhrī ed. Ḥikmat p. 94, ed. ʿAbd Allāh om. (p. 15912), tr. Qazwīnī ed. Ḥikmat p. 269); Tārīkh i Rashīdī (quoted in *Mélanges asiatiques* ix p. 348); *Gulzār i abrār* no. 233. For some of his descendants see *Maʾāthir al-umarāʾ* iii p. 117.

No. 20, 1st par., ult. *Read* 910/1504–5.

No. 20 (1), MSS. **Bānkīpūr** Pers. Hand-list 1131–2 = **Bānkīpūr** xiv 1124–5.

No. 20 (1), MSS. [*Jawāhir al-tafsīr.*] Also **Yeñi** 19 (S. i–iv. AH 967, transcribed from an autograph), **Qarah Muṣṭafā** 100 (S. i–iv. AH 1031), Nūr i ʿUthmānīyah 279 (S. i–iv. AH 1062 ?), [Ritter, *OLZ*. 1928 col. 1125], **Mashhad** i, *fṣl.* 3, MSS., nos. 75–77 (of which 75 is dated 979/1571–2), iv p. 432, nos. 317 (S. i. AH 1118/1706), 318 (S. i), **Majlis** ii 808 (AH 983/1575–6) **Sipahsālār** i p. 113, nos. 171 (S. i–iv 81. 16th cent.), 172 (S. i–iii), **Āṣafīyah** iii p. 230 (beautiful MS.), **Leningrad** Univ. (Salemann-Rosen p. 14).

No. 20 (1), 2nd par., end. Nūr i ʿUthmānīyah 279 and Yeñī 19 are the *Jawāhir al-tafsīr* (see the Additions to No. 20 (1), MSS. above): Bāyazīd 145 is the *Mawāhib i ʿAlīyah.* [Ritter, *OLZ*. 1928 col. 1125.] Tashkent 8 (17th cent.) is the *Mawāhib i ʿAlīyah*, as the opening words show.

No. 19, penult. par., footnote. [Muʿīn al-Dīn Farāhī] For a Persian abridgment, *Khulāṣah i Baḥr al-durar*, see *OCM*. xi/2 (Feb. 1935) p. 76 (Lahore, Panjāb Univ. AH 1213/1798).

---

2 Possibly with the intention of ascribing the work to S. ʿAbd Allāh *al-maʿrūf bi*-Nuqrah-kār (cf. Ḥ. Kh. iv p. 534^{3}, Brockelmann i p. 305^{24}, *Supptbd.* ii pp. 14^{29}, 21).

No. 20 (2), 2nd par. [*Mawāhib i ʿalīyah.*] **Bānkīpūr** Pers. Hand-list 1145–56 = **Bānkīpūr** xiv 1126–37.

No. 20 (2), 3rd par., end. [*Mawāhib i ʿalīyah.* Editions.] Also **Ṭihrān** AHS 1317/1938 (2 Vols. See Mas̲h̲had cat. iv p. 503).

No. 20 (2), penult. par., end. *Insert*: A Ṣūfī commentary on Sūrah xii divided into sixty *fuṣūl* and entitled *Jāmiʿ al-sittīn* (beg. *al-Ḥ. l. al-K̲h̲āliq al-Akbar*) is described briefly in **Sipahsālār** i pp. 100–1 no. 163 (defective. 19th cent.), where it is stated that according to the [spurious ?] preface the subject matter was taken down by a number of hearers from the dictation of Ḥusain Kās̲h̲ifī, who then furnished the work with a preface. It seems probable that this commentary is identical with the *Jāmiʿ laṭāʾif al-basātīn* recorded below (no. 49 (*a*) (10). See also Additions and corrections to that record).

No. 20, last par. [Ḥusain Kās̲h̲ifī.] Also *Majālis al-nafāʾis* (tr. Fak̲h̲rī, ed. Hikmat p. 93, ed. ʿAbd Allāh p. 158, tr. Qazwīnī, ed. Ḥikmat p. 268); *K̲h̲azīnah i ganj i Ilāhī* (Sprenger p. 74); *K̲h̲azīnat al-aṣfiyāʾ* ii pp. 326–7.

No. 20, end. *Insert*:

20*a*. ʿImād [al-Dīn] M. [b. Maḥmūd] **Ṭārumī**; born at Ṭārum, migrated to Gujrāt and died there in 941/1534–5. [*Ẓafar al-wālih* (in Arabic) i p. 246.]

Risālah i firdausīyah, a commentary (dealing with *īmān* and *taubah*) on Sūrah vi 159 ("... *yauma yaʾtī baʿḍu āyāti Rabbika* ..."), written by order of S̲h̲ams al-Dīn Abū 'l-Naṣr Muẓaffar S̲h̲āh [II] b. Maḥmūd S̲h̲āh [of Gujrāt, AH 917–32/1511–26]: **Mas̲h̲had** iv p. 440 no. 340 (defective at end).

No. 21, 1st par. [Abū 'l-Fatḥ al-Ḥusaini.] Mīr Abū 'l-Fatḥ S̲h̲arafī S̲h̲arīfī Ḥusainī ʿArab-S̲h̲āhī b. S. M. b. Mak̲h̲dūm b. S. S̲h̲arīf Jurjānī (cf. no. 53 *supra*), a pupil of ʿIṣām al-Dīn Ibrāhīm [b. M. b. ʿArab-S̲h̲āh al-Isfarāʾīnī (cf. Brockelmann *Sptbd.* ii p. 571), was educated in Transoxiana but settled eventually at Ardabīl, where he died in 976/1568–9 (see Ḥasan Rūmlū ed. Seddon p. 443[9], Seddon's trans., p. 192). He was a convert to S̲h̲īʿsm, his father having been an Anti-S̲h̲īʿite (Mas̲h̲had cat. i, *fṣl.* 1, MSS., nos. 180, 271). Among his works, of which several are mentioned by Ḥasan Rūmlū, was an Arabic commentary, *Miftāḥ al-lubāb*, composed in 955/1548 (Mas̲h̲had i, *fṣl.* 1, MSS., nos. 180, 271, I.H. 1772), on *al-Bāb al-ḥādī-ʿas̲h̲ar* (cf. Brockelmann *Sptbd.* i p. 707[22]). Although a *ḥās̲h̲iyah bar Tahd̲h̲īb i manṭiq* (in addition to a *ḥas̲h̲iyah bar Kubrā*[3]) is mentioned by Ḥasan

---

3 Cf. Ivanow Curzon 513, Ḥ.K̲h̲. iii p. 446[7].

Rūmlū among Mīr Abū 'l-Fatḥ's works, it seems at least doubtful whether he can be identical (as is stated in the Mashhad catalogue, i, *fṣl.* 3, MSS., p. 18[5], and the Sipahsālār catalogue, i p. 129[4]) with Mīr Abū 'l-Fatḥ S. M. b. Abī Sa'īd al-Ḥusainī known as Tāj i Sa'īdī, who annotated and completed Dawānī's unfinished commentary on Taftāzānī's *Tahdhīb al-manṭiq* (Mashhad i, *fṣl.* 2, MSS., no. 34, I'jāz Ḥusain 858) and who, according to those catalogues, was a pupil of Qāḍī-zādah i Rūmī[2] and died in 950 (or, according to I.Ḥ., about 950).

No. 21, 2nd par., MSS. [*Tafsīr i Shāhī.*] Also **Mashhad** i, *fṣl.* 2, MSS., nos. 49–51 (three copies, one dated 974/1566–7), **Sipahsālār** i p. 129 no. 193.

No. 22 (1), MSS. **Bānkīpūr** Pers. Hand-list 1112–13 = **Bānkīpūr** xiv 1144–5.000

No. 22 (1), MSS. [*Tarjamat al-khawāṣṣ.*] **Bashīr Āghā** 37, 38 and 39 contain respectively Sūrahs i–xvii (quite modern, though dated 882 (!)), xix–xxxv (defective at end. N.d.) and xxxvi–cxiv (defective at beginning, AH 1113). 37 is certainly Zawārī's commentary, 38 possibly so, 39 probably so. [Ritter, *OLZ.* 1928 col. 1125.] Also **Mashhad** i, *fṣl.* 3, MSS., nos. 15–18 (all defective. 18 dated 1020/1611–12), iv p. 412 no. 263, **Lahore** Panjāb Univ. ("Pt I"; dated 1089/1678–9, "Pt. II"; dated 1061/1651. See *OCM.* xi/2 (Feb. 1935) p. 76), **Majlis** ii 798 (S. xix–cxiv. AH 1074/1663–4), 797 (S. i–xvii. AH 1083/1672–3), 796 (S. i–xviii. 17th cent.).

No. 22 (5), footnote. For al-Faḍl al-Ṭabarsī see *Tārīkhi Baihaq* pp. 242–3, where the date of his death is given as 523.

No. 22 (9). [*Tarjamah i tafsīr i Imām Ḥasan i 'Askarī.*] This is the *Āthār al-akhyār* (not *al-akhbār*) mentioned no. 49 (*a*) (4) *infra*: see Mashhad iv p. 401, where a slightly defective MS. of 1265/1849 is described.

No. 22, end. *Insert*:

22*a*. S. **'Azīz Allāh** Ḥusainī wrote in 967/1559–60 for Shāhzādah Sulṭānum Ṣafawīyah[5] an Arabic commentary on Sh. Ṭūsī's *Uṣūl i dīn* (Mashhad i *fṣl.* 1, MSS., no. 194). For the same princess he wrote in Persian—

Tafsīr i Kalimah i Tahlīlīyah: **Mashhad** i, *fṣl.* 3, MSS., no. 59 (AH 963/1555–6).

4 Qāḍī-zādah's death is mentioned in the *Zīj* of Ulugh Bēg, who died in 853/1449. Mīr Abū 'l-Fatḥ Sharīfī cannot therefore have been a pupil of his.

5 Daughter of Shah Isma'īl, b. 925, d. 969 (see Ḥasan Rūmlū p. 418, Seddon's trans. p. 182).

No. 22 (10), footnote. [Ibn Ṭā'ūs.] Also *Qiṣaṣ al-ʿulamāʾ* p. 315; Brockelmann i p. 498, *Sptbd.* i pp. 911–13.

No. 22 (11), footnote. For the *ʿUddat al-dāʿī*, see also Gotha Arab. cat. i no. 771 (1) (?), I.H. 2110, Brockelmann *Sptbd.* ii p. 210.

No. 22 (11), footnote. [Ibn Fahd.] Also *Majālis al-muʾminīn* p. 249 penult.; *Qiṣaṣ al-ʿulamāʾ* p. 336 ult. For Brockelmann i 498 *read* Brockelmann *Sptbd.* ii p. 210.

No. 23 (1), MSS. [*Manhaj al-ṣādiqīn.*] Also **Mashhad** iv p. 456 nos. 381 (acephalous, S. xxv (end only)–xxxv. AH 983/1575), 380 (S. xix–xxv, defective at end. Same hand. According to the catalogue the composition of this volume, the fourth, was completed on 28 Muḥarram 982), i, *fṣl.* 3, MSS., no. 213 (S. iv–viii), **Sipahsālār** i pp. 177–8 nos. 239 (S. ix–xviii = *Jild* iii. N.d.), 240 (S. xxxvi–lv. N.d.).

No. 23 (1), 2nd par. [*Manhaj al-ṣādiqīn.* Editions.] Also **Tabrīz** 1314/ 1896–7 (see Mashhad iv p. 502 and Harrassowitz's *Bücher- Katalog* 415 (1928) no. 3319, the latter of which gives Ṭihrān as the place of publication).

No. 23 (2), MSS. **Bānkīpūr** Pers. Hand-list 1133–6 = **Bānkīpūr** xiv 1146–9.

No. 23 (2), MSS. [*Khulāṣat al-Manhaj.*] Also **Mashhad** i, *fṣl.* 3, MSS., nos. 119–28 (one of which is dated 989/1581), **Sipahsālār** i pp. 123–7 nos. 186–9 (of which 187 is dated 1067/1656–7), **Majlis** ii 809 (AH 1114–15/1702–4), **Ellis Coll.** M. 113 (AH 1128/1716), **Ivanow** 2nd Suppt. 989 (S. i–vi. AH 1153/1740), **ʿAlīgaṛh** Subḥ. MSS. p. 6 nos. 16 (S. i–xix. AH 1251/1835–6), 17 (S. xix–cxiv), **Bānkīpūr** Suppt. ii 2057 (last *juzʾ*(?) AH 1255/1839), **Caetani** 25.

No. 24, last par. [Fakhr al-Dīn Sammākī] Also Ḥasan Rūmlū p. 490 (his death on 9 Dhū 'l-Qadah 984/28 Jan. 1577), Seddon's trans. p. 209; Brockelmann *Sptbd.* ii p. 587.

No. 25, last par. [Jalāl al-Dīn T'hānēsarī.] Also *Akhbār al-akhyār* p. 285; *Ṭabaqāt i Akhbarī*; ii p. 473; *Akbar-nāmah* iii p. 341, Beveridge's trans. iii p. 500; *Gulzār i abrār* no. 560.

No. 27, end. *Insert*:

27*a*. ʿ**Abd al-Ḥaqq** b. Saif al-Dīn al-Turk **al-Dihlawī** al-Bukhārī died in 1052/1642–3 (see no.s 243, 1298, etc., *supra*).
Tafsīr i Āyat al-Nūr (S. xxiv 35); **Rieu** ii 863 (18th cent.).

27*b*. Shāh[6] **Qāḍī Yazdī**

Tafsīr āyāt al-aḥkām, completed in 1021/1612 for Sulṭān Muḥammad Quṭb-Shāh (AH. 1020–35/1612–26): IH 518 (*Tarjamat āyāt al-aḥkām*), 612 (*Tafsīr ā. al-a.*), 1765 (*Sharḥ ā. al-a.*), **Āṣafīyah** iii p. 230 no. 436.

27*c*. **Aḥmad b. Zain al-ʿĀbidīn** al-ʿAlawī **al-ʿĀmilī** al-Iṣfahānī, a cousin (*ibn khālah, Rauḍāt al-jannāt* p. 116[15]) and pupil of M. Bāqir Dāmād (who died in 1041/1631–2: see Browne *Lit. Hist.* iv p. 406) and the recipient of an *ijāzah* written in 1018/1609–10 by Bahāʾ al-Dīn al-ʿĀmilī (IḤ 23), is best known as the author of two anti-Christian works (neither of them mentioned by IḤ), *al-Lawāmiʿ al-rabbānīyah fī radd al-shubah al-Naṣrānīyah* completed in 1031/ 1621 (MSS.: Browne Pers. Cat. 7, 8, Blochet i 54, Edinburgh 372, Vatican 22) and the *Miṣqal i ṣafā dar tajliyah i Āʾīnah i ḥaqq-numā* completed in 1032/1622 (MSS.: Blochet i 52, 53, Mashhad i, *fṣl.* 1, nos. 256, 257, Rieu i 28*b*, Vatican 72 (5)). He wrote also *Kashf al-ḥaqāʾiq fī sharḥ Taqwīm al-īmān*, annotations (in Arabic) on the *Taqwīm al-īmān* of M. Bāqir Dāmād (IḤ 853, Mashhad i, *fṣl.* 1, MSS., no. 222) and *Miftāḥ al-Shifāʾ wa-ʾl-ʿurwat al-wuthqā*, annotations on the *ilāhīyāt of the Shifāʾ* of Ibn Sīnā (IH 3034).

Laṭāʾif i ghaibī (beg. *Baʿd az ḥamd i Mubdiʿī kih sabʿah i muʿallaqāt*), a commentary on those verses of the *Qurʾān* relating to the person and attributes of God and other points of dogma,[7] begun in 1033/1623–4 and dedicated to Iʿtimād al-Daulah Abū ʾl-Ḥasan: **Bodleian** 1819 (transcribed from an autograph), **Mashhad** i, *fṣl.* 3, MSS., no. 181 (defective at end).

27*d*. **Yūsuf Miṣrī**

ʿIqd i gauhar, a metrical commentary written in 1035/ 1625–6 for Shāh ʿAbbās I: **Princeton** 447 foll. 1–23*b* (beginning only. AH 1123/1711).

27*e*. **Muʿizz al-Dīn Ardistānī** b. Ẓahīr al-Dīn Mīr Mīrān al-Ḥusainī.

Tafsīr i Sūrah i Hal atā [i.e. S. lxxvi presumably], completed in 1044/1634 at the suggestion of M. b. Khātūn (cf. no. 84, 1st par. *supra*) and dedicated to ʿAbd Allāh Quṭb-Shāh: **Mashhad** i, *fṣl.* 3, MSS., no. 55 (apparently autograph).

---

6 It is not clear whether this word is here a title or part of the name. In the former case the *Tafsīr āyāt al-aḥkām* may possibly be an early work of Mīrzā Qāḍī b. Kāshif al-Dīn Yazdī, who died at Ardabīl in 1075/1664–5 (see Rieu ii 844*a*).

7 This account of the subject of the work is based on that given in the Mashhad catalogue. In the Bodleian catalogue it is described as "a rich collection of traditions, with Persian paraphrase and detailed explanation".

No. 28, last par. [Mullā S͟hāh.] See also no. 1332, 3rd par., footnote *supra*; *Pādshāh-nāmah* i, 1, p. 333, ii p. 754; *Hamīshah bahār* (Sprenger p. 128); K͟hāfī K͟hān i p. 549.

No. 28, end. *Insert*:

28*a*. Bahā' al-Dīn M. b. Tāj al-Dīn Ḥasan al-Iṣfāhanī, surnamed **al-Fāḍil al-Hindī**, died at Iṣfahān in 1137/1725 (see no. 279 *supra*).

> *al-Baḥr al-mawwāj*, a translation and commentary: **Majlis** ii 790 (no preface. 18th cent.).

No. 29, end. *Insert*:

29*a*. **Bahā' al-Dīn M. b. S͟haik͟h-'Alī S͟harīf Lāhījī.** *Tarjamat al-Qur'ān*, a Shī'ite translation and commentary completed at Patnah [?] in 108- (perhaps 1086: corruptly in the colophon as quoted "*min sanati wa-thamānīna wa-alf*"): **Mas͟hhad** iv p. 414 nos. 267 (S. ii 4–xvii), 268 (S. xviii–cxiv. AH 1260 (?)/1844).

No. 30, 2nd par. [*Zēb i tafāsīr.*] Cf. *Ma'āthir i 'Ālamgīrī* p. 539.

No. 32, end. *Insert*:

32*a*. **M. Riḍā b. M. Mahdī b. M. Bāqir Sabzawari.**
> *Tarjamat al-Sulṭānī*, an annotated translation of Sūrah xviii (*al-Kahf*) completed in 1115/1704 at the request of S͟hāh Sulṭān-Ḥusain Ṣafawī: **Mas͟hhad** iv p. 413 no. 264 (ornate MS.).

No. 33, 2nd par. [*Mawā'id al-Raḥmān.*] Presumably identical with the (apparently untitled) translation prepared by order of Nādir S͟hāh, which is preserved in **Blochet** iv 2210 (written circ. AD 1740 for Nādir S͟hāh's library). For the Bombay lithograph see also Mas͟hhad iv p.502.

No. 33, 2nd par., 2nd footnote. [Ḥusain K͟hwānsārī. Also *Ātash-kadah* (Bodleian 384 no. 434).

No. 33, last par. [Jamāl al-Dīn K͟hwānsārī.] Also "Ḥazīn's"; *Tad͟hkirat al-aḥwāl* p. 53 penult., Belfour's trans. p. 59; *Nujūm al-samā'* p. 191.

No. 34, end. *Insert*:

34*a*. **Zain al-ʿĀbidīn Birādar "Diwān"**, presumably a Dak'hanī, since he wrote verses in Dak'hanī Urdū, is the author of a commentary (apparently in Persian) on Muḥibb Allāh Bihārī's *Sullam al-ʿulūm* (see Brockelmann ii p. 421, *Sptbd.* ii p. 622), which he completed in 1150/1737–8 and which is preserved together with his *dīwān* (*Dīwān i Dīwān*) and thirty-five other works, mostly short tracts, in an India Office MS.

(1) ***Fuyūḍāt al-Fatiḥah***, a commentary on Sūrah i: **Ethé** 1700 (1).

(2) ***Ḥāshiyah i risālah i Fuyūḍāt al-Fātiḥah***, notes on the preceding: **Ethé** 1700 (2).

No. 35 (1), 1st par., MSS. [*Fatḥ al-Raḥmān.*] Also **Bānkīpūr** xvii 1655 (*Muqaddamah* only. AH 1251/1835), 1654 (?) (*Muqaddamah fī qawānīn al-tarjamah*), **ʿAlīgaṛh** Subḥ. MSS. p. 6 no. 14. **Bānkīpūr** Pers. Hand-list 1140–1 = **Bānkīpūr** xiv 1157–8.

No. 35 (2), 1st par. [*al-Fauz al-kabīr.*] For a description of this work see Zubaid Aḥmad *The contribution of India to Arabic literature* pp. 28–31.

No. 35 (2), 1st par., MSS.[*al-Fauz al-kabīr.* MSS.] Also **Bānkīpūr** xvii 1601.

No. 35 (2), 2nd par., end.[*al-Fauz al-kabīr.* Editions.] Also **Cairo** 1346/ 1927–8 (as an appendix to M. Munīr's *Irshād al-rāghibīn fī 'l-kashf ʿan āy al-Qurʾān al-mubīn.* See *Der Islam* xix p. 74 no. 168).

No. 35 (2), 3rd par. For the *Fatḥ al-Khabīr* see Zubaid Aḥmad *The contribution of India to Arabic literature* pp. 19–20.

No. 35, last par. [Walī Allāh Dihlawī] Also *Khazīnat al-aṣfiyāʾ* ii p. 373; *Ḥayāt i Walī* (in Urdu. 360 pp.), by M. Raḥīm-Bakhsh, Delhi 1319/1901–2*; Bānkīpūr xiv p. 134; Brockelmann *Sptbd.* ii pp. 614–15: Zubaid Aḥmad *The contribution of India to Arabic literature* pp. 19–20, 246, etc. For an anonymous work defending Walī Allāh against the charge that he had insufficient respect for the Imams see Bānkīpūr xvii 1619.

No. 36 (4), 2nd par. [Qamar al-Dīn Aurangābādī.] Also Brockelmann *Sptbd.* ii p. 616; Zubaid Aḥmad *The contribution of India to Arabic literature* p. 314.

No. 36, end. *Insert*:

36*a*. Āqā M. **Hāshim** "Hāshim" b. Mīrzā Ismāʿīl **Shīrāzī** Dhahabī was a *mustaufī* in the service of the Zands, but resigned in order to lead the life of a Ṣūfī. He became the disciple, son-in-law and *khalīfah* of S. Quṭb al-Dīn Nairīzī, one of the *mashāyikh* of the Silsilah i Dhahabīyah i Kubrawīyah. He died in 1199/1785 and was buried in the Ḥāfiẓīyah at Shīrāz. [*Riyāḍ al-ʿārifīn* pp. 624–6; *Ṭarāʾiq al-ḥaqāʾiq* hi p. 98; Mashhad cat. iv pp. 501–2].

Manāhil al-taḥqīq, a commentary on the words "*A-lā ilā 'llāhi tasīru 'l-umūr*" (Sūrah xlii 53) containing Ṣūfī reflexions on *mabdaʾ* and *maʿād*: **Ṭihrān** 1323/1905 (followed by a Ṣūfī tract, *risālaʾī dar sulūk*, by Mīrzā Abū 'l-Qāsim known as (*maʿrūf bi-*) Mīrzā Bābā Dhahabī Shīrāzī. See Mashhad iv p. 501 no. 286).

No. 38. [*Laṭāʾif al-tafsīr.*] "Die Zuweisung des Werkes an Naḥīfī lässt sich aus dem Codex ohne weiteres nicht rechtfertigen. Offenbar die Kladde des Verfassers. Der eigentliche Text scheint fol. 3*b* zu beginnen:

بسمله ... المناجاة الرحمانية ای معبود شاهان و ای مسجود پادشاهان

Nähere Untersuchung war mir nicht möglich." [Ritter. *OLZ*. 1928 col. 1125.]

No. 39 (1). [*Durr al-naẓīm.*] Presumably identical with the *Durr i naẓīm i Khāqānī* (beg. *Jāmiʿtarīn kalāmī*) written by Mullā M. Riḍā "Kauthar" Hamadānī for Fatḥ-ʿAlī Shāh, of which a MS. (pt. 1 only, on the verses relating to *tauhīd*, in a *muqaddamah*, five *aṣls* and a *khātimah*. AH 1223/ 1808–9) is described in Mashhad iv p. 439 no. 338. Edition (pts. 1 and 2): **Ṭihrān** (see Mashhad iv p. 488. Probably the edition of 1279).

No. 40, 1st par., footnote. Ghulām-Ḥalīm is the chronogrammatic pseudonym used by ʿAbd al-ʿAzīz in his *Tuḥfah i Ithnā-ʿAsharīyah*, whether or not it was (as Raḥmān ʿAlī implies) the *nām i tārīkhī* given to him by his father. Cf. Blochmann *Contributions to Persian lexicography* (in *JASB*. 37/1 (1868)) p. 63: *nām i tārīkhī*, an additional name which parents give their children, in order to remind them of the year in which they were born—a very necessary thing in the East, where few people know their correct age.

No. 40 (5), 1st par., MSS. **Bānkīpūr** Pers. Hand-list 1142–4—**Bānkīpūr** xiv 1159–61.

No. 40 (5), 1st par., MSS. [*Fatḥ al-ʿAzīz.*] Also **ʿAlīgaṛh** Subḥ. MSS. p. 5 no. 8 (S. lxvii–cxiv), **Ivanow** 2nd Suppt. 990 (S. lxxviii–cxiv. 19th cent.).

No. 40 (5), 2nd par.[*Fatḥ al-ʿAzīz*. Editions.] Also **Delhi** 1267/1851 (Bibl. Orient. Sprengeriana 449–50, Zenker ii 1069). An edition of 1264/1848 is recorded (without specification of the place of publication) in Āṣafīyah iii p. 230 no. 441. P. 24, l. 31. [ʿAbd al-ʿAzīz Dihlawī] Also *Khazīnat al-aṣfiyāʾ* ii pp. 388–9; Brockelmann *Sptbd.* ii p. 615.

No. 40, end. *Insert*:

40*a*. **Ḥusain Riḍā** b. ʿAlī b. Yaʿqūb **Afshār**.

Tafsīr i ʿAlawī, a Shīʿite commentary written in 1202/ 1787–8: **Calcutta Madrasah** 108–9 (AH 1207–8/1792–4).

No. 41 (2), end of par. [*Risālah i shaqq al-qamar*.] For a lithographed edition (pp. 16. Asʿad al-akhbār Pr., Āgrah, 1268/1852) see Arberry p. 435.

No. 41, end. [Rafīʿ al-Dīn Dihlawī] Also *Fihrist i muṣannafāt i Maulānā Shāh Rafīʿ al-Dīn Dihlawī* (in Urdu), by M. Shafīʿ (in OCM. ii/1 (Nov. 1925) pp. 42–9).

No. 41, end. *Insert*:

41*a*. **M. Bāqir** (*mashhūr bah*) **Nawwāb** b. M. Lāhījānī (by origin) Iṣfahānī (by residence), the author of a Persian translation of the *Nahj al-balāghah* (Sipahsālār ii pp. 17–19), wrote his *Tuḥfat al-Khāqān* in 1230/1815 at the request of Fatḥ-ʿAlī Shāh.

Tuḥfat al-Khāqān, a commentary in which the expositions are classified under the headings (1) *qiṣaṣ*, (2) *aḥkām*, (3) *maʿārif*, (4) *mawāʿiẓ* and (5) *mawāʿid*: **Sipahsālār** i pp. 97–8 no. 161 (vol. i only, on the verses relating to the Prophets and the Imāmate. Possibly autograph), **Majlis** ii p. 8 no. 794 (vol. i only. AH 1230/1815).

No. 43, 2nd par., MSS. **Bānkīpūr** Pers. Hand-list 1101 = **Bānkīpūr** xiv 1168.

No. 44, last par. [M. Saʿīd Aslamī] Also *Ḥadīqat al-marām* (in Arabic) p. 3.

No. 45, 1st par. More fully S. Rajab ʿAlī Khān Bahādur Ḥusainī Ḥasanī Naqawī Bhakkarī Dihlawī Lāhaurī (see Mashhad iv p. 492, where the Lahore edition of the *Sirr i akbar* is described).

No. 45 (1). More fully *K. al-gh. ʿan wujūh āyāt Hal atā* (see Mashhad iv p. 495).

No. 47 (1). *Read Ḥaḍrat-Shāhī.*

No. 41 (1), footnote. [M. Ḥasan Amrōhawī] Also *Nukhbat al-tawārīkh* p. 63.

No. 47, end. *Insert*:

47*a*. **Ḥaidar ʿAlī Faiḍābādī**, a dogmatic theologian and an Anti-Shīʿite controversialist, spent the last few years of his life at Ḥaidarābād in receipt of a stipend from the Niẓām and he died there about 1890. His *Muntahā 'l-kalām* was published at [Lucknow] in 1282/1865 (cf. Edwards col. 240).

Fuyūḍāt i Ḥaidarīyah, a *tafsīr*: **Āṣafīyah** iii p. 230 nos. 573–8 (6 vols.). [Raḥmān ʿAlī p. 55.]

No. 48, 1st par. *Read* Qinnaujī.

No. 48, 1st par., footnote. *Read* Qinnaujī.

No. 48, 2nd par., ult. 29 Jumādā ii 1307/20 Feb. 1890 is the date given in the *Maʾāthir i Ṣiddīqī* iii p. 200[2].

No. 48 (1). [*Ifādat al-shuyūkh.*] This work is a treatise on the abrogating and abrogated verses of the *Qurʾān*, not a *tafsīr*.

No. 48, last par. Also Brockelmann *Sptbd.* ii pp. 859–61.

No. 48, end. *Insert*:

48*a*. **M. Bāqir Bawānātī**, surnamed Ibrāhīm Jān Muʿaṭṭar, an eccentric poet, who had "travelled through half the world"; and had "been successively a Shíʿte Muhammadan, a dervish, a Christian, an atheist, and a Jew" before elaborating his own "Islamo-Christianity", was resident in London for some years as an old man and there had E. G. Browne as a pupil in Persian. Having left London towards the end of 1884 he lived for a time at Bairūt and returned thence to Persia, where he died about 1890. His *Shumaisah i Landanīyah*, a *qaṣīdah* of 366 verses, was published in London (with a similar poem, the *Sudairah i nāsūtīyah*) in 1882*. Twenty-nine verses from the former poem were printed with an English translation by E. G. Browne in *The press and poetry of modern Persia*, pp. 168–74.

Rauḍāt i Landanī u fauḥāt i anjumanī kināyat az Qurʾān i Muʿaṭṭar, a metrical commentary composed in 1883 on twenty-six sūrahs believed by the commentator to have been revealed in the first year of the Prophet's mission: **Browne** Coll. A. 3 (autograph).

[Browne *A year amongst the Persians* pp. 12–15. Portrait in *The press and poetry of modern Persia*, facing p. 168.]

48*b*. Ḥasan b. M. Bāqir Iṣfāhanī, surnamed (*mulaqqab*) **Ṣafī ʿAlī-Shāh** and, as a poet, calling himself "Ṣafī", was an eminent member of the Niʿmat-Allāhī order.[8] Devoted from boyhood to the society of Ṣūfīs, he went at the age of twenty from Iṣfahān to visit Mīrzā Kūchak[9] at Shīrāz, was accepted by him as a disciple and later accompanied him to Kirmān. In 1280/1863–4 he went by way of India on a pilgrimage to Mecca. On his return to India he stayed there for four years and published at Bombay a metrical work entitled *Zubdat al-asrār* (*dar asrār i shahādat*), which he had begun at Kirmān on the suggestion of Mīrzā Kūchak. He then went to Karbalāʾ and from there to Yazd, but in consequence of disagreements with the *ahl i ḥāl u qāl* he returned to India, intending to spend the rest of his life in the Deccan. After two years, however, he went back to Persia and settled in Tihrān, where he died on 24 Dhī-Qaʿdah 1316/5 April 1899. In addition to the *Zubdat al-asrār* and the *tafsīr*, works by him entitled *ʿIrfān al-ḥaqq*, *Baḥr al-ḥaqāʾiq* and *Mīzān al-maʿrifah* are mentioned in the *Ṭarāʾiq al-Ḥaqāʾiq* (iii p. 204[34]).

Tafsīr i Ṣafī, a metrical (*mathnawī*) Ṣūfī commentary on the whole of the *Qurʾān* begun in 1306/1888–9 and completed in 1308/1890–1: **Ṭihrān** 1308/1890–1 (see Mashhad iv p. 474).

[*al-Maʾāthir wa-'l-āthār* (quoted in the *Ṭarāʾiq al-ḥaqāʾiq*); *Ṭarāʾiq al-ḥaqāʾiq* iii p. 204; Rashīd Yāsimī *Adabīyāt i muʿāṣir* p. 66 (portrait); Mashhad cat. iv p. 474.]

48*c*. Ākhūnd Mullā **Ḥusain** b. ʿAlī **Sijāsī** Zanjānī.

Wasīlat al-najāh, a commentary on the Sūrah i Wa-'l-shams (xci), begun on 2 Dhī-Ḥijjah 1321/19 Feb. 1904: **Tabrīz** 1323/1905 (see Mashhad iv p. 504).

48*d*. **Zain al-ʿĀbidīn Khān Kirmānī.**

Ajwibat al-masāʾil, explanations of certain Qurʾānic verses in answer to questions from Ḥājj Mīrzā ʿAlī Akbar Āqā-yi Jaurābchī Tabrīzī, completed

8 According to a brief autobiography summarised in the *Ṭarāʾiq al-ḥaqāʾiq* he was born on 3 Shaʿbān 1251/24 Nov. 1835, but this date is inconsistent with the statement that he was twenty years old (*dar bīst-sālagī*) when he became a disciple of Mīrzā Kūchak [who died in 1262/1846].

9 For Mīrzā Kūchak "Wiṣāl" see Browne *Lit. Hist*, iv p. 316.

in 1339/1921; **Tabrīz** 1344/1925–6 (appended to the same author's *Tanzīh al-anbiyā'* and *Tamyīz al-auṣiyā'*. See Mashhad iv p. 463).

48*e*. Sh. **Asad Allāh "Shams" Gulpāyagānī** was living at the time when his *Asrār al-'ishq* was published.

Asrār al-'ishq, a Ṣūfī *mathnawī* in explanation of the Sūrah i Yūsuf (xii): **Iṣfahān** 1343/1924–5 (Mashhad IV p. 464).

48*f*. S. **Ḥusain b. Naṣr Allāh** b. Ṣādiq Mūsawī **'Arab-Bāghi**.

(1) ***Īqān dar awāmir u nawāhī i Qur'ān***, a translation of the Qur'ānic verses containing commands and prohibitions, completed in 1345/1927: **Urūmiyah** 1346/1927–8 (see Mashhad iv p. 466).

(2) ***Manāhij al-mu'minīn***, an exposition of the Qur'ānic verses relating to the Prophet's family, divided into eighteen *manāhij* and a *khātimah* and completed in 1358/1939 (see Mashhad iv p. 501, where the date and place of publication are not mentioned but a reference is given to the [not yet published ?] section of the catalogue dealing with *Akhbār* under *Manāhij al-'ārifīn*).

48*g*. **'Abbās 'Alī Kaiwān Qazwīnī**.

Tafsīr i Kaiwān:**Ṭihrān** 1350/1931–2 (pts. 1–3, extending to S. iv 109. See Mashhad iv p. 480).

48*h*. S. M. 'Aṣṣār, i.e. S. M. b. Maḥmūd Ḥusainī Ṭihrānī Lawāsānī i *ma'rūf bi-***'Aṣṣār** *mutakhalliṣ bah* "Āshuftah", was born at Tihrān in 1264/1848 or 1265/1849 and died at Mashhad on 9 Muḥarram 1356/22 March 1937 (see Mashhad iii p. 22[18]). Autograph MSS. of several works by him are preserved at Mashhad.

Nāsikh al-tafāsīr, a commentary of which the first volume (probably the only one ever written) was begun in 1351/1932 and completed towards the end of 1355/ 1936–7: **Mashhad** iv p. 457 no. 383 (S. i xxxix 6. Autograph).

48*j*. **Muḥsin 'Imād** *mudarris i* **Ardabīlī** *mutakhalliṣ bi-* "Ḥālī."

Āyāt al-raj'ah, a commentary on the verses bearing on the doctrine of *raj'at*, completed in 1357/1938: **Tihrān** AHS 1318/1939–40 (see Mashhad iv p. 462).

48*k*. S. **Kāẓim** [b. S. M.] **'Aṣṣār** is described in the Mashhad catalogue as a Professor in the University of Tihrān.

Tafsīr *[i Saiyid Kāẓim i 'Aṣṣār]*, exegetical lectures from a Ṣūfī standpoint delivered in the Mu'assasah i Wa'ẓ u Khiṭābah in the years AHS 1315 and 1317 and extending only to the verse *Māliki yaumi 'l-dīn* [*az āyah i Māliki yaumi 'l-dīn tajāwuz na-kardah*]: **Tihrān** AHS 1315–17/1936–9 (see Mashhad iv p. 468).

48*l*. Ḥājj Sh. **Sharī'at** b. Ḥājj Sh. Hasan b. Mīrzā Riḍā- Qulī **Sanglajī**, having studied Law, Theology, Philosophy and Ṣūfism under eminent instructors in Tihrān, spent four years in the prosecution of his studies at Najaf. He died at Tihrān on 9 Muḥarram 1363/5 Jan. 1944 at the age of fifty-three.

Kilīd i fahm i Qur'ān, on some preliminary matters relating to *tafsīr* (*kitāb barkhī maṭālib i muqaddamātī i tafsīr ast*): **Tihrān** 1361/1942 (see Mashhad iv p. 495).

48*m*. Sh. **Muḥammad** (b. Ḥājj Sh. Ḥasan) **Sanglajī Tihrānī**.

(1) ***Tafsīr i Sūrah i Ḥamd u Ikhlāṣ***, a concise commentary on Sūrahs i and cxii completed in 1361/ 1942: **Tihrān** (Tābān Pr.) (see Mashhad iv p. 472, where the date of publication [not later than AHS 1323/1944, the date of purchase] is not stated).

(2) ***Tafsīr i Sūrah i Ḥamd***, a later edition of the first of the above-mentioned commentaries: **Tihrān** (Majlis Pr.) AHS 1325/1946–7 (see Mashhad iv p. 472).

48*n*. 'Aṭā' Allāh **Shihāb-pūr** is described in the Mashhad catalogue as a contemporary author.

Āyāt i Dhū 'l-Qarnain, a commentary on the verses relating to Dhū 'l-Qarnain: **Tihrān** AHS 1323/1944 (2nd ed. Anjuman i Tablīghāt i Islāmī. See Mashhad iv p. 462).

48*o*. Sh. **M. Bāqir Kamara'ī**

Kānūn i ḥikmat i Qur'ān, a commentary on Sūrah xxxi (Luqmān) completed on 20 Ādhar-māh 1323 [*sic*, but this seems to be a misprint for 1322[10]]: **Tihrān** 1323/ 1945 (see Mashhad iv p. 494).

48*p*. Sh. M. **Khāliṣī-zādah.**

Tafsīr i Qur'ān: **Tihrān** AHS 1323/1945 (*muqaddamah*. See Mashhad iv p. 479).

10 According to the Mashhad catalogue the work was published in Isfand 1323 and purchased in Farwardīn 1324.

48*q*. **Khalīl b. Abū Ṭālib Kamara'ī** was born in 1317/1899–1900. Having received his early education at Khwānsār and elsewhere, he went in 1337/1918–19 to Sulṭānābād and from 1340/1921–2 to 1354/1935–6 he studied and taught at Qum. Since AHS 1314/1935–6 he has been resident in Tihrān.

Tafsīr i Sūrah i Nūr: **Tihrān** AHS 1324–5/1945–6 (pts. 1–2, of which the second, completed in 1365/1946, extends to verse 35 (36), "*Allāhu nūr al-samāwāt.*" See Mashhad iv p. 473).

No. 49 (*a*) (2). The *Anīs al-murīdīn wa-rauḍat al-muḥibbīn*, written at Balkh in 475/1082–3, is in forty *majālis* and forms part of the *Tāj al-qiṣaṣ* (see no. 196 *supra* and Bānkīpūr vi p. 75). **Bānkīpūr** Pers. Hand-list 1103 = **Bānkīpūr** xiv 1111 (AH 1001/1592–3).

No. 49 (*a*) (2), end. *Insert*:

(2*a*). ***Anīs*** (or ***Uns***) ***al-murīdīn wa-shams al-majālis*** (beg. *al-Ḥ. l. 'l. abda'a wujūd al-insān* ..., some lines after which there follows (in Ethé 1778 at any rate: see *JRAS*. 1928 p. 103) a Persian doxology beginning *Ḥ. u sp. mar Ṣāni'ī rā kih bulbul i khwash-nawā-yi balāghat*): a Ṣūfī exposition of the Qur'ānic story of Joseph, ascribed incorrectly (see R. Levy's article in *JRAS*. 1929 pp. 103–6) to 'Abd Allāh Anṣārī (for whom see no. 1245 *supra*): H. Kh. i p. 453 (reading *Uns*), **Ethé** 1778 (AH 1013/1605), **Mashhad** iv p. 408 no. 255 (defective at both ends), **Browne** Coll. D. 7 (modern).

No. 49 (*a*) (3). [*Aṣdaq al-bayān fī qiṣaṣ al-Qur'ān wa-mawā'iẓ al-Raḥmān*]. **Bānkīpūr** Hand-list 1102 = **Bānkīpūr** xiv 1151 (S. vii–xviii. Described on a fly-leaf as the second quarter of the *Ḥadā'iq al-tafsīr*, but the title given above occurs in a (spurious ?) preface. The work contains references to the *Yūsuf u Zalīkhā* of Jāmī, who is described as "deceased". AH 1038/1629).

No. 49 (*a*) (4). [***Āthār al-akhyār*** (so, not *al-akhbār*, in the Mashhad cat., doubtless correctly).] Also **Mashhad** iv p. 401 no. 230 (slightly defective. AH 1265/1849. According to the catalogue this is the translation made by 'Alī b. Ḥasan al-Zawārī (cf. no. 22 *supra*)).

No. 49 (*a*) (4), end. *Insert*:

(4*a*). ***Āyāt al-wilāyah***, a commentary by Mīrzā Abū 'l-Qāsim Dhahabī Shīrāzī on 1001 verses regarded as referring to the Prophet's family: **Tihrān** 1323/1905 (2 vols. See Mashhad iv pp. 462–3).

No. 49 (*a*) (5), MSS. [*Baḥr al-asrār*.] Also **Mashhad** iv p. 409 nos. 256 (AH 1278/1862), 257. Edition: **Kirmān** 1329/1911 (see Mashhad iv p. 466).

According to the Mashhad catalogue, which refers to *Bustān al-siyāḥah* p. 483 and *Ṭarā'iq al-ḥaqā'iq* iii [p. 93], Mīrzā M. Taqī b. M. Kāẓim Kirmānī *mulaqqab bi-* Muẓaffar ʿAlī-Shāh died in 1215/1800–1 and was buried outside the East Gate of Kirmānshāhān.

No. 49 (*a*) (6). The *Baḥr al-maʿānī* is a commentary on S. lxxviii–cxiv. **Bānkīpūr** Hand-list 1104 = **Bānkīpūr** xiv 1153. The former writes *al-madʿū bi-* KhWĀWND Miyān, the latter *al-madʿū bi-*KhWND Miyān (transliterated Khund Miân).

No. 49 (*a*) (7), end. *Insert*:
(7*a*). ***Fātiḥah u maʿnā-yi ān***, a translation by ʿAbbās Rāsikhī of M. ʿAbduh's *Tafsīr Sūrat al-Fātiḥah wa-mushkilāt al-Qur'ān* (for which see Brockelmann *Sptbd.* iii p. 320): **Rasht** [AHS 1325/1946 (?), that being the year in which the translator presented the work to the Mashhad library. See Mashhad iv p. 494].

No. 49 (*a*) (8). Ṭā-Hā Quṭb al-Dīn Qādirī Kairānawī[11] (not Katānawī) is the subject of the penultimate biography in the *Taḥā'if i Rashīdīyah* and the *Tārīkh i Qādirīyah* (see no. 1351 *supra*). Presumably he lived in the second half of the 17th century.

No. 49 (*a*) (9). Read *Istiqṣā' al-ifḥām* (with dotted ḥ)...*fī jawāb Muntahā 'l-kalām*. The work is a reply to the Anti-Shīʿite *M. al-k.* ([Lucknow] 1282/1865°) of Ḥaidar ʿAlī Faiḍābādī (cf. above, *ad* no. 47, end) and doubtless has no very strong claim to appear in this section. Another edition: 1276/1859–60 (Āṣafīyah ii p. 1330 where the place of publication [probably Lucknow] is not mentioned).

No. 49 (*a*) (10). [*Jāmiʿ laṭā'if al-basātīn.*] **Bāyazīd** 287, dated 841 and containing 317 foll., begins *Sipās mar Khudhāwandī rā kih Āfrīdhgār u Qādir i bar kamāl-ast ... chunīn gūyad Khwājah i Imām Tāj al-Dīn Saif al-Naẓar Jamāl al-Ayimmah Abū Bakr Aḥmad b. M. b. Yazīd al-Ṭūsī.* **Bāyazīd** 288 is an Arabic *ḥāshiyah* on Baiḍāwī (*daftar* incorrect). **Asʿad** 94 (43 foll., undated) begins *Qāl al-Saiyid al-Imām Tāj al-Dīn Saif al-Naẓar Imām Aḥmad b. M. b. Zaid al-Ṭūsī Nīkūtarīn i ʿilmhā pand u ḥikmat-ast.* It deals with Sūrah xii but could not at the most be more than a mere abridgment of the work contained in Bāyazīd 287. [Ritter, OLZ. 1928 col. 1125.] The title as given by Ivanow is *Kitāb sittīn jāmiʿu 'l-laṭā'if (wa') l-basātīn.* **Ivanow** 1241 (late 15th or early 16th cent.) begins *Sp. mar Khudāwandī rā kih Qādir i bar kamāl ast.* Probably another MS. of this work

11 For Kairānah see no. 1351, 1st par. *supra*.

is **Sipahsālār** i pp. 100–1 no. 163 (see Additions and corrections ad no. 20 (2), penult. par., end.).

No. 49 (*a*) (10), end. *Insert*:

(10*a*). ***Jawāhir al-īmān***, a translation of the *tafsīr* ascribed to the 11th Imām, al-Ḥasan al-ʿAskarī, (cf. no. 49 (*a*) (4) *supra*, with Additions and corrections) by Āg͟hā M. Bāqir Yazdī. Edition: 1320/1902–3 (see Āṣafīyah iii p. 230, where the place of publication is not stated).

No. 49 (*a*) (11). **Peshawar** 155 (*sic lege*) is described as a 15th cent. MS.

No. 49 (*a*) (12). [*Jalā*ʾ[12] *al-adhhān*.] Also **Mas͟hhad** i, *fṣl*. 3, MSS., nos. 78 (S. i–xxxv. AH 972/1564–5), 79 (S. vii–xxxv. AH 1010/1601–2), 80 (S. xxxvi–cxiv. AH 1011/1602–3), **Majlis** ii 803 (S. ii 148–vi (?). AH 1009/1600–1), 804 (S. vii–xvii. AH 1011/1602–3), 805 (S. xix–xxxv. 17th cent.), 806 (S. xxxvi–cxiv. AH 1069/1658–9), 807 (S. i–xvii. 17th cent.), **Sipahsālār** i pp. 101–6 nos. 164 (S. i–xviii (?). AH 1038/1628–9), 165 (?) (S. xix–cxiv. AH 1093/1682. The cataloguer gives reasons for doubting whether this volume is a part of the *Jalā*ʾ *al-adhhān*).

No. 49 (*a*) (12). *Insert*:

(12*a*). ***al-Kalām al-aʿlā fī tafsīr Sūrat al-Aʿlā bi-aḥādīt͟h al-Muṣṭafā***, by Maulawī Mus͟htāq Aḥmad Ḥanafī C͟hish͟tī Amēṭʾhawī.[13] Edition: **Ḥaidarābād** (Āṣafīyah iii p. 230, where the date is not mentioned).

No. 49 (*a*) (14). Asʿad 145 and 146 are the *Kas͟hf al-asrār wa-ʿuddat al-abrār* of Ras͟hīd al-Dīn A. b. M. Maibudī (see above *ad* no. 5, end.). [Ritter, OLZ. col. 1124[24].]

No. 49 (*a*) (15). The *Lawāmiʿ al-tanzīl* was begun in 1296/1879 according to Mas͟hhad i, *fṣl*. 3, ptd. bks., no. 35 (vol. i. AH 1301/1883–4).

No. 49 (*a*) (15), end.. *Insert*: (15*a*). ***Lubb al-fawāʾid***: **ʿAlīgaṛh** Subḥ. MSS. p. 6 no. 25.

No. 49 (*a*) (18). [*Majmaʿ al-biḥār*.] For Muẓaffar ʿAlī Niʿmatallāhī see the Additions and corrections to no. 49 (*a*) (5). Another MS.: **Mas͟hhad** iv p. 450 no. 364 (AH 1268/1852). According to the Mas͟hhad catalogue this is a prose

12 This vocalisation is more probable than *Jilā*ʾ.

13 For Amēṭʾhī see no. 639, 1st par., footnote *supra*.

version of the same author's *Baḥr al-asrār*, a Ṣūfī commentary on Sūrah i (cf. no. 49 (*a*) (5) *supra*, with Additions and corrections).

Edition: [**Persia**] 1323/1905 (title incorrectly given as *Jāmiʿ al-biḥār* at beginning. See Mas͟hhad iv p. 496).

No. 49 (*a*) (19). **Bānkīpūr** Pers. Hand-list 1129 = **Bānkīpūr** xiv 1169 (vol. iii, apparently the last, in 136 chapters. 19th cent.). Neither the author's name nor the title occurs in the text of the Bānkīpūr MS., but in several places a later hand has written *Tafsīr i Maẓhar al-Ḥaqq*. "The arrangement is that all the verses relating to a particular subject, such as prayer, the reading of the Qurân, etc., are grouped in a chapter, and then commented on."

No. 49 (*a*) (19), end. *Insert*:

(19*b*.) ***Miftāḥ al-ʿirfān fī tartīb suwar al-Qurʾān***, probably by M. Bāqir Bawānatī (for whom see ad no. 48, end *supra*): **Browne** Coll. Y. 9 (4).

No. 49 (*a*) (20), end. *Insert*:

(20*a*.) ***Mubīn***, a concise commentary in the nature of a literal translation, by Nūr al-Dīn M. birādar-zādah i Faiḍ: **Mas͟hhad** i, *fṣl.* 3, MSS., no. 182 (AH 1274/1857–8).

No. 49 (*a*) (22). [***al-Mustak͟hlaṣ***]. See Additions to no. 50, end.

No. 49 (*a*) (24), end. *Insert*:

(24*a*.) (***Qiṣṣah i Yūsuf***), an anonymous commentary beginning *al-Ḥ. l. R. al-ʿā. wa-'l-ʿāqibatu ... Faṣl. Bi-dān-ki īn kitāb jamʿ kardah āmad dar bayān i qiṣṣah i Yūsuf*: **Skutari** Hudāʾī 77 (AH 849). [Ritter, *OLZ*. 1928 col. 1126[7].] Probably also **Bānkīpūr** xiv 1171 (19th cent. Cf. 49 (*a*) (61), with Additions).

(24*b*.) (***Qiṣṣah i Yūsuf***), in 57 chapters, perhaps translated from an Arabic original: **Blochet** i 395 (acephalous, beginning in Ch. XII. AH 898/1492).

No. 49 (*a*) (27), end. *Insert*:

(27*a*.) ***Risālah i nūrīyah***, a commentary on the *Āyah i nūr* (S. xxiv 35), by Ḥājj M. Raḥīm K͟hān Kirmānī. Edition: place ? date ? (see Mas͟hhad iv p. 488).

(27*b*.) ***Rislāh i Qalandarīyah***, on S. xxxv 1: **Cambridge** Trin. Coll. R. 13, 45 (19) (Palmer p. 115).

No. 49 (*a*) (33). S. Nāṣir al-Dīn M. **Abū 'l-Manṣūr** Dihlawī b. S. M. ʿAlī b. S. Fārūq ʿAlī, noted in his day as an Anti-Christian controversialist, was born at Nāgpūr, where his father was *Mīr Munshī* to the British Residency. When Raḥmān ʿAlī wrote about him (presumably in, or shortly before 1894), he had reached the age of sixty-four and was resident in Delhi, engaged in the composition of his Persian *tafsīr*. Raḥman ʿAlī mentions the titles of twenty-eight other works by him, most of them, if not all, presumably in Urdu and many of them replies to the works of Indian and other Christians (see also the index to Blumhardt's catalogue of Hindustani books in the India Office Library under Muḥammad Abū al-Manṣūr). [*Kalimat al-ḥaqq*, an Urdu biography, by M. Nuṣrat ʿAlī, Delhi 1870*, 1876* *ʿAin al-yaqīn*, an Urdu account of his writings, by S. Mahdī Ḥasan, Delhi 1873* Raḥmān ʿAlī p. 232.]

No. 49 (*a*) (33), end. *Insert*:

(33*a*.) ***Tafsīr al-Qurʾān***, a translation by S. M. Taqī Fakhr-Dāʿī Gīlānī of S. Aḥmad Khān's Urdu translation and commentary (for which see no. 654, 5th par. *supra*): **Ṭihrān** (pt. 1 (to Sūrah ii 80), apparently undated but presented by the publishers to the Mashhad Library AHS 1318/ 1939–40. See Mashhad iv p. 479).

(33*b*.) ***Tafsīr fī maʿnā 'l-tauḥīd***, on the last (30th) section: **Princeton** 79 (acephalous, AH 1264/1848).

No. 49 (*a*) (36), end. *Insert*:

(36*a*.) ***Tafsīr i Āyat al-Kursī*** (beg. *al-Ḥ. l. 'l anzala ʿalā ʿabdihi 'l-kitāb ... Baʿd az imlā-yi ṣahāʾif i ilāhī*), a Sunnī commentary written apparently in the 10th/16th century and divided into a *muqaddamah*, two *maqālahs* and a *khātimah*: **Majlis** ii 802 (AH 962/1555).

No. 49 (*a*) (37). Delete the query after al-Majlisī. The work is dedicated to Shāh Sulaimān Ṣafawī. **Bānkīpūr** Pers. Hand-list 1114 = **Bānkīpūr** xiv 1154 (19th cent.).

No. 49 (*a*) (42). The *Tafsīr i Dalīl al-Raḥmān* is a large Shīʿite commentary begun in Rajab 1214/1799 in Shah-ʿĀlam's reign. **Bānkīpūr** Pers. Hand-list 1115–20 = **Bānkīpūr** xiv 1162–7.

No. 49 (*a*) (43) should be deleted. **Nūr i ʿUthmaniyah** 444 is the *Kashf al-asrār wa-ʿuddat al-abrār* of Rashīd al-Dīn A. b. M. Maibudī (see Additions to no. 5, end.). [Ritter, OLZ. 1928 col. 1124[27].]

No. 49 (*a*) (47), an Arabic work, should be deleted. [Ritter, OLZ. 1928 col. 1125.]

No. 49 (*a*) (57), end. *Insert*:
(57*a*.) ***Tafsīr i Sūrah i Wa-'l-ḍuḥā*** (xciii), by M. ʿAlī Qādirī: **Āṣafīyah** iii p. 230 no. 513 (AH 1130/1718).

No. 49 (*a*) (60). **Asʿad** 101, dated 1028, is defective at the beginning (first words: *u bayān ba-ṣaub i Sūrah i Āl i ʿImrān mutawajjih shud*). [Ritter, *OLZ*. 1928, col. 1125.]

No. 49 (*a*) (61). ***Tafsīr i Sūrah i Yūsuf*** (beg. *al-Ḥ. l. R. al-ʿā.... Bi-dān-kih īn kitāb jamʿ kardah āmad dar bayān i Yūsuf b. Yaʿqūb ... bā āyathā-yi Qurʾān*. Cf. ad no. 49 (a) (24), end, (24*a*): **Bānkīpūr** Pers. Hand-list 1127 = **Bānkīpūr** xiv 1171 (19th cent.).

No. 49 (*a*) (62). ***Tafsīr i Sūrah i Yūsuf*** (beg. *Ḥamd i bī-ḥadd u bī-nihāyat u madḥ i bī-ʿadd u bī-ghāyat ḥadrat i jalāl*), a Shīʿite work: **Chelebi ʿAbd Allāh** 19 (AH 667). [Ritter, *OLZ*. 1928 col. 1125.]

No. 49 (*a*) (64), end. *Insert*:
(64*a*) ***Tafsīr i Sūrah i Yūsuf:*** **Lindesiana** p. 222 no. 537 (circ. AD 1750).
(64*b*) ***Tafsīr i Sūrah i Yūsuf***, by Miyān[14] Jān Muḥammad b. Abū Saʿīd Anṣārī Jāland'harī:[15] **Lahore** Panjāb Univ. (AH 1277/1860. See *OCM*. xi/2 p. 77).

No. 49 (*a*) (69) should be deleted. Qarah Muṣṭafā 100 (AH 1031) is the *Jawāhir al-tafsīr* (for which see no. 20 (1) *supra*, with Additions and corrections to that entry). [Ritter, *OLZ*. 1928 col. 1125[6].]

No. 49 (*a*) (69). *Insert*:
(69a) ***Tarkīb al-Qurʾān*** (beg. *Naḥmaduka 'llāhumma yā man alhamanā ... Bar alwāḥ i ṣāfiyah*), grammatical analysis and Persian translation of the *Qurʾān* by an anonymous Shīʿite apparently of the Ṣafawī period: **Majlis** ii 800 (S. i–ii only. With a marginal commentary by another Shīʿite apparently contemporary with the author, AH 1120/1708).

No. 49 (*a*) (70). The *Tauḍīḥ* (beg. *Ḥamd ān Khudāʾī rā kih bi-firistād bar Paighāmbar i mā Qurʾān i muzhdah-dihandah*) is a concise anonymous commentary based on the *Kashshāf*, the *Tafsīr i Zāhidī* (see no. 5, 2nd. par., with

14 Cf. no. 1321 (2), 1st footnote.
15 Jaland'har = "Jullundur" in the Panjāb.

Additions), Dīnawarī, etc. Other MSS.: **Bānkīpūr** xiv 1150 [= no. (72) below. 16th cent.], **Mashhad** i, *fṣl.* 3, MSS., no. 32 (old).

No. 49 (*a*) (72). **Bānkīpūr** Pers.Hand-list 1130 = **Bānkīpūr** xiv 1150. This is the same work as no. (70) above.

No. 49 (*a*) (73). *Insert*:

(73*a*) *'Urwat al-muttaqīn*, a Shī'ite commentary on the *Āyat al-Kursī* (S. ii 256) and the two succeeding verses, by M. b. Ḥaidar 'Alī *ma'rūf bi*-Ashraf Warnūsfādarānī: **Mashhad** iv p. 443 no. 346 (acephalous).

No. 49 (*b*) (8), end. *Insert*: (9) **Mashhad** i, *fṣl.* 3, MSS., no. 34 (beg. Basmalah *Āghāz kardam ba-nām i Khudāwand i Rūzīdihandah i Amurzandah Al-Ḥamdu li-llāhi* ... Old), (10) **Mashhad** i, *fṣl.* 3, MSS., no. 43 (defective at both ends. The author quotes Persian verses by Sa'dī and others. Old).

No. 49 (*c*), 2nd par., MSS. **Vatican** 20 (55) = **Vatican** Pers. 55 (Rossi p. 81. Cf. Vatican Pers. 51, Rossi p. 77).

No. 50, 2nd par., MSS. [*Tarājim al-a'ājim.*] Of the Āyā Ṣōfyah MSS. only 4665 is the *T. al-a.* 4664*a* and 4666*a* are the *Mustakhlaṣ* of Ḥāfiẓ al-Dīn Bukhārī [see below, ad no. 50, end]. The rest of those two MSS. is devoted to a commentary on a *qaṣīdah* of Dhū 'l-Rummah. [Ritter, *OLZ*. 1928 col. 1125.]

No. 50, 2nd par., MSS. *Read* **Fātiḥ** 5177 (the number given in the *defter* is incorrect). [Ritter, *ibid.*]

No. 50, end. *Insert*:

50*a*. **Ḥāfiẓ al-Dīn** Abū 'l-Faḍl M. b. M. b. Naṣr **Bukhāri** was born at Bukhārā in 615/1218 and died there in 693/1294 (see *al-Jawāhir al-muḍī'ah* ii pp. 121–2, *al-Fawā'id al-bahīyah* p. 199).

al-Mustakhlaṣ (beg. *al-Ḥ. l. wa-salām 'alā 'ibādihi 'lladhīna 'ṣṭafā 'alā 'l-khuṣūṣ wa-'l-khulūṣ*), a Qur'ānic glossary: **Āyā Ṣōfyah** 4664*a* (AH 757), 4666*a* (AH 772), 4837*a*, **Fātiḥ** 645*a*. [Ritter, *OLZ*. 1928 col. 1125, *ad* p. 31 no. 22.]

No. 53, 2nd par., MSS. 'Āshir p. 175 no. 428 (dated 925) is 'Ādil Shīrāzī's alphabetical rearrangement of the work. [Ritter, *OLZ*. 1928 col. 1126.]

No. 53, 2nd par., MSS. [*Tarjumān al-Qur'ān.*] Also 'Alīgaṛh Subḥ. MSS. p. 56 no. 15 (AH 952 ?), **Mashhad** iii, *faṣl.* 11, MSS., no. 9.

No. 53, Rearrangements (2). 'Ādil Shīrāzī (cf. Ritter *OLZ.* 1928 col. 1126) wrote Persian metrical paraphrases of 'Alī's *Ṣad kalimah* (see Sipahsālār ii pp. 68–72; Bodleian 1432–4; etc.) and of the *Nathr al-la'āli'* (Krafft p. 182 no. 478, probably also Berlin 9 foll. 126–156 and de Slane 2770 fol. 135*b seq.* Edition: Ṭihrān 1306/1888–9 (see Sipahsālār ii p. 69[11])) as well as a commentary on Abū 'l-Fatḥ Bustī's *qaṣīdah* [*al-nūnīyah* presumably] (MS. in the possession of S. Naṣr Allāh Taqawī. See Sipahsālār ii p. 69[5]).

No. 53, Rearrangements (2), MSS, end. [*Tarjumān al-Qur'ān.* 'Ādil's rearrangement.] Also **'Āshir** p. 175 no. 428 (beg. *Bi-dān aiyadaka 'llāh kih tarjumān ta'rīb i tar-zafān-ast u dar wai sih lughat ast.* AH 925). [Ritter, *OLZ.* 1928 col. 112617], probably also **Āyā Ṣōfyah** 85 (contains no mention of author, but opening words agree with 'Āshir p. 175 no. 428. Undated. Ritter, *OLZ.* 1928 col. 1126[11]).

Insert:

(3) anonymous epitome rearranged alphabetically; **Ellis Coll.** M. 84 (3) (probably AH 1101/1690).

No. 53, last par., end. [al-Jurjānī] Also Bānkīpūr Arab. Cat. v p. 86; Brockelmann *Sptbd.* ii p. 305.

No. 54. These lines should be deleted. Āyā Ṣōfyah 85 (undated) contains no mention of the author, but the opening words (which agree with those of 'Āshir p. 175 no. 428) seem to show that it is the *Tarjumān al-Qur'ān* of al-Jurjānī [as rearranged by 'Ādil Shīrāzī]. [Ritter, *OLZ.* 1928 col. 1126[11].]

No. 57 (1). Āyā Ṣōfyah 4837 (1) should be deleted. This is the *Mustakhlaṣ of Ḥāfiẓ al-Dīn Bukhārī* (see below, ad no. 50, end). [Ritter, *OLZ.* 1928 col. 1125, *ad* p. 31 (22).]

No. 57 (5). [*Khulāṣah i Mustakhlaṣ al-ma'ānī.*] Also **Lindesiana** p. 178 no. 498 (circ. AD 1650).

No. 57 (5). **Bānkīpūr** Pers. Hand-list 1164 = **Bānkīpūr** xiv 1174.

No. 57 (6), end. *Insert*:

(6*a*) ***Risālah i lughat al-Qurʾān ba-Fārisī*** (beg. *wa-baʿdu fa-innī tarjamtu lughāt al-Qurʾān ʿalā abwāb mufaṣṣalah bi-ʾl-ḥurūf al-muʿjamah*): **Majlis** 607 (1) (16th cent.?).
(6*b*) ***Tarjamah i lughāt i Qurʾān*** (beg. *Sūrat al-Nās. al-Qaul guftan*): **Sipahsālār** i pp. 185–6 no. 251 (16th cent.).

No. 57 (7). *Read* (7) ***Tarjumān al-Qurʾān*** (beg. *al-Ḥ. l. ʾl. arsala ʾl-rusul*): **Berlin** 232 (8) (fragment), **Majlis** 54.

No. 58 (*b*) (3). [*Kashf al-amānī* ...] "Nr. 58 (3) (926h.) 379 foll. ist ein selbständiges Buch, wenn auch auf der *Šāṭibīje* beruhend. Anfang: ...

اما بعد حمد الله على نواله

[Ritter, *OLZ*. 1928 col. 1126.]

No. 58 (*b*) (5). "Nr. (5) ist eine *Terjeme, kein Šarḥ*." [Ritter, *OLZ*. 1928 col. 1126.]

No, 58 (*b*) (6). Kamānkash 15 bis (undated) contains (1) the *Shāṭibīyah* with interlinear Persian translation beginning *Āghāz kardam ba-kalimah i Bi-smi ʾllāh jamʿ al-awwal naqīḍ al-ākhir*. [Another MS.: **ʿAtīq Wālidah** 20*a* (old naskhī of 7th–8th/13th–14th cent.)], (2) a Persian tract of 9 foll, on *tajwīd* beginning *al-Ḥ. l. ʾl. taqaddasa ʿan al-aulād wa-ʾl-ajnād*, (3) a Persian work on the interpretation of dreams (*al-bāb al-awwal fī adab al-muʿabbir wa-tamyīz al-ruʾyā*). [Ritter, *OLZ*. 1928 col. 1126.]

No, 58 (*b*) (6), end. *Insert*:
(6*a*) ***Sharḥ i Shāṭibīyah***, dedicated to Fatḥ-ʿAlī Shāh and his heir apparent ʿAbbās Mīrzā (cf. no. 434, footnote *supra*) by M. Qāsim b. Muḥsin b. ʿAlī Ḥusainī Tabrīzī: **Majlis** ii 812.

No, 58 (*b*) (8). **Bānkīpūr** Pers. Hand-list 1167 = **Bānkīpūr** xiv 1175.

No. 59, 1st par. In Majlis ii p. 31[14] the name is given as M. b. Maḥmūd b. M. b. Aḥmad b. ʿAlī Sharīf Samarqand [ī?] Hamadānī ʾl-aṣl "Ḥāfiẓ" takhalluṣ. The Vatican catalogue (p. 93) adds to the *nisbahs* al-Baghdādī (by residence).

Cf. Brockelmann *Sptbd*. i p. 727. He wrote also in Arabic *al-Qaṣīdat al-fāʾiḥah fī tajwīd al-Fātiḥah* (Ḥ. Kh. iv p. 545, Vatican Pers. 70 (3), Rossi p. 93).

No. 59 (1). *al-Mabsūṭ fī ʾl-qirāʾat* [*sic*] *al-sabʿ wa-ʾl-maḍbūṭ min iḍāʿat al-ṭabʿ* is the form in which the title occurs in the preface of the Majlis MS. The work is divided into three *kitābs*, of which the second and third are in Arabic. Opening words: *al-Ḥ. l. 'l. adhāqa qulūb*. Other MSS.: **Vatican** Pers. 70 (4) (AH 754/1353. Rossi p. 93), **Majlis** ii 817 (AH 865/1460–1), **Mashhad** ii, *fṣl.* 7, MSS., no. 38 (AH 1019/ 1610–11).

No. 59 (1), MSS. *Read* Aḥmad Allāh.

No. 59 (2). *al-Multaqaṭ min maʿānī Ḥirz al-amānī fī tajrīd al-tajwīd* is the full title according to Majlis ii p. 39. The work is a *qaṣīdah* in forty-four verses. Opening words: *al-Ḥ. l. 'l. anzala 'l-Qur'āna tanzīl^an^*. Another MS.: **Majlis** ii 821–2 (with a metrical commentary by the author in 400 verses. In the same hand as Majlis ii 817, which is dated 865/1460–1).

No. 59 (2), last par. The *"kitāb i qirā'at"* (beg. *al-Ḥ. l. R. al-ʿā ... Iʿlam hadāka 'llāh*) by *bandah i ḍaʿīf Samarqandī* is in ten *bābs*.

No. 59 (2), end. *Insert*:

(3) (***Risālah dar ikhtilāf i Abū Bakr b. ʿAbbās u Ḥafṣ dar qirā'at***) (beg. *al-Ḥ. l. 'l. j. ṣūduranā khazā'in*): **Mashhad** ii, *fṣl.* 7, MSS., no. 13.

No. 61, 2nd par. [*Farā'id al-fawā'id.*] **Bānkīpūr** Pers. Hand-list 1168 (*b*) = **Bānkīpūr** xiv 1180 foll. 71–133. Also **ʿAlīgaṛh** Subḥ. MSS. p. 5 (AH 1079/1668–9).

No. 61, 4th par., MSS. **Bānkīpūr** Pers. Hand-list 1168 = **Bānkīpūr** xiv 1180 (AH 1145/1733).

No. 61, end. Another commentary on al-Jazarī's *Muqaddimah* is ***Taisīr al-bayān fī tajwīd al-Qur'ān***: **Āṣafīyah** iii p. 748.

No. 62, 2nd par. *Khulāṣat al-tanzīl fī adā' al-ḥurūf li-l-tartīl* is the full title according to Palmer. Opening words: *Ai ba-nām i Tu iftitāḥ i kalām*. Also **ʿAlīgaṛh** Subḥ. MSS. p. 5 (AH 1079/1668–9), **Cambridge** Trinity R. 13. 45 (16) (Palmer p. 114) and apparently also **Mashhad** ii, *fṣl.* 7, MSS., nos. 12 (*Risālah dar makhārij al-ḥurūf*, by Ibn ʿImād, written in 809 [so, not 803] and beginning as above, AH 1017/1608–9), 41 (*Manẓūmah dar tajwīd*, by Ibn ʿImād, beginning as above).

No. 63, 1st par. [Ṭāhir Iṣfahānī.] Cf. Brockelmann *Sptbd.* ii p. 274.

No. 63 (1), MSS. [*Durr al-farīd.*] Also **Mashhad** ii, *fṣl.* 7, MSS., no. 10 (AH 1018/1609–10).

No. 63 (2), 1st par. *Manhal al-ʿaṭshān fī rasm aḥruf al-Qurʾān* (so Ritter, OLZ. 1928 col. 1126, and also Peshawar 1095).

No. 63 (2), 1st par., MSS. ʿ**Umūmī** 208, dated 878, contains (1) *Manhal al-ʿaṭshān* ... (beg. *Ḥ. u sp. i bī-ḥadd u q. Pādshāhī rā*), (2) the same author's *Nihāyat al-itqān fī tajwīd al-Qurʾān* (so according to the colophon. Beg. *A. b. chunīn guyad faqīr i ḥaqīr i jānī Ṭāhir i Ḥāfiẓ i Iṣfahānī kih īn mukhtaṣar mushtamil ast bar qāʿidaʾī u ḍābiṭaʾī chand dar tajwīd u taṣḥīḥ i Qurʾān i ʿAẓīm*). Possibly identical with no. 82 (*b*) (7). [Ritter, OLZ. 1928 col. 1126.]

No. 63 (2), 2nd par. **Āyā Ṣōfyah** 44 (undated) is an anonymous work on *tajwīd*, the ascription of which to Ṭāhir is quite arbitrary. It begins *Ḥ. i bī-ḥ. u thanā-yi lā-yuʿadd Khudāwandī rā sazad kih nuqūsh i ḥurūf jawāhir i Qurʾān bar lauḥ i qalb*. [Ritter, OLZ. 1928 col. 1126.]

No. 63 (2), 2nd par. ʿ**Umūmī** 213 (AH 894) contains (1) a monograph on Ḥamzah's reading, especially his treatment of the *hamz*, beginning *Chunīn gūyad faqīr i ḥaqīr i jānī Ṭāhir b. ʿArab* [so: cf. Ḥ. Kh. iv p. 546[6]] *b. Ibrāhīm al-Iṣfahānī kih baʿḍī az dūstān ... bayān i madhhab i Ḥamzah b. Ḥabīb al-Zaiyāt i Kūfī rā dar waqf bar hamz* ..., (2) *Nihāyat al-itqān fī tajwīd al-Qurʾān*. [Ritter, OLZ. 1928 col. 1126.]

No. 63 (2), 2nd par., end. **Mashhad** ii, *fṣl.* 7, MSS., no. 11 (acephalous) is a *Risālah dar wuqūf* described in the catalogue as by M. Ṭāhir Ḥāfiẓ Iṣfahānī.

No. 64, 2nd par., MSS. **Bānkīpūr** Pers. Hand-list 1171–2 = **Bānkīpūr** xiv 1177–8.

No. 64, 2nd par., MSS. [*Qawāʿid al-Qurʾān.*] Also **Mashhad** ii, *fṣl.* 7, MSS., no. 27 (AH 930 [*sic* ?]), **Majlis** ii 815 (17th cent.), **Blochet** iv 2213, **Peshawar** 1953 (5), **Princeton** 448 (fragments), 450 (fragment).

No. 65 2nd. par., MSS. [*Tuḥfah i Shāhī.*] Also **Mashhad** ii, *fṣl.* 7, MSS., no. 5 (AH 1087/1676–7), **Princeton** 447 (AH 1123/ 1711), **Blochet** iv 2169 (AH 1133/1721).

No. 65, penult. par. **Bānkīpūr** Pers. Hand-list 1170 = **Bānkīpūr** xiv 1181 (beg. *al-Ḥ. l. R. al-ʿa....chunīn gūyad aqallu ʿibādi ʾllāh wa-aḥwajuhum ilā ʿafwi ʾllāh*. Divided into a *muqaddamah*, twelve *faṣls* and a *khātimah*).

No. 65, penult. par., end. Also by ʿImād al-Dīn al-Astarābādī is:—

Risālah dar qirā'at i 'Āṣim (beg. *Ḥ. i bī-ḥ. u sp. i bī-q.*), in the manner of the *Shāṭibīyah* (*"īn risālah ba-ṭarīq i Shāṭibīyah ast"*): **Mashhad** ii, *fṣl.* 7, MSS., no. 16.

No. 68, 2nd par., MSS. [*Maqṣūd al-qārī'.*] Also **Lahore** Panjab Univ. (AH 1275/1858–9. See *OCM*. xi/2 p. 78).

No. 68, last par. [*Maqṣūd al-qārī'.*] *Read* Editions: **Bombay** (Ḥaidarī Pr.) 1290/1873* (in *Majmū'ah: al-Bayān al-jazīl ...*, a collection of nine short Urdu, Persian and Arabic works on the *Qur'ān* and its recitation, the first being *al-Bayān al-jazīl li-l-tartīl*, in Urdu, the second *M. al-q.* 92 pp.); **Lucknow** (Asadī Pr.) 1290/1873°* (in *Majmū'ah: al-B. al-j. li-l-t,., M. al-q ...*; another edition of the same, or perhaps nearly the same, collection. 72 pp.).; (Majma' al-'ulum Pr.) 1293/1876* (72 pp.); (N.K.) 1886† (a similar *Mamjmū'ah.* 62 pp.); (Dilpadhīr Pr.) 1308/1891° (in *Majmū'ah i bīst rasā'il i qirā'at*, the first nine (?) being those contained in the *Majmū'ah: al-Bayān al-jazīl ...* 108 pp.); (Qādirī Pr.) 1895† (the same twenty works. 108 pp.).

No. 69, end. *Insert*:

69*a*. S. **Qāsim b.** Mīr **Nūr Allāh.** ***Maṭla' al-shams***, a metrical work written in 1045/1635–6 at Ḥaidarābād: **Mashhad** ii, *fṣl.* 7, MSS., no. 32.

No. 70, 1st par. Saiyid Abū 'l-Qāsim *mutakhalliṣ bi-*Qārī says in his preface that he wrote in the reign of Shāh 'Abbās i Thānī i Ṣafawī (see Majlis ii p. 39).

No. 70, 2nd par., MSS. [*Naẓm al-la'ālī ...*]. Also **Majlis** ii, p. 39 no. (819) (*Manẓūma'ī dar tajwīd*). No formal title is mentioned in the Majlis catalogue, which, however, quotes a verse in which *Naẓm i la'ālī* occurs as a chronogram (= 1061 or 1062).

The work is metrical, consists of 89 verses and begins *Ai kalām az intiẓām i nām i dhātat bar niẓām*. Perhaps it is identical with the *Naẓm i la'ālī* published on the margin of S. Ḥasan Lak'hnawī's *Rashḥah i faiḍ*; (see below, ad no. 80, end, 80*c*).

No. 71, 1st par. Mullā Muṣṭafā Qārī Tabrīzī Shī'ī Imāmī according to the Sipahsālār catalogue.

No. 71 (2). [*Tuḥfat al-qurrā'.*] According to Majlis ii p. 10 the work was begun at Mecca, completed at al-Madīnah and after the author's return to Persia was shown to Mullā M. Bāqir Khurāsānī, one of the *ʿulamāʾ* of Iṣfahān, who made some additions.

No. 71 (2), MSS. [*Tuḥfat al-qurrāʾ*.] For (13) *read* (1–3). Also **Sipahsālār** i p. 184 no. 250 (AH 1072/1661–2), **Majlis** ii 795 (AH 1087/1676), **Mashhad** ii, *fṣl.* 7, MSS., no. 6 (AH 1088/ 1677), **ʿAlīgaṛh** Subḥ. MSS. p. 5 (AH 1122/1710), and possibly **Ivanow** 1st Suppt. 818 (defective). Edition: **Bombay** 1302/1884–5 (Āṣafīyah iii p. 154).

No. 71 (3). The *Irshād al-qāriʾ* (beg. *Ai Fātiḥah i muṣḥaf i ḥamdat tauḥīd*), was begun at the tomb of ʿAlī, completed in 1078/1668 at the shrine of Ḥusain and dedicated to Maulānā M. Bāqir. **Bānkīpūr** Pers. Hand-list 1165 == **Bānkīpūr** xiv 1179.

No. 72, 2nd par., MSS. [*Ḥilyat al-qāriʾ*.] Also **Āṣafīyah** iii p. 154 no. 128.

No. 76, end. *Insert*:

76*a*. In 1180/1766–7 at Ḥaidarābād was written:—
(***Risālah dar tajwīd***): **Rehatsek** p. 195 no. 42.

No. 78. This entry should be deleted. The *Mukhtaṣar al-tajwīd*, though described in the List as Persian, is an Urdu work written in 1242 and published at Delhi in 1285*, when the author was still alive.

No. 79, end. *Insert*:

79*a*. **Mukhtār** Aʿmā **Iṣfahānī**. ***Mukhtār al-qurrāʾ***, written in 1240 (but see further on): **Mashhad** ii, *fṣl.* 7, MSS., nos 33–4 (the latter dated 1230 !), **Majlis** ii p. 35 nos. 818–19 (AH 1274/1857–8).

No. 80, end. *Insert*:

80*a*. S. **Maḥmūd b. ʿAbd Allāh** Mūsawī **Dizfūlī**.

(1) ***Qawāʿid al-tajwīd fī tartīl al-Qurʾān al-Majīd***, begun in 1238/1822–3, completed in 1239/1823–4 and divided into a *muqaddamah*, twelve *bābs* and a *khātimah*: **Majlis** ii 813 (AH 1240/1824–5).

(2) ***Tuḥfat al-ikhlāṣ***, an abridgment of the preceding work, completed in 1244/1828–9, divided similarly and dedicated to the Shāh-zādah Ḥusām al-Salṭanah: **Majlis** ii 793 (same hand).

(3) *Mukhtaṣar al-tajwīd*, completed in 1240/1824–5 and divided into ten *faṣls*: **Majlis** ii p. 36 no. 814 (same hand).

80*b*. S. **M. b. Mahdī Ḥusainī** dedicated to Muḥammad Sh̲āh Qājār (AH 1250–64/1834–48) a Qurʾānic concordance (with a Persian preface) entitled *Kash̲f al-āyāt i Muḥammad-Sh̲āhī* (a chronogram = 1251/1835–6), which has been published at Tabrīz [date ? See Mash̲had ii, *fṣl.* 7, ptd., bks., no. 2] and, appended to the *Tafsīr al-Jalālain*, at Ṭihrān in 1276/1859–60 [see Ellis ii col. 160, Mash̲had iv p. 495].

Maẓāhir i Maḥmūdīyah:Ṭihrān 1264/1848 (see Mash̲had ii, *fṣl.* 7 (*Tajwīd*), ptd. bks., no. 3, where the precise subject is not stated).

80*c*. S. **Ḥasan Lak'hnawī**.

Rash̲ḥah i faiḍ, composed in 1264/1848. Edition: **Lucknow** (Āṣafīyah iii p. 154 no. 132, where the date is not mentioned. With *Naẓm i lāʾālī* (cf. no. 70 ?) on margin).

80*d*. **M. b. Asad Allāh b. ʿAlī-Riḍā Qārīʾ Māzandāranī**.

Maẓamir [*sic*, apparently for *Maẓāhir*] *i Muḥammadīyah*, dedicated to Nāṣir al-Dīn Sh̲ah: **Mash̲had** ii, *fṣl.* 7, MSS., no. 40.

No. 81, end. [Saʿd Allāh Murādābādī.] Also Bānkīpūr ix pp. 57–8.

Insert:

81*a*. **Maḥmūd b. M. ʿAlawī Fāṭimī Ḥasanī Ḥusainī Ḥāfiẓ Tabrīzī** was Warden of the tomb of the Walī-ʿahd and Nāʾib al-Salṭanah [i.e. presumably ʿAbbās Mīrzā: cf. no. 434, footnote *supra*, *Ency. Isl.* under ʿAbbās Mīrzā] as well as Instructor and Head of the *Ḥuffāẓ*, *Qurrāʾ*, *Ṣudūr* and *Kh̲uṭabāʾ* at the shrine of the Imam Riḍā [at Mash̲had]. He was the author of an Arabic work entitled *Jawāhir al-Qurʾān*, which was published at Tabrīz in 1287/1870–1 with a marginal Persian translation by the author (cf. Brockelmann *Sptbd.* ii p. 830, where the date given for his death, 1270/1853, seems to be incorrect).

Mafātiḥ al-tanzīl, on *tajwīd* and other matters relating to the *Qurʾān*, in a *muqaddamah*, twelve *bābs* and a *kh̲ātimah*, but perhaps never continued beyond the tenth *bāb*, which was completed in 1297/1880: **Majlis** ii 820 (*Muqaddamah* and *Bābs* i–x).

No. 82 (*a*) (1), end. *Insert*:

(1*a*). ***Baḥr al-nūr***, on the *qirā'āt i Sab'ah* in eight *bābs* and a *khātimah*, by 'Alī b. Ḥasan 'Alī Kūsārī (cf. no. 82 (*a*) (5)): **Majlis** ii 791 (part of the first *faṣl* and a fragment of the *khātimah*. Circ. AH 1117/1705–6 ?).

No. 82 (*a*) (4). *Ḥall i mutashābih i mamzūj* is a chronogram = 882/ 1477–8.

No. 82 (*a*) (4), MSS. **Bānkīpūr** Pers. Hand-list 1169 = **Bānkīpūr** xiv 1176.

No. 82 (*a*) (5). [*Ḥayāt al-fu'ād*.] Beg. *al-Ḥ. l. al-'Alī 'l. rafa'a ahlahu*. Also **Majlis** II p. 22 no. 792 (lacunae, AH 1117/1705–6. Title given here as *Ḥayāt al-qulūb*). For another work by the same author, *Baḥr al-nūr*, see above, ad no. 82 (*a*) (1), end.

No. 82 (*a*) (7). [*Qaṣīdah* by 'Izz al-Dīn M.] **Decourdemanche** ii S.P. 1673 (12) = **Blochet** iv 2213, fol. 161*b* (author's name given as Émir 'Izz ed-Din ibn Mohammed ibn Béha ed-Din el-Djouri). **Decourdemanche** ii S.P. 1673 (6) = **Blochet** iv 2213 fol. 79*b*. Another MS. of M. Ṣādiq's commentary: **Ethé** ii 3058 (9) (AH 1135/1722).

No. 82 (*a*) (10), end. *Insert*:

(10*a*). *Khulāṣat al-qirā'ah*, by M. Mu'min b. 'Abd al-Karīm Qāri' (who quotes Bahā' al-Dīn al-'Āmilī (d. 1030/ 1621)): **Sipahsālār** i p. 186 no. 252.

(10*b*). ***Khulāṣat al-tajwīd***, anonymous: **Blochet** iv 2213 fol. 162*b*.

No. 82 (*a*) (15), end. *Insert*:

(15*a*). ***Majma' al-gharā'ib***, by Dūst-Muḥammad b. Yādgār: **Leningrad** Univ. no. 556 (Salemann-Rosen p. 18).

(15*b*). ***Marta' al-ghizlān***, on *tajwīd*, composed in 1212/ 1797–8 by Ḥaidar: **Lahore** Panjab Univ. (AH 1275/1858. See *OCM*. xi/2 p. 77).

(15*c*). ***Minhāj al-nashr fī 'l-qirā'āt al-'ashr***, by Ḥusain b.'Uthmān: **I.O.** 4594 (17th cent. See *JRAS*. 1939 p. 376).

No. 82 (*a*) (16), end. *Insert*:

(16*a*). ***Mukhtaṣar***, by M. b. 'Alī b. M. al-Ḥusainī [possibly identical with no. (17) and with p. 48 (5)]: **'Alīgaṛh** Subḥ. MSS. p. 5.

No. 82 (*a*) (17) [*Mukhtaṣar fī bayān* ...]. See the preceding addition.

No. 82 (*a*) (18), end. *Insert*:

18*a*. **Nūr i sarmadī az mis͟hkāt i Muḥammadī**. Edition: 1261/1845 (Āṣafīyah iii p. 154 no. 129, where the place of publication is not stated).

Delete No. 82 (*a*) (22) **Taisīr al-qārī** etc. This is evidently Nūr al-Ḥaqq Dihlawī's commentary on al-Buk͟hārī's Ṣaḥīḥ.

No. 82 (*a*) (26), MSS. [*Tuḥfat al-ḥuffāẓ*.] Also **Mas͟hhad** ii, *fṣl.* 7, MSS., no. 4.

No. 82 (*a*) (27). *Tuḥfat al-Raḥmānī dar tajwīd i Qur'ānī* (so "in the conclusion";), a short tract in five chapters. **Bānkīpūr** Pers. Hand-list 1166 = **Bānkīpūr** xiv 1182.

No. 82 (*a*) (28). [*Zīnat al-qāri'*.] Also **Lahore** Panjāb Univ. (AH 1224/ 1808–10. See *OCM*. xi/2 p. 78), **Bānkīpūr** xvii 1561. The opening words given in the different catalogues vary considerably.

No. 82 (*b*) (5). Possibly identical with the *Muk͟htaṣar fī bayān tajwīd al-Furqān*, 82 (*a*) (17) (see also above, ad no. 82 (*a*) (16), end).

No. 82 (*b*) (11), end. *Insert*:
(12) **Risālah i tajwīd** (beg. *al-Ḥ. l. 'l. faḍḍala 'l-'ilma fī 'l-a'ṣār*), metrical, with an Arabic preface in prose, by 'Abd Allāh b. Aḥmad Bāyazīd al-Kultānī: **Bānkīpūr** Suppt. ii 2215 (19th cent.).
(13) **Risālah dar 'ilm i tajwīd**, in twelve *bābs*, by Aḥmad b. Ḥusain, a descendant of Burair (or Barīr ?) b. K͟huḍair (or K͟haḍīr ?) Hamadānī: **Majlis** 66 (AH 753/1352).
(14) **Risālah i tajwīd** (beg. *al-Ḥ. l. al-'Alī al-'Aẓīm allad͟hī nazzala 'l-Kitāb*), by Ḥāfiẓ G͟hulām-Muṣṭafā: **Bānkīpūr** Suppt. ii 2214 (19th cent.).
(15) **Risālah i tajwīd** (beg. *al-Ḥ. l. R. al-'ā ... a. b. īn risālah īst muk͟htaṣar dar bayān i ḍarūrīyāt*), in a *muqaddamah*, eight *faṣls* and a *k͟hātimah*, by M. Muḥsin b. Samī': **Sipahsālār** i p. 187 no 253 (AH 1228/1813).

No. 82 (*c*) I. (9), end. *Insert*:
(10) **Risālah dar qirā'at** (beg. *al-Ḥ. l. R. al-'ā. Bi- dān-kih barāy i tartīb i adā' i naẓm i Qur'ān*), composed probably towards the end of the 8th/14th century: **Sipahsālār** i pp. 187–8 no. 254 (AH 1046/1636–7).
(11) **Risālah fī tajwīd al-Qur'ān** (beg. *al-Ḥ. l. R. al-'ā. al-Malik al-'Allām wa-jā'il al-nūr wa-'l-ẓalām*); **Princeton** 80 (AH 1083/1672, said to have been transcribed from a MS. written at Simnān in 876/1471–2).

(12) Several untitled works; **Blochet** iv 2213.
(13) Salemann-Rosen p. 15 no. 406.

No. 82 (*c*) II. (*a*) (6). Cf. **Rehatsek** p. 195 no. 42.

No. 82 (*c*) II. (*a*) (7), end. *Insert*:
(8) ***Wuqūf i Kalām Allāh i Sharīf*** (beg. *Baʿd az-ān āram bayānī az wuqūf*): **Lahore** Panjāb Univ. (AH 1275/1858. See *OCM*. xi/2 p. 78).

No. 84, 1st par. M. ʿAlī Karbalāʾī is the subject of a brief notice in the *Nujūm al-samāʾ*, p. 134, where, however, there is little information beyond some words about *al-Wāḍiḥah* (for which see Brockelmann *Sptbd.* ii p. 610).

No. 84, 2nd and 3rd par. Full title: *Hādiyah i Quṭb-Shāhī dar istikhrāj i āyāt i kalām i ilāhī*. [Ritter, *OLZ*. 1928 col. 1126 penult.] Also **Āṣafiyah** iii p. *bāʾ*, no. 112. Bāyazīd 14, Nūr i ʿUthmānīyah 135 and Salīmīyah 7 are copies of the *Hādiyah i Quṭb-Shāhī*. [Ritter, *OLZ*. 1928, col. 1127.]

No. 85, 1st par. Muṣṭafā Khān Kāshī (*kih shīʿah īst* [read *shuʿbah īst*?] *az ulūs i Afāghinah, Maʾāthir al-umarāʾ* iii p. 637) was in the service of Prince M. Aʿẓam, Aurangzēb's third son and became his intimate friend and counsellor, but by order of Aurangzēb, who distrusted him, he was dismissed and sent on a pilgrimage to Mecca. The rest of his life was spent in seclusion at Aurangābād. See Khāfī Khān ii pp. 439–43; *Maʾāthir al-umarāʾ* iii pp. 637–9.

No. 85 (1), MSS. **Bānkīpūr** Pers. Hand-list 1162–3 = **Bānkīpūr** xiv 1172–3.

No. 85 (1), 2nd par. [*Nujūm al-Furqān*.] Other editions: **Ṭihrān** 1274/ 1857–8 (Mashhad i, *fṣl.* 3, ptd. bks., no. 51); **Lucknow** 1886†.

No. 86, 1st par., end. Delete the full stop after 1795–6.

No. 84, 1st par., footnote. For M. b. Khātūn see also Ṭāhir Naṣrābādī p. 159.

No. 86, 3rd par. ʿUmūmī 190 (dated 1088) deals with the division of the text into tenths and fifths and begins *al-Ḥ. l. R. al-ʿā. ḥamd*^{an} *dāʾim*^{an} *li-rubūbīyatihi … a.b. bi-dān-kih Imām … Tāj al-Dīn* MṢDR [*Muṣaddar* ?] *Bukhārī dar-īn nuskhah dhikr i āyāt u aʿshār u akhmās kardah ast u har sūrah rā guftah ast kih chand ʿushr ast u ʿadad i aʿshār ba- ḥisāb i handasah nawishtah ast*. [Ritter, *OLZ*. 1928 col. 1127.]

No. 87, end. *Insert*:

87a. Ṣadr al-ʿulamāʾ Mīrzā **ʿAbd al-Muḥammad** b. S̲h̲ams al-ʿulamāʾ Ḥajj Mīrzā Fatḥ-ʿAlī **Lāhījānī**.

Manẓūmah i nūrānīyah, a metrical list of the sūrahs, etc., completed in 1341/1922: Ṭihrān 1341/1922–3 (see Mas̲h̲had iv p. 502).

No. 89, 3rd par., end. [*al-Durr al-naẓīm*.] *Insert*:
Persian translation completed in 926/1519–20 by Aḥmad b. Ḥājjī M. al-Sakkākī al-Ṭabasī: **Princeton** 77 (17th cent.), **Majlis** ii 799 (AH 1249/1833–4).

No. 90, 1st par., footnote. For ʿAbd al-ʿAlī Birjandī see also *Haft iqlīm* no. 830; Brockelmann *Sptbd*. ii p. 591. According to the Mas̲h̲had cat., iii, *fṣl*. 17, MSS., no. 115, he died in 934.

No. 90, 2nd par., end. [ʿAbd al-ʿAlī's work on the *K̲h̲awāṣṣ al-Qurʾān*.] Also **Ivanow** 1st Suppt. 909 (acephalous. Early 19th cent.), **Lahore** Panjāb Univ. (see *OCM*. xi/2 p. 76, where the title is given as *Jauhar al-Qurʾān*).

New edition in which the verses are arranged in the same order as in the Qurʾān: *K̲h̲izānat al-asrār* (beg. *al-Ḥ.l. ʾl. anzala ʾl-Q. ʿalā ʿabdihi li-yakūna* ...), prepared in 962/1554–5 by Maẓhar al-Dīn M. al-Qāriʾ b. Bahāʾ al-Dīn ʿAlī and divided into twenty chapters: **Būhār** 192 (defective at end and elsewhere. 17th cent.).

No. 93, 2nd par., MSS. [*Ḍiyāʾ al-ʿuyūn*.] Also **Ivanow** 1st Suppt. 911 (late 18th cent.), 2nd Suppt. 1096 (1) (defective).

No. 94 (1). *al-Mirʾāt al-ʿiyānīyah* was composed for Prince Bāyazīd b. Sulaimān [1]. Ā.Ṣ. 407 is a "Dedikations exemplar". [Ritter, *OLZ*. 1928, col. 1127.]

No. 94 (2), footnote. For the *K̲h̲awāṣṣ al-Qurʾān* of al-Tamīmī see also Brockelmann *Sptbd*. ii p. 985.

No. 94 (2), 1st sentence. M. b. M. Sabzawārī is presumably identical with M. b. S̲h̲. M. b. Saʿīd al-Harawī, author of the *Baḥr al-g̲h̲arāʾib* (Edition: place ? 1299/1882 (Āṣafīyah i p. 54 no. 213, under Adʿiyah)) and with M. b. S̲h̲. M. Harawī, author of the *Waẓāʾif al-ṣāliḥīn* (MS.: Āṣafīyah i p. 64 no. 18 (AH 1272/1855–6), under Adʿiyah).

No. 94 (2), MSS. *Read* **Bānkīpūr** xvi 1427 (18th cent.).

No. 94 (2), MSS. [*Tuḥfat al-gharā'ib.*] Also **'Alīgaṛh** Subḥ. MSS. p. 20 no. 18, **Āṣafiyah** i p. 54 no. 147.

No. 94 (2), end. *Insert*:

Urdu translation (?): *Tuḥfat al-gharā'ib*, by M. b. Sh. M. Arḍ Bīlī [*sic*, presumably for Ardabīlī]: 1305/1887–8 (Āṣafiyah i p. 66, where the place of publication is not mentioned).

No. 95, 1st par., (1). **Āyā Ṣōfyah** 424 is ascribed to the Imām Shāfi'ī. [Ritter, *OLZ*. 1924 col. 1127.]

No. 95, 1st. par., end. *Insert*: (19) **Princeton** 71 (2) (S. xxxvi), 71 (3) (S. lxxiii).

No. 96 (1), end. [*Fal-nāmah i Ja'far al-Ṣādiq.*] Also **Ivanow** 1st Suppt. 913–14, 2nd Suppt. 1096 (6), **Edinburgh** New Coll. p. 11, **Upsala** Zetterstéen 395 (6), **Ethé** 3075.

No. 99, end. *Insert*:

99*a*. **Sh. M. Riḍā b. Asad Allāh Yazdī.**

Rajā' al-ghufrān fī muhimmāt al-Qur'ān, completed in 1331/1913: **Shīrāz** 1331/1913 (see Mashhad iv p. 488).

99*b*. S. **Mahdī Badā'i'-nigār** "Lāhūtī" Tafrīshī.

Badā'i' al-bayān fī jāmi' [*sic* ?] ***al-Qur'ān***, a concise introduction to the *Qur'ān* completed in 1346/1927: **Ṭihrān** AHS 1319/1940–1 (see Mashhad iv p. 466).

No. 100 (1), end. *Insert*:

(1*a*) ***Ghāyat al-taḥqīq***, on the number of sūrahs, their occasion, the number of verses, letters and *rukū'āt* in them, etc., by Niẓām al-Dīn al-Banārasī: **Blochet** iv 2155 (17th-cent.).

(1*b*) ***I'jāz i Qur'ān u balāghat i Muḥammad***, a translation of Muṣṭafā Ṣādiq al-Rāfi'ī's *I'jāz al-Qur'ān wa-'l-balāghat al-Nabawīyah* (Brockelmann *Sptbd.* iii p. 75) by 'Abd al-Ḥusain b. al-Dīn [*sic* ?]: **Ṭihrān** AHS 1320/ 1941–2 (see Mashhad iv p. 465).

No. 100 (2). This entry should be deleted. The *'Ilm al-kitāb* by Khwājah Mīr "Dard" does not deal with the *Qur'ān* but is a commentary on the author's Ṣūfī work *Wāridāt* (see Bānkīpūr xvi 1408).

No. 100 (5), end. *Insert*:

(5*a*) ***Maẓhar al-tibyān fī tarjamat al-Itqān***, a translation of al-Suyūṭī's *Itqān* (see Brockelmann ii p. 154, *Sptbd.* ii p. 179) made by S. 'Alī Akbar b. Murtaḍā Ṭabāṭabā'ī Yazdī, *Mudarris* in the Madrasah i Manṣūrīyah at Shīrāz (cf. *Fārs-nāmah i Nāṣirī* i p. 97), by request of Mu'tamad al-Daulah Farhād Mīrzā (for whom see no. 259 *supra*): **Mashhad** iv p. 454 no. 376 (pt. 1 only. AH 1298/1881).

No. 100 (9), end. *Insert*:

(9*a*) ***Tārīkh i Qur'ān***, a translation by Abū 'l-Qāsim Saḥāb (cf. no. 1484A *supra*) of the (unpublished ?) *Ta'rīkh al-Qur'ān* of Abū 'Abd Allāh Zanjānī (Professor in the University of Ṭihrān, b. AH 1309/1891–2, d. AHS 1320/1941): **Ṭihrān** AHS 1317/1938–9 (see Mashhad iv p. 467).

No. 101, 2nd par., MSS. [*Tarjamah i Tārīkh i Ṭabarī.*] Also **Bānkīpūr** Suppt I 1744 (AH 1012/1604), **Caetani** 31 (AH 1034/1624), **Aumer** 361 (in the *Ergänzungsheft*. AH 1038/1628–9), **Leningrad** Pub. Lib. (3 copies. See *Mélanges asiatiques* iii (St. Petersburg 1859) p. 726), **Majlis** 231.

No. 101, French translations (1). [*Tarjamah i Tārīkh i Ṭabarī.*] A copy of Dubeux's translation preserved in the Cambridge University Library contains pp. 1–368, breaking off abruptly in the account of the Exodus. [J. D. Pearson, in a letter.] The copies at the British Museum and the India Office contain only pp. 1–280.

No. 102, 3rd par., end. [*Zain al-akhbār.*] Another edition: **Ṭihrān** AHS 1315/1936–7 [R. Lescot, *B.E.O.I.F. de Damas* vii–viii p. 281].—"Some extracts from Gardīzī's chapter on the Turks have been re-edited and translated by Marquart in his *Das Volkstum d. Komanen* (1914) and some more translations by the said author lie in MS. in the library of the Istituto biblico pontificale in Rome." [Minorsky, *BSOS*. viii p. 256.]

No. 102, Descriptions (3), end. *Insert*:

(4) [The chapter on India (English)] *Gardīzī on India. By V. Minorsky* (in *BSOAS*. xii/3–4 (1948) pp. 625–40).

No. 103, 2nd par., MSS. [*Mujmal al-tawārīkh wa-'l-qiṣaṣ.*] Also **Istānbūl** Prof. M. Fuad Köprülü (AH 751/1350. See *Die Welt des Islams* 12 (1930–1) p. 104 and *JRAS*. 1938 p. 563), **Heidelberg** P. 118 (circ. AD 1500. See *Zeitschrift für Semitistik* 6/3 (1928) p. 233). Edition: **Ṭihrān** AHS 1318/1939–40 (ed. Malik al-Shuʿarāʾ "Bahār").

No. 104, 1st par. *For* Niyāltigīn *read* Yināl-tigīn. [Minorsky, *BSOS*. viii/1 (1935) p. 257].—l. 22. *Read* Uchh.

No. 104, 2nd par., MSS. [*Ṭabaqāt i Nāṣirī.*] Also **Leningrad** Asiat. Mus. (a good old MS. See Barthold's article *O nekotorykh vostochnykh rukopisakh* in *Prilozhenie k. prot. X. zasyed. Otd. Istor. Nauk i Fil. Ross. Akad. ot* 17 *Sent.* 1919 *g.*, pp. 923–30. Cf. *Islamica* iii p. 316), **Blochet** iv 2327 (*Ṭabaqahs* xvii–xxii. 17th cent.).

No. 104, penult. par., end. [*Ṭabaqāt i Nāṣirī.*] Russian translation of extracts relating to the Golden Horde: *Sbornik materialov otnosyash-chikhsya k istorii Zolotoi Ordy.* ii:[16] *Izvlecheniya iz persidskikh sochinenii sobrannye V. G. Tizengauzenom i obrahotannye A. A. Romskevichem i S. L. Volinym*, **Leningrad** 1941 (Akademiya Nauk SSSR, Institut Vostokovedeniya), pp. 13–19.

No. 104, last par. [Minhāj Jūzjānī] Also *Ẓafar al-wālih* (in Arabic) by ʿAbd Allāh M. al-Makkī ed. E. D. Ross, London 1910–28 (see index).

No. 104, last par., end. Also *ʿAhd i Shamsī kā ēk muʾarrikh shāʿir*, by Āghā ʿAbd al-Sattār Khān (in *OCM*. xiv/3 (May 1938) pp. 11–24).

No. 105, 2nd par., end. [*Niẓām al-tawārīkh.*] Also **Princeton** 53A (early 14th cent.), **Blochet** iv 2162 (1) (AH 1081/1670).

No. 105, 4th par., end. Another edition: **Ṭihrān** AHS 1313/1931 [Lescot, *B.E.O.I.F. de Damas* vii–viii p. 281].

No. 106, 1st par. [*al-Majmūʿat al-Rashīdīyah.*] For other MSS. see Brockelmann *Sptbd.* ii p. 273.

No. 106, p. 54, penult. *For* ancien fonds, persan 107 *read* **Blochet** iv 2217. Ancien fonds, persan 107 (= Blochet iv 2154) is a volume containing *inter alia* the same

16 Vol. i, containing extracts from Arabic authors, was published by Tiesenhausen (d. 15.2.1902) at St. Petersburg in 1884.

attestations of the orthodoxy of Rashīd al-Dīn's works as occur in de Slane 2324. Cf. Krafft 148.

No. 106, p. 54, bottom. [*Munsha'āt i Rashīdī.*] Edition: *Mukātabāt i Rashīdī,* **Lahore** 1947 (ed. M. Shafīʿ. See the list of abbreviations prefixed to M. Shafīʿ's edition of the *Maṭlaʿ i saʿdain,* vol. ii, pts. 2–3, Lahore 1949). For an account of six of these letters (nos. 12, 29, 43, 34, 52 and 47) see *Letters of Rashīd al-Dīn Faḍlullāh relating to India,* by M. Shafīʿ (in the *Woolner commemoration volume,* Lahore 1940, pp. 236–40). Reasons for doubting the genuineness of the collection have been given by R. Levy in an article entitled *The Letters of Rashīd al-Dīn Faḍl-Allāh* in *JRAS.* 1946 pp. 74–8.

No. 106, 2nd par., MS Blochet i 255. [*Dhail i Jāmiʿ al-tawārīkh.*] Extracts relating to the Golden Horde have been published on the basis of Blochet i 255 and a Leningrad MS. (Institut Vostoko-vedeniya D 66 (a)) with a Russian translation in *Sbornik materialov otnosyashchikhsya k istorii Zolotoi Ordy, II* ... **Leningrad** 1941 (cf. ad no. 104, penult. par., end. *supra*) pp. 243–7 (trans. pp. 139–43).

No. 106, 2nd par., MSS. [*Jāmiʿ al-tawārīkh.* MSS.] Also **Blochet** iv 2279 (most of vol. ii. AH 830/1426/7), 2280 (part of vol. i, viz. the account of the Mongol tribes and of Chingiz Khān's ancestors and the greater part of the life of Chingiz Khān. 16th cent.).

No. 106, 4th par. (1), end. [*Jāmiʿ al-tawārīkh.* Extracts.] *Add:*

(1a) [part of (?) *Faṣl* 1 of *Bāb* 1 of vol. i (on the origin of the Turkish tribes)]. *Das Kudatku Bilik des Jusuf Chass-Hadschib aus Bälasagun. Theil I. Der Text in Transscription herausgegeben von ... W. Radloff.* **St. Petersburg** 1891, pp. xiv–xxviii (Persian text with German translation by C. Salemann).

No. 106, 4th par. (2), end. [*Jāmiʿ al-tawārīkh.* Extracts.] *Insert:*

(2a) Reprint of the bare Persian text from Blochet's edition: **Ṭihrān** AHS 1313/1934–5.

No. 106, 4th par. (1), footnote. For replies to Blochet's condemnation of Berezin's edition see Barthold's review mentioned in no. 106, Descriptions (6) *supra* and Minorsky's remarks in *BSOS.* viii/1 (1935) p. 256.

No. 106, 4th par., end. [*Jāmiʿ al-tawārīkh.* Extracts.] *Insert:*

(7) [the reigns of Abāqā, Tikūdār, Arghūn and Gaikhātū from vol. i, *Bāb* 2] *Taʾrīḫ-i-mubārak-i-Ġāzānī des Rašīd al-Dīn Faḍl Allāh Abī-l-Ḫair.*

Geschichte der Ilḫāne Abāġā bis Gaiḫātū (1265–1295). *Kritische Ausgabe ... von Karl Jahn.* **Prague** 1941 (Abhandlungen der Deutschen Gesellschaft der Wissenschaften und Künste in Prag, phil.-hist. Abteilung, i. Heft).

(8) [The reign of Ghāzān, from vol. i, *Bāb* 2.] *Geschichte Ġāzān-Ḫān's aus dem Ta'rīḫ-i-mubārak-i-Ġāzānī des Rašīd al-Dīn Faḍlallāh ... herausgegeben ... von Karl Jahn.* **London**~1940 (Gibb Memorial, N.S. xiv).

(9) *The account of the Ismāʿīlī doctrines in the* Jāmiʿ al-Tawārīkh *of Rashīd al-Dīn Fadlallāh. By R. Levy* (in JRAS. 1930 pp. 509–36 (Persian text with English translation)).

No. 106, 5th par., end. [*Jāmiʿ al-tawārīkh.* Translations.] *Add:*

(8) [English translation of extracts concerning the Ismāʿīlī doctrines] *The account of the Ismāʿīlī doctrines in the* Jāmiʿ al-Tawārīkh *of Rashīd al-Dīn Faḍlallāh. By R. Levy* (in JRAS. 1930 pp. 509–36. With the Persian text).

(9) [Russian translation of passages relating to the Golden Horde] *Sbornik materialov otnosyashchikhsya k istorii Zolotoi Ordy. II ...* **Leningrad** 1941 (cf. ad no. 104, penult. par., end *supra*) pp. 27–79.

(10) [Russian translation extending from the reign of Hulāgū to that of Ghāzān] *Sbornik letopisei. Tom III.*[17] *Perevod s persidskago A.K. Arendsa, pod redaktsiyei* (†) *A. A. Romaskevicha* [who had the largest share in the work], *E. E. Bertelsa i A. Y. Yakobovskago.* **Leningrad** 1946 (Akademiya Nauk SSSR. 340 pp. The translation, in the preparation of which seven MSS. were consulted, was ready before the war). [Minorsky, in a letter.]

No. 106, last par. [Rashīd al-Dīn.] Also *Durrat al-akhbār* (*takmilah*) pp. 126–30; *Dastūr al-wuzarā'* pp. 315–21.

No. 107, 2nd par., end. [*Zubdat al-tawārīkh.*] For a description see Blochet *Introduction à l'histoire des Mongols* pp. 140–57.

No. 108, end. [Nīkpay's history.] *Insert:*

Extracts relating to the Sāmānids derived from al-ʿUtbī's *Yamīnī: Description topographique et historique de Boukhara par Mohammed Nerchakhy ... Texte persan publié par C. Schefer,* **Paris** 1892°*, pp. 111–22.

17 Vol. i, according to the original plan, was to contain the introduction on the Turkish and Mongol tribes (cf. no. 106, Extracts (1) *supra*), vol. ii the history of Ogedey etc. (= Blochet) and vol. iv a commentary and indexes, but at the moment there is no question of completing the work.

No. 109, 2nd par., MSS. [*Rauḍat ūlī 'l-albāb.*] Also **Tashkent** Univ. 56 (AH 1275/1858–9).

No. 109, 2nd par., MSS. *Delete*: **ʿĀshir** p. 114 no. 254.

No. 109, 2nd par., MSS. Nūr i ʿUthmānīyah 3088 is Maḥmūd al-Ījī's history (see *PL.* no. 266) and should be deleted. [Rypka, *Archiv Orientální* x/1–2 (1938) p. 359.]

No. 110, 2nd par., end. Hindūshāh b. Sanjar completed at Tabrīz in 707/ 1308 the Arabic work *Mawārid al-adab* (for which see Brockelmann ii p. 192, *Sptbd.* ii p. 256). For the scanty autobiographical information obtainable from the *Tajārib al-salaf* see the editor's introduction to the edition and *Dānishmandān i Ādharbāyjān* p. 399. Kīrān (evidently an arabicised form of Gīrān, since the *nisbah* is spelt al-Jīrānī in the preface to the *Mawārid al-adab*) is described in the *Nafthat al-maṣdūr* p. 42 n. and the *Dānishmandān i Ādharbāyjān* p. 399 n. as a town between Tabrīz and Bailaqān. For a place of this name near Iṣfahān see Samʿānī fol. 147*a* (where it is spelt Jairān) and *Tāj al-ʿarūs* iii p. 116, l. 8 *ab infra.*

No. 110. 3rd par., end. [*Tajārib al-salaf.*] Edition: *T. al-s.... taʾlīf i Hindūshāh ... Ṣāḥibī Nakhjuwānī ... bi-taṣḥīḥ u ihtimām i ʿAbbās Iqbāl*, **Ṭihrān** AHS 1313/1934. Extract [life of Niẓām al-Mulk]: *Siasset Namèh ... Texte persan édité par C. Schefer. Supplément*, pp. 1–21.

No. 111 (2), 1st par., MSS. [*Tārīkh i Guzīdah.*] Also **Blochet** iv 2282 (AH 989/1581), **Tashkent** Univ. 59 (defective. 17th cent.). **Leningrad** Asiat. Mus. (at least two in addition to the MS. of 847/1443 mentioned on p. 82: see *Mélanges asiatiques* ii (1852–6) p. 56 (a MS. of 1244/1828), iv (1860–3) p. 54), Pub. Lib. (at least two copies: see *Mélanges asiatiques* iii (1859) p. 727, vi (1873) p. 93), **Caetani** 13 (AH 1296/ 1878).

No. 111 (2), 3rd par. *Delete the entry* (3).

No. 111 (2), 4th par., end. [*Tārīkh i Guzīdah.*] *Add*:

(7) [Russian translation of passages relating to the Golden Horde] *Sbornik materialov....* (cf. ad no. 104, penult. par., end *supra*), ii ... **Leningrad** 1941 pp. 90–8 (Persian text pp. 219–27).

No. 112, 2nd par., MSS. **Ethé** 22 is dated 1127/1715.

No. 112, end. *Insert*:

112*a*. **Abū Bakr al-Quṭbī al-Aharī.**

Tārīkh i Shaikh Uwais, a general history dedicated to Sulṭān Shaikh Uwais, the Jalā'ir, who reigned 756–76/1355–74: **Leyden** v p. 228 no. 2634 (defective. N.d.).

Extracts relating to the Golden Horde: *Sbornik materialov* ... (cf. ad no. 104, penult. par., end *supra*) ii ..., **Leningrad** 1941 pp. 228–31 (Russian translation pp. 99–103).

No. 114, 2nd par., end. [*Firdaus al-tawārīkh.*] *Insert*:

Extract (passage on the Great Lur): *Chèref-Nâmeh ou Fastes de la Nation Kourde ... Traduits ... par F. B. Charmoy* (cf. PL. no. 490, 4th par.) i/2 pp. 328–37.

No. 115, first line. *For* an unknown author *read* **Muʿīn al-Dīn Naṭanzī** (cf. Daulat-Shāh p. 371[15]).

No. 115, 2nd par., beginning. *Read*: (1) ***A general history*** to AH 815/1412 (called by Barthold "The Anonym of Iskandar", but subsequently (in *Comptes-rendus de l'Acad. des Sciences de l'U.R.S.S.*, 1927, pp. 115–16)[18] identified by him as the work of Muʿīn al-Dīn Naṭanzī).

No. 115, end. *Insert*:

Extracts relating to the Golden Horde: *Sbornik materialov* ... (cf. ad no. 104, penult. par., end *supra*) ii ... **Leningrad** 1941 pp. 232–42 (Russian translation pp. 126–38). (2) ***Muntakhab al-tawārīkh i Muʿīnī***, a sketch of general history to the end of Tīmūr's reign presented to Muʿīn al-Dunyā wa-'l-Dīn Abū 'l-Fatḥ Shāh-Rukh Bahādur at Harāt on 22 Rajab 817/1414 and shown by Barthold ("*Yeshche ob anonyme Iskendera*" in *Bulletin de l'Acad. des Sciences de l'U.R.S.S.*, 1929 pp. 165–80) to be virtually identical, apart from the change of dedication,[19] with the "Anonym of Iskandar": **Blochet** iv 2283 (transcribed from an autograph and corrected by the author).

French translation of extracts: *Les exploits d'Emîrzâdé 'Omar Cheikh fils de Timour, à Kachghar, en Ferghana et en Mongolie*, by L. Zimin (in *Revue du Monde Musulman*, 28 (Paris, 1914) pp. 244–58).

---

18 Cf. *BSOS*. viii/1 (1935) p. 256 (Minorsky) and *ZDMG*. 90/2 (1936) pp. 361–3.

19 "... its only difference is that all the passages referring to the former dedicatee Iskandar have been abridged and his title reduced from *ḥaḍrat-i Sulṭān* to *amīr-zāda*" (Minorsky, *BSOS*. viii/1 (1935) p. 257, Cf. Hinz, *ZDMG*. 90/2 (1936) pp. 362–3).

No. 116, beginning. In a passage translated by W. Hinz (ZDMG. 90/2 (1936) pp. 376–7) from the Leningrad MS. (see below) the author calls himself Jaʿfarī b. M. al-Ḥusainī and uses "Jaʿfarī" as his *takhalluṣ*.

No. 116, end. [*Tārīkh i Jaʿfarī*.] Also **Leningrad** Pub. Lib., Pers. nov. ser. 201 (defective at both ends. 16th cent. See W. Barthold's article *Novy istochnik po istorii Timuridov* in *Zapiski Instituta Vostokovedeniya* v (Leningrad 1936) pp. 5–42 and W. Hinz's summary of the article in ZDMG. 90/2 (1936) pp. 373–98).

No. 117 (2) (*f*) For the spelling of the name Kart see no. 467, 1st footnote.

No. 117, 1st par., footnote. For other MSS. see K. Bayānī's preface to his edition of the *Dhail i Jāmiʿ al-tawārīkh*.

No. 117 (2), MSS. [*Majmūʿah i Ḥāfiẓ i Abrū*.] Also **Blochet** iv 2284 (apparently the *Dhail i Jāmiʿ al-tawārīkh*, the history of the Muẓaffarids, the *Ẓafar-nāmah* and the *Dhail i kitāb i Ẓafarnāmah*. Circ. AD 1530. Mistakenly described by Blochet as the last part of the *Zubdat al-tawārīkh*).

No. 117 (2), end. [*Majmūʿah i Ḥāfiẓ i Abrū*.] *Insert*:

Edition of 2(*h*): *Dhail i Jāmiʿ al-tawārīkh i Rashīdī taʾlīf i Shihāb al-Dīn ʿAbd Allāh ... al-madʿū bi-Ḥāfiẓ i Abrū ... Bakhsh i nukhustīn* [pt. 2 is the French translation] *bā muqaddamah u ḥawāshī u taʿlīqāt i Duktur Khān-Bābā Bayānī*. **Ṭihrān** 1317/1939‡.

Translation of the years 703–58/1303–57[20] from 2 (*h*): *Ḥâfiz-i Abrû. Chronique des Rois Mongols en Iran. Texte persan édité et traduit par K. Bayani ...* II. *Traduction et notes.* **Paris** 1936‡ (reviewed by Minorsky in BSOS. ix/1 (1937) pp. 235–6).

Edition of 2(*k*): *Continuation du Ẓafarnāma de Niẓāmuddīn Šāmī par Ḥāfiẓ-i Abrū éditée d'après les manuscrits de Stamboul par Felix Tauer* (in *Archiv Orientální*, vi (**Prague** 1934) pp. 429–65).

No. 117 (3), 1st par., MSS., end. [*Majmaʿ al-tawārīkh*.] Majlis 257 contains *Rubʿ* ii. For some other MSS. see K. Bayānī's preface to his edition of the *Dhail i Jāmiʿ al-tawārīkh* pp. *lām-alif-tā*.

No. 117 (3), 2nd par., end. [*Majmaʿ al-tawārīkh*. Extracts.] *Add*:

20 The first date expressly mentioned in the narrative (p. 14[16]) is 706.

(2) *Safar-nāmah i Chīn sanah 1419* [*ʿĪsawī*] *tā sanah 1422* [*ʿĪsawī*] *yaʿnī maḍmūn u muḥaṣṣal i rūz-nāmchah i Khwājah Ghiyāth al-Dīn i naqqāsh īlchī i Bāysunghur Mīrzā b. Shāh-Rukh ... kih Ḥāfiẓ i Abrū dar Zubdat al-tawārīkh darj numūdah* [edited with notes and index by M. Shafīʿ] (in the *Oriental College Magazine*, vol. vii, no. 1 (Lahore, Nov. 1930), pp. 1–66).

(3) *A Persian embassy to China; being an extract from Zubdatu't Tawarikh of Hafiz Abru. Translated* [and edited] *by K. M. Maitra.* **Lahore** 1934*.

No. 117 (3) 3rd par., end. [*Majmaʿ al-tawārīkh*. Descriptions.] *Add*:
(4) Barthold *Turkestan*, London 1928, pp. 55–6.

No. 117 (3), last par. The Persian text of the passage in the *Mujmal i Faṣīḥī* is quoted in Rosen Institut p. 325.

No. 118, end. [*Tārīkh i khairāt.*] Cf. W. Hinz, ZDMG. 90/2 (1936) pp. 363–5.

No. 119, 1st par. *Read* Būndēlk'haṇḍ.

No. 119, 1st par. For Yūsuf Bud'h (if that is the correct spelling) see *Sawāṭiʿ al-anwār* (Ethé col. 332); *Gulzār i abrār* no. 160; *Khazīnat al-aṣfiyāʾ* i pp. 383–4; Raḥmān ʿAlī p. 256; Rieu, iii p. 1079*a*; Bānkīpūr xvi p. 49; etc.

No. 120, first line. *Read either* **Khwāfī** *without the article or* **al-Khawāfī**, *that being the Arabic form of the word.*

No. 121, 2nd par., MSS. [*Jāmiʿ al-tawārīkh i Ḥasanī.*] Also **Ṭihrān** National Lib. (AH 880/1475–6. See p. 5 of Mahdī Bayānī's introduction to his edition of the *Badāʾiʿ al-azmān*).

No. 122, 1st par. *Read* 861/1456–7.

No. 122, 1st par., end. For a MS. of the *Manhaj* (so?) *al-rashād* see Leyden iv p. 299 no. 2110.

No. 123, 1st par. For Burhān al-Dīn Khāwand-Shāh see *Haft iqlīm* no. 1494.

No. 123, 1st par. According to *Ḥabīb al-siyar* iii, 3, p. 339[16], Mīr Khwānd died on 2 Dhī Qaʿdah 903. Rajab seems to be a slip of Rieu's.

No. 123, 2nd par., MSS, **Browne**, end: 14. *Read* Naudhar.

No. 123, 2nd par. (7). [*Rauḍat al-ṣafāʾ*.] The *khātimah* was written in 900/1494–5 according to a statement ("in most copies") at the end of the article on Khwārazm (Rieu iii p. 1079*b*). Other MSS.: **Princeton** 462 (vol. i AH 909/1503–4), 463–7 (three more copies of vol. i and two of vol. iii), 55 (vol. vi), **Tashkent Univ.** 62 (AH 977/1569), **Aumer** 202 (*Khātimah*. AH 994/1586), **Bānkīpūr** Suppt. i 1745 (vol. iv. AH 997/1588–9), **Blochet** iv 2286–90, etc. No. 123, 2nd par., MSS, **Browne**, end:

Read Naudhar.

No. 123, 3rd par. *Read* 1265–6 *instead of* 1266 *and* 1853–7° *instead of* 1853–6°. "2 vols." is doubtless correct as regards the B. M. and I.O. copies, but the ten unpaginated *jilds* are separable and are not always bound in two.

No. 123, 4th par. (8). [*Rauḍat al-ṣafāʾ*.] The extract published by Mitscherlich in 1814 relates to the kings of Nīmrūz, the descendants of Ṭāhir b. M. b. Ṭāhir b. Khalaf. [A. G. Ellis, orally.]

No. 123, 4th par. (15). [*Mirchondi Historia Seldschukidarum*.] In the Cambridge University Library there is another issue published at Giessen in 1838 (in libraria J. Rickeri) identical with the previous issue except for the title-page. [J. D. Pearson, in a letter.]

No. 123, 7th par., end. [*Rauḍat al-ṣafāʾ*.] For an Eastern-Turkish translation made by M. Yūsuf, called al-Rājī, b. Qāḍī Khwājam-birdī al-Khuwārazmī in the reign of Abū 'l-Ghāzī M. Amīn Khwārazm-Shāh (AH 1261–71/1845–55) see *Mélanges asiatiques* vii (St. Petersburg 1876) p. 411.

No. 123, Translations of extracts, footnote. Amberes = Antwerp.

No. 123, 8th par., no. (13). For the meaning of "the Ṭāhirids" in this case see above, ad no. 123, 4th par. (8).

No. 123, last par. [Mīr Khwānd.] Also *Laṭāʾif-nāmah* pp. 159–60.

No. 124, 2nd par. Read 887/1482.

No. 125, 1st par., end. [Khwānd-Amīr.] According to the *Sanawāt al-atqiyā'*, fol. 282*a*, he died in 946.

No. 125, 2nd par., end. The India Office MS. is D.P. 435B.

No. 125 (2), MSS.[*Khulāṣat al-akhbār.*] Also **Caetani** 10, **Leningrad** Mus. Asiat. (see *Mélanges asiatiques* ii (St. Petersburg 1852–6) p. 57).

No. 125 (3), beginning. [*Ḥabīb al-siyar.*] See Rieu iii 1079*b*: "In an appendix found in some copies only, and quoted at length in Mir'āt i Jahān-numā, fol. 345, Khwānd-Amīr records his journey to India, AH 934, and his introduction to Bābar, AH 935. He adds that he accompanied the emperor on his expedition to Bengal, working on the road, as circumstances and his enfeebled health would allow, at his great history, and that he completed the work (or its final revision) at a place near the confluence of the Siru with Ganges (in the month of Sha'bān, AH 935; see Bābar's Memoirs, p. 411). A translation of the main part of that appendix is to be found in Elliot's History of India, vol. iv, pp. 143, 155."

No. 125 (3), MS **Lindesiana** nos. 809–11. *Read* 1063/1652–3.

No. 125 (3), MSS. [*Ḥabīb al-siyar.*] Also **Blochet** iv 2291 (complete. AH 1010/1601–2), **Princeton** 56 (*Iftitāḥ* and vol. i. 18th cent.).

No. 125 (3), Editions. According to Dorn (*Mélanges asiatiques* vi (St. Petersburg 1873) p. 119) the Ṭihrān edition omits "mehrere gerade für Russland interessante Capitel".

No. 125 (3), Extracts, end.[*Ḥabīb al-siyar.*] *Insert*:

(10) [Life of Niẓām al-Mulk] *Siasset Naméh ... Texte persan édité par C. Schefer ... supplément*, pp. 22–48.

(11) *Rijāl i kitāb i Ḥabīb al-siyar az ḥamlah i Mughūl tā marg i Shāh Ismā'īl i Awwal*, **Ṭihrān** AHS 1324/1945–6 (ed. 'Abd al-Ḥusain Nawā'ī. Supplement to the periodical *Yādgār*, Year 1. Cf. *Oriens* iii/2 (1950) p. 330).

No. 125 (3), Translations of extracts, (14). Cf L. Bouvat *L'empire mongol* (*2ème phase*), Paris 1927, p. 163 n. 2: "La notice de Sultân Hoseïn Baykara occupe les pp. 239–283 du t. iii de Khondémir; M. H. Ferté en a traduit la premiere partie, allant jusqu'à la page 254 ..."

No. 125, last par. [Khwānd-Amīr.] Also *Laṭā'if-nāmah*) p. 157; *Akbarnāmah* i p. 120, Beveridge's trans. i p. 281.

No. 126. 'Abd al-Karīm al-Namīdīhī is doubtless identical with the author whose name Horn spells 'Abd al-Karīm Namīdahī and whose work *Kanz al-ma'ānī* is preserved at Istānbūl in the 'Āshir Efendī Library (no. 884. See Horn *Pers. Hss.* p. 501 no. 952).

No. 127, 1st par., end. [Faiḍ Allāh Banbānī.] For further information about him and his works, which include the *Majma' al-nawādir* completed in 903/1497–8, see an Urdu article entitled *Majma' al-nawādir* by M. Iqbāl in OCM. xv/4 (Aug. 1939) pp. 98–106. Cf. Brockelmann *Sptbd.* ii p. 610.

No. 127 2nd par., MSS., **Rieu**, first reference. *Read* 86 *b*.

No. 129, 1st par. For Naqīb Khān see no. 135, 1st footnote.

No. 129. 2nd par., MSS. [*Lubb al-tawārīkh.*] Also **Ellis Coll.** M. 244 (AH 967/1559–60), M. 245 (defective. 17th cent.), **Vatican** Pers. 16 (AH 986/1578. Rossi p. 42), **Blochet** iv 2177 (2) (18th cent.).

No. 129, 2nd par., end. Vatican 48 = Vatican Pers. 16 (AH 986/1578. Rossi p. 42). *Insert*:

Editions: (1) **Bombay** 1302/1884 (264 pp. See Fahmi Edhem Karatay *Istanbul Üniversitesi Kütüphanesi Farsça Basmalar Katalogu* p. 192). (2) [**Ṭihrān**] AHS 1314/1936 ‡ (ed. S. Jalāl al-Dīn Ṭihrānī. 264 pp.).

No. 129, 5th par., end. *Insert*:

French translation: **Paris** Bibl. Nat. fonds français 19027 (see Blochet iv 2177).

No. 129, 7th par. *For* 134 *read* 129–34.

No. 130, 2nd par., MSS. [*Tārīkh i Ibrāhīmī.*] Also **Leningrad** Mus. Asiat. (see Semenov *Ukazatel'* p. 30).

No. 130, end. *Insert*:

130*a*. A history entitled *Takmilat al-akhbār*, of which no MSS. seem to be recorded in the published catalogues of libraries, is cited several times as an authority in the *Dānishmandān i Ādharbāyjān*, on p. 76 of which it is said to have been composed in 997 [*sic*, but read 967/1559] and dedicated to Shāh Ṭahmāsp's daughter Parī Khān Khānum by Khwājah 'Alī mulaqqab bah Zain al-'Ābidīn ma'rūf bah 'Abdī Bēg b. 'Abd al-Mu'min Ṣadr al-Dīn Shīrāzī, who at first used "Nuwīdī" and later "'Abdī" as his *takhalluṣ*. [P.S. Of this history, a general history to 967/1559 with a section on the Ṣafawīs, there is a MS., defective at the end, in the possession of Prof. B. N. Zakhoder according to his statement on p. 7 of his translation of Qāḍī Aḥmad's "*Traktat o kalligrafakh i khudozhnikakh*" [cf. no. 1431 *supra*]. V. Minorsky, in a letter.]

No. 131, 2nd par., MS **Āṣafīya**. *Read* no. 1330 (portion only).

No. 131, 2nd par., end. *For* 133 *read* 134 *b*.

No. 131, end. [Khwur-Shāh b. Qubād.] Also *Ency. Isl.* under Niẓām-Shāhī (Minorsky).

No. 132 (1), MSS. MS. I.O. 3939 is dated 1074/1664.

No. 132 (1), MSS. [*Nigāristān*.] Also **Madras** 319 (AH 1015/1606), **Ellis Coll.** M. 120 (AH 1043/1633), **Oxford** Ind. Inst. MS. Whinfield 48 (AH 1070/1659), **Heidelberg** P. 222 (AH 1102/1690. PICTURES. See *ZDMG*. 91/2 (1937) p. 376), **Blochet** iv 2292 (late 17th cent.), **Tashkent Univ.** 39 (AH 1274/1857–8), **Ivanow** 1st Suppt. 776 (AH 1300/ 1883?).

No. 132 (2), 1st par.,. MS. **I.O.** D.P. *Read* 999/1591.

No. 132 (2), 1st par., end. [*Nusakh i jahān-ārā*.] *Insert*:

Text and Russian translation of passages relating to the Golden Horde: *Sbornik materialov* ... (cf. ad no. 104, penult. par., end *supra*) II ... **Leningrad** 1941, pp. 269–71, 210–12.

No. 132, 3rd par., end. Also (3) Elliot *Bibliographical index* pp. 136–8.

No. 132 (2), last par. [Aḥmad Ghaffārī.] Also *Safīnah i Khwushgū* ii no. 204; *Makhzan al-gharā'ib* no. 205; *Tadhkirah i khwushnawīsān* pp. 82–3.

No. 133, last par. [Muṣliḥ al-Dīn Lārī.] Also Ḥasan Rūmlū xii p. 454, Seddon's trans. p. 197; *Tārīkh i Ma'ṣūmī* p. 204; Brockelmann *Sptbd.* ii p. 620.

No. 134, end. *Insert*:

134*a*. **ʿAbd Allāh Kābulī.** ***Tadhkirat al-tawārīkh***, written in 990/1582: **Bukhārā** Semenov 46.

No. 135, 1st footnote, 2nd par. [Naqīb Khān.] Also *Ṭabaqāt i Akbarī* ii p. 450: *Iqbāl-nāmah* pp. 75–6.

No. 135, 2nd footnote, end. [Fatḥ Allāh Shīrāzī.] Also *Maʾāthir al-umarāʾ*, Beveridge's trans. pp. 543–6.—3rd footnote *Delete the word* Mīr.—3rd footnote, end. [Ḥakīm Humām.] Also *Haft iqlīm* no. 1219; *Maʾāthir al-umarāʾ* i pp. 563–5.—4th footnote, end. [Ḥakīm ʿAlī Gīlānī] Also *Haft iqlīm* no. 1214; *Maʾāthir al-umarāʾ* i pp. 568–73, Beveridge's trans. pp. 180–4; Brockelmann *Sptbd.* ii p. 626.—8th footnote, end. [Aḥmad Tattawī.] Also *Muntakhab al-tawārīkh* iii pp. 168–9.

No. 135, 1st par., footnote 65, 2nd par. [Āṣaf Khān (Jaʿfar Bēg).] Also *Tadhkirah i Naṣrābādī* pp. 53–5; *Maʾāthir al-umarāʾ*, Beveridge's trans. pp. 282–7.

No. 135, 2nd par., MSS. [*Tārīkh i alfī*.] Also **Bombay** Univ. 93 (from Riḥlat 505 to a little after Shāh Ṭahmāsp's death), **Madras** 286 (AH 501–840. N.d.). See also *Discovery of a portion* [how much is not stated, but the pages reproduced deal with Ma'mūn, Muʿtaṣim and Wāthiq] *of the original illustrated manuscript* ["in large folio size" with "magnificent miniatures on each leaf"] *of the Tarikh-i-alfi written for the Emperor Akbar* (*in the collection of Mr. Ajit Ghose, Calcutta*), by M. Maḥfūẓ al-Ḥaqq (in *Islamic culture* v/3 (July 1931) pp. 462–71, with reproductions of two pages).

No. 135, 5th par., first line. Read *al-ghuṣaṣ*.

No. 136, 3rd par., end ["Wuqūʿī."] Also *Nafāʾis al-maʾāthir* (Sprenger p. 54); *Haft iqlīm* no. 763. There seems to have been some confusion between M. Sharīf "Wuqūʿī" Nīshāpūrī and "Wuqūʿī" Tabrīzī [see *Nafāʾis al-maʾāthir* (Sprenger p. 54), *Haft iqlīm* no. 1346, *Dānishmandān i Ādharbāyjān* pp. 394–5]. *Insert*:

136*a*. Sh. **Kabīr b. Munawwar Lāhaurī**, a scholar of Akbar's reign, accompanied Murtaḍā Khān (Sh. Farīd Bukhārī. d. 1025/1616) to the siege of Kāngrah in 1025/1616 and died at Aḥmadābād in 1026/1617 or 1027/1618 [Badāʾūnī iii p. 106; *Ṭabaqāt i Shāh-Jahānī; Mirʾāt al-ʿālam; Āʾīn i Akbarī* tr. Blochmann p. 547; Rieu iii p. 1097*a*].

Tārīkh i Murtaḍā 'l-dahr, a (general?) history composed in 1006/1597–8: **Rieu** iii 1037*b* (extracts only. Circ. AD 1850).

No. 137, 1st par., end. [Ṭāhir M. Sabzawārī.] For abridged paraphrases of the *Mahābharata* and of two other Sanskrit works made by him at Akbar's request see Rieu iii 1043*a*, Ethé 1955.

No. 137, 2nd par., end. [*Rauḍat al-ṭāhirīn.*] Also **I.O.** 4588 (defective. AH 1131/1719. See *JRAS.* 1939 p. 374), **Bānkīpūr** Suppt. i 1749 (defective. 18th cent.) 1748 (AH 1228/1813).

No. 138, last par., end. [Ḥasan Bēg Khākī.] Also *Akbar-nāmah* iii p. 834; *Makhzan al-gharā'ib* no. 721.

No. 140, 3rd par., end. [*Tārīkh i Ḥaidarī.*] *Add*:

(3) [Passages relating to the Golden Horde] *Sbornik materialov* ... (cf. ad no. 104, penult. par., end *supra*) ii ... **Leningrad** 1941 pp. 272–4 (Russian trans. pp. 213–15).

No. 142, 2nd par., beginning. [*Ṣubḥ i ṣādiq.*] *For* ten centuries *read* eleven centuries.

No. 142, 2nd par., MSS. Also **'Alīgaṛh** Subḥ. MSS. p. 57 no. 10 (vol. ii. AH 1159/1746), **Vatican** Pers. 93–7 (vols. ii–iii. AH 1196/1782. Rossi p. 109)

No. 143, last par. *Tadhkirah i Ṭāhir i Naṣrābādī* p. 64 in the Ṭihrān edition (his father, M. Ṣāliḥ, p. 452).

No. 145, 2nd par. The *Mīzān al-ḥaqq* is in Turkish, not Arabic.

No. 145, 3rd par., MSS. [*Taqwīm al-tawārīkh.*] Also **Blochet** iv 2293 (mid 17th cent.).

No. 146, end. [*Afṣaḥ al-akhbār.*] Also **Rieu** iii 1017*b* (extracts only. Circ. AD 1850).

No. 147, end. *Insert*:

147*a*. **M. Afḍal Ḥusainī.** ***Zubdat al-tawārīkh*** (beg. *Ba'd az sp. u st. i Parwardgār i 'ālamiyān u durūd i nā-ma'dūd i ḥaḍrat i Saiyid al-Mursalīn*), a concise general history, including a detailed account of the Ṣafawīs, to AH 1063/1652, similar in contents and arrangement to the *Z. al-t.* of Kamāl Khān[21] [and possibly a plagiarism]: **Bānkīpūr** Suppt. i 1750 (19th cent.).

147*b*. **M. Barārī** Ummī b. M. Jamshēd b. Jabbārī Khān b. Majnūn Khān Qāqshāl is the author of a scientific encyclopaedia entitled *ʿUqūl i ʿasharah,* which he completed in 1084/1673–4 (see Bānkīpūr ix 914, Berlin 97, Bodleian 1495, Būhār 222, Flügel i 27, Ivanow 1500 (2), Ivanow Curzon 485, Lindesiana p. 193 no. 714). His great-grandfather and his grandfather were both grandees of Akbar's time (see *Āʾīn i Akbarī* tr. Blochmann pp. 369–70, *Maʾāthīr al-umarāʾ* iii pp. 207–11).

Mujmal i mufaṣṣal, a concise general history to AH 1037/ 1628 (Shāh-Jahān's accession), transcribed from the original drafts in 1065/1655 (according to a statement near the beginning of Ivanow 43) but not completed apparently until 1079/1668, since that is given as the date of the second volume (on the Persian and Indian Tīmūrids): **Bodleian** 101 (defective at beginning and concluding with AH 1020/1611. Identified by Ivanow), 242 (vol. ii only. AH 1079/1668 (?), apparently autograph), **Ivanow** 43 AH 1100/1688–9, transcribed for the author), **Madras** i 317 (AH 1171/1757–8).

No. 149, first sentence, end. M. Yūsuf "Wālih" was subsequently appointed to the *wizārat i sarkār i tūp-khānah i mubārakah.*

No. 149, 2nd par., end. [*Khuld i barīn.*] *Insert*:

Extract (Shāh Ṣafī's reign from the sixth year onwards): *Dhail i Tārīkh i ʿĀlam-ārāy i ʿAbbāsī taʾlīf i Iskandar Bēg Turkmān ... u M. Yūsuf i muʾarrikh ba-taṣḥīḥ i Suhailī i Khwānsārī,* **Tihrān** AHS 1317/1938–9 (Iskandar Bēg's account of Shāh Ṣafī's first five years (see *PL.* no. 391) followed (p. 146[8]) by the narrative of the remainder of the reign from the *Khuld i barīn* on the basis of a MS. in the Kitāb-khānah i Millī i Malik. Cf. *BSOS.* x/2 (1940) p. 540).

No. 149, last par., end. [M. Yūsuf "Wālih."] Also *Tadhkirah i Naṣrābādī* i p. 82.

No. 151 (2), MSS. [*Mirʾāt al-ʿālam.*] Also **Bānkīpūr** Suppt. i 1751 (19th cent.).

No. 151 (2), 1st par., end.[*Mirʾāt al-ʿālam.*] *Insert*:

21 The opening words of Kamāl Khān's work are *Baʿd az ḥamd u thanā-yi P. u d. i bī-pāyān bar Aḥmad i Mukhtār.*

Extracts (lives of calligraphists, painters, etc.): OCM. x/4 (Aug. 1934) pp. 33–65 (ed. M. Shafīʿ). Description etc. by Maulawī Ṣiddīq Ḥusain: OCM. v/1 (Nov. 1928) pp. 7–8.

No. 151 (3) (*a*), MSS. [*Mirʾāt i jahān-numā.*] Also **Ellis Coll.** M. 259 (AH 1142/1729–30).

No. 151 (3) (*b*), 2nd par., end. [*Mirʾāt i jahān-numā.*] Another description: OCM. v/1 (Nov. 1928) pp. 8–22 (an article by Maulawī Ṣiddīq Ḥusain).

No. 158, 2nd par., MSS. [*Jannāt al-firdaus.*] Also **Ellis Coll.** M. 246 (with a continuation to AH 1244/1828–9 by Tajammul Ḥusain. Early 19th cent.).

No. 161, 2nd par. [*Tārīkh i Qipchāq-Khānī.*] See also Validov *O sobr. rkp. v Bukh. khan.* pp. 258–9.

No. 162, beginning. M. Muḥsin calls himself *Mustaufī i sarkār i faiḍ- āthār*, which may perhaps mean that he was *Mustaufī* of the estates of the Mashhad sanctuary (see Minorsky's commentary to the *Tadhkirat al-mulūk*, p. 146). "It may be added that Muḥammad Muḥsin in his *Zubdat al-tavarīkh* (f. 205*b*) states that in 1132/1720 he was in attendance on the Nāẓir of the Cathedral Mosque of Mashhad and enjoyed the rank of vazīr ʿ in the same department' ..." (Minorsky, *ibid.*).

No. 164, beginning. *Read* **M. ʿAlī** b. M. Ṣādiq Ḥusainī Nīshāpūrī Najafī **Burhānpūrī**.

No. 164, 6th par., MSS. [*Mirʾāt al-ṣafāʾ.*] Also **Ellis Coll.** M. 258 (AH 1176/1762–3, apparently autograph).

No. 164, 6th par., end. *Read* **Āṣafīyah** iii.

No. 164, last par. The *Tārīkh i rāḥat-afzā*, a history of the Tīmūrids from 736/1335–6 to 1173/1759–60, the date of compilation, was published in 1947 at Ḥaidarābād (Deccan) with an Urdu preface by S. Khwurshēd ʿAlī. [J. D. Pearson, in a letter.]

No. 165, 2nd, 3rd, and 4th par. [*Tuḥfat al-kirām.*] See the amended account of this work in no. 828 (1).

No. 166, 2nd par., MSS. [*Jām i jahān-numā.*] Also **Bānkīpūr** Suppt. i 1752–3 (AH 1018 [*sic*! Read 1180?]. Described as autograph).

No. 168, 1st par. *Read* 1182/1768–9.

No. 168, 2nd par., MSS. [*Farḥat al-nāẓirīn.*] Also **Kapūrt'halah** 35 (see *OCM*. iii/4 (Aug. 1927) p. 16).

No. 169, 1st par. *Read*: and the *Muntakhab al-tawārīkh* of Ḥasan Bēg Khākī (see no. 138 2nd par. *supra*) very deficient.

No. 169, 2nd par., MSS. [*Tārīkh i Muḥammadī.*] If Rieu's statement that the author completed this work in 1190 is based only on the fact that the necrologies in the B.M. MS. end with that year, it should not be accepted without further evidence. In I.O. 3980 the necrologies extend to 1208. Doubtless the copyists or owners of different MSS. continued the series of dates to their own times.

No. 169, 2nd par., MSS. [*Tārīkh i Muḥammadī.*] I.O. 3889 and 3890 contain only the necrologies. I.O. 3980 contains only the preface and the necrologies from 1150 to 1208.

No. 170, beginning. [M. b. Muʿtamad Khān.] See also the autobiography of his cousin "Āshōb" (MS.: I.O. 4034) fol. 14*b*.

No. 170, 2nd par. **Rehatsek** p. 99 no. 52 (*Risālah i Kaptān Jōnātan* [*sic*] *dar aḥwāl i Farang* "composed AH 1211") seems to be a later version of Jonathan Scott's account of Europe.

No. 171, 1st par. Mavī = MWY, the vocalisation being conjectural.

No. 171, 2nd par., MSS. [*Jām i jahān-numā.*] Also **Rieu** iii 1051*a* (extracts only).

No. 172, 2nd par., end. *Read*: **I.O.** 3994 (reigns of Farrukh-siyar, Rafīʿ al-Darajāt etc. and M. Shāh., probably from the *B. al-m.*[22] AD 1891), 3983 (Nādir Shāh and Aḥmad Shāh Durrānī. AD 1895), 3883 (reigns of Aḥmad Shāh and ʿĀlamgīr II, probably from the *B. al-m.* 18th cent.).

22 So far as Indian Tīmūrid history is concerned the *B. al-m.* and the *Tārīkh i Muẓaffarī* (cf. *PL*. no. 688) are practically identical (see Bānkīpūr vii p. 108, l. 5 *ab infra*).

No. 173, last par. [*Khulāṣat al-afkār.*] The preface and *khātimah* are summarized in *JRAS*. 1848 pp. 154–7.

No. 173, last par. [Abū Ṭālib Khān.] Also *Dānishmandān i Ādharbāyjān* pp. 243–4.

No. 174, 1st and 2nd par. "*Ardalān* is a better form for *Ardilān* (p. 146), in spite of the *E.I.*" (Minorsky, *BSOS*. viii/1 (1935) p. 257[17]).

No. 175, beginning. *Read* **Dihlawī.**

No. 175, 2nd par., MSS. [*Mir'āt i āftāb-numā.*] Also **Bodleian** 121 (n.d.), **Ellis Coll.** M. 373 (early 19th cent.).

No. 177, beginning. ["Bandah" Tabrīzī.] Although apparently his name is written Riḍā (رضا) in the B.M. MS. Rieu i 135 (cf. Browne Coll. G. 16 and Majlis 258, but not Rieu Suppt. 39), the biographers seem to be unanimous in calling him Mīrzā (M.) Raḍī.

No. 177, last par., end. ["Bandah" Tabrīzī.] Also *Tadhkirah i Muḥammad-Shāhī* (Rieu Suppt. 124) fol. 183*a*; *Rauḍat al-ṣafā-yi Nāṣirī* vol. ix, eleventh page from end; *Dānishmandān i Ādhar- bāyjān* pp. 70–1; Berthels *Ocherk istorii persidskoi literatury* p. 82.

No. 180, beginning. Ṭabāṭabā, not Ṭabāṭabā'ī, seems to be the form preferred by M. Riḍā himself.

No. 180 (1), MSS. [*Zubdat al-gharā'ib.*] Also **Ellis Coll.** M. 280 (vol. i. AH 1238/1823).

No. 184, 1st par. Mirzā Jahāngir and Mirzā Bābur were sons of M. Akbar Shāh (cf. Blumhardt's *Catalogue of Hindustani MSS. in the ... India Office* p. 93); *Read* Hamīrpūr *with undotted h.*

No. 184, end. *Insert:*

184*a*. Faiḍ i Ḥaqq Chishtī Qādirī, known as (*'urf*) **M. Faiḍ Allāh** Munshī, entitled (*mukhāṭab*) **Faḍl i 'Alī Khān Ṣiddīqī Āṣaf-Jāhī** has already been mentioned (*PL.* i no. 1037) as the author of histories entitled *Waqā'i' i Dakan* and *Gauhar i shāhwār*.

Khizānah i Rasūl-Khānī, a general history to AH 1251/ 1835, the date of completion, with a special history of the Quṭb-Shāhs and Niẓāms, dedicated to Nawwāb Ghulām-Rasūl Khān: **Bānkīpūr** Suppt. i 1755 (AH 1296/1879).

No. 186 should follow no. 188.

No. 186, last par. There is a portrait of T. W. Beale in the possession of the Royal Asiatic Society of Bengal (see *JASB*. 1925 p. xcvi).

No. 188, beginning.. M. Ṣādiq "Akhtar" i.e. doubtless M. Ṣ. "A." Hūglawī, for whom see no. 940.

No. 188, end. *Insert*:

188*a*. Rājah **Kundan Lāl "Ashkī"** b. Mannūn Lāl "Falsafī" Dihlawī was the author of an encyclopædia entitled *Nuzhat al-nāẓirīn* (Lindesiana p. 172), of the *Zīj i Ashkī* composed in 1231/1816 (Āṣafīyah i p. 814) and of the Arabic work *al-Qisṭās* composed at Delhi in 1237/1821–2 at the age of twenty-four[23] (Brockelmann *Sptbd.* iii p. 1312, Zubaid Aḥmad *The contribution of India to Arabic literature* p. 383).

Muntakhab i Tanqīḥ al-akhbār,[24] "historical tables" (general or Indian?): Sulṭān al-maṭābiʿ [**Lucknow**?[25]] 1267/1851*.

No. 189, last line. *Read* 1853–7°. For a description of the *Rauḍat al-ṣafā-yi Nāṣirī* see *A traveller's narrative written to illustrate the episode of the Bâb, edited ... and translated ... by E. G. Browne*, ii (Cambridge 1891) pp. 188–92.

No. 190, 1st par. [S. Ilāhī Bakhsh.] An account of this author and his *Kh. i j-n.* is given in an appendix to M. ʿĀbid ʿAlī Khān's *Memoirs of Gaur and Pandua*, Calcutta 1931 (cf. *JRAS*. 1933 pp. 169–71).

---

23 If he was twenty-four in 1237, he must have been only eighteen in 1231, the date given for the composition of his *Zīj*.

24 For a volume of a work entitled *Tanqīḥ al-akhbār* see no. 193 (*a*) (12). A work of that title is ascribed to Rājah Kundan Lāl in the Urdu dictionary *Jāmiʿ al- lughāt* (under Kundan Laʿl).

25 For a Sulṭān al-maṭābiʿ at Lucknow see Arberry pp. 288, 452 and 518.

No. 191, 1st par., end. M. Taqī "Sipihr" died on 17 Rabīʿ ii 1297 [29 March 1880] according to *al-Maʾāthir wa-'l-āthār* p. 188*a*, l. 2.

No. 191, 2nd par. [*Nāsikh al-tawārīkh*.] The words "published (originally, it appears) in 14 volumes" should be deleted. According to the volumes preserved in the Cambridge University Library (about which information has kindly been supplied by Mr. J. D. Pearson) and the descriptions in the Mashhad catalogue (vol. iii, *fṣl.* 14, nos. 193–207, where, however, nothing is said about a division into *kitābs* and a continuous numeration is given to the *jilds*) the work is divided as follows:—

Kitāb I (from Ādam to the Hijrah) in two *jilds* ((1) *"kih maʿrūf ast ba-Hubūṭ"* (M[26]), to the birth of Christ, **Ṭihrān** 1273/1857 (C,[27] probably also BM.), 1285/1868–9 (*Ency. Isl.* under Sipihr), 1306/1888–9 (M., Ā[28]), 1321/1903 (C), (2) to the Hijrah, **Ṭihrān** [1860? °], 1285/1868–9 (*Ency. Isl.* under Sipihr), 1310/1892–3 (Ā), 1320/1902 (C), published also, it seems, in two parts (a) *"mashhūr ba-Aḥwālāt i ḥaḍrat i ʿĪsā"* (M), 2nd ed. **Ṭihrān** 1303/1885–6 (M), (b) *"kih mutaʿalliq ast ba-tārīkh i ḥaḍrat i khatmī-martabat"* (M), i.e. Muḥammad's life [to the Hijrah presumably], 2nd ed. **Ṭihrān** 1301/1883–4 (M).

Kitāb II, from the Hijrah to the author's time, but only the following *jilds* seem to have been published, (1) [called vol.[29] 3 in M] Muḥammad, from the Hijrah to his death, 1st ed. **Ṭihrān** 1285/1868–9 (M), 1310/1892–3 (Ā) 1314/ 1896–7 (C), (2) ["vol. 4", M] the first three Caliphs, **Ṭihrān** 1280/1863–4 ("1st ed.", M), 1305/1888 (date of index. C), 1306/1888–9 (identical with the preceding? Ā), (3) ["vol. 5", M] ʿAlī, n.d.? (Ā), 1319/1901–2 (C), 1323/1905–6 (M), (4) ["vol. 6", M) Fāṭimah, 1308/1890–1 (Ā); 1319/1901 (C); **Tabrīz** 1320/1902–3 (M), (5) ["vol. 7", M] Ḥasan, **Ṭihrān** 1302/1884–5 (M), 1309/1891–2 (C), (6) ["vol. 8", M] Ḥusain, place? 1307/1889–90 (Ā), **Bombay** 1309/1892 (M, C (?)), (7) ["vol. 9", M] Zain al-ʿĀbidīn, pt. 1,[30] **"Persia"** 1313/1895–6 (Āṣafīyah iii p. 110 no. 1530, where a copy (apparently of this volume) is called *N. al-t.* (*takmilah*), *jild i awwal* and ʿAbbās-Qulī Khān is given (incorrectly?) as the author), **Qafqāz** 1324/1906 (M), (8) ["vol. 10", or *Mishkāt al-adab i Nāṣirī*, M] Zain al-ʿĀbidīn, pt. 2, composed in 1304/1886–7, by ʿAbbās-Qulī Khān (cf. PL. no. 309), **Ṭihrān** 1316/1898–9

26 M = Mashhad catalogue.

27 Cambridge University Library.

28 A = Āṣafīyah catalogue.

29 The letter *jīm*, apparently an abbreviation for *jild*, rather than *juzʾ* in this catalogue.

30 According to the Mashhad catalogue, iii, *fṣl.* 14, ptd. bks., p. 41, M. Taqī "Sipihr" wrote eight (complete) volumes of the *N. al-t.* and half of the biography of Zain al-ʿĀbidīn.

(M), **"Persia"** 1322/1904 (Āṣafīyah iii p. 110 no. 1530, where this volume (apparently) is called *N. al-t.* (*takmilah*), *jild i duwum*), (9) ["vol. 11", M] Bāqir, pt. 1, composed (in 1315 according to Āṣafīyah cat.) by ʿAbbās-Qulī Khān, **Ṭihrān** 1315/1897–8 '(M), **"Persia"** 1318/1900–1 (Āṣafīyah iii p. 110 no. 1532, where this volume (apparently) is called *N. al-t.* (*takmilah*) *jild i awwal*), (10) ["vol. 12", M] Bāqir, pt. 2, compiled (by ʿAbbāṣ-Qulī Khān) in 1324 (so M)[31] under the superintendence (*ba-ihtimām*) of ʿAin al-Daulah, **Majlis** 563 (*"N. al-t. Mutammim i jild i duwum i aḥwāl i … M. Bāqir."* 338 foll.). Edition: **Ṭihrān** 1324/1906 (M. Cf. Āṣafīyah iii p. 110 no. 1533, where this volume is called *N. al-t.* (*takmilah*), *jild i duwum*, and ʿAbbās-Qulī Khān is given as the author. Cf. *PL.* i no. 309), together with the *Tārīkh i Qājārīyah* (*"az mujalladāt i N. al-t."*) in three *jilds* (1) the early Qājārs to Fatḥ-ʿAlī Shāh, (2) Muḥammad Shāh, (3) Nāṣir al-Dīn Shāh, **Ṭihrān** 1273/1856–7 (C. Only *Jild* 1 has this date: the other *jilds* have copyists' names but no date), 1304/1886–7 (C, A), 1315/1897–8 (M, C), **Tabrīz** 1319/1901–2 (M, C. Date in all three vols. Cf. *PL.* i no. 441).

No. 191, last par., end. (M. Taqī "Sipihr".] Also *al-Maʾāthir wa-'l-āthār* pp. 187–8.

No. 192, last par., end. [Iʿtimād al-Salṭanah.] Also Browne *The Persian revolution* p. 405; *Dānishmandān i Ādharbāyjān* pp. 43–5; *Tārīkh i jarāʾid* i pp. 311–12. Portraits in Feuvrier *Trois ans à la cour de Perse*, Paris [circ. 1894?], pp. 49, 80.

No. 193 (*a*) (3), end. *Insert*:

(3*a*) ***Khulāṣat al-tawārīkh***, by M. b. Yūsuf Miftāḥ al-Mulk: **Ṭihrān** 1325/1907. [R. Lescot, *B.E.O.I.F. de Damas*, vii–viii, p. 281].

No. 193 (*a*) (9), end. *Insert*:

(9*a*) ***Muntakhab al-tawārīkh i Muẓaffarī***, by Ibrāhīm Khān Ṣadīq [Ṣiddīq?] al-Mamālik: **Ṭihrān** 1323/1905 [R. Lescot, *ibid.*]. [P.S. See an article by Jahāngīr Qāʾimmaqāmī in *Yādgār* IV/1–2 (1947) pp. 19–34.]

No. 193 (*a*) (10), end. *Insert*:

(10*a*) ***Rāḥat al-qulūb***, a sketch of general history, with a special history of Bengal to 1207/1792–3, the date of composition, by M. Rāḥat: **Bānkīpūr** Suppt. i 1754 (AD 1840).

31 At the end of Majlis 563 the author gives 1323 as the date of the completion of the *baqīyah i jild i duwum i aḥwāl i … M. Bāqir.*

(10*b*) ***Rāḥat al-qulūb***, by Faiḍ Allāh Khān: **Lindesiana** p. 136 no 420 (AH 1134–40/1721–8).

No. 193 (*a*) (11), end. [*Subḥat al-akhyār.*] Also **Philadelphia** Lewis Coll. 37.

No. 193 (*a*) (13), end. *Insert*:

(13*a*) ***Tārīkh i 'umūmī dar qarn i hafdahum u hizhdahum***, by Naṣr Allāh Khān "Falsafī":[32] **Ṭihrān** AHS 1316/1937–8 [R. Lescot, *B.E.O.I.F. de Damas* vii–viii, p. 281].

(13*b*) ***Tārīkh i 'umūmī dar qarn i nūzdahum u bīstum***, by the same: **Ṭihrān** AHS 1310/1931–2 [R. Lescot, *ibid.*].

(13*c*) ***Tārīkh i 'umūmī i qurūn i wusṭā***, by 'Abd al-Ḥusain Shaibānī, 3 vols. **Ṭihrān** AHS 1312–15/1933–7*. [R. Lescot, *ibid.*].

No. 193 (*a*) (14), end. The date is 1329–43 according to Harrassowitz's *Bücher-Katalog* 430 no. 933.

No. 193 (*c*) (1), end. [Ethé 120.] **Bānkīpūr** Suppt. i 1747 (17th cent.) seems to be another copy.

No. 197, 2nd par., end. *Read* **Āṣafīyah** ii p. 880 no. 55; also **Edinburgh** New Coll. p. 7.

No. 198, 1st par., last line. [*al- Bashāghirī.*] This *nisbah*, used of a different person, is spelt Pashāghirī in *Rashaḥāt* p. 215 (*az qaryah i PSHĀGHR būdah and kih dīhī buzurg ast az wilāyat i Samarqand miyān i sharq u shamāl u az-ānjā tā shahr duwāzdah farsang ast*).

No. 198, 2nd par., end. [*Kashf al-ghawāmiḍ.* Al-Ṣābūnī's abridgment.] A MS. at Cairo (Catalogue, 2nd ed., v p. 265) is mentioned by Brockelmann (*Sptbd.* ii p. 262).

No. 199, 2nd par., MSS. [*Maqāṣid al-auliyā'.*] "Opus ... Sultanoe gente Selgukidarum 'Abû-l-Muzaffer ... dedicatum est" (Mehren); **Decourdemanche** S.P. 1852 = **Blochet** iv 2295 (late 17th cent.). Another MS.: **'Alīgaṛh** Subḥ. MSS. p. 60 no. 19 (old).

---

32 b. Ṭihrān a.h. 1319/1901–2 (see Ishaque *Modern Persian poetry* pp. 12, 31; Īraj Afshār *Nathr i Fārsī i mu'āṣir* pp. 225–31 (portrait)). Cf. ad no. 405 (4) *infra*.

No. 201, 2nd par., MSS. [*Zarātusht-nāmah.*] Also **Bombay** Univ. p. 331 (AY 1164/1794–5), **Brelvi-Dhabhar** p. xxix no. 16.

No. 202, beginning. For Abū 'l-Ḥasan b. al-Haiṣam al-Būshanjī see Brockelmann *Sptbd.* i p. 592, probably also *Haft iqlīm* no. 616.

No. 202, 2nd par. M. b. Asʿad b. ʿAbd Allāh al-Ḥanafī al-Tustarī, an author of Ūljāytū's time, wrote an abridgment of the *Jawāmiʿ al-ḥikāyāt* (*Muntakhab i Jāmiʿ* [*sic*] *al-ḥikāyāt*, as Khwānd-Amīr calls it) in 723/1323 (MS. (?): Vatican Pers. 71 (2) = Rossi p. 94). See *Tārīkh i Guzīdah* p. 811; *Ḥabīb al-siyar* iii, 1, p. 113; Niẓām al-Dīn *Introduction to the Jawámiʿu 'l-Ḥikáyát* pp. 31[19], 123[20]; H. W. Duda *Ferhād und Schīrīn* p. 180.

No. 202, 2nd par. *Read* J. 21 (12).

No. 202, 2nd par., end. [al-Būshanjī's *Qiṣaṣ al-anbiyā'*.] *Insert*:
Extract: *A parallel to the story in the Mathnawí of Jalálu 'd-Dín Rúmí, of the Jewish king who persecuted the Christians. By E. G. Browne* (in *Islamica* ii/1 (Leipzig 1926) pp. 129–34).

No. 202, 2nd par. [***Tārīkh i Mūsawī***]. Other quasititles are *Qiṣṣah i Mūsā* and *Mūsā-nāmah*.

No. 203, last line. *Read* **Madras** i 299, 300, 531.

No. 205, (1), MSS. [*Mir'āt al-quds.*] Also **Vatican** Pers. 48 (defective. 18th cent. Rossi p. 75).

No. 205, (2), MSS. [*Dāstān i aḥwāl i Ḥawāriyān.*] Also **Vatican** Pers. 81 (17th cent. Rossi p. 99).

No. 211 (*a*) (4), end. *Insert*:
(4*a*) ***Anīs al-murīdīn wa-shams al-majālis***, an account of Joseph in fourteen *majālis* incorrectly ascribed to the celebrated ʿAbd Allāh Anṣārī of Harāt, who died in 481/ 1088 (see *Ency. Isl.* under Anṣārī, Brockelmann i 433, *Rauḍāt al-jannāt* 450, *Haft iqlīm*, no. 619, *Safīnat al-auliyā'* p. 165 (no. 300) and the authorities cited in the *Ency. Isl.* and in *J.R.A.S.*, 1929, p. 105): Ḥ.Kh. i, no. 1339, **Ethé** 1778 (AH 1013/1605), **Browne** Coll. D. 7 (modern). For a discussion of the authorship see *A prose version of the Yūsuf and Zulaikha*

legend, ascribed to Pīr-i Anṣār of Harāt. By Reuben Levy (in J.R.A.S., 1929, pp. 103–6).

No. 211 (a) (34). [*Qiṣaṣ al-anbiyā'*.] MSS.: **I.O.** D.P. 698A (AH 1063/1651), 698B, 698C, 700.

No. 211 (*a*) (41), end.. *Insert*:

(41*a*) ***Qiṣṣah i Yūsuf***, in 57 chapters: **Blochet** i 395 (lacking preface and Ch. i–ix. AH 898/1492).

(41*b*) ***Qiṣṣah i Yūsuf***, by Qāḍī S.... 'Alī Amīr-al-Zamānī: **Blochet** iv 2125 (*Majālis* 4–38 with lacunæ. 15th cent.).

No. 211 (*a*) (42). [*Tadhkirat al-anbiyā'*, by Ghulām-Muḥammad.] Possibly also **Rehatsek** p. 190 (n.d.).

No. 211 (*b*) (1), end. *Insert*:

(2) History of Alexander the Great in prose: **Blochet** iv 2374 (AH 1115/1704).

No. 212, 3rd par., MSS. [*Tarjamah i Siyar al-Nabī*.] Also **'Alīgaṛh** Subḥ. MSS. p. 61 nos. 33–5 (AH 985/1577–8).

No. 213, 1st par. *For* in al-Ruṣāfah *read* or al-Ruṣāfah. "According to Le Strange, *Baghdad during the Abbasid Caliphate*, p. 189, the two were identical" [R. Levy, JRAS. 1936 p. 524].

No. 215 (2), MSS. [*Tarjamah i Shamā'il al-Nabī*, completed in 988.] Also **Manchester** Rylands Lib. no. 133.

No. 215 (5), end.. [*Shamā'il al-Nabī*.] *Insert*:

(6) By "'Allāmah Niẓām al-Dīn": **Āṣafīyah** iii p. 270 no. 967 (extending to the *Bāb al-kuḥl*).

(7) Verse translation dedicated to Akbar by Ḥāfiẓ [M. b. Bāqir] Harawī, who wrote also a Persian prose translation entitled *Khaṣā'il*: **Princeton** 58 (17th cent.).

No. 216 (3). [*Sharaf al-Nabī*.] See Niẓámu'd-Dīn *Introduction to the Jawámi'u 'l-Ḥikáyāt*, G.M.S., London, 1929, p. 87, where it is pointed out that Rieu Arabic Suppt. 509 lacks nearly half of the ninety chapters and that Blochet i 371 contains only sixty-one of them.

No. 216 (3), MSS. [*Tarjamah i Sharaf al-Nabī.*] For Blochet i 371 see the preceding note.

No. 217, last par. Abu Bakr b. M. Bharūchī is the author of a Persian translation of *al-Ḥiṣn al-ḥaṣīn* (Brockelmann ii p. 203, *Sptbd.* ii, p. 277) completed in 910/1505 for Sulṭān Maḥmūd Shāh [Bēgarah] of Gujrāt (MSS.: Ethé 2641, Ivanow 992).

No. 217, last par., end.[*al-Shifā'*]. *Insert*:
Commentary by Shihāb Efendī: **Āṣafīyah** iii p. 270 no. 932.

No. 218, beginning. [*al-Ṭabarsī.*] The common pronunciation and the usual explanation (that the word is equivalent to Ṭabaristānī or Ṭabarī) appear to be incorrect, since according to his contemporary 'Alī b. Zaid al-Baihaqī (*Tārīkh i Baihaq*, p. 242) al-Faḍl b. al-Ḥasan came originally from ṬBRS (apparently like Ṭabrish (*Tārīkh i Qum* pp. 78, 117, etc.) an Arabicised form of Tafrish, for according to Baihaqī ṬBRS is *manzilī miyān i Qāshān u Iṣfahān*) and the correct pronunciation would therefore seem to be Ṭabrasī or Ṭabrisī (see Aḥmad Bahmanyār's discussion of the word in his edition of the *Tārīkh i Baihaq*, pp. 347–53).

No. 218 (3), MSS. [*Tarjamah i Makārim al-akhlāq*, completed in 1064.] Also **Bānkīpūr** xiv 1219, **Ivanow** 2nd Suppt. 1021.

No. 218 (4), end. *Add*:
(5) [*Tarjamah i*] *Makārim al-akhlāq*, probably one of those already mentioned: **Lindesiana** p. 109 no. 680 (AH 1180/1766–7).

No. 218, end. *Insert*:

218*a*. Quṭb al-Dīn Abū 'l-Ḥasan **Sa'īd b. Hibat Allāh al-Rāwandī** died in 573/1177–8.
***al-Kharā'ij wa-'l-jarā'iḥ**, fī 'l-mu'jizāt* (in Arabic), on the miracles of Muḥammad and the Imāms (see I.Ḥ. 1046, Brockelmann *Sptbd.* i p. 624).
Persian translation: ***Kifāyat al-mu'minīn***, by M. Sharīf al-Khādim: **Āṣafīyah** iii p. 662.

No. 219, beginning. For 'Abd al-Salām al-Andarasfānī see Brockelmann *Sptbd.* i p. 624.

No. 219, 3rd par. For biographies of Kamāl al-Dīn Khwārazmī see *PL*. nos. 1284, 1287, 1288. Cf. *Laṭā'if-nāmah* p. 17; *Majālis al-mu'minīn* pp. 321–9.

No. 219, last par., MSS. [*al-Maqṣad al-aqṣā.*] Also **Heidelberg** P. 434 (16th cent. See *Zts.f. Semit.* x/1–2 (1935) p. 85).

No. 222, 4th par., end. [*Surūr al-maḥzūn.*] MSS.: **Princeton** 60 (AH 1256/1840), **'Alīgaṛh** Subḥ. MSS. p. 60 no. 14.

No. 223, 1st par., end. [Sa'īd al-Kāzarūnī.] For other works by him see Brockelmann *Sptbd.* ii p. 262.

No. 223, beginning. [Sa'īd al-Kāzarūnī.] Also *Haft iqlīm* p. 209 (no. 166).

No. 224, 2nd par., beginning. [*Sufar al-sa'ādah.*] The authority for vocalizing *Sufar* with *ḍammah* is Gotha 33, dated 884, in which the *sīn* is repeatedly so vocalized.

No. 224, 2nd par., MSS.[*Sufar al-sa'ādah.*] Also **Princeton** 81 (AH 1261/ 1845), 82 (extracts. 18th cent.).

No. 224, 4th par., MSS. [*Sufar al-sa'ādah.* Arabic trans.] For other MSS. and editions see Brockelmann *Sptbd.* ii p. 235.

No. 224, 6th par., *The words* (corrected by the author himself) *should be deleted.*

No. 225 (3), line 5. *Read* 8th/14th century.

No. 225, 3rd par. [Ḥasan b. Ḥusain Sabzawārī] *Delete the words in square brackets.* By Blochet the dedicatee is described, no doubt correctly, as "l'un des souverains sarbédarides du Khorasan, Nizam ed-Din Yahya ibn Shams ed-Din Khadjè Karabi,[33] qui regna de 753 à 759 de l'hégire (1352–1358 ..."). Ḥasan Sabzawārī must therefore have been an author of the 8th/14th century.

No. 225, 3rd par., MSS. [*Rāḥat al-arwāḥ.*] Also **Blochet** iv 2296 (AH 930/1523–4), **Ivanow** 2nd Suppt. 1041 (2) (AH 1125/1713).

33 *Sic*, but Karrāb *bar wazn i ḍarrāb* is, or was, a village three parasangs from Khusraujird (see *Tārīkh i Baihaq*, ed. Bahmanyār, p. 343).

No. 225, 4th par. [*Bahjat al-mabāhij.*] *Read* 578A. I.O.D.P. 578B (*sic lege*) breaks off in the *faṣl* on al-Bāqir.

No. 228, beginning. *Read*: S. **Muḥammad b.... Jaʿfar ... Makkī.**

No. 228. last par.[M. b. Jaʿfar Makkī.] Also *Akhbār al-akhyār* pp. 136–41.

No. 230, 2nd par., MSS. [*al-Tuḥfat al-Salāmīyah.*] Also **Āṣafīyah** iii p. 380 no. 184 (AH 1252/1836–7).

No. 232, 2nd par., MSS. [*Bayān i ḥaqāʾiq i aḥwāl i Saiyid al-Mursālīn.*] Also Sprenger 296 (A.S.B.), **Leningrad** Univ. 1175c (*Miṣbāḥ al-a.* only. Romaskewicz p. 14), 1198 (*F. al-a.* only. Romaskewicz p. 11), **Majlis** ii 1135 (1) (*F. al-a.* only. Late 15th cent.), 1132 (1) (*F. al-a.* AH 1235/1820), 1132 (2) (fragment of *F. al-a.* AH 1252/1836–7).

No. 232, last par.[Pīr Jamāl.] Also Ilāhī (Sprenger p. 74); *Ātash- kadah* no. 362; *Riyāḍ al-ʿārifīn*, 2nd ed., pp. 85–91.

No. 234, 2nd par., MSS. [*Shawāhid al-nubuwwah.*] Also **Blochet** iii 1676 (AH 895/1490, from an autograph), iv 2300 (3) (AH 968/ 1561), **Browne** Coll. B. 4 (before AH 970/1562–3), **Princeton** 85 (16th cent.), **Lahore** Panjāb Univ. (AH 1010/1601–2 (?). See *OCM*. viii/3 (May 1932) p. 142), ʿ**Alīgaṛh** Subḥ. MSS. p. 15 no. 69, p. 16 no. 80, **Ivanow** 612 (1).

No. 234, 3rd par. *Read* **Bombay** 1288/1872 (see Karatay p. 36).

No. 234, 3rd par., end. [*Shawāhid al-nubuwwah.*] *Insert*: Description: Browne *Lit. Hist.* iii p. 513.

No. 235 (1), MSS. [*Maʿārij al-nubuwwah.*] Also **Tashkent Univ.** 13 (AH 896/1490–1, from an autograph), **Blochet** iv 2298 (*Rukns* iii–iv and *Khātimah.* Early 16th cent.) **Berlin** 545 (AH 998/1589–90), 546, 547 (*Muqaddimah* and *Rukns* i–ii. AH 1066/1655), **Ellis Coll.** M. 286 (AH 1004/1596), M. 285, ʿ**Alīgaṛh** Subḥ. MSS. p. 59 nos. 2–3, p. 61 no. 31.

No. 235, 4th par., MSS. [*Dalāʾil i nubuwwat.*] Also **Lindesiana** p. 259 no. 112, **Upsala** 310.

No. 236 (1), beginning. [*Rauḍat al-aḥbāb.*] Ethé's account of the divisions of this work has been provisionally accepted here and the contents of other MSS. have been described in accordance therewith, but possibly a further examination of good old MSS. might lead to some modification of Ethé's statements.

No. 236 (1), MSS. [*Rauḍat al-aḥbāb.*] Also **Blochet** iv 2300 (1) (*Maqṣad* i only. AH 968/1561), 2299 (16th cent.), **Vatican** Pers. 111 (*Maqṣad* ii. AH 977/1569. Rossi p. 120), **ʿAlīgaṛh** Subḥ. MSS. p. 57 no. 5 (AH 999/1590–1), p. 56 no. 4, **Brelvi and Dhabhar** p. 62 no. 1 (*Maqṣad* i. AH 1084/ 1673–4).

No. 236 (1), Turkish translation. [*Rauḍat al-aḥbāb.* Turkish trans.] MS.: **Heidelberg** T 417 (see *Zts. f. Semit.* x/1–2 (1935) p. 84).

No. 236, last par., end. [Jamāl al-Ḥusainī.] Also *Ḥadāʾiq al-Ḥanafīyah* pp. 368–9; Brockelmann *Sptbd.* ii p. 262.

No. 240, first line. The word Ganāʾī (or Kanāʾī, whichever is the correct spelling) is explained as meaning *nawīsandah* in the *Wāqiʿāt i Kashmīr* p. 66 (cf. p. 143).

No. 240. last par. Read: *Muntakhab al-tawārīkh* iii pp. 142–9, 259–60, 403[6].

No. 240. last par. Read: *Wāqiʿāt i Kashmīr* pp. 110–11.

No. 240. last par. [Yaʿqūb "Ṣarfī".] Also *Āʾīn i Akbarī* p. 250, Blochmann's trans. pp. 581–2; *Ḥadāʾiq al-Ḥanafīyah* p. 394.

No. 241, beginning. [*Maṭāliʿ al-anwār.*] It is pointed out by Sh. ʿAbd al-Qādir i Sarfarāz (Bombay Univ. cat. p. 18) that the *M. al-a.* was one of the works used by M. Bihāmad-Khānī for his *Tārīkh i Muḥammadī* (cf. no. 119 *supra*) and must therefore have been composed before 842/1438–9. That it is later than 700/1300–1 seems to be shown by a reference to Ṣighnāqī's commentary on the *Hidāyah* (Brockelmann i p. 377[21], *Sptbd.* i, p. 644, l. 9 *ab infra*), which occurs on fol. 90*a* in the I.O. MS. D.P. 741.

No. 241, 2nd par., first line. Full title: *Maṭāliʿ al-anwār fī tarjamat al-āthār.*

No. 241, 2nd par., MSS. [*Maṭāliʿ al-anwār.*] Also **Lahore** Panjāb Univ. (AH 1011/1602–3. See *OCM.* viii/3 (May 1932) p. 142), **Bombay** Univ. p. 18 (AH 1210/1796).

No. 241, 2nd par., MS. I.O. D.P. *Read* 1122/1710.

No. 243, beginning. 'A bd al-Ḥaqq Dihlawī seems usually to call himself 'A al-Ḥ. b. S. al-D. al-Turk [not al-Turkī] al-Dihlawī al-Bukhārī, but in a note appended to his commentary on the *Mishkāt*, (Rieu i p. 14*b*) he calls himself 'A. al-Ḥ. b. S. al-D. al-Dihlawī *waṭan*^{an} al-Bukhārī, *aṣl*^{an} al-Turkī *nasab*^{an}.

No. 243, 2nd par., MSS. [*Madārij al-nubuwwah.*] Also **Princeton** 84 (extracts only).

No. 243, 3rd par. *For* [**Lucknow?**] *read* [**Madrās**].

No. 243, 4th par. ['Abd al-Ḥaqq Dihlawī] The *Ḥilyah* (beg. *Bi-smi 'llāh wa-'l-ḥ. l. 'alā jūdihi.* Other MSS.: **Rieu** ii 863*b*, **I.O.** D.P. 654A) was extracted by the author from the *Madārij al-nubuwwah* just after its completion. The (*Ādāb i libās i Rasūl*) (beg. *Ba'd i ḥ. u st. i Ilāhī*) appears to be independent. Other MSS.: **Ivanow** 1st Suppt. 923 (3) (late 18th cent.), **Bānkīpūr** Suppt. ii 2169 (19th cent.).

No. 243, last par., beginning. 'Abd al-Ḥaqq Dihlawī's list of his works has been published also by Hidāyat Ḥusain in *JASB*. xxii (1926) pp. 43–60. Another MS.: **Āṣafīyah** iii p. 34.

No. 243, last par., end. ['Abd al-Ḥaqq Dihlawī] Also *Ṭabaqāt i Akbarī* ii p. 464; *Gulzār i abrār* no. 571; *Tūzuk i Jahāngīrī* p. 282, l. 5 *ab infra*, English trans. ii p. Ill; *'Amal i Ṣāliḥ* iii pp. 384–5; *Muntakhab al-lubāb* i pp. 239–40, ii p. 551; *Safīnah i Khwushgū* no. 321; *Subḥat al-marjān* pp. 52–3; Elliot *Bibliographical index* pp. 273–6; *Ḥadā'iq al-Ḥanafīyah* p. 409; Brockelmann *Sptbd.* ii p. 603.

No. 246, 3rd par. ["Masīḥ" Kairānawī] Also *Kalimāt al-shu'arā'* (Sprenger p. 114); *Safīnah i Khwushgū* no. 688.

No. 247, 1st par., antepenult. The *Zād al-ma'ād* is classed among M. Bāqir's Persian works, though the actual prayers are in Arabic.

No. 247, 1st par., end.[List of M. Bāqir's works,] Also **Ivanow** 2nd Suppt. 1039 and probably **'Alīgaṛh** Subḥ. MSS. p. 3.

No. 247 (1), MSS. [*Ḥayāt al-qulūb.*] **I.O.** D.P. 632B contains vol. ii, only.

No. 247 (1). MSS. [*Ḥayāt al-qulūb.*] Also **Edinburgh** New Coll. p. 7.

No. 247 (1), end. *Insert*:

Continuation: *Ṣaḥīfat al-muttaqīn wa-manhaj al-yaqīn* (*dar dhikr i imāmat takmilah i Ḥ. al-q.*), by Raḍī al-Dīn M. b. M. Naṣīr birādar-zādah i ʿAllāmah i Majlisī: I.Ḥ. 2060 (where the author is called M. Raḍī b. M. N. al-Majlisī and the work is stated to have been composed in the reign of Shāh Sulṭān-Ḥusain), **Āṣafīyah** iii p. 380 no. 261 (AH 1212/1797–8).

No. 247 (2), first line. **Jalā'** should probably be read rather than **Jilā'**.

No. 247 (2), MSS. [*Jalā' al-ʿuyūn*.] Also **Bānkīpūr** Suppt. i 1758 (damaged. AH 1107/1696), **ʿAlīgaṛh** Subḥ. MSS. p. 59 no. 1.

No. 247 (3), end. [M. Bāqir Majlisī.] Also *al-Faiḍ al-qudsī fī aḥwāl al-Majlisī*, a detailed biography (in Arabic apparently) by Ḥusain Nūrī Tabarsī (19th century: see Brockelmann ii p. 832), which according to Majlis ii p. 53 n. 2 has been printed at the beginning of the *Biḥār al-anwār*; Brockelmann *Sptbd.* ii pp. 572–4.

No. 248, end. [Ḥakīm M. Kāẓim.] Also Zubaid Aḥmad *The contribution of India to Arabic literature* p. 386.

No. 249, first line. *Read* Qinnaujī; last line 1st par. *Read* Qinnauj.

No. 250, 2nd par., MSS. [*Ḥamlah i Ḥaidarī*.] Also **ʿAlīgaṛh** Subḥ. MSS. p. 39 no. 22 (AH 1137/1724–5), p. 57 no. 7, **I.O.** D.P. 631 (with Najaf's continuation).

No. 250, 2nd par. MSS., **Ross and Browne**. *Read* 175.

No. 250, 3rd par., Editions. According to Sprenger the *Ḥamlah i Ḥaidarī* was "lithographed at Lucnow, AH 1268, 2 vols. folio 238 and 329 pp. of 50 bayts". The 1267 edition has 238 and 333 pages. It is without any continuation.

No. 250, last par. ["Bādhil."] Also *Maʾāthir al-umarā'* iii p. 940; Sprenger no 153; *Nujūm al-samā'* p. 220.

No. 250, end. *Insert*:

250*a*. **ʿAbd al-Aḥad** b. M. Saʿīd b. Aḥmad **Sirhindī** died in 1142/1729–30. He was a grandson of the celebrated saint Aḥmad Sirhindī (for whom see *PL.* no. 1316

(1), 1st footnote). His father, Sh. M. Saʿīd, surnamed Khāzin al-raḥmah, was born in 1005/1597 (see *Ḥaḍarāt al-quds*, I.O. D.P. 630, fol. 99*a*) and died in 1070/1659–60 (see *Khazīnat al-aṣfiyā'* i 639, where he is called Aḥmad Saʿīd).

Khazā'in i nubuwwat[34] (a chronogram = 1126/1714), a short biography of Muḥammad: **I.O.** D.P. 636 (18th cent.).

[*Khazīnat al-aṣfiyā'* i p. 662.]

No. 253, 1st par.The bracket after Tīmūrids should be a comma.

No. 256. For ʿAbd al-Raḥīm Ṣafīpūrī's works see Brockelmann *Sptbd.* ii p. 853.

No. 256, end. *Insert*:

Mīr **ʿAlī** b. Ḥāfiẓ M. ʿAlī **Riḍawī Dihlawī.**

Mā'idah i pur-thimār tarjamah i Nuzul al-abrār, "biographical notes concerning the Prophet and the Shīʿite Imāms," being a translation made in 1252/1836–7 of the *N. al-a.* ["by Abu-Ṭālib al-Makkī † 386 [AD 996]," according to the Princeton catalogue, possibly the anonymous work of this title which was published at [Bombay] in [1880] and which is described in Ellis ii p. 447 as "biographies of the Caliph ʿAlī, his wife Fāṭimah and his two sons al-Ḥasan and al-Ḥusain"], to which the translator has added a concluding chapter on the Twelve Imāms based on Jāmī's *Shawāhid al-nubuwwah*: **Princeton** 61 (AH 1280/1863).

No. 257, last par. [ʿAlī Akbar "Bismil".] Also *Madā'iḥ al-Muʿtamadīyah* (Rieu Suppt. 127) fol. 57*a*; *Riyāḍ al-ʿārifīn* pp. 423–4; *Ṭarā'iq al-ḥaqā'iq* iii p. 156.

No. 259, last par. [Farhād Mīrzā.] Also *Majmaʿ al-fuṣaḥā'* i pp. 46–52; *al-Ma'āthir wa-'l-āthār* p. 195; Rieu Suppt. p. 221; Berthels *Ocherk istorii persidskoi literatury* pp. 102–3.

No. 260 (*a*) (5), end. *Insert*:

(5*a*) ***Jām i gītī-numā***, a metrical account of the Prophet's expeditions, by M. b. Ismāʿīl Khwānsārī. Edition: **Ṭihrān** 1303/1885–6 (Āṣafīyah iii p. 100).

No. 260 (*a*) (7), end *Insert*:

34 *Khazā'in al-nubuwwat* in the MS., but the title is said to be a chronogram and in this form it would give a date later than the author's death.

(7*a*) ***Kunūz al-rumūz***, on the merits and exploits of Muḥammad in forty *maqāmahs*, by Ḥusām b. M. al-Mashshāṭī: **Gotha** 4 (2) (AH 889/1484).

(7*b*) ***Laṭā'if al-akhbār fī siyar al-Mukhtār***, by Sh. Ibrāhīm b. Ismā'īl Tattawī: **Āṣafīyah** iii p. 380 no. 275 (Pt. I only).

No. 260 (*a*) (15), end *Insert*:

(15*a*) ***Mi'rāj-nāmah***: **Ivanow** 1st Suppt. 837 (1) (AH 1134/1722).

(15*b*) ***Mi'rāj-nāmah*** (beg. *'Aun mī-khwāhad dilam az Khāliq i Jān-āfrīn*), metrical, by a certain "'Aṭṭār": **Blochet** ii 1050 (4).

No. 260 (*a*) (16), end *Insert*:

(16*a*) ***Mu'jizāt i Ān-Ḥaḍrat ṣl'm muntakhab az kutub i siyar***, by S. Nūr 'Alī al-mukhāṭab bah Qudrat-Jang b. Qādir al-Daulah Bahādur: **Āṣafīyah** iii p. 380.

No. 260 (*a*) (22). *Read*: (22) ***Nathr al-jawāhir***, a translation by S. 'Alīm Allāh b. 'Atīq Allāh Ḥusainī Jāland'harī[35] (d. 1202/1787–8) of the Arabic *Naẓm al-durar wa-'l-marjān* (cf. Bānkīpūr Arab. cat. xv 1033, Āṣafīyah ii p. 874, Brockelmann *Sptbd.* ii p. 603), a, life of Muḥammad completed in 1091/1680 by Auḥad al-Dīn Mīrzā Jān (or Khān) Brkī Jāland'harī. Edition: **Lahore** 1902°.

No. 260 (*a*) (23). *Read*: ***Naẓm al-durar wa-'l-marjān***.

No. 260 (*a*) (24), end. *Insert*:

(24*a*) ***Nūr-nāmah***: **Bānkīpūr** xvii 1660 (*Aṣl* vii only, on the Mi'rāj. 1127 *Faṣlī*).

(24*b*) ***Risālāh dar bayān i khilqat i Nūr i Muḥammadī***: **Āṣafīyah** iii p. 380.

No. 260 (*a*) (27), end. *Insert*:

(27*a*) ***Shamā'il-nāmah***; **Blochet** iv 2219 (19th cent.).

(27*b*) ***Shamā'il-nāmah***, metrical: **Āṣafīyah** iii p. 380 no. 191 (AH 1277/1860–1).

No. 260 (*a*) (32), end. *Insert*:

(32*a*) ***Taṣwīr i balāghat*** (*ḥilyat al-Nabī*), by Nawwāb 'Azīz-Jang (for whom see no. 1045). Edition: place? 1340/ 1921–2 (Āṣafīyah iii p. 380).

(32*b*) ***Tawallud-nāmah***: **Ivanow** 1st Spt. 837 (2) (AH 1134/1722).

No. 260 (*a*) (33). *Read* 1847°, [1869*], 1877*.

---

35 I.e. of "Jullundur" in the Panjāb. According to *Khazīnat al-aṣfiyā'* i p. 505 and Raḥmān 'Alī p. 147 he was a disciple of Shāh Abū 'l-Ma'ālī and a *khalīfah* of S. Bhīk'h.

No. 260 (*a*) (34), end. *Insert*:

(35) ***Wasīlat al-faqīr sharḥ asmā' al-Rasūl al-Bashīr***, by M. Hāshim b. [ʿAbd?] al-Ghafūr Sind'hī: **Āṣafīyah** iii p. 380.

No. 260 (*b*) (2). Delete these lines. See no. 231, 2nd par..

No. 260 (*b*) (4), end. *Insert*:

(4) Work on the Prophet's birth in 9 sections: **Blochet** iv 2350 (15th cent.).

No. 261. [Ibn Aʿtham.] Cf. Brockelmann *Sptbd.* i p. 220. According to the Mashhad cat., iii, *fṣl.* 14, MSS. no. 11, the *Futūḥ* was composed in 204/819–20.

No. 261, 2nd par., first line. M. b. Aḥmad b. Abī Naṣr b. Aḥmad al Mustaufī al-mulaqqab al-Raḍī al-Kātib according to the preface of Browne Coll. G. 1 (1).

No. 261, 2nd par., antepenult. [al-Mābarnābādī.] For Mābīzhanābād (spelling and vocalization uncertain, but zh, not r, seems to be correct) see *Tārīkh i jahan-gushā-yi Juwainī* ii p. 134^{19}, with Qazwīnī's note, and *Tatimmat Ṣiwān al-ḥikmah*, Arabic text, ed. M. Shafīʿ, p. 158^{4}. It was evidently near Khwāf.

No. 261, 3rd par., MSS. [*Futūḥ i Ibn i Aʿtham.*] Also **Browne** Coll. G. 1 (1) (defective at both ends and extending to ʿUthman's murder), G. 1 (2) (from ʿUthmān's murder to al-Ḥusain's death. AH 924/1518).

No. 261, last line. [Ibn Aʿtham.] Also Brockelmann i p. 516, *Sptbd.* i p. 220.

No. 262, 4th par. (1), MSS. [*Tuḥfah i Malikī*[36]] Also **Āṣafīyah** iii p. 270 (AH 1230/1815).

No. 262, end. *Insert*:

(3) ***Tarjamah i ʿUyūn akhbār al-Riḍā***, a translation made at Mashhad in 1075/1664–5 by M. Ṣāliḥ b. M. Bāqir Qazwīnī: **Sipahsālār** i p. 225 no. 290.

No. 263, 4th par. (1), 1st line. [*Tarjamat al-manāqib.*] The date 938 is that given in the *Rauḍāt al-jannāt*, but the translator's colophon as quoted in the Sipahsālār catalogue i p. 229^{12} gives 968. No date is mentioned in the Bānkīpūr and Aberystwyth catalogues.

36 In spite of Arabic grammatical rules this is doubtless the correct form of the title.

No. 263, 4th par. (1), MSS. [*Tarjamat al-manāqib.*] Also **Āṣafīyah** iii p. 662, **Sipahsālār** i p. 228 no. 294 (late 18th cent.).

No. 263, last par. [al-Irbilī.] Also *Āthār al-Shīʿat al-Imāmīyah* iv p. 165; Brockelmann *Sptbd.* i p. 713.

No. 264, 2nd par. [*Aḥsan al-kibār.*] It appears from a statement on fol. 95*b* (seven lines from the beginning of *Bāb* 5) in I.O. MS. D.P. 573 that in 728/1327–8 the author, having returned from Sulṭānīyah to Iṣfahān and thence to Fīrūzān, became resident in the last place and began to write the *Aḥsan al-kibār* in 739/1338–9.

No. 264, 2nd par., MSS. **I.O.** D.P. 573 contains only the first twelve of the seventy-eight *bābs.*

No. 265, 2nd par., MSS., **I.O.** D.P. *Read* 109A.

No. 265, 2nd par., MSS. [*Manāqib al-Sādāt.*] Also **Ivanow** Curzon 371 (AH 1103/1691), **ʿAlīgaṛh** Subḥ. MSS. p. 16 no. 82, **Mashhad** i, *fṣl.* 14, MSS., no. 35 (defective at end). This work is a Sunnī *arbaʿīn* with Persian translation and commentary and is misplaced in this section. The title does not occur in the text.

No. 268, 2nd par., MSS. [*Rauḍat al-shuhadāʾ.*] Also **Tashkent Univ.** 73 (16th cent.), **Blochet** iv 2301 (defective. Late 16th cent.), **Princeton** 457 (AH 1080/1669–70), **Vatican** Pers. 159 (1) (AH 1105/1693. Rossi p. 152), **Bānkīpūr** Suppt. i 1757 (AH 1240/1825), **ʿAlīgaṛh** Subḥ. MSS. p. 57 no. 8 (AH) 1243/1827–8), no. 9, p. 56 nos. 1–2 (AH 1251–2/1835–7), **Ethé** 159, **Āṣafīyah** iii p. 102 no. 1161, p. 104 nos. 1163, 1516.

No. 268, 3rd par. [*Rauḍat al-shuhadāʾ* Editions.] Also **Bombay** 1285/1868–9 (**Āṣafīyah** iii p. 104).

No. 268, 4th par., MSS. (10). [*Dah majlis.*] Also **I.O.** D.P. 656 (AH 1159/1746), 646 (AH 1223/1808), **Blochet** iv 2305 (AH 1245/1829–30), **Bombay** Univ. p. 245 no. 167, **Āṣafīyah** iii p. 102 (metrical), **T.C.D.** 1590.

No. 268, 5th par., MSS. [*Ḥadīqat al-suʿadāʾ.*] Also **Dresden** p. 84 no. 80 (Wolfenbüttel), **R.A.S.** T 6 (?) (*Saʿādat-nāmah*).

No. 270, 2nd line. For Sifarghābād, evidently a village near Jām, cf. *JRAS*. 1917 p. 355[11], where it is spelt and p. 335[15], where a person named Akhī ʿAlī is mentioned. These passages occur in the biography of Aḥmad i Jām edited by W. Ivanow (cf. *PL*. no. 1266).

No. 273, 2nd par. The *Aḥwāl al-Aʾimmah al-Ithnai-ʿashar*, as the author calls it in his *Taʾlīf qalb al-alīf*, was completed in 1010/1601–2 and based mainly on the *Faṣl al-khiṭāb* of M. Pārsā (for whom see *PL*. no. 13). The opening words are *Sp. i bī-andāzah Āfrīdgārī rā*. Other MSS.: **Rieu** ii 863*b* ult. (18th cent.), **Bānkīpūr** xvii 1736 (18th cent.), probably also **Āṣafīyah** iii p. 662 (*Faḍāʾil i A. i I.-ʿa.*, composed in 1008 (*sic*?). Author not stated[37]).

No. 274, 1st par. [M. Ṣāliḥ "Kashfī".] For "Subḥānī" the *ʿAmal i Ṣāliḥ* has "Sujān" (a Hindī word meaning "well-informed", "wise", "intelligent": cf. *PL*. no. 622, 2nd footnote), which is much more probable.

No. 274 (1), MSS. The date of I.O. 4425 is 1067/1656.

No. 274, last par. *Read: Pādshāh-nāmah* ii 505 etc.; *ʿAmal i Ṣāliḥ* iii p. 444.

No. 276, 2nd par. [A work on the Imāms.] This work was completed in 1058/1648. Other MSS.: **Būhār** 117 (A.H. 1081/1670–1), 118–19, **I.O.** D.P. 307A, **Rieu** i 32*b*.

No. 278, last line. *Read* 1295/1878°.

No. 279, last par. [al-Fāḍil al-Hindī.] Also "Ḥazīn" *Tadhkirat al-aḥwāl* p. 130, Belfour's trans. p. 143; *Nujūm al-samāʾ* p. 211.

No. 281, first line. [An anonymous author.] In the preface of Ivanow 2nd Suppt. 1042 he gives his name as M. Riḍā b. M. Muʾmin al-Imāmī al-Khātūnābādī al-mudarris. The work was begun in 1125/1713 and completed in 1127/ 1715.

No. 281, 2nd par. [*Jannāt al-khulūd*.] Tables giving the names of God with explanations, the names and brief accounts of the ancient Prophets, Muḥammad, the Imāms, Caliphs, some eminent Shīʿites, holy days, anniversaries and festivals, prayers, etc. Other MSS.: **Ellis Coll.** M. 279 (AH 1259/ 1843), **Ivanow** 2nd Suppt. 1042 (AH 1267/1851), **Mashhad** iii, *fṣl.* 14, MSS., no. 26. Editions:

37 ʿAbd al-Ḥaqq's name does not appear in the preface to the *A. i A. i I.-ʿa*, but his *takhalluṣ* "Ḥaqqī" occurs in a *rubāʿī* at the end. No title is mentioned in the preface.

Ṭihrān 1264/1848°, 1268/1852°. It has repeatedly been printed according to the Mashhad catalogue.

No. 282, 1st par., penult. Read *Dil-gushā-nāmah.*

No. 282, end. *Insert*:

282*a*. **M. Mashhadī.** ***Ansāb al-aṭhār***, lives of the Panj Tan and the Imāms, completed in 1146/1733–4: **Madras** 437.

No. 285, 2nd par., MSS. [*Qurrat al-ʿainain.*] Also **Bānkīpūr** xiv 1288.

No. 287, 2nd par., MSS. [*Muḥarriq al-qulūb.*] Also **Blochet** iv 2297 (AH 1234/1819).

No. 287, 3rd par. Other editions: place? 1284/1867–8 (with Ḥasan Yazdī's *Muhaiyij al-aḥzān* (cf. *PL*. no. 311 (32)) on margin. See Mashhad i, *fṣl.* 4, ptd. bks., no. 127); **Persia** 1294/1877 (see Āṣafīyah iii p. 108).

No. 287, last par. [M. Mahdī Nirāqī.] Also *Nujūm al-samāʾ* p. 319; Brockelmann *Sptbd.* ii p. 824.

No. 291, 1st line. More fully M. Ikrām al-Dīn b. Niẓām al-Dīn b. Muḥibb al-Ḥaqq.

No. 291, 2nd par. The *Saʿādat al-kaunain* is based mainly on the Arabic *Miftāḥ al-najāʾ fī manāqib Āl al-ʿAbāʾ* of M. b. Muʿtamad Khān (see *PL*. no. 169, 1st par.).

No. 292 (1), 1st line. [*Ḥamlah i Ḥaidarī.*] *Read* on the lives of Muḥammad and ʿAlī.

No. 292, last par. [Bamūn ʿAlī "Rājī".] Also *Majmaʿ al-fuṣaḥāʾ* ii pp. 147–50.

No. 293, 2nd par. *Muḥīṭ al-ʿazāʾ* (i.e. presumably "the ocean of mourning") is doubtless the correct reading.

No. 294, 2nd par., MSS. [*Riyāḍ al-shahādah.*] Also **Ellis Coll.** M. 263 (AH 1244/1826).'

No. 296, 3rd par. [*Mātam-kadah.*] For an edition without place or date of publication (282 pp.) see Harrassowitz's *Bücher-Katalog* 430 (1912) no. 821.

No. 297, 1st par. [Ṣibghat Allāh.] See also *PL*. no. 652.

No. 297, end. [*Dāstān i gham.*] Another edition: AH 1311/ 1893–4 (Āṣafīyah i p. 240 no. 298, where the place of publication is not mentioned).

No. 299, 2nd par. [ʿAbd al-ʿAzīz Dihlawī.] *Read*: (i) ***Sirr al-shahādatain.***

No. 299, 3rd par., end. [Salāmat Allāh "Kashfī".] See also *Shamʿ i anjuman* pp. 405–6.

No. 299, 3rd par., end. [*Taḥrīr al-shahādatain.*] MS.: **ʿAlīgaṛh** Subḥ. MSS. p. 60 no. 8, probably also **Bānkīpūr** xvii 1624 (*Tarjamah i Sirr al-shahādatain*, without preface or translator's name, but transcribed at Cawnpore (Salāmat Allāh's place of residence) in 1259/1843).

No. 299, last par., end. [ʿAbd al-ʿAzīz Dihlawī.] *Insert*:
(2) ***Qirān al-saʿdain i dhū 'l-nūrain dar dhikr i shahādat i Imām Ḥusain***: **Āṣafīyah** iii p. 106 no. 1021 (defective at end).

No. 300, 1st line. For M. Ṣāliḥ Burghānī, who was a brother of the *Shahīd i Thālith*, M. Taqī Burghānī (for whom see the next addendum), and who died at Karbalāʾ on a date apparently unrecorded, see *Qiṣaṣ al-ʿulamāʾ* pp. 74–6; *Nujūm al-samāʾ* pp. 416–17; *Aḥsan al-wadīʿah* i pp. 35–8.

No. 300, end. *Insert*:

300*a*. **M. Taqī** b. M. **Burghānī** Qazwīnī, called *Shahīd i Thālith*, was born at Burghān, near Ṭihrān, and settled at Qazwīn, where he was murdered in 1264/1848 by Bābīs, who resented his *takfīr* (see no. 1574, 2nd par., last footnote *supra*).

Majālis al-muttaqīn, composed in 1258/1842, dedicated to Muḥammad Shāh Qājār and evidently of rather miscellaneous contents, since according to the *Nujūm al-samāʾ* p. 409[10] *mushtamil ast bar mawāʿiẓ u ḥikam u ḥall i aḥādīth u tafsīr i āyāt u taṭbīq i ān ba-maṣāʾib i Saiyid al-Shuhadāʾ ʿm balkih ʿumdah i maqṣūdash dar ān-kitāb dhikr i maṣāʾib i ān-ḥaḍrat ast.*[38] Edition: **Persia** 1270/1854° (cf. Āṣafīyah iii p. 108 no. 1015. According

38 In the Āṣafīyah catalogue, therefore, it occurs in the section *Tārīkh i fārisī*, whereas Edwards describes it as "a work on Shīʿah doctrine and morals".

to *Aḥsan al-wadīʿah* i p. 33^{12}, where it is inadvertently called *Majālis al-muʾminīn*, it has been lithographed several times (*mirār*^{an}) in Persia).

300*b*. Mullā **M. b. ʿAlī Akbar Khurāsānī** known (*al-mashhūr*) as Firishtah, is described as *marḥūm* on the title-page of his *Mātam-kadah*.

__Mātam-kadah__, on the Imāms, etc., begun in 1261/1845 and divided, according to the preface, into fourteen *mātamkadahs* and a *khātimah* [but probably left unfinished]: **Calcutta** 1270/1854 (*Mātam-kadahs* i–iv (Muḥammad, Fāṭimah, ʿAlī, Ḥasan) only. Imāmīyah Pr. Pp. 413, misprinted 414. SOAS.).

No. 301, end. *Insert*:

301*a*. **"Rājī"** (evidently, if the date given below is correct, a different person from Bamūn ʿAlī "Rājī" Kirmānī, who, as stated in no. 292 *supra*, died some years before 1270).

__Ḥaqāʾiq__, or, according to the heading, *Tārīkh i Muḥammadī* (beg. *Ḥaqāʾiq-shināsān i rāh i hudā*), a long metrical biography of Muḥammad, completed in 1270/1853–4, dedicated to Nāṣir al-Dīn Shāh and divided into 291 *ʿunwāns*: **Ivanow** 2nd Suppt. 987 (AH 1272/1856).

301*b*. In 1270/1853–4 Maulawī S. **Najaf ʿAlī** and **Ṣafdar ʿAlī** b. Ḥaidar ʿAlī Riḍawī (cf. no. 43 *supra*) wrote their *Tadhkirat al-aṣfiyāʾ* at the suggestion of Nawwāb Dilēr al-Daulah Dilāwar al-Mulk Mīrzā M. ʿAlī Khān Fīrōz-Jang.

__Tadhkirat al-aṣfiyāʾ__: **Āṣafīyah** iii p. 380 no. 186 (under *Siyar i fārisī*, but the precise subject is not stated. *a.h.* 1270/1853–4).

No. 308, footnote. *Read* broker (*dallāl*).

No. 308, footnote, end. [A. b. M. al-Yamanī al-Shirwānī.] Also Sarkis *Dictionnaire encyclopédique de bibliographie arabe* coll. 1120–1; *Dānishmandān i Ādharbāyjān* p. 31.

No. 308, last par. [M. ʿAbbās "Rifʿat" Shirwānī.] Also *Ṣubḥ i gulshan* pp. 180–2.

No. 309 (1). [*Aḥwāl i ḥaḍrat i Bāqir*, or rather, to judge from Edwards's quotation from the title-page, *Sharḥ i aḥwāl i ... ḥaḍrat i Bāqir*.] For this work, written in continuation of the *Nāsikh al-tawārīkh*, see the Additions to no. 191, 2nd par.

No. 309 (2), 2nd par. [*Ṭirāz al-mudhahhab i Muẓaffarī*.] Also [**Ṭihrān**] 1315/1898 (see Karatay p. 186).

No. 311 (*a*) (5). Ismāʿīl K͟hān "Sarbāz" was a poet of Nāṣir al-Dīn S͟hāh's reign (see *al-Maʾāt͟hir wa-'l-āt͟hār* p. 207).

No. 311 (*a*) (11). [*Bait al-aḥzān.*] Another edition: **Persia** 1325/1907 (Āṣafīyah iii p. 94, where 1262 is given as the date of composition).

No. 311 (*a*) (13), end. *Insert*:

(13*a*)   *D͟kikr i s͟hahādat i ḥaḍrat i Imām Ḥusain mausūm bah Ṣaḥīfah i d͟hahabīyah*, by M. ʿAbd al-Qādir b. Mīrān S. Ḥasan b. S. M. al-Ḥusainī al-Qādirī: **Āṣafīyah** iii p. 102 (AH 1165/1752).

No. 311 (*a*) (14), MSS. [*Durr baḥr al-manāqib.*] Also **Blochet** iv 2302 (doubtless the abridgment, though Blochet describes it as the *B. al-m.* Circ. AD 1525), **Majlis** ii 831 (AH 1046/1636-7).

No. 311 (*a*) (15). *Read* Mas͟hhad, *fṣl.* 4, ptd., bks., no. 112.

No. 311 (*a*) (16), end. *Insert*:

(16*a*)   *Faḍl i Ṣafdarī*, on the merits of ʿAlī, by M. Najm al-Dīn Qādirī: **Arrah** 1294/1877*.

(16*b*)   *G͟ham-namah i ḥaḍrat i Imām Ḥusain*, composed in the time of Nawwāb M. G͟haut͟h K͟hān of the Carnatic (1842–55) by G͟hulām-Yaḥyā Naqawī Ḥusainī:[39] **Āṣafīyah** iii p. 106.

No. 311 (*a*) (20–23), last par. [*Kanz al-ansāb.*] Also [Ṭihrān?] 1297/1880‡.

No. 311 (*a*) (23), end. *Insert*:

(23*a*)   *Kanz al-g͟harāʾib fī qiṣaṣ al-ʿajāʾib*, on the history and merits of the first four Caliphs, al-Ḥasan and al-Ḥusain, by Najm al-Dīn Qāsim b. M. Mad͟hmakīnī (?): **Blochet** iv 2141 (AH 882/1478).

(23*b*)   *Kanz al-maṣāʾib*, by S. M. Ḥasan al-Ḥusainī al-s͟hahīr bah Āqā K͟hān: **Āṣafīyah** iii p. 108.

No. 311 (*a*) (25). For Jaʿfar S͟hūs͟htarī, who died in 1303/1885, see *Aḥsan al-wadīʿah* i pp. 92–9, where it is stated that the *K͟haṣāʾiṣ al-Ḥusainīyah* has been lithographed more than once in Persia.

No. 311 (*a*) (25), end. *Insert*:

---

[39]   A pupil of Irtaḍā ʿAlī K͟hān (for whom see no. 1381 *supra*).

(25*a*) ***Khulāṣat al-akhbār*** (subject?), by S. M. Mahdī b. S. M. Jaʿfar al-Mūsawī. Edition: **Persia** 1282/1865–6 (Āṣafīyah iii p. 380).

No. 311 (*a*) (30), end. *Insert*:

(30*a*) ***Manāqib i Maʿṣūmīn***, by ʿAbd al-Khāliq b. ʿAbd al-Karīm Yazdī Mashhadī. Edition: **Persia** 1313/1895–6 (Āṣafīyah iii p. 662).

No. 311 (*a*) (32), end. [*Muhaiyij al-aḥzān*.] Also 1284/1867–8 (place? On margin of Mahdī Nirāqī's *Muḥarriq al-qulūb* (cf. no. 287, 2nd par. *supra*). See Mashhad i, *fṣl*. 4, ptd. bks., no. 127).

No. 311 (*a*) (38), end. *Insert*:

(38*a*) ***Mukhtār-nāmah***: **Ellis Coll.** M. 54 (18th cent.).

No. 311 (*a*) (48), end.*Insert*:

(48*a*) ***Nukhbah i Sipihrī*** (subject?), by ʿAbd al-Raḥīm b. Abī Ṭālib Tabrīzī. Edition: 1322/1904–5 (place? See Āṣafīyah iii p. 380). [P.S. According to Browne *Press and poetry* p. 161 this is a life of the Prophet abridged from the *Nāsikh al-tawārīkh*.]

No. 311 (*a*) (58), end. *Insert*:

(58*a*) ***Safīnah i Ahl i Bait***, dates of birth and death, compiled in the reign of ʿAlī ʿĀdil-Shāh:[40] **Āṣafīyah** iii p. 104 no. 997 (AH 1331/1913).

(58*b*) ***Ṣaḥīfah i dhahabīyah*** (*Dhikr i shahādat i ḥaḍrat i Imām Ḥusain mausūm bah Ṣ. i dh.*), by M. ʿAbd al-Qādir b. Mīrān S. Ḥasan b. S. M. Ḥusainī Qādirī: **Āṣafīyah** iii p.102 (AH 1165/1752).

No. 311 (*a*) (63), end. *Insert*:

(63*a*) ***Tadhkirat al-Sādāt***, the names, surnames, dates of birth and death and similar matters connected with Muḥammad, Fāṭimah and the Twelve Imāms, by Aḥmad b. Maḥmūd Muḥammadī Akbarābādī: **Allahabad** 1880*.

(63*b*) ***Tadhkirat al-shuhadā'***, lives of Muḥammad, Abū Bakr, Fāṭimah, ʿUmar, ʿ Uthmān, ʿAlī, al-Ḥusain and al-Ḥasan, by M. Ḥusain b. Bāqī Bukhārī: **Blochet** iv 2303 (19th cent.).

---

40 The two Sulṭāns of this name reigned 965–87/1557–79 and 1070–97/ 1660–86 respectively.

No. 311 (*a*) (65), MSS.[*Tārīkh i ʿUmarī.*] Also **Āṣafīyah** iii p. 96 no. 999 (where the work is called *T. i ʿU. al-maʿrūf bah Ḥiṣār al-Islām* and the author's (translator's) name is given as M. Ḥusain [b.] ʿUmar [b.] M. [b.?] ʿAbd al-Salām Harawī).

No, 311 (*a*) (65), end. *Insert*:
(65*a*) ***Tarjīḥ al-faḍāʾil*** (subject?): **Āṣafīyah** iii p. 662 (under *Manāqib*).

No. 311 (*a*) (66). M. Ibrāhīm "Jauharī" died in 1253/1837–8 (see S. Jalāl al-Dīn Ṭihrānī's *Iṣfahān* (in *Gāh-namah i 1312* (cf. no. 340 (1), editions (3) *supra*) p. 135)).

No. 311 (*a*) (66), end. *Insert*:
(66*a*) ***Tuḥfat al-abrār dar dhikr i ḥālāt i Aʾimmah i akhyār***, a short work in a *muqaddamah*, twelve *bābs* and a *khātimah*: **Vatican** Pers. 12 (2) (17th cent. Rossi p. 39).

No. 311 (*a*) (69). Naurūz ʿAlī Bisṭāmī is described in *al-Maʾāthir wa-ʾl-āthār* (p. 214) as a scholar (*ʿālim*) and preacher (*wāʿiẓ*) resident at Mashhad.

No. 311 (*a*) (69), end. *Insert*:
(69*a*) ***Wasāʾil i Muẓaffarī***, *dar maṣāʾib*, by ʿAlī al-ʿAlawī al-Yazdī b. Murtaḍā al-Ṭabāṭabāʾī. Edition: **Ṭihrān** 1320/1902–3 (Āṣafīyah iii p. 112).

No. 311 (*a*) (71), end. *Insert*:
(72) ***Zubdat al-akhbār dar faḍāʾil u manāqib i Aṭhār***, by M. Qāsim b. M. Sharīf: **Āṣafīyah** iii p. 662.

No. 316, 1st line. ʿAlī-Qulī Mīrzā was *Wazīr i ʿUlūm*, the first person to be so called (*al-Maʾāthir wa-ʾl-āthār* p. 193*b* antepenult.). He was *Mudīr* of the Dār al-Funūn from 1272/1855–6 until his death in 1298/1880 (*op. cit.* p. 19) and *Wazīr i Tijārah* and *Wazīr i Ṣanāʾiʿ* from the fourteenth year of Nāṣir al-Dīn Shāh's reign (*ibid.*). He died on 10 Muḥarram 1298/13 December 1880.

No. 316, 3rd par., end. [ʿAlī-Qulī Mīrzā.] Also *Majmaʿ al-fuṣaḥāʾ* i p. 41 (under his *takhalluṣ* "Fakhrī"); *al-Maʾāthir wa-ʾl-āthār* pp. 193–4; *Ṭarāʾiq al-ḥaqāʾiq* iii p. 278. For a portrait see Rieu Suppt. 412 (vi).

No. 318, 1st par. Jalāl al-Dīn, the fifty-fifth son of Fatḥ-ʿAlī Shāh, was eight years old at his father's death (*Majmaʿ al-fuṣaḥāʾ* i p. 21).

No. 316 (2), footnote. For a portrait of Mānekjī see Feuvrier *Trois ans à la cour de Perse*, Paris [circ. 1894?], p. 273.

No. 318, 3rd par., end. [*Nāmah i khusrawān*.] Also **Lucknow** 1931* ("Part 1, dealing with the Sāsānian dynasty" (Arberry). Ed. Ṣābir ʿAlī Khān). See also Browne *Lit. Hist.* ii p. 6.

No. 319, 1st par., beginning. The name of "Furūghī's ' ' father was given incorrectly as M. ʿAlī on the authority of the British Museum catalogue, in which works by more than one "Furūghī" are grouped under the heading "Muḥammad Ḥusain ibn Muḥammad ʿAlī, called Furūghī and Adīb i Iṣfahānī". M. Ḥasan Khān Marāghī, who was an intimate friend of Mīrzā M. Ḥusain Adīb i Iṣfahānī mashhūr bi-laqab i Furūghī, says that he was the son of M. Mahdī Arbāb (*al-Maʾāthir wa-ʾl-āthār* p. 189). He mentions that at the time of writing he was Director of the Dār al-Ṭibāʿah i Khāṣṣah (the Royal Press) and of the Dār al-Tarjamah and that his *dīwān* was then in the press.

No. 319, 1st par. M. Ḥusain Khān "Furūghī" died in 1325/1907 (*Bīst maqālah i Qazwīnī*, pt. 1, p. 8 n. 2). P.S. Exact date: 15 Ramaḍān/22 October.

No. 319, 2nd par. ["Furūghī's" *Tārīkh i Īrān*] Also **Ṭihrān** 1318/ 1900–1. [R. Lescot, *Bull. E.O.I.F. de Damas*, vii–viii p. 281.]

No. 319, last par., end. [M. Ḥusain "Furūghī".] Also *al-Maʾāthir wa-ʾl-āthār* p. 189; *Tārīkh i jarāʾid* ... ii pp. 122–4.

No. 320, 1st par., end. M. ʿAlī Khān Furūghī was born in 1873 (so *The Times*) or 1875 (so *Indo-Iranica*) and died on 26–27 November 1942 (obituary notice in *The Times* of 1.12.42; portrait in *Indo-Iranica* i/2 (Calcutta, Oct. 1946), facing p. 37). See also Īraj Afshār *Nathr i Fārsī i muʿāṣir* pp. 67–74 (portrait).

No. 321 (*a*) (7), end. *Insert*:

(7*a*) ***Tārīkh i Īrān***, by M. Ḥasan Khān Iʿtimād al-Salṭanah (for whom see no. 192 *supra*): **Ṭihrān** 1293/ 1876. [R. Lescot, *Bull. E.O.I.F. de Damas* vii–viii, p. 281.]

No. 321 (*a*) (11), end. *Insert*:

(11*a*) ***Tārīkh i pādshāhān i ʿAjam***, metrical, by Mīrzā Ṣadīq [Ṣādiq?] Qāʾim-maqām: **Ṭihrān** 1324/1906. [R. Lescot, *ibid.*].

No. 321 (*a*) (12). [*Tārīkh i Shaikh Uwais.*] This is a general history and is misplaced here. Extracts relating to the Golden Horde: *Sbornik materialov* ... ii ... **Leningrad** 1941 (cf. ad no. 104, penult. par., end *supra*) pp. 228–31 (Russian translation, pp. 99–103).

No. 324, 2nd par. [*Tajārib al-umam.*] This is evidently a translation of the Arabic work *Nihāyat al-arab fī akhbār al-Furs wa-'l-'Arab*, which was described by E. G. Browne in *JRAS*. 1900 pp. 195–259. [N. C. Sainsbury and, independently, A. J. Arberry, in letters.] Cf. Brockelmann *Sptbd.* i p. 235. There is another MS. (dated 811/1409) in the possession of Mr. Wilfred Merton. According to that MS. the ruler for whom the translation was made was Nuṣrat al-Dīn Aḥmad [Atābak of Luristān from 696/1296 to 733/1333. Cf. no. 110, 2nd par. *supra*]. The translator's name does not appear in the text but on the title-page the work is ascribed to Ḥamd Allāh Mustaufī. The names Aiyūb b. Qirrīyah, 'Abd Allāh b. al-Muqaffa' and "Atābak i sa'īd Sa'd b. Zangī" occur in their correct forms. In view of this new information the Āyā Ṣōfyah MS. cannot be regarded as an autograph. [A. J. Arberry, in a letter.]

No. 330, 2nd par., penult. sentence. For a MS. containing forty-two of these fictitious letters see Majlis 772, where they are called *Ṣad khiṭābah* and where it is stated that they appear to have been printed in the eleventh or twelfth year of the Calcutta newspaper *Ḥabl al-matīn*.

No. 330 (2). The *Nāmah i bāstān* was completed at Trebizond in 1313/1895–6 (see Browne *The Persian Revolution* p. 409).

No. 330 (2), 2nd par. [*Sālār-nāmah.*] Another edition: **Kirmān** 1316/ 1898–9. [R. Lescot, *Bull. E.O.I.F. de Damas* vii–viii p. 9 281.]

No. 332 (*a*) (2). [Ḥasan Pīrniyā.] Cf. V. Minorsky in *Acta Orientalia* xvi p. 49 n.2:, "Comme travail populaire il faut signaler l'histoire du monde ancien en trois volumes de Ḥasankhān Pīrniyā (ex-Mušīr al-daula, mort le 23 novembre 1935); c'est une vue d'ensemble très méritoire basée sur les bonnes sources européennes." See also Īraj Afshār *Nathr i Fārsī i mu'āṣir* pp. 50–6.

No. 332 (*a*) (3), end. *Insert*:

(3*a*) ***Īrān-nāmah***, by Mīrzā 'Abbās b. M. 'Alī Sostarī [Shushtarī?]: **Mysore** 1925. [R. Lescot, *Bull. E.O.I.F. de Damas* vii–viii p. 282.]

(3*b*) ***Jang-hā-yi haft-ṣad-sālah i Īrān u Rūm***, by Colonel Ghulām-Ḥusain Muqtadir: **Ṭihrān** AHS 1315/ 1936–7. [R. Lescot, *ibid.*].

No. 332 (*a*) (5), end. *Insert*:

(6)   *Qushūn-kashī ba-mamālik i Tūrān*, a study of the S͟hāh-nāmah from the strategic point of view, by Jamīl Qūzānlū: Ṭihrān AHS 1310/1931–2. [R. Lescot, *ibid.*]

(7)   *Tārīk͟h i Niẓāmī i jang i ʿArab bā ʿAjam*, by Jamīl Qūzānlū: Ṭihrān AHS 1311/1932–3. [R. Lescot, *ibid.*]

(8)   *Tārīk͟h i Niẓāmī i jang i Īrān u Makidōniyah*, by Jamīl Qūzānlū: Ṭihrān AHS 1311/1932–3. [R. Lescot, *ibid.*]

(9)   *Tārīk͟h i pādshāhān i ʿAjam yā Siyāq al-tawārīk͟h*: anonymous: Ṭihrān 1292/1875. [R. Lescot, *ibid.*]

(10) *Yād-dās͟ht-hā-yi K͟husrau i awwal Anūshīrwān*, by Ibrāhīm-Zādah Ṣafawī: Ṭihrān 1310/1892–3. [R. Lescot, *ibid.*]

(11) *Yazdgird i siwwum*, anonymous: Ṭihrān AHS 1312/ 1933–4. [R. Lescot, *ibid.*]

No. 333, Persian translations (2), footnote. For C͟handū Lāl see no. 1475.

No. 334, 2nd par., end. [*Tārīk͟h i Baihaqī.*] Also **Ellis Coll. M. 21** (AH 1281/1864–5).

No. 334, 3rd par., end. Other editions: (**3**) Ṭihrān AHS 1319/1940 (vol. i, 600 pp. corresponding to the first 614 out of the 868 pages of the Calcutta edition, edited with textual notes by Saʿīd Nafīsī), 1326/1947 (vol. ii, pp. 601–968 i.e. the remainder of the text and the explanatory notes on pp. 1–39), *in progress*. (**4**) Ṭihrān AHS 1324/1945 (ed. G͟hanī and Faiyāḍ).

No. 334, last par. [Abū ʾl-Faḍl Baihaqī.] The passage in the *Tārīk͟h i Baihaq* occurs on pp. 175–8 in Aḥmad Bahmanyār's edition and is quoted in M. Shafīʿ's edition of the *Tatimmat Ṣiwān al-ḥikmah*, fasc. 1, pp. 179–83. See also *Āt͟hār i gum-shudah i Abū ʾl-Faḍl i Baihaqī*, by Saʿīd Nafīsī, Ṭihrān AHS 1315/1936‡.

No. 335, 1st par., end. [Anūshirwān b. K͟hālid.] Also *Dastūr al-wuzarāʾ* pp. 210–11.

No. 339 (2). [*al-Tawassul ilā ʾl-tarassul.*] Also Ḥ. K͟h. ii p. 463, **Yenī 1000, Nūr i ʿUt͟hmānīyah 4300**.

No. 340 (1), 1st par., MSS. [*Tārīk͟h i Jahān-gus͟hāy i Juwainī.*] Also **Ellis Coll. M. 214** (vol. i and part of vol. ii. 16th cent.), **M. 215** (vol. i and large part of vol. ii. 18th cent.).

No. 340 (1), 4th par., end. [*Tārīkh i Jahān-gushāy i Juwainī.* Translations of extracts.] *Add*:

(6) [On the Golden Horde. (Russian.).] *Sbornik materialov* … ii …, **Leningrad** 1941 (cf. ad no. 104, penult. par., end *supra*), pp. 20–24.

No. 342, 1st and 2nd par. [*Tārīkh i Uljāytū Sulṭān.*] "The question of Qāshānī's authorship is studied by Barthold in his review of Blochet's book, in *Mir Islama*, i, 1, 1912, pp. 56–107 …" [Minorsky, *BSOS*. ix/1 (1937) p. 254).

No. 343, 2nd par. "The most detailed description of Aqsarā'ī's history now available is found in Barthold's *O nekotorikh vostoch. rukopisakh Konstantinopol'a, Zapiski*, xviii (1908), pp. 0124–0137 (numerous quotations)." [Minorsky, *ibid.*] P.S. See ad no. 580, end *infra*.

No. 344, 1st par. [Waṣṣāf.] For a MS. at Cairo containing selections from his poems and prose works [presumably in Arabic] see Brockelmann *Sptbd.* ii p. 53.

No. 344, 2nd par., MSS. [*Tārīkh i Waṣṣāf.*] Also **Ivanow** 1st Suppt. 757 (lacks vol. v. AH 1246/1831, **Ellis Coll.** M. 418–M. 421.

No. 344, 3rd par. Also **Bombay** 1241/1826 (707 pp. See Karatay p. 1).

No. 344, 3rd par., editions, Tabrīz. *Read* 1314/1896–7*.

No. 344, 7th par., end.[*Tārīkh i Waṣṣāf.*] *Insert*:

Russian translation of passages relating to the Golden Horde: *Sbornik materialov* … ii, Leningrad 1941 (cf. ad no. 104, penult. par., end *supra*), pp. 80–89.

No. 348 (2), 2nd par., end. [*Shajarat al-Atrāk.* Extracts.] *Add*: (2) [Passages relating to the Golden Horde.] *Sbornik materialov* … ii … **Leningrad** 1941 (cf. ad no. 104, penult. par., end *supra*) pp. 262–8 (with Russian translation, pp. 202–9).

No. 348, last par. [Ulugh Bēg.] Also *Laṭā'if-nāmah* p. 207.

No. 349, 1st par., antepenult. *For* no. 83 ("Diwan des Ahmad Jasawi" [sic]) *read* no. 88 (Geschichte von Fīrūz Šāh in Versen (Mesnewi) [sic]).

No. 349, 1st par., end. See *Ein türkisches Werk von Haydar-Mirza Dughlat. Von Ahmet-Zeki Validi* (in *BSOS*. viii/4 (1937) pp. 985–9).

No. 349, 2nd par., beginning. [*Tārīkh i Rashīdī.*] As the *T. i R.* is not concerned with the Mongols of Persia, it is inappropriately placed here and should be regarded as transferred to the subsection on KĀSHGHAR (nos. 542 and 543 *infra*).

No. 349, 2nd par., 1st line.The correct date seems to be 953 (see Ethé 2848 and Ross's translation).

No. 349, 7th par., end. [*Tārīkh i Rashīdī.* Translations of extracts.] *Add*:

(3) *Mīrzā Muḥammad Ḥaydar Dughlāt on the Harāt school of painters,* [an English translation] *by T. W. Arnold* (in *BSOS*. v/4 (1930) pp. 671–4).

No. 351, 2nd par., end. [*Mawāhib i Ilāhī.*] Also **Ellis Coll.** M. 287 (autograph? 14th cent.).

Edition: **Tihrān** 1326/1947 ("vol. i", about half of the work. Ed. Saʿīd Nafīsī).

No. 353, 2nd par. [*Rūz-nāmah i ghazawāt i Hindūstān.*] See the remarks of W. Hinz in *ZDMG*. 90/2 (1936) pp. 358–9.

No. 354, 1st par., 3rd footnote. "It is a question whether Shanb-i-Ghāzān (p. 278) is correct; Rizā Qulī Khān in the Farhang-i-Nāṣirī spells the word Shumb." [C. N. Seddon, *JRAS*. 1938 p. 569.]

No. 354, 5th par., end. [Niẓām Shāmī's *Ẓafar-namah.*] Russian translation of passages relating to the Golden Horde: *Sbornik materialov* ... ii ..., **Leningrad** 1941 (cf. ad no. 104, penult. par., end *supra*), pp. 104–25.

No. 354, last par.. Read *Ẓafar-nāmah* iv p. 248.

No. 355, 2nd par., MSS. **Houtum-Schindler** 54 (3) = **Browne** Coll. R. 1 (3) (abridged or incomplete. 19th cent.).

No. 355, 2nd par., MSS. [*Malfūẓāt i Tīmūrī.*] Also **Calcutta Madrasah** 176 (3) (17th cent.), **ʿAlīgaṛh** Subḥ. MSS. p. 60 no. 12 (AH 1252/1836–7), **Tashkent Univ.** 65 (AH 1303/1885–6).

No. 355, 3rd par., end. *Add*:

(5) *Tūzuk i Tīmūrī u Tūzuk i Napōliyōn*, **Bombay** 1308/1890–1 [R. Lescot, *Bull. E.O.I.F. de Damas*, vii–viii, p. 282].

No. 355, antepenult. par., MSS. [*Malfūẓāt i Ṣāḥib-Qirān.*] **Ellis Coll.** M. 257 (18th cent.).

No. 356 (1), MSS. [Sharaf al-Dīn's *Ẓafar-nāmah.*] Also **Rāmpūr** (AH 843/1439–40. See *OCM.* ii/2 (Feb. 1926) p. 12), **Princeton** 54 (AH 872/1467–8. PICTURES by Bihzād), **Tashkent Univ.** 63 (AH 1112/1700–1), **Leningrad** Univ. 1122* (Romaskewicz p. 10).

No. 356 (1), MSS. **Dorn** A.M. p. 375 = **Dorn** 295.

No. 356 (1), Extracts, end. [*Ẓafar-nāmah.* Extracts.] *Add*:

(2) [the *dībāchah* and the first few lines of the *muqaddamah*] *OCM.* xv/4 (Aug. 1939), *ḍamīmah*, pp. 3–28 (ed. M. Shafīʿ).

(3) [Passages from the *muqaddamah* relating to the Golden Horde] *Sbornik materialov* ... ii ... **Leningrad** 1941 (cf. ad no. 104, penult. par., end *supra*) pp. 248–50.

No. 356 (1), Translations of extracts, end. [*Ẓafar-nāmah.* Translations of extracts.] *Add*:

(4) [Passages relating to the Golden Horde (Russian).] **Sbornik materialov** ... ii ... **Leningrad** 1941 (cf. ad no. 104, penult. par., end *supra*) pp. 144–89.

No. 356, last par. *Read: Mirʾāt al-khayāl* p. 67 (no. 51).

No. 356, last par., end. [Sharaf al-Dīn ʿAlī Yazdī.] Also *Riyāḍ al-ʿārifīn* pp. 363–4; "Āyatī" *Tārīkh i Yazd* pp. 295–6.

No. 358 (4), MSS. [*Tīmūr-nāmah i Hātifī.*] Also **Majlis** ii 905 (AH 957/ 1550), **Vatican** Barb. Orient. 104 (1) (AH 967/1559–60. Rossi p. 159), **Ellis Coll.** M. 141 (AH 976/1568–9), **Blochet** iii 1536 (AH 978/1571), **Sipahsālār** ii 1154 (AH 980/ 1572–3), 1152–3 (both mid 10th/16th cent.), **Philadelphia** Lewis Coll. p. 53 (AH 991/1583), **Calcutta Madrasah** 145 (early 18th cent.), **Rāghib** 1095 (n.d. See Duda *Ferhād und Schīrīn* p. 181).

No. 358 (4), MSS. *Read* **Madras** I 101.

No. 358 (4), MSS. [*Ẓafar-nāmah i Hātifī.* Editions.] Also **Lucknow** 1896‡ (2nd ed.).

No. 358 last par. ["Hātifī."] Also *Laṭā'if-nāmah* pp. 105–6; *Khulāṣat al-afkār* no. 304.

No. 358, last par. *Khulāṣat al-kalām* (Bodleian 390) no. 76 = Bānkīpūr viii 705 no. 56 (p. 146).

No. 359 (2), end. *Insert*:

(2*a*) ***Tārīkh i Ṣāḥib-Qirān Amīr Tīmūr Kūrkān*** (beg. *Ḥ. u sp. u sh. u st. ḥaḍrat i Pādshāhī rā tuwānad būd*), composed in 1124/1712 (the same date as the preceding work) by an author who calls himself "Rumūz" [*sic*?]: **Tashkent Univ.** 58 (AH 1261–5/1845–9. Cf. Kahl pp. 17–18).

No. 360. The "Anonym of Shāh-Rukh" is identical with Tāj al-Salmānī's history [W. Hinz, *Quellenstudien zur Geschichte der Timuriden* (*ZDMG*. 90/2 (1936)) pp. 367–8]. The B.M. MS. contains two-fifths of the work. [Hinz, *ibid.*, p. 369 penult.]

No. 361, 1st par. Tāj al-Salmānī went from Shīrāz to Tīmūr at Samarqand in 800/1397–8. For the little autobiographical information given by him in his history see W. Hinz, *ZDMG*. 90/2 (1936) pp. 368–9. He is doubtless the same person as the calligraphist Khwājah T. al-S., of Iṣfahān, who is described as the first to write *Ta'līq* with elegance or even as its inventor [Majnūn Rafīqī *Khaṭṭ u sawād, Bāb* ii (*OCM*. x/4 (Aug. 1934) p. 18); Aḥmad Ibrāhīmī *Khulāṣat al-tawārīkh* (?), *Qism* ii, at end (*OCM*. x/4 (Aug. 1934) p. 29); Idem, (*Tadhkirah i khwush-nawīsān*) (cf. no. 1431, 2nd par. *supra*), Zakhoder's trans. p. 89].

No. 361, 2nd par. *Read*:

(***Dhail i Ẓafar-nāmah***) or (***Tārīkh i Tāj i Salmānī***), an untitled history of the end of Tīmūr's reign and the early years of Shāh-Rukh's (to 811/1409): Ḥ. Kh. iv p. 176 l. 3, **Lālā Ismā'īl** 304 = Tauer 414 (very slightly defective at beginning, AH 988/1580. See W. Hinz *ZDMG*. 90/2 (1936) pp. 367–73), **Rieu** i 180*b* (beg. *Afḍal i ḥ. u sp. u akmal i sh. i bī-q*. About two-fifths of the work, lacking nearly all of the *sabab i ta'līf i kitāb* and extending to the defeat of Pīr Muḥammad by Khalīl in Ramaḍān 808/Feb. 1406. 15th cent. Cf. W. Hinz *ZDMG*. 90/2 (1936) pp. 357–8, 366–71), **Āyā Ṣōfya** 3028–9 (?) (see W. Hinz *ibid.* p. 367 n. 3, where these two MSS. are described on the authority of Aḥmad Zakī Valīdī as a further copy (so, not two copies) of Tāj i Salmānī's history. In the *defter* they do indeed appear as *Tārīkh i Tīmūr* by Tāj al-Salmānī, but Tauer describes these MSS. (nos. 409 and

401 in his list) as copies of Sharaf al-Dīn Yazdī's *Ẓafar-nāmah* (cf. no. 356 (1) MSS. *supra*) and, to judge by the number of leaves (586 and 366), this would seem to be correct), **Fātiḥ** 4305 = Tauer 415 (about three-quarters of the work. 12th/18th cent.).

No. 361, end. Insert here the article of no. 364 (*Muʿizz al-ansāb*) below.

No. 362, 3rd par. "Qāsimī" died in 982/1574–5 (see Ḥasan Rūmlū i p. 462[1], Seddon's trans. p. 201).

No. 362, end. ["Qāsimī."] Also *Mai-khānah* pp. 141–52; *Haft āsmān* pp. 136–8.

No. 363, 2nd par., MSS. [*Maṭlaʿ i saʿdain.*] Also **Ellis Coll.** M. 14 (*Daftar* ii. AH 970/1563), M. 12 (apparently AH 807–30 from *Daftar* ii. 17th cent.), M. 13 (*Daftar* i. 18th cent.).

No. 363, 3rd par., end. [*Maṭlaʿ i saʿdain.*] The publication of M. Shafīʿ's [first] edition was resumed in *OCM*. xiv/2 (Feb. 1938), pp. 193–224, and continued in succeeding issues, but this edition may be regarded as superseded by M. Shafīʿ's second edition, of which the first volume (*Jild* ii, *juzʾ* 1. AH 807–33. Pp. 655 [?]) was published at **Lahore** in 1360/1941 [Information concerning this volume from V. Minorsky, in a letter] and the second volume (*Jild* ii, *juzʾ* 2–3. AH 833–75. Pp. 621–1558) at the same place (Gīlānī Press) in 1368/1949‡. A volume of indexes is in preparation.

No. 363, 5th par. (4), footnote. Also in *A Persian embassy to China; being an extract from Zubdatu't-tawarikh of Hafiz Abru* [*sic*]. *Translated* [and edited] *by K. M. Maitra*. Lahore, 1934*.

No. 363, 5th par., end. [*Maṭlaʿ i saʿdain.* Extracts.] *Add*: (7) [Passages relating to the Golden Horde.] *Sbornik materialov* ... ii ... **Leningrad** 1941 (cf. ad no. 104, penult. par., end *supra*) pp. 251–61.

No. 363, 6th par., end. [*Maṭlaʿ i saʿdain.* Translations of extracts.] *Add*: (**14**) [Passages relating to the Golden Horde. (Russian.)] *Sbornik materialov* ... ii ... **Leningrad** 1941 (cf. ad no. 104, penult. par., end *supra*), pp. 190–201.

No. 364 should follow no. 361.
Before no. 370, *Insert*:

369*a*. **Jalāl al-Dīn** M. b. Asʿad Ṣiddīqī **Dawānī**, well known as the author of the *Akhlāq i Jalālī*, was born at Dawān, near Kāzarūn, in 830/1426–7, became *Qāḍī* of Fārs and Professor in the Dār al-Aitām madrasah at Shīrāz and died in 908/1502–3 (see *Majālis al-nafāʾis* (tr. Fakhrī ed. ʿAbd Allāh p. 229, ed. "Ḥikmat" p. 141, tr. Qazwīnī ed. "Ḥikmat" p. 309; Ḥasan Rūmlū p. 71, Seddon's trans. p. 31; *Majālis al-muʾminīn* p. 347 (4th biography from end of *Majlis* vii); *Haft iqlīm* i p. 209 (no. 167); *al-Fawāʾid al-bahīyah* p. 89 n. 2; *Ency. Isl.* under Dawwānī (Brockelmann); Brockelmann ii p. 217, *Sptbd.* ii p. 306; etc.).

ʿArḍ-nāmah, an account of a parade held by Sulṭān Khalīl in 881/1476 near Band i Mīr or Band i Amīr ("a short distance to the south of the ruins of Persepolis", Minorsky) in Fārs, when he was Governor of the province on behalf of his father Ūzūn Ḥasan, including a list of civil and military officers in Fars and interesting statistical data: **I.O.** D.P. 952 (*d*) (AH 900/1495), **Bānkīpūr** Suppt. ii 2120 (AH 1077/1667), **Ḥamīdīyah** 1438 (in the *Kullīyāt* of Dawānī).

Edition: *Milli tatabbuʿlar mejmuʿasi, jild* ii, *say* 5, **Istānbūl** 1331/1913, pp. 273–305 (corrections, pp. 385–6. Edited by Kilisli Rifʿat. See *BSOS*. x/1 (1939) p. 141 n. 1).

Abridged translation with notes: *A civil and military review in Fārs in 881/1476. By V. Minorsky* (*BSOS*. x/1 (1939) pp. 141–78).

No. 370, first line. *Read* Rūzbihān.

No. 370, 1st par., last sentence. *Read Mīhmān-nāmah.*

No. 370, 1st par., last line. *Read* 915/1509.

No. 370, 2nd par., last three lines. [*Tārīkh i ʿālam-ārāy i Amīnī*]. These three lines should be deleted. The two Cairo MSS., though described in the catalogue (evidently through a misuse of Ḥ. Kh.) as the *ʿĀlam-ārāy* of Faḍl Allāh, are parts of the *ʿĀlam-ārāy i ʿAbbāsī* (see no. 387, 2nd par. *infra*), as the opening words show. "The Eton MS. described as *Tārīkh-i ʿĀlam-ārā* in fact consists of two quite distinct volumes: Vol. i is the first of the *Afḍal al-tawārīkh* by Faḍlī Iṣfahānī, of which the Br. Mus. MS. described in Rieu, Supp. p. 56 (Professor Storey's 385) forms the immediate continuation; Vol. ii is the second part of Iskandar Munshī's *ʿĀlam-ārā* down to the year 1023." [V. Minorsky, *BSOS*. ix/1 (1937) p. 254.]

No. 372, 1st line. ["Banāʾī"] "I have little doubt that Bannāʾī is the correct form of the *nisba*. In words like *saqqā, nakhkhās*, etc., Persian verse writers often drop the *tashdīd* for metrical reasons." [R. A. Nicholson, in a letter.] In an Edinburgh MS. containing a selection of "Banā'ī's" *ghazals* (New Coll. Or. (Pers.) 35 (*b*)) the form with *tashdīd* seems never to occur.

No. 372, 5th par. [*Dīwān i Banā'ī*.] Also Bānkīpūr Suppt. i 1879, Blochet iii 1769.

No. 372, last par. *Tuḥfah i Sāmī*, Ṭihrān ed., pp. 98–100.

No. 372, last par., end.["Banā'ī."] Also *Zapiski Vost. Otd. Russ. Arkh. Obshch.* xix p. 0164 seqq. (an article by Samoilovich referred to by Barthold in *Mir-Ali-Shir* p. 160); Barthold *Herāt* tr. Hinz, pp. 85–6.

No. 373, 2nd par., MSS. [*Shāh-nāmah i Hātifī*.] Also **Rāghib** 1095 (see Duda *Ferhad und Schirin* p. 181).

No. 376, 2nd par. [(*Tārīkh i Shāh Ismā'īl*).] "Many of the facts reported in the anonymous 376 have been utilized in Ḥasan-i Rūmī's *Aḥsan al-tawārīkh*" [Minorsky, *BSOS*. ix/1 (1937) p. 254], See also *BSOS*. x/4 (1942) p. 1026, where in a review of Ghulām Sarwar's *History of Shāh Ismā'īl Ṣafawī* Minorsky remarks "As regards the sources, he establishes two interesting facts with regard to the anonymous B.M. Or. 3248, which the lamented Sir E. D. Ross studied in his thesis (published in *JRAS*., April 1896): (1) he contradicts the idea that Or. 3248 is identical with the *Futūḥāt* of Ṣadr al-Dīn Harawī, and (2) suggests that the real author's name appears in a marginal note as Bījan. The note has been mutilated at the bookbinder's and cannot be read entirely, but the suggestion merits our attention."

No. 378, 2nd par., MSS. [*Tārīkh i Maḥmūd b. Khwānd-Amīr*.] Also **Ellis Coll.** M. 232 (AH 1047/1637).

No. 379 (1), MSS. [*Shāh-nāmah i Ismā'īl*.] Also **Blochet** iii 1828 (AH 993/1585 or thereabouts), **Majlis** ii 1103 (AH 1060/ 1650), **Madrās** 129, 257 (*b*).

No. 379 (2), MSS. [*Shāh-nāmah i Ṭahmāsp*.] Also **Madrās** 129, 257 (*b*).

No. 380 (2), 1st par. footnote. "The origin of Shāh Tahmāsp's Memoir was first and fully discussed and established by Zhukovsky in *Zap*. vi, 1891, pp. 377–383." [Minorsky, *BSOS*. ix/1 (1937) p. 254.]

No. 380 (2), 1st par., MSS. [*Tadhkirah i Shāh Ṭahmāsp.*] Also **Ellis Coll.** M 375 (AH 1289/1872).

No. 380 (2), 2nd par., penult. *Read* 1343/1924* (See Arberry p. 509).

No. 381, first sentence. Ḥasan Rūmlū was born at Qum in 937/1530–1 according to his own statement (*Aḥsan al-tawārīkh* p. 238[17], Seddon's trans. p. 110).

No. 381, 2nd par., MSS. [*Aḥsan al-tawārīkh.*] Also **Ellis Coll.** M 138 (vol. xii. Mainly 17th cent.), M 445 (vol. xii).

No. 382, end. *Insert:*

382*a*. Qāḍī **Aḥmad Ibrāhīmī** Ḥusainī [Qummī] b. Mīr Munshī Sharaf al-Dīn has already been mentioned (no. 1431 *supra*) in connexion with his *tadhkirah* of calligraphists and painters composed about 1006/1597–8.

Khulāṣat al-tawārīkh, a work[41] of which the fifth and last volume[42] contains a history of the Ṣafawīs undertaken by order of Shāh Ismāʿīl II (AH 984–5/1576–8), "completed" down to 999/1590–1, dedicated to Shāh ʿAbbās and extending to 1592 in the Berlin MS., which is defective at the end: **Berlin** Preussische Staatsbibliothek 2°, 2202, **Majlis** (see *Oriens* 3/1 (1950) p. 159).

Description: *Eine neuentdeckte Quelle zur Geschichte Irans im 16. Jahrhundert. Von Walther Hinz* (in ZDMG. 89/3–4 (1935) pp. 315–28).

No. 384, 2nd par., MSS. [(*Tārīkh i ʿAbbāsī*).] Also **Madrās** 295 (?) (a fragment of 86 pp. Not identified in the catalogue, but beginning with the same words). A German translation by W. Hinz was described by him in *ZDMG.* 89/3–4 (1935) p. 315 n. 2 as nearly completed in manuscript.

No. 385, first line. The author of the *Afḍal al-tawārīkh* is Faḍlī Iṣfahānī. [Minorsky, *BSOS.* ix/1 (1937) p. 254.]

41 To quote the author's words as summarised by W. Hinz: "ein neues Werk (*nosḫä-yĕ tāzä*) über die Geschichte der ṣafavīdischen Herrschaft und der Fürsten dieses Hauses ..., zugleich mit einem Überblick über die den ʿAlīden anhangenden Herrscher in einer Reihe von Bänden vom Beginn der Schöpfung bis zum Aufkommen des jetzigen Herrscherhauses.

42 Possibly the only volume ever written.

No. 385, MSS. [*Afḍal al-tawārīkh.*] Also **Eton** 172 (*a*) (vol. i, of which Rieu Suppt. 56 is the immediate continuation). [Minorsky, *ibid.*]

No. 386 (1). [*Jang-nāmah i Kishm.*] Vatican p. 27 no. 66 = **Vatican** Pers. 30 (AH 1032/1622. Rossi p. 56). An earlier edition (?): "*Gengnamé Kesciem, poemetto persiano c. nota di L. Bonelli.* Torino (1886)" (Harrassowitz's Bücher-Katalog 352 (1912) no. 1525).

No. 387, 1st par., end. Iskandar probably died in 1043/1633–4, having dealt with the first five years of Shāh Ṣafī's reign in his *Dhail i Tārīkh i ʿĀlam-ārāy i ʿAbbāsī* (see no. 391, 4th par. *supra* and the Additions and Corrections to that record).

No. 387, 2nd par., MSS. [*Tārīkh i ʿĀlam-ārāy i ʿAbbāsī.*] Also **Cairo** p. 505 (two copies of *Ṣaḥīfah* i, one dated AH 1001/1592–3, wrongly described in the catalogue as copies of the *Tārīkh i ʿĀlamārāy i Amīnī*), **Eton** 173 (*Ṣaḥīfah* ii, *Maqṣad* i to AH 1023/ 1614. See Minorsky *BSOS*. ix/1 (1937) p. 254. Wrongly described in the catalogue), **Madrās** 297 (*Ṣaḥīfah* ii), **Lincei** (see *Rendiconti* 1912 p. 116), **Caetani** 24 (AH 1256/1840).

No. 387, last par. [Iskandar Munshī.] Also *Makhzan al-gharāʾib* no. 1069.

No. 391. "In the previous fascicle (p. 313, No. 391) Professor Storey gave expression to the view that the history of the Safavid Shāh-Ṣafī by Muḥammad Maʿṣūm b. Khwājagī (Aumer 31) may be identical with the *Khulāṣat al-siyar* which Dorn, *As. Mus.*, p. 382, described as the continuation of Iskandar-munshi's *ʿĀlam-ārā*. Some light on the question is now thrown by Romaskevich (*Materialī po istorii Turkmen*, ii, 1938, p. 12) who confirms the view that Muhammad Maʿṣūm's biography is found in the MS. (a detail overlooked by Dorn). The only point still obscure is how much of the book belongs respectively to Iskandarmunshī and Muhammad B. Maʿṣūm. In the introduction of the book it is stated that when Iskandar-munshi brought his *ʿĀlam-ārā* to completion, he was requested to extend his famous annals over the reign of Shah ʿAbbās I's successor, Ṣafī I. After some hesitation, the aged historian (then 70 years old) started on this new work, which he began by describing the accession of Ṣafī I and by a paragraph on the education which ʿAbbās I gave to the future ʿAbbās II. The style of the work does not allow to discriminate between its two parts but, as Ṣafī I ruled 14 years, while Muhammad b. Maʿṣūm says that he wrote the history of his 10 years, it would seem, Professor Romaskevich remarks, that the first four years of this shah (namely 1038–1042/1628–32) were written by Iskandar-munshi. If so, the famous historian must have lived to the age of 74 years, at least. The

Khulāṣat al-siyar stops at the accession of ʿAbbās II (1052/1642), but M. b. Maʿṣūm records his appointment as vazīr to the governor of Qarabāgh (Ganja) Murtaḍa-quli khan Ziyādoghlī, in the fourth year of ʿAbbas II. M. b. Maʿṣūm's previous employment recorded by Professor Storey: *ishrāf-i iṣṭabl-i nāmvār* points only to his employment as mushrif ("controller") in the administration of the Amīrakhorbāshī (the real Master of the Horse!)." [Minorsky, *BSOS*. x/2 (1940) p. 540.]

No. 391, 2nd par., end. *Read* **Aumer** 231 (AH 1074/1663–4).

No. 391, 4th par., 1st sentence, end. Edition of Iskandar Bēg's own continuation: *Dhail i Tārīkh i ʿĀlam-ārāy i ʿAbbāsī taʾlīf i Iskandar Bēg Turkmān ... u M. Yūsuf i muʾarrikh ba-taṣḥīḥ i Suhailī Khwānsārī*, **Tihrān** AHS 1317–18/1938–9 (Iskandar probably died in 1043, having dealt with the first five years of Shāh Ṣafī. The editor has completed the reign (p. 146[8] onwards) from the *Khuld i barīn* (see *PL*. no. 149, 2nd par.) on the basis of a MS. in the Kitāb-khānah i Millī i Malik).

No. 392, 4th par., MSS. [*ʿAbbās-nāmah*.] Also **Madrās** 293 (AH 1184/1771), **Ellis Coll.** M 406 (18th cent.), M 405 (AH 1284/1868–9), **Leningrad** Univ. 1031 (Romaskewicz p. 4).

No. 392, last par.*Tadhkirah i Naṣrābādī*, Ṭihrān ed., pp. 17–20.

No. 394, first line. "Iwāghlī is undoubtedly Ev-oghlı (of this name there is a village to the north-east of Khoy, and four villages in Transcaucasia; the term seems to correspond to the Ottoman *ev-oghlan*)." [Minorsky, *BSOS*. ix/1 (1937) p. 255. Cf. *BSOS*. x/4 (1942) p. 1028[1].]

No. 394, 2nd par., MSS. [*Majmaʿ al-inshāʾ*.] Possibly also **Lindesiana** p. 109 no 834 (*Murāsalāt i pādshāhān*, by Ibn Abū 'l-Qāsim Iṣfahānī. Iṣfahān, AH 1096/1684).

No. 395, end.[Walī-Qulī Shāmlū.] See *Tadhkirah i Naṣrābādī* pp. 93–4.

No. 397, 4th par., beginning. *Read* Description.

No. 397, 2nd par. Read *Yasāwul*. [Minorsky, *BSOS*. ix/1 (1937) p. 255.]

No. 399, footnote. Read *nisbah*.

No. 399, end. *Insert*:

399*a*. ***Tārīkh i sulṭānī***, an anonymous history of the Ṣafawids, the last date mentioned being 1163/1750: **Ellis Coll.** M 59 (AH 1205/1790).

No. 401, 2nd par., end. [*Majmaʿ al-tawārīkh.*] *Read* **I.O.** 3750 (circ. AD 1906). *Insert*:

Edition: **Ṭihrān** AHS 1328/1950 (ed. ʿAbbās Iqbāl).

No. 402, 2nd par., MSS. [*Fawāʾid i Ṣafawīyah.*] Also **Ellis Coll.** M 23 (continued to AH 1231. Early 19th cent.).

No. 404, 2nd par., beginning.. *Zabūr i Āl i Dāwud* is without doubt the correct reading. [ʿAbbās Iqbāl's introduction to the *Majmaʿ al-tawārīkh* (see addendum to no. 401, 2nd par., end *supra*), p. *dāl* n. 3.]

No. 405 (1), end. *Insert*:

(1*a*) ***Makātīb i zamānah i salāṭīn i Ṣafawīyah***, by ʿAbd al-Ḥusain b. Adham Naṣīrī Ṭūsī: **Āṣafīyah** iii p. 110 no. 1214, **Blochet** iv 2338, **D.M.G.** 69 (2) (preface only).

No. 405 (2), beginning. Read *dār al-salṭanah i Tabrīz.*

No. 405 (2), end. [*Tārīkh i pādshāhān i Ṣafawīyah.*] Presumably identical with **Madras** i 294, a history of the Ṣafawids to Sulṭān-Ḥusain beginning *Subḥāna 'llāhi dhī 'l-mulk wa-'l-malakūt.*

No. 405 (4), end. *Insert*:

(5) ***Sharḥ i tāj-gudhārī i Shāh Sulaimān i Ṣafawī***, by Chardin, tr. ʿAlī-Riḍā Khān. Edition: Ṭihrān (date? See Mashhad iii, fṣl. 14, ptd. bks., no. 135).

(6) *Tārīkh i rawābiṭ i Īrān u Urōpā dar daurah i Ṣafawīyah*, by Naṣr Allāh "Falsafī":[43] Vol. i. **Ṭihrān** AHS 1316/1937–8. [R. Lescot, *Bull. E.O.I.F. de Damas*, vii–viii p. 282. Cf. *Luzac's Oriental list* 1938 p. 9.]

No. 407, beginning. Mahdī Khān was appointed "Historiographer" in 1736 according to Catholicos Abraham (Brosset's trans. p. 312, cited by Minorsky, *Tadhkirat al-mulūk*, comm, p. 121[24]).

---

43 b. AH 1319/1901 at Ṭihrān. See D. J. Irani *Poets of the Pahlavi regime* pp. 515–41 (portrait); M. Ishaque *Sukhanvarān i Īrān* i pp. 414–17 (portrait facing p. 412), *Modern Persian poetry* pp. 12, 21. Cf. ad 193 (*a*) (13) *supra*.

No. 407, 1st par., last line. Read *Mabānī 'l-lughah.*

No. 407 (1), 1st par., MSS. [*Tārīkh i Nādirī.*] Also **Philadelphia** Lewis Coll. p. 64 (AH 1187/1773), **Strassburg** 17 (defective), **Edinburgh** New Coll. p. 6. Other editions: **Tabrīz** 1264/1848 (R. Lescot, *Bull. E.O.I.F. de Damas*, vii–viii p. 282), **Bombay** 1309/1892 (*ZDMG*. 85 (1931) p. *20* no. 19033).

No. 407 (2), 1st par., MSS. [*Durrah i nādirah.*] Also **Heidelberg** p. 367 (AH 1252/1836. See *Zts.f. Semit.* x/1–2 (1935) p. 97), **Leningrad** Univ. 1091 (AH 1255/1839–40. Romaskewicz p. 6).

No. 407 (2), 2nd par., 1st line. *Read* 1854–5*.

No. 407 (2), 2nd par., end. [*Durrah i nādirah.* Editions.] Also **Tihrān** AHS 1324/1945 (abridged and printed as pp. 7–60 of a volume entitled *Nādir Shāh.* which contains also (pp. 61–130) the *Tadhkirat al-aḥwāl* of "Ḥazīn", similarly abridged).

No. 408, penult. Read *Akademii.*

No. 410 (3), end. [Note on the Persian invasions of India.] Also **Bānkīpūr** Suppt. ii 2240.

No. 411, 2nd par. *Instead of* ... i 231*b* (Add. and corrections) (latter part of the work only. End of 18th cent.), 6564 (sic lege pro 6567) foll. 457*a*–490*b*. See Rieu's Additions ... *read* ... i 231*b* (Add. 6564 (sic lege pro 6567) foll. 457*a*–490*b*. See Rieu's Additions and corrections) (latter part of the work only. End of 18th cent.),...

No. 412 (7). *Read* Malcolm's.

No. 412 (8). *Read* Khudāwandī.

No. 412 (11), end. *Insert:*

(11*a*) ***Nādir Shāh***, by S. M. 'Alī, Professor, Niẓām's College, Ḥaidarābād. Edition: 1332/1914 (place? See Āṣafīyah iii p. 110).

No. 412 (14), 2nd footnote, end. See also *Note on James Fraser....*, by W. Irvine, in *JRAS*. 1899 pp. 214–20.

No. 412 (14), end. *Insert:*

(14*a*) ***Tarīkh i Niẓāmī i jang i Īrān u Hind***, by Jamīl Qūzānlū: **Ṭihrān** AHS 1307/1928–9 [R. Lescot, *Bull. E.O.I.F. de Damas* vii–viii p. 282].

No. 415, 2nd par., MSS. [*Mujmal al-tārīkh i ba'd-i-Nādirīyah.*] Also **Ellis Coll.** M 22 (AH 1245/1829).

No. 415, 3rd par., end. [*Mujmal al-tārīkh....*] Another edition: *Mujmal al-tawārīkh i pas az Nādir*, **Ṭihrān** (date? See *Luzac's Oriental list* 1942 p. 9).

No. 416, 2nd par., end. *Insert*:

Edition: *Tārīkh i Gītī gushā*, **Ṭihrān** AHS 1317/1938–9 (with continuations by 'Abd al-Karīm b. 'Alī Riḍā al- Sharīf (p. 276) and M. Riḍā Shīrāzī (p. 374). Edited by Sa'īd Nafīsī).

No. 419, 2nd par., MSS. [*Tārīkh i Zandīyah* Also **Leningrad** Univ. 1136 (Romaskewicz p. 4).

No. 424, 1st line. *For* M. Nadīm "Nadīm" *read* Mīrzā M. "Nadīm

No. 424, last par. [M. "Nadīm".] Also *Rauḍat al-ṣafā-yi Nāṣirī* ix fol. 178b (fifth page from end).

No. 425, 2nd par., MSS. [*Shahanshāh-nāmah.*] Also **Majlis** ii 1104, **Āṣafīyah** iii p. 106 no. 1538 (?) (*Fatḥ-nāmah i Ghāzī.* A different recension? Defective), **Bānkīpūr** Suppt. i 1989 (1) (selections only), **Heidelberg** p. 249 (circ. AD 1850. See *Zts. f. Semit.* x/1–2 (1935) p. 94).

No. 425, last par. ["Ṣabā" Kāshānī] Also *Rauḍat al-ṣafā-yi Nāṣirī* ix, 8th page from end; Berthels *Ocherk istorii persidskoi literatury* pp. 82–6.

No. 426 (1), MSS. *Read* **Madrās** i 316 (AH 1245/1829–30).

No. 426, last par. ['Abd al-Razzāq Dunbulī.] Also *Rauḍat al-ṣafā-yi Nāṣirī* ix, 7th page from end; *Dānishmandān i Ādharbāyjān* pp. 353–7.

No. 427, last par. [M. Ṣādiq "Humā".] Also *Rauḍat al-ṣafā-yi Nāṣirī* ix, 9th page from end.

No. 428, 2nd par., MSS. [*Tārīkh i Ṣāḥib-qirānī.*] Also **Leningrad** Univ. 1142 (Romaskewicz p. 4).

No. 428, last par. [Maḥmūd Qājār.] Also ZDMG. 45 (1891) p. 403 (Vambéry. Cf. no. 1195 (3) *supra*). *Insert*:

428*a*. **M. Mahdī Iṣfahānī**, known as al-Muḥibb.
Ḥikāyāt al-salāṭīn, a history of the Zands and of the Qājārs to Fatḥ-ʿAlī Shāh, a compilation from sources for the most part already known: **Edinburgh** New Coll. p. 6.

No. 429 (1), MSS. [*Tārīkh i Dhū 'l-Qarnain*.] Also **Leningrad** Univ. 1164* (Romaskewicz p. 4).

No. 429, last par.["Khāwarī" Shīrāzī] Also *Rauḍat al-ṣafā-yi Nāṣirī* ix, 7th page from end.

No. 430, last par. [M. Taqī ʿAlī-ābādī.] Also *Rauḍat al-ṣafā-yi Nāṣirī* ix fol. 175*b* ult. (11th page from end).

No. 432, last par. [Abū 'l-Qāsim Farāhānī.] Also *Rauḍat al-ṣafā-yi Nāṣiri* x fol. 5*a* antepenult.; *Ṭarā'iq al-ḥaqā'iq* ii p. 123.

No. 433.. For Riḍā-Qulī Mīrzā's journey see no. 1615.

No. 434, 1st line. *Read* Fatḥ-ʿAlī's second and eldest surviving son.

No. 435, 1st line. *Read* ʿ**Aḍud.**

No. 436, 1st par. Jahāngīr Mīrzā was made Governor of Sāliyān in 1243/1827–8 (*Rauḍat al-ṣafā-yi Nāṣirī* ix fol. 137*a*). For a reference to the *Tārīkh i nau* see *R. al-ṣ. i N.* ix fol. 139*a*.

No. 436, 2nd par., end. [*Tārīkh i nau.*] Edition: **Ṭihrān** AHS 1327/1949 (see *Oriens* iv/1 (1951) p. 187).

No. 437, 4th par., end. [*Nuqṭat al-kāf.*] *Insert*:
Commentary on E. G. Browne's introduction to his edition:
Risālah i Saiyid Mahdī i Dahajī:[44] **Browne** Coll. F. 57 (vol. i only. Autograph. Cf. Browne *Materials for the study of the Bábí religion* pp. 231–3 and 237).

44 Dahaj is near Shahr i Bābak.

No. 437, last par. [Mīrzā Jānī Kāshānī.] Also *Ency. Isl.* under Kāshānī (T. W. Haig).

No. 438 (4). The Persian original of ʿAbd al-Aḥad Zanjānī's reminiscences is Browne Coll. F. 25 (6).

No. 439, first visit. *Read* ***Rūz-nāmah.*** This is apparently the untitled edition of the Ḥakīm al-Mamālik's journal (see no. 1491, 2nd par. *supra*, Mashhad cat. iii *fṣl.* 14, ptd. bks., no. 122, where it is called *Safar-nāmah i Khurāsān*, and Āṣafīyah iii p. 250 no 98, where it is called *Rūz-nāmah i Ḥakīm al-Mamālik*).

No. 439, antepenult. [*Safar i ʿIrāq.*] Edition: **Ṭihrān** 1311/1893–4 (see Mashhad iii, *fṣl.* 14, ptd. bks., no. 120).

No. 439, last par. [Nāṣir al-Dīn Shāh.] Also Zaidān *Mashāhīr al-sharq* (in Arabic) pp. 133–5.

No. 440 (1), ult. *Read* 1273/1856.

No. 440 (1), 2nd par. *Read* Langues.

No. 440 (1), 2nd. par. *Read* 1853–7°.

No. 441. [*Tārīkh i Qājārīyah.*] See also the Additions and Corrections to no. 191, 2nd par. *supra*.

No. 442, 2nd par. For Farrukh Khān see also no. 1421, 1st footnote.

No. 443, end. *Insert*:

443*a*. **Aḥmad b. Abū 'l-Ḥasan Sharīfī Shīrāzī.** (***Tārīkh i Qājārīyah***), a history of Persia from 1212/1805 to 1286/1869: MS. in the possession of Khān Bahādur Āghā Mīrzā Muḥammad, C.I.E. Description with English translation of some extracts: *Some new notes on Babiism.* By Kh. B. Ā. M. M., C.I.E. (in *JRAS*. 1927, pp. 443–70).

No. 444, 3rd par. *Read* ending with Tihrān (spelt with tā, not ṭā).

No. 444 (2), 1st par. [*al-Maʾāthir wa-l-āthār.*] For a more adequate description see no. 1661.

No. 444 (2), 2nd par. [*al-Maʾāt͟hir wa-ʾl-āt͟hār.*] *Read*: Edition: [**Ṭihrān**] 1306–7/1889°* (the date 1306 is given on the title-page, but 8 Muḥarram 1307 in the colophon on p. 294).

No. 445, 2nd par., end. [*Tārīk͟h i jadīd.*] Also **Browne** Coll. Sup. 7 (transcribed by Browne from Browne Coll. F. 55 and collated with Rieu Suppt. 15).

No. 447, end. *Insert*:—

447*a*. S͟hāh-zādah ʿ**Abbās Mīrzā Mulk-ārā** b. Muḥammad S͟hāh Qājār was born in Rajab 1255/Sept.-Oct. 1839 and was thus eight years younger than his brother Nāṣir al-Dīn S͟hāh (for whom see no. 439 *supra*). Being regarded by the latter as an enemy and as a potential claimant to the throne, he was banished to Bag͟hdād towards the end of 1268/1852 and it was not until the end of 1294/1877 that he received permission to return to Persia. Nāṣir al-Dīn S͟hāh then conferred upon him the title of Mulk-ārā and appointed him Governor of Zanjān. Subsequently he held the Governorships of Qazwīn and Gīlān. Having resigned in 1313/1895–6, he was sent as Envoy Extraordinary to congratulate the Tsar Nicholas II on his accession [which occurred in November 1894]. After the assassination of Nāṣir al-Dīn S͟hāh [1 May 1896] he was again sent to Russia. In 1314/1896 he was appointed Minister of Justice and in 1316/1898–9 he died at Ṭihrān and was buried at Qum.

(***S͟harḥ i ḥāl i ʿAbbās Mīrzā Mulk-ārā***), an autobiography extending to the author's return from Russia in 1314/1896: MS. in the possession of Dr. Qāsim G͟hanī (cf. no. 1238 *supra*) transcribed from an autograph.

Edition: [**Ṭihrān**] AHS 1325/1946 (ed. ʿAbd al-Ḥusain Nawāʾī. With an introduction by ʿAbbās Iqbāl (cf. no. 1453 *supra*). Nas͟hrīyāt i Anjuman i Nas͟hr i Āt͟hār i Īrān, no. 1).

N. 448, 3rd par. *Read* 1915°*.

No. 450, 3rd par. [*Tārīk͟h i bīdārī i Īrāniyān.*] The place and date are Ṭihrān 1328 [1910] according to Berthels *Ocherk istorii persidskoi literatury* p. 202.

No. 451 (4), end. *Insert*:

(5) ***Dawn-breakers, The; Nabíl's[45] narrative of the early days of the Baha'i revelation ... Translated from the original Persian and edited by Shoghi Effendi*: New York** (Kingsport, Tennessee, printed) 1932* (685 pp.).

45 "Nabīl" Zarandī died in 1892 (see Browne *Lit. Hist*, iv pp. 151 n., 187 n., etc.).

(6) ***Fārs u jang i bain al-milal***, by Rukn-zādah Ādamīyat: **Ṭihrān** AHS 1312/1933*.

(7) ***Inqilāb u taḥawwul i Ād͟harbāyjān***, the history of Sattār K͟hān.[46] etc., by Ḥusain Farzād: **Ṭihrān** (see *Luzac's O.L.* 1946 p. 104, where the date is not mentioned).

(8) ***Īrān u Ingilīs***, by Mahdī Mujtahidī: AHS 1326/1947 (see the same author's *Rijāl i Ād͟harbayjān*, fly-leaf at end).

(9) ***Fulūs i Muẓaffarī***, on the events connected with the accession of Muẓaffar al-Dīn S͟hāh: **Majlis** 678.

(10) ***Kitāb i sabz i bī-ṭarafī i Īrān***: **Ṭihrān** 1336–7/ 1917–19 (2 vols. See R. Lescot, *Bull. E.O.I.F. de Damas* vii–viii p. 282).

(11) ***Muk͟htaṣarī az zindagānī i siyāsī i Sulṭān Aḥmad S͟hāh Qājār***, by Ḥusain Makkī: **Ṭihrān** AHS 1323/1944–5 (see an unsigned review in the periodical *Suk͟han*. Yr. ii/2 (Bahman 1323) p. 152).

(12) ***Rawābiṭ i Napōliyōn u Īrān***, by ʿAbbās Mīrzā: **Ṭihrān** n.d. [R. Lescot, *Bull. E.O.I.F. de Damas* vii–viii p. 282.]

(13) ***Taḥawwulāt i siyāsī i niẓām i Īrān***, by Qāʾimmaqāmī: **Ṭihrān** AHS 1326/1947 (see Probsthain's *Orientalia nova* 2 (1946–8) p. 27).

(14) ***Tārīk͟h i ijtimāʿī u idārī i daurah i Qājār***, by ʿAbd Allāh Mustaufī:[47] **Ṭihrān** AHS 1324/1945 onwards, (vol. i, 728 pp., Probsthain's *Orientalia nova* 1 (1944–6) p. 16, "Part 2" (= vol. ii?). 720 pp., *Luzac's O.L.* 1945 p. 79, vol. iii, pt. 2 (1300–4), 539 pp., Probsthain's *Orientalia nova* 2 (1946–8) p. 28, *Luzac's O.L.* 1948 p. 12.) Cf. no. 1665, 2nd par. *supra*.

(15) ***Tārīk͟h i inqilāb i mas͟hrūṭīyat i Īrān***, by Mahdī Malik-zādah, in 7 vols.: **Ṭihrān** AHS 1328/1949–, *in progress* (vol. i 1328, vol. ii 1329).

(16) ***Tārīk͟h i jang i Ingilīs u Īrān*** (mentioned, without author's name or date, in the list of the *Intis͟hārāt i majallah i Yādgār* on the back cover of the *Simṭ al-ʿulā*).

(17) ***Tārīk͟h i jarāʾid u majallāt i Īrān***, an alphabetical dictionary of newspapers and periodicals, by M. Ṣadr Hās͟hīmī: **Iṣfahān** AHS 1327/1948-*in progress* (vol. i (*Alif*), 351 pp., vol. ii (*Bāʾ* to *Rāʾ*), 339 pp., AHS 1328/1950).

(18) ***Tārīk͟h i mas͟hrūṭah i Īrān*** by S. Aḥmad Kasrawī Tabrīzī (for whom see nos. 321 3.1.1 (5) and 489 *supra*): **Ṭihrān** (2nd ed. See *Luzac's O.L.* 1942 p. 9, where the date is not mentioned, and Mahdī Mujtahidī's *Rijāl i Ād͟harbāyjān* p. 129).

46 For whom see Browne *History of the Persian revolution*; *Yādgār v/1–2* pp. 96–99 (a biography by M. Qazwīnī); *Rijāl i Ād͟harbāyjān* pp. 85–7.

47 A work by this author entitled *Inqilāb i Farānisah* is mentioned in Yāsimī's *Adabīyāt i muʿāṣir* p. 113.

(19) ***Tārīkh i rawābiṭ i siyāsī i Īrān ba-dunyā***, by Najaf-Qulī Muʿizzī[48] (Ḥusām al-Daulah): **Ṭihrān**(See *Luzac's Oriental list* 1946 p. 105, where the date is not mentioned.)

(20) ***Tārīkh i rawābiṭ i siyāsī i Īrān u Ingilīs dar qarn i nūzdahum i mīlādī***, by Maḥmūd i Maḥmūd: **Ṭihrān** (vol. i. See *Luzac's Oriental list* 1950 p. 38 (date not mentioned), vol. ii, see *LOL*. 1950 p. 59 (date not mentioned).)

(21) ***Wāqiʿāt i dū-sālah yā Tārīkh i bad-bakhtī i Iran***, by Ḥājjī Āqā Shīrāzī: **Ṭihrān** 1330/1912 [R. Lescot, *Bull. E.O.I.F. de Damas* vii–viii p. 282]

(22) ***Yāddāshthā'ī az zindagānī i khuṣūṣī i Nāṣir al-Dīn Shāh***, by Dūst-ʿAlī Khān Muʿaiyir al-Mamālik (b. Dūst-Muḥammad Khān Muʿaiyir al-Mamālik), whose mother was ʿIṣmat al-Daulah, a daughter of Nāṣir al-Dīn Shāh: [**Ṭihrān**, 1946?] (188 pp.).

No. 452. ʿAbd Allāh Khān Amīr Ṭahmāsb, having skilfully pacified Ādharbāyjān, was appointed Minister of War by Riḍā Shāh Pahlawī and subsequently Minister of Roads. He was murdered by Lurs on the road between Khurramābād and Burūjird, when on a visit of inspection. See Ḥabīb Allāh Mukhtārī's *Tārīkh i bīdārī i Īrān* pp. 349⁹–351 (portrait).

No. 452, end. *Insert*:

452*a*. **M. R. Hazār.**

Daurān i Pahlawī: **Shirāz** AH 1336/1917–18. [R. Lescot, *Bull. E.O.I.F. de Damas* vii–viii p. 282.]

452*b*. Ḥabīb Allāh **"Naubakht"**, *nigārandah i majallah i Qushūn*, was born at Shīrāz in 1284/1905. Among his publications are the educational works *Qānūn i fikr* and *ʿIlm i ṭabāʾiʿ*.

(1) ***Shāhanshāh i Pahlawī***: **Ṭihrān** n.d. (Pt. i, years 1301–8/1923–30. Pp. 320, 7). [Minorsky, *BSOS*. ix/1 (1937) p. 254; R. Lescot, *Bull. E.O.I.F. de Damas* vii–viii p. 282; *Dharīʿah* iii p. 259.]

(2) ***Shāh-nāmah***, or ***Pahlawī-nāmah***, a history of Persia, in verse, from the fall of the Sāsānians to the beginning of the Pahlawī dynasty in six parts: vol. i (= pts. 1–3) **Ṭihrān** [1932*] (cf. *Luzac's O.L.* 1933 p. 14).

[Irani *Poets of the Pahlavi regime* pp. 619–25; Yāsimī *Adabīyāt i muʿāṣir* pp. 99, 113, 116; Ishaque *Modern Persian poetry* pp. 105, 112, 116; M. Ṣadr Hāshimī *Tārīkh i jarāʾid u majallāt i Īrān* ii pp. 32–6 (portrait).]

48 Works by this author entitled *Tārīkh i Amrīkā* and *Sukhanwarān i ʿaṣr i Pahlawī* are mentioned in Yāsimī's *Adabīyāt i muʿāṣir* p. 113.

452*c*. **Jaʿfar Saiyāḥ.**

Pahlawī-namah, in verse: **Ṭihrān** AHS 1313/1934–5. [R. Lescot, *Bull. E.O.I.F. de Damas* vii–viii p. 282.]

452*d*. **Ḥabīb Allāh Mukhtārī** Mukhtār al-Salṭanah, the son of Karīm Khān Mukhtār al-Salṭanah Sardār i Manṣūr, has held various military commands and administrative appointments connected with the Persian army (for some details see *Tārīkh i bīdārī i Īrān* p. [923] and for a portrait *op. cit.* p. 1).

Tārīkh i bīdārī i Īrān, a history of Persia under the Pahlawī dynasty to 1946 preceded by a summary account of the last thirty years of Qājār rule: **Ṭihrān** 1326/1947 (923 pp. Many illustrations).

452*e*. Other works:[49]—

(1) ***Pīsh-rafthā-yi Īrān***, by Saʿīd Nafīsī (cf. no. 1236 *supra*): **Ṭihrān** (see *Luzac's O.L.* 1939 p. 177, where the date is not mentioned).

(2) ***Az Shahrīwar tā fājiʿah i Ādharbāyjān u Zanjān***, on the events of AHS 1320/1941 and the following years, by Ḥusain Kūhī Kirmānī: **Ṭihrān** n.d. [1947. See Probsthain's *Orientalia nova* 2 (1946–8) p. 27 no. 424].

(3) ***Siyāsat i daulat i Shūrawī dar Īrān az*** 1296 [1917–18] *tā 1306* [1927–8], by M. ʿA. Manshūr Garakānī: **Ṭihrān** AHS 1326/1948‡ (vol. i).

(4) ***Tārīkh i bīst-sālah i Īrān***, by Ḥusain Makkī: **Ṭihrān** AHS 1323–4/1944–5 (vol. i: the coup d'etat of 1299, vol. ii: the change of dynasty. See Probsthain's *Orientalia nova*, i (1944–6) p. 16). Cf. ad no. 1483. *infra*.

(5) ***Tārīkh i mukhtaṣar i aḥzāb i siyāsī i Īrān***, by Malik al-Shuʿarāʾ "Bahār":[50] **Ṭihrān** AHS 1323/1944 (vol. i (the fall of the Qājār dynasty). See *Luzac's O.L.* 1945 p. 6, where the date is not mentioned, Probsthain's *Orientalia nova* 1 (1944–6) p. 15, and a review by B. S. in the periodical *Sukhan*, Yr. ii/2 (Bahman 1323/1945) p. 151). Cf. Machalski in *Rocz. Orient*, xv pp. 107–8.

No. 453, end. *Insert*:

Description: *An account of the Tārīkhi Qumm, by Ann K. S. Lambton* (in *BSOAS*. xii/3–4 (1948) pp. 586–96).

---

49 No attempt has been made to deal at all fully with the publications of contemporary Persian historians, which scarcely fall within the scope of the present work.

50 Mīrzā M. Taqī, the son of M. Kāẓim "Ṣabūrī" Kāshānī, was born at Mashhad in 1304/1886–7. See Browne *The press and poetry of modern Persia* pp. 260–89 (portraits), etc., *Lit. Hist*, iv p. 345; D. J. Irani *Poets of the Pahlavi regime* pp. 196–226 (portrait); M. Ishaque *Sukhanvarān-i-Īrān* i pp. 358–403 (portrait), *Modern Persian poetry* pp. 10, 24, etc.; Rashīd Yāsimī *Adabīyāt i muʿāṣir* pp. 30–32 (portrait).

No. 454, 1st line. *Read* S̲h̲. **M. ʿAlī b. Ḥusain** b. ʿAlī b. Bahāʾ al-Dīn, a resident of Qum.

No. 454, 1st par.. *For* wrote in 1302/1884–5 *read* began in 1325/1907.

No. 454, 2nd par. The title, not formally mentioned in the preface, is given on the title-page as *Tārīkh i Qum musammā bi-Anwār al-Mus̲h̲aʿs̲h̲aʿīn*. P. 2 is headed *Hād̲h̲ā jild* [sic] *al-awwal min kitāb Anwār al-Mus̲h̲aʿs̲h̲aʿīn fī s̲h̲arāfat al-Qum* [sic] *wa-ʾl-Qummīyīn* ... In the first of the publisher's two colophons the work is called *Tārīkh i Qum* and in the second *Anwār al-Mus̲h̲aʿs̲h̲iʿīn* [sic]. The volume is described by the author as vol. i. There is a copy in the Cambridge University Library.

No. 454, end. *Insert*:

454a. S. **ʿAlī Akbar "Kās̲h̲if"** b. S. Raḍī **Burqaʿī Qummī**, already mentioned as the author of the *Kāk̲h̲ i dil-āwīz* (no. 1582 (1) *supra*), was born at Qum in AHS 1278/1899–1900 (see *Suk̲h̲anwarān i nāmī i muʿāṣir*, by his son, S. M. Bāqir Burqaʿī, p. 190).

Rāhnumā-yi Qum, "History and Geography of Qum": Ṭihrān (see *Luzac's O.L.* 1939 p. 177, where the date is not mentioned).

No. 455, 3rd par. *Read* al-ʿAlawī al-Āwī *according to the printed text, p. 1 penult.*

No. 455, 3rd par., end.[*Maḥāsin i Iṣfahān.*] *Insert*:
Edition of the Persian translation: *T. i M. i I.*, Ṭihrān AHS 1328/1949‡ (ed. ʿAbbās Iqbāl).

No. 456, 1st line. M. Mahdī Arbāb b. M. Riḍā Iṣfahānī, the father of M. Ḥusain K̲h̲ān "Furūg̲h̲ī" (see *PL.* no. 319 and the corrigenda to that record) died in 1314/1896–7 (see ʿAbd al-Karīm Jazī's *Rijāl i Iṣfahān* p. 232).

No. 456, 2nd par., end.[*Niṣf i jahān.*] Also **London** S.O.A.S. Per. 28 (AH 1315/1897). *Insert*:

456a. **Ḥasan** b. ʿAlī b. Maḥmūd **Jābirī Anṣārī** Iṣfahānī was born in 1287/1870–1 and was still alive [in 1950?] when S. Muṣliḥ al-Dīn Mahdawī gave a brief account of him in his preface to ʿAbd al-Karīm Jazī's *Rijāl i Iṣfahān* (p. hā). His works amount to more than twenty.

(1) ***Nīm-jahān***, a concise history of Iṣfahān composed in 1333/1915 and containing at the end biographies of its celebrities together with a sketch of universal history (*"wa-fī dhailihi ta'rīkh 'umūmī nāfi' mufīd"*, *Dharī'ah* iii p. 233[4]). Edition: 1333/1915 (see *Dharī'ah* iii p. 232, where the place of publication, doubtless Iṣfahān, is not mentioned).
(2) ***Tārīkh i niṣf i jahān u hamah i jahān***, probably identical with the preceding or a new edition of it: **Iṣfahān** n.d. [R. Lescot *Bull. E.O.I.F. de Damas*, vii–viii p. 282].
(3) ***Tārīkh i Iṣfahān u Rai*** (mentioned by S. Muṣliḥ al-Dīn Mahdawī, *loc. cit.*, without specification of the date and place of publication).

456*c*. Mīr S. **'Alī Janāb** b. M. Bāqir b. M. Ḥusain (Mīr S. 'A. b. M. B. b. M. Ḥ. *al-mushtahir bi-*Janāb) was born at Iṣfahān in 1287/1870–1 and died at Tihrān in Shawwāl 1349/Feb.–March 1931 (see 'Abd al-Karīm Jazī *Rijāl i Iṣfahān*, editor's preface, p. *dāl*).

al-Iṣfahān [*sic*], an account, historical, topographical, statistical, etc., begun in Shawwāl 1342/May 1924: **Iṣfahān** AHS 1303/1924J (vol. i only. Cf. *Dharī'ah* iii p. 233).

456*d*. **Ḥusain Nūr Ṣādiqī** was born on 24 Shawwāl 1328/29 October 1910 (see 'Abd al-Karīm's *Rijāl i Iṣfahān*, editor's preface, p. *wāw*).

Iṣfahān: **Ṭihrān** "1938" (see Harrassowitz's *Litterae orientales* Oct. 1938 p. 15 and *Luzac's O.L.* 1938, p. 71).

After 3.17 ***Kāshān*** *Insert*:

457*a*. **Aḥmad b. Ḥusain b. 'Alī** al-Kātib wrote in the reign of Jahān-Shāh [of the Qarā-Quyūnlū, AH 839–72/1435–67].

Tārīkh i jadīd, extending to 862/1458: **Majlis** (not in the published catalogues, but see "Āyatī's" *Tārīkh i Yazd* p. 17[20]).

Edition: *T. i j. i Yazd*: **Yazd** AHS 1317/1938‡.

457*b*. **M. Mufīd** Mustaufī b. Najm al-Dīn Maḥmūd Bāfqī **Yazdī** (see no. 461 *supra*).

Jāmi' i Mufīdī (see no. 461, 2nd par., where this work is erroneously placed, since Yazd, though anciently in Fārs and so treated, for example, in the *Fārs-nāmah* and by Yāqūt, has for some centuries been regarded as a part of 'Irāq i 'Ajamī).

457*c*. **M. Ṭāhir Mālmīrī.**

Tārīkh i Shuhadā i Yazd: **Cairo** 1342/1923–4 [R. Lescot, *Bull. E.O.I.F. de Barms* vii–viii p. 283],

457*d.* **ʿAbd al-Ḥusain "Āyatī"** (formerly "Āwārah") b. Ḥajj Sh. M. was born at Taft in 1288/1871. In 1320/1902–3 he became a convert to Bahāism and for a number of years he travelled extensively as a missionary of that faith. In 1923 he published at Cairo a history entitled *al-Kawākib al-durrīyah fī maʾāthir al-Bahāʾīyah*,[51] but he later abandoned Bahāism and published a three-volume attack on it under the title *Kashf al-ḥiyal*. The monthly periodical *Namakdān* founded by him in 1929 was edited by him until its discontinuance in 1935.

Tārīkh i Yazd (on the wrapper, but not on the title-page, is added *yā Ātash-kadah i Yazdān*), completed AHS 1317/1938–9: **Yazd** AHS 1317/1938–9.

[Autobiography in *Tārīkh i Yazd* p. 277 (portrait); M. Ishaque *Sukhanvarān-i-Īrān* ii pp. 8–14 (portrait), *Modern Persian poetry* pp. 9, 18, 41, 196, etc.]

457*e.* **Aḥmad Ṭāhirī.**

Tārīkh i Yazd: **Ṭihrān** (See *Luzac's O.L.* 1939 p. 75, where the date is not mentioned.)

No. 459, 2nd par., MSS. [*Shīrāz-nāmah.*] Also **I.O.** 4615 (AH 1075/1665. See *JRAS*. 1939 p. 384), **Ellis Coll. M.** 183 (AH 1287/1871).

No. 459, 2nd par., MSS.Dorn 305 and Dorn A.M. p. 374 are the same MS.

No. 461. [*Jāmiʿ i Mufīdī*] This article is misplaced: see above, the addenda to **3.17 *Kāshān***, (457*b*).

No. 464, 2nd par., after 1st sentence. [*Fārs-nāmah i Nāṣirī.*] *Insert*:

Abridged translation of the two sections relating to the tribes in the final chapter: *Hajji Mirza Hasan-i-Shirazi on the nomad tribes of Fars in the Fars-nameh-i-Nasiri. By D. Austin Lake* (in *JRAS*. 1923 pp. 209–31).

No. 465, 1st line. M. Naṣīr "Furṣat" b. "Bahjat" Ḥusainī Shīrāzī entitled (*mulaqqab*) Furṣat al-Daulah was born in 1271/ 1854–5 according to Majlis 323, where a collection of his poems (*Ashʿār i Furṣat*) is described. Cf. Ishaque *Modern Persian poetry* pp. 33 n., 82, where the date of his death is given as 1339/1920. A collection of his poems, *Dabistān al-furṣah*, was published at Bombay in 1334/1916* with a biography by Ibrāhīm Adīb "Sākit". Presumably he is identical with the Furṣat Shīrāzī whose *Āthār i salāṭīn i ʿaẓīm al-shaʾn i ʿahd i qadīm i bāstān i*

51 An Arabic translation from the (doubtless unpublished) Persian: see Brockelmann *Sptbd.* ii p. 847 [11–13], where the date is given as 1343/1924.

mamlakat i Īrān was published at Ṭihrān in 1354/1935 (see Harrassowitz's *Litterae Orientates*, Oct. 1938 p. 10 no. 823).

No. 465, 2nd par. *For* south-eastern *read* south-western.

No. 465, end. *Insert*:

465*a*. **Rukn-zādah "Ādamīyat".** ***Fārs u jang i bain al-milal*: Ṭihrān** AHS 1312/1933*.

No. 466, first sentence. ['Alī b. Zaid Baihaqī.] The correct date of his birth is 493 (see *Tārīkh i Baihaq*, editor's preface, p. YB).

No. 466, 1st par., Arabic works (2). A fragmentary MS. of the *Wishāḥ Dumyat al-qaṣr* preserved in the Chelebī Ḥusain Library at Brusa was described by O. Rescher in *ZDMG*. 68 (1914) p. 52.

No. 466, Persian works (2), end. [*Tārīkh i Baihaq*.] Edition: **Ṭihrān** AHS 1317/1937‡ (ed. Aḥmad Bahmanyār. With prefaces by the editor and by M. Qazwīnī).
Extracts: (1) [concerning the author's family] *OCM*. ix/2 (Feb. 1933) pp. 107–20 (ed. M. Shafī'). (2) [concerning the Niẓām al-Mulk and his family] *OCM*. v/1 (Nov. 1928) pp. 76–80, v/2 (Feb. 1929) pp. 85–94 (ed. M. Shafī').

No. 466, last par. ['Alī b. Zaid Baihaqī.] The reference to the *Kharīdat al-qaṣr* [*sic lege*] should be deleted. The person whose biography occurs in that work, and to whom 'Imād al-Dīn erroneously ascribes the *Wishāḥ Dumyat al-qaṣr* is Sharaf al-Dīn 'Alī b. al-Ḥasan al-Baihaqī, of whom there is a notice in the *Tārīkh i Baihaq*, pp. 225–6. See M. Shafī''s remarks in *Islamic culture* vi/4 (Oct. 1932) pp. 595–6.

No. 466, last par.['Alī b. Zaid Baihaqī.] Also *The author of the oldest biographical notice of 'Umar Khayyam & the notice in question*, by M. Shafī' (in *Islamic culture* vi/4 (Oct. 1932) pp. 586–623); M. Shafī''s introduction to his edition of the *Tatimmat Siwān al-ḥikmah* (cf. no. 1485, editions (2) *supra*); Brockelmann *Sptbd.* i pp 557–8; M. Qazwīnī's preface to the *Tārīkh i Baihaq*, Ṭihrān AHS 1317/1937.

No. 467, 2nd par. end. [*Tārīkh i Mulūk i Kart.*] Also **Kābul** State Library (see *Journal asiatique*, Jan. 1924, p. 150). [Minorsky, *BSOS*. ix/1 (1937) p. 255.]

No. 468 (1), MSS. [*Rauḍāt al-jannāt.*] Also **Ellis Coll.** M. 288 (AH 1073/1663).

No. 469, 2nd par. [*Maqṣad al-iqbāl al-Sulṭānīyah.*] Presumably this is the same work as

Mazārāt i Harāt, by ʿAbd Allāh b. ʿAbd al-Raḥmān Ḥusainī: **Harāt** AHS 1310/1931–2 (with a supplement by ʿUbaid Allāh Abū Saʿīd Harawī). [R. Lescot, *Bull. E.O.I.F. de Damas*, vii–viii p. 283.]

No. 471, 2nd par., penult. *Read* 1301/1884°*–1303/1886°*.

No. 471, end. *Insert*:

471*a*. Other works relating to Khurāsān:—

(1) ***Āthār i Harāt***,[1] by Khalīl Afghān: **Harāt** AHS 1309–10/1930–2 (3 vols.). [R. Lescot, *Bull. E.O.I.F. de Damas* vii–viii p. 283.]

(2) ***Faḍāʾil i Balkh***,[52] an anonymous translation made at the request of the Qāḍī *Majlis i ʿālī Ṣadr i kabīr* Fakhr al-Dīn Abū Bakr ʿAbd Allāh b. Abū ʾl-Farīd al-Balkhi (but this name, written in place of a name erased, may not be genuine) from an Arabic work in three sections ((1) traditions concerning the superiority of Balkh, (2) a description of the town, (3) biographies of seventy celebrated *shaikhs* connected with the neighbourhood) completed at Balkh on 1 Ramaḍān 610/14 January 1214 by the Shaikh al-Islām Abū Bakr b. ʿAbd Allāh [b.] ʿUmar b. Dāwud al-Wāʿiẓ Ṣafī al-Dīn al-Balkhī (but this name, occurring in the translator's preface, has likewise been written in place of a name erased): **Blochet** i 519 (lacks last six "sections" (biographies?). Late 15th cent.). Edition of Sections i and ii: Schefer *Chrestomathie persane*, tome i (3).

(3) ***Tārīkh i inqilāb i Ṭūs***, by M. Ḥasan Harawī: **Mashhad** 1339/1920–1. [R. Lescot, *Bull. E.O.I.F. de Damas*, vii–viii p. 283.]

(4) ***Tārīkh i mazārāt i Balkh***, written in the reign of ʿAbd al-Muʾmin Khān b. ʿAbd Allāh Khān Uzbak [AH 1006–7/1598–9] by M. Ṣāliḥ b. Amīr ʿAbd Allāh b. Amīr ʿAbd al-Raḥmān: **Kābul** National Library (see A. Z. Validi in *Journal asiatique*, Jan.-March 1924 p. 150). [Minorsky, BSOS. ix/1 (1937) p. 255.]

(5) ***Tārīkh i muḥāṣarah u fatḥ i Harāt*** on the taking of Harāt by the Persians in the Anglo-Persian War, by Mīrzā Ibrāhīm Badāʾiʿ-nigār: **Ṭihrān** 1273/1856–7. [R. Lescot, *Bull. E.O.I.F. de Damas* vii–viii p. 283.]

52 Both Harāt and Balkh are of course now in Afghānistān.

(6) ***Tārīkh i wāqiʿah i Mashhad i Muqaddas***, on the bombardment of Mashhad by the Russians, anonymous: **Mashhad** 1330/1912. [R. Lescot, *ibid.*]

No. 472 (1), end. [*Badāʾiʿ al-azmān.*] *Insert*:

Incomplete reconstruction of the work from quotations in the *Jāmiʿ al-tawārīkh i Ḥasanī* (cf. no. 121, 2nd par. *supra*) and M. b. Ibrāhīm's *Tārīkh i Saljūqiyān i Kirmān* (cf. no. 474, 2nd par. *supra*): *Tārīkh i Afḍal yā Badāʾiʿ al-azmān fī waqāʾiʿ Kirmān ... farāham āwardah i Duktur Mahdī Bayānī*, **Ṭihrān** AHS 1326/1948 (Intishārāt i Dānishgāh i Ṭihrān, 15).

No. 473, 2nd par., end. [*Simṭ al-ʿulā.*] Edition: **Ṭihrān** AHS 1328/1949 (ed. ʿAbbās Iqbāl with help from M. Qazwīnī).

No. 476, end. *Insert*:

476*a*. Major **Sykes** (i.e. presumably Sir Percy Sykes, b. 1867, d. 11.6.1945,[53] who became British Consul for Kirmān and Persian Balūchistān in 1894 and who is best known for his *History of Persia* (2 vols., London 1915, 2nd ed. 1921, 3rd ed. 1930), of which the first volume (at least) has appeared in a Persian translation[54] (see *Luzac's O.L.* 1945 p. 79)).

Tārīkh i Kirmān, translated by Mīr Naṣr Allāh Khān Nawwāb Shīrāzī from the unpublished English original: **Kirmān** 1322/1904–5. [R. Lescot, *Bull. E.O.I.F. de Damas* vii–viii p. 283.]

No. 477, 2nd par., end. [Ibn Isfandiyār's *Tārīkh i Ṭabaristān.*] Edition: **Ṭihrān** AHS 1320/1941–2 (Pt. 1, 331 pp. Cf. *Luzac's O.L.* 1942 p. 66, 1947 p. 39).

No. 477, 3rd par., footnote, end. Cf. also *Acta Orientalia* x (1931) pp. 45–55 (Christensen).

No. 481, 3rd par., end. [*Tārīkh i Gīlān.*] Another edition: **Rasht** AHS 1315/1936–7. [R. Lescot, *Bull. E.O.I.F. de Damas* vii–viii p. 283.]

53 For obituary notices see *The Times* 12.6.1945; *Luzac's O.L.* 1945 p. 28; etc.

54 His *Ten thousand miles in Persia* (London 1902) has been translated by Ḥusain Saʿādat Nūrī under the title *Hasht sāl dar Irān yā dah hazār mīl sair dar kishwar i Shāhanshāhī* (2 vols. Iṣfahān and Ṭihrān a.h.s. 1315–16/1936–7, See Harrassowitz's *Litterae orientales* April-July 1939 p. 18).

No. 486, 2nd par., MSS. [*Tādhhirah i Shūshtarīyah.*] Also **Ellis Coll.** M. 9 (AH 1322/1904).

No. 488, end. *Insert*:

488*a*. S. **Ṣadr al-Dīn Ẓahīr-al-Islām-zādah Dizfūlī.**

Shakaristān dar tārīkh i sih-hazār-sālah i Khūzistān: Ṭihrān AHS 1308/1929–30. [R. Lescot, *Bull. E.O.I.F. de Damas* vii–viii p. 283.]

No. 489, 1st par., end. S. Aḥmad Kasrawī was murdered in Ṭihrān towards the end of AHS 1324/1945–6. See *Rijāl i Ādharbāyjān*, by Mahdī Mujtahidī, pp. 126–31, 223–4, and, for a portrait, the frontispiece to *Maqālāt i Kasrawi* (*Essays from Kasrawi, collected by Y. Zoka*), pt. 1 (Ṭihrān AHS 1327/1948).

No. 489, 2nd par., end. [*Tārīkh i pānṣad-sālah i Khūzistān.*] "On the rare sources utilized by Kasravī in his book on Khūzistān see my review in *BSOS*. viii 4, p. 1173." [Minorsky, *BSOS*. ix/1 (1937) p. 255.]

No. 489, end. *Insert*:

3.25 *The Bakhtyārīs*

489*a*. **'Abd al-Ḥusain Khān Lisān al-Salṭanah** Malik al-Mu'arrikhīn.

(1) ***Tārīkh i Bakhtyārī***, a history covering the years 1004–1299/1692–1882 composed in 1327/1909 by order of Ḥājjī 'Alī-Qulī Khān Sardār i As'ad Wazīr i Jang b. Ḥusain-Qulī Khān Īlkhānī Bakhtyārī: Maṭba'ah i Mīrzā 'Alī Aṣghar [place?] n.d. (Camb. Univ. Lib. Moh. 591.A.3).

(2) ***Khulāṣat al-a'ṣār fī ta'rīkh al-Bakhtiyār***: **Ṭihrān** 1333/1915. [R. Lescot, *Bull. E.O.I.F. de Damas* vii–viii p. 283.]

3.26 *Ādharbāyjān*

489*b*. **'Abd al-Razzāq** Bēg b. Najaf-Qulī Khān **Dunbulī** died in 1243/1827–8 (see no. 426, 1st par. *supra*).

Tārīkh i Danābilah (cf. no. 426, 1st par., and *BSOS*. ix/1 (1937) p. 254, where Minorsky remarks "Under 'local histories' Ādharbāyjān ought to be represented by the history of the Dunbulī rulers of Khoy and Tabrīz by 'Abd al-Razzāq Dunbulī ...", but no MSS. or editions seem to be recorded in the catalogues. According to *Dharī'ah* iii p. 253 the title of the work is *Riyāḍ al-jannah*).

489*c*. **Nādir Mīrzā** b. Badīʿ al-Zamān b. M.-Qulī b. Fatḥ-ʿAlī S͟hāh **Qājār** wrote a work on Persian cookery (title?) and another entitled *Nawādir i Nādirī* on Arabic proverbs (see *Dānis͟hmandān i Ād͟harbāyjān* p. 367; Īraj Afs͟hār *Nat͟hr i Fārsī i muʿāṣir* pp. 12, 14–16 (portrait)).

Tārīk͟h u jug͟hrāfiyā-yi dār al-salṭanah i Tabrīz: **Tihrān** [AH 1323 (1905) according to Īraj Afs͟hār, but according to Minorsky (*Acta Orientalia* xxi (1951) p. 122) the work, edited in 1905 [1323] by "Sipihr" [cf. *PL*. no. 309], was not published until circ. 1940].

489*d*. Ḥajjī **M. Bāqir**.

Tārīk͟h i inqilāb i Ād͟harbāyjān u balwā-yi Tabrīz: **Tabrīz** 1326/1908. [R. Lescot, *Bull. E.O.I.F. de Damas* vii–viii p. 283.]

489*e*. S. Aḥmad **Kasrawī Tabrīzī** (see no. 489 *supra* and Addendum to that record).

(1) ***Tārīk͟h i hijdah-sālah i Ād͟harbāyjān***: **Tabrīz** AHS 1314–16/1935–8. [R. Lescot, *ibid.*]

(2) ***S͟hahriyārān i gum-nām*** (see no. 321 (*a*) (5) *supra*).

No. 494, 2nd par. "The histories of the vālīs of Ardalān are in Persian: *Ḥadīqa-yi Nāṣirī* by ʿAlī-Akbar (towards AH 1310) and the history of Mastūra (= Māh-sharaf khānum). Of the latter I possessed a copy which was said to be an autograph; the MS. was stolen from me in Tehran." [Minorsky, *BSOS*. ix/1 (1937) p. 255.]

"Māh-i-Sharaf Khānūm, connue en poésie sous le *takhalloṣ* de Mastūre fī 'l-wāqiʿ (elle aurait laissé un diwan de 20,000 vers), morte en 1264 à 44 ans, est l'auteur d'une histoire des émirs d'Ardelan, composée en 1247. Un manuscrit de cet ouvrage est conservé dans la bibliothèque du Dr. Saʿīd Khān (Téhéran). II est daté de 1339. Les premières pages manquent." [R. Lescot, *Bull. E.O.I.F. de Damas* vii–viii p. 283.]

"Mīrzā ʿAlī Akbar Monshī Vaqāʾiʿ Negār, *Ḥadīqe-i-nāṣerīye*. Histoire des émirs d'Ardelan composée en 1309 lunaire. Le Dr. Saʿīd Khān en possède une copie executée en 1316." [R. Lescot, *ibid.*]

No. 494, end. *Insert*:

494*a*. **ʿAlī Aṣg͟har Hamadānī.**

Kurdistān: **Tabrīz** 1312/1894–5. [R. Lescot, *ibid.*]

No. 495, 2nd par., MSS. [*Tārīkh i Bukhārā.*] Also **Tashkent Univ.** 68 (2) (AH 1304/1886–7).

No. 495, 3rd par., end. [*Tārīkh i Bukhārā.*] Another edition (of M. b. Zufar's abridgment): **Tihrān** [1939] (preface dated Isfandmāh 1317 [1939]. Ed. Mudarris Riḍawī 128 (not 178) pp. Cf. *Luzac's OL.* 1939 p. 75).

No. 496, 4th par., MSS.[*Qandīyah.* Persian trans.] Also **Upsala** Zetterstéen 402 (defective).

No. 497, 1st line. *Read* **"Banā'ī"**. Cf. ad no. 372, 1st line *supra.*

No. 498, 2nd par. *Read* Babur's.

No. 499, 2nd par. *Read* ***Mīhmān-nāmah.***

No. 501. ["Wāṣifī", *Badā'i' al-waqā'i'.*] See an article by A. N. Boldyrev in the *Trudy* of the Oriental Section of the Hermitage Museum at Leningrad, vol. ii (1940) pp. 203–70, in which "Wāṣifī's" memoirs are studied in detail and from which it appears that "Wāṣifī", a professional poet, was born at Harāt in 889/1485 and lived there until April 1512, when he went to Central Asia. [Minorsky, in a letter.]

No. 503, last par. ["Mushfiqī."] Also *Ṭabaqāt i Akbarī* ii p. 497; *Ātash-kadah* no. 724; *Khulāṣat al-afkār* no. 442.

No. 504, 2nd par., beginning. "The terms 'pompous and verbose' hardly do justice to Ḥāfiẓ Tanish's history, which has been highly praised by many scholars." [Minorsky, *BSOS.* ix/1 (1937) p. 255.]

No. 504, 2nd par., MSS. [*Sharaf-nāmah i shāhī.*] Also **Ellis Coll.** M. 408 (18th cent.).

No. 506, 4th par., MSS. [*Tārīkh i Rāqimī.*] Also **Tashkent Univ.** 57 (AH 1244/1828–9).

No. 506, 4th par., antepenult. *Read* P. 162.

No. 509, 2nd par., 2nd line. *Read* etc.) and.

No. 509, 2nd par., MSS. [*Tadhkirah i Muqīm-Khānī.*] Also **Tashkent Univ.** 61 (AH 1225/1810), **Leningrad Univ.** 964*b* (AH 1238? See Romaskewicz p. 5), **Caetani** 4.

No. 516, 2nd par. [*Tārīkh i Badakhshān.*] Another MS.: **Kābul** National Library (see A. Z. Validi in *Journal asiatique,* Jan.–March 1924, p. 150). [Minorsky, *BSOS.* ix/1 (1937) p. 255],

No. 521, 2nd par.[A history of the Manghits.] This MS. is in the Asiatic Museum (see *Islamica* iii/3 (1927) p. 316).

No. 522, last line. *Read* Semenov.

No. 528 (12) Wapkandi. Possibly Wābkanawī (from Wābkanah, 3 farsakhs from Bukhārā: see Barthold *Turkestan* p. 132).

No. 537, 1st line. *Read* **Shighā'ul.** [Minorsky, in *BSOS.* ix/1 (1937) p. 255[23].] Cf. Minorsky in *BSOS.* ix/1 (1937) p. 243: "... *Shiqā'ul,* or *Shighā'ul,* a Turkish rank = Pers. *mihmāndār,* "master of ceremonies," cf. Budagov *Slovaŕ* p. 668."

No. 538, 2nd par., end. *Read* 385).

No. 541. This entry should be deleted. For Eton 175 see no. 698, Persian translations (3), MSS.

No. 541, end. *Insert*:

541*a*. M. **Ḥaidar Dūghlāt** died in 958/1551 (see no. 349 *supra*).
Tārīkh i Rashīdī: see no. 349 *supra.*

No. 543 (1), penult. Read *v* xvi *v*.

No. 543 (3). The *Tadhkirah i Khwājagān* of M. Ṣādiq Kāshgharī, being apparently a Turkī work on the lives of certain Central-Asian saints, should be deleted. See *Manuscrits turcs de l'Institut des Langues Orientales décrits par W. D. Smirnov* St. Petersburg 1897) pp. 156–60. Even if it exists also in Persian, the work should appear under Biography, not History.

No. 544 (1), MSS. [*Tārīkh i Khān-i-Jahānī.*] Also **Kapūrt'halā** 36 (not an autograph. See M. Shafīʿ in *OCM.* iii/4 (Aug. 1927) p. 18), **Āṣafīyah** iii p. 94 no. 1073 (defective). For some further MSS. as well as for descriptions of some of those already mentioned see the article by S. M. Imām al-Dīn in *Islamic culture* referred to in the second addition to 544 (1) below.

No. 544 (1), end. [*Tārīkh i Khān-i-Jahānī.*] *Insert*:

Edition: in preparation by S. M. Imāmu'd-Dīn (see *Islamic culture* xxii/3 (July 1948) p. 294). Description: *The Tārīkh Khān-i-Jahānī-wa-Makhzan-i-Afghānī*, by S. M. Imamuddin (in *Islamic culture* xxii/2 (April 1948) pp. 128–42, xxii/3 (July 1948) pp. 280–94).

No. 544 (2), MSS. [*Makhzan i Afghānī.*] Also **Princeton** 57 (AH 1159/ 1746), **Āṣafīyah** iii p. 108 no. 1052. For some further MSS. as well as for descriptions of some of those already mentioned see the article by S. M. Imāmu'd-Dīn referred to above (ad no. 544 (1), end.).

No. 544, 4th par., antepenult. *Read* (AH 1181/1767–8. Christ's).

No. 544, end. *Insert*:

544*a*. "The manuscripts of some historical works in Persian by Khushḥāl Khān Khaṭak[55] have been discovered by Miss Khadijah Begam Feroz ud-Din and are discussed in her (unpublished) Lahore thesis on the "Life and Works of the Illustrious Khushḥāl Khān, Chief of the Khaṭaks" [G. Morgenstierne, *AO*. xvii p. 239.]

No. 547, 1st par. *Read* Mannū.

No. 549, 2nd par., MSS. [*Tārīkh i Aḥmad-Shāhī.*] Also **Ellis Coll.** M. 233 (apparently complete. Late 18th cent.).

No. 550, 2nd par. "The expression 'Yūsuf-zai (i.e. Bāyazīd Anṣārī)'... is not correct" [G. Morgenstierne, *Acta Orientalia* xvii p. 238.]

No. 551, 2nd par. "According to Darmesteter, Chants populaires des Afghans, p. clxxxv, the Tārīkh i Hāfiẓ-Raḥmat (No. 551) was written in 1770."

55 Warrior and poet, b. 1022/1613, imprisoned for seven years at Gwalior by Aurangzēb, d. "a.d. 1691, in the 78th year of his age". (Blumhardt *Catalogue of the Marathi ... Pushtu, and Sindhi manuscripts in ... the British Museum* p. 15 (based on Raverty's *Selections from the poetry of the Afghans*); *Ency. Isl.* under Khushḥāl Khān (R. B. Whitehead); etc.)

[G. Morgenstierne, *AO*. xvii p. 238.] If this is correct, the date of I.O. 3733 cannot be AH 1176.

No. 552, 2nd par., MSS. [*Khulāṣat al-ansāb*.] Also **Ellis Coll.** M. 130 (early 19th cent.).

No. 555, 2nd par., MSS. [*Bhāō-nāmah*.] Also probably **Blochet** iv 2331 fol. 136 (?) (late 18th cent.). According to the *Cambridge History of India* iv p. 591 "the original MS. has now been discovered by Sir Jadunath Sarkar and a revised translation appeared in the *Indian historical quarterly*, 1934.

No. 557, end. *Insert*:

557*a*. (***Tārīkh i Aḥmad Shāh***), without preface or title: **Blochet** iv 2382 (18th cent.).

No. 558, end. [*Ḥusain-Shāhī*.] *Insert*:
Fragment of an early draft (?): **I.O.** 4035.

No. 561. *Read* Durrānīs.

No. 566, 2nd par.For a short account of Akbar Khān (d. 1849) see Buckland's *Dictionary of Indian biography* p. 9.

No. 566, MSS. [*Akbar-nāmah*.] Also **Ellis Coll.** M. 133 (late 19th cent.).

No. 567, 2nd par., MSS. [*Ẓafar-nāmah i Kābul*.] Also **Ellis Coll.** M. 331 (late 19th cent.).

No. 570 (2), 1st par., MSS. [*Tārīkh i Aḥmad*.] Probably also **Āṣafīyah** iii p. 94 no. 1317 (described as *Tārīkh i Durrānī*, by Ḥājjī [*sic*?] 'Abd al-Karīm).

No. 570, end. *Insert*:

570*a*. S. **Badr al-Dīn** was a resident of Aḥmadnagar.
Kaifīyat i jang i Kābul (beg. *Aḥwalāt i safar i Kābul kih jam'īyat i Ingilīs*), a short (9 foll.) account of the British march to Kābul and the battle of Lahore with the Sik'hs, ending with 21 April 1845: **Bombay** Univ. p. 228.

No. 572, 2nd par. penult. *Read* composition, and.

No. 574, 3rd par. *Read* Editions.
[*Fatḥ-nāmah i Kāfiristān.*] The date of the first edition is given by Arberry as 1313 (1896).

No. 575, 5th par. [Amīr ʿAbd al-Raḥmān's autobiography.] There were apparently two editions of the Persian retranslation, (1) **Lahore-Mashhad** 1319/1901–2 (title: *Tāj al-tawārīkh* etc. 2 vols. See Semenov *Ukazatel'* p. 10); (2) **Bombay,** Faiḍ-rasān Press, 1322/1904 (title: *Tāj al-tawārīkh* etc. 2 vols. Pp. 244; 220. See F. E. Karatay *Istanbul Üniversitesi Kütüphanesi Farsça Basmalar Kataloğu* p. 5. Described by C. N. Seddon (*JRAS*. 1938 p. 569) as "a lithographed edition prepared by M. Jaʿfar Mawlā and M. Ḥusain Lārī, AH 1322".[56])

No. 575, last par. [Amīr ʿAbd al-Raḥmān Khān.] Also Zaidān *Mashāhīr al-sharq* (in Arabic) i pp. 142–52; *Who was who 1897–1915* p. 2.

No. 576, end. *Insert*:

576*a*. **Maḥmūd Ṭarzī** was born in 1285/1870 (see *PL*. no. 1629).
Sirāj al-tawārīkh, a detailed history of the Afghāns: **Kābul** (vol. i (only?). Date? See Peshawar cat. p. 291).

No. 577 (1), last line. *Read* Ṣafawids): Rieu.

No. 577 (11), end. *Insert*:
(11*a*) (***Tārīkh i Badakhshān***), a history of the years 1068–1223/1658–1808: **Kābul** National Library (see A. Z. Validi in *Journal asiatique*, Jan.-March 1924, p. 150). [Minorsky, *BSOS*. ix/1 (1937) p. 255], See also no. 516 *supra*.

No. 577, end. For some works relating to Balkh, Harāt, etc., now in Afghānistān, see the section History of Persia: Khurāsān.

No 578. "On Ibn Bībī see now Duda, *ZDMG*. [N.F.], Band 14 [89], Heft 3/4 [1935], p. 19." [Minorsky, *BSOS*. ix/1 (1937) p. 255.]

56 These two persons, however, are not mentioned as the translators but as those by whose order (*farmāyish*) and under whose superintendence (*ihtimām*) the work was printed. Ghulām-Murtaḍā Khān is described (vol. ii, *khātimah* p. 219) as the *muʾallif u mutarjim* of the book, and it is stated that he completed the translation at the end of Dhī Qaʿdah 1319. Mīrzā ʿAbd al-Raḥmān Khān was assistant translator of vol. i, and, having died just after the completion of that volume, was succeeded by Ḥusain ʿAlī Shīrāzī. There is a copy of the Bombay edition in the Cambridge University Library.

No. 578, last par. Schefer's *Quelques chapitres* occupy pp. 1–102 of the first volume of the *Recueil de textes et de traductions.*

No. 578, end. [*Mukhtaṣar i Saljūq-nāmah.*] *Insert*:
Russian translation of extracts relating to the Golden Horde: *Sbornik materialov* ... ii ... Leningrad 1941 (cf. ad no. 104, penult. par., end *supra*) pp. 25–6.

No. 579, end.. [*Tārīkh i āl i Saljūq.*] *Insert*:
Facsimile with Turkish translation: *Histoire des Seldjoukides d'Asie Mineure par un anonyme depuis l'origine de la dynastie jusqu'á la fin du regne de Sultan Alâ-ed-Din Keikoubad* IV. *fils de Soleimanshah.* 765/1364. *Texte persan publié d'aprés le* MS. *de Paris par Prof. Dr. Feridoun Nâfiz Uzluk.* **Ankara** 1952 (*Tārīkh i āl i Selchūq dar Ānāṭōlī.* Pp. 95, 80. Anadolu Selçuklulari gününde Mevlevi Bitikleri, 5: Anadolu Selçuklulari Devleti Tarihi, iii).

No. 580, 2nd par. *Read* Caliphs.

No. 580, end. [Aqsarā'ī's history.] Edition: *Musāmarat al-akhbār*[57] *wa-musāyarat al-akhyār ta'līf i Maḥmūd ... al-Aqsarā'ī ... bā muqaddamah u taṣḥīḥ u ḥawāshī i Duktur 'Uthmān Tūrān,* **Ankara** 1944 (Türk Tarih Kurumu Yayınlardan iii. seri, no. 1). [V. Minorsky, in a letter.]

No. 582, 1st line. [*Bāyazīd-nāmah.*] The author is Maḥmūd "Niẓāmī" Malik-zādah. [F. Babinger, in a letter.]

No. 587, 3rd par., 1st line. Read ***Hasht bihisht.***

No. 587, 3rd par., MSS. [*Hasht bihisht.*] Also **Ellis Coll.** M. 186 (*Katībahs* i–vi. 18th cent.), M. 187 (*K.* vi–viii. 19th cent.), **Bombay Univ.** 35 (part of *K.* vii).

No. 587, 8th par. [*Dhail i Hasht bihisht.*] The author's son, i.e. Abū 'l-Faḍl M. Daftarī (cf. no. 105, penult. par. *supra* and no. 587, Continuation *infra*).

No. 587, 8th par., antepenult. *Read* Tauer 525.

57 *al-aḥbār?*

No. 588, 1st par., antepenult. *For* may be *read* is. Aẓhar al-Dīn; so Ḥ. Kh., but Ẓahīr al-Dīn is correct. For Kabīr b. Uwais see no. 1645 (2), 2nd footnote *infra*.

No. 594 (2), MSS. [*Shahanshāh-nāmah i ... Sulṭān Murād Khān.*] For the illustrations in the Yildiz MS. see Edhem and Stchoukine *Les manuscrits orientaux illustrés de la Bibliothéque de l'Université de Stamboul*, Paris 1933, pp. 3–6.

No. 595, 2nd par., MSS. [*Futūḥāt al-ʿAjam.*] Also **Rieu** ii 665*a*.

No. 597, MSS. [*Fatḥ-nāmah i Khūnkār i Rūm.*] Also **Ethé** 859 (2).

No. 599, 1st par. Ibrāhīm Efendī, i.e. Dr. Ibrāhīm b. Najjār according to F. E. Karatay *Istanbul Üniversitesi Kütüphanesi Farsça Basmalar Kataloğu* p. 84.

No. 599, last par. *Read* § 600.

No. 601 (2). [*Tārīkh i Āyā Ṣōfyah.*] For a short anonymous tract on the foundation of the Ā.Ṣ. see Blochet iii 1976 fol. 177 (AH 947/1540–1).

No. 601 (3), end. *Insert*:
(3*a*) ***Tārīkh i Rūm u Farang***, a history of Turkey and Europe, by ʿAbd al-ʿAzīz Dihlawī (for the best-known person of this name see no. 41 *supra*): **Ellis Coll.** M.2. (incomplete. Autograph?).

No. 602, 3rd par., 1st footnote. *Read* Alikhanov-Avarski. [Minorsky, *BSOS.* ix/1 (1937) p. 255.] l. 28. Read *Alikhanova-Avarskogo.*

No. 602, Russian translations (2). Read *Alikhanova-Avarskogo.*

No. 603, 4th par. "Bacharly is a German transcription from Russian for Bahārlī." [Minorsky, *BSOS.* ix/1 (1937) p. 255.]

No. 603, last par. [ʿAbbās-Qulī Aghā.] Also *Dānishmandān i Ādharbāyjān* pp. 305–6; *Abbaskulu ağa Bakihanli*, by M. F. Köprülü (in *Türk amaci* i (1942–3) pp. 145–50. Cf. *Oriens* i/2 (1948) p. 346).

No. 606, last par., MSS. [*Akhbār i ḥasīnah.*] Also **Ivanow** Curzon 90 (18th cent.).

No. 607, 2nd par., MSS. [*Jadhb al-qulūb.*] Also **Ellis Coll.** M. 4 (AH 1109/1697–8), **Princeton** 64 (18th cent.), **ʿAlīgaṛh** Subḥ. MSS. p. 61 no. 36 (pt. i only), **Peshawar** 1462 (3), 1437.

No. 608 (1), end. *Insert*:

(1*b*) ***Īrān i kunūnī u Khalīj i Fārs***, by Ismāʿīl Nūr-zādah Būshahrī: **Tihrān** (216 pp. See *Luzac's OL*. 1946 p. 104).

No. 608 (2), end. *Insert*:

(2*a*) *Mafātīḥ al-adab fī tawārīkh al-ʿArab*, by M. ʿAlī Sadīd al-Salṭanah: place? n.d. [R. Lescot, *Bull. E.O.I.F. de Damas* vii–viii p. 283*b*.]

No. 608 (3), end. *Insert*:

(3*a*) ***Naft u marwārīd***, by M. ʿA. Manshūr Garakānī: (cf. ad no. 452, 452*e* (3)) **Tihrān** 1946 (189 pp. See Probsthain's *Orientalia nova* 2 (1946–8) p. 27 no. 425; *Luzac's OL*. 1946 p. 105 (title given as *Siyāsat i Ingilīs dar Khalīj i Fārs u jughrāfiyāyi jazāʾir i Baḥrain*), 1947 p. 101).

(3*b*) ***Naẓarī bah Īrān u Khalīj i Fārs***, by Nūr-zādah (i.e. presumably Ismāʿīl N.-Z. Būshahrī mentioned above under (1*b*)): **Tihrān** (128 pp. See *Luzac's OL*. 1945 p. 79, 1946 p. 6).

No. 608 (5). [*Short account of the Wahhābī incursions*.] Published by R. B. Serjeant and G. M. Wickens in *Islamic culture* xxiii/4 (Oct. 1949) pp. 308–9.

No. 609, 2nd par., end. *Insert*:

[England.] ***Tārīkh i guzīdah i Farīdūn Malkum***, by Farīdūn Malkum [son of Prince Malkom Khān Nāẓim al-Daulah (for whom see Browne *The press and poetry of modern Persia* pp. 18–19, etc., *Lit. Hist*, iv pp. 463, 468)]: **Paris** 1324/1908 (407 pp. See F. E. Karatay *Istanbul Üniversitesi Kütüphanesi Farsça Basmalar Kataloğu* p. 52; Browne *The press and poetry of modern Persia* p. 162).

No. 609, 3rd and 4th par., first lines. *Read* ***Ingilistān***.

No. 609, 11th par. Read *Piṭr*. [Minorsky, BSOS. ix/1 (1937) p. 255.]

No. 609, 14th par. For the name Āwānus cf. no. 1150, 1st par. and E. Rossi's *Elenco dei manoscritti persiani della Biblioteca Vaticana* p. 80, where the transcription Oannes [presumably an Armenian name[58]] is suggested with a query.

No. 609, 14th par., end. *Insert*:

58 That Āwānus is an Armenian name seems highly probable. An Armenian called "Agha Wanus" was in the service of the Bēgam Samrū (see Brajendranath Banerji *Begam Samru* p. 67).

[Russia.] ***Āʾīnah i Sikandarī***, a biography of Alexander III (b. 1845, acc. 1881, d. 1894), by Ḥasan Khān Iʿtimād al-Salṭanah (cf. no. 192 *supra*): **Mashhad** iii, *fṣl.* 14, MSS., no. 4 (AH 1313/1895–6).
[Russia.] ***Qaiṣar-nāmah*** a *mathnawī* on the Russo-Turkish war, by ʿAzīz al-Dīn "ʿAzīz" (so Āṣafīyah) or "ʿAzīzī" (so Edwards) Lak'hnawī: [**Cawnpore**] 1296/1879°.

No. 609, 15th par. Read ***Piṭr*** [cf. correction to no. 609, 11th par. *supra*].

No. 609, 4th par. from end. The *Mīkādō-nāmah* is a verse according to Arberry.

No. 609, 3rd par. from end. For Maḥmūd Ṭarzī see no. 1629 *infra*.

No. 609, 3rd par. from end. The date as given by Arberry is 1334–5/1916–17*.

No. 610, 1st line. For Surkhkat see Barthold *Turkestan* pp. 120 n. 6, 131.

No. 610, 1st par. For ʿAlī Akbar Khiṭāʾī see *Islam Ansiklopedisi* under Alî Ekber (A. Zeki Yelidi Togan); P. Kahle *Eine islamische Quelle über China um 1500* (in *Acta Orientalia* xii/2).

No. 611 (1). The *Mīkādō-nāmah* is in verse according to Arberry.

No. 611 (4). For Maḥmūd Ṭarzī see no. 1629 *infra*.

No. 611 (4). The date, as given by Arberry, is 1334–5/1916–17*.

No. 613, last par. Also *Life and work of Khwāja Nizāmuddīn Ahmad Bakhshī. By Baini Prashad* (in *JASB.*, Letters, iv/4 (1938) pp. 769–94).

No. 614, 3rd footnote. The hemistich *Wa-awwalu arḍ*^{in} etc. is quoted in the *Tāj al-ʿarūs* under TMM and is there ascribed to Raqqāʿ or Raffāʿ b. Qais al-Asadī Cf. Lane *s.v.* ʿaqqa, *Irshād al-arīb* ii p. 12, Ibn Baṭṭūṭah iv p. 327.

No. 614, 1st footnote: Instead of معاعل, read مفاعل.

No. 614, 2nd par., penult. sentence. [ʿAbd al-Qādir Badāʾūnī] Of the dates given for his death 1024/1615 must be nearest to the truth, if the reference to the death of "Ẓuhūrī" and "Malik" Qummī is not a later insertion in the notice of "Ẓuhūrī" in the *Muntakhab al-tawārīkh*, iii p. 269.

No. 614, 4th par. (10). For the *Baḥr al-asmār* see *'Abd al-Qādir Badā'ūnī and the Kathā-sarit-sāgara*, by C. A. Storey (in *Woolner commemoration volume*, Lahore 1940, pp. 249–50).

No. 616, 1st line. [Nūr al-Ḥaqq Dihlawī.] "Mashriqī" was his *takhalluṣ*.

No. 616, 3rd par.[Nūr al-Ḥaqq Dihlawī.] Another passage from the *Farḥat al-nāẓirīn* giving a brief notice of N. al-Ḥ. "Mashriqī" as a poet is quoted in OCM. iv/4 (Aug. 1928) p. 105.

No. 620, 1st par. penult. *Read* 1877°* *and delete* 1887°.

No. 620, penult. par., MSS. [*Rājāwalī*.] Also **Madrās** i 276 (?) (described as *Aḥwāl i rājagān* by 'Abd al-Karīm b. Ilyās, but the opening words agree with those of the *Rājāwalī*). A similar work is **Madrās** i 292 (*Tārīkh i rājagān*, beginning *Ḥamd u thanāy Muqaddirī rā kih qudratash*).

No. 621, 2nd par., MSS. [*Lubb al-tawārīkh i Hind.*] Also **Ellis Coll.** M. 351 (AH 1105/1094).

No. 622, 2nd par., MSS. [*Khulāṣat al-tawārīkh.*] Also **Ellis Coll.** M. 392 (18th cent.).

No. 627, 5th par. before end, ***Muntakhhab al-lubāb***, MSS. [*Muntakhhab al-lubāb.*] Also **Madrās** i 318 (vol. iii. AH 1197/1783), **Ellis Coll.** M. 220 (vol. ii. 18th cent.).

No. 641, 1st par., end. [Lachhmī Narāyan "Shafīq".] Another work of his is the *Nakhlistān*, a collection of tales written in 1218/ 1803–4 (MSS.: Rehatsek p. 233 no. 56, Ross-Browne 253).

No. 641 (1), MSS. [*Ḥaqīqat-hā-yi Hindustān.*] Also **Rehatsek** p. 104 no. 60, **Madrās** i 533 (AD 1936).

No. 643, 2nd par., MSS. [*Ṣaḥīḥ al-akhbār.*] Also **Rieu** iii 1052*a* (extracts only).

No. 649, 2nd par., MSS. [*Chahār chaman.*] Also **Ellis Coll.** M. 91 (?) (*Chahār gulshan* (*sic*?)).

No. 654, 5th par. *Insert a second bracket after* the *Journal asiatique* 1860–1).

No. 654, 5th par. [*Tafsīr al-Qurʾān*.] The first part (to S. ii v. 80) of a Persian translation by S. M. Taqī Fakhr-Dāʿī Gīlānī has been published in Tihrān (presumably in or shortly before AHS 1318/1939–40, the date of presentation to the Mashhad library. See Mashhad iv p. 479).

No. 654, 4th par. from end.[*Jām i Jam*.] Also **Ellis Coll.** M. 390.

No. 654, last par. [S. Aḥmad Khān.] Also *Eminent Mussalmans* (anon., pub. Natesan, Madras, 1926) pp. 1–37; L. Bevan Jones *The people of the mosque*, London, 1932 pp. 208–11; W. C. Smith *Modern Islām in India*, Lahore 1943, pp. 6–23; J. M. S. Baljon *The reforms and religious ideas of Sir Sayyid Aḥmad Khân*, Leyden 1949.

No. 664, 2nd par., MSS. [*Tāj al-Maʾāthir*.] Also **Leningrad** Univ. 1157 (AH 987/1579), 1093 (AH 1288/1871–2. See Romaskewicz p. 4).

No. 665 (1) ***Qirān al-saʿdain***, MSS. Also **Leningrad** Univ. 1114*a* (AH 982/1574–5. See Romaskewicz p. 11), 1172 (AH 1041/ 1631–2?), **Majlis** ii 1129 (17th cent.?), **Vatican** Pers. 153 (AH 1257/1841. Rossi p. 149), **Edinburgh** New Coll. p. 8.

No. 665 (1) ***Qirān al-saʿdain***, MSS., penult. *Read* **Madrās** i 131 (AH 1173/1760).

No. 665 (1) ***Qirān al-saʿdain***, Commentaries. Also (4) *Sharḥ i Qirān al-saʿdain*, by "ʿAfwī" Dihlawī: **ʿAlīgaṛh** Subḥ. MSS. p. 48 no. 3 (AH 1157/ 1744).

No. 665 (3) ***Khazāʾin al-futūḥ***, 2nd. par. For a review of this edition, with numerous corrections, by "Sh." [= M. Shafīʿ?] see *OCM*. xi/4 (Aug. 1935) pp. 105–19.

No. 665 (4) ***Duwal Rānī Khaḍir Khān***, 1st line. DWL, according to the poet (cf. Rieu ii p. 612*b*), is to be pronounced like the plural of *daulat*, possibly therefore Diwal, which, of the plurals of *daulat*, is nearest in sound to Dēval, if that was the first element in the name of the Rājah's daughter.

No. 665 (4) ***Duwal Rānī Khaḍir Khān***, 2nd line. *Read*: The pronunciation Khiḍr occurs occasionally in the poem, but much less frequently than Khaḍir.

No. 665 (4) ***Duwal Rānī Khaḍir Khān***, 1st par., MSS. Also **Majlis** ii 934 (AH 989/1581).

No. 665 (4) ***Duwal Rānī Khaḍir Khān***, 1st par., penult. *Read* **Madrās** i 111.

No. 665 (5), ***Nuh sipihr***, 1st par., end. *Insert*:
Edition: **Oxford Univ. Press** 1950 (ed. M. Waḥīd Mirzā. Islamic Research Association Series, 12).

No. 665 (6), ***Tughluq-nāmah***, 2nd par. For a review by M. Shafīʿ see OCM. x/2 (Feb. 1934) pp. 148–51 and for corrections of the text of this edition see an Urdu article by M. Waḥīd Mirzā in OCM. xi/1 (Nov. 1934) pp. 116–46.

No. 665, last par. [Khusrau Dihlawī.] Also Jāmī *Bahāristān*, near end of *Rauḍah* vii; *Riyāḍ al-ʿārifīn* pp. 112–15; *Nuzhat al-khawāṭir* pp. 38–41; Raḥmān ʿAlī p. 57; Berthels *Ocherk istorii persidskoi literatury* pp. 39–43.

No. 666, 6th par., MSS. [*Tārīkh i Fīrōz-Shāhī.*] Also **Ellis Coll.** M. 101 (early 19th cent.), **Madrās** i 298 (defective).

No. 666, last par. [Ḍiyāʾ al-Dīn Baranī.] Also *Kalimāt al-ṣādiqīn* no 61; *Maṭlūb al-ṭālibīn* (Ethé col. 325); *Nuzhat al-khawāṭir* p. 64.

No. 667, 3rd par. Another edition: *Futūḥāt-i-Fīrūzshāhī* [Persian text edited from a transcript of a MS. belonging to ʿAlīgaṛh Muslim University]. *By N. B. Roy* (in *JRASB.*, Letters, vol. vii/1 (1941) pp. 61–89).

No. 667, 4th par. Another translation: *The victories of Sulṭān Fīrūz Shāh of Tughluq Dynasty* (752–90 *h.*). *English translation of Futūhāt-i-Fīrūz Shāhī. By N. B. Roy* (in *Islamic culture* 15/4 (Oct. 1941) pp. 449–64).

No. 667, last par. [Fīrōz Shāh Tughluq.] Also *Nuzhat al-khawāṭir* pp. 110–13.

No. 668, 2nd par., end. [*Sīrat i Fīrōz-Shāhī*]. *Insert*:
Extracts: (1) *A memoir on Kotla Firoz Shah, Delhi. By J. A. Page ... with* [the Persian text and] *a translation of* [an extract, viz. foll. 91*b*–105*b* in the Bānkīpūr MS., from] *Sirat-i-Firozshahi by Moh. Hamid Kuraishi.* (Memoirs of the Archæological Survey of India, no. 52 (Delhi 1937) pp. 3–25 (text), 33–42 (translation).) (2) *Jajnagar expedition of Sulṭān Fīrūz Shāh—English translation and text of an extract from ʿSīrat-i-Fīrūz Shāhī'. By N. B. Roy* (in *JRASB.*, Letters, viii/1 (1942) pp. 57–98).

No. 672, 2nd line. Ḥasnū: so Rieu, but presumably Ḥasanū (i.e. Ḥasan with the diminutive termination -ū) is correct.

No. 674, 2nd par., end. [*Tārīkh i salāṭīn i Afāghinah.*] *Insert*:

Edition: *Tārīkh-i-Shāhī (also known as Tārīkh-i-Salāṭīn-i-Afāghina) of Aḥmad Yādgār ... Edited by M. Hidayat Hosain.***Calcutta** 1939 (Bibliotheca Indica, no. 257. Cf. *JRAS*. 1939 p. 684).

No. 684, 2nd par., MSS. [*Malāḥat i maqāl.*] Also **Lahore** Panjāb Univ. (defective. See *OCM*. ix/1 p. 23).

No. 686, 1st line. For the names Ṣūfī Ṣan'ān and Mirzā Bābā cf. *Ḥabīb al-siyar* iii, 3, p. 342 (Sh. Ṣūfī 'Alī) and *'Ālam-ārāy i 'Abbāsī* p. 122 (Mīrzā Bābā).

No. 692, 1st line. [Apūrva Krishna, or, to use the Hindī forms, Apūrb Kishan.] "Kunwar," Apūrb Kishan's *takhalluṣ*, is a Hindī word meaning "prince".

No. 694, last par. ["Ghālib."] Also *Āthār al-ṣanādīd* (cf. no. 654, 5th par.), Lucknow 1876, pt. 4, pp. 74–82; *Madhhab i Ghālib* (in Urdu), a discussion of "Ghālib's" religious views, by S. Aulād Ḥusain "Shādān" Bilgrāmī (in *OCM*. viii/3 (May 1932) pp. 123–9); *Ghālib kē jadīd tadhkirōṅ par ēk naẓar*, by S. M. 'Abd Allāh (in *OCM*. xv/4 (Aug. 1939) pp. 3–25).

No. 697 (2), end. *Insert*:

(2*a*) ***Tārīkh i bādshāhān i Dihlī***, by Akbar 'Alī b. S. M. 'Alī al-Bukhārī.

Edition: place 1273/1856–7 (Āṣafīyah iii p. 94).

No. 698, 4th par., 2nd footnote, ult. *Read JASB*.

No. 698, Persian translations (1), 1st par., end. (Zain al-Dīn Khwāfī.] Also Raḥmān 'Alī p. 68.

No. 698, Persian translations (2), 3rd line. *Read* Bihrōz.

No. 698, Persian translations (3), MSS. [*Wāqi'āt i Bāburī.*] Also **Madrās** i 301.

No. 700, 1st par., end. *Insert*:

Edition: *Qānūn-i-Humāyūnī (also known as Humāyūn Nāma) of Khwāndamīr. Edited by M. Hidayat Hosain.* **Calcutta** 1940 (Bibliotheca Indica, no. 260. See *JRAS*. 1941 p. 96).

No. 702, 1st footnote. For the Bayāt tribe see also Malcolm *History of Persia* ii, London, 1829, p. 140 n.4.

No. 702, 2nd par., end. [*Tārīkh i Humāyūn.*] No formal title is given to the book by the author, who refers to it as *īn tadhkirah* and *īn mukhtaṣar*. The title given to the work by Ethé seems to come from the copyist's colophon, where it is called *Tawārīkh i ḥaḍrat i Humāyūn Bādshāh* (Hidayat Hosain's edition p. 378). *Insert*:

Edition: *Tadhkira-i-Humāyūn wa Akbar of Bāyazīd Biyāt* [*sic*]. *Edited by M. Hidayat Hosain.* **Calcutta** 1941* (Bibliotheca Indica, 264).

No. 702, 3rd par., end. According to Hidayat Hosain (preface, p. vii) Prof. Banārsi Prasād Saksēna published "in the same *Journal*" [i.e. apparently the *Allahabad University Studies*] in 1939 (History Section, pp. 1–82) the translation of another part (unspecified) of the Memoirs. "The translation of about one-third of the work still remains to be published."

No. 702, last par. [Bāyazīd Bayāt.] Also *Journal of Indian history,* iv/1–3 (Madras 1926) pp. 43–60 (an account of the author and his work by B. P. Saksēna. See Hidayat Hosain's preface, p. vii).

No. 706, 1st line. Read **"Faiḍī"**.

No. 709, 3rd par., 6th line from foot. [*Mukātabāt i ʿAllāmī, daftar* iv.] See also next entry.

No. 709, 3rd par., last two lines [*Ruqaʿāt i Abū 'l-Faḍl.*] *For* "Editions have been published at Calcutta in 1238/1822–3* 1238* and at Cawnpore in 1872*" *read* "An edition was published at Calcutta in 1238* of the Bengali (Faṣlī) era." The work published by Nawal Kishōr at Cawnpore in 1876* (not 1872) and reprinted at least three times under the title *Ruqaʿāt i Abū 'l-Faḍl* is the work referred to above as the fourth *daftar* of the *Mukātabāt i ʿAllāmī.*

No. 709 (1). Read *Āʾīn i Akbarī.*

No. 709 (1), 5th footnote, end. [*Akbar-nāmah.*] The Chester Beatty MS. is presumeably the subject of the Roxburghe Club's *Chronicle of Akbar the Great. A description* [by Sir Thomas Arnold and J. V. S. Wilkinson] *of a manuscript of the Akbar-nama illustrated by the court painters* (Oxford 1937. Impl. folio, with coloured frontispiece and 33 plates, 5 of which are coloured. See Bernard

Quaritch's Catalogue No. 562 (1939) p. 4, where a copy was offered at £25, and Luzac's Supplement No. 6 (March 1941) p. 2).

No. 709 (1), 1st par., MSS. [*Akbar-nāmah.*] Also **Vatican** Pers. 90–92 (*Daftar* i, pt. 2, and *Daftar* ii. Rossi p. 107), 109 (*Daftar* i, pt. 1. Rossi p. 119).

No. 709 (1), 1st par., penult. *Read* **Madrās** i 281–4.

No. 709 (1), Abridged English translations (3). [*Akbar-nāmah.*] This translation is by W. Erskine.

No. 709 (1), Translated extracts. [*Akbar-nāmah.*] *Insert*:
Description of a MS.: see addendum to no. 709 (1), 5th footnote, end.

No. 709 (2), 4th par., end. [*Āʾīn i Akbarī.* English translations.] *Insert*:
The Āʾīn-i Akbarī ... Translated ... by H. Blochmann ... Second edition, revised by D. C. Phillott, **Calcutta** 1927–39. *ʿAin* [*sic*]-*i-Ākbari* [*sic*] ... *Vol. iii ... Translated ... by Colonel H. S. Jarrett ... revised and further annotated by Sir Jadu-Nath Sarkar*, **Calcutta** 1948 (Bibliotheca Indica). Vol. ii, the first of Jarrett's two volumes, seems to have been omitted from this re-edition. Blochmann's volume contains the first two of the five *daftars*, "vol. iii" contains the last two.

No. 709 (2), antepenult. par. Maulawī M. Najaf ʿAlī K͟hān Jhajjarī *al-muk͟hāṭab bah* Tāj al-ʿulamāʾ, son of a Qāḍī of Jhajjar (i.e., according to M. Idrīs, the place of that name near Rohtak) was in the service of M. ʿAlī K͟hān, Nawwāb of Ṭōnk, from whom in 1295/1878 he received instructions to write commentaries in Arabic, Persian and Urdu on each of the three poems, *Bānat Suʿād, Qaṣīdah i Burdah* and *Qaṣīdah i Amālī*. Among his many works in Arabic, Persian and Urdu were *Takmilah i Ṣaulat i Fārūqī* (cf. PL. no. 786, 2nd par.) in 50,000 verses and commentaries on the *Maqāmāt* of Ḥarīrī (in words consisting entirely of undotted letters), the *Dīwān of* Mutanabbī, the *Ḥamāsah* and the *Dasātīr*. See Raḥmān ʿAlī p. 236, M. Idrīs p. 91. Both of these authors, the latter of whom completed the *Taṭyīb al-ik͟hwān* in 1313/1895, speak of Najaf ʿAlī K͟hān as still alive.

No. 709 (2), antepenult. par. Jhajar seems to be an obsolete English spelling for Jhajjar.

No. 709 (2), last par. [Abū ʾl-Faḍl.] Autobiography also in *Mukātabāt i ʿAllāmī, daftar* 3 (according to Bombay Univ. p. 282).

No. 711, 2nd par. According to the printed text of the *Ma'āthir i Raḥīmī* (vol. iii p. 1698 penult.) the date of collation was 1026. The note relating to this is followed by another dated 1031.

No. 711, last par. *Read* Āqā Bābā.

No. 712, 3rd par. B. W. Chapman [Rieu iii 980*a*, l. 2] seems to be a mistake for R[obert] B[arclay] Chapman (see Rieu iii, preface p. xxiv).

No. 713, 2nd line. S. Amīr Ḥaidar "Amīr" b. S. Nūr al-Ḥusain b. Mīr Ghulām-'Alī "Āzād" Bilgrāmī was born in 1165/ 1751–2 and was only three years old when his father was accidentally drowned. Educated first at Bilgrām by his relative S. M. "Shā'ir" Bilgrāmī (for whom see no. 952 *supra*) and after his death [in 1185/1772] by his grandfather Ghulām-'Alī "Āzād" (for whom see no. 1162 *supra*) at Aurangābād, he returned to Bilgrām after the latter's death [in 1200/1786] and was subsequently appointed *Muftī* to the *'Adālat i Kull*, or Supreme Court, in the Presidency of Bengal. On p. 4 of his *Persian moonshee* (London 1801) Gladwin expresses acknowledgments to "Mowlawy Ameer Hyder, Mufty to the Sudder Nizamut and Dewanny Adawlats" [i.e. the Supreme Courts of Criminal and Civil Justice].

No. 713, last par. [S. Amīr Ḥaidar Bilgrāmī.] Also *Mi'rāj al-khayāl; Khāzin al-shu'arā'* fol. 45*b* (where the biography in Walī Allāh's *Tārīkh i Farrukhābād* is summarized); *Ṣubḥ i gulshan* p. 39; Maqbūl Aḥmad *Ḥayāt i Jalīl* (cf. no. 952, footnote *supra*) ii p. 174 note 132.

No. 714, 2nd par. [*Nāfi' al-ṭālibīn.*] Also **Ivanow** Curzon 135 (AD 1797–8).

No. 717, 3rd par. 1st sentence. *Read* the first two rarer).

No. 717, 3rd par., MSS. [*Iqbāl-nāmah i Jahāngīrī.*] For a discussion of the pictures in the Philadelphia MS. see an article entitled *Late Mughul illustrations to the Iqbāl-Nāmah* by M. A. Simsar and W. Norman Brown in *JAOS*. 58/2 (June 1938).

No. 717, footnote 626. This note should be deleted.

No. 717, 3rd par., MSS, **'Alīgaṛh**. *Read* p. 60 no. 21 (vol. ii).

No. 717, 3rd par., MSS, antepenult. *Read* p. 52), **Madrās** i 278–80.

No. 717, 3rd par., MSS. [*Iqbāl-nāmah i Jahāngīrī.*] Also **Brelvi and Dhabhar** p. xiii (AH 1137/1724–5. Wrongly described in the catalogue as the *Maʾāthir i Jahāngīrī*), **Rehatsek** p. 76 no. 12.

No. 718, 2nd par., MSS. [*Maʾāthir i Jahāngīrī.*] **Brelvi and Dhabhar** p. xiii and **Rehatsek** p. 76 no 12 should be deleted. These are evidently copies of the *Iqbāl-nāmah* (as is shown by the opening words quoted in the former catalogue).

No. 723, 1st par., 6th line from foot. *Read* Young)].

No. 725, last par. Read *Tadhkirah i Ṭāhir i Naṣrābādī* p. 227.

No. 727, 2nd par., MSS. [*Ẓafar-nāmah i Shāh-Jahānī.*] Also **Leningrad** Univ. 1063*a* (AH 1082? Romaskewicz p. 11).

No. 727, last par., 2nd line. Read *ʿAmal i Ṣāliḥ* iii pp. 397–401.

No. 727, last. par., 6th line. Read *Wāqiʿāt i Kashmīr* p. 150.

No. 730, 3rd par., MSS. [*Chār chaman i Barahman.*] *Read* **Madrās** i 315 and 336*a* (both *Qawāʿid al-salṭanat i Shāh-Jahān*). Also **Madrās** i 306 (*Chār chaman.* AH 1134/ 1721–2), **Ellis Coll.** M. 79 (*Ch. ch.*. Early 19th cent.), 80 (AH 1241/1826), **Rehatsek** p. 66 no. 17 (apparently *Ch. ch.*), presumably also **Lahore** Panjāb Univ. (*Q. al-s. i Sh-J.* AH 1249–50/1834. See OCM. vii/4 (Aug. 1931) p. 69).

No. 730, 4th par., MSS. [*Guldastah i Chār chaman.*] Also **Blochet** iv 2328 (early 18th cent.).

No. 730, last par. Read *ʿAmal i Ṣāliḥ* iii pp. 434–5, 443.

No. 730, last par. ["Barahman".] Also *Shamʿ i anjuman* p. 92.

No. 731, last par. ["Kalīm."] Read *ʿAmal i Ṣāliḥ* iii pp. 402–4; *Tadhkirah i Ṭāhir i Naṣrābādī* (Sprenger p. 90; Ṭihrān ed. pp. 220–3).

No. 732, 1st par. Read *Īzadī.*

No. 734, last line. *Read* Rieu i 260, iii 934*b*.

No. 738 (1), 1st par. MSS. [*ʿAmal i Ṣāliḥ.*] Possibly also **Eton** 190 (see addendum to no. 755 (4).).

No. 738 (1), 2nd par. *Read* 1912–39°*.

No. 741 (2), end. *Insert*:

(3) ***Iqbāl-nāmah i Dhū 'l-Faqār-Khānī***, an account of Nawwāb Dhū 'l-Faqār Khān's expedition against Maʿṣūm Khān, composed in 1068/1657–8 "during the reign of Aurangzeb" at the request of Mirzā M. Ṭāhir: **Calcutta Madrasah** 182 (2) (AH 1069/1658–9).

No. 742, end. [*Tārīkh i Shāh-Shujāʿī.*] For some remarks on this history see J. Sarkar *History of Aurangzib* ii p. 303.

No. 743, 5th par. [*Tārīkh i Āshām.*] The date is given (incorrectly) by Edwards as 1264 [1847] and by Arberry more correctly as 1265/1848–9. The year occurs both on the title-page and in the colophon. In the latter place the day of the month, 1 Rajab, is added. Consequently the correct date is 1265/ 1849°*.

No. 745, 2nd par., MSS. [*ʿĀlamgīr-nāmah.*] Also **Ellis Coll.** M. 268 (18th cent.).

No. 745, 2nd par., MSS. *Read* **Madrās** i 311 (AH 1133/1720), 312, 313.

No. 748, 3rd par., end. [*Futūḥāt i ʿĀlamgīrī.*] Cf. also Sarkar *History of Aurangzib* ii p. 305.

No. 750, penult. par., end. [*Dilgushā.*] Cf. also Sarkar *History of Aurangzib* ii p. 304.

No. 751, 3rd par., penult. *Read* [1873?°],

No. 751, 4th par., end. Niʿmat Khān's *tafsīr*, the *Niʿmat i ʿuẓmā*, has been mentioned in no. 32 *supra*.

No. 751 (1), 1st par., 1st line. Read ***jihād i Ḥaidarābād***.

No. 751 (1), 1st par., MSS. *Read* **Madrās** i 273–4.

No. 751 (2), 1st par., MSS. [*Jang-nāmah.*] Also **Lahore** Panjāb Univ. Lib. (AH 1256/1840. See *OCM*. vii/3 (May 1931) p. 62).

No. 752, 2nd par., MSS., **Eton** 189. AH 1180 is an "owner's date".

No. 752, 3rd par., end. *Insert*:

English translation: *Maāsir-i-Ālamgiri ... of Sāqi Must'ad* [*sic*] *Khan. Translated ... and annotated by Sir Jadunath Sarkar....* **Calcutta** 1947 (Bibliotheca Indica).

No. 752, last par., 2nd line. *Read* 936*b*, 1083*b*.

No. 753, 1st par., end. For the meaning of Maʿmūrī see *Maʾāthir al-umarāʾ* iii p. 376, where it is stated that Muẓaffar Khān Mīr ʿAbd al-Razzāq Maʿmūrī was by descent a Saiyid of Maʿmūrābād "*kih mauḍiʿī-st az Najaf i Ashraf*".

No. 754, 3rd par., end description, before MSS. [*Aḥkām i ʿĀlamgīrī.*] "The volume contains not fully written out letters but only a precis of the points which the Emperor dictated to his secretary for inclusion in the letters. But they are not so brief and obscure as the contents of 31 [i.e. the *Kalimāt i ṭaiyibāt*]. The persons addressed are usually named. The contents refer to the last decade of Aurangzib's reign. I have used the Rampur State Library MS., a fine copy which must have belonged to the Delhi Palace Library, and collated it with the Khuda Bakhsh MS., a neatly written copy of the 18th century. No other MS. of it is known to exist." (Jadunath Sarkar *History of Aurangzib* ii (Calcutta 1912) p. 310.)

No. 755 (2), end. For the *Aurang-nāmah* (composed in 1072/1661–2) see a description entitled *An unpublished contemporary history of Aurangzeb's accession in verse* by M. Abdulla Chughtai in *Islamic culture* vi/1 (Jan. 1932) pp. 157–60, where the date of the Āṣafīyah MS. is given as 1116/1704.

No. 755 (4). Margoliouth writes *Gulshān*. The date of composition (1070) suggests that this is a MS. of the *ʿAmal i Ṣāliḥ* (see no. 738 (1) *supra*).

No. 755 (4), footnote, 1st line. *For* his *read* the.

No. 758 (2), ult. *Read* **Browne** Suppt. 189 (n.d. King's 47).

No. 760, 5th par., 2nd line, bracketed text. *Read* Ḥaidarābād.

No. 761, 1st par., 2nd half, [AH 1227 apparently]. *Read* [AH 1127 apparently].

No. 769, 2nd par., 2nd line. *Read* death, to.

No. 770 (1). *Read* 19 June 1707.

No. 777, 1st par. For *infra* read *supra.*

No. 778, footnote 691, penult. "Some 200 Sanskrit and Zend MSS." (Buckland.) The Fraser MSS. in the Bodleian include a considerable number in Persian (see Ethé's *Catalogue of the Persian ... manuscripts in the Bodleian Library, Pt. II*, coll. 1373–6).

No. 779 (1), MSS. [*Mirʾāt i wāridāt.*] *Read* **Rieu** i 275*b* (*Ṭabaqah* i. Late 18th cent.).

No. 780, 1st line. [Ānand Rām.] Ānanda, with a long *ā* in the first syllable, is the Sanskrit form, but in Hindī the first syllable can be shortened and this shortened form seems to be used by most Indian writers in speaking of "Mukhliṣ".

No. 780, 2nd par. (4). *Delete* I.O. D.P. 491 (*e*).

No. 780, 2nd par. (8), end. *Insert*:
(8*a*) *Rāḥat al-afrās*, on farriery (MSS.: Lindesiana p. 113, Rāmpūr (Nadhīr Aḥmad 260)).

No. 780 (9) and (10). *Read*:
(9) ***Badāʾiʿ i waqāʾiʿ***, memoirs of the author's life and of contemporary events in northern India, written at different dates[59] and incorporating three or four sections ((1) the account of Nādir Shāh's invasion[60] (beg. *Wāqiʿah īst nādir*) = foll. 114*b*–169*b* in the Panjāb Univ. MS., (2) *Aḥwāl i sīzdah-rūzah safar i Gaṛh Muktēsar* [in Dhū 'l-Qaʿdah 1156[61]] = foll. 180*a*–192*b* in the

59 AH 1152 and the 29th regnal year [a.h. 1159] are mentioned as dates of composition on foll. 116 and 234 of the Panjāb University MS.

60 The title *Tadhkirah i Anand Rām Mukhliṣ* given by Elliot (and Sarkār) to this part (and the two succeeding parts?) of the work came doubtless from Nawwāb Ḍiyāʾ al-Dīn Khān's MS., but it may have no good authority. The extracts translated from that MS. by Perkins for Elliot relate only to Nādir Shāh's invasion, but there is nothing to show whether the last words of Perkins's translation were the end of the MS.

61 I.e. Dec.-Jan. 1743. W. Irvine gives the date as 1747, which would correspond to 1160.

Panjāb Univ. MS., (3) *Aḥwāl i safar i Bingaṛh*[62] [in Muḥ.-Jum. I 1158[63]] = foll. 193*a*–229 in the Panjāb Univ. MS.) and (4) *Nuskhah i sawāniḥ i aḥwāl*, on events in the Panjāb from Jumādā II 1158/ July 1745 to Jumādā II 1161/ June 1748 = foll. 229*b* 243*a* in the Panjāb Univ. MS.), which may have originated as separate tracts: **Lahore** Panjāb Univ. (286 foil., beginning with events of 1145 and ending with 1161, the only complete copy hitherto recorded. See M. Shafīʿ's detailed description mentioned below), **Rāmpūr** (= Nadhīr Aḥmad 61, beg. *Aḥwāl i mutawajjih shudan i … M. Shāh, … samt i Gaḍh Muktēsar … Bīst u sīwum i Muḥarram al-Ḥarām sāl i 1158*. AH 1158/1745, autograph), ʿ**Alīgaṛh** Muslim Univ. Akh. 112 (71 foll., containing only the account of Nādir Shāh's invasion, the *Nuskhah i sawāhiḥ i aḥwāl*, and the *Aḥwāl i sīzdah-rūzah i safar i Gaḍh Muktēsar*. See M. Shafī's article p. 89), **Delhi** K.B.Ẓafar Ḥasan's private library (complete? See Aẓhar ʿAlī's edition p. 41[8]), **Ethé** 2724 (the journey to Muktēsar in 1156 only. 16 foil. Description on fol. *1a*: *Waqāʾiʿ i sair i Gangā*).

Edition of the account of the march to Bingaṛh: *Safar-nāmah i Mukhliṣ … ba-taṣḥīḥ u taḥshiyah i …* *Saiyid* **Aẓhar ʿAlī, Rāmpūr** 1946 (*Silsilah i maṭbūʿāt i Kitāb-khānah i Riyāsat i Rāmpūr*, no. 7. Persian text (108 pp.) with Urdu introduction (140 pp.), notes and indexes).

Description of the work with a full list of the headings and an edition of the *Nuskhah i sawāniḥ i aḥwāl*: *Iqtibās az Badāʾiʿ i waqāʾiʿ*, by M. Shafīʿ (in *OCM*. xviii/1 (Nov. 1941) pp. 89–124).

Description of a portion of the work (from a MS. belonging to Nawwāb Ḍiyāʾ al-Dīn Khān of Lōhārū) with 22 pp. of translated extracts: Elliot and Dowson *History of India* viii 76–98.

English translation of the account of the pilgrimage to Muktēsar: see no. 780 (10), 2nd par..

No. 780, last par. [Anand Rām "Mukhliṣ."] Also *Majmūʿah i naghz* ii p. 176; S. Aẓhar ʿAlī's introduction to the *Safar-nāmah* pp. 7–39.

No. 786 (5) (*Sawāniḥ i aḥwāl i Āshōb*) and (6) (*Tārīkh i shahādat i Farrukh-siyar …*) are of course in prose and should not have been included in a list of poetical works by "Āshōb".

62 A journey "undertaken with the object of shooting and hunting as well as to punish one ʿAlī Muḥammad Rohilla" (Nadhīr Aḥmad). The route led first to Muktēsar, but this journey is quite different from that to Muktēsar fair in 1156.

63 The 27th and (from 1 Rabīʿ ii) 28th years of Muḥammad Shāh's reign. The date 1150/1737 given by Nadhīr Aḥmad is obviously a slip, since his quotation from the Persian text gives 1158.

No. 791, 1st line. Farshūrī, or rather, it would seem, Farshaurī (or Firshaurī?) i.e. connected with Peshawar. Cf. *Ṭabaqāt i Akbarī* i p. 37[3] (*Pashāwar kih dar kutub i salaf bah Bikrām u* PRSWR *u* FRSHWR *mashhūr ast*); "ʿIṣāmī" *Futūḥ al-salāṭīn* p. 410, l. 7863: *Shunīdam kih khwad ham ba-Lāhaur mānd Sarān i sipah rā ba-*FRSHWR *rānd* (cf. ll. 7866, 7870); ʿAbd al-Ḥaiy Lak'hnawī *Nuzhat al-khawāṭir* (in Arabic) p. 146[13] (*M. b. M. al-Junaidī … al-*FRSHWRĪ *… wulida bi-madīnat Pashāwar*); Yule and Burnell *Hobson Jobson* under Peshawar. Yāqūt spells the name Farshābūr.

No. 795, 1st par. Shākir Khān was born at Pānīpat in 1128/1716 according to his own statement in his encyclopedia *Ḥadīqah i ḥādiq i ganjīnah i Ṣādiq* (Ethé 2228, Bānkīpūr Suppt. ii 2022).

No. 798 (1). For James Browne (not Brown) see no. 844 *infra*.

No. 798 (2), antepenult. *Read* Kōl, and.

No. 799, end. According to "Rangīn's" Persian preface to his *Dīwān i rékhtah* (Blumhardt *Catalogue of Hindustani manuscripts in the … India Office*, no. 185) Ṭahmās Bēg Khān reached India at the age of seven with Nādir Shāh's invading army. He eventually became a *haft-hazārī*.

No. 800, 1st par. The words "who created him a Khān" should be deleted. It was Tīmūr Shāh who raised him to the rank of Khān, changing his original name of Tīmūr to Ṭahmās Khān.

No. 802, 2nd footnote. *Tawallud*: so in the printed texts. Perhaps *maulid* should be read. Read *dār al-khilāfah i*.

No. 808, 1st par., (2). ["Aẓfarī."] For the Persian translation of the *Maḥbūb al-qulūb* see an article entitled *ʿAlī-Shēr kī ēk kitāb kā qalamī nuskhah yaʿnī Marghūb al-fuʾād tarjamah i Maḥbūb al-qulūb* [in the Panjāb Univ. Lib.], by S. M. ʿAbd Allāh in *OCM*. xi/4 (Aug. 1935) pp. 41–8.

No. 808, 1st par., end.["Aẓfarī."] For his *Mīzān i Turkī*, a Turkī grammar, see Madrās i 459 (AH 1209/1794–5, autograph).

No. 808, 2nd par., end. [*Wāqiʿāt i Aẓfarī.*] *Read* **Madrās** i 450 (AH 1243/ 1828), 451.

No. 808, last par. ["Aẓfarī."] Also OCM. xi/4 (Aug. 1935) pp. 41–8 (in the article referred to above).

No. 809, 2nd par., MSS. [*Shāh-ʿĀlam-nāmah.*] Also **Ellis Coll.** M. 293 (slightly defective at end).

No. 814, 1st par. Faḍl i ʿAẓīm "ʿAẓīm" Khairābādī was a son of Maulawī Faḍl i Imām Khairābādī (for whom see Raḥmān ʿAlī p. 162) and an elder brother of the well known scholar Faḍl i Ḥaqq Khairābādī (for whom see Raḥmān ʿAlī p. 164, Brockelmann *Sptbd.* ii p. 854). The brief and dateless notices of him given in the *Shamʿ i anjuman* (p. 328) and the *Ṣubḥ i gulshan* (p. 288) do not mention the titles of any of his works.

No. 816, 1st par. For "Farānsū" see an article entitled *Urdū kā Jarman shāʿir "Farānsū" aur us kī taṣnīfāt* by S. M. ʿAbd Allāh in OCM. xx/3 (May 1944) pp. 3–30, where information is drawn from MSS. (apparently not autographs[64]) of "Farānsū's" works in the Panjāb University Library. His name as given by himself (but not without some later corruption) is Farānsū KWYN[65] walad i Jān[66] Kārlīw[67] KWYN (*Masarrat-afzā*, preface, and *Guldastah i ḥusn u ʿishq*, preface, OCM. xx/3 p. 5, l. 4 from foot, and p. 20[11]), Farānsū KWYN … nām i wālid Jān Kādlīb[68] KWYN (*Mirʾāt i ḥusn u ʿishq*, colophon, OCM. xx/3 p. 5[8]) Farāsū Gāḍlīb KWYN (*Gulbun i tamannā*, preface, OCM. xx/3 p. 22 penult.). In "Shōr's" *Waqāʾiʿ i Ghadr* it is stated that Misṭar Farānsis [Kō'ins?] died suddenly of old age in July 1861 (OCM. xx/3 p. 7 ult., quoting from an article on "Farānsū" by Pyārē Lāl "Shākir" Mīraṭ'hī in the *sāl-nāmah* of the *Adabī dunyā* (Lahore) for 1939). The correct form of the surname could probably be ascertained by examination of the Indian newspapers for July 1861. His father went to India from Poland at the age of sixteen or seventeen and married a Frenchwoman, to whom Farānsū KWYN was born at Shāhjahānābād on 15 March 1777 (*Mirʾāt i ḥusn u ʿishq*, colophon, OCM. xx/3 p. 5). He became a Captain in the service of the Bēgam Samrū (for whom see no. 900 *infra*) and after her death (in 1836) went to Harchandpūr, where he suffered grievously at the time of the Mutiny.

64 Except perhaps one MS. of the *dīwān* (OCM. xx/3 p. 25[6]).

65 This is evidently the name which appears elsewhere as Gūst, Gūstīn, Akden, etc. If Gādlīb had not occurred by its side in these MSS., it might have been supposed to be itself a corruption of Gōtlīb.

66 I.e. John.

67 Apparently a corruption of Gādlīb.

68 I.e. presumably Gādlīb = Gottlieb.

No. 816, 2nd par., MSS. [*Fatḥ-nāmah i Angrēz.*] A defective MS. beginning with the "capture of Benares" and ending with the title only of the section "Return of the government to Calcutta" is in the Phillipps collection (cf. ad no. 881, 2nd par., 5th line from foot *infra*). [G. M. Wickens, in a letter.]

No. 820, last par. For Nawwāb Amīr ʿAlī see also the *Chār dīwār* of his son S. Ashraf al-Dīn Aḥmad (Calcutta 1894*).

No. 823, 2nd par., 1st line. [*Chach-nāmah.*] According to C. N. Seddon (*JRAS*. 1941 p. 172) the title of the Arabic original was *Minhāj al-dīn wa-'l-mulk*.

No. 823, 3rd par., end. *Insert*:

Edition: *Fatḥ-nāmah i Sind* (*Chach-nāmah*) *by ʿAlī ibn Ḥāmid ... al-Kūfī. Edited by Dr. ʿUmar ibn Muḥammad Dāūdpōtā*, **Ḥaidarābād**. Deccan, [Delhi printed] 1939 (Persian MSS. Society Series, no. 3. For a review by C. N. Seddon see *JRAS*. 1941 pp. 171–2. The wording of the title-page may not be precisely as given above).

No. 824, 3rd par., MSS. [*Tārīkh i Maʿṣūmī.*] Also **I.O.** 4563 (2) (AH 1242/ 1826. See *JRAS*. 1939 p. 356).

No. 824, 4th par. For *Sazzid* read *Sayyid.*

No. 824, last par. [*M. Maʿṣūm "Nāmī".*] Also *Islamic culture* ix/3 (July 1935) p. 417 (a notice from the *Dhakhīrat al-khawānīn* translated by M. Abdulla Chughtai); *OCM*. xiii/4 (Aug. 1937) pp. 90–110 (the inscription on his tomb and some other inscriptions connected with him and his family in an article entitled *Sind'h kē baʿḍ kitbē* by M. Shafīʿ).

No. 825, 2nd par., MSS. [*Bēg-Lār-nāmah.*] Also **Ellis Coll.** M. 185 (AH 1233/1817).

No. 828, 1st pat., ult. *For* Mount Maklī *read* Maklī hill.[69]

No. 828 (1). [*Tuḥfat al-kirām.*] An autograph MS. (doubtless in private possession) was used by M. Shafīʿ for his article *Khaṭṭāṭān i Sind* (cf. no. 1436 *infra*) in *OCM*. xi/2 (Feb. 1938) pp. 131–4.

69 On Maklī hill, two miles N.W. of Tattah, is a vast necropolis covering an area of six square miles.

No. 828 (1), MSS. **I.O.** 4535 was formerly **I.O.** MSS. Per. D. 4.

No. 828, (1), 2nd par., end.[*Tuḥfat al-kirām.*] *Insert*:
Extract relating to the calligraphists of Sind (= vol. iii p. 241 in the lithograph): *OCM*. xi/2 (Feb. 1935) pp. 131–4 (ed. M. Shafīʿ).

No. 835 (2), end. *Insert*:
(3) ***Tārīkh i Sind***, an anonymous epitome to 1207/ 1792–3: **I.O.** 4563 (1) (AH 1242/1826. See *JRAS*. 1939 p. 356).

No. 840, last par., penult. *Read* p. 472.

No. 843, 1st par., ult. *Read probably* [? Hindie].

No. 846, last par. *Read* 294*a*); Amar.

No. 847, 2nd par., MSS. [*Aḥwāl i firqah i Sik'hān.*] Also **Ellis Coll.** M. 224 (AH 1224/1809).

No. 856 (1), end. *Insert*:
Analysis: *A notice of the ʿUmdatu 't-tawarikh. By the late E. Rehatsek* (in *The Indian antiquary* xxiii (1894) pp. 57–72).

No. 857, 2nd line. Jamūn: so Rieu (iii p. 955), but Jammūn in Khwājah ʿAbd al-Majīd's Urdu dictionary *Jāmiʿ al-lughāt.*

No. 860, 2nd par., footnote. For the Sit'hānah and Malkah campaign see also W. W. Hunter *The Indian Musalmans*, London, 1871, pp. 1–43 (cf. G. F. I. Graham *Life and work of Syed Ahmed Khan*, London 1885, pp. 228–9, etc.); *The Punjaub and North-West Frontier of India. By an old Punjaubee*, London 1878 pp. 47–61; R. R. Sethi *Events leading to the Ambela Expedition, 1863* (in *Bengal: past and present*, 46/1 (July–Sept. 1930) pp. 14–22).

No. 870, last par.. [*Rāja-taraṅgiṇī.*] For Shāh-Muḥammad Shāhābādī's translation see *Āʾīn i Akbarī* tr. Blochmann p. 106.

No. 874, 1st par., penult. [Ḥaidar Malik.] According to the *Wāqiʿāt i Kashmir*, p. 125, the title given to Ḥaidar Malik was Raʾīs al-Mulk i Chaghatāʾī.

No. 877, 2nd par., MSS. [Narāyan Kaul's *Tārīkh i Kashmīr.*] Also **Ellis Coll.** M. 299 ("with the continuation of Pandit Bīrbal." AH 1267/1851), M. 298 (with the continuation to 1262/ 1846).

No. 880, last par. [M. Aʿẓam.] Also *Ḥadāʾiq al-Ḥanafīyah* p. 450.

No. 881, 2nd par., 5th line from foot.[*Gauhar i ʿālam.*] An undated MS. (367 foll., 8¼ × 6½ in., 15 or 16 ll.) formerly in the collection of Sir Thomas Phillipps (1792–1872) and now in another private collection contains both the sixth *ṭabaqah* and the *khātimah* (marvels, etc., to the number of forty-five) and brings the history down to 1191/1777. [G. M. Wickens, in a letter.]

No. 882, 2nd par. *Read* Paklī *instead of* Paglē.

No. 883, 2nd par., MSS. [*Majmaʿ al-tawārīkh.*] Also **Ellis Coll.** M. 317 (*Majmūʿat* [so, fol. 7] *al-tawārīkh.* Samwat 1927/1870), M. 316 (19th cent.). See also the addendum to no. 877, 2nd par., MSS.

No. 886 (1), 1st par., end. [*Gulzār i Kashmīr.*] MS.: **Ellis Coll.** M. 225 (mid 19th cent.).

No. 887 (5), end. *Insert*:

(5a) ***Mūjaz al-tawārīkh***, a sketch of the history of Kashmīr in tabular form, by M. Saif al-Dīn Kashmīrī: **Amritsar** (Khādim i Panjāb Press) 1324/1907* (*Tārīkh i jadwalī i Kashmīr mausūm bah M. al-t.* 28 pp.).

No. 890, 2nd par. *Read* 1825.

No. 893, end.*Insert*:

893a. Pandit **Shankar Nāt'h "Nādir"** (AD 1826).

Jangnāmah i Bharatpūr, or ***Nuṣrat u Ẓafar***, an account of Durjan Sāl's deposition: **Lahore** Panjāb Univ. (AH 1260/1841. See *OCM*. vii/4 p. 68).

No. 895, 1st line. For Francis Gottlieb "Farānsū" see the addenda to no. 816, 1st par. *supra*.

No. 909, line above.[The Rohillas.] According to M. Longworth Dames's article on Ḥāfiẓ Raḥmat Khān in the *Ency. Isl.* "the name Rohilla (properly Rōhēlā) or Highlander" is an Eastern Pandjābī adjective from *rōh* "a hilly country". In Khwājah 'Abd al-Majīd's Urdu dictionary *Jāmi' al-lughāt* (iii p. 248) the word is spelt Rōhīlā with *ī* not *ē* and with a short first syllable. Presumably that is the correct pronunciation in Urdu.

No. 909, first line. Ghulām-Muḥyī 'l-Dīn[70] S. 'Abd al-Laṭīf is the author of three mystical works, (1) *Laṭā'if i Laṭīfī*, (2) *Risālah i taufīq* and (3) *Miftāḥ al-asrār*, which are preserved in an India Office MS. (I.O. 4570. See *JRAS*. 1939 p. 360). For another work of his, *Dār al-khuld*, a collection of letters mainly on Ṣūfī subjects, see Ivanow 415. He died in 1194/1780 (see *Guldastah i Karnātak* (Ivanow 1st Suppt. p. 8): *Ṣubḥ i waṭan* 76).

No. 910, 1st par. Nūr al-Dīn Ḥusain was at one time an officer in the household of 'Imād al-Mulk Ghāzī al-Dīn Khān (for whom see no. 1372 *supra*) and later became *Munshī* and trusted diplomatic agent to Sir Charles Malet, the British Resident at Poona [Jadunath Sarkar in *Islamic culture* x/4 (Oct. 1936) p. 648].

No. 912, 2nd par., MSS. [*Tārīkh i faiḍ-bakhsh*.] Also **Ellis Coll.** M. 294 (18th cent.).

No. 912, end. *Insert*:

912*a*. **Bihārī Lāl** Munshī.

Lives of (1) *Najīb al-Daulah*,[71] (2) *Ḍābiṭah Khān*,[72] (3) *'Alī Muḥammad Khān, Ḥāfiẓ Raḥmat Khān*,[73] *Dūṅdē Khān*[74] *and other Rohillas*, written in 1787 at Camp Fatḥgaṛh for Captain "Ustar":[75] MS. discovered (at some place unspecified) by Jadunath Sarkar.

Translation of the first section: *Najib-ud-daulah, Ruhela chief. A unique Persian manuscript.* [Translated in part by] *Jadunath Sarkar* (in *Islamic culture* x/4 (Oct. 1936) pp. 648–58).

70 For names of this type consisting of the word *ghulām* followed by the name of a saint cf. no. 1354, footnote.

71 Cf. no. 910, 2nd par.

72 Cf. no. 911, 2nd par.

73 Cf. no. 913, 1st par.

74 Cf. no. 815, footnotes 745 and 746.

75 Believed by Sarkār to be "a copyist's error for *Istur=Stuart*, meaning that Col. Stuart who was kidnapped by the Sikhs when hunting near Anupshahar and afterwards released for a ransom through the mediation of Begam Samru in 1788". But if "Ustar" was a captain in 1787, he is unlikely to have been a colonel in 1788.

No. 915 (1), MSS. [*Durr i manẓūm.*] Also **Princeton** 59 (but this MS. of 15 foll. is apparently a fragment from the beginning of the poem, since it is described as "a poetical description of the nocturnal journey of the Prophet and of his personal appearance").

No. 919, 3rd par. *Read* 1899°*.

No. 922, end. *Insert*:

922*a*. Another account of Chait Sing'h's rebellion is contained in Sanbhau Lāl's *Miftāḥ i khazā'in* (a chronogram=1197/ 1783. See Rieu iii 1016*b*, 1026*a*, 1056*b*).

No. 923, 2nd par., MSS. [*Tuḥfah i tāzah.*] Also **Ellis Coll.** M. 221 (AH 1238/1821).

No. 930, end. *Insert*:

930*a*. For the *Waqā'iʿ i Shujāʿī* see no. 801, 2nd par. *supra*.
No 938, 3rd par., MSS. [*ʿImād al-saʿādat.*] Also **Ellis Coll.** M. 126 (19th cent.).

No. 940, 1st par. (2). An edition of the *Ṣubḥ i ṣādiq* was lithographed at Meerut in 1292/1875* (26 pp.). Sprenger's description of this work as an autobiography is incorrect, since it is a string of reflections in ornate prose and verse on the trials of human life and the wickedness of contemporary humanity.

No. 940, last par. [Ṣādiq Khān "Akhtar".] Also Garcin de Tassy i p. 184 (where his father's name is given as Qāḍī M. Laʿl and where he is said to have been still alive in 1854); *Miʿrāj al-khayāl* (Ivanow Curzon p. 67); *Khāzin al-shuʿarā'* fol. 46*a*, l. 4; R. B. Saksēna *History of Urdu literature* p. 122 (where it is stated that, having lost the favour of Wājid ʿAlī Shāh, he left Lucknow and became a *Taḥṣīldār* at Etawah, where he died in 1858); T. Grahame Bailey *History of Urdu literature* p. 67.

No. 941, 1st par. John Doeswell Shakespeare: so Rieu, but J. Dowdeswell Shakespear is correct (cf. W. W. Hunter *The Thackerays in India* p. 147).

No. 941, 1st par. ʿAbd al-Aḥad "Rābiṭ" b. M. Fā'iq, a resident of Amēṭ'hī, was a "Sarishtedar" in the office of the British Resident at Lucknow and died at Ameṭ'hī in 1268/1851–2 (see M. Taqī Aḥmad's translation, p. l n., where no authority is mentioned). P.S. See *Nigāristān i sukhan* p. 28.

No. 941, end. [*Waqā'iʿ i dil-padhīr.*] *Insert*:

Translation: *Tarikh Badshah Begam (a Persian manuscript on the history of Oudh) translated by Muhammad Taqi Ahmad* [from a MS. formerly in the possession of "the late Maharajah of Balrampur"]. **Allahabad** 1938 (cf. *JRAS*. 1939 p. 351).

No. 942, 2nd par., MSS. *Read* iii 1052*b* (extracts only), 1053*b* (extracts only. Circ. AD 1850).

No. 946, 1st par., 1st date. *For* AH 1197/1782–3 *read* on 23 Muḥarram 1197/ 29 December 1782 (see *OCM*. iii/3 (May 1927) p. 49).

No. 946, last par. [Ratan Sing'h "Zakhmī".] Also *Ṣubḥ i gulshan* p. 189, where the date of his death is given as 1267 [1850–1].

No. 952, 1st par., footnote. [ʿAbd al-Jalīl Bilgrāmī.] Also *Safīnah i Khwushgū* (Bānkīpūr viii p. 97); *Khulāṣat al-kalām* (Bkp. viii p. 143).

No. 952, last par. [M. b. ʿAbd al-Jalīl Bilgrāmī]. Also *Khizānah i ʿāmirah* pp. 284–6.

No. 952, last par., ult. *Read* 1929, ii pp. 159–63.

No. 953, 2nd par. *For* village *read* small town.

No. 955, last par. [*Bahāristān i Ghaibī.*] *Read* **Gauhati** 1936 (see *JRAS*. 1937 p. 581 and Sir R. Burn's review in *JRAS*. 1941 pp. 70–2).

No. 960, 2nd par., MSS. [*Tārīkh i Mahābat-Jang.*] Also **Ellis Coll.** M. 429 (AH 1185/1772).

No. 975, 2nd par., end. [*Ṭabaqāt i Muḥsinīyah. Read* 57 foll.): **Calcutta** 1889*.

No. 975, 2nd par., footnote. There was a portrait of Ḥājjī M. Muḥsin in Room 195 at the India Office and a reproduction of it in *Bengal: past and present*, v p. 159.

No. 976 (4). For Munnī (not Manī) Bēgam see *Amīr-nāmah* p. 32 and Beale's *Oriental biographical dictionary* p. 280.

No. 982, 3rd par., end. *Insert*:

Urdu translation: *Tarikh-i-Gujrat. By Abu Turab Vali. Translated ... into Urdu, with introduction, by Shabeah* [*sic*?] *Ahmad*. **Allahabad** 1945 (see Probsthain's *Orientalia nova* i (1944–6) no. 614 and *Luzac's OL*. 1945 p. 58, in which latter place the language of the translation is not specified).

No. 983, 1st line. *Read* **Sikandar** ibn M. **Manjhū.**

No. 984, 2nd par., 2nd line. Read *Aḥmadābād i Gujrāt.*

No. 990, 1st line.[S̲h̲āh-Jahān Bēgam.] *Read* "S̲h̲īrīn", afterwards "Tājwar". See *Ḥayāt i S̲h̲āh-Jahānī*, tr. Ghosal, p. 241.

In her Persian poetry, however, she seems to have called herself "S̲h̲āh i Jahān", which is given as her *tak̲h̲alluṣ* in the *S̲h̲amʿ i anjuman*, the *Nigāristān i suk̲h̲an* and the *Ṣubḥ i guls̲h̲an.*

No. 990, 2nd par. For these and other works see *Ḥayāt i S̲h̲āh-Jahānī*, tr. Ghosal, pp. 241–6.

No. 990, last par. [S̲h̲āh-Jahān Bēgam.] Also *Nigāristān i suk̲h̲an* pp. 45–7; *Ṣubḥ i guls̲h̲an* pp. 217–20; *Hayat-i-Shahjehani, life of ... Nawab Shahjehan Begum ..., by Her Highness Nawab Sultan Jehan Begum ... Translated by B. Ghosal.* Bombay 1926.

No. 994, 1st line. *Read* **Ḥiṣārī.**

No. 1001, 2nd par. Read ***Wāqiʿah i Jhōjhār Sing'h.***

No. 1006 (4), end. *Insert*:

(4*a*) ***Tūdah i ṭūfān i Mac̲h̲hlī-bandar***, an account of an inundation at Masulipatam (cf. no. (1) above) in 1281/ 1864–5, by Qādir Muḥyī 'l-Dīn: **Āṣafīyah** iii p. 100.

No. 1007, last par., end. [ʿAlī b. ʿAzīz Allāh Ṭabāṭabā.] *Insert*:
[*Haft iqlīm* no. 1147?]

No. 1009, 3rd par., end. [*Fatḥ-nāmah i S̲h̲ōlāpūr.*]

Edition: *Conquest of Sholāpūr by Burhān Niẓām Shāh I* (*914–961* A.H., *1508–1553*) *as described by Shāh Ṭāhir. By M. Hidayat Hosain* (in *JRASB.*, Letters, v/l (1939) pp. 133–53).

No. 1009, last par. [Shāh Ṭāhir Dak'hanī.] Also *Haft iqlīm* no. 1305; *Khazīnah i ganj i Ilāhī* (Sprenger p. 80[20]); *Hamīshah bahār* (Sprenger p. 125); *Safīnah i Khwushgū* no. 70; *Khulāṣat al-afkār* no. 162; *Makhzan al-gharā'ib* no. 1453 (?); article by Hidayat Hosain in the Denison Ross *Festschrift*.

No. 1011, 1st par. The *Jāmiʿ al-ʿulūm* was completed on 14 Muḥarram 1173/8 Sept. 1759 according to Brockelmann *Sptbd.* ii p. 628.

No. 1015, 2nd par., MSS. [*Futūḥāt i ʿĀdil-Shāhī.*] Also **Ellis Coll.** M. 119 (17th cent.).

No. 1015, last par. ["Fuzūnī".] Also *Ṣubḥ i gulshan* p. 317.

No. 1015, end. *Insert*:

1015*a*. **M. Ẓuhūr ibn** Maulawī **Ẓuhūrī** was presumably a son of the poet "Ẓuhūrī" Turshīzī (who died in 1025/1616 or thereabouts: see Browne *Lit. Hist*, iv p. 253; *Ency. Isl.* under Ẓuhūrī (Huart); Bānkīpūr cat. iii pp. 32–4; etc.).

Muḥammad-nāmah, on the reign of Muḥammad ʿĀdil-Shāh: **Ellis Coll.** M. 282 (AH 1183/1769–70), **Kapurthala** 31 (24 year of Shāh-ʿĀlam (AH 1196–7). See *OCM*. iii/4 (Aug. 1927) p. 15).

No. 1016, 2nd par. "The University Library of Belfast possesses an incomplete history of Bījāpūr (especially of the Khāqān-i Sikandar-iqbāl = Muḥammad, 1035–70/1626–60?), beginning: *shukr-va-sipās-va sitāyish-i bī-qiyās ḥaḍrat-i pādshāh-i ʿalal-iṭlāq*. It must be identical with Abul-Qāsim's *Guldasta-yi gulshan-i rāz*, Browne Coll. H. 17 (13) which begins *ḥamd- va-sipās-i bi-qiyās*" [Minorsky, *BSOS*. x/2 (1940) p. 540]. This identification seems improbable, since the opening words of the *Guldastah i gulshan i rāz* (?) (this title comes merely from a fly-leaf) are *Ḥ. u sp. i bī-qiyās mar dhāt i mustajmaʿ i jamīʿ i ṣifāt i kamāl*.

No. 1017, 2nd par., MSS. [*Tārīkh i ʿAlī ʿĀdil-Shāh.*] Also **Madrās i** 213 (*a*) (*Tārīkh i ʿĀdil-Shāh*, by Nūr Allāh ..., described as a history of Ibrāhīm ʿĀdil-Shāh, presumably therefore the earlier part (84 pp. only) of the *T. i ʿA. Ā.-Sh.*).

No. 1028, 2nd par., MSS. [*Tārīkh i futūḥāt i Āṣafī.*] Probably also **Madrās** i 127 (*Mathnawī i Futūḥāt i Āsafī*. "Author, Asafi." Beg. *Ba-nām i Shahanshāh i mulk i baqā*).

No. 1034, 1st line. [Mīr-ʿĀlam.] For this form of title cf. Mīrzā-yi ʿālamiyān Mīrzā M. Shafīʿ (*ʿĀlam-ārāy i ʿAbbāsī* p. 568[9]).

No. 1034 (1), 1st par., footnote, 4th line from foot. *For* be *read* he.

No. 1034 (1), 2nd par. *Read* 1266/1850°*.

No. 1034, last par. [Mīr-ʿĀlam.] Also *A memoir of Sir Salar Jang, G.C.S.I.*, by Syed Hossain Bilgrami, Bombay 1883, pp. 9–12.

No. 1034, last par., last line. *Read* Ḥaidarābād 1930 (see *JRAS*. 1933 pp. 194–6).

No. 1038, 1st par. For Chandū Lāl no. 1475 *infra*.

No. 1042, 2nd par., end. [*Gulzār i Āṣafīyah.*] For an autograph MS. in the private library of Maulawī ʿUmar Yāfiʿī [presumably at Ḥaidarābād] see *Islamic culture* xxii/4 (Oct. 1948) p. 400.

No. 1042, 2nd par., footnote. On p. 111 the 2nd of Muḥarram 1260 is called *al-ān*.

No. 1043, 2nd par. (5). For the *Bayāḍ i dil-gushā*, incorrectly described here (on the authority of Steingass's card-catalogue) as an anthology, see no. 1389, 2nd par. *infra*.

No. 1043, last par. [Naṣr Allāh Khān.] Also *Gulshan i hamīshah- bahār* pp. 92–4 (autobiography. Cf. no. 1219, 2nd par. *infra*); *Ṣubḥ i gulshan* p. 519.

No. 1045, 1st par. For the Nāʾiṭī tribe see nos. 1451 and 1452 *infra* and *Maʾāthir al-umarāʾ* iii p. 562 (Beveridge's trans. i p. 164).

No. 1045, last par. [Nawwāb ʿAziz-Jang.] Also a short autobiography prefixed to the *Kullīyāt i naẓm i Wilā* (Ḥaidarābād 1328/ 1910*).

No. 1046 (2), end. *Insert*:

(2a) ***Gazēṭīr i ḍilʿ i Ēlgandal***, composed in 1289 *Faṣlī* [AH 1297/1880?] by Mānik-Shāh Bābūjī, formerly 2nd Taʿalluqdār of the Elgandal District: **Āṣafīyah** iii p. 102 (AH 1297/1880).

No. 1046 (10). For the *Tārīkh i rāḥat-afzā* see *supra*, addendum to no. 164, last par..

No. 1046 (11). [*Waqā'iʿ i shūrish i Afghānīyah.*] It is not clear whether the Ḥaidarābād referred to is Ḥaidarābād, Sind, or Ḥaidarābād, Deccan.

No. 1046 (11), end. *Insert*:
(12) ***Waṣīyat-nāmah i Nawwāb Āṣaf-Fāh Bahādur***: **Bodleian** 2020.

No. 1047, one line above: **12.40** ***The Marāṭ'hās***
In spite of the preference of certain Orientalists for the form *Marhaṭṭah* (with a doubled *ṭ*) it appears doubtful whether this form is even permissible in Urdu and in the Persian of India. At any rate the usual Urdu pronunciation seems to be with a single *ṭ*. In 'Abd al-Majīd's *Jāmiʿ al-lughāt* (an Urdu dictionary) *Marhaṭā* and *Marhaṭah* are given as the Urdu spellings and *Marhaṭṭā* as a Hindī spelling. Another pronunciation (the only one mentioned in the *Farhang i Āṣafīyah*) is *Marahṭā* or *Marahṭah*. Presumably therefore the spelling *Marhaṭṭah* should be corrected in nos. 1049 2nd par., 1054 2nd and 5th par., 1057 2nd par. and 1062 (1) and (2).

No. 1056, last par. *Read* Ghulām-Ṣamadānī.

No. 1056, last par., end. [*Bisāṭ al-ghanā'im.*] *Insert*:
English translation by Colonel J. W. Watson: **Ethé** ii 3018 marg.

No. 1062 (1). [*Aḥwāl i Bhā'ō Marhaṭah.*] *For* Circ. AD 1808 (?) *read* 2 copies, one dated 1197/1783.

No. 1062 (3), MSS..[*Aḥwāl i ḥasab u nasab i Janūbiyān.*] Also **Ellis Coll.** M. 47.

No. 1070, 2nd par., last line on p. 605. *Delete* this.

No. 1070 (2), 1st line. *Read* ***Letters***.

No. 1070 (3), 1st par. For a transcript of Ethé 3001 see Blochet iv 2119.

No. 1070 (3), 1st par. Read *infra cit*.

No. 1070, last par. Read *Tippoo*.

No. 1075, last par., end. *Read* [*sic*, for 1844].

No. 1076, 2nd par. Read *Kirdgār kārsāz i rūzgār.*

No. 1078, 3rd par. In the Calcutta Madrasah catalogue, p. 105, the *Kār-nāmah i Ḥaidarī* is spoken of as a work of ʿAbd al-Raḥīm Gōrak'hpūrī (who went to Afghānistān with Mountstuart Elphinstone and W. Fraser, translated some English mathematical works into Persian and died in Calcutta).

No. 1078, last par. *Read* Calcutta 1854.

No. 1079 (7). Read *Srī-Rang-Paṭan* [with a single *ṭ*. Dr. Khiḍr ʿAlī Khān, orally].

No. 1079 (7), end. *Insert*:
(8) ***Tārīkh i Ṭīpū Sulṭān*** (beg. *Sulṭān i nash'atain*): **Madrās** i 288.
(9) ***Waqāʾiʿ i Ḥaidarī*** (beg. *Shāyistah-tarīn kalāmī*), a brief history of Ḥaidar ʿAlī and Ṭīpū: **Madrās** i 320–1.

No. 1083, 1st par., penult. *Read* 1162/1749.

No. 1083, 3rd par., end. *Insert*:
Edition: *Anwar Nāma of Abjadi. Edited by Muhammad Husain Mahvi.* **Madrās** 1944 (Madras Univ. Islamic Series, no. 8. See *JRAS*. 1946 p. 210).

No. 1084, 2nd par., MSS. *Read* **Madrās** i 304.

No. 1084, 3rd par., end. [*Tūzuk i Wālā-Jāhī.*] Part ii of Nainar's translation was published in 1939 (see *JRAS*. 1940 p. 398, 1942 p. 71).

No. 1086, 2nd par., MSS. [*Sawāniḥāt i mumtāz.*] Also **Madrās** i p. 546 no. 535, p. 486 no. 447 (AH 1350/1931,[76] probably transcribed from the preceding MS.).

No. 1087, (1), end. *Insert*:
(1*a*) ***Bahār i Aʿẓam-Jāhī***, an account of Nawwāb Aʿẓam-Jāh's journey to Nagūr and back in 1238/1822–3 by Ghulām-ʿAbd al-Qādir "Nāẓir" entitled Qādir

76 The words "Appearance, old" in the description of the MS. are presumably a *lapsus calami* for "Appearance, new".

ʿAẓīm Khān (for whom see no. 1451): **Madrās** i 529 (AH 1239/ 1823–4, autograph).

(1*b*) ***Sharaf-nāmah***, or *Tārīkh i Ḥafīẓ-Allāh-Khānī*, a history of the Nawwābs of the Carnatic from ʿAẓīm al-Daulah to Ghulām-Ghauth, by M. Auliyā, entitled Ḥafīẓ Allāh Khān: **Madrās** i 530 (AH 1354/1935).

No. 1091, end.. *Insert*:

1091 *a*. For the *Badāʾiʿ al-waqāʾiʿ* of "Wāṣifī" see no. 501, 2nd par.

No. 1094, 3rd par., 1st footnote. [*Dīwān i Fānī.*] Also **Majlis** ii 1035 (between 901/1495–6 and 906/1500–1).

No. 1094, Persian translations (4), 2nd par. *Read*: pp. 155–7); *Tuḥfah i Sāmī*.

No. 1099, 2nd par., 5th footnote, end. Shujāʿ Bēg Arghūn, or Amīr Shāh-Shujāʿ Arghūn was not another son of Dhū 'l-Nūn but the same person as Shāh-Bēg Arghūn (see *Ency. Isl.* under Arghūn dynasty of Sind, Firishtah ii p. 620 penult.).

No. 1100, 2nd par., MSS. [*Tuḥfah i Sāmī.*] Also **Vatican** Pers. 106 (AH 977/1569 or 997/1588. Rossi p. 116), **Ellis Coll.** M. 367 (AH 1026/1617).

No. 1105, end. *Insert*:

1105*a*. Ṣādiq Bēg **"Ṣādiqī" Afshār,** poet and painter, was born at Tabrīz in 940/1533–4 and became Librarian to Shāh ʿAbbās (985–1038/1587–1629). According to the *Dānishmandān i Adharbāyjān* he prepared in 1010/1601–2 at Iṣfahān a collected edition of his works in Persian and Turkī prose and verse, which included a Persian *mathnawī* entitled *Fatḥ-nāmah i ʿAbbās i nāmdār* as well as the *Majmaʿ al-khawāṣṣ*. For his *Ḥaẓẓīyāt*, a small Persian work on Ṣūfism, see Berlin 12 (7), Bodleian 1243 (2) and *Dānishmandān i Adharbāyjān* p. 213 (10).

Majmaʿ al-khawāṣṣ, dateless Turkī notices of contemporary poets composed [*circa* 1000/1592[77]] in the reign of Shāh ʿAbbās (985–1038/1587–1629) and divided into eight *majmaʿ*s ((1) kings, p. 7, (2) princes, p. 21, (3) nobles of Turkish race (*arkān i salṭanat az Turkān*), p. 29, (4) nobles of Persian race, p. 39, (5) sons of Turkish and Persian nobles, p. 63, (6) Saiyids, p. 74, (7) Turkish poets who wrote in Turkish, Persian and Arabic, p. 102,

77 At the end of the work there is a chronogram for the circumcision of Ṣafī Mīrzā in 1003.

(8) contemporary Persian poets, p. 131), and a *khātimah* (verses by the author): Ḥ. Kh. ii p. 263, v p. 401, **Istānbūl** Univ. Lib. 4085 (AH 1016/1607–8), 4097 (AH 1037/1627–8), **Nūr i ʿUthmānīyah** 3720 (AH 1021/1612), **Gotha** Turkish cat. p. 139 no. 168.

Edition with Persian translation: *Tadhkirah i Majmaʿ al-khawāṣṣ ba-zabān i Turkī i Chaghatāy taʾlīf i Ṣādiqī i Kitābdār u tarjamah i ān ba-zabān i Fārsī ba-khāmah i Duktur ʿAbd al-Rasūl Khayyām-pūr muʿallim i Dānishgāh i Tabrīz*, **Tabrīz** AHS 1327/1948–9 (327 pp.).

List of the 342[78] poets in the Gotha MS.: Gotha Turkish cat. pp. 140–8. [Autobiographical statements collected in editor's preface, pp. *ḥā* to *yā*; *Tadhkirah i Naṣrābādī* pp. 39–40; *ʿĀlam- ārāy i ʿAbbāsī* p. 127; *Khulāṣat al-kalām* no. 39; *Makhzan al-gharāʾib* no. 1299; *Shamʿ i anjuman* p. 256; *Dānishmandān i Ādharbāyjān* pp. 212–13; *Armaghān* xii pp. 15–21, 185–99.]

No. 1137, last par. Read *raʿnā*.

No. 1147, 1st par., beginning. Lakzī is the Arabic form (cf. Samʿānī fol. 495, l. 19, Suyūṭī *Lubb al-Lubāb* p. 230, *Tāj al-ʿarūs* iv p. 78; l. 5 from foot) and it may possibly be used also in Persia, but the word is spelt Lagzī in the *Farhang i Niẓām*.

No. 1149, Abridgments, MSS. [*Muntakhab i Majmaʿ al-nafāʾis.*] Also **Ellis Coll.** M. 50 (early 19th cent.).

No. 1150, 2nd par., 6th footnote. The spelling Sīwistān may be incorrect. Yāqūt writes Sīwastān.

No. 1150 (1), Editions, end. [*Tadhkirat al-aḥwāl.* Editions.] Also **Ṭihrān** AHS 1324/1945 (abridged by Muḥammadī and published under the title *Safar-nāmah i Shaikh Muḥammad ʿAlī Ḥazīn* as pp. 61–130 (last) of the volume entitled *Nādir Shāh*, of which pp. 7–60 are an abridgment of M. Mahdī's *Durrah i Nādirī* [*sic*]).

No. 1150, last par., beginning. ["Ḥazīn."] A brief note by "Ḥazīn", in Arabic, on the teachers whose lectures he attended and on the books studied by him is preserved in Ivanow 1778 (3).

---

78 The number is 333 in the Istānbūl MSS. used by ʿAbd al-Rasūl Khaiyām-pūr (see his preface p. *zāy*, n. 1). According to the *Dānishmandān i Ādharbāyjān* the number of biographies is 480 [presumably in a later edition].

No. 1162, 1st par., twice. The spelling Sīwistān may be incorrect. Yāqūt writes Sīwastān.

No. 1162, Arabic works (2), 1st par. [*Subḥat al-marjān.*] Cf. Zubaid Aḥmad *The contribution of India to Arabic literature* pp. 180–2.

No. 1162, Arabic works (2), last par., penult. sentence. *For* (12) *read* (11).

No. 1162, Arabic works (3). For "Āzād's" *dīwāns* see also Zubaid Aḥmad *The contribution of India to Arabic literature* pp. 213–19, 428.

No. 1162, Arabic works (4).[*Maẓhar al-barakāt.*] See also Zubaid Aḥmad *The contribution of India to Arabic literature* p. 428.

No. 1162, Persian works (15). The spelling Sīwistān may be incorrect. Yāqūt writes Sīwastān.

No. 1170, 4th par., MSS. [*Ātash-kadah.*] Also **Majlis** ii 886 (AH 1217/1802–3), **Ellis Coll.** M. 231 (ornate MS. Late 18th cent.).

No. 1170, penult. par. [*Tadhkirah i Isḥāq.*] Also **Majlis** ii 897 (AH 1217/ 1802–3).

No. 1174, 2nd par., MSS. [*Anīs al-aḥibbā'.*] Also **Majlis** ii 893 (AH 1203/ 1788–9).

No. 1176 (1), 1st par. [*Gulzār i Ibrāhīm.*] For an autograph MS. of the second half (*sīn* to *yā'*) in the private library of Maulawī 'Umar Yāfi'ī [presumably at Ḥaidarābād] see *Islamic culture* xxii/4 (Oct. 1948) p. 403.

No. 1176 (1), 2nd par. [*Gulzār i Ibrāhīm*. Urdu trans.] According to *Islamic culture* xxii/4 (Oct. 1948) p. 403 "Later in 1212 AH Mirza 'Alī Luṭf translated a selection of it in Urdu. This was published by Muhammad 'Abdullah Khān (late Nazim of the Āṣafia Library) with a foreword by Maulvi 'Abdul Ḥaq, B.A., in 1906, as Gulshan-i-Hind. Some time back the Tadhkira was corrected and edited by Dr. Zore [i.e. "Zōr"] and was published by the Anjuman-i-Tarraqi [*sic*]-i-Urdu, and forms No. 72 of its publication series."

No. 1187, 1st par., last sentence. Read *Ṣād i daftar i ashwāq* (a chronogram=1187/1773. See Rieu ii 723*b*).

No. 1187 (1), MSS.[*Bāgh i gulhā-yi ḥusn.*] Also **Rieu** ii 723*b* ii (AH 1191/1777). The work, however, does not belong to this section: it contains "descriptions of the various points of female beauty, in ornate prose, with appropriate verses, partly due to the author, partly to other poets not named" (Rieu).

No. 1187, last par. ["'Ishq."] Also Garcin de Tassy ii p. 45; Rieu ii 723*b*.

No. 1194, 2nd par., MSS. [*Anjuman i Khāqān.*] Also **Majlis** ii 892.

No. 1195, end. *Insert*:

1195*a*. S. Ḥasan (or Ḥusain?) **"Thamar" Nā'īnī** is mentioned briefly in the *Anjuman i Khāqān* as one of the Ṭabāṭabā'ī Saiyids of Nā'īn. He is mentioned also in the *Bayān i Maḥmūd*.

Tadhkirah i Thamar i Nā'īnī, notices of forty panegyrists of Ḥājj M. Ḥusain Khān Niẓām al-Daulah Iṣfahānī, who succeeded Mīrzā Shafī' as Ṣadr i A'ẓam and who died in 1238/1822–3, in a *muqaddamah*, two *bābs* and a *khātimah*: **Majlis** ii 898 (lacks *Muqaddamah* and perhaps part of *Khātimah*. Autograph?).

No. 1199 (1), end. ['Abd al-Razzāq Bēg Dunbulī] *Insert*:

(1*a*) ***Ḥadā'iq al-udabā'***, twenty-three *ḥadīqahs* dedicated in 1232/1817 to 'Abbās Mīrzā Nā'ib al-Salṭanah and dealing, in the words of the cataloguer, with "*munsha'āt u muṭāraḥāt i shu'arā-yi 'Arab u 'Ajam u faṣāḥat u balāghat i aqwāl i ānān u siyāsat i mulūk u ādāb i wuzarā' u uṣūl i dīn u akhlāq u tawārīkh u lughāt u ghair az īnhā*": **Majlis** ii 915 (a large fragment (322 foll.) containing biographies of Persian poets and selections from their Arabic poems. Autograph?).[79]

No. 1200, last par. ["Rā'iq."] Also *Sham' i anjuman* p. 181.

No. 1204, 2nd par., MSS. [*Tadhkirat al-salāṭīn.*] For the Majlis MS. see now **Majlis** ii 894.

No. 1205, 2nd par., MSS. [*Tadhkirah i Muḥammad-Shāhī.*] Also **Majlis** ii 902 (AH 1249/1833–4), 903 (AH 1251/1835–6).

79 A (complete?) MS. of this work was seen by the cataloguer in the library of the late Thiqat al-Islām.

No. 1207, last par. [Muṣṭafā Khān "Shēftah".] Also *Āthār al-ṣanādīd* (cf. no. 654, 5th par. *supra*), Lucknow 1876, pt. 4, pp. 110–11.

No. 1214, 2nd par., MSS. [*Madā'iḥ al-Mu'tamadīyah.*] Also **Majlis** ii 1192 (autograph?).

No. 1225 (20), 2nd par. [*Majma' al-fuṣaḥā'.*] Another edition: [**Ṭihrān**, n.d.] (657 pp. See F. E. Karatay *Istanbul Üniversitesi Kütüphanesi Farsça Basmalar Kataloğu*, p. 151).

No. 1225, end. *Insert*:

1225*a*. **"Kāẓim"** wrote at least part of his *tadhkirah* at Zanjān.

Tadhkirah i Kāẓim, notices of a few poets and poetesses, nearly all ancient, composed in 1286–7/1869–70: **Majlis** ii 901 (307 foll. AH 1286–7, autograph).

No. 1228, 1st par. Nawwāb Shams al-'Ulamā' 'Alī Ḥasan Khān is mentioned incidentally in S. Najīb Ashraf Nadwī's *Muqaddamah i ruqa'āt i 'Ālamgīr* (in Urdu), A'ẓamgaṛh [1930*] p. 108[3], where he is described as Nāẓim i Nadwah, Lak'hna'ū [i.e. presumably Director (?) of the educational society Nadwat al-'Ulamā' founded at Lucknow in 1894 or of the school maintained by that society or both (see R. B. Saksēna *History of Urdu literature* p. 290)]. In the autobiography printed under the *takhalluṣ* "Salīm" (evidently a *takhalluṣ* still earlier than "'Āshiqī" mentioned above) in the *Ṣubḥ i gulshan*, pp. 208–11, it is stated that he was born on 4 Rabī' al-Ākhir 1283/16 August 1866 at Bhōpāl. He was thus twelve years old when he published that work and must have received a great deal of assistance from the collaborator mentioned in his preface, Maulawī S. M. Yūsuf 'Alī, *Kār- pardāz i āstānah i 'alīyah i walī-'ahd i riyāsat.*

No. 1231, end. *Insert*:

1231*a*. **Ibrāhīm b. Mahdī.**

Tadhkirah i majdīyah, poems by members of Nāṣir al-Dīn Shāh's court and high officials, with notices of the authors and portraits: **Ṭihrān** 1302/1885° (52 foll.); 1303/1885–6 (81 pp. See Karatay p. 84).

1231*b*. From statements made here and there in his *tadhkirah* it appears that **"Mumaiyiz"** was at one time auditor at Nihāwand (*sālī kih bandah ma'mūr* *bi-ta'dīl i Nihāwand būdam,*[80] p. 209), that in 1250/1834–5 he was at Tabrīz (p. 184), that in 1262/1846 he was staying in Tihrān (p. 114) and that in 1299/1881–2 he saw Mūsā Khān "Sarhang" and took down some verses of his.

Tadhkirah i Mumaiyiz, notices of contemporary poets: **Majlis** ii 904 (AH 1306/1888–9, apparently autograph).

No. 1235, end. *Insert*:

1235*a*. **'Alī Aṣghar "Ḥikmat"** b. Ḥishmat al-Mamālik Aḥmad 'Alī Mustaufī, member of a distinguished medical family and on his mother's side the grandson of Ḥasan Fasā'ī (see no. 464 *supra*), was born at Shīrāz on 23 Ramaḍān 1310/10 April 1893 and was educated at the American High School [in Ṭihrān] and the University of Paris. He has been Professor of Persian Literature in the University of Ṭihrān since 1931 and was Minister of Foreign Affairs in the cabinet of 1948. He had previously held several other ministries, including that of education. Among his works are didactic *mathnawīs* and translations of plays by Shakespeare. His edition of two translations of the *Majālis al-nafā'is* has already been mentioned (no. 1094, Persian translations (1) Editions (2), and (2) Edition *supra*).

Jāmī, *mutaḍammin i taḥqīqāt dar tārīkh i aḥwāl u āthār i manẓūm u manthūr i khātam al-shu'arā Nūr al-Dīn 'Abd al-Raḥmān i Jāmī*: **Tihrān** 1320/1942 (413 pp.).

[Rashīd Yāsimī *Adabīyāt i mu'āṣir* pp. 41–4 (portrait); M. Ishaque *Modern Persian poetry* pp. 11, 26, etc.; Ḥabīb Allāh Mukhtārī *Tārīkh i bīdārī i Īrān* pp. 270–1 (portrait); *International Who's who* 1950 under Hekmat; Īraj Afshār *Nathr i Fārsī i mu'āṣir* pp. 132–7 (portrait)].

No. 1236, 1st par. Sa'īd Nafīsī is one of the Professors of Persian Literature in the University of Ṭihrān (see *The world of learning* 1950). Also *Tārīkh i jarā'id u majallāt i Īrān* iii pp. 70–1 (portrait); Īraj Afshār *Nathr i Fārsī i mu'āṣir* pp. 169–92 (portrait).

No. 1237, 1st par. "Rashīd" Yāsamī is Professor of the History of Īrān in the University of Ṭihrān (see *The world of learning*, 1950, where Yāsamī is so spelt (officially?)). See also Berthels *Ocherk istorii persidskoi literatury* pp. 167–9; S. M. Bāqir Burqa'ī *Sukhanwarān i nāmī i mu'āṣir* pp. 89–93 (portrait); Īraj Afshār *Nathr i Fārsī i mu'āṣir* pp. 149–56 (portrait).

---

80 From these words the cataloguer infers that he "*maqām i ta'dīl i mālīyāt yā mumaiyizī dāshtah*".

No. 1238, last par. [Qāsim Ghanī.] Also Īraj Afshār *Nathr i Fārsī i mu'āṣir* pp. 193–204 (portrait).

No. 1239, 1st par. B. al-Z. Furūzān-far is Professor of the History of Persian Literature in the University of Ṭihrān (see *The world of learning* 1950).

No. 1239, last par. [Badī' al-Zamān Furūzān-far.] Also Burqa'ī *Sukhanwarān i nāmī i mu'āṣir* pp. 22–4 (portrait. His name is given here as M. Ḥasan B. al-Z. F.-f.); Īraj Afshār *Nathr i Fārsī i mu'āṣir* pp. 212–14 (portrait).

No. 1240, end. *Insert*:

1240*a*. S. **Ḥusain Shajarah "Bīnā"** b. 'Abd al-Rasūl Shajarah was born at Iṣfahān in 1318/1900–1.

(1) ***Shakhsīyat i Maulawī***, on Jalāl al-Dīn Rūmī and his work: **Ṭihrān** AHS 1316/1937–8.

(2) ***Taḥqīq dar rubā'īyāt u zindagānī i Khaiyām***: **Ṭihrān** (see *Luzac's Oriental List* 1942 p. 11, where the date is not mentioned).

[Ishaque *Sukhanvarān-i-Īrān* ii pp. 220–4 (portrait), *Modern Persian poetry* pp. 12, 30.]

No. 1241, last par. ["Ḥabīb" Yaghmā'ī] Also D. J. Irani *Poets of the Pahlavi regime* p. 271; Burqa'ī *Sukhanwarān i nāmī i mu'āṣir* p. 57 (portrait).

No. 1242, end. *Insert*:

1242*a*. S. **M. Bāqir Burqa'ī** is the son of S. 'Alī Akbar "Kāshif" Burqa'ī Qummī.[81]
Sukhanwarān i nāmī i mu'āṣir, alphabetically arranged notices of poets who were alive in AHS 1300/1920–1 or later years, with a final notice of the earlier poet "Amīrī" (M. Ṣādiq Adīb al-Mamālik, for whom see Browne *Lit. Hist.* iv pp. 346–9): [**Ṭihrān** AHS 1329/1950–1 (date of preface).] (Mu'assasah i Maṭbū'ātī i Amīr i Kabīr.)

No. 1243 (1), end. *Insert*:

81 For whom see *Sukhanwarān i nāmī i mu'āṣir* pp. 190–6, where it is stated that he was born at Qum a.h.s. 1278/1899–1900 and where twelve published works of his are mentioned. For one of these works, the *Kākh i dil-āwīz*, see no. 1582 (1) *supra*. Another is the *Rāhnumā-yi Qum*.

(1*a*) ***Ḥayāt i Saʿdī***, translated from the Urdu of Alṭāf Ḥusain "Ḥālī"[82] by S. Naṣr Allāh "Surūsh": **Tihrān** AHS 1316/1937 (see *Luzac's OL*. 1938 p. 127 and Harrassowitz's *Litterae orientales* July 1938 p. 9).

No. 1243 (2). For Aḥmad "Suhailī" b. Ghulām-Riḍā Khān Khwānsārī (b. AHS 1291/1912–13 at Tihrān, Librarian of the Kitāb-khānah i Millī i Malik[83] and editor of the *Dhail i Tārīkh i ʿĀlam-ārāy i ʿAbbāsī*) see Burqaʿī *Sukhanwarān i nāmī i muʿāṣir* pp. 127–8 (portrait).

No. 1243 (2), end. *Insert*:

(2*a*) ***Iqbāl i Lāhaurī***,[84] *shāʿir i Pārsī-gūy i Pākistān. Baḥth dar aḥwāl u afkār i ū nigārish i Mujtabā Mīnuwī*.[85] **Ṭihrān** AHS 1327/1948–9 (*Az intishārāt i majallah i Yaghmā*. 75 pp.).

No. 1243 (4), end.. *Insert*:

(4*a*) ***Saʿdī-nāmah***, essays (and some poems) on Saʿdī by M. Qazwīnī, ʿAbbās Iqbāl, Furūzān-far and others, mostly Professors in the University of Ṭihrān: **Ṭihrān** AHS 1316/1938‡ (nos. 11–12 of the periodical *Taʿlīm u tarbiyat*, vol. (year) vii, but published also as an independent work).

No. 1243 (7). *Read* notices.

No. 1245, 3rd par. The Mashhad and Sipahsālār MSS. are evidently portions of the *Kashf al-asrār wa-ʿuddat al-abrār* of Rashīd al-Dīn Aḥmad b. M. Maibudī (see *supra*, addendum to no. 5).

No. 1245, end. *Insert*:

1245*a*. **Abū Bakr Muḥammad al-Khaṭīb,** i.e. Abū Bakr M. b. ʿAbd al-Karīm b. ʿAlī b. Saʿd al-Khaṭīb, died in 502/1109.

82 For "Ḥālī" (1837–1914) see nos. 654, last par. and 694, last par. *supra*; R. B. Saksēna *History of Urdu literature* pp. 210–19, 279–82; T. Grahame Bailey *History of Urdu literature* pp. 88, 94.

83 For an account of this library, collected by Ḥājj Ḥusain Āqā Malik [al-Tujjār, who was still alive in a.h.s. 1318/1939, when "Suhailī" Khwānsārī wrote his preface to the *Dhail i Tārīkh i ʿĀlam-ārāy i ʿAbbāsī*], see ʿAbd al-ʿAzīz Jawāhir al-Kalām's *Kitāb-khānahā-yi Īrān* (cf. PL. no. 1581), pp. 79–85, where it is described as the most important of the libraries of Persia at the present time. In *The world of learning* and the *Index generalis* it is called the Hadji Malek Library.

84 For "Iqbāl" (1875–1938) see T. Grahame Bailey *History of Urdu literature* pp. 103–4; etc., etc.

85 Born in 1320/1902–3 at Tihrān, now Professor in the Faculty of Adabīyāt at Tihrān: see Īraj Afshār *Nathr i Fārsī i muʿāṣir* pp. 215–24 (portrait).

(*Aḥwāl al-Shaikh Abī Isḥāq al-Kāzarūnī*),[86] an Arabic biography of A. I. al-K. (for whom see no. 1254 I, Persian translations, 2nd footnote, *Der Islam* xix p. 18 *sqq.* (M. F. Köprülü and P.Wittek) and *Ency. Isl.*, suppt., under Kāzerūnī (Wittek)): no MSS. recorded.

Persian translations (expanded):

(1) ***Firdaus al-murshidīyah fī asrār al-ṣamadīyah***, completed in 728/1327 by Maḥmūd b. ʿUthmān: **Āyā Ṣōfyah** 3254.

Edition: *Die Vita des Scheich Abū Isḥāq al-Kāzarūnī in der persischen Bearbeitung von Maḥmūd b. ʿUṯmān, herausgegeben und eingeleitet von F. Meier*, **Leipzig** 1948 (Bibliotheca Islamica, 14).

(2) ***Marṣad al-aḥrār ilā siyar al-murshid al-abrār***, composed circ. 750/1349 by Rajāʾ Muḥammad b. ʿAbd al-Raḥmān b. ʿAbd al-Raḥīm al-Kāzarūnī surnamed (*al-mulaqqab bah*) ʿAlāʾ [al-Dīn], apparently one of the saint's disciples: **A. Chester Beatty's** private library (AH 830/ 1427).

Description: *The biography of Shaikh Abū Isḥāq al-Kāzarūnī. By A. J. Arberry* (in *Oriens* 3/2 (1950) pp. 163–82).

No. 1251, 2nd par., footnote. [ʿAbd al-Qādir Jilānī] Also M. A. Ayni and F. J. Simore-Munir *Seyyid Abd-al-Kadir Guilani, un grand saint de l'Islam*, Paris 1938 (Les grandes figures de l'Orient, vi. See *Luzac's OL.* 1939 p. 21); *Saiyedena Hazrat Ghaus- ul-Azam*, by Saiyed Abdus Salik, Calcutta (see *Luzac's OL.* 1939 pp. 118, 126).

No. 1254, 2nd par., 2nd footnote. [Abū Isḥāq Kāzarūnī.] Also p. 1343^{1-19}; *Der Islam* xix p. 18 *sqq.* (M. F. Köprülü and P. Wittek); *Ency. Isl.*, suppt., under Kāzerūnī (Wittek).

No. 1259, 1st par., 1st footnote. [Mīr (i?) Khwurd.] Cf. also *Ātash-kadah* no. 189: "Mîr Khurd, with the takhalluṣ Malâlî, brother of Mîr Kalân of Sabzwâr."

No. 1259, 1st par., 4th footnote, beginning. [Niẓām al-Dīn Auliyā kī bastī.] See *A guide to Niẓāmu-d Dīn*, by Maulvi Zafar Hasan, Calcutta 1922 (Memoirs of the Archæological Survey of India, no. 10).

No. 1260, 2nd par., MSS. [*Safar-nāmah i Makhdūm i Jahāniyān.*] **Berlin** 536 (2) (58 foll. AH 1236/1821. "Allerhand fabelhafte Erzählungen von meist fabelhaften Ländern," beginning with the Masjid i Aqṣā) seems to be a part of this work.

86 The title, if it has one, is not mentioned in Arberry's article, the source of most of the information given here.

No. 1263, 1st par., footnote. [ʿAlāʾ al-Dīn ʿAṭṭār.] Also no. 1411 (78) *infra; Ḥabīb al-siyar* iii, 3, p. 87.

No. 1266, 2nd par. [*Khulāṣat al-maqāmāt.*] For a work entitled *Maqāmāt i Aḥmad i Jām* by Muḥammad al-Ishasnawī see Ellis Coll. M. 266 (16th cent.).

No. 1274, 2nd par., MSS. [*Nafaḥāt al-uns.*] Also **Ellis Coll.** M. 209 (AH 901/1496).

No. 1274, Commentaries (1), MSS. [*Ḥāshiyah i Nafaḥāt al-uns.*] Also **Majlis** ii 914 (AH 1036/1626–7).

No. 1277, 2nd par., last footnote. The abridgment seems to be the *Tuḥfah i Khānī* (see Ivanow Curzon 648).

No. 1277, Persian commentary. M. Ḥusain b. M. Hādī is the author of several medical works, which include the *Majmaʿ al-jawāmiʿ*, composed in 1185/1771–2, and the well-known *Makhzan al-adwiyah*, and of a commentary on Muḥsin Kāshī's *Kalimāt i maknūnah* (Brockelmann *Sptbd.* ii p. 584).

No. 1298, 1st par., footnote. He usually calls himself al-Turk (not al-Turkī) but nevertheless in a note at the end of his commentary on the *Mishkāt* he calls himself ʿA. al-Ḥ. b. S. al-D. al-Dihlawī *waṭan^{an}* al-Bukhārī *aṣl^{an}* al-Turkī *nasab^{an}* al-Ḥanafī *madhhab^{an}* al-Ṣūfī *mashrab^{an}* al-Qādirī *ṭarīqat^{an}* (see Rieu i p. 14).

No. 1298 (1), MSS. [*Akhbār al-akhyār.*] Also **Ellis Coll.** M. 5 (AH 1168/1755), M. 6 (18th cent.).

Editions: also [**Bombay**] Hāshimī Pr., 1280/1864 (310 pp. See F. E. Karatay, Istanbul Univ. cat. p. 3).

No. 1316 (1), 1st footnote, 2nd part, sources. [Aḥmad Sirhindī.] Also *Gulzār i asrār al-Ṣūfīyah* (Ethé 1901), *Bāb* iv, and probably *Manāqib i Aḥmadīyah u maqāmāt i Saʿdīyah*, by M. Maẓhar al-Dīn Fārūqī, Delhi 1847 (see F. E. Karatay, Istanbul Univ. cat. p. 127).

No. 1320, 2nd par., 3rd footnote. [Ādam Banūrī.] Also *Gulzār i asrār al-Ṣūfīyah* (Ethé 1901), *Bāb* iv; S. Shams Allāh Qādirī *Qāmūs al-aʿlām* (in Urdu), pt. I (Ḥaidarābād 1935), col. 12.

No. 1344, 2nd par., 1st footnote. [Saʿdī Lāhaurī.] Also *Gulzār i asrār al-Ṣūfīyah* (Ethé 1901), *Bāb* iv.

No. 1381, 1st par. The first element in the name of this author seems to have been, not Irtiḍā', as might have been expected, but Irtaḍā (ارتضى), the third person singular of the perfect tense. It will be noticed that on the title-page of his "*Furaiz- i-Irtazeeah*", printed at Madrās in his lifetime (see no. 1381, 1st par. (4), footnote), his name is spelt Irtaza Alee.

No. 1402, 1st par. M. Bāqir Wā'iẓ Māzandarānī died in 1313/1895–6 according to Mashhad iii, *fṣl.* 14, ptd. bks., no. 61. It seems that Māzandarānī, rather than Ṭihrānī, should be in thick type.

No. 1411 (3), end. *Insert*:

(3*a*) ***Aḥwālāt i marḥūm Shaikh Aḥmad b. Zain al-Dīn al-Aḥsā'ī***,[87] by M. Ṭāhir.
Edition: place? 1310/1892–3 (Āṣafīyah iii p. 362).

No. 1411 (9). The *Badā'i' al-āthār* is in two volumes according to the *Kitāb i Ṣubḥī* p. 141,[88] where there is some information about Maḥmūd Zarqānī.

No. 1411 (12), end. *Insert*:

(12*a*) ***Bisṭām u Bāyazīd i Bisṭāmī***, by Iqbāl Yaghmā'ī: **Ṭihrān** (see *Luzac's OL*. 1938 p. 183).

No. 1411 (16). Imdād Allāh, a prominent Ṣūfī resident at T'hānah Bhawan (18 miles N.W. of Muẓaffarnagar), emigrated to Mecca at the time of the Indian Mutiny and was still there, lecturing on Rūmī's *Mathnawī* in the Ḥaram i Sharīf, when Raḥmān 'Alī wrote a notice of him on pp. 28–9 of his *Tadhkirah i 'ulamā' i Hind* [published in 1894].

No. 1411 (19), end. *Insert*:

(19*a*) ***Ghazzālī-nāmah***, a life of al-Ghazzālī, by Jalāl [al-Dīn Khān "Sanā"] Humā'ī[2]: **Ṭihrān** (see *Luzac's OL*. 1940 pp. 63, 108).

No. 1411 (26). [*Ḥikāyāt al-ṣāliḥīn*.] MS. (without title and author's name but divided as described by Ḥ. Kh.): **Rieu** Suppt. 393 (beg. *Th. u st. mar Khudāy-rā kih Āfrīdgār i jahān-ast u Āfrīdgār i hamah jānwarān ast*. Breaks off towards

87 Cf. no. 1411 (73), (99*a*) [Additions], (116).
88 For whom see no. 1668 (17) *infra*, footnote.

end of second *ḥikāyat* in *Bāb* xx. 153 foll. 13th cent.). "The author was a Sunni, living apparently in the fifth century of the Hijrah" (Rieu).

No. 1411 (36), end. *Insert*:

(36*a*) ***Makhzan al-aʿrās***, by Sh. Sharaf al-Dīn [b.?] Qāḍī Sh. M. Shahrawānī: **Āṣafīyah** iii p. 106 (AH 1156/1743).

(36*b*) ***Makhzan al-wilāyah wa-'l-jamāl li-ḥuṣūl al-maʿrifah wa-'l-kamāl***, an account of Chishtī Niẓāmī *shaikhs*, by M. Wilāyat ʿAlī Khān: **Lucknow** 1300/1883° (on title-page 1286. 164 pp.).

No. 1411 (43), end. *Insert*:

(43*a*) ***Manāqib i Aḥmadīyah u maqāmāt i Saʿdīyah***,[89] by M. Maẓhar al-Dīn Fārūqī: **Delhi** 1847 (288 pp. See F. E. Karatay *Istanbul Üniversitesi Kütüphanesi Farsça Basmalar Kataloğu* p. 127).

No. 1411 (63), end. *Insert*:

(63*a*) ***Naẓm al-durar fī silk al-siyar***, a life of S. Amīr, a Naqshbandī saint, by Ṣafī Allāh called Mullā-yi Bāndah:[90] **Delhi** [1888°] (332 pp.).

No. 1411 (99), end. *Insert*:

(99*a*) **(*Sharḥ i hāl al-Shaikh Aḥmad* [*b.*] *Zain al-Dīn al-Aḥsāʾī*)**:[91] **Bombay** n.d. (Browne *Materials for the study of the Bábí religion* p. 194).

No. 1411 (114), end. *Insert*:

(114*a*) ***Tadhkirah i Shāh-Ālam***,[92] **by S. ʿAbd al-Raḥmān**, commonly called (*ʿurf*) Shāh Buddah [BDH?]: **Āṣafīyah** i p. 318.

No. 1411 (116). *Read* Aḥmad [b.] Zain al-Dīn.

No. 1411 (116), end. *Insert*:

(116*a*) ***Tadhkirat al-qubūr***, on the saints and other celebrities buried at Iṣfahān, by ʿAbd al-Karīm b. Mahdī Iṣfahānī: **Iṣfahān** 1324/1906

89 The combination of *Aḥmadīyah* in the title with Fārūqī in the name of the author suggests that this work is concerned with Aḥmad Fārūqī Sirhindī (for whom see no. 1316 (1) *supra*) and presumably with Saʿdī Lāhaurī (for whom see no. 1344, last par., 1st footnote *supra*).

90 i.e., presumably, of Bāndah ("Banda") in Būndēlk'hand.

91 Cf. ad no. 1411 (3) [1411 (3*a*)], no. 1411 (73), no. 1411 (116).

92 The work may possibly relate to the Gujrātī saint Shāh-ʿĀlam [d. 880/1475 see *Gulzār i abrār* (Ivanow 259) no. 183 and no. 1321 (1) 1st part *supra*].

[R. Lescot, *Bull. E.O.I.F. de Damas* vii–viii p. 282], See also Addendum ad no. 1539, 1539 (*b*) *infra*.

No. 1411 (119), end. *Insert*:

(119*a*) ***Tiqṣār juyūd al-aḥrār min tidhkār junūd al-abrār***, biographies of Ṣūfīs, by Nawwāb M. Ṣiddīq Ḥasan Khān (d. 1890: see no. 48 *supra*): **Bhōpāl** 1295/1878 (295 pp. See F. E. Karatay Istanbul Univ. cat. p. 131).

No. 1411 (124), end. *Insert*:

(124*a*) ***Wāqiʿāt i Rashīdī***, an account of various spiritual experiences of the author, Maulawī M. Rashīd al-Dīn Khān: **Lucknow** 1923* (with Urdu translation by Taqī Ḥaidar Qalandar).

No. 1438, 1st par., end. [Sanglākh.] For works by S. entitled *Burj i zawāhir* (Istānbūl 1276/1859, 176 pp.) and *Durj i zawāhir* (*sic*; read *jawāhir*? Cairo 1272/1855, 147 pp.), see F. E. Karatay *Istanbul Üniversitesi Kütüphanesi Farsça Basmalar Kataloğu*, p. 161.

No. 1438, 2nd par., end. [*Imtiḥān al-fuḍalāʾ*.] Other editions: [**Persia**] 1288/1871 (2 vols. See F. E. Karatay, *op. cit.* p. 161); **Istānbūl** 1291/1874 (104 pp. [*sic*?]. *Vid. ibid.*).

No. 1438, 3rd par. [Sanglākh.] Also *Yādgār* v/1–2 pp. 106–8 (biog. by M. Qazwīnī).

No. 1439, 1st par. ʿAbd al-Muḥammad Khān Īrānī died at Cairo on 5 Ābān-māh AHS 1314/27 October 1935 (see M. Ṣadr Hāshimī *Tārīkh i jarāʾid u majallāt i Īrān* ii p. 197, where a biography and a portrait (p. 198) will be found). For a work of his entitled *Zardusht i bāstānī u falsafah i ū* (212 pp.) see Harrassowitz's *Litterae orientales* 57 (Jan. 1934) p. 15, where the place and date of publication are given (doubtless incorrectly[93]) as Teheran 1933.

No. 1444, 1st par., (4) and (5). [Qāsim ʿAlī Khān "Āfrīdī"]. For his Pashtō *dīwān* see also Blumhardt *Catalogue of the Marathi, ... Pushtu, and Sindhi manuscripts in ... the British Museum* pp. 23–4 nos. 38–9.

93 The same place and date are given on the same page for the publication of the *Paidāyish i khaṭṭ u khaṭṭāṭān*.

No. 1444, end. *Insert*:

13.6.2a The Bakhtyārīs

1444*a*. **ʿAbd al-Ḥusain Khān Lisān al-Salṭanah** Malik al-muʾarrikhīn.
(1) ***Tārīkh i Bakhtyārī***,[94] covering the period 1004–1299/1692–1882 and composed in 1327/1909 by command of Ḥājjī ʿAlī-Qulī Khān Sardār i Asʿad Wazīr i Jang: Maṭbaʿah i Mīrzā ʿAlī Aṣghar [**Ṭihrān**? n.d.].
(2) ***Khulāṣat al-aʿṣār fī taʾrīkh al-Bakhtiyār***: **Ṭihrān** 1333/1914–15. [R. Lescot, *Bull. E.O.I.F. de Damas* vii–viii p. 283.]

No. 1451, 2nd par., footnote. For the Nāʾiṭī tribe see also *Maʾāthir al-umarāʾ* iii p. 562, Beveridge's trans. i p. 164.

No. 1453, last par. [ʿAbbās Iqbāl, b. 1314/1896–7.] See Īraj Afshār *Nathr i Fārsī i muʿāṣir* pp. 157–68 (portrait).

No. 1454 (1), end. *Insert*:
(1*a*) ***Risālah dar ḥāl i āmadan i Sādāt i Mutaʿallawī [Mustaʿlawī?] dar Sind***: **Āṣafīyah** iii p. 756.
(1*b*) ***Shajarah i khānadān i Bambah***, a pedigree of certain descendants of the Caliph ʿUthmān, compiled by Mīr M. ʿAlī Muẓaffarābādī and edited by Khudā-bakhsh Bambah: **Rāwal Pindī** 1338/1920* (Shāntī Steam Press. 30 pp.).

No. 1457, end. *Insert*:

1457*a*. **Mujtabā Mīnovī**[95] and **Ṣādiq Hidāyat.** ***Māziyār*** (English title: *Māziyār*. (1) *His life and activities*. (2) *A historical drama in 3 acts*): **Ṭihrān** AHS 1312/ 1933* (128 pp.).

No. 1459, 1st par., beginning. [*Sīrat al-Sulṭān Jalāl al-Dīn Mankubirnī*.] For a Persian translation by M. ʿAlī Khān "Nāṣiḥ"[96] published at Ṭihrān (presumably in 1945) see *Luzac's OL*. 1946 p. 6.

94 This title is given in the preface.
95 Cf. ad no. 1243 (4) supra.
96 Born at Ṭihrān in 1316/1898–9: see Ishaque *Sukhanvarān-i-Īrān* ii pp. 341–9 (portrait), *Modern Persian poetry* pp. 12, 29; Irani *Poets of the Pahlavi regime* pp. 598–9; M. Bāqir Burqaʿī *Sukhanwarān i nāmī i muʿāṣir* pp. 220–2 (portrait).

No. 1472, end. *Insert*:

1472*a*. Mīrzā **Muḥammad b. Abī 'l-Qāsim** was ten years old at the time of his father's death early in 1142/1729. He was appointed *Kalāntar* of Fārs in 1170/1756 by Karīm Khān Zand and he died at Iṣfahān in 1200/1786.

(***Rūznāmah i Mīrzā Muḥammad***), an autobiography extending to the year 1199/1785; **Ṭihrān** National Library (AH 1299/1882), Prof. Sa'īd Nafīsī's private library (AH 1324/1906), Royal Library.

Edition: *Rūznāmah i Mīrzā Muḥammad Kalāntar i Fārs*, **Ṭihrān** AHS 1325/1946 (ed. 'Abbās Iqbāl (cf. no. 1453 *supra*). Supplement to the periodical *Yādgār*, year 2).

No. 1483, end. *Insert*:

1483*a*. **Ḥusain Makkī** (pseud. **Farīdūn Ādamīyat**[97]) has already been mentioned as the author of the *Tārīkh i bīst-sālah i Īrān*[98] (ad no. 452 [452*e* (4)] *supra*) and of *Mukhtaṣarī az zindagānī i siyāsī u khuṣūṣī i Sulṭān Aḥmad Shāh Qājār*[99] (ad no. 451 (4)[451 (11)] *supra*).

Amīr i Kabīr[100] ***u Īrān yā waraqī az tārīkh i siyāsī i Īrān***, a Ṭihrān University doctoral dissertation published originally under the pseudonym Farīdūn Ādamīyat: **Ṭihrān** AHS 1323–4/1944–5 (3 vols. See Machalski, *Rocz. Orient.*, xv p. 101, n. 2); 2nd edition, Ṭihrān (see *Luzac's OL*. 1951 p. 30, where the title is given as *Amīr i Kabīr: ba-munāsabat i ṣadumīn sāl i qatl i Amīr i Kabīr* and the number of pages as 326. Presumably this is the same work as that called *Zindagī i Mīrzā Taqī Khān Amīr i Kabīr* in the select list of publications of the *Mu'assasah i Maṭbū'atī i Amīr i Kabīr* printed on the back cover of S. M. Bāqir Burqa'ī's *Sukhanwarān i nāmī i mu'āṣir*).

Description: F. Machalski *Quelques remarques sur l'état actuel de l'historiographie persane* (in *Rocznik Orientalistyczny* xv (1939–49)) pp. 101–2.

1483*b*. **Mahdī Mujtahidī** (cf. ad 1493, 1493*a* *infra*).

---

97 Cf. F. Machalski in *Rocz. Orient*, xv (1939–49) p. 101, where the names are reversed (Ādamīyat Farīdūn), and Maḥmūd Farhād Mu'tamad's *Sipahsālār i A'ẓam* p. 5 n.

98 Vol. i, *Kūditā-yi 1299*, Ṭihrān A.H.S. 1323/1944, vol. ii, *Muqaddamāt i taghyīr i salṭanat*, Ṭihrān A.H.S. 1324/1945 (cf. Machalski, *loc. cit.*, p. 102).

99 Cf. Machalski, *loc. cit.*, p. 103[1].

100 M. Taqī Farāhānī, Nāṣir al-Dīn Shāh's first Prime Minister, who was put to death by his order on 9 January 1852 (see Watson *History of Persia* pp. 364 *sqq.*, 398–406; Browne *Lit. Hist*, iv pp. 152–3; Sykes *History of Persia*, 3rd ed., ii pp. 339–40, 344–5; Ḥallāj *Tārīkh i nahḍat i Irān* p. 20 (portrait)).

Tārīkh i zindagānī i Taqī-zādah:[101] **Ṭihrān** AHS 1322/ 1944 (see the same author's *Rijāl i Adharbāyjān*, fly-leaf at end).

1483*c*. **Maḥmūd Farhād Mu'tamad.**
Tārīkh i siyāsī i daurah i ṣadārat i Mīrzā Ḥusain-Khān Mushīr al-Daulah Sipahsālār i A'ẓam, an account of Mīrzā Ḥusain Khān b. Nabī Khān, who was Sipahsālār i A'ẓam from Rajab to Sha'bān 1288/Sept.-Nov. 1871 and Prime Minister from Nov. 1871 to 1290/1873: **Ṭihrān** AHS 1325 [-6/1947‡].

No. 1485, 4th par., end. [*Tatimmat Ṣiwān al-ḥikmah.* Arabic text.] Another edition: *Ta'rīkh ḥukamā' al-Islām,* **Damascus** 1946 (Arab. Academy. Ed. M. Kurd 'Alī. See *JRAS*. 1948 p. 72).

No. 1487, Persian translation, MSS. [*Nuzhat al-arwāḥ.* Maqṣūd 'Alī's trans.] Also **Ellis Coll.** M. 238 (17th cent.).

No. 1487, Persian translation, end. [*Nuzhat al-arwāḥ.*] Another Persian translation: *Kanz al-ḥikmah tarjamah i N. al-a.* **Ṭihrān** AHS 1316/ 1938 (a modern translation by Ḍiyā' al-Dīn Durrī 2 vols. See *Oriens* iii/2 (1950) p. 330).

No. 1487, Persian translation, end. [*Tarjamah i Ta'rīkh al-ḥukamā'.*] Āṣafīyah i p. 346 no. 102 is a work of this title composed, according to the catalogue, in 1152/1739–40. If this date is correct, the work must be different from Maqṣūd 'Alī's translation of Shahrazūrī.

No. 1491, 2nd par. [*Rūz-nāmah i Ḥakīm al-Mamālik.*] See the addendum to no. 439, first visit (1867), and also M. Ṣadr Hāshimī *Tārīkh i jarā'id u majallāt i Īrān* ii pp. 327–9.

No. 1491, last par. ['Alī Naqī Ḥakīm al-Mamālik.] Also Browne *Press and poetry of modern Persia* p. 91; M. Ṣadr Hāshimī *op. cit.* p. 328, where a reference is given to *Yādgār* iii/1.

No. 1491, end. *Insert*:

1491*a*. Dr. **Maḥmūd Najmābādī.**
Sharḥ i ḥāl u maqām i Muḥammad i Zakarīyā i Rāzī pizishk i nāmī i Īrān: **Ṭihrān** (396 pp. See *Luzac's OL*. 1939 p. 76).

101 Cf. no. 321 (*a*) (1) *supra*; Īraj Afshār *Nathr i Fārsī i mu'āṣir* pp. 75–86 (portrait).

1491*b*. Dr. **Qāsim G͟hanī** was born in 1316/1898–9 at Sabzawār (see no. 1238 *supra* and Īraj Afs͟hār *Nath͟r i Fārsī i Muʿāṣir* pp. 193–204 (portrait)).
 Ibn i Sīnā: Ṭihrān (see *Luzac's OL*. 1937 p. 208).

1491*c*. **ʿAlī Akbar K͟hān "Dih-k͟hudā"**, or "Dak͟hau", Qazwīnī was born at Ṭihrān in 1297/1880 and is well known as the author of *Amth͟āl u ḥikam* (4 vols., Ṭihrān AHS 1310/1931–2) and of the enormous *Lug͟hat-nāmah* now in progress, to say nothing of his other claims to fame.
 Zindagānī i Abū Raiḥān al-Bīrūnī: Ṭihrān (see *Luzac's OL*. 1946 p. 43).
[Browne *Lit. Hist*, iv pp. 469–82, *Press and poetry of modern Persia* pp. 190, 200–4 (portrait); Berthels *Ocherk istorii persidskoi literatury* pp. 125–6; D. J. Irani *Poets of the Pahlavi regime* pp. 277–80 (portrait); Ishaque *Suk͟hanwarān-i-Īrān* i pp. 84–91 (portrait), *Modern Persian poetry* pp. 10, 21, etc.; Ras͟hīd Yāsimī *Adabīyāt i muʿāṣir* pp. 50–2 (portrait); Burqaʿī *Suk͟hanwarān i nāmī i muʿāṣir* pp. 77–9 (portrait); Īraj Afs͟hār *Nath͟r i Fārsī i muʿāṣir* pp. 93–6 (portrait).]

No. 1493, 1st par. M. ʿAlī K͟hān "Tarbiyat" died on 26 Dai 1318/–January 1940 (see Mahdī Mujtahidī *Rijāl i Ād͟harbāyjān* p. 31).

No. 1493, end. *Insert*:

1493*a*. **Mahdī Mujtahidī** is the author of a work entitled *Īrān u Ingilīs* (see ad no. 451, (8) *supra*).
 (1)   *Rijāl i Ād͟harbāyjān dar ʿaṣr i mas͟hrūṭīyat*: [Ṭihrān] AHS 1327/1948‡.
 (2)   *Tārīk͟h i zindagānī i Taqī-zādah*: see ad no. 1483, 1483 (*b*) *supra*.

No. 1508, end. For "Āzād's" *S͟hajarah i ṭaiyibah* see no. 1162, Persian works (12) *supra*.

No. 1532, last par. [Dargāh-Qulī K͟hān.] Also *S͟hamʿ i anjuman* p. 148.

No. 1533, end. *Insert*:

13.12.20a Gīlān

1533*a*. **Ḥasan S͟hams Gīlānī**, the son of a well-known k͟haṭīb, Ḥājj Iʿtimād, was born at Ras͟ht on 29 Ṣafar 1343/29 September 1924 and educated at Ras͟ht, Qum and Najaf.
 Tārīk͟h i ʿulamāʾ u s͟huʿarā-yi Gīlān, composed AHS 1325/1946 and divided into a *muqaddamah* (autobiography, p. 4), two *faṣl*s ((1) on Gīlān and its

towns, p. 21, (2) scholars, poets, etc., of Gīlān, p. 29) and a *khātimah* (on the poets of Qum, p. 134): **Ṭihrān** AHS 1327–8/ 1949‡ (152 pp.).

No. 1539, end. *Insert*:

1539*a*. Other works:—
(1) ***Mukhtaṣar i siyar i Hindūstān***, a short dictionary of celebrities who were born or flourished in India, by M. Waḥīd Allāh Sabzawārī: **Delhi** 1270/1854° (95 pp.), apparently also **Āgrah** 1892† (Ḥaidarī Pr.).

13.12.24a Iṣfahān

1539*b*. Ākhund Mullā **ʿAbd al-Karīm b. Mahdī Jazī**[102] [or Gazī] Iṣfahānī died on 13 Dhū 'l-Ḥijjah 1339/18 August 1921.

Tadhkirat al-qubūr, on the celebrities buried at Iṣfahān: **Iṣfahān** 1324/1906. [R. Lescot *Bull. E.O.I.F. de Damas* vii–viii p. 282]; AHS 1328/1949–50 (title: *Rijāl i Iṣfahān yā Tadhkirat al-qubūr*. 2nd ed., with notes and additions by the author's son S. Muṣliḥ al-Dīn Mahdawī. 260 pp.).

1539*c*. **S. Jalāl al-Din Ṭihrāni**, a teacher of astronomy and mathematics, has published editions of several Persian and Arabic texts (cf. nos. 340 Editions (3), 453 last par. and 455 2nd par. *supra* and, for a list, *Gāh-nāmah i 1314* pp. 2–3), some of them as appendices to his almanacs for the years AHS 1310–14/1931–6.

Iṣfahān, mainly on its buildings and the celebrities buried there: **Ṭihrān** AH 1351/ AHS 1311/1933 (in *Gāh-nāmah i 1312* pp. 76–160).

No. 1556, end. *Insert*:

13.12.33a Quhistān

1556*a*. Sh. Ḍiyāʾ al-Dīn **M. Ḥusain "Āyatī"** Khurāsānī.

Bahāristān dar tārīkh u tarājim i rijāl i Qaʾināt u Quhistān, completed in 1364/1945: **Ṭihrān** AHS 1327/ 1948–9‡ (393 pp.). Cf. no. 1243 (9).

No. 1567, end. *Insert*:

13.12.39a Ṭabaristān

102 Gaz (or, in its arabicised form, Jaz) is a village in the *bulūk* of Barkhwār, north of Iṣfahān.

1567*a*. ʿ**Abbās Shāyān** is *Raʾīs i idārah i āmār u thabt i aḥwāl i Tihrān* (see *Māzandarān*, vol. ii, title-page, and, for a portrait, vol. ii p. 199).

Māzandarān,, vol. ii (contemporary celebrities of Māzandarān) **Ṭihrān** AHS 1327/1949 (199 pp.).[103]

No. 1574, 3rd par., beginning. For Arabic works by Nūr Allāh Shūshtarī see also Zubaid Aḥmad *The contribution of India to Arabic literature* pp. 237–8, 255, 275–6, 323–5, 348, 405.

No. 1574, 4th par., MSS. [*Majālis al-muʾminīn*.] Also **Ellis Coll. M.** 313 (AH 1093/1682), 314 (1st half. 19th cent,).

No. 1576, 2nd par., footnote. For S. Dildār ʿAlī see also *Nujūm al-samāʾ* pp. 346–51 and *Kashf al-ḥujub* (in Arabic, by Iʿjāz Ḥusain Kintūrī), editor's preface, p. 4, n. 1.

No. 1578, 2nd par. [*Majmūʿah i Ḥaidar-Shukōh*.] Cf. *Risālah i Ḥaidarī dar ʿaqāʾid i salāṭīn i Tīmūrī* ("*dar bayān i nadhr gudharānīdan i ʿalam ba-dargāh i ḥaḍrat i ʿAbbās ʿm.*"), by Shāhzādah M. Ḥ.-Sh. b. Mīrzā M. K.-b. Edition: Lucknow (date? with the mathnawī *Shaukat i Ḥaidarī*. Āṣafīyah iii p. 102).

No. 1575, last par. [M. b. Sulaimān Tunakābunī.] Also *Tārīkh i ʿulamā u shuʿarā-yi Gīlān* p. 58, where the date of his death is given as 28 Jumādā II 1302.

No. 1581, beginning. "Jawāhir al-Kalām": so on the title-pages of the *Āthār al-Shīʿat al-Imāmīyah* and the *Kitāb-khānahā-yi Īrān*, but Jawāhir-kalām on the title-page of the *Fihrist i Kitāb-khānah i ʿUmūmī i Maʿārif* (Pt. i, AHS 1313, Pt. ii, AHS 1314).

No. 1586, last par. [*Bustān al-muḥaddithīn*.] Also **Delhi,** Mujtabāʾī Pr., 1898 (132 pp. See F. E. Karatay, Istanbul Univ. cat. p. 3).

No. 1615, 1st par., end. [Journey of the Persian princes.] *Insert*:
Persian text [?]: see no. 433 *supra*.

No. 1631 (7), end. *Insert*:
(7*a*) ***Musāfarat i Tiflīs***, by Mīrzā Taqī Khān: **Leningrad** Univ. 1120 (AH 1288/1871. Romaskewicz p. 14).

103 Vol. i (geography and history) has been printed (according to vol. ii p. 199) but may not yet have reached Europe, vol. iii is to deal with tribes, local customs, supplementary biographies, etc.

(7*b*) ***Musāfir***, an account in verse of a visit to Afghānistān in October 1933, with poems written on that occasion, by M. Iqbāl Lāhaurī, the well-known Urdu and Persian poet: **Lahore,** Gīlānī Electric Pr., 1934* (59 pp.).

No. 1631 (13). **Ambala**: so Arberry, but according to the U.P. Quarterly Catalogue (1909/1) the book, published by a resident of Ambala, was printed at the Mashriq al-ʿUlūm Press, **Bijnaur.**

No. 1643 (2), end. *Insert*:

(3) ***Taṣwīr i ʿibrat***, a biography of Bībī Khūrī Jān, by M. ʿAbd al-Qādir Khān: **Madrās** 1922* (92 pp.).

No. 1645 (2), 2nd footnote. [Kabīr b. Uwais.] Also *Majālis al-nafāʾis* tr. Shāh-Muḥammad Qazwīnī pp. 396–7.

No. 1649, 2nd. par., MSS. [*Haft iqlīm.*] Also **Ellis Coll.** M. 41 (AH 1089/ 1678. Now in Cambridge Univ. Lib.), M. 42, M. 43.